CH. #	CHAPTER TITLE	FOCUS COMPANY	MANAGERIAL FOCUS	CONTRAST COMPANIES	KEY RATIOS
8	Reporting and Interpreting Cost of Goods Sold and Inventory	**DELL INC.** Dell Inc. (Direct-sale computer vendor)	Manufacturing management	Gateway IBM	**Inventory Turnover**
9	Reporting and Interpreting Property, Plant, and Equipment; Natural Resources; and Intangibles	*WESTJET* WestJet Airlines Ltd. (Major Canadian airline)	Planning productive capacity	Southwest Airlines Jet Blue Airways	**Fixed Asset Turnover**
10	Reporting and Interpreting Liabilities	**PETRO-CANADA** Petro-Canada (Oil and gas company)	Capital structure	Suncor Energy Imperial Oil	**Current Ratio Accounts Payable Turnover**
11	Reporting and Interpreting Bonds	**PLACER DOME INC.** Placer Dome Inc. (Gold mining company)	Long-term debt financing	Barrick Gold Newmont Mining	**Financial Leverage Times Interest Earned**
12	Reporting and Interpreting Owners' Equity	*Bell Canada Enterprises* BCE Inc. (Canada's largest communications company)	Corporate ownership	Shaw Communications TELUS	**Dividend Yield Dividend Payout**
13	Analyzing Financial Statements	THE HOME DEPOT The Home Depot Inc. (Home improvement retailer)	Financial statement analysis	Canadian Tire Lowe's	**Ratio Summary**

Financial Accounting

SECOND CANADIAN EDITION

Robert Libby

Cornell University

Patricia A. Libby

Ithaca College

Daniel G. Short

Miami University

George Kanaan

Concordia University

Maureen Gowing

University of Windsor

Toronto   Montréal   Boston   Burr Ridge, IL   Dubuque, IA   Madison, WI   New York
San Francisco   St. Louis   Bangkok   Bogotá   Caracas   Kuala Lumpur   Lisbon   London
Madrid   Mexico City   Milan   New Delhi   Santiago   Seoul   Singapore   Sydney   Taipei

McGraw-Hill
Ryerson

Financial Accounting
Second Canadian Edition

Copyright © 2006, 2003, by McGraw-Hill Ryerson Limited, a Subsidiary of The McGraw-Hill Companies. © 2007, 2004, 2001, 1998, 1996, by The McGraw-Hill Companies, Inc. All rights reserved. No part of this publication may be reproduced or transmitted in any form or by any means, or stored in a data base or retrieval system, without the prior written permission of McGraw-Hill Ryerson Limited, or in the case of photocopying or other reprographic copying, a license from The Canadian Copyright Licensing Agency (Access Copyright). For an Access Copyright licence, visit www.accesscopyright.ca or call toll free to 1-800-893-5777.

ISBN: 007088952X

1 2 3 4 5 6 7 8 9 10   TCP   0 9 8 7 6

Printed and bound in Canada

Care has been taken to trace ownership of copyright material contained in this text; however, the publisher will welcome any information that enables them to rectify any reference or credit for subsequent editions.

Publisher, Business and Economics: Nicole Lukach
Marketing Manager: Charlotte Liu
Developmental Editor: Suzanne Simpson Millar
Senior Editorial Associate: Christine Lomas
Copy Editor: Kelli Howey
Production Coordinator: Janie Deneau
Cover Design: Dave Murphy/Valid Design and Layout
Cover Image Credits: Times Square, New York City, Electric Stock Ticker, Getty Images Grant Faint; Mobile Phone, Getty Images, Pete Gardner; Snowboarding, Getty Images, Karl Weatherly; Airplane Detail, PhotoLink/Getty Images; Golf Ball, PhotoDisc/Getty Images; Coffee, © Royalty-Free/Corbis (Image # 42-15557412)
Page Layout: Chris Hudson/Bookman Typesetting Co. Inc.
Printer: Transcontinental Printing Limited

Library and Archives Canada Cataloguing in Publication

Financial accounting / Robert Libby ... [et al.]. — 2nd Canadian ed.

Includes index.
ISBN 0-07-088952-X

1. Accounting—Textbooks.   2. Corporations—Accounting—Textbooks.   3. Financial statements—Textbooks.   I. Libby, Robert

HF5635.F43 2006   657   C2005-907115-X

Robert Libby

Robert Libby is the David A. Thomas Professor of Management at the Johnson Graduate School of Management at Cornell University, where he teaches the introductory financial accounting course. He has previously taught at the University of Illinois, Pennsylvania State University, University of Texas at Austin, University of Chicago, and University of Michigan. He received his B.S. from Pennsylvania State University and his M.A.S. and Ph.D. from the University of Illinois; he is also a CPA. Bob is a widely published author specializing in behavioural accounting.

Patricia A. Libby

Patricia Libby is Chair of the Department of Accounting and Associate Professor of Accounting at Ithaca College, where she teaches the undergraduate financial accounting course. She has previously taught graduate and undergraduate financial accounting at Eastern Michigan University and the University of Texas. Before entering academe, she was an auditor with Price Waterhouse (now Pricewaterhouse-Coopers) and a financial administrator at the University of Chicago. She received her B.S. from Pennsylvania State University, her M.B.A. from DePaul University, and her Ph.D. from the University of Michigan; she is also a CPA. Pat conducts research on using cases in the introductory course and other parts of the accounting curriculum.

Daniel G. Short

Daniel Short is Professor of Accounting and Dean of the M.J. Neeley School of Business at Texas Christian University in Fort Worth, Texas. Formerly, he was Dean at the Richard T. Farmer School of Business at Miami University (Ohio) and the College of Business at Kansas State University. Prior to that, he was Associate Dean at the University of Texas at Austin, where he taught the undergraduate and graduate financial accounting courses. He has also taught at the University of Michigan and the University of Chicago. Dan received his undergraduate degree from Boston University and his M.B.A. and Ph.D. from the University of Michigan. He has won numerous awards for his outstanding teaching abilities and has published articles.

George Kanaan

George Kanaan is Associate Dean at the John Molson School of Business at Concordia University, where he teaches the introductory financial accounting course. George previously taught undergraduate and graduate courses at McMaster University. He received his B.A. from the Lebanese University, his M.A. from Southern Illinois University at Carbondale, and his Ph.D. from the University of Wisconsin–Madison. He has conducted research on disclosures related to pension accounting, deferred income taxes, and the effects of changing prices. George's research has been published in *The Journal of Accounting, Auditing and Finance,* and *Managerial Finance*. During his tenure as Chair of the Department of Accountancy, the John Molson School of Business became the first Canadian business school to receive accreditation of its accounting programs by AACSB International—the Association to Advance Collegiate Schools of Business.

Maureen Gowing

Maureen Gowing is Assistant Professor of Accounting at the Odette School of Business at the University of Windsor. She has taught accounting research methods at the Ph.D. level, as well as financial and managerial accounting and accounting theory at both the M.B.A. and undergraduate levels. She has co-authored and published articles on ethics in accounting in the *Journal of Business Ethics*, and the *International Journal of Business Research*. Maureen has also conducted research on the effectiveness of technological and pedagogical strategies in teaching different content in accounting courses. She is also the Canadian author of a managerial accounting text. She worked for several years as an analyst in the oil and securities industries and at the Vancouver Stock Exchange doing forensic accounting. Maureen obtained her B.A. from Carleton University, her M.B.A. from the University of Toronto, and her Ph.D. from Queen's University.

Contents in Brief

Contents

CHAPTER **FOUR**

Adjustments, Financial Statements, and the Quality of Earnings   163

FOCUS COMPANY: VAN HOUTTE, INC.—THE BUSIEST TIME OF THE FISCAL YEAR   163

CHAPTER **FIVE**

Reporting and Interpreting Cash Flows   227

CHAPTER **SIX**

Communicating and Interpreting Accounting Information   283

CHAPTER **SEVEN**

Reporting and Interpreting Sales Revenue, Receivables, and Cash   343

FOCUS COMPANY: GILDAN ACTIVEWEAR INC.—
PRODUCT DEVELOPMENT, PRODUCTION, AND
WORKING CAPITAL MANAGEMENT: KEYS TO
GROSS PROFIT   343

CHAPTER **EIGHT**

Reporting and Interpreting Cost of Goods Sold and Inventory   405

CHAPTER **TEN**

Reporting and Interpreting Liabilities   527

CHAPTER **ELEVEN**

Reporting and Interpreting Bonds   589

CHAPTER **TWELVE**

Reporting and Interpreting Owners' Equity   633

FOCUS COMPANY: BCE, INC.: FINANCING
CORPORATE GROWTH WITH CAPITAL SUPPLIED
BY OWNERS   633

CHAPTER **THIRTEEN**

Analyzing Financial Statements 683

FOCUS COMPANY: HOME DEPOT: FINANCIAL
ANALYSIS: BRINGING IT ALL TOGETHER 683

Finally, a textbook on which both students and instructors can agree. The authors of *Financial Accounting*, second Canadian edition, continue to make financial accounting more relevant and interesting to students. How? By helping the instructor and student become partners in learning, using a remarkable learning approach that keeps students engaged and involved in the material from the first day of class.

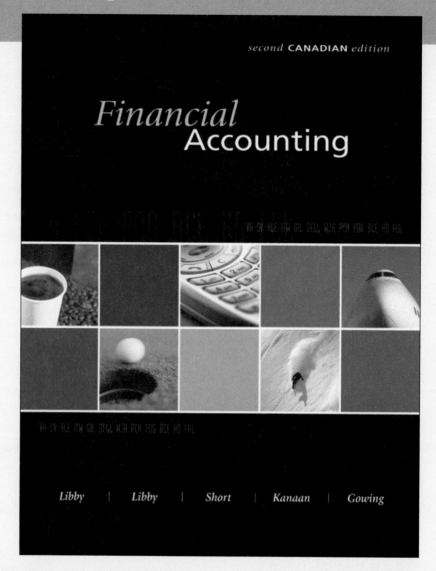

second **CANADIAN** *edition*

Financial Accounting

Libby | *Libby* | *Short* | *Kanaan* | *Gowing*

Financial Accounting's distinctive focus-company method motivates students by involving them in the business decisions of a real company, demonstrating how financial accounting makes a difference in the success of a firm. That, combined with pedagogical features and technology assets that serve a variety of learning styles, makes Libby/Libby/Short/Kanaan/Gowing the textbook that both students and instructors agree is the best of its kind on the market today.

# of students and instructors alike.

Financial Accounting's success is based on three key attributes:

RELEVANCE. The authors' use of real-world focus companies is the best tool for demonstrating the relevance of financial accounting topics. Ethics continues to be a crucial topic within accounting, and *Financial Accounting* integrates coverage of ethical issues throughout the book. Furthering its real-world applicability, the end-of-chapter cases tie into the annual reports of Van Houtte Inc. and the Forzani Group Limited. This gives students valuable practice in reading and interpreting real financial data. Finally, Real-World Excerpts expand important chapter topics with insight into how real firms use financial accounting to their competitive advantage.

CLARITY. Do students complain that their textbook is hard to read? They don't if they're reading *Financial Accounting*, which is the proven choice for presenting financial accounting in a clear, relevant approach that keeps students engaged throughout the course. To continue to meet the changing needs of financial accounting instructors and students, the organization of the material has been refined to ensure maximum readability for students, and flexibility for instructors.

TECHNOLOGY AIDS. Today's students have diverse learning styles and numerous time commitments, and they want technology supplements that help them study more efficiently and effectively. Lyryx Assessment, algorithmic test banks, narrated PowerPoint® presentations, self-study multimedia files and more, provide your students with powerful tools tied directly to *Financial Accounting* second Canadian edition. These tools will help them maximize their study time and make their learning experience more enjoyable.

CHOICE. *Financial Accounting*, second Canadian edition, is the proven choice for presenting financial accounting with a clear, relevant approach that keeps students engaged throughout your course. Read on for more insight into what has made this textbook such a success with faculty and students.

Proven Learning Solutions

Financial Accounting offers a host of pedagogical tools that complement the way you like to teach and the ways your students like to learn. Some offer information and tips that help you in presenting a complex subject; others highlight issues relevant to what your students read online and in the papers, or see on television. Either way, *Financial Accounting's* pedagogical support will make a real difference in your course and in your students' learning.

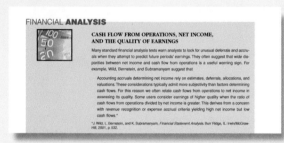

FINANCIAL ANALYSIS

The **Financial Analysis** sections tie important chapter concepts covered in each chapter to real-world decision-making examples. They also highlight alternative viewpoints and add to the critical thinking skills and decision-making focus of the text. In a recent survey of the types of services that will be required of accounting graduates in the future, financial analysis was given top ranking by the accounting practitioners who participated in the survey.[1]

INTERNATIONAL PERSPECTIVE

As our Canadian instructors are acutely aware, the harmonization of Canadian with U.S. and international accounting standards is a top priority of the Canadian Institute of Chartered Accountants. Because of the rapid increase in global competition, the **International Perspective** sections make students aware of the differences in accounting methods used around the world. International issues are included in the end-of-chapter material as well.

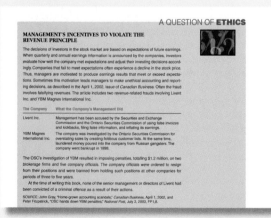

A QUESTION OF ETHICS

In every business, decision makers are occasionally confronted with ethical dilemmas that require them to make choices that will have different effects on different groups of people. **A Question of Ethics** boxes appear throughout the text, conveying to students the importance of acting responsibly in business practice. The more students are exposed to ethical situations, the more likely they will consider the effects their choices will have on others. Recent events in the accounting profession have made ethics awareness more crucial than ever.

---

[1] W.S. Albrecht and R.J. Sack. *Accounting Education: Charting the Course through a Perilous Future.* Sarasota, FL: AAA, 2000, p. 15.

SELF-STUDY QUIZZES

This learning feature engages the student, provides interactivity, and promotes efficient learning. Research shows that students learn best when they are actively engaged in the learning process. These **Self-Study Quizzes** ask students to pause at strategic points throughout each chapter to ensure they understand key points before moving ahead.

FOCUS ON CASH FLOWS

Each chapter includes **Focus on Cash Flows**, a discussion and analysis of changes in the cash flow of the focus company and explores the decisions that caused those changes. The early and consistent coverage of cash flows encourages students to think more critically about the decisions they will face as managers and the impact those decisions will have on the company's cash flow.

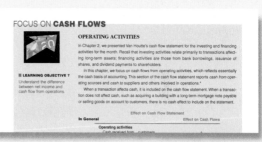

KEY RATIO ANALYSIS

Students will be better prepared to use financial information if they learn to evaluate financial performance as they learn how to measure and report them. For this reason, we include relevant key ratios in the **Key Ratio Analysis** sections. Each Key Ratio Analysis box presents a ratio analysis for the focus company in the chapter as well as for comparative companies. Cautions are also provided to help students understand the limitations of certain ratios.

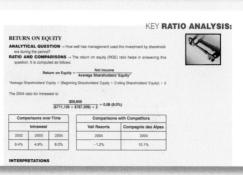

REAL WORLD EXCERPT

These insightful excerpts appear throughout the text and include annual report information from the focus companies as well as numerous other companies, news articles from various publications, analysts' reports, and press releases.

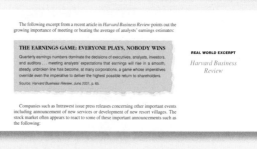

Proven Learning Solutions

ORGANIZATION OF THE CHAPTER SCHEMATIC

A unique feature of Libby *Financial Accounting*, this visual framework provides a powerful visual schematic of each chapter's content, easily enabling students to identify the topics covered.

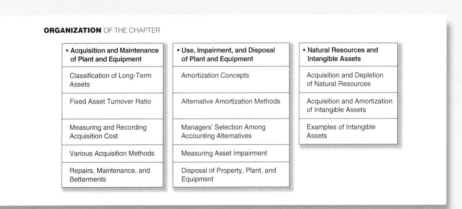

ORGANIZATION OF THE CHAPTER

• Acquisition and Maintenance of Plant and Equipment	• Use, Impairment, and Disposal of Plant and Equipment	• Natural Resources and Intangible Assets
Classification of Long-Term Assets	Amortization Concepts	Acquisition and Depletion of Natural Resources
Fixed Asset Turnover Ratio	Alternative Amortization Methods	Acquisition and Amortization of Intangible Assets
Measuring and Recording Acquisition Cost	Managers' Selection Among Accounting Alternatives	Examples of Intangible Assets
Various Acquisition Methods	Measuring Asset Impairment	
Repairs, Maintenance, and Betterments	Disposal of Property, Plant, and Equipment	

ALL JOURNAL ENTRIES TIED TO THE ACCOUNTING EQUATION

Journal entries in early chapters marked with (A), (L), (SE), (R), (E), or X, (if a contra account) and + and − signs assist students in transaction analysis. In addition, following each journal entry is a summary of the effects of each transaction on the fundamental accounting equation.

LEARNING OBJECTIVES CROSS-REFERENCED

Outlined at the beginning of each chapter, these Learning Objectives are cross-referenced to the end-of-chapter material.

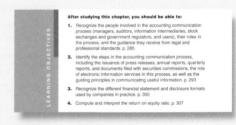

LEARNING OBJECTIVES

After studying this chapter, you should be able to:

1. Recognize the people involved in the accounting communication process (managers, auditors, information intermediaries, stock exchanges and government regulators, and users), their roles in the process, and the guidance they receive from legal and professional standards. p. 285

2. Identify the steps in the accounting communication process, including the issuance of press releases, annual reports, quarterly reports, and documents filed with securities commissions, the role of electronic information services in this process, as well as the guiding principles in communicating useful information. p. 293

3. Recognize the different financial statement and disclosure formats used by companies in practice. p. 300

4. Compute and interpret the return on equity ratio. p. 307

 • International: Assignment that includes an international perspective.

 • Ethics: An ethical dilemma that the student must solve.

 • Cash Flows: Requires the student to work cash flow analyses.

 • Ratio Analysis: Assignment that includes ratio analysis.

 • WWW: Guides the student to additional articles, exercises, and Internet links.

 • Written Communication: Assignment that requires the student to do written work.

 • Team Project: Assignments that are to be done by student teams.

 • SPATS: Spreadsheet Application Template Software uses Excel® templates to solve selected end-of-chapter assignments.

Flexible End-of-Chapter Content and Organization

Each chapter is followed by an extensive selection of end-of-chapter assignments that examine single concepts or integrate multiple concepts presented in the chapter. To maintain the real-world flavour of the chapter material, they are often based on real Canadian, U.S., and international companies, and require analysis, conceptual thought, calculation, and written communication. Assignments suitable for written individual or group projects and oral presentations are included in strategic locations.

Chapter Take-Aways   Bulleted, end-of-chapter summaries that correspond with the learning objectives outlined at the beginning of the chapter.

Key Ratios   Summary of the key ratios presented in the chapter.

Finding Financial Information   Highlights the chapter's key concepts in an easy-to-review graphic. The graphic includes Balance Sheet, Income Statement, Cash Flow Statement, and Note Information.

Key Terms   Key terms introduced in each chapter are referenced to the chapter text.

Questions   Allow students and faculty to ensure that chapter concepts have been grasped.

Multiple Choice   Questions that allow for a quick check of basic concepts.

Exercises   Assignments that cover multiple learning objectives from each chapter.

Problems   Detailed assignments that integrate various topics discussed in the chapter. They are cross-referenced in blue to the Alternate Problems.

Alternate Problems   Similar in level and content to the end-of-chapter problems. They are cross-referenced in blue to the Problems.

Cases and Projects   This section includes Finding and Interpreting Financial Information, Financial Reporting and Analysis Cases, Critical Thinking Cases, and a Financial Reporting and Analysis Team Project.

Instructors will find several ways to identify end-of-chapter materials to use when achieving the learning objectives. Accordingly, we have:

- Added applicable Learning Objective numbers in the margin.
- Arranged assignments by increasing the level of difficulty in learning objective order.
- Included a number of assignments that focus on understanding the effects of transactions, rather than producing journal entries.
- Included user-oriented analytical materials.
- Incorporated themes: International, ethics, cash flows, ratio analysis, real world, written communication, team project, broadening research skills, comparing companies within and across industries and over time, finding financial information, and interpreting the financial press.

What's New in the Second Canadian Edition?

The primary goals for this second Canadian edition are to streamline the presentation of material while making it clearer to students what they should take away from each chapter; to reorganize the material covered in specific chapters so as to provide instructors more flexibility in key topical coverage; to reflect recent changes that have taken place in the accounting environment; and to update and revise end-of-chapter material to better match instructors' needs. Common changes to all chapters include the addition of 10 multiple-choice questions per chapter, elimination of the mini-exercises, elimination of all but one of the Financial Analysis and Reporting Projects, and updating the real-world data used in the problems. Additional changes specific to each chapter are noted below.

Chapter 1
- Changed the focus company from Maxidrive, a fictitious company, to Unibroue, a Quebec-based microbrewery
- Reorganized the overview of financial statements to focus on the basic structure and elements of each statement
- Introduced new graphics to reinforce key concepts
- Consolidated the Financial Analysis related to the balance sheet elements
- Added Exhibit 1.6 to illustrate the relationships among the financial statements
- Expanded the discussion about ethics and legal liability
- provided a brief introduction to the requirements of the Sarbanes-Oxley Act

Chapter 2
- Changed the focus company to Van Houtte Inc., one of North America's leading gourmet coffee companies
- Expanded the coverage of the classified balance sheet
- Replaced the financial leverage ratio with the debt-to-equity ratio and shifted ratio analysis earlier to motivate the use of balance sheet information
- Added more visual illustrations of key concepts
- Strengthened and simplified the coverage of cash flows
- Added new end-of-chapter exercises and problems

Chapter 3
- Changed the focus company to Van Houtte Inc.
- Introduced the multiple-step income statement
- Added more visual illustrations of key concepts
- Added Exhibit 3.2 to illustrate the timing of revenue recognition
- Eliminated the unadjusted financial statements, which are not prepared in actual practice
- Shortened the coverage of segmented information
- Introduced a comparison of accrual versus cash bases of accounting
- Moved ratio analysis earlier to motivate the use of income statement information and added the return on assets ratio
- Substantially revised end-of-chapter material

Chapter 4
- Changed the chapter title to reflect coverage of the quality of earnings
- Changed the focus company to Van Houtte Inc.
- Revised the section on adjusting entries to add clarity
- Added more visual illustrations of key concepts
- Introduced the concept of materiality and its role in the adjustment process
- Illustrated the use of adjustments on the trial balance worksheet (Exhibit 4.3)

- Reduced the coverage of cash flows
- Added many new and revised end-of-chapter exercises and problems

Chapter 5
- Shifted the coverage of cash flows from Chapter 13 to Chapter 5
- Updated all information for Sleeman Breweries Ltd.
- Eliminated the overview of financial statement relationships (covered in Chapter 4)
- Substantial revision allowing use of either the direct method or indirect method (or both) to prepare the operating section
- Extensive use of T-accounts and graphics to illustrate the process for direct and indirect methods
- Added new summary tables for reinforcement

Chapter 6
- Updated all information for Intrawest Corporation
- Shifted the section on Players in the Accounting Communication Process to the beginning of the chapter
- Moved the classified balance sheet and the multiple-step income statement to Chapters 2 and 3
- Expanded coverage of qualitative characteristics of accounting information
- Substantially revised end-of-chapter material; addition of new problems based on WestJet Airlines, RONA, and Danier Leather

Chapter 7
- Updated all information on Gildan
- Added more visual illustrations of key concepts
- Introduced a section on internal control and management responsibility
- Strengthened the discussion of internal control of cash.
- Many new and revised end-of-chapter exercises and problems

Chapter 8
- Updated all information on Dell and real-world excerpts
- New FIFO and LIFO inventory graphics
- Shifted the discussion of cash flows to the end of the chapter
- Eliminated Financial Analysis boxes that were not essential

Chapter 9
- Reorganized the chapter to improve the flow of topics
- Updated all information on WestJet Airlines
- Shifted ratio analysis earlier to reinforce the use of accounting information in analytical decisions
- Shortened and shifted the cash flow analysis section to the end of the chapter
- Refocused the coverage of revenue and capital expenditures and used the WorldCom scandal for illustration purposes

- Moved discussion of changes in accounting estimates to a chapter supplement to simplify the content
- Revised material on intangible assets, included recent CICA recommendations, and provided real-world examples
- Added new end-of-chapter exercises and problems

Chapter 10
- Changed the focus company to Petro-Canada
- Reorganized discussion of current liabilities
- Revised discussion of estimated liabilities and expanded on coverage of warranty liability
- Expanded discussion of lease liabilities
- Focused cash flow discussion on accounts payable and accrued liabilities, and changed location to provide users with greater flexibility
- Expanded discussion of long-term notes
- Expanded discussion of future income tax assets and liabilities, and moved it to chapter supplement
- Moved discussion of retirement benefits to chapter supplement
- Improved on the presentation of present values and future values
- Added new end-of-chapter exercises and problems related to leases, warranty liabilities, and contingent liabilities

Chapter 11
- Changed the focus company to Placer Dome Inc.
- Reorganized the chapter to focus primarily on bonds
- Improved graphics to enhance understanding
- Added discussion about the bond market
- Added discussion on early retirement of bonds
- Eliminated discussion of debt issued at variable interest rates

Chapter 12
- Updated all information on BCE, Inc.
- Moved discussion of repurchase of shares to chapter supplement
- Moved cash flow discussion to end of chapter
- Expanded discussion related to employee compensation
- Many new and revised end-of-chapter exercises and problems

Chapter 13
- Updated all information on Home Depot
- Improved graphics to support discussions
- Improved focus of discussion of individual ratios, and added the payable turnover ratio

Teaching and Learning

Financial Accounting's technology learning solutions complement the textbook every step of the way, giving students the extra help they need while providing instructors with tools for teaching a stimulating and rewarding class.

LYRYX ASSESSMENT FOR FINANCIAL ACCOUNTING

A COMPLETE ONLINE ASSESSMENT SYSTEM

Lyryx Assessment for *Financial Accounting* second Canadian edition, is a web-based teaching, learning and assessment tool that has captured the attention of post-secondary institutions across the country while improving student success in financial accounting.

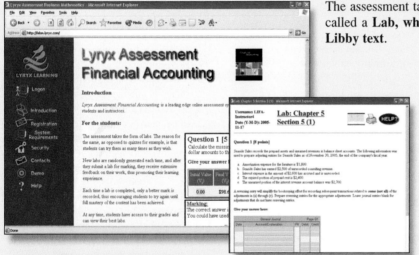

The assessment takes the form of a homework assignment called a **Lab, which corresponds to the chapters in the Libby text**.

The Labs are **algorithmically generated and automatically graded**, so students get instant scores and feedback—no need to wait until the next class to find out how well they did!

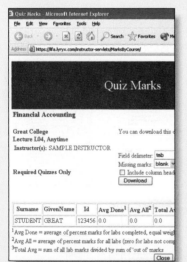

New Labs are randomly generated each time, providing the student with unlimited opportunities to try a type of question. After they submit a Lab for marking, students receive **extensive feedback** on their work, thus promoting their learning experience. Student motivation is high with these Labs because they can be **tied to assessment** and because they can try as many times as they want prior to the due date, with only their best grade being recorded.

After registering their course with us, instructors can create Labs of their choice by selecting problems from our test bank, and setting a deadline for each one. Instructors have access to all the students' marks and can view their best Labs. Instructors can download the class grades at any time to analyze individual and class performance.

If students do their financial accounting practice and homework, they *will* improve their performance in the course. Recent research regarding the use of Lyryx has shown that when Labs are tied to assessment, even if worth only a small percentage of the total grade for the course, students will do their homework—and more than once. *The result is improved student success in introductory financial accounting!*

Please contact your *iLearning Sales Specialist* for additional information on the Lyryx Interactive Financial Accounting system.

with Technology

ONLINE LEARNING CENTRE

McGraw-Hill Ryerson offers you an online resource that combines the best content with the flexibility and power of the Internet. Organized by chapter, the Libby Online Learning Centre (OLC) offers the following features to enhance your learning and understanding of Financial Accounting:

For the Instructor Access instructor supplements including the Instructor's Manual, PowerPoint presentation slides, Solutions Manual, Excel Templates tied to the end-of-chapter material, and solutions to Excel template problems, all organized by chapter.

For the Student The student section of the site includes Topic Tackler multimedia content, self-quizzes, learning objectives, chapter outlines, chapter takeaways, glossary, Excel templates, Web links, demo cases, and digital flashcards.

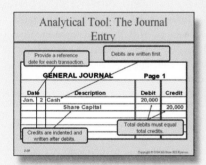

ANNUAL REPORTS

Annual Reports of two dynamic Canadian companies that are referenced in the text's problem material are posted online for student study.

ALGORITHMIC TEST BANK

If you've ever thought that no test bank, however well made, could have all the problems you could possibly need, think again. The Algorithmic Test Bank available with *Financial Accounting*, 2nd Canadian edition, includes a problem generator that replicates the structure of text problems while populating them with fresh numbers. Create unique versions of every homework assignment, every quiz, every test—or use it to provide dozens of similar but distinct problems for students to practise on.

Supplements for the Instructor

INSTRUCTOR'S CD-ROM

This integrated CD-ROM allows you to access most of the text's ancillary materials. You no longer need to keep track of the various supplements that accompany your text. Instead, almost everything is available on one convenient CD-ROM:

- **PowerPoint® Presentations.** These slides for use in your classroom are completely customized for the second Canadian edition of *Financial Accounting*. Also available on the Online Learning Centre.

- **Solutions Manual.** Provides solutions for end-of-chapter questions, mini-exercises, exercises, problems, and cases. Only available on the Instructor's CD-ROM.

- **Instructor's Manual.** The supplements, including the Test Bank, Study Guide, and PowerPoint® slides, are topically cross-referenced in the Instructor's Manual to help instructors direct students to specific ancillaries to reinforce key concepts. Also available on the Online Learning Centre.

- **Algorithmic Test Bank.** Add and edit questions; create up to 99 versions of each test; attach graphic files to questions; import and export test in Rich Text Format for paper-based use; and select questions by type, level of difficulty, or learning objective. This software includes password protection for saved tests or questions databases, and is able to run on a network.

- **Instructor's Excel® Templates.** These Excel templates allow students to develop important spreadsheet skills by using them to solve selected end-of-chapter assignments. Also available on the Online Learning Centre.

ONLINE LEARNING CENTRE

www.mcgrawhill.ca/college/libby
(See page xxv for details.)

WEB CT/BLACKBOARD

Content cartridges are available for the course management systems **WebCT** and **Blackboard**. These platforms provide instructors with user-friendly, flexible teaching tools. Please contact your local McGraw-Hill Ryerson *i*Learning Sales Specialist for details.

www.blackboard.com

PAGEOUT

Visit www.mhhe.com/pageout to create a Web page for your course using our resources. **PageOut** is the McGraw-Hill Ryerson Web site development centre. This Web-page generation software is free to adopters and is designed to help faculty create an online course, complete with assignments, quizzes, links to relevant Web sites, and more—all in a matter of minutes.

PRIMIS CUSTOM PUBLISHING CASE OPTIONS

Through McGraw-Hill Ryerson's custom publishing division, **Primis**, instructors are able to select cases to accompany *Financial Accounting* in a number of ways. Create your own case set, or browse the selection of cases that correspond to the chapter material. Contact your McGraw-Hill Ryerson *i*Learning Sales Specialist for more information.

*i*LSS

Your **Integrated *i*Learning Sales Specialist** is a McGraw-Hill Ryerson representative who has the experience, product knowledge, training, and support to help you assess and integrate any of the above-noted products, technology, and services into your Financial Accounting course for optimum teaching and learning performance. Whether it's using our test bank software, helping your students improve their grades, or putting your entire course online, your *i*Learning Sales Specialist is there to help you do it. Contact your *i*Learning Sales Specialist today to learn how to maximize all of McGraw-Hill Ryerson's resources.

*i*LEARNING SERVICES PROGRAM

McGraw-Hill Ryerson offers a unique *i*Services package designed for Canadian faculty. Our mission is to equip providers of higher education with superior tools and resources required for excellence in teaching. For additional information, visit www.mcgrawhill.ca/highereducation/iservices.

Supplements for the Student

ONLINE LEARNING CENTRE

www.mcgrawhill.ca/college/libby
(See page xxv for details)
Multiple Choice, True/False Quizzes, Essay Questions, Flashcards, a searchable glossary, matching questions, up-to-date articles and more.

Chapter-Specific Online Supplements   Supplemental topics specific to chapter content are also included on the OLC, for instructors who wish to cover this material.

- *The Formal Recordkeeping System:* This appendix, supplemental for Chapters 2 to 4, describes and illustrates the use of the General Journal and General Ledger during the accounting period, the construction of the worksheet at year-end, and the use of reversing entries at the beginning of the next accounting period.

- *Comparison of the Direct and Indirect Methods of Preparing the Cash Flow from Operating Activities Section of the Cash Flow Statement:* For use in Chapter 5, this simplified example—both a mini-chapter and an illustrative Excel spreadsheet, illustrates the difference between the computation of cash flow from operating activities using two methods: the direct method and the indirect method.

- *Canadian Capital Markets:* To supplement Chapter 6, this document helps define capital markets and the role of capital markets in Canada.

- *Financial Instruments:* After reading this supplement to Chapter 10, students will understand the important differences among financial instruments.

- *Accounting for Goodwill and Other Intangible Assets:* For use with Chapter 9, this supplement explains how businesses generate goodwill and account for it over time.

- *Expanding the ROE Profit Driver Analysis: The Scott Formula:* To supplement Chapter 13. This expanded analysis of the ROE model provides additional insights into the operating, investing and financing activities of a business.

EXCEL TEMPLATES

These templates are tied to selected end-of-chapter material and are available on the OLC.

WORKING PAPERS

Contains all the forms necessary for completing end-of-chapter assignments.

MBA COMPANION

This supplement includes expended material on topics prominent in MBA-level programs, including leases and income taxes.

Acknowledgements

Writing and adapting a successful textbook requires a team effort and we have enjoyed working with excellent teammates. Throughout the process, many people stepped forward with tremendous efforts that allowed us to accomplish our goals. First and foremost, we are deeply indebted to Robert Libby, Patricia Libby, and Daniel Short, the authors of the U.S. text for developing the pedagogical approach used in this book. Their approach helped us tremendously in shaping this second Canadian edition. We would also like to recognize the devoted efforts of those who added their input to the development of this book. We received invaluable advice and suggestions during the revision process, and for this, we thank the following colleagues:

SECOND EDITION REVIEWERS

Teresa Anderson	University of Ottawa
Rick Bates	University of Guelph
Hilary Becker	Carleton University
Sandra Daga	University of Toronto
Greg Dunning	University of Windsor
Gerry Dupont	Carleton University
Dave Eliason	Southern Alberta Institute of Technology
Larry Goldsman	McGill University
Elizabeth Grasby	University of Western Ontario
Melissa Harty	University of Western Ontario
Ian Hutchinson	Acadia University
Heather Johnston	Brandon University
Hilary Johnston	Brandon University
Stuart Jones	University of Calgary
Duane Kennedy	University of Waterloo
Michael Konopaski	Trent University
Valorie Leonard	Laurentian University
Jingyu Li	Brock University
Marie Madill-Payne	George Brown College
Vanessa Magness	Ryerson University
David McConomy	Queen's University
Muriel McKenna	Seneca College
Cameron Morrill	University of Manitoba
Joe Pidutti	Durham College
Jo-Anne Ryan	Nipissing University
Mervat Saleh	Concordia University
Catherine Seguin	University of Toronto
Bob Sproule	University of Waterloo
Carol Tristani	Seneca College
Mike Welker	Queen's University
Elisa Zuliani	University of Toronto

FIRST EDITION REVIEWERS

Cecile Ashman	Algonquin College
Rick Bates	University of Guelph
David Carter	University of Waterloo
Don Drury	McGill University
Gary Dupont	Carleton University
Gary Entwistle	University of Saskatchewan
Leo Gallant	St. Francis Xavier University
Marilyn Glynn	Ryerson University
Mahlon Harvey	University of Winnipeg
David Herauf	Carleton University
David Hiscock	University of Waterloo
Stuart Jones	University of Calgary
Valorie Leonard	Laurentian University
Carol McKeen	Queen's University
Cameron Morrill	University of Manitoba
Fred Phillips	University of Saskatchewan
Lloyd Seguin	Wilfrid Laurier University
Mohamed Shehata	McMaster University
Chris Wright	Lakehead University

We have also received invaluable input an support through the years from present and former colleagues and students.

We are also indebted to the following individuals who helped adapt, critique, and shape the ancillary package for the Canadian market: Hilary M. Becker, Carleton University; Michael L Hockenstein, Vanier College; Ian Feltmate, Acadia University; Deborah Mortimer, University of Manitoba.

The extraordinary efforts of a talented group of individuals at McGraw-Hill Ryerson made all of this come together. We especially thank Nicole Lukach for her guidance throughout this project; Suzanne Simpson Millar, who worked tirelessly managing the whole process from the initial development stage until the final printing; Kelly Dickson, who managed the final production of this book; and all the marketing and sales people who helped bring this book to both instructors and students. We also thank all those who worked behind the scenes to ensure the successful completion of this book. Special thanks to Kelli Howey, who edited our work.

We thank Van Houtte Inc. and The Forzani Group Ltd. for permitting us to use their annual reports to provide students with real-world examples of financial statements and accompanying notes. We are also grateful to all the focus companies that allowed us to use excerpts from their financial statements.

Special thanks go to our families for their support, patience, and understanding while we worked on completing this second edition. We dedicate the book to them.

George Kanaan
Maureen Gowing

TO OUR STUDENT READERS

This book is aimed at two groups of readers:

1. *Future managers*, who will need to interpret and use financial statement information in business decisions.
2. *Future accountants*, who will prepare financial statements for those managers.

Future managers need a firm basis for using financial statement information in their careers in marketing, finance, banking, manufacturing, human resources, sales, information systems, or other areas of management. Future accountants need a solid foundation for further professional study.

Both managers and accountants must understand how to *use financial statements in making real business decisions* to perform their duties successfully. The best way to learn this is to study accounting in real business contexts. This is the key idea behind our *focus company approach*, which we introduce in the first chapter. Each chapter's material is integrated with a focus company, its decisions, and its financial statements. The focus companies are drawn from 10 different industries, providing you with a broad range of experience with realistic business

and financial accounting practices. In each chapter, *you will actually work with these real companies' statements* and those of additional contrast companies.

When you complete this book, you will be able to read and understand financial statements of real companies. We help you achieve this goal by:

1. Selecting learning objectives and content based on the way that seasoned managers use financial statements in modern businesses. *We emphasize the topics that count.*

2. Recognizing that students using this book have no previous exposure to accounting and financial statements and often little exposure to the business world. We take you through the financial statements three times at increasing levels of detail (in Chapter 1, Chapters 2 through 5, and Chapters 6 through 13). This is the secret to our *"building block approach."*

3. Helping you *"learn how to learn"* by teaching efficient and effective approaches for learning the material. Keep these learning hints in mind throughout.

4. Providing regular feedback in *Self-Study Quizzes*, which occur throughout each chapter. *Complete the quizzes before you move on.* Then check your answers against the solution provided at the end of the chapter. If you are still unclear about any of the answers, refer back to the chapter material before moving on.

5. Highlighting the *Key Terms* in bold print and repeating their definitions in the margins. You should pay special attention to the definitions of these terms and review them at the end of the chapter. A handy glossary is provided at the end of the book.

6. Introducing the *Key Financial Ratios* used to assess different elements of financial performance at the same time you are learning how to measure and report those elements. These will show you what kinds of accounting information managers use and how they interpret it.

At the end of each chapter, test what you have learned by working the Demonstration Cases. *Working problems is one of the keys* to learning accounting. Good luck in your first accounting course.

After studying this chapter, you should be able to:

1. Recognize the information conveyed in each of the four basic financial statements and how it is used by different decision makers (investors, creditors, and managers). p. 5

2. Identify the role of generally accepted accounting principles (GAAP) in determining the content of financial statements. p. 19

3. Distinguish the roles of managers and auditors in the accounting communication process. p. 21

4. Appreciate the importance of ethics, reputation, and legal liability in accounting. p. 23

Financial Statements and Business Decisions

In June 2004, Sleeman Breweries Ltd., a leading brewer and distributor of premium beer in Canada, purchased Unibroue Inc.—the largest microbrewery in Quebec—for $40 million. The price Sleeman paid was decided by considering the value of the economic resources owned by Unibroue, its debts to others, its ability to sell goods for more than the cost to produce them, and its ability to generate the cash necessary to pay its current bills. Much of this assessment was based on financial information that Unibroue provided to Sleeman in the form of financial statements.

FOCUS COMPANY:

Unibroue Inc.

VALUING AN ACQUISITION USING FINANCIAL STATEMENT INFORMATION

THE OBJECTIVES OF *FINANCIAL ACCOUNTING*

Determining the price that Sleeman was willing to pay for Unibroue is typical of the economic decisions that are made based on financial statements. Businesses use financial statements as the primary means to communicate financial information to parties outside the organization. The purpose of this text is to help you develop the ability to read and interpret financial statements of business organizations and understand the system that produces those statements. This book is aimed at two groups of readers: *future managers*, who will need to interpret and use financial statement information in business decisions, and *future accountants*, who will prepare financial statements for those managers. The book provides future managers with a firm basis for using financial statement information in their careers in marketing, finance, banking, manufacturing, human resources, sales, information systems, and other areas of management. It also provides future accountants with a solid foundation for further professional study.

Both managers and accountants must understand *financial statements* (what the statements tell you and what they do not tell you about a business enterprise), *business operations*, and *the use of financial statements in decision making* to perform their duties successfully. As a consequence, we integrate actual business practice in our discussions, starting with Chapter 1. We examine the fundamentals of financial accounting in a variety of business contexts relevant to your future careers. Each chapter's material is integrated around a *focus company* (in this chapter, Unibroue). The focus companies are drawn from 10 different industries, providing you with a broad range of experience with realistic business and financial accounting practices. When appropriate, the focus company's operations and financial statements are then compared to those of the *contrast companies*. When you complete this book, you will be able to read and understand financial statements of real companies.

The way that seasoned managers use financial statements in modern businesses has guided our selection of learning objectives and content. At the same time, our teaching approach recognizes that students using this book have no previous exposure to accounting and financial statements and often little exposure to the business world. The book also is aimed at helping you learn how to learn by teaching efficient and effective approaches for learning the material.

UNDERSTANDING THE BUSINESS

THE PLAYERS

Unibroue was founded in 1990 by André Dion and Serge Racine, who saw great potential in the craft beer market. These beers are produced and sold locally, and are often filtered but not pasteurized. Other mass produced beers are pasteurized and sold nationally and internationally. Predicting the rise in demand for craft beer, the founders started the company to produce specialty craft beer. They invested a major portion of their savings, becoming the sole owners of Unibroue Inc. As is common in new businesses, the founders also functioned as managers of the business (they were *owner-managers*).

In the spring of 1992, Unibroue marketed its first beer, Blanche de Chambly, which was well-received by consumers. As a result of their first success, the founders soon discovered that they needed additional money to develop their business. So they borrowed money from a local bank and other lenders, or *creditors,* and used the funds to expand the business by introducing new brands to the market, such as Maudite, La Fin du Monde, U2, and 2004. Unibroue's annual launching of new specialty beers helped the company grow its sales from $4.9 million in 1993 to $25.6 million in 2003. The company's success attracted the attention of its competitors. On April 20, 2004, Sleeman Breweries Ltd. announced its intention to buy Unibroue; Sleeman subsequently acquired the company in June 2004.

Investors—such as Sleeman, which bought an entire company, or individuals who buy small percentages of large corporations—make their purchases hoping to gain in two ways. They hope to receive a portion of what the company earns in the form of cash payments called *dividends,* and they hope to eventually sell their share of the company at a higher price than they paid.

THE BUSINESS OPERATIONS

To understand any company's financial statements, you must first understand its operations. As noted, Unibroue develops and markets specialty craft beers for personal consumption. Unibroue's beers are manufactured from natural ingredients including water, malted barley, malted or raw wheat, corn, spices, sugar, and yeast. Unibroue purchases some of these ingredients from other companies, referred to as *suppliers.* These ingredients are brewed into beer in a five-step process that starts with fermentation and proceeds to filtration/clarification, bottling and kegging, and, if necessary, refermentation in the bottle in a specially designed holding room.

Unibroue distributes its beers both through its own distribution network and through independent distributors. In 2003 its customers were large supermarket chains, such as Loblaws, convenience stores, cafés, and other licensed establishments.

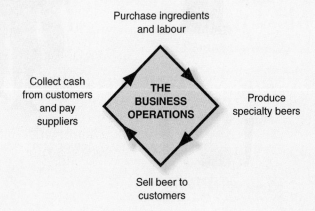

THE ACCOUNTING SYSTEM

Like all businesses, Unibroue has an **accounting** system that collects and processes financial information about an organization and reports that information to decision makers. Unibroue's managers (often called *internal decision makers*) and parties outside the firm such as the managers at Sleeman Breweries and the bank's loan officer (often called *external decision makers*) use reports produced by this system. Exhibit 1.1 outlines the two parts of the accounting system. Internal managers typically require continuous detailed information because they must plan and manage the day-to-day operations of the organization. Developing accounting information for internal decision makers is called *managerial* or *management accounting* and is the subject of a separate accounting course. The focus of this text is accounting for external decision makers, called *financial accounting*, and the four basic financial statements and related disclosures that are the output of that system.

We begin this process with a brief but comprehensive overview of the four basic financial statements and the people and organizations involved in their preparation and use. This overview provides you with a context in which you can learn the more detailed material that is presented in the following chapters. In particular, we focus on how two primary users of the statements, investors (owners) and creditors (lenders), relied on each of Unibroue's four basic financial statements in their decisions to invest in or lend money to Unibroue. Later in the chapter, we begin to discuss a broader

ACCOUNTING is a system that collects and processes (analyzes, measures, and records) financial information about an organization and reports that information to decision makers.

■ **LEARNING OBJECTIVE 1**

Recognize the information conveyed in each of the four basic financial statements and how it is used by different decision makers (investors, creditors, and managers).

EXHIBIT **1.1**

The Accounting System and Decision Makers

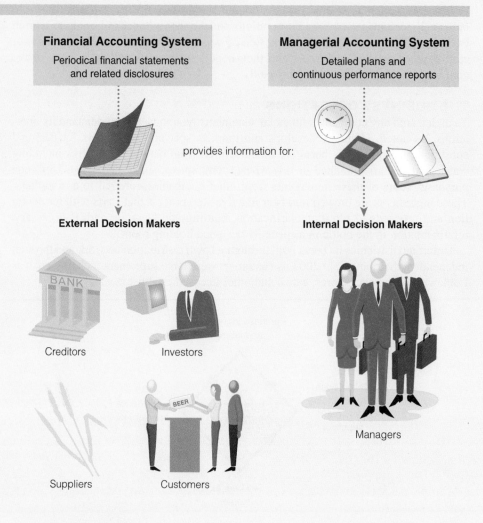

Financial Accounting System
Periodical financial statements and related disclosures

Managerial Accounting System
Detailed plans and continuous performance reports

provides information for:

External Decision Makers

Internal Decision Makers

Creditors

Investors

Suppliers

Customers

Managers

range of uses of financial statement data in marketing, management, human resources, and other business contexts.

To understand the way that Sleeman Breweries used Unibroue's financial statements in its decision, we must first understand what specific information is presented in the four basic financial statements for a company such as Unibroue.

We present many new business and financial statement terms in this chapter. Instead of trying to memorize the definitions of every term used in this chapter, focus your attention on learning the general structure and content of the statements. Specifically, you should focus on these questions:

1. What categories of items (often called *elements*) are reported on each of the four statements? (What type of information does a statement convey, and where can you find it?)

2. How are the elements within a statement related? These *relationships* are usually described by an equation that tells you how the elements fit together.

3. Why is each element important to managers', owners', or creditors' decisions? (How important is the information to decision makers?)

The *Self-Study Quizzes* that occur throughout the chapter will test your ability to answer these questions. Remember that since this chapter is an overview, each concept discussed in this chapter will be discussed again in Chapters 2 through 6.

ORGANIZATION OF THE CHAPTER

• **The Basic Financial Statements**
The Balance Sheet
The Income Statement
The Statement of Retained Earnings
The Cash Flow Statement
Relationships among the Statements
Notes

• **Using Financial Statements to Determine Unibroue's Value**
Determining Unibroue's Purchase Price

• **Responsibilities for the Accounting Communication Process**
Generally Accepted Accounting Principles (GAAP)
Management Responsibility and the Demand for Auditing
Ethics, Reputation, and Legal Liability

THE FOUR BASIC FINANCIAL STATEMENTS: AN OVERVIEW

The four basic financial statements include the *balance sheet,* the *income statement,* the *statement of retained earnings,* and the *cash flow statement.*[1] These are the basic statements normally prepared by profit-oriented corporations for use by investors, creditors, and other external decisions makers. They summarize the financial activities of the business. They can be prepared at any point in time and can apply to any time span (such as one year, one quarter, or one month). Like most companies, Unibroue prepares financial statements for investors and creditors at the end of each quarter (known as *quarterly reports*) and at the end of the year (known as *annual reports*).

The organization for which financial data are to be collected, called an **accounting entity**, must be precisely defined. The business entity itself, not the business owners, is viewed as owning the resources it uses and as owing its debts.

THE BALANCE SHEET

The purpose of the **balance sheet** is to report the financial position (amount of assets, liabilities, and shareholders' equity) of an accounting entity at a particular point in time. We can learn a lot about what the balance sheet reports just by reading the statement from the top. The balance sheet of Unibroue Inc. presented by its former owners to Sleeman Breweries is shown in Exhibit 1.2.

Structure   The *heading* of the balance sheet identifies four significant items related to the statement:

1. *name of the entity*—Unibroue Inc.
2. *title of the statement*—Balance Sheet
3. *specific date of the statement*—At December 31, 2003
4. *unit of measure*—(in thousands of dollars)

An **ACCOUNTING ENTITY** is the organization for which financial data are to be collected.

A **BALANCE SHEET (STATEMENT OF FINANCIAL POSITION)** reports the financial position (assets, liabilities, and shareholders' equity) of an accounting entity at a point in time.

---

[1]The income statement and the statement of retained earnings are sometimes combined into the statement of earnings and retained earnings.

EXHIBIT **1.2**

Balance Sheet

	UNIBROUE INC.	
	Balance Sheet	
	At December 31, 2003	
	(in thousands of dollars)	

amount of cash in the company's bank accounts
shares and treasury bills purchased with excess cash
amounts owed by customers from prior sales
ingredients and bottled but unsold beer
rent and insurance paid in advance
factories and production machinery
land on which the factories are built

Assets

Cash	$ 1,120
Short term investments	401
Accounts receivable	4,219
Inventories	3,800
Prepaid expenses	1,348
Plant and equipment	22,717
Land	550
Total assets	$34,155

amounts owed to suppliers for prior purchases
amount of taxes owed to the government
amounts owed on written debt contracts
liabilities that resulted from complex accounting rules

Liabilities

Accounts payable	$ 1,312	
Income taxes payable	310	
Notes payable	7,327	
Future income taxes	2,818	
Total liabilities		$11,767

amounts invested in the business by shareholders
past earnings not distributed to shareholders

Shareholders' Equity

Share capital	$ 9,238	
Retained earnings	13,150	
Total shareholders' equity		22,388
Total liabilities and shareholders' equity		$34,155

The notes are an integral part of these financial statements.
This balance sheet is an adaptation of Unibroue's actual balance sheet.

The balance sheet is like a financial snapshot indicating the entity's financial position *at a specific point in time*—in this case, December 31, 2003—which is stated clearly on the balance sheet. Financial reports are normally denominated in the currency of the country in which they are located, in this case Canadian dollars. Similarly, U.S. companies report in U.S. dollars and Mexican companies in Mexican pesos. Medium-sized companies often report in thousands of dollars; that is, they round the last three digits to the nearest thousand. The cash amount of $1,120 on Unibroue's balance sheet actually means $1,120,000.

Unibroue's balance sheet first lists the company's assets, followed by liabilities and shareholders' equity. Assets are economic resources legally controlled by the entity and financed either by creditors (which creates liabilities) or owners (which creates shareholders' equity). Because Unibroue is a corporation, its owners' equity is designated shareholders' equity.

BASIC ACCOUNTING EQUATION (BALANCE SHEET EQUATION):
Assets = Liabilities + Shareholders' Equity.

Since each asset must have a source of financing, a company's assets must, by definition, equal the sum of its liabilities and shareholders' equity.[2] The **basic accounting equation**, often called the **balance sheet equation**, is written as

---

[2]A corporation is a business that is incorporated under the federal or provincial laws. The owners are called *shareholders* or *stockholders*. Ownership is represented by shares of capital that usually can be bought and sold freely. The corporation operates as a separate legal entity, separate and apart from its owners. The shareholders enjoy limited liability; they are liable for the debts of the corporation only to the extent of their investments. Chapter Supplement A discusses forms of ownership in more detail.

Assets	=	**Liabilities + Shareholders' Equity**

Economic resources (e.g., cash, inventory)

Sources of financing for the economic resources
Liabilities: from creditors
Shareholders' Equity: from shareholders

The basic accounting equation shows what we mean when we refer to a company's *financial position:* the economic resources that the company owns and the sources of financing for those resources.

Elements   *Assets* are economic resources controlled by the entity as a result of past transactions and from which future economic benefits can be obtained. Unibroue's assets include seven major items. The exact items listed as assets on a company's balance sheet depend on the nature of its operations. The seven items listed by Unibroue are the economic resources needed to produce and sell beer to its customers. Each of these economic resources is expected to provide future benefits to the company. To prepare for the fermentation process, Unibroue first needed *cash* to purchase *land* on which to build manufacturing facilities and install production machinery (*buildings and equipment*). Unibroue needs to have insurance to protect its resources against potential losses; advance payment of any insurance premiums gave rise to *prepaid expenses*. Unibroue then began purchasing ingredients, which led to the balance assigned to *inventories*. When Unibroue sells its beers to supermarkets and convenience stores, it sells them on credit and receives promises to pay called *accounts receivable*, which are collected in cash later. When the amount of cash exceeds the company's needs in the near future, Unibroue invests the excess cash in *short-term investments* (e.g., shares issued by other companies).

Every asset on the balance sheet is initially measured at the total cost incurred to acquire it. For example, the balance sheet for Unibroue reports Land, $550; this is the amount paid (in thousands) for the land when it was acquired. Balance sheets do not generally show the amounts for which the assets could currently be sold.

Liabilities are the entity's obligations that result from past transactions. They arise primarily from the *purchase of goods or services* on credit and through *cash borrowings* to finance the business.

There are four types of liabilities listed on Unibroue's balance sheet. The accounts payable arise from the purchase of goods and services from suppliers on credit without a formal written contract (or note). The income taxes payable represent an amount due to the taxation authorities as a result of the company's profitable operations in 2003. The notes payable result from cash borrowings based on formal written debt contracts with lending institutions such as banks.

The term "future income taxes" arises because the governments that collect tax require companies to calculate their income tax using the federal and provincial tax laws instead of specific accounting standards. Future income taxes represent the amount that would be paid to the federal and provincial governments if they ceased to require a separate calculation of taxable income that differs from the accounting income that is reported in the income statement to other external users.

Shareholders' equity indicates the amount of financing provided by owners of the business and earnings. Shareholders' equity arises from two sources: (1) *share capital*, or the investment of cash and other assets in the business by the owners, and (2) *retained earnings*, or the amount of earnings reinvested in the business (and thus not distributed to shareholders in the form of dividends).

In Exhibit 1.2, the Shareholders' Equity section reports two items. Unibroue's shareholders invested a total of $9,238,000 in the business and received over 4 million shares of capital in exchange for their contributions. This is reported as share capital.[3] Unibroue's total earnings (or losses incurred) less all dividends paid to the shareholders since formation of the corporation equalled $13,150,000 and is reported as *retained earnings*. Total shareholders' equity is the sum of the proceeds received on issuing shares to owners plus the retained earnings.

FINANCIAL **ANALYSIS**

INTERPRETING ASSETS, LIABILITIES, AND SHAREHOLDERS' EQUITY ON THE BALANCE SHEET

Assessment of Unibroue assets was important to its creditors, and to its prospective investor, Sleeman Breweries, because assets provide a basis for judging whether the company has sufficient resources available to operate the business.

Sleeman Breweries was interested in Unibroue's debts because of its concern whether the company had sufficient sources of cash to pay its debts. Unibroue's debts were also relevant to its bankers' decisions to lend money to the company because existing creditors share the bankers' claims against Unibroue's assets. If a business does not pay its creditors, they may force the sale of assets sufficient to meet their claims. The sale of assets often fails to cover all of a company's debts, and some creditors may take a loss.

Unibroue's shareholders' equity or net worth is important to creditors because their claims legally come before those of owners. If Unibroue goes out of business and its assets are sold, the proceeds of that sale must be used to pay back creditors before the owners receive any money. Thus, creditors consider shareholders' equity a protective cushion.[4]

A Note on Format   A few additional formatting conventions are worth noting here. Assets are listed on the balance sheet by ease of conversion into cash. Liabilities are listed by their maturity (due date). Most financial statements include the monetary unit sign (in Canada, the $) beside the first dollar amount in a group of items (e.g., the cash amount in the assets). Also, it is common to place a single underline below the last item in a group before a total or subtotal (e.g., land). A dollar sign is also placed beside group totals (e.g., total assets) and a double underline below. The same conventions are followed in all four basic financial statements. We will discuss alternative balance sheet formats in more detail in Chapter 2.

SELF-STUDY **QUIZ 1-1**

1. Unibroue's *assets* are listed in one section and *liabilities* and *shareholders' equity* in another. Notice that the two sections balance in conformity with the basic accounting equation. In the following chapters, you will learn that the basic accounting equation is the basic building block for the entire accounting process. Your task here is to verify that the shareholders' equity of $22,388,000 is correct, using the numbers for assets and liabilities presented in Exhibit 1.2 and the basic accounting equation in the form

Assets − Liabilities = Shareholders' Equity

---

[3]It should be noted that the amounts in share capital on Unibroue's balance sheet did not change when Unibroue's shareholders sold their shares to Sleeman Breweries since the transaction did not involve an additional contribution of cash or other assets to Unibroue. This transaction, which took place between Unibroue's original owners and Sleeman, occurred outside of the accounting entity, Unibroue, and thus was not recorded by its accounting system.

[4]Case CP1–5 (p. 43) considers various possibilities when a company goes out of business.

2. Learning which items belong in each of the balance sheet categories is an important first step in understanding their meaning. Mark each balance sheet item in the following list as an asset (A), liability (L), or shareholders' equity (SE), without referring to Exhibit 1.2.

_____ Accounts payable

_____ Accounts receivable

_____ Cash

_____ Share capital

_____ Plant and equipment

_____ Inventories

_____ Land

_____ Notes payable

_____ Retained earnings

After you complete your answers, check them with the solutions on page 27. If you are unclear about any of the answers, you should refer back to the chapter material preceding the quiz before moving on.

THE INCOME STATEMENT

Structure The **income statement (statement of income, statement of earnings**, or **statement of operations)** reports the accountant's primary measure of performance of a business: revenues generated less expenses incurred during the accounting period. While the term *profit* is commonly used in our language for this measure of performance, accountants prefer to use the technical terms *net income* or *net earnings*. Unibroue's net income measures its success in selling beer for more than it cost to generate those sales.

A quick reading of Unibroue's income statement (Exhibit 1.3) provides an indication about its purpose and content. The heading of the income statement again identifies the name of the entity, the title of the statement, and the unit of measure used in the statement. Unlike the balance sheet, which reports financial information as of a certain date, the income statement reports information for a *specified period of time* (for the year ended December 31, 2003). The time period covered by the financial statements (one year in this case) is called an **accounting period**.

The **INCOME STATEMENT (STATEMENT OF INCOME, STATEMENT OF EARNINGS, STATEMENT OF OPERATIONS)** reports the revenues less the expenses of the accounting period.

The **ACCOUNTING PERIOD** is the time period covered by the financial statements.

EXHIBIT **1.3**

Income Statement

UNIBROUE INC.
Income Statement
For the Year Ended December 31, 2003
(in thousands of dollars)

Revenues			*name of the entity*
Sales revenue	$25,598		*title of the statement*
			accounting period
Total revenues		$25,598	*unit of measure*
Expenses			*revenue earned from sale of beer*
Cost of goods sold	15,443		*cost to produce the beer sold*
Selling, distribution, and market development			*expenses related to sales distribution and market*
expense	6,334		*development*
Administrative expense	1,345		*operating expenses not related to production*
Interest expense	736		*cost of using borrowed funds*
Total expenses		23,858	
Income before income taxes		1,740	
Income tax expense		596	*income taxes on the period's pretax income*
Net income		$1,144	

The notes are an integral part of these financial statements.
This income statement is an adaptation of Unibroue's actual income statement for 2003.

Notice that Unibroue's income statement has three major captions: revenues, expenses, and net income. The income statement equation that describes this relationship is

$$\text{Revenues} - \text{Expenses} = \text{Net Income}$$

Elements Companies earn *revenues* from the sale of goods or services to customers (in Unibroue's case, from the sale of beer). Revenues are normally reported on the income statement when the goods or services are sold to customers whether or not they have been paid for. Retail stores such as Wal-Mart or McDonald's often receive cash at the time of sale. However, when Unibroue sells its beer to supermarkets and convenience stores, it receives a promise of future payment called an *account receivable,* which is collected in cash at a later date. In either case, the business recognizes total sales (cash and credit) made during a specific accounting period as revenue for that period. Various terms are used in financial statements to describe different sources of revenue (e.g., provision of services, sale of goods, rental of property). Unibroue lists only one source, *sales revenue,* for beer delivered to customers.

Expenses represent the dollar amount of resources the entity used up, or consumed, to earn revenues during the period. Unibroue lists five items as expenses on the income statement. The *cost of goods sold* is the total cost to Unibroue to produce the beer delivered to customers during the year. These include the costs of ingredients used in production, wages paid to the factory workers, and even a portion of the cost of factories and equipment used to produce the goods that were sold (called *amortization*). *Selling expenses* include a variety of expenses such as the salaries of sales staff and expenses related to distribution of beer and the development of new markets. *Administrative expenses* also include many items such as the salaries of management personnel, plus other general costs of operating the company not directly related to production.

Unibroue also reported *interest expense,* which reflects the cost of using borrowed funds. Finally, as a corporation, Unibroue must pay income tax based on pretax income. Unibroue's income tax expense is approximately 34 percent of its pretax income.

Expenses may require the immediate payment of cash, a payment of cash at a future date, or the use of some other resource such as an inventory item that may have been paid for in a previous period. For accounting purposes, the expense reported in one accounting period may actually be paid for in another accounting period. Nevertheless, the company recognizes all expenses (cash and credit) incurred during a specific accounting period regardless of the timing of the cash payment. For example, let us assume that Unibroue owes $50,000 in sales commissions to salespeople who sold beer to supermarkets in December 2003, but did not pay the $50,000 until January 2004. In this case, the sales commissions would be recognized as expenses for the accounting period ending on December 31, 2003, because during December 2003 the salespeople exerted the efforts that resulted in commissions for their success at selling beer.

Net income or net earnings (often called *profit* or *the bottom line*) is the excess of total revenues over total expenses. If total expenses exceed total revenues, a net loss is reported. (Net losses are normally noted by parentheses around the income figure.) When revenues and expenses are equal for the period, the business has operated at breakeven.

We noted earlier that revenues are not necessarily the same as collections from customers and expenses are not necessarily the same as payments to suppliers. As a result, net income normally does not equal the net cash generated by operations. This latter amount is reported on the cash flow statement discussed later in the chapter.

FINANCIAL **ANALYSIS**

ANALYZING THE INCOME STATEMENT: BEYOND THE BOTTOM LINE

Investors such as Sleeman and creditors closely monitor a firm's net income because it indicates the firm's ability to sell goods and services for more than they cost to produce and deliver. Investors buy the company's shares when they believe that future earnings will improve and lead to a higher share price. Lenders also rely on future earnings to provide the resources to repay loans. The details of the statement also are important. For example, Unibroue had to sell more than $25 million worth of beer to make just over $1 million. The beer industry is very competitive. If a competitor were to lower prices just 10 percent, forcing Unibroue to do the same, or if Unibroue had to triple market development to catch up to a competitor, its net income could easily turn into a net loss. These factors and others help investors and creditors estimate the company's future earnings.

SELF-STUDY **QUIZ 1-2**

1. Learning which items belong in each of the income statement categories is an important first step in understanding their meaning. Mark each income statement item in the following list as a revenue (R) or an expense (E) without referring to Exhibit 1.3.

   _____ Cost of goods sold   _____ Sales

   _____ Administrative   _____ Selling and distribution

2. During the year 2003, Unibroue delivered beer to customers for which the customers paid or promised to pay in the future amounts totalling $25,598,000. During the same year, it collected $25,270,000 in cash from its customers. Without referring to Exhibit 1.3, indicate which of the two numbers will be shown on Unibroue's income statement as *sales revenue* for 2003. Explain.

3. During the year 2003, Unibroue *produced* beer with a total cost of production of $15,115,000. During the same year, it *delivered* to customers beer that had cost a total of $15,443,000 to produce. Without referring to Exhibit 1.3, indicate which of the two numbers will be shown on Unibroue's income statement as *cost of goods sold* for 2003. Explain.

After you complete your answers, check them with the solutions on page 27.

THE STATEMENT OF RETAINED EARNINGS

Structure   Unibroue prepares a separate **statement of retained earnings**, shown in Exhibit 1.4. The heading identifies the name of the entity, the title of the statement, and the unit of measure used. Like the income statement, the statement of retained earnings covers a specific period of time (the accounting period), which in this case is one year. The statement of retained earnings reports the way that net income and the distribution of dividends affected the company's financial position during the accounting period. Net income earned during the year increases the balance of retained earnings. The declaration of dividends to the shareholders decreases retained earnings.[5] The retained earnings equation that describes these relationships is

Beginning Retained Earnings + Net Income − Dividends = Ending Retained Earnings

The **STATEMENT OF RETAINED EARNINGS** reports the way that net income and the distribution of dividends affected the financial position of the company during the accounting period.

---

[5]Net losses are subtracted. The complete process of declaring and paying dividends is discussed in a later chapter.

EXHIBIT **1.4**

Statement of Retained Earnings

name of the entity
title of the statement
accounting period
unit of measure

last period ending retained earnings
net income reported on the income statement
dividends declared during the period
ending retained earnings on the balance sheet

UNIBROUE INC.	
Statement of Retained Earnings	
For the Year Ended December 31, 2003	
(in thousands of dollars)	
Retained earnings, January 1, 2003	$12,506
Net income for 2003	1,144
Dividends for 2003	(500)
Retained earnings, December 31, 2003	$13,150

The notes are an integral part of these financial statements.
This statement is an adaptation of Unibroue's actual statement of retained earnings for 2003.

Elements   The statement begins with Unibroue's retained earnings at January 1, 2003 (the beginning of the accounting period). The net income reported on the income statement for the current period is added and dividends declared during the year are subtracted from this amount. During 2003, Unibroue earned $1,144,000, as shown in Exhibit 1.3. Also during 2003, Unibroue declared and paid a total of $500,000 in dividends to its shareholders.[6] The net result is that retained earnings at December 31, 2003 (the end of the accounting period) increased by $644,000 (= $1,144,000 − $500,000), or the portion of net income reinvested in the business.

The ending retained earnings amount of $13,150,000 is the same as that reported in Exhibit 1.2 on Unibroue's balance sheet. Thus, the statement of retained earnings shows the relationship between the income statement and the balance sheet.

FINANCIAL **ANALYSIS**

INTERPRETING RETAINED EARNINGS

Reinvestment of earnings, or retained earnings, is an important source of financing for Unibroue, representing more than one-third of its financing. Creditors closely monitor a firm's statement of retained earnings because the firm's policy on dividend payments to its shareholders affects its ability to repay its debts. Every dollar Unibroue pays to shareholders as a dividend is not available for use in paying back its debt to creditors. Investors examine retained earnings to determine whether the company is reinvesting a sufficient portion of earnings to support future growth.

THE CASH FLOW STATEMENT

Structure   Unibroue's cash flow statement is presented in Exhibit 1.5. The cash flow statement divides Unibroue's cash inflows (receipts) and outflows (payments) into three primary categories of cash flows in a typical business: cash flows from operating, investing, and financing activities. The heading identifies the name of the entity, the title of the statement, and the unit of measure used. Like the income statement, the cash flow statement covers a specified period of time (the accounting period), which in this case is one year.

As discussed earlier in this chapter, reported revenues do not always equal cash collected from customers because some sales may be on credit. Also, expenses reported on the income statement may not be equal to the cash paid out during the period

---

[6]Unibroue did not declare dividends since its formation, preferring to reinvest earnings in the business in order to sustain its growth. Nevertheless, we assume that dividends were declared in 2003 for illustrative purposes.

EXHIBIT **1.5**

Cash Flow Statement

UNIBROUE INC.		
Cash Flow Statement		
For the Year Ended December 31, 2003		
(in thousands of dollars)		
Cash flows from operating activities		
Cash collected from customers	$25,270	
Cash paid to suppliers and employees	(22,329)	
Cash paid for interest	(422)	
Cash paid for taxes	(41)	
Net cash flow from operating activities		$ 2,478
Cash flows from investing activities		
Cash paid to purchase short-term investment	(401)	
Cash paid to purchase manufacturing equipment	$ (1,694)	
Net cash flow from investing activities		(2,095)
Cash flows from financing activities		
Repayment of notes payable	$ (1,063)	
Cash paid for dividends	(500)	
Net cash flow from financing activities		(1,563)
Net decrease in cash during the year		$ (1,180)
Cash at beginning of year		2,300
Cash at end of year		$ 1,120

name of the entity
title of the statement
accounting period
unit of measure
directly related to earning income

purchase/sale of productive assets

from investors and creditors

change in cash during the period
last period's ending cash balance
ending cash on the balance sheet

The notes are an integral part of these financial statements.
This statement is an adaptation of Unibroue's actual cash flow statement for 2003.

because expenses may be incurred in one period and paid for in another. As a result, net income (revenues minus expenses) does *not* usually equal the amount of cash received minus the amount paid during the period. Because the income statement does not provide any information concerning cash flows, accountants prepare the **cash flow statement** to report inflows and outflows of cash.

The cash flow statement equation describes the causes of the change in cash reported on the balance sheet from the end of the last period to the end of the current period:

> **Change in Cash = Cash Flows from Operating Activities**
> **+ Cash Flows from Investing Activities**
> **+ Cash Flows from Financing Activities**

Note that each of the three cash flow sources can be positive or negative.

Elements *Cash flows from operating activities* are cash flows that are directly related to earning income. For example, when Loblaws and other customers pay Unibroue for the beer it has delivered to them, Unibroue lists the amounts collected as cash collected from customers. When Unibroue pays salaries to its salespeople or pays bills received from suppliers of malted barley or corn, it includes the amounts in cash paid to suppliers and employees.[7]

Cash flows from investing activities include cash flows related to the acquisition or sale of the company's productive assets. This year, Unibroue had two cash outflows for investing activities: the purchase of additional manufacturing equipment to meet the growing demand for its beer, and the purchase of short-term investments. *Cash flows from financing activities* are directly related to the financing of the company itself. They involve both receipts and payments of cash to investors and creditors (except for suppliers). This year, Unibroue paid $1,063,000 on notes payable, and $500,000 in dividends to the company's shareholders.

The **CASH FLOW STATEMENT** reports cash inflows and outflows that are related to operating, investing, and financing activities during the accounting period.

---

[7]Alternative ways to present cash flows from operating activities are discussed in Chapter 5.

FINANCIAL **ANALYSIS**

INTERPRETING THE CASH FLOW STATEMENT

Many analysts believe that the cash flow statement is particularly useful for predicting future cash flows that may be available for payment of debt to creditors and dividends to investors. Bankers often consider the Operating Activities section to be most important because it indicates the company's ability to generate cash from sales to meet its current cash needs. Any amount left can be used to repay the bank debt or expand the company.

Shareholders will invest in a company if they believe that it will eventually generate more cash from operations than it uses so that cash will become available to pay dividends and to expand. The Investing Activities section shows that Unibroue has made heavy investments in new manufacturing capacity, a good sign if demand continues to increase. The Financing Activities section indicates that Unibroue was able to pay dividends to shareholders and repay part of its notes payable because it generated cash from operating activities.

SELF-STUDY **QUIZ 1-3**

1. During the year 2003, Unibroue delivered beer to customers that paid or promised to pay in the future amounts totalling $25,598,000. During the same year, it collected $25,270,000 in cash from its customers. Without referring to Exhibit 1.5, indicate which of the two numbers will be shown on Unibroue's cash flow statement for 2003.

2. Learning which items belong in each cash flow statement category is an important first step in understanding their meaning. Mark each item in the following list as a cash flow from operating activities (O), investing activities (I), or financing activities (F), without referring to Exhibit 1.5. Also place parentheses around the letter only if it is a cash *outflow*.

    _____ Cash paid for dividends

    _____ Cash paid for interest

    _____ Cash received from bank loan

    _____ Cash paid for taxes

    _____ Cash paid to purchase manufacturing equipment

    _____ Cash paid to suppliers and employees

    _____ Cash collected from customers

After you complete your answers, check them with the solutions on page 27.

RELATIONSHIPS AMONG THE STATEMENTS

Our discussion of the four basic financial statements focused on the different elements reported in the statements, how the elements are related through the equation for each statement, and how the elements are important to the decisions of investors, creditors, and other external users. We have also discovered how the statements, all of which are outputs from the same system, are related to one another. In particular, we learned that:

1. Net income from the income statement results in an increase in ending retained earnings on the statement of retained earnings.

2. Ending retained earnings from the statement of retained earnings is one of the two components of shareholders' equity on the balance sheet.

3. The change in cash on the cash flow statement added to the cash balance at the beginning of the year equals the balance of cash at the end of the year, which appears on the balance sheet.

Thus, as external users, we can think of the income statement as explaining, through the statement of retained earnings, how the operations of the company improved its

EXHIBIT **1.6**

Relationships among Unibroue's Statements

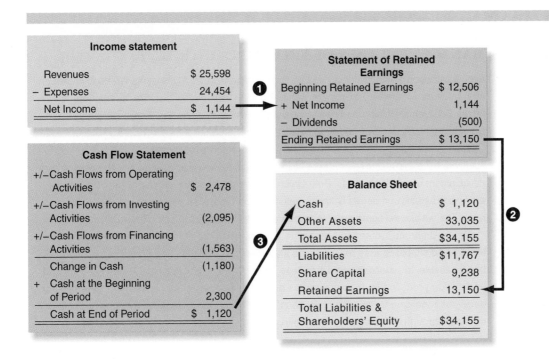

financial position during the year. The cash flow statement explains how the operating, investing, and financing activities of the company affected the cash balance on the balance sheet during the year. These relationships are illustrated in Exhibit 1.6 for Unibroue's financial statements.

NOTES

At the bottom of each of Unibroue's four basic financial statements is this statement: *"The notes are an integral part of these financial statements."* This is the accounting equivalent of the warning on a package of cigarettes. It warns users that failure to read the **notes** (or **footnotes**) to these financial statements will result in an incomplete picture of the company's financial health. Notes provide supplemental information about the financial condition of a company, without which the financial statements cannot be fully understood.

There are three basic types of notes. The first type provides descriptions of the accounting rules applied in the company's statements. The second presents additional detail about a line on the financial statements. For example, Unibroue's inventory note indicates the costs of ingredients, beer that is in the process of being fermented, and bottled beer that is ready for sale to customers. The third type of note presents additional financial disclosures about items not listed on the statements themselves. For example, Unibroue leases one of its production facilities; terms of the lease are disclosed in a note. We will discuss many note disclosures throughout the book because understanding their content is critical to understanding the company.[8]

NOTES (FOOTNOTES) provide supplemental information about the financial condition of a company, without which the financial statements cannot be fully understood.

---

[8]The four basic financial statements and related notes are part of more elaborate documents called *annual reports* that are produced by public companies. Annual reports are normally split into two sections. The first section is a non-financial section that usually includes a letter to shareholders from the chairperson of the company's board of directors and the chief executive officer; descriptions of the company's management philosophy, products, its successes (and occasionally its failures); exciting prospects and challenges for the future; as well as beautiful photographs of products, facilities, and personnel.

The second section includes the core of the report. The principal components of this financial section include summarized financial data for 5 or 10 years, management's discussion and analysis of the company's financial condition and results of operations, the four financial statements and related notes, the auditor's report, recent stock price information, a summary of quarterly financial data, and a list of directors and officers of the company.

FINANCIAL **ANALYSIS**

MANAGEMENT USES OF FINANCIAL STATEMENTS

In our discussion of financial analysis thus far, we have focused on the perspectives of *investors* and *creditors*. In addition, managers within the firm often make direct use of financial statements. For example, Unibroue's *marketing managers* and *credit managers* use customers' financial statements to decide whether to extend credit to them for their purchases of bottled beer. Unibroue's *purchasing managers* analyze financial statements of suppliers to judge whether the suppliers have the resources to meet Unibroue's demand for ingredients and to invest in the development of new ingredients. Both Unibroue's *human resource managers* and the *employees' union* use the company's financial statements as a basis for contract negotiations over pay rates. The net income figure even serves as a basis for computing employees' *bonuses*.

When Unibroue's managers examine the financial statements of the company's customers and suppliers, they rely on these statements as the best source of financial information available to external users because they do not have access to internal financial information produced by their customers and suppliers. However, when they make internal decisions regarding Unibroue's operations, they rely on more detailed financial information obtained through the company's managerial accounting system.

USING FINANCIAL STATEMENTS TO DETERMINE UNIBROUE'S VALUE

DETERMINING UNIBROUE'S PURCHASE PRICE

Even at this early stage of your study of accounting, we can illustrate part of the process Sleeman Breweries went through to determine the price it was willing to pay for Unibroue Inc. The price Sleeman paid was decided by considering a variety of factors, including the value of Unibroue's assets, its debts to others, its ability to sell goods for more than their production cost, and its ability to generate the cash necessary to pay its current bills. These factors are the subject matter of the balance sheet, income statement, and cash flow statement.

One method for estimating the value of a company is with a *price/earnings ratio* (or *P/E ratio* or *P/E multiple*). The P/E ratio measures the multiple of current year's earnings that investors are willing to pay for the company's shares. All other things being equal, a high P/E ratio means that investors have confidence in the company's ability to produce higher profits in future years. As in the Unibroue case, competitors' P/E ratios often serve as a starting point in analyzing the price that should be paid for a company or its shares.

A key to Sleeman's decision to buy Unibroue was the fact that other companies in the same industry with similar performance and past growth were selling for 18 times their current year's earnings. Accordingly, the price Sleeman paid could be determined using the following computation:

$$\text{Price/Earnings Ratio} = \frac{\text{Market Price}}{\text{Net Income}}$$

$$
\begin{aligned}
\text{Market (Purchase) Price} &= \text{P/E Ratio} \times \text{Net Income} \\
&= 18 \times \text{Net Income} \\
&= 18 \times \$1,144,000 \\
&= \$20,592,000
\end{aligned}
$$

The price that Sleeman paid to acquire Unibroue—$40 million—is much higher than the price suggested by the above formula. In some cases, companies are willing to pay a higher amount in order to acquire special assets that are valuable to the acquiring company. In this case, Sleeman had been looking for a Québec foothold for some time. The acquisition of Unibroue, which has a loyal customer base for its European-style beers, gives Sleeman a significant manufacturing presence in Québec, the country's second largest beer market. Sleeman paid more than 18 times last year's earnings because they believe that this acquisition will improve Unibroue's earnings in future years.

A difficult part of this analysis is deciding what price/earnings multiplier is appropriate for this situation. Sleeman carefully considered this issue, and its analysis involved more than this simple formula. However, the P/E ratio provides an estimation of the market value of Unibroue's net assets.[9]

RESPONSIBILITIES FOR THE ACCOUNTING COMMUNICATION PROCESS

Effective communication means that the recipient understands what the sender intends to convey. For the decision makers at Sleeman to use the information in Unibroue's financial statements effectively, they had to understand what information each statement conveys.

They also needed to know that the amounts reported in the statements fairly represent what is claimed. Financial statements that do not represent what they claim to are meaningless and cannot be used effectively to make decisions. For example, if the balance sheet lists $2,000,000 for a factory that does not exist, that part of the statement does not convey useful information.

Decision makers also needed to understand the *measurement rules* applied in computing the numbers on the statements. A swim coach would never try to evaluate a swimmer's time in the "100 freestyle" without first asking if the time was for a race in metres or in yards. Likewise, a decision maker should never attempt to use accounting information without first understanding the measurement rules that were used to develop the information. These measurement rules are called **generally accepted accounting principles**, or **GAAP**. These encompass not only specific rules, practices, and procedures relating to particular circumstances, but also broad principles and conventions of general application.

GENERALLY ACCEPTED ACCOUNTING PRINCIPLES (GAAP)

How Are Generally Accepted Accounting Principles Determined? The accounting system that we use today has a long history. Its foundations are normally traced back to the works of an Italian monk and mathematician, Fr. Luca Pacioli. In 1494, he described an approach developed by Italian merchants to account for their activities as owner-managers of business ventures. Many others wrote works on accounting after Pacioli, but prior to 1933, each company's management largely determined its financial reporting practices. Thus, little uniformity in practice existed among companies.

Following the dramatic stock market decline of 1929, the Securities Act of 1933 and The Securities Exchange Act of 1934 were passed into law by the U.S. Congress. These acts created the **Securities and Exchange Commission (SEC)** and gave it broad powers to determine the measurement rules for financial statements that companies must provide to shareholders. In Canada, provincial securities legislation created securities commissions, most notably the **Ontario Securities Commission (OSC)**, to regulate the flow of financial information provided by publicly traded companies whose shares trade on Canadian stock exchanges, such as the Toronto Stock Exchange. Similar to the SEC, the OSC plays an influential role in promoting sound accounting practices by publicly traded companies.

Since their establishment, these securities commissions have worked with organizations of professional accountants to establish groups that are given the primary responsibilities to work out the detailed rules that become generally accepted accounting

■ **LEARNING OBJECTIVE 2**
Identify the role of generally accepted accounting principles (GAAP) in determining the content of financial statements.

GENERALLY ACCEPTED ACCOUNTING PRINCIPLES (GAAP) are the measurement rules used to develop the information in financial statements.

The **SECURITIES AND EXCHANGE COMMISSION (SEC)** is the U.S. government agency that determines the financial statements that public companies must provide to shareholders and the measurement rules that they must use in producing those statements.

The **ONTARIO SECURITIES COMMISSION (OSC)** is the most influential Canadian regulator of the flow of financial information provided by publicly traded companies in Canada.

---

[9]The role of net income in determining the value of a company will be discussed in more detail in your corporate finance course and more advanced courses in financial statement analysis. See, for example, K.R. Palepu, P.M. Healy, and V.B. Bernard, *Business Analysis and Valuation*. Cincinnati, OH: South-Western, 2000, Chapter 11.

The **ACCOUNTING STANDARDS BOARD (AcSB)** is the private-sector body given the primary responsibility to work out the detailed rules that become accepted accounting standards.

principles. The current Canadian group that has this responsibility is the **Accounting Standards Board (AcSB)** of the Canadian Institute of Chartered Accountants. The AcSB is responsible for establishing standards of accounting and reporting by Canadian companies and not-for-profit organizations. These standards or recommendations, which are published in the *CICA Handbook*, have expanded over time because of the increasing diversity and complexity of current business practices.

Most managers do not need to learn all of the details included in these standards. Our approach is to focus on those details that have the *greatest impact on the numbers presented in financial statements* and are appropriate for an introductory course.

Why Is GAAP Important to Managers and External Users? Generally accepted accounting principles (GAAP) are of great interest to the companies that must prepare the statements and to the readers of these statements. GAAP provide guidance to companies in selecting the accounting methods that best reflect the results of their operations and financial situation. At the same time, generally accepted accounting methods help prevent managers from deliberately manipulating income figures that serve their interests by using accounting practices that are not in conformity with GAAP. Widely divergent accounting practices reduce the comparability of financial information produced by different companies; hence, GAAP limits the number of acceptable alternative accounting methods in order to enhance the comparability of financial information across companies and over time. Furthermore, understanding GAAP enables external users to assess the quality of the information presented in the financial statements and related notes.

Companies and their managers and owners are most directly affected by the information presented in the financial statements. Companies incur the cost of preparing the statements and bear the major economic consequences of their publication. These economic consequences include, among others:

1. effects on the selling price of a company's shares.
2. effects on the amount of bonuses received by management and employees.
3. loss of competitive advantage over other companies.

Recall that the amount that Sleeman was willing to pay to purchase Unibroue was determined in part by net income computed in accordance with GAAP. This presents the possibility that changes in accounting standards can affect the price buyers are willing to pay for companies.

Employees who receive part of their pay based on reaching stated targets for net income are directly concerned with any changes in how net income is computed. Managers and owners often are concerned that publishing more information in financial statements will give away trade secrets to other companies that compete with them. As a consequence of these and other concerns, changes in accounting standards are actively debated, political lobbying often takes place, and the accounting standards that are eventually issued are often a compromise among the wishes of interested parties.

INTERNATIONAL PERSPECTIVE

REAL WORLD EXCERPT

Telus

ANNUAL REPORT

ARE GENERALLY ACCEPTED ACCOUNTING PRINCIPLES SIMILAR IN OTHER COUNTRIES?

While businesspeople compete in a single global economy, different sets of generally accepted accounting principles have developed within particular countries. Differences in political, cultural, and economic histories have produced a great number of cross-national differences in practice. These differences do affect the numbers presented in the financial statements. For example, Telus Corporation, the second largest Canadian provider of telecommunication products and services, is required to prepare two sets of financial statements in compliance with both Canadian and U.S. accounting rules because its shares are traded on Canadian and U.S. stock exchanges. Since Canadian and U.S. accounting rules differ with respect to measuring and reporting certain business transactions, the two sets of Telus's financial statements, which summarize the same business transactions, provide different financial results. The annual report of Telus for the year 2003 included the following:

Years ended December 31 (millions)	2003	2002
Net income (loss) in accordance with Canadian GAAP	$331.5	$ (229.0)
Net income (loss) in accordance with U.S. GAAP	329.0	(1,925.9)

Telus's net income (loss) for the years 2002 and 2003 is not the same under Canadian and U.S. GAAP because the accounting rule makers have produced different sets of generally accepted accounting standards that are commensurate with the legal, political, economic, and business environments in these two countries. You will discover in later chapters that accounting is not an exact science and that generally accepted accounting principles can lead to different sets of standards that can, in practice, produce different sets of financial statements.

The International Accounting Standards Committee (IASC) and others are attempting to eliminate these differences. But currently, managers and users of financial statements who cross national borders must be aware of the specific nature of these reporting differences to interpret financial statements successfully. Although our primary focus is on Canadian GAAP, we briefly discuss practice in other countries when appropriate.

MANAGEMENT RESPONSIBILITY AND THE DEMAND FOR AUDITING

Who is responsible for the accuracy of the numbers in Unibroue's financial statements? Two documents taken from Unibroue's annual report provide us with much of the answer to this question.

The **report of management**, shown in Exhibit 1.7, makes two points clear. First, primary responsibility for the information in the financial statements lies with management, as represented by the highest officer of the company and its highest financial

■ **LEARNING OBJECTIVE 3**

Distinguish the roles of managers and auditors in the accounting communication process.

EXHIBIT **1.7**

Report of Management

REAL WORLD EXCERPT

Unibroue Inc.

ANNUAL REPORT

Management's Report Concerning Financial Statements

Unibroue Inc.'s consolidated financial statements and the financial information included in this annual report are the responsibility of management. These financial statements have been prepared in accordance with generally accepted accounting principles in Canada and have been approved by the Board of Directors.

Unibroue Inc. maintains accounting and internal control systems which, in the opinion of management, ensure the reasonable accuracy of the financial information as well as the orderly and efficient conduct of the company's business.

Mainly through its Audit Committee, the Board of Directors assumes its responsibilities regarding the financial statements found in this annual report. This Committee which holds annual meetings with management and the external auditors has reviewed the financial statements of Unibroue Inc. and has recommended their approval by the Board of Directors.

The attached financial statements have been audited by the Chartered Accountants Raymond Chabot Grant Thornton, General Partnership.

André Dion, FCA
Chairman of the Board, President
and Chief Executive Officer

The **REPORT OF MANAGEMENT** indicates management's primary responsibility for financial statement information and the steps to ensure the accuracy of the company's records.

The **AUDIT REPORT (REPORT OF INDEPENDENT AUDITORS)** describes the auditors' opinion of the fairness of the financial statement presentations and the evidence gathered to support that opinion.

officer. Second, the managers take three important steps to ensure the accuracy of the company's records: (1) they maintain a system of controls over both the records and the assets of the company, (2) they hire outside independent auditors to attest to the fairness of the statement presentations, and (3) they form a committee of the board of directors to review these two safeguards. These safeguards are listed in the report of management.

The role of the independent auditor is described in more detail in the **audit report**, or **report of independent auditors** (Exhibit 1.8). The **audit report** describes the auditor's opinion of the fairness of the financial statement presentations and the evidence gathered to support that opinion. It is important to note that the main difference between the report of management and the report of the independent auditors concerns the responsibility for the financial information included in the company's annual report. As the report of the independent auditors indicates, the auditor's responsibility is to express an opinion on the Unibroue financial statements that have been prepared by its accounting personnel and reviewed by the *audit committee* of the *board of directors* that assumes responsibility for these financial statements.

In Canada, an accountant may be licensed as a *Chartered Accountant* (CA), a *Certified General Accountant* (CGA), or a *Certified Management Accountant* (CMA). These accounting designations are granted by the respective professional accounting organizations on completion of specific educational programs and experience requirements.[10] Professional accountants can offer various accounting services to the public, but only CAs and CGAs (in most Canadian provinces[11]) are permitted to issue audit reports of

EXHIBIT 1.8

Auditors' Report

REAL WORLD EXCERPT

Unibroue Inc.

ANNUAL REPORT

Auditors' Report to the Shareholders of Unibroue Inc.

We have audited the consolidated balance sheets of Unibroue Inc. as at December 31, 2003 and 2002, and the consolidated statements of earnings and retained earnings, and of cash flows for the years then ended. These financial statements are the responsibility of the Company's management. Our responsibility is to express an opinion on these financial statements based on our audits.

We conducted our audits in accordance with Canadian generally accepted auditing standards. Those standards require that we plan and perform an audit to obtain reasonable assurance whether the financial statements are free of material misstatement. An audit includes examining, on a test basis, evidence supporting the amounts and disclosures on the financial statements. An audit also includes assessing the accounting principles used and significant estimates made by management, as well as evaluating the overall financial statement presentation.

In our opinion, these consolidated financial statements present fairly, in all material respects, the financial position of the company at December 31, 2003 and 2002, and the results of its operations and its cash flows for the years then ended, in conformity with Canadian generally accepted accounting principles.

Raymond Chabot Grant Thornton
General Partnership
Chartered Accountants

---

[10]Refer to the following Web sites for details of the educational and experience requirements for the respective designations:

Chartered Accountant: www.cica.ca
Certified General Accountant: www.cga-canada.org
Certified Management Accountant: www.cma-canada.org

[11]At the date of publication of this book, CGAs were not permitted to perform audits in the provinces of Nova Scotia and Prince Edward Island, and had limited audit rights in Québec. In British Columbia, CMAs are permitted to do assurance audits upon successful application to the Audit Certification Board.

publicly traded companies because they have certain responsibilities that extend to the general public as well as to the specific business that pays for their services.

An **audit** involves the examination of the financial reports (prepared by the management of the entity) to ensure that they represent what they claim and conform with GAAP. In performing an audit, the independent auditor examines the underlying transactions and the accounting methods used to account for these transactions. Because of the enormous number of transactions involving a major enterprise such as Wal-Mart that total billions of dollars each year, the auditor does not examine each transaction. Rather, professional approaches are used to ascertain beyond reasonable doubt that transactions were measured and reported properly.

Many unintentional and intentional opportunities exist for managers to prepare misleading financial reports. An audit performed by an independent auditor is the best protection available to the public. When that protection fails, however, the independent auditor is sometimes found liable for losses incurred by those who rely on the statements. You can learn more about auditing and other information assurance services in auditing courses.

> An **AUDIT** is an examination of the financial reports to ensure that they represent what they claim and conform with generally accepted accounting principles.

ETHICS, REPUTATION, AND LEGAL LIABILITY

If financial statements are to be of any value to decision makers, users must have confidence in the fairness of the information. These users will have greater confidence in the information if they know that the people who were associated with auditing the financial statements were required to meet professional standards of ethics and competence.

The three Canadian professional accounting organizations require all of their members to adhere to professional codes of ethics. These broad principles are supported by specific rules that govern the performance of audits by members of these organizations. These organizations stress how important it is for each member to behave in ways that enhance the reputation of the profession by voluntarily complying with ethical codes. For example, the Canadian Institute of Chartered Accountants places ethical behaviour and professionalism as the most important of the pervasive competencies possessed by its members.[12] The Certified General Accountants Association of Canada notes in its *Code of Ethical Principles and Rules of Conduct* that an accountant's actions will have an influence not only on the welfare of society but also on that of the profession.[13] The Society of Management Accountants of Canada has also issued a few publications related to ethical conduct, such as *Codes of Ethics, Practice and Conduct* and *Implementing Ethics Strategies within Organizations.*[14] Failure to comply with professional rules of conduct can result in serious penalties for professional accountants, including rescinding the professional designation of an offending member. The potential economic effects of damage to reputation and malpractice liability, however, provide even stronger incentives to abide by professional standards. Thus, the profession recognizes that its members' reputations for ethical conduct and competence are their most important assets.

Financial statements fraud is a fairly rare event, due in part to the diligent efforts of practising professional accountants. In fact, many such frauds are first identified by the firm's accounting staff or its external auditors who advise regulatory authorities of possible wrongdoing. In doing so, these "whistle blowers" place the interest of the public at large ahead of their own interests and act accordingly. However, in case of malpractice, independent auditors may be held liable for losses suffered by those who relied on the audited financial statements.

> ■ **LEARNING OBJECTIVE 4**
>
> Appreciate the importance of ethics, reputation, and legal liability in accounting.

[12]*The CA Competency Map.* The Canadian Institute of Chartered Accountants, Toronto: Canada, 2004, pp. 17–21, accessible through the CICA's Web site: www.cica.ca.

[13]*Code of Ethical Principles and Rules of Conduct.* Certified General Accountants Association of Canada, Vancouver: Canada, 2004, accessible through the CGA's Web site: www.cga-online.org.

[14]These publications are accessible through the Society's Web site: www.cma-canada.org.

It is important to note that the vast majority of managers and owners do act in an honest and responsible manner. However, when the top officers in an organization collude to deceive other parties, they may temporarily succeed. In many cases, even the most diligent audit may not immediately uncover the results of fraud involving collusion of the top officers of a corporation, such as occurred in a number of well-publicized cases like YBM and Livent in Canada, Enron and WorldCom in the United States, and Parmalat in Italy. However, those who were involved in fraudulent behaviour were eventually identified and were sanctioned for their behaviour by the appropriate legal authorities.

Misrepresentations by managers highlight the crucial importance of the public accounting profession in ensuring the integrity of the financial reporting system. The recent failures in publicly disclosing financial information that is not in conformity with existing accounting standards cost billions of dollars to the shareholders, creditors, and employees of these companies. In addition, these fraudulent cases raised many questions about the integrity of managers and auditors. More importantly, these spectacular financial reporting failures led to significant reforms of the accounting profession and the imposition of new government regulations both in Canada and the United States that make it more difficult and costly for company managers to engage in fraudulent activities.[15]

DEMONSTRATION **CASE**

At the end of most chapters, one or more demonstration cases are presented. These cases provide an overview of the primary issues discussed in the chapter. Each demonstration case is followed by a recommended solution. You should read the case carefully and then prepare your own solution before you study the recommended solution. **This self-evaluation is highly recommended.**

The introductory case presented here reviews the elements reported on the income statement and the balance sheet and how the elements within the statements are related.

ABC Service Corporation was organized by Able, Baker, and Casella on January 1, 2006. On that date, the investors exchanged $36,000 cash for all of the shares of the company. On the same day, the corporation borrowed $10,000 from a local bank and signed a three-year note, payable on December 31, 2008. Interest of 10 percent is payable each December 31. On January 1, 2006, the corporation purchased service supplies for $20,000 cash. Operations started immediately.

---

[15]In the wake of the wave of U.S. corporate scandals, the U.S. Congress passed in 2002 a significant piece of legislation known as the Sarbanes-Oxley Act, or Sarbox for brevity. Sarbox requires companies to comply with a series of measures intended to improve on corporate governance in order to discourage corporate fraud by managers. To achieve this, companies are required to evaluate their internal controls and financial reporting procedures on an annual basis. Public companies must now present standardized summaries of their internal control procedures in their annual report, stating that management is responsible for adequate internal control structures. Furthermore, the company's independent auditor must issue a report attesting to management's assertion on the effectiveness of the company's internal controls and procedures. At the time of writing this text, Canadian regulators and standard setters had adopted similar requirements for Canadian public companies. For example, the Ontario Securities Commission had put in place new rules that are similar to those required by the Sarbanes-Oxley legislation, but tailored to specific Canadian circumstances and priorities. Under these rules, chief executive officers and chief financial officers of publicly traded companies are required to (1) certify the fair presentation of annual reports, (2) have an audit committee that is independent of management and includes members who are financially literate, and (3) have their external audit conducted by a public accounting firm registered with the Canadian Public Accountability Board, the new independent watchdog for public company auditors (Ontario Securities Commission, Annual Report 2004). Moreover, the Auditing and Assurance Standards Board of the Canadian Institute of Chartered Accountants has recently introduced a new section of the *CICA Handbook* that provides the guidance necessary to issue a report on the effectiveness of an entity's internal control over financial reporting in conjunction with a financial statement audit.

At the end of 2006, the corporation had completed the following additional business transactions (summarized):

(a) Performed services and billed customers for $100,000, of which $94,000 was collected by year-end.

(b) Used up $5,000 of service supplies while rendering services.

(c) Paid $54,000 for other service expenses.

(d) Paid $1,000 in annual interest expense on the note payable.

(e) Paid $8,000 of income taxes to the Canada Revenue Agency.

Required:

Complete the following two financial statements for 2006 by entering the correct amounts. The suggested solution follows the blank statements.

ABC SERVICE CORPORATION
Income Statement
_____ (date)
(in dollars)

		Computation
Revenues		
Service revenue	$_____	_____
Expenses		
Service expenses	$_____	_____
Interest expense	_____	_____
Total pretax expenses	_____	
Income before income tax	$_____	
Income tax expense	_____	_____
Net Income	$_____	

ABC SERVICE CORPORATION
Balance Sheet
_____ (date)
(in dollars)

		Computation
Assets		
Cash	$_____	_____
Accounts receivable	_____	_____
Service supplies	_____	_____
Total assets	$_____	
Liabilities		
Note payable (10%)	$_____	_____
Total liabilities	$_____	
Shareholders' Equity		
Share capital	$_____	_____
Retained earnings	_____	_____
Total shareholders' equity	_____	
Total liabilities and shareholders' equity	$_____	

We strongly recommend that you prepare your own answers to these requirements and then check your answers with the suggested solution.

SUGGESTED SOLUTION

ABC SERVICE CORPORATION
Income Statement
For the Year Ended December 31, 2006
(in dollars)

			Computation
Revenues			
Service revenue		$100,000	*Total billed to customers*
Expenses			
Service expenses	$59,000		*$5,000 + $54,000*
Interest expense	1,000*		
Total pretax expenses		60,000	
Income before income tax		$ 40,000	
Income tax expense		8,000	
Net Income		$ 32,000	

*This amount equals 10 percent of the amount borrowed ($10,000 $\times$ 10%).

Note that the *income before income tax* is the difference between revenues and pretax expenses, and that income tax expense is deducted from income before income tax to arrive at *net income*.

ABC SERVICE CORPORATION
Balance Sheet
At December 31, 2006
(in dollars)

			Computation
Assets			
Cash		$ 57,000	*$36,000 + $10,000*
			− $20,000 + $94,000
			− $54,000 − $1,000
			− $8,000
Accounts receivable		6,000	*$100,000 − $94,000*
Service supplies		15,000	*$20,000 − $5,000*
Total assets		$ 78,000	
Liabilities			
Note payable (10%)	$10,000		*Given, bank loan*
Total liabilities		$ 10,000	
Shareholders' Equity			
Share capital	$36,000		*Given*
Retained earnings	32,000*		*From income statement*
Total shareholders' equity		68,000	
Total liabilities and shareholders' equity		$ 78,000	

*Given that ABC Service Corporation started on January 1, 2006, and there were no dividends declared in 2006, the ending balance of retained earnings equals the net income for 2006. Hence, there is no need to prepare the statement of retained earnings for 2006.

SOLUTIONS TO **SELF-STUDY QUIZZES**

Self-Study Quiz 1-1

1. Assets ($34,155,000) − Liabilities ($11,767,000) = Shareholders' Equity ($22,388,000).

2. L, A, A, SE, A, A, A, L, SE (reading down the columns).

Self-Study Quiz 1-2

1. E, E, R, E (reading down the columns).

2. Sales revenue in the amount of $25,598,000 is recognized because sales revenue is normally reported on the income statement when the goods or services have been delivered to customers who have either paid or promised to pay for them in the future.

3. Cost of goods sold is $15,443,000 because expenses are the dollar amount of resources used up to earn revenues during the period. Only the beer that has been delivered to customers is used up. The beer still on hand is part of the asset inventory.

Self-Study Quiz 1-3

1. $25,270,000 is recognized on the cash flow statement because this number represents the actual cash collected from customers related to current and prior years' sales.

2. (F), (O), F, (O), (I), (O), O.

CHAPTER **TAKE-AWAYS**

1. **Recognize the information conveyed in each of the four basic financial statements and how it is used by different decision makers (investors, creditors, and managers).   p. 5**

   The *balance sheet* is a statement of financial position that reports dollar amounts for the assets, liabilities, and shareholders' equity at a specific point in time.

   The *income statement* is a statement of operations that reports revenues, expenses, and net income for a stated period of time.

   The *statement of retained earnings* explains changes to the retained earnings balance that occurred during the reporting period.

   The *cash flow statement* reports inflows and outflows of cash for a specific period of time.

   The statements are used by investors and creditors to evaluate different aspects of the firm's financial position and performance.

2. **Identify the role of generally accepted accounting principles (GAAP) in determining the content of financial statements.   p. 19**
   GAAP are the measurement rules used to develop the information in financial statements. Knowledge of GAAP is necessary for accurate interpretation of the numbers in financial statements.

3. **Distinguish the roles of managers and auditors in the accounting communication process.   p. 21**
   Management has primary responsibility for the accuracy of a company's financial information. Auditors are responsible for expressing an opinion on the fairness of the financial statement presentations based on their examination of the reports and records of the company.

4. **Appreciate the importance of ethics, reputation, and legal liability in accounting.   p. 23**
   Users will have confidence in the accuracy of financial statement numbers only if the people associated with their preparation and audit have reputations for ethical behaviour and competence. Management and auditors can also be held legally liable for fraudulent financial statements and malpractice.

In this chapter, we studied the basic financial statements that communicate financial information to external users. Chapters 2, 3, 4, and 5 will provide a more detailed look at financial statements and examine how to translate data about business transactions into these statements. Learning the relationship between business transactions and financial statements is the key to using financial statements in planning and decision making. Chapter 2 begins our discussion of how the accounting function collects data about business transactions and processes the data to provide periodic financial statements, with emphasis on the balance sheet. To accomplish this purpose, Chapter 2 discusses key accounting concepts, the accounting model, transaction analysis, and analytical tools. We examine typical business activities of an actual service-oriented company to demonstrate the concepts in Chapters 2, 3, 4, and 5.

Chapter Supplement A

Types of Business Entities

This textbook emphasizes *accounting for profit-making business entities*. The three main types of business entities are sole proprietorship, partnership, and corporation. A *sole proprietorship* is an unincorporated business owned by one person; it usually is small in size and is common in the service, retailing, and farming industries. Often the owner is the manager. Legally, the business and the owner are not separate entities. However, accounting views the business as a separate entity that must be accounted for separately from its owner.

A *partnership* is an unincorporated business owned by two or more persons known as *partners*. Some partnerships are large in size (e.g., international public accounting firms and law firms). The agreements between the owners are specified in a partnership contract that deals with matters such as division of income among partners and distribution of resources of the business on termination of its operations. A partnership is not legally separate from its owners. Legally, each partner in a general partnership is responsible for the debts of the business (each general partner has *unlimited liability*). The partnership, however, is a separate business entity to be accounted for separately from its several owners.

A *corporation* is a business incorporated federally under the Canada Business Corporations Act or provincially under similar provincial Acts. The owners are called *shareholders* or *stockholders*. Ownership is represented by shares of capital that usually can be bought and sold freely. When an approved application for incorporation is filed by the organizers, a charter is issued by either the federal or the provincial government. This charter gives the corporation the right to operate as a legal entity, separate from its owners. The shareholders enjoy *limited liability*. Shareholders are liable for the corporation's debts only to the extent of their investments. The corporate charter specifies the types and amounts of share capital that can be issued. Most provinces require a minimum of two shareholders and a minimum amount of resources to be contributed at the time of organization. The shareholders elect a governing board of directors, which in turn employs managers and exercises general supervision of the corporation. Accounting also views the corporation as a separate business entity that must be accounted for separately from its owners.

In terms of economic importance, the corporation is the dominant form of business organization in Canada. This dominance is caused by the many advantages of the corporate form: (1) limited liability for the shareholders, (2) continuity of life, (3) ease in transferring ownership (shares), and (4) opportunities to raise large amounts of money by selling shares to a large number of people. The primary disadvantages of a corporation are (1) the loss of control by shareholders, (2) complex reporting procedures for a variety of government agencies, and (3) that income may be subject to double taxation (it is taxed when it is earned and again when it is distributed to shareholders as dividends). In this textbook, we emphasize the corporate form of business. Nevertheless, the accounting concepts and procedures that we discuss also apply to other types of businesses.

Specific aspects of the three types of business entities are compared in Exhibit 1.9.

Chapter Supplement B

Employment in the Accounting Profession Today

Since 1900, accounting has attained the stature of professions such as law, medicine, engineering, and architecture. As with all recognized professions, accounting is subject

EXHIBIT **1.9**

Comparison of Three Types of Business Entities

	Proprietorship	Partnership	Corporation
Number of owners	One owner	Two or more owners	Many owners
Legal status of entity	Not separate from that of its owner(s)		Separate legal entity
Responsibility of owners for debts of business entity	Unlimited legal liability		Owners' liability is limited to their investment.
Accounting status	Each entity is separate from its owner(s) for accounting purposes		

to professional competence requirements, is dedicated to service to the public, requires a high level of academic study, and rests on a common body of knowledge. As indicated earlier, three Canadian accounting designations are available to an accountant: CA, CGA, and CMA. These designations are granted only on completion of requirements specified by the respective professional organizations. Although specific requirements vary among the three professional organizations, they include a university degree with a specified number of accounting courses, good character, a minimum of two years of relevant professional experience, and successful completion of a professional examination. Similar accounting designations exist in other countries, most notably the *Certified Public Accountant* (CPA) in the United States.

Accountants usually are engaged in professional practice or are employed by businesses, government entities, and not-for-profit organizations. The accounting profession is continuously changing. While many accountants still provide traditional accounting and tax services to businesses, individual clients, and government organizations, other areas of practice have become increasingly common in the accounting profession today. Demand for value-added accounting services (e.g., financial analysis, evaluation and implementation of new information technology and business processes, management advisory and consulting services, forensic accounting, and environmental accounting) is reshaping the nature of educational programs that prepare students to become professional accountants.[16]

PRACTICE OF PUBLIC ACCOUNTING

Although an individual may practise public accounting, usually two or more individuals organize an accounting firm in the form of a partnership (in many cases, a limited liability partnership, or LLP). Accounting firms vary in size from a one-person office, to regional firms, to the Big Four firms (Deloitte & Touche, Ernst & Young, KPMG Peat Marwick, and PricewaterhouseCoopers), which have hundreds of offices located worldwide. Accounting firms usually render three types of services: assurance services, management consulting services, and tax services.

Assurance Services　Assurance services are independent professional services that improve the quality of information, or its context, for decision makers. The most important assurance service performed by professional accountants in public practice is financial statement auditing. The purpose of an audit is to lend credibility to the financial reports, that is, to ensure that they fairly represent what they claim. An audit involves an examination of the financial reports (prepared by the management of the entity) to ensure that they conform with GAAP. Other areas of assurance services include integrity and security of electronic commerce and reliability of information systems.

Management Consulting Services　Many independent accounting firms offer management consulting services. These services usually are accounting-based and

---

[16]Refer to the following Web site for more details about the types of services and skills that should be provided by accountants in the future: **www.nextgenaccountant.com/research_hili/research_sum.html.**

encompass such activities as the design and installation of accounting, data processing, and profit-planning and control (budget) systems; financial advice; forecasting; inventory controls; cost-effectiveness studies; and operational analysis. This facet of public accounting practice has grown rapidly. The perceived influence of offering such services on auditor independence has recently caused large accounting firms to dissociate their consulting practice from their audit function.

Tax Services   Accountants in public practice usually provide income tax services to their clients. These services include both tax planning as a part of the decision-making process and the determination of the income tax liability (reported on the annual income tax return). Because of the increasing complexity of provincial and federal tax laws, a high level of competence is required, which accountants specializing in taxation can provide. The accountant's involvement in tax planning often is quite significant. Most major business decisions have significant tax impacts; in fact, tax-planning considerations often govern certain business decisions.

EMPLOYMENT BY ORGANIZATIONS

Many accountants, including CAs, CGAs, and CMAs, are employed by profit-making and not-for-profit organizations. An organization, depending on its size and complexity, may employ from a few to hundreds of accountants. In a business enterprise, the chief financial officer (usually a vice-president or controller) is a member of the management team. This responsibility usually entails a wide range of management, financial, and accounting duties.

In a business entity, accountants typically are engaged in a wide variety of activities, such as general management, general accounting, cost accounting, profit planning and control (budgeting), internal auditing, and computerized data processing. A primary function of the accountants in organizations is to provide data that are useful for internal managerial decision making and for controlling operations. The functions of external reporting, tax planning, control of assets, and a host of related responsibilities normally are also performed by accountants in industry.

EMPLOYMENT IN THE PUBLIC AND NOT-FOR-PROFIT SECTORS

The vast and complex operations of governmental units, from the local to the international level, create a need for accountants. The same holds true for other not-for-profit organizations such as charitable organizations, hospitals, and universities. Accountants employed in the public and not-for-profit sectors perform functions similar to those performed by their counterparts in private organizations.

A survey of positions occupied by accounting professionals and related salaries is available at www.accountemps.com.

FINDING FINANCIAL INFORMATION

BALANCE SHEET
Assets = Liabilities + Shareholders' Equity

INCOME STATEMENT
Revenues
− Expenses
———
Net Income

STATEMENT OF RETAINED EARNINGS
Retained Earnings, beginning of the period
+ Net Income
− Dividends
———
Retained Earnings, end of the period

CASH FLOW STATEMENT
Cash Flow from Operating Activities
+ Cash Flow from Investing Activities
+ Cash Flow from Financing Activities
———
Net Change in Cash

KEY **TERMS**

Accounting p. 5

Accounting Entity p. 7

Accounting Period p. 11

Accounting Standards Board (AcSB) p. 20

Audit p. 23

Audit Report (Report of Independent Auditors) p. 22

Balance Sheet (Statement of Financial Position) p. 7

Basic Accounting Equation (Balance Sheet Equation) p. 8

Cash Flow Statement p. 15

Generally Accepted Accounting Principles (GAAP) p. 19

Income Statement (Statement of Income, Statement of Earnings, or Statement of Operations) p. 11

Notes (Footnotes) p. 17

Ontario Securities Commission (OSC) p. 19

Report of Management p. 22

Securities and Exchange Commission (SEC) p. 19

Statement of Retained Earnings p. 13

QUESTIONS

1. Define *accounting*.
2. Briefly distinguish financial accounting from managerial accounting.
3. The accounting process generates financial reports for both internal and external users. Identify some of the groups of users.
4. Briefly distinguish investors from creditors.
5. What is an accounting entity? Why is a business treated as a separate entity for accounting purposes?
6. Complete the following:

Name of Statement	Alternative Title
a. Income statement	*a.* _____
b. Balance sheet	*b.* _____
c. Audit report	*c.* _____

7. What information should be included in the heading of each of the four primary financial statements?
8. What are the purposes of (a) the income statement, (b) the balance sheet, (c) the cash flow statement, and (d) the statement of retained earnings?
9. Explain why the income statement and the cash flow statement are dated "For the Year Ended December 31, 2005," whereas the balance sheet is dated "At December 31, 2005."
10. Briefly explain the importance of assets and liabilities to the decisions of investors and creditors.
11. Briefly define the following: *net income* and *net loss*.
12. Explain the accounting equation for the income statement. Define the three major items reported on the income statement.
13. Explain the accounting equation for the balance sheet. Define the three major components reported on the balance sheet.
14. Explain the accounting equation for the cash flow statement. Explain the three major components reported on the statement.
15. Explain the accounting equation for the statement of retained earnings. Explain the four major items reported on the statement of retained earnings.
16. Financial statements discussed in this chapter are aimed at *external* users. Briefly explain how a company's *internal* managers in different functional areas (e.g., marketing, purchasing, human resources) might use financial statement information.
17. Briefly describe how accounting measurement rules (generally accepted accounting principles) are determined in Canada.
18. Briefly explain the responsibility of company management and the independent auditors in the accounting communication process.
19. (Supplement A) Briefly differentiate among a sole proprietorship, a partnership, and a corporation.
20. (Supplement B) List and briefly explain the three primary services that accountants in public practice provide.

MULTIPLE-CHOICE **QUESTIONS**

1. Which of the following is *not* one of the four basic financial statements?
   a. balance sheet
   b. audit report
   c. income statement
   d. cash flow statement

2. As stated in the audit report, or *Report of Independent Accountants,* the primary responsibility for a company's financial statements lies with
   a. the owners of the company
   b. independent financial analysts
   c. the auditors
   d. the company's management

3. Which of the following is true?
   a. AcSB created OSC
   b. GAAP created AcSB
   c. OSC created CICA
   d. AcSB created GAAP

4. Which of the following statements is false?
   a. Retained earnings is increased by net income and decreased by a net loss.
   b. Retained earnings is a component of shareholders' equity on the balance sheet.
   c. Retained earnings is an asset on the balance sheet.
   d. Retained earnings represents earnings not distributed to shareholders in the form of dividends.

5. Which of the following is *not* one of the four items required to be shown in the heading of a financial statement?
   a. the financial statement preparer's name
   b. the title of the financial statement
   c. the unit of measure in the financial statement
   d. the name of the business entity

6. How many of the following statements are true?
   • The cash flow statement separates cash inflows and outflows into three major categories: operations, investing, and financing.
   • The ending cash balance shown on the cash flow statement must agree with the amount shown on the balance sheet at the end of the same fiscal period.
   • The total increase or decrease in cash shown on the cash flow statement must agree with the "bottom line" (net income or net loss) reported on the income statement.
   a. none
   b. one
   c. two
   d. three

7. Which of the following is *not* a typical footnote included in an annual report?
   a. A note describing the auditor's opinion of the management's past and future financial planning for the business
   b. A note providing more detail about a specific item shown in the financial statements
   c. A note describing the accounting rules applied in the financial statements
   d. A note describing financial disclosures about items not appearing in the financial statements

8. Which of the following statements is true?
   a. The income statement is sometimes called the statement of operations.
   b. The income statement reports revenues, expenses, and liabilities.
   c. The income statement reports only revenue for which cash was received at the point of sale.
   d. The income statement reports the financial position of a business at a particular point in time.

9. Which of the following statements is false?
   a. The accounts shown on a balance sheet represent the basic accounting equation for a particular business entity.
   b. The retained earnings balance shown on the balance sheet must agree to the ending retained earnings balance shown on the statement of retained earnings.
   c. The balance sheet reports the changes in specific account balances over a period of time.
   d. The balance sheet reports the amount of assets, liabilities, and shareholders' equity of an accounting entity at a point in time.

10. Which of the following statements regarding GAAP is true?
    a. Canadian GAAP is the body of accounting knowledge followed by all countries in the world.
    b. Changes in GAAP can affect the interests of managers and shareholders.

c. GAAP is the abbreviation for generally accepted auditing procedures.

d. Changes to GAAP must be approved by the Senate Finance Committee.

For more practice with multiple-choice questions, go to our Web site at www.mcgrawhill.ca/college/libby, click on "Student Edition" in the upper left menu, click on this chapter's name and number from the list of contents, and then click on "Multiple-Choice Quiz" from the menu on the left.

EXERCISES

E1–1 Matching Definitions with Terms or Abbreviations   ■ **LO1, 2**

Match each definition with its related term or abbreviation by entering the appropriate letter in the space provided.

Term or Abbreviation	Definition
_____ (1) OSC	A. A system that collects and processes financial information about an organization and reports that information to decision makers.
_____ (2) Audit	
_____ (3) Sole proprietorship	
_____ (4) Corporation	B. Measurement of information about an entity in the monetary unit of the country—dollars or other national currency.
_____ (5) Accounting	
_____ (6) Separate entity	C. An unincorporated business owned by two or more persons.
_____ (7) Audit report	
_____ (8) Cost principle	D. The organization for which financial data are to be collected (separate and distinct from its owners).
_____ (9) Partnership	
_____ (10) CGA	E. An incorporated entity that issues shares as evidence of ownership.
_____ (11) AcSB	
_____ (12) CA	F. Initial recording of financial statement elements at acquisition cost.
_____ (13) Unit of measure	
_____ (14) GAAP	G. An examination of the financial reports to ensure that they represent what they claim and conform with generally accepted accounting principles.
_____ (15) Publicly traded	
	H. Chartered Accountant.
	I. An unincorporated business owned by one person.
	J. A report that describes the auditors' opinion of the fairness of the financial statement presentations and the evidence gathered to support that opinion.
	K. Ontario Securities Commission.
	L. Accounting Standards Board.
	M. A company that can be bought and sold by investors on established stock exchanges.
	N. Generally accepted accounting principles.
	O. Certified General Accountant.

E1–2 Matching Financial Statement Items to Financial Statement Categories   ■ **LO1**

Procter & Gamble

According to its annual report, "Procter & Gamble markets a broad range of laundry, cleaning, paper, beauty care, health care, food and beverage products in more than 140 countries around the world, with leading brands including Tide, Ariel, Crest, Crisco, Vicks and Max Factor." The following are items taken from its recent balance sheet and income statement. Note that different companies use slightly different titles for the same item. Mark each item in the following list as an asset (A), liability (L), or shareholders' equity (SE) that would appear on the balance sheet or a revenue (R) or expense (E) that would appear on the income statement.

_____ (1) Accounts payable

_____ (2) Accounts receivable

_____ (3) Cash and cash equivalents

_____ (4) Cost of products sold

_____ (5) Property, plant, and equipment

_____ (6) Income taxes

_____ (7) Interest expense

_____ (8) Inventories

_____ (9) Land

_____ (10) Marketing, administrative, and other operating expenses

_____ (11) Long-term debt

_____ (12) Net sales

_____ (13) Notes payable

_____ (14) Retained earnings

_____ (15) Taxes payable

■ **LO1**

Tootsie Roll

E1–3   Matching Financial Statement Items to Financial Statement Categories

Tootsie Roll Industries is engaged in the manufacture and sale of candy. Major products include Tootsie Roll, Tootsie Roll Pops, Tootsie Pop Drops, Tootsie Flavor Rolls, Charms, and Blow Pop lollipops. The following items were listed on Tootsie Roll's recent income statement and balance sheet. Mark each item from the balance sheet as an asset (A), liability (L), or shareholders' equity (SE) and each item from the income statement as a revenue (R) or expense (E).

_____ (1) Accounts payable	_____ (10) Buildings
_____ (2) Accounts receivable	_____ (11) Cash and cash equivalents
_____ (3) Cost of goods sold	_____ (12) Land
_____ (4) Distribution and warehousing	_____ (13) Machinery and equipment
_____ (5) Dividends payable	_____ (14) Marketing, selling, and advertising
_____ (6) General and administrative	_____ (15) Net sales
_____ (7) Income taxes payable	_____ (16) Notes payable to banks
_____ (8) Inventories	_____ (17) Provision for income taxes*
_____ (9) Investments	_____ (18) Retained earnings

■ **LO1**

Honda Motor Co.

E1–4   Preparing a Balance Sheet

Established less than 50 years ago, Honda Motor Co., Ltd., of Japan is a leading international manufacturer of automobiles and the largest manufacturer of motorcycles in the world. As a Japanese company, it follows Japanese GAAP and reports its financial statements in millions of yen (the sign for yen is ¥). A recent balance sheet contained the following items (in millions). Prepare a balance sheet as at March 31, 2004, solving for the missing amount.

Cash and cash equivalents	¥ 724,421
Share capital	291,204
Accounts payable and other current liabilities	3,334,819
Inventories	765,433
Investments	541,066
Long-term debt	1,394,612
Net property, plant, and equipment	1,435,531
Other assets	846,943
Other liabilities	724,937
Retained earnings	2,583,196
Total assets	8,328,768
Total liabilities and shareholders' equity	?
Trade accounts, notes, and other receivables	4,015,374

■ **LO1**

E1–5   Completing a Balance Sheet and Inferring Net Income

Terry Lloyd and Joan Lopez organized Read More Store as a corporation; each contributed $50,000 cash to start the business and received 4,000 shares of capital. The store completed its first year of operations on December 31, 2006. On that date, the following financial items were determined: cash on hand and in the bank, $42,900; amounts due from customers from sales of books, $36,000; unused portion of store and office equipment, $43,000; amounts owed to publishers for books purchased, $8,000; one-year note for $1,000, signed on January 15, 2006 and payable to a local bank. No dividends were declared or paid to the shareholders during the year.

Required:

1. Complete the following balance sheet as at December 31, 2006.

2. What was the amount of net income for the year?

_____

_____

_____

_____

*In Canada and the United States, "provision for income taxes" is most often used as a synonym for "income tax expense."

Assets			Liabilities		
Cash	$ ____		Accounts payable	$ ____	
Accounts receivable	____		Note payable	____	
Store and office equipment	____		Interest payable	120	
			Total liabilities		$ ____
			Shareholders' Equity		
			Share capital	$ ____	
			Retained earnings	12,780	
			Total shareholders' equity		____
Total assets	$ ____		Total liabilities and shareholders' equity		$ ____

E1–6 Analyzing Revenues and Expenses and Preparing an Income Statement ▨ **LO1**

Assume that you are the owner of The Collegiate Shop, which specializes in items that interest students. At the end of September 2007, you find (for September only) the following:

a. Sales, per the cash register tapes, of $120,000, plus one sale on credit (a special situation) of $2,000.

b. With the help of a friend (who majored in accounting), you determined that all of the goods sold during September had cost $45,000 to purchase.

c. During the month, according to the chequebook, you paid $38,000 for salaries, rent, supplies, advertising, and other expenses; however, you have not yet paid the $600 monthly utilities for September.

Required:

On the basis of the data given, what was the amount of income for September (disregard income taxes)? Show computations. (*Hint*: A convenient form to use has the following major side captions: Revenue from Sales, Expenses, and the difference—Net Income.)

E1–7 Preparing an Income Statement and Inferring Missing Values ▨ **LO1**

Wal-Mart Stores, Inc., is the largest retail chain in the United States, operating more than 2,000 stores. A recent annual income statement contained the following items (in millions). Solve for the missing amounts and prepare a condensed income statement for the year ended January 31, 2004. (*Hint:* First order the items as they would appear on the income statement and then solve for the missing values.)

Wal-Mart

Cost of sales	$198,747
Interest costs	832
Net income	?
Net sales	258,681
Operating, selling, and general and administrative expenses	44,909
Provision for income taxes*	5,118
Other expenses	21
Total costs and expenses	?
Total revenues	?
Income before income tax	?

E1–8 Analyzing Revenues and Expenses and Completing an Income Statement ▨ **LO1**

Home Realty, Incorporated, has been operating for three years and is owned by three investors. J. Doe owns 60 percent of the 9,000 shares that are outstanding, and is the

---

*In Canada and the United States, "provision for income taxes" is a common synonym for "income tax expense."

managing executive in charge. On December 31, 2006, the following financial items for the entire year were determined: commissions earned and collected in cash, $150,000; rental service fees earned and collected, $15,000; expenses paid including salaries, $62,000; commissions, $35,000; payroll taxes, $2,500; rent, $2,200; utilities, $1,600; promotion and advertising, $8,000; income taxes, $18,500; and miscellaneous expenses, $500. At December 31, there were $16,000 of commissions earned but not collected yet, and the rent for December was not paid. Complete the following income statement:

Revenues		
Commissions	$ _____	
Rental service fees	_____	
Total revenues		$ _____
Expenses		
Salaries	$ _____	
Commission	_____	
Payroll tax	_____	
Rent	_____	
Utilities	_____	
Promotion and advertising	_____	
Miscellaneous	_____	
Total expenses (excluding income taxes)		_____
Income before income taxes		$ _____
Income tax expense		_____
Net income		$ 50,500

LO1

E1–9 Inferring Values Using the Income Statement and Balance Sheet Equations
Review the chapter explanations of the income statement and the balance sheet equations. Apply these equations in each independent case to compute the two missing amounts for each case. Assume that it is the end of 2005, the first full year of operations for the company.
(*Hint:* Organize the listed items as they are presented in the balance sheet and income statement equations and then compute the missing amounts.)

Independent Cases	Total Revenues	Total Expenses	Net Income (Loss)	Total Assets	Total Liabilities	Shareholders' Equity
A	$100,000	$82,000	$	$150,000	$70,000	$
B		80,000	12,000	112,000		60,000
C	80,000	86,000		104,000	26,000	
D	50,000		13,000		22,000	77,000
E		81,000	(6,000)		73,000	28,000

LO1

E1–10 Preparing an Income Statement and Balance Sheet
Huang Corporation was organized by five individuals on January 1, 2006. At the end of January 2006, the following monthly financial data are available:

Total revenues	$130,000
Total expenses (excluding income taxes)	80,000
Income tax expense (all unpaid as at January 31)	15,000
Cash balance, January 31, 2006	30,000
Receivables from customers (all considered collectable)	15,000
Merchandise inventory (by inventory count at cost)	42,000
Payables to suppliers for merchandise purchased from them (will be paid during February 2006)	11,000
Share capital (2,600 shares)	26,000

No dividends were declared or paid during 2006.

Required:

Complete the following two statements:

HUANG CORPORATION
Summary Income Statement
For the Month of January 2006

Total revenues	$ _____
Less: Total expenses (excluding income tax)	_____
Income before income tax	_____
Less: Income tax expense	_____
Net income	_____

HUANG CORPORATION
Balance Sheet
As at January 31, 2006

Assets

Cash	$ _____
Receivables from customers	_____
Merchandise inventory	_____
Total assets	$ _____

Liabilities

Payables to suppliers	$ _____
Income taxes payable	_____
Total liabilities	_____

Shareholders' equity

Share capital	$ _____	
Retained earnings	_____	
Total shareholders' equity		_____
Total liabilities and shareholders' equity		$ _____

E1–11   **Analyzing and Interpreting an Income Statement and Price/Earnings Ratio**   ▦ **LO1**

Pest Away Corporation was organized by three individuals on January 1, 2005, to provide insect extermination services. At the end of 2005, the following income statement was prepared:

PEST AWAY CORPORATION
Income Statement
For the Year Ended December 31, 2005

Revenues		
Service revenue (cash)	$204,000	
Service revenue (credit)	24,000	
Total revenues		$228,000
Expenses		
Salaries	$ 78,000	
Rent	21,000	
Utilities	12,000	
Advertising	14,000	
Supplies	25,000	
Interest	8,000	
Total expenses		158,000
Income before income tax		$ 70,000
Income tax expense		21,000
Net income		$ 49,000

Required:

1. What was the average amount of monthly revenue?
2. What was the amount of monthly rent?
3. Explain why supplies are reported as an expense.
4. Explain why interest is reported as an expense.
5. What was the average income tax rate for Pest Away Corporation?
6. Can you determine how much cash the company had on December 31, 2005? Explain.
7. If the company had a market value of $588,000, what is its price/earnings ratio?

LO1

Dell Computer

E1–12 Focus on Cash Flows: Matching Cash Flow Statement Items to Categories

Dell Computer is a leading designer and manufacturer of personal computers. The following items were taken from its recent cash flow statement. Note that different companies use slightly different titles for the same item. Without referring to Exhibit 1.5, mark each item in the list as a cash flow from operating activities (O), investing activities (I), or financing activities (F). Place parentheses around the letter only if it is a cash outflow.

_____ (1) Cash paid to suppliers and employees
_____ (2) Cash received from customers
_____ (3) Income taxes paid
_____ (4) Interest and dividends received
_____ (5) Interest paid
_____ (6) Proceeds from sale of investment in Conner Peripherals, Inc.
_____ (7) Purchases of property, plant, and equipment
_____ (8) Repayment of borrowings

LO1

E1–13 Preparing a Cash Flow Statement

NITSU Manufacturing Corporation is preparing the annual financial statements for the shareholders. A cash flow statement must be prepared. The following data on cash flows were developed for the entire year ended December 31, 2006: cash inflow from operating revenues, $270,000; cash expended for operating expenses, $180,000; sale of unissued NITSU shares for cash, $30,000; cash dividends declared and paid to shareholders during the year, $22,000; and payments on long-term notes payable, $80,000. During the year, a tract of land was sold for $15,000 cash (which was the same price that NITSU had paid for the land in 2005), and $38,000 cash was expended for two new machines. The machines were used in the factory. The beginning-of-the-year cash balance was $63,000.

Required:

Prepare a cash flow statement for 2006. Follow the format illustrated in the chapter.

LO1

E1–14 Analyzing Cash Flows from Operations

Paul's Painters, a service organization, prepared the following special report for the month of January 2005:

Service Revenue, Expenses, and Income

Service revenue		
Cash services (per cash register tape)	$115,000	
Credit services (per charge bills; not yet collected by end of January)	20,500	
		$135,500
Expenses:		
Salaries and wages expense (paid by cheque)	$ 60,000	
Salaries for January not yet paid	3,000	
Supplies used (taken from stock, purchased for cash during December)	2,000	
Estimated cost of using company-owned truck for the month (called *amortization*)	500	
Other expenses (paid by cheque)	16,000	81,500
Income before income tax		54,000
Income tax expense (not yet paid)		13,500
Income for January		$ 40,500

Required:

1. The owner (who knows little about the financial part of the business) asked you to compute the amount by which cash had increased in January 2005 from the operations of the company. You decided to prepare a detailed report for the owner with the following major captions: Cash Inflows (collections), Cash Outflows (payments), and the difference—Net Increase (or Decrease) in Cash.

2. Reconcile the difference—net increase (or decrease) in cash—you computed in requirement 1 with the income for January 2005.

PROBLEMS

P1–1 Preparing an Income Statement and a Balance Sheet (AP1–1) ■ **LO1**

Assume that you are the president of Nuclear Company. At December 31, 2005, the end of the first year of operations, the following financial data for the company are available:

Cash	$ 22,000
Receivables from customers (all considered collectable)	12,000
Inventory of merchandise (based on physical count and priced at cost)	90,000
Equipment owned, at cost less used portion	45,000
Accounts payable owed to suppliers	44,370
Salary payable for 2005 (on December 31, 2005, this was owed to an employee who was away because of an emergency and will return around January 10, 2006, at which time the payment will be made)	2,000
Total sales revenue	140,000
Expenses, including the cost of the merchandise sold (excluding income taxes)	89,100
Income taxes expense (at 30% of pretax income); all paid during 2005	?
Share capital, 7,000 shares outstanding	87,000
No dividends were declared or paid during 2005.	

Required (show computations):

1. Prepare a summarized income statement for the year ended December 31, 2005.

2. Prepare a balance sheet at December 31, 2005.

P1–2 Analyzing a Student's Business and Preparing an Income Statement (AP1–2) ■ **LO1**

While pursuing her undergraduate studies, Brigitte Lebeau needed to earn sufficient money for the coming academic year. Unable to obtain a job with a reasonable salary, she decided to try the lawn care business for three months during the summer. After a survey of the market potential, Brigitte bought a used pick-up truck on June 1 for $1,500. On each door she painted "Brigitte's Lawn Service, Phone 471-4487." She also spent $900 for mowers, trimmers, and tools. To acquire these items, she borrowed $2,500 cash by signing a note payable, promising to pay the $2,500 plus interest of $75 at the end of the three months (ending August 31).

At the end of the summer, Brigitte realized that she had done a lot of work, and her bank account looked good. This fact prompted her to become concerned about how much profit the business had earned.

A review of the cheque stubs showed the following: bank deposits of collections from customers totalled $12,600. The following cheques had been written: gas, oil, and lubrication, $920; truck repairs, $210; mower repair, $75; miscellaneous supplies used, $80; helpers, $4,500; payroll taxes, $175; payment for assistance in preparing payroll tax forms, $25; insurance, $125; telephone, $110; and $2,575 to pay off the note including interest (on August 31). A notebook kept in the truck, plus some unpaid bills, reflected that customers still owed her $800 for lawn services rendered and that she owed $200 for gas and oil (credit card charges). She estimated that the cost for use of the truck and the other equipment (called *amortization*) for three months amounted to $500.

Required:

1. Prepare a quarterly income statement for Brigitte's Lawn Service for the months of June, July, and August 2005. Use the following main captions: Revenues from Services,

Expenses, and Net Income. Because this is a sole proprietorship, the company will not be subject to income tax.

2. Do you see a need for one or more additional financial reports for this company for 2005 and thereafter? Explain.

LO1

P1–3 Comparing Income with Cash Flow (A Challenging Problem)

New Delivery Company was organized on January 1, 2006. At the end of the first quarter (three months) of operations, the owner prepared a summary of its operations as shown in the first row of the following tabulation:

Summary of Transactions	Computation of	
	Income	Cash
a. Services performed for customers, $66,000, of which one-sixth remained uncollected at the end of the quarter.	+$66,000	+$55,000
b. Cash borrowed from the local bank, $25,000 (one-year note).		
c. Small service truck purchased for use in the business: cost, $9,000; paid 30% down, balance on credit.		
d. Expenses, $36,000, of which one-sixth remained unpaid at the end of the quarter.		
e. Service supplies purchased for use in the business, $3,000, of which one-fourth remained unpaid (on credit) at the end of the quarter. Also, one-fifth of these supplies were unused (still on hand) at the end of the quarter.		
f. Wages earned by employees, $20,000, of which one-half remained unpaid at the end of the quarter.		

Based only on the above transactions, compute the following for the quarter:
  Income (or loss)
  Cash inflow (or outflow)
	══════	══════

Required:

1. For each of the six transactions given in this tabulation, enter what you consider to be the correct amounts. Enter a zero when appropriate. The first transaction is illustrated.

2. For each transaction, explain the basis for your responses.

LO1

P1–4 Evaluating Data to Support a Loan Application (A Challenging Problem)

On January 1, 2006, three individuals organized West Company as a corporation. Each individual invested $10,000 cash in the business. On December 31, 2006, they prepared a list of resources owned (assets) and a list of the debts (liabilities) to support the company's request for a loan of $70,000 submitted to a local bank. None of the three investors had studied accounting. The two lists prepared were as follows:

Company resources	
Cash	$ 12,000
Service supplies inventory (on hand)	7,000
Service trucks (four practically new)	76,000
Personal residences of organizers (three houses)	190,000
Service equipment used in the business (practically new)	30,000
Bills due from customers (for services already completed)	17,000
Total	$332,000
Company obligations	
Unpaid wages to employees	$ 19,000
Unpaid taxes	8,000
Owed to suppliers	10,000
Owed on service trucks and equipment (to a finance company)	50,000
Loan from organizer	10,000
Total	$ 97,000

Required:

Prepare a short memo indicating:

1. Which of these items do not belong on the balance sheet (bear in mind that the company is considered to be separate from the owners)?

2. What additional questions would you raise about measurement of items on the lists? Explain the basis for each question.

3. If you were advising the local bank on its loan decision, which amounts on the lists would create special concerns? Explain the basis for each concern and include any recommendations that you have.

4. In view of your responses to (1) and (2), calculate the amount of shareholders' equity as at December 31, 2006. Show your computations.

ALTERNATE PROBLEMS

AP1–1 **Preparing an Income Statement and a Balance Sheet** (P1–1)   ■ **LO1**

Assume that you are the president of McClaren Corporation. At June 30, 2007, the end of the first year of operations, the following financial data for the company are available:

Cash	$13,150
Receivables from customers (all considered collectable)	9,500
Inventory of merchandise (based on physical count and priced at cost)	61,000
Equipment owned, at cost less used portion	36,000
Accounts payable owed to suppliers	35,500
Salary payable for 2007 (on June 30, 2007, this was owed to an employee who was away because of an emergency and will return around July 7, 2007, at which time the payment will be made)	1,500
Total sales revenue	90,000
Expenses, including the cost of the merchandise sold (excluding income taxes)	60,500
Income taxes expense (at 30% of pretax income); all paid during 2007	?
Share capital, 5,000 shares outstanding	62,000
No dividends were declared or paid during 2007.	

Required (show computations):

1. Prepare a summarized income statement for the year ended June 30, 2007.

2. Prepare a balance sheet at June 30, 2007.

AP1–2 **Analyzing a Student's Business and Preparing an Income Statement** (P1–2)   ■ **LO1**

Upon graduation from high school, John Abel immediately accepted a job as an electrician's assistant for a large local electrical repair company. After three years of hard work, John received an electrician's licence and decided to start his own business. He had saved $12,000, which he invested in the business. First, he transferred this amount from his savings account to a business bank account for Abel Electric Repair Company, Incorporated. His lawyer had advised him to start as a corporation. He then purchased a used panel truck for $9,000 cash and second-hand tools for $1,500; rented space in a small building; inserted an ad in the local paper; and opened the doors on October 1, 2005. Immediately, John was very busy; after one month, he employed an assistant.

Although John knew practically nothing about the financial side of the business, he realized that a number of reports were required and that costs and collections had to be controlled carefully. At December 31, 2005, prompted in part by concern about his income tax situation, John recognized the need for financial statements. His wife Jane developed some financial statements for the business. On December 31, 2005, with the help of a friend, she gathered the following data for the three months just ended. Bank account deposits of collections for electric repair services totalled $32,000. The following cheques had been written: electrician's assistant, $8,500; payroll taxes, $175; supplies purchased and used on jobs, $9,500; oil, gas, and maintenance on truck, $1,200; insurance, $700; rent, $500; utilities and telephone, $825; and miscellaneous expenses (including advertising), $600. Also, uncollected bills to customers for electric repair services amounted to $3,000. The $200 rent for December had not been paid. The average income tax rate is 30 percent. John estimated the cost of using the truck and tools (*amortization*) during the three months to be $1,200.

Required:

1. Prepare a quarterly income statement for Abel Electric Repair Company, Incorporated, for the three months of October through December 2005. Use the following main captions: Revenue from Services, Expenses, Income before Income Taxes, and Net Income.

2. Do you think that John may have a need for one or more additional financial reports for 2005 and thereafter? Explain.

CASES AND PROJECTS

FINDING AND INTERPRETING FINANCIAL INFORMATION

■ **LO1, 3**   **CP1–1 Finding Financial Information**

Van Houtte Inc.

Refer to the financial statements of Van Houtte Inc. in Appendix B at the end of this book.

Required:

1. What is the amount of net income for the current fiscal year?
2. What amount of revenue was earned in the current fiscal year?
3. How much inventory does the company have at the end of the current fiscal year?
4. By what amount did cash and cash equivalents* change during the year?
5. Who is auditor for the company?

■ **LO1, 3**   **CP1–2 Finding Financial Information**

The Forzani
Group Ltd.

Refer to the financial statements of The Forzani Group Ltd. on the Online Learning Centre Web site at **www.mcgrawhill.ca/college/libby/studentresources**.

Required:

Read the annual report. Look at the income statement, balance sheet, and cash flow statement closely and attempt to infer the types of information they report. Then answer the following questions based on the report.

1. What types of products does the company sell?
2. Did the chief executive officer (CEO) believe that the company had a good year?
3. On what day of the year does its fiscal year end?
4. For how many years does it present complete
   a. balance sheets?
   b. income statements?
   c. cash flow statements?
5. Are its financial statements audited by independent accountants? How do you know?
6. Did its total assets increase or decrease over the last year?
7. What was the ending balance of inventories?
8. Write out its basic accounting (balance sheet) equation in dollars at year-end.

■ **LO1**   **CP1–3 Comparing Companies**

Van Houtte
vs.
The Forzani Group

Refer to the financial statements and the accompanying notes of Van Houtte Inc. given in Appendix B and of The Forzani Group Ltd. on the Online Learning Centre Web site at **www.mcgrawhill.ca/college/libby/student/resources**.

Required:

1. Both companies report "basic" earnings per share on their income statements and the market price per share of their stock either in their annual reports or on their Web sites. Using current year's earnings per share and the highest stock price per share reported for the most recent year, compute the price/earnings ratio. Which company provided the highest price/earnings ratio for the current year? (*Note:* For Van Houtte, use a market price of $23.50 per share.)
2. Which company do investors believe will have the higher growth in earnings in the future?

FINANCIAL REPORTING AND ANALYSIS CASES

■ **LO1**   **CP1–4 Using Financial Reports: Identifying and Correcting Deficiencies in an Income Statement and a Balance Sheet**

Performance Corporation was organized on January 1, 2005. At the end of 2005, the company had not yet employed an accountant; however, an employee who was "good with numbers" prepared the following statements at that date:

Cash equivalents are short-term investments readily convertible into cash and whose value is unlikely to change.

PERFORMANCE CORPORATION
December 31, 2005

Income from sales of merchandise	$175,000
Total amount paid for goods sold during 2005	(90,000)
Selling costs	(25,000)
Amortization (on service vehicles used)	(10,000)
Income from services rendered	47,000
Salaries and wages paid	(57,000)

PERFORMANCE CORPORATION
December 31, 2005

Resources		
Cash		$ 32,000
Merchandise inventory (held for resale)		42,000
Service vehicles		50,000
Retained earnings (profit earned in 2005)		30,000
Grand total		$154,000
Debts		
Payable to suppliers		$ 22,000
Note owed to bank		25,000
Due from customers		20,000
Total		$ 67,000
Supplies on hand (to be used in rendering services)	$ 8,000	
Accumulated amortization* (on service vehicles)	10,000	
Share capital, 6,500 shares	65,000	
Total		83,000
Grand total		$150,000

Required:

1. List all of the deficiencies that you can identify in these statements. Give a brief explanation of each one.

2. Prepare a proper income statement for Performance Corporation for 2005 (correct net income is $30,000) and a proper balance sheet at December 31, 2005 (correct total assets are $142,000).

CP1–5 Using Financial Reports: Applying the Balance Sheet Equation to Liquidate a Company ▉ **LO1**
On June 1, 2007, Bland Corporation prepared a balance sheet just prior to going out of business. The balance sheet totals showed the following:

Assets (no cash)	$90,000
Liabilities	50,000
Shareholders' equity	40,000

Shortly thereafter, all of the assets were sold for cash.

Required:

1. How would the balance sheet appear immediately after the sale of the assets for cash for each of the following cases? Use the format given here.

Balances Immediately after Sale

	Cash Received for the Assets	Assets	−	Liabilities	=	Shareholders' Equity
Case A	$ 90,000	$_____		$_____		$_____
Case B	80,000	$_____		$_____		$_____
Case C	100,000	$_____		$_____		$_____
Case D	35,000	$_____		$_____		$_____

Accumulated amortization represents the cost related to the used portion of the asset and should be subtracted from the asset balance.

2. How should the cash be distributed in each separate case? (*Hint:* Creditors must be paid in full before owners receive any payment.) Use the format given here:

	To Creditors	To Shareholders	Total
Case A	$_____	$_____	$_____
Case B	$_____	$_____	$_____
Case C	$_____	$_____	$_____
Case D	$_____	$_____	$_____

CRITICAL THINKING CASES

LO1, 3 **CP1–6** **Making Decisions as a Manager: Reporting the Assets and Liabilities of a Business**
Elizabeth Watkins owns and operates Liz's Boutique (a sole proprietorship). An employee prepares a financial report for the business at each year-end. This report lists all of the resources (assets) owned by Watkins, including such personal items as the home she owns and occupies. It also lists all of the debts of the business, but not her personal debts.

Required:

1. From an accounting point of view, do you disagree with what is being included in and excluded from the report of business assets and liabilities? Explain.

2. Upon questioning, Watkins responded, "Don't worry about it; we use it only to support a loan from the bank." How would you respond to this comment?

LO3 **CP1–7** **Making Decisions as an Owner: Deciding about a Proposed Audit**
You are one of three partners who own and operate Mary's Maid Service. The company has been operating for seven years. One of the other partners has always prepared the company's annual financial statements. Recently you proposed that the statements be audited each year because it would benefit the partners and preclude possible disagreements about the division of profits. The partner who prepares the statements proposed that his Uncle Ray, who has a lot of financial experience, can do the job and at little cost. Your other partner remained silent.

Required:

1. What position would you take on the proposal? Justify your response.

2. What would you strongly recommend? Give the basis for your recommendation.

LO3, 4 **CP1–8** **Evaluating an Ethical Dilemma: Ethics and Auditor Responsibilities**
A key factor that an auditor provides is independence. The *codes of professional conduct* typically state that a member in public practice should be independent in fact and appearance when providing auditing and other attestation service.

Required:
Do you consider the following circumstances to suggest a lack of independence? Justify your position. (Use your imagination. Specific answers are not provided in the chapter.)

1. Karl Ottman is a partner with a large audit firm and is assigned to the Ford audit. Karl owns 10 shares of Ford.

2. Jane Winkler has invested in a mutual fund company that owns 500,000 shares of Sears Canada Inc. She is the auditor of Sears.

3. Bob Franklin is a clerk/typist who works on the audit of BCE Inc. He has just inherited 50,000 shares of BCE. (Bob enjoys his work and plans to continue despite his new wealth.)

4. Nancy Chen worked on weekends as the controller for a small business that a friend started. Nancy quit the job in midyear and now has no association with the company. She works full-time for a large accounting firm and has been assigned to do the audit of her friend's business.

5. Sylvie Karam borrowed $100,000 for a home mortgage from First City National Bank. The mortgage was granted on normal credit terms. Sylvie is the partner in charge of the First City audit.

FINANCIAL REPORTING AND ANALYSIS TEAM PROJECT

CP1–9   **Team Project: Examining an Annual Report**

■ **LO1, 3**

As a team, select an industry to analyze. *Reuters* provides lists of industries and their make-up at www.investor.reuters.com. Each group member should acquire the annual report for one publicly traded company in the industry, with each member selecting a different company. (Library files, the SEDAR service at www.sedar.com, or the company's Web site are good sources. The Annual Report Gallery at www.reportgallery.com provides links to the Web sites of well-known companies.) On an individual basis, each group member should write a short report answering the following questions about the selected company.

1. What types of products or services does it sell?

2. On what day of the year does its fiscal year end?

3. For how many years does it present complete
   a. balance sheets?
   b. income statements?
   c. cash flow statements?

4. Are its financial statements audited by independent auditors? If so, by whom?

5. Did its total assets increase or decrease over the last year?

6. Did its net income increase or decrease over the last year?

Discuss any patterns that you observe as a team. Then, as a team, write a short report comparing and contrasting your companies, using the six attributes listed above.

LEARNING OBJECTIVES

Investing and Financing Decisions and the Balance Sheet

2

Van Houtte, founded in 1919, provides more than 100 different flavours of gourmet coffee and Bigelow teas by the cup to Chevron stations, Couche-Tard outlets, hotels, hospitals, and offices from Halifax to Nanaimo in Canada and from Los Angeles, California to Golfstown, New Hampshire in the United States. Its current network includes more than 3,575 points of sale in Canada and roughly 725 in the United States. Van Houtte purchases, roasts, and merchandises coffee beans online and in grocery stores across Canada. You can also enjoy a cup of espresso in one of its 74 café bistros in Quebec. Since 1993, Van Houtte has invested $260 million to grow through acquiring other companies, and more than $230 million to grow through purchasing coffee brewers, roasters, and distributing and retailing facilities.

Van Houtte exercises a social conscience in the area of coffee production and has been one of the first to market Fair Trade coffees, whereby farmers in Africa, Asia, and Central and South America are paid a premium for their product. In a joint initiative with Care Canada it launched a gourmet coffee from Honduras to help producers become self-sufficient. As part of its social responsibility, Van Houtte merchandises a line of organic coffees, the Coffee Lovers brand, and donates a percentage of its revenues from these sales to improve the lives of children of families living in coffee-growing communities.

Van Houtte achieved $348.8 million in sales in the fiscal year ending April 2, 2005. The company's growth in sales and total assets since 1994 is shown in the graph in millions of dollars and it has promised continued growth in the future.

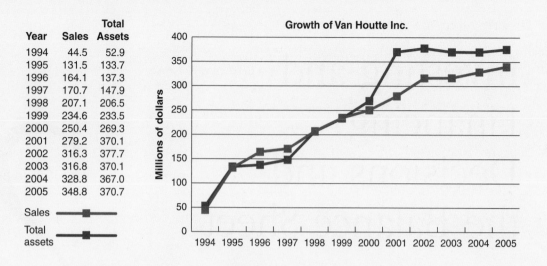

Year	Sales	Total Assets
1994	44.5	52.9
1995	131.5	133.7
1996	164.1	137.3
1997	170.7	147.9
1998	207.1	206.5
1999	234.6	233.5
2000	250.4	269.3
2001	279.2	370.1
2002	316.3	377.7
2003	316.8	370.1
2004	328.8	367.0
2005	348.8	370.7

UNDERSTANDING THE BUSINESS

Coffee is a global industry. Coffee consumed by North Americans is produced in and exported from some of the world's poorest countries. Kraft Foods, Nestlé, Sara Lee, and Procter & Gamble capture most of the $65-billion retail coffee market in North America. For the relatively small $3-billion retail market in coffee services, whether they sell by the cup in a convenience store or by the bag online, Green Mountain Coffee Roasters, Starbucks, and Van Houtte compete ferociously. Van Houtte distinguishes itself by its unique, single-cup coffee dispensing systems used in offices, gas stations, hotels, and university and college campuses. The most recent dispensing system, Espresso Café™, brews and dispenses cappuccinos and other specialty coffees in less than a minute. The company relies on a strategy of quality for both its products and its services, keeping its business simple and focused on coffee. It has grown both by acquiring related businesses and by controlling quality at each step in its supply chain. Financial statements help users understand how well the company has implemented its strategy and to assess future growth potential.

Financial statements for Canadian companies contain estimates of financial value that are developed in accordance with generally accepted accounting principles. Financial statements are intended to communicate the economic facts, measured in dollars and cents, in a standardized, formal way. Therefore, by applying accounting rules consistently, accountants formally communicate reliable estimates that faithfully represent important economic facts of a company like Van Houtte. As explained in Chapter 1, financial statements include four components: the balance sheet, the income statement, the statement of retained earnings, and the cash flow statement. In this chapter we focus on the balance sheet, and we examine how this financial statement communicates the results or consequences of Van Houtte's strategy by answering the following questions:

- What type of business activities cause changes in balance sheet amounts from one period to the next?
- How do specific activities affect each of the balance sheet amounts?
- How do companies keep track of these balance sheet amounts?

Once we have answered these questions, we will be able to perform two key analytical tasks:

1. To analyze and predict the effects of Van Houtte's business decisions on its financial statements.
2. To use financial statements of other competing companies to identify and evaluate activities that other managers engaged in during a past period. These latter inferences are a key to *financial statement analysis*.

In this chapter, we begin with the balance sheet as we focus on typical asset acquisition activities (often called *investing activities*) in which Van Houtte engages, along with the related *financing activities* such as borrowing funds from creditors and receiving funds from investors to acquire the assets. When we finish we will know the approximate financial value of what Van Houtte owns as well as where the money came from to make these investments. We examine activities affecting only balance sheet amounts. In Chapters 3 and 4 we discuss operating activities affecting both income statement and balance sheet amounts. Although these activities are all related, we separate them initially to aid your understanding.

ORGANIZATION OF THE CHAPTER

• Overview of the Conceptual Framework	• What Type of Business Activities Cause Changes in Balance Sheet Amounts?	• How Do Transactions Affect Accounts?	• How Do Companies Keep Track of Account Balances?	• How Is the Balance Sheet Prepared?
Concepts Emphasized in Chapter 2	Nature of Business Transactions	Principles of Transaction Analysis	The Direction of Transaction Effects and the Debit-Credit Framework	Some Misconceptions
Elements of the Classified Balance Sheet	Accounts	Analyzing Van Houtte's Transactions	Analytical Tools: The Journal Entry The T-account	
			Transaction Analysis Illustrated	

Let us begin our answers to the three questions by returning to the basic concepts introduced in Chapter 1.

OVERVIEW OF THE CONCEPTUAL FRAMEWORK

■ **LEARNING OBJECTIVE 1**
Define the objective of financial reporting and the related key accounting assumptions and principles.

The key accounting terms and concepts we defined in Chapter 1 are part of a framework, a coherent set of interrelated objectives and fundamental concepts. The framework is intended to lead to applying standards in a consistent manner in accounting practice. It prescribes the nature, function, and limitations of both financial accounting and financial statements. The essential elements of this framework are embodied in section 1000 of the *CICA Handbook,* which is a comprehensive set of accounting standards developed in Canada. The framework is synthesized from financial accounting theory developed over many years and has been published by the U.S. Financial Accounting Standards Board (FASB). The essential elements are outlined in Exhibit 2.1 and will be discussed gradually in each of the next four chapters as we introduce various aspects of the accounting process.

An understanding of the accounting concepts will be helpful as you study. It is much easier to learn and remember *how* the accounting process works if you know *why* it works a certain way. A clear understanding will also help you in future chapters as we examine more complex business activities.

CONCEPTS EMPHASIZED IN CHAPTER 2

Objective of Financial Reporting The top of the pyramid in Exhibit 2.1 indicates the **primary objective of external financial reporting**, which guides the remaining sections of the conceptual framework. The primary objective of financial reporting is to provide useful economic information about a business to help external parties,

The **PRIMARY OBJECTIVE OF EXTERNAL FINANCIAL REPORTING** is to provide useful economic information about a business to help external parties make sound financial decisions.

EXHIBIT **2.1**

Financial Accounting and
Reporting Conceptual
Framework

Primary Objective of External Financial Reporting [Ch. 2]

To provide useful economic information to external users for decision
making (for assessing future cash flows)

Elements of Financial Statements

Asset, Liability, Shareholders' Equity
  [Ch. 2]
Revenue, Expense, Gain, Loss [Ch. 3]

Qualitative Characteristics

Understandability, Relevance, Reliability,
  Comparability [Ch. 5]

Assumptions

Separate Entity [Ch. 2]
Continuity (Going Concern)
  [Ch. 2]
Unit of Measure [Ch. 2]
Periodicity [Ch. 3]

Principles

Historical Cost [Ch. 2]
Revenue Recognition [Ch. 3]
Matching [Ch. 3]
Full Disclosure [Ch. 5]

Constraints

Cost Benefit [Ch. 5]
Materiality [Ch. 4]

primarily investors and creditors, make sound financial decisions. The users of
accounting information are identified as *decision makers*. These decision makers
include average investors, creditors, and experts who provide financial advice. They
are all expected to have a reasonable understanding of accounting concepts and procedures (this may be one of the reasons why you are studying accounting). Of course,
as we discussed in Chapter 1, many other groups, such as suppliers and customers, also
use external financial statements.

Users are most interested in information to assist them in projecting the future cash
inflows and outflows of a business. For example, creditors and potential creditors need
to assess an entity's ability to pay interest over time and pay back the initial amount
borrowed, called the *principal*. Investors and potential investors want to assess the
entity's ability to pay dividends in the future. They also want to judge the future success of the company so that as the stock price rises, investors can then sell the stock for
more than the price they paid to buy it.

Underlying Assumptions of Accounting   The assumptions of accounting are
primarily based on the business environment in which accounting operates. They
reflect the scope of accounting and the expectations that set certain limits on how
accounting information is reported. Three of these assumptions were discussed in
Chapter 1. Under the **separate-entity assumption**, each business must be accounted
for as an individual organization, separate and apart from its owners, all other persons,
and other entities. Separation of the owners' resources (and obligations) from those of
the business entity is necessary for legal purposes and for a proper evaluation of the
entity's results of operations and its financial position. For example, a building purchased by one of the owners of a real estate development and management company
should not be mixed with buildings owned by the company. Under the **unit-of-
measure assumption**, each business entity accounts for and reports its financial results
primarily in terms of the national monetary unit (dollars in Canada, yen in Japan, pesos
in Mexico, etc.), even if the entity has business operations in many countries.

The use of a specific unit of measure allows for meaningful aggregation of financial
amounts. Furthermore, accountants assume that the unit of measure has a stable value
over time, even though we recognize that the price we pay to purchase a specific item,
such as a candy bar, tends to increase over time. Van Houtte's balance sheet includes
many assets measured in Canadian dollars from the 1970s, 1980s, and 1990s. The stable monetary unit assumption allows accountants to combine different dollar amounts,
even though the purchasing power of the dollar has changed over time.

For accounting purposes, a business normally is assumed to continue operating long
enough to meet contractual commitments and plans. This **continuity assumption** is some-

The **SEPARATE-ENTITY
ASSUMPTION** states that
business transactions are
separate from the transactions
of the owners.

The **UNIT-OF-MEASURE
ASSUMPTION** states that
accounting information should
be measured and reported in
the national monetary unit.

The **CONTINUITY (GOING-
CONCERN) ASSUMPTION**
states that businesses are
assumed to continue to operate
into the foreseeable future.

times called the *going-concern assumption* because we expect a business to continue to operate into the foreseeable future. Violation of this assumption means that assets and liabilities can be valued and reported on the balance sheet as if the company were to be liquidated (that is, discontinued, with all assets sold and all debts paid). In all future chapters, unless indicated otherwise, we assume that businesses meet the continuity assumption.

Basic Accounting Principle   The historical **cost principle** states that the cash-equivalent cost needed to acquire an asset (the historical cost) should be used for initial recognition (recording) of all financial statement elements. Under the cost principle, cost is measured on the date of the transaction as the cash paid plus the current dollar value of all non-cash considerations (any assets, privileges, or rights) also given in the exchange. For example, if you trade your computer plus cash for a new car, the cost of the new car is equal to the cash paid plus the market value of the computer. Thus, in most cases, cost is relatively easy to determine and can be verified. A disadvantage is that, subsequent to the date of acquisition, the continued use of historical cost on the balance sheet does not reflect any changes in market value.

Van Houtte Inc. owns land that cost $1,571,000 when it was acquired several years ago. Although the market price or economic value of the land has risen over time, its recorded value remains unchanged at $1,571,000, because this amount is an objective measure based on an actual exchange that occurred in the past. It would be desirable to show on the balance sheet the land's current value; that is, the price at which it could either be sold or replaced instead of its outdated historical cost. However, the land's current value may not be reliable if different real estate appraisers produce different values for the same piece of land. For this reason, accountants continue to rely on historical cost measures for reporting purposes because they are factual though they may not be useful for specific decision-making purposes.

Assets, liabilities, and shareholders' equity are the key elements of a corporation's balance sheet, as we learned in Chapter 1. Let us review the definitions.

> The **COST PRINCIPLE** requires assets to be recorded at the historical cash-equivalent cost, which on the date of the transaction is cash paid plus the current dollar value of all non-cash considerations also given in the exchange.

ELEMENTS OF THE CLASSIFIED BALANCE SHEET

When we classify, we group similar things together and arrange them in a specific order. There are three major groups or classifications on a *classified balance sheet:* assets, liabilities, and shareholders' equity. Each of these three large groups is divided into subgroups.

Let us explore Van Houtte's simplified balance sheet, presented in Exhibit 2.2. First, notice the title of the statement, Consolidated Balance Sheet. *Consolidated* means that the classified elements of Van Houtte's balance sheet are combined with those of other companies under its control (e.g., VKI Technologies).[1] For convenience, the amounts for the various balance sheet elements are shown in *thousands of dollars*. Two amounts are shown for each element: one at April 2, 2005, and the other at April 3, 2004, one year earlier. This system allows investors to compare at a glance the value of each classified element from year to year, and then analyze these changes to understand if the company's financial position has improved or deteriorated over time.

Van Houtte's balance sheet is shown in *column* or *report* format, with assets listed first, followed by liabilities, and then shareholders' equity. Other companies may choose an account format with the assets listed on the left hand side and liabilities and shareholders' equity listed on the right. Both formats are standard ways of communicating the same information. We will now explain the various elements that appear on Van Houtte's balance sheet.

Assets are economic resources controlled by an entity as a result of past transactions or events and from which future economic benefits may be obtained. In other words, these are the resources that the entity has and can use to operate in the future. When reporting conservative information to users, managers use judgment (and past experience) to determine the most likely future benefit. For example, a company may have a

> ■ **LEARNING OBJECTIVE 2**
>
> Define the elements of a classified balance sheet.

> **ASSETS** are economic resources controlled by an entity as a result of past transactions or events and from which future economic benefits may be obtained.

---

[1]The rules for consolidation of financial statements are covered in advanced accounting courses.

EXHIBIT **2.2**

Van Houtte's Balance Sheet

VAN HOUTTE INC.
Consolidated Balance Sheet
(in thousands of dollars)

Assets	April 2, 2005	April 3, 2004
Current assets		
Cash	$ 5,400	$ 7,300
Accounts receivable	41,300	36,400
Inventories	28,000	26,800
Prepaid expenses	3,300	3,300
Other current assets	1,700	2,500
Total current assets	79,700	76,300
Investments	18,900	18,100
Fixed assets, net	115,800	117,000
Goodwill	141,700	140,900
Other long term assets	14,600	17,800
Total assets	**$370,700**	**$370,100**
Liabilities and shareholders' equity		
Current liabilities		
Accounts payable	$ 31,900	$ 25,500
Accrued liabilities	9,700	7,600
Current portion of long term debt	28,000	22,700
Total current liabilities	69,600	55,800
Long term notes payable	60,300	84,800
Other long term liabilities	9,400	10,300
Total liabilities	139,300	150,900
Shareholders' equity		
Share capital	130,300	127,100
Retained earnings	101,100	92,100
Total shareholders' equity	231,400	219,200
Total liabilities and shareholders' equity	**$370,700**	**$370,100**

Note: These balance sheets are adaptations of Van Houtte's actual balance sheets at those dates. Some of the actual balance sheet elements were combined for illustrative purposes.

list of customers who owe $10,000. However, past experience suggests that only $9,800 will be collected. The more probable or conservative figure is reported to users for projecting future cash flows.

Exhibit 2.2 presents Van Houtte's balance sheet, with amounts rounded to the nearest hundred thousand dollars. Notice that Van Houtte's fiscal year ends on the last Saturday in March, or the first Saturday in April, which was March 29 in 2003 and April 3 in 2004. The choice of year-ends will be discussed in Chapter 4.

Typically, the assets of a company include:

1. Current assets (short term)
   a. Cash and cash equivalents
   b. Short-term investments
   c. Accounts receivable
   d. Inventory
   e. Prepaid expenses (i.e., expenses paid in advance of use)
   f. Other current assets

2. Non-current assets (long term)
   a. Long-term investments
   b. Property, plant, and equipment (at cost less accumulated amortization)
   c. Intangible assets
   d. Other (miscellaneous) assets

Assets are divided into two subgroups, current and non-current assets. **Current assets**, also known as *short-term assets,* are those economic resources that Van Houtte will either transform into cash or use within one year of the balance sheet date or one operating cycle of the company's business, whichever is longer. Assets are listed on the balance sheet *in order of liquidity,* which means how soon they can be transformed into cash. Under current assets, *Cash and cash equivalents* (highly liquid investments) appear first because they are the most liquid assets. It should be emphasized that each of the items reported on the balance sheet, such as cash and cash equivalents, is a combination of a number of similar items. For Van Houtte, there were no cash equivalents at April 2, 2005. Furthermore, Van Houtte did not report any *short-term investments,* such as shares of other companies purchased as investments of excess cash.

Any *receivable* represents an amount of money owed to Van Houtte. *Accounts receivable* represent amounts owed by customers who purchased products and services on credit. These amounts are normally collected within one year of the balance sheet date.

Inventory refers to goods that (1) are held for sale to customers in the normal course of business, or (2) are used to produce goods or services for sale. Inventory is always considered to be a current asset, no matter how long it takes to produce and sell. Van Houtte's inventory would include green and roasted coffee beans not yet sold to distributors, coffee brewing equipment purchased but not yet sold to customers wanting its coffee services, as well as bags of ground coffees and teas. *Prepaid expenses* (e.g., insurance premiums and rent paid in advance of use of a building) reflect available benefits (e.g., monthly insurance protection, office space) that the company will use within one year. *Other assets,* when reported, will include a number of assets with smaller balances that are combined together.

CURRENT ASSETS are assets that will be used or turned into cash, normally within one year. Inventory is always considered to be a current asset, regardless of the time needed to produce and sell it.

FINANCIAL **ANALYSIS**

ANALYSIS OF CHANGES IN INVENTORY AND ACCOUNTS RECEIVABLE

Investors analyze the financial statements of a company to decide whether or not to purchase its shares or to lend it money. One important decision factor is how easily a company can access cash to pay both its debts to creditors and its dividends to shareholders. In a normal business cycle, Van Houtte would produce roasted coffee beans for sale to distributors such as Safeway and Provigo. But there is a gap between the time the beans are roasted and the date they are sold. During this time the beans are called *inventory.* The less time the beans remain unsold in inventory, the faster this inventory is transformed into cash from sales. Let us assume for simplicity that Van Houtte's inventory represents these unsold coffee beans, and examine the company's ability to access cash.

At first glance the cash has decreased from $7.3 million at April 3, 2004 to $5.4 million at April 2, 2005. An investor would also observe that the accounts receivable increased from $36.4 million at April 3, 2004 to $41.3 million at April 2, 2005, indicating that the company has collected less cash from customers who bought merchandise on credit. Investors would examine the cash flow statement for further explanation of how events in the past year resulted in the change in cash (see Chapter 5). For the moment, based on this brief analysis, an investor would be reassured that the first two elements reported on the balance sheet are relevant to answering an important question about how easily Van Houtte can access cash to pay its debts and dividends.

NON-CURRENT ASSETS are considered to be long term because they will be used or turned into cash over a period longer than the next year.

Following the Current assets section, Van Houtte reports a number of **non-current assets**. These assets are considered to be long term because they will be used or turned into cash over a period longer than the next year. *Investments* are long-term assets such as shares issued by other companies that will not be used to produce goods and services. *Property, plant, and equipment* includes all land, buildings, machinery, and equipment such as tools, furniture, and other fixtures that will be used to produce Van Houtte's goods and services. These are also called *fixed assets* or *capital assets*—they have a physical form you can touch, and therefore each asset is *tangible*.

Intangible assets have no physical existence but have a long life. They usually are not acquired for resale but are directly related to the operations of the business. Intangible assets include such items as franchises, patents, trademarks, copyrights, and goodwill. Their values arise from the *legal rights* and *privileges* of ownership, and can be identified only as a result of a purchase that transfers ownership. For example, if Van Houtte develops and patents a process for brewing coffee, the value of this intangible asset will not appear on its balance sheet because no transaction with an external party has occurred that lets the accountant identify and verify the asset's value in the marketplace. Van Houtte does report goodwill, a special type of intangible asset related to its purchases of other companies over the years. Intangible assets, including goodwill, are discussed in more detail in Chapter 9.

Other assets, when reported, will include a number of assets that are combined together because of their relatively small values.

LIABILITIES are probable debts or obligations of the entity that result from past transactions, which will be paid with assets or services.

Liabilities are a corporation's debts and obligations arising from past transactions. They represent future outflows of assets (mainly cash) or services to the *creditors* that provided the corporation with the resources needed to conduct its business. When the corporation borrows money, creditors receive not only full payment of the amount owed to them, but also interest on the borrowed amount.

Typically, the liabilities of a company include:

1. Current liabilities (short term)
   a. Bank indebtedness
   b. Accounts payable
   c. Accrued liabilities
   d. Current portion of long-term debt
   e. Other current liabilities

2. Non-current liabilities (long term)
   a. Notes and mortgages payable
   b. Lease obligations
   c. Bonds payable
   d. Other long-term liabilities

CURRENT LIABILITIES are obligations that will be paid in cash (or other current assets) or satisfied by providing service within the coming year.

Like assets, liabilities are divided into two subgroups, current and non-current. They are listed by *order of time to maturity,* which means how soon an obligation must be paid. **Current liabilities**, known as short-term liabilities, must be paid within the next year or the operating business cycle of the company, whichever is longer. Normally the cash from converting current assets is used to pay current liabilities. The first current liability represents short-term loans from banks. Bank loans are common when the company does not have a sufficient amount of cash to pay its creditors. The second current liability is *Accounts payable,* which represents the total amount owed to suppliers of the raw materials used in making coffee. The third liability, *Accrued liabilities,* is the total amount owed to suppliers for various types of services such as payroll, rent, and other obligations. Current liabilities also include borrowings from banks and other financial institutions that must be repaid within a year. When an entity has long-term debt, the portion that becomes payable within the next year is called the *current portion of long-term debt. Other current liabilities,* when reported, will include a number of liabilities with relatively small amounts that are combined together.

FINANCIAL **ANALYSIS**

ANALYSIS OF CHANGE IN ACCOUNTS PAYABLE

Using both current assets and current liabilities for Van Houtte, we can improve our analysis of how accessible cash will be to repay debts to creditors and dividends to shareholders.

The company's current liabilities shows that Van Houtte owes $13.8 million more in current liabilities at April 2, 2005 than it did at April 3, 2004. As investors, we would tentatively conclude that the company has relied further on suppliers of goods and services to finance its current assets. However, investors must learn far more about the business cycle for coffee services, the outlook for the coffee industry, and Van Houtte's main competitors before coming to a firm conclusion.

At the beginning of this chapter we stated that investors are most interested in relevant information that helps them predict future cash inflows and outflows. From this very preliminary analysis, investors can predict that because Van Houtte has increased its current liabilities by $13.8 million, a larger amount of cash is needed next year to repay the outstanding debt to creditors than in the current year.

Long-term liabilities are a company's debts having maturities that extend beyond one year from the balance sheet date. They include long-term bank loans, bonds, mortgages, pension liabilities, and lease obligations, among others. At April 2, 2005 Van Houtte's balance sheet showed various types of long-term liabilities, which will be covered in future chapters.

LONG-TERM LIABILITIES are a company's debts that have maturities that extend beyond one year from the balance sheet date.

A QUESTION OF **ETHICS**

ENVIRONMENTAL LIABILITIES

Due to changing legal requirements and concerns for social responsibility, companies are facing significant pressure to estimate and disclose environmental liabilities, such as the clean-up of hazardous waste sites and site restoration and reclamation costs. Determining the amounts and likelihood of environmental obligations, though, can be very difficult when the costs of remediation are not clearly evident.

Recent studies suggest that many companies face environmental liabilities, yet most fail to disclose the financial risk involved in complying with environmental regulations. In a study of 13 pulp and paper companies, at least half could have negative financial impacts between 5 percent and 10 percent of the market value of the companies' equity; however, few had adequately disclosed the financial risk in their financial reports.* Likewise, financial reports by semiconductor manufacturers facing potential liabilities from the environmental impact of using chemicals in the manufacturing process were also reviewed. The study found "no reporting at all on environmental performance."

The reporting of environmental performance and accounting for environmental obligations is an important issue in Canada because of the country's richness in natural resources. Companies that operate in the oil, mining, pharmaceuticals, and chemical industries need to identify potential environmental liabilities, estimate their magnitude, and disclose them in their financial reports. As an example, PotashCorp, which is the world's largest producer of crop nutrients and industrial nitrogen, included an amount of US$81.3 as "accrued reclamation costs" to restore sites used for production purposes.

*Bryan Lee, "SEC Urged to Up Compliance," Dow Jones Newswires, January 31, 2001, Article 6.

SHAREHOLDERS' EQUITY (OWNERS' EQUITY OR STOCKHOLDERS' EQUITY) is the financing provided by the owners and the operations of the business.

Shareholders' equity (owners' equity or stockholders' equity) is the financing provided to the corporation by both its owners and the operations of the business. One key difference between owners and creditors is that creditors are entitled to settlement of their legal claims on the corporation's assets before the owners receive a penny, even if this consumes all the corporation's assets. Consequently, owners have a residual claim on the corporation's assets.

Owners *invest* (purchase shares) in a company because they expect to receive two types of cash flow: dividends, which are a distribution of the corporation's earnings (a return on shareholders' investment), and gains from selling their shares for more than they paid (known as *capital gains*).

Typically the shareholders' equity of a corporation includes:

1. Share capital (or capital stock)
2. Retained earnings (accumulated earnings that have not been declared as dividends)

SHARE CAPITAL results from owners providing cash (and sometimes other assets) to the business.

Share capital reflects the proceeds received when the corporation issued the shares. Occasionally, shareholders will contribute resources for which they do not receive shares; such contributions are called *contributed surplus*. The sum of share capital and contributed surplus represents the *contributed capital* of the corporation. The 2004 edition of *Financial Reporting in Canada* reports that approximately 45 percent of the 200 companies surveyed had disclosed contributed surplus in their 2002 financial statements.[2] Van Houtte's share capital of $130.3 million has resulted from selling shares to investors at different points in the company's history.

RETAINED EARNINGS refers to the cumulative earnings of a company that are not distributed to the owners and are reinvested in the business.

Most companies that operate profitably retain part of their earnings for reinvestment in their business. The other part is distributed as dividends to shareholders. The annual earnings that are not distributed to shareholders are called **retained earnings**. Van Houtte's retained earnings equal $101.1 million at April 2, 2005 and represent the net amount of earnings that have not been distributed to shareholders since the company was incorporated in 1980.

A Note on Ratio Analysis   Users of financial information compute a number of ratios in analyzing a company's past performance and financial condition as input in predicting its future potential. For example, using the elements and classification in the balance sheet, creditors can assess a company's ability to pay off its debt, or see what the company's trend is in taking on more debt.

The change in ratios over time and how they compare to the ratios of the company's competitors provide valuable information for users' decisions. We begin our look at ratio analysis by examining the debt-to-equity ratio in this chapter. This ratio and many others will be presented throughout the rest of this textbook, with a final summary of ratio analysis in Chapter 13.

KEY **RATIO ANALYSIS:**

THE DEBT-TO-EQUITY RATIO

ANALYTICAL QUESTION → As an investor who must decide whether or not to buy shares, it is important to know how much of the company's assets is financed by creditors and how much is financed by the owners. The *debt-to-equity ratio* is used to assess the debt capacity of a business. It is computed as follows:

$$\text{Debt-to-Equity Ratio} = \frac{\text{Total Liabilities}}{\text{Total Shareholders' Equity}}$$

■ **LEARNING OBJECTIVE 3**

Compute and interpret the debt-to-equity ratio.

---

[2]C. Byrd, I. Chen, and J. Smith, *Financial Reporting in Canada* 2004. Toronto: CICA, 2004, p. 320.

The 2005 ratio for Van Houtte is:

$$\$139,300 \div \$231,400 = 0.60$$

RATIO AND COMPARISONS

Comparisons over Time			Comparisons with Competitors*	
Van Houtte Inc.			Starbucks	Green Mountain Coffee Roasters
2003	2004	2005	2004**	2004
0.74	0.69	0.60	0.37	0.76

INTERPRETATIONS

In General → The debt-to-equity ratio indicates how much debt has been used to finance the company's acquisition of assets relative to equity financing that is supplied by shareholders. A high ratio normally suggests that a company relies heavily on funds provided by creditors. Managers use the ratio to decide if they should finance any additional acquisitions using debt. Creditors use this ratio to assess the risk that a company may not be able to meet its financial obligations during a business downturn. Investors use this ratio to assess the level of financial risk associated with the expected cash flows from their investment (dividends and appreciation in the share value).

Focus Company Analysis → Van Houtte's debt-to-equity ratio decreased significantly from 0.74 in 2003 to 0.69 in 2004, and again to 0.60 in 2005. This indicates that Van Houtte's assets at April 2, 2005 are financed with $0.60 in debt for every $1 of equity. Van Houtte's balance sheet shows that in 2005, the company increased its equity by $12.2 million while its total liabilities decreased by $11.6 million. These financing decisions helped reduce the ratio to 0.60. An investor would also read other reports, such as the company's *Annual Information Form,* and carefully review the "Management Discussion and Analysis" section in Van Houtte's annual report to discover why these changes have occurred.

> **SELECTED FOCUS COMPANY DEBT-TO-EQUITY RATIOS**
>
> WestJet Airlines Ltd.   2.18
> Gildan Activewear   0.49
> Intrawest Corporation   1.86

Investors look not only at ratios over time for Van Houtte, but also at the debt-to-equity ratio of competitors for comparison purposes. The debt-to-equity ratio of Green Mountain Coffee Roasters is higher than Van Houtte's, but Starbucks' ratio is significantly lower than both. This suggests that Van Houtte has a higher financial risk than Starbucks, and may not be in as good a financial position as Starbucks to generate the cash necessary to meet its financial obligations in case of a business downturn.

A Few Cautions → The debt-to-equity ratio tells only part of the story with respect to risks associated with debt. The ratio is a good indication of debt capacity, but it does not help the investor understand whether the company's operations can support the amount of debt that it has. Remember that debt carries with it the obligation to make cash payments for interest and principal. As a result, most investors would evaluate the debt-to-equity ratio within the context of the amount of cash the company is able to generate from operating activities. While the current ratio indicates whether the accessibility of cash has improved or not, investors can complete a more detailed analysis of relevant information on the cash flow statement, which we introduce later in this chapter.

---

*Investors cannot always compare closest competitors. Some companies are privately owned and their financial information is not publicly available. Other close competitors are owned by larger corporations. For example, Tim Hortons seems a natural competitor for Van Houtte's café–bistros, but it is owned by a U.S. company, Wendy's International Inc. Another, Second Cup, is owned by a Canadian company, Cara Foods Ltd., which has recently become a private company. Kraft, Nestlé, and Sara Lee compete to sell ground coffee in grocery stores where Van Houtte also sells its coffee; however, these U.S. companies all sell much more than simply coffee.
**The ratios for Van Houtte's competitors are shown for 2004 instead of 2005 because the three companies have different fiscal year-ends.

SELF-STUDY QUIZ 2-1

Wendy's International

Wendy's International, Inc., had the following balances on a recent balance sheet (in thousands):

Liabilities—$876,934; Shareholders' equity—$1,758,606

Compute Wendy's debt-to-equity ratio:

What does this tell you about Wendy's financing strategy?

After you complete your answers, check them with the solutions on page 78.

As you can see, using the relevant financial information from financial statements to calculate a single ratio is only the first step toward understanding whether a company is healthy enough to merit your investment dollar. The real challenges are discovering why the ratios have changed over time, comparing to competitors' ratios, developing a keen understanding of the industry and businesses, and using all this knowledge to predict the future for a company.

Now that we have reviewed several of the basic accounting concepts and terms, we need to understand the economic activities of a business that result in changes in amounts reported in financial statements and the process used in generating the financial statements.

WHAT TYPE OF BUSINESS ACTIVITIES CAUSE CHANGES IN BALANCE SHEET AMOUNTS?

NATURE OF BUSINESS TRANSACTIONS

■ **LEARNING OBJECTIVE 4**

Identify what constitutes a business transaction and identify common balance sheet account titles used in business.

A **TRANSACTION** is (1) an exchange between a business and one or more external parties to a business or (2) a measurable internal event such as *adjustments* for the use of assets in operations.

Accounting focuses on specific events that have an economic impact on the entity. These are called **transactions** and are recorded as a part of the accounting process. The first step in translating the results of business events to financial statement numbers is determining which events are and are not transactions. Only transactions are reflected in the statements. Note that the definitions of *assets* and *liabilities* indicate that only economic resources and debts *resulting from past transactions* are recorded on the balance sheet. A broad definition includes two types of transactions:

1. *External events:* These are *exchanges* of assets and liabilities between the business and one or more other parties. Examples include the purchase of a machine, the sale of merchandise, the borrowing of cash, and the investment in the business by the owners. These types of transactions will be discussed in this chapter as they affect the balance sheet elements and in Chapter 3 as they affect income statement elements.

2. *Internal events:* These events are not exchanges between the business and other parties but have a direct and measurable effect on the accounting entity. Examples include losses due to fire or other natural disasters and *adjustments* such as those to record the use of property, plant, and equipment in operations and interest expense on money that was borrowed. Adjustments will be discussed in Chapter 4.

Throughout this textbook, the word *transaction* will be used in the broad sense to include both types of events.

At the same time, some important events that have an economic impact on the company are not reflected in Van Houtte's statements. In most cases, signing a contract, which involves no cash, goods, services, or property changing hands, is not considered to be a transaction because it involves only the exchange of promises, not of assets or liabilities. For example, if Van Houtte hires a new regional manager and signs an employment contract, no transaction occurs from an accounting perspective because no exchange of assets or liabilities has occurred. Each party to the contract has made promises (the manager agrees to work; Van Houtte agrees to pay in exchange for the manager's work). For each day the new manager works, however, the exchange of services by the employee results in a transaction that Van Houtte must record (as an obligation to pay the manager's salary).

How does the accounting staff at Van Houtte record external and internal events that cause changes in the company's balance sheet amounts? The recording of transactions has evolved over time. Advances in computer hardware and software technology have paved the way for efficient recording of transactions and instantaneous preparation of financial statements. However, the basic system of recording transactions has withstood the test of time, and has been in use for the past 500 years. This initial system was documented by Fr. Luca Pacioli, an Italian monk, who wrote a book in 1494 that included the rudiments of the recordkeeping system that entities use today.

Even prior to Pacioli's treatise, merchants devised their own systems to keep track of their business dealings. Accounting historians have researched the practices previously used in various countries and reported interesting and fascinating methods of recording transactions that attest to the ingenuity of the human mind.

The basic tenets of manual and computerized recording systems are discussed in this chapter and elaborated on further in Chapters 3 and 4.

ACCOUNTS

An **account** is a standardized format that organizations use to accumulate the dollar effects of transactions on each financial statement item. The resulting balances are kept separate for financial statement purposes. Each company must establish a chart of accounts to facilitate recording transactions. A *chart of accounts* is the list of all of the account names, usually organized by financial statement element. That is, asset accounts are listed first (such as Cash, Inventory, Accounts Receivable, Equipment, and Land) followed by liability accounts (such as Accounts Payable, Notes Payable, and Taxes Payable), shareholders' equity accounts (Share Capital and Retained Earnings), revenue accounts (such as Sales Revenue), and expense accounts (such as Payroll Expense). The account names listed here are quite common and are used by most companies.

You have probably already noticed some regularities in how accounts are named:

1. Accounts with "receivable" in the title are always assets, representing amounts owed to the corporation.

2. Accounts with "payable" in the title are always liabilities, representing amounts the corporation owes to its creditors.

The chart of accounts also lists a unique number for each account that is used when entering data into the accounting system. For example, 1-111 could be the account number for Cash, 1-146 for Supplies Inventory, 2-221 for Long-Term Notes Payable, 3-111 for Share Capital, 4-235 for Rent Revenue, and 5-138 for Salaries Expense. In formal recordkeeping systems, including computerized accounting systems, use of appropriate account numbers is important.

The accounts you see in the financial statements are actually summations (or aggregations) of a number of more detailed accounts in a company's accounting system. For example, Van Houtte keeps separate inventory accounts for paper supplies, food, and

An **ACCOUNT** is a standardized format that organizations use to accumulate the dollar effects of transactions on each financial statement item.

beverages but combines them as Inventories on the balance sheet. Since our aim is to understand financial statements, we focus on aggregated accounts as presented in the statements.

INTERNATIONAL **PERSPECTIVE**

The News Corporation Limited

UNDERSTANDING THE MEANING OF ACCOUNT TITLES IN FOREIGN FINANCIAL STATEMENTS

Chapter 1 states that differences in the political, cultural, and economic environment of other countries have produced significant variations in accounting and reporting rules. Foreign companies often use different account titles than Canadian companies use. Some also use additional accounts for financial statement items not normally reported under Canadian accounting rules. For example, an Australian company, The News Corporation Limited, headed by K. Rupert Murdoch, follows A-GAAP (Australian generally accepted accounting principles). The principal activities of The News Corporation Limited include printing and publishing books, newspapers, and magazines, television broadcasting, and film production and distribution. Similar Canadian corporations include CanWest Global Communications Corp. and Quebecor Inc. The titles of accounts in a recent financial report are similar to those used by Canadian companies, except for liabilities and shareholders' equity:

Australian Accounts	Canadian Equivalents
Liabilities	
Borrowings	Similar to Notes and Bonds Payable
Creditors	Relates to what is owed to suppliers and others, similar to Accounts Payable
Provision	A summary of payables for income tax, dividends, payroll, and other liabilities
Shareholders' Equity	
Retained Profits	Similar to Retained Earnings

Every company has a different chart of accounts, depending on the nature of its business activities. For example, a small lawn care service may have an asset account called Lawn Mowing Equipment, but it is unlikely that the Royal Bank of Canada would need such an account. These differences will become more apparent as we examine the balance sheets of various companies.

Because each company has a different chart of accounts, you should *not* try to memorize a typical chart of accounts. **When you prepare homework problems, either you will be given the account names the company uses or you should select appropriate descriptive names.** Once a name is selected for an account, the exact name must be used in all transactions that affect the account.

SELF-STUDY **QUIZ 2-2**

Wendy's International

The following is a list of accounts from a recent balance sheet for Wendy's International, Inc. Indicate on the line provided whether each of the following is an asset (A), liability (L), or shareholders' equity account (SE).

____ Salaries and Wages Payable   ____ Long-Term Capital Lease Obligations

____ Buildings   ____ Restaurant Equipment

____ Notes Receivable   ____ Retained Earnings

____ Accounts and Drafts Payable   ____ Short-Term Investments

After you complete the schedules, check them with the answers on page 78.

HOW DO TRANSACTIONS AFFECT ACCOUNTS?

Managers make business decisions that often result in transactions affecting financial statements. Typical decisions are to expand the number of stores, advertise a new product, change employee benefit packages, and invest excess cash. Keeping a historical record (like a diary of important events) allows managers to evaluate the effects of past decisions and plan future business activities. In planning, managers are interested in how the implementation of their plans (their decisions) will be reflected on the financial statements. For example, the decision to purchase additional inventory for cash in anticipation of a major sales initiative increases the inventory and decreases cash. If the demand for the inventory does not occur, a lower cash balance reduces the company's flexibility and ability to pay other obligations. Business decisions often involve an element of risk that should be assessed. Therefore, it is necessary for business managers to understand how transactions impact the accounts on the financial statements. The process for determining the effects of transactions is called *transaction analysis* and is discussed next.

■ **LEARNING OBJECTIVE 5**

Apply transaction analysis to simple business transactions in terms of the accounting model: Assets = Liabilities + Shareholders' Equity.

PRINCIPLES OF TRANSACTION ANALYSIS

Transaction analysis is the process of studying a transaction to determine its economic effect on the entity in terms of the accounting equation (A = L + SE, also known as the *accounting model*). We will outline the process in this section of the chapter and create a visual tool representing the process (the transaction analysis model). The basic accounting equation and two fundamental concepts are the foundation for the transaction analysis model. The two concepts underlying the transaction analysis process are that:

TRANSACTION ANALYSIS is the process of studying a transaction to determine its economic effect on the business in terms of the accounting equation.

1. Every transaction affects at least two accounts (duality of effects); it is critical to identify correctly the accounts affected and the direction of the effect (increase or decrease).

2. The accounting equation must remain in balance after each transaction.

Success in performing transaction analysis depends on a clear understanding of how the transaction analysis model is constructed, based on these concepts. **Study this material well. You should not move on to a new concept until you understand and can apply all prior concepts.**

Duality of Effects   The first concept is that every transaction has *at least two effects* on the basic accounting equation. This is known as the *duality of effects,* which is the foundation of the *double-entry system* of recordkeeping. Most transactions with external parties involve an *exchange* of assets, liabilities, and/or equity between the entity and the external party. For example, suppose that Van Houtte purchased some paper napkins for cash.

Transaction	Van Houtte Received	Van Houtte Gave
Purchased paper napkins for cash	Supplies (increased)	Cash (decreased)

In analyzing this transaction, we determined that the accounts affected were Supplies and Cash. As we discussed in Chapter 1, however, most supplies are purchased on credit (that is, money is owed to suppliers). In that case, Van Houtte would engage in *two* transactions: (1) the purchase of an asset on credit and (2) the eventual payment. In the first transaction, Van Houtte would receive supplies (an increase in an asset) and would give in return a promise to pay later (an increase in a liability). In the second transaction, Van Houtte would eliminate or receive back its promise to pay (a decrease in the accounts payable liability) and would give up cash (a decrease in an asset).

Transaction	Van Houtte Received	Van Houtte Gave
(1) Purchased paper napkins on credit	Supplies (increased)	Accounts Payable (increased) [a promise to pay]
(2) Paid on its accounts payable	Accounts Payable (decreased) [a promise was eliminated]	Cash (decreased)

As noted earlier, not all important business activities result in a transaction that affects the financial statements. Most important, signing a contract involving the exchange of two promises to perform a future business transaction does not result in an accounting transaction that is recorded at the date of signing the contract. For example, consider the case in which Van Houtte and Xerox sign an agreement, with Xerox promising to provide repair service on Van Houtte's copy machines at a price of $50 for each visit during the next year and Van Houtte promising to pay for the service when Xerox provides it. No accounting transaction has taken place yet because Van Houtte and Xerox have exchanged only promises.[3] When Xerox provides service, however, a transaction occurs since service is exchanged for a promise to pay.

Similarly, if Van Houtte sent an order to its paper supplier for more napkins and the supplier accepted the order, which will be filled the following week, no transaction has taken place for accounting purposes. Only two promises have been exchanged. From the supplier's perspective, the same holds true. No transaction has taken place, so the supplier's financial statements are unaffected. As soon as the napkins are shipped to Van Houtte, however, the supplier has given up inventory in exchange for a promise from Van Houtte to pay for the napkins, and Van Houtte has exchanged its promise to pay for the napkins that it received as ordered. *One promise* has been exchanged for *goods*, so a transaction has taken place, and both Van Houtte and the supplier's statements will be affected.

---

[3]Contracts of this nature that are likely to result in significant future liabilities must be noted in the financial statements as commitments.

Balancing the Accounting Equation The accounting equation must remain in balance after each transaction. Total assets must equal total liabilities and shareholders' equity. If the correct accounts have been identified and the appropriate direction of the effect on each account has been determined, then the equation should remain in balance. Therefore, in performing the transaction analysis process, you should complete the following steps in this order:

1. *Accounts and effects*
   a. **Identify the accounts affected**, making sure that the duality concept is met. Ask yourself what is given and what is received.
   b. **Classify each account** as an asset (A), liability (L), or shareholders' equity (SE).
   c. **Determine the direction of the effect** (amount of increase [+] or decrease [−] on each account).

2. *Balancing*
   d. **Determine that the accounting equation (A = L + SE) remains in balance.**

ANALYZING VAN HOUTTE'S TRANSACTIONS

Let us consider typical transactions and events of Van Houtte, and most other businesses, as examples to illustrate the use of this process. As we stated earlier, only transactions affecting balance sheet accounts are presented in this chapter. Assume that Van Houtte has the following transactions during April 2005 (the month following the balance sheet in Exhibit 2.2). The month will end on April 30. Accounts titles are based on that balance sheet and are summarized in Exhibit 2.3. As stated earlier, each account has a unique number, but these numbers are omitted for simplicity.

EXHIBIT **2.3**

Van Houtte's Chart of Accounts

Chart of Accounts (to be used in our Van Houtte example)	To account for
Assets (A)	
Cash	— Cash on hand
Accounts Receivable	— Amounts owed by customers, franchisees, and affiliates
Inventories	— Food, beverage, and paper products supplies on hand
Prepaid Expenses	— Benefits or rights to be received in the future (e.g., insurance coverage, rent)
Other Current Assets	— Summary of a number of accounts with smaller balances (current in nature)
Investments	— Amounts invested in securities of other entities
Fixed Assets	— The cost of land, buildings, and equipment to be used in operations in the future
Notes Receivable	— Funds lent to others (e.g., affiliates, employees)
Other Long-Term Assets	— Summary of a number of accounts with smaller balances (long-term in nature)
Liabilities (L)	
Accounts Payable	— Amount owed to suppliers (e.g., for coffee beans, for utility usage)
Accrued Liabilities	— Amount to be paid to others (e.g., wages to employees, interest on debt)
Other Current Liabilities	— Summary of a number of accounts with smaller balances (current in nature)
Long-Term Notes Payable	— Amounts borrowed from banks
Other Long-Term Liabilities	— Summary of a number of accounts with smaller balances (long-term in nature)
Shareholders' Equity (SE)	
Share Capital	— Amount paid by investors in exchange for the company's shares
Retained Earnings	— Accumulated net income not distributed to shareholders as dividends

All of the amounts used in this illustration are in thousands of dollars.

(a) **Van Houtte issues shares to new investors in exchange for $1,300 in cash.**

1. Identify and classify accounts and effects.	*Cash (A) is received + $1,300. Share certificates are given, Share Capital (SE) + $1,300.*
2. Is the accounting equation in balance?	*Yes. There is a $1,300 increase on the left side and a $1,300 increase on the right side of the equation.*

Assets	=	Liabilities	+	Shareholders' Equity
Cash				**Share Capital**
(a) +1,300	=			+1,300

(b) **The company borrows $1,000 from its local bank, signing a promissory note to be paid in two years.**

1. Identify and classify accounts and effects.	*Cash (A) is received + $1,000. A written promise to pay is given to the bank, Notes Payable (L) + $1,000.*
2. Is the accounting equation in balance?	*Yes. There is a $1,000 increase on the left side and a $1,000 increase on the right side of the equation.*

	Assets	=	Liabilities	+	Shareholders' Equity
			Long-Term		
	Cash		**Notes Payable**		**Share Capital**
(a)	+1,300	=			+1,300
(b)	+1,000	=	+1,000		

Transactions *(a)* and *(b)* are *financing* transactions. Companies that need cash for *investing* purposes (to buy or build additional facilities as part of their plans for growth) often seek funds by selling shares to investors, as in Transaction *(a)*, or borrowing from creditors, usually banks, as in Transaction *(b)*.

(c) **For expansion, Van Houtte opened two new company-owned café–bistros. The company purchased $2,200 of new coffee brewers, counters, refrigerators, and other equipment (fixed assets), paying $1,500 in cash and signing a note for $700, payable to the equipment manufacturer in two years.**

1. Identify and classify accounts and effects.	*Property and Equipment (A) is received +$2,200. Cash (A) −$1,500 is given and a written promise to pay is also given to the manufacturer, Notes Payable (L) +$700.*
2. Is the accounting equation in balance?	*Yes, there is a $700 increase on the left side of the equation and a $700 increase on the right side.*

Notice that more than two accounts were affected by this transaction.

	Assets		=	Liabilities	+	Shareholders' Equity
		Fixed		**Long-Term**		**Share**
	Cash	**Assets**		**Notes Payable**		**Capital**
(a)	+1,300		=			+1,300
(b)	+1,000		=	+1,000		
(c)	−1,500	+2,200	=	+ 700		

The analysis of Transactions *(d)* through *(f)* follows. The effects are listed in the chart at the end of Self-Study Quiz 2-3. For Transactions *(g)* and *(h)*, space is left in the chart for your answers to the quiz that follows Transaction *(f)*.

(d) **Van Houtte lends $450 to new franchisees who sign notes agreeing to repay the loans in 18 months. The franchisees open 25 new restaurants.**

1. Identify and classify accounts and effects.	*Cash (A) is given −$450.* *Written promises from the franchisees are received, Notes Receivable (A) +$450.*
2. Is the accounting equation in balance?	*Yes. The equation remains the same because assets increase and decrease by the same amount.*

(e) **Van Houtte purchases $3,000 of shares issued by other companies as a long-term investment.**

1. Identify and classify accounts and effects.	*Cash (A) is given −$3,000.* *Share certificates from the other companies are received, Investments (A) +$3,000.*
2. Is the accounting equation in balance?	*Yes. The equation remains the same because assets increase and decrease by the same amount.*

(f) **Van Houtte's board of directors has not declared dividends for shareholders. However, for illustration purposes, we will assume that the first dividend for $200 is declared and paid.**

1. Identify and classify accounts and effects.	*Cash (A) is given −$200.* *In this transaction, earnings retained in the business are distributed to investors, Retained Earnings (SE) −$200.*
2. Is the accounting equation in balance?	*Yes. There is a $200 decrease on the left side of the equation and a $200 decrease on the right side.*

SELF-STUDY **QUIZ 2-3**

The most effective way to develop your transaction analysis skills is to practise with many transactions. The key is repeating the steps until they become a natural part of your thought process. Therefore, beginning with the analysis in Transactions (*a*) through (*f*), complete the transaction analysis steps and following chart for Transactions (*g*) and (*h*).

(g) **Van Houtte collects $300 cash on notes receivable from a number of franchisees.** (*Hint:* **Think about what is received and what is given back.**)

1. Identify and classify accounts and effects.
2. Is the accounting equation in balance?

(h) **Van Houtte paid $400 on the promissory note owed to the local bank.**

1. Identify and classify accounts and effects.
2. Is the accounting equation in balance?

Complete the following chart.

		Assets			=	Liabilities	+	Shareholders' Equity	
	Cash	Notes Receivable	Investments	Property and Equipment		Long-Term Notes Payable		Share Capital	Retained Earnings
(*a*)	+1,300				=			+1,300	
(*b*)	+1,000				=	+1,000			
(*c*)	−1,500			+2,200	=	+700			
(*d*)	−450	+450			=				
(*e*)	−3,000		+3,000		=				
(*f*)	−200				=				−200
(*g*)	☐	☐			=				
(*h*)	☐				=	☐			

After you complete the chart, check it with the solution on page 78.

(i) Van Houtte's board of directors approved the opening of four café–bistros at a meeting in April 2005 and the granting of $200 of loans to new franchisees who plan to open new café–bistros in May 2005.

Unlike Transactions *(a)* through *(h)*, which reflect exchanges between Van Houtte and external parties, these two decisions of the board of directors are not transactions because no exchanges have taken place yet. The company's board of directors made commitments that will likely translate into actions in May 2005. Specific balance sheet accounts will be affected only when the actual exchanges occur in May 2005. However, such commitments will normally be disclosed in a financial statement note.

HOW DO COMPANIES KEEP TRACK OF ACCOUNT BALANCES?

■ **LEARNING OBJECTIVE 6**

Determine the impact of business transactions on the balance sheet using two basic tools: journal entries and T-accounts.

Because companies have significantly more transactions every day than those illustrated, recording transaction effects and keeping track of account balances in the manner used in the preceding illustration is impractical for most organizations. We will now expand the transaction analysis model and develop two very important tools that aid in reflecting the results of transaction analysis and performing other financial analysis tasks: journal entries and T-accounts.

These analytical tools are more efficient mechanisms for reflecting the effects of transactions and for determining account balances for financial statement preparation. These efficiencies are important from the standpoint of accounting systems design. **As future business managers, you should develop your understanding and use of these tools in financial analysis. For those studying accounting, this knowledge is the foundation for understanding the accounting system and future coursework.** After we learn to perform transaction analysis using these tools, we will illustrate their use in financial analysis.

THE DIRECTION OF TRANSACTION EFFECTS AND THE DEBIT-CREDIT FRAMEWORK

As we saw earlier, transactions change assets, liabilities, and shareholders' equity. To reflect these effects efficiently, we need to structure the transaction analysis model in a manner that shows the *direction* of the effects. In Exhibit 2.4, notice that:

- The increase symbol + is located on the left side of the T for accounts that appear on the left side of the accounting equation, and on the right side of the T for accounts that are on the right side of the equation.

DEBIT means the left side of an account.

- The symbols **dr** or **debit**, and **cr** or **credit** are always written on the left and the right of each account, respectively. Debit means the left side of an account and credit means the right.

From this transaction analysis model, we can observe the following:

- Asset accounts normally have debit balances (their positive, or increase, side).

CREDIT means the right side of an account.

- Liabilities and shareholders' equity accounts normally have credit balances (their positive, or increase, side).

EXHIBIT **2.4**

Transaction Analysis Model

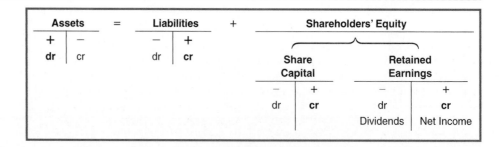

As you are learning to perform transaction analysis, you should refer to this model often until you can construct it on your own without assistance. We build on this model in Chapter 3 when we add transactions affecting operations.

Many students have trouble with accounting because they forget that the only meaning for **debit** is the left side of an account and the only meaning for **credit** is the right side of an account. Perhaps someone once told you that you were a credit to your school or your family. As a result, you may think that there is "goodness" attached to credits and perhaps a "badness" attached to debits. Such is not the case. Just remember that **debit means left** and **credit means right**.

If the correct accounts and effects have been identified through transaction analysis, the accounting equation will remain in balance. What will also be true is that **the total dollar value of all debits equals the total dollar value of all credits** in a transaction. Therefore, this equality check (Debits = Credits) should be added to the transaction analysis process.

ANALYTICAL TOOL: THE JOURNAL ENTRY

In a bookkeeping system, transactions are initially recorded in chronological order in a *journal* (see our Web site at **www.mcgrawhill.ca/college/libby/student/resources** for a detailed illustration of formal recordkeeping procedures). After analyzing the business documents that describe a transaction, the bookkeeper prepares the formal entry in the journal. Using debits and credits, the bookkeeper writes a journal entry for each transaction. The **journal entry** provides a summary of a transaction and its effects on various accounts, using the double-entry bookkeeping system explained previously. The journal entry for Transaction (*c*) in the Van Houtte illustration is written as follows:

A **JOURNAL ENTRY** provides a summary of a transaction and its effects on various accounts, using the double-entry bookkeeping system.

Date	Accounts and explanation	Debit	Credit
	Fixed assets (+A)	2,200	
	Cash (−A)		1,500
	Long-term notes payable (+L)		700
	Purchased fixed assets paying part in cash and signing a note for the rest.		

Notice the following:

- A date for each transaction is useful for future reference.
- The debits are written first (on top); the credits are written below all of the debits and are indented to the right (both words and amounts). The order of the debits or credits does not matter, as long as the debits are on top and the credits are on the bottom and indented.
- Total debits ($2,200) equal total credits ($1,500 + $700).
- Any journal entry that affects more than two accounts is called a *compound entry*. Three accounts are affected by this transaction. Although this is the only transaction in the preceding illustration that affects more than two accounts, many transactions in future chapters will require compound journal entries.

While you are learning to perform transaction analysis, use the symbols A, L, and SE next to each account title, as is done in the preceding journal entry, including all homework problems. Specifically identifying accounts as assets (A), liabilities (L), or shareholders' equity (SE) makes using the transaction analysis model clearer and journal entries easier. In the next few chapters, we will also include the direction of the effect with the symbol. For example, if Cash is to be increased, we will write Cash (+A).

We have found that many students try to memorize journal entries without understanding or using the transaction analysis model. The task becomes increasingly difficult as new detailed transactions are presented in subsequent chapters. However, **memorizing, understanding, and using the transaction analysis model** presented here will save you time and prevent confusion.

ANALYTICAL TOOL: THE T-ACCOUNT

By themselves, journal entries do not provide the balances in accounts. After the journal entries have been recorded, the bookkeeper posts (transfers) the dollar amounts to each account that was affected by the transaction to determine account balances. In most computerized accounting systems, this happens automatically upon recording the journal entry. As a group, the accounts are called a *ledger*. In a manual accounting system used by some small organizations, the ledger is often a three-ring binder with a separate page for each account. In a computerized system, accounts are part of a database and stored on a disk. See Exhibit 2.5 for an illustration of a journal page and the related Cash ledger page. Note that the cash effects from the journal entries have been posted to the Cash ledger page.

The **T-ACCOUNT** is a tool for summarizing transaction effects for each account, determining balances, and drawing inferences about a company's activities.

One very useful tool for summarizing the transaction effects and determining the balances for individual accounts is a **T-account**, a simplified representation of a ledger account. The T-accounts for the Cash and Long-Term Notes Payable accounts for Van Houtte, based on Transactions (*a*) through (*h*), are presented in Exhibit 2.6. Notice that increases in cash (an asset) are on the left and decreases are on the right side of the T-account. For Long-Term Notes Payable, however, increases are on the right and decreases are on the left since the account is a liability. Also notice that the ending balance is indicated on the positive side and is double-underlined.

T-accounts can be written as equations that yield balances for financial statement purposes:

	Beginning balance	+	Increases	−	Decreases	=	Ending balance
Cash	$ 5,400	+	2,600	−	5,550	=	$ 2,450
Long-Term Notes Payable	$60,300	+	1,700	−	400	=	$61,600

The words *debit* and *credit* are used as verbs, nouns, and adjectives. For example, we can say that (1) Van Houtte's Cash account was debited (verb) when shares were issued to investors; (2) to credit (verb) an account means to put the amount on the right side of the T-account; (3) a debit (noun) is the left side of an account; and (4) Long-Term Notes Payable is a credit account (adjective). These terms will be used instead of *left* and *right* throughout the rest of the textbook. The next section illustrates the steps you should follow in using the model to analyze the effects of transactions, record the effects in journal entries, and determine account balances by using T-accounts.

TRANSACTION ANALYSIS ILLUSTRATED

The typical monthly transactions of Van Houtte presented earlier will be used to demonstrate transaction analysis and the use of journal entries and T-accounts. We

EXHIBIT **2.5**

Illustration of a Journal Page and a Ledger Account in Columnar Format

GENERAL JOURNAL

Page ___1___

Date	Account Titles and Explanations	Posted Ref.	Debit	Credit
4/1/2005	Cash	101	9,000	
	Share capital	301		9,000
	Issued 1,500 shares to investors (names).			
4/3/2005	Equipment	110	600	
	Cash	101		200
	Notes payable	201		400
	Purchased hand tools (supplier and invoice data			
	indicated), paying part in cash (cheque number			
	indicated) and part on account.			

GENERAL LEDGER

Account Title ___Cash___   Account Number ___101___

Date	Explanation	Posted Ref.	Debit	Credit	Balance
4/1/2005	Investments by owners	1	9,000		9,000
4/3/2005	Hand tools purchased	1		200	8,800
4/4/2005	Land purchased	1		5,000	3,800
4/5/2005	Fuel purchased	1		90	3,710
4/6/2005	Revenue in advance	2	1,600		5,310
4/8/2005	Insurance purchased	2		300	5,010
4/10/2005	Collection from customers	2	3,500		8,510
4/14/2005	Wages paid	3		3,900	4,610
4/18/2005	Note and interest paid	3		740	3,870
4/21/2005	Suppliers paid	3		100	3,770
4/29/2005	Collection from city	4	1,262		5,032

EXHIBIT **2.6**

T-Accounts Illustrated

	+ **Cash (A)** −			− **Long-Term Notes Payable (L)** +	
Beginning balance	5,400		Beginning balance	60,300	
(a)	1,300	(c) 1,500	−400 { (h) 400	(b)	1,000
+2,600 { (b)	1,000	(d) 450		(c)	700
(g)	300	(e) 3,000 } −5,550			
		(f) 200			
		(h) 400			
Ending balance	2,450		Ending balance	61,600	

+1,700

analyze each transaction, checking that the accounting equation remains in balance and debits equal credits. In the T-accounts, located together at the end of the illustration, the amounts from Van Houtte's balance sheet at April 2, 2005, have been inserted as the beginning balances in each account. After reviewing or preparing each journal entry, trace the effects to the appropriate T-accounts using the transaction letters as a reference. The first transaction has been highlighted for you.

Study this illustration carefully (including the explanations of transaction analysis). Careful study of the illustration is *essential* to the understanding of (1) the accounting model, (2) transaction analysis, (3) recording the dual effects of each transaction, and (4) the dual-balancing system. **The most effective way to learn these critical concepts that affect material throughout the rest of the textbook is to practise, practise, practise**.

(a) **Van Houtte issues shares to new investors in exchange for $1,300 in cash.**

Cash (+A)	1,300	
Share capital (+SE)		1,300

Assets	=	Liabilities	+	Shareholders' Equity	
Cash	+1,300 dr			Share capital	+1,300 cr

These effects were posted to the appropriate T-accounts in Self-Study Quiz 2-4 (see the shaded amounts). To post, copy the debit or credit amount on each line to the appropriate T-account indicated in order to accumulate balances for each account. For example, the $1,300 debit is listed in the debit (increase) column of the Cash T-account.

(b) **The company borrows $1,000 from its local bank, signing a promissory note to be paid in two years.**

Cash (+A)	1,000	
Long-term notes payable (+L)		1,000

Assets	=	Liabilities	+	Shareholders' Equity
Cash	+1,000 dr	Long-term notes payable	+1,000 cr	

(c) **For expansion, Van Houtte opened two new company-owned café–bistros. The company purchased $2,200 of new coffee brewers, counters, refrigerators, and other equipment (fixed assets), paying $1,500 in cash and signing a note for $700, payable to the equipment manufacturer in two years.**

Fixed assets (+A)	....	2,200	
Cash (−A)	....		1,500
Long-term notes payable (+L)	....		700

Assets		=	Liabilities		+	Shareholders' Equity
Fixed assets	+2,200 dr		Long-term	+700 cr		
Cash	−1,500 cr		notes payable			

(d) **Van Houtte lends $450 to franchisees who sign notes agreeing to repay the loans in 18 months.**

| Notes receivable (+A) | .... | 450 | |
| Cash (−A) | .... | | 450 |

Assets		=	Liabilities	+	Shareholders' Equity
Cash	−450 cr				
Notes receivable	+450 dr				

(e) **Van Houtte purchases $3,000 of shares issued by other companies as a long-term investment.**

| Investments (+A) | .... | 3,000 | |
| Cash (−A) | .... | | 3,000 |

Assets		=	Liabilities	+	Shareholders' Equity
Cash	−3,000 cr				
Investments	+3,000 dr				

(f) **Van Houtte's board of directors has not declared dividends for shareholders. However, for illustration purposes, we will assume that the first dividend for $200 is declared and paid.**

| Retained earnings (−SE) | .... | 200 | |
| Cash (−A) | .... | | 200 |

Assets		=	Liabilities	+	Shareholders' Equity	
Cash	−200 cr				Retained earnings	−200 dr

SELF-STUDY **QUIZ 2-4**

For Transactions (*g*) and (*h*), fill in the missing information, including postings to the T-accounts.

(g) **Van Houtte collects $300 cash on notes receivable from a number of franchisees.**

Write the journal entry →   [Post to the T-accounts.]

Assets		=	Liabilities	+	Shareholders' Equity
Cash	+300 dr				
Notes receivable	−300 cr				

(h) **Van Houtte paid $400 on the promissory note owed to the local bank.**

| Long-term notes payable (−L) .... | 400 | | [Post to the |
| Cash (−A) .... | | 400 | T-accounts.] |

Assets	=	Liabilities	+	Shareholders' Equity

The following are the T-accounts that changed during the period because of these transactions. The balances of all other accounts remained the same. The account balances from Van Houtte's balance sheet at April 2, 2005, have been included as the beginning balances:

Assets = **Liabilities + Shareholders' Equity**

Cash (A)

+ (dr)		− (cr)	
Beg. bal.	5,400		
(a)	1,300	(c)	1,500
(b)	1,000	(d)	450
(g)	☐	(e)	3,000
		(f)	200
		(h)	☐
End. bal.	2,450		

Fixed Assets (A)

+ (dr)		− (cr)
Beg. bal.	115,800	
(c)	2,200	
End. bal.	118,000	

Investments (A)

+ (dr)		− (cr)
Beg. bal.	18,900	
(e)	3,000	
End. bal.	21,900	

Notes Receivable (A)

+ (dr)		− (cr)	
Beg. bal.	0		
(d)	450	(g)	☐
End. bal.	150		

Long-Term Notes Payable (L)

− (dr)		+ (cr)	
		Beg. bal.	60,300
(h)	☐	(b)	1,000
		(c)	700
		End. bal.	61,600

Share Capital (SE)

− (dr)	+ (cr)	
	Beg. bal.	130,300
	(a)	1,300
	End. bal.	131,600

Retained Earnings (SE)

− (dr)		+ (cr)	
		Beg. bal.	101,100
(f)	200		
		End. bal.	☐

You can verify that you posted the entries properly by adding the increase side and subtracting the decrease side and then comparing your answer to the ending balance given in each of the T-accounts. You can check your answers with the solutions on page 78.

FINANCIAL **ANALYSIS**

INFERRING BUSINESS ACTIVITIES FROM T-ACCOUNTS

T-accounts are useful primarily for instructional purposes and as a financial analysis tool. In many cases, we will use this tool to determine what transactions a company engaged in during a period. For example, the primary transactions affecting Accounts Payable for a period are purchases of assets on account and cash payments to suppliers. If we know the beginning and ending balances of Accounts Payable and all of the amounts that were purchased on credit during a period, we can determine the amount of cash paid. The T-account will include the following:

Accounts Payable (L)

− (dr)		+ (cr)	
		Beg. bal.	600
Cash		Purchases	
payments	?	on account	1,500
		End. bal.	300

SOLUTION:

Beginning balance	+	Purchases	−	Cash payments	=	Ending balance
$600	+	$1,500	−	p	=	$300
		$2,100	−	p	=	$300
				p	=	$1,800

HOW IS THE BALANCE SHEET PREPARED?

■ **LEARNING OBJECTIVE 7**

Prepare and analyze a simple balance sheet.

It is possible to prepare a balance sheet at any point in time from the balances in the accounts. Exhibit 2.7 was prepared using the new balances shown in the T-accounts in the preceding Van Houtte illustration (shaded lines in the exhibit) plus the original balances in the accounts that did not change. It compares the account balances at April 30, 2005, with those at April 2, 2005. Notice that when multiple periods are presented, the most recent balance sheet amounts are usually listed on the left.

At the beginning of the chapter, we presented the changes in Van Houtte's balance sheets from the beginning of the year to the end of the year. We questioned what made the accounts change and what the process was for reflecting the changes. Now we can see that the accounts have changed again in one month due to the transactions illustrated in this chapter:

	Assets	=	Liabilities	+	Shareholders' Equity
April 30, 2005	$373,100		$140,600		$232,500
April 2, 2005	370,700		139,300		231,400
Change	+$ 2,400		+$ 1,300		+$ 1,100

EXHIBIT **2.7**

Van Houtte's Balance Sheet

VAN HOUTTE INC.
Consolidated Balance Sheet
(in thousands of dollars)

Assets	April 30, 2005	April 2, 2005
Current assets		
Cash	$ 2,450	$ 5,400
Accounts receivable	41,300	41,300
Inventory	28,000	28,000
Prepaid expenses	3,300	3,300
Other current assets	1,700	1,700
Total current assets	78,050	79,700
Note receivable	150	—
Investments	21,900	18,900
Fixed assets, net	118,000	115,800
Goodwill	141,700	141,700
Other long-term assets	14,600	14,600
Total assets	**$373,100**	**$370,700**
Liabilities and shareholders' equity		
Current liabilities		
Accounts payable	$ 31,900	$ 31,900
Accrued liabilities	9,700	9,700
Current portion of long-term debt	28,000	28,000
Total current liabilities	69,600	69,600
Long-term notes payable	61,600	60,300
Other long-term liabilities	9,400	9,400
Total liabilities	140,600	139,300
Shareholders' equity		
Share capital	131,600	130,300
Retained earnings	100,900	101,100
Total shareholders' equity	232,500	231,400
Total liabilities and shareholders' equity	**$373,100**	**$370,700**

FOCUS ON **CASH FLOWS**

INVESTING AND FINANCING ACTIVITIES

The eight transactions we have analyzed for Van Houtte included issuing shares, borrowing from a bank, purchasing fixed assets, lending to franchisees, purchasing shares in other companies, declaring and paying dividends, collecting cash payment on a note receivable, and paying down a bank loan (see Exhibit 2.8). All these transactions affected cash. As we indicated at the beginning of Chapter 1, investors are vitally interested in learning how the company obtained cash and how it was used. Information about cash inflows and outflows is so important that it is presented in a separate financial statement, the *cash flow statement,* which is discussed in detail in Chapter 5.

■ **LEARNING OBJECTIVE 8**

Identify investing and financing transactions and how they are reported on the cash flow statement.

For the moment, let us divide the eight transactions into two sets—one set related to investment activities and another set related to financing activities—and then assess how each set affects cash.

The first set includes one transaction that created cash inflow and three transactions that caused cash outflow. The collection on notes receivable increased cash by $300. On the other hand, the payment of $1,500 in cash for the purchase of fixed assets; the long-term loan to franchisees for $450; and the investment in shares of other companies for $3,000 resulted in a total cash outflow of $4,950. The net change to cash from investment activities is an outflow of *$4,650.*

The second set of transactions relates to financing activities and includes two transactions that created cash inflow and two transactions that caused cash outflow. The issuance of shares for $1,300 and the borrowing of $1,000 from the bank caused a total cash inflow of $2,300. In contrast, the payment of dividends of $200 and the partial repayment on a bank loan of $400 resulted in a total cash outflow of $600 during the same period. The net change to cash from financing activities is an inflow of *$1,700.* In summary, the change in the cash balance of $5,400 at the beginning of the period to $2,450 at the end of the period can be explained as follows:

Cash from (used for) investment activities	$(4,650)
Cash from (used for) financing activities	1,700
Net change in cash flow	(2,950)
Beginning balance in cash	5,400
Ending balance in cash	$ 2,450

Now we can see how the painstaking transaction analysis we completed helped us produce a complete and separate summary of how cash was affected by investment and financing decisions. This summary is relevant because it provides information that not only shows the sources and uses of cash but also helps both investors and creditors predict future cash flows for Van Houtte and make appropriate financial decisions.

EXHIBIT **2.8**

Van Houtte's Cash Flow Statement

Items are referenced to events *(a)* through *(h)* illustrated in this chapter.

VAN HOUTTE INC. Consolidated Cash Flow Statement For the Month Ended April 30, 2005 (in thousands of dollars)	
Operating Activities	
(none in this chapter)	
Investing Activities	
Purchased of fixed assets *(c)*	$(1,500)
Purchased long-term investments *(e)*	(3,000)
Lent funds to franchisees *(d)*	(450)
Received payment on loans to franchisees *(g)*	300
Net cash used in investing activities	**(4,650)**
Financing Activities	
Issued shares *(a)*	1,300
Borrowed from banks *(b)*	1,000
Repaid loan from bank *(h)*	(400)
Paid dividends *(f)*	(200)
Net cash provided by financing activities	**1,700**
Net decrease in cash	**(2,950)**
Cash at beginning of month	5,400
Cash at end of month	**$ 2,450**

Agrees with the cash balance reported on the balance sheet.

SELF-STUDY **QUIZ 2-5**

Lance, Inc.

Lance, Inc., manufactures and sells snack products. From a recent annual cash flow statement, indicate whether the transaction affected the cash flow as an investing (I) activity or a financing (F) activity and indicate the direction of the effect on cash (+ = increases cash; − = decreases cash):

Transactions	Type of Activity (I or F)	Effect on Cash Flows (+ or −)
1. Paid dividends.	_____	_____
2. Sold property.	_____	_____
3. Sold marketable securities (investments).	_____	_____
4. Purchased vending machines.	_____	_____
5. Repurchased its own shares.	_____	_____

After you complete your work, check it with the solution on page 78.

SOME MISCONCEPTIONS

Some people confuse bookkeeping with accounting. In effect, they confuse a part of accounting with the whole. Bookkeeping involves the routine, clerical part of accounting and requires only minimal knowledge of accounting. A bookkeeper may record the repetitive and uncomplicated transactions in most businesses and may maintain the simple records of a small business. In contrast, the accountant is a highly trained professional, competent in the design of information systems, analysis of complex transactions, interpretation of financial data, financial reporting, auditing, taxation, and management consulting.

Another prevalent misconception is that all transactions are subject to precise and objective measurement and that the accounting results reported in the financial statements are exactly what happened during that period. In reality, accounting numbers are influenced by estimates, as subsequent chapters will illustrate. Some people believe that financial statements report the entity's market value (including its assets), but they do not. To understand and interpret financial statements, the user must be aware of their limitations as well as their usefulness. One should understand what the financial statements do and do not try to accomplish.

Finally, financial statements are often thought to be inflexible because of their quantitative nature. As you study accounting, you will learn that it requires considerable *professional judgment* on the part of the accountant to capture the economic essence of complex transactions. Accountants develop professional judgment after years of experience in analyzing business transactions and in applying generally accepted accounting principles in preparing and auditing financial reports. Accounting is stimulating intellectually; it is not a cut-and-dried subject. It calls on your intelligence, analytical ability, creativity, and judgment. Accounting is a communication process involving an audience (users) with a wide diversity of knowledge, interest, and capabilities; therefore, it will call on your ability as a communicator. The language of accounting uses concisely written phrases and symbols to convey information about the resource flows measured for specific organizations.

To understand financial statements, you must have a certain level of knowledge of the concepts and the measurement procedures used in the accounting process. You should learn what accounting is really like and appreciate the reasons for using certain procedures. This level of knowledge cannot be gained by reading a list of the concepts and a list of the misconceptions. Neither can a generalized discussion of the subject matter suffice. A certain amount of involvement, primarily problem solving (similar to the requirement in mathematics courses), is essential in the study of accounting focused on the needs of the user. Therefore, we provide problems aimed at the desirable knowledge level for the user as well as the preparer of financial statements.

DEMONSTRATION **CASE**

On April 1, 2005, three ambitious college students started Terrific Lawn Maintenance Corporation. Completed transactions (summarized) through April 30, 2005, for Terrific Lawn Maintenance Corporation follow:

(*a*) Issued $9,000 of shares in total to the three investors in exchange for cash. Each investor received 500 shares.

(*b*) Acquired rakes and other hand tools (equipment) with a list price of $690 for $600; paid $200 cash and signed a note for the balance with the hardware store.

(*c*) Ordered three lawn mowers and two edgers from XYZ Lawn Supply, Inc., for $4,000.

(*d*) Purchased four acres of land as a future building site of a storage garage. Paid cash, $5,000.

(*e*) Received the mowers and edgers that had been ordered, signing a note to pay XYZ Lawn Supply the amount owed in 30 days.

(*f*) Sold one acre of land to the city for a park. The city signed a note to pay Terrific Lawn Maintenance Corp. $1,250, the cost of the land, by the end of the month.

(*g*) Paid $700 on the notes owed to XYZ Lawn Supply and the hardware store.

(*h*) Collected cash on note owed by the city.

(*i*) One of the owners borrowed $3,000 from a local bank for personal use.

Required:

1. Set up T-accounts for Cash, Notes Receivable (from the city), Equipment (for hand tools and mowing equipment), Land, Notes Payable (to equipment supply companies), and Share Capital. Beginning balances are $0; indicate these beginning balances in the T-accounts. Analyze each transaction using the process outlined in the chapter. Prepare journal entries in chronological order. Enter the effects of the transactions on the accounting model in the appropriate T-accounts. Identify each amount with its letter in the preceding list.

2. Use the amounts in the T-accounts developed in requirement 1 to prepare a classified balance sheet for Terrific Lawn Maintenance Corporation at April 30, 2005. The April 30, 2005, balance sheet requires use of the account balances for all assets, liabilities, and shareholders' equity. The transaction analysis model is presented for your use:

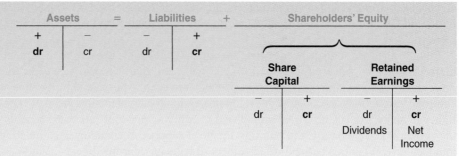

3. Prepare the investing and financing sections of the cash flow statement.

We strongly recommend that you prepare your own answers to these requirements and then check your answers with the solution provided below.

SUGGESTED SOLUTION

1. **Transaction analysis, journal entries, and T-accounts:**

(a)   Cash (+A)   9,000
            Share capital (+SE)   9,000

Assets		=	Liabilities	+	Shareholders' Equity	
Cash	+9,000 dr				Share capital	+9,000 cr

(b)   Equipment (+A)   600
            Cash (−A)   200
            Notes payable (+L)   400

Assets		=	Liabilities		+	Shareholders' Equity
Equipment	+600 dr		Notes payable	+400 cr		
Cash	−200 cr					

The **cost principle** states that assets should be recorded at the amount paid on the date of the transaction. This is $600, not the list price of $690.

(c) **This is not an accounting transaction; no exchange has taken place. No accounts are affected.**

(d)   Land (+A)   5,000
            Cash (−A)   5,000

Assets		=	Liabilities	+	Shareholders' Equity
Land	+5,000 dr				
Cash	−5,000 cr				

(e)   Equipment (+A)   4,000
            Notes payable (+L)   4,000

Assets		=	Liabilities		+	Shareholders' Equity
Equipment	+4,000 dr		Notes payable	+4,000 cr		

(f)   Notes receivable (+A)   1,250
            Land (−A)   1,250

Assets		=	Liabilities	+	Shareholders' Equity
Notes receivable	+1,250 dr				
Land	−1,250 cr				

| (g) | Notes payable (−L) .... | 700 | |
| | Cash (−A) .... | | 700 |

Assets	=	Liabilities	+	Shareholders' Equity
Cash −700 cr		Notes payable −700 dr		

| (h) | Cash (+A) .... | 1,250 | |
| | Notes receivable (−A) .... | | 1,250 |

Assets	=	Liabilities	+	Shareholders' Equity
Cash +1,250 dr				
Notes receivable −1,250 cr				

(*i*) This is not a transaction that involves the company. The separate-entity assumption states that transactions of the owners are separate from transactions of the business.

| Assets | | = | Liabilities + Shareholders' Equity |

Cash (A)

+ (dr)		− (cr)	
Beg. bal.	0		
(a)	9,000	(b)	200
(h)	1,250	(d)	5,000
		(g)	700
End. bal.	4,350		

Notes Receivable (A)

+ (dr)		− (cr)	
Beg. bal.	0		
(f)	1,250	(h)	1,250
End. bal.	0		

Notes Payable (L)

− (dr)		+ (cr)	
		Beg. bal.	0
(g)	700	(b)	400
		(e)	4,000
		End. bal.	3,700

Share Capital (SE)

− (dr)		+ (cr)	
		Beg. bal.	0
		(a)	9,000
		End. bal.	9,000

Equipment (A)

+ (dr)		− (cr)	
Beg. bal.	0		
(b)	600		
(e)	4,000		
End. bal.	4,600		

Land (A)

− (dr)		− (cr)	
Beg. bal.	0		
(d)	5,000	(f)	1,250
End. bal.	3,750		

2. Balance sheet:

TERRIFIC LAWN MAINTENANCE CORPORATION
Balance Sheet
At April 30, 2005

Assets		Liabilities	
Cash	$ 4,350	Notes payable	$ 3,700
Equipment	4,600		
Land	3,750	**Shareholders' Equity**	
		Share capital	9,000
Total assets	$12,700	Total liabilities and shareholders' equity	$12,700

Notice that balance sheets presented earlier in the text listed assets on the top and liabilities and shareholders' equity on the bottom. This is called the **report form**. Preparing a balance sheet with assets on the left side and liabilities and shareholders' equity on the right side, such as the preceding one, is called the **account form**. Both are used in practice.

Two common balance sheet forms:

REPORT FORM lists assets on the top, liabilities and shareholders' equity on the bottom.

ACCOUNT FORM lists assets on the left, liabilities and shareholders' equity on the right.

3. Investing and financing effects of the cash flow statement:

TERRIFIC LAWN MAINTENANCE CORPORATION
Cash Flow Statement
For the Month Ended April 30, 2005

Operating Activities	
(none in this case)	
Investing Activities	
Purchased land (*d*)	$(5,000)
Purchased equipment (*b*)	(200)
Received payment on notes receivable (*h*)	1,250
Net cash used in investing activities	**(3,950)**
Financing Activities	
Issued shares (*a*)	9,000
Payments on borrowings (*g*)	(700)
Net cash provided by financing activities	**8,300**
Change in cash	**4,350**
Beginning cash balance	0
Ending cash balance	**$4,350**

SOLUTIONS TO **SELF-STUDY QUIZZES**

Self-Study Quiz 2-1

$876,934 ÷ $1,758,606 = 0.50.

Wendy's is following a slightly less risky financing strategy. The ratio is lower than Van Houtte's. This means that for every dollar of shareholders' equity, creditors supplied $0.50 to acquire assets.

Self-Study Quiz 2-2

Column 1: L; A; A; L. Column 2: L; A; SE; A.

Self-Study Quiz 2-3

(*g*) Cash (A) is received +$300. The franchisees' written promises to pay are "given back" (paid off), Notes Receivable (A) −$300. The equation remains the same because assets increase and decrease by the same amount.

(*h*) Cash (A) is given −$400. Van Houtte's written promise to the bank is "given back" (paid off), Long-Term Notes Payable −$400. There is a $400 decrease on the left side of the equation and a $400 decrease on the right side.

If your answers did not agree with ours, we recommend that you go back to each transaction to make sure that you have completed each of the steps for each transaction.

Self-Study Quiz 2-4

(*g*) Journal entry:

Cash (+A)	300	
Notes receivable (−A)		300

(*h*) Effects on the Accounting Equation:

Assets		=	Liabilities		+	Shareholders' Equity
Cash	−400 cr		Long-term notes payable	−400 dr		

Self-Study Quiz 2-5

1. F −   2. I +   3. I +   4. I −   5. F −

CHAPTER **TAKE-AWAYS**

1. **Define the objective of financial reporting and the related key accounting assumptions and principles.** **p. 49**
   - The primary objective of external financial reporting is to provide useful economic information about a business to help external parties, primarily investors and creditors, make sound financial decisions.
   - Key accounting assumptions and principles:
     - *a.* Separate-entity assumption—transactions of the business are accounted for separately from transactions of the owner.

    b. Unit-of-measure assumption—financial information is reported in the national monetary unit.

    c. Continuity (going-concern) assumption—a business is expected to continue to operate into the foreseeable future.

    d. Historical cost principle—financial statement elements should be recorded at their cash-equivalent cost on the date of the transaction.

2. **Define the elements of a classified balance sheet.**   **p. 51**

    • Elements of the balance sheet:

    a. Assets—probable future economic benefits owned by the entity as a result of past transactions.

    b. Liabilities—probable debts or obligations of the entity as a result of past transactions, which will be paid with assets or services.

    c. Shareholders' equity—the financing provided by the owners and the operations of the business.

3. **Compute and interpret the debt-to-equity ratio.**   **p. 56**

    The debt-to-equity ratio (Total Liabilities ÷ Shareholders' Equity) measures the relationship between total liabilities and the shareholders' capital that finance the assets. The higher the ratio, the more debt is used to finance assets. As the ratio (and thus debt) increases, risk increases.

4. **Identify what constitutes a business transaction and identify common balance sheet account titles used in business.**   **p. 58**

    A transaction includes:

    • An exchange between a business and one or more external parties to a business.

    or

    • A measurable internal event such as adjustments for the use of assets in operations.

    An account is a standardized format that organizations use to accumulate the dollar effects of transactions of each financial statement item. Typical balance sheet account titles include the following:

    • Assets: Cash, Accounts Receivable, Inventory, Prepaid Expenses, and Property and Equipment.

    • Liabilities: Accounts Payable, Notes Payable, Accrued Liabilities, and Taxes Payable.

    • Shareholders' equity: Share Capital and Retained Earnings.

5. **Apply transaction analysis to simple business transactions in terms of the accounting model: Assets = Liabilities + Shareholders' Equity.**   **p. 61**

    To determine the economic effect of a transaction on the entity in terms of its accounting equation, each transaction is analyzed as to the accounts (at least two) that are affected. In an exchange, the company receives something and gives something. If the accounts, direction of the effects, and amounts are correctly analyzed, the accounting equation must stay in balance. The transaction analysis model is

6. **Determine the impact of business transactions on the balance sheet using two basic tools, journal entries and T-accounts.**   **p. 66**

    • Journal entries express the effects of a transaction on accounts using the debit-credit framework. The accounts and amounts to be debited are listed first. Then the accounts and amounts to be credited are listed below the debits and indented, resulting in debits on the left and credits on the right.

    (date)   Account   xxx
                  Account   xxx

• T-accounts summarize transaction effects for each account. These tools can be used to determine balances and draw inferences about a company's activities.

+	Asset	−		− Liability and Shareholders' Equity +	
Beginning balance					Beginning balance
Increases		Decreases	Decreases		Increases
Ending balance					Ending balance

7. **Prepare and analyze a simple balance sheet.   p. 72**
Classified balance sheets are structured with
• Assets categorized as "current assets" (those to be used or turned into cash within the year, with inventory always considered to be a current asset) and non-current assets such as long-term investments, property and equipment, and intangible assets.
• Liabilities categorized as "current liabilities" (those that will be paid with current assets) and long-term liabilities.

8. **Identify investing and financing transactions and how they are reported on the cash flow statement.   p. 73**
A cash flow statement reports the sources and uses of cash for the period by the type of activity that generated the cash flow: operating, investing, and financing. Investing activities are purchasing and selling long-term assets, making loans, and receiving payment from loans to others. Financing activities are borrowing and repaying loans to banks, issuing and repurchasing shares, and paying dividends.

In this chapter, we discussed the fundamental accounting model and transaction analysis. Journal entries and T-accounts were used to record the results of transaction analysis for investing and financing decisions that affect balance sheet accounts. In Chapter 3, we continue our detailed look at financial statements, in particular the income statement. The purpose of Chapter 3 is to build on your knowledge by discussing concepts for the measurement of revenues and expenses and by illustrating transaction analysis for operating decisions.

KEY **RATIO**

The **debt-to-equity ratio** measures the relationship between total liabilities and the shareholders' capital that finance the assets. The higher the ratio, the more debt is assumed by the company to finance assets. It is computed as follows (p. 56):

$$\text{Debt-to-Equity Ratio} = \frac{\text{Total Liabilities}}{\text{Shareholders' Equity}}$$

BALANCE SHEET

Current Assets	*Current Liabilities*
Cash	Bank
Accounts and notes	indebtedness
receivable	Accounts payable
Inventory	Notes payable
Prepaid expenses	Accrued liabilities
Non-Current Assets	payable
Long-term	*Non-Current*
investments	*Liabilities*
Fixed assets	Long-term debt
Intangibles	*Shareholders'*
	Equity
	Share capital
	Retained earnings

INCOME STATEMENT
To Be Indicated in Chapter 3

CASH FLOW STATEMENT
Under Investing Activities
+ Sales of non-current assets for cash
− Purchases of non-current assets for cash
− Loans to others
+ Receipt of cash on loans to others
Under Financing Activities
+ Borrowing from banks
− Repayment of loans from banks
+ Issuance of shares
− Repurchasing shares
− Payment of dividends

NOTES
Under Summary of Significant Accounting Policies
Description of management's choice for fiscal year.

KEY **TERMS**

Account p. 59

Account Form p. 77

Assets p. 51

Continuity (Going-Concern) Assumption p. 50

Cost Principle p. 51

Credits p. 66

Current Assets p. 53

Current Liabilities p. 54

Debits p. 66

Journal Entry p. 67

Liabilities p. 54

Long-Term Liabilities p. 55

Non-current Assets p. 54

Primary Objective of External Financial Reporting p. 49

Report Form p. 77

Retained Earnings p. 56

Separate-Entity Assumption p. 50

Share Capital p. 56

Shareholders' Equity (Owners' Equity or Stockholders' Equity) p. 56

T-account p. 68

Transaction p. 58

Transaction Analysis p. 61

Unit-of-Measure Assumption p. 50

QUESTIONS

1. What is the primary objective of financial reporting for external users?
2. Define the following:
   a. *Asset.*
   b. *Current asset.*
   c. *Liability.*
   d. *Current liability.*
   e. *Share capital.*
   f. *Retained earnings.*
3. Explain what the following assumptions and principle mean in accounting:
   a. *Separate-entity assumption.*
   b. *Unit-of-measure assumption.*
   c. *Continuity assumption.*
   d. *Cost principle.*

4. Why are accounting assumptions necessary?
5. How is the debt-to-equity ratio computed and how is it interpreted?
6. For accounting purposes, what is an account? Explain why accounts are used in an accounting system.
7. What is the fundamental accounting model?
8. Define a business transaction in the broad sense and give an example of the two different kinds of transactions.
9. Explain what *debit* and *credit* mean.
10. Briefly explain what is meant by *transaction analysis*. What are the two steps in transaction analysis?
11. What two equalities in accounting must be maintained in transaction analysis?
12. What is a *journal entry*?
13. What is a *T-account?* What is its purpose?
14. What transactions are classified as investing activities in a cash flow statement? What transactions are classified as financing activities?
15. What is the difference between a bookkeeper and an accountant?
16. What is meant by cash flows from investing activities?

MULTIPLE-CHOICE **QUESTIONS**

1. If a publicly traded company is trying to maximize its perceived value to decision makers external to the corporation, the company is most likely to *understate* which of the following on its balance sheet?
   a. assets
   b. liabilities
   c. retained earnings
   d. share capital

2. Which of the following is not an asset?
   a. short-term investments in shares
   b. land
   c. prepaid expense
   d. share capital

3. Which of the following is false if a company's debt-to-equity ratio is increasing over time?
   a. The amount of shareholders' equity is decreasing relative to total liabilities.
   b. The amount of total liabilities is increasing relative to shareholders' equity.
   c. The company is decreasing its risk related to required interest payments associated with debt.
   d. The company is increasing its risk related to required interest payments associated with debt.

4. Total assets on a balance sheet prepared on any date must agree with
   a. the sum of total liabilities and net income as shown on the income statement
   b. the sum of total liabilities and share capital
   c. the sum of total liabilities and retained earnings
   d. the sum of total liabilities and shareholders' equity

5. The "duality of effects" can best be described as follows:
   a. When one records a transaction in the accounting system, at least two effects on the basic accounting equation will result.
   b. When an exchange takes place between two parties, both parties must record the transaction.
   c. When a transaction is recorded, both the balance sheet and the income statement must be affected.
   d. When a transaction is recorded, one account will always increase and one account will always decrease.

6. The T-account is a tool commonly used for analyzing
   a. increases and decreases to a single account in the accounting system
   b. debits and credits to a single account in the accounting system
   c. changes in specific account balances over a time period
   d. all of the above

7. Assets are listed on the balance sheet
   a. in alphabetical order
   b. in order of magnitude, from lowest value to highest value

   c. from most liquid to least liquid

   d. from least liquid to most liquid

  8. Which of the following is not a financing activity on the cash flow statement?

   a. when the company lends money

   b. when the company issues shares to shareholders

   c. when the company pays dividends

   d. when the company borrows money

  9. How many of the following statements are true regarding *debits* and *credits?*

   • In any given transaction, the total amount of the debits and the total amount of the credits must be equal.

   • Debits decrease certain accounts and credits decrease certain accounts.

   • Liabilities and shareholders' equity accounts usually end in credit balances, while assets usually end in debit balances.

   a. none   b. one   c. two   d. three

 10. How many of the following statements are true regarding the balance sheet?

   • One cannot determine the true "fair market value" of a company by reviewing its balance sheet.

   • Certain internally generated assets, such as a trademark, are reported on a company's balance sheet.

   • A balance sheet shows only the ending balances, in a summarized format, of all "balance sheet accounts" in the accounting system as of a particular date.

   a. none   b. one   c. two   d. three

For more practice with multiple-choice questions, go to our Web site at www.mcgrawhill.ca/college/libby, click on "Student Edition" in the upper left menu, click on this chapter's name and number from the list of contents, and then click on "Multiple-Choice Quiz" from the menu on the left.

EXERCISES

E2–1 Matching Definitions with Terms   ■ **LO1**

Match each definition with its related term by entering the appropriate letter in the space provided. There should be only one definition per term (there are more definitions than terms).

Term	Definition
_____ (1) Separate-entity assumption	A. = Liabilities + Shareholders' Equity.
_____ (2) Cost principle	B. Reports assets, liabilities, and shareholders' equity.
_____ (3) Credits	C. Accounts for a business separate from its owners.
_____ (4) Assets	D. Increase assets; decrease liabilities and shareholders' equity.
_____ (5) T-account	E. An exchange between an entity and other parties.
_____ (6) Journal entry	F. The concept that businesses will operate into the foreseeable future.
_____ (7) A = L + SE, and Debits = Credits	G. Decrease assets; increase liabilities and shareholders' equity.
_____ (8) Liabilities	H. The concept that assets should be recorded at cash-equivalent cost.
	I. A standardized format used to accumulate data about each item reported on financial statements.
	J. Accounting model.
	K. The two equalities in accounting that aid in providing accuracy.
	L. The results of transaction analysis in accounting format.
	M. The account that is credited when money is borrowed from a bank.
	N. Economic resources owned or controlled by an entity.
	O. Every transaction has a least two effects.
	P. Probable debts or obligations to be paid with assets or services.

■ **LO1, 2**

E2–2 Matching Definitions with Terms

Match each definition with its related term by entering the appropriate letter in the space provided. There should be only one definition per term (that is, there are more definitions than terms).

Term	Definition
_____ (1) Transaction	A. Economic resources to be used or turned into cash within one year.
_____ (2) Continuity assumption	B. Reports assets, liabilities, and shareholders' equity.
_____ (3) Balance sheet	C. Accounts for a business separate from its owners.
_____ (4) Liabilities	D. Increase assets; decrease liabilities and shareholders' equity.
_____ (5) Assets = Liabilities + Shareholders' Equity	E. An exchange between an entity and other parties.
_____ (6) Current assets	F. The concept that businesses will operate into the foreseeable future.
_____ (7) Note payable	G. Decrease assets; increase liabilities and shareholders' equity.
_____ (8) Duality	H. The concept that assets should be recorded at cash-equivalent cost.
_____ (9) Retained earnings	I. A standardized format used to accumulate data about each item reported on financial statements.
_____ (10) Debits	J. The accounting model.
	K. The two equalities in accounting that aid in providing accuracy.
	L. The account that is credited when money is borrowed from a bank.
	M. Cumulative earnings of a company that are not distributed to the owners.
	N. Every transaction has at least two effects.
	O. Probable debts or obligations to be paid with assets or services.

■ **LO4**

E2–3 Identifying Events as Accounting Transactions

For each of the following events, which result in an exchange transaction for O'Brien Company (Y for yes and N for no)?

_____ (1) O'Brien purchased a machine and signed a note payable in six months.

_____ (2) Six investors in O'Brien Company sold their stock to another investor.

_____ (3) The company lent $150,000 to a member of the board of directors.

_____ (4) O'Brien Company ordered supplies from Office Max to be delivered next week.

_____ (5) The founding owner, Meaghan O'Brien, purchased additional shares in another company.

_____ (6) The company borrowed $1,000,000 from a local bank.

■ **LO4**

E2–4 Identifying Account Titles

The following are independent situations.

a. A company orders and receives 10 personal computers for office use for which it signs a note promising to pay $22,000 within three months.

b. A company purchases a new delivery truck that has a list, or sticker, price of $24,000 for $21,000 cash.

c. A women's clothing retailer orders 30 new display stands for $300 each for future delivery.

d. A new company is formed and sells 100 shares for $15 per share to investors.

e. A manufacturing company signs a contract for the construction of a new warehouse for $500,000. At the signing, the company writes a cheque for $50,000 as a deposit on the future construction.

f. A publishing firm purchases the copyright (an intangible asset) to a manuscript for an introductory accounting text from the author for $40,000.

g. A manufacturing firm pays dividends of $100,000 to shareholders in cash.

h. A company purchases 100 shares of BCE Inc. for $5,000 cash.

i. A company purchases a piece of land for $50,000 cash. An appraiser for the buyer valued the land at $53,000.

j. A manufacturing company purchases the patent (an intangible asset) on a new digital satellite system for television reception for $500,000 cash and a note for $400,000, payable in one year at an annual interest of 10 percent.

k. A local company is a sole proprietorship (one owner); its owner buys a car for $10,000 for personal use. Answer from the company's point of view.

l. A company signs a six-month note for a $1,000 loan on June 30, 2005, to be paid back on December 31, 2005, with 10-percent annual interest.

m. A company pays $1,500 principal on its note payable.

Required:

1. Indicate the appropriate account titles, if any, affected in each of the preceding events. Consider what is given and what is received.

2. At what amount would you record the truck in (*b*)? The land in (*i*)? What measurement principle are you applying?

3. What accounting concepts did you apply for situations (*c*) and (*k*)?

E2–5 Classifying Accounts and Their Usual Balances ■ **LO4, 6**

As described in a recent annual report, Polaroid Corporation designs, manufactures, and markets worldwide a variety of products primarily in instant image recording fields, including instant photographic cameras and films, electronic imaging recording devices, conventional films, and light-polarizing filters and lenses.

Required:

For each of the following accounts from Polaroid's recent balance sheet, complete the following chart by indicating whether the account is classified as a current asset (CA), non-current asset (NCA), current liability (CL), non-current liability (NCL), or shareholders' equity (SE), and whether the account usually has a debit or credit balance.

Account	Balance Sheet Classification	Debit or Credit Balance
1. Land	_____	_____
2. Retained earnings	_____	_____
3. Notes payable (due in 3 years)	_____	_____
4. Prepaid expenses	_____	_____
5. Long-term investments	_____	_____
6. Share capital	_____	_____
7. Machinery and equipment	_____	_____
8. Accounts payable	_____	_____
9. Short-term investments	_____	_____
10. Taxes payable	_____	_____
11. Accounts Receivable	_____	_____
12. Buildings	_____	_____
13. Cash	_____	_____
14. Merchandise Inventory	_____	_____
15. Supplies Inventory	_____	_____
16. Wages Payable	_____	_____

E2–6 Identifying Effects on Balance Sheet Elements ■ **LO5**

Complete the following table by entering either the word *increases* or *decreases* in columns (1) and (2), and either the word *debit* or *credit* in columns (3) and (4).

	(1) Debit	(2) Credit	(3) Increases	(4) Decreases
Assets	_____	_____	_____	_____
Liabilities	_____	_____	_____	_____
Shareholders' equity	_____	_____	_____	_____

■ **LO5**   **E2–7 Determining Financial Statement Effects of Several Transactions**
The following events occurred for Favata Company:

a. Received investment of cash by organizers, $20,000.

b. Borrowed cash from a bank and signed a note for $8,000.

c. Purchased $12,000 in land; paid $2,000 in cash and signed a mortgage note with a local bank for the balance (due in 15 years).

d. Loaned $300 to an employee who signed a note due in three months.

e. Paid the bank the amount borrowed in (b).

f. Purchased $8,000 of equipment, paying $3,000 in cash and signing a note due to the manufacturer.

Required:
For each of the events (a) through (f), perform transaction analysis and indicate the account, amount, and direction of the effects (+ for increase and − for decrease) on the accounting equation. Check that the accounting equation remains in balance after each transaction. Use the following headings:

Event	Assets	=	Liabilities	+	Shareholders' Equity

■ **LO5**   **E2–8 Determining Financial Statement Effects of Several Transactions**

Nike Inc.

Nike, Inc., with headquarters in Beaverton, Oregon, is one of the world's leading manufacturers of athletic shoes and sports apparel. The following activities occurred during a recent year. The amounts are rounded to millions of dollars.

a. Purchased $216.3 in property, plant, and equipment; paid $5 in long-term debt and the rest in cash.

b. Issued $21.1 in additional shares for cash.

c. Declared $100 in dividends; paid $78.8 during the year, with the rest payable in the following year.

d. Several Nike investors sold their own shares to other investors on the stock exchange for $21.

e. Repaid $3.2 in principal on long-term debt obligations.

f. Received cash for sale investments in other companies at their cost of $1.4.

Required:

1. For each of these events, perform transaction analysis and indicate the account, amount, and direction of the effects on the accounting equation. Check that the accounting equation remains in balance after each transaction. Use the following headings:

Event	Assets	=	Liabilities	+	Shareholders' Equity

2. Explain your response to Transaction (d).

■ **LO6**   **E2–9 Recording Investing and Financing Activities**
Refer to E2–7.

Required:
For each of the events in E2–7, prepare journal entries, checking that debits equal credits.

■ **LO6**   **E2–10 Recording Investing and Financing Activities**
Refer to E2–8.

Required:

1. For each of the events in E2–8, prepare journal entries, checking that debits equal credits.

2. Explain your response to Transaction (d).

■ **LO6**   **E2–11 Analyzing the Effects of Transactions in T-Accounts**
Mulkeen Service Company, Inc., was organized by Conor Mulkeen and five other investors. The following activities occurred during the year:

a. Received $60,000 cash from the investors; each was issued 6,000 shares.

b. Purchased equipment for use in the business at a cost of $12,000; one-fifth was paid in cash, and the company signed a note for the balance, payable in six months.

c. Signed an agreement with a cleaning service to pay it $150 per week for cleaning the corporate offices.

d. Lent $2,000 to one of the investors who signed a note due in six months.

e. Issued shares to additional investors who contributed $4,000 in cash and a lot of land valued at $10,000.

f. Paid the amount of the note payable in (b).

g. Conor Mulkeen borrowed $10,000 for personal use from a local bank and signed a note payable in one year.

Required:

1. Create T-accounts for the following accounts: Cash, Note Receivable, Equipment, Land, Note Payable, and Share Capital. Beginning balances are zero. For each of the preceding transactions, record the effects of the transaction in the appropriate T-accounts. Include good referencing and totals for each T-account.

2. Using the balances in the T-accounts, fill in the following amounts for the accounting equation:

   Assets $_____ = Liabilities $_____ + Shareholders' Equity $_____

3. Explain your responses to Transactions (c) and (g).

E2–12 **Inferring Investing and Financing Transactions, and Preparing a Balance Sheet**   ■ **LO5, 7**
During its first week of operations, January 2–7, 2006, Fullem Fine Furniture Company completed seven transactions with the dollar effects indicated in the following T-accounts:

	Cash				Short-Term Note Receivable				Store Fixtures	
(1)	12,000	4,000	(3)	(4)	3,000	2,000	(7)	(5)	7,000	
(2)	50,000	3,000	(4)							
(7)	2,000	7,000	(5)							
		3,000	(6)							

	Land				Short-Term Note Payable				Share Capital	
(3)	12,000			(6)	3,000	50,000	(2)		12,000	(1)
						8,000	(3)			

Required:

1. Write a brief explanation of Transactions 1 through 7. Explain any assumptions that you made.

2. Compute the ending balance in each account and prepare a classified balance sheet for Fullem Fine Furniture Company on January 7, 2006.

E2–13 **Inferring Investing and Financing Transactions, and Preparing a Balance Sheet**   ■ **LO5, 7**
During its first month of operations, March 2006, Faye's Fashions, Inc., completed seven transactions with the dollar effects indicated in the following T-accounts:

	Cash				Short-Term Investments				Short-Term Note Receivable	
(1)	50,000	4,000	(2)	(4)	6,000	2,000	(6)	(3)	4,000	
(6)	2,000	4,000	(3)							
		6,000	(4)							
		3,000	(5)							

	Computer Equipment				Delivery Truck				Long-Term Note Payable	
(7)	4,000			(2)	25,000			(5)	3,000	21,000	(2)

	Share Capital	
	50,000	(1)
	4,000	(7)

Required:

1. Write a brief explanation of Transactions 1 through 7. Explain any assumptions that you made.

2. Compute the ending balance in each account and prepare a classified balance sheet for Faye's Fashions, Inc., at the end of March 2006.

■ LO6   **E2–14**   **Recording Journal Entries**

Boyce Corporation was organized on May 1, 2005. The following transactions occurred during the first month.

a. Received $60,000 cash from the three investors who organized Boyce Corporation.

b. Borrowed $10,000 cash and signed a 12-percent note due in two years.

c. Purchased $10,000 in equipment, paying $2,000 in cash and signing a six-month note for the balance.

d. Ordered $16,000 in store fixtures.

e. Paid the amount of the note signed in (*c*).

f. Lent $1,000 to an employee who signed a note to repay the loan in three months.

g. Received and paid for the store fixtures ordered in (*d*).

Required:

Prepare journal entries for each transaction. Be sure to use good referencing and categorize each account as an asset (A), liability (L), or shareholders' equity (SE). If a transaction does not require a journal entry, explain the reason.

■ LO6   **E2–15**   **Recording Journal Entries**

Philippine Long Distance Telephone Company

In an annual report, Philippine Long Distance Telephone Company describes itself as "the largest of 63 entities furnishing telephone services in the Philippines. It has a network of 145 central office exchanges serving the Metro Manila area and 146 other cities and municipalities throughout the country." The monetary unit is the Philippine peso (₱). The following transactions were adapted from the annual report. Amounts are in millions of pesos.

a. Declared ₱1,115.8 in dividends to be paid next month.

b. Ordered ₱450 in equipment.

c. Paid ₱1,115.8 in dividends previously declared in (*a*).

d. Issued additional shares for ₱6,127.1 in cash.

e. Sold land at its cost for cash, ₱3,549.9.

f. Received the equipment ordered in Transaction (*b*), paying ₱120 in cash and signing a note for the balance.

g. Purchased temporary investments for ₱745.6.

h. Paid ₱4,642.6 in principal on long-term debt.

Required:

Prepare journal entries for each transaction. Be sure to use good referencing and categorize each account as an asset (A), liability (L), or shareholders' equity (SE). If a transaction does not require a journal entry, explain the reason.

■ LO3, 6   **E2–16**   **Analyzing the Effects of Transactions Using T-Accounts, Preparing a Balance Sheet, and Interpreting the Debt-to-Equity Ratio as a Manager of the Company**

Doane Company has been operating for one year (2005). You are a member of the management team investigating expansion ideas, all of which will require borrowing funds from banks. At the start of 2006, Doane's T-account balances were as follows:

Assets:

Cash		Short-Term Investments		Property and Equipment	
4,000		1,000		4,000	

Liabilities:

Short-Term Notes Payable		Long-Term Notes Payable	
	300		600

Shareholders' Equity:

Share Capital	Retained Earnings
6,100	2,000

Required:

1. Using the data from these T-accounts, complete the balance sheet equation on January 1, 2006:

   Assets $_____ = Liabilities $_____ + Shareholders' Equity $_____.

2. Enter in the T-accounts the following transactions that occurred in 2006:

   (*a*) Paid one-half of the principal on the long-term note payable.

   (*b*) Sold $500 of the investments for $500 cash.

   (*c*) Paid in full the principal on the short-term notes payable.

   (*d*) Sold one-fourth of the property and equipment for $1,000 in cash.

   (*e*) Borrowed $1,600 at 10 percent from the bank (signing a note); the principal and interest are due in three years.

   (*f*) Paid $600 in dividends to shareholders.

3. Compute ending balances in the T-accounts to complete the balance sheet on December 31, 2006:

   Assets $_____ = Liabilities $_____ + Shareholders' Equity $_____.

4. Using the ending balances in the T-accounts, prepare a classified balance sheet at December 31, 2006, in good form.

5. Calculate the debt-to-equity ratio at December 31, 2006. If the industry average for the debt-to-equity ratio is 1.00, what does your computation suggest to you about Doane Company? Would you support expansion by borrowing? Why or why not?

E2–17   **Analyzing the Effects of Transactions Using T-Accounts, Preparing a Balance Sheet, and Evaluating the Debt-to-Equity Ratio over Time as a Bank Loan Officer**   ▪ **LO3, 6, 7**

At the beginning of year 2007, Lee Delivery Company, Inc., which was organized in 2006, applied to your bank for a $100,000 loan to expand the business. The vice-president of the bank asked you to review the information and make a recommendation on lending the funds. The following transactions occurred during year 2006 (the company's first year of operations):

(*a*) Received cash from the organizers, $40,000.

(*b*) Purchased land for $15,000 and signed a one-year note (at a 10-percent annual interest rate).

(*c*) Bought two used delivery trucks for operating purposes at the start of the year at a cost of $10,000 each; paid $2,000 cash and signed a promissory note for the balance, payable over the next three years (at an annual interest rate of 11 percent).

(*d*) Sold one-third of the land for $5,000 to Birkins Moving, which promised to pay in six months.

(*e*) Paid $2,000 cash to a truck repair shop for a new motor for one of the trucks. (*Hint:* Increase the account you used to record the purchase of the trucks since the usefulness of the truck has been improved.)

(*f*) Traded the other truck and $6,000 cash for a new one.

(*g*) Shareholder Jonah Lee paid $22,000 cash for a vacant lot (land) for his personal use.

(*h*) Collected the amount of the note due from Birkins Moving in (*d*).

(*i*) Paid one-third of the principal of the note due for the delivery trucks in (*c*).

Required:

1. Set up appropriate T-accounts with beginning balances of $0 for Cash, Short-Term Notes Receivable, Land, Equipment, Short-Term Notes Payable, Long-Term Notes Payable, and Share Capital. Using the T-accounts, record the effects of these transactions on Lee Delivery Company.

2. Prepare a classified balance sheet for Lee Delivery Company at the end of 2006.

3. At the end of the next two years, Lee Delivery Company reported the following amounts on its balance sheets:

	End of 2008	End of 2007
Assets	$120,000	$90,000
Liabilities	70,000	40,000
Shareholders' Equity	50,000	50,000

Compute the company's debt-to-equity ratio for 2007 and 2008. What is the trend and what does this suggest about the company?

4. What recommendation would you make to the bank's vice-president about lending the money to Lee Delivery Company?

LO6

E2–18 Explaining the Effects of Transactions on Balance Sheet Accounts Using T-Accounts
Heavey and Lovas Furniture Repair Service, a company with two shareholders, began operations on June 1, 2006. The following T-accounts indicate the activities for the month of June.

Cash (A)				Notes Receivable (A)				Tools and Equipment (A)			
(a)	17,000	(b)	10,000	(c)	1,500	(d)	500	(a)	3,000	(f)	800
(d)	500	(c)	1,500								
(f)	800	(e)	1,000								

Building (A)		Notes Payable (L)				Share Capital (SE)		
(b)	50,000	(e)	1,000	(b)	40,000		(a)	20,000

Required:
Explain Transactions (a) through (f), which resulted in the entries in the T-accounts. That is, what activity made the account increase or decrease?

LO6

E2–19 Inferring Typical Investing and Financing Activities in Accounts
The following T-accounts indicate the effects of normal business transactions:

Equipment			Note Receivable			Notes Payable		
1/1	300		1/1	75			130	1/1
	250	?		?	290	?	170	
12/31	450		12/31	50			180	12/31

Required:

1. Describe the typical investing and financing transactions that affect each T-account. That is, what economic events occur to make these accounts increase or decrease?

2. For each T-account, compute the missing amounts.

LO8

The Forzani
Group Ltd.

E2–20 Identifying Investing and Financing Activities Affecting Cash Flows
The Forzani Group Ltd. (FGL) is Canada's largest sporting goods retailer, with 217 company-owned stores under the Forzani's, Sport Chek, Coast Mountain Sports, and Sport Mart banners. FGL also boasts 174 franchised stores under the Sport Experts, Atmosphere, Intersport, RnR, Econosports, and Tech Shop names. The stores sell name-brand and private-label sports equipment, footwear, and apparel. The following are several of FGL's investing and financing activities that were reflected in a recent annual cash flow statement.

a. Principal repayment of long-term debt.

b. Purchase of investments.

c. Issuance of shares.

d. Addition to capital assets (property, plant, and equipment).

e. Issuance of long-term debt.

f. Repurchase of shares.

g. Disposal of other assets.

Required:
For each of these, indicate whether the activity is investing (I) or financing (F) and the direction of the effect on cash flows (+ = increases cash; − = decreases cash).

E2–21 Preparing the Investing and Financing Section of the Cash Flow Statement

■ **LO8**

Hilton Hotels

Hilton Hotels Corporation constructs, operates, and franchises domestic and international hotel and hotel-casino properties. Information from the company's recent annual cash flow statement indicates the following investing and financing activities during that year (simplified):

Additional borrowing from banks	$438.5
Purchase of investments	282.2
Sale of property (assume sold at cost)	5.4
Issuance of shares	2.9
Purchase and renovation of properties	274.5
Payment of debt	32.2
Receipt of payment on a note receivable	5.4

Required:

Prepare the Investing and Financing sections of the cash flow statement for Hilton hotels. Assume that the company's year-end is December 31, 2005.

E2–22 Finding Financial Information as a Potential Investor

■ **LO4, 7, 8**

You are considering investing the cash you inherited from your grandfather in various company shares. You have received the annual reports of several major companies.

Required:

For each of the following, indicate where you would locate the information in an annual report. (*Hint:* The information may be in more than one location.)

1. Total current assets.

2. Principal amount of debt repaid during the year.

3. Summary of significant accounting policies.

4. Cash received from sales of non-current assets.

5. Amount of dividends paid during the year.

6. Short-term obligations.

7. Date of the statement of financial position.

PROBLEMS

P2–1 Identifying Accounts on a Classified Balance Sheet and Their Normal Debit or Credit Balances (AP2–1)

■ **LO1, 4**

Petro-Canada

Petro-Canada is a major Canadian integrated oil and gas company that explores, produces, refines, markets, and supplies crude oil and petroleum products. Its operations include refineries in Alberta, Ontario, and Québec and almost 1,600 gas stations across Canada. The following are several of the accounts that appeared on a recent balance sheet of Petro-Canada.

(1) Cash and Short-Term Investments	(7) Inventories
(2) Accounts Receivable	(8) Accounts Payable
(3) Share Capital	(9) Retained Earnings
(4) Long-Term Debt	(10) Property, Plant, and Equipment
(5) Prepaid Expenses	(11) Long-Term Investments
(6) Income Tax Payable	

Required:

For each account, indicate how it normally should be categorized on a classified balance sheet. Use CA for current asset, NCA for non-current asset, CL for current liability, NCL for non-current liability, and SE for shareholders' equity. Also indicate whether the account normally has a debit or credit balance.

P2–2 Determining Financial Statement Effects of Various Transactions (AP2–2)

■ **LO4, 5**

Lester's Home Healthcare Services was organized on January 1, 2006, by four friends. Each organizer invested $10,000 in the company and, in turn, was issued 8,000 shares. To date, they are the only shareholders. During the first month (January 2006), the company completed the following six transactions:

a. Collected a total of $45,000 from the organizers and, in turn, issued the shares.

b. Purchased a building for $65,000, equipment for $16,000, and three acres of land for $12,000; paid $13,000 in cash, and signed a 10-percent mortgage for the balance payable to the local bank in 15 years. (*Hint:* Five different accounts are affected.)

c. One shareholder reported to the company that he sold 700 shares to another shareholder for a cash consideration of $7,000.

d. Purchased short-term investments for $5,000 cash.

e. Sold one acre of land costing $4,000 to another company for $4,000 cash.

f. Loaned one of the shareholders $5,000 for moving costs, in exchange for a signed note due in one year.

Required:

1. Was Lester's Home Healthcare Services organized as a sole proprietorship, a partnership, or a corporation? Explain the basis for your answer.

2. During the first month, the records of the company were inadequate. You were asked to prepare a summary of the preceding transactions. To develop a quick assessment of the transaction effects on Lester's Home Healthcare Services, you have decided to complete the tabulation that follows and to use plus (+) for increases and minus (−) for decreases for each account. The first transaction is used as an example.

	Assets					=	Liabilities	+	Shareholders' Equity	
Cash	Short-Term Investments	Notes Receivable	Land	Building	Equipment		Notes Payable		Share Capital	Retained Earnings
(a) +45,000						=			+45,000	

3. Did you include the transaction between the two shareholders—Transaction (*c*)—in the tabulation? Why?

4. Based only on the completed tabulation, provide the following amounts at January 31, 2006 (show computations):
   a. Total assets.
   b. Total liabilities.
   c. Total shareholders' equity.
   d. Cash balance.
   e. Total current assets.

■ **LO3, 6, 7**

P2–3 **Recording Transactions in T-Accounts, Preparing a Balance Sheet, and Evaluating the Debt-to-Equity Ratio** (AP2–3)

Patrie Plastics Company has been operating for three years. At December 31, 2005, the accounting records reflected the following:

Cash	$35,000	Intangibles	$5,000
Short-term investments	3,000	Accounts payable	25,000
Accounts receivable	5,000	Accrued liabilities payable	3,000
Inventory	40,000	Short-term note payable	12,000
Long-term note receivable	2,000	Long-term note payable	80,000
Equipment	80,000	Share capital	150,000
Factory building	150,000	Retained earnings	50,000

During the year 2006, the following summarized transactions were completed:

a. Purchased equipment that cost $30,000; paid $10,000 cash and signed a one-year note for the balance.

b. Issued 2,000 shares for $24,000 cash.

c. Loaned $12,000 to a supplier who signed a two-year note.

d. Purchased $10,000 in investments.

e. Paid $5,000 on the note in Transaction (*a*).

f. Borrowed $20,000 cash on December 31, 2006, from a local bank and signed a note, payable June 30, 2007.

g. Purchased a patent (an intangible asset) for $5,000 cash.

h. Built an addition to the factory for $45,000; paid $15,000 in cash and signed a three-year note for the balance.

i. Hired a new president at the end of the year. The contract was for $125,000 per year plus options to purchase company shares at a set price based on company performance.

j. Returned defective equipment to the manufacturer, receiving a cash refund of $2,000.

Required:

1. Create T-accounts for each of the accounts on the balance sheet and enter the balances at the end of 2005 as beginning balances for 2006.

2. Record each of the transactions for 2006 in T-accounts (including referencing) and determine the ending balances.

3. Explain your response to Transaction (*i*).

4. Prepare a classified balance sheet at December 31, 2006.

5. Compute the debt-to-equity ratio for 2006. What does this ratio suggest about Patrie Plastics Company?

P2–4 Identifying Effects of Transactions on the Cash Flow Statement (AP2–4)
Refer to P2–3.

■ **LO8**

Required:
Using the transactions (*a*) through (*j*) in P2–3, indicate whether each transaction is an investing (I) or financing (F) activity for the year and the direction of the effect on cash flows (+ for increase and − for decrease). If there is no effect on cash flows, write NE.

P2–5 Recording Transactions, Preparing Journal Entries, Posting to T-Accounts, Preparing a Balance Sheet, and Evaluating the Debt-to-Equity Ratio
Bayer AG, with headquarters in Leverkeusen, Germany, is an international research-based group of companies active in health, agriculture, polymers, and chemicals. Popular products include Bayer Aspirin, Alka-Seltzer, and One-A-Day vitamins. The following is Bayer's (simplified) balance sheet from a recent year:

■ **LO3, 6, 7**

Bayer AG

BAYER AG	
Balance Sheet	
At December 31, 2003	
(in millions of euros)	
ASSETS	
Current assets	
Cash	€ 2,863
Receivables and other assets	8,925
Inventories	5,885
	17,673
Non-current assets	
Investments	1,781
Property, plant, and equipment	9,937
Intangible assets	6,514
Other assets	1,540
Total assets	**19,772**
	€37,445
LIABILITIES AND SHAREHOLDERS' EQUITY	
Current liabilities	
Accounts payable	€ 2,265
Other short-term obligations	7,122
	9,387
Long-term liabilities	**15,845**
Shareholders' equity	
Share capital	4,812
Retained earnings	7,401
	12,213
Total liabilities and shareholders' equity	**€37,445**

Assume that the following transactions occurred in 2004:

a. Issued additional shares for €1,200 in cash.

b. Borrowed €3,952 from banks due in two years.

c. Declared and paid €953 in dividends to shareholders.

d. Purchased additional intangibles for €45 cash.

e. Purchased property, plant, and equipment; paid €2,647 in cash and €5,410 with additional long-term bank loans.

f. Acquired additional investments; paid €160 in cash.

g. Lent €250 to an affiliate that signed a six-month note.

h. Sold investments costing €115 for the same amount in cash.

Required:

1. Prepare a journal entry for each transaction.

2. Create T-accounts for each balance sheet account and include the December 31, 2003, balances. Post each journal entry to the appropriate T-accounts.

3. Prepare a balance sheet for Bayer based on the T-account ending balances at December 31, 2004.

4. Compute Bayer's debt-to-equity ratio for 2004. What does this suggest about the company?

■ **LO8**

Foster's Brewing

P2–6 Preparing the Investing and Financing Sections of a Cash Flow Statement (AP2–6)
Refer to P2–5.

Required:

Based on the transactions that occurred in 2004, prepare the Investing and Financing sections of the cash flow statement of Bayer's for 2004.

■ **LO3, 7**

McDonald's Corporation

P2–7 Using Financial Reports: Preparing a Classified Balance Sheet and Analyzing the Debt-to-Equity Ratio (AP2–5)
The accounts below, in alphabetical order, are adapted from a recent McDonald's Corporation balance sheet (amounts are in millions of dollars):

	Current Year	Prior Year		Current Year	Prior Year
Accounts and notes receivable	796.5	708.1	Long-term debt	7,843.9	5,632.4
Accounts payable	684.9	585.7	Notes payable (short term)	275.5	1,073.1
Accrued liabilities	1,046.0	1,068.7	Other long-term liabilities	2,274.3	2,437.4
Cash and equivalents	421.7	419.5	Other non-current assets	705.9	822.4
Current maturities of long-term debt	354.5	546.8	Prepaid expenses and other current assets	344.9	362.0
Intangible assets, net	1,443.4	1,261.8	Property and equipment, net	17,047.6	16,324.5
Inventories	99.3	82.7	Retained earnings	7,746.0	8,334.2
Investments in and advances to affiliates	824.2	1,002.2	Share capital	1,458.4	1,304.9

Required:

1. Construct, in good form, a classified balance sheet (with two years reported) for McDonald's Corporation.

2. Compute the company's debt-to-equity ratio for the current year. How do you interpret this ratio for McDonald's?

ALTERNATE PROBLEMS

■ **LO1, 2, 4**

Celestica Inc.

AP2–1 Identifying Accounts on a Classified Balance Sheet and Their Normal Debit or Credit Balances (P2–1)
According to a recent annual report of Celestica Inc., the company is a "key player in the new technology-driven global economy." The company provides a broad range of services

including "design, prototyping, assembly, testing, product assurance, supply chain management, worldwide distribution and after-sales service." The following are several of the accounts from a recent balance sheet:

(1) Accounts Receivable

(2) Short-Term Borrowings

(3) Share Capital

(4) Long-Term Debt

(5) Prepaid Expenses and Other Assets

(6) Intangible Assets

(7) Property, Plant, and Equipment

(8) Retained Earnings

(9) Accounts Payable

(10) Cash and Short-Term Investments

(11) Accrued Liabilities

(12) Other Long-Term Liabilities

(13) Inventories

(14) Income Taxes Payable

Required:

Indicate how each account normally should be categorized on a classified balance sheet. Use CA for current asset, NCA for non-current asset, CL for current liability, NCL for non-current liability, and SE for shareholders' equity. Also indicate whether the account normally has a debit or credit balance.

AP2–2 Determining Financial Statement Effects of Various Transactions and Interpreting the Debt-to-Equity Ratio (P2–2)

■ **LO4, 5**

Malamud Incorporated is a small manufacturing company that makes model trains to sell to toy stores. It has a small service department that repairs customers' trains for a fee. The company has been in business for five years. At the end of the most recent year, 2005, the accounting records reflected total assets of $550,000 and total liabilities of $250,000. During the current year, 2006, the following summarized transactions were completed:

a. Issued 10,000 shares for $100,000 cash.

b. Borrowed $130,000 cash from the bank and signed a 10-year, 12-percent note.

c. Built an addition onto the factory for $210,000 and paid cash to the contractor.

d. Purchased equipment for the new addition for $30,000, paying $3,000 in cash and signing a note due in six months for the balance.

e. Purchased $85,000 in long-term investments.

f. Returned a defective piece of the equipment purchased in transaction (*d*); received a reduction of $4,000 on the note payable.

g. Paid $12,000 of the principal due on the note in (*b*).

h. Purchased a delivery truck (equipment) for $12,000; paid $5,000 cash and signed a short-term note for the remainder.

i. Loaned the company president, Jennifer Malamud, $2,000 cash. Ms. Malamud promised to pay the amount and annual interest at the rate of 10 percent within one year.

j. A shareholder sold some of her shares in Malamud Incorporated to her neighbour for $6,000.

k. Received $250 cash from Ms. Malamud on the note due, Transaction (*i*).

Required:

1. Prepare a summary of the preceding transactions. To develop a quick assessment of the transaction effects on Malamud Incorporated, you have decided to complete the tabulation that follows and to use plus (+) for increases and minus (−) for decreases for each account. The first transaction is used as an example.

		Assets			=	Liabilities		+	Shareholders' Equity	
Cash	**Notes Receivable**	**Long-Term Investments**	**Equipment**	**Building**		**Short-Term Notes Payable**	**Long-Term Notes Payable**		**Share Capital**	**Retained Earnings**
(a) +100,000					=				+100,000	

2. Did you include Transaction (*j*) in the tabulation? Why?

3. Based on beginning balances plus the completed tabulation, calculate the following amounts at the end of 2006 (show computations):

   a. Total assets.

   b. Total liabilities.

   c. Total shareholders' equity.

4. Compute the company's debt-to-equity ratio. What does this ratio suggest to you about Malamud Incorporated?

■ **LO3, 6, 7** **AP2–3** **Recording Transactions in T-Accounts, Preparing a Balance Sheet, and Evaluating the Debt-to-Equity Ratio** (P2–3)

Spar Aerospace
Limited

Spar Aerospace Limited specializes in aviation services. The following is adapted from a recent annual financial report (assume that the fiscal year ends on December 31, 2004). Dollars are in thousands.

Cash and cash equivalents	$34,395	Intangibles	$22,354
Short-term investments	0	Other assets	1,738
Accounts receivable	33,740	Accounts payable and	
Short-term note receivable	36,482	accrued expenses	41,498
Inventories	20,423	Other current liabilities	16,617
Prepaid expenses and		Long-term debt	19,531
other current assets	723	Share capital	79,719
Property, plant, and equipment	23,364	Retained earnings	20,854
Long-term investments and			
notes receivable	5,000		

Assume that the following transactions occurred in the first quarter ended March 31, 2005:

a. Received $630 on long-term receivables owed by affiliates.

b. Paid $12,340 in principal on long-term debt.

c. Purchased $3,400 in additional intangibles.

d. Sold equipment at its cost for $4,020 cash.

e. Purchased short-term investments of $2,980.

f. Issued additional shares for $1,020 in cash.

g. Purchased property, plant, and equipment; paid $1,830 in cash and $9,400 with additional long-term bank loans.

h. Sold at cost other assets for $310 cash.

i. Declared and paid $300 in dividends.

Required:

1. Create T-accounts for each of the accounts on the balance sheet; enter the balances at December 31, 2004.

2. Record each of the transactions for the first quarter ended March 31, 2005, in the T-accounts (including referencing) and determine the ending balances.

3. Prepare a classified balance sheet at March 31, 2005.

4. Compute the debt-to-equity ratio for the quarter ended March 31, 2005. What does this suggest about Spar Aerospace Limited?

■ **LO8** **AP2–4** **Identifying Effects of Transactions on the Cash Flow Statement** (P2–4)

Spar Aerospace
Limited

Refer to AP2–3.

Required:

Using the transactions (*a*) through (*i*) in AP2–3, indicate whether each transaction is an investing (I) or financing (F) activity for the year and the direction of the effect on cash flows (+ for increase and − for decrease). If there is no effect on cash flows, write NE.

■ **LO3, 7** **AP2–5** **Using Financial Reports: Preparing a Classified Balance Sheet and Analyzing the Debt-to-Equity Ratio** (P2–7)

The accounts below, in alphabetical order, are adapted from Danier Leather Inc.'s recent balance sheet (amounts in thousands of dollars):

	Current Year	Prior Year		Current Year	Prior Year
Accounts payable and accrued liabilities	9,425	9,350	Other non-current assets	5,078	1,018
Accounts receivable	634	683	Prepaid expenses and		
Cash	23,000	7,254	other current assets	1,030	1,257
Income taxes payable	952	-0-	Property & equipment, net	30,212	34,246
Inventories	29,915	37,029	Retained earnings	36,902	43,999
Non-current liabilities	18,205	4,143	Share capital	24,385	23,995

Required:

1. Prepare, in good form, a classified balance sheet (with two years reported) for Danier Leather Inc. Assume the current year ends on June 30, 2005.

2. Compute the company's debt-to-equity ratio for the current year. How do you interpret this ratio for Danier Leather?

CASES AND PROJECTS

FINDING AND INTERPRETING FINANCIAL INFORMATION

CP2–1 Finding Financial Information

■ **LO1, 2, 3, 4, 5, 8**

The Forzani Group

Refer to the financial statements and the accompanying notes of The Forzani Group Ltd., available on the Online Learning Centre Web site at www.mcgrawhill.ca/college/libby/ student/resources.

Required:

1. Is the company a corporation, a partnership, or a proprietorship? How do you know?

2. Use the company's balance sheet to determine the amounts in the accounting equation (A = L + SE).

3. The company shows on the balance sheet that inventories are reported at $278,631,000. Does this amount represent the expected selling price? Why or why not?

4. What is the company's fiscal year-end? Where did you find the exact date?

5. What are the company's long-term obligations?

6. Compute the company's debt-to-equity ratio and explain its meaning.

7. How much cash did the company spend on purchasing property, plant, and equipment each year (capital expenditures)? Where did you find the information?

CP2–2 Comparing Companies

■ **LO3, 4, 8**

Van Houtte vs. The Forzani Group

Refer to the financial statements and the accompanying notes of The Forzani Group Ltd., available at the Online Learning Centre Web site www.mcgrawhill.ca/college/libby/ student/resources, and of Van Houtte Inc., given in Appendix B.

Required:

1. Which company is larger in terms of total assets?

2. Compute the debt-to-equity ratio for both companies. Which company is assuming more risk? Why do you think that?

3. In the most recent year, what were the net cash flows (that is, the increases in cash minus the decreases in cash) related to the buying, maturing, and selling of investments (marketable securities) for each company?

4. How much did each company pay in dividends for the most recent year?

5. What account title does each company use to report any land, buildings, and equipment it may have?

FINANCIAL REPORTING AND ANALYSIS CASES

CP2–3   **Broadening Financial Research Skills: Locating Financial Information on the SEDAR Database**

The Securities Commissions regulate companies that issue shares on the stock market. They receive financial reports from public companies electronically under a system called *SEDAR* (System for Electronic Document Analysis and Retrieval). Using the Internet, anyone may search the database for the reports that have been filed. A similar system is available for retrieval of financial information about U.S. public companies. It is known as *EDGAR* (Electronic Data Gathering and Retrieval Service).

Using your Web browser, access the SEDAR database at www.sedar.com. To search the database, select "English," then "Company Profiles"; click on the letter V to get a list of all company names that start with V. Select Van Houtte Inc., then click on "View this company's public documents" at the lower left corner of the next screen.

Required:

To look at SEDAR filings:

1. Click on the interim financial statements — English. Then locate the Balance Sheet.
   a. What was the amount of Van Houtte's total assets at the end of the most recent quarter reported?
   b. Did long-term debt increase or decrease for the quarter?
   c. Compute the debt-to-equity ratio. How does it compare to the ratio indicated for Van Houtte in this chapter? What does this suggest about the company?

2. Look at the "Cash Flow Statement" in the interim report.
   a. What amount did Van Houtte spend on capital expenditures for the most recent quarter reported?
   b. What was the total amount of cash flows from (used in) financing activities for the most recent quarter reported?

CP2–4   **Interpreting the Financial Press**

The May 24, 1999, edition of *Fortune* magazine includes an article entitled "A Crash Course for Online Investors: The SEC Can't Always Protect You."* You can access the article on the Online Learning Centre Web site at www.mcgrawhill.ca/college/libby/student/resources.

Required:

Read the article and then answer the following questions:

1. What is a *cyberinvestor* according to the article?

2. What investment risk do cyberinvestors face?

3. List the rules suggested in the article to minimize risk from investing online.

CP2–5   **Using Financial Reports: Evaluating the Reliability of a Balance Sheet**

Betsey Jordan asked a local bank for a $50,000 loan to expand her small company. The bank asked Betsey to submit a financial statement of the business to supplement the loan application. Betsey prepared the following balance sheet.

Balance Sheet June 30, 2005	
Assets	
Cash and GICs (investments)	$ 9,000
Inventory	30,000
Equipment	46,000
Personal residence (monthly payments, $2,800)	300,000
Other assets	20,000
Total assets	**$405,000**
Liabilities	
Short-term debt to suppliers	$ 62,000
Long-term debt on equipment	38,000
Total debt	100,000
Shareholders' equity	**305,000**
Total liabilities and shareholders' equity	**$405,000**

---

*© 1999 Time Inc. All rights reserved.

Required:

The balance sheet has several flaws. However, there is at least one major deficiency. Identify it and explain its significance.

CP2–6 Using Financial Reports: Analyzing the Balance Sheet

Research In Motion Limited is a Canadian enterprise that designs, manufactures, and markets wireless products for the mobile communications industry. Recent (adapted) balance sheets for the company are presented below.

■ **LO3, 6, 7**

Research in Motion
Limited

Research In Motion Limited Consolidated Balance Sheets (in thousands of U.S. dollars)	February 28 2004	March 1 2003
Assets		
Current		
Cash and cash equivalents	$1,192,680	$340,681
Trade receivables	95,213	40,803
Other receivables	12,149	4,538
Inventory	42,836	31,275
Other current assets	12,527	11,079
	1,355,405	428,376
Investments	333,886	190,030
Capital assets	147,709	161,183
Intangible assets	64,269	51,479
Goodwill	30,109	30,588
Total assets	$1,931,378	$861,656
Liabilities		
Current		
Accounts payable	$ 35,570	$ 18,594
Accrued liabilities	154,930	105,117
Income taxes payable	1,684	4,909
Deferred revenue	16,498	14,336
Current portion of long-term debt	193	6,143
	208,875	149,099
Long-term debt	6,240	5,776
Total liabilities	215,115	154,875
Shareholders' equity		
Share capital	1,829,388	874,377
Retained earnings (Accumulated deficit)	(113,125)	(167,596)
Total shareholders' equity	1,716,263	706,781
Total liabilities and shareholders' equity	$1,931,378	$861,656

Required:

1. Is Research In Motion a corporation, sole proprietorship, or partnership? Explain briefly.

2. Use the company's balance sheet to determine the amounts in the accounting equation (A = L + SE) at the end of the fiscal years 2003 and 2004.

3. Calculate the company's debt-to-equity ratio at the end of fiscal 2004. Interpret the ratio that you calculated. What other information would make your interpretation more useful?

4. Prepare the journal entry for the payment of the principal on the long-term debt if it were due at the end of February 2005.

5. Does the company appear to have been generally profitable during its years in business? Explain.

6. If no dividends were declared, how much was the net income (loss) for the fiscal year ended February 28, 2004? What other information do you need to be sure of your answer?

■ LO3, 7 **CP2–7** **Using Financial Reports: Analyzing the Balance Sheet**

Smiley Corp. and Tsang Inc. were organized in 2002. Both companies operate in the same line of business. The balance sheets of the two companies at December 31, 2005 are as follows:

Smiley Corp. Balance Sheet December 31, 2005			Tsang Inc. Balance Sheet December 31, 2005		
Assets			**Assets**		
Cash		$ 17,000	Cash		$ 7,200
Accounts receivable		30,000	Accounts receivable		14,400
Inventory		16,000	Inventory		7,600
Property, plant, and equipment		117,600	Property, plant, and equipment		244,400
Total		$180,600	Total		$273,600
Liabilities and Shareholders' Equity			**Liabilities and Shareholders' Equity**		
Liabilities:			Liabilities:		
Notes payable (short-term)		$ 18,600	Notes payable (short-term)		$ 33,600
Accounts payable		14,400	Accounts payable		64,800
Total liabilities		33,000	Total liabilities		98,400
Shareholders' equity:			Shareholders' equity:		
Share capital		90,000	Share capital		108,000
Retained earnings		57,600	Retained earnings		67,200
Total shareholders' equity		147,600	Total shareholders' equity		175,200
Total		$180,600	Total		$273,600

Required:

1. Eric Frechette wants to invest in one of these two companies by purchasing all of its shares. As a financial adviser to Mr. Frechette, which company would you select as an investment? Provide justification for your selection.

2. Each company applied to Development Bank for a loan of $20,000, payable in four months. As a bank loan officer, would you lend each company the requested amount? Explain.

CRITICAL THINKING CASES

■ LO1, 2, 7 **CP2–8** **Making a Decision as a Financial Analyst: Preparing and Analyzing a Balance Sheet**

Your best friend from home writes you a letter about an investment opportunity that has come her way. A company is raising money by issuing shares and wants her to invest $20,000 (her recent inheritance from her great-aunt's estate). Your friend has never invested in a company before and, knowing that you are a financial analyst, asks that you look over the balance sheet and send her some advice. An *unaudited* balance sheet, in only moderately good form, is enclosed with the letter:

DEWEY, CHEETUM, AND HOWE, INC. Balance Sheet For the Year Ending December 31, 2005	
Accounts receivable	$ 8,000
Cash	1,000
Inventory	8,000
Furniture and fixtures	52,000
Delivery truck	12,000
Buildings (estimated market value)	98,000
Total assets	**$179,000**
Accounts payable	$ 16,000
Payroll taxes payable	13,000
Long-term notes payable	15,000
Mortgage payable	50,000
Total liabilities	**$ 94,000**
Share capital	$ 80,000
Retained earnings	5,000
Total shareholders' equity	**$ 85,000**

There is only one footnote, and it states that the building was purchased for $65,000, has been amortized by $5,000 on the books, and still carries a mortgage (shown in the liability section). The footnote further states that, in the opinion of the company president, the building is "easily worth $98,000."

Required:

1. Draft a new balance sheet for your friend, correcting any errors you note. (If any of the account balances need to be corrected, you may need to adjust the retained earnings balance correspondingly.) If no errors or omissions exist, state so.

2. Write a letter to your friend explaining the changes you made to the balance sheet, if any, and offer your comments on the company's apparent financial condition based only on this information. Suggest other information your friend might want to review before coming to a final decision on whether to invest.

CP2–9 Manipulation of Financial Statements: Ethical Considerations ■ LO4

Technology N Motion is a publicly traded company that is facing financial difficulties. To survive, the company needs large new bank loans. As the chief financial officer of the company you approached several banks, but each has asked for your audited financial statements for 2006, the most recent fiscal year. You called for a meeting with other corporate officers to discuss how the financial statements could be improved. The suggestions made by your colleagues include:

1. We owe $20 million to our suppliers. We could show half this amount as a liability on our balance sheet and report the other half as share capital. This will improve our financial position.

2. We own land that is worth at least $8 million in today's market, but it cost us only $3 million when we bought it. Why not show the land at $8 million on the company's balance sheet, which increases both the total assets and shareholders' equity by $5 million?

3. We owe FirstRate Software $2 million, due in 30 days. I can ask their chief financial officer to let us delay the payment of this debt for a year, and our company could sign him a note that pays 8 percent interest.

Required:

Evaluate each of these three proposals to improve Technology N Motion's financial statements by considering both accounting and ethical issues.

CP2–10 Evaluating an Ethical Dilemma: Analyzing Management Incentives ■ LO4

In 1993, Leslie Fay Companies, manufacturer of women's apparel, filed for bankruptcy protection shortly after a scandal erupted over fraudulent accounting information. As reported in *The Wall Street Journal* (March 28, 1995, p. B1, B16), the company's audit committee report sharply criticized top management, suggesting that "it would have been difficult for senior management not to spot the extensive inventory and sales fraud."

Leslie Fay

There were numerous ways in which Leslie Fay committed the fraud, according to the report: to boost sales and lower costs, mid-level company officials forged inventory tags, ignored expected inventory shrinkage, multiplied the value of items in inventory, improperly inflated sales, and made up phantom inventory. These officials also constantly altered records to meet sales targets. In March 1995, Leslie Fay's independent auditors, BDO Seidman, filed charges against Leslie Fay management, suggesting a cause of the fraudulent activity was due to senior management's adoption of unrealistic budgets: "Senior management created an environment which encouraged and rewarded the cooking of Leslie Fay's books and records" (*The Wall Street Journal,* March 29, 1995).

Required:

1. Describe the parties who were harmed or helped by this fraud.

2. Explain how adopting unrealistic budgets may have contributed to the fraud.

3. Why do you think the independent auditor filed charges against its former client?

FINANCIAL REPORTING AND ANALYSIS
TEAM PROJECT

LO3, 4, 8   CP2–11   Team Project: Analysis of Balance Sheets and Ratios

As a team, select an industry to analyze. Using a Web browser, each team member should acquire the annual report for one publicly traded company in the industry, with each member selecting a different company.

Required:

1. On an individual basis, each team member should write a short report that lists the following information.
   a. The date of the balance sheet.
   b. The asset accounts.
   c. The major investing and financing activities for the most recent period.
   d. The financial leverage ratio for the most recent period.

2. Then, as a team, write a short report comparing and contrasting your companies using the preceding attributes. Discuss any patterns across the companies that you as a team observe, and provide potential explanations for any differences discovered.

LEARNING OBJECTIVES

After studying this chapter, you should be able to:

1. Describe a typical business operating cycle and explain the necessity for the periodicity assumption. p. 106

2. Explain how business activities affect the elements of the classified income statement. p. 108

3. Compute and interpret the total asset turnover ratio. p. 112

4. Explain the accrual basis of accounting and apply the revenue and matching principles to measure income. p. 113

5. Compute and interpret the return on assets ratio. p. 119

6. Apply transaction analysis to examine and record the effects of operating activities on the financial statements. p. 120

7. Understand the difference between net income and cash flow from operations. p. 128

Operating Decisions and the Income Statement

3

Van Houtte ranks among the largest and most integrated gourmet coffee companies in the North American coffee industry. Van Houtte operates the largest office coffee services network in North America, with an approximate 50-percent market share in Canada and an estimated 3 percent of the highly fragmented U.S. market. The company serves the office coffee market through its subsidiaries Filterfresh in the United States, Red Carpet in Ontario and Western Canada, and Selena in Québec and Eastern Canada. It is estimated that office coffee service operations account for approximately 65 percent of Van Houtte's total revenues. The remaining 35 percent of revenues are generated by the manufacture and sale of single-cup coffee brewers, as well as through roasting and distribution of gourmet coffees through various retail channels, including Van Houtte's Café Bistro division. The presence of Van Houtte's 74 Café Bistros in the foodservice channel plays a role in the company's overall branding strategy, albeit mainly in Québec, as there are no Café Bistros outside of the province.

Over the years, Van Houtte expanded its business operations by investing in many companies, including VKI Technologies, which designs and manufactures its own single-cup coffee equipment, and Keurig, which develops and holds patents for various single-cup brewing equipment. Together, VKI and Keurig boast the largest number of single-cup brewers installed in North America, with more than 60,000 brewing units installed, of which Van Houtte has more than 40,000 installations among its various office coffee services operations.

Van Houtte is the leading roaster of gourmet coffee in the retail channel in Canada, servicing grocery stores, superstores, convenience stores, drugstores, and restaurants. Currently, more than 3,575 supermarkets are serviced across Canada, roughly half outside of Québec. In the United States, Van Houtte distributes its coffees in roughly 725 grocery stores.

Van Houtte had revenues of $348.8 million in fiscal year 2005 and roasts roughly 25 million pounds of coffee per year.

UNDERSTANDING THE BUSINESS

To become the number-one coffee services company, Van Houtte develops strategies and plans (or expectations), and identifies measurable indicators of progress toward its goal. In developing operating and growth strategies, companies such as Van Houtte plan their companywide operations in terms of the elements of the income statement (specific revenues and expenses).

Financial analysts, creditors, and shareholders also develop their own set of expectations about Van Houtte's future performance. The published income statement provides the primary basis for comparing these plans or projections to actual results of operations. We discuss these comparisons and the stock market's reactions to Van Houtte's results throughout this chapter as we learn about income recognition and measurement. To understand how business plans and the results of operations are reflected on the income statement, we need to answer the following questions:

1. What type of business activities affect the income statement?
2. How are these activities recognized and measured?
3. How are these activities reported on the income statement?

In this chapter, we focus on Van Houtte's operating activities, which include sales of roasted coffee beans to retailers; packaged tea and coffee to bistros, hotels, and restaurants; and supplies to franchisees. The results of these activities are reported on the income statement.

ORGANIZATION OF THE CHAPTER

• How Do Business Activities Affect the Income Statement?	• How Are Operating Activities Recognized and Measured?	• The Expanded Transaction Analysis Model	• Comparison of Accrual and Cash Bases of Accounting
The Operating Cycle	Accrual Accounting	Transaction Analysis Rules	
Elements on the Classified Income Statement	The Revenue Principle	Analyzing Van Houtte's Transactions	
Total Asset Turnover Ratio	The Matching Principle		

HOW DO BUSINESS ACTIVITIES AFFECT THE INCOME STATEMENT?

THE OPERATING CYCLE

■ **LEARNING OBJECTIVE 1**

Describe a typical business operating cycle and explain the necessity for the periodicity assumption.

The **OPERATING CYCLE** is the time it takes for a company to pay cash to suppliers, sell those goods and services to customers, and collect cash from customers.

The long-term objective for any business is *to turn cash into more cash*. For companies to stay in business, this excess cash must be generated from operations (that is, from the activities for which the business was established), not from borrowing money or selling long-term assets.

Companies acquire inventory and the services of employees, and then sell inventory or services to customers. The length of time between the payment of cash to suppliers of inventory and to employees, and the collection of cash from customers (known as the operating cycle), depends on the nature of the business.

The operating cycle for Van Houtte is relatively short. It spends cash to purchase green coffee beans; roasts and packages them according to its own blends and recipes; distributes the coffee through distribution channels that reach consumers at home, at work, and at play; and then collects cash from customers. In some companies, inventory is paid for well before it is sold. Toys "R" Us, for example, builds its inventory for months preceding the year-end holiday season. It borrows funds from banks to pay for the inventory and repays the loans with interest when cash is received from customers. In other companies, cash is received from customers well after a sale takes place. For example, car dealerships often sell cars over time, with monthly payments from customers due over several years. Companies attempt to shorten the operating cycle by creating incentives to encourage customers to buy sooner or pay faster in order to improve the company's cash flows.

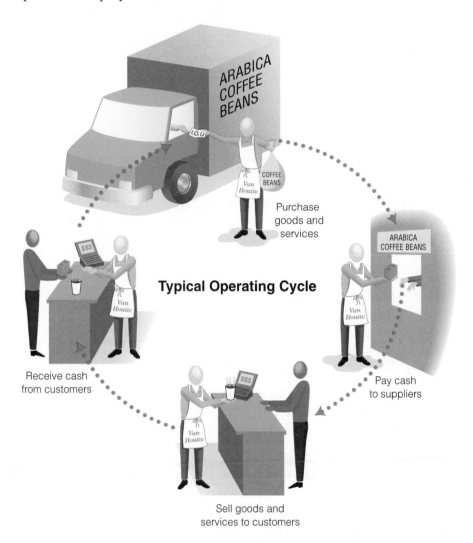

Typical Operating Cycle

Purchase goods and services

Pay cash to suppliers

Sell goods and services to customers

Receive cash from customers

FINANCIAL **ANALYSIS**

SHORT-TERM DEBT FINANCING AND THE OPERATING CYCLE

From the timing of the cash outflows and inflows shown in the illustration above, we can see that many businesses must pay suppliers and employees before they receive cash from customers, causing them to seek short-term financing. Then when the companies receive cash from customers, they pay off the liability. In addition, if a company plans to grow—say, to sell twice as many goods as in the prior period—it may not have collected enough cash from the prior period's customers to purchase the quantity of inventory needed in the next period. Sources of financing include suppliers and financial institutions (banks and commercial credit companies).

The **PERIODICITY ASSUMPTION** indicates that the long life of a company can be reported in shorter periods.

■ **LEARNING OBJECTIVE 2**

Explain how business activities affect the elements of the classified income statement.

Managers know that reducing the time needed to turn cash into more cash (that is, shortening the operating cycle) means higher profits and faster growth. With the excess cash, managers may purchase additional inventory or other assets for growth, repay debt, or distribute it to owners.

Until a company ceases activities, the operating cycle is repeated continuously. However, decision makers require periodic information about the financial condition and performance of a business. To measure income for a specific period of time, accountants follow the **periodicity assumption**, which assumes that the long life of a company can be reported in shorter time periods, such as months, quarters, and years.[1] The measurement of net income for a short period, such as one year of the company's life, requires accountants to make certain assumptions. The resulting amount is not an exact true income, but the accountant's best estimate of the true income. Two types of issues arise in reporting periodic income to users:

1. Recognition issues: *When* should the effects of operating activities be recognized (recorded)?

2. Measurement issues: *What amounts* should be recognized?

Before we examine the rules accountants follow in resolving these issues, let us review the elements of financial statements that are affected by operating activities.

ELEMENTS ON THE CLASSIFIED INCOME STATEMENT

Exhibit 3.1 shows a recent income statement for Van Houtte simplified for the purposes of this chapter.[2]

The income statement (also known as statement of earnings or statement of operations)[3] includes up to four major sections:

1. Results of continuing operations

2. Results of discontinued operations

3. Extraordinary items
   Net income (the sum of 1, 2, and 3)

4. Earnings per share

All companies report information for sections 1 and 4, while some companies report information in sections 2 and 3 depending upon their particular circumstances. The bottom line, *Net income,* is the sum of sections 1, 2, and 3. First, we will focus on the most common and most relevant section, *Continuing operations.*

Continuing Operations   This section of the classified income statement presents the results of continuing operations. It can be presented in one of two common formats:

1. The single-step format, which lists all revenue items followed by all expense items and then shows the difference between revenues and expenses,[4] or

---

[1]In addition to the audited annual statements, most businesses prepare quarterly financial statements (also known as *interim reports* covering a three-month period) for external users. The securities commissions require public companies to do so.

[2]For presentation purposes, dollar amounts have been rounded to the nearest one hundred thousand dollars, and several elements in the original statements have been simplified. However, for illustrative purposes one item in the actual statement, Cost of goods sold and net operating expenses, has been separated into three different items: Cost of goods sold, Selling expenses, and General and administrative expenses. Industry information was used in estimating the amounts of these three items. Van Houtte presents income statement information for two consecutive years, but many companies present such details for three years.

[3]A survey of 200 companies showed that 61 companies used the title *Income Statement*, 83 used the title *Statement of Earnings,* 48 used the title *Statement of Operations*, and 8 used other titles in their 2003 annual reports. C. Byrd, I. Chen, and J. Smith, *Financial Reporting in Canada, 2004*. Toronto: CICA 2004, p. 92.

[4]Only four of the 200 companies surveyed in *Financial Reporting in Canada, 2004* used the single-step format. C. Byrd, I. Chen, and J. Smith, *Financial Reporting in Canada, 2004*. Toronto: CICA 2004, p. 92.

EXHIBIT **3.1**

Income Statement

CONSOLIDATED STATEMENTS OF EARNINGS
Years ended April 2, 2005, April 3, 2004, and March 29, 2003
(in thousands of dollars, except for earnings per share)

	2005	2004	2003
Revenue	348,800	328,400	316,800
Cost of goods sold	177,900	167,900	168,800
Gross profit	170,900	160,500	148,000
Operating expenses			
Selling	80,800	77,800	65,000
General and administrative	24,400	23,200	21,200
Depreciation and amortization	31,000	31,000	30,000
	136,200	132,000	116,200
Operating income	34,700	28,500	31,800
Interest expense	3,900	4,900	5,400
Non-recurring charges	—	—	5,200
Earnings before income taxes	30,800	23,600	21,200
Income taxes	7,000	4,600	5,000
Earnings before other items	23,800	19,000	16,200
Investment income	100	100	100
Non-controlling interest	(2,100)	(500)	(300)
Earnings from continuing operations	21,800	18,600	16,000
Discontinued operations (net of taxes, $406)	—	—	(1,300)
Net earnings	21,800	18,600	14,700
Earnings per share	1.01	0.87	0.68
Weighted average number of shares outstanding (in thousands)	21,598	21,428	21,517

Note: This statement of earnings is an adaptation from Van Houtte's actual statement of earnings. The statement of earnings for 2003 is added for illustrative purposes.

2. The multiple-step format, with cost of goods sold deducted from sales to present gross margin (or gross profit) as a subtotal. Other operating expenses are then deducted to show operating profit (income) as a second subtotal. Classification of the various income statement items helps financial statement users in assessing the company's operating performance and in predicting the company's future profitability.

Like most companies, Van Houtte uses a multiple-step format in reporting income statement information.

Revenues **Revenues** result from selling goods or services as part of a company's normal ongoing operations. Van Houtte earns revenue when it sells coffee and equipment to customers or earns royalties from franchisees. When revenues are earned, assets, usually cash or receivables, often increase. Sometimes, a company receives cash in exchange for a promise to provide goods or services in the future. At that point, revenue is not earned, but a liability account, usually a deferred or unearned revenue, is created. When the company provides the promised goods or services to the customer, revenue is recognized and the liability is settled. We can say, then, that revenues are increases in assets or settlements of liabilities from *ongoing operations*.

Like most companies, Van Houtte generates revenues from a variety of sources:

1. *Selling coffee services to offices, hotels, hospitals, campuses.* Van Houtte indicated in its 2005 annual report that it has captured 50 percent of the coffee services market in Canada, which is the largest source of the company's sales. Using this information, we can infer that $174.4 million of the total revenue ($348.8 million) for

REVENUES are increases in assets or settlements of liabilities from ongoing operations.

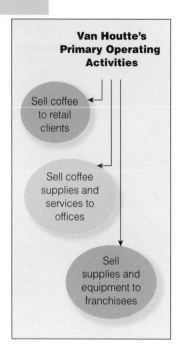

Van Houtte's Primary Operating Activities

Sell coffee to retail clients

Sell coffee supplies and services to offices

Sell supplies and equipment to franchisees

2005 came from providing coffee services in Canada. The company also estimated it has 3 percent of the U.S. market for coffee services, estimated at US$3 billion for 2005. Hence, sales in the U.S. market contributed about $90 million in revenue. Together these two sources provided roughly $264.4 million, or 75.8 percent of the total revenue for 2005.

2. *Selling coffee supplies and equipment to café–bistros.* The smallest source of revenue for Van Houtte is provided by its franchise royalties and fees. In 1997, the company reported $37 million in revenue from 104 outlets. But by 2005 the network had decreased to 74 outlets. If we assume the revenue decrease was proportional to the reduction in number of outlets, then we can estimate revenue from this source at $26.3 million. To open a Van Houtte café–bistro, a franchisee must pay a fee for the right to use the logo, supplies, and trademarks of the company in a specified location. The franchise contract also requires the franchisee to periodically pay Van Houtte franchise royalties of 5 percent of revenue. A quick calculation reveals that the gross revenue for these franchisees was approximately $526 million, about $7.1 million per outlet.

3. *Selling coffee to retailers.* The company's next largest source of sales is to retailers that sell Van Houtte's roasted coffee to consumers. Although the company provides no estimate of this source of revenue, it does note that its network of café–bistros provides only marginal revenue, which can be estimated at $26.3 million for 2005 based on information disclosed by the company in 1997. This leaves approximately $58.1 million of total revenue in 2005 arising from the sale of coffee to retailers.

EXPENSES are decreases in assets or increases in liabilities to generate revenues during the period.

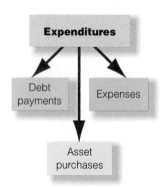

Expenditures

Debt payments

Expenses

Asset purchases

Expenses Some students confuse the terms *expenditures* and *expenses*. An expenditure is any outflow of money for any purpose, whether to buy equipment or pay off a loan. An expense is more narrowly defined. It results when a cost such as advertising is incurred or an asset such as inventory is used *to generate revenues during a period.* Therefore, not all expenditures are expenses, which are necessary to generate revenues.

Van Houtte pays employees to sell its coffee products and provide services to clients, uses electricity to operate equipment and light facilities, advertises its coffee services, and uses coffee and paper supplies. Without incurring these expenses, Van Houtte could not generate revenues. Although some of the expenses may result from expenditures of cash at the time they are incurred, some may be incurred after cash was paid in the past, and other expenses may be incurred before cash is paid in the future. When an expense occurs, *either* assets (such as supplies inventory and cash) decrease, *or* liabilities (such as salaries or utilities payable) increase. Expenses can therefore be defined as decreases in assets or increases in liabilities to generate revenues during the period.

The following are Van Houtte's primary expenses:

1. *Cost of goods sold* is the cost of products sold to customers. This includes the cost of green beans and other supplies that are part of the asset Inventories and are used to produce and package the roasted and ground coffee beans. This expense also includes the cost of coffee beans, supplies, and equipment, also part of Inventories, that are sold to franchisees. In companies with a manufacturing or merchandising focus, the cost of goods sold (also called cost of sales) is usually the most significant expense. The cost of goods sold for Van Houtte is estimated at $177.9 million and represents about 51 percent of the revenues for 2005. We present additional discussion of accounting for the cost of goods sold in Chapter 8. The difference between sales revenues and cost of goods sold is known as **gross profit** or **gross margin**.

GROSS PROFIT (or gross margin) is net sales less cost of goods sold.

2. *Operating expenses* are the usual expenses incurred in operating a business during a specific accounting period. The expenses reported will depend on the nature of the company's operations. *Selling expenses* usually include salaries and benefits to employees as well as advertising and promotion expenses. *General and administrative expenses* would include salaries for employees who support the sales effort such as legal counsel, accountants, and computer technicians as well as rent, utilities,

and insurance expenses, among others. The *depreciation and amortization expense* refers to the cost of using long-term assets such as buildings and equipment that are used in roasting, grinding, packaging, and distributing the company's coffee products during the period.[5] Another subtotal, **Operating income**, also called Income from Operations, is computed by subtracting operating expenses from gross profit.

Non-operating Items Not all activities affecting an income statement are central to continuing operations. Using excess cash to purchase shares in other companies is an investing activity for Van Houtte. Any interest or dividends earned on the investment is called *investment income*. Likewise, borrowing money is a financing activity. The cost of using that money is called *interest expense*. Except for financial institutions, incurring interest expense or earning investment income are not the central operations of most businesses, including Van Houtte. We say that these are *peripheral* (normal but not central) *transactions*.

Similarly, companies sell property, plant, and equipment occasionally and replace them with new assets to modernize their facilities. Selling land for more than the original purchase price results in a *gain,* not in revenue, because the sale of land is not a central operating focus for the business. The **gain** results in an increase in assets or decrease in liabilities from a peripheral transaction. In contrast, **losses** are decreases in assets or increases in liabilities from peripheral transactions. The non-recurring charges (or losses) in Van Houtte's income statement for 2003 resulted primarily from a reduction in the benefits expected from the use of coffee-service equipment and vending machines following an in-depth review in 2002 of the future use of these assets in light of changes in market conditions and evolution of the technology. Further discussion of the impairment of long-term assets is covered in Chapter 9.

Van Houtte's income statement lists another non-operating item: *Non-controlling interest*. Van Houtte has invested in many businesses by purchasing all, or in some cases most, of the shares issued by these companies. Purchase of all or a majority of other companies' shares allows Van Houtte to control their operating, investing, and financing decisions. When Van Houtte owns a majority of the shares of another company, it becomes a *controlling* shareholder. The other shareholders are then known as *non-controlling* shareholders, and are entitled to a proportionate share of the earnings of the company in which they invested. Hence, non-controlling interest refers to the portion of the consolidated income that is attributable to non-controlling shareholders.[6]

The non-operating items that are subject to income taxes are added or subtracted from operating income to obtain **income before income taxes**, also called *Pretax Earnings*. The deduction of applicable income taxes and the addition or subtraction of other non-operating items not subject to income tax leads to *income from continuing operations* of the business.

Income Tax Expense Income Tax Expense is the last expense listed on the income statement. All profit-making corporations are required to compute income taxes owed to federal, provincial, and foreign governments. Income tax expense is calculated as a percentage of the difference between revenues and expenses determined by applying federal and provincial tax rates. Van Houtte's effective tax rate in 2005 was 22.7 percent (Income Tax Expense $7,000 ÷ Income Before Income Taxes $30,800). This indicates that for every dollar of profit that Van Houtte made in 2005, the company paid almost $0.23 to taxation authorities.

Discontinued Operations **Discontinued operations** can result from either abandoning or selling a major business segment. Information related to discontinued operations is disclosed separately on the income statement with details of the disposal presented in a

---

Van Houtte's Primary Expenses

OPERATING INCOME (income from operations) equals net sales less cost of goods sold and other operating expenses.

GAINS are increases in assets or decreases in liabilities from peripheral transactions.

LOSSES are decreases in assets or increases in liabilities from peripheral transactions.

INCOME BEFORE INCOME TAXES (pretax earnings) equals revenues minus all expenses except income tax expense.

DISCONTINUED OPERATIONS result from the disposal of a major segment of the business and are reported net of income tax effects.

---

[5]This expense is discussed in detail in Chapters 4 and 9.

[6]Intercorporate investments is a complex topic that is covered in advanced accounting courses.

note to the financial statements. Separate reporting informs users that the results of discontinued operations are less useful as predictors of the company's future profitability.

In 2003, Van Houtte sold one of its investments in shares of other companies. The sale resulted in a net loss of $1,300,000, net of income tax effects, as reported in Exhibit 3.1. The company included details of the discontinued operations in a note to its financial statements.

EXTRAORDINARY ITEMS are gains or losses that are considered unusual in nature, infrequent in occurrence, and not dependent primarily on decisions by management or owners. They are reported net of tax on the income statement.

Extraordinary Items   **Extraordinary items** are gains or losses incurred by the company that are considered unusual in nature, infrequent in occurrence, and not dependent primarily on decisions by management or owners. Examples include losses suffered from natural disasters such as floods and hurricanes in geographic areas where such disasters rarely occur. These items must be reported separately on the income statement, net of income tax effects. Separate reporting informs decision makers that the items are not likely to recur; hence, they are less relevant to predicting the company's future performance. Note disclosure is needed to explain the nature of the extraordinary item.

The reporting of extraordinary items is rare. In fact, a recent survey of 200 companies indicated that none of these companies reported extraordinary events in their 2001, 2002, or 2003 annual reports.[7]

Earnings Per Share   Corporations are required to disclose earnings per share on the income statement or in the notes to the financial statements. This ratio is widely used in evaluating the operating performance and profitability of a company. A steady increase in earnings per share is a signal of good management. To compute earnings per share, we divide net income by the weighted average number of shares outstanding during the period. The calculation of the denominator is complex and is presented in advanced accounting courses.

Van Houtte has reported growth in earnings per share from 2003 to 2005. Although this appears to be good news, investors would want to check the historical trend of earnings per share for at minimum a period of five years. More importantly, investors need to compare Van Houtte's performance to its competitors during the same time period. Finally, it should be noted that overreliance on this ratio for investment decisions can lead to inadvisable decisions.

KEY **RATIO ANALYSIS:**

■ **LEARNING OBJECTIVE 3**

Compute and interpret the total asset turnover ratio.

THE TOTAL ASSET TURNOVER RATIO

ANALYTICAL QUESTION → How effective is management in generating sales from assets (resources)?

RATIO AND COMPARISONS → The total asset turnover ratio is useful in answering this question. It is computed as follows:

$$\text{Total Asset Turnover Ratio} = \frac{\text{Sales (or Operating) Revenues}}{\text{Average Total Assets}}$$

The 2005 ratio for Van Houtte is:

$$\frac{\$348,800}{(\$370,100 + \$370,700)/2} = 0.94$$

[7]C. Byrd, I. Chen, and J. Smith. *Financial Reporting in Canada*, 29th edition. Toronto: The Canadian Institute of Chartered Accountants, 2004, p. 419. An example of an extraordinary item was reported by Le Groupe Vidéotron Ltée in the company's 1998 annual report. A note to the financial statements stated: "The Company incurred expenses related to the ice storm that hit the province of Québec in January 1998, for a total of $13,695,000, net of an estimated amount set up for the recovery from the insurers in this matter."

Comparisons over Time			Comparisons with Competitors*	
Van Houtte Inc.			Starbucks	Green Mountain Coffee Roasters
2003	2004	2005	2004	2004
0.85	0.90	0.94	1.45	2.00

INTERPRETATIONS

In General → The total asset turnover ratio measures the sales generated per dollar of assets. A high asset turnover signifies efficient management of assets and a low asset turnover ratio signifies an inefficient one. A company's products and business strategy contribute significantly to its resulting ratio. However, when competitors are similar, management's ability to control the firm's assets is also vital in determining success. Financial performance improves as the ratio increases.

Creditors and security analysts use this ratio to assess a company's effectiveness at controlling current and non-current assets. In a well-run business, creditors expect fluctuations in the ratio due to seasonal upswings and downturns. For example, as inventory is built up preceding a high sales season, companies need to borrow funds. The asset turnover ratio will decline from the increase in assets. Then the high season sales provide the cash needed to repay the loans. The asset turnover ratio accordingly increases from the increase in sales.

Focus Company Analysis → Van Houtte's total asset turnover ratio increased gradually from 2003 to 2005, suggesting an increase in management effectiveness in using assets to generate sales. Van Houtte's 2005 total asset turnover ratio is lower than those of the competitors listed above. The main reason for the significant differences in these ratios is attributed to the sizable amount of goodwill on Van Houtte's balance sheet compared to the amounts reported for goodwill on the balance sheets of Starbucks and Green Mountain. Goodwill results from Van Houtte's acquisition of other businesses, and is not an asset that is used like equipment and inventories to generate sales. The exclusion of goodwill from Van Houtte's total assets would increase the total asset turnover ratio to 1.53 in 2005 instead of 0.94.

A Few Cautions → The total asset turnover ratio may decrease due to seasonal fluctuation. However, a declining ratio may also be caused by changes in corporate policies, such as more lax collection efforts in accounts receivable, that cause assets to rise. A detailed analysis of the changes in the key components of assets provides additional information on the nature of the change in the asset turnover ratio and thus management's decisions. Remember that any one ratio is not sufficient as a basis for investment decisions.

*The ratios for Van Houtte's competitors are shown for 2004 instead of 2005 because the three companies have different fiscal year-ends.

> **SELECTED FOCUS COMPANY TOTAL ASSET TURNOVER RATIOS**
>
> | Intrawest Corporation | 0.65 |
> |---|---|
> | WestJet Airlines | 0.63 |
> | Gildan Activewear | 1.16 |

HOW ARE OPERATING ACTIVITIES RECOGNIZED AND MEASURED?

You probably determine your personal financial position by the cash balance in your bank account. Your financial performance is measured as the difference between your cash balance at the beginning of the period and the balance at the end of the period (that is, whether you end up with more or less cash). If you have a higher cash balance, cash receipts exceeded cash disbursements for the period. Measuring income in this manner is called the **cash basis of accounting**, in which revenues are recorded when cash is received, and expenses are recorded when cash is paid, regardless of when the revenues are earned or the expenses incurred. Many small retailers, medical offices, and other small businesses use the cash basis of accounting. This basis is often quite adequate for these organizations that usually do not have to report to external users.

ACCRUAL ACCOUNTING

Net income measured on a cash basis can be misleading. For example, a company using the cash basis can report higher net income in one period simply because (1) a customer paid cash in advance of receiving a good or service or (2) the company

> **CASH BASIS Income Measurement**
>
> Revenues (= cash receipts)
> − Expenses (= cash payments)
> Net Income

CASH BASIS ACCOUNTING records revenues when cash is received and expenses when cash is paid.

■ **LEARNING OBJECTIVE 4**

Explain the accrual basis of accounting and apply the revenue and matching principles to measure income.

ACCRUAL BASIS
Income Measurement

Revenues (= when earned)
– Expenses (= when incurred)

Net Income

ACCRUAL BASIS ACCOUNTING records revenues when earned and expenses when incurred, regardless of the timing of cash receipts or payments.

postponed the payment of utility bills until the next period. In the first case, the company has not performed the service or exchanged a good to earn a revenue. In the second case, the company has already used gas, electricity, and phone service to generate revenues (creating an expense), but the expense is not recorded because payment occurs in the next period.

Since financial statements created under the cash basis of accounting normally postpone or accelerate recognition of revenues and expenses long before or after goods and services are produced and delivered, they also do not necessarily reflect all assets and liabilities of a company on a particular date. For these reasons, cash basis financial statements are not very useful to external decision makers. Therefore, generally accepted accounting principles require the **accrual basis of accounting** for financial reporting purposes. This means that assets, liabilities, revenues, and expenses should be recognized when the transaction that causes them occurs, not necessarily when cash is received or paid. *Revenues are recognized when they are earned and expenses when they are incurred.*

The two basic accounting principles that determine when revenues and expenses are to be recorded under the accrual basis of accounting are the *revenue principle* and the *matching principle.*

THE REVENUE PRINCIPLE

The **REVENUE PRINCIPLE** states that revenues are recognized when the earnings process is complete or nearly complete, an exchange has taken place, and collection is reasonably assured.

Under the **revenue principle**, three criteria must normally be met for revenue to be recognized (that is, recorded). If *any* of the following conditions is *not* met, revenue normally is *not* recognized and should not be recorded.

1. *The earnings process is complete or nearly complete.* This means that the company has performed or substantially performed the acts promised to the customer by providing goods or services.

2. *An exchange transaction takes place.* In exchange for the company's performance, the customer provides cash or a promise to pay cash (a receivable) that is measureable.

3. *Collection is reasonably assured.* Companies establish credit policies to reduce the risk of extending credit to customers who fail to pay. Since there is always some risk that payment will not be received in the future, normal credit risk is taken into consideration in determining whether collection from customers is reasonably assured.

Van Houtte earns half of its revenue from contracts with companies that provide brewed coffee by the cup to their employees. A sale is completed when the equipment, coffee, tea, and supplies are delivered to customers. Van Houtte can then recognize revenue if there is reasonable assurance that payment will be received in the future.

The company also sells franchises, although since 1997 it has actively restructured and reorganized its café–bistro network to reduce the number of outlets. When a new franchisee is approved, the franchisee pays Van Houtte a fee *before* obtaining any startup support services or supplies. The company should not record the amount received as revenue because it has not yet performed on any promises. Instead, the company records the amount received as a liability, *unearned or deferred revenue*. This deferred or unearned revenue account represents the amount of goods and services owed to the franchisees.

Revenue is recorded according to the revenue principle when the three conditions are met, *regardless of when cash is received.* Cash may be received either before or after revenue recognition, each resulting in two transactions—one on the date of cash receipt and one on the date the revenue is earned.

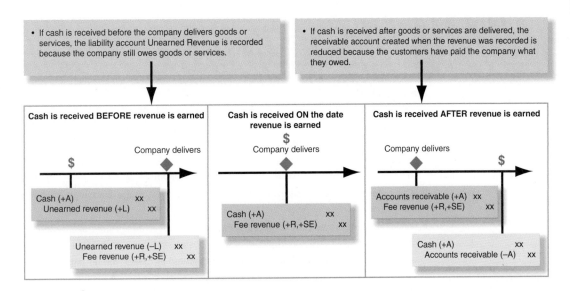

Companies usually disclose their revenue recognition practices in a note to the financial statements. The following excerpt from Van Houtte's note describes how it recognizes its revenue:

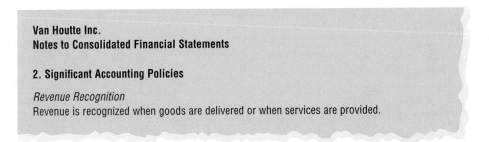

Van Houtte Inc.
Notes to Consolidated Financial Statements

2. Significant Accounting Policies

Revenue Recognition
Revenue is recognized when goods are delivered or when services are provided.

Exhibit 3.2 shows the revenue recognition practices used by other companies that offer different types of products and services. Note that the completion of the earnings process depends on the nature of the products sold and services provided by the company.

EXHIBIT **3.2**

Timing of Revenue Recognition

Company Name	Product or Service	Typical Timing of Revenue Recognition
WestJet Airlines	Air transportation	Passenger revenue is recognized when air transportation is provided. Tickets sold but not yet used are included in the balance sheet as advance ticket sales under current liabilities.
CanWest Global Communications Corp.	Radio and television broadcasting, publication of magazines and newspapers	Revenue derived from broadcasting activities related to the sale of airtime is recognized at the time commercials are broadcast. Circulation and advertising revenue from publishing activities is recognized when the newspaper is delivered. Subscription revenue is recognized on a straight-line basis over the term of the subscription.
Intrawest Corporation	Development and operation of village-centred resorts	Revenue from the sale of properties is recorded generally when title to the completed unit is conveyed to the purchaser, the purchaser becomes entitled to occupancy, and has made a payment that is appropriate in the circumstances. Management service revenue is recognized as the service is provided. Commission revenue from real estate brokerage operations is recognized at the time an offer of sale is closed by the purchaser or all other contractual obligations have been satisfied.
Teckcominco	Mining (production of metallurgical coal, zinc, copper, and gold)	Sales are recognized and revenues are recorded at market prices upon the delivery of the product to the customer when title transfer and the rights and obligations of ownership pass to the customer. A number of the company's products are sold under pricing arrangements where final prices are determined by quoted market prices in a period subsequent to the date of sale. Subsequent variations in the price are recognized as revenue adjustments as they occur until the price is finalized.

SELF-STUDY **QUIZ 3-1**

This self-study quiz allows you to practise applying the revenue principle under accrual accounting. We recommend that you refer back to the three *revenue recognition criteria* presented earlier as you answer each question. It is important to complete this quiz now to make sure you can apply this principle.

The following transactions are samples of typical monthly operating activities of Van Houtte.

1. Indicate the account titles that are affected and the type of account for each (A for asset, L for liability, and R for revenue).

2. Identify the amount of revenue that is recognized in April, the revenue that has been earned in March, and the revenue that will be earned in future periods (unearned revenue).

3. Compute the revenue recognized in April and compare it to the amount of cash received in April.

4. Which amount—revenue recognized in April or cash received in April—is a better measure of Van Houtte's operating performance? Explain.

Refer to the Van Houtte chart of accounts presented in Exhibit 3.4 on page 122 for account titles. *Note:* All dollar amounts are in thousands.

After you complete the quiz, check your answers with the solutions on page 132.

Activity	Accounts Affected and Type of Account	Cash Received in April	Amount of Revenue Earned in		Unearned Revenue
			March	April	
(a) In April, Van Houtte sold coffee supplies to office services customers for $35,200 cash.					
(b) In April, Van Houtte sold roasted coffee beans to retail outlets for $30,200, of which $20,200 was in cash and the rest was on account.					
(c) In April, franchisees paid Van Houtte $3,450 in cash for royalties, of which $750 related to March sales.					
(d) In April, Van Houtte signed contracts with new clients and received $500 in cash. The company provided $400 in services to these clients during April; the remainder of the services will be provided over the next three months.					
(e) In April, retail outlets paid $1,200 on account to Van Houtte. This amount covers sales of roasted coffee beans in March.					
Totals					

A QUESTION OF **ETHICS**

MANAGEMENT'S INCENTIVES TO VIOLATE THE REVENUE PRINCIPLE

The decisions of investors in the stock market are based on expectations of future earnings. When quarterly and annual earnings information is announced by the companies, investors evaluate how well the company met expectations and adjust their investing decisions accordingly. Companies that fail to meet expectations often experience a decline in the stock price. Thus, managers are motivated to produce earnings results that meet or exceed expectations. Sometimes this motivation leads managers to make unethical accounting and reporting decisions, as described in the April 1, 2002, issue of *Canadian Business.* Often the fraud involves falsifying revenues. The article includes two revenue-related frauds involving Livent Inc. and YBM Magnex International Inc.

The Company	What the Company's Management Did
Livent Inc.	Management has been accused by the Securities and Exchange Commission and the Ontario Securities Commission of using false invoices and kickbacks, filing false information, and inflating its earnings.
YBM Magnex International Inc.	The company was investigated by the Ontario Securities Commission for overstating sales by creating fictitious customer lists. At the same time, laundered money poured into the company from Russian gangsters. The company went bankrupt in 1998.

The OSC's investigation of YBM resulted in imposing penalties, totalling $1.2 million, on two brokerage firms and five company officials. The company officials were ordered to resign from their positions and were banned from holding such positions at other companies for periods of three to five years.

At the time of writing this book, none of the senior management or directors of Livent had been convicted of a criminal offence as a result of their actions.

SOURCE: John Gray, "Home-grown accounting scandals," *Canadian Business*, April 1, 2002, and Peter Fitzpatrick, "OSC hands down YBM penalties," *National Post*, July 3, 2003, FP1,8.

THE MATCHING PRINCIPLE

The **matching principle** requires that when the period's revenues are properly recognized according to the revenue principle, all of the resources consumed in earning those revenues should be recorded in that same period, *regardless of when cash is paid.* Thus, expenses are "matched" to revenues and recorded in the same period as the related revenues. For example, when Van Houtte provides coffee services to customers, it earns revenue. The costs of generating the revenue include expenses incurred such as:

The **MATCHING PRINCIPLE** requires that expenses be recorded when incurred in earning revenue.

• Salaries to employees who *worked during the period* (Salaries expense)

• Utilities for the electricity *used during the period* (Utilities expense)

• Ground coffee beans *used during the period* (Cost of goods sold)

• Facilities *rented during the period* (Rent expense)

• *Use* of roasting and packaging equipment *during the period* (Amortization expense)

Some of these expenses are matched directly to sales revenue, such as the cost of goods sold and sales commissions. Other expenses, such as utilities, rent of facilities, insurance, and interest, may not be identifiable with specific sources of revenue but need to be incurred in order to generate revenue during the period.

As with revenues and cash receipts, expenses are recorded as incurred, **regardless of when cash is paid.** Cash may be paid before or after expense recognition, resulting in two transactions: one on the date of the cash payment and one on the date the expense is incurred in generating revenue:

- For example, green coffee beans and packaging supplies are acquired prior to their use. These items are recorded as inventory, an asset, when they are purchased, but are not expensed until they are used. Similarly, companies usually pay for rent in advance of using rental property and record the cash outlay in the asset account, Prepaid Expenses, representing future benefits to the company. This asset is allocated over time to Rent Expense as the property is used. In addition, part of the cost of long-term assets, such as equipment used in operations, needs to be matched with the revenues generated in the period. The portion of the assets that was used up is recognized as Amortization Expense.

- In some cases, resources are used to generate revenues prior to a cash outlay. Van Houtte's payroll expense represents the amount earned by managers and employees who prepare and serve the coffee and tea. It is an expense for that period. While employees are usually paid after they provide their services, Wages Expense and Wages Payable should be recorded when the service is provided by the employees.

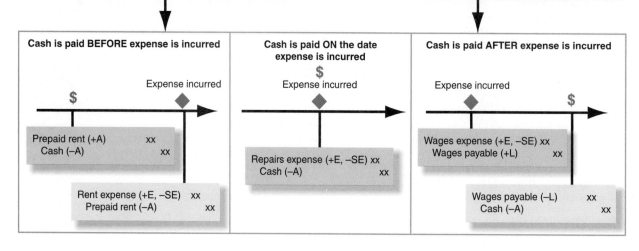

SELF-STUDY **QUIZ 3-2**

This self-study quiz allows you to practise applying the *matching principle* under accrual accounting. It is important to complete this quiz now to make sure you can apply this principle.

The following transactions are samples of typical monthly operating activities of Van Houtte.

1. Indicate the account titles that are affected and the type of account for each (A for asset, L for liability, and E for expense).

2. If an expense is to be recognized in *April,* indicate the amount. If an expense is not to be recognized in April, indicate why.

3. Compute the amount of expenses recognized in April and compare this amount to the cash paid in April.

Refer to the Van Houtte chart of accounts presented in Exhibit 3.4 on page 122 for account titles. *Note:* All dollar amounts are in thousands.

After you complete the quiz, check your answers with the solutions on page 133.

Activity	Accounts Affected and Type of Account	Cash Paid in April	Amount of Expense Incurred in April OR Why an Expense Is Not Recognized
(a) In April, Van Houtte paid $10,000 to suppliers on account for coffee supplies received in March. These supplies were not yet sold to customers.			
(b) In April, the cost of roasting and packaging the beans sold to retail outlets was $14,000.			
(c) On April 5, Van Houtte paid $4,500 for office rent for April, May, and June.			
(d) In April, the cost of coffee supplies sold to coffee services customers was $19,600. These coffee supplies were purchased in previous months.			
(e) In late April, Van Houtte received a utility bill for $500 payable in May for electricity used in April.			
Totals			

FINANCIAL **ANALYSIS**

THE FEEDBACK VALUE OF ACCOUNTING INFORMATION AND STOCK MARKET REACTION

A company can experience difficulty even if it does not report a net loss. Any unexpected deviation of actual performance from the operating plan, such as lower than expected quarterly earnings, needs to be explained. Stock market analysts and investors use accounting information to make investment decisions. The stock market, which is based on investors' expectations about future company performance, often reacts negatively (that is, with a reduction in the company's stock price) to lower than expected operating results.

On June 3, 2004, Van Houtte announced both the results of its fourth quarter and of its fiscal year ending April 3, 2004. On the day of the announcement, the price per share closed at $15.25, an increase of $0.27 over the closing price on the previous day. Van Houtte's year-end results showed an increase of earnings per share (EPS) by $0.19 (from $0.68 per share for 2003 to $0.87 per share for 2004). The company attributed this growth to a 17.8-percent increase in revenue generated in the U.S. market, and a growth of 3 percent in Canada.* The increase in share price suggests that the reported EPS figure is higher than investors' expectations.

This is a clear example of how the release of financial data provides relevant information to investors who revise their expectations about the company performance, causing a change in the price per share. Accounting information has a pervasive effect on the economic decisions that investors and creditors make.

*Van Houtte's Web site: http://investor.vanhoutte.com, accessed July 16, 2004.

KEY **RATIO ANALYSIS:**

RETURN ON ASSETS (ROA)

ANALYTICAL QUESTION → How well has management used the total invested capital provided by debtholders and shareholders during the period?

RATIO AND COMPARISONS → Analysts refer to the rate of return on assets (ROA) as a useful measure in addressing this issue. It is computed* as follows:

$$\text{Return on Assets} = \frac{\text{Net Income}}{\text{Average Total Assets**}}$$

■ **LEARNING OBJECTIVE 5**

Compute and interpret the return on assets ratio.

Both the total asset turnover ratio (covered earlier in this chapter) and the return on assets measure management's effectiveness in utilizing the company's resources: the first in generating revenue during the period, the second in generating income after expenses are deducted from revenues.

*In more complex return on total asset analyses, interest expense (net of tax) and non-controlling interest are added back to net income in the numerator of the ratio, since the measure assesses return on capital, independent of its source.

**Average Total Assets = (Beginning Total Assets + Ending Total Assets) ÷ 2

The 2005 ratio for Van Houtte is:

$$\frac{\$21,706}{(\$370,100 + \$370,700) \div 2} = 0.058\ (5.8\%)$$

Comparisons over Time			Comparisons with Competitors*	
Van Houtte Inc.			Starbucks	Green Mountain Coffee Roasters
2003	2004	2005	2004	2004
3.9%	5.1%	5.8%	12.7%	11.4%

*The ratios for Van Houtte's competitors are shown for 2004 instead of 2005 because the three companies have different fiscal year-ends.

INTERPRETATIONS:

In General → ROA measures how much the firm earned for each dollar of investment. It is the broadest measure of profitability and management effectiveness, independent of financing strategy. ROA allows investors to compare management's investment performance against alternative investment options. Firms with higher ROA are doing a better job of selecting new investments, all other things being equal. Company managers often compute the measure on a division-by-division basis and use it to evaluate division managers' relative performance.

Focus Company Analysis → Van Houtte appears to have done well in fiscal year 2005 (which includes nine months of 2004) compared to both 2003 and 2004. Examination of the company's income statement shown in Exhibit 3.1 indicates that sales increased in 2005 compared to 2004, but this increase in sales required an increase in selling expenses. Other expense items in 2005 did not change significantly from those of the previous year, except for interest expense, which decreased by $1,000. At the same time, the company's total assets did not change significantly during the past two years. These changes caused ROA to increase in 2005. However, Van Houtte's ROA is much lower than those of its competitors. For this reason, the company's management needs to review its operations to improve on its effectiveness in utilizing the company's resources.

A Few Cautions → Effective analysis of ROA requires an understanding of why ROA differs from prior levels and from the ROA of the company's competitors. Analysis of the differences in ROA over time and across companies can be facilitated by a decomposition of this ratio into two other ratios, as shown later in Chapter 13.

THE EXPANDED TRANSACTION ANALYSIS MODEL

■ LEARNING OBJECTIVE 6

Apply transaction analysis to examine and record the effects of operating activities on the financial statements.

Now that we have seen the variety of business activities affecting the income statement and how they are measured, we need to determine how these business activities are recorded in the accounting system and reflected in the financial statements. Chapter 2 covered investing and financing activities affecting assets, liabilities, and share capital. We now expand the transaction analysis model presented in that chapter to include operating activities.

TRANSACTION ANALYSIS RULES

The complete transaction model presented in Exhibit 3.3 includes all five elements: Assets, Liabilities, Shareholders' Equity, Revenues, and Expenses. Recall that the Retained Earnings account is the accumulation of all past revenues and expenses minus any income distributed as dividends[8] to shareholders (that is, earnings not retained in the business). When net income is positive, Retained Earnings increases; when a net loss occurs, Retained Earnings decreases. These relationships among financial statement elements are summarized in the upper part of Exhibit 3.3.

In constructing this complete model, we maintain the direction rule and the debit-credit framework described in Chapter 2:

Assets	
DR +	

Liabilities	
	CR +

Shareholders' Equity Accounts	
	CR +

Revenue and Gains	
	CR +

Expenses and Losses	
DR +	

- For accounts on the left side of the accounting equation, the increase symbol is written on the left side of the T-account. For accounts on the right side of the accounting equation, the increase symbol is written on the right side.

- Debits (dr) are written on the left side of each T-account and credits (cr) are written on the right.

The expanded transaction analysis model simply replaces net income with two additional elements, revenues and expenses. When revenues increase, both net income and retained earnings increase; hence, the increase in any revenue account is reported on

---

[8]Instead of reducing Retained Earnings directly when dividends are declared, companies may use the account Dividends Declared. It has a debit balance.

EXHIBIT **3.3**

Transactional Analysis Model

Assets = Liabilities + Shareholders' Equity

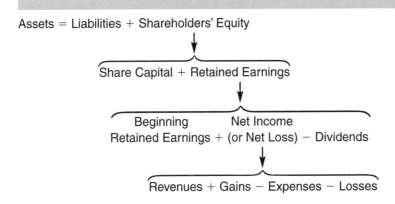

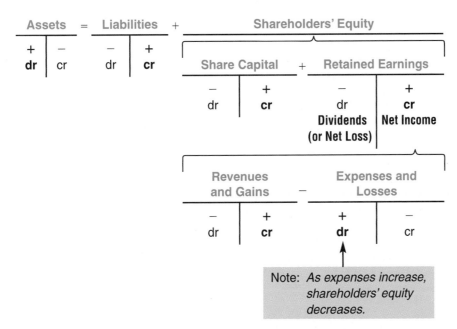

Note: *As expenses increase, shareholders' equity decreases.*

the credit side of the account. Conversely, when expenses increase, both net income and retained earnings decrease. Since the decrease in retained earnings is reported on the debit side of the account, the increase in any expense account is, equivalently, reported on the debit side of the account. Consequently, revenues normally have credit balances and expenses normally have debit balances.

As presented in Chapter 2,

1. Every transaction affects at least two accounts (duality of effects); it is critical to identify correctly the accounts affected and the direction of the effect (increase or decrease).

2. The accounting equation must remain in balance after each transaction.

3. The total dollar value of the debits in the transaction should equal the total dollar value of the credits.

Since revenues are defined as inflows of net assets, then, by definition, recording a revenue results in either increasing an asset or decreasing a liability. In like manner, when recording an expense, an asset is decreased or a liability is increased. Revenues and expenses normally are not recorded in the same journal entry.

You should refer to the transaction analysis model until you can construct it on your own without assistance. Study the following illustration carefully to make sure that you understand the impact of operating activities on both the balance sheet and the income statement.

ANALYZING VAN HOUTTE'S TRANSACTIONS

We begin with Van Houtte's April 2, 2005, balance sheet presented at the end of Chapter 2, which included the effects of the transactions illustrated in that chapter. We use the account titles listed in that balance sheet and those shown on the income statement in Exhibit 3.1 as we analyze a summary of the operating activities. A list of revenue and expense accounts is also provided in Exhibit 3.4.

EXHIBIT **3.4**

Van Houtte's Partial Chart of Accounts

Chart of Accounts (to be used in our Van Houtte example)	To account for
Revenues and Gains (R)	
Sales Revenue—Office Services	— Sales of coffee and other products to office services customers
Sales Revenue—Retail Outlets	— Sales of coffee and other products to retail outlet customers
Franchise-Related Revenue	— Amounts earned from franchises through franchise agreements
Investment Income	— Amounts earned on investments (e.g., dividends and interest)
Expenses and Losses (E)	
Cost of Goods Sold	— Cost of green beans and other products sold to customers
Salaries Expense	— Amount earned by the employees for work performed to generate revenue
Advertising Expense	— Amount incurred for advertising and promotions to generate revenue
Rent Expense	— Amount incurred for renting leased facilities during the period
General and Administrative Expense	— Amount of insurance and utilities used during the period
Amortization Expense	— Estimated cost of buildings and equipment used during the period
Interest Expense	— Cost of using borrowed funds during the period
Income Tax Expense	— Amount of tax related to the income generated during the period

Now let us apply the complete transaction analysis model and rules to our continuing Van Houtte's illustration. All amounts are in thousands of dollars.

(*a*) **Van Houtte sold coffee products to office services clients for $35,200 in cash. The cost of these sales was $19,600. [*Note:* This requires two entries, one for the revenue earned and one for the expense incurred in generating the revenue.]**

Cash (+A)	35,200	
Sales revenue—office services (+R → +SE)		35,200
Cost of goods sold (+E → − SE)	19,600	
Inventories (−A)		19,600

Assets		=	Liabilities	+	Shareholders' Equity	
Cash	+35,200				Sales revenue—office	
Inventories	−19,600				services	+35,200
					Cost of goods sold	−19,600

Notice that when the revenue is increased, we also indicate the effect on total shareholders' equity with the following notation: +R → +SE. Similar notation will be used for expenses, which decrease shareholders' equity.

These effects are posted to the appropriate T-accounts in Exhibit 3.5 on page 125 (see the shaded amounts).

(b) Van Houtte sold roasted coffee beans to retail outlets for $30,200; $20,200 was received in cash and the rest was due from the outlets. The cost of the beans sold was $14,000.

Cash (+A)		20,200	
Accounts receivable (+A)		10,000	
Sales revenue—retail outlets (+R → +SE)			30,200
Cost of goods sold (+E → −SE)		14,000	
Inventories (−A)			14,000

Assets		=	Liabilities	+	Shareholders' Equity	
Cash	+20,200				Sales revenue—	
Accounts					retail outlets	+30,200
receivable	+10,000				Cost of goods sold	−14,000
Inventories	−14,000					

(c) Van Houtte received $3,450 in royalties from franchisees; $750 of the amount was due from franchisees' sales in March and the rest from April sales.

Cash (+A)		3,450	
Accounts receivable (−A)			750
Franchise-related revenue (+R → +SE)			2,700

Assets		=	Liabilities	+	Shareholders' Equity	
Cash	+3,450				Franchise—related	
Accounts					revenue	+2,700
receivable	−750					

(d) Van Houtte signed contracts with new office services clients and received $500 cash. The company earned $400 immediately by performing services for these clients; the rest will be earned over the next several months.

Cash (+A)		500	
Sales revenue—office services (+R → +SE)			400
Unearned revenue (+L)			100

Assets		=	Liabilities		+	Shareholders' Equity	
Cash	+500		Unearned			Sales revenue—	
			revenues	+100		office services	+400

(e) Van Houtte paid $7,400 for prepaid expenses: $1,600 for insurance for the next four months, $4,500 for rent in shopping centres for the next three months, and $1,300 for advertising in May.

| Prepaid expenses (+A) | | 7,400 | |
| Cash (−A) | | | 7,400 |

Assets		=	Liabilities	+	Shareholders' Equity
Cash	−7,400				
Prepaid expenses	+7,400				

(f) Van Houtte paid $7,310 for utilities, repairs, and fuel for delivery vehicles, all considered general and administrative expenses.

| General and administrative expenses (+E → −SE) | | 7,310 | |
| Cash (−A) | | | 7,310 |

Assets		=	Liabilities	+	Shareholders' Equity	
Cash	−7,310				General and administrative	
					expenses	−7,310

(g) Van Houtte ordered and received $29,000 in supplies inventories; $9,000 was paid in cash and the rest was on account with suppliers.

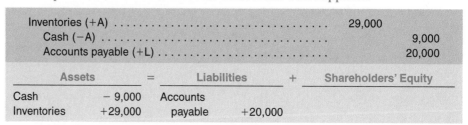

	Assets	=	Liabilities	+	Shareholders' Equity
Cash	− 9,000	Accounts			
Inventories	+29,000	payable	+20,000		

(h) Van Houtte paid $13,500 in cash to employees for work in April: $9,500 related to sales personnel, and $4,000 for employees in the corporate headquarters, considered general and administrative expenses.

Salaries expense—sales personnel (+E → −SE) 9,500
General and administrative expense (+E → −SE) 4,000
   Cash (−A) 13,500

	Assets	=	Liabilities	+	Shareholders' Equity

Cash	−13,500				Salaries expense—
					    sales personnel −9,500
					General and administrative
					    expenses −4,000

SELF-STUDY **QUIZ 3-3**

For transactions (i) through (k), fill in the missing information. Be sure to post journal entries to the T-accounts at the end of the illustration.

(i) Van Houtte sold $4,300 in coffee-brewing equipment to office services customers who signed notes due in 18 months. The cost of the equipment was $3,800. (*Note:* This requires two entries, one for the revenue and one for the expense incurred in generating the revenue.)

Write the journal entry; post the effects to the T-accounts →

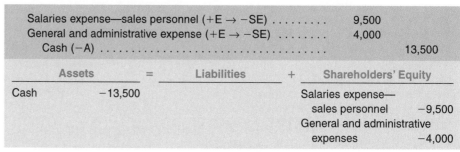

	Assets	=	Liabilities	+	Shareholders' Equity
Notes rec.	+4,300				Sales revenue— office services +4,300
Inventories	−3,800				Cost of goods sold −3,800

(j) Van Houtte paid $10,000 on accounts owed to suppliers.

Write the journal entry; post the effects to the T-accounts →

Show the effects on the accounting equation →

	Assets	=	Liabilities	+	Shareholders' Equity

(k) **Van Houtte sold land for $3,500. The cost of the land is $500.**

Cash (+A)	3,500	
Fixed assets (−A)		500
Gain on sale of land (Gain → +SE)		3,000

Assets	=	Liabilities	+	Shareholders' Equity

← Show the effects on the accounting equation

After you complete the quiz, check your answers with the solution on page 133.

Exhibit 3.5 shows the T-accounts that changed during the period because of transactions *(a)* through *(k)*. The balances of all other accounts remained the same. The amounts from Van Houtte's balance sheet at the end of Chapter 2 have been included as the beginning balances. At the beginning of every period, income statement accounts have zero beginning balances; therefore, no balances exist in the revenue and expense accounts at the beginning of the month.

You can verify that you posted the entries properly by adding the increase side and subtracting the decrease side and then comparing your answer to the ending balance given in each of the T-accounts.

Based on the April transactions that have been posted in the T-accounts, we can now begin the process of preparing financial statements reflecting the operating, investing, and financing activities recorded in April. This process requires a few additional steps that are covered in Chapter 4.

EXHIBIT **3.5**

T-Accounts

The beginning balances of balance sheet accounts are taken from Exhibit 2.7.

ASSETS

+	Cash (A)		−
Beg. bal.	2,450		
a	35,200	e	7,400
b	20,200	f	7,310
c	3,450	g	9,000
d	500	h	13,500
k	3,500	j	
End. bal.	18,090		

+	Accounts Receivable (A)		−
Beg. bal.	41,300		
b	10,000	c	750
End. bal.	50,550		

+	Inventories (A)		−
Beg. bal.	28,000	a	19,600
		b	14,000
g	29,000	i	
End. bal.	19,600		

+	Prepaid Expenses (A)		−
Beg. bal.	3,300		
e	7,400		
End. bal.	10,700		

+	Notes Receivable (A)		−
Beg. bal.	150		
i			
End. bal.	4,450		

+	Fixed Assets, net		−
Beg. bal.	118,000	k	500
End. bal.	117,500		

LIABILITIES

−	Unearned Revenue (L)		+
		d	100
		End. bal.	100

−	Accounts Payable (L)		+
		Beg. bal.	31,900
j		g	20,000
		End. bal.	41,900

(continued on next page)

EXHIBIT **3.5**

T-Accounts *(continued)*

REVENUES AND GAINS

−	Sales Revenue— Office Services (R)	+
	a	35,200
	d	400
	End. bal.	35,600

−	Franchise-Related Revenue (R)	+
	c	2,700
	End. bal.	2,700

−	Sales Revenue— Retail Outlets (R)	+
	b	30,200
	i	
	End. bal.	34,500

−	Gain on Sale of Land	+
	k	3,000
	End. bal.	3,000

EXPENSES

+	Cost of Goods Sold (E)	−
a	19,600	
b	14,000	
i		
End. bal.	37,400	

+	General and Administrative Expenses (E)	−
f	7,310	
h	4,000	
End. bal.	11,310	

+ Salaries Expense—Sales Personnel (E) −		
h	9,500	
End. bal.	9,500	

FINANCIAL **ANALYSIS**

REPORTING FINANCIAL INFORMATION BY GEOGRAPHIC AND OPERATING SEGMENTS

Many companies, especially very large ones, operate in multiple geographic segments. These companies are often called *multinationals*. The Van Houtte income statement presented at the beginning of the chapter is based on aggregated data and may not prove as useful to investors seeking to assess possible risks and returns from companies operating in foreign markets. This is also true if a company operates in more than a single business. For example, a manufacturing operation in a South American country suffering from political unrest is riskier than a manufacturing facility located in Ontario. Therefore, the financial statements show the geographic sources of revenues and operating earnings, as well as Van Houtte's dependence on foreign markets for its revenues and earnings. The annual report of Van Houtte Inc. for the year ended April 3, 2004, included the following details in note 21, Segmented Information.

Extracts from Note 21, Segmented Information

Business Segments

Revenues	
Canada	$229,126
United States	88,523
	$317,649

Operating Earnings before Depreciation and Amortization, Financial Expenses, and Non-recurring Items

Canada	$50,691
United States	13,005
	$63,696

The segmentation of a company's revenues and earnings should be consistent with management's segregation of its revenues and earnings for internal decision making purposes. For example, Van Houtte consolidated all of its roasting operations, distribution channels, coffee services, and retail networks into a single operating unit. It also created another operating unit for its U.S. distribution channels. Hence, the segmentation of its revenues and earnings into two business segments: Canada and the United States.

COMPARISON OF ACCRUAL AND CASH BASES OF ACCOUNTING

We have indicated earlier in the chapter that generally accepted accounting principles require companies to measure income based on accrual accounting instead of the cash basis of accounting. Exhibit 3.6 lists the operating activities that occurred in April and compares the effects of these operating transactions on both the accrual and cash bases of accounting. Accrual income reflects the difference between revenues earned and expenses incurred during April, whereas cash income is simply the difference between cash receipts and payments for operating activities. These two income amounts are rarely equal.

EXHIBIT **3.6**

Operating Activities, April

Transaction	Effect on Accrual Income	Effect on Cash Income
(a) Van Houtte sold coffee products to office services clients for $35,200 in cash. The cost of these sales was $19,600.	$35,200 (19,600)	$35,200
(b) Van Houtte sold roasted coffee beans to retail outlets for $30,200; $20,200 was received in cash and the rest was due from the outlets. The cost of the beans was $14,000.	30,200 (14,000)	20,200
(c) Van Houtte received $3,450 in royalties from franchisees; $750 of the amount was due from franchisees' sales in March and the rest from April sales.	2,700	3,450
(d) Van Houtte signed contracts with new office services clients and received $500 cash. The company earned $400 immediately by performing services for these clients; the rest will be earned over the next several months.	400	500
(e) Van Houtte paid $7,400 for prepaid expenses: $1,600 for insurance for the next four months, $4,500 for rent in shopping centres for the next three months, and $1,300 for advertising in May. Part of the prepaid insurance and prepaid rent were used up in April.	(1,900)	(7,400)
(f) Van Houtte paid $7,310 for utilities, repairs, and fuel for delivery vehicles, all considered general and administrative expenses.	(7,310)	(7,310)
(g) Van Houtte ordered and received $29,000 in supplies inventories; $9,000 was paid in cash and the rest was on account with suppliers.		(9,000)
(h) Van Houtte paid $13,500 in cash to employees for work in April: $9,500 related to sales personnel and $4,000 for employees in the corporate headquarters, considered general and administrative expenses.	(13,500)	(13,500)
(i) Van Houtte sold $4,300 in coffee-brewing equipment to office services customers who signed notes due in 18 months.	4,300	
(j) The cost of the equipment was $3,800.	(3,800)	
(k) Van Houtte paid $10,000 on accounts owed to suppliers.		(10,000)
	$12,690	$12,140

FOCUS ON **CASH FLOWS**

■ LEARNING OBJECTIVE 7

Understand the difference between net income and cash flow from operations.

OPERATING ACTIVITIES

In Chapter 2, we presented Van Houtte's cash flow statement for the investing and financing activities for the month. Recall that investing activities relate primarily to transactions affecting long-term assets; financing activities are those from bank borrowings, issuance of shares, and dividend payments to shareholders.

In this chapter, we focus on cash flows from operating activities, which reflects essentially the cash basis of accounting. This section of the cash flow statement reports *cash from* operating sources and *cash to* suppliers and others involved in operations.*

When a transaction affects cash, it is included on the cash flow statement. When a transaction does not affect cash, such as acquiring a building with a long-term mortgage note payable or selling goods on account to customers, there is no cash effect to include on the statement.

Effect on Cash Flow Statement

In General		**Effect on Cash Flows**
Operating activities		
Cash received from	customers	+
	investments	+
Cash paid	to suppliers	−
	to employees	−
	for interest	−
	for income taxes	−
Investing activities (from Chapter 2)		
Financing activities (from Chapter 2)		

Focus Company Analysis: The Operating Activities section of the cash flow statement for Van Houtte is based on the transactions illustrated in this chapter, while the investing and financing activities relate primarily to transactions from Chapter 2. This section of the statement reports the sources and uses of cash for operating purposes. Remember that only the transactions that affect cash are reported.

	VAN HOUTTE INC.		
	Partial Consolidated Cash Flow Statement		
	For the Month of April 2005		
	(in thousands of dollars)		
	Operating Activities		
($35,200 + 20,200 + 500)	Cash received: from customers (*a* + *b* + *d*)	$55,900	
	from franchisees (*c*)	3,450	
	Operating cash inflow		$59,350
($9,000 + 10,000)	Cash paid: to suppliers (*g* + *j*)	$19,000	
	to employees (*h*)	13,500	
	for general and		
($7,400 + $7,310)	administrative expenses (*e* + *f*)	14,710	
	Operating cash outflow		$47,210
	Net cash flow provided by operating activities		$12,140

*When operating cash inflows and outflows are presented, the company is using the *direct method* of reporting cash flows from operations. However, most companies report cash from operations using the *indirect method* that will be discussed in Chapter 5 and later chapters.

The transactions recorded in this chapter increased the cash balance by $15,640, from a beginning balance of $4,350 to an ending balance of $19,990. The difference of $3,500 between the increase in the cash balance ($15,640) and the cash flows from operating activities is the cash received for the sale of land, an investing activity that is reported in the Investing Activities section of the cash flow statement.

To remain in business in the long run, companies must generate positive cash flows from operations. Cash is needed to pay suppliers and employees. When cash from operations is negative over a period of time, the only other ways to obtain the necessary funds are to (1) sell long-term assets (which reduces future productivity), (2) borrow from creditors (at increasing rates of interest as risk of default rises), or (3) issue additional shares (where investor expectations about poor future performance drives the stock price down). There are clearly limits on how many of these activities companies can undertake.

Van Houtte has realized positive operating cash flows over the past five years as shown below. This represents a conservative approach to reporting revenues and expenses that builds analysts' confidence as to the reliability of the income information reported.

	2001	2002	2003	2004	2005
Cash flow from operations	$52,543	$45,891	$46,892	$45,564	$60,684
Net earnings	21,789	5,176	14,728	18,564	21,706

These operating cash flows are more than double the amount of net income reported by the company during each of the past five years.

SELF-STUDY **QUIZ 3-4**

CANADIAN TIRE CORPORATION LIMITED

Canadian Tire Corporation Limited is a leading hard goods retailer with more than 400 stores across Canada. The transactions below are taken from a recent annual cash flow statement. Indicate whether the transaction affected cash flow as an operating (O), investing (I), or financing (F) activity, and indicate the direction of the effect on cash (+ for increases; − for decreases):

Transactions	Type of Activity (O, I, or F)	Effect on Cash Flows (+ or −)
1. Distribution to shareholders		
2. Receipt of cash from customers		
3. Additions to property		
4. Payment of income taxes		
5. Payment of cash to suppliers		
6. Repayment of long-term debt		
7. Receipt of interest on investments		
8. Borrowings of long-term debt		
9. Issuance of shares		
10. Payment of interest on debt		
11. Payment of cash to employees		
12. Sale of property		

After you complete the schedule, check your solution with the answers on page 133.

DEMONSTRATION **CASE**

This case is a continuation of the Terrific Lawn Maintenance Corporation introduced in Chapter 2. The company was established with supplies, property, and equipment purchased ready for business. The balance sheet at April 30, 2005, based on investing and financing activities is as follows:

TERRIFIC LAWN MAINTENANCE CORPORATION
Balance Sheet
At April 30, 2005

Assets		Liabilities	
Cash	$ 4,350	Notes payable	$ 3,700
Equipment	4,600		
Land	3,750	Shareholders' Equity	
		Share capital	9,000
Total assets	$12,700	Total liabilities and shareholders' equity	$12,700

The following completed activities occurred during April 2005:

a. Purchased and used gasoline for mowers and edgers, paying $90 in cash at a local gas station.

b. In early April, received from the city $1,600 cash in advance for lawn maintenance service for April through July ($400 each month). The entire amount was recorded as Unearned Revenue.

c. In early April, purchased insurance costing $300 covering six months, April through September. The entire payment was recorded as Prepaid Expenses.

d. Mowed lawns for residential customers who are billed every two weeks. A total of $5,200 of service was billed in April.

e. Residential customers paid $3,500 on their accounts.

f. Paid wages every two weeks. Total cash paid in April was $3,900.

g. Received a bill for $320 from the local gas station for additional gasoline purchased on account and used in April.

h. Paid $100 on accounts payable.

Required:

1. On a separate sheet of paper, set up T-accounts for Cash, Accounts Receivable, Equipment, Land, Prepaid Expenses, Accounts Payable, Unearned Revenue (same as deferred revenue), Notes Payable, Share Capital, Retained Earnings, Mowing Revenue, Fuel Expense, and Wages Expense. Beginning balances for balance sheet accounts should be taken from the preceding balance sheet. Beginning balances for operating accounts are $0. Indicate these balances on the T-accounts.

2. Analyze each transaction using the steps outlined in Chapter 2. Please refer to the expanded transaction analysis model presented in this chapter.

3. On a separate sheet of paper, prepare journal entries to record the transactions above in chronological order and indicate their effects on the accounting model (Assets = Liabilities + Shareholders' Equity). Include the equality checks: (1) Debits = Credits and (2) the accounting equation is in balance.

4. Enter the effects of each transaction in the appropriate T-accounts. Identify each amount with its letter in the list of activities.

5. Compute balances in each of the T-accounts.

We strongly recommend that you prepare your own answers to these requirements and then check your answers with the following solution.

SUGGESTED SOLUTION

1. **Journal entries, effects on accounting equation, equality checks, and T-accounts:**

(*a*) Fuel expense (+E → −SE)   90
     Cash (−A)   90

Assets	=	Liabilities	+	Shareholders' Equity	
Cash	−90			Fuel expense	−90

(*b*) Cash (+A)   1,600
     Unearned revenue (+L)   1,600

Assets	=	Liabilities	+	Shareholders' Equity	
Cash	+1,600	Unearned revenue	+1,600		

(*c*) Prepaid expenses (+A)   300
     Cash (−A)   300

Assets	=	Liabilities	+	Shareholders' Equity	
Cash	−300				
Prepaid expenses	+300				

(*d*) Accounts receivable (+A)   5,200
     Mowing revenue (+R → +SE)   5,200

Assets	=	Liabilities	+	Shareholders' Equity	
Accounts receivable	+5,200			Mowing revenue	+5,200

(*e*) Cash (+A)   3,500
     Accounts receivable (−A)   3,500

Assets	=	Liabilities	+	Shareholders' Equity	
Cash	+3,500				
Accounts receivable	−3,500				

(*f*) Wages expense (+E → −SE)   3,900
     Cash (−A)   3,900

Assets	=	Liabilities	+	Shareholders' Equity	
Cash	−3,900			Wages expense	−3,900

(*g*) Fuel expense (+E → −SE)   320
     Accounts payable (+L)   320

Assets	=	Liabilities	+	Shareholders' Equity	
		Accounts payable	+320	Fuel expense	−320

(*h*) Accounts payable (−L)   100
     Cash (−A)   100

Assets	=	Liabilities	+	Shareholders' Equity	
Cash	−100	Accounts payable	−100		

T-Accounts

The beginning balances of the balance sheet accounts are taken from the solutions to the demonstration case in Chapter 2 (page 76).

ASSETS

+	Cash (A)		−
Beg. bal.	4,350		
b	1,600	a	90
e	3,500	c	300
		f	3,900
		h	100
End. bal.	5,060		

+	Accounts Receivable (A)		−
d	5,200	e	3,500
End. bal.	1,700		

+	Prepaid Expenses (A)	−
c	300	
End. bal.	300	

+	Equipment (A)	−
Beg. bal.	4,600	
End. bal.	4,600	

+	Land (A)	−
Beg. bal.	3,750	
End. bal.	3,750	

LIABILITIES

−	Accounts Payable (L)		+
h	100	g	320
		End. bal.	220

−	Unearned Revenue (L)		+
		b	1,600
		End. bal.	1,600

−	Notes Payable (L)		+
		Beg. bal.	3,700
		End. bal.	3,700

SHAREHOLDERS' EQUITY

−	Share Capital (SE)		+
		Beg. bal.	9,000
		End. bal.	9,000

−	Retained Earnings (SE)	+

REVENUES

−	Mowing Revenue (R)		+
		d	5,200
		End. bal.	5,200

EXPENSES

+	Wages Expense (E)	−
f	3,900	
End. bal.	3,900	

+	Fuel Expense (E)	−
a	90	
g	320	
End. bal.	410	

SOLUTIONS TO **SELF-STUDY QUIZZES**

Self-Study Quiz 3-1

Accounts Affected and Type of Account	Amount of Cash Received	Amount of Revenue Earned in March	Amount of Revenue Earned in April	Unearned Revenue
(a) Cash (A) Sales Revenue—Office Services (R)	$35,200		$35,200	
(b) Cash (A) Accounts Receivable (A) Sales Revenue—Retail Outlets (R)	20,200		30,200	
(c) Cash (A) Franchise-Related Revenue (R) Accounts Receivable (A)	3,450	$ 750	2,700	
(d) Cash (A) Franchise-Related Revenue (R) Unearned Revenue (L)	500		400	$100
(e) Cash (A) Accounts Receivable (A)	1,200	1,200		
Totals	$60,550		$68,500	

The total cash received in April, $60,550, is not equal to the amount of revenue recognized for April, $68,500. The cash received in April includes two amounts for revenue recorded for March and $100 for revenue to be recognized in the future. On the other hand, the revenues for April include $10,000 to be collected at a later date. Revenues reflect the efforts made in April, not earlier or later and are therefore a better measure of operating performance than cash receipts.

Self-Study Quiz 3-2

Accounts Affected and Type of Account	Cash Paid in April	Amount of Expense Recognized in January OR Why an Expense Is Not Recognized
(a) Cash (A) Accounts Payable (L)	$10,000	March purchase, paid in April; supplies expensed when used or sold.
(b) Inventories (A) Cost of Goods Sold (E)		$14,000 (of used inventory).
(c) Cash (A) Rent Expense (E) Prepaid Expenses (A)	$ 4,500	$1,500 incurred in April. $3,000 not yet incurred until future months.
(d) Inventories (A) Cost of Goods Sold (E)		$19,600 (of used inventory).
(e) Accounts Payable (L) General and Administrative Expense (E)		$500 incurred in April to be paid in the future.
Totals	**$14,500**	**$35,600 expenses for April.**

The amount of expenses incurred in April provides a better measure of the resources consumed or used in the process of generating revenues in April.

Self-Study Quiz 3-3

(i)	Notes receivable (+A)	4,300	
	Sales revenue—office services (+R → +SE)		4,300
	Cost of goods sold—equipment (+E → −SE)	3,800	
	Inventories (−A)		3,800
(j)	Accounts payable (−L)	10,000	
	Cash (−A)		10,000

Assets		=	Liabilities	+	Shareholders' Equity
Cash	−10,000		Accounts payable −10,000		

(k)	Assets		=	Liabilities	+	Shareholders' Equity
	Cash	+3,500				Gain on sale of land +3,000
	Fixed assets	−500				

Self-Study Quiz 3-4

1. F − 2. O + 3. I − 4. O − 5. O − 6. F −
7. O + 8. F + 9. F + 10. O − 11. O − 12. I +

CHAPTER **TAKE-AWAYS**

1. **Describe a typical business operating cycle and explain the necessity for the periodicity assumption. p. 106**
   - Operating cycle—the cash-to-cash cycle is the time it takes to purchase goods or services from suppliers, sell the goods or services to customers, and collect cash from customers.
   - Periodicity assumption—to measure and report financial information periodically, we assume the long life of the company can be cut into shorter periods.

2. **Explain how business activities affect the elements of the classified income statement. p. 108**
   - Elements on the classified income statement:
     a. Revenues—increases in assets or settlements of liabilities from ongoing operations.
     b. Expenses—decreases in assets or increases in liabilities from ongoing operations.
     c. Gains—increases in assets or settlements of liabilities from peripheral activities.
     d. Losses—decreases in assets or increases in liabilities from peripheral activities.

3. **Compute and interpret the total asset turnover ratio. p. 112**
   The total asset turnover ratio (Sales ÷ Average Total Assets) measures the sales generated per dollar of assets. The higher the ratio, the more efficient the company is at managing assets.

4. **Explain the accrual basis of accounting and apply the revenue and matching principles to measure income.   p. 113**

   When applying accrual accounting concepts, revenues are recognized (recorded) when earned and expenses are recognized when incurred to generate the revenues.
   - Revenue principle—recognize revenues when the earnings process is complete or nearly complete, an exchange has taken place, and collection is probable.
   - Matching principle—recognize expenses when incurred in earning revenue.

5. **Compute and interpret the return on assets ratio.   p. 119**

   The return on assets ratio measures how much the company earned for each dollar of assets. It provides information on profitability and management's effectiveness in utilizing assets. An increasing ratio over time suggests increased efficiency. ROA is computed as net income divided by average total assets.

6. **Apply transaction analysis to examine and record the effects of operating activities on the financial statements.   p. 120**

   The expanded transaction analysis model includes revenues and expenses:

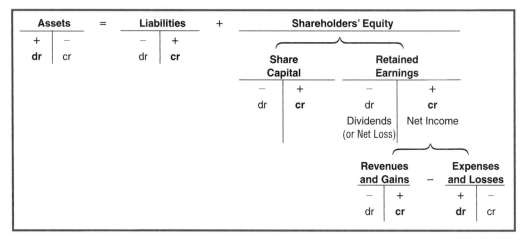

7. **Understand the difference between net income and cash flow from operations.   p. 128**

   Net income is the difference between revenues and expenses, whereas cash flow from operations equals the difference between cash receipts and cash payments related to operations. Net income differs from cash flow from operations because the revenue recognition and matching principles result in the recognition of revenues and related expenses that are independent of the timing of cash receipts and payments.

   In this chapter, we discussed the operating cycle and accounting concepts relevant to income determination: the periodicity assumption, definitions for the income statement elements (revenues, expenses, gains, and losses), the revenue principle, and the matching principle. These accounting principles are defined in accordance with the accrual basis of accounting, which requires revenues to be recorded when earned and expenses to be recorded when incurred in generating revenues during the period. We expanded the transaction analysis model introduced in Chapter 2 by adding revenues and expenses. In Chapter 4, we discuss the activities at the end of the accounting period: the adjustment process, the preparation of adjusted financial statements, and the closing process.

KEY **RATIO**

The total asset turnover ratio measures the sales generated per dollar of assets. A high ratio suggests that the company is managing its assets (resources used to generate revenues) efficiently. It is computed as follows (p. 112):

$$\text{Total Asset Turnover Ratio} = \frac{\text{Sales (or Operating) Revenues}}{\text{Average Total Assets}}$$

"Average" is (Last Year's Value + This Year's Value) ÷ 2.

BALANCE SHEET

Current Assets	*Current Liabilities*
Cash	Accounts payable
Accounts and notes	Notes payable
receivable	Accrued liabilities
Inventory	payable
Prepaid expenses	*Non-Current*
Non-Current Assets	*Liabilities*
Long-term	Long-term debt
investments	*Shareholders'*
Fixed assets	*Equity*
Intangibles	Share capital
	Retained earnings

INCOME STATEMENT

Revenues
    Sales (from various operating activities)
    Investment income
Expenses
    Cost of goods sold (used inventory)
    Rent, wages, interest, amortization,
        insurance, etc.
Pretax Income
    Income tax expense
Net Income

CASH FLOW STATEMENT

Under Operating Activities
    + Cash from customers
    + Cash from interest and dividends
    − Cash to suppliers
    − Cash to employees
    − Cash for interest
    − Cash for income taxes

NOTES

Under Summary of Significant Accounting Policies
    Description of company's revenue
        recognition policy.

KEY **TERMS**

Accrual Basis Accounting p. 114

Cash Basis Accounting p. 113

Discontinued Operations p. 111

Expenses p. 110

Extraordinary Items p. 112

Gains p. 111

Gross Profit (Gross Margin) p. 110

Income before Income Taxes p. 111

Losses p. 111

Matching Principle p. 117

Operating Cycle p. 106

Operating Income p. 111

Periodicity Assumption p. 108

Revenues p. 109

Revenue Principle p. 114

QUESTIONS

1. Explain a typical business operating cycle.
2. Explain what the periodicity assumption means in accounting.
3. Indicate the income statement equation and define each element.
4. Explain the difference between
    a. revenues and gains.
    b. expenses and losses.
5. Define *accrual accounting*. Contrast it with cash basis accounting.
6. What three conditions normally must be met for revenue to be recognized under the accrual basis of accounting?
7. Explain the matching principle.
8. Explain why shareholders' equity is increased by revenues and decreased by expenses.
9. Explain why revenues are recorded as credits and expenses as debits.
10. Complete the following matrix by entering either *debit* or *credit* in each cell:

Item	Increase	Decrease
Revenues		
Expenses		
Gains		
Losses		

11. Complete the following matrix by entering either *increase* or *decrease* in each cell:

Item	Debit	Credit
Revenues		
Expenses		
Gains		
Losses		

12. Identify whether each of the following transactions results in a cash flow effect from operating, investing, or financing activities, and indicate the effect on cash (+ for increase and − for decrease). If there is no cash flow effect, write "None":

Transaction	Operating, Investing, or Financing Effect	Direction of the Effect
Cash paid to suppliers		
Sale of goods on account		
Cash received from customers		
Purchase of investments for cash		
Cash paid for interest		
Issuance of shares for cash		

13. State the equation for the total asset turnover ratio, and explain how it is interpreted.

MULTIPLE-CHOICE QUESTIONS

1. Which of the following is *not* a specific account in a company's chart of accounts?
   - *a.* Gains
   - *b.* Net income
   - *c.* Revenue
   - *d.* Unearned revenue
2. Which of the following is *not* one of the three conditions that normally must be met for revenue to be recognized according to the revenue principle for accrual basis accounting?
   - *a.* The price is determinable.
   - *b.* Services have been performed.
   - *c.* Cash has been collected.
   - *d.* Clear evidence of arrangement for customer payment.
3. The matching principle controls
   - *a.* where on the income statement expenses should be presented.
   - *b.* how costs are allocated between Cost of Goods Sold (sometimes called Cost of Sales) and general and administrative expenses.
   - *c.* the ordering of current assets and current liabilities on the balance sheet.
   - *d.* when costs are recognized as expenses on the income statement.
4. You have observed that the asset turnover ratio for a retail chain has increased steadily over the last three years. The *most* likely explanation is that
   - *a.* a successful advertising campaign increased sales companywide, but no new store locations were added over the last three years.
   - *b.* salaries for upper management as a percentage of total expenses have decreased over the last three years.
   - *c.* new stores were added throughout the last three years, and sales increased as a result of the additional new locations.
   - *d.* the company began construction of a new, larger main office location three years ago that was put into use at the end of the second year.
5. Cash payments for salaries are reported in what section of the Cash Flow Statement?
   - *a.* Financing
   - *b.* Operating
   - *c.* Investing
   - *d.* None of the above
6. A company collects $100 cash on an account receivable from a customer for a sale last period. How would the receipt of cash impact the following two financial statements this period?

	Income Statement	Cash Flow Statement
a.	Revenue + $100	Inflow from investing
b.	No impact	Inflow from financing

    c. Revenue − $100   Inflow from operations

    d. No impact   Inflow from operations

7. When expenses exceed revenues in a given period,
    a. retained earnings is not impacted.
    b. retained earnings is increased.
    c. retained earnings is decreased.
    d. one cannot determine the impact on retained earnings without additional information.

8. Which account is *least* likely to be debited when revenue is recorded?
    a. Accounts Payable   *c.* Cash
    b. Accounts Receivable   *d.* Unearned Revenue

9. Which is the most likely goal of a business with regard to its operating cycle?
    a. To sustain its current operating cycle
    b. To expand its current operating cycle
    c. To shorten its current operating cycle
    d. To ignore its current operating cycle

10. Which of the following is the entry to be recorded by a law firm when it receives a retainer from a new client at the initial client meeting?
    a. *debit* to Accounts Receivable; *credit* to Sales Revenue
    b. *debit* to Unearned Revenue; *credit* to Sales Revenue
    c. *debit* to Cash; *credit* to Unearned Revenue
    d. *debit* to Unearned Revenue; *credit* to Cash

For more practice with multiple-choice questions, go to our Web site at www.mcgrawhill.ca/college/libby, click on "Student Edition" in the upper left menu, click on this chapter's name and number from the list of contents, and then click on "Multiple-Choice Quiz" from the menu on the left.

EXERCISES

E3–1 Matching Definitions with Terms   ■ **LO1, 2, 4**

Match each definition with its related term by entering the appropriate letter in the space provided. There should be only one definition per term (that is, there are more definitions than terms).

Term	Definition
_____ (1) Expenses	A. Report the long life of a company in shorter periods.
_____ (2) Gains	B. Record expenses when incurred in earning revenue.
_____ (3) Revenue principle	C. The time it takes to purchase goods or services from suppliers, sell goods or services to customers, and collect cash from customers.
_____ (4) Cash basis accounting	
_____ (5) Unearned revenue	D. A liability account used to record cash received before revenues have been earned.
_____ (6) Operating cycle	
_____ (7) Accrual basis accounting	E. Increases in assets or decreases in liabilities from peripheral transactions.
_____ (8) Prepaid expenses	F. Decreases in assets or increases in liabilities from ongoing operations.
_____ (9) Revenues − Expenses = Net Income	G. Record revenues when earned and measurable (an exchange takes place, the earnings process is complete or nearly complete, and collection is reasonably certain).
_____ (10) Ending Retained Earnings = Beginning Retained Earnings + Net Income − Dividends	H. Decreases in assets or increases in liabilities from peripheral transactions.
_____ (11) Losses	I. Record revenues when received and expenses when paid.
_____ (12) Matching principle	J. The income statement equation.
	K. An asset account used to record cash paid before expenses have been incurred.
	L. The retained earnings equation.
	M. Record revenues when earned and expenses when incurred.
	N. Increases in assets or decreases in liabilities from peripheral transactions.

LO2   **E3–2 Inferring Income Statement Values**

Supply the missing dollar amounts for the 2006 income statement of Ultimate Style Company for each of the following independent cases:

	Case A	Case B	Case C	Case D	Case E
Sales revenue	$900	$700	$410	$?	$?
Selling expense	?	150	80	400	250
Cost of goods sold	?	380	?	500	310
Income tax expense	?	30	20	40	30
Gross margin	400	?	?	?	440
Income before income tax	200	90	?	190	?
Administrative expense	150	?	60	100	80
Net income	170	?	50	?	80

LO2   **E3–3 Preparing a Multiple-Step Income Statement**

The following data were taken from the records of Village Corporation at December 31, 2006:

Sales revenue	$70,000
Gross profit	24,500
Selling (distribution) expense	8,000
Administrative expense	?
Income before income tax	12,000
Income tax rate	30%
Number of shares outstanding	3,000

Required:

Prepare a complete multiple-step income statement for the company (showing both gross profit and income from operations). Show all computations. (*Hint:* Set up the side captions starting with sales revenue and ending with earnings per share; use the amounts and percentages given to infer missing values.)

LO2   **E3–4 Preparing Single- and Multiple-Step Income Statements**

The following data were taken from the records of Kimberley Appliances, Incorporated, at December 31, 2005:

Sales revenue	$120,000
Administrative expense	10,000
Selling (distribution) expense	18,000
Income tax rate	25%
Gross profit	48,000
Number of shares outstanding	2,000

Required:

1. Prepare a complete single-step income statement for the company. Show all computations. (*Hint:* Set up the side captions or rows starting with sales revenue and ending with earnings per share; use the amounts and percentages given to infer missing values.)

2. Prepare a complete multiple-step income statement for the company (showing both gross profit and income from operations).

LO3, 5   **E3–5 Computing and Explaining the Total Asset Turnover Ratio**

The following data are from annual reports of Justin's Jewellery Company:

	2006	2005	2004
Total assets	$ 60,000	$ 50,000	$ 40,000
Total liabilities	12,000	10,000	5,000
Total shareholders' equity	48,000	40,000	35,000
Sales	154,000	144,000	130,000
Net income	5,000	3,800	25,000

Compute Justin's total asset turnover ratio and its return on assets for 2005 and 2006. What do these results suggest to you about Justin's Jewellery Company?

E3–6 Reporting Cash Basis versus Accrual Basis Income   ■ LO4

Mostert Music Company had the following transactions in March:

a. Sold instruments to customers for $10,000; received $6,000 in cash and the rest on account.

b. Determined that the cost of the instruments sold was $7,000.

c. Purchased $4,000 of new instruments inventory; paid $1,000 in cash and the rest on account.

d. Paid $600 in wages for the month.

e. Received a $200 bill for utilities that will be paid in April.

f. Received $1,000 from customers as deposits on orders of new instruments to be sold to customers in April.

Complete the following statements:

Cash Basis Income Statement		Accrual Basis Income Statement	
Revenues	$.	Revenues	$. . . . .
Cash sales	. . . .	Sales to customers	. . . .
Customer deposits			
Expenses		Expenses	
Inventory purchases	. . . .	Cost of sales	. . . .
Wages paid	. . . .	Wages expense	. . . .
		Utilities expense	. . . .
Net income		Net income	

Does the cash basis or the accrual basis of accounting provide a better indication of the operating performance of Mostert Music Company in March? Explain.

E3–7 Identifying Revenues   ■ LO2, 4

Revenues are normally recognized when the earnings process is complete or nearly complete, a transaction has taken place, and collection is reasonably assured. The amount recorded is the cash-equivalent sales price. The following events and transactions occurred in September 2005:

a. A customer orders and receives 10 personal computers from Gateway 2000; the customer promises to pay $20,000 within three months. Answer from Gateway's standpoint.

b. Sam Shell Dodge sells a truck with a list, or sticker, price of $24,000 for $21,000 cash.

c. The Hudson's Bay Company orders 1,000 men's shirts from Gildan Activewear Inc. for $18 each for future delivery. The terms require payment in full within 30 days of delivery. Answer from Gildan's standpoint.

d. Gildan Activewear completes production of the shirts described in (c) and delivers the order. Answer from Gildan's standpoint.

e. Gildan receives payment from the Hudson's Bay Company for the order described in (c). Answer from Gildan's standpoint.

f. A customer purchases a ticket from WestJet for $435 cash to travel the following January. Answer from WestJet's standpoint.

g. General Motors issues $26 million in new shares.

h. Hall Construction Company signs a contract with a customer for the construction of a new $500,000 warehouse. At the signing, Hall receives a cheque for $50,000 as a deposit on the future construction. Answer from Hall's standpoint.

i. On September 1, 2005, a bank lends $10,000 to a company. The loan carries a 12-percent annual interest rate, and the principal and interest are due in a lump sum on August 31, 2006. Answer from the bank's standpoint.

j. A popular ski magazine company receives a total of $1,800 from subscribers on September 30, the last day of its fiscal year. The subscriptions begin in the next fiscal year. Answer from the magazine company's standpoint.

k. Sears Canada, a retail store, sells a $100 lamp to a customer who charges the sale on his store credit card. Answer from the standpoint of Sears.

Required:

For each of the September transactions,

1. Indicate the account titles that are affected and the type of each account (A for asset, L for liability, SE for shareholders' equity, and R for revenue).

2. If a revenue is to be recognized in September, indicate the amount. If a revenue is not to be recognized in September, indicate which of the revenue recognition criteria are not met.

Use the following headings in structuring your solution:

Event or Transaction	Accounts Affected and Type of Account	Amount of Revenue Earned in September OR Revenue Criteria Not Met

LO2, 4

E3–8 Identifying Expenses

Revenues are normally recognized when goods or services have been provided and payment or promise of payment has been received. Expense recognition is guided by an attempt to match the costs associated with the generation of those revenues to the same time period. The following events and transactions occurred in January 2006:

a. Gateway 2000 pays its computer service technicians $85,000 in salary for the two weeks ended January 7. Answer from Gateway's standpoint.

b. Turner Construction Company pays $4,500 in workers' compensation insurance for the first three months of the year.

c. McGraw-Hill Ryerson Limited uses $1,200 worth of electricity and natural gas in its headquarters building for which it has not yet been billed.

d. Gildan Activewear Inc. completes production of 500 men's shirts ordered by Bon Ton's Department Store at a cost of $9 each and delivers the order. Answer from Gildan's standpoint.

e. The campus bookstore receives 500 accounting textbooks at a cost of $70 each. The terms indicate that payment is due within 30 days of delivery.

f. During the last week of January, the campus bookstore sold 450 accounting textbooks received in (e) at a sales price of $100 each.

g. Sam Shell Dodge pays its salespersons $3,500 in commissions related to December automobile sales. Answer from Sam Shell Dodge's standpoint.

h. On January 31, Sam Shell Dodge determines that it will pay its salespersons $4,200 in commissions related to January sales. The payment will be made in early February. Answer from Sam Shell Dodge's standpoint.

i. A new grill is installed at a McDonald's restaurant. On the same day, payment of $14,000 is made in cash.

j. On January 1, 2006, Carousel Mall had janitorial supplies costing $1,000 in storage. An additional $600 worth of supplies was purchased during January. At the end of January, $900 worth of janitorial supplies remained in storage.

k. A Concordia University employee works eight hours, at $15 per hour, on January 31; however, payday is not until February 3. Answer from the university's point of view.

l. Wang Company paid $3,600 for a fire insurance policy on January 2. The policy covers the current month and the next 11 months. Answer from Wang's point of view.

m. Amber Incorporated has its delivery van repaired in January for $280 and charges the amount on account.

n. Ziegler Company, a farm equipment company, receives its phone bill at the end of January for $230 for January calls. The bill has not been paid to date.

o. Spina Company receives and pays in January a $2,100 invoice from a consulting firm for services received in January.

p. Felicetti's Taxi Company pays a $600 invoice from a consulting firm for services received and recorded in Accounts Payable in December.

Required:

For each of the January transactions:

1. Indicate the account titles that are affected and the type of each account (A for asset, L for liability, SE for shareholders' equity, and E for expense).

2. If an expense is to be recognized in January, indicate the amount. If an expense is not to be recognized in January, indicate why.

Use the following headings in structuring your solution:

Event or Transaction	Accounts Affected and Type of Account	Amount of Expense Incurred in January OR Why an Expense Is Not Recognized

E3–9 Identifying Revenues and Expenses
LO2, 4, 7

Bob's Bowling, Inc. operates several bowling centres for games and equipment sales. The following transactions occurred in July 2005.

Required:

1. For each transaction, indicate in the appropriate column the account titles that are affected and the type of account (A for asset, L for liability, R for revenue, and E for expense), and the amount of cash received or paid.

2. If a revenue or an expense is to be recognized in July, indicate the amount. If a revenue or expense is not to be recognized in July, indicate why.

3. Explain why the difference between revenues and expenses is not equal to the net cash flow during July 2005.

Activity	Accounts Affected and Type of Account	Cash Received (Paid) in July	Amount of Revenue Earned or Expense Incurred in July OR Why a Revenue or an Expense Is Not Recognized
(a) Bob's collected $10,000 from customers for games played in July.			
(b) Bob's sold bowling equipment inventory for $5,000; received $3,000 in cash and the rest on account. The cost of sales is $2,800.			
(c) Bob's received $1,000 from customers on account who purchased merchandise in June.			
(d) The men's and women's bowling leagues gave Bob's a deposit of $1,500 for the upcoming fall season.			
(e) Bob's paid $2,000 for the June electricity bill and received the July bill for $2,200, which will be paid in August.			
(f) Bob's paid $4,000 to employees for work in July.			
(g) Bob's purchased and paid for $1,200 in insurance for coverage from July 1 to October 1.			
(h) Bob's paid $1,000 to plumbers for repairing a broken pipe in the restrooms.			
Totals			

E3–10 Determining the Financial Statement Effects of Operating Activities Involving Revenues
LO6

Bob's Bowling, Inc., operates several bowling centres (for games and equipment sales). For each of the following transactions, complete the tabulation, indicating the amount and effect (+ for increase and − for decrease) of each transaction. (Remember that A = L + SE, R − E = NI, and NI affects SE through Retained Earnings.) Write NE if there is no effect. The first transaction is provided as an example.

	Balance Sheet			Income Statement		
Transaction	Assets	Liabilities	Shareholders' Equity	Revenues	Expenses	Net Income
a. Bob's collected $10,000 from customers for games played in July.	+10,000	NE	+10,000	+10,000	NE	+10,000
b. Bob's sold $5,000 in bowling equipment inventory; received $3,000 in cash and the rest on account. The cost of sales is $2,800.						

	Balance Sheet			Income Statement		
Transaction	Assets	Liabilities	Shareholders' Equity	Revenues	Expenses	Net Income
c. Bob's received $1,000 from customers on account who purchased merchandise in June.						
d. The men's and women's bowling leagues gave Bob's a deposit of $1,500 for the upcoming fall season.						
e. Bob's paid $2,000 for the June electricity bill and received the July bill for $2,200 to be paid in August.						
f. Bob's paid $4,000 to employees for work in July.						
g. Bob's purchased $1,200 in insurance for coverage from July 1 to October 1.						
h. Bob's paid $1,000 to plumbers for repairing a broken pipe in the restrooms.						

■ **LO6**

E3–11 Determining Financial Statement Effects of Various Transactions

The following transactions occurred during a recent year:

a. Issued shares to organizers for cash (example).

b. Borrowed cash from the local bank.

c. Purchased equipment on credit.

d. Earned revenue, collected cash.

e. Incurred expenses, on credit.

f. Earned revenue, on credit.

g. Paid cash on account.

h. Incurred expenses, paid cash.

i. Earned revenue, collected three-fourths in cash and the rest on credit.

j. Experienced theft of $100 cash.

k. Declared and paid cash dividends.

l. Collected cash from customers on account.

m. Incurred expenses, paid four-fifths in cash and the rest on credit.

n. Paid income tax expense for the period.

Required:

Complete the tabulation below for each of the transactions, indicating the effect (+ for increase and − for decrease) of each transaction. (Remember that A = L + SE, R − E = NI, and NI affects SE through Retained Earnings.) Write NE if there is no effect. The first transaction is provided as an example.

	Balance Sheet			Income Statement		
Transaction	Assets	Liabilities	Shareholders' Equity	Revenues	Expenses	Net Income
(a) (example)	+	NE	+	NE	NE	NE

■ **LO6**

Wolverine World Wide, Inc.

E3–12 Determining Financial Statement Effects of Various Transactions

Wolverine World Wide, Inc., manufactures military, work, sport, and casual footwear and leather accessories under a variety of brand names, such as Hush Puppies, Wolverine, and Bates, to a global market. The following transactions occurred during a recent year. Dollars are in thousands.

a. Issued $48,869 in shares to investors (example).

b. Purchased $297,804 of additional inventory of raw materials on account.

c. Borrowed $58,181 on long-term notes.

d. Sold $413,957 of products to customers on account; the cost of the products sold was $279,673.

e. Declared and paid cash dividends of $2,347.

f. Purchased $18,645 of additional property, plant, and equipment for cash.

g. Incurred $88,396 in selling expenses with two-thirds paid in cash and the rest on account.

h. Earned $1,039 interest on investments, received 90 percent in cash.

i. Incurred $4,717 in interest expense (not yet paid).

Required:

Complete the tabulation below for each of the transactions, indicating the effect (+ for increase and − for decrease) of each transaction. (Remember that A = L + SE, R − E = NI, and NI affects SE through Retained Earnings.) Write NE if there is no effect. The first transaction is provided as an example.

	Balance Sheet			Income Statement		
Transaction	Assets	Liabilities	Shareholders' Equity	Revenues	Expenses	Net Income
(a) (example)	+48,869	NE	+48,869	NE	NE	NE

E3–13 Recording Journal Entries

Sysco, formed in 1969, is the largest U.S. marketer and distributor of food service products, serving nearly 250,000 restaurants, hotels, schools, hospitals, and other institutions. The following summarized transactions are typical of those that occurred in a recent year.

LO6

Sysco

a. Borrowed $80 million from a bank, signing a short-term note.

b. Provided $10.02 billion in service to customers during the year, with $9.5 billion on account and the rest received in cash.

c. Purchased plant and equipment for $173.4 million in cash.

d. Purchased $9,736 billion inventory on account.

e. Paid $1.02 billion in salaries during the year.

f. Received $410 million on account paid by customers.

g. Purchased and used fuel of $352 million in delivery vehicles during the year (paid for in cash).

h. Declared and paid $48.8 million in dividends for the year.

i. Paid $820 million cash on accounts payable.

j. Incurred $25 million in utility usage during the year; paid $15 million in cash and the rest on account.

Required:

Prepare a journal entry to record each of the transactions. Determine whether the accounting equation remains in balance and debits equal credits after each entry.

E3–14 Recording Journal Entries

Intrawest Corporation operates many ski resorts in North America. The company sells lift tickets, ski lessons, and ski equipment. It operates several restaurants and rents townhouses to vacationing skiers. The following hypothetical December transactions are typical of those that occur at one of its resorts.

LO6

Intrawest

a. Borrowed $600,000 from the bank on December 1 with a six-month note at 12-percent annual interest to finance the beginning of the new season. The principal and interest are due on the maturity date.

b. Purchased a new snowplough for $30,000 cash on December 1. The plough is estimated to have a five-year life and a $5,000 residual value.

c. Purchased and received $10,000 of ski equipment on account to sell in the ski shop.

d. Incurred $22,000 in routine maintenance expenses for the chair-lifts; paid cash.

e. Sold $84,000 of season passes in advance and received cash.

f. Sold daily lift passes for a total of $93,000 in cash.

g. Sold 10 pairs of skis for $350 each on account. (The cost of each pair was $250.)

h. Received a $400 deposit on a townhouse to be rented for five days in January.

i. Paid half of the amount of the transaction in (c).

j. Received $2,000 on account from the customer in (g).

k. Paid $67,000 in wages to employees for the month of December.

Required:

1. Prepare a journal entry to record each transaction. (Remember to check that debits equal credits and that the accounting equation is in balance after each transaction.)

2. Assume that Intrawest had a $1,200 balance in Accounts Receivable at the beginning of the year. Determine the ending balance in the Accounts Receivable account. Show your work in T-account format.

LO6   **E3–15 Recording Journal Entries**

Rowland & Sons Air Transport Service, Inc., has been in operation for three years. The following transactions occurred in February:

February 1   Paid $1,900 for rent of hangar space in February.
February 2   Purchased fuel costing $450 on account for the next flight to Winnipeg.
February 4   Received customer payment of $950 to ship several items to Montréal next month.
February 7   Flew cargo from Ottawa to Edmonton; the customer paid $1,240 for the air transport.
February 10   Paid pilot $4,000 in wages for flying in January.
February 14   Paid $600 for an advertisement in the local paper to run on February 19.
February 18   Flew cargo for two customers from Regina to Calgary for $1,800; one customer paid $500 cash and the other asked to be billed.
February 25   Purchased spare parts for the planes costing $1,350 on account.
February 27   Declared a $1,300 cash dividend to be paid in March.

Required:

Prepare a journal entry to record each transaction. Be sure to categorize each account as an asset (A), liability (L), shareholders' equity (SE), revenue (R), or expense (E).

LO4, 6, 7   E3–16 Analyzing the Effects of Transactions in T-Accounts, and Computing Cash Basis versus Accrual Basis Net Income

Sbrocchi's Piano Rebuilding Company has been operating for one year (2004). At the start of 2005, its income statement accounts had zero balances and its balance sheet account balances were as follows:

Cash	$ 5,000	Accounts payable	8,000
Accounts receivable	25,000	Deferred revenue (deposits)	3,200
Supplies	1,200	Note payable (due in three years)	40,000
Equipment	8,000	Share capital	8,000
Land	6,000	Retained earnings	18,000
Building	32,000		

Required:

1. Create T-accounts for the balance sheet accounts and for these additional accounts: Rebuilding Fees Revenue, Rent Revenue, Wages Expense, and Utilities Expense. Enter the beginning balances.

2. Enter the following January 2005 transactions in the T-accounts, using the letter of each transaction as the reference:
   a. Received a $500 deposit from a customer who wanted her piano rebuilt.
   b. Rented a part of the building to a bicycle repair shop; received $300 for rent in January.
   c. Delivered 10 rebuilt pianos to customers who paid $16,000 in cash.
   d. Received $6,000 from customers as payment on their accounts.
   e. Received an electric and gas utility bill for $420 to be paid in February.
   f. Ordered $800 in supplies.
   g. Paid $1,700 on account to suppliers.
   h. Received from the home of Ms. Sbrocchi, the major shareholder, an $850 tool (equipment) to use in the business.
   i. Paid $9,000 in wages to employees for work in January.
   j. Declared and paid a cash dividend of $3,000.
   k. Received and paid for the supplies ordered in (f).

3. Using the data from the T-accounts, calculate the amounts for the following on January 31, 2005:

   Revenues, $_____ − Expenses, $_____ = Net Income, $_____

   Assets, $_____ = Liabilities, $_____ + Shareholders' Equity, $_____

4. Calculate the company's net income for January using the cash basis of accounting. Why does this differ from the accrual basis net income (in part 3 above)?

E3–17 **Analyzing the Effects of Transactions on the Cash Flow Statement** ■ **LO6**
Refer to E3-16.

Required:
Use the following chart to identify whether each of the transactions in E3-16 results in a
cash flow effect from operating (O), investing (I), or financing (F) activities, and indicate the
direction and the effect on cash (+ for increase and − for decrease). If there is no cash flow
effect, write *none*. The first transaction is provided as an example.

Transaction	Operating, Investing, or Financing Effect	Direction and Amount of the Effect
(a)	O	+ 500

E3–18 **Analyzing the Effects of Transactions in T-Accounts** ■ **LO6**
Karen Gorewit and Pat Nally had been operating a catering business, Travelling Gourmet,
for several years. In March 2006, the partners were planning to expand by opening a retail
sales shop and decided to form the business as a corporation called Travelling Gourmet, Inc.
The following transactions occurred in March 2006:

a. Received $10,000 cash from each of the two shareholders to form the corporation,
in addition to $2,000 in accounts receivable, $5,300 in equipment, a van (equipment)
appraised at a fair market value of $14,500, and $1,200 in supplies.

b. Purchased a vacant store in a good location for $60,000 with a $12,000 cash down
payment and a mortgage from a local bank for the remainder.

c. Borrowed $25,000 from the local bank on a 10 percent, one-year note.

d. Purchased for cash and used food and paper products costing $8,830.

e. Made and sold food at the retail store for $10,900 in cash.

f. Catered four parties in March for $3,200; $2,000 was billed, and the rest was received
in cash.

g. Received a $320 telephone bill for March to be paid in April.

h. Paid $314 for gas to use the van in March.

i. Paid $5,080 for wages of employees who worked in March.

j. Paid a $300 dividend from the corporation to each owner.

k. Paid $15,000 to purchase equipment (refrigerated display cases, cabinets, tables, and chairs),
and $9,870 to renovate and decorate the new store (added to the cost of the building).

Required:
1. Set up appropriate T-accounts for Cash, Accounts Receivable, Supplies, Equipment,
Building, Accounts Payable, Note Payable, Mortgage Payable, Share Capital, Retained
Earnings, Food Sales Revenue, Catering Sales Revenue, Cost of Food and Paper
Products, Utilities Expense, Wages Expense, and Gasoline Expense.

2. Record in the T-accounts the effects of each transaction for Travelling Gourmet, Inc.,
in March. Identify the amounts with the letters starting with (*a*).

E3–19 **Analyzing the Effects of Transactions on the Cash Flow Statement** ■ **LO6**
Refer to E3–18.

Required:
Use the following chart to identify whether each of the transactions in E3-18 results in a
cash flow effect from operating (O), investing (I), or financing (F) activities, and indicate the
direction and the effect on cash (+ for increase and − for decrease). If there is no cash flow
effect, write *none*. The first transaction is provided as an example.

Transaction	Operating, Investing, or Financing Effect	Direction and Amount of the Effect
(a)	F	+ 20,000

E3–20 **Inferring Operating Transactions and Preparing an Income Statement and a** ■ **LO2, 4, 6**
Balance Sheet
Kiernan Kite Company (a corporation) sells and repairs kites from manufacturers around
the world. Its stores are located in rented space in malls and shopping centres. During its

first month of operations ended April 30, 2006, Kiernan Kite Company completed eight transactions with the dollar effects indicated in the following schedule:

| Accounts | Dollar Effect of Each of the Eight Transactions | | | | | | | | Ending Balance |
	(a)	(b)	(c)	(d)	(e)	(f)	(g)	(h)	
Cash	$50,000	$(10,000)	$(5,000)	$ 7,000	$(2,000)	$(1,000)		$3,000	
Accounts receivable				3,000					
Inventory			20,000	(3,000)					
Prepaid expenses					1,500				
Store fixtures		10,000							
Accounts payable			15,000				1,200		
Unearned revenue								2,000	
Share capital	50,000								
Sales revenue				10,000				1,000	
Cost of sales				3,000					
Wages expense						1,000			
Rent expense					500				
Utilities expense							1,200		

Required:

1. Write a brief explanation of transactions (*a*) through (*h*). Explain any assumptions that you made.

2. Compute the ending balance in each account and prepare an income statement for the company for April 2006 and a classified balance sheet as at April 30, 2006.

▨ LO3, 6

E3–21 **Analyzing the Effects of Transactions Using T-Accounts and Interpreting the Total Asset Turnover Ratio as a Financial Analyst**

Internet Marketing Inc. (IMI), which has been operating for three years, provides marketing consulting services worldwide for dot-com companies. You are a financial analyst assigned to report on the effectiveness of IMI's management team at managing its assets. At the start of 2005 (its fourth year), IMI's T-account balances were as follows. Dollars are in thousands.

ASSETS

Cash		Accounts Receivable		Long-Term Investments	
3,000		10,000		8,000	

LIABILITIES

Accounts Payable		Unearned Revenue		Long-Term Notes Payable	
	3,000		6,000		2,000

SHAREHOLDERS' EQUITY

Share Capital		Retained Earnings	
	6,000		4,000

REVENUES

Consulting Fee Revenue		Investment Income	

EXPENSES

Wages Expense		Travel Expense		Utilities Expense	

Rent Expense	

Required:

1. Using the data from these T-accounts, complete the accounting equation on January 1, 2005.

    Assets $_____ = Liabilities $_____ + Shareholders' Equity $_____

2. Enter the following 2005 transactions in the T-accounts:
    a. Received $7,700 cash from clients on account.
    b. Provided $70,000 in services to clients; received $50,000 in cash and the rest on account.
    c. Received $500 in income on investments.
    d. Paid $20,000 in wages, $21,800 in travel, $12,000 rent, and $2,000 on accounts payable.
    e. Received a utility bill for $1,300 for the current month.
    f. Paid $600 in dividends to shareholders.
    g. Received $2,000 in cash from clients in advance of services that IMI will provide next year.

3. Compute ending balances in the T-accounts to determine the missing amounts on December 31, 2005:

    Revenues $_____ − Expenses $_____ = Net Income $_____

    Assets $_____ = Liabilities $_____ + Shareholders' Equity $_____

4. Calculate the total asset turnover ratio for 2005. If the company had an asset turnover ratio of 2.00 in 2004 and of 1.80 in 2003, what does your computation suggest to you about IMI? What would you state in your report?

E3–22 Inferring Transactions and Computing Effects Using T-Accounts   ■ **LO6**

A recent annual report of a leading business and financial news company included the following accounts. Dollars are in millions.

Accounts Receivable			Prepaid Expenses			Unearned Revenue		
1/1	313		1/1	25			240	1/1
	2,573	?		43	?	?	328	
12/31	295		12/31	26			253	

Required:

1. Describe the typical transactions that affect each T-account (that is, the economic events that occur to make these accounts increase and decrease).

2. Compute the missing amounts for each T-account.

PROBLEMS

P3–1 Recording Non-Quantitative Journal Entries (AP3–1)   ■ **LO6**

The following list includes a series of accounts for Heiss Corporation, which has been operating for three years. These accounts are listed and numbered for identification, and followed by a series of transactions. For each transaction, indicate the account(s) that should be debited and credited by entering the appropriate account number(s) to the right of each transaction. If no journal entry is needed, use number 16. The first transaction is used as an example.

Account No.	Account Title	Account No.	Account Title
1	Cash	9	Wages payable
2	Accounts receivable	10	Income taxes payable
3	Supplies inventory on hand	11	Share capital
4	Prepaid expense	12	Retained earnings
5	Equipment	13	Service revenue
6	Patents	14	Operating expenses
7	Accounts payable	15	Income tax expense
8	Note payable	16	None of the above

Transactions	Debit	Credit
a. Example: Purchased equipment for use in the business; paid one-third cash and signed a note payable for the balance.	5	1, 8
b. Issued shares to new investors.	——	——
c. Paid cash for salaries and wages earned this period.	——	——
d. Collected cash for services performed this period.	——	——
e. Collected cash on accounts receivable for services previously performed.	——	——
f. Performed services this period on credit.	——	——
g. Paid operating expenses incurred this period.	——	——
h. Paid cash on accounts payable for expenses previously incurred.	——	——
i. Incurred operating expenses this period to be paid next period.	——	——
j. Purchased supplies inventory to be used later; paid cash.	——	——
k. Used some of the supplies inventory for operations.	——	——
l. Purchased a patent (an intangible asset); paid cash.	——	——
m. Made a payment on the equipment note in (a); the payment was part principal and part interest expense.	——	——
n. Paid three-fourths of the income tax expense for the year; the balance will be paid next year.	——	——
o. On the last day of the current period, paid cash for an insurance policy covering the next year.	——	——

■ **LO6**   **P3–2 Recording Journal Entries** (AP3–2)

Chad Polovick organized a new company, CollegeCaps, Inc. The company operates a small store in an area mall and specializes in baseball-type caps with logos printed on them. Chad, who is never without a cap, believes that his target market is college students. You have been hired to record the transactions occurring in the first two weeks of operations.

May 1	Issued 1,000 shares for $30 per share.
May 1	Borrowed $40,000 from the bank to provide additional funding to begin operations. The interest rate is 14 percent annually; principal and interest are due in 24 months.
May 1	Paid $1,200 for the current month's rent and another $1,200 for next month's rent.
May 1	Paid $1,800 for a one-year fire insurance policy (recorded as a prepaid expense).
May 3	Purchased furniture and fixtures for the store for $15,000 on account. The amount is due within 30 days.
May 4	Purchased a supply of University of Waterloo, York University, and Saint Mary's University baseball caps for the store for $1,800 cash.
May 5	Placed advertisements in local college newspapers for a total of $360 cash.
May 9	Sold caps totalling $400, half of which was charged on account. The cost of the caps sold was $150.
May 10	Made full payment for the furniture and fixtures purchased on account on May 3.
May 14	Received $100 from a customer on account.

Required:

Prepare a journal entry to record each of the transactions. Be sure to categorize each account as an asset (A), liability (L), shareholders' equity (SE), revenue (R), or expense (E).

■ **LO6**   **P3–3 Determining Financial Statement Effects of Various Transactions, and Identifying Cash Flow Effects** (AP3–3)

Wendy's
International Inc.

According to its annual report, Wendy's serves "the best hamburgers in the business" and other fresh food including salads, chicken sandwiches, and baked potatoes in more than 4,000 restaurants worldwide. The following activities were inferred from a recent annual report.

a. Purchased additional investments.

b. Served food to customers for cash. Ignore the using up of food supplies until (*h*).

c. Declared and paid cash dividends.

  d. Incurred restaurant operating costs in company-owned facilities; paid part in cash and the rest on account.

  e. Sold franchises, receiving part in cash and the remainder in notes due from franchisees.

  f. Paid interest on debt for the current year.

  g. Purchased food and paper products; paid part in cash and the rest on account.

  h. Used food and paper products.

Required:

  1. Complete the tabulation below for each of the transactions, indicating the effect (+ for increase and − for decrease) of each transaction. (Remember that A = L + SE, R − E = NI, and NI affects SE through Retained Earnings.) Write NE if there is no effect. The first transaction is provided as an example.

	Balance Sheet			**Income Statement**		
Transaction	Assets	Liabilities	Shareholders' Equity	Revenues	Expenses	Net Income
(*a*) (example)	+/−	NE	NE	NE	NE	NE

  2. Indicate where each transaction would be reported on the cash flow statement. Use O for operating activities, I for investing activities, F for financing activities, and NE if the transaction would not be included on the statement.

P3–4 Analyzing the Effects of Transactions Using T-Accounts, Preparing an Income Statement, Evaluating the Total Asset Turnover Ratio and the Return on Assets as a Manager (AP3–4)

■ **LO3, 5, 6**

Paula Abboud, a connoisseur of fine chocolate, opened Paula's Passions Inc. in Collegetown on February 1, 2005. The shop specializes in a selection of gourmet chocolate candies and a line of gourmet ice cream. You have been hired as manager. Your duties include maintaining the store's financial records. The following transactions occurred in February 2006, the first month of operations.

  a. Received contributions of $16,000 in total from four shareholders to form the corporation.

  b. Paid store rent for three months at $800 per month (recorded as prepaid expenses).

  c. Purchased supplies for $300 cash.

  d. Purchased on account and received candy for $5,000, due in 60 days.

  e. Obtained a $10,000 loan at the bank and signed a note at 12-percent annual interest. The principal and interest are due in a lump sum in two years.

  f. Used the money from (*e*) to purchase a computer for $2,500 (for recordkeeping and inventory tracking). The rest was used to buy furniture and fixtures for the store.

  g. Placed a grand opening advertisement in the local paper for $425 cash.

  h. Made sales on Valentine's Day totalling $1,800; $1,525 was in cash and the rest on accounts receivable. The cost of the candy sold was $1,000.

  i. Made a $500 payment on accounts payable.

  j. Incurred and paid employee wages of $420.

  k. Collected accounts receivable of $50 from customers.

  l. Made a repair on one of the display cases for $118 cash.

  m. Made cash sales of $2,000 during the rest of the month. The cost of the goods sold was $1,100.

Required:

  1. Set up appropriate T-accounts for Cash, Accounts Receivable, Supplies, Merchandise Inventory, Prepaid Rent, Equipment, Furniture and Fixtures, Accounts Payable, Notes Payable, Share Capital, Sales Revenue, Cost of Goods Sold (Expense), Advertising Expense, Wages Expense, and Repair Expense. All accounts begin with zero balances.

2. Record in the T-accounts the effects of each transaction for Paula's Passions in February, referencing each transaction in the accounts with the transaction letter. Show the ending balances in the T-accounts.

3. Prepare an income statement for February 2006.

4. Write a short memo to Paula offering your opinion on the results of operations during the first month of business.

5. After three years in business, you are being evaluated for a promotion. One measure is how efficiently you managed the assets of the business. The following data are available:

	2008*	2007	2006
Total assets	$80,000	$45,000	$35,000
Total liabilities	45,000	20,000	15,000
Total shareholders' equity	35,000	25,000	20,000
Total sales	85,000	75,000	50,000
Net income	20,000	10,000	4,000

*At the end of 2008, Paula decided to open a second store, requiring loans and inventory purchases prior to the opening in early 2008.

Compute the total asset turnover ratio and the return on assets for 2007 and 2008 and evaluate the results. Do you think you should be promoted? Why?

■ **LO6**   **P3–5**   **Analyzing the Effects of Transactions on the Cash Flow Statement**
Refer to P3–4.

Required:
Use the following chart to identify whether each of the transactions in P3–4 results in a cash flow effect from operating (O), investing (I), or financing (F) activities, and indicate the direction and the effect on cash (+ for increase and − for decrease). If there is no cash flow effect, write *none*. The first transaction is provided as an example.

Transaction	Operating, Investing, or Financing Effect	Direction and Amount of the Effect
(a)	F	16,000

■ **LO3, 5**   **P3–6**   **Analyzing the Effects of Transactions Using T-Accounts, Preparing Financial**

Canada Post

Statements, and Evaluating the Total Asset Turnover Ratio (AP3–6)
The following are several March 31, 2006, account balances (in millions of dollars) from a recent annual report of Canada Post Corporation, followed by several typical transactions. The corporation's vision is described in the annual report as follows:

Canada Post will be a world leader in providing innovative physical and electronic delivery solutions, creating value for our customers, employees, and all Canadians.

Account	Balance	Account	Balance
Long-term assets	$1,733	Equity of Canada	$1,182
Accounts payable	296	Receivables	535
Prepaid expenses	101	Other non-current assets	833
Accrued expenses payable	127	Cash	913
Long-term debt	92	Investments	443
Deferred revenues	153	Other non-current liabilities	2,708

These accounts are not necessarily in good order and have normal debit or credit balances. The following hypothetical transactions (in millions of dollars) occurred the next month (from April 1, 2006, to April 30, 2006):

a. Provided delivery service to customers, receiving $720 in accounts receivable and $60 in cash.

b. Purchased new equipment costing $816; signed a long-term note.

c. Paid $74 cash to rent equipment, with $64 for rental this month and the rest for rent for the next few days.

d. Spent $396 cash to maintain and repair facilities and equipment during the month.

e. Collected $652 from customers on account.

f. Borrowed $90 by signing a long-term note.

g. Paid employees $380 during the month.

h. Purchased for cash and used $49 in supplies.

i. Paid $184 on accounts payable.

j. Ordered $72 in spare parts and supplies.

Required:

1. Set up T-accounts for the preceding list and enter the respective balances. (*Note:* A deficit reflects accumulated losses instead of accumulated profits as in retained earnings.) (You will need additional T-accounts for income statement accounts.)

2. For each transaction, record the effects in the T-accounts. Label each using the letter of the transaction. Compute ending balances.

3. Prepare in good form a multiple-step income statement for April 2006.

4. Prepare in good form a classified balance sheet as at April 30, 2006.

5. Compute the company's total asset turnover ratio and its return on assets. What do these ratios suggest to you about Canada Post?

P3–7 Recording Journal Entries and Identifying Cash Flow Effects

■ **LO5, 6**

Cedar Fair

Cedar Fair, L. P. (Limited Partnership), owns and operates four seasonal amusement parks: Cedar Point in Ohio, Valleyfair near Minneapolis/St. Paul, Dorney Park and Wildwater Kingdom near Allentown, Pennsylvania, and Worlds of Fun/Oceans of Fun in Kansas City. The following are summarized transactions similar to those that occurred in 2005 (amounts in thousands of dollars):

a. Guests at the parks paid $89,664 cash in admissions.

b. The primary operating expenses (such as employee wages, utilities, and repairs and maintenance) for the year 2005 were $66,347, with $60,200 paid in cash and the rest on account.

c. Interest paid on long-term debt was $6,601.

d. The parks sell food and merchandise and operate games. The cash received in 2005 for these combined activities was $77,934.

e. The cost of products sold for cash during the year was $19,525.

f. Cedar Fair purchased and built additional buildings, rides, and equipment during 2005, paying $23,813 in cash.

g. The most significant assets for the company are land, buildings, rides, and equipment. Therefore, a large expense for Cedar Fair is amortization expense (related to the using of these assets to generate revenues during the year). In 2005, the amount was $14,473 (credit Accumulated Amortization).

h. Guests may stay at accommodations owned by the company at the parks. In 2005, Accommodations Revenue was $11,345; $11,010 was paid by the guests in cash and the rest was on account.

i. Cedar Fair paid $2,900 on notes payable.

j. The company purchased $19,100 in food and merchandise inventory for the year, paying $18,000 in cash and the rest on account.

k. The selling, general, and administrative expenses (such as the president's salary and advertising for the parks, those not classified as operating expenses) for 2005 were $21,118; $19,500 was paid in cash and the rest was on account.

l. Cedar Fair paid $8,600 on accounts payable during the year.

Required:

1. Prepare a journal entry to record each of these transactions. Use the letter of each transaction as its reference.

2. Use the following chart to identify whether each transaction results in a cash flow effect from operating (O), investing (I), or financing (F) activities, and indicate the direction and amount of the effect on cash (+ for increase and − for decrease). If there is no cash flow effect, write *none*. The first transaction is provided as an example.

Transaction	Operating, Investing, or Financing Effect	Direction and Amount of the Effect
(a)	O	+89,664

ALTERNATE PROBLEMS

LO6   **AP3–1 Recording Non-Quantitative Journal Entries** (P3–1)

The following is a series of accounts for Ortiz & Ortiz, Incorporated, which has been operating for two years. The accounts are listed and numbered for identification, followed by a series of transactions. For each transaction, indicate the account(s) that should be debited and credited by entering the appropriate account number(s) to the right of each transaction. If no journal entry is needed, write *none* after the transaction. The first transaction is given as an example.

Account No.	Account Title	Account No.	Account Title
1	Cash	9	Wages payable
2	Accounts receivable	10	Income taxes payable
3	Supplies inventory	11	Share capital
4	Prepaid expense	12	Retained earnings
5	Buildings	13	Service revenue
6	Land	14	Operating expenses
7	Accounts payable	15	Income tax expense
8	Mortgage payable		

Transactions	Debit	Credit
a. Example: Issued shares to new investors.	1	11
b. Performed services this period on credit.		
c. Purchased (but did not use) supplies this period on credit.		
d. Prepaid a fire insurance policy this period to cover the next 12 months.		
e. Purchased a building this period with a 20-percent cash down payment and a mortgage loan for the balance.		
f. Collected cash this year for services rendered and recorded in the prior year.		
g. Paid cash this period for wages earned and recorded last period.		
h. Paid cash for operating expenses charged on accounts payable in the prior period.		
i. Paid cash for operating expenses charged on accounts payable in the current period.		
j. Incurred and recorded operating expenses on credit to be paid next period.		
k. Collected cash at the point of sale for services rendered.		
l. Used supplies from inventory to clean the offices.		
m. Recorded income taxes for this period to be paid at the beginning of the next period.		
n. Declared and paid a cash dividend this period.		
o. Made a payment on the building, which was part principal repayment and part interest.		
p. A shareholder sold some shares this period to another person for an amount above the original issuance price.		

AP3–2 Recording Journal Entries (P3–2)

■ LO6

Rhonda Bennett is the president of ServicePro, Inc., a company that provides temporary employees for not-for-profit companies. ServicePro has been operating for five years; its revenues are increasing with each passing year. You have been hired to help Rhonda in analyzing the following transactions for the first two weeks of April:

April 2 Purchased office supplies for $500 on account.
      3 Received the telephone bill for $245.
      5 Billed United Way $1,950 for temporary services provided.
      8 Paid $250 for supplies purchased and recorded on account last period.
      8 Placed an advertisement in the local paper for $400 cash.
      9 Purchased a new computer for the office costing $2,300 cash.
    10 Paid employee wages of $1,200. Of this amount, $200 had been earned and recorded in the prior period.
    11 Received $1,000 on account from United Way.
    12 Purchased land as the site of a future office for $10,000. Paid $2,000 down and signed a note payable for the balance. The note is due in five years and has an annual interest rate of 10 percent.
    13 Issued 2,000 additional shares for $40 per share in anticipation of building a new office.
    14 Billed Family & Children's Service $2,000 for services rendered.

Required:
Prepare a journal entry to record each of the transactions. Be sure to categorize each account as an asset (A), liability (L), shareholders' equity (SE), revenue (R), or expense (E).

AP3–3 Determining Financial Statement Effects of Various Transactions and Identifying Cash Flow Effects (P3–3)

■ LO6

Casual Look, Inc. is a specialty retailer of quality casual apparel for men and women. The following activities were inferred from a recent annual report.

a. Example: Incurred expenses, paid part cash and part on credit.

b. Sold merchandise to customers on account. (*Hint*: Also reduce inventory for the amount sold.)

c. Declared and paid cash dividends.

d. Collected cash on account.

e. Used supplies.

f. Repaid long-term debt principal and interest.

g. Purchased equipment; paid part cash and part on credit.

h. Paid cash on account.

i. Issued additional shares.

j. Paid rent to mall owners.

k. Received dividends and interest on investments.

Required:

1. Complete the tabulation below for each of the transactions, indicating the effect (+ for increase and − for decrease) of each transaction. (Remember that A = L + SE, R − E = NI, and NI affects SE through Retained Earnings.) Write NE if there is no effect. The first transaction is provided as a sample.

| | **Balance Sheet** | | | **Income Statement** | | |
	Assets	Liabilities	Shareholders' Equity	Revenues	Expenses	Net Income
Transaction						
(a) (example)	−	+	−	NE	+	−

2. Indicate where each transaction would be reported on the cash flow statement, if at all. Use O for operating activities, I for investing activities, F for financing activities, and NE if the transaction would not be included on the statement.

LO5, 6

AP3–4 **Analyzing the Effects of Transactions Using T-Accounts, Preparing an Income Statement, Evaluating the Total Asset Turnover Ratio and the Return on Assets as a Manager** (P3–4)

Green Stables, Inc., was established on April 1, 2005. The company provides stables, care for animals, and grounds for riding and showing horses. You have been hired as the new assistant controller. The following transactions for April 2005 are provided for your review.

a. Received contributions from five investors of $50,000 in cash ($10,000 each), a barn valued at $100,000, land valued at $75,000, and supplies valued at $2,000. Each investor received 3,000 shares.

b. Built a small barn for $50,000. The company paid half the amount in cash and signed a three-year note payable for the balance on April 1, 2005.

c. Provided animal care services, all on credit, for $15,260.

d. Rented stables to customers who cared for their own animals and received cash payment of $13,200.

e. Received from a customer $1,500 to board her horse in April, May, and June (record as unearned revenue).

f. Purchased straw (a supply inventory) on account for $3,210.

g. Paid $840 in cash for water utilities expense incurred in the month.

h. Paid $1,700 on accounts payable for previous purchases.

i. Received $3,000 from customers on accounts receivable.

j. Paid $4,000 in wages to employees who worked during the month.

k. Purchased a one-year insurance policy for $1,800 at the end of the month.

l. Received an electric utility bill for $1,740 for usage in April; the bill will be paid next month.

m. Paid $500 cash dividend to each of the investors at the end of the month.

Required:

1. Set up appropriate T-accounts. All accounts begin with zero balances.

2. Record in the T-accounts the effects of each transaction for Green Stables in April, referencing each transaction in the accounts with the transaction letter. Show the ending balances in the T-accounts.

3. Prepare an income statement and a statement of retained earnings at the end of April, 2005, as well as a balance sheet as at April 30, 2005.

4. Write a short memo to the five owners offering your opinion on the results of operations during the first month of business.

5. After three years in business, you are being evaluated for a promotion to chief financial officer. One measure is how efficiently you managed the assets of the business. The following data are available:

	2007*	2006	2005
Total assets	$480,000	$320,000	$300,000
Total liabilities	125,000	28,000	30,000
Total shareholders' equity	355,000	292,000	270,000
Total sales	450,000	400,000	360,000
Net income	50,000	30,000	(10,000)

*At the end of 2007, Green Stables decided to build an indoor riding arena for giving lessons year-round. The company borrowed construction funds from a local bank and the arena was opened in early 2008.

Compute the total asset turnover ratio and the return on assets and evaluate the results. Do you think you should be promoted? Why?

AP3–5 Analyzing the Effects of Transactions on the Cash Flow Statement
Refer to AP3–4.

■ **LO6**

Required:
Use the following chart to identify whether each of the transactions in AP3–4 results in a cash flow effect from operating (O), investing (I), or financing (F) activities, and indicate the direction and the effect on cash (+ for increase and − for decrease). If there is no cash flow effect, write *none*. The first transaction is provided as an example.

Transaction	Operating, Investing, or Financing Effect	Direction and Amount of the Effect
(a)	F	+ 50,000

AP3–6 Analyzing the Effects of Transactions Using T-Accounts, Preparing Financial Statements, and Evaluating the Total Asset Turnover Ratio (P3–6)
The following are the summary account balances from a recent balance sheet of Petro-Canada. The accounts are followed by a list of hypothetical transactions for the month of January 2006. The following accounts are shown in millions of dollars.

■ **LO5, 6**

Petro-Canada

Cash	$ 635	Accounts payable	$1,822
Long-term debt	2,229	Income tax payable	300
Accounts receivable	1,503	Prepaid expenses	16
Inventories	551	Retained earnings	4,266
Future income taxes (credit)	2,518	Other long-term assets	1,126
Property and equipment, net	10,759	Share capital	3,455

The accounts have normal debit or credit balances, but they are not necessarily listed in good order.

a. Purchased new equipment costing $150 million by issuing long-term debt.

b. Received $900 million on accounts receivable.

c. Received and paid the telephone bills for $1 million.

d. Earned $500 million in sales to customers on account; cost of sales was $300 million.

e. Paid employees $100 million for wages earned in January.

f. Paid half of the income taxes payable.

g. Purchased inventory for $23 million on account.

h. Prepaid rent for February for a warehouse for $12 million.

i. Paid $10 million of long-term debt and $1 million in interest on the debt.

j. Purchased a patent (an intangible asset) for $8 million cash.

Required:

1. Set up T-accounts for the preceding list and enter the respective balances. (You will need additional T-accounts for income statement accounts.)

2. For each transaction, record the effects in the T-accounts. Label each using the letter of the transaction. Compute ending balances.

3. Prepare in good form a multiple-step income statement, and a statement of retained earnings for the month of January 2006, as well as a classified balance sheet as at January 31, 2006.

4. Compute the company's total asset turnover ratio and its return on assets. What do these ratios suggest to you about Petro-Canada?

CASES AND PROJECTS

FINDING AND INTERPRETING ACCOUNTING INFORMATION

■ **LO2, 3, 5, 6** CP3–1

The Forzani
Group Ltd.

Finding Financial Information

Refer to the financial statements and the accompanying notes of The Forzani Group Ltd. (FGL), available on the Online Learning Centre Web site at www.mcgrawhill.ca/college/libby/student/resources.

Required:

1. State the amount of the largest expense on the 2005 income statement and describe the transaction represented by the expense.

2. Prepare the journal entry for interest expense for the year ended January 30, 2005 (for this question, assume that the amount has not yet been paid).

3. Assuming that all net sales are on credit, how much cash did FGL collect from customers? (*Hint:* Use a T-account of accounts receivable to infer collection.)

4. A shareholder has complained that "dividends should be paid because the company had net earnings of $21.55 million. Since this amount is all cash, more of it should go to the owners." Explain why the shareholder's assumption that earnings equal net cash inflow is valid. If you believe that the assumption is not valid, state so and support your position concisely.

5. Describe and contrast the purpose of an income statement versus a balance sheet.

6. Compute the company's total asset turnover ratio and its return on assets for 2005. Explain their meaning.

■ **LO2, 4, 7** CP3–2

The Forzani Group
vs. Van Houtte

Comparing Companies

Refer to the financial statements and the accompanying notes of Van Houtte Inc. given in Appendix B, and of The Forzani Group Ltd. on the Online Learning Centre Web site at www.mcgrawhill.ca/college/libby/student/resources.

Required:

1. What title does each company call its income statement? Explain what the term *consolidated* means.

2. Which company had higher net income at the end of its fiscal year?

3. What were the primary causes of the change in sales as reported by the company in the Management Discussion and Analysis section of the annual report?

4. Compute the total asset turnover ratio and the return on assets for each company for the most recent year. Which company is utilizing assets more effectively to generate sales and net income? Explain.

5. How much cash was provided by operating activities by each company during the most recent year? What was the percentage change in operating cash flows for each company during the most recent year? (*Hint*: Percentage Change = [Current Year Amount − Prior Year Amount] ÷ Prior Year Amount.)

6. How much did each company pay in income taxes during the last fiscal year reported in the financial statements? Where did you find this information?

7. What segments does The Forzani Group report in the notes? What does Van Houtte report about segments?

■ **LO3** CP3–3

Van Houtte

Comparing a Company over Time

Refer to the annual report for Van Houtte Inc. (in Appendix B).

Required:

1. At the beginning of the Management's Discussions and Analysis section of Van Houtte's annual report, the Financial Highlights provide selected financial data for the past three years. Compute the total asset turnover ratio for fiscal years 2004 and 2005.

2. In Chapter 2, we discussed the debt-to-equity ratio. Compute this ratio for fiscal years 2004 and 2005.

3. What do your results from the trends in the two ratios suggest to you about Van Houtte?

FINANCIAL REPORTING AND ANALYSIS CASES

CP3–4 Interpreting the Financial Press

■ **LO4**

Fortune

The August 2, 1999, edition of *Fortune* presented numerous articles on accounting irregularities and fraud. One article entitled "Lies, Damned Lies, and Managed Earnings: The Crackdown Is Here" discusses the implications of unethical managerial decisions. You can access a portion of the article at **www.mcgrawhill.ca/college/libby/student/resources**.

Required:

Read the article and then answer the following questions:

1. From Chapter 1, what is the SEC and what is its role?

2. What are the three criteria for recording revenue under the revenue recognition principle?

3. What actual or alleged fraudulent activities were committed by the three companies mentioned in the article? What accounting concepts were violated in each case?

CP3–5 Finding Financial Information as an Investor

■ **LO5**

You are evaluating your current portfolio of investments to determine those that are not performing to your expectations. You have all of the companies' most recent annual reports.

Required:

For each of the following, indicate where you would locate the information in an annual report. (*Hint:* The information may be in more than one location.)

1. Description of a company's primary business(es).

2. Income taxes paid.

3. Accounts receivable.

4. Cash flow from operating activities.

5. Description of a company's revenue recognition policy.

6. Inventory sold during the year.

7. The data needed to compute the total asset turnover ratio.

CP3–6 Using Financial Reports: Interpreting Challenging International Financial Statements

■ **LO5, 6**

Volkswagen

Your cousin, an engineering major, has inherited some money and wants to invest in an auto company. She has never taken an accounting course and has asked you to help her compare a North American automaker's financial statements to those of German automaker Volkswagen. Find below the (adapted) comparative income statement and balance sheet of the Volkswagen Group for a recent fiscal year.

Required:

Write a letter to your cousin explaining the similarities and differences you would expect to find if you compared Volkswagen's financial statements to those of a company based in North America. Do you think that the underlying accounting principles in Germany and North America would be similar or different? Explain.

**Statement of Earnings (adapted) of the Volkswagen Group
for the Fiscal Year Ended December 31, 2003 and 2002
(in millions of €)**

	2003	2002
Sales	87,153	86,948
Cost of sales	76,493	72,950
Gross profit	**+ 10,660**	**+ 13,998**
Distribution expenses	7,846	7,560
Administrative expenses	2,724	2,155
Other operating income	4,403	4,137
Other operating expenses	3,163	3,659
Operating profit	**+ 1,780**	**+ 4,761**
Share of profit and losses of Group companies	+ 511	+ 534
Interest results	+ 93	− 466
Other financial result	− 855	− 843
Financial result	**− 251**	**− 775**
Profit before tax	**+ 1,529**	**+ 3,986**
Income tax expense	411	1,389
Profit after tax	**+ 1,118**	**+ 2,597**
Minority interests	− 23	− 13
Net profit attributable to shareholders	**+ 1,095**	**+ 2,584**

**Balance sheet (adapted) of the Volkswagen Group
At December 31, 2003 and 2002
(in million of €)**

	2003	2002
Assets		
Fixed assets		
Intangible assets	8,202	7,736
Tangible assets	23,852	22,842
Investment in Group companies	3,360	3,397
Other financial assets	607	588
	36,021	34,563
Leasing and rental assets	8,906	8,445
Current assets		
Inventories	11,670	10,677
Receivables and other assets	50,063	47,314
Securities	3,148	3,192
Cash and cash equivalents	7,536	2,987
	72,417	64,170
Prepayments and deferred charges	1,792	1,718
Total assets	119,136	108,896
Equity and liabilities		
Capital and reserves		
Subscribed capital	1,089	1,089
Capital reserve	4,451	4,451
Revenue reserves	14,171	13,905
Accumulated profits	4,719	5,189
	24,430	24,634
Minority interests	104	57
Provisions	22,810	22,349
Deferred tax liabilities	2,472	2,558
Liabilities	68,998	58,965
Deferred income	322	333
Total equity and liabilities	119,136	108,896

CRITICAL THINKING CASES

CP3–7   **Making a Decision as a Bank Loan Officer: Analyzing and Restating Financial Statements That Have Major Deficiencies (A Challenging Case)**

■ **LO4, 6**

Tom Martinez started and operated a small boat repair service company during 2006. He is interested in obtaining a $100,000 loan from your bank to build a dry dock to store boats for customers in the winter months. At the end of the year, he prepared the following statements based on information stored in a large filing cabinet:

MARTINEZ COMPANY
Profit for 2006

Service fees collected during 2006		$55,000
Cash dividends received		10,000
Total		$65,000
Expense for operations paid during 2006	$22,000	
Cash stolen	500	
New tools purchased during 2006 (cash paid)	1,000	
Supplies purchased for use on service jobs (cash paid)	3,200	
Total		26,700
Profit		$38,300

Assets Owned at the End of 2006

Cash in chequing account	$ 29,300
Service garage (at current market value)	32,000
Tools and equipment	18,000
Land (at current market value)	30,000
Shares in ABC Industrial	130,000
Total	$239,300

The following is a summary of completed transactions:

(*a*) Received the following contributions to the business from the owner when it was started in exchange for 1,000 shares in the new company:

Building	$21,000	Land	$20,000
Tools and equipment	17,000	Cash	1,000

(*b*) Earned service fees during 2006 of $87,000; of the cash collected, $20,000 was for deposits from customers on work to be done by Martinez during 2007.

(*c*) Received the cash dividends on shares of ABC Industrial purchased by Tom Martinez as a personal investment six years earlier.

(*d*) Incurred expenses during 2006, $61,000.

(*e*) Determined amount of supplies on hand (unused) at the end of 2006, $700.

Required:

1. Did Martinez prepare the income statement on a cash basis or an accrual basis? Explain how you can tell. Which basis should be used? Explain why.

2. Prepare an accrual-based income statement for 2006 and a balance sheet at the end of 2006. Explain (using footnotes) the reason for each change that you make to the income statement.

3. What additional information would assist you in formulating your decision regarding the loan to Mr. Martinez?

4. Based on the revised statements and additional information needed, write a letter to Mr. Martinez explaining your decision at this time regarding the loan.

CP3–8   **Proper Measurement of Income**

■ **LO4, 6**

Paula Manolakos purchased La Forêt Inc., a bakery, from Gianni Fiori. The purchase agreement included a provision that required Paula to pay Gianni 25 percent of the bakery's net income in each of the next five years. The agreement stated that the bakery's net income would be measured in a "fair and reasonable manner," but did not state that it would be measured in accordance with generally accepted accounting principles. Neither Paula nor Gianni was familiar with accounting concepts.

In measuring net income, Paula used the following accounting policies:

a. Revenue was recognized when cash was received from customers. Because of the nature of the business, most customers paid in cash, but a few customers purchased merchandise on account and were allowed to pay in 30 days.

b. Paula set her annual salary at $60,000, which Gianni has agreed was reasonable. She also paid $30,000 per year to her spouse and to each of her two teenaged children. These family members did not work in the business on a regular basis, but they did help during busy periods.

c. Weekly expenditures for eggs, milk, flour, and other supplies were charged directly to Supplies Expense, as were the weekly groceries for Paula's family.

d. The bakery had modern baking equipment valued at $50,000 at the time Paula purchased the company. The income statement for the first year included a $50,000 equipment expense related to these assets.

e. Income taxes expense included the amount paid by the corporation (which was computed correctly), as well as the personal income taxes paid by various members of Paula's family on the salaries they earned for working in the business.

Gianni was disappointed, however, when Paula reported a net income for the first year that was far below his expectations.

Required:

1. Discuss the fairness and reasonableness of Paula's accounting policies. Identify the accounting principle or assumption that may have been violated.

2. Do you think that the net cash flow from operations (cash receipts minus cash payments) is higher or lower than the net income reported by Paula? Explain.

3. What advice would you give Gianni to ensure that the bakery's net income would be measured properly in future years?

■ **LO4**   **CP3–9   Evaluating an Ethical Dilemma**

Mike Kruk is the manager of a Vancouver regional office for an insurance company. As the regional manager, his compensation package comprises a base salary, commissions, and a bonus when the region sells new policies in excess of its quota. Mike has been under enormous pressure lately, stemming largely from two factors. First, he is experiencing a mounting personal debt due to a family member's illness. Second, compounding his worries, the region's sales of new policies have dipped below the normal quota for the first time in years.

You have been working for Mike for two years, and like everyone else in the office, you consider yourself lucky to work for such a supportive boss. You also feel great sympathy for his personal problems over the last few months. In your position as accountant for the regional office, you are only too aware of the drop in new policy sales and the impact this will have on the manager's bonus. While you are working late at year-end, Mike stops by your office.

Mike asks you to change the manner in which you have accounted for a new property insurance policy for a large local business. A cheque for the premium, substantial in amount, came in the mail on December 31, the last day of the reporting year. The premium covers a period beginning on January 5. You deposited the cheque and correctly debited cash and credited an *unearned revenue* account. Mike says, "Hey, we have the money this year, so why not count the revenue this year? I never did understand why you accountants are so picky about these things anyway. I'd like you to change the way you have recorded the transaction. I want you to credit a *revenue* account. And anyway, I've done favours for you in the past, and I am asking for such a small thing in return." With that, he leaves for the day.

Required:

How should you handle this situation? What are the ethical implications of Mike's request? Who are the parties who would be helped or harmed if you complied with the request? If you fail to comply with his request, how will you explain your position to him in the morning?

FINANCIAL REPORTING AND ANALYSIS
TEAM PROJECT

CP3–10   **Team Project: Analysis of Income Statements and Ratios**

■ **LO2, 3, 4, 7**

As a team, select an industry to analyze. Using a Web browser, each team member should acquire the annual report for one publicly traded company in the industry, with each member selecting a different company.

Required:

1. On an individual basis, each team member should write a short report that lists the following information:

   a. The major revenue and expense accounts on the most recent income statement.

   b. Computation of the total asset turnover ratio and the return on assets.

   c. Description of revenue recognition policy, if reported.

   d. The ratio of cash from operating activities to net income for each year presented. This measures how liberal (that is, speeding up revenue recognition or delaying expense recognition) or conservative (that is, taking care not to record revenues too early or expenses too late) a company's management is in choosing among various revenue and expense recognition policies. A ratio above 1.0 suggests more conservative policies and below 1.0, more liberal policies.

2. Then, as a team, write a short report comparing and contrasting your companies using these attributes. Discuss any patterns across the companies that you as a team observe. Provide potential explanations for any differences discovered.

LEARNING OBJECTIVES

After studying this chapter, you should be able to:

1. Explain the purpose of a trial balance in the preparation of financial statements. p. 165

2. Analyze the adjustments necessary at the end of the period to update balance sheet and income statement accounts. p. 167

3. Present an income statement with earnings per share, a statement of retained earnings, and a balance sheet. p. 181

4. Compute and interpret the net profit margin ratio. p. 185

5. Explain the closing process. p. 186

Adjustments, Financial Statements, and the Quality of Earnings

4

FOCUS COMPANY:

Van Houtte, Inc.

THE BUSIEST TIME OF THE FISCAL YEAR

Van Houtte, Inc., defines its fiscal year-end as the Saturday closest to March 31 each year. Van Houtte's 2004 fiscal year ended on Saturday, April 3, 2004; the 2005 fiscal year ended on Saturday, April 2, 2005. As this focus company illustrates, a firm's fiscal year does not have to conform to the calendar year. In a recent survey of 200 companies, 61 (39 percent) did not use a December year-end in 2003,* including 16 companies that chose a fiscal year-end defined as, for example, "the last Saturday of the month" or "the Saturday closest to the end of the month," which results in financial information in some years covering 52 weeks and in other years 53 weeks.

Many companies use a natural business year-end, which occurs at the lowest point in their annual business cycle. Retail stores, for example, tend to experience much seasonal fluctuation in business activity. The holiday shopping period in November and December and merchandise returns in January are usually the months of highest activity, followed immediately by several months of low activity. For this reason, retail stores may use a January 31 year-end. The following lists a number of well-known companies and their year-end dates:

---

*C. Byrd, I. Chen, and J. Smith, *Financial Reporting in Canada,* 29th edition. Toronto: The Canadian Institute of Chartered Accountants, 2004, p. 6.

Company	Industry	Year-End
Canadian Tire Corporation	Consumer products	Saturday closest to December 31
Dell Computer Corporation	Computer hardware	Friday nearest January 31
The Gap	Clothing—retail	January 31
Gildan Activewear Inc.	Consumer products	First Sunday following September 28
Honda Motor Co. Ltd.,	Auto manufacturers	March 31
Hudson's Bay Company	Merchandising	January 31
Intrawest Corporation	Real estate management	June 30
McDonald's	Fast-food restaurants	December 31
Molson Inc.	Beverages	March 31
Nortel Networks Corp.	Telecommunications products	December 31
Royal Bank of Canada	Banking	October 31

For any company, whatever fiscal year-end is chosen, it is the busiest and most critical time from an accounting standpoint—the accounts are adjusted, financial statements are prepared, and the books are closed. It is also the point at which the external auditor completes audit work and issues an opinion on the fairness of the financial statements, which can then become available to external users. For Van Houtte, even though 2005 operations ended on April 2, 2005, the company's auditor, KPMG, LLP, completed the audit and signed the opinion on May 20, 2005 (seven weeks later). The auditor's work is performed gradually over time, but is not completed until the company has prepared its financial statements and the related notes at the end of the period.

UNDERSTANDING THE BUSINESS

Managers are responsible for preparing financial statements that are useful to investors, creditors, and others. Financial information is most useful for analyzing the past and predicting the future when it is considered by users to be of *high quality*. High-quality information is relevant (makes a difference in the decision process, and is available in a timely manner) and reliable (represents economic reality, is verifiable, and is unbiased).

Users expect revenues and expenses to be reported in the proper period based on the revenue and matching principles discussed in Chapter 3. Revenues must be recorded when earned, and expenses must be recorded when incurred, regardless of when cash is received or paid. Because many operating activities take place over a period of time, *adjustments* must be made at the end of the reporting period to record related revenues and expenses in the correct period. These entries update the records and are the focus of this chapter. Often, measuring revenues and expenses requires managers to make estimates and judgments, such as Van Houtte did in estimating its amortization expense.

Analysts, creditors, and investors assess how *conservative* the management's estimates and judgments are so they can determine the quality of financial information. When alternative methods to measure and report assets, liabilities, revenues, and expenses are available to management, the choices that produce the lower asset and revenue amounts, or the higher liability or expense amounts, would lead to lower net income and are considered to be conservative. Conservative estimates and judgments lead to higher-quality financial information. The information must not mislead the users in anticipating that the company will have a stronger financial position or higher earnings potential than actually exists. The effects of management's choices among alternative accounting methods and the use of estimates are presented throughout the rest of this text.

In this chapter, we emphasize the use of the T-accounts and journal entries (the analytical tools introduced in Chapters 2 and 3) to help you understand how the necessary adjustments are analyzed and recorded at the end of the accounting period. Then we prepare financial statements using adjusted accounts. Finally, we illustrate the process of "closing the books" to prepare the accounting records for the next accounting period.

ORGANIZATION OF THE CHAPTER

• Adjusting Revenues and Expenses
Accounting Cycle
Unadjusted Trial Balance
Analysis of Adjusting Entries
Deferred Revenues and Deferred Expenses
Accrued Revenues and Accrued Expenses
Van Houtte's Illustration
Materiality and Adjusting Entries

• Preparing Financial Statements
Income Statement
Statement of Retained Earnings
Balance Sheet
Net Profit Margin Ratio

• Closing the Books
End of the Accounting Cycle
Post-closing Trial Balance

ADJUSTING REVENUES AND EXPENSES

ACCOUNTING CYCLE

The **accounting cycle** is the process used by entities to analyze and record transactions, adjust the records at the end of the period, prepare financial statements, and prepare the records for the next cycle. *During the accounting period,* transactions that result in exchanges between the company and other external parties are analyzed and recorded (in the general journal in chronological order), and the related accounts are updated (in the general ledger), similar to our Van Houtte illustrations in Chapters 2 and 3. In this chapter, we examine the end-of-period steps that focus primarily on adjustments to record revenues and expenses in the proper period and to update the balance sheet accounts for reporting purposes. Exhibit 4.1 presents the fundamental steps in the accounting cycle.

The **ACCOUNTING CYCLE** is the process used by entities to analyze and record transactions, adjust the records at the end of the period, prepare financial statements, and prepare the records for the next cycle.

UNADJUSTED TRIAL BALANCE

The first step normally taken at the end of the accounting period is to create a trial balance, also known as an *unadjusted trial balance.* A **trial balance** is a list of individual accounts in one column, usually in financial statement order, with their ending debit or credit balances in the next two columns. Debit balances are indicated in the left column and credit balances are indicated in the right column. Then the two columns are totalled to provide a check on the equality of the debits and credits. In fact, that is all

▇ LEARNING OBJECTIVE 1

Explain the purpose of a trial balance in the preparation of financial statements.

A **TRIAL BALANCE** is a list of all accounts with their balances to provide a check on the equality of the debits and credits.

EXHIBIT **4.1**

The Accounting Cycle

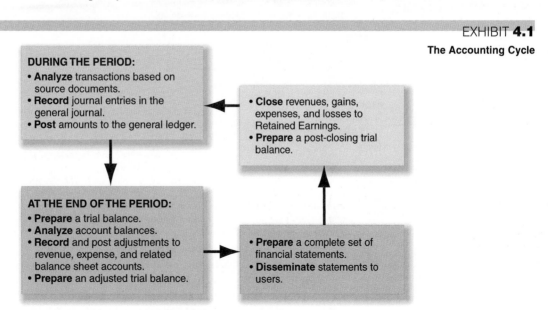

that the trial balance reflects. A trial balance can be produced manually or, more often, generated by computerized software. However, errors in a computer-generated trial balance may still exist even though debits equal credits when wrong accounts and/or amounts are used in the journal entries.[1]

A trial balance is a schedule prepared for internal purposes and is not considered to be a financial statement for external users. Exhibit 4.2 presents an unadjusted trial

EXHIBIT **4.2**

Trial Balance for Van Houtte Inc.

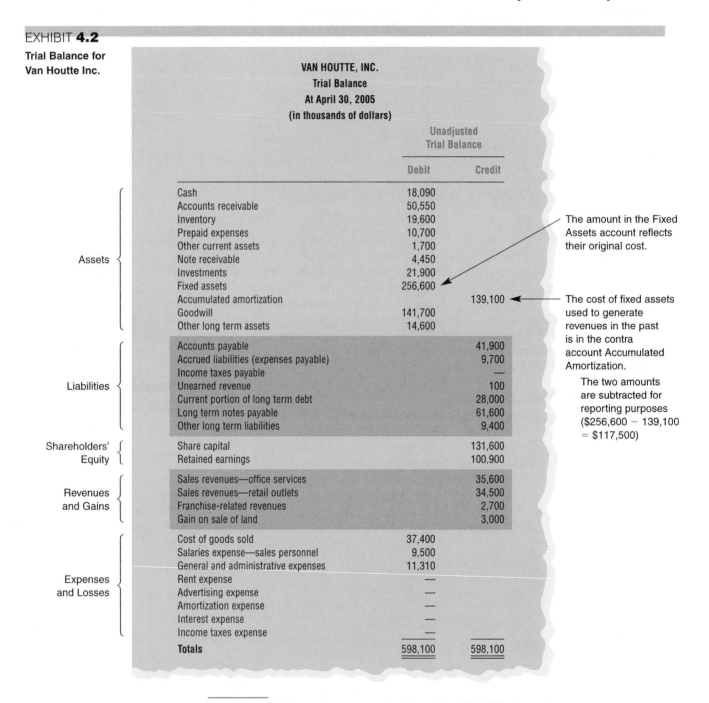

VAN HOUTTE, INC.
Trial Balance
At April 30, 2005
(in thousands of dollars)

	Unadjusted Trial Balance	
	Debit	Credit
Cash	18,090	
Accounts receivable	50,550	
Inventory	19,600	
Prepaid expenses	10,700	
Other current assets	1,700	
Note receivable	4,450	
Investments	21,900	
Fixed assets	256,600	
Accumulated amortization		139,100
Goodwill	141,700	
Other long term assets	14,600	
Accounts payable		41,900
Accrued liabilities (expenses payable)		9,700
Income taxes payable		—
Unearned revenue		100
Current portion of long term debt		28,000
Long term notes payable		61,600
Other long term liabilities		9,400
Share capital		131,600
Retained earnings		100,900
Sales revenues—office services		35,600
Sales revenues—retail outlets		34,500
Franchise-related revenues		2,700
Gain on sale of land		3,000
Cost of goods sold	37,400	
Salaries expense—sales personnel	9,500	
General and administrative expenses	11,310	
Rent expense	—	
Advertising expense	—	
Amortization expense	—	
Interest expense	—	
Income taxes expense	—	
Totals	**598,100**	**598,100**

Assets

Liabilities

Shareholders' Equity

Revenues and Gains

Expenses and Losses

The amount in the Fixed Assets account reflects their original cost.

The cost of fixed assets used to generate revenues in the past is in the contra account Accumulated Amortization.

The two amounts are subtracted for reporting purposes ($256,600 − 139,100 = $117,500)

---

[1]Errors in a trial balance also may occur in a manual recordkeeping system when wrong accounts and/or amounts are posted from correct journal entries. If the two columns are not equal, errors have occurred in one or more of the following:

- In preparing journal entries when debits do not equal credits.
- In posting the correct dollar effects of transactions from the journal entry to the ledger.
- In computing ending balances in accounts.
- In copying ending balances in the ledger to the trial balance.

These errors can be traced and should be corrected before adjusting the records.

balance for Van Houtte at April 30, 2005 based on the balances of the T-accounts illustrated in Chapters 2 and 3.

Notice that the Fixed Assets account is stated at original cost of $256,600 in the trial balance but was stated at $117,500 (original cost minus the portion allocated to past operations) in previous chapters. For long-term assets such as equipment used in operations, individual account balances remain at original cost to preserve the historical information. To reflect the used-up portion of the assets' cost, a **contra account** is created. *Any contra account is directly related to another account but has a balance on the opposite side of the T-account.* As a contra account increases, the net amount (the account balance less the contra account balance) decreases. For fixed assets, the contra asset is called Accumulated Amortization.[2] It has a credit balance of $139,100. We will discuss many contra accounts in other chapters and will designate contra accounts with an *X* in front of the type of account to which it is related (e.g., Accumulated Amortization [XA] for contra asset).

The difference between an asset's acquisition cost and accumulated amortization is called **book value** (**net book value** or **carrying value**). The book value does *not* represent the current market value of the asset because accounting for amortization is a cost allocation process rather than a market valuation process. As do many other companies, Van Houtte subtracts the balance in Accumulated Amortization from the cost in the Fixed Assets account, reporting the net amount on the balance sheet. The balance of each individual account is disclosed in a footnote to the financial statements. The note disclosure from a recent Van Houtte's annual report follows:

A **CONTRA ACCOUNT** is an account that is an offset to, or reduction of, the primary account.

BOOK VALUE (NET BOOK VALUE, CARRYING VALUE) of an asset is the difference between its acquisition cost and accumulated amortization, its related contra account.

Note 8

Fixed assets

	Cost	2004 Accumulated depreciation	Net book value
Land	$ 1,571	$ —	$ 1,571
Buildings	15,229	5,098	10,131
Coffee service equipment and vending equipment	153,020	84,644	68,376
Machinery and equipment	41,107	22,394	18,713
Furniture, computer equipment and leasehold improvements	25,844	16,412	9,432
Rolling stock	18,164	10,582	7,582
	$254,935	$139,130	$115,805

Adjustments to the balances of many accounts listed on the trial balance are made at the end of the accounting period, before preparing the financial statements.

ANALYSIS OF ADJUSTING ENTRIES

We learned in Chapter 3 that under accrual accounting, revenues are recorded when earned (the revenue principle) and expenses are matched with the related revenues during the same period (the matching principle). Operating income for a period, therefore, is determined by identifying and recording *all* revenues and expenses for that period regardless of when cash is received or paid. Often **adjusting entries** are necessary at the end of the accounting period to meet this objective. In reality, nearly all asset and liability accounts need to be analyzed and adjusted at year-end to measure income properly and provide appropriate amounts for assets, liabilities, and shareholders' equity on the balance sheet. The analysis involves determining whether (1) cash was received or paid *in the past* but has become earned or incurred over time, or

■ **LEARNING OBJECTIVE 2**

Analyze the adjustments necessary at the end of the period to update balance sheet and income statement accounts.

ADJUSTING ENTRIES are entries necessary at the end of the accounting period to identify and record all revenues and expenses of that period.

---

[2]The term *amortization* refers to the cost of using up all types of long-term assets, consistent with the recommendations of the *CICA Handbook*. Some companies use the term *depreciation*, which refers to the cost of buildings and equipment used up over time in generating revenues. In this book we use the term amortization, except when actual company statements use the term depreciation.

(2) cash will be received or paid *in the future* after revenues have been earned or expenses incurred during the current period.

DEFERRED REVENUES AND DEFERRED EXPENSES

When cash is received prior to revenue recognition, the company records a journal entry to debit Cash and credit an Unearned Revenue account (a liability). For example, the receipt of cash from a tenant in advance of occupancy of the premises is recorded as a credit to Unearned Rent Revenue. Similarly, the receipt of cash for annual subscriptions to a magazine is recorded as a credit to Unearned Subscriptions Revenue. In such situations, the receiving company promises to perform services or deliver goods in the future. Revenue recognition is deferred until the company meets its obligation. Unearned revenue is essentially a **deferred revenue** account. At the end of the accounting period, the unearned revenue account needs to be reduced and a revenue account needs to be increased by the amount of revenue earned during the period.

When cash is paid prior to incurring an expense, the company records a journal entry to debit an asset account and credit Cash. The company purchases a resource with probable future benefits that are expected to be received over time to generate revenue. For example, cash paid for insurance coverage for a specified future period is recorded as a debit to Prepaid Insurance Expense. Likewise, cash paid for supplies for future use is recorded as a debit to Supplies Inventory. These are common examples of **deferred expenses.** Expense recognition is deferred until the asset is used. At the end of the accounting period, the deferred expense account needs to be reduced and an expense account needs to be increased by the amount of expense incurred during the period.

The following time line helps in visualizing the preceding discussion.

DEFERRED REVENUES are previously recorded liabilities that need to be adjusted at the end of the accounting period to reflect the amount of revenues earned.

DEFERRED EXPENSES are previously acquired assets that need to be adjusted at the end of the accounting period to reflect the amount of expense incurred in using the assets to generate revenue.

ACCRUED REVENUES AND ACCRUED EXPENSES

Unlike deferred revenues that were recorded because cash was received in the past, **accrued revenues** have not yet been recorded at the end of the accounting period even though revenue has been earned over time. For example, a long-term loan to an affiliated company earns interest over time. If interest is paid at the maturity date of the loan, then interest earned during the period would not have been recorded by the company as revenue yet. No account exists to be adjusted. Since another entity owes the company money, a Receivable account needs to be created along with the related revenue account in an adjusting entry. In the case of earned interest, a journal entry is recorded with a debit to Accrued Interest Receivable and a credit to Interest Revenue. When cash is received in the future, the Receivable account is reduced.

Likewise, numerous expenses are often incurred in the current period that companies pay for in the next period. For example, employees may earn their salaries during the accounting period but may not be paid until the next accounting period. Such

ACCRUED REVENUES are previously unrecorded revenues that need to be recorded at the end of the accounting period to reflect the amount earned and its related receivable account.

unrecorded **accrued expenses** require an adjustment entry to create a payable account along with the related expense account. In this case, a journal entry is recorded with a debit to Salaries Expense and a credit to Salaries Payable. Other common examples of accrued expenses are Interest Expense incurred on debt, and Utilities Expense for bills received from utility suppliers. When the cash amounts are paid in the future, the payable accounts are reduced.

The following time line illustrates the process of accrual of revenues and expenses.

ACCRUED EXPENSES are previously unrecorded expenses that need to be recorded at the end of the accounting period to reflect the amount incurred and its related payable account.

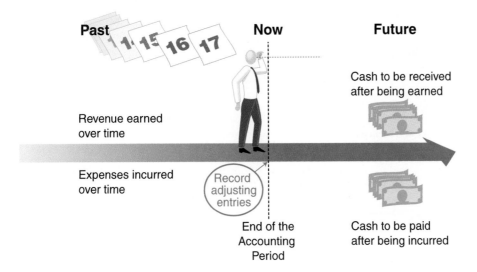

The process for determining the proper adjusting entry in each case is slightly more complex for deferred revenues and expenses than for accrued revenues and expenses.

To illustrate the process, we first apply it to a simplified scenario involving a dental office, and then use the same process to make the necessary adjustments to Van Houtte's accounts at the end of April 2005.

Let us assume that the fiscal year for a dental office ends on December 31. The dentist maintains her accounting records on an accrual basis. Upon reviewing her trial balance at the end of the year, she identified four items that require adjustment:

1. Unearned dental fees representing cash she *received in the past* in advance from local businesses to provide dental care to their employees in the future (insurance coverage and dental services are assumed to occur evenly over time unless otherwise indicated)—a deferred revenue.

2. Professional liability insurance *paid in the past* that provides for insurance coverage in the future—a deferred expense.

3. Interest she will *receive in the future* from a loan made during the year to an employee—an accrued revenue.

4. Wages she will *pay in the future* to employees who worked for her until year-end—an accrued expense.

The following three steps will assist you in the process of adjusting the accounts at the end of the accounting period:

Step 1. *Review the journal entry that was made when the cash was received or paid.*

Step 2. *Draw a time line to visualize the events related to the amount of revenue or expense that should be recognized during the accounting period.* Indicate all relevant dates and amounts for each period involved.

Step 3. *Record the adjusting journal entry (AJE).* (The title of the revenue or expense account should be related to the asset or liability account. For example, Interest Expense is related to Interest Payable.)

The following examples illustrate the application of these steps.

Deferred Revenues On December 1, the dental office accepted a $2,400 payment from local businesses to provide dental care to their employees over the next three months. By December 31, the dentist had provided one month of service and thus had earned revenue of $800 ($2,400 ÷ 3 months).

Step 1. On December 1, the amount received represents future obligations (dental service) owed by the dental office. This is the definition of a liability. The journal entry to record this transaction is:

Cash (+A)	2,400	
Unearned dental fee revenue (+L)		2,400

Step 2. As time passes after receiving the fees, a portion of the liability is settled and revenue is earned.

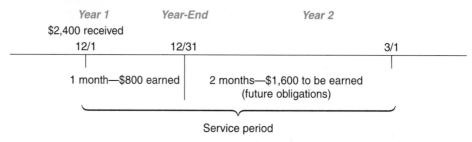

Year 1	*Year-End*	*Year 2*
$2,400 received		
12/1	12/31	3/1

1 month—$800 earned | 2 months—$1,600 to be earned (future obligations)

Service period

Unearned Dental Fee Revenue (L)

	2,400	12/1
*AJE 800 earned		
	1,600	12/31

Dental Fee Revenue (R)

	0	12/1
	800	AJE
	800	12/31

*AJE = adjusting journal entry

Step 3. The earned portion ($800) of the liability Unearned Dental Fee Revenue is a revenue. The remaining unearned portion ($1,600) is service due in the future. The adjusting journal entry and transaction effects follow:

12/31 AJE— Unearned dental fee revenue (−L)	800	
Dental fee revenue (+R, +SE)		800

Assets	=	Liabilities	+	Shareholders' Equity
		Unearned dental fee revenue −800		Dental fee revenue +800

Deferred Expenses Now we consider the second situation when, on November 1, the dentist paid $1,800 for six months of insurance coverage (from November 1 of this year to May 1 of next year). This results in $300 coverage each full month ($1,800 ÷ 6 months). On December 31, two months have passed, and two of the six months of insurance coverage have been used during the year. To reflect incurring this expense in the current period, an adjusting entry is necessary. The process follows:

Step 1. On November 1, the amount paid represents future benefits (insurance coverage) to the dental office. This is the definition of an asset. The journal entry to record this transaction is:

Prepaid insurance expense (+A)	1,800	
Cash (−A)		1,800

Step 2. As time passes after paying for the insurance, a portion of the asset is used during the period representing coverage received by the dentist.

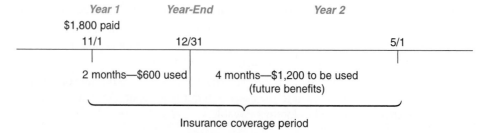

Year 1	*Year-End*	*Year 2*
$1,800 paid		
11/1	12/31	5/1

2 months—$600 used | 4 months—$1,200 to be used (future benefits)

Insurance coverage period

Step 3. The used-up portion ($600) of the asset Prepaid Insurance Expense is an expense. The remaining unused portion ($1,200) provides future benefits into next year. The adjusting entry and transaction effects follow:

Prepaid Insurance Expense (A)		
11/1	1,800	
		600 used AJE
12/31	1,200	

12/31 AJE—	Insurance expense (+E, −SE)	600	
	Prepaid insurance expense (−A)		600

Assets		=	Liabilities	+	Shareholders' Equity	
Prepaid insurance expense	−600				Insurance expense	−600

Insurance Expense (E)		
11/1	0	
AJE	600	
12/31	600	

By December 31 (the end of the accounting period), the dentist will have received two months of coverage ($600). Therefore, for the current year, Insurance Expense (E) should be $600 with $1,200 in the Prepaid Insurance Expense (A) account on the balance sheet.

Accrued Revenues   We assume that the dental office loaned $2,000 to an employee on September 1 for which the employee signed a note to pay the principal and interest at a 12-percent annual rate in six months. Any borrowing or lending of money involves two cash flows: one for the principal and one for the interest. Interest is the cost of borrowing money; it is an expense to the borrower and revenue to the lender. As each day passes until the principal is paid, more interest accumulates.

On September 1, an entry is made to reflect the lending of cash (principal) to the employee, but no interest revenue is recorded since none is earned on the day the note is signed. By the end of the year, however, four months have passed, so the dental office has earned four months of interest revenue that will not be received until March 1.

Step 1.   When the money was loaned, the dental office increased the asset Note Receivable and decreased Cash for $2,000. However, no entry was made at that date to recognize interest revenue because interest was not earned yet.

Step 2.   Interest is calculated by the following formula:

$$\text{Principal} \times \text{Annual Interest Rate} \times \frac{\text{\# of months of interest}^3}{12}$$

$2,000 \times .12 \times 4/12 = 80 interest earned in the first period.

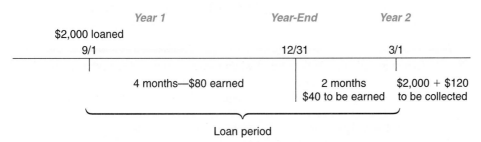

Step 3.   To recognize revenues in the period earned, an adjusting journal entry is needed. The effect is an increase in an asset and an increase in a revenue related to interest.

Accrued Interest Receivable (A)		
AJE	80	
12/31	80	

12/31AJE—	Accrued interest receivable (+A)	80	
	Interest revenue (+R, +SE)		80

Assets		=	Liabilities	+	Shareholders' Equity	
Accrued interest receivable	+80				Interest revenue	+80

Interest Revenue (R)		
	80	AJE
	80	12/31

T-accounts are not necessary since the amount is computed directly. They are presented here for illustration.

[3]In practice, interest calculations are based on the exact number of days, but in this textbook, we use the number of months for convenience.

Since the accrued revenue has not yet been recorded until the end of the period, the adjusting entry increases a receivable account and increases a revenue account by the computed amount. When the employee pays the principal and interest on March 1 of the next period, the entry is as follows:

March 1	Cash (+A)	2,120	
	Note receivable (−A)		2,000
	Accrued interest receivable (−A)		80
	Interest revenue (+R, +SE)		40

Assets		=	Liabilities	+	Shareholders' Equity	
Cash	+2,120				Interest revenue	+40
Note receivable	−2,000					
Accrued interest receivable	− 80					

The $2,120 received in cash on March 1 includes $2,000 in principal repayment and $120 for interest. Four months of interest were recognized in the preceding year as interest revenue and the other two months of interest ($40) are recognized as interest revenue this year.

Accrued Expenses Now assume that all employees are paid a total of $3,000 biweekly. Payment for 10 working days is made on the second Friday. The last payment for the year was on Friday, December 27. The employees continued to work through December 31, the end of the accounting period, but they will not be paid until January 10.

Step 1. No entry was made in the past for this expense, which was incurred during the year but has not yet been paid (an accrual).

Step 2. The amount of wages owed to employees per day is $300 ($3,000 paid for 10 working days). By December 31, employees are owed $600 for two workdays, December 30 and December 31.

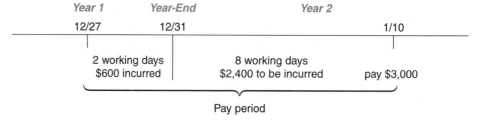

Accrued Wages Payable (L)

		600	AJE
		600	12/31

Wages Expense (E)

AJE	600	
12/31	600	

T-accounts are not necessary since the amount is computed directly. They are presented here for illustration.

Step 3. To match expenses in the period when incurred to generate revenue, an adjusting journal entry is needed. The effect is an increase in a liability and an increase in an expense related to wages.

12/31 AJE— Wages expense (+E, −SE)	600	
Accrued wages payable (+L)		600

Assets	=	Liabilities	+	Shareholders' Equity	
		Accrued wages payable	+600	Wages expense	−600

To complete the analysis, consider the entry on the next payday, January 10 in the next period:

January 10	Wages expense (+E, −SE)	2,400	
	Accrued wages payable (−L)	600	
	Cash (−A)		3,000

Assets	=	Liabilities	+	Shareholders' Equity	
Cash	−3,000	Accrued wages payable	−600	Wages expense	−2,400

The $3,000 is paid, but only $2,400 relates to the expense incurred in the second period. The $600 was properly recorded as an expense in the prior period and is now paid (the liability is reduced). Because the year ended between paydays, a portion of the total paid in the second period is an expense in the first year and the rest is an expense in the second year. Thus, expenses were properly matched in the appropriate period.

The following summarizes this process.

Deferrals: Deferred accounts already exist at the end of the accounting period from a previous entry involving cash receipt or payment. Due to the passage of time, an asset (usually, Prepaid Expenses, Supplies, Buildings, and Equipment) or a liability (Unearned Revenue) is overstated at year-end and must be *decreased;* its related revenue or expense account is understated and must be *increased*. We compute the correct ending balance in the account and adjust the balance to that amount. In each case, T-accounts and time lines can be quite useful.

Accruals: Since no previous entry has been made, expense accruals *increase* an expense and a payable, and revenue accruals *increase* a revenue and a receivable. As a consequence, we directly compute the amount of the needed adjustment.

Overall: It is important to note that adjusting entries *do not affect the Cash account.*

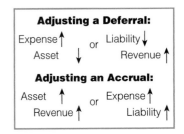

When adjustments are completed, an adjusted trial balance is prepared and the adjusted balances are used to prepare financial statements, which is the next step of the accounting cycle. Before we illustrate a complete set of financial statements for Van Houtte, we need to adjust the company's accounts at the end of April 2005.[4]

FINANCIAL **ANALYSIS**

ACCRUALS AND DEFERRALS: JUDGING EARNINGS QUALITY

Most of the adjustments discussed in this chapter, such as the allocation of prepaid insurance or the determination of accrued interest revenue, involve direct calculations and require little judgment on the part of the company's management. In later chapters, we will discuss many other adjustments that involve difficult and complex estimates about the future. These include, for example, estimates of customers' ability to make payments to the company for purchases on account, the useful lives of new machines, and future amounts that a company may owe on warranties of products sold in the past. Each of these estimates and many others can have significant effects on the stream of net earnings that companies report over time.

When attempting to value firms based on their balance sheet and income statement data, analysts also evaluate the estimates that form the basis for the adjustments. Those firms that make relatively pessimistic estimates that reduce current income are judged to follow *conservative* financial reporting strategies, and their reports of performance are given more credence. The earnings numbers reported by these companies are often said to be of "higher quality" because they are less influenced by management's natural optimism. Firms that consistently make optimistic estimates that result in reporting higher net income, however, are judged to be *aggressive*. Analysts judge these companies' operating performance to be of lower quality.

VAN HOUTTE'S ILLUSTRATION

We illustrate common adjusting entries by updating the accounts of Van Houtte based on the account balances and transactions in Chapters 2 and 3. As we review Van

---

[4]Companies can choose fiscal periods other than actual month-ends, and financial statements can cover different accounting periods (month, quarter, or year). Adjusting entries may be prepared monthly, quarterly, and/or annually to ensure that proper amounts are included on the financial reports presented to external users.

Houtte's trial balance in Exhibit 4.2, we can identify several deferral accounts that will need to be analyzed and may need to be adjusted:

Prepaid Expenses	All or a portion of the prepaid rent, insurance, and advertising may have been used by month-end.
Fixed Assets	These long-term assets have been used during the month to generate revenue. A portion of their historical acquisition cost is recorded as an expense.
Unearned Revenue	All or a portion may have been earned by month-end.

In addition, the unadjusted trial balance includes a number of receivables and payables that suggest there may be revenues earned and expenses incurred that have not yet been recorded. Adjusting entries are needed to accrue the revenues and expenses for April.

Accounts Receivable	Franchisees may owe additional royalties to Van Houtte for the last week of April's sales.
Accrued Expenses Payable	Any wages due to employees for work during the last week of April and amounts due for utilities used during the month but not yet billed to Van Houtte need to be recorded as expenses for the month.
Long-Term Notes Payable	Van Houtte owes interest on any borrowed funds.
Income Taxes Payable	Income tax expense needs to be recorded for the period.

Study the following illustration carefully to understand the steps in the adjustment process, paying close attention to the computation of the amounts in the adjustment and the effects on the account balances. First we adjust the deferred revenues and expenses and then the accrued revenues and expenses utilizing the three-step process previously discussed: (1) identify the original entry, (2) create a time line with relevant dates and amounts, and (3) identify the necessary adjusting entry.

Prepaid Expenses

(a) **In April 2004, Van Houtte paid a total of $7,400 for future expenses including insurance ($1,600), rent ($4,500), and advertising ($1,300). The payment for insurance covers four months—one month has passed (April), and three months of future insurance benefits remain. The payment for rent covers three months—one month has passed, and two months of future rent benefits remain. The payment for advertising relates to May 2005 and has not been used yet. In addition to the payment of $7,400 in April, Van Houtte has paid an amount of $3,300 prior to April 2005 to cover future expenses as reflected on its balance sheet at April 2, 2005. For illustrative purposes, we assume that this amount relates entirely to prepaid advertising expenses, and that $2,700 was used in April.**

Step 1. The journal entries made in the past to record the prepaid expenses are:

Prepaid expenses (+A)	7,400	
Cash (−A)		7,400

Step 2. As time passes, prepaid expenses are used up during April.

	April		Month-End		May and Beyond
	During the month		4/30		
Insurance	Expense incurred	$ 400	To be incurred		$1,200
Rent:	Expense incurred	$1,500	To be incurred		$3,000
Advertising:	Expense incurred	$2,700	To be incurred ($1,300 + $3,300 − $2,700)		$1,900

Step 3. The used-up portion of the asset Prepaid Expenses is an expense. The unused portion provides benefits in future periods. In this case, three expense accounts are affected by the adjustment—Insurance Expense, Rent Expense, and Advertising Expense, with Insurance Expense categorized as general and administrative expense on the income statement. The adjusting entry and transaction effects follow:

Prepaid Expenses (A)			
Beg.	3,300		
Purchased	7,400	4,600	Used
End.	6,100		

4/30—Adjusting Journal Entry

General and administrative expenses (+E, −SE)	400	
Rent expense (+E, −SE)	1,500	
Advertising expense (+E, −SE)	2,700	
Prepaid expenses (−A)		4,600

Assets	=	Liabilities	+	Shareholders' Equity
Prepaid expenses −4,600				General and administrative expenses − 400
				Rent expense −1,500
				Advertising expense −2,700

General and Administrative Expenses (E)			
Bal.	11,310		
AJE	400		
End.	11,710		

Rent Expense (E)			
Ch. 3 bal.	0		
AJE	1,500		
End.	1,500		

Advertising Expense (E)			
Ch. 3 bal.	0		
AJE	2,700		
End.	2,700		

Fixed Assets (and Accumulated Amortization) When buildings and equipment are used over time to generate revenue, a part of their cost should be expensed in the same period (the matching principle). Accountants say that buildings and equipment are amortized over time as used. The accounting process of amortization involves the systematic and rational allocation of the cost of a long-term asset over its useful life to the periods in which the asset is used to generate revenues.

A common misconception held by students and others unfamiliar with accounting terminology is that amortization reflects the asset's decline in market value. In accounting, amortization is a *cost allocation* concept, not a way of reporting a reduction in market value. As previously discussed, a contra account, Accumulated Amortization, is used to accumulate the amount of the historical cost allocated to prior periods. It is directly related to the Fixed Assets account but has the opposite balance (a credit balance).

The purpose of setting up an Accumulated Amortization account, instead of reducing the Fixed Assets account directly for periodic amortization, is to provide financial statement users with additional information that helps them estimate the average useful life and the relative age of the property and equipment owned by the company.

Amortization will be discussed in greater detail in Chapter 9. To simplify matters until we reach that chapter, we assume that long-term assets used in operations provide benefits to the company evenly over time. Therefore, the historical cost is amortized in equal amounts each period. This is known as the *straight-line* method.

(b) Fixed assets have a historical cost of $256,600 at the end of the month. The accumulated amortization of $139,100 is the used-up portion of the historical cost prior to this month. These assets have an average useful life of 10 years and an estimated residual value (the assets' estimated sales prices at the end of their useful lives to the company) of $28,600.

Step 1. The journal entry made in the past to record the purchase of fixed assets is:

Fixed Assets (+A)	(many purchases)	
Cash (−A) [or a liability]		(many purchases)

Step 2. As time passes, fixed assets are used during the period. The straight-line formula for computing the estimated amount of long-term assets used during the period is as follows:

$$\frac{(\text{Cost} - \text{Residual value})}{\text{Useful life}} = \text{Amortization expense for the period}$$

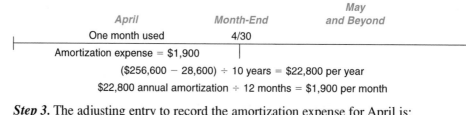

Amortization expense = $1,900

($256,600 − 28,600) ÷ 10 years = $22,800 per year

$22,800 annual amortization ÷ 12 months = $1,900 per month

Step 3. The adjusting entry to record the amortization expense for April is:

Accumulated Amortization—Fixed Assets (XA)		
	139,100	Ch. 3 bal.
	1,900	**Used**
	141,000	End.

4/30—Adjusting Journal Entry

Amortization expense (+E, −SE) 1,900

Accumulated amortization—

fixed assets (+XA→−A) 1,900

Amortization Expense (E)		
Ch. 3 bal.	0	
AJE	**1,900**	
End	1,900	

Assets	=	Liabilities	+	Shareholders' Equity
Accumulated amortization— fixed assets −1,900				Amortization expense −1,900

Note that increasing the contra-asset account decreases total assets.

SELF-STUDY **QUIZ 4-1**

Unearned Revenues

(c) Van Houtte has provided $100 in additional services to new office services clients that had previously paid initial fees to Van Houtte (unearned revenue at the time).

Step 1. The entry made in the past is:

Cash (+A) 100

Unearned revenue (+L) 100

Because cash was received in the past, the account to be adjusted is (circle one)

an accrual   a deferral.

Step 2. The unadjusted trial balance (Exhibit 4.2) shows that the balance in Unearned Revenue is $100 at April 30. This amount, $100, has been earned in April.

Unearned Revenue (L)		
	100	Ch. 3 bal.
AJE ☐		
	0	End.

Step 3. Record the adjusting journal entry (AJE).

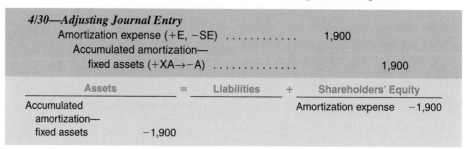

Sales Revenue— Office Services (R)		
	35,600	Ch. 3 bal.
	☐	AJE
	35,700	End.

4/30—Adjusting Journal Entry

Record the entry →

Assets	=	Liabilities	+	Shareholders' Equity
		Unearned Revenue −100		Sales revenue—office services +100

After you complete your answers, check them with the solution on page 194.

Receivables

(d) Van Houtte's franchisees reported that they owe Van Houtte $900 in additional royalties for sales in the last week of April.

Step 1. No entry was made in the past.

Step 2. The time line shows that the $900 earned in April will be collected in the future.

		May
April	*Month-End*	*and Beyond*
During the last week	4/30	
$900 revenue earned		To be collected

Step 3. The adjusting entry to recognize the royalties earned in April and the related increase in Accounts Receivable follows:

4/30—Adjusting Journal Entry
Accounts receivable (+A)   900
    Franchise-related revenue (+R, +SE)   900

Assets	=	Liabilities	+	Shareholders' Equity	
Accounts receivable +900				Franchise-related revenue	+900

Accounts Receivable (A)

Ch. 3 bal.	50,550		
Earned	**900**		
End.	51,450		

Franchise-Related Revenue (R)

		2,700	Ch. 3 bal.
		900	**AJE**
		3,600	End.

Accrued Expenses Payable (such as Utilities, Salaries, and Interest)

(e) On April 30, Van Houtte received a utility bill for $500 for use of natural gas and electricity in the headquarters building during April. The bill will be paid in May.

Step 1. No entry was made in the past.

Step 2. The time line shows that the $500 expense incurred in April will be paid in the future.

		May
April	*Month-End*	*and Beyond*
During the month	4/30	
$500 expense incurred		To be paid

Step 3. Since using utilities was necessary for the company to generate revenues in April, the amount should be recorded as an April expense. The adjusting journal entry and transaction effects follow:

4/30—Adjusting Journal Entry
General and administrative expenses (+E, −SE)   500
    Accrued expenses payable (+L)   500

Assets	=	Liabilities	+	Shareholders' Equity	
		Accrued expenses payable +500		General and administrative expenses	−500

Accrued Expenses Payable (L)

		9,700	Ch. 3 bal.
		500	**Incurred**
		10,200	End.

General and Administrative Expenses (E)

Bal. from (a)	11,710		
AJE	**500**		
End.	12,210		

(f) Van Houtte owed its employees salaries for the last week in April: $1,500 for salespersons and customer service employees, and $1,600 to administrative employees working at the headquarters. The salaries will be paid during the first week in May.

Step 1. No entry was made in the past.

Step 2. The time line shows that the wages earned by employees in April are payable in the following period.

		May
April	*Month-End*	*and Beyond*
During the last week	4/30	
$3,100 expense incurred		To be paid

Accrued Expenses Payable (L)

	10,200 Bal. from (e)
	3,100 Incurred
	13,300 End.

Salaries Expense—Sales Personnel (E)

Ch. 3 bal.	9,500
AJE	**1,500**
End.	11,000

General and Administrative Expenses (E)

Bal. from (e)	12,210
AJE	**1,600**
End.	13,810

Step 3. Since the employees worked and generated revenues during April, the amount owed to them should be recorded as an April expense. The adjusting journal entry and transaction effects are:

4/30—Adjusting Journal Entry

Salaries expense—sales personnel (+E, −SE) ..	1,500	
General and administrative expenses (+E, −SE)	1,600	
Accrued expenses payable (+L)		3,100

Assets	=	Liabilities	+	Shareholders' Equity
		Accrued expenses payable +3,100		General and administrative expenses −1,600
				Salaries expense— sales personnel −1,500

SELF-STUDY **QUIZ 4-2**

(g) **Van Houtte borrowed $1,000 at the beginning of April from a local bank, signing a note payable in two years with interest of 12 percent payable at the end of each year.**

Step 1. No entry for interest was made in the past.

Because cash is to be paid in the future, the account to be adjusted is (circle one)

an accrual   a deferral.

Step 2. The time line shows that the interest expense incurred in April is payable in the future.

	April	Month-End	May and Beyond
	During the month	4/30	
	$[ ] expense incurred		To be paid

Accrued Expenses Payable (L)

	13,300 Bal. from (f)
	[ ] Incurred
	[ ] End.

Interest Expense (E)

Ch. 3 bal.	0
AJE	[ ]
End.	[ ]

Step 3. Compute interest using the formula below and record the adjusting journal entry.

$$\text{Interest} = \text{Principal} \times \text{Annual Rate} \times \frac{\text{\# of months}}{12}$$

4/30—Adjusting Journal Entry

Record the entry → [   ]

Assets	=	Liabilities	+	Shareholders' equity
		Accrued expenses payable + [ ]		Interest expense − [ ]

After you complete your answers, check them with the solutions on page 194.

Income Taxes Expense   The final adjusting journal entry is to record the accrual of income taxes that will be paid in the next quarter (an unrecorded expense). This adjusting entry is recorded last because all other adjustments should be incorporated in computing income before income taxes, which is based on the adjusted balances:

All revenues	$76,800	Unadjusted total	$75,800 + 900 + 100
− All expenses	68,320	Unadjusted total	$58,210 + 4,600 + 1,900 + 500 + 3,100 + 10
Pretax income	$ 8,480		

(h) Van Houtte's average income tax rate is 25 percent.

Step 1. No entry was made in the past.

Step 2. The time line indicates that the income tax expense for April is payable in the future.

		May
April	Month-End	and Beyond
During the month	4/30	

$8,480 pretax income
× 25% tax rate
$2,120 (rounded) tax expense incurred

To be paid

Step 3. The adjusting journal entry to record the income tax expense follows:

Income Taxes Payable (L)

	0	Ch. 3 bal.
	2,120	Incurred
	2,120	End.

> **4/30—Adjusting Journal Entry**
> Income tax expense (+E, −SE) 2,120
>   Income taxes payable (+L)   2,120

Assets	=	Liabilities	+	Shareholders' Equity
		Income taxes payable +2,120		Income tax expense −2,120

Income Tax Expense (E)

Ch. 3 bal.	0	
AJE	2,120	
End.	2,120	

MATERIALITY AND ADJUSTING ENTRIES

The term *materiality* refers to the relative importance of an item. An item is material if knowledge of the item is likely to influence the decisions of financial statement users. The concept of **materiality** allows accountants to use estimated amounts and even to ignore other accounting principles if the results of these actions do not have a material effect upon the financial statements.

The process of making adjusting entries can be simplified if we account for immaterial items in the easiest and most convenient manner. For example, businesses purchase many assets that provide benefits for a long period of time. Some of these assets have a very low cost such as pencil sharpeners and wastebaskets. The proper accounting treatment for such assets is to amortize their cost to expense over their useful lives. However, the cost of such assets can be directly charged to expense accounts, rather than to asset accounts in accordance with the materiality concept. Thus, the need for an adjusting entry to record periodic amortization expense is eliminated. Furthermore, adjusting entries to record accrued expenses or revenues may be ignored if the dollar amounts are immaterial.

The accountant's decision to treat a specific item as immaterial depends on a number of considerations and is a matter of professional judgment. Traditional rules of thumb in the auditing profession imply that an item is material if it exceeds 1 to 1.5 percent of total assets or sales, or 5 to 10 percent of net income. Materiality depends upon the nature of the item, as well as its dollar value. If an employee has been stealing small amounts of money systematically, then these amounts should not be judged as immaterial because they indicate a weakness in the company's internal control system that should be corrected.[5] Accountants must also consider the combined effect of numerous immaterial events. While each item may be immaterial when considered by itself, the combined effect of many items may be material.

MATERIALITY suggests that minor items that would not influence the decisions of financial statement users are to be treated in the easiest and most convenient manner.

---

[5]In fact, a bank employee was able to accumulate a large sum of money by altering a computer program to round off amounts of exchange transactions to the nearest cent and transferring the fractional amounts to a specific account under his control. Even though the amounts involved per transaction were very small, the volume of banking transactions resulted in the accumulation of a relatively large amount. Fortunately, the employee's fraud was detected a few years later and an appropriate penalty was imposed on him.

FINANCIAL **ANALYSIS**

MANAGEMENT'S JUDGMENT IN YEAR-END ADJUSTMENTS: SIGNALS FOR ANALYSTS AND AUDITORS

Unlike the fairly routine procedures followed to record transactions based on supporting documentation during the accounting period, *knowledge* and *judgment* are primary inputs in determining end-of-period adjustments to revenues and expenses. As such, the accounts most subject to year-end adjustment are of considerable interest to external users of the financial statements. Investors, creditors, and analysts recognize that management's judgment plays the most important role in determining year-end adjustments and that these judgments may provide important signals of management's expectations for the future. Since end-of-period adjustments are the most complex portion of the annual recordkeeping process, they are prone to error. As noted in Chapter 1, external auditors (independent accountants) examine the company's records on a test, or sample, basis. To maximize the chance of detecting any errors significant enough to affect users' decisions, auditors allocate more time to test transactions that are most likely to be in error. You must understand the mechanics of the adjustment process before you can understand the information that adjustments contain and the errors that can occur.

A QUESTION OF **ETHICS**

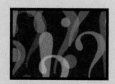

ADJUSTMENTS AND MANAGEMENT INCENTIVES

Owners and managers of companies are most directly affected by the information presented in financial statements. If the financial performance and condition of the company appear strong, the company's stock price rises. Shareholders usually receive dividends and the value of their investment increases. Managers often receive bonuses based on the strength of a company's financial performance, and many in top management are compensated with options to buy their company's shares at prices below market.* The higher the market value, the more compensation they earn. When actual performance lags behind expectations, managers and owners may be tempted to manipulate accruals and deferrals to make up part of the difference. For example, managers may record cash received in advance of being earned as revenue in the current period or may fail to accrue certain expenses at year-end.

Evidence from studies of large samples of companies indicates that some do engage in such behaviour. This research is borne out by enforcement actions of the Securities Commission against companies and sometimes against their auditors. These enforcement actions most often relate to accrual of revenue and receivables that should be deferred to future periods. In many of these cases, the firms involved, their managers, and their auditors are penalized for such actions. Furthermore, owners suffer because the company's share price is affected negatively by news of an investigation by a securities commission.

For example, in June 2004 the Ontario Securities Commission (OSC) charged four top management personnel of Atlas Cold Storage Income Trust with misleading investors after the warehouse operator restated two years of earnings. The OSC indicated that in preparing Atlas Cold's financial statements the four executives understated some costs and expenses and recorded some expenses in the wrong periods. These errors resulted in overstatements of net income for 2001, 2002, and the second quarter of 2003. The restatement (correction) of the company's financial results erased a total of $42.6 million of earnings in 2001 and 2002, widened the loss for the third quarter of 2003, and caused suspension of payments to investors. At the time of writing this textbook, the four executives were scheduled to appear in an Ontario Court.**

*P. Healy and J. Whalen, "A Review of the Earnings Management Literature and Its Implications for Standard Setting," *Accounting Horizons*, December 1999, Vol. 13, No. 4.
***Four Ex-Atlas Officials Misled Investors, OSC Charges*, Bloomberg, June 4, 2004.

PREPARING FINANCIAL STATEMENTS

The next step of the accounting cycle is to prepare a complete set of adjusted financial statements. The account balances that are reported in these financial statements appear in Exhibit 4.3, which shows the updated trial balance after all end-of-period adjustments have been posted to the ledger accounts.

■ **LEARNING OBJECTIVE 3**

Present an income statement with earnings per share, a statement of retained earnings, and a balance sheet.

EXHIBIT **4.3**

Van Houtte, Inc. Trial Balance

VAN HOUTTE INC.
Trial Balance
At April 30, 2005
(in thousands of dollars)

		Unadjusted Trial Balance		Adjustments		Adjusted Trial Balance	
		Debit	Credit	Debit	Credit	Debit	Credit
Assets	Cash	18,090				18,090	
	Accounts receivable	50,550		(d) 900		51,450	
	Inventory	19,600				19,600	
	Prepaid expenses	10,700			(a) 4,600	6,100	
	Other current assets	1,700				1,700	
	Note receivable	4,450				4,450	
	Investments	21,900				21,900	
	Fixed assets	256,600				256,600	
	Accumulated amortization		139,100		(b) 1,900		141,000
	Goodwill	144,700				141,700	
	Other long term assets	14,600				14,600	
Liabilities	Accounts payable		41,900				41,900
	Accrued liabilities (expenses payable)		7,600		(e) 500		13,310
					(f) 3,100		
					(g) 10		
					(h) 2,120		
	Income taxes payable		—				2,120
	Unearned revenue		100	(c) 100			—
	Current portion of long term debt		28,000				28,000
	Long term notes payable		61,600				61,600
	Other long term liabilities		9,400				9,400
Shareholders' Equity	Share capital		131,600				131,600
	Retained earnings		100,900				100,900
Revenues and Gains	Sales revenues—office services		35,600		(c) 100		35,700
	Sales revenues—retail outlets		34,500				34,500
	Franchise-related revenues		2,700		(d) 900		3,600
	Gain on sale of land		3,000				3,000
Expenses and Losses	Cost of goods sold	37,400				37,400	
	Salaries expense—sales personnel	9,500		(f) 1,500		11,000	
	General and administrative expenses	11,310		(a) 400		13,810	
				(e) 500			
				(f) 1,600			
	Rent expense	—		(a) 1,500		1,500	
	Advertising expense	—		(a) 2,700		2,700	
	Amortization expense	—		(b) 1,900		1,900	
	Interest expense	—		(g) 10		10	
	Income taxes expense	—		(h) 2,120		2,120	
	Totals	598,100	598,100	13,230	13,230	606,630	606,630

The four financial statements are interrelated. That is, the numbers in one statement flow into the next statement, as illustrated in Exhibit 4.4.

EXHIBIT **4.4**

Relationships of the Financial Statements

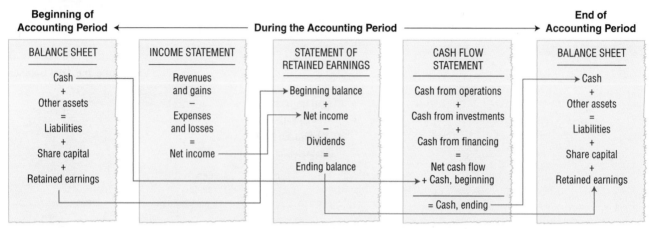

The company starts the accounting period with a set of asset, liability, and shareholders' equity account balances. Its operations during the period are summarized in the income statement and the statement of retained earnings, which are connected by the net income (or loss) for the period. The ending balance of

retained earnings is then reported in the shareholders' equity section of the balance sheet at the end of the period. Finally, the cash flow statement provides details of the cash inflows and outflows that explain the change in cash between the two balance sheet dates.

INCOME STATEMENT

The income statement is prepared first because net income is a component of Retained Earnings. The April income statement for Van Houtte is based on transactions in Chapters 2 and 3 and adjustments in this chapter.

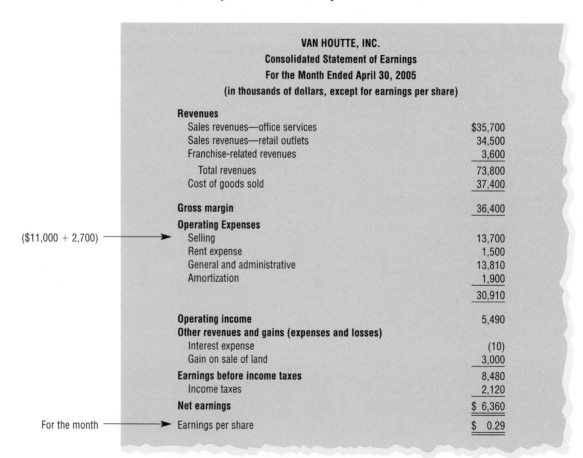

VAN HOUTTE, INC.
Consolidated Statement of Earnings
For the Month Ended April 30, 2005
(in thousands of dollars, except for earnings per share)

Revenues	
Sales revenues—office services	$35,700
Sales revenues—retail outlets	34,500
Franchise-related revenues	3,600
Total revenues	73,800
Cost of goods sold	37,400
Gross margin	36,400
Operating Expenses	
Selling	13,700
Rent expense	1,500
General and administrative	13,810
Amortization	1,900
	30,910
Operating income	5,490
Other revenues and gains (expenses and losses)	
Interest expense	(10)
Gain on sale of land	3,000
Earnings before income taxes	8,480
Income taxes	2,120
Net earnings	$ 6,360
Earnings per share	$ 0.29

($11,000 + 2,700) →

For the month →

You will note that the ratio earnings per share (EPS) is reported on the income statement. It is widely used in evaluating the operating performance and profitability of a company and is the only ratio required to be disclosed on the statement or in the notes to the statements. Earnings per share is computed as follows:

$$\text{Earnings per Share} = \frac{\text{Net Income Available to the Common Shareholders}}{\begin{array}{c}\text{Weighted-Average Number of Common Shares}\\\text{Outstanding during the Period}\end{array}}$$

The calculation of the denominator is complex and is presented in other accounting courses. Based on Van Houtte's actual annual report for 2005, the weighted-average number of common shares outstanding was approximately 21,598,000. For simplicity, we use this same denominator in the computations of the earnings per share shown on the income statement. Additional EPS disclosures will be discussed in Chapter 6.

EPS = $6,360,000 Net Income ÷ 21,598,000 Shares = $0.29

STATEMENT OF RETAINED EARNINGS

The final amount from the income statement, net income, is carried forward to the statement of retained earnings. If dividends had been declared during April 2005, they would be deducted to arrive at the ending balance at April 30, 2005.

VAN HOUTTE, INC.
Consolidated Statement of Retained Earnings
For the Month Ended April 30, 2005
(dollars in thousands)

Beginning balance, April 2, 2005	$100,900
Net income	6,360
Dividends	–0–
Ending balance, April 30, 2005	**$107,260**

BALANCE SHEET

The balance for retained earnings flows into the balance sheet. You will notice that the contra-asset account, Accumulated Amortization, has been subtracted from the Fixed Assets account to reflect net book value (or carrying value) at month-end for balance sheet purposes. Recall that assets are listed in order of liquidity, while liabilities are listed in order of due date. Current assets are those used or turned into cash within one year. Current liabilities are obligations to be paid with current assets within one year.

VAN HOUTTE INC.
Consolidated Balance Sheet
April 30, 2005
(in thousands of dollars)

Assets	
Current assets	
Cash	$ 18,090
Accounts receivable	51,450
Inventory	19,600
Prepaid expenses	6,100
Other current assets	1,700
Total current assets	96,940

(continued)

Notes receivable	4,450
Investments	21,900
Fixed assets (net of accumulated amortization of $141,000)	115,600
Goodwill	141,700
Other long term assets	14,600
Total assets	**$395,190**
Liabilities and shareholders' equity	
Current Liabilities	
Accounts payable	$ 41,900
Accrued liabilities	13,310
Income taxes payable	2,120
Current portion of long term debt	28,000
Total Current Liabilities	85,330
Long term notes payable	61,600
Other long term liabilities	9,400
Total liabilities	156,330
Shareholders' equity	
Share capital	131,600
($100,900 + 6,360) ⟶ Retained earnings	107,260
Total shareholders' equity	238,860
Total liabilities and shareholders' equity	**$395,190**

In addition to preparing the basic financial statements, companies provide further information about specific elements of these statements in notes that follow these statements. The additional details supporting the reported numbers facilitate analysis of the company's operating performance and financial condition. A closer look at note disclosures related to financial statements is provided in Chapter 6.

FOCUS ON **CASH FLOWS**

DISCLOSURE

As presented in the previous chapters, the cash flow statement explains the difference between the ending and beginning balances in the Cash account on the balance sheet during the accounting period. Put simply, the cash flow statement is a categorized list of all transactions of the period that affected the Cash account. The three categories are operating, investing, and financing activities. Since the adjustments made in this chapter did not affect cash, the components of the cash flow statement presented in Chapters 2 and 3 have not changed.

Further discussion of the cash flow statement is presented in Chapter 5.

FINANCIAL **ANALYSIS**

CASH FLOW FROM OPERATIONS, NET INCOME, AND THE QUALITY OF EARNINGS

Many standard financial analysis texts warn analysts to look for unusual deferrals and accruals when they attempt to predict future periods' earnings. They often suggest that wide disparities between net income and cash flow from operations is a useful warning sign. For example, Wild, Bernstein, and Subramanyam suggest that

Accounting accruals determining net income rely on estimates, deferrals, allocations, and valuations. These considerations typically admit more subjectivity than factors determining cash flows. For this reason we often relate cash flows from operations to net income in assessing its quality. Some users consider earnings of higher quality when the ratio of cash flows from operations divided by net income is greater. This derives from a concern with revenue recognition or expense accrual criteria yielding high net income but low cash flows.*

*J. Wild, L. Bernstein, and K. Subramanyam, *Financial Statement Analysis.* Burr Ridge, IL: Irwin/McGraw-Hill, 2001, p. 532.

KEY **RATIO ANALYSIS:**

NET PROFIT MARGIN RATIO

ANALYTICAL QUESTION → How effective is management in generating profit on every dollar of sales?

RATIO AND COMPARISONS → The net profit margin ratio is useful in answering this question. It is computed as follows:

$$\text{Net Profit Margin} = \frac{\text{Net Income}}{\text{Net Sales*}}$$

The 2005 ratio for Van Houtte:

$$\frac{\$21,706}{\$348,755} = 0.62 \ (6.2\%)$$

*Net sales is sales revenue less any returns from customers and other reductions. For companies in the service industry, total operating revenues equal net sales.

■ **LEARNING OBJECTIVE 4**

Compute and interpret the net profit margin ratio.

Comparisons over Time			Comparisons with Competitors	
Van Houtte Inc.			**Starbucks**	**Green Mountain Coffee Roasters**
2003	2004	2005	2004	2004
4.6%	5.6%	6.2%	8.8%	5.7%

INTERPRETATIONS

In General → Net profit margin measures how much profit is earned from every sales dollar generated during the period. A rising net profit margin signals more efficient management of sales and expenses. Differences among industries result from the nature of the products or services provided and the intensity of competition. Differences among competitors in the same industry reflect how each company responds to changes in competition (and demand for the product or service) and changes in managing sales volume, sales price, and costs. Financial analysts expect well-run businesses to maintain or improve their net profit margin over time.

Focus Company Analysis → Van Houtte's net profit margin has steadily increased over the past three years. Despite a reorganization in 2003 and the introduction of a new espresso machine in fiscal 2004, the company kept $0.062 on each revenue dollar in 2005 compared to $0.046 in 2003.

Compared to its competitors, Van Houtte has a slightly better performance than Green Mountain, but did not achieve as good a ratio as Starbucks. Despite the improvement in Van Houtte's ratio over the past three years, its management should analyze the various expense items in an effort to better control these costs and continue to improve on its performance.

A Few Cautions → The decisions that management makes to maintain the company's net profit margin in the current period may have negative long-run implications. Analysts should perform additional analysis of the ratio to identify trends in each component of revenues and expenses. This involves dividing each line on the income statement by net sales. Statements presented with these percentages are called *common-sized income statements*; they are discussed more fully in Chapter 13. Changes in the percentages of the individual components of net income provide information on shifts in management's strategies.

SELECTED FOCUS COMPANY NET PROFIT MARGINS

Intrawest Corporation	3.9%
Dell Inc.	6.2%
WestJet Airlines Ltd.	−1.6%

CLOSING THE BOOKS

END OF THE ACCOUNTING CYCLE

■ **LEARNING OBJECTIVE 5**

Explain the closing process.

PERMANENT (REAL) ACCOUNTS are the balance sheet accounts whose ending balances are carried into the next accounting period.

The balance sheet accounts are updated continuously throughout the accounting period, and the ending balance for the current period becomes the beginning account balance for the next period. The balances in these accounts, called **permanent** or **real accounts**, are not reduced to zero at the end of the accounting period. For example, the ending Cash balance of one accounting period must be the beginning Cash balance of the next accounting period. The only time a permanent account has a zero balance is when the item represented is no longer owned or owed.

In contrast, revenue, expense, gain, and loss accounts are often called **temporary** or **nominal accounts** because they are used to accumulate data for the *current accounting period only*. At the end of each period, their balances are transferred, or closed, to the Retained Earnings account so that the company starts with zero balances in these accounts at the beginning of the next accounting period. This periodic clearing of the balances of the income statement accounts into Retained Earnings is done by recording a closing entry.

TEMPORARY (NOMINAL) ACCOUNTS are income statement (and sometimes dividends declared) accounts that are closed to Retained Earnings at the end of the accounting period.

The closing entry has two purposes:

1. To transfer net income or loss to Retained Earnings.
2. To establish a zero balance in each of the temporary accounts to start the accumulation in the next accounting period.

CLOSING ENTRIES transfer balances in temporary accounts to Retained Earnings and establish zero balances in temporary accounts.

Accounts with credit balances are closed by debiting the total amount; accounts with debit balances are closed by crediting the total amount. The net amount of all account balances is then closed directly to Retained Earnings (although companies may close income statement accounts to a special temporary summary account, called **Income Summary,** which is then closed to Retained Earnings). In this way, the income statement accounts are again ready for their temporary accumulation function for the next period.

INCOME SUMMARY is a temporary account used only during the closing process to facilitate closing temporary accounts.

Closing entries are dated the last day of the accounting period, entered in the usual format in the journal, and immediately posted to the ledger (or T-accounts). We illustrate the closing process by preparing the closing entry for Van Houtte at April 30, 2005, although in practice companies close their records only at the end of the fiscal year.

Sales revenues—office services (−R)	35,700	
Sales revenues—retail outlets (−R)	34,500	
Franchise-related revenues (−R)	3,600	
Gain on sale of land (−R)	3,000	
Cost of goods sold (−E)		37,400
Salaries expense—sales personnel (−E)		11,000
General and administrative expenses (−E)		13,810
Rent expense (−E)		1,500
Advertising expense (−E)		2,700
Amortization expense (−E)		1,900
Interest expense (−E)		10
Income taxes expense (−E)		2,120
Retained earnings (+SE)		6,360

POST-CLOSING TRIAL BALANCE

POST-CLOSING TRIAL BALANCE should be prepared as the last step of the accounting cycle to check that debits equal credits and all temporary accounts have been closed.

After the closing process is complete, all of the income statement accounts have a zero balance. These accounts are then ready for recording revenues and expenses in the new accounting period. The ending balance in Retained Earnings now is up to date (matches the amount on the balance sheet) and is carried forward as the beginning balance for the next period. As the last step of the accounting information processing cycle, a **post-closing trial balance** (Exhibit 4.5) should be prepared as a check that debits equal credits and that all temporary accounts have been closed.

EXHIBIT **4.5**

Post-Closing Trial Balance
for Van Houtte, Inc.

VAN HOUTTE INC.
Trial Balance
At April 30, 2005
(in thousands of dollars)

| | Adjusted Trial Balance | | Post-Closing Trial Balance | |
	Debit	Credit	Debit	Credit
Assets				
Cash	18,090		18,090	
Accounts receivable	51,450		51,450	
Inventory	19,600		19,600	
Prepaid expenses	6,100		6,100	
Other current assets	1,700		1,700	
Note receivable	4,450		4,450	
Investments	21,900		21,900	
Fixed assets	256,600		256,600	
Accumulated amortization		141,000		141,000
Goodwill	141,700		141,700	
Other long term assets	14,600		14,600	
Liabilities				
Accounts payable		41,900		41,900
Accrued liabilities (expenses payable)		13,310		13,310
Income taxes payable		2,120		2,120
Unearned revenue		—		—
Current portion of long term debt		28,000		28,000
Long term notes payable		61,600		61,600
Other long term liabilities		9,400		9,400
Shareholders' Equity				
Share capital		131,600		131,600
Retained earnings		100,900		107,260
Revenues and Gains				
Sales revenues—office services		35,700		0
Sales revenues—retail outlets		34,500		0
Franchise-related revenues		3,600		0
Gain on sale of land		3,000		0
Expenses and Losses				
Cost of goods sold	37,400		0	
Salaries expense—sales personnel	11,000		0	
General and administrative expenses	13,810		0	
Rent expense	1,500		0	
Advertising expense	2,700		0	
Amortization expense	1,900		0	
Interest expense	10		0	
Income taxes expense	2,120		0	
Totals	606,630	606,630	529,830	529,830

DEMONSTRATION **CASE**

We take our final look at the accounting activities of Terrific Lawn Maintenance Corporation by illustrating the activities at the end of the accounting cycle: the adjustment process, financial statement preparation, and the closing process. Chapter 2 presented investing and financing activities, and Chapter 3 presented operating activities. No adjustments had been made to the accounts to reflect all revenues earned and expenses incurred in April, however. The trial balance for Terrific Lawn on April 30, 2005, based on the unadjusted balances in Chapter 3, is as follows:

TERRIFIC LAWN MAINTENANCE CORPORATION
Unadjusted Trial Balance
At April 30, 2005

	Debit	Credit
Cash	5,060	
Accounts receivable	1,700	
Prepaid expenses	300	
Equipment	4,600	
Accumulated amortization		0
Land	3,750	
Accounts payable		220
Unearned revenue		1,600
Notes payable		3,700
Accrued utilities payable		0
Wages payable		0
Interest payable		0
Income tax payable		0
Share capital		9,000
Retained earnings		0
Mowing revenue		5,200
Fuel expense	410	
Wages expense	3,900	
Insurance expense	0	
Utilities expense	0	
Amortization expense	0	
Interest expense	0	
Income tax expense	0	
Totals	19,720	19,720

In reviewing the trial balance, three deferral accounts (Unearned Revenue, Prepaid Expenses, and Equipment) may need to be adjusted and additional accruals may be necessary for interest on Notes Payable, Wages Expense, income taxes, and other expense or revenue accounts. The following information is determined at the end of the accounting cycle:

Deferred Accounts

a. $1,600 cash received from the city at the beginning of April (recorded as Unearned Revenue) for four months of service (April through July) has been partially earned by the end of April.

b. Insurance costing $300 for six months (April through September) paid by Terrific Lawn at the beginning of April (Prepaid Expenses) has been partially used in April.

c. Mowers, edgers, rakes, and hand tools (equipment) have been used and need to be amortized. They have a total cost of $4,600 and an estimated useful life of 10 years. No residual value is expected. The company uses straight-line amortization.

Accrued Accounts

d. Wages have been paid through April 29. Wages earned in April by the employees but not yet paid accrue at $130 per day.

e. An extra telephone line was installed in April. The telephone bill for $52, including hook-up and usage charges, was received on April 30 and will be paid in May.

f. Interest accrued on the outstanding notes payable at an annual rate of 12 percent. The $3,700 in principal has been outstanding all month.

g. The estimated income tax rate for Terrific Lawn is 35 percent for both federal and provincial income taxes.

Required:

1. Analyze each deferral and each accrual using the process outlined in this chapter. Include T-accounts for both accruals and deferrals and compute ending balances.

2. Prepare an adjusted trial balance.
3. Use the adjusted account balances from requirement 2 to prepare an income statement and a statement of retained earnings for the month ended April 30, 2005, as well as a balance sheet at April 30, 2005. Include earnings per share on the income statement. The company issued 1,500 shares.
4. Prepare the closing entry for April 30, 2005.
5. Compute the company's net profit margin for the month.

We strongly recommend that you prepare your own answers to these requirements and then check your answers with the following solution.

SUGGESTED SOLUTION

1. Analysis of deferrals and accruals, adjusting entries, and T-accounts:

Unearned Revenue

(a) **$1,600 cash received from the city at the beginning of April (recorded as Unearned Revenue) for four months of service (April through July) has been partially earned by the end of April.**

Step 1. The journal entry made in the past is:

Cash (+A)	1,600	
Unearned revenue (+L)		1,600

Step 2. The amount of revenue that should be recognized in April is $400 ($1,600 ÷ 4 months). The remaining amount will be earned gradually in future periods.

	April	Month-End	Beyond April
$1,600 received			
	During the month	4/30	
	$400 revenue earned		$1,200 to be earned

Step 3. The adjusting journal entry to recognize the revenue earned in April is:

4/30—Adjusting Journal Entry		
Unearned revenue (−L)	400	
Mowing revenue (+R, +SE)		400

Assets	=	Liabilities	+	Shareholders' Equity
		Unearned revenue −400		Mowing revenue +400

Unearned Revenue (L)

		1,600	Bal.
Earned	400		
		1,200	End.

Mowing Revenue (R)

		5,200	Bal.
		400	AJE
		5,600	End.

Prepaid Expenses

(b) **Insurance costing $300 for six months (April through September) paid by Terrific Lawn at the beginning of April (Prepaid Expenses) has been partially used in April.**

Step 1. The journal entry made in the past is:

Prepaid expenses (+A)	300	
Cash (−A)		300

Step 2. The amount of insurance expense that should be recognized in April is $50 ($300 ÷ 6 months). The remaining amount, $250, will be recognized as expense gradually over the next five months.

	April	Month-End	Beyond April
$300 paid			
	During the month	4/30	
	$50 expense incurred		$250 to be incurred

Prepaid Expenses (A)

Bal.	300		
		50	Used
End.	250		

Insurance Expense (E)

Bal.	0		
AJE	50		
End.	50		

Accumulated Amortization (XA)

		0	Bal.
		38	Used
		38	End.

Amortization Expense (E)

Bal.	0		
AJE	38		
End.	38		

Wages Payable (L)

		0	Bal.
		130	Incurred
		130	End.

Wages Expense (E)

Bal.	3,900		
AJE	130		
End.	4,030		

Step 3. The adjusting journal entry to recognize the insurance expense for April is:

4/30—Adjusting Journal Entry
Insurance expense (+E, −SE) 50
  Prepaid expenses (−A) 50

Assets	=	Liabilities	+	Shareholders' Equity	
Prepaid expenses −50				Insurance expense	−50

Equipment (and Accumulated Amortization)

(c) Mowers, edgers, rakes, and hand tools (equipment) have been used and need to be amortized. They have a total cost of $4,600 and an estimated useful life of 10 years. No residual value is expected. The company uses straight-line amortization.

Step 1. The journal entry made in the past is:

Lawn equipment (+A) 4,600
  Cash (−A) 200
  Notes Payable (+L) 4,400

Step 2. The amortization expense for April 2002 is $38 ($4,600 ÷ 120 months). The remaining amount will be recognized in future periods as the equipment is used.

	April	Month-End	Beyond April

$4,600 paid

		4/30	
	$38 expense incurred		The rest incurred in the future when the assets are used.

Step 3. The adjusting journal entry to record the amortization expense is:

4/30—Adjusting Journal Entry
Amortization expense (+E, −SE) 38
  Accumulated amortization (+XA→−A) 38

Assets	=	Liabilities	+	Shareholders' Equity	
Accumulated amortization −38				Amortization expense	−38

Accrued Expenses Payable (such as Wages, Utilities, and Interest)

(d) Wages have been paid through April 29. Wages earned in April by the employees but not yet paid accrue at $130 per day.

Step 1. No entry was made in the past.

Step 2. The amount of wages expense incurred in April will be paid in the next accounting period.

	April	Month-End	Beyond April

	1 day worked	4/30	
	$130 expense incurred		To be paid

Step 3. The adjusting journal entry to record the wages expense is:

4/30—Adjusting Journal Entry
Wages expense (+E, −SE) 130
  Wages payable (+L) 130

Assets	=	Liabilities	+	Shareholders' Equity	
		Wages payable +130		Wages expense	−130

(e) **An extra telephone line was installed in April. The telephone bill for $52, including hook-up and usage charges, was received on April 30 and will be paid in May.**

Step 1. No entry was made in the past.

Step 2. The amount of the telephone bill should be recognized in April and will be paid in May.

April	Month-End	Beyond April
	4/30	
$52 expense incurred		To be paid

Step 3. The adjusting journal entry to record the utilities expense is:

4/30—Adjusting Journal Entry
Utilities expense (+E, −SE)   52
    Accrued utilities payable (+L)   52

Assets	=	Liabilities	+	Shareholders' Equity
		Accrued utilities payable +52		Utilities expense −52

Accrued Utilities Payable (L)

	0	Bal.
	52	Incurred
	52	End.

Utilities Expense (E)

Bal.	0	
AJE	52	
End.	52	

(f) **Interest accrued on the outstanding notes payable at an annual rate of 12 percent. The $3,700 in principal has been outstanding all month.**

Step 1. The notes payable were recorded when signed. The interest incurred has not yet been recorded.

Step 2. The interest expense that should be recognized in April is $37 [$3,700 × .12 × (1/12)]. This amount is payable in a future period.

April	Month-End	Beyond April
	4/30	
$37 expense incurred		To be paid

Step 3. The adjusting journal entry to record the interest expense is:

4/30—Adjusting Journal Entry
Interest expense (+E, −SE)   37
    Interest payable (+L)   37

Assets	=	Liabilities	+	Shareholders' Equity
		Interest payable +37		Interest expense −37

Interest Payable (L)

	0	Bal.
	37	Incurred
	37	End.

Interest Expense (E)

Bal.	0	
AJE	37	
End.	37	

Income Taxes Payable

(g) **The estimated income tax rate for Terrific Lawn is 35 percent for both federal and provincial income taxes.**

Step 1. No entry was made in the past.

Step 2. The income tax expense that should be recognized in April is $344, calculated as follows:

Chapter 3 Totals + Adjustments

All revenues $5,600 = $5,200 + 400
All expenses   −4,617 = 4,310 + 50 + 38 + 130 + 52 + 37
Pretax income $ 983 × 0.35 tax rate = $344 tax expense (rounded)

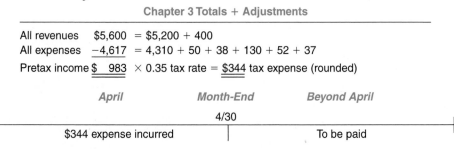

April	Month-End	Beyond April
	4/30	
$344 expense incurred		To be paid

Income Taxes Payable (L)

	0	Bal.
	344	Incurred
	344	End.

Income Tax Expense (E)

Bal.	0	
AJE	344	
End.	344	

Step 3. The adjusting journal entry to record the income tax expense follows:

4/30—Adjusting Journal Entry
Income tax expense (+E, −SE) 344
   Income taxes payable (+L) 344

Assets	=	Liabilities	+	Shareholders' Equity
		Income taxes payable +344		Income tax expense −344

2. Adjusted trial balance.

TERRIFIC LAWN MAINTENANCE CORPORATION
Trial Balance
At April 30, 2005
(in thousands of dollars)

	Unadjusted Trial Balance		Adjustments				Adjusted Trial Balance	
	Debit	Credit	Debit		Credit		Debit	Credit
Cash	5,060						5,060	
Accounts receivable	1,700						1,700	
Prepaid expenses	300			(b)	50		250	
Equipment	4,600						4,600	
Accumulated amortization		0		(c)	38			38
Land	3,750						3,750	
Accounts payable		220						220
Unearned revenue		1,600	(a)	400				1,200
Notes payable		3,700						3,700
Accrued utilities payable		0		(e)	52			52
Wages payable		0		(d)	130			130
Interest payable		0		(f)	37			37
Income taxes payable		0		(g)	344			344
Share capital		9,000						9,000
Retained earnings		0						—
Mowing revenue		5,200		(a)	400			5,600
Fuel expense	410						410	
Wages expense	3,900		(d)	130			4,030	
Insurance expense	0		(b)	50			50	
Utilities expense	0		(e)	52			52	
Amortization expense	0		(c)	38			38	
Interest expense	0		(f)	37			37	
Income tax expense	0		(g)	344			344	
Totals	19,720	19,720	1,051		1,051		20,321	20,321

3. Financial statements

TERRIFIC LAWN MAINTENANCE CORPORATION
Income Statement
For the Period Ended April 30, 2005

Revenues:

Mowing revenue	$5,600
Total revenues	5,600

Expenses:

Fuel	410
Wages	4,030
Insurance	50
Utilities	52
Amortization	38
Interest	37
Total expenses	4,617
Income before income taxes	983
Income tax expense	344
Net Income	$ 639
Earnings per share	$0.426

$639 Net Income ÷ 1,500 Shares Outstanding

TERRIFIC LAWN MAINTENANCE CORPORATION
Statement of Retained Earnings
For the Period Ended April 30, 2005

Beginning balance	$ 0
Net income	639
Dividends	0
Ending balance	$639

TERRIFIC LAWN MAINTENANCE CORPORATION
Balance Sheet
At April 30, 2005

Assets			Liabilities	
Current Assets:			**Current Liabilities:**	
Cash		$ 5,060	Accounts payable	$ 220
Accounts receivable		1,700	Unearned revenue	1,200
Prepaid expenses		250	Wages payable	130
Total current assets		7,010	Accrued utilities payable	52
Equipment	$4,600		Interest payable	37
Less: Accumulated amortization	38	4,562	Income taxes payable	344
Land		3,750	Notes payable	3,700
			Total current liabilities	5,683
			Shareholders' Equity	
			Share capital	9,000
			Retained earnings	639
			Total shareholders' equity	9,639
Total assets		$15,322	Total liabilities and shareholders' equity	$15,322

4. Closing entry

Mowing revenue (−R)	5,600	
Fuel expense (−E)		410
Wages expense (−E)		4,030
Insurance expense (−E)		50
Utilities expense (−E)		52
Amortization expense (−E)		38
Interest expense (−E)		37
Income tax expense (−E)		344
Retained earnings (+SE)		639

5. Net Profit Margin:

$$\frac{\text{Net Income}}{\text{Net Sales}} = \$639 \div \$5,600 = 11.41\% \text{ for the month of April.}$$

SOLUTION TO **SELF-STUDY QUIZZES**

Self-Study Quiz 4-1

(c) The account to be adjusted is a deferral.

Unearned revenue (−L)	100	
Sales revenue—office services (+R, +SE)		100

Self-Study Quiz 4-2

(g) The principal was recorded when the note was signed. However, the bank's money was used during the month. Using money borrowed from others entails interest expense for the period of use until the principal is repaid.

$1,000 principal × 12% annual interest rate × 1 month/12 = $10 interest expense

Both Accrued Expenses Payable (L) and Interest Expense (E) are increased by $10, resulting in $10 balances for each.

Interest expense (+E, −SE)	10	
Accrued expenses payable (+L)		10

Chapter Supplement

An Optional Recordkeeping Efficiency

In the examples on pages 170–171, cash received or paid prior to revenue or expense recognition was recorded in a balance sheet account. This approach is consistent with accrual accounting since, on the cash exchange date, either an asset or a liability exists. Payments or receipts are often recorded, however, as expenses or revenues on the transaction date. This is done to simplify recordkeeping since revenues or expenses are frequently earned or incurred by the end of the accounting period. When the full amount is not completely incurred or earned, an adjustment is necessary in these cases also. Note that, regardless of how the original entry is recorded, the same correct ending balances in the Unearned Dental Fee Revenue and Dental Fee Revenue accounts result after the adjustment. The adjusting entry is different, however, in each case.

For example, for the December 1 illustration, the original entry could have been recorded in a revenue account and adjusted as follows:

Step 1. On December 1, the amount received could have been recorded as revenue.

Cash (+A)	2,400	
Dental fee revenue (1R, 1SE)		2,400

Step 2. As time passes after receiving the fees, only a portion of the fees are earned and the rest is due as service in the future.

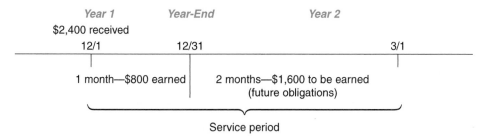

Step 3. The unearned portion ($1,600) of the revenue is a liability, with service due in the future. The remaining portion ($800) is revenue earned in the current period. The adjusting entry and translation effects follow.

	Unearned Dental Fee Revenue (L)	
	0	12/1
	1,600	AJE
	1,600	12/31

12/31 AJE— Dental fee revenue (−R, −SE)	1,600	
Unearned dental fee revenue (+L)		1,600

Assets	=	Liabilities	+	Shareholders' Equity	
		Unearned dental fee revenue	+1,600	Dental fee revenue	−1,600

	Dental Fee Revenue (R)	
	2,400	12/1
AJE 1,600		
	800	12/31

CHAPTER **TAKE-AWAYS**

1. **Explain the purpose of a trial balance in the preparation of financial statements. p. 165**
   A trial balance is a list of all accounts with their debit or credit balances indicated in the appropriate column to provide a check on the equality of the debits and credits. The trial balance may be
   • Unadjusted—before adjustments are made.
   • Adjusted—after adjustments are made.
   • Post-closing—after revenues and expenses are closed to Retained Earnings.

2. **Analyze the adjustments necessary at the end of the period to update balance sheet and income statement accounts. p. 167**
   • Adjusting entries are necessary at the end of the accounting period to measure income properly and provide for appropriate amounts for balance sheet accounts. The analysis involves
   (1) Identifying deferrals (accounts created in the past when cash was received or paid before being earned or incurred) and accruals (revenues earned and expenses incurred before cash is to be received or paid in the future).
   (2) Drawing a time line with relevant dates, amounts, and any computations included for each deferral or accrual.
   (3) Recording the adjusting entry needed to obtain the appropriate ending balances in the accounts.
   The effect is summarized as follows:

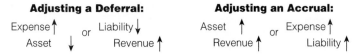

   • Recording adjusting entries has no effect on the Cash account.

3. **Present an income statement with earnings per share, a statement of retained earnings, and a balance sheet. p. 181**
   Adjusted account balances are used in preparing the following financial statements:
   • Income Statement → Revenues − Expenses = Net Income (including earnings per share computed as net income available to the common shareholders divided by the weighted-average number of common shares outstanding during the period).
   • Statement of Retained Earnings → Beginning Retained Earnings + Net Income − Dividends = Ending Retained Earnings.
   • Balance Sheet → Assets = Liabilities + Shareholders' Equity.

- Cash Flow Statement → Change in Cash = Cash Flows from Operating Activities +/− Cash Flows from Investing Activities +/− Cash Flows from Financing Activities.

4. **Compute and interpret the net profit margin ratio. p. 185**
   The net profit margin ratio (Net Income ÷ Net Sales) measures how much profit each dollar of sales generated during the period. A rising net profit margin signals more efficient management of sales and expenses.

5. **Explain the closing process. p. 186**
   Temporary accounts (revenues, expenses, gains, and losses) are closed to a zero balance at the end of the accounting period to allow for the accumulation of income items in the following period. To close these accounts:
   - Debit each revenue and gain account and credit Retained Earnings.
   - Credit each expense and loss account and debit Retained Earnings.

Each year, many companies report healthy profits but file for bankruptcy. Some investors consider this situation to be a paradox, but sophisticated analysts understand how this situation can occur. These analysts recognize that the income statement is prepared under the accrual concept (revenue is reported when earned and the related expense is matched with the revenue). The income statement does not report cash collections and cash payments. Troubled companies usually file for bankruptcy because they cannot meet their cash obligations (for example, they cannot pay their suppliers or meet their required interest payments). The income statement does not help analysts assess the cash flows of a company. The cash flow statement discussed in Chapter 5 is designed to help statement users evaluate a company's cash inflows and outflows.

KEY **RATIO**

> **The net profit margin ratio** measures how much profit each sales dollar generated during the period. A high or rising ratio suggests that the company is managing its sales and expenses efficiently. It is computed as follows (p. 185):
>
> $$\text{Net Profit Margin} = \frac{\text{Net Income}}{\text{Net Sales}}$$

FINDING FINANCIAL INFORMATION

BALANCE SHEET

Current Assets	*Current Liabilities*
Accruals include	Accruals include
Interest	Interest payable
receivable	Wages payable
Rent receivable	Utilities
Deferrals include	payable
Inventory	Income tax
Prepaid expenses	payable
Non-Current Assets	Deferrals include
Deferrals include	Deferred
Property and	revenue
equipment	
Intangibles	

INCOME STATEMENT

Revenues
  Include end-of-period adjustments
Expenses
  Include end-of-period adjustments
Income before Income Taxes
  Income tax expense

Net Income

NOTES
In Various Notes If Not on the Balance Sheet
  Details of accrued expenses payable

KEY **TERMS**

Accounting Cycle p. 165

Accrued Expenses p. 169

Accrued Revenues p. 168

Adjusting Entries p. 167

Book Value (Net Book Value, Carrying Value) p. 167

Closing Entries p. 186

Contra Account p. 167

Deferred Expenses p. 168

Deferred Revenues p. 168

Income Summary p. 186

Materiality p. 179

Permanent (Real) Accounts p. 186

Post-Closing Trial Balance p. 186

Temporary (Nominal) Accounts p. 186

Trial Balance p. 165

QUESTIONS

1. Explain the accounting information processing cycle.
2. Identify, in sequence, the phases of the accounting information processing cycle.
3. What is a trial balance? What is its purpose?
4. Briefly explain adjusting entries. List the four types of adjusting entries, and give an example of each type.
5. Explain estimated residual value. Why is it important in measuring amortization expense?
6. What is a contra asset? Give an example of one.
7. Explain why adjusting entries are entered in the journal on the last day of the accounting period and then are posted to the ledger.
8. Explain how the financial statements relate to each other.
9. What is the equation for each of the following statements: (a) income statement, (b) balance sheet, (c) cash flow statement, and (d) statement of retained earnings?
10. Explain the effect of adjusting entries on cash.
11. How is earnings per share computed and interpreted?
12. Contrast an unadjusted trial balance with an adjusted trial balance. What is the purpose of each?
13. What is the purpose of closing entries? Why are they recorded in the journal and posted to the ledger?
14. Differentiate among (a) permanent, (b) temporary, (c) real, and (d) nominal accounts.
15. Why are the income statement accounts closed but the balance sheet accounts are not?
16. What is a post-closing trial balance? Is it a useful part of the accounting information processing cycle? Explain.
17. How is the net profit margin ratio computed and interpreted?

MULTIPLE-CHOICE QUESTIONS

1. Which of the following accounts would not appear in a closing entry?
   a. Interest Revenue
   b. Accumulated Amortization
   c. Retained Earnings
   d. Salary Expense
2. Which account is least likely to appear in an adjusting journal entry?
   a. Cash
   b. Interest Receivable
   c. Property Tax Expense
   d. Salaries Payable
3. When a concert promoting company collects cash for ticket sales two months in advance of the show date, the following account is credited.
   a. Accrued Expense
   b. Accrued Revenue
   c. Deferred Expense
   d. Deferred Revenue
4. On December 31 (fiscal year-end), an adjustment is made to reclassify a portion of unearned revenue as earned revenue. How many accounts on the year-end balance sheet will be affected by this entry?
   a. None
   b. One
   c. Two
   d. Three
5. Failure to make an adjusting entry to recognize accrued salaries payable would cause
   a. an overstatement of assets and shareholders' equity.
   b. an overstatement of assets and liabilities.
   c. an understatement of expenses, liabilities, and shareholders' equity.
   d. an understatement of expenses and liabilities and an overstatement of shareholders' equity.

6. An adjusted trial balance
   a. shows the ending balances in a "debit" and "credit" format before posting the adjusting journal entries.
   b. is prepared after closing entries have been posted.
   c. is a tool used by financial analysts to review the performance of publicly traded companies.
   d. shows the ending balances resulting from the adjusting journal entries in a "debit" and "credit" format.

7. Which of the following statements regarding amortization of a building is false?
   a. Amortization represents the decline in the value of the building over time.
   b. Amortization is an estimated expense to be recorded over the building's estimated useful life.
   c. As amortization is recorded, shareholders' equity is reduced.
   d. As amortization is recorded, assets are reduced.

8. Which of the following columns in a trial balance are used as a source for preparing the income statement?
   a. Unadjusted Trial Balance   c. Adjusted Trial Balance
   b. Adjustments   d. Post-Closing Trial Balance

9. What ratio is required by GAAP to be reported on the financial statements or in the notes to the statements?
   a. Return on equity ratio   c. Current ratio
   b. Net profit margin ratio   d. Earnings per share ratio

10. If a company is successful in reducing selling and administrative expenses while maintaining sales volume and the sales price of its product, then the net profit margin ratio
    a. will not change.   c. will decrease.
    b. will increase.   d. will either decrease or remain unchanged.

For more practice with multiple-choice questions, go to our Web site at www.mcgrawhill.ca/college/libby, click on "Student Edition" in the upper left menu, click on this chapter's name and number from the list of contents, and then click on "Multiple-Choice Quiz" from the menu on the left.

EXERCISES

■ **LO1**

E4–1 Preparing a Trial Balance

Swanson Company has the following adjusted accounts and balances at year-end (June 30, 2005):

Accounts payable	200	Cash	120	Land	200
Accounts receivable	400	Cost of sales	820	Long-term debt	1,300
Accrued expenses		Income taxes		Prepaid expenses	40
payable	150	expense	110	Rent expense	400
Accumulated		Income taxes		Retained earnings	170
amortization	250	payable	30	Salaries expense	660
Amortization expense	110	Interest expense	80	Sales revenue	2,400
Buildings and		Interest income	50	Share capital	300
equipment	1,400	Inventories	610	Unearned fees	100

All these accounts have normal debit or credit balances.

Required:
Prepare an adjusted trial balance in good form for the Swanson Company at June 30, 2005.

■ **LO2**

E4–2 Matching Definitions with Terms

Match each definition with its related term by entering the appropriate letter in the space provided.

Definition	Term
_____ 1. At year-end, wages payable of $3,600 had not been recorded or paid.	A. Accrued expense
_____ 2. Supplies for office use were purchased during the year for $500, and $100 of the office supplies remained on hand (unused) at year-end.	B. Deferred expense
	C. Accrued revenue
_____ 3. Interest of $250 on a note receivable was earned at year-end, although collection of the interest is not due until the following year.	D. Deferred revenue
_____ 4. At year-end, service revenue of $2,000 was collected in cash but was not yet earned.	

E4–3 Identifying Adjusting Entries from Unadjusted Trial Balance   ■ **LO1,2**

As stated in its annual report, Unik Computer Corporation is an information technology
company, developing and marketing hardware, software, solutions, and services. Following
is a hypothetical trial balance listing account that Unik uses. Assume that the balances are
unadjusted at the end of a recent fiscal year ended December 31.

UNIK COMPUTER CORPORATION
Unadjusted Trial Balance
At December 31, 2006
(millions of dollars)

	Debit	Credit
Cash	$ 4,091	
Accounts receivable	6,998	
Inventories	2,005	
Prepaid expenses	624	
Property, plant, and equipment	5,223	
Accumulated amortization		$ 2,321
Intangible assets	3,641	
Other assets	3,414	
Accounts payable		4,237
Accrued liabilities		1,110
Income taxes payable		282
Pension obligations		545
Other liabilities		5,104
Share capital		7,270
Retained earnings		8,633
Product revenue		27,372
Services revenue		3,797
Cost of products sold	21,383	
Cost of services sold	2,597	
Selling, general, and administrative expenses	4,978	
Research and development costs	1,353	
Other operating expenses	4,283	
Income tax expense	81	
	60,671	60,671

Required

1. Based on the information in the unadjusted trial balance, list the balance sheet deferral
   accounts that may need to be adjusted at December 31 and the related income statement
   account in each case (no computations are necessary).

2. Based on the information in the unadjusted trial balance, list the balance sheet accrual
   accounts that may need to be recorded at December 31 and the related income statement
   account in each case (no computations are necessary).

▨ LO2

E4–4 Recording Adjusting Entries and Determining Financial Statement Effects (Deferral Accounts)

Consider the following transactions for Liner Company.

  a. Collected $900 rent for the period December 1, 2005, to March 1, 2006, which was credited to Deferred Rent Revenue on December 1, 2005.

  b. Paid $1,200 for a one-year insurance premium on July 1, 2005; debited Prepaid Insurance for that amount.

  c. Purchased a machine for $10,000 cash on January 1, 2004; estimated a useful life of five years with a residual value of $2,000.

Required:

  1. Prepare the adjusting entries required for the year ended December 31, 2005, using the process illustrated in the chapter.

  2. For each of the transactions above, indicate the amounts and direction of effects of the adjusting entry on the elements of the balance sheet and income statement. Using the following format, indicate + for increase, − for decrease, and NE for no effect.

	Balance Sheet			**Income Statement**		
Transaction	Assets	Liabilities	Shareholders' Equity	Revenues	Expenses	Net Income
a.						
b.						
c.						

▨ LO2

E4–5 Recording Adjusting Entries and Determining Financial Statement Effects (Accrual Accounts)

Consider the following transactions for Liner Company.

  a. Received a $220 utility bill for electricity usage in December to be paid in January 2006.

  b. Owed wages to 10 employees who worked three days at $150 each per day at the end of December. The company will pay employees at the end of the first week of January 2006.

  c. On September 1, 2005, loaned $5,000 to an officer who will repay the loan in one year at an annual interest rate of 12 percent.

Required:

  1. Prepare the adjusting entries required for the year ended December 31, 2005, using the process illustrated in the chapter:

  2. For each of the transactions above, indicate the amounts and direction of effects of the adjusting entry on the elements of the balance sheet and income statement. Using the following format, indicate + for increase, − for decrease, and NE for no effect.

	Balance Sheet			**Income Statement**		
Transaction	Assets	Liabilities	Shareholders' Equity	Revenues	Expenses	Net Income
a.						
b.						
c.						

▨ LO2

E4–6 Recording Adjusting Entries

Evans Company completed its first year of operations on December 31, 2004. All of the 2004 entries have been recorded, except for the following:

  a. At year-end, employees earned wages of $6,000, which will be paid on the next payroll date, January 6, 2005.

  b. At year-end, the company had earned interest revenue of $3,000. The cash will be collected March 1, 2005.

Required

  1. What is the annual reporting period for this company?

2. Identify whether each transaction above is a deferral or an accrual. Using the process illustrated in the chapter, prepare the required adjusting entry for Transactions (*a*) and (*b*). Include appropriate dates and write a brief explanation of each entry.

3. Why are these adjustments made?

E4–7 Recording Adjusting Entries and Reporting Balances in Financial Statements   ■ **LO2, 3**

Dion, Ltée is making adjusting entries for the year ended December 31, 2006. In developing information for the adjusting entries, the accountant learned the following:

a. Paid a one-year insurance premium of $3,000 on September 1, 2006, for coverage beginning on that date.

b. At December 31, 2006, obtained the following data relating to shipping supplies from the records and supporting documents. The company uses a large amount of shipping supplies that are purchased in volume, stored, and used as needed.

Shipping supplies on hand, January 1, 2006	$15,000
Purchases of shipping supplies during 2006	70,000
Shipping supplies on hand, per inventory December 31, 2006	11,000

Required

1. What amount should be reported on the 2006 income statement for Insurance Expense? For Shipping Supplies Expense?

2. What amount should be reported on the December 31, 2006, balance sheet for Prepaid Insurance? For Shipping Supplies Inventory?

3. Using the process illustrated in the chapter, record the adjusting entry for insurance at December 31, 2006, assuming that the bookkeeper debited the full amount paid on September 1, 2006, to Prepaid Insurance.

4. Using the process illustrated in the chapter, record the adjusting entry for shipping supplies at December 31, 2006, assuming that the purchases of shipping supplies were debited in full to Shipping Supplies Inventory.

E4–8 Recording Seven Typical Adjusting Entries   ■ **LO2**

Crawford's Department Store is completing the accounting process for the year just ended, December 31, 2006. The transactions during 2006 have been journalized and posted. The following data with respect to adjusting entries are available:

a. Office supplies inventory at January 1, 2006, was $350. Office supplies purchased and debited to Office Supplies Inventory during the year amounted to $800. The year-end inventory showed $300 of supplies on hand.

b. Wages earned during December 2006, unpaid and unrecorded at December 31, 2006, amounted to $2,700. The last payroll date was December 28; the next pay date will be January 6, 2007.

c. Three-fourths of the basement of the store is rented for $1,300 per month to another merchant, M. Riesman. Riesman sells compatible, but not competitive, merchandise. On November 1, 2006, the store collected six months' rent in the amount of $7,800 in advance from Riesman and credited the amount to Unearned Rent Revenue.

d. The remaining basement space is rented to Rita's Specialty Shop for $520 per month, payable monthly. On December 31, 2006, the rent for November and December 2006 was neither collected nor recorded. Collection is expected on January 10, 2007.

e. The store used delivery equipment that cost $30,000 and was estimated to have a useful life of four years and a residual value of $6,000 at the end of the four years. Assume amortization for a full year for 2006. The asset will be amortized evenly over its useful life.

f. On July 1, 2006, a one-year insurance premium amounting to $1,800 was paid in cash and debited to Prepaid Insurance. Coverage began on July 1, 2006.

g. Crawford's operates an alteration shop to meet its own needs. The shop also does alterations for M. Riesman. At the end of December 31, 2006, Riesman had not paid for alterations completed, amounting to $750. This amount has not yet been recorded as Alteration Shop Revenue. Collection is expected during January 2007.

Required

1. Identify each of these transactions as a deferred revenue, deferred expense, accrued revenue, or accrued expense.

2. Using the process illustrated in the chapter, prepare for each situation the adjusting entry that should be recorded for Crawford's at December 31, 2006.

■ **LO2, 3**   **E4–9 Determining Financial Statement Effects of Seven Typical Adjusting Entries**
Refer to E4–8.

Required:

For each of the transactions in E4–8, indicate the amount and direction of effects of the adjusting entry on the elements of the balance sheet and income statement. Using the following format, indicate + for increase, − for decrease, and NE for no effect.

	Balance Sheet			Income Statement		
Transaction	Assets	Liabilities	Shareholders' Equity	Revenues	Expenses	Net Income
a.						
b.						
c.						
etc.						

■ **LO2, 4**   **E4–10 Recording Transactions Including Adjusting and Closing Entries (Non-Quantitative)**
The following accounts are used by Kelsey's Kitchen, Inc.

Codes	Accounts	Codes	Accounts
A	Cash	J	Share capital
B	Office supplies inventory	K	Retained earnings
C	Revenue receivable	L	Service revenue
D	Office equipment	M	Interest revenue
E	Accumulated amortization	N	Wage expense
F	Note payable	O	Amortization expense
G	Wages payable	P	Interest expense
H	Interest payable	Q	Supplies expense
I	Unearned service revenue	R	None of the above

Required:

For each of the following nine independent situations, record the journal entry by entering the appropriate code(s) and amount(s).

		Debit		Credit	
	Independent Situations	Code	Amount	Code	Amount
a.	Accrued wages, unrecorded and unpaid at year-end, $400 (example).	N	400	G	400
b.	Service revenue collected in advance, $800.				
c.	Dividends declared and paid during year, $900.				
d.	Amortization expense for year, $1,000.				
e.	Service revenue earned but not yet collected at year-end, $600.				
f.	Office Supplies Inventory account at beginning of the year, $400; inventory of supplies on hand at year-end, $150. (No purchases during the year.)				
g.	At year-end, interest on note payable not yet recorded or paid, $220.				
h.	Balance at year-end in Service Revenue account, $62,000. Record the closing entry at year-end.				
i.	Balance at year-end in Interest Expense account, $420. Record the closing entry at year-end.				

E4–11 Determining Financial Statement Effects of Three Adjusting Entries   ■ LO2, 3

Kwan Corp. started operations on January 1, 2006. It is now December 31, 2006, the end of the fiscal year. The part-time bookkeeper needs your help to analyze the following three transactions:

a. On January 1, 2006, the company purchased a special machine for a cash cost of $15,000. The machine has an estimated useful life of 10 years and no residual value.

b. During 2006, the company purchased office supplies that cost $1,600. At the end of 2006, office supplies worth $400 remained on hand.

c. On July 1, 2006, the company paid cash of $600 for a one-year premium on an insurance policy on the machine. Coverage began on July 1, 2006.

Required:

Complete the following schedule of the amounts that should be reported for 2006:

Selected Balance Sheet Amounts at December 31, 2006	Amount to Be Reported
Assets	
Equipment	$ _____
Accumulated amortization	_____
Carrying value of equipment	_____
Office supplies inventory	_____
Prepaid insurance	_____
Selected Income Statement Amounts for the Year Ended December 31, 2006	
Expenses	
Amortization expense	$ _____
Office supplies expense	_____
Insurance expense	_____

E4–12 Inferring Transactions   ■ LO2

Deere & Company is the world's leading producer of agricultural equipment; a leading supplier of a broad range of industrial equipment for construction, forestry, and public works; a producer and marketer of a broad line of lawn and grounds care equipment; and a provider of credit, managed health care plans, and insurance products for businesses and the general public. The following information is taken from an annual report (in millions of dollars):

Deere & Company

Income Taxes Payable				Dividends Payable				Interest Payable		
		Beg. bal.	71			Beg. bal.	43		Beg. bal.	45
(a)	?	(b)	332	(c)	?	(d)	176	(e) 297	(f)	?
		End. bal.	80			End. bal.	48		End. bal.	51

Required:

1. Identify the nature of each of the Transactions (a) through (f). Specifically, what activities cause the accounts to increase and decrease?

2. Compute the amounts of Transactions (a), (c), and (f).

E4–13 Analyzing the Effects of Errors on Financial Statement Items   ■ LO2, 3

Scarletti and Long, Inc., publishers of movie and song trivia books, made the following errors in adjusting the accounts at year-end (December 31):

a. Did not record amortization on equipment costing $130,000 with a residual value of $30,000 and a 10-year useful life.

b. Failed to adjust the Unearned Revenue account to reflect that $3,000 was earned by the end of the year.

c. Recorded a full year of accrued interest expense on a $15,000, 10-percent note payable that has been outstanding since November 1 of the current year.

d. Failed to adjust Insurance Expense to reflect that $400 relates to future insurance coverage.

e. Did not accrue $800 owed to the company by another company renting part of the building as a storage facility.

Required:

1. For each error, prepare (a) the adjusting journal entry that was made, if any, and (b) the entry that should have been made at year-end.

2. Using the following headings, indicate the effect of each error and the amount of the effect (that is, the difference between the entry that was or was not made and the entry that should have been made). Use O if the effect overstates the item, U if the effect understates the item, and NE if there is no effect.

	Balance Sheet			Income Statement		
Transaction	Assets	Liabilities	Shareholders' Equity	Revenues	Expenses	Net Income
a.						
b.						
c.						
etc.						

3. Explain the concept of materiality and how it might affect the adjusting entries you prepared in requirement 1.

LO2, 3   **E4–14   Analyzing the Effects of Adjusting Entries on the Income Statement and Balance Sheet**

On December 31, 2005, Cohen and Company prepared an income statement and balance sheet but failed to take into account four adjusting entries. The income statement, prepared on this incorrect basis, reflected pretax income of $30,000. The balance sheet (before the effect of income taxes) reflected total assets, $90,000; total liabilities, $40,000; and shareholders' equity, $50,000. The data for the four adjusting entries follow:

a. Amortization for the year on equipment that cost $75,000 was not recorded. The equipment's useful life is 10 years and its residual value is $5,000.

b. Wages amounting to $17,000 for the last three days of December 2005 were not paid and not recorded (the next pay date is January 10, 2006).

c. An amount of $4,500 was collected on December 1, 2005, for rental of office space for the period December 1, 2005, to February 28, 2006. The $4,500 was credited in full to Unearned Rent Revenue when collected.

d. Income taxes were not recorded. The income tax rate for the company is 30 percent.

Required:

Complete the following tabulation to correct the financial statements for the effects of the four errors (indicate deductions with parentheses):

Items	Net Income	Total Assets	Total Liabilities	Shareholders' Equity
Balances reported	$30,000	$90,000	$40,000	$50,000
Effect of amortization				
Effect of wages				
Effect of rent revenue				
Adjusted balances				
Effect of income taxes				
Correct balances				

LO2, 3, 4   **E4–15   Reporting a Correct Income Statement with Earnings per Share to Include the Effects of Adjusting Entries and Evaluating the Net Profit Margin as an Auditor**

Barton, Inc., completed its first year of operations on December 31, 2006. Because this is the end of the fiscal year, the company bookkeeper prepared the following tentative income statement:

Income Statement, 2006		
Rental revenue		$114,000
Expenses:		
Salaries and wages expense	$28,500	
Maintenance expense	12,000	
Rent expense (on location)	9,000	
Utilities expense	4,000	
Gas and oil expense	3,000	
Miscellaneous expenses (items not listed elsewhere)	1,000	
Total expenses		57,500
Income		$ 56,500

You are an independent accountant hired by the company to audit its accounting systems and review its financial statements. In your audit, you developed additional data as follows:

a. Unpaid wages for the last three days of December amounting to $330 were not recorded.

b. The unpaid $400 telephone bill for December 2006 has not been recorded.

c. Amortization on rental autos, amounting to $22,000 for 2006, was not recorded.

d. Interest on a $20,000, one-year, 9-percent note payable dated October 1, 2006, was not recorded. The full amount of interest is payable on the maturity date of the note.

e. The Unearned Rental Revenue account has a balance of $4,000 as at December 31, 2006 which represents rental revenue for the month of January 2007.

f. Maintenance expense includes $1,000, which is the cost of maintenance supplies still on hand at December 31, 2006. These supplies will be used in 2007.

g. The income tax expense is $7,300. Payment of income tax will be made in 2007.

Required:

1. For each item (*a*) through (*g*) what adjusting entry, if any, do you recommend that Barton should record at December 31, 2006? If none is required, explain why.

2. Prepare a correct income statement for 2006 in good form including earnings per share, assuming that 7,000 shares are outstanding. Show computations.

3. Compute net profit margin based on the corrected information. What does this ratio suggest? If the industry average for net profit margin is 18 percent, what might you infer about Barton?

E4–16 Evaluating the Effect of Adjusting Unearned Subscriptions on Cash Flows and Performance as a Manager

■ **LO3**

You are the regional sales manager for Weld News Company. Weld is making adjusting entries for the year ended March 31, 2006. On September 1, 2005, $12,000 cash was received from customers in your region for two-year magazine subscriptions beginning on that date. The magazines are published and mailed to customers monthly. These were the only subscription sales in your region during the year.

Required:

1. What amount should be reported as cash from operations on the 2006 cash flow statement?

2. What amount should be reported on the 2006 income statement for subscriptions revenue?

3. What amount should be reported on the March 31, 2006, balance sheet for unearned subscriptions revenue?

4. Prepare the adjusting entry at March 31, 2006, assuming that the subscriptions received on September 1, 2005, were recorded for the full amount in Unearned Subscriptions Revenue.

5. The company expects your region's annual revenue target to be $4,000.
   a. Evaluate your region's performance, assuming that the revenue target is based on cash sales.
   b. Evaluate your region's performance, assuming that the revenue target is based on accrual accounting.

■ **LO2**

E4–17 Recording Adjusting Entries, Completing a Trial Balance, and Preparing Financial Statements

Cayuga Ltd. prepared the following trial balance at the end of its first year of operations ending December 31, 2007. To simplify the case, the amounts given are in thousands of dollars. Other data not yet recorded at December 31, 2007:

a. Insurance expired during 2007, $4.

b. Amortization expense for 2007, $4.

c. Wages payable, $8.

d. Income tax expense, $9.

Account Titles	Unadjusted		Adjustments		Adjusted	
	Debit	Credit	Debit	Credit	Debit	Credit
Cash	38					
Accounts receivable	9					
Prepaid insurance	6					
Machinery (20-year life, no residual value)	80					
Accumulated amortization		8				
Accounts payable		9				
Wages payable						
Income taxes payable						
Share capital (4,000 shares)		68				
Retained earnings (deficit)	4					
Revenues (not detailed)		84				
Expenses (not detailed)	32					
Totals	169	169				

Required:

1. Prepare the adjusting entries for 2007.

2. Complete the trial balance Adjustments and Adjusted columns.

3. Using the adjusted balances, complete the following income statement and statement of retained earnings for 2007, and the balance sheet at December 31, 2007.

Income Statement
For the Year Ended December 31, 2007
(in thousands except for earnings per share)

Revenues (not detailed)	$ _____
Expenses (not detailed)	_____
Income before income tax	_____
Income tax expense	_____
Net income	$ _____
Earnings per share	$ _____

Statement of Retained Earnings
For the Year Ended December 31, 2007
(in thousands)

Beginning balance, January 1, 2007	$ _____
Net income	_____
Dividends declared	_____
Ending balance, December 31, 2007	$ _____

Balance Sheet
December 31, 2007
(in thousands)

Assets		Liabilities	
Cash	$ _____	Accounts payable	$ _____
Accounts receivable	_____	Wages payable	_____
Prepaid insurance	_____	Income taxes payable	_____
Machinery	_____	Total liabilities	_____
Accumulated amortization	_____		
		Shareholders' Equity	
		Share capital	_____
	_____	Retained earnings	_____
		Total liabilities and	
Total assets	$ _____	shareholders' equity	$ _____

E4–18 Recording Closing Entries   ■ **LO5**

Refer to E4–17.

Required:

Using the adjusted balances in E4–17, prepare the closing entries for 2007. What is the purpose of "closing the books" at the end of the accounting period?

E4–19 Preparing Financial Statements and Analyzing Net Profit Margin   ■ **LO3, 5**

Liner Company has the following adjusted trial balance at December 31, 2006. No dividends were declared; however, 400 additional shares were issued during the year for $2,000:

	Debit	Credit
Cash	$ 2,700	
Accounts receivable	3,000	
Interest receivable	120	
Prepaid insurance	600	
Notes receivable	3,000	
Equipment	12,000	
Accumulated amortization		$ 2,000
Accounts payable		1,600
Accrued expenses payable		3,820
Income taxes payable		2,900
Deferred rent revenue		600
Share capital (500 shares)		2,400
Retained earnings		1,000
Sales revenue		45,000
Interest revenue		120
Rent revenue		300
Wages expense	20,600	
Amortization expense	2,000	
Utilities expense	1,220	
Insurance expense	600	
Rent expense	10,000	
Income tax expense	3,900	
Total	$59,740	$59,740

Required:

1. Prepare an income statement in good form for 2006. Include earnings per share.
2. Prepare a statement of retained earnings in good form for 2006.
3. Prepare a balance sheet in good form at December 31, 2006.
4. Compute Liner Company's net profit margin for the year. What does this ratio mean?

■ **LO2**

E4–20 Inferring Adjusting Entries from Incomplete Trial Balance

The trial balance of PQ Ltd. included the following accounts at January 31, 2006.

	Unadjusted Trial Balance		Adjusted Trial Balance	
	Debit	Credit	Debit	Credit
Cash	$ 4,580		$ 4,580	
Accounts receivable	4,000		4,750	
Office supplies	500		180	
Office equipment	8,000		8,000	
Accumulated amortization— office equipment		3,500		3,625
Accounts payable		1,750		1,750
Salaries payable				780
Unearned consulting revenue		600		250
Share capital		12,000		12,000
Retained earnings		1,650		1,650
Dividends declared	500		500	
Consulting revenue		6,380		7,480
Salaries expense	6,500		7,280	
Office supplies expense			320	
Rent expense	1,800		1,800	
Amortization expense			125	

Required:

1. Determine which accounts have been adjusted on January 31 by comparing the unadjusted account balances to the adjusted balances.

2. Prepare the adjusting journal entries that must have been made to cause these changes in account balances. Include an explanation as part of each adjusting entry.

PROBLEMS

■ **LO1**

Dell Inc.

P4–1 Preparing a Trial Balance (AP4–1)

Dell Inc. is the world's largest computer systems company selling directly to customers. Products include desktop computer systems, notebook computers, workstations, network server and storage products, and peripheral hardware and software. The following is a list of accounts and amounts reported in recent financial statements. The accounts have normal debit or credit balances and the dollars are rounded to the nearest million. Assume the year ended on January 29, 2006.

Accounts payable	$ 7,316	Investments	$ 6,770	Research and development expense	$	464
Accounts receivable	3,635	Long-term debt	505			
Accrued expenses payable	3,580	Other current assets	1,910	Retained earnings		?
Accumulated amortization	1,133	Other income	180	Sales revenue		41,444
Cash	4,317	Other non-current liabilities	1,630	Selling, general, and		
Cost of sales	33,892	Property, plant, and		administrative expenses		3,544
Income tax expense	1,079	equipment	2,650	Share capital		149
Inventories	327			Short-term investments		835

Required:

Prepare an adjusted trial balance at January 29, 2006. How did you determine the amount for retained earnings?

■ **LO2, 3**

P4–2 Recording Adjusting Entries (AP4–2)

McGraw Company's fiscal year ends on December 31. It is December 31, 2005, and all of the 2005 entries have been made, except the following adjusting entries.

a. On September 1, 2005, McGraw collected six months' rent of $5,400 on storage space. At that date, McGraw debited Cash and credited Unearned Rent Revenue for $5,400.

b. The company earned service revenue of $2,000 on a special job that was completed December 29, 2005. Collection will be made during January 2006; no entry has been recorded.

c. On November 1, 2005, McGraw paid a premium of $4,200 for a one-year property insurance policy, for coverage starting on that date. Cash was credited and Prepaid Insurance was debited for this amount.

d. At December 31, 2005, wages earned by employees totalled $1,500. The employees will be paid on the next payroll date, January 15, 2006.

e. Amortization must be recognized on a service truck that cost $12,000 on July 1, 2005 (estimated useful life is six years with no residual value).

f. Cash of $1,500 was collected on November 1, 2005, for services to be rendered evenly over the next year beginning on November 1 (Unearned Service Revenue was credited).

g. On December 27, 2005, the company received a tax bill of $450 from the city for property taxes on land for 2005. The amount is payable during January 2006.

h. On October 1, 2005, the company borrowed $12,000 from a local bank and signed a 10-percent note for that amount. The principal and interest are payable on September 30, 2006.

Required:

1. Indicate whether each transaction relates to a deferred revenue, deferred expense, accrued revenue, or accrued expense.

2. Prepare the adjusting entry required for each transaction at December 31, 2005.

P4–3 **Recording Adjusting Entries and Determining Their Financial Statement** ■ **LO2, 3**
Effects (AP4–3)

Handy Haulers Company is at the end of its fiscal year, December 31, 2006. The following data were developed from the company's records and related documents:

a. On July 1, 2006, a one-year insurance premium on equipment in the amount of $1,200 was paid and debited to Prepaid Insurance. Coverage began on July 1.

b. During 2006, office supplies amounting to $900 were purchased for cash and debited in full to Supplies Inventory. At the end of 2005, the inventory of supplies remaining on hand (unused) amounted to $200. The inventory of supplies on hand at December 31, 2006, showed $300.

c. On December 31, 2006, Bert's Garage completed repairs on one of the company's trucks at a cost of $800; the amount is not yet recorded and by agreement will be paid during January 2007.

d. In December 2006, a tax bill for $1,500 on land owned during 2006 was received from the city. The taxes, which have not been recorded, are due on February 15, 2007.

e. On December 31, 2006, the company completed a contract for another company. The bill was for $8,000 payable within 30 days. No journal entry has been made for this transaction.

f. On July 1, 2006, the company purchased a new hauling van at a cash cost of $23,600. The estimated useful life of the van was 10 years, with an estimated residual value of $2,000. No amortization has been recorded for 2006 (compute amortization for six months in 2006).

g. On October 1, 2006, the company borrowed $10,000 from the local bank on a one-year, 9-percent note payable. The principal plus interest is payable on September 30, 2007.

h. The income before any of the adjustments or income taxes was $30,000. The company's income tax rate is 30 percent. Compute the adjusted income after considering the effects of Transactions (a) through (g) to determine the income tax expense for 2006.

Required:

1. Indicate whether each transaction relates to a deferred revenue, deferred expense, accrued revenue, or accrued expense.

2. Prepare the adjusting entry required for each transaction at December 31, 2006.

3. Using the following headings, indicate the effect of each adjusting entry and the amount of each. Use + for increase, − for decrease, and NE for no effect.

	Balance Sheet			Income Statement		
Transaction	Assets	Liabilities	Shareholders' Equity	Revenues	Expenses	Net Income
a.						
b.						
c.						
etc.						

LO3

P4–4 **Computing Amounts on Financial Statements and Finding Financial Information** (AP4–4)
The following transactions and events are provided by the records of South Hill Apartments (a corporation) at the end of its fiscal year, December 31, 2005:

> Revenue
> *a.* Rent revenue collected in cash during 2005 for occupancy in 2005 — $512,000
> *b.* Rent revenue earned for occupancy in December 2005; not collected until 2006 — 16,000
> *c.* Rent collected in December 2005 in advance of occupancy in January 2006 — 12,000
>
> Salaries
> *d.* Cash payment in January 2005 for employee salaries earned in December 2004 — 4,000
> *e.* Salaries incurred and paid during 2005 — 62,000
> *f.* Salaries earned by employees during December 2005 that will be paid in January 2006 — 3,000
> *g.* Cash advance to employees in December 2005 for salaries that will be earned in January 2006 — 1,500
>
> Supplies
> *h.* Maintenance supplies inventory on January 1, 2005 (balance on hand) — 3,000
> *i.* Maintenance supplies purchased for cash during 2005 — 8,000
> *j.* Maintenance supplies inventory on December 31, 2005 — 1,700

Required:
Using T-accounts, compute the amounts that should be reported in South Hill's 2005 financial statements for the following items, and indicate on which financial statement the item is reported. For Cash, create one T-account and label each effect to determine the amounts affecting cash as indicated here (from tenants, to suppliers, to employees):

1. Rent revenue
2. Salary expense
3. Maintenance supplies expense
4. Cash from tenants
5. Rent receivable
6. Cash to suppliers
7. Receivables from employees
8. Maintenance supplies inventory
9. Unearned rent revenue
10. Salaries payable
11. Cash to employees

LO1, 2, 4, 5 **P4–5** **Inferring Year-End Adjustments, Computing Earnings per Share and Net Profit Margin, and Recording Closing Entry** (AP4–5)
Willenborg Company is completing the information processing cycle at its fiscal year-end, December 31, 2007. Following are the correct account balances at December 31, 2007, both before and after the adjusting entries for 2007.

	Trial Balance, December 31, 2007					
	Before Adjusting Entries		Adjustments		After Adjusting Entries	
Items	Debit	Credit	Debit	Credit	Debit	Credit
a. Cash	$ 9,000				$ 9,000	
b. Service revenue receivable					400	
c. Prepaid insurance	600				400	
d. Equipment	120,200				120,200	
e. Accumulated amortization, equipment		$31,500				$ 40,000
f. Accrued advertising payable						4,700
g. Share capital		80,000				80,000
h. Retained earnings, January 1, 2007		14,000				14,000
i. Service revenue		46,000				46,400
j. Salary expense	41,700				41,700	
k. Amortization expense					8,500	
l. Insurance expense					200	
m. Advertising expense					4,700	
	$171,500	$171,500			$185,100	$185,100

Required:

1. Compare the amounts in the columns before and after the adjusting entries to reconstruct the adjusting entries made in 2007. Provide an explanation for each adjustment.

2. Compute the amount of income, assuming that it is based on the amounts (a) before adjusting entries and (b) after adjusting entries. Which income amount is correct? Explain.

3. Compute the earnings per share, assuming that 4,000 shares are outstanding.

4. Compute the net profit margin. What does this suggest to you about the company?

5. Record the closing entries at December 31, 2007.

P4–6 Recording Adjusting and Closing Entries and Preparing a Balance Sheet and an Income Statement Including Earnings per Share (AP4–6) ■ **LO1, 2, 3, 5**

Mostert, Inc., a small service company, keeps its records without the help of an accountant. After much effort, an outside accountant prepared the following unadjusted trial balance as at the end of the company's fiscal year, December 31, 2006:

Data not yet recorded at December 31, 2006, include:

a. The supplies inventory on December 31, 2006, reflected $200 remaining on hand.

b. Insurance expired during 2006, $400.

c. Amortization expense for 2006, $4,000.

d. Wages earned by employees not yet paid on December 31, 2006, $1,100.

e. Income tax expense was $7,350.

Account Titles	Debit	Credit
Cash	60,000	
Accounts receivable	13,000	
Service supplies inventory	800	
Prepaid insurance	1,000	
Service trucks (5-year life, no residual value)	20,000	
Accumulated amortization, service trucks		12,000
Other assets	11,200	
Accounts payable		3,000
Note payable (3 years; 10% each December 31)		20,000
Share capital (5,000 shares outstanding)		28,200
Retained earnings		7,500
Service revenue		77,000
Other expenses, excluding income tax	41,700	
Totals	147,700	147,700

Required:

1. Record the adjusting entries at December 31, 2006.

2. Prepare an income statement for 2006 and a balance sheet at December 31, 2006, including the effects of the preceding five transactions.

3. Assume that you forgot to adjust the balance of the service supplies inventory account. How would this error affect the amount of net income? Does this error lead to a material effect on net income? Explain.

4. Record the closing entry at December 31, 2006.

■ **LO1, 2, 3, 4, 5**   **P4–7   Comprehensive Review Problem: From Recording Transactions (including Adjusting and Closing Entries) to Preparing a Complete Set of Financial Statements and Performing Ratio Analysis (see Chapters 2, 3, and 4)** (AP4–7)

Brothers Hadi and Hamid Gaber began operations of their tool and die shop (H & H Tool, Inc.) on January 1, 2005. The company's fiscal year ends on December 31. The trial balance on January 1, 2006, was as follows (the amounts are rounded to thousands of dollars):

Account No.	Account Titles	Debit	Credit
01	Cash	3	
02	Accounts receivable	5	
03	Service supplies inventory	12	
04	Land		
05	Equipment	60	
06	Accumulated amortization (equipment)		6
07	Other assets (not detailed to simplify)	4	
11	Accounts payable		5
12	Notes payable		
13	Wages payable		
14	Interest payable		
15	Income taxes payable		
21	Share capital (65,000 shares)		65
31	Retained earnings		8
35	Service revenue		
40	Amortization expense		
41	Income tax expense		
42	Interest expense		
43	Other expenses		
	Totals	84	84

Transactions and events during 2006 (summarized in thousands of dollars) follow:

a. Borrowed $10 cash on a 12-percent note payable, dated March 1, 2006.

b. Purchased land for future building site, paid cash, $9.

c. Earned revenues for 2006, $160, including $50 on credit.

d. Sold 3,000 additional shares for $1 cash per share (show dollars in thousands).

e. Recognized other expenses for 2006, $85, including $20 on credit.

f. Collected accounts receivable, $24.

g. Purchased additional assets, $10 cash (debit Other Assets).

h. Paid accounts payable, $13.

i. Purchased service supplies on account, $18 (debit to Account No. 03).

j. Signed a $25 service contract to start February 1, 2007.

k. Declared and paid cash dividend, $15.

Data for adjusting entries:

l. Service supplies inventory on hand at December 31, 2006, $12 (debit Other Expenses).

m. The equipment's useful life is 10 years; no residual or scrap value.

n. Accrued interest on notes payable (to be computed).

o. Wages earned since the December 24 pay date, but not yet paid, $15.

p. Income tax expense payable in 2007, $8.

Required:

1. Set up T-accounts for the accounts on the trial balance and enter their beginning balances.

2. Record Transactions (*a*) through (*k*) and post them to the T-accounts.

3. Record and post the adjusting entries (*l*) through (*p*).

4. Prepare an income statement (including earnings per share) and a statement of retained earnings for 2006, as well as a balance sheet at December 31, 2006.

5. Record and post the closing entries.

6. Prepare a post-closing trial balance.

7. Compute the following ratios for 2006:
    a. Debt-to-equity.
    b. Total asset turnover
    c. Net profit margin

P4–8 Recording Journal Entries and Inferring Adjustments   ■ **LO2**

Stay'N Shape was started by Jennifer Long several years ago to provide physical fitness services to its customers. The following balances were extracted from the company's general ledger as at the following dates:

	May 31, 2006	April 30, 2006
Unearned revenue	$ 4,500	$ 3,000
Accounts receivable	44,000	59,000
Prepaid rent	?	4,900
Prepaid insurance	?	1,200
Notes payable	20,000	20,000
Supplies inventory	?	7,200
Supplies expense	17,200	

Additional information about several transactions that occurred in May is provided below:

a. Some customers pay for services in advance. The remaining customers are billed for services used and are allowed one month to pay their bills. During May, the company received from customers a total of $62,000 in cash, including an amount of $7,000 which was paid by customers in advance.

b. At the end of April, the company had paid rent for the next five months and recorded the amount as Prepaid rent.

c. The balance of Prepaid insurance at April 30 represents the cost of insuring the company's premises and equipment for one month. In May, the company received an invoice from the insurance company for a renewal of the company's insurance policy for one year. The insurance premium was increased by 10 percent over the amount of the premium of the previous year because the company filed a few insurance claims. The company paid the one-year insurance premium.

d. The note payable carries interest at 6 percent and is due on June 30, 2006 along with accrued interest. The company recognizes interest expense on a monthly basis.

e. An invoice for $780 pertaining to advertising work done during May was received on May 2.

f. Supplies amounting to $17,200 were purchased on account during May and debited to the Supplies expense account. A physical count of supplies on hand on May 31 valued the inventory at $11,500.

Required:

Prepare journal entries to record the following transactions and events:

1. The receipt of cash from customers and the recognition of all revenues earned in May.

2. Rent expense for May.

3. Payment of the premium for the new insurance policy.

4. Interest expense that accrued in May.

5. The invoice for advertising work, received on May 2.

6. The adjustment to the Supplies inventory account.

ALTERNATE PROBLEMS

■ **LO1**

Starbucks
Corporation

AP4–1 Preparing a Trial Balance (P4–1)

Starbucks Corporation purchases and roasts high-quality, whole-bean coffees and sells them along with fresh-brewed coffees, Italian-style espresso beverages, a variety of pastries and confections, coffee-related accessories and equipment, and a line of premium teas. In addition to sales through its company-operated retail stores, Starbucks also sells coffee and tea products through other channels of distribution. The following is a simplified list of accounts and amounts reported in financial statements. The accounts have normal debit or credit balances and the dollars are rounded to the nearest million. Assume the year ended on September 30, 2005.

Accounts payable	$ 169	Income tax expense	$ 168	Other operating expenses	$ 141
Accounts receivable	114	Interest revenue	50	Prepaid expenses	55
Accrued liabilities	440	Inventories	343	Property, plant, and	
Accumulated amortization	1,050	Long-term investments	280	equipment	2,376
Cash	201	Long-term liabilities	38	Retained earnings	?
Cost of sales	1,686	Net sales revenues	4,075	Share capital	998
Amortization expense	239	Other current assets	61	Short-term investments	149
General and administrative		Other long-term assets	140	Store operating expenses	1,379
expenses	244				

Required:

Prepare an adjusted trial balance at September 30, 2005. How did you determine the amount for retained earnings?

■ **LO2, 3**

AP4–2 Recording Adjusting Entries and Determining Their Financial Statement Effects (P4–2)

Chandra Company's fiscal year ends on June 30. It is June 30, 2006, and all of the 2006 entries have been made, except the following adjusting entries:

a. On March 30, 2006, Chandra paid $2,800 for a six-month premium for property insurance starting on that date. Cash was credited and Prepaid Insurance was debited for this amount.

b. At June 30, 2006, wages of $900 were earned by employees but not yet paid. The employees will be paid on the next pay date, July 15, 2006.

c. On June 1, 2006, Chandra collected maintenance fees of $520 for two months. At that date, Chandra debited Cash and credited Unearned Maintenance Revenue for $520.

d. Amortization must be recognized on a service truck that cost $19,000 on July 1, 2005. The truck's estimated useful life is four years with a $3,000 residual value.

e. Cash of $4,200 was collected on May 1, 2006, for services to be rendered evenly over the next year, beginning on May 1 (Unearned Service Revenue was credited).

f. On February 1, 2006, the company borrowed $20,000 from a local bank and signed a 9-percent note for that amount. The principal and interest are payable on January 31, 2007.

g. On June 15, 2006, the company received from the city a tax bill for $500 covering property taxes on land for the first half of 2006. The amount is payable during July 2006.

h. The company earned service revenue of $2,000 on a special job that was completed on June 29, 2006. Collection will be made during July 2007; no entry has been recorded.

Required:

1. Indicate whether each transaction relates to a deferred revenue, deferred expense, accrued revenue, or accrued expense.

2. Prepare the adjusting entry required for each transaction at June 30, 2006.

3. Using the following headings, indicate the effect of each adjusting entry and the amount of the effect. Use + for increase, − for decrease, and NE for no effect.

	Balance Sheet			Income Statement		
Transaction	Assets	Liabilities	Shareholders' Equity	Revenues	Expenses	Net Income
a.						
b.						
c.						
etc.						

AP4–3   Recording Adjusting Entries and Determining Their Financial Statement Effects (P4–3)

■ **LO2, 3**

Sophie's Catering Company is at its fiscal year-end, December 31, 2006. The following data were developed from the company's records and related documents:

a. During 2006, office supplies amounting to $1,400 were purchased for cash and debited to Supplies Inventory. At the beginning of 2006, the inventory of supplies on hand (unused) amounted to $350. The inventory of supplies on hand at December 31, 2006, was $400.

b. On December 31, 2006, the company catered an evening gala for a local celebrity. The $7,500 bill was payable by the end of January 2007. No cash has been collected, and no journal entry has been made for this transaction. (Ignore cost of goods sold.)

c. On December 15, 2006, repairs on one of the company's delivery vans were completed at a cost of $700; the amount is not yet recorded and will be paid at the beginning of January 2007.

d. On October 1, 2006, a one-year insurance premium on equipment in the amount of $1,500 was paid and debited to Prepaid Insurance. Coverage began on November 1.

e. In November 2006, Sophie's signed a lease for a new retail location, providing a down payment of $2,100 for the first three months. The amount was debited to Prepaid Rent. The lease began on December 1, 2006.

f. On July 1, 2006, the company purchased new refrigerated display counters at a cash cost of $18,000. The estimated useful life of the equipment is five years, with an estimated residual value of $3,000. No amortization has been recorded for 2006 (compute amortization for six months in 2006).

g. On November 1, 2006, the company loaned $4,500 to one of its employees who signed a one-year, 10-percent note. The principal and interest are payable on October 31, 2007.

h. The income before any of the adjustments or income taxes was $22,400. The company's income tax rate is 30 percent. Compute the adjusted income, taking into consideration Transactions (a) through (g) to determine the income tax expense for 2006.

Required:

1. Indicate whether each transaction relates to a deferred revenue, deferred expense, accrued revenue, or accrued expense.

2. Prepare the adjusting entry required for each transaction at December 31, 2006.

3. Using the following headings, indicate the effect of each adjusting entry and the amount of each. Use + for increase, − for decrease, and NE for no effect.

	Balance Sheet			Income Statement		
Transaction	Assets	Liabilities	Shareholders' Equity	Revenues	Expenses	Net Income
a.						
b.						
c.						
etc.						

AP4–4   Computing Amounts on Financial Statements and Finding Financial Information (P4–4)

■ **LO3**

The following transactions and events are provided by the records of Deerfield Cleaning (a corporation) at the end of its fiscal year, December 31, 2006:

Cash Receipts and Revenue

a. Collected cash in January 2006 for the only cleaning contracts completed in past years that were not yet paid by customers — $ 11,000

b. Service revenue collected in cash during 2006 for cleaning contracts in 2006 — 213,000

c. Service revenue earned for contracts in December 2006 but not collected until 2007 — 14,000

d. Amount collected in advance in December 2006 for service to be provided in January 2007 — 19,000

Salaries

e. Cash payment made in January 2006 for employee salaries earned in 2005; no other amounts were due to employees for past periods — 1,500

f. Salaries incurred and paid during 2006 — 78,000

g. Salaries earned by employees during December 2006 that will be paid in January 2007 — 1,900

Supplies

h. Cleaning supplies inventory on January 1, 2006 — 1,800

i. Cleaning supplies purchased for cash during 2006 — 14,500

j. Cleaning supplies inventory on December 31, 2006 — 2,700

Required:

Using T-accounts, compute the amounts that should be reported in Deerfield's 2006 financial statements for the following items, and indicate on which financial statement the item is reported. For cash, create one T-account and label each effect to determine the amounts affecting cash as indicated here (from customers, to suppliers, to employees):

1. Service revenue
2. Cash to employees
3. Cleaning supplies expense
4. Accounts receivable
5. Cash to suppliers

6. Cleaning supplies inventory
7. Wages expense
8. Cash from customers
9. Unearned revenue
10. Wages payable

LO1, 2, 4, 5 AP4–5   **Inferring Year-End Adjustments, Computing Earnings per Share and Net Profit Margin, and Recording Closing Entries** (P4–5)

Gilca Ltd. is completing the information processing cycle at the end of its fiscal year, December 31, 2006. The correct account balances at December 31, 2006, both before and after the adjusting entries for 2006, are shown below:

	Trial Balance, December 31, 2006						
	Before Adjusting Entries		Adjustments		After Adjusting Entries		
Items	Debit	Credit	Debit	Credit	Debit	Credit
a. Cash	$ 18,000				$ 18,000	
b. Service revenue receivable					1,500	
c. Prepaid rent	1,200				800	
d. Property, plant, and equipment	210,000				210,000	
e. Accumulated amortization, PP&E		$52,500				$ 70,000
f. Income taxes payable						6,500
g. Deferred revenue		16,000				8,000
h. Share capital		110,000				110,000
i. Retained earnings, January 1, 2006		21,700				21,700
j. Service revenue		83,000				92,500
k. Salary expense	54,000				54,000	
l. Amortization expense					17,500	
m. Rent expense					400	
n. Income tax expense					6,500	
	$283,200	$283,200			$308,700	$308,700

Required:

1. Compare the amounts in the columns before and after the adjusting entries to reconstruct the adjusting entries made in 2006. Provide an explanation for each adjustment.

2. Compute the amount of income assuming that it is based on the amounts (a) before adjusting entries and (b) after adjusting entries. Which income amount is correct? Explain.

3. Compute the earnings per share, assuming that 5,000 shares are outstanding.

4. Compute the net profit margin. What does this suggest to you about the company?

5. Record the closing entries at December 31, 2006.

AP4–6 Recording Adjusting and Closing Entries and Preparing a Balance Sheet and an Income Statement Including Earnings per Share (P4–6)

■ **LO1, 2, 3, 5**

Vialdi Co., a small service repair company, keeps its records without the help of an accountant. After much effort, an outside accountant prepared the following unadjusted trial balance as at the end of the company's fiscal year, December 31, 2006:

Account Titles	Debit	Credit
Cash	19,600	
Accounts receivable	7,000	
Supplies inventory	1,300	
Prepaid insurance	900	
Equipment (5-year life, no residual value)	27,000	
Accumulated amortization, equipment		12,000
Other assets	5,100	
Accounts payable		2,500
Note payable (2 years; 12% each December 31)		5,000
Share capital (4,000 shares outstanding)		16,000
Retained earnings		10,300
Service revenue		48,000
Other expenses, excluding income tax	32,900	
Totals	93,800	93,800

Data not yet recorded at December 31, 2006, include:

a. Amortization expense for 2006, $2,000.

b. Insurance expired during 2006, $540.

c. Wages earned by employees not yet paid on December 31, 2006, $1,100.

d. The supplies inventory on December 31, 2006, reflected $500 remaining on hand.

e. Income tax expense was $2,950.

Required:

1. Record the adjusting entries at December 31, 2006.

2. Prepare an income statement for 2006 and a balance sheet at December 31, 2006. Include the effects of the preceding five transactions.

3. Compute the net income assuming that you did not make an adjustment to the balance of the supplies inventory account. Does this error cause a material change in net income? Explain.

4. Record the closing entries at December 31, 2006.

AP4–7 Comprehensive Review Problem: From Recording Transactions (including Adjusting and Closing Entries) to Preparing a Complete Set of Financial Statements and Performing Ratio Analysis (see Chapters 2, 3, and 4) (P4–7)

■ **LO1, 2, 3, 4, 5**

Serena and Bill Davis began operations of their furniture repair shop (Rumours Furniture, Inc.) on January 1, 2004. The company's fiscal year ends December 31. The trial balance on January 1, 2005, was as follows (the amounts are rounded to thousands of dollars):

Account No.	Account Titles	Debit	Credit
01	Cash	5	
02	Accounts receivable	4	
03	Supplies inventory	2	
04	Small tools inventory	6	
05	Equipment		
06	Accumulated amortization (equipment)		
07	Other assets (not detailed to simplify)	9	
11	Accounts payable		7
12	Notes payable		
13	Wages payable		
14	Interest payable		
15	Income taxes payable		
16	Deferred revenue		
21	Share capital (15,000 shares)		15
31	Retained earnings		4
35	Service revenue		
40	Amortization expense		
41	Income tax expense		
42	Interest expense		
43	Other expenses		
	Totals	26	26

Transactions during 2005 (summarized in thousands of dollars) follow:

a. Borrowed $25 cash on an 8-percent note payable, dated July 1, 2005.

b. Purchased equipment for $18 cash on July 1, 2005.

c. Sold 5,000 additional shares for $1 cash per share (show dollars in thousands).

d. Earned revenues for 2005, $74, including $15 on credit.

e. Recognized other expenses for 2005, $35, including $9 on credit.

f. Purchased additional small tools inventory, $3 cash.

g. Collected accounts receivable, $8.

h. Paid accounts payable, $11.

i. Purchased supplies on account, $10 (debit to Account No. 03).

j. Received a $3 deposit on work to start January 15, 2007.

k. Declared and paid cash dividend, $12.

Data for adjusting entries:

l. Service supplies inventory of $4 and small tools inventory of $9 were on hand at December 31, 2005 (debit Other Expenses).

m. The equipment's useful life is four years and its residual value is $2.

n. Accrued interest on notes payable (to be computed).

o. Wages earned since the December 24 pay date but not yet paid, $4.

p. Income tax expense payable in 2007, $4.

Required:

1. Set up T-accounts for the accounts on the trial balance and enter their beginning balances.

2. Record Transactions (*a*) through (*k*) and post them to the T-accounts.

3. Record and post the adjusting entries (*l*) through (*p*).

4. Prepare an income statement (including earnings per share) and a statement of retained earnings for 2005, as well as a balance sheet at December 31, 2005.

5. Record and post the closing entries.

6. Prepare a post-closing trial balance.

7. Compute the following ratios for 2005:
    a. Debt-to-equity
    b. Total asset turnover
    c. Net profit margin

CASES AND PROJECTS

FINDING AND INTERPRETING FINANCIAL INFORMATION

CP4–1 Finding Financial Information

LO2, 3, 4, 5

The Forzani Group

Refer to the Online Learning Centre Web site at **www.mcgrawhill.ca/college/libby/student/ resources** for the financial statements of The Forzani Group Ltd. (FGL).

Required:

1. How much is in the Prepaid Expenses account at the end of the 2005 fiscal year?
2. What did the company report for Long-Term Receivables at January 30, 2005? Where did you find this information?
3. How much did the company pay in interest for the 2005 fiscal year? Where did you find this information?
4. To what account is Accumulated Amortization related?
5. What company accounts would not appear on a post-closing trial balance?
6. Prepare the closing entry for Prepaid Expenses.
7. What is the company's basic earnings per share for the two years reported?
8. Compute the company's net profit margin for the two years reported. What does the trend suggest to you about FGL?

CP4–2 Comparing Companies Over Time

LO2, 5

The Forzani Group vs. Van Houtte

Refer to the Online Learning Centre Web site at **www.mcgrawhill.ca/college/libby/student/ resources** for the financial statements of The Forzani Group Ltd. and to Appendix B for the financial statements of Van Houtte, Inc.

Required:

1. What was the Cost of Sales for each company's most recent fiscal year? Where did you find the information? What reasons would a company have for not reporting the cost of sales? Explain.
2. Compute the percentage of Cost of Sales to Sales for each company if possible. Are you able to calculate the same ratios for the previous two fiscal years? If so, show computations. If not, explain why.
3. Compute each company's net profit margin for the years shown in its annual report. What do your results suggest about each company over time and in comparison to each other?

FINANCIAL REPORTING AND ANALYSIS CASES

CP4–3 Using Financial Reports: Inferring Adjusting Entries and Information Used in Computations and Recording Closing Entries

LO1, 2, 4

The T-accounts of Longhorn Company at the end of the third year of operations, December 31, 2006, follow. The adjusting entries at December 31 are identified by letters.

Cash			Note Payable 8%			Share Capital (8,000 shares)		
Bal.	20,000			1/1/2005	10,000		Bal.	56,000

Inventory, Maintenance Supplies			Interest Payable			Retained Earnings		
Bal.	500	(a) 300		(b)	800		Bal.	9,000

Service Equipment			Income Taxes Payable			Service Revenue		
1/1/2004	90,000			(f)	13,020	(c) 6,000	Bal.	220,000

Accumulated Amortization, Service Equipment			Wages Payable			Expenses		
		Bal. 18,000		(e)	500	Bal.	160,000	
		(d) 9,000				(a)	300	
						(b)	800	
						(d)	9,000	
						(e)	500	
						(f)	13,020	

Other Assets			Unearned Revenue		
Bal.	42,500			(c)	6,000

Required:

1. Develop three trial balances of Longhorn Company at December 31, 2006, using the following format:

Account	Unadjusted Trial Balance		Adjusted Trial Balance		Post-Closing Trial Balance	
	Debit	Credit	Debit	Credit	Debit	Credit

2. Write an explanation for each adjusting entry for 2006.

3. Record the closing journal entries.

4. What was the apparent useful life of the service equipment? What assumptions must you make to answer this question?

5. What was the average income tax rate for 2006?

6. What was the average issue (sale) price per share of the share capital?

■ **LO2**   **CP4–4**   **Using Financial Reports: Analyzing the Effects of Adjustments**

Seneca Land Company, a closely held corporation, invests in commercial rental properties. Seneca's fiscal year ends on December 31. At the end of each year, numerous adjusting entries must be made because many transactions completed during the current and prior years have economic effects on the financial statements of the current and future years. Assume that the current year is 2006.

Required:

This case concerns four transactions that have been selected for your analysis. Answer the questions for each.

TRANSACTION (*a*): On July 1, 2003, the company purchased office equipment costing $14,000 for use in the business. The company estimates that the equipment will have a useful life of 10 years and no residual value.

1. Over how many accounting periods will this transaction directly affect Seneca's financial statements? Explain.

2. Assuming straight-line amortization, how much amortization expense was reported on the 2003 and 2004 income statements?

3. How should the office equipment be reported on the balance sheet at December 31, 2005?

4. Would Seneca make an adjusting entry at the end of each year during the life of the equipment? Explain your answer.

TRANSACTION (*b*): On September 1, 2006, Seneca collected $24,000 for rent of office space. This amount represented rent for a six-month period, September 1, 2006, through February 28, 2007. Unearned Rent Revenue was increased (credited), and Cash was increased (debited) for $24,000.

1. Over how many accounting periods will this transaction affect Seneca's financial statements? Explain.

2. How much rent revenue on this office space should Seneca report on the 2006 income statement? Explain.

3. Did this transaction create a liability for Seneca as of the end of 2006? Explain. If yes, how much?

4. Should Seneca make an adjusting entry on December 31, 2006? Explain. If your answer is yes, prepare the adjusting entry.

TRANSACTION (*c*): On December 31, 2006, Seneca owed employees wages of $7,500 because the employees worked the last three days in December 2006. The next payroll date is January 5, 2007.

1. Over how many accounting periods does this transaction affect Seneca's financial statements? Explain.

2. How would this $7,500 amount affect Seneca's income statement for 2006 and the balance sheet at December 31, 2006?

3. Should Seneca make an adjusting entry on December 31, 2006? Explain. If your answer is yes, prepare the adjusting entry.

TRANSACTION (d): On January 1, 2006, Seneca agreed to supervise the planning and subdivision of a large tract of land for a customer, J. Ray. This service job that Seneca will perform involves four separate phases. By December 31, 2006, three phases had been completed to Ray's satisfaction. The remaining phase will be done during 2007. The total price for the four phases (agreed on in advance by both parties) was $60,000. Each phase involves about the same amount of services. On December 31, 2006, Seneca had not collected any cash for the services already performed.

1. Should Seneca record any service revenue on this job for 2006? Explain. If yes, prepare the adjusting entry to record the revenue.

2. What entry will Seneca make when it completes the last phase, assuming that the full contract price is collected on the completion date, February 15, 2007?

CP4–5 Using Financial Reports: Inferring Adjusting and Closing Entries and Answering Analytical Questions

■ **LO1, 2, 4, 5**

Rowland Company was organized on January 1, 2005. At the end of the first year of operations, December 31, 2005, the bookkeeper prepared the following trial balances (amounts in thousands of dollars):

Account No.	Account Titles	Unadjusted Trial Balance		Adjustments		Adjusted Trial Balance	
		Debit	Credit			Debit	Credit
11	Cash	40				40	
12	Accounts receivable	17				17	
13	Prepaid insurance	2				1	
14	Rent receivable					2	
15	Property, plant, and equipment	46				46	
16	Accumulated amortization						11
17	Other assets	6				6	
18	Accounts payable		27				27
19	Wages payable						3
20	Income taxes payable						5
21	Unearned rent revenue						4
22	Note payable (10%; dated January 1, 2005)		20				20
23	Share capital (1,000 shares)		30				30
24	Retained earnings	3				3	
25	Revenues (total)		105				103
26	Expenses (total including interest)	68				83	
27	Income tax expense					5	
	Totals	182	182			203	203

Required:

1. Based on inspection of the two trial balances, prepare the 2005 adjusting entries recorded by the bookkeeper (provide brief explanations).

2. Based on these data, prepare the 2005 closing entries with brief explanations.

3. Answer the following questions (show computations):
   a. How many shares were outstanding at year-end?
   b. What was the estimated useful life of the property, plant, and equipment, assuming a residual value of $2,000 and a purchase date of January 1, 2005?
   c. What was the amount of interest expense included in the total expenses?
   d. What was the balance of Retained Earnings on December 31, 2005?
   e. What was the average income tax rate?
   f. How would the two accounts Rent Receivable and Unearned Rent Revenue be reported on the balance sheet?
   g. Explain why cash increased by $40,000 during the year even though net income was comparatively very low.

h. What was the amount of earnings per share for 2005?

i. What was the average selling price of the shares?

j. When was the insurance premium paid and over what period of time did the coverage extend?

k. What was the net profit margin for the year?

■ **LO2, 3**   **CP4–6   Using Financial Reports: Analyzing Financial Information in a Sale of a Business— A Challenging Case**

John Place, a local massage therapist, decided to sell his practice and retire. He has had discussions with a therapist from another province who wants to relocate. The discussions are at the complex stage of agreeing on a price. The financial statements of Place's practice, Halcyon Stress Reduction, played an important role in this process. Place's secretary, Kelsey, maintained the records, under his direction. Each year, Kelsey developed a statement of profits on a cash basis from the records she maintained but she did not prepare a balance sheet. Upon request, Place provided the other therapist with the following statements for 2006 prepared by Kelsey:

HALCYON STRESS REDUCTION		
Statement of Profits		
2006		
Therapy fees collected		$115,000
Expenses paid:		
Rent for office space	$13,000	
Utilities expense	360	
Telephone expense	2,200	
Office salaries expense	16,500	
Office supplies expense	900	
Miscellaneous expenses	2,400	
Total expenses		35,360
Profit for the year		$79,640

Upon agreement of the parties, you have been asked to examine the financial figures for 2006. The other therapist said, "I question the figures because, among other things, they appear to be on a 100-percent cash basis." Your investigations revealed the following additional data at December 31, 2006:

a. Of the $115,000 in therapy fees collected in 2006, $30,000 was for services performed prior to 2006.

b. At the end of 2006, therapy fees of $8,000 for services performed during the year were uncollected.

c. Office equipment owned and used by Place cost $5,000 and had an estimated useful life of 10 years.

d. An inventory of office supplies at December 31, 2006, reflected $300 worth of items purchased during the year that were still on hand. Also, the records for 2005 indicate that the supplies on hand at the end of that year were about $125.

e. At the end of 2006, the secretary whose salary is $18,000 per year had not been paid for December because of a long trip that extended to January 15, 2007.

f. The $140 phone bill for December 2006 was not paid until January 11, 2007.

g. The payment for office rent was for 13 months, including January 2007.

Required:

1. Prepare a correct income statement for 2006 based on the information above. Show your computations for any amounts changed from those in the statement prepared by Place's secretary. (Suggested solution format—use four-column headings: Items; Cash Basis per Halcyon's Statement, $; Explanation of Changes; and Corrected Basis, $.)

2. Write a memo to support your schedule prepared in requirement 1. The purpose should be to explain the reasons for your changes and to suggest other important items that should be considered in the pricing decision.

CP4–7 Using Financial Reports: Preparing Income Statements for Different Periods

■ **LO2, 3**

Wong's Insurance Agency adjusts its accounts at the end of each month. The adjusted balances of the revenue and expense accounts at two different dates of the year appear below. The company's fiscal year starts on July 1.

	March 31, 2007	December 31, 2006
Commissions earned	$72,000	$45,000
Salaries expense	18,000	12,000
Rent expense	11,250	7,500
Amortization expense	1,350	900
Advertising expense	14,000	7,500

The company is subject to an income tax rate of 40 percent.

Required:

Prepare income statements for two separate time periods: the quarter ending March 31, 2007, and the 9-month period ending March 31, 2007. Explain how you determined the amounts for each time period and show supporting computations.

CP4–8 Using Financial Reports: Analyzing Financial Information from Real Financial Statements

■ **LO2, 3**

The current liabilities of WestJet Airlines include an account titled Advance Ticket Sales. The company's recent annual reports show the following trend in the balance of this account over a three-year period.

	2001	2002	2003
Advance ticket sales (in thousands)	28,609	44,195	58,086

The first note to the company's financial statements, titled *Significant accounting policies*, includes the following disclosure about revenue recognition:

> Guest revenue is recognized when air transportation is provided. Tickets sold but not used are included in the balance sheet as advance ticket sales under current liabilities.

Required:

1. What does the balance in the account Advance Ticket Sales represent?

2. Why does WestJet recognize guest revenue when transportation is provided, rather than when cash is received?

3. How does WestJet Airlines normally settle this liability?

4. Should WestJet recognize flight expenses, such as jet fuel, salaries of flight crew, and cost of food and beverage, in the period when the flights occur or during the period when tickets are sold? Explain.

5. Explain the most probable reason for the increase in the amount of this liability from 2001 to 2003.

6. Based on the trend in the amount of this liability, would you expect the annual amounts of guest revenue to increase, decrease, or remain stable over the three-year period? Explain.

CRITICAL THINKING CASES

CP4–9 Using Financial Reports: Evaluating Financial Information as a Bank Loan Officer

■ **LO2, 3, 4**

Meadville Corporation has been in operation since January 1, 2006. It is now December 31, 2006, the end of the company's fiscal year. The company has not done well financially during the first year, although revenue has been fairly good. The three shareholders manage the company, but they have not given much attention to recordkeeping. In view of a serious cash shortage, they have applied to your bank for a $20,000 loan. You requested a complete set of financial statements. The following annual financial statements for 2006 were prepared by a clerk and then were given to the bank.

MEADVILLE CORPORATION

Income Statement		Balance Sheet	
For the Period Ended December 31, 2006		**At December 31, 2006**	
Transportation revenue	$85,000	**Assets**	
Expenses:		Cash	$2,000
Salaries expense	17,000	Receivables	3,000
Maintenance expense	12,000	Inventory of maintenance supplies	6,000
Other expenses	18,000	Equipment	40,000
Total expenses	$47,000	Prepaid insurance	4,000
Net income	$38,000	Other assets	27,000
		Total assets	$82,000
		Liabilities	
		Accounts payable	$9,000
		Shareholders' Equity	
		Share capital (10,000 shares outstanding)	35,000
		Retained earnings	38,000
		Total liabilities and shareholders' equity	$82,000

After briefly reviewing the statements and looking into the situation, you requested that the statements be redone (with some expert help) to "incorporate amortization, accruals, inventory counts, income taxes, and so on." As a result of a review of the records and supporting documents, the following additional information was developed:

a. The inventory of maintenance supplies of $6,000 shown on the balance sheet has not been adjusted for supplies used during 2006. An inventory count of the maintenance supplies on hand (unused) on December 31, 2006, showed $1,600. Supplies used should be debited to Maintenance Expense.

b. The insurance premium paid in 2006 was for years 2006 and 2007; therefore, the prepaid insurance at December 31, 2006, amounted to $2,000. The total insurance premium was debited to Prepaid Insurance when paid in 2006.

c. The equipment cost $40,000 when purchased January 1, 2006. It had an estimated useful life of five years (no residual value). No amortization has been recorded for 2006.

d. Unpaid (and unrecorded) salaries at December 31, 2006, amounted to $2,700.

e. At December 31, 2006, transportation revenue collected in advance amounted to $7,000. This amount was credited to Transportation Revenue when the cash was collected.

f. The company is subject to an income tax rate of 25 percent.

Required:

1. Record the six adjusting entries required on December 31, 2006, based on the preceding additional information.

2. Recast the preceding statements after taking into account the adjusting entries. Use the following format for the solution:

	Amounts	CHANGES		Correct
Items	Reported	Plus	Minus	Amounts
(List here each item from the two statements)				

3. Omission of the adjusting entries caused:
   a. Net income to be overstated or understated (select one) by $_____.
   b. Total assets to be overstated or understated (select one) by $_____.
   c. Total liabilities to be overstated or understated (select one) by $_____.

4. Use both the unadjusted and adjusted balances to calculate the following ratios for the company: (a) earnings per share and (b) net profit margin. Explain the causes of the differences and the impact of the changes on financial analysis.

5. Write a letter to the company explaining the results of the adjustments, your analysis, and your decision regarding the loan.

FINANCIAL REPORTING AND ANALYSIS TEAM PROJECT

CP4–10 **Team Project: Analysis of Accruals, Earnings per Share, and Net Profit Margin**

■ **LO2, 3, 5**

Using your Web browser, as a team select an industry to analyze. Each team member should then use the Internet to obtain the annual report for one Canadian publicly traded company in the industry, with each member selecting a different company.

Required:

1. On an individual basis, each team member should write a short report listing the following:
   a. The company's earnings per share for each year.
   b. The company's net profit margin for each year.
   c. The amount of accrued expenses (a liability) on the balance sheet and the ratio of accrued expenses to total liabilities.
   d. Summaries of any notes to the financial statements that describe accrued expenses in detail.

2. Discuss any patterns that you as a team observe. Then, as a team, write a short report comparing and contrasting your companies according to the preceding attributes. Provide potential explanations for any differences discovered.

Reporting and Interpreting Cash Flows

In 1834, John H. Sleeman established himself as an Ontario brewer. His business expanded over the years, and successive generations of the Sleeman family managed it until the operations were closed and sold during the Great Depression of the 1930s. The business resumed in 1985 as Sleeman Brewing & Malting Co. Ltd.; in 1988 the company constructed a brewing facility in Guelph, Ontario, and began producing Sleeman Cream Ale using the original Sleeman family recipe developed 100 years earlier.

After several expansions, the brewing facilities can currently produce 1.4 million hectolitres of beer per year—1 hectolitre fills 12.2 cases of beer, each containing 24 bottles. The company, known today as Sleeman Breweries Ltd., has also grown through purchases of niche Canadian breweries whose products have strong, popular regional appeal, such as Okanagan Spring in British Columbia and Unibroue in Québec. Sleeman Breweries Ltd. also licensed the rights to import and distribute U.S., European, U.K., and Japanese beers such as Samuel Adams Boston Lager, Grolsch, Newcastle Brown, and Sapporo. Recently the company established a strategic partnership with Boston Beer Company to export its brands to the United States. Many readily recognize Sleeman Honey Brown Lager and Cream Ale because, in 2003, Sleeman's sales volume reached 1,255,000 hectolitres of beer—more than 350 million bottles of beer.

Sleeman's net income for 2003 exceeded 12 million—but as impressive as this net income is, cash flow is critical to any company's survival. Growing, profitable operations such as Sleeman's do not always generate positive cash flow. Seasonal fluctuations in sales, purchases of inventory, and advertising may cause high *net profits* but net cash *out*flows in some quarters, and *losses* but net cash *in*flows in others. As a consequence, Sleeman must carefully manage cash flows as well as profits. Financial analysts consider the information provided on Sleeman's cash flow statement as well as its income statement and balance sheet in order to assess the amount, timing, and uncertainty of future cash flows to determine whether investment in Sleeman's shares will return more or less cash than the original investment.

UNDERSTANDING THE BUSINESS

Clearly, net income is an important indicator of performance, but cash flow is also critical to a company's success. Cash flow permits a company to expand its operations, replace worn assets, take advantage of market opportunities, and pay dividends to its owners. Some financial analysts go as far as saying that "cash flow is king." Both managers and analysts need to understand the various sources and uses of cash that are associated with business activity.

The cash flow statement focuses attention on a firm's ability to generate cash internally, its management of current assets and current liabilities, and the details of its investments, as well as external financing. It is designed to help both managers and analysts answer important cash-related questions such as these:

- Will the company have enough cash to pay its short-term debts to suppliers, employees, taxation authorities, and other creditors without additional borrowing?

- Is the company adequately managing its accounts receivable, inventory, and other current assets?

- Has the company made necessary investments in new productive capacity?

- Did the company generate enough cash flow internally to finance necessary investments, or did it rely on external financing?

- Is the company changing the proportion of debt and equity in its capital structure?

Sleeman is a particularly good example to illustrate the importance of the cash flow statement for two reasons. First, like all companies in its industry, Sleeman's inventory purchases and sales vary with the seasons. This seasonal variation has surprising effects on cash flows and net income. Second, an important element of its business strategy is the outsourcing of some of its production of value brands (called *contract brewing*). This dramatically affects its investments in plant and equipment and the need for external financing to support growth.

We begin our discussion with an overview of the cash flow statement. We then use the cash flow statement taken from a quarterly report for Sleeman Breweries Ltd. to provide detailed coverage of the preparation, reporting, and interpretation of information in the cash flow statement.

ORGANIZATION OF THE CHAPTER

• Classification of Cash Flows	• Reporting and Interpreting Cash Flows from Operating Activities	• Reporting and Interpreting Cash Flows from Investing Activities	• Reporting and Interpreting Cash Flows from Financing Activities	• Additional Cash Flow Disclosures
Cash Flows from Operating Activities	**Part A:** Reporting Cash Flows from Operating Activities —Direct Method **OR**	Reporting Cash Flows from Investing Activities	Reporting Cash Flows from Financing Activities	Non-Cash Investing and Financing Activities
Cash Flows from Investing Activities	**Part B:** Reporting Cash Flows from Operating Activities —Indirect Method	Interpreting Cash Flows from Investing Activities	Interpreting Cash Flows from Financing Activities	Supplemental Cash Flow Information
Cash Flows from Financing Activities		Capital Acquisitions Ratio		
Net Increase (Decrease) in Cash	Interpreting Cash Flows from Operations			
Relationships to the Balance Sheet and Income Statements	Quality of Income Ratio			

CLASSIFICATION OF CASH FLOWS

Basically, the cash flow statement explains how the cash balance at the beginning of the period changed to another cash balance at the end of the period. For purposes of this statement, the definition of *cash* includes cash and cash equivalents. **Cash equivalents** are short-term, highly liquid investments that are both

1. readily convertible to known amounts of cash.
2. so near their maturity that they present insignificant risk of changes in value because of changes in interest rates.

Generally, an investment qualifies as a cash equivalent only when it has a short maturity of three months or less from the date of accquisition. Examples of cash equivalents are Treasury bills (a form of short-term government debt), money market funds, and commercial paper (short-term notes payable issued by large corporations).

As you can see in Exhibit 5.1, the cash flow statement reports cash inflows and outflows based on three broad categories: (1) operating activities, (2) investing activities,

■ **LEARNING OBJECTIVE 1**

Classify cash flow statement items as part of net cash flows from operating, investing, and financing activities.

A **CASH EQUIVALENT** is a short-term, highly liquid investment with an original maturity of less than three months.

EXHIBIT **5.1**

Consolidated Cash Flow Statement

REAL WORLD EXCERPT

Sleeman Breweries Inc.

QUARTERLY REPORT

SLEEMAN BREWERIES INC.
Consolidated Statements of Cash Flows—Unaudited
As at September 27, 2003
(all amounts in 000s)

	3 Months Ended September 27, 2003
Net inflow (outflow) of cash related to the following activities:	
OPERATING	
Net earnings	$ 4,359
Items not affecting cash:	
Depreciation and amortization	1,648
Future income taxes	1,590
	7,597
Changes in non-cash operating working capital items	2,531*
	10,128
INVESTING	
Additions to property, plant, and equipment	(1,350)
Proceeds from long-term investments	248
	(1,102)
FINANCING	
Net repayments of bank operating loans	(4,653)
Stock options exercised	27
Long-term obligations—principal repayments	(2,430)
	(7,056)
NET CASH FLOW AND CASH BALANCE, END OF PERIOD	1,970

See accompanying notes to the consolidated financial statements.
These financial statements should be read in conjunction with the audited annual financial statements.

*Changes in non-cash operating working capital items:	
Decrease in accounts receivable	$ 5,209
Decrease in inventories	440
Decrease in prepaid expenses	881
Decrease in accounts payable**	(2,295)
Decrease in accrued liabilities	(1,704)
	$ 2,531

**Sleeman, like many companies, combines the balances of accounts payable and accrued liabilities (accrued expenses) on its balance sheet. We split the total amount reported in two amounts arbitrarily for illustrative purposes.

and (3) financing activities. To improve comparability, section 1540 of the *CICA Handbook* defines each category included in the required statement. These definitions (with explanations) are presented in the following sections.

CASH FLOWS FROM OPERATING ACTIVITIES

Cash flows from operating activities (cash flows from operations) are the cash inflows and cash outflows that directly relate to revenues and expenses reported on the income statement. These cash flows are not affected by accruals, deferrals, and allocations that result from the timing of revenue and expense recognition. There are two alternative approaches for presenting the operating activities section of the statement:

1. The **direct method** reports the components of cash flows from operating activities listed as gross receipts and gross payments

Inflows	Outflows
Cash received from	*Cash paid for*
Customers	Purchase of goods for resale and
Dividends and interest on investments	services (electricity, etc.)
	Salaries and wages
	Income taxes
	Interest on liabilities

The difference between the inflows and outflows is called the *net cash inflow (outflow) from operating activities*. Sleeman experienced a net cash inflow of $10,128,000 from its operations for the third quarter of 2003. The *CICA Handbook* recommends the direct method, but it is rarely seen in practice. Many financial executives have reported that they do not use it because it is more expensive to implement than the indirect method.

2. The **indirect method** starts with net income and then eliminates non-cash items to arrive at net cash inflow (outflow) from operating activities.

Net income
+/− Adjustments for non-cash items
Net cash inflow (outflow) from operating activities

Notice in Exhibit 5.1 that in the third quarter of 2003, Sleeman reported net income of $4,359,000 but generated positive cash flows from operating activities of $10,128,000. Recall that the income statement is prepared under the accrual concept, whereby revenues are recorded when earned without regard to when the related cash is collected. Similarly, expenses are matched with revenues and recorded in the same period as the revenues without regard to when the related cash payments are made.

In this chapter, we present computations of net cash inflow (outflow) from operating activities using both the direct and indirect methods. However, we will emphasize the indirect method in the remaining chapters because of the extensive use of this method in actual financial reporting.[1]

For now, the most important thing to remember about the two methods is that they are simply alternative ways to compute the same amount. The total amount of cash flows from operating activities is *always the same* (an inflow of $10,128,000 in Sleeman's case) regardless of whether it is computed using the direct or indirect method.

CASH FLOWS FROM INVESTING ACTIVITIES

Cash flows from investing activities are cash inflows and outflows related to the purchase and disposal of long-term productive assets and investments in the securities of

---

CASH FLOWS FROM OPERATING ACTIVITIES (CASH FLOWS FROM OPERATIONS) are cash inflows and outflows directly related to earnings from normal operations.

The **DIRECT METHOD** of presenting the Operating Activities section of the cash flow statement reports components of cash flows from operating activities as gross receipts and gross payments.

The **INDIRECT METHOD** of presenting the Operating Activities section of the cash flow statement adjusts net income to compute cash flows from operating activities.

CASH FLOWS FROM INVESTING ACTIVITIES are cash inflows and outflows related to the acquisition or sale of productive facilities and investments in the securities of other companies.

---

[1]A recent survey of 200 companies revealed that only two companies used the direct method in their 2003 annual reports. C. Byrd, I. Chen, and J. Smith, *Financial Reporting in Canada 2004*. Toronto, CICA, 2004, p. 106.

other companies. Under this classification, the cash outflows represent the entity's "investments" of cash to acquire these assets. The cash inflows occur only when cash is received from disposal (sale or collection) of prior investments. Typical cash flows from investing activities include:

Inflows	Outflows
Cash received from	Cash paid for
Sale or disposal of property, plant, and equipment	Purchase of property, plant, and equipment
Sale or maturity of investments in securities	Purchase of investments in securities

The difference between these cash inflows and outflows is called *net cash inflow (outflow) from investing activities*.

For Sleeman, this amount was an outflow of $1,102,000 for the third quarter of 2003. The Investing Activities section of the statement shows Sleeman's long-term investment strategy. The Management Discussion and Analysis (MD&A) section of the report indicates that the company was continuing to invest in expanding its production facilities. These investments allow Sleeman to bottle and can more of its products in-house.

CASH FLOWS FROM FINANCING ACTIVITIES

Cash flows from financing activities include both cash inflows and outflows from external sources (owners and creditors) to finance the enterprise and its operations. Under this classification, the cash inflows represent the financing activities that obtain cash from owners and creditors. The cash outflows occur only when cash is paid back to the owners and creditors for their previous cash-providing activities. Usual cash flows from financing activities include these:

CASH FLOWS FROM FINANCING ACTIVITIES are cash inflows and outflows related to external sources of financing (owners and creditors) for the enterprise.

Inflows	Outflows
Cash received from	Cash paid for
Borrowing on notes, mortgages, bonds, etc., from creditors	Repayment of principal to creditors (excluding interest, which is an operating activity)
Issuing equity securities to shareholders	Repurchasing equity securities from owners
	Dividends to shareholders

The difference between these cash inflows and outflows is called *net cash inflow (outflow) from financing activities*. For Sleeman, this amount was an outflow of $7,056,000 for the third quarter of 2003. The Financing Activities section of the statement shows that Sleeman repaid $7,083,000 to its creditors during the period and raised only $27,000 from shareholders.

NET INCREASE (DECREASE) IN CASH

The combination of **the net cash flows from operating activities, investing activities, and financing activities must equal the net increase (decrease) in cash** for the reporting period. For the third quarter of 2003, Sleeman reported a net increase in cash of $1,970,000 which explains the change in cash on the balance sheet from the beginning balance of zero to the ending balance of $1,970,000.

	(in thousands)
Net cash provided by operating activities	$10,128
Net cash used in investing activities	(1,102)
Net cash used in financing activities	(7,056)
Net increase in cash and cash equivalents	1,970
Cash and cash equivalents at beginning of period	0
Cash and cash equivalents at end of period	$ 1,970

SELF-STUDY QUIZ 5-1

Canadian Tire Corporation

Canadian Tire Corporation is a network of businesses engaged in retail, financial services, and petroleum. A listing of some of its cash flows follows. Indicate whether each item is disclosed in the Operating Activities (O), Investing Activities (I), or Financing Activities (F) section of the statement. (Refer to Exhibit 5.1 as a guide.)

_____ a. Purchase of short-term investments

_____ b. Net income

_____ c. Change in trade accounts receivable

_____ d. Additions to property and equipment

_____ e. Change in prepaid expenses and other current assets

_____ f. Change in inventories

_____ g. Change in accrued liabilities

_____ h. Depreciation and amortization

_____ i. Issuance of common shares

_____ j. Change in trade accounts payable

After you complete your answers, check them with the solutions on page 256.

To give you a better understanding of the cash flow statement, we now discuss in more detail Sleeman's statement and the way that it relates to the balance sheet and income statement. Then we examine the way that each section of the statement describes a set of important decisions that Sleeman's management made. We also discuss the way financial analysts use each section to evaluate the company's performance.

RELATIONSHIPS TO THE BALANCE SHEET AND INCOME STATEMENTS

Preparing and interpreting the cash flow statement require analyzing the balance sheet and income statement accounts that relate to the three sections of the cash flow statement. As we discussed in previous chapters, accountants record transactions as journal entries that are posted to specific ledger accounts and the balances of these accounts are then used to prepare the income statement and the balance sheet. Companies cannot prepare the cash flow statement by using amounts recorded in the specific accounts because these amounts are based on accrual accounting. Instead, accountants must analyze the amounts recorded under the accrual basis and adjust them to a cash basis. To prepare the cash flow statement, they need the following data:

1. **Comparative balance sheets** that are used in computing the cash flows from all activities (operating, investing, and financing). To ease the preparation process, we recommend that you compute the change from the beginning to the end of the period for each balance sheet item.

2. A **complete income statement,** which is used primarily in identifying cash flows from operating activities.

3. **Additional details** concerning selected accounts that reflect different types of transactions and events. Analysis of individual accounts is necessary because often the net change in an account balance during the year does not reveal the underlying nature of the cash flows.

Our approach to preparing and understanding the cash flow statement focuses on the changes in the balance sheet accounts. It relies on a simple algebraic manipulation of the balance sheet equation

$$\text{Assets} = \text{Liabilities} + \text{Shareholders' Equity}$$

First, assets can be split into cash and non-cash assets:

$$\text{Cash} + \text{Non-Cash Assets} = \text{Liabilities} + \text{Shareholders' Equity}$$

If we move the non-cash assets to the right side of the equation, then

$$\text{Cash} = \text{Liabilities} + \text{Shareholders' Equity} - \text{Non-Cash Assets}$$

Given this relationship, the change in cash (Δ) between the beginning and end of the period must equal the changes (Δ) in the amounts on the right side of the equation:

$$\Delta \text{ Cash} = \Delta \text{ Liabilities} + \Delta \text{ Shareholders' Equity} - \Delta \text{ Non-Cash Assets}$$

Thus, any transaction that changes cash must be accompanied by a change in liabilities, shareholders' equity, or non-cash assets. Exhibit 5.2 illustrates this concept for selected cash transactions.

EXHIBIT **5.2**

Selected Cash Transactions and Their Effects on Other Balance Sheet Accounts

Category	Transaction	Cash Effect	Other Account Affected
Operating	Collect accounts receivable	+Cash	−Accounts Receivable (A)
	Pay accounts payable	−Cash	−Accounts Payable (L)
	Prepay rent	−Cash	+Prepaid Rent (A)
	Pay interest	−Cash	−Retained Earnings (SE)
	Sale for cash	+Cash	+Retained Earnings (SE)
Investing	Purchase equipment for cash	−Cash	+Equipment (A)
	Sell investment securities for cash	+Cash	−Investments
Financing	Pay back debt to bank	−Cash	−Notes Payable—Bank (L)
	Issue shares for cash	+Cash	+Share Capital (SE)

In the next sections of this chapter, we will classify each of these other balance sheet changes as relating to operating (O), investing (I), or financing (F) activities, based on quarterly financial statements of Sleeman Breweries Ltd.

REPORTING AND INTERPRETING CASH FLOWS FROM OPERATING ACTIVITIES

Since the operating section can be prepared in one of two formats, we discuss them separately. Part A describes the direct method, and part B the indirect method. Your instructor may choose to assign either method, or both. After you have completed the part(s) assigned, you should move to the discussion of interpreting cash flow from operations.

Remember that:

1. Cash flow from operating activities is always the same regardless of whether it is computed using the direct or indirect method.

2. The investing and financing sections are always presented in the same manner regardless of the format of the operating section.

PART A: REPORTING CASH FLOWS FROM OPERATING ACTIVITIES—DIRECT METHOD

Exhibit 5.3 shows Sleeman's comparative balance sheets at the end of the second and third quarters of 2003, and its income statement for the third quarter of 2003. Recall that the direct method reports gross cash receipts and gross cash payments related to operating activities. It presents a summary of all operating transactions that resulted in either a debit or a credit to cash.

■ **LEARNING OBJECTIVE 2A**

Report and interpret cash flows from operating activities using the direct method.

EXHIBIT **5.3**

**Sleeman Breweries Ltd.:
Comparative Balance Sheet
and Current Income Statement
(in thousands)**

SLEEMAN BREWERIES LTD.

Consolidated Balance Sheet—unaudited

(in thousands of dollars)

Related Cash Flow Section		Sept. 27, 2003	June 28, 2003	Change
	Assets			
	Current Assets			
	Cash	$ 1,970		
O	Accounts receivable	32,139	$ 37,348	−5,209
O	Inventories	27,506	27,946	−440
O	Prepaid expenses	1,495	2,376	−881
	Total current assets	63,110	67,670	
I*	Property, plant, and equipment (net)	72,693	72,359	334
I	Long-term investments	7,338	7,586	−248
I	Intangible assets	85,880	86,512	−632
	Total assets	$229,021	$234,127	
	Liabilities			
	Current liabilities			
F	Bank indebtedness	—	$ 4,653	−4,653
O	Accounts payable	$ 16,515	18,810	−2,295
O	Accrued liabilities	11,654	13,358	−1,704
F	Current portion of long-term debt	11,629	10,405	1,224
	Total current liabilities	39,798	47,226	
F	Long-term obligations	79,058	82,712	−3,654
O	Future income taxes	10,465	8,875	1,590
	Total liabilities	129,321	138,813	
	Shareholders' Equity			
F	Share capital	44,943	44,916	27
O and F	Retained earnings	54,757	50,398	4,359
	Total shareholders' equity	99,700	95,314	
	Total liabilities and shareholders' equity	$229,021	$234,127	

The balances of certain accounts have been adjusted to simplify the presentation.

*The accumulated amortization account is also related to operations because amortization expense is added back to net income.

SLEEMAN BREWERIES LTD.

Consolidated Statement of Earnings—Unaudited

(in thousands of dollars)

	Quarter ended Sept. 27, 2003
Net revenue	$53,091
Cost of goods sold	26,576
Gross margin	26,515
Selling, general and administrative	16,985
Depreciation and amortization	1,648
Earnings before interest and taxes	7,882
Interest expense	1,373
Income before taxes	6,509
Provision for income taxes	2,150
Net income	**$ 4,359**

Cash Flows from Operating Activities

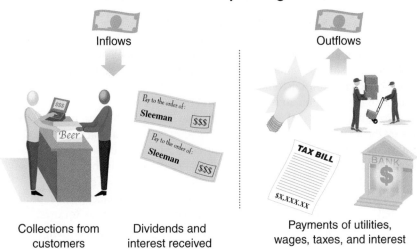

Inflows	Outflows
Collections from customers	Dividends and interest received	Payments of utilities, wages, taxes, and interest

The computation of cash receipts and payments requires adjusting each item on the income statement from an accrual basis to a cash basis. To facilitate this process, we use the following steps:

Step 1: Mark the changes in the balance sheet accounts related to earning income (operating items) with an O. These accounts include the following:

- Current assets (other than cash and short-term investments, which relate to investing activities).
- Current liabilities (other than amounts owed to investors and financial institutions,[2] all of which relate to financing activities).
- Other asset, liability, or shareholders' equity accounts that relate to operations.

In Exhibit 5.3, all of the relevant asset, liability, and shareholders' equity accounts have been marked with an O. These items include Accounts receivable, Inventories, Prepaid expenses, Accounts payable, Accrued liabilities, Future income taxes, and Retained earnings.

Step 2: Convert the revenue and expense items from an accrual basis to a cash basis. We can compute the amount of cash receipts and cash payments by examining the changes in the balances of current assets and current liabilities. Analysis of the changes in any balance sheet account is facilitated by examining the type of transactions that affect the account and then determining the amount of cash received or paid during the accounting period using the following equation:

$$\text{Beginning Balance} + \text{Increases} - \text{Decreases} = \text{Ending Balance}$$

We will use this relationship to analyze the changes in the current asset and liability accounts.

Converting Revenues to Cash Inflows When sales are recorded, accounts receivable increase, and when cash is collected, accounts receivable decrease. Hence, the change from the beginning balance of Accounts Receivable (AR_B) to the ending balance (AR_E) can be represented as follows:

$$AR_B + \text{Sales revenue} - \text{Cash collections} = AR_E$$

---

[2]Examples of the accounts excluded are Dividends Payable, Short-Term Borrowing (or Bank Indebtedness), and Current Portion of Long-Term Debt (representing long-term debt with an original term longer than one year that is due within one year of the statement date).

We can rearrange this equation as follows:

$$\textbf{Cash collections} = \textbf{Sales revenue} + \textbf{AR}_B - \textbf{AR}_E$$

The beginning and ending balances of accounts receivable are reported on the balance sheet, and sales revenue is reported on the income statement. However, the amount collected from customers is not reported on either statement, but can be derived from the equation above.[3]

The beginning balance of accounts receivable increases the cash received from customers on the assumption that all amounts owed to the company at the beginning of the period are collected during the period. In contrast, the ending balance of accounts receivable is deducted from sales revenue because these receivables have already been included in sales revenue, but have not yet been collected from customers.

Using information from Sleeman's income statement and balance sheet presented in Exhibit 5.3, we can compute the cash collected from customers as follows:

$$\textbf{Cash collections} = \$53,091 + \$37,348 - \$32,139 = \$58,300$$

Accounts Receivable

Beg.	37,348		
Sales	53,091	Collections	**58,300**
End.	32,139		

Converting Cost of Goods Sold to Cash Paid to Suppliers   The cost of goods sold during the accounting period may be greater or smaller than the amount of cash paid to suppliers of merchandise during the period. The computation of the cash paid to suppliers is a two-stage process. First, we analyze the change in the Inventory (INV) account to determine the amount of merchandise purchases during the period, and then we analyze the change in the Accounts Payable (AP) account to compute the amount of cash payments to suppliers using the following equations:

$$\textbf{INV}_B + \textbf{Merchandise purchases} - \textbf{Cost of goods sold} = \textbf{INV}_E$$

$$\textbf{AP}_B + \textbf{Merchandise purchases} - \textbf{Cash payments to suppliers} = \textbf{AP}_E$$

Rearranging these two equations yields:

$$\textbf{Merchandise purchases} = \textbf{Cost of goods sold} + \textbf{INV}_E - \textbf{INV}_B$$

$$\textbf{Cash payments to suppliers} = \textbf{Merchandise purchases} + \textbf{AP}_B - \textbf{AP}_E$$

The beginning and ending balances of inventory and accounts payable are reported on the balance sheet, and the cost of goods sold is reported on the income statement. However, the amount of merchandise purchases and the payments to suppliers are not reported on either statement, but can be derived from the equations above.[4]

The ending balance of inventory is added to cost of goods sold to determine the cost of goods that were available for sale during the period. Given that part of the merchandise was available at the beginning of the period (INV_B), it is deducted from the goods available to determine the amount of purchases during the period.

The beginning balance of accounts payable is added to merchandise purchases to determine the total amount payable to suppliers. The ending balance of accounts payable is then deducted from that total because these payables have not been paid to suppliers yet.

---

[3]We assume that all sales are made on account. However, the amount of cash collected from customers is the same regardless of the mix of cash and credit sales. To be sure, assume that sales are 20-percent cash and 80-percent on account, and compute the amount of cash collected from customers during the period. You can use other percentages as well.

[4]We assume that all purchases are made on account. However, the amount of cash paid to suppliers is the same regardless of the mix of cash and credit purchases. To be sure, assume that purchases are 10-percent cash and 90-percent on account, and compute the amount of cash paid to suppliers during the period. You can use other percentages as well.

Using information from Sleeman's income statement and balance sheet presented in Exhibit 5.3, we can compute the cash paid to suppliers as follows:

$$\text{Merchandise purchases} = \$26{,}576 + \$27{,}506 - \$27{,}946 = \$26{,}136$$

$$\text{Cash payments to suppliers} = \$26{,}136 + \$18{,}810 - \$16{,}515 = \$28{,}431$$

Converting Other Operating Expenses to a Cash Outflow The total amount of any operating expense on the income statement may differ from the cash payment for that expense during the accounting period. Some expenses are paid before they are recognized as expenses (e.g., prepaid rent). When prepayments are made, the balance in the asset Prepaid Expenses increases; when prepaid expenses are used up and recognized as expenses for the period, the account balance decreases. Other expenses are paid for after they are recognized in the same or previous periods. In this case, when expenses are recorded, the balance in the account Accrued Liabilities increases; when payments are made, the account balance decreases. The computation of the cash paid for operating expenses is therefore a two-stage process. First, we analyze the change in the Prepaid Expenses (PE) account to determine the amount of cash paid during the period, and then we analyze the change in the Accrued Liabilities (AL) account to compute the amount of cash that was paid during the period for various other expenses, as shown below.

$$PE_B + \text{Prepayments} - \text{Prepayments that expired during the period} = PE_E$$

$$AL_B + \text{Accrued expenses} - \text{Cash payments for other expenses} = AL_E$$

Rearranging these two equations yields:

$$\text{Prepayments} = \text{Prepayments that expired during the period} + PE_E - PE_B$$

$$\text{Cash payments for other expenses} = \text{Accrued expenses} + AL_B - AL_E$$

The beginning and ending balances of prepaid expenses and accrued liabilities are reported on the balance sheet; the prepayments that expired during the period and the accrued expenses are both reported on the income statement as operating expenses (or general, selling and administrative expenses). However, the amounts paid for these expenses during the period are not reported on either statement, but they can be derived from the equations above.

Using information from Sleeman's income statement and balance sheet presented in Exhibit 5.3, we can compute the cash paid for other expenses as follows:

Cash paid for other expenses = $16,985 (general, selling, and administrative expenses, reflecting prepayments that expired during the quarter and accrued expenses)

  +   1,495 (prepaid expenses, end of quarter)

  −   2,376 (prepaid expenses, beginning of quarter)

  + 13,358 (accrued liabilities, beginning of quarter)

  − 11,654 (accrued liabilities, end of quarter)

  = $17,808

Similar analysis can be applied to computing the cash payments for interest and income taxes. Sleeman reports interest expense of $1,373. Since there is no balance in Interest Payable, interest paid must be equal to interest expense.

Inventory

Beg.	27,946		
Purchases	26,136	Cost of goods sold	26,576
End.	27,506		

Accounts Payable

		Beg.	18,810
Cash payments	28,431	Purchases	26,136
		End.	16,515

Prepaid Expenses

Beg.	1,495	Prepayments that expired	1,495
Cash payments	2,376		
End.	2,376		

Accrued Liabilities

Cash payments	13,358	Beg.	13,358
		Unpaid expenses	11,654
		End.	11,654

Sleeman's income tax expense equals $2,150. This expense usually consists of two components: an amount that is currently payable to the federal and provincial taxation authorities, and another amount labelled Future Income Taxes. Future income taxes result from temporary differences that exist between the accounting principles that underlie financial reporting and tax rules that govern the preparation of tax returns. These differences relate to the timing of recognition of revenues and expenses for financial reporting (that is based on accrual accounting) compared to taxation rules that essentially use a cash basis of accounting.

The computation of cash paid for income taxes should take into consideration changes in two accounts: Income Taxes Payable and Future Income Taxes. Since there is no balance in Income Taxes Payable, income taxes paid is computed as follows:

Income tax expense	$2,150
Change in income taxes payable	0
	2,150
Increase in future income tax liability	1,590
Cash payments for income taxes	$ 560

The operating cash inflows and outflows are accumulated in Exhibit 5.4.

EXHIBIT **5.4**

Sleeman Breweries Ltd.
Schedule of Net Cash Flow
From Operating Activities,
Direct Method (in thousands)

Cash flows from operating activities		
Cash collected from customers		$58,300
Cash payments		
–to suppliers	$28,431	
–for other operating expenses	17,808	
–for interest	1,373	
–for income taxes	560	48,172
Net cash provided by operating activities		$10,128

To summarize, the following adjustments must commonly be made to convert income statement items to the related operating cash flow amounts:

Income Statement Account	+/– Change in Balance Sheet Account(s)	= Operating Cash Flow
Sales revenue	+ Beginning accounts receivable – Ending accounts receivable	= Collections from customers
Cost of goods sold	– Beginning inventory + Ending inventory + Beginning accounts payable – Ending accounts payable	= Payments to suppliers of inventory
Other operating expenses	– Beginning prepaid expenses + Ending prepaid expenses + Beginning accrued liabilities – Ending accrued liabilities	= Payments to suppliers of services (e.g., rent, utilities, wages)
Interest expense	+ Beginning interest payable – Ending interest payable	= Payments for interest
Income tax expense	+ Beginning income taxes payable – Ending income taxes payable +/– Changes in future incomes tax assets and liabilities	= Payments for income taxes

INTERNATIONAL **PERSPECTIVE**

AUSTRALIAN PRACTICES

Foster's Brewing is the first name in Australian beer and a major player in world beverage markets. Following Australian GAAP, which require use of the direct method of presentation, Foster's cash flow from operations is presented as follows:

STATEMENT OF CASH FLOWS FOR THE YEAR ENDED 30 JUNE 2003 ($M)	
Operating Activities	
Receipts from customers	7,150.0
Payments to suppliers, employees, principals	(6,039.7)
Interest received	146.8
Borrowing costs	(303.6)
Income taxes paid	(257.0)
Net cash flows from operating activities	696.5

REAL WORLD EXCERPT

Foster's Brewing

ANNUAL REPORT

Note that Foster's combines payments to suppliers, employees, and principals (officers), but other companies report these items separately. Like Canadian companies that choose the direct method, Foster's reports the indirect presentation in a note to the financial statements.

PART B: REPORTING CASH FLOWS FROM OPERATING ACTIVITIES—INDIRECT METHOD

We have learned that under accrual accounting, revenues are recognized when earned and expenses are recognized when incurred to generate revenues (the matching principle), regardless of the timing of cash receipts and payments. Consequently, net income includes both cash and non-cash elements related to revenues, expenses, gains, and losses.

■ **LEARNING OBJECTIVE 2B**

Report and interpret cash flows from operating activities using the indirect method.

$$\text{Net income} = \text{Cash elements} +/- \text{Non-cash elements}$$

The direct method focuses on the cash elements of net income by computing cash receipts and cash payments to arrive at net cash flows from operating activities. In contrast, the indirect method starts with net income and eliminates non-cash elements to arrive at the same result.

$$\text{Cash elements} = \text{Net income} +/- \text{Non-cash elements}$$

Keeping track of all the additions and subtractions made to convert net income to cash flows from operating activities is facilitated by setting up a schedule to record the computations. We construct such a schedule for Sleeman in Exhibit 5.5 on page 241.

Preparation of the operating section using the indirect method involves the following steps:

Step 1: Mark the changes in the balance sheet accounts related to earning income (operating items) with an O. These accounts include the following:

- Current assets (other than cash and short-term investments that relate to investing activities).
- Current liabilities (other than amounts owed to investors and financial institutions,[5] all of which relate to financing activities).

---

[5]Examples of the accounts excluded are Short-Term Debt to Financial Institutions, Current Portion of Long-Term Debt, and Dividends Payable. The current portion of long-term debt is debt with an original term of more than one year that is payable within one year of the balance sheet date.

- Retained earnings because it increases by the amount of net income, which is the starting point for the Operating section. (Retained earnings also decreases by dividends paid, which is a financing outflow noted by an F.)

Property, plant, and equipment (net) is relevant to the computation of cash flows from both Operating Activities and Investing Activities (noted by an I) because it is affected by amortization expense.

In Exhibit 5.3, all of the relevant assets, liability, and shareholders' equity accounts have been marked with an O. These items include Accounts receivable, Inventories, Prepaid expenses, Accounts payable, Accrued liabilities, Future income taxes, and Retained earnings.

As we have noted, retained earnings and property, plant, and equipment are also relevant to operations.

Step 2: **Begin the Operating Activities section with net income reported on the income statement.** We begin our schedule presented in Exhibit 5.5 with net income of $4,359 taken from Sleeman's income statement (Exhibit 5.3).

Step 3: **Adjust net income for the effects of items marked O that reflect differences in the timing of accrual basis net income and cash flows.** The following adjustments are the ones most frequently encountered:

Income Statement Amounts or Balance Sheet Changes	Impact on the Cash Flow Statement
Net Income	Starting point for computation
Amortization expense	Added
Decreases in current assets	Added
Increases in current liabilities	Added
Increases in current assets	Subtracted
Decreases in current liabilities	Subtracted

This step is completed in two parts:

Step 3a: **Adjust net income for amortization expense.** Recording amortization expense does not affect the cash account (or any other current asset or liability). It affects a noncurrent asset (such as Equipment, net). **Since amortization expense is subtracted in computing net income, but does not affect cash, we always add it back** to convert net income to cash flow from operating activities.[6] In the case of Sleeman, we need to remove the effect of amortization expense by adding back $1,648 to net income (see Exhibit 5.5).[7]

Step 3b: **Adjust net income for changes in current assets and current liabilities.** Each **change** in current assets (other than cash and short-term investments) and current liabilities (other than amounts owed to owners and financial institutions) causes a difference between net income and cash flow from operating activities. When converting net income to cash flow from operating activities, apply the following general rules:

---

[6]The fact that amortization is added back to net income may lead the reader to conclude that amortization expense is a source of cash. Nothing could be further from the truth! In fact, amortization is a process of allocation of the cost of assets that have been amortized in the past regardless of the timing of payments for the assets.

[7]Gains and losses on sales of equipment and investments are dealt with in a similar manner and are discussed in Chapter Supplement A. Other similar additions and subtractions are discussed in more advanced accounting courses.

- **Add the change when a current asset decreases or current liability increases.**
- **Subtract the change when a current asset increases or current liability decreases.**

Understanding what makes these current assets and current liabilities increase and decrease is the key to understanding the logic of these additions and subtractions.

EXHIBIT **5.5**

Sleeman Breweries: Schedule for Net Cash Flow from Operating Activities, Indirect Method (in thousands)

Conversion of net income to net cash flow from operating activities:

Items	Amount	Explanation
Net income, accrual basis	$ 4,359	From income statement.
Add (subtract) to convert to cash basis:		
Depreciation and amortization expense	+1,648	Add because depreciation and amortization expense is a non-current accrued expense.
Future income tax expense	+1,590	Add because the future income tax expense is a non-current accrued expense.
Decrease in accounts receivable	+5,209	Add because cash collected from customers is more than accrual basis revenues.
Decrease in inventory	+440	Add because cost of goods sold expense is less than purchases.
Decrease in prepaid expenses	+881	Add because accrual basis expenses are more than cash prepayments for expenses.
Decrease in accounts payable	−2,295	Subtract because purchases on account (due to suppliers) are less than cash payments to suppliers.
Decrease in accrued liabilities	−1,704	Subtract because accrual basis expenses are less than the cash payments for expenses.
Net cash inflow from operating activities	$10,128	Reported on the cash flow statement.

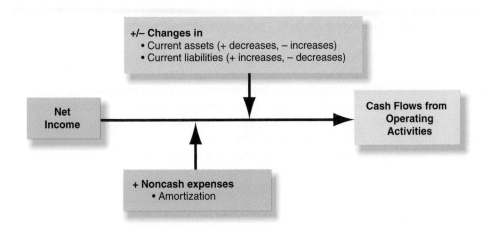

Change in Accounts Receivable We illustrate this logic with the first operating item (O) listed on Sleeman's Balance sheet (Exhibit 5.3), accounts receivable. Remember that the income statement reflects sales revenue, but the cash flow statement must reflect cash collections from customers. As the following accounts receivable

T-account illustrates, when sales revenues are recorded, accounts receivable increases, and when cash is collected from customers, accounts receivable decreases.

Accounts Receivable (A)			
Beginning balance	37,348		
Sales revenue (on account)	53,091	Collections from customers	58,300
Ending balance	32,139		

Change −5,209 {

In the Sleeman example, sales revenue on account reported on the income statement is lower than cash collections from customers by $58,300 − $53,091 = $5,209.[8] Since more money was collected from customers, this amount must be added to net income to convert to cash flows from operating activities. Note that this amount is also the same as the **change** in the accounts receivable account:

Ending balance	$32,139
−Beginning balance	37,348
Change	−$ 5,209

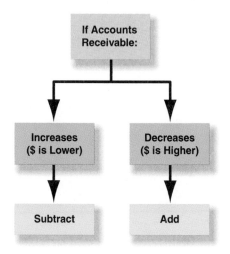

If Accounts Receivable:

Increases ($ is Lower) → Subtract

Decreases ($ is Higher) → Add

This same underlying logic is used to determine adjustments for the other current assets and liabilities.

To summarize, the income statement reflects revenues of the period, but cash flow from operating activities must reflect cash collections from customers. Sales on account increase the balance in accounts receivable, and collections from customers decrease the balance.

Accounts Receivable (A)			
Beg.	37,348		
		Decrease	5,209
End.	32,139		

The balance sheet for Sleeman Breweries indicates a **decrease** in accounts receivable of $5,209 for the period, which means cash collected from customers is higher than revenue. To convert to cash flows from operating activities, the amount of the decrease must be **added** to net income in Exhibit 5.5. (An increase is subtracted from net income.)

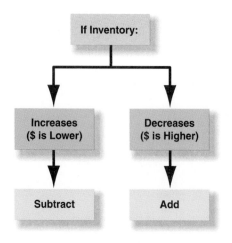

If Inventory:

Increases ($ is Lower) → Subtract

Decreases ($ is Higher) → Add

Change in Inventory The income statement reflects merchandise sold for the period, whereas cash flow from operating activities must reflect cash purchases.

Both the change in inventory and the change in accounts payable (borrowing from suppliers) determine the magnitude of this difference. It is easiest to think about the change in inventory in terms of the simple case in which the company pays cash to suppliers of inventory. We address the added complexity involved when purchases are made on account when we discuss the adjustment for the change in accounts payable.

Since purchases of goods increase the balance in inventory and cost of goods sold decreases the balance in inventory, the change in inventory is the difference between purchases and the cost of goods sold.

---

[8]The amount of cash collected from customers is the same, regardless of the mix of cash sales and credit sales. To make sure, assume that sales are 20 percent cash and 80 percent on account, and calculate the amount of cash collected from customers during the period.

Inventories (A)			
Beg.	27,946		
		Decrease	440
End.	27,506		

Sleeman's balance sheet indicates that inventory **decreased** by $440, which means that the amount of purchases is lower than the amount of merchandise sold. The decrease must be **added** to net income to convert to cash flow from operating activities in Exhibit 5.5. (An increase is subtracted from net income.)

Change in Prepaid Expenses   The income statement reflects expenses of the period, but cash flow from operating activities must reflect the cash payments. Cash prepayments increase the balance in prepaid expenses, and expenses recognized during the period decrease the balance in prepaid expenses.

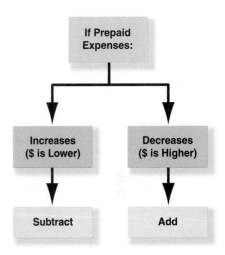

Prepaid Expenses (A)			
Beg.	2,376		
		Decrease	881
End.	1,495		

The Sleeman balance sheet indicates a **decrease** of $881 in prepaid expenses, which means that the amount of expenses is more than new cash prepayments. The decrease (the extra expenses) must be **added** back to net income in Exhibit 5.5. (An increase is subtracted from net income.)

Change in Accounts Payable   Cash flow from operations must reflect cash purchases, but not all purchases are for cash. Purchases on account increase accounts payable, and cash paid to suppliers decreases accounts payable.

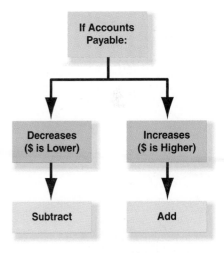

Accounts Payable (L)			
		Beg.	18,810
Decrease	2,295		
		End.	16,515

Sleeman's accounts payable **decreased** by $2,295, which means that cash payments were more than purchases on account, and this decrease (the extra payments) must be **subtracted** from net income in Exhibit 5.5. (An increase is added to net income.)

Change in Accrued Liabilities   The income statement reflects all accrued expenses, but the cash flow statement must reflect actual payments for those expenses. Recording accrued expenses increases the balance in Accrued liabilities and cash payments for the expenses decrease Accrued liabilities.

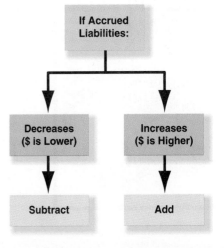

Accrued Liabilities (L)			
		Beg.	13,358
Decrease	1,704		
		End.	11,654

Sleeman's accrued liabilities **decreased** by $1,704, which indicates that accrual-basis expenses are lower than cash paid for the expenses. The decrease must be **subtracted** from net income in Exhibit 5.5. (An increase is added back to net income.)

Summary   We can summarize the typical additions and subtractions that are required to reconcile net income with cash flow from operating activities as follows:

Item	ADDITIONS AND SUBTRACTIONS TO RECONCILE NET INCOME TO CASH FLOW FROM OPERATING ACTIVITIES	
	When Item Increases	When Item Decreases
Amortization	+	
Accounts receivable	−	+
Inventory	−	+
Prepaid expenses	−	+
Accounts payable	+	−
Accrued expenses (liabilities)	+	−

Notice in this table that an *increase in an asset or a decrease in a liability* is always *subtracted* to reconcile net income to cash flows from operating activities. A *decrease in an asset or an increase in a liability* is always *added* to reconcile net income to cash flows from operating activities. The cash flow statement for Sleeman Breweries Ltd. (Exhibit 5.1) shows the same additions and subtractions to reconcile net income to cash flows from operating activities described in Exhibit 5.5.

It is important to note again that the net cash inflow or outflow is the same regardless of whether the direct or indirect method of presentation is used (in this case, an inflow of $10,128). The two methods differ only in terms of the details reported on the statement.[9]

SELF-STUDY **QUIZ 5-2**

Canadian Tire Corporation

Indicate which of the following items taken from Canadian Tire Corporation's cash flow statement would be added (+), subtracted (−), or not included (0) in the reconciliation of net income to cash flow from operations.

_____ *a.* Increase in inventories.

_____ *b.* Net borrowings from bank.

_____ *c.* Depreciation and amortization.

_____ *d.* Decrease in trade accounts receivable.

_____ *e.* Increase in trade accounts payable and accrued expenses.

_____ *f.* Increase in prepaid expenses and other current assets.

After you complete your answers, check them with the solutions on page 256.

INTERPRETING CASH FLOWS FROM OPERATIONS

The Operating Activities section of the cash flow statement focuses attention on the firm's ability to generate cash internally through operations and its management of working capital (current assets minus current liabilities). Many analysts regard this as the most important section of the statement because, in the long run, operations are the only source of cash. Investors should not invest in a company if they believe that it will not be able to pay them dividends or make reinvestments with cash generated from operations. Similarly, creditors should not lend money if they believe that cash generated from operations will not be available to pay back the loan. For example, many

---

[9]A more detailed illustration showing both the direct and indirect methods of computing cash flows from operations is available on the Online Learning Centre Web site at www.mcgrawhill.ca/college/libby/student/resources.

Internet-based companies crashed when investors lost faith in their ability to turn business ideas into cash from operations.

A common rule followed by financial and credit analysts is to stay away from firms with rising net income but falling cash flow from operations. Rapidly rising inventories require the use of cash until goods are sold. Similarly, rapidly rising accounts receivable also delay the collection of cash. Rising inventories and accounts receivable often predict a future slump in profits as revenues fall. This increases the need for external financing as overall cash inflows from operations decline. In the first quarter of 2003, Sleeman exhibited just such a pattern. Is this a sign of troubled waters ahead for the leader of the craft beer industry? Why, as indicated in the following chart, did net income increase slightly in the following quarter, but cash flow from operations showed a significant rebound?

	Net Income		Cash Flows from Operations
1st quarter	$1,906	>	(6,942)
2nd quarter	$2,049	<	$7,479

To answer these questions, we must carefully analyze how Sleeman's operating activities are reported in the cash flow statement. At the same time, we also must learn more about the brewing industry to properly interpret this information.

Fluctuating Cash Flows from Operations: A Warning Sign?   In the first quarter, Sleeman's net income was $1,906 (in thousands), yet it reported a use of cash for operations of $6,942. Does this suggest that Sleeman may be facing more difficult times?

Analysts who cover the beverage industry know that this is a result of seasonal fluctuations in beer sales to distributors. They recognize that beer sales are low in the first quarter (January to March) because of winter, and that sales are high during the second quarter (April to June) in anticipation of summer. The higher sales volume in the second quarter requires a buildup of inventories over time to meet demand in the summer months, which leads to cash payments to suppliers and employees exceeding cash collections from customers. The imbalance in cash inflows and outflows increases the need for external financing. However, the use of cash for operations during the first quarter is followed by a net cash inflow from operations in the second quarter, when sales and collections from customers increase. This normal seasonal fluctuation in sales is clearly not a sign of problems for Sleeman.

Analyzing Inventory Changes   An unexpected increase in inventory can be another cause for net income to outpace cash flow from operations. Such inventory growth can be a sign that planned sales growth did not materialize. A decline in inventory can be a sign that the company is anticipating lower sales in the next quarter. Many analysts compute the quality of income (or quality of earnings) ratio as a general warning sign of these and similar problems.

FINANCIAL **ANALYSIS**

CLASSIFICATION OF CASH FLOWS

We indicated in Chapter 4 that managers may speed up the recognition of revenues or delay the recognition of expenses in order to increase the reported net income, which would reflect positively on their performance and compensation. For this reason, analysts also examine the cash flow from operations, because cash receipts and payments are less susceptible to manipulation. However, the reported operating cash flow can be influenced by classifying certain operating cash flows as investing cash flows.

Certain companies, such as Nortel Networks Limited, General Motors Corp., and Harley-Davidson Inc., provide loans or other financial assistance to their customers to help them buy the companies' products. These loans reduce cash and increase the amount of receivables. The reduction in cash and corresponding increase in receivables are the result of an operating transaction. But these companies tended to classify these transactions as investing activities rather than operating activities in order to avoid their negative effects on operating cash flows. Recently, the U.S. Securities and Exchange Commission required that cash flows resulting from vendor financing be classified as operating cash flows instead of investing cash flows. This requirement has resulted in significant reductions of operating cash flows for companies that followed this practice. For example, the operating cash flows of General Motors Corp. and Ford Motor Company for the year 2003 declined by US$4.4 billion and US$2.1 billion, respectively. The reclassification of cash flows has implications for a proper evaluation of operating cash flows and related analyses, such as the quality of income ratio discussed below.

Source: Michael Rapoport, "Cash flow takes an SEC hit," *National Post*, March 24, 2005, p. FP15.

KEY **RATIO ANALYSIS:**

QUALITY OF INCOME RATIO

ANALYTICAL QUESTION → How much cash does each dollar of net income generate?
RATIO AND COMPARISONS → The quality of income ratio is useful in answering this question. It is computed as follows:

$$\text{Quality of Income Ratio} = \frac{\text{Cash Flow from Operating Activities}}{\text{Net Income}}$$

■ LEARNING OBJECTIVE 3

Analyze and interpret the quality of income ratio.

Sleeman's ratio for the third quarter of 2003 is:

$$\frac{\$10,128}{\$4,359} = 2.32 \ (232\%)$$

Comparisons over Time				Comparisons with Competitors	
Sleeman Breweries (annual)				Molson Inc.	Boston Beer
2001	2002	2003		2003	2003
1.94	1.00	1.11		1.10	1.86

INTERPRETATIONS

Selected Focus Company Comparisons

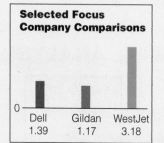

Dell	Gildan	WestJet
1.39	1.17	3.18

IN GENERAL → The quality of income ratio measures the portion of income that was generated in cash. All other things being equal, a higher quality of income ratio indicates a greater ability to finance operating and other cash needs from operating cash inflows.[10] A higher ratio also indicates that it is less likely that the company is using aggressive revenue recognition policies to increase net income. When this ratio does not equal 1.0, analysts must establish the source of the difference to determine the significance of the findings. There are four potential causes of any difference:

1. *The corporate life cycle (growth or decline in sales).* When sales are increasing, receivables and inventory normally increase faster than accounts payable. This often reduces operating cash flows below income, which, in turn, reduces the ratio. When sales are declining, the opposite occurs, and the ratio increases.

---

[10]When a net loss is reported, a more negative ratio indicates greater ability to finance the company from operations.

2. *Seasonality.* As was the case for Sleeman, seasonal variations in sales and purchases of inventory can cause the ratio to deviate from 1.0.

3. *Changes in revenue and expense recognition.* Aggressive revenue recognition or failure to accrue appropriate expenses will inflate net income and reduce the ratio.

4. *Changes in management of operating assets and liabilities.* Inefficient management will increase operating assets and decrease liabilities, which will reduce operating cash flows and reduce the ratio. More efficient management will have the opposite effect.

FOCUS COMPANY ANALYSIS → Sleeman's quality of income ratio has ranged from 1.00 to 1.94 during the last three years. As we noted earlier, the difference between net income and cash flow from operations in the case of Sleeman for the first quarter of 2003 was not a cause for alarm. It was due to normal seasonal changes in sales and receivables. The annual results for 2003 support this conclusion, indicating a slight increase in the quality of income ratio from 2002. Its ratio is also quite similar to that of Molson Inc. but lower than the quality of income ratio achieved by Boston Beer. The wide variation in Sleeman's ratio would prompt analysts to contact management to determine its causes.

A FEW CAUTIONS → The quality of income ratio can be interpreted only based on an understanding of the company's business operations and strategy. For example, a low ratio can be due simply to normal seasonal changes. However, it also can indicate obsolete inventory, slowing sales, or failed expansion plans. Analysts often analyze this ratio in tandem with the accounts receivable turnover and inventory turnover ratios to test for these possibilities.*

*K. G. Palepu, P. M. Healy, and V. L. Bernard, *Business Analysis and Valuation Using Financial Statements,* 2e. Cincinnati, OH: South-Western, 2000.

A QUESTION OF **ETHICS**

FRAUD AND CASH FLOWS FROM OPERATIONS

The cash flow statement often gives outsiders the first hint that financial statements may contain errors and irregularities. The importance of this indicator as a predictor is receiving more attention following the corporate scandals in the United States, as *Forbes* reported:

REAL WORLD EXCERPT

Forbes

> From July 1997 to July 2002 the SEC launched 227 investigations of suspected financial misreporting, 126 of them relating to revenue recognition. Improper timing of sales is the biggest offense—borrowing from the next quarter in a desperate effort to make the analysts happy for the quarter. The SEC also found 80 cases of utterly fictitious revenues and 21 cases of improperly valued revenues . . .
>
> . . . How do you protect yourself as an investor? Spend as much time with the cash flow statement as with the profit-and-loss statement that precedes it. If a company is counting dubious transactions in its revenues, in all likelihood the buyers haven't paid yet, and the cash flow from operations will be anemic in relation to reported profit.*

As noted in earlier chapters, unethical managers sometimes attempt to reach earnings targets by manipulating accruals and deferrals of revenues and expenses to inflate income. Since these adjusting entries do not affect the cash account, they have no effect on the cash flow statement. As a consequence, a growing difference between net income and cash flow from operations can be a sign of such manipulations. This early warning sign has been evident before some famous bankruptcies, such as that of W. T. Grant. This company had inflated income by failing to make adequate accruals of expenses for uncollectable accounts receivable and obsolete inventory. The growing difference between net income and cash flow from operations that resulted was noted by the more astute analysts who recommended selling the stock long before the bankruptcy.

*Source: Andrew T. Gillies, "Is That Revenue for Real," *Forbes,* April 14, 2003, p. 161.

REPORTING AND INTERPRETING CASH FLOWS FROM INVESTING ACTIVITIES

REPORTING CASH FLOWS FROM INVESTING ACTIVITIES

Preparing this section of the cash flow statement requires analyzing the accounts related to property, plant, and equipment; intangible assets; and investments in the securities of other companies, and lending to other than customers. Normally, the relevant balance sheet accounts include short-term investments and long-term asset accounts such as Long-Term Investments and Property, Plant, and Equipment. The following relationships are the ones that you will encounter most frequently:

Related Balance Sheet Account(s)	Investing Activity	Cash Flow Effect
Property, plant, and equipment and intangible assets (e.g., patents)	Purchase of property, plant, and equipment or intangible assets for cash	Outflow
	Sale of property, plant, and equipment or intangible assets for cash	Inflow
Short- or long-term investments in shares and bonds issued by other companies	Purchase of investment securities for cash	Outflow
	Sale (maturity) of investment securities for cash	Inflow

Typical investing activities include the following:

1. Cash expenditures that include the acquisition of tangible productive assets such as buildings and equipment or intangible assets such as trademarks and patents. Only purchases paid for with cash or cash equivalents are included. Purchases made using debt issued to the seller, for example, are excluded.

2. Cash proceeds from the sale of productive assets or intangible assets. This is the amount of cash that was received from the sale of assets, regardless of whether the assets were sold at a gain or a loss.

3. Purchase of short- or long-term investments for cash. These investments can include shares or bonds issued by other companies, guaranteed investment certificates, or government securities with maturities of more than three months. (Remember that those with maturities of three months or less are cash equivalents.)

4. Cash proceeds from the sale or maturity of short- or long-term investments. Again, this is the amount of cash that was received from the sale, regardless of whether the assets were sold at a gain or a loss.

In the case of Sleeman Breweries, the analysis of changes in the balance sheet (shown in Exhibit 5.3) indicates that three long-term assets (noted with an I) have changed during the period: Property, Plant, and Equipment (net), Long-Term Investments, and Intangible Assets. Company records would then be searched to determine the causes of changes in these assets.

Property, Plant, and Equipment (net)   The company's Property, Plant, and Equipment (PPE) increased by an amount of $334, net of accumulated amortization. Typically, the net change in PPE is the result of three main changes: (1) purchase of new assets, (2) disposal of old assets, and (3) periodic amortization of these assets. The purchase of assets increases the balance of PPE, the disposal of assets decreases the balance of PPE by the net book value (original cost − accumulated amortization) of the assets disposed of, and the periodic amortization increases the accumulated amortization, which in turn reduces the balance of PPE.

During the third quarter of 2003, Sleeman purchased new property, plant, and equipment for cash in the amount of $1,350, which is a cash outflow. This amount less the amortization expense of $1,016, which is added to the net income in the Operations section of the cash flow statement,[11] explains the net increase in PPE of $334.

Property, Plant, and Equipment (net)

Beg.	72,359	Amortization	1,016
Purchases	1,350		
End.	72,693		

Cash purchases and sales of plant and equipment are listed separately on the cash flow statement.

Long-Term Investments   Sleeman's records indicate that it sold long-term investments during the quarter and received $248 in cash. This transaction explains the decrease in the account balance.

Long-Term Investments (A)

Beg.	7,586	Sale	248
End.	7,338		

Intangible Assets   Finally, Sleeman's intangible assets decreased by $632. This net change is the result of the recording of amortization expense that does not affect cash but is added to net income to compute the cash flow from operating activities.

Intangible Assets (A)

Beg.	86,512	Amortization	632
End.	85,880		

These investing items are listed in the schedule of investing activities in Exhibit 5.6, and result in a cash outflow of $1,102.

EXHIBIT **5.6**

Sleeman Breweries Ltd.: Schedule for Net Cash Flow from Investing Activities (in thousands)

Items from Balance Sheet and Account Analysis	Cash Inflow (Outflows)	Explanation
Additions to property, plant, and equipment	($1,350)	Payment in cash for buildings and equipment.
Proceeds from long-term investments	248	Receipt of cash for sale of investments.
Net cash inflow (outflow) from investing activities	($1,102)	Reported on the cash flow statement.

INTERPRETING CASH FLOWS FROM INVESTING ACTIVITIES

Two common ways of assessing a company's ability to finance its expansion needs from internal sources are the capital acquisitions ratio and free cash flow.

---

[11]This amount is part of the depreciation and amortization expense that the company reported on its income statement. The other component, $632, relates to the amortization of intangible assets.

KEY **RATIO ANALYSIS:**

■ **LEARNING OBJECTIVE 5**

Analyze and interpret the capital acquisitions ratio.

CAPITAL ACQUISITIONS RATIO

ANALYTICAL QUESTION → To what degree was the company able to finance purchases of property, plant, and equipment with cash provided by operating activities?

RATIO AND COMPARISONS → Since capital expenditures for plant and equipment often vary greatly from year to year, this ratio is often computed over longer periods of time than one year, such as the three-year period used here. It is computed as follows:

$$\text{Capital Acquisitions Ratio} = \frac{\text{Cash Flow from Operating Activities}}{\text{Cash Paid for Property, Plant, and Equipment}}$$

The 2001 through 2003 ratio for Sleeman is:

$$\frac{\$45,971}{\$28,315} = 1.62$$

Comparisons over Time		Comparisons with Competitors	
Sleeman		**Molson Inc.**	**Boston Beer**
1998–2000	2001–2003	2001–2003	2001–2003
0.89	1.62	4.04	7.19

INTERPRETATIONS

In General → The capital acquisitions ratio reflects the portion of purchases of property, plant, and equipment financed from operating activities without the need for outside debt or equity financing or the sale of other investments or fixed assets. A high ratio indicates less need for outside financing for current and future expansion. This provides the company with opportunities for strategic acquisitions, avoids the cost of additional debt, and reduces the risks of bankruptcy that come with additional leverage (see Chapter 11).

Focus Company Analysis → Although Sleeman's ratio has increased from 0.89 to 1.62 in recent years, Sleeman's capital acquisitions ratio is significantly lower than its competitors. To many, the tangible nature of plant and equipment may suggest that it is a low-risk investment. When companies in an industry build more productive capacity than is necessary to meet customer demand, however, the costs of maintaining and financing idle plant can drive a company to ruin. The brewing industry currently has significant excess capacity. Sleeman reduces the risks of overbuilding plant and equipment investments by outsourcing the production of its value brands to other brewers. This practice, called *contract brewing,* gives Sleeman advantages through lower borrowing and amortization costs and through lower costs of transportation. Sleeman also obtains these cost savings by producing beer in each region for niche markets; thus, it owns most of its capacity and this strategy is reflected in its ratio. In contrast, Boston Beer follows a strategy of outsourcing and avoids the risk of excess capacity. The effects of the alternative strategies are made evident by this ratio.

A Few Cautions → Since the needs for investment in plant and equipment differ dramatically across industries (for example, airlines versus pizza delivery restaurants), a particular firm's ratio should be compared only with its prior years' figures or with other firms in the same industry. Also, a high ratio may indicate a failure to update plant and equipment, which can limit a company's ability to compete in the future.

Selected Focus Company Comparisons

Dell 11.74

Gildan 1.47

WestJet Airlines 0.40

FINANCIAL **ANALYSIS**

FREE CASH FLOW

Managers and analysts also often calculate **free cash flow** as a measure of the firm's ability to pursue long-term investment opportunities. It is normally calculated as follows:

$$\text{Free Cash Flow} = \text{Cash Flows from Operating Activities} - \text{Dividends} - \text{Capital Expenditures}$$

Any positive free cash flow is available for additional capital expenditures, investments in other companies, and mergers and acquisitions, without the need for external financing. While free cash flow is considered a positive sign of financial flexibility, it also can represent a hidden cost to shareholders. Sometimes managers use free cash flow to pursue unprofitable investments just for the sake of growth or for perquisites for management use (such as fancy offices and corporate jets). In these cases, the shareholders would be better off if free cash flow were paid as additional dividends or used to repurchase the company's shares in the open market.

FREE CASH FLOW =
Cash Flows from Operating Activities − Dividends − Capital Expenditures

REPORTING AND INTERPRETING CASH FLOWS FROM FINANCING ACTIVITIES

REPORTING CASH FLOWS FROM FINANCING ACTIVITIES

Financing activities are associated with generating capital from creditors and owners. This section reflects changes in two current liabilities, *notes payable to financial institutions* (often called *short-term debt*), *current portion of long-term debt,* as well as changes in *long-term liabilities and shareholders' equity accounts.* These balance sheet accounts relate to the issuance and retirement of debt, repurchase of shares, and the payment of dividends. The following relationships are the ones that you will encounter most frequently:

■ **LEARNING OBJECTIVE 6**

Report and interpret cash flows from financing activities.

Related Balance Sheet Account(s)	Cash Flow Financing Activity	Effect
Short-term debt (notes payable)	Borrowing cash from bank or other financial institution	Inflow
	Repayment of loan principal	Outflow
Long-term debt	Issuance of long-term debt for cash	Inflow
	Repayment of principal on long-term debt	Outflow
Share capital	Issuance of shares for cash	Inflow
	Repurchase (retirement) of shares with cash	Outflow
Retained earnings	Payment of cash dividends	Outflow

Financing activities are associated with generating capital from creditors and owners. Typical financing activities include the following:

1. *Proceeds from issuance of short- and long-term debt.* This represents cash received from borrowing from banks and other financial institutions, and issuance of long-term debt (e.g., notes, debentures, bonds) to the public. If the debt is issued for other than cash (for example, issued directly to a supplier of equipment to pay for a purchase), it is not included on the statement.

2. *Principal payments on short- and long-term debt.* Cash outflows associated with debt include the periodic repayment of principal as well as the early retirement of debt. As you saw in previous chapters, most debt requires periodic payments of both principal and interest. The portion of the cash payment associated with principal is listed as a cash flow from financing activities. The portion that is associated with interest is a cash flow from operating activities.

3. *Proceeds from the issuance of common shares.* This represents cash received from the sale of common shares to investors. If the shares are issued for other than cash (for example, issued directly to an employee as part of salary), the amount is not included in the statement.

4. *Purchase of shares for retirement.* This cash outflow includes cash payments for repurchase of the company's own shares from shareholders.

5. *Cash portion of dividends.* This is the amount of cash dividends paid to shareholders during the year. Some students wonder why cash payments made to creditors

(interest) are shown as an operating activity but cash payments to owners (dividends) are shown as a financing activity. Remember that interest is reported on the income statement and is, therefore, directly associated with earning income (it is an operating activity). Dividend payments are not reported on the income statement because they represent a distribution of income. Dividends are more appropriately shown as a financing activity.

To compute cash flows from financing activities, you should review changes in debt and shareholders' equity accounts. In the case of Sleeman Breweries, analysis of changes in the balance sheet account balances indicates that bank operating loans, share capital, and long-term obligations changed during the period (noted with an F).

Short-Term Debt Company records indicate that the change in bank indebtedness resulted from the repayment of $4,653 in cash. This item is listed in Exhibit 5.7.

		Bank Indebtedness (L)	
		Beg.	4,653
Payment	4,653		
		End.	0

Share Capital The change in share capital resulted from an issue of common shares to key executives who were granted stock options in the past. These executives paid $27 in exchange for the shares issued.

	Share Capital (SE)	
	Beg.	44,916
	Issue of shares	27
	End.	44,943

Long-Term Debt The company's long-term debt, including the current portion, decreased from $93,117 to $90,687. Therefore, Sleeman repaid $2,430 of its long-term debt during the third quarter of 2003, as shown in Exhibit 5.7.

		Long-Term Obligations (L)	
		Beg.	93,117
Payment	2,430		
		End.	90,687

When Sleeman retires some of its own shares, it will report them as cash outflows in the Financing section for that period. If Sleeman ever decides to pay dividends, it would also list them as financing cash outflows.

EXHIBIT 5.7

Sleeman Breweries Ltd.: Schedule for Net Cash Flow from Financing Activities (in thousands)

Items from Balance Sheet and Account Analysis	Cash Inflow (Outflows)	Explanation
Net repayments of bank operating loans	($4,653)	Repayment of borrowing from bank
Stock options exercised	27	Cash inflow from company executives who purchased common shares
Long-term obligations—principal repayments	(2,430)	Repayment of the principal amount of long-term debt, including the current portion
Net cash outflow for investing activities	($7,056)	Reported on the cash flow statement

INTERPRETING CASH FLOWS FROM FINANCING ACTIVITIES

The long-term growth of a company is normally financed from three sources: internally generated funds (cash from operating activities), the issuance of shares, and money borrowed on a long-term basis. As we discuss in Chapter 11, companies can adopt a number of different capital structures (the balance of debt and equity). The financing sources that management uses to fund growth will have an important impact on the firm's risk and return characteristics. The cash flow statement shows how management has elected to fund its growth. This information is used by analysts who wish to evaluate the capital structure and growth potential of a business.

FINANCIAL **ANALYSIS**

INTERPRETATION OF CASH FLOW PATTERNS

The cash flow statement depicts the relationships among the operating, investing, and financing activities. Throughout this chapter, we have illustrated the reporting and interpretation of Sleeman's cash flows for the third quarter of 2003. These cash flows are specific to one company for a specified time period. To generalize, the table below shows the eight possible patterns of cash flows generated from (used for) operating, investing, and financing activities. A general explanation for each observed pattern is also provided.

Table 1

Analysis of Cash Flow Statements: Patterns

	1	2	3	4	5	6	7	8
Cash Flow from Operating	+	+	+	+	−	−	−	−
Cash Flow from Investing	+	−	+	−	+	−	+	−
Cash Flow from Financing	+	−	−	+	+	+	−	−

General explanation of each pattern:

1. The company is using cash generated from operations, from the sale of long-term assets, and from financing to build its cash reserves. This is a very liquid company, possibly looking for acquisitions. This pattern is very unusual.

2. The company is using cash generated from operations to buy long-term assets and to reduce its debt or distribute cash dividends to shareholders. This pattern reflects a mature, successful firm.

3. The company is using cash from operations and from the sale of fixed assets to reduce its debt or distribute cash dividends to shareholders. It is actually downsizing its operations.

4. The company is using cash from operations and from borrowing (or from equity investment) to expand. This pattern is typical of many growing companies.

5. The company's operating cash flow problems are covered by the sale of long-term assets and by borrowing or shareholder contributions. The company is selling its fixed assets to stay in business, and the fact that investors are willing to supply the financing indicates that they apparently expect a turnaround in operating cash flows.

6. The company experiences a shortfall in cash flow from operations and from investing activities. The deficiency in cash is financed by long-term debt or investments by shareholders. This pattern is most typical of a young, fast-growing company.

7. The company is financing operating cash flow shortages, paying its debtholders and/or its shareholders via the sale of long-term assets. The company is actually shrinking.

8. The company is using cash reserves to finance operations, pay long-term creditors and/or investors, and acquire new long-term assets. This unusual scenario is possible only if cash previously accumulated is being used to meet these cash outflows.

Source: Adapted from M. T. Dugan, B. E. Gup, and W. D. Samson, "Teaching the Statement of Cash Flows," *Journal of Accounting Education*, Vol. 9, 1991, pp. 33–52.

SELF-STUDY **QUIZ 5-3**

Canadian Tire Corporation

Indicate which of the following items taken from Canadian Tire Corporation's cash flow statement would be reported in the Investing section (I) or Financing section (F) and whether the amount would be an inflow (+) or an outflow (−).

_____ *a.* Net payments on borrowings from bank.

_____ *b.* Purchase of property and equipment for cash.

_____ *c.* Purchase of other (intangible) assets for cash.

_____ *d.* Proceeds from sale (issuance) of common shares.

After you complete your answers, check them with the solutions on page 256.

ADDITIONAL CASH FLOW DISCLOSURES

■ **LEARNING OBJECTIVE 7**

Explain the impact of additional cash flow disclosures.

The formal cash flow statement for Sleeman Breweries is shown in Exhibit 5.1. As you can see, it is a simple matter to construct the statement after the detailed analysis of the accounts and transactions has been completed (shown in Exhibits 5.4, 5.5, 5.6, and 5.7). As you would expect, the preparation of the statement for a larger, more complex company is more difficult than was the case for Sleeman. Despite the added complexity, the preparation of the statement for all companies is based on the same analytical approach that we have just discussed. Companies also must provide two other disclosures related to the cash flow statement.

NON-CASH INVESTING AND FINANCING ACTIVITIES

NON-CASH INVESTING AND FINANCING ACTIVITIES are transactions that do not have direct cash flow effects; they are reported as a supplement to the cash flow statement in narrative or schedule form.

Certain transactions are important investing and financing activities but have no cash flow effects. These are called **non-cash investing and financing activities**. For example, the purchase of a $100,000 building with a $100,000 mortgage given by the former owner does not cause either an inflow or an outflow of cash. As a result, these non-cash activities are not listed in the three main sections of the cash flow statement. Section 1540 of the *CICAHandbook* requires supplemental disclosure of these transactions in either narrative or schedule form. Sleeman's cash flow statement does not list any non-cash investing and financing activities. The following schedule from the 2003 annual report of Gildan Activewear Inc. provides examples of these non-cash transactions.

REAL WORLD EXCERPT

Gildan Activewear

ANNUAL REPORT

b) Supplemental cash flow disclosure

	2003	2002	2001
Non-cash transactions			
Acquisition of fixed assets through the assumption of debt and settlement of amounts due to the Company	—	—	6,800,000
Additions to fixed assets included in accounts payable and accrued liabilities	3,145,138	6,470,616	1,337,900

Source: Gildan Activewear Inc., annual report 2003, page 49

SUPPLEMENTAL CASH FLOW INFORMATION

Companies such as Sleeman that use the indirect method of presenting cash flows from operations also must provide two other figures: cash paid for interest and for income taxes. These are normally listed at the bottom of the statement or in the notes.

DEMONSTRATION **CASE**

Redhook Ale Brewery

During the year ended December 31, 2005, Redhook Ale Brewery, a craft brewer, reported net income of $3,182 (all numbers in thousands), and cash and cash equivalents of $472 at the beginning and $24,676 at the end of the year. It also engaged in the following activities:

a. Paid $18,752 in principal on debt.
b. Received $46,202 in cash from initial public offering of common shares.
c. Incurred other non-current accrued operating expenses of $857.
d. Paid $18,193 in cash for purchase of fixed assets.
e. Accounts receivable increased by $881.
f. Borrowed $16,789 from various lenders.
g. Refundable deposits payable increased by $457.
h. Inventories increased by $574.
i. Made cash deposits on equipment of $5,830.
j. Income tax refund receivable decreased by $326.
k. Sold (issued) shares to employees for $13 in cash.
l. Accounts payable decreased by $391.
m. Received $4 from other investing activities.
n. Accrued expenses increased by $241.
o. Prepaid expenses increased by $565.
p. Recorded amortization of $1,324.
q. Paid $5 cash for other financing activities.

Required:

Based on this information, prepare the cash flow statement for the year ended December 31, 2005. Use the indirect method to compute the cash flow from operating activities.

We strongly recommend that you prepare your own answer to this requirement and then check it with the solution below.

SUGGESTED SOLUTION

REDHOOK ALE BREWERY
CASH FLOW STATEMENT
FOR THE YEAR ENDED DECEMBER 31, 2005 (IN THOUSANDS)

Operating activities	
Net income	$ 3,182
Add (deduct) items not affecting cash:	
Amortization	1,324
Other non-current accrued expenses	857
Increase in accounts receivable	(881)
Increase in inventories	(574)
Decrease in income taxes receivable	326
Increase in prepaid expenses	(565)
Decrease in accounts payable	(391)
Increase in accrued expenses	241
Increase in refundable deposits payable	457
Net cash flow from operating activities	3,976
Investing activities	
Expenditures for fixed assets	(18,193)
Deposits on equipment	(5,830)
Other	4
Net cash flow from investing activities	(24,019)
Financing activities	
Proceeds from debt	16,789
Repayment of debt	(18,752)
Proceeds from sale of shares (IPO)	46,202
Proceeds from sale of shares (options)	13
Other	(5)
Net cash flow from financing activities	44,247
Increase in cash and cash equivalents	24,204
Cash and cash equivalents:	
Beginning of year	472
End of year	$24,676

SOLUTIONS TO **SELF-STUDY QUIZZES**

Self-Study Quiz 5-1

a. I, *b.* 0, *c.* 0, *d.* I, *e.* 0, *f.* 0, *g.* 0, *h.* 0, *i.* F, *j.* 0.

Self-Study Quiz 5-2

a. −, *b.* 0, *c.* +, *d.* +, *e.* +, *f.* −.

Self-Study Quiz 5-3

a. F−, *b.* I−, *c.* I−, *d.* F+.

Chapter Supplement A

Spreadsheet Approach—Cash Flow Statement: Indirect Method

As situations become more complex, the analytical approach that we used to prepare the cash flow statement for Sleeman Breweries Ltd. becomes cumbersome and inefficient. In actual practice, most companies use a spreadsheet approach to prepare the cash flow statement. The spreadsheet is based on the same logic that we used in our previous illustration. Its primary advantage is that it offers a more systematic way to keep track of data. You may find it useful even in simple situations because it minimizes the possibility of errors.

Exhibit 5.8 shows the spreadsheet to prepare Sleeman's cash flow statement. It is organized as follows:

1. Four columns to record dollar amounts are established. The first column is for the beginning balances for items reported on the balance sheet; the next two columns reflect debit and credit changes to those balances; the final column contains the ending balances for the balance sheet accounts.

2. On the left of the top half of the spreadsheet, each account name from the balance sheet is entered.

3. On the left of the bottom half of the spreadsheet, the name of each item that will be reported on the cash flow statement is entered.

Changes in the various balance sheet accounts are analyzed in terms of debits and credits in the top half of the spreadsheet, with the offsetting debits and credits being recorded in the bottom half of the spreadsheet in terms of their impact on cash flows. Each change in the non-cash balance sheet accounts explains part of the change in the Cash account. To illustrate, let us examine each of the entries on the spreadsheet for Sleeman Breweries shown in Exhibit 5.8. You will note that they follow each of the items presented in the schedule to prepare the cash flow statement shown in Exhibits 5.5, 5.6, and 5.7.

a. This entry is used to start the reconciliation; net income is shown as an inflow in the Operating Activities section to be reconciled by the non-cash entries. The credit to Retained Earnings reflects the effects of the original closing entry. This is the starting point for the reconciliation.

b. Depreciation and amortization expense is a non-cash expense. It is added back to net income because this type of expense does not cause a cash outflow when it is recorded. The credit to Accumulated Amortization reflects the effects of the original entry to record amortization.

c. This entry reconciles the accrual of future income tax liabilities with payments for these liabilities. It is added because cash payments for these liabilities were less than new accruals.

d. This entry reconciles the change in accounts receivable during the period with net income. It is added to net income because cash collections from customers exceeded sales revenue.

e. This entry reconciles the purchases of inventory with cost of goods sold. It is added to net income because less inventory was purchased than was sold.

EXHIBIT **5.8**

Spreadsheet to Prepare Cash
Flow Statement, Indirect Method

SLEEMAN BREWERIES LTD.
Quarter Ended September 27, 2003
(in thousands of dollars)

Items from Balance Sheet	Beginning Balances June 28, 2003	Analysis of Change Debit	Analysis of Change Credit	Ending Balances September 27, 2003
Cash and cash equivalents				
Accounts receivable	37,348		(d) 5,209	32,139
Inventories	27,946		(e) 440	27,506
Prepaid expenses	2,376		(f) 881	1,495
Property, plant and equipment (net)	72,359	(i) 1,350	(b) 1,016	72,693
Long term investments	7,586		(j) 248	7,338
Intangible assets	86,512		(b) 632	85,880
Accounts payable	18,810	(g) 2,295		16,515
Accrued liabilities	13,358	(h) 1,704		11,654
Current portion of long term debt	10,405		(m) 1,224	11,629
Bank indebtedness	4,653	(k) 4,653		—
Long term obligations	82,712	(m) 3,654		79,058
Future income taxes	8,875		(c) 1,590	10,465
Share capital	44,916		(l) 27	44,943
Retained earnings	50,398		(a) 4,359	54,757

	Inflows	Outflows	Subtotals
Cash Flow Statement			
Cash flows from operating activities			
Net income	(a) 4,359		
Adjustments to reconcile net income to net cash provided by operating activities:			
Depreciation and amortization	(b) 1,648		
Future income taxes	(c) 1,590		
Changes in noncash working capital items			
Accounts receivable	(d) 5,209		
Inventory	(e) 440		
Prepaid expenses	(f) 881		
Accounts payable		(g) 2,295	
Accrued liabilities		(h) 1,704	
			10,128
Cash flows from investing activities			
Additions to fixed assets		(i) 1,350	
Proceeds from long term investments	(j) 248		
			(1,102)
Cash flows from financing activities			
Repayment of bank operating loans		(k) 4,653	
Stock options exercised	(l) 27		
Repayment of long-term debt		(m) 2,430	
			(7,056)
Net increase (decrease) in cash and cash equivalents			1,970
	14,402	12,432	

f. This entry reconciles the prepayment of expenses with their expiration. It is added to net income because new cash prepayments are less than the amounts that expired and were recorded as expenses during the period.

g. This entry reconciles cash paid to suppliers with purchases on account. It is subtracted because more cash was paid than was borrowed during the period.

h. This entry reconciles the accrual of expenses with related payments. It is added to net income because cash payments for these expenses were less than the accrued liabilities.

i. This entry records the purchases of new plant and equipment for cash.

j. This entry records the decrease in long-term investments.

k. This entry records the repayment of bank indebtedness.

l. This entry records cash contributions made by executives to purchase shares.

m. This entry shows the repayment of principal on long-term debt, including the current portion.

The preceding entries complete the spreadsheet analysis because all accounts are reconciled. The net increase or decrease reported on the cash flow statement is the same as the change in the cash balance on the balance sheet during the period. The formal cash flow statement can be prepared directly from the spreadsheet.

Preparing a cash flow statement is more difficult than preparing an income statement or a balance sheet. To develop the cash flow statement, it is necessary to analyze changes in various accounts to determine the cash flow effects. The other statements can be prepared easily by taking the balances from various accounts in the ledger.

The analytical technique that you have learned for preparing the cash flow statement will help you deal with other significant business problems. For example, this type of analysis is useful for developing cash budgets for a business. Many small businesses that experience rapid sales growth get into serious financial difficulties because they did not forecast the cash flow effects associated with credit sales and large increases in inventory.

CHAPTER **TAKE-AWAYS**

1. **Classify cash flow statement items as part of net cash flows from operating, investing, and financing activities.   p. 229**
    The statement has three main sections: Cash Flows from Operating Activities, which are related to earning income from normal operations; Cash Flows from Investing Activities, which are related to the acquisition and sale of productive assets; and Cash Flows from Financing Activities, which are related to external financing of the enterprise. The net cash inflow or outflow for the year is the same amount as the increase or decrease in cash and cash equivalents for the year. Cash equivalents are highly liquid investments with original maturities of less than three months.

2a. **Report and interpret cash flows from operating activities using the direct method. p. 233**
    The direct method for reporting cash flows from operating activities accumulates all of the operating transactions that result in either a debit or a credit to cash into categories. The most common inflows are cash received from customers and dividends and interest on investments. The most common outflows are cash paid for purchase of services and goods for resale, salaries and wages, income taxes, and interest on liabilities. It is prepared by adjusting each item on the income statement from an accrual basis to a cash basis.

2b. **Report and interpret cash flows from operating activities using the indirect method. p. 239**
    The indirect method for reporting cash flows from operating activities reports a conversion of net income to net cash flow from operating activities. The conversion involves additions and subtractions for (1) non-current accruals including expenses (such as amortization expense) and revenues that do not affect current assets or current liabilities, and (2) changes in each of the individual current assets (other than cash and short-term investments) and current liabilities (other than short-term debt to financial institutions and current portion of long-term debt, which relate to financing), that reflect differences in the timing of accrual basis net income and cash flows.

3.   **Analyze and interpret the quality of income ratio.   p. 246**
    The quality of income ratio (Cash Flow from Operating Activities ÷ Net Income)
    measures the portion of income that was generated in cash. A higher quality of income
    ratio indicates greater ability to finance operating and other cash needs from operating
    cash inflows. A higher ratio also indicates that it is less likely that the company is using
    aggressive revenue recognition policies to increase net income.

4.   **Report and interpret cash flows from investing activities.   p. 248**
    Investing activities reported on the cash flow statement include cash payments to acquire
    property, plant, and equipment, and short- and long-term investments. They also include
    cash proceeds from the sale of these assets.

5.   **Analyze and interpret the capital acquisitions ratio.   p. 250**
    The capital acquisitions ratio (Cash Flow from Operating Activities ÷ Cash Paid
    for Property, Plant, and Equipment) reflects the portion of purchases of property,
    plant, and equipment financed from operating activities without the need for outside
    debt or equity financing or the sale of other investments or other long-term assets. A
    high ratio is beneficial because it provides the company with opportunities for strategic
    acquisitions.

6.   **Report and interpret cash flows from financing activities.   p. 251**
    Cash inflows from financing activities include cash proceeds from issuance of short- and
    long-term debt and share capital. Cash outflows include principal payments on short-
    and long-term debt, cash paid for the repurchase of the company's shares, and dividend
    payments. Cash payments associated with interest relate to operating activities.

7.   **Explain the impact of additional cash flow disclosures.   p. 254**
    Non-cash investing and financing activities are investing and financing activities that
    do not involve cash. They include, for example, purchases of long-term assets with
    long-term debt or shares, exchanges of long-term assets, and exchanges of debt for
    shares. These transactions are disclosed only as supplemental disclosures to the cash
    flow statement.

   The previous five chapters discussed the important steps in the accounting process
that lead to the preparation of the four basic financial statements. The end to the internal portions of the accounting process, however, is just the beginning of the process of
communicating accounting information to external users. In Chapter 6, we discuss the
important players in this communication process, the many statement format choices
available, the additional note disclosures required for both private and public companies, and the process, manner, and timing of the transmission of this information to
users. At the same time, we discuss common uses of the information in investment
analysis, debt contracts, and management compensation decisions. These discussions
will help you consolidate much of what you have learned about the financial reporting
process from previous chapters. It will also preview many of the important issues we
will address later in the book.

KEY **RATIOS**

The **quality of income ratio** indicates what portion of income was generated in cash.
It is computed as follows (p. 246):

$$\text{Quality of Income Ratio} = \frac{\text{Cash Flow from Operating Activities}}{\text{Net Income}}$$

The **capital acquisitions ratio** measures the ability to finance purchases of property,
plant, and equipment from operations. It is computed as follows (p. 250):

$$\text{Capital Acquisitions Ratio} = \frac{\text{Cash Flow from Operating Activities}}{\text{Cash Paid for Property, Plant, and Equipment}}$$

FINDING
FINANCIAL
INFORMATION

BALANCE SHEET
Changes in Assets, Liabilities, and Shareholders' Equity

INCOME STATEMENT
Net Income and Accruals

CASH FLOW STATEMENT
Cash Flows from Operating Activities
Cash Flows from Investing Activities
Cash Flows from Financing Activities
Separate Schedule (or note):
    Non-cash investing and financing activities
    Interest and taxes paid

NOTES
Under Summary of Significant Accounting Policies
    Definition of cash equivalents
Under Separate Note
    If not listed on cash flow statement:
        Non-cash investing and financing
            activities
        Interest and taxes paid

KEY **TERMS**

Cash Equivalent p. 229

Cash Flows from Financing Activities
    p. 231

Cash Flows from Investing Activities
    p. 230

Cash Flows from Operating Activities
    (Cash Flows from Operations) p. 230

Direct Method p. 230

Free Cash Flow p. 251

Indirect Method p. 230

Non-Cash Investing and Financing
    Activities p. 254

QUESTIONS

1. Compare the purposes of the income statement, the balance sheet, and the cash flow statement.
2. What information does the cash flow statement report that is not reported on the other required financial statements? How do investors and creditors use that information?
3. What are cash equivalents? How are purchases and sales of cash equivalents reported on the cash flow statement?
4. What are the major categories of business activities reported on the cash flow statement? Define each of these activities.
5. What are the typical cash inflows from operating activities? What are the typical cash outflows for operating activities?
6. Under the indirect method, amortization expense is added to net income to compute cash flows from operating activities. Does amortization cause an inflow of cash?
7. Explain why cash paid during the period for purchases and for salaries is not specifically reported as cash outflows on the cash flow statement under the indirect method.
8. Explain why a $50,000 increase in inventory during the year must be included in developing cash flows for operating activities under both the direct and indirect methods.
9. Compare the two methods of reporting cash flows from operating activities in the cash flow statement.
10. What are the typical cash inflows from investing activities? What are the typical cash outflows for investing activities?
11. What are the typical cash inflows from financing activities? What are the typical cash outflows for financing activities?
12. What are non-cash investing and financing activities? Give two examples. How are they reported on the cash flow statement?

MULTIPLE-CHOICE QUESTIONS

1. Most companies use the indirect method of computing the change in cash from operating activities because of the following reason(s):

a. The *CICA Handbook* recommends use of the indirect method.
b. It is less costly to prepare than the direct method.
c. The indirect method arrives at a higher cash inflow amount.
d. Both (a) and (b) are correct.

2. In what order do the three sections of the cash flow statement appear when reading from top to bottom?
   a. Financing, Investing, Operating
   b. Investing, Operating, Financing
   c. Operating, Financing, Investing
   d. Operating, Investing, Financing

3. Total cash inflow in the operating section of the cash flow statement should include:
   a. cash received from customers at the point of sale
   b. cash collections from customer accounts receivable
   c. cash received in advance of revenue recognition (unearned revenue)
   d. All of the above.

4. If the balance in prepaid expenses increased during the year, how should this be reflected on the cash flow statement when following the indirect method, *and why*?
   a. The change in the account balance should be subtracted from net income because the net increase in prepaid expenses did not impact net income but did reduce the cash balance.
   b. The change in the account balance should be added to net income because the net increase in prepaid expenses did not impact net income but did increase the cash balance.
   c. The net change in prepaid expenses should be subtracted from net income to reverse the income statement effect that had no impact on cash.
   d. The net change in prepaid expenses should be added to net income to reverse the income statement effect that had no impact on cash.

5. Which of the following would not appear in the investing section of the cash flow statement?
   a. purchase of shares issued by other corporations
   b. sale of obsolete equipment used in the factory for cash
   c. purchase of land for cash
   d. gain on sale of building

6. Which of the following items would not appear in the financing section of the cash flow statement?
   a. the repurchase of the company's own shares
   b. the receipt of dividends
   c. the repayment of debt
   d. the payment of dividends

7. Which of the following is not added to net income when computing cash flows from operations under the indirect method?
   a. the net increase in accounts payable
   b. the net decrease in accounts receivable
   c. amortization expense reported on the income statement
   d. all of the above are added

8. If a company engages in a non-cash material transaction, which of the following is required?
   a. The company must include an explanatory narrative or schedule along with the cash flow statement.
   b. No disclosure is necessary.
   c. The company must include an explanatory narrative or schedule along with the balance sheet.
   d. It must be reported in the investing and financing section of the cash flow statement.

9. The change in cash shown *in the operating section* of the cash flow statement should equal which of the following?
   a. net income on the income statement
   b. the change in accounts receivable
   c. the change in accounts payable
   d. none of the above

10. The *total* change in cash as shown near the bottom of the cash flow statement for the year should equal
    a. the difference in retained earnings when reviewing the comparative balance sheets.
    b. net income or net loss as found on the income statement.
    c. the difference in cash when reviewing the comparative balance sheets.
    d. none of the above.

For more practice with multiple-choice questions, go to our Web site at www.mcgrawhill.ca/college/libby, click on "Student Edition" in the upper left menu, click on this chapter's name and number from the list of contents, and then click on "Multiple-Choice Quiz" from the menu on the left.

EXERCISES

LO1, 2A

Adolph Coors

E5–1 Matching Items Reported to Cash Flow Statement Categories (Direct Method)

Adolph Coors Company was founded in 1873. Its tie to the magical appeal of the Rocky Mountains is one of its most powerful trademarks. Some of the items included in its annual consolidated cash flow statement presented using the *indirect method* are listed below. Indicate whether each item is disclosed in the Operating Activities (O), Investing Activities (I), or Financing Activities (F) section of the statement or (NA) if the item does not appear on the statement.

_____ 1. Proceeds from sale of properties.

_____ 2. Purchase of stock. [This involves the company's repurchase of its own shares.]

_____ 3. Depreciation, depletion, and amortization.

_____ 4. Cash payments to suppliers.

_____ 5. Inventories (decrease).

_____ 6. Principal payment on long-term debt.

LO1, 2B

Nike

E5–2 Matching Items Reported to Cash Flow Statement Categories (Indirect Method)

Nike, Inc., is the best-known sports shoe, apparel, and equipment company in the world because of its association with sports legends such as Michael Jordan, teams such as the Michigan Wolverines, and events such as the Olympics. Some of the items included in its annual consolidated cash flow statement presented using the *indirect method* are listed below.

Indicate whether each item is disclosed in the Operating Activities (O), Investing Activities (I), or Financing Activities (F) section of the statement or (NA) if the item does not appear on the statement.

_____ 1. Amortization.

_____ 2. Additions to property, plant, and equipment.

_____ 3. Increase (decrease) in notes payable. (The amount is owed to financial institutions.)

_____ 4. (Increase) decrease in other current assets.

_____ 5. Proceeds from disposal of property, plant, and equipment.

_____ 6. Reductions in long-term debt, including current portion.

_____ 7. Repurchase of stock.

_____ 8. (Increase) decrease in inventory.

_____ 9. Net income.

_____ 10. Additions to long-term debt.

LO1

Leon's Furniture

E5–3 Determining Cash Flow Statement Effects of Transactions

Leon's Furniture Limited is an Ontario-based retailer of home furnishings. For each of the following first-quarter transactions, indicate whether *net cash inflows (outflows)* from operating activities (O), investing activities (I), or financing activities (F) are affected and whether the effect is an inflow (+) or outflow (−), or (NE) if the transaction has no effect on cash. (*Hint:* Determine the journal entry recorded for the transaction. The transaction affects net cash flows if, and only if, the account Cash is affected.)

_____ 1. Paid cash to purchase new equipment.

_____ 2. Purchased raw materials inventory on account.

_____ 3. Collected cash from customers.

_____ 4. Recorded an adjusting entry to record an accrued salaries expense.

_____ 5. Recorded and paid interest on debt to creditors.

_____ 6. Repaid principal on revolving credit loan from the bank.

_____ 7. Paid rent for the following period.

_____ 8. Sold used equipment for cash at book value.

_____ 9. Made payment to suppliers.

_____ 10. Declared and paid cash dividends to shareholders.

LO1

Dell Inc.

E5–4 Determining Cash Flow Statement Effects of Transactions

Dell Inc. is a leading manufacturer of personal computers and servers for the business and home markets. For each of the following transactions, indicate whether *net cash inflows (outflows)* from operating activities (O), investing activities (I), or financing activities (F) are affected and whether the effect is an inflow ($+$) or outflow ($-$), or (NE) if the transaction has no effect on cash. (*Hint:* Determine the journal entry recorded for the transaction. The transaction affects net cash flows if, and only if, the account Cash is affected.)

_____ 1. Recorded and paid income taxes to the federal government.

_____ 2. Issued common shares for cash.

_____ 3. Paid rent for the following period.

_____ 4. Recorded an adjusting entry for expiration of a prepaid expense.

_____ 5. Paid cash to purchase new equipment.

_____ 6. Issued long-term debt for cash.

_____ 7. Collected cash from customers.

_____ 8. Purchased raw materials inventory on account.

_____ 9. Recorded and paid salaries to employees.

_____ 10. Purchased new equipment by signing a three-year note.

E5–5 Interpreting Amortization Expense from a Management Perspective   ■ **LO2B**

QuickServe, a chain of convenience stores, was experiencing some serious cash flow difficulties because of rapid growth. The company did not generate sufficient cash from operating activities to finance its new stores, and creditors were not willing to lend money because the company had not produced any income for the previous three years. The new controller for QuickServe proposed a reduction in the estimated life of store equipment to increase amortization expense; thus, "we can improve cash flows from operating activities because amortization expense is added back on the cash flow statement." Other executives were not sure that this was a good idea because the increase in amortization would make it more difficult to have positive earnings: "Without income, the bank will never lend us money."

Required:
What action would you recommend for QuickServe? Why?

E5–6 Comparing the Direct and Indirect Methods   ■ **LO2A, 2B**

To compare the computation of cash flow from operations under the direct and indirect methods, enter check marks to indicate which items are used with each method.

Cash Flows (and Related Changes)	Method of Computing Cash Flows from Operations	
	Direct	Indirect
1. Collections from customers		
2. Increase or decrease in accounts receivable		
3. Payments to suppliers		
4. Increase or decrease in inventory		
5. Increase or decrease in accounts payable		
6. Payments to employees		
7. Increase or decrease in wages payable		
8. Amortization expense		

E5–7 Reporting Cash Flows from Operating Activities (Direct Method)   ■ **LO2A**

The following information pertains to Day Company:

Sales		$75,000
Expenses		
Cost of goods sold	$45,000	
Amortization	6,000	
Salaries	10,000	61,000
Net income		$14,000
Increase in accounts receivable	$ 5,000	
Decrease in merchandise inventory	7,000	
Increase in salaries payable	500	

Required:

Present the Operating Activities section of the cash flow statement for Day Company using the direct method.

■ **LO2A, 2B** **E5–8** **Reporting and Interpreting Cash Flows from Operating Activities from an Analyst's Perspective (Direct and Indirect Method)**

Kane Company completed its income statement and balance sheet for 2007 and provided the following information:

Service revenue		$50,000
Expenses		
Salaries	$42,000	
Amortization	7,300	
Utilities	7,000	
Other	1,700	58,000
Net loss		($ 8,000)
Decrease in accounts receivable	$11,000	
Purchase of a small service machine	5,000	
Increase in salaries payable	9,000	
Decrease in unearned service revenue	6,000	

Required:

1. Present the Operating Activities section of the cash flow statement for Kane Company using both the direct and indirect methods.

2. What were the major reasons that caused Kane to report a net loss but positive cash flow from operations? Why are the reasons for the difference between cash flow from operations and net income important to financial analysts?

■ **LO2B** **E5–9** **Reporting and Interpreting Cash Flows from Operating Activities from an Analyst's Perspective (Indirect Method)**

Sizzler International, Inc.

Sizzler International, Inc., operates 700 family restaurants around the world. The company's annual report contained the following information (in thousands):

	2004
Net loss	$(8,782)
Depreciation and amortization	32,915
Increase in receivables	170
Decrease in inventories	643
Increase in prepaid expenses	664
Decrease in accounts payable	2,282
Decrease in accrued liabilities	719
Increase in income taxes payable	1,861
Reduction of long-term debt	12,691
Additions to equipment	29,073

Required:

1. Based on this information, compute the cash flow from operating activities using the indirect method.

2. What were the major reasons that caused Sizzler to report a net loss but positive cash flow from operations? Why are the reasons for the difference between cash flow from operations and net income important to financial analysts?

■ **LO2B** **E5–10** **Inferring Balance Sheet Changes from the Cash Flow Statement**

Colgate-Palmolive

A cash flow statement for Colgate-Palmolive reported the following information (in millions):

Operating Activities	Current Year
Net income	$477.0
Amortization	192.5
Cash effect of changes in	
Receivables	(38.0)
Inventories	28.4
Other current assets	10.6
Payables	(10.0)
Other	(117.8)
Net cash provided by operations	$542.7

Required:

Based on the information reported on the cash flow statement for Colgate-Palmolive, determine whether the following accounts increased or decreased during the year: Receivables, Inventories, Other Current Assets, and Payables.

E5–11 Inferring Balance Sheet Changes from the Cash Flow Statement ■ **LO2B**

A cash flow statement for Apple Computer contained the following information (in thousands):

Apple Computer, Inc.

Operations	Current Year
Net income	$310,178
Amortization	167,958
Changes in assets and liabilities	
Accounts receivable	(199,401)
Inventories	418,204
Other current assets	33,616
Accounts payable	139,095
Income taxes payable	50,045
Other current liabilities	39,991
Other adjustments	(222,691)
Cash generated by operations	$736,995

Required:

For each of the asset and liability accounts listed on the cash flow statement, determine whether the account balances increased or decreased during the current year.

E5–12 Analyzing Cash Flows from Operating Activities; Interpreting the Quality of Income Ratio ■ **LO2B, 3**

An annual report for PepsiCo contained the following information (in millions):

PepsiCo

Net income	$1,637.9
Depreciation and amortization	1,444.2
Increase in accounts receivable	161.0
Increase in inventory	89.5
Decrease in prepaid expenses	3.3
Increase in accounts payable	143.2
Decrease in taxes payable	125.1
Decrease in other current liabilities	96.7
Cash dividends paid	476.6
Repurchase of shares	463.5

Required:

1. Compute the cash flows from operating activities for PepsiCo using the indirect method.
2. Compute the quality of income ratio.
3. What were the major reasons why Pepsi's quality of income ratio did not equal 1.0?

■ **LO4, 6**   **E5–13 Reporting Cash Flows from Investing and Financing Activities**

Pan American
Silver Corp.

Pan American Silver Corp. is a mining company based in British Columbia. In a recent quarter, it reported the following activities:

Net loss	$45,878
Purchase of property, plant, and equipment	1,077
Shares issued for cash	4,649
Proceeds from bank loans	10,043
Cash collection from customers	30,085
Purchase of mineral property	17,815
Acquisition of shares of subsidiary	65
Interest paid	326
Payments for products and services	26,700
Proceeds from sale of short-term investments	14

Required:

Based on this information, present the Investing and Financing Activities sections of the cash flow statement.

■ **LO4, 6**   **E5–14 Reporting and Interpreting Cash Flows from Investing and Financing Activities with Discussion of Management Strategy**

Sobeys

Sobeys Inc. is one of Canada's two national retail grocery and food distributors. The company owns or franchises more than 1,300 corporate and franchised stores in all 10 provinces under retail banners that include Sobeys, Garden Market IGA, IGA, IGA Extra, and Price Chopper. In a recent year, it reported the following activities (in millions):

Net income	$115.9
Purchases of property and equipment	424.2
Decrease in accounts payable and accrued liabilities	77.8
Issue of shares	8.6
Depreciation and amortization	136.1
Proceeds from sale of discontinued operations	412.7
Repayment of long-term debt	147.5
Increase in accounts receivable	2.8
Payment of dividends	15.8

Required:

1. Based on this information, present the Investing and Financing Activities sections of the cash flow statement.

2. What do you think was management's plan for the use of the cash generated by the sale of discontinued operations?

■ **LO5**   **E5–15 Analyzing and Interpreting the Capital Acquisitions Ratio**

Boston Beer

A recent annual report for Boston Beer Company contained the following data for the three most recent years (in millions):

	2005	2004	2003
Cash flow from operating activities	$ 19.6	$13.8	$19.3
Cash flow from investing activities	15.0	(30.2)	4.3
Cash flow from financing activities	(27.4)	(8.8)	(3.5)

Assume that all investing activities involved acquisition of new plant and equipment.

Required:

1. Compute the capital acquisitions ratio for the three-year period in total.

2. What portion of Boston Beer's investing activities was financed from external sources or pre-existing cash balances during the three-year period?

3. What do you think is the likely explanation for the large amount of cash flow from financing activities during 2005?

E5–16 Reporting Non-Cash Transactions on the Cash Flow Statement; Interpreting the Effect on the Capital Acquisitions Ratio

■ **LO7**

An analysis of Martin Corporation's operational asset accounts provided the following information:

a. Acquired a large machine that cost $26,000, paying for it by signing a $15,000, 12-percent interest-bearing note due at the end of two years, and 500 common shares with a market value of $22 per share.

b. Acquired a small machine that cost $8,700. Full payment was made by transferring a tract of land that had a book value of $8,700.

Required:

1. Show how this information should be reported on the cash flow statement.

2. What would be the effect of these transactions on the capital acquisitions ratio? How might these transactions distort interpretation of the ratio?

E5–17 (Supplement B) Preparing a Cash Flow Statement, Direct and Indirect Methods: Complete Spreadsheet

An analysis of accounts showed the following:

a. Purchased an operational asset, $20,000, and issued common shares in full payment.

b. Purchased a long-term investment for cash, $15,000.

c. Paid cash dividend, $12,000.

d. Sold operational asset for $2,000 cash (cost, $21,000, accumulated amortization, $19,000).

e. Sold 500 shares at $12 per share cash.

	Beginning Balances 12/31/2004	Analysis of Change		Ending Balances 12/31/2005
List of Accounts		Debit	Credit	
Income statement items				
Sales			$140,000	
Cost of goods sold		$59,000		
Amortization expense		7,000		
Wage expense		28,000		
Income tax expense		9,000		
Interest expense		5,000		
Other expenses		15,800		
Net income		16,200		
Balance sheet items				
Cash	$ 16,500			$ 11,200
Accounts receivable	22,000			22,000
Merchandise inventory	68,000			75,000
Long-term Investments				15,000
Operational assets	114,500			113,500
Total debits	$221,000			$236,700
Accumulated amortization	$ 32,000			$ 20,000
Accounts payable	17,000			14,000
Wages payable	2,500			1,500
Income taxes payable	3,000			4,500
Bonds payable	54,000			54,000
Share capital	100,000			126,000
Retained earnings	12,500			16,700
Total credits	$221,000			$236,700

	Inflows	Outflows
Cash flow statement		
Cash flows from operating activities:		
Cash flows from investing activities:		
Cash flows from financing activities:		
Net increase (decrease) in cash		
Totals		

Required:

1. Complete the spreadsheet for the cash flow statement using the indirect method to compute the cash flows from operating activities.

2. Prepare the Operating Activities section of the cash flow statement using the direct method.

PROBLEMS

LO1, 2A, 2B, 4, 6, 7

P5–1 Preparing the Cash Flow Statement (AP5–1)

Selected financial information for Frank Corporation is presented below.

Selected 2005 Transactions:

a. Purchased investment securities for $5,000 cash.

b. Borrowed $15,000 on a two-year, 8-percent interest-bearing note.

c. During 2005, sold machinery for its net book value; received $11,000 in cash.

d. Purchased machinery for $50,000; paid $9,000 in cash and signed a four-year note payable to the dealer for $41,000.

e. At December 31, 2005, declared and paid a cash dividend of $10,000.

Selected account balances at December 31, 2004 and 2005 are as follows:

	December 31	
	2004	2005
Cash	$21,000	$76,000
Accounts receivable	12,000	17,000
Inventory	60,000	52,000
Accounts payable	10,000	7,000
Accrued wages payable	1,000	800
Income taxes payable	3,000	5,000

One-fourth of the sales and one-third of the purchases were made on credit.

FRANK CORPORATION
Income Statement
For the Year Ended December 31, 2005

Sales revenue		$400,000
Cost of goods sold		268,000
Gross profit		132,000
Expenses		
Salaries and wages	$51,000	
Amortization	9,200	
Rent (no accruals)	5,800	
Interest (no accruals)	12,200	
Income tax	$11,800	
Total expenses		90,000
Net income		$ 42,000

Required:

1. Prepare a cash flow statement for the year ended December 31, 2005, using the schedule approach. Compute the cash flow from operating activities using the indirect method. Include any additional required note disclosures.

2. Prepare the Operating Activities section of the cash flow statement using the direct method.

3. Which method of reporting cash flow from operating activities is easier to prepare? Explain.

4. Which method of reporting cash flow from operating activities is easier to understand? Why?

P5–2 Preparing Cash Flow Statement (Indirect Method)   ■ LO2B

The comparative balance sheets of Mikos Inc. as at December 31, 2005 and 2006, and its income statement for the year ended December 31, 2006, are presented below.

MIKOS INC.
Comparative Balance Sheets
December 31

	2006	2005
Assets		
Cash	$ 9,000	$ 17,000
Short-term investments	45,000	20,000
Accounts receivable	68,000	26,000
Inventories, at cost	54,000	40,000
Prepaid expenses	4,000	6,000
Land	45,000	70,000
Buildings and equipment, net	280,000	179,000
Intangible assets	24,000	28,000
	$529,000	$386,000
Liabilities and Shareholders' Equity		
Accounts payable	$ 17,000	$ 40,000
Income tax payable	6,000	1,000
Accrued liabilities	10,000	-0-
Long-term notes payable	110,000	150,000
Share capital	200,000	60,000
Retained earnings	186,000	135,000
	$529,000	$386,000

MIKOS INC.
Income Statement
For the Year Ended December 31, 2006

Sales		$850,000
Cost of goods sold	$430,000	
Amortization expense—intangible assets	4,000	
—buildings and equipment	33,000	
Operating expenses	221,000	
Interest expense	12,000	700,000
Income before income taxes		150,000
Income tax expense		45,000
Net income		$105,000

Additional information:

a. Land was sold for cash at book value.

b. The short-term investments will mature in February 2007.

c. Cash dividends were declared and paid in 2006.

d. New equipment with a cost of $166,000 was purchased for cash, and old equipment was sold at book value.

e. Long-term notes of $10,000 were paid in cash, and notes of $30,000 were converted to shares.

f. Accounts payable pertain to merchandise suppliers.

Required:

1. Prepare a cash flow statement for Mikos Inc. for the year ended December 31, 2006. Use the indirect method to report cash flow from operating activities.

2. Assume the role of a bank loan officer who is evaluating this company's cash flow situation. Analyze the cash flow statement you prepared in requirement 1.

3. What additional information does the cash flow statement provide that is not available on either the balance sheet or the income statement? Explain.

■ **LO2A, 2B**   **P5–3** **Comparing Cash Flows from Operating Activities (Direct and Indirect Methods)** (AP5–2)
Beta Company's accountants just completed the financial statements for the year and have provided the following information (in thousands):

Income Statement for 2005		
Sales revenue		$20,600
Expenses and losses:		
Cost of goods sold	$9,000	
Amortization	2,000	
Salaries	5,000	
Rent	2,500	
Insurance	800	
Utilities	700	
Interest	600	20,600
Net income		$ 0

Selected Balance Sheet Accounts		
	2004	**2005**
Merchandise inventory	$ 60	$ 82
Accounts receivable	450	380
Accounts payable	210	240
Salaries payable	20	29
Rent payable	6	2
Prepaid rent	7	2
Prepaid insurance	5	14

Other Data:
The company signed long-term notes for $20,000 during the year.

Required:

1. Prepare the Operating Activities section of the cash flow statement for 2005 using:
   a. the direct method.
   b. the indirect method.

2. As a financial analyst, would you prefer to see the cash flow from operations reported using either the direct method or the indirect method? Justify your answer.

3. As the accountant who prepares the company's cash flow statement, would you prefer to use the direct or the indirect method to report the cash flow from operations? Explain.

P5–4 **(Supplement A) Preparing Cash Flow Statement Spreadsheet, Cash Flow Statement, and Schedules Using the Indirect Method** (AP5–3)
Hunter Company is developing its annual financial statements at December 31, 2005. The statements are complete except for the cash flow statement. The completed comparative balance sheets and income statement are summarized:

	2004	2005
Balance sheet at December 31		
Cash	$ 18,000	$ 44,000
Accounts receivable	29,000	27,000
Merchandise inventory	36,000	30,000
Property, plant, and equipment (net)	72,000	75,000
	$155,000	$176,000

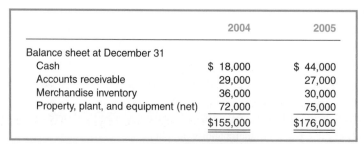

Accounts payable	$ 22,000	$ 25,000
Wages payable	1,000	800
Note payable, long term	48,000	38,000
Share capital	60,000	80,000
Retained earnings	24,000	32,200
	$155,000	$176,000
Income statement for 2005		
Sales		$100,000
Cost of goods sold		(61,000)
Other expenses		(27,000)
Net income		$ 12,000

Additional Data:

a. Bought equipment for cash, $9,000.

b. Paid $10,000 on the long-term note payable.

c. Issued common shares for $20,000 cash.

d. Declared and paid a $3,800 cash dividend.

e. Incurred expenses that included amortization, $6,000; wages, $10,000; taxes, $3,000; other, $8,000.

Required:

1. Prepare a cash flow statement spreadsheet using the indirect method to report cash flows from operating activities.

2. Prepare the cash flow statement for the year ended December 31, 2005.

3. Prepare a schedule of non-cash investing and financing activities, if necessary.

4. Evaluate the company's use of the cash flow generated from (or used for) operations.

ALTERNATE PROBLEMS

AP5–1 Preparing the Cash Flow Statement (Direct and Indirect Methods) (P5–1)   ■ **LO1, 2A, 2B, 4, 6, 7**
Stonewall Company was organized on January 1, 2004. During the year ended December 31, 2004, the company provided the following data:

Income Statement	
Sales revenue	$ 80,000
Cost of goods sold	(35,000)
Amortization expense	(4,000)
Other expenses	(32,000)
Net income	$ 9,000
Balance Sheet	
Cash	$ 48,000
Accounts receivable	18,000
Merchandise inventory	15,000
Machinery (net)	25,000
Total assets	$106,000
Accounts payable	$ 10,000
Accrued expenses (liabilities)	21,000
Dividends payable	2,000
Note payable, short term	15,000
Share capital	54,000
Retained earnings	4,000
Total liabilities and shareholders' equity	$106,000

Analysis of Selected Accounts and Transactions:

a. Issued 3,000 common shares for cash, at $18 per share.

b. Borrowed $15,000 on a one-year, 8-percent interest-bearing note; the note was dated June 1, 2004.

c. Paid $29,000 to purchase machinery.

d. Purchased merchandise for resale at a cost of $50,000; paid $40,000 cash and the balance on account. The company uses a perpetual inventory system.

e. Exchanged plant machinery with a book value of $2,000 for office machines with a market value of $2,000.

f. Declared a cash dividend of $5,000 on December 15, 2004 payable to shareholders on January 15, 2005.

g. Because this is the first year of operations, all account balances are zero at the beginning of the year; therefore, the changes in the account balances are equal to the ending balances.

Required:

1. Prepare a cash flow statement for the year ended December 31, 2004, using the schedule approach. Use the indirect method to report cash flow from operating activities.

2. Prepare the Operating Activities section of the cash flow statement using the direct method.

3. Which method of reporting cash flows from operations is easier to prepare? Explain.

4. Which method of reporting cash flows from operations is easier to understand? Explain.

■ **LO2A, 2B**   **AP5–2**   **Comparing Cash Flows from Operating Activities (Direct and Indirect Methods)** (P5–3)

Pan American Silver Corp.

The accountants of Pan American Silver Corp. completed the balance sheet at September 30, 2005, and the income statement for the quarter ended on that date and have provided the following information (in thousands):

Income Statement		
Sales revenue		$26,382
Investment income, net		94
Gain on sale of assets		3,523
		29,999
Expenses		
Operating	$28,448	
Depreciation and amortization	3,020	
Reclamation	330	
Exploration	438	
General and administration	1,452	33,688
Net loss		($3,689)

Selected Balance Sheet Accounts		
	June 30 2005	**Sept. 30 2005**
Short-term investments	$ 13	$ 513
Accounts receivable	4,877	2,067
Inventories	7,595	5,369
Prepaid expenses	5,595	5,615
Accounts payable	10,302	8,414
Accrued liabilities	8,793	5,343
Current portion of bank loans	4,209	1,975

Required:

1. Prepare the Operating Activities section of the cash flow statement using the direct method.

2. Prepare the Operating Activities section of the cash flow statement using the indirect method.

3. Companies that use the direct method to report cash flows from operations are also required to disclose in the notes a reconciliation of net income to cash flows from operating activities. What additional information does this disclosure requirement provide to users of financial statements? Explain.

AP5–3   **(Supplement A) Preparing Cash Flow Statement Spreadsheet and Cash Flow Statement Using the Indirect Method: Includes Non-Cash Investing and Financing Activity and Sale of an Asset at Book Value** (P5–4)

Choo-Foo Company is developing its 2005 annual report. The following information is provided:

	2004	2005
Cash	$21,000	$22,400
Accounts receivable	18,000	21,000
Inventory	35,000	32,000
Prepaid insurance	2,400	1,400
Long-term investments	12,500	9,300
Property, plant, and equipment (net)	31,100	59,600
Patent	2,000	1,500
Accounts payable	27,000	15,000
Wages payable	4,000	1,000
Income taxes payable	2,000	2,200
Note payable, long term	20,000	10,000
Share capital	53,000	86,000
Retained earnings	16,000	33,000

Other Information:

a. Sold long-term investments at book value for $3,200 cash. Purchased machinery by issuing 3,000 shares that had a market value of $11 per share.

b. Revenues for the year totalled $150,000.

c. Expenses for the year included: amortization, $5,000; insurance, $2,000; wages, $48,500; income taxes, $7,000; and cost of goods sold, $62,000.

Required:

1. Prepare a cash flow statement spreadsheet using the indirect method to report cash flows from operating activities.

2. Prepare the cash flow statement for the year ended December 31, 2005.

3. Prepare a schedule of non-cash investing and financing activities.

4. Evaluate the company's use of the cash flow generated from (or used for) operations.

CASES AND PROJECTS

FINDING AND INTERPRETING FINANCIAL INFORMATION

CP5–1 Finding Financial Information

Refer to the financial statements of Van Houtte Inc. given in Appendix B of this book.

■ LO2B, 4, 6

Van Houtte

Required:

1. Which of the two basic reporting approaches for the cash flows from operating activities did the company adopt?

2. What amount of cash did the company pay for taxes during the current year?

3. Explain why the gain on disposal of fixed assets was deducted in the reconciliation of net income to net cash provided by operating activities.

4. What was the amount of free cash flow for the year ended April 2, 2005?

5. Has the company paid cash dividends during the last two years? How did you know?

CP5–2 Finding Financial Information

Refer to the Online Learning Centre Web site at **www.mcgrawhill.ca/college/libby/student/resources** for the financial statements of The Forzani Group Ltd.

■ LO2B, 4, 6

The Forzani Group

Required:

1. What were the three largest adjustments to reconcile net income to the net cash provided by operating activities? Refer to the cash flow statement and to note 8. Explain the direction of the effect of each adjustment in the reconciliation.

2. What have been The Forzani Group's major uses of cash over the past two years? What have been its major sources of cash for these activities?

3. What was the amount of free cash flow for the year ended January 30, 2005? What does this imply about the company's financial flexibility?

LO3, 5   **CP5–3**   **Comparing Companies**

Van Houtte

Refer to the Online Learning Centre Web site at **www.mcgrawhill.ca/college/libby/student/resources** for the financial statements of The Forzani Group Ltd. and to Appendix B of this book for the financial statements of Van Houtte Inc.

Required:

1. Compute the quality of income ratio for both companies for the current year. How might the difference in their sales growth rates explain the difference in the ratio? Sales Growth Rate = (Current Year's Sales − Prior Year's Sales) ÷ Prior Year's Sales.

2. Compute the capital acquisitions ratio for both companies for the current year. Compare their abilities to finance purchases of property, plant, and equipment with cash provided by operating activities.

FINANCIAL REPORTING AND ANALYSIS CASES

LO2A, 4, 6   **CP5–4**   **Using Financial Reports: Analyzing Nortel's Cash Flow Statement**

Nortel Networks

Nortel Networks Corporation grew quickly during the boom years of the communications technology industry in the 1990s, achieving its growth through acquisitions of other companies. The company's shares rose to a high of $124.50 per share before tumbling down following the collapse of investments in the technology sector in early 2001. The assets that Nortel acquired were mostly in-process research and development and goodwill, which were amortized over short periods of time not exceeding five years. The amortization of goodwill and other intangible assets, and subsequent write-off of these assets, were sizeable and caused the company to suffer net losses during the past few years. However, the company's management tried to focus investors' attention on its earnings from operations, downplaying the significance of the recurring net losses.

Nortel revenues, earnings from operations before income taxes, and net losses for the years 1998, 1999, and 2000 are shown below, along with its cash flow statements for these years (on page 275).

	2000	1999	1998
Revenues	$30,293	$22,217	$17,575
Earnings from operations before income taxes	3,580	2,405	1,668
Net loss	(2,957)	(197)	(569)

Required:

1. Analyze Nortel's cash flows from operating activities during the years 1998, 1999, and 2000, paying particular attention to the main sources of difference between net loss and net cash flow from operating activities.

2. Would you expect Nortel's cash flows from operations for the year 2001 to be positive or negative? Justify your response.

3. Analyze Nortel's cash flows from investing activities. What conclusions can you draw from the information presented in that section of the cash flow statement?

4. Obtain a copy of Nortel's cash flow statement for the year 2001 through the company's Web site or the SEDAR service (www.sedar.com). Did the company's cash flow situation in 2001 improve or deteriorate relative to previous years? Explain.

NORTEL NETWORKS CORPORATION
Consolidated Statements of Cash Flows
Years Ended December 31

(millions of U.S. dollars)	2000	1999	1998
Cash flows from (used in) operating activities			
Net loss	$(2,957)	$(197)	$(569)
Adjustments to reconcile net loss to net cash from (used in) operating activities, net of effects from acquisitions and divestitures of businesses:			
Amortization	7,095	2,651	2,259
Equity in net loss of associated companies	34	13	19
Stock option compensation	99	—	—
Tax benefit from stock options	447	—	—
Future income taxes	(520)	31	59
Other liabilities	77	67	37
Gain on sale of businesses and investments	(856)	(264)	(441)
Other—net	(45)	(180)	77
Change in operating assets and liabilities:			
Accounts receivable	(777)	(1,481)	(236)
Inventories	(2,057)	(1,363)	185
Income taxes payable	(179)	240	98
Accounts payable and accrued liabilities	362	1,417	230
Other operating assets and liabilities	(733)	12	(203)
Net cash from (used in) operating activities	(10)	946	1,515
Cash flows from (used in) investing activities			
Expenditures for plant and equipment	(1,887)	(823)	(649)
Proceeds on disposals of plant and equipment	33	24	27
Increase in long-term receivables	(1,574)	(1,101)	(651)
Decrease in long-term receivables	779	193	295
Acquisitions of investments and businesses— net of cash acquired	(128)	(697)	115
Proceeds on sale of investments	1,688	993	751
Net cash used in investing activities	(1,089)	(1,411)	(112)
Cash flows from (used in) financing activities			
Dividends on common shares	(223)	(204)	(178)
Increase in notes payable—net	109	70	6
Proceeds from long-term debt	255	194	56
Repayments of long-term debt	(67)	(116)	(281)
Decrease in capital leases payable	(37)	(8)	(3)
Issuance of common shares	479	521	125
Common shares purchased for cancellation	—	(14)	(224)
Net cash from (used in) financing activities	516	443	(499)
Effect of exchange rate changes on cash and cash equivalents	(25)	(2)	6
Net increase (decrease) in cash and cash equivalents	(608)	(24)	910
Cash and cash equivalents at beginning of period—net	2,257	2,281	1,371
Cash and cash equivalents at end of period—net	$1,649	$2,257	$2,281

CP5–5 Using Financial Reports: Analyzing Van Houtte's Cash Flow Statement

Van Houtte Inc. is the largest gourmet coffee roasting organization in Canada, and one of the leading coffee service specialists in North America. Its cash flow statements for fiscal years 2004 and 2003 and the related note are shown below.

■ **LO2B, 3, 4, 5, 6**

Van Houtte

CONSOLIDATED STATEMENTS OF CASH FLOWS
Years ended April 3, 2004 and March 29, 2003
(in thousands of dollars)

	2004	2003
Cash flows from operating activities		
Net earnings from continuing operations	$18,564	$15,988
Adjustments for:		
Depreciation of fixed assets	28,881	28,310
Amortization of other assets	2,149	1,459
Amortization of financial expenses	478	599
Future income taxes	(3,194)	(400)
Non-controlling interest	476	343
Share in net earnings of companies subject to significant influence, net of dividends received of $81 in 2003	(39)	(23)
Write-down and write-off of fixed assets	—	2,911
Loss on disposal of investment	—	1,740
(Gain) loss on disposal of fixed assets	(91)	2
Gain on disposal of businesses	(393)	(85)
Gain on foreign exchange	(126)	(182)
	46,705	50,662
Net change in non-cash balances related to operations *(Note 18)*	(1,141)	(3,810)
	45,564	46,852
Cash flows from investing activities		
Business acquisitions *(Note 19)*	(13,884)	(5,024)
Additions to fixed assets	(23,116)	(32,256)
Proceeds from disposal of fixed assets	1,503	1,610
Proceeds from disposal of investment	—	1,504
Acquisitions of investments	(1,139)	(410)
Increase in other assets	(2,801)	(2,216)
	(39,437)	(36,792)
Cash flows from financing activities		
Issue of subordinate voting shares *(Note 14)*	285	495
Redemption of subordinate voting shares for cancellation *(Note 14)*	(710)	(2,131)
Increase in long-term debt	51	1,579
Dividends	(4,719)	(4,308)
Dividends paid to non-controlling shareholders of subsidiaries	(830)	(551)
	(5,923)	(4,916)
Effect of exchange rate changes on cash denominated in foreign currency	(2,011)	(596)
Effect of discontinued operations on cash and cash equivalents	—	(148)
Net (decrease) increase in cash	(1,807)	4,400
Cash, beginning of year	9,148	4,748
Cash, end of year	$ 7,341	$ 9,148

See accompanying notes to consolidated financial statements.

NOTE 18
Additional information on cash flows

	2004	2003
Operating activities		
Changes in non-cash operating working capital items:		
(Increase) decrease in the undernoted items:		
Accounts receivable	$ (2,744)	$ 4,198
Income taxes payable	1,655	(401)
Inventories	(2,372)	(512)
Prepaid expenses	384	795
(Decrease) increase in the undernoted items:		
Accounts payable and accrued liabilities	2,865	(6,535)
Employee future benefits	(1,212)	(903)
Working capital acquired	283	(452)
	$ (1,141)	$ (3,810)
Cash payments of interest and income taxes were as follows:		
Cash interest payments	$ 4,765	$ 5,174
Cash payments for income taxes	$ 6,211	$ 4,979
Purchases of fixed assets financed by accounts payable	$ 1,644	$ 632

Source: Van Houtte Inc., annual report 2004, page 43.

Required:

1. The cash flows from operating activities show that "depreciation of fixed assets" is added to "net earnings from continuing operations." Is depreciation (or amortization) a source of cash? Explain.
2. Was the cash collected from customers during fiscal year 2004 higher or lower than Van Houtte's sales revenue for that year? Explain.
3. Explain why Van Houtte's cash flow from operations decreased in 2004 compared to 2003, while its net earnings from continuing operations increased during the same year?
4. Did Van Houtte expand during 2003 and 2004? If so, how did the company pay for its expansion? Explain.
5. Compute and analyze Van Houtte's quality of income ratio, capital acquisitions ratio, and free cash flow for both years.

CP5–6 Using Financial Reports: Analyzing Research In Motion's Cash Flow Statement

■ **LO2B, 3, 4, 5, 6**

Research in Motion

Research In Motion (RIM) is a leading designer, manufacturer, and marketer of innovative wireless solutions for the worldwide mobile communications market. Its products are used around the world and include the BlackBerry® wireless platform, software development tools, and software/hardware licensing agreements. RIM's cash flow statements for fiscal years 2004, 2003, and 2002 are shown below.

CONSOLIDATED STATEMENT OF CASH FLOWS
For the years ended February 28, 2004, March 1, 2003, and March 2, 2002

For the year ended	February 28, 2004	March 1, 2003	March 2, 2002
	US GAAP (note 1)		
Cash flows from operating activities			
Net income (loss)	$ 51,829	$(148,857)	$ (28,321)
Items not requiring an outlay of cash:			
Amortization	54,529	31,147	17,497
Deferred income taxes	—	29,244	(16,836)
Loss on disposal of capital assets	223	502	—
Loss (gain) on foreign currency translation of long-term debt	859	(339)	4
Write-down of investments	—	—	5,350
Net changes in working capital items:			
Trade receivables	(54,410)	1,958	7,607
Other receivables	(7,611)	1,473	7,918
Inventory	(11,561)	6,202	30,567
Other current assets	512	(525)	(3,467)
Accounts payable	16,976	7,059	1,834
Accrued liabilities	16,123	17,555	(2,333)
Accrued litigation and related expenses	33,690	50,702	—
Increase in restricted cash	(36,261)	—	—
Income taxes payable	(3,225)	2,106	(1,018)
Deferred revenue	2,162	4,563	(1,097)
	63,835	2,790	17,705
Cash flows from financing activities			
Issuance of share capital and warrants	994,640	1,155	1,491
Financing costs	(39,629)	—	—
Buyback of common shares pursuant to Common Share Purchase Program (note 11(a))	—	(24,502)	(5,525)
Repayment of debt	(6,130)	(614)	(303)
	948,881	(23,961)	(4,337)
Cash flows from investing activities			
Acquisition of investments	(186,989)	(190,030)	—
Proceeds on sale or maturity of investments	43,746	—	—
Acquisition of capital assets	(21,815)	(39,670)	(73,917)
Acquisition of intangible assets	(32,252)	(30,997)	(7,106)
Acquisition of subsidiaries (note 8)	478	(21,990)	(9,709)
Acquisition of short-term investments	(24,071)	(41,900)	(925,885)
Proceeds on sale and maturity of short-term investments	24,071	345,983	834,907
	(196,832)	21,396	(181,710)
Foreign exchange effect on cash and cash equivalents	(146)	(20)	(4)
Net increase (decrease) in cash and cash equivalents for the year	815,738	205	(168,346)
Cash and cash equivalents, beginning of year	340,681	340,476	508,822
Cash and cash equivalents, end of year	$1,156,419	$ 340,681	$ 340,476

See notes to the consolidated financial statements.
Source: Research In Motion's annual report for 2004, page 33.

Required:

1. Have RIM's trade receivables increased or decreased during fiscal year 2004? By how much have its trade receivables changed during the past three years? Explain.
2. How does the change in inventory during fiscal year 2004 affect cash? Explain.
3. Explain why RIM shows positive cash flow from operations in 2003 and 2002 while it reported net losses in both years.
4. How did the company finance the acquisition of long-term assets during 2002 and 2004? Explain.
5. What additional information does the cash flow statement provide that is not available on either the balance sheet or the income statement?

■ **LO2B, 3,**   **CP5–7** **Using Financial Reports: Analyzing Celestica's Cash Flow Statement**
4, 5, 6
Celestica Inc. is a world leader in providing electronics manufacturing services to original
Celestica Inc.
equipment manufacturers, communications, and other industries. Celestica provides a wide variety of products and services to its customers, including complex printed circuit board assemblies such as PC motherboards and communication and networking cards. These assemblies end up in servers, workstations, personal computers, peripherals, and communications devices. Celestica also offers supply chain management, as well as design, global distribution, and post-sales repair services. Celestica operates facilities in the Americas, Europe, and Asia.

CONSOLIDATED STATEMENTS OF CASH FLOWS
(in millions of U.S. dollars)
Year ended December 31

	2001	2002	2003
Cash provided by (used in)			
Operations			
Net loss	$ (39.8)	$ (445.2)	$ (265.8)
Items not affecting cash:			
Depreciation and amortization	319.5	311.0	222.1
Deferred income taxes	(27.9)	(107.8)	27.1
Non-cash charge for option issuances	—	—	0.3
Restructuring charges (note 11)	98.6	194.5	(2.3)
Other charges (note 11)	36.1	292.1	80.5
Other	1.7	(6.1)	(14.0)
Changes in non-cash working capital items:			
Accounts receivable	887.2	297.4	14.4
Inventories	822.5	623.9	(252.6)
Other assets	45.7	26.1	(43.2)
Accounts payable and accrued liabilities	(854.0)	(202.7)	65.2
Income taxes payable	0.9	(0.4)	9.8
Non-cash working capital changes	902.3	744.3	(206.4)
Cash provided by (used in) operations	1,290.5	982.8	(158.5)
Investing			
Acquisitions, net of cash acquired	(1,299.7)	(111.0)	(0.5)
Purchase of capital assets	(199.3)	(151.4)	(175.9)
Proceeds on sale of capital assets	—	71.6	7.3
Other	1.4	(0.7)	(0.4)
Cash used in investing activities	(1,497.6)	(191.5)	(169.5)
Financing			
Bank indebtedness	(2.8)	(1.6)	—
Repayments of long-term debt	(56.0)	(146.5)	(3.5)
Debt redemption fees (note 11(f))	—	(6.9)	—
Deferred financing costs	(3.9)	(2.6)	(1.6)
Repurchase of convertible debt (note 8)	—	(100.3)	(223.5)
Issuance of share capital	737.7	7.4	5.1
Share issue costs, pre-tax	(10.0)	—	—
Repurchase of capital stock (note 9)	—	(32.5)	(274.9)
Other	1.1	(0.1)	4.2
Cash provided by (used in) financing activities	666.1	(283.1)	(494.2)
Increase (decrease) in cash	459.0	508.2	(822.2)
Cash, beginning of year	883.8	1,342.8	1,851.0
Cash, end of year	$ 1,342.8	$1,851.0	$1,028.8

Cash is comprised of cash and short-term investments.
Supplemental cash flow information (note 19)
See accompanying notes to consolidated financial statements.
Source: Celestica Inc., annual report 2003, page 33.

Required:

1. The cash flows from operating activities show that "depreciation and amortization" is added to "net loss." Are depreciation and amortization a source of cash? Explain.
2. How does the change in inventory during 2003 affect cash? Explain.
3. Compare the changes in non-cash working capital items across the three years. What conclusions can you draw from this comparison?
4. Compute and analyze Celestica's capital acquisitions ratio and free cash flow for the three years.
5. Has Celestica become more or less risky during 2003? What other financial statement might include information that would help you confirm your answer? Explain.
6. Analyze the company's pattern of cash flows from operating, investing, and financing activities over the three years. What conclusion can you draw from the changing pattern of cash flows? Explain.
7. Obtain a copy of Celestica's cash flow statement for the year 2004 through the company's Web site (www.celestica.com) or the SEDAR service (www.sedar.com). Did the company's cash flow situation in 2004 improve or deteriorate relative to previous years? Explain.
8. As a potential investor in Celestica's shares, what additional information would you need before making your decision?

CP5–8 Using Financial Reports: Analyzing a U.K. Cash Flow Statement

■ **LO1, 2B**

Scottish & Newcastle serves up Courage by the pint. The U.K.'s largest brewer makes a number of popular beers, including Courage, John Smith's, Newcastle, and Kronenbourg. It also brews licensed beers such as Foster's and Miller. The Edinburgh-based company follows U.K. generally accepted accounting principles. Its cash flow statement prepared according to those principles follows, along with one of the related notes.

Scottish & Newcastle

GROUP CASH FLOW STATEMENT Eight months ended 31 December 2003					
		8 months to December 2003		12 months to April 2003	
	Notes	£m	£m	£m	£m
Net cash inflow from operating activities	35		241		509
Dividends received from joint ventures			10		19
Returns on investments and servicing of finance					
Interest received		9		8	
Interest paid		(138)		(146)	
Dividends paid to minorities		—		(23)	
Net cash outflow for returns on investments and servicing of finance			(129)		(161)
Taxation			(18)		(58)
Capital expenditure and financial investment					
Purchase of tangible fixed assets		(150)		(458)	
Purchase of investments		(64)		(147)	
Sale of tangible fixed assets		33		68	
Realisation of investments		73		114	
Net cash outflow for capital expenditure and financial investment			(108)		(423)
Acquisitions and disposals					
Purchase of businesses		(314)		(1,586)	
Net cash acquired with businesses		7		6	
Disposal of businesses		2,446		—	
Net cash sold with businesses		(24)		—	
Purchase of and loans to joint ventures		(23)		(24)	
Net cash inflow (outflow) for acquisitions and disposals			2,092		(1,604)
Equity dividends paid			(178)		(252)

(continued)

GROUP CASH FLOW STATEMENT *(continued)*

	Notes	8 months to December 2003 £m	£m	12 months to April 2003 £m	£m
Net cash inflow/(outflow) before use of liquid resources and financing			1,910		(1,970)
Management of liquid resources					
Movement in short term deposits with banks			(9)		139
Financing					
Issues of ordinary share capital		3		4	
Proceeds of loan capital		878		4,311	
Repayment of loan capital		(2,707)		(2,593)	
Capital element of finance lease repayments		(9)		(7)	
Net cash inflow/(outflow) from financing			(1,835)		1,715
Increase/(decrease) in cash in the period	36		66		(116)

Liquid resources comprise term deposits of less than one year.
Source: Scottish & Newcastle, annual report 2004, page 48.

NOTE 35
Net cash inflow from operating activities

	December 2003 £m	April 2003 £m
Group operating profit	232	348
Exceptional charges against operating profit	54	90
Depreciation—normal	124	169
Amortisation of goodwill	88	75
Defined benefit operating profit charge less contributions paid	(67)	(25)
Provisions against investments	1	—
(Increase)/decrease in stocks	35	(14)
(Increase)/decrease in debtors	(74)	9
Decrease in creditors	(95)	(52)
Net cash inflow from ordinary operating activities	298	600
Reorganisation and onerous contract costs	(57)	(91)
Net cash inflow from operating activities	241	509

The net cash flow from operating activities includes a £35m contribution to the Managed Retail pension scheme prior to disposal.
Source: Scottish & Newcastle, annual report 2004, page 69.

Required:

1. Which of the two basic reporting approaches for the cash flow statement did the company adopt?

2. Compare Scottish & Newcastle's statement with that of Sleeman Breweries presented in Exhibit 5.1. What differences do you see between the U.K. and Canadian versions of the statement?

CRITICAL THINKING CASE

■ **LO2B**

Carlyle Golf, Inc.

CP5–9 **Making a Decision as a Financial Analyst: Analyzing Cash Flow for a New Company**
Carlyle Golf, Inc., was formed in September 1992. The company designs, contracts for the manufacture of, and markets a line of men's golf apparel. A portion of the cash flow statement for Carlyle follows:

	1993
Cash flows from operating activities	
Net income	$(460,089)
Depreciation	3,554
Non-cash compensation (stock)	254,464
Deposits with suppliers	(404,934)
Increase in prepaid assets	(42,260)
Increase in accounts payable	81,765
Increase in accrued liabilities	24,495
Net cash flows	$(543,005)

Management expects a solid increase in sales in the near future. To support the increase in sales, it plans to add $2.2 million to inventory. The company did not disclose a sales forecast. At the end of 1993, Carlyle had less than $1,000 in cash. It is not unusual for a new company to experience a loss and negative cash flows during its start-up phase.

Required:
As a financial analyst recently hired by a major investment bank, you have been asked to write a short memo to your supervisor evaluating the problems facing Carlyle. Emphasize typical sources of financing that may or may not be available to support the expansion.

FINANCIAL REPORTING AND ANALYSIS TEAM PROJECT

CP5–10 Team Project: Analyzing Cash Flows

■ **LO1, 2A, 3, 4, 5, 6**

As a team, select an industry to analyze (industry lists can be found at www.marketguide.com/mgi/industry/industry.html and www.hoovers.com; click on Companies & Industries. Each team member should acquire the annual report for one publicly traded company in the industry, with each member selecting a different company. (Library files, the SEDAR service at www.sedar.com, or the company itself are good sources.) On an individual basis, each team member should then write a short report answering the following questions about the selected company.

1. Which of the two basic reporting approaches for cash flows from operating activities did the company adopt?

2. What is the quality of income ratio for the most current year? What were the major causes of differences between net income and cash flow from operations?

3. What is the capital acquisitions ratio for the three-year period presented in total? How is the company financing its capital acquisitions?

4. What portion of the cash from operations in the current year is being paid to shareholders in the form of dividends?

Discuss any patterns across the three companies that your team observes. Then, as a team, write a short report comparing and contrasting your companies using these attributes. Provide potential explanations for any differences discovered.

After studying this chapter, you should be able to:

1. Recognize the people involved in the accounting communication process (managers, auditors, information intermediaries, stock exchanges and government regulators, and users), their roles in the process, and the guidance they receive from legal and professional standards. p. 285

2. Identify the steps in the accounting communication process, including the issuance of press releases, annual reports, quarterly reports, and documents filed with securities commissions, the role of electronic information services in this process, as well as the guiding principles in communicating useful information. p. 293

3. Recognize the different financial statement and disclosure formats used by companies in practice. p. 300

4. Compute and interpret the return on equity ratio. p. 307

Communicating and Interpreting Accounting Information

If you are a skier or snowboarder, you may have visited the Whistler Blackcomb mountain resort in British Columbia, Panorama in the Canadian Rockies, Blue Mountain in Ontario, or Tremblant in Québec. Intrawest has developed these mountain resorts into all-season playgrounds that offer a variety of sports activities. The company also owns and operates many other resorts and residential villages to accommodate visitors in Canada, the United States, and France.

Intrawest Corporation was formed in the mid-1970s by Joe Houssian as a Vancouver-based real estate development company. Over time, it evolved into North America's largest resort real estate company and largest ski resort operator. The 2010 Winter Olympics and Paralympic Games that will be held in Vancouver and Whistler will help build on the company's reputation.

Intrawest became a public company in 1990, when its shares were listed for trading on the Toronto Stock Exchange (TSX). This move required the preparation of detailed, audited financial information in compliance with both the listing rules of the TSX and the securities regulations of the Ontario Securities Commission (OSC). In 1997, after further expanding its operations into the United States, Intrawest also listed its shares for trading on the New York Stock Exchange (NYSE). This cross-listing of the company's shares requires that Intrawest's financial disclosure also conform to generally accepted accounting principles that are applicable in the United States, as well as the listing rules for the NYSE and the securities regulations of the Securities and Exchange Commission (SEC).

Clear and timely communication of the company's financial situation enables the company to comply with exchange rules and regulations of securities commissions. It also informs Intrawest's customers, investors, creditors, and other users of financial statements of the company's success in implementing its business strategy.

UNDERSTANDING THE BUSINESS

Intrawest's success formula starts with a resort and then builds an animated village so visitors stay longer. As more satisfied customers visit the resort more often, they spend more money and bring their friends. Then Intrawest adds attractions to draw more people to its destinations. This leads to the expansion of year-round facilities that maximize the use of shops, hotels, convention facilities, and restaurants. As occupancy and room rates climb, so does the demand for resort real estate, which creates a surge in real estate sales. All of this results in a total resort experience that brings year-round destination visitors, increases the company's revenues, and leads to the development of more resorts. Intrawest's management understands that the company's financial success depends on operating actively used resorts that meet the customers' desire for a range of activities.

Successful companies such as Intrawest learn to match their financial reporting to their business strategies. Marketing and communication are fundamental to both. As Intrawest strives to become a leading integrated leisure company, it continues to seek opportunities to innovate in response to its customers' needs. Intrawest's investments in new resorts, the results of operating existing resorts, and the company's financial condition are communicated to shareholders, creditors, and other interested parties through press releases, conference calls with shareholders and the media together with financial analysts, and periodic reporting of financial information.

Intrawest knows that when investors lose faith in the truthfulness of a firm's accounting numbers, they also normally punish the company's stock. The accounting scandals at Enron and WorldCom are the best recent examples. They have even caused investors to question the accounting practices at other companies, as suggested by this front-page story in *The Wall Street Journal*.

REAL WORLD EXCERPT

Wall Street Journal

BURDEN OF DOUBT: STOCKS TAKE A BEATING AS ACCOUNTING WORRIES SPREAD BEYOND ENRON

It's not the economy anymore, stupid. It's the accounting.

Yesterday was the day that the smoldering corporate accounting scandal, which started with Enron Corp. . . . reached a wide group of U.S. companies and seriously singed their stock prices. Accounting problems surfaced in sectors ranging from banking to oil, prompting fears of new mini-Enrons and spurring a sell-off of shares at the slightest whiff of such trouble.

As a result, . . . the stock market took a tumble, with shares falling to their lowest levels in three months.

Source: *The Wall Street Journal*, January 30, 2002.

Chapters 2 through 5 focused on the mechanics of preparing the four basic financial statements: balance sheet, income statement, statement of retained earnings, and cash flow statement. In these chapters, we explained the importance of generally accepted accounting principles (e.g., historical cost, revenue recognition, and matching) in generating the information disclosed in these statements. We also learned to compute and interpret some financial ratios to analyze and understand how creditors and investors use the information that accountants report to justify financial investment decisions.

In this chapter, we discuss the disclosure process itself and the supporting roles played by important participants who regulate this formal process. We also focus on specific disclosures provided in annual reports to help you learn how to find relevant information in the reports.

ORGANIZATION OF THE CHAPTER

• **Players in the Accounting Communication Process**	• **The Disclosure Process**	• **A Closer Look at Financial Statements and Notes**	• **Return-on-Equity Analysis**
Managers (CEO, CFO, and Accounting Staff)	Press Releases	Overview of Intrawest's Financial Statements	
Auditors	Annual Reports	Notes to Financial Statements	
Information Intermediaries: Analysts and Information Services	Quarterly Reports	Voluntary Disclosures	
Stock Exchanges and Government Regulators	Reports to Securities Commissions		
Users: Institutional and Private Investors, Creditors, and Others	Guiding Principles for Communicating Useful Information		
	Constraints of Accounting Measurement		

PLAYERS IN THE ACCOUNTING COMMUNICATION PROCESS

Exhibit 6.1 summarizes the accounting communication process in terms of the people involved, their roles in the process, and the guidance they receive from legal and professional standards.

MANAGERS (CEO, CFO, AND ACCOUNTING STAFF)
As noted in Chapter 1, the primary responsibility for the information in Intrawest's financial statements and related disclosures lies with management as represented by the highest officer in the company, often called the *president and chief executive officer*[1] (CEO) and the highest officer associated with the financial and accounting side of the business, often called the *chief financial officer* (CFO). These two officers must sign the statement of management responsibility that is included in the annual report. For public companies, the same officers are responsible for the principal reports filed

■ **LEARNING OBJECTIVE 1**

Recognize the people involved in the accounting communication process (managers, auditors, information intermediaries, stock exchanges and government regulators, and users), their roles in the process, and the guidance they receive from legal and professional standards.

---

[1]For most U.S. and Canadian companies, the chief executive officer is also the *chairman* of the board of directors. In contrast, in the United Kingdom these two functions should not be held by the same individual in order to ensure that there is a clear division of responsibility for running the company's business. In this regard, the board of directors is likely to be more independent of management if the two functions are held by different individuals. Separation of these two functions could potentially lead to more transparent communication of accounting information by the company. The recent emphasis on corporate governance in both the U.S. and Canada has led a number of Canadian companies to split the two functions. In fact, all the Canadian banks have done so in the past few years.

EXHIBIT 6.1

**The Accounting
Communication Process**

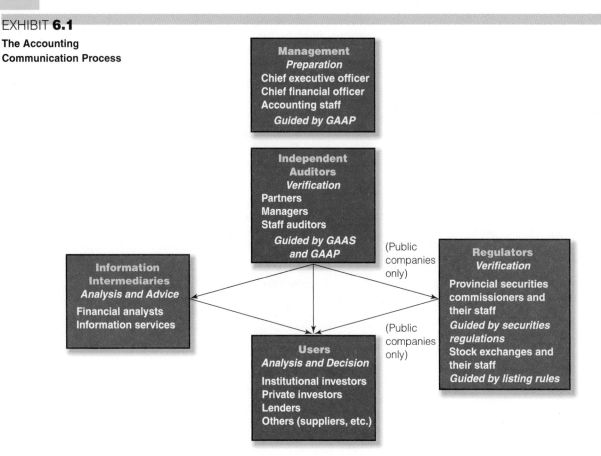

with the provincial securities commissions. At Intrawest, Joe Houssian, president and CEO, and John Currie, CFO, had that responsibility for fiscal year 2004. They were responsible for the conformance of the statements and related disclosures with GAAP.

REAL WORLD EXCERPT

Intrawest

ANNUAL REPORT

MANAGEMENT'S RESPONSIBILITY

The consolidated financial statements of Intrawest Corporation have been prepared by management and approved by the Board of Directors of the Company. Management is responsible for the preparation and presentation of the information contained in the consolidated financial statements. The Company maintains appropriate systems of internal control, policies and procedures that provide management with reasonable assurance that assets are safeguarded and that financial records are reliable and form a proper basis for preparation of financial statements.

The Company's independent auditors, KPMG LLP, have been appointed by the shareholders to express their professional opinion on the fairness of the consolidated financial statements. Their report is included below.

The Board of Directors ensures that management fulfills its responsibilities for financial reporting and internal control through an Audit Committee which is composed entirely of outside directors. This committee reviews the consolidated financial statements and reports to the Board of Directors. The auditors have full and direct access to the Audit Committee.

Joe S. Houssian   John E. Currie
Chairman, President and Chief Executive Officer   Chief Financial Officer
September 2, 2004

The members of the *accounting staff* who actually prepare the details of the reports also have professional responsibility for the accuracy of this information, although their legal responsibility is smaller. Indeed, their future professional success depends heavily on their reputations for honesty and competence.

AUDITORS

As we discussed in Chapter 1, the provincial securities commissions require publicly traded companies to have their statements audited by professional independent accountants following generally accepted auditing standards (GAAS). Many privately owned companies also have their statements audited. By signing an *unqualified*, or **clean**, **audit opinion**, the audit firm assumes responsibility for the fairness of the financial statements and related presentations.

CLEAN AUDIT OPINION
Auditors' statement that the financial statements are fair presentations in all material respects in conformity with GAAP.

REAL WORLD EXCERPT

Intrawest

ANNUAL REPORT

AUDITORS' REPORT TO THE SHAREHOLDERS

We have audited the consolidated balance sheets of Intrawest Corporation as at June 30, 2004 and 2003 and the consolidated statements of operations, retained earnings, and cash flows for the years then ended. These financial statements are the responsibility of the Company's management. Our responsibility is to express an opinion on these financial statements based on our audits.

We conducted our audits in accordance with Canadian generally accepted auditing standards. Those standards require that we plan and perform an audit to obtain reasonable assurance whether the financial statements are free of material misstatement. An audit includes examining, on a test basis, evidence supporting the amounts and disclosures in the financial statements. An audit also includes assessing the accounting principles used and significant estimates made by management, as well as evaluating the overall financial statement presentation.

In our opinion, these consolidated financial statements present fairly, in all material respects, the financial position of the Company as at June 30, 2004 and 2003 and the results of its operations and its cash flows for the years then ended in accordance with Canadian generally accepted accounting principles.

KPMG LLP
Chartered Accountants
Vancouver, Canada
September 2, 2004

This opinion adds credibility to the statements and often is required by agreements with lenders and private investors.[2] Intrawest was initially financed through investments by Mr. Houssian and loans from financial institutions (e.g., banks and commercial finance companies). By voluntarily subjecting the company's statements to independent verification, Intrawest reduced the risk to the private investors and financial institutions that the company's condition was not as represented in the statements. As a consequence, rational investors and lenders should lower the rate of return (interest) they charge for providing capital.

KPMG is currently Intrawest's auditor. KPMG, Deloitte & Touche, Ernst & Young, and PricewaterhouseCoopers are the largest audit firms that employ thousands of

---

[2]In some cases, the auditor may not be satisfied that the company's financial statements are in compliance with GAAP. A *qualified* opinion would then be issued if the company's management is not willing to modify the financial reports as per the auditor's recommendation. If the exceptions to GAAP are very serious, then the auditor may issue an *adverse* opinion if the company's management cannot be persuaded to rectify the problems to avoid such an opinion. In extreme cases, the auditor may deny the issuance of an opinion if insufficient information is available to express an opinion. These latter types of opinions are rarely issued by auditors.

professional accountants in offices scattered throughout the world. They audit the great majority of publicly traded companies and many privately held companies. Some public companies and most private companies are audited by audit firms of smaller size. A list of well-known companies and their auditors at the time this chapter was written follows.

Company	Industry	Auditor
Honda Motor Co. Ltd. (Japan)	Automobiles	KPMG
Nortel Networks Corporation	Computer equipment	Deloitte & Touche
Singapore Airlines (Singapore)	Airline	Ernst & Young
Wendy's (United States)	Fast food	PricewaterhouseCoopers

Companies often hire financial managers from their audit firms because of their broad financial experience as well as their specific company knowledge gained during prior years' audits.

A QUESTION OF **ETHICS**

WHERE WERE THE AUDITORS?

Most professional accountants act in an honest and ethical manner, abiding by the codes of ethics developed by the professional accounting organizations. Nevertheless, a few accountants act in their own interest and disregard ethical conduct. They even become accomplices in spectacular fraud cases and subsequent company bankruptcies. For example, Enron Corp., a U.S. energy trading company, intentionally inflated its net earnings by hiding assets and related debts from 1997 to 2001. Throughout this period, the auditors of Arthur Andersen LLP, a global accounting services company with revenues in excess of $500 million, should have known that the financial statements issued by Enron's management were fraudulent.

The collapse of Enron, the largest unexpected bankruptcy in U.S. history at that time, caused tremendous losses to the company's shareholders, creditors, employees, and other stakeholders. Furthermore, Enron's bankruptcy in December 2001 caused the collapse of Arthur Andersen. More than 300 clients left the firm within 90 days, taking with them $250 million of potential revenue to other audit firms. This audit failure led to calls for improved accountability by managers and auditors. This generated considerable discussion among securities regulators, financial analysts, investors, and creditors for stricter regulation of the accounting profession.

The Sarbanes-Oxley Act (SOX) approved by the U.S. Congress in July 2002 was a direct response to the Enron and other scandals that occurred in the United States. This new law has set higher standards of responsibility on the officers and directors of publicly listed companies as well as auditors. Canadian companies that are listed on U.S. stock exchanges, such as Intrawest, must comply with the SOX requirements.

INFORMATION INTERMEDIARIES: ANALYSTS AND INFORMATION SERVICES

Students often view the communication process between companies and financial statement users as a simple process of mailing the report to individual shareholders who read the report and then make investment decisions based on what they have learned. This simple picture is far from today's reality. Now most investors rely on sophisticated financial analysts and information services to gather and analyze information.

Financial Analysts   Financial analysts receive accounting reports and other information about the company from electronic information services. They also gather information through conversations with company executives and visits to company facilities. The results of these analyses along with information about competitors, the overall economy, and even population trends are combined into analysts' reports.

Analysts' reports normally include forecasts of share price and future quarterly and annual earnings per share; a buy, sell, or hold recommendation for the company shares; and explanations for these judgments.[3] In making these **earnings forecasts**, the analysts rely heavily on their knowledge of how the accounting system translates business events into the numbers on a company's financial statements, which is the subject matter of this text. This knowledge includes an understanding of the alternative accounting methods available to companies to account for different transactions and specialized industry practices that may be applied to a particular industry. Analysts are regularly evaluated based on the accuracy of their forecasts, as well as the profitability of their stock picks.[4]

Analysts often work in the research departments of brokerage and investment banking houses such as RBC Dominion Securities, mutual fund companies such as the Investors Group, and investment advisory services such as Standard & Poor's, that sell their advice to others. Individual analysts often specialize in particular industries (such as sporting goods or energy companies). For example, Irene Nattel of RBC Dominion Securities and Felicia Kantor of Lehman Brothers (both brokerage and investment banking companies) are among 10 analysts who follow Intrawest at both Canadian and U.S. brokerage houses. With other analysts at their firms, they write reports that analyze the company's future prospects.

Analysts' employers either use the reports directly or sell them to other investors. As a consequence, the analyst transfers his or her knowledge of accounting, the company, and the industry to others who lack this expertise. Many believe that decisions made based on analysts' advice cause stock market prices to react quickly to accounting information announcements. A quick, unbiased reaction to information is called *market efficiency* in finance. It is highly unlikely that unsophisticated investors can glean more information from financial statements than the sophisticated analysts have already learned. Careful analysis does not lead all analysts to the same conclusions, however. These differences of opinion are reflected in the following earnings (per share) forecasts and stock recommendations made by a number of analysts at the time of writing this book.

EARNINGS FORECASTS are predictions of earnings for future accounting periods.

INTRAWEST CORPORATION EARNINGS FORECAST		
	For fiscal 2005	For fiscal 2006
Average forecast	$1.46	$1.71
Lowest forecast	1.19	1.55
Highest forecast	1.82	1.99
Number of analysts	10	10

REAL WORLD EXCERPT

Yahoo.com

Analysts make recommendations to buy, hold, or sell a company's shares based on their earnings forecasts. In the case of Intrawest, one analyst recommended "strong buy," three analysts recommended "buy," four analysts recommended "hold," and two analysts recommended "sell" at the time of writing this book.

---

[3]For further discussion of analysts' forecasts, see R. K. Bowen, A. K. Davis, and D. A. Matsumuto, "Do Conference Calls Affect Analysts' Forecasts?" *The Accounting Review*, April 2002, pp. 387–404, and M. Earnes, S. Glover, and J. Kennedy, "The Association between Trading Recommendations and Analysts' Earnings Forecasts," *Journal of Accounting Research*, 2003, 40, 1, pp. 85–104.

[4]See M. B. Mikhail, B. R. Walther, and R. H. Willis, "Does Forecast Accuracy Matter to Security Analysts?" *The Accounting Review*, April 1999, pp. 185–200.

In general, financial analysts tend to make optimistic earnings forecasts in order to maintain a good relationship with the company's management. The reason is that managers provide analysts with vital information for their analysis. Optimistic earnings forecasts, however, put additional pressure on management to meet and even exceed analysts' forecasts in order to please investors. The drive to meet analysts' earnings expectations has led the management of some companies to adopt accounting policies that result in premature recognition of revenue and/or deferral of expenses in order to increase reported earnings.

A QUESTION OF **ETHICS**

IT PAYS TO BE A WARY INVESTOR

Occasional unethical behaviour on the part of financial analysts and investment advisers suggest that savvy investors should apply a healthy dose of skepticism along with their accounting knowledge when reading or listening to investment advice. Alleged ethical lapses, questionable business practices, and illegal activity by representatives of some of the largest, most highly respected brokerage and investment banking houses have recently made the news. These activities include the rigging of prices in securities auctions, excess trading of customers' accounts to generate higher commissions, insider trading, the sale of securities without full disclosure of their risks, issuance of flattering research recommendations, and executing trades for some customers at more advantageous prices than others. Most analysts, brokers, and investment bankers act in an honest and ethical fashion; however, they earn profits by charging commissions on securities transactions. When brokers let their need to earn commissions cloud their investment advice, this can lead to questionable or even unethical behaviour. For example, in 2004 the mutual funds industry paid fines in excess of US$2.3 billion in restitution, penalties, and reduced fees to customers for trading abuses.[5]

The information services discussed in the next section allow investors to gather their own information about the company and to monitor the recommendations of a variety of analysts.

Information Services   Canadian companies actually can file financial statements and other securities-related forms electronically with SEDAR (System for Electronic Document Analysis and Retrieval), which is the official site for the filing of documents by public companies as required by securities laws in Canada.[6] SEDAR is currently a free service available on the Web at www.sedar.com.

To look at SEDAR, just type the address on your Web browser. Select French or English, depending on your preference, then select Company Profiles followed by the letter of the alphabet that corresponds to the first letter of the company's name. You will then see a list of companies that includes the selected company. Many of the financial statement examples used in this book were downloaded from this Web site. Many companies also provide access to their financial statements and other information over the Web. Intrawest's financial information is available at www.intrawest.com/investor/index.asp.

Financial analysts obtain much of the information they use from the wide variety of commercial online information services. Services such as Lexis-Nexis (www.lexis nexis.com), Compustat (www.compustat.com), and CanWest Interactive Inc. (www.fp infomart.ca) provide broad access to financial statements and related news information.

---

[5]*Washington Post,* May 31, 2004.

[6]Canadian companies that have shares traded on U.S. stock exchanges can file SEC forms electronically with EDGAR (Electronic Data Gathering and Retrieval) sponsored by the SEC.

Some of the services provide specialized information. For example, First Call provides consensus (average) and analyst-by-analyst earnings forecasts for more than 18,000 domestic and foreign companies. More than 800 research analysts contribute earnings forecasts to the service. Samples of the consensus forecasts can be accessed on its Web site: www.thomson.com.

More general information services include the Dow Jones Interactive (www.djnr.com) and Bloomberg (www.bloomberg.com), as well as the financial sections of national newspapers such as *The Globe and Mail* and *National Post*. Dow Jones provides access to news stories about companies, as well as current and historical stock prices and company press releases, including the initial announcements of annual and quarterly financial results. The Bloomberg service also provides the ability to combine these sources of information in sophisticated analyses.

A growing number of other resources offer a mixture of free and fee-based information on many companies on the Web. These include www.investor.reuters.com, www.hoovers.com, and finance.yahoo.com.

FINANCIAL ANALYSIS

INFORMATION SERVICES: USES IN MARKETING, CLASSWORK, AND JOB SEARCHES

Information services have become the primary tool used not only by sophisticated analysts but also by marketing strategists to analyze competing firms. Sales representatives also use the services to analyze potential customers' needs and creditworthiness. Growing, creditworthy companies are the most profitable targets for the sales representative's efforts.

Information services are an important source of information to students for their term papers and job searches. Potential employers expect top job applicants to demonstrate knowledge about their company during an interview. To learn more about electronic information services, contact the business or reference librarian at your college or university library or explore some of the preceding Websites.

STOCK EXCHANGES AND GOVERNMENT REGULATORS

Companies that are listed on Canadian and U.S. stock exchanges must disclose financial information to the investing public in compliance with securities regulations. Stock exchanges provide an essential quality assurance service to listed companies by undertaking ongoing surveillance of their reporting and trading activities. When they suspect non-compliance with accounting standards, the stock exchanges undertake independent investigations, and share information with securities commissions; Canada Revenue Agency, which collects income taxes from corporations; and other law-enforcement agencies such as the Royal Canadian Mounted Police (RCMP). As intermediaries, the stock exchanges may also enforce their rules through penalties ranging from temporary cease-trade orders to fines and delisting of companies.

Securities commissions also provide oversight of financial disclosure. In Canada, the provincial securities and exchange commissions have legal authority to enforce provincial government regulations assuring the timeliness and quality of financial disclosure. The most prominent is the Ontario Securities Commission (OSC), which sets additional reporting standards for firms whose debt or equity securities are publicly traded. The OSC staff reviews these reports for compliance with OSC standards, investigates irregularities, and punishes violators of OSC regulations. Many OSC investigations are reported in the business press, such as the *National Post* or the *Globe and Mail*. The OSC also publishes this information online each month at www.oscbulletin.carswell.com.

USERS: INSTITUTIONAL AND PRIVATE INVESTORS, CREDITORS, AND OTHERS

INSTITUTIONAL INVESTORS are managers of pension funds, mutual funds, endowment funds, and other funds that invest on behalf of others.

Institutional investors include private pension funds (associated with unions and employees of specific companies); public pension funds (for provincial and municipal employees); mutual funds; and endowment, charitable foundation, and trust funds (such as the endowment of your college or university). These institutional shareholders usually employ their own analysts who also rely on the information intermediaries just discussed. Institutional shareholders control the majority of publicly traded shares of Canadian companies. For example, at the time of writing this book, institutional investors owned approximately 80 percent of Intrawest's outstanding shares.

PRIVATE INVESTORS include individuals who purchase shares in companies.

Private investors include large individual investors such as Joe Houssian and some of the company's directors, as well as small retail investors who, like most individuals, buy a small number of shares of publicly traded companies through brokers such as BMO Nesbitt Burns and TD Waterhouse. Retail investors normally lack the expertise to understand financial statements and the resources to gather data efficiently. As a consequence, they often rely on the advice of information intermediaries or turn their money over to the management of mutual and pension funds (institutional investors).

LENDERS (CREDITORS) include suppliers and financial institutions that lend money to companies.

Lenders, or **creditors**, include suppliers, banks, commercial credit companies, and other financial institutions that lend money to companies. Lending officers and financial analysts in these organizations use these same public sources of information. In addition, when companies borrow money from financial institutions, they often agree to provide additional financial information (e.g., monthly statements) as part of the lending contract. Lenders are often the primary external user group for financial statements of private companies. Institutional and private investors also become creditors when they buy a company's publicly traded bonds and debentures.[7]

A QUESTION OF **ETHICS**

REAL WORLD EXCERPT

Analyst's Accounting Observer

CONFLICTING INTERESTS OF MANAGERS, SHAREHOLDERS, AND CREDITORS

The economic interests of managers, shareholders, and creditors often differ. For example, paying dividends to shareholders benefits the shareholders but leaves less money available to pay creditors. Refurnishing the offices occupied by managers benefits them but leaves less money to pay dividends. Ethical conduct and mutual trust play a major role in balancing these differing interests.

Accounting and financial statements also play a major role in enforcing these relationships of trust. Compliance with agreements (contracts) between managers and shareholders and between shareholders and creditors are monitored with financial statement data.* Enron, WorldCom, and other recent cases have made the wisdom of famed analyst Jack Ciesielski's warning for managers, shareholders, directors, creditors, and analysts more evident:

> One usual answer to the question "why does accounting matter?" is that it helps to avoid "blow-ups": the unpleasant outcome when a stock crashes because the firm's management engaged in accounting chicanery that subsequently becomes visible. Actually, common sense and a good working knowledge of basic finance ("rising receivables and inventory are not a good thing") can help avoid blow-ups; but understanding accounting

*Research that examines the use of accounting in contracting is called *agency theory*.

---

[7]*Debentures* are debt securities that are not secured with specific collateral (no specific assets are pledged as security for the debt). *Bonds* normally are secured by specific collateral such as investments in shares of other companies. Chapter 11 provides more details about bonds and debentures.

can help an analyst assess management candor with shareholders. And it can help an analyst understand more about the drivers of earnings and their sustainability; the analyst who understands accounting matters will know precisely where the "soft spots" are in financial reporting, the ones that can be manipulated in order to meet an expected earnings target or avoid breaking a loan covenant.

Source: Analyst's Accounting Observer, www.aaopub.com, August 2000.

Financial statements play an important role in the relationships between customers and suppliers. Customers evaluate the financial health of suppliers to determine whether they will be able to provide a reliable, up-to-date source of supply. Suppliers evaluate their customers to estimate their future needs and ability to pay their debts to the suppliers. Competitors also attempt to learn useful information about a company from its statements. The potential loss of competitive advantage is one of the costs to the preparer of public financial disclosures. Accounting regulators consider these costs as well as the direct costs of preparation when they require new disclosures.

SELF-STUDY **QUIZ 6-1**

Match the players involved in the accounting communication process with their roles or the guiding principles for communicating information with their definitions.

1. Relevant information	*a.* Management primarily responsible for accounting information.
2. CEO and CFO	*b.* An independent party who verifies financial statements.
3. Financial analyst	*c.* Information that influences users' decisions.
4. External auditor	*d.* Only information that provides benefits in excess of costs should be reported.
5. Cost–benefit constraint	*e.* An individual who analyzes financial information and provides advice.

After you complete the quiz, check your answers with those on page 313.

THE DISCLOSURE PROCESS

As noted in our discussion of information services and information intermediaries, the accounting communication process includes more steps and participants than one would envision in a world in which annual and quarterly reports are simply mailed to shareholders.

PRESS RELEASES

To provide timely information to external users and to limit the possibility of selective leakage of information, Intrawest and most public companies announce quarterly and annual earnings through a **press release** as soon as the audited annual figures (or reviewed quarterly figures) are available. Intrawest normally issues its earnings press releases within six weeks of the end of the accounting period. The announcements are sent electronically to the major print and electronic news services, which make them immediately available to subscribers. An excerpt of a quarterly press release for Intrawest is reprinted in Exhibit 6.2. It includes key financial figures and an invitation to interested parties to access a live webcast concerning the company's quarterly results. Attached to the release are condensed income statements and balance sheets (unaudited) that are included in the formal quarterly report to shareholders mailed after the press release.

■ **LEARNING OBJECTIVE 2**

Identify the steps in the accounting communication process, including the issuance of press releases, annual reports, quarterly reports, and documents filed with securities commissions, the role of electronic information services in this process, as well as the guiding principles in communicating useful information.

A **PRESS RELEASE** is a written public news announcement normally distributed to major news services.

INTRAWEST REPORTS FISCAL 2004 THIRD-QUARTER RESULTS

All Dollar Amounts Are in U.S. Currency

Vancouver, May 11, 2004—Intrawest Corporation, the world's leading operator and developer of village-centered resorts, announced today its results for the fiscal 2004 third quarter ended March 31, 2004. Total revenue for the quarter was $437.3 million compared with $402.5 million for the same period last year. Total Company EBITDA (earnings before interest, income taxes, non-controlling interest, depreciation and amortization) was $128.1 million compared with $125.5 million in the same quarter last year. Income from continuing operations was $56.2 million or $1.17 per share (all per share amounts are fully diluted) compared with $56.8 million or $1.19 per share in the same quarter last year.

. . .

"We have shown significant improvement in cash flow this year," said Joe Houssian, Intrawest's chairman, president and chief executive officer. "With the recent creation of our leisure and travel group, all the pieces are now in place to increase the profitability of our resort operations and grow our resort real estate business while driving down debt."

. . .

Intrawest's Board of Directors today declared a dividend of Cdn$0.08 per common share payable on July 21, 2004 to shareholders of record on July 7, 2004.

The term EBITDA does not have a standardized meaning prescribed by generally accepted accounting principles (GAAP) and may not be comparable to similarly titled measures presented by other publicly traded companies. A reconciliation between net earnings as determined in accordance with Canadian GAAP and EBITDA is presented in the Statistical Supplement included below.

A conference call is scheduled for Tuesday, May 11, 2004 at 2:30 p.m. ET (1:30 p.m. CT, 11:30 a.m. PT) to review Intrawest's fiscal 2004 third quarter results. The call will be webcast live on Intrawest's Web site at www.intrawest.com. Access to the call can also be obtained by calling 1-888-202-2787 (media and retail investors) and 1-888-458-1598 (analysts and institutional investors), using the access code 88228, before the scheduled start time. A playback version of the conference call will be available until May 18, 2004 at 1-877-653-0545. The password to access the playback version is 228774.

For additional information, contact Stephen Forgacs, manager, investor relations and corporate communications, at (604) 623-6620 or at sforgacs@intrawest.com. If you would like to receive future news releases by email, please contact investor_relations @intrawest.com.

Press releases related to annual earnings and quarterly earnings often precede the issuance of the quarterly or annual report by 15 to 45 days. This time is necessary to prepare the additional detail and to print and distribute those reports.

Many companies, including Intrawest, follow these press releases with a conference call at which senior managers answer questions about the quarterly results from analysts. These calls are open to the investing public. Listening to these recordings is a good way to learn about a company's business strategy and its expectations for the future, as well as key factors that analysts consider when they evaluate a company. Intrawest's most recent quarterly conference call can be accessed at www.intrawest.com/investor/webcasts.asp.

For actively traded stocks such as those of Intrawest, most of the stock market reaction (share price increases and decreases from investor trading) to the news in the press release usually occurs quickly. Recall that a number of analysts follow Intrawest and regularly predict the company's earnings. When the actual earnings are published, the market reacts *not* to the amount of earnings but to *unexpected earnings*, the difference between actual earnings and expected earnings. For example, Intrawest's share price increased slightly from $20.05 to $20.80 on the day of the press release, which implies that the fiscal 2004 third-quarter earnings exceeded analysts' expectations.

The following excerpt from a recent article in *Harvard Business Review* points out the growing importance of meeting or beating the average of analysts' earnings estimates:

THE EARNINGS GAME: EVERYONE PLAYS, NOBODY WINS

Quarterly earnings numbers dominate the decisions of executives, analysts, investors, and auditors . . . meeting analysts' expectations that earnings will rise in a smooth, steady, unbroken line has become, at many corporations, a game whose imperatives override even the imperative to deliver the highest possible return to shareholders.

Source: *Harvard Business Review*, June 2001, p. 65.

Companies such as Intrawest issue press releases concerning other important events including announcement of new services or development of new resort villages. The stock market often appears to react to some of these important announcements such as the following:

INTRAWEST SELLING STAKE IN NINE RESORT VILLAGES

VANCOUVER—Intrawest Corp. said Thursday it is selling an 80 per cent stake in the commercial properties at nine of its resort villages to CNL Income Properties Inc., a Florida-based real estate investment trust. The commercial properties have a total value of $160 million, Intrawest said, adding that it will continue as property and leasing manager of all of the retail and commercial space involved. The commercial properties include restaurants, retail and specialty shops. Resort lodging is not included in the deal.

"Creation of this partnership is another significant step in our transition to a management-intensive structure from a more capital-intensive one," said Joe Houssian, chairman, president and chief executive officer of Intrawest. "This transaction will provide a significant recovery of capital as well as a partnership for future commercial development," Houssian said.

. . .

The deal is scheduled to close before the end of December 2004.
Shares of Intrawest gained 25 cents, closing at $19.95 on the TSX.

Source: www.cbc.ca/stories/2004/08/12/business/intrawest_040812.

Investors reacted positively to the sale of property because it reflects the company's strategy of focusing on managing properties rather than owning them. The sales price allows the company to reduce its debt.

ANNUAL REPORTS

For privately held companies, *annual reports* are relatively simple documents photocopied on white paper. They normally include the following:

1. Four basic financial statements: income statement, balance sheet, statement of retained earnings, and cash flow statement.
2. Related notes (footnotes).
3. Report of independent accountants (auditor's opinion).

The annual reports of public companies are significantly more elaborate, both because of additional reporting requirements imposed on these companies by securities commissions and because many companies use their annual reports as public relations tools to communicate non-accounting information to shareholders, customers, the press, and others.

The annual reports of public companies are normally split into two sections: the first, "non-financial," section usually includes a letter to shareholders from the chairman and CEO; descriptions of the company's management philosophy, products, its successes (and occasionally its failures); and exciting prospects and challenges for the future. Beautiful photographs of products, facilities, and personnel often are included. The second, "financial," section includes the core of the report. Securities regulators set minimum disclosure standards for the financial section of the annual reports of public companies. The principal components of the financial section include:

1. Summarized financial data for a 5- or 10-year period.
2. Management's Discussion and Analysis of financial condition and results of operations.
3. The basic financial statements.[8]
4. Notes (Footnotes).
5. Report of Independent Accountants (Auditor's Opinion) and sometimes the Report of Management Responsibility.
6. Recent stock price information.
7. Summaries of the unaudited quarterly financial data (described later).
8. Lists of directors and officers of the company and relevant addresses.

The order of these components varies.

Length of MD&A Section	Number of Companies
1–5 pages	8
6–10	31
11–15	39
16–20	43
21–25	26
26 or more pages	51

Most of these components except for Management's Discussion and Analysis (MD&A) have been discussed in earlier chapters. This component includes management's discussion and explanation of key figures in the financial statements and risks the company faces in the future. The MD&A section contains important non-financial and strategic information to help users interpret the financial statements. Many companies devote a sizeable portion of their annual reports to the MD&A section, as the chart in the margin shows.[9] For example, Intrawest devoted 15 pages of its 2004 annual report for a detailed analysis of its various sources of revenue and related expenses for that year. In addition, management provided non-financial information enabling readers to compare the number of skier visits in 2004 and 2003, which allows investors to determine whether the revenue per skier visit has increased or decreased for this segment of the business. Intrawest's MD&A section also includes a review of the company's liquidity, capital resources, and contractual obligations. A complete annual report from Van Houtte Inc., which includes all of these sections, is reprinted in Appendix B of this textbook. As noted earlier, many companies make their annual reports available on the Web.

QUARTERLY REPORTS

Quarterly reports normally begin with a short letter to shareholders. This is followed by a condensed income statement for the quarter, which often shows less detail than the annual income statement, and a condensed balance sheet dated at the end of the quarter (e.g., March 31 for the first quarter). These condensed financial statements are not audited and so are marked *unaudited*. Also, the cash flow statement, statement of retained earnings, and some notes to the financial statements often are not included. Private companies also normally prepare quarterly reports for lenders. Intrawest's quarterly reports are issued about seven weeks after the end of each quarter.

---

[8]The Canadian Accounting Standards Board has recently approved *CICA Handbook* section 1530, "Comprehensive Income," which requires companies to prepare a new Statement of Comprehensive Income. This statement would include all changes in equity during a period except those resulting from investments by shareholders and distributions to shareholders. An introduction to this new statement is available on the Online Learning Centre Web site at www.mcgrawhill.ca/college/libby/studentresources.

[9]C. Byrd, I. Chen, and J. Smith, *Financial Reporting in Canada 2004*. Toronto: Canadian Institute of Chartered Accountants, 2004, p. 49.

REPORTS TO SECURITIES COMMISSIONS

Public companies must also file periodic reports with the OSC and other provincial securities commissions. These reports include the annual report, quarterly reports, an annual information form, and an information circular.

The annual information form provides a more detailed description of the business, including such items as the company's corporate structure, the industry in which it operates, the products and services it offers, product and project development, sales and marketing, manufacturing, and competition. The form also lists the properties owned and leased by the company, and significant contracts that the company has signed.

The information circular is a legal document that is forwarded to the company's shareholders prior to the annual general or special meeting of shareholders. It provides information about the items that the shareholders will be asked to consider and vote on during the meeting, including election of new directors, appointment of independent auditors, and other matters of a legal nature. The circular also provides details of the monetary compensation of key management personnel.

In addition to these periodic reports, companies file other types of reports as the need arises. These include a short-form prospectus that provides details of the equity and/or debt securities that they plan to issue to investors, and press releases concerning new developments. The SEDAR Web site www.sedar.com lists all of the reports, documents, and news items that Intrawest and other corporations have filed.[10]

GUIDING PRINCIPLES FOR COMMUNICATING USEFUL INFORMATION

Information presented in financial reports is useful if it makes a difference in the context of making a decision. Several qualitative characteristics determine the usefulness of accounting information for decision making.[11] These were introduced in Chapter 2 (Exhibit 2.1) and are presented in more detail in Exhibit 6.3.

First of all, information cannot be useful if it is not properly understood. Users of accounting information are assumed to have a reasonable understanding of business and economic activities and accounting, and be willing to study the information with reasonable diligence.[12]

Second, information is useful for decision making if it is both **relevant** and **reliable**. Relevant information is of little value if it is not reliable, and reliable information is useless if it is not relevant for a specific decision context.

Relevance Information disclosed in financial statements is relevant if it can influence users' decisions by helping them assess the impact of past activities and/or predict future events. For example, the various elements of an income statement have predictive value if they help users predict future levels of net income or its subcomponents, such as operating income. The *predictive value* of the income statement is

RELEVANT INFORMATION can influence a decision; it is timely and has predictive and/or feedback value.

RELIABLE INFORMATION is verifiable, unbiased, and accurate.

---

[10]U.S., Canadian, and international companies that have shares trading on U.S. securities exchange markets are required to file a number of reports with the SEC. These include Form 10-K, which provides a detailed description of the business, and more detailed schedules concerning various figures reported in the annual financial statements, and Form 10-Q, which is essentially a quarterly report to shareholders. Intrawest is a "foreign private issuer" as defined by U.S. securities legislation. This allows Intrawest to use disclosure documents prepared under Canadian securities regulations instead of filing Forms 10-K and 8-K. For example, Intrawest files with the SEC its annual information form instead of producing Form 10-K. Furthermore, Intrawest does not prepare its financial statements in accordance with U.S. GAAP, but it provides a note that reconciles its Canadian financial statements to U.S. GAAP.

[11]Section 1000 "Financial Statement Concepts" of the *CICA Handbook* describes these characteristics.

[12]To help users better understand the contents of its financial reports, IBM includes on its Web site a glossary of terms and provides basic explanations of the information contained in financial statements (www.ibm.com/investor/tools/financials.phtml).

EXHIBIT **6.3**

Qualitative Characteristics of Accounting Information

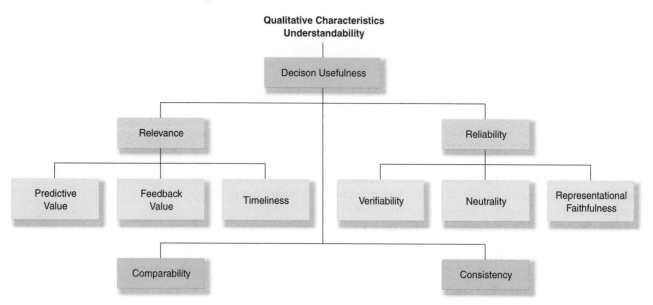

enhanced if non-recurring items are presented separately on a multiple-step income statement, because these items are transient in nature. Similarly, information presented on the income statement has *feedback value* if it confirms prior expectations about earnings.

Information that is not available to users in a timely manner loses its relevance because it would not be considered in making decisions. *Timeliness* of accounting information enhances both its predictive and feedback values. The relevance of accounting information for decision making declines as time passes. For this reason, companies produce quarterly reports and issue press releases to convey timely information to investors, creditors, and other user groups.

Reliability   Information presented in financial statements is reliable when it is verifiable, unbiased, and accurate. *Verifiability, neutrality*, and *representational faithfulness* characterize the reliability of accounting information. Accounting information is verifiable if independent accountants can agree on the nature and amount of the transaction. For example, the historical cost of a piece of land that is reported on Intrawest's balance sheet on June 30, 2004 is usually highly verifiable. The cost of acquisition is based on the purchase price and related costs that result from actual exchanges with external parties. However, the market value of the land at that date is a subjective estimate that reflects the appraiser's past experience. It is not verifiable because it is not based on an exchange transaction. If Intrawest is considering the sale of land, its market value would be relevant for that decision even though it is less reliable than the land's historical cost.

Neutrality relates to the measurement and presentation of information. The usefulness of accounting information is enhanced when it is neutral; that is, free from bias in its measurement and presentation. Bias in measurement occurs when the item being measured is consistently understated or overstated. For example, a consistent understatement of amortization expense leads to a biased higher net income. In this context, the development of accounting standards for measurement and reporting of transaction effects should not result in favouring one group of users over others. For example, the measurement and reporting of liabilities should not result in consistent underreporting of liabilities on the balance sheet because this would favour owners over creditors, and may influence investment and credit decisions of financial statement users.

Information provided in financial statements should reflect the substance of the underlying transactions. For example, the inventory account of a company that sells computer equipment would include items that are held for sale to customers. If inventory included also desktop and laptop computers used by employees in their daily work, then the inventory balance does not faithfully represent the cost of goods available for sale. Similarly, unearned revenue that is recognized prematurely as revenue for the period causes the amount of revenue reported on the income statement to be overstated, thus lacking representational faithfulness.

Comparability and Consistency *Comparability* of **accounting information** enables users to identify similarities and discrepancies between two sets of financial reports produced by two different companies. This quality is also important when comparing information provided by the same company over time.

The comparability of financial reports is enhanced if there is **consistency** in using the same accounting methods over time. Changes in accounting methods reduce the comparability of information and necessitate disclosure of the effects of the change in order to maintain comparability.

ACCOUNTING INFORMATION can be compared across businesses when similar accounting methods have been applied.

CONSISTENT INFORMATION can be compared over time because similar accounting methods have been applied.

CONSTRAINTS OF ACCOUNTING MEASUREMENT

Accurate interpretation of financial statements requires that the statement reader be aware of three important constraints of accounting measurement. First, although items and amounts that are of low significance must be accounted for, they do not have to conform precisely to specified accounting guidelines or be separately reported if they would not influence reasonable decisions. Accountants usually designate such items and amounts as *immaterial*. Determining **material amounts** is often very subjective.

Second, companies produce and disseminate accounting information to users with the expectation that the benefits to users from using such information exceed the cost of producing it. The perceived benefits of new information relate to its usefulness in decision making. Such benefits may be difficult to measure, but the costs of producing additional information can be estimated with reasonable accuracy. When standards setters, like the Accounting Standards Board, require companies to disclose specific information, known as *mandatory* disclosure, they would have determined implicitly that the benefits to users exceed the costs that the company will incur to produce the information. For example, a recently introduced regulation by the Canadian Securities Administrators concerning internal control over financial reporting[13] imposed additional costs on companies to evaluate their internal control procedures in order to discourage corporate fraud by managers. These additional expenditures are expected to lead to improvements in internal control procedures that would curb the misappropriation of assets by managers and other employees. The perceived benefits of this new regulation are increased reliability and decision usefulness of the accounting information disclosed in financial statements. While the cost of improving internal control procedures can be estimated, the related benefits to users of financial statements may be difficult to measure.

In other cases, the company's managers may decide that *voluntary* disclosure of information about specific aspects of the company's operations would be beneficial to users. In such cases, the costs of disclosure should not exceed the expected benefits. In this context, the **cost–benefit constraint** plays an important role in determining whether new information should be produced and communicated to users.

Finally, **conservatism** requires that special care be taken to avoid (1) overstating assets and revenues and (2) understating liabilities and expenses. Users of financial statements often want to know about possible sources of trouble for the company. For example, creditors need to know how secure their investments will be if the company's fortunes deteriorate, but they may not be interested in whether the company might do exceptionally well. They care more about the downside risk than the upside potential. For this reason, financial statements that show assets at historical cost, but reduce these amounts when current

MATERIAL AMOUNTS are amounts that are large enough to influence a user's decision.

The **COST–BENEFIT CONSTRAINT** suggests that information should be produced only if the perceived benefits of increased decision usefulness exceed the expected costs of providing that information.

CONSERVATISM suggests that care should be taken not to overstate assets and revenues or understate liabilities and expenses.

---

[13]Reporting on Internal Control over Financial Reporting, Multilateral Instrument 52-111, Canadian Securities Administrators, February 4, 2005, as posted on CSA's Web site: http://www.csa-acvm.ca, accessed on March 11, 2005.

values are significantly lower, help satisfy the needs of creditors. This lower-of-cost-or-market guideline attempts to offset managers' natural optimism about their business operations, which sometimes creeps into the financial reports that they prepare. More companies have perished through excessive optimism than through excessive caution.

A CLOSER LOOK AT FINANCIAL STATEMENTS AND NOTES

LEARNING OBJECTIVE 3

Recognize the different financial statement and disclosure formats used by companies in practice.

To make financial statements more useful to investors, creditors, and analysts, specific *classifications* of information are included in the statements. Various classifications are used in practice. You should not be confused when you notice different formats used by different companies. You will find that each format is consistent with the principles discussed in this text.

OVERVIEW OF INTRAWEST'S FINANCIAL STATEMENTS

Exhibits 6.4, 6.5, 6.6, and 6.7 show the financial statements of Intrawest for fiscal year 2004.

EXHIBIT **6.4**

Balance Sheet of Intrawest Corporation

REAL WORLD EXCERPT

Intrawest Corporation

ANNUAL REPORT

Consolidated Balance Sheets
June 30, 2004 and 2003
(in thousands of United States dollars)

	2004	2003
Assets		
Current Assets:		
Cash and cash equivalents	$ 109,816	$ 126,832
Amounts receivable (note 7)	142,427	126,725
Other assets (note 8(a))	94,105	123,610
Resort properties (note 6)	412,343	662,197
Future income taxes (note 13)	18,638	10,619
	777,329	1,049,983
Resort operations (note 5)	940,949	918,727
Resort properties (note 6)	368,309	405,100
Amounts receivable (note 7)	52,958	76,842
Investment in and advances to Leisura (note 20)	50,899	—
Other assets (note 8(b))	65,306	65,070
	$2,255,750	$2,515,722
Liabilities and Shareholders' Equity		
Current Liabilities:		
Amounts payable	$ 209,037	$ 223,832
Deferred revenue and deposits (note 10)	87,649	134,878
Bank and other indebtedness (note 9)	109,685	287,176
	406,371	645,886
Bank and other indebtedness (note 9)	849,132	973,743
Deferred revenue and deposits (note 10)	82,211	43,609
Future income taxes (note 13)	87,461	94,986
Non-controlling interest in subsidiaries	43,266	46,359
	1,468,441	1,804,583
Shareholders' equity:		
Capital stock (note 12)	463,485	460,742
Retained earnings	318,883	264,640
Foreign currency translation adjustment	4,941	(14,243)
	787,309	711,139
	$2,255,750	$2,515,722

Contingencies and commitments (note 15)
Subsequent event (note 23)
See accompanying notes to consolidated financial statements.

EXHIBIT **6.5**

**Income Statement of
Intrawest Corporation**

REAL WORLD EXCERPT

*Intrawest
Corporation*

ANNUAL REPORT

Consolidated Statements of Operations
For the years ended June 30, 2004 and 2003
(in thousands of United States dollars, except per share amounts)

	2004	2003
Resort operations		
Revenue	$ 541,315	$ 499,885
Expenses	436,184	387,450
Resort operations contribution	105,131	112,435
Management services		
Revenue	124,394	88,202
Expenses	96,909	77,223
Management services contribution	27,485	10,979
Real estate development		
Revenue	878,195	512,695
Expenses	788,504	444,438
	89,691	68,257
Income from equity accounted investment	1,683	—
Real estate development contribution	91,374	68,257
Income before undemoted items	223,990	191,671
Interest and other income	6,117	2,417
Interest expense	(45,766)	(47,142)
Corporate general and administrative expenses	(20,369)	(14,889)
Depreciation and amortization	(68,626)	(67,516)
Call premium and unamortized costs of senior notes redeemed	(12,074)	—
Write-down of technology assets (note 8(b))	—	(12,270)
Income before income taxes and non-controlling interest	83,272	52,271
Provision for income taxes (note 13)	(10,434)	(6,243)
Non-controlling interest	(12,889)	(11,274)
Income from continuing operations	59,949	34,754
Results of discontinued operations (note 4)	—	(578)
Net income	$ 59,949	$ 34,176
Net income per common share (note 12(h))		
Basic	$ 1.26	$ 0.73
Diluted	1.25	0.73

See accompanying notes to consolidated financial statements.

EXHIBIT **6.6**

**Statement of Retained Earnings
of Intrawest Corporation**

REAL WORLD EXCERPT

*Intrawest
Corporation*

ANNUAL REPORT

Consolidated Statements of Retained Earnings
For the years ended June 30, 2004 and 2003
(in thousands of United States dollars)

	2004	2003
Retained earnings, beginning of year	$ 264,640	$ 235,515
Net income	59,949	34,176
Dividends	(5,706)	(5,051)
Retained earnings, end of year	$ 318,883	$ 264,640

See accompanying notes to consolidated financial statements.

EXHIBIT **6.7**

**Cash Flow Statement of
Intrawest Corporation**

REAL WORLD EXCERPT

*Intrawest
Corporation*

ANNUAL REPORT

**Consolidated Statements of Cash Flows
For the years ended June 30, 2004 and 2003
(in thousands of United States dollars)**

	2004	2003
Cash provided by (used in)		
Operations		
Income from continuing operations	$ 59,949	$ 34,754
Items not affecting cash:		
Depreciation and amortization	68,626	67,516
Future income taxes	(1,240)	(3,914)
Income from equity accounted investment	(1,683)	—
Amortization of financing costs	6,441	3,479
Loss on asset disposals, net of write-offs	1,388	858
Stock-based compensation	290	—
Amortization of benefit plan	1,992	2,097
Write-down of technology assets	—	12,270
Non-controlling interest	12,889	11,274
Funds from continuing operations	148,652	128,334
Recovery of costs through real estate sales	743,405	433,011
Acquisition and development of properties held for sale	(487,659)	(601,524)
Changes in amounts receivable, net	42,396	(10,109)
Changes in non-cash operating working capital (note 21)	(23,929)	29,269
Cash provided by (used in) continuing operating activities	422,865	(21,019)
Cash provided by discontinued operations	—	140
	422,865	(20,879)
Financing		
Proceeds from bank and other borrowings	537,286	599,112
Repayments of bank and other borrowings	(841,332)	(469,234)
Issue of common shares for cash, net of issuance costs	461	2,684
Redemption and repurchase of non-resort preferred shares (note 12(a))	—	(6,697)
Dividends paid	(5,706)	(5,051)
Distributions to non-controlling interest	(16,543)	(6,923)
	(325,834)	113,891
Investments		
Expenditures on:		
Resort operations assets	(69,342)	(64,546)
Other assets	(23,321)	(15,257)
Investment in Leisura (note 20)	(37,260)	—
Business acquisitions (note 3)	—	(2,849)
Proceeds from asset disposals	15,876	39,783
	(114,047)	(42,869)
Increase (decrease) in cash and cash equivalents	(17,016)	50,143
Cash and cash equivalents, beginning of year	126,832	76,689
Cash and cash equivalents, end of year	$ 109,816	$ 126,832

Cash flow information (note 21)
See accompanying notes to consolidated financial statements.

As we have seen in previous chapters, the items presented in these statements are classified in order to provide useful information to users. The assets and liabilities on Intrawest's balance sheet are split between current and non-current portions. Also, the income statement includes a number of sections and subtotals to aid the user in identifying the company's operating income for the year and to highlight the effect of other items on net income.

The presentation of information in Intrawest's income statement reflects the nature of the company's business operations. Unlike other companies that produce and sell specific consumer products, Intrawest derives its revenue from three primary sources: resort operations, management services, and real estate development. Intrawest's income statement does not show cost of goods sold, as we see in a typical income statement. Instead, the company reports the revenues and expenses that are directly related to each of its three business segments as well as the contribution that each business segment has made to covering the company's other expenses that are not directly attributable to each segment, such as interest expense and amortization. This helps the income statement user in assessing the relative contribution of each business segment to Intrawest's overall profitability. For example, resort operations contributed the most to Intrawest's profitability in both fiscal years 2003 and 2004. However, the relative contribution of this segment declined in 2004 compared to the contributions of the other two segments: management services and real estate development.

Lastly, Intrawest's cash flow statement shows the sources and uses of cash that resulted from its operating, investing, and financing activities during the past two fiscal years. Such a categorization of the cash flows is important, especially those resulting from operating activities. Companies can not survive for a long time without generating positive cash flows from their operations.

Intrawest's financial statements are condensed reports where each financial statement item is a combination of a number of accounts used in the company's accounting system. While the amounts reported on the various financial statements provide important information, users require additional details to facilitate their analysis. Such details are typically disclosed in notes that follow the financial statements. Standards setting organizations, like the Canadian Accounting Standard Board, and securities commissions, such as the Ontario Securities Commission, require public companies to provide a minimum set of detailed information to assist the users of financial statements in making informed investment and credit decisions. In addition, companies may provide other information voluntarily if management believes that such information will reflect positively on the company. In general, management refrains from disclosing information that may have a negative effect on the company's future profitability and financial condition—hence the need for a minimum set of disclosures that are typically provided in notes to financial statements. Intrawest included 23 notes to its 2004 financial statements covering both mandatory and voluntary disclosures. Excerpts from Intrawest's notes are illustrated below along with our discussion of selected elements of the company's financial statements.

NOTES TO FINANCIAL STATEMENTS

Notes to financial statements include three types of information:

1. Description of the key accounting policies (rules) applied to the company's statements.

2. Additional details supporting reported amounts in the financial statements.

3. Relevant financial information not disclosed in the statements.

Accounting Policies Applied in the Company's Statements The first or second note is typically a summary of significant accounting policies. As you will see in your study of subsequent chapters, generally accepted accounting principles (GAAP) permit companies to select from alternative methods for measuring the effects of transactions. The summary of significant accounting policies tells the user which accounting methods the company has adopted.

NOTE 2

SIGNIFICANT ACCOUNTING POLICIES

Revenue Recognition

(i) Resort operations revenue is recognized as the service is provided.

(ii) Revenue from the sale of properties is recorded generally when title to the completed unit is conveyed to the purchaser, the purchaser becomes entitled to occupancy and the purchaser has made a payment that is appropriate in the circumstances.

(iii) Points revenue associated with membership in the vacation ownership business of Club Intrawest (which revenue is included in real estate sales) is recognized when the purchaser has paid the amount due on closing, all contract documentation has been executed and all other significant conditions of sale are met.

(iv) Management service revenue is recognized as the service is provided. Reservation fee revenue is recorded at the net of the amount charged to the customer and the amount paid to the supplier.

(v) Commission revenue from real estate brokerage operations is recognized at the time an offer of sale is closed by the purchaser or all other contractual obligations have been satisfied.

This note provides information about the timing of recognition of Intrawest's different types of revenue. Without an understanding of the various accounting methods used, it is impossible to analyze a company's financial results effectively.

FINANCIAL **ANALYSIS**

ALTERNATIVE ACCOUNTING METHODS AND GAAP

Many people mistakenly believe that GAAP permit only one accounting method to be used to compute each value in the financial statements (e.g., inventory). Actually, GAAP often allow selection of an accounting method from a menu of acceptable methods. This permits a company to choose the methods that most closely reflect its particular economic circumstances (economic reality). This flexibility complicates the financial statement users' task—they also must understand how the company's choice of accounting methods affects its financial statement presentations. As Gabrielle Napolitano and Abby Joseph Cohen of the investment banking firm of Goldman, Sachs & Co. note in a research report,

There are numerous legitimate ways in which company accounts can be made obscure. Further, investors must be wary of the means by which reported earnings can be manipulated or smoothed. Users of financial statements (e.g., shareholders, creditors, and others) are often forced to wrestle with dramatic differences in reporting practices between firms.*

*Gabrielle Napolitano and Abby Joseph Cohen, "The Quality of Reported Earnings Has Improved, But . . . Pointers on What to Look for in Company Reports," *U.S. Research* (New York: Goldman, Sachs & Co., January 2, 1997).

For example, before analyzing two companies' statements prepared using different accounting methods, one company's statements must be converted to the other's methods to make them comparable. Otherwise, the reader is in a situation similar to comparing distances in kilometres and miles without conversion to a common scale. In chapters 8 and 9, we discuss alternative accounting methods and their effects on financial statements.

Additional Detail Supporting Reported Amounts The second category of notes provides supplemental information concerning the data shown in the financial statements. Among other information, these notes may show revenues broken down by geographic region of business segments, unusual transactions, or expanded detail on a specific classification.

Intrawest's balance sheet (Exhibit 6.4) lists four items under both the current and non-current categories: Resort properties, Amounts receivable, Deferred revenue, and Bank and other indebtedness. These items are interrelated and reflect the nature of the company's business. Since Intrawest develops resort villages and sells a variety of housing units to interested customers, properties that are available for sale as well as those under development are classified as current assets. To develop properties, Intrawest receives deposits from buyers of housing units (a deferred revenue) and borrows funds from banks and other creditors. The portions of these financing sources that relate to current resort properties are classified as current liabilities. Intrawest also finances the sale of properties and receives payments from property buyers over an extended period of time. Hence, a portion of the amounts receivable is classified as non-current.

Note 2 to Intrawest's financial statements explains the accounting policies that have been used in measuring and reporting these items.[14] Details of amounts reported on the balance sheet are provided in subsequent notes. For example, Note 7 shows details of the amounts receivable and the breakdown of the total amount between current and non-current portions. It also informs the reader of the interest rate on the loans, mortgages, and notes receivable. It further indicates that part of the amounts receivable are used as collateral for the settlement of the company's debts.

REAL WORLD EXCERPT

*Intrawest
Corporation*

ANNUAL REPORT

NOTES TO CONSOLIDATED FINANCIAL STATEMENTS

NOTE 7: AMOUNTS RECEIVABLE

	2004	2003
Receivables from sales of real estate	$ 47,869	$ 54,576
Resort operations trade receivables	31,483	34,427
Loans, mortgages and notes receivable	85,777	89,189
Funded senior employee share purchase plans (note 12(e))	4,019	4,445
Other accounts receivable	26,237	20,930
	195,385	203,567
Current portion	142,427	126,725
	$ 52,958	$ 76,842

Amounts receivable from sales of real estate primarily comprise sales proceeds held in trust which are generally paid out to the Company or to construction lenders within 60 days.

Total payments due on amounts receivable are approximately as follows:

Year ending June 30,	
2005	$ 142,427
2006	15,968
2007	2,773
2008	2,512
2009	6,988
Subsequent to 2009	24,717
	$ 195,385

---

[14]Additional discussion of accounting rules related to amounts receivable, long-term assets, deferred revenue, and long-term debt is provided in later chapters.

> The loans, mortgages and notes receivable bear interest at both fixed and floating rates which averaged 11.59% per annum as at June 30, 2004 (2003 – 10.71%). Certain of these amounts have been pledged as security for the Company's bank and other indebtedness (note 9).

Relevant Financial Information Not Disclosed on the Statements The final category of notes includes information that impacts the company financially but is not shown on the statements. Examples include information on stock option plans, legal matters, and any material event that occurred subsequent to year-end but before the financial statements are published. In Note 9, Intrawest disclosed that its ability to raise additional debt is subject to specific limitations.

REAL WORLD EXCERPT

*Intrawest
Corporation*

ANNUAL REPORT

> ## NOTES TO CONSOLIDATED FINANCIAL STATEMENTS
>
> *9. Bank and Other Indebtedness*
>
> . . .
>
> The Company is subject to certain covenants in respect of some of the bank and other indebtedness which require the Company to maintain certain financial ratios. The Company is in compliance with these covenants at June 30, 2004.

VOLUNTARY DISCLOSURES

GAAP and securities regulations set only a minimum level of required financial disclosures. Many companies, including Intrawest, provide important disclosures beyond those required. Such voluntary disclosures may appear in the annual report, in documents filed with securities commissions, in press releases, or on the company's Web site.

RETURN ON EQUITY ANALYSIS

■ LEARNING OBJECTIVE 4

Compute and interpret the return on equity ratio.

Evaluating company performance is the primary goal of financial statement analysis. Company managers, as well as competitors, use financial statements to better understand and evaluate a company's business strategy. Analysts, investors, and creditors use these same statements to evaluate performance as part of their share valuation and credit evaluation judgments. Our discussion of the financial data contained in accounting reports has now reached the point where we can evaluate the performance of the company in relation to the investment made by shareholders.

KEY **RATIO ANALYSIS:**

RETURN ON EQUITY

ANALYTICAL QUESTION → How well has management used the investment by shareholders during the period?

RATIO AND COMPARISONS → The return on equity (ROE) ratio helps in answering this question. It is computed as follows:

$$\text{Return on Equity} = \frac{\text{Net Income}}{\text{Average Shareholders' Equity*}}$$

*Average Shareholders' Equity = (Beginning Shareholders' Equity + Ending Shareholders' Equity) ÷ 2

The 2004 ratio for Intrawest is:

$$\frac{\$59,949}{(\$711,139 + \$787,309) \div 2} = 0.08 \ (8.0\%)$$

Comparisons over Time		
Intrawest		
2002	2003	2004
9.4%	4.9%	8.0%

Comparisons with Competitors	
Vail Resorts	Compagnie des Alpes
2004	2004
−1.2%	10.1%

INTERPRETATIONS

In General → ROE measures how much the firm earned for each dollar of shareholders' investment. In the long run, firms with higher ROE are expected to have higher share prices than firms with lower ROE, all other things equal. Managers, analysts, and creditors use this ratio to assess the effectiveness of the company's overall business strategy (its operating, investing, and financing strategies).

Focus Company Analysis → The preceding computation indicates that Intrawest's ROE is relatively low in 2003 compared to both 2002 and 2004. Intrawest noted that the decrease in net income in 2003 is due to higher amortization and interest expense as well as a write-down of technology assets. Intrawest performed significantly better than Vail Resorts, North America's second-ranking ski resort operator, which operates resorts mainly in Colorado and Wyoming, but did not perform as well as the Compagnie des Alpes, one of the largest ski-lift operators in Europe, which operates ski resorts in the French and Italian Alps.

A Few Cautions → An increasing ROE can also indicate that a manufacturing company is failing to invest in research and development or modernization of plant and equipment. While such a strategy will decrease expenses and thus increase ROE in the short run, it normally results in future declines in ROE as the company's products and plant and equipment reach the end of their life cycles. As a consequence, experienced decision makers evaluate ROE in the context of a company's business strategy. Intrawest has expanded its real estate development in recent years, which increased expenses and decreased ROE.

More detailed analysis of ROE and its relationship to other financial ratios are covered in Chapter 13.

FINANCIAL **ANALYSIS**

ACCOUNTING-BASED EXECUTIVE BONUSES

Many companies believe that good performance by executives can be motivated by tying their compensation to the financial performance of the company. The basic idea is to link the compensation of executives to a measure of income. As a result, the financial interests and motivations of the management team become aligned with those of the company's shareholders. Details of a company's executive compensation are disclosed in the Information Circular or Management Proxy Circular that is forwarded to shareholders prior to the annual general meeting of the company's shareholders.

The annual compensation of key executives consists typically of three components: a base salary, a bonus, and other compensation. The bonus is usually based on achieving a predetermined level of performance. For example, Gildan Activewear Inc., the focus company of Chapter 7, pays its executives a bonus if the actual return on assets attains or exceeds specific performance targets and if other employees attain specific objectives. For a recent fiscal year, the five executive officers earned $2,217,583 in salaries and $2,787,093 in bonuses. (Source: Gildan Activewear Inc., Management Proxy Circular, December 17, 2004, p. 8.)

The connection between performance-based compensation and income measures provides managers with an incentive to adopt accounting policies that increase the reported income measures. As reported net income goes up, compensation to the company's executives will also increase. Some skeptics also believe that performance-based pay that is tied to the financial statements gives managers an incentive to distort the amounts reported in the financial statements in order to increase their total compensation.

SELF-STUDY **QUIZ 6-2**

Assume that Intrawest's executives receive bonuses if the current year's net income exceeds the previous year's net income by 20 percent. Use Exhibit 6.5 to check whether Intrawest's executives earned any bonuses in fiscal year 2004.

Computations _____

_____

Discuss why Intrawest might choose to pay executives based on performance and why it uses the same accounting numbers in reports to shareholders to measure the executives' performance.

_____

After you complete your work, check your solution with the answer on page 313.

FINANCIAL **ANALYSIS**

DIFFERENT EARNINGS FOR DIFFERENT PURPOSES

In recent years, many companies reported different measures of *earnings* in addition to net income as determined by GAAP. When companies report non-GAAP measures of earnings, they divert investors' attention away from the financial results of continuing operations.

For example, in discussing its annual and quarterly results of operations, Intrawest's management focuses investors' and analysts' attention on EBITDA (earnings before interest, income taxes, non-controlling interest, depreciation, and amortization). Comparison of the revenue, net income, and EBITDA for the years 2000–2004 shows clearly why investors and analysts should be cautious about interpreting this measure of income (amounts in millions of U.S. dollars).

	2000	2001	2002	2003	2004
Revenue	$810.5	$922.8	$986.0	$1,086.6	$1,543.9
EBITDA	165.4	200.3	211.2	209.2	268.3
Net income	52.1	63.5	58.6	34.8	59.9

Revenue increased by 90 percent over the five-year period, with a corresponding increase of 62 percent in EBITDA. However, net income increased by only 15 percent over the same period.

DEMONSTRATION **CASE**

Sleeman Breweries Ltd., which was introduced in Chapter 5, makes several beers, including its best-selling Sleeman Cream Ale and Honey Brown Lager. The company also owns the Canadian rights to the Stroh's family of beers and imports various international brands from the United States, England, and Japan. Sleeman's financial statements for the years 2002 and 2003 are shown below.

SLEEMAN BREWERIES LTD.
Consolidated Balance Sheets
(in thousands of dollars)

	December 27, 2003	December 28, 2002
Assets		
Current		
Accounts receivable—Trade	$ 30,322	$ 25,454
—Other (note 4)	7,556	3,910
Income taxes recoverable	—	190
Inventories (note 5)	31,054	22,843
Prepaid expenses	5,379	1,677
	74,311	54,074
Note receivable (note 4)	2,166	3,072
Property, plant and equipment (note 6)	74,691	70,120
Long-term investment and executive loans (note 7)	6,337	7,586
Intangible assets (note 8)	86,443	86,581
	$243,948	$221,433

(continued)

SLEEMAN BREWERIES LTD.
Consolidated Balance Sheets *(continued)*

	December 27, 2003	December 28, 2002
Liabilities		
Current		
Bank indebtedness (note 9)	555	10,461
Accounts payable and accrued liabilities	40,492	28,847
Income taxes payable	2,284	—
Current portion of long-term debt (note 10)	13,374	9,672
	56,705	48,980
Long-term debt (note 10)	71,916	73,950
Future income taxes (note 11)	11,527	8,306
	140,148	131,236
Shareholders' Equity		
Share capital (note 12)	45,075	43,753
Contributed surplus	28	—
Retained earnings	58,697	46,444
	103,800	90,197
	$243,948	$221,433

SLEEMAN BREWERIES LTD.
Consolidated Statements of Earnings and Retained Earnings
(in thousands of dollars except per share amounts)

	Fiscal Year Ended	
	December 27, 2003	December 28, 2002
Net revenue	$185,036	$157,053
Cost of goods sold	96,703	79,059
Gross margin	88,333	77,994
Gain on sale of agency agreement	—	3,595
Gain on settlement of obligation (note 3)	591	—
Selling, general and administrative	55,523	51,659
Earnings before the undernoted	33,401	29,930
Depreciation and amortization	6,301	5,402
Interest expense—net	6,097	6,017
Earnings before income taxes	21,003	18,511
Income taxes (note 11)	8,750	6,190
Net earnings	12,253	12,321
Retained earnings, beginning of year	46,444	34,123
Retained earnings, end of year	$ 58,697	$ 46,444
Earnings per share (note 14)		
Basic	$ 0.77	$ 0.79
Diluted	$ 0.76	$ 0.77

SLEEMAN BREWERIES LTD.
Consolidated Statements of Cash Flows
(in thousands of dollars except per share amounts)

	Fiscal Year Ended	
	December 27, 2003	December 28, 2002
Net inflow (outflow) of cash related to the following activities:		
Operating		
Net earnings	$ 12,253	$ 12,321
Items not affecting cash		
Depreciation and amortization	6,301	5,402
Future income taxes	3,221	2,000
Gain on sale of agency agreement	—	(3,595)
Gain on settlement of obligation (note 3)	(591)	—
Non cash interest charges in income	(90)	(69)
Stock-based compensation expense	28	—
Loss (gain) on disposal of equipment	4	(388)
	$ 21,126	$ 15,671
Changes in non-cash operating working capital items (note 15)	(7,533)	(2,277)
	13,593	13,394
Investing		
Business acquisitions	—	(52)
Proceeds from sale of agency agreement	980	351
Additions to property, plant and equipment	(8,652)	(6,986)
Additions to intangible assets	(2,105)	(7,975)
Proceeds from executive loans	249	504
Proceeds from disposal of equipment	19	839
	(9,509)	(13,319)
Financing		
Net decrease in bank operating loans	(9,906)	(5,602)
Stock options exercised	1,322	2,288
Long-term debt—proceeds	90,000	11,161
Long-term debt—principal repayments	(85,500)	(7,922)
	(4,084)	(75)
Net cash flow and cash balance, end of year	$ —	$ —
Supplemental disclosures of cash flows:		
Interest paid	$ 6,121	$ 6,028
Income taxes paid, net of cash refunds of $885 (2002 – $221)	$ 3,332	$ 7,158

Required:

1. Examine Sleeman's balance sheets. Identify the six largest changes in the book value of assets, liabilities, and shareholders' equity between the balance sheet dates. Based on what you have learned so far, what type of transactions could have caused the changes in the book value of these items?

2. Access Note 6 to the financial statements from the company's Web site (www.sleeman.ca) and identify the specific changes to the Property, Plant, and Equipment account.

3. Compute the following ratios for fiscal years 2002 and 2003: debt-to-equity, total asset turnover, return on assets, return on equity, and net profit margin. Use the results of your computations to comment on the company's financial situation and profitability of its operations in both years. Sleeman's total assets and shareholders' equity at December 29, 2001 amounted to $197,642 and $73,088, respectively.

4. Sleeman's operations generated significant amounts of cash during both the years 2002 and 2003. The company also made significant investments in property, plant, and equipment, and in intangible assets. How did the company finance the acquisition of these assets in 2003?

5. Compute and interpret the quality of income ratio and the capital acquisitions ratio for both 2002 and 2003.

6. Access finance.yahoo.com, search for Sleeman Breweries Ltd. (ALE.TO), and look up "Analysts' Estimates" under "Analyst Coverage." What is the average analysts' estimate of Sleeman's earnings per share (EPS) for the next two fiscal years? Do analysts expect Sleeman's EPS to increase or decrease in the future? What information did the analysts take into consideration in computing their EPS estimates for the next two years?

SUGGESTED SOLUTION

1. The six balance sheet items that had the largest changes in their book values, and the typical reasons for these changes, are summarized below (amounts in thousands of dollars):

Balance sheet item	Change	Typical reasons for change
Accounts receivable—trade	+$4,868	Increase in sales to customers on credit.
Inventories	+ 8,211	Purchase of ingredients to make beer, increase in the beer that has been produced and ready for sale.
Property, plant, and equipment	+ 4,571	Acquisition of new assets, disposal of old asset, net of amortization of assets for the year.
Bank indebtedness	− 9,906	Repayment of amounts due to banks.
Accounts payable and accrued liabilities	+11,645	Increase in the amounts payable to trade suppliers, and in accrued expenses.
Retained earnings	+12,253	This increase reflects the net income for the year.

2. Note 6 to the financial statements shows that Sleeman's property, plant, and equipment includes Land, Plant, Capital projects in process, Machinery and equipment, Office equipment, and Leasehold improvements. These assets have increased by $8,626. At the same time, amortization of the Plant, Machinery and equipment, Office equipment, and Leasehold improvements increased by $4,055 during the year, which reduces the book value of these assets.

3.

Ratio	2002	2003
Debt to equity = Total liabilities ÷ Total shareholders' equity	1.45	1.35
Total asset turnover = Net sales ÷ Average total assets	0.75	0.79
Return on assets = Net income ÷ Average total assets	5.9%	5.3%
Return on equity = Net income ÷ Average shareholders' equity	15%	13%
Net profit margin = Net income ÷ Net sales	7.8%	6.6%

Computations:

2002

D/E = \$131,236 ÷ \$90,197 = 1.45
TAT/O = \$157,053 ÷ [(\$197,642 + \$221,433)/2] = 0.75
ROA = \$12,321 ÷ [(\$197,642 + \$221,433)/2] = 0.059
ROE = \$12,321 ÷ [(\$73,088 + \$90,197)/2] = 0.15
NPM = \$12,321 ÷ \$157,053 = 0.078

2003

D/E = \$140,148 ÷ \$103,800 = 1.35
TAT/O = \$185,036 ÷ [(\$221,433 + \$243,948)/2] = 0.79
ROA = \$12,253 ÷ [(\$221,433 + \$243,948)/2] = 0.053
ROE = \$12,253 ÷ [(\$90,197 + \$103,800)/2] = 0.13
NPM = \$12,253 ÷ \$185,036 = 0.066

The debt-to-equity ratio decreased from 1.45 to 1.35, suggesting a relative decrease in liabilities and an improvement in the company's financial risk. The total asset turnover ratio increased slightly, suggesting a slight improvement in the utilization of the company's assets to generate revenue. The three profitability ratios—return on assets, return on equity, and net profit margin—have decreased because net income for 2003 was almost equal to that of 2002, while total assets, shareholders' equity, and net sales increased during 2003. This suggests that management should pay closer attention to the expenses and attempt to reduce them in the future.

4. Sleeman's cash flow statement shows that the company spent $9,509 on investments during 2003. The financing activities also caused a net cash outflow of $4,084. The cash generated from operations, totalling $13,593, provided the necessary financing for the company's investments.

5. Quality of income ratio = Cash Flow from Operating Activities ÷ Net income

    2002: $13,394 ÷ $12,321 = 1.087
    2003: $13,593 ÷ $12,253 = 1.109

The ratios indicate that there is close correspondence between the cash generated from operations and net income, which assures the user that deferral and accruals of revenues and expenses do not result in a significant difference between cash from operations and net income.

$$\text{Capital acquisitions ratio} = \frac{\text{Cash Flow from Operating Activities}}{\text{Cash Paid for Property, Plant, and Equipment}}$$

    2002: $13,394 ÷ ($6,986 − $839) = 2.18
    2003: $13,593 ÷ ($8,652 − $ 19) = 1.57

In both years, the company generated enough cash from its operations to cover the payments needed for the additional investments made during these two years.

6. The average analysts' estimate of Sleeman's EPS for fiscal year 2004 is $0.91 and $1.06 for fiscal year 2005. These average EPS estimates are based on individual estimates of 9 and 8 analysts, respectively.

    Sleeman's basic EPS for fiscal year 2003 is $0.77, as disclosed in its income statement. Analysts expect the company to improve on its performance in the next two years.

    Analysts use a variety of information sources to arrive at their EPS estimates. First, they need to develop a very good understanding of the industry, and Sleeman's role in the industry. Their information sources would include examination of the company's financial statements, analysis of population trends and expectations of future demand for beer in general and the company's products in particular, analysis of the company's strategies and future plans, conversations with company executives, and information about the company's competitors.

SOLUTIONS TO **SELF-STUDY QUIZZES**

Self-Study Quiz 6-1

1*c*, 2*a*, 3*e*, 4*b*, 5*d*.

Self-Study Quiz 6-2

Change in net income = $59,949 − $34,176 = $25,773

Percentage change in net income = $25,773 ÷ $34,176 = 75% (greater than 20%)

They did earn their bonuses. Paying Intrawest executives a bonus for increasing earnings helps align the interests of the executives with those of the shareholders. In addition, companies often pay executives bonuses based on the numbers in the annual report because the auditors have independently verified those numbers.

CHAPTER **TAKE-AWAYS**

1. **Recognize the people involved in the accounting communication process (managers, auditors, information intermediaries, stock exchanges and government regulators, and users), their roles in the process, and the guidance they receive from legal and professional standards.   p. 285**
Management of the reporting company must decide on the appropriate format (categories) and level of detail to present in its financial reports. Independent audits increase the credibility of the information. Financial statement announcements from public companies usually are first transmitted to users through electronic information services. The securities commission staff reviews public reports for compliance with legal and professional standards, investigates irregularities, and punishes violators. Analysts play a major role in making financial statements and other information available to average investors through their stock recommendations and earnings forecasts.

2. **Identify the steps in the accounting communication process, including the issuance of press releases, annual reports, quarterly reports, and documents filed with securities commissions, the role of electronic information services in this process, as well as the guiding principles in communicating useful information.   p. 293**
Earnings are first made public in press releases. Companies follow these announcements with annual and quarterly reports containing statements, notes, and additional information. Public companies must also file additional reports with the securities commissions (e.g., OSC, SEC), which contain more details about the company. Electronic information services are the key source of dissemination of this information to sophisticated users.

3. **Recognize the different financial statement and disclosure formats used by companies in practice.   p. 300**
Most statements are classified and include subtotals that are relevant to analysis. On the balance sheet, the most important distinctions are between current and non-current assets and liabilities. On the income statement and cash flow statement, the separation of operating and non-operating items is most important. The notes to the statements provide descriptions of the accounting rules applied and more information about items disclosed in the statements, as well as information about economic events not disclosed in the statements.

4. **Compute and interpret the return on equity ratio.   p. 307**
ROE measures how well management used the investment by shareholders during the period. Managers, analysts, and creditors use this ratio to assess the effectiveness of the overall business strategy (its operating, investing, and financing strategies).

In Chapter 7, we begin our in-depth discussion of financial statements. We will begin with two of the most liquid assets—cash and accounts receivable—and transactions that involve revenue, adjustments to revenues, and certain selling expenses that relate to recording cash and accounts receivable. Many analysts and the securities regulators believe that accuracy in revenue recognition and the related recognition of cost of goods sold (discussed in the next chapter) are the most important determinants of the accuracy—and, thus, the usefulness—of financial statement presentations. We will also introduce concepts related to the management and control of cash and receivables, which is a critical business function. A detailed understanding of these topics is crucial to future managers, accountants, and financial analysts.

KEY **RATIO**

Return on equity (ROE) measures how much the firm earned for each dollar of shareholders' investment. It is computed as follows (p. 307):

$$\text{Return on Equity} = \frac{\text{Net Income}}{\text{Average Shareholders' Equity}}$$

BALANCE SHEET
Key Classifications
   Current and non-current assets and
      liabilities
   Contributed capital and retained earnings

INCOME STATEMENT
Key Subtotals
   Gross profit
   Income from operations
   Net income
   Earnings per share

CASH FLOW STATEMENT
Under Operating Activities (indirect method)
   Net Income
   ± Items Not Affecting Cash
   = Cash Provided by Operating Activities

NOTES
Key Classifications
   Descriptions of accounting rules applied
      in the statements
   Additional detail supporting reported
      numbers
   Relevant financial information not
      disclosed on the statements

KEY **TERMS**

Accounting Information p. 299
Clean Audit Opinion p. 287
Comparability p. 299
Conservatism p. 299
Consistency p. 299
Cost–Benefit Constraint p. 299
Earnings Forecasts p. 289

Institutional Investors p. 292
Lenders (Creditors) p. 292
Material Amounts p. 299
Press Release p. 293
Private Investors p. 292
Relevance p. 297
Reliability p. 297

QUESTIONS

1. Describe the roles and responsibilities of management and independent auditors in the financial reporting process.
2. Define the following three users of financial accounting disclosures and the relationships among them: *financial analysts, private investors,* and *institutional investors.*
3. Briefly describe the role of information services in the communication of financial information.
4. Explain why information must be relevant and reliable to be useful.
5. What basis of accounting (accrual or cash) does GAAP require on (a) the income statement, (b) the balance sheet, and (c) the cash flow statement?
6. Briefly explain the normal sequence and form of financial reports produced by private companies in a typical year.
7. Briefly explain the normal sequence and form of financial reports produced by public companies in a typical year.
8. List the six major classifications reported on a balance sheet.
9. What are the three major classifications on a cash flow statement?
10. What are the three major categories of notes or footnotes presented in annual reports? Cite an example of each.
11. Briefly define *return on equity* and what it measures.

MULTIPLE-CHOICE QUESTIONS

1. If average total assets increase, but net income, net sales, and average shareholders' equity remain the same, the impact on the return on equity ratio would
   a. increase
   b. decrease
   c. remain the same
   d. Increase or decrease depending on additional information.
2. If a company plans to differentiate its products by offering low prices and discounts for items packaged in bulk (such as a discount retailer that requires memberships for its customers), which ratio is the company attempting to boost?

    a. Net profit margin   c. Return on equity

    b. Asset turnover   d. All of the above

3. Accounting information is relevant if it has the capacity of making a difference to the decision makers who use it. Which of the following qualities should accounting information have in order to be relevant?

    a. Timeliness and feedback value   c. Predictive value and verifiability

    b. Neutrality and timeliness   d. Representational faithfulness and verifiability

4. Which of the following statements is *not* consistent with the concept of materiality?

    a. Financial statements should be accurate to the nearest dollar, but need not show cents.

    b. The concept of materiality is based upon what users of financial statements consider important in making their decisions.

    c. The concept of materiality permits accountants to ignore other generally accepted accounting principles in certain situations.

    d. The concept of materiality permits accountants to use the easiest and most convenient means of accounting for events that are immaterial.

5. Which of the following reports is filed annually with the securities commission?

    a. Quarterly report   c. Annual report

    b. Press release   d. All of the above

6. Which of the following concepts has the least influence in determining the amortization expense reported on the income statement?

    a. Matching   c. Historical cost

    b. Relevance   d. Reliability

7. Which of the following is *not* a normal function of a financial analyst?

    a. Issue earnings forecasts

    b. Examine the records underlying the financial statements to certify their conformance with GAAP

    c. Make buy, hold, and sell recommendations on companies' stock

    d. Advise institutional investors on their securities holdings

8. The classified balance sheet format allows one to identify quickly

    a. the most valuable asset of the company

    b. the specific due date for all liabilities of the company

    c. the amount of liabilities that must be paid within the upcoming year

    d. All of the above.

9. Which of the following statements provides the best definition of earnings per share (EPS)?

    a. EPS equals the increase in cash during the accounting period divided by the average number of shares outstanding during the period.

    b. EPS equals net income divided by the average number of shares outstanding during the accounting period.

    c. EPS equals retained earnings at the end of the accounting period divided by the average number of shares outstanding during the accounting period.

    d. EPS equals net income divided by the average shareholders' equity during the accounting period.

10. What type of audit report does a client hope to include with its annual report?

    a. Conservative   c. Comparable

    b. Qualified   d. Unqualified

For more practice with multiple-choice questions, go to our Web site at **www.mcgrawhill.ca/college/libby**, click on "Student Edition" in the upper left menu, click on this chapter's name and number from the list of contents, and then click on "Multiple-Choice Quiz" from the menu on the left.

EXERCISES

LO1

E6–1 Matching Players in the Accounting Communication Process with Their Definitions

Match each player with the related definition by entering the appropriate letter in the space provided.

Players	Definitions
____ (1) OSC	A. Adviser who analyzes financial and other economic information to form forecasts and stock recommendations.
____ (2) Independent auditor	
____ (3) Institutional investor	

_____ (4) CEO and CFO

_____ (5) Creditor

_____ (6) Financial analyst

_____ (7) Private investor

_____ (8) Information service

B. Financial institution or supplier that lends money to the company.

C. Chief executive officer and chief financial officer who have primary responsibility for the information presented in financial statements.

D. Independent accountant who examines financial statements and attests to their fairness.

E. Ontario Securities Commission, which regulates financial disclosure requirements.

F. A company that gathers, combines, and transmits (paper and electronic) financial and related information from various sources.

G. Individual who purchases shares in companies.

H. Manager of pension, mutual, and endowment fund that invests funds on behalf of others.

E6–2 Finding Financial Information: Matching Information Items to Financial Reports ■ **LO2**

Following are information items included in various financial reports. Match each information item with the report(s) where it would most likely be found by entering the appropriate letter(s) in the space provided.

Information Item	Report
_____ (1) Summarized financial data for 5- or 10-year period.	A. Annual report
_____ (2) Initial announcement of quarterly earnings.	B. Annual information form
_____ (3) Complete quarterly income statement, balance sheet, and cash flow statement.	C. Press release
_____ (4) The four basic financial statements for the year.	D. Quarterly report
_____ (5) Detailed discussion of the company's competition.	E. None of the above
_____ (6) Notes to financial statements.	
_____ (7) Identification of those responsible for the financial statements.	
_____ (8) Initial announcement of hiring of new vice-president for sales.	

E6–3 Understanding the Disclosure Process through the Intrawest Web Site ■ **LO2**

Using your Web browser, contact Intrawest at its Web site (www.intrawest.com). Examine the most recent quarterly earnings press release and the related interim report.

Intrawest

Required:

Based on the information provided on the site, answer the following questions.

1. What were the release dates of the quarterly earnings press release and the interim report?

2. What additional information was provided in the interim report that was not reported in the earnings press release?

E6–4 Information Provided on Company Web Sites ■ **LO2, 3**

Using your Web browser, contact Van Houtte Inc. at its Web site (www.vanhoutte.com).

Van Houtte

Required:

Based on the information provided on the site, answer the following questions.

1. Which document(s) provided the most recent information on quarterly earnings?

2. For the most recent quarter, what was the change in sales revenue compared to the same quarter one year earlier? What was management's explanation for the change (if any)?

3. What was the annual earnings per share, stock price per share, and price–earnings ratio (see Chapter 1) on the day of the most recent fourth-quarter earnings press release?

E6–5 Earnings per Share and Stock Prices ■ **LO1**

The following news story appeared in the _Financial Post_ on September 11, 2001 after Intrawest released its results of operations for fiscal year 2001.

INTRAWEST KEEPS PROFIT GROWTH STREAK ALIVE

B.C.-based resort operator's revenue up 16.5%

VANCOUVER—Intrawest Corp., operator of such major North American mountain resorts as British Columbia's Whistler Blackcomb, yesterday posted a 16.5% rise in profit for the past fiscal year.

Income hit US$60.59 million or US$1.45 a share compared with US$51.99 million (US$1.20) in fiscal 2000, the Vancouver-based company reported. . . . On the Toronto stock market yesterday, Intrawest shares closed at $28.05, down 30¢.

Source: *Financial Post*, September 11, 2001, page C7.

Required:
Intrawest's earnings per share increased from $1.20 to $1.45, but its share price dropped by $0.30. Explain why the price per share decreased even though the company announced an increase in its earnings per share.

■ LO1   **E6–6** **Earnings per Share and Share Prices**
The following news story appeared in the *Globe and Mail* on July 23, 2004 after Microsoft Corporation released its results of operations for fiscal year 2004.

Microsoft fell 97 cents (U.S.) to $28.03 on the Nasdaq stock exchange after it reported earnings Thursday that missed analyst targets by a penny, although sales topped expectations. Profit at the world's largest software maker climbed to $2.69 billion (U.S.) or 25 cents a share from $1.48 billion or 14 cents a share a year earlier. In addition, Microsoft said it expects to earn 30 cents a share in its first quarter, excluding a 5-cent stock compensation charge, on revenue of between $8.9 billion and $9.0 billion. Analysts were forecasting first-quarter earnings of 32 cents a share on revenue of $8.8 billion.

Source: http://www.bellzinc.theglobeandmail.com/servlet/story/RTGAM.20040723.wSTOCKS 0723/business/Business/businessBN/

Required:
Microsoft's earnings per share increased from 14 cents to 25 cents. Yet its share price dropped by 97 cents. Explain why the price per share decreased even though the company announced an increase in its earnings per share.

■ LO2   **E6–7** **Guiding Principles for Communicating Useful Information**
Match each qualitative characteristic of useful accounting information with the related definition by entering the appropriate letter in the space provided.

Qualitative Characteristics	Definitions
_____ (1) Relevance	A. Application of the same accounting methods over time.
_____ (2) Timeliness	
_____ (3) Predictive value	B. Agreement between what really happened and the disclosed information.
_____ (4) Feedback value	
_____ (5) Reliability	C. The information is available prior to the decision.
_____ (6) Verifiability	D. The accounting information does not favour a particular group.
_____ (7) Representational faithfulness	E. The information helps reduce the uncertainty in the future.
_____ (8) Neutrality	F. The information provides input to evaluate previous expectations.
_____ (9) Comparability	G. The information allows the evaluation of one alternative against another alternative.
_____ (10) Consistency	

H. The information has a bearing on a specific decision.

I. The information can be depended upon.

J. Implies that qualified persons working independently arrive at similar conclusions.

E6–8 Assessing the Relevance and Reliability of Information ■ **LO2**

Paula Romanov is the credit manager of Pinnacle Inc. She is considering whether to extend credit to Mak Inc., a new customer. Pinnacle sells most of its goods on credit, but is very careful in extending credit to new customers. Tim Mak, the owner of Mak Inc., provided the following documents to Paula to assist her in her evaluation:

1. A detailed analysis of the sales revenue and net income that Mak Inc. expects to achieve within the next 12 months.

2. Projections of the company's sales during the next five years.

3. The company's monthly bank statements for the past three years.

4. A report of the company's credit history prepared by Mak's employees.

5. A letter signed by all four company officers indicating that they are prepared to personally guarantee the amount of credit that Pinnacle approves.

6. Brief résumés of the four company officers along with descriptions of the functions they perform in the company.

7. Eight letters of reference from close friends and relatives of the four company officers.

Required:

Analyze each of the items above with respect to the characteristics of relevance (predictive value, feedback value, and timeliness) and reliability (verifiability, neutrality, and representational faithfulness). Explain whether or not each item possesses these characteristics.

E6–9 Finding Financial Information: Matching Financial Statements with the Elements of Financial Statements ■ **LO3**

Match each financial statement with the items presented in it by entering the appropriate letter in the space provided.

Elements of Financial Statements	Financial Statements
_____ (1) Liabilities	A. Income statement
_____ (2) Cash from operating activities	B. Balance sheet
_____ (3) Losses	C. Cash flow statement
_____ (4) Assets	D. None of the above
_____ (5) Revenues	
_____ (6) Cash from financing activities	
_____ (7) Gains	
_____ (8) Shareholders' equity	
_____ (9) Expenses	
_____ (10) Assets owned by a shareholder	

E6–10 Ordering the Classifications on a Typical Balance Sheet ■ **LO3**

A list of classifications on the balance sheet is shown below. Number the classifications in the order in which they normally appear on a balance sheet.

No.	Title
_____	Current liabilities
_____	Long-term liabilities
_____	Long-term investments
_____	Intangible assets
_____	Property, plant, and equipment
_____	Current assets
_____	Retained earnings
_____	Share capital
_____	Other non-current assets

■ **LO3**

Shaw
Communications

E6–11 **Preparing and Interpreting a Classified Balance Sheet with Discussion of Terminology (Challenging)**

Shaw Communications Inc. is a diversified Canadian communications company whose core business is providing broad-band cable television, Internet, and satellite services to approximately 2.8 million customers. Shaw also has significant interests in telecommunications, Internet infrastructure, and interactive television companies. The following is a list of items presented in the company's recent balance sheet. The items are listed in alphabetical order and the amounts are in millions of Canadian dollars.

Accounts payable and accrued liabilities	$ 335.0
Accounts receivable, net	89.5
Bank indebtedness	27.0
Current portion of long-term debt	187.3
Deferred charges (long term)	152.9
Deferred credits (long term)	541.6
Deferred income taxes (credit balance)	184.9
Income taxes payable	2.0
Investments and other assets	1,068.4
Long-term debt	1,590.3
Non-controlling interest	17.8
Prepaid expenses and other	9.3
Property, plant, and equipment, net	1,683.4
Retained earnings (including cumulative translation adjustment)	254.5
Share capital	2,136.0
Subscriber base and broadcast licences, net	2,318.4
Unearned revenue	45.5

Required:

1. Prepare a classified consolidated balance sheet for Shaw Communications Inc. as at the end of the current year (August 31), using the categories presented in the chapter.

2. Three of the items end in the term *net*. Explain what this term means in each case.

■ **LO3**

Power Corporation

E6–12 **Inferring Share Issuances and Cash Dividends from Changes in Shareholders' Equity**

Power Corporation recently reported the following December 31 balances in its shareholders' equity accounts (in millions):

	Current Year	Prior Year
Share capital	$ 564	$ 551
Retained earnings	3,392	2,885
Total shareholders' equity	$3,956	$3,436

During the current year, Power Corp. reported net income of $657 million. Assume that the only other transactions that affected shareholders' equity during the current year were the issuance of shares and the declaration and payment of cash dividends.

Required:

Re-create the two journal entries reflecting the issuance of shares and the declaration and payment of dividends.

■ **LO4**

Lands' End

E6–13 **Analyzing and Interpreting Return on Equity**

Lands' End Inc. is a mail-order and Internet-based direct merchant of traditionally styled casual clothing accessories, shoes, soft luggage, and products for the home. Selected income statement and balance sheet amounts (in thousands) for two recent years are presented below.

	Current Year	Prior Year
Net income	$ 31,185	$ 64,150
Average shareholders' equity	349,211	338,092

Required:

Compute the ROE for the current and prior years and explain the meaning of the change.

E6–14 **Analyzing and Evaluating Return on Equity from a Security Analyst's Perspective**   ■ **LO4**
Papa John's is one of the fastest-growing pizza delivery and carry-out restaurant chains.
Selected income statement and balance sheet amounts (in thousands) for two recent years
are presented below.

Papa John's

	Current Year	Prior Year
Net income	$ 26,853	$ 18,614
Average shareholders' equity	232,988	196,352

Required:

1. Compute the ROE for the current and prior years and explain the meaning of the change.

2. Would security analysts more likely increase or decrease their estimates of share value
   on the basis of this change? Explain.

PROBLEMS

P6–1 **Matching Transactions with Concepts**   ■ **LO1, 2**
The concepts of accounting covered in Chapters 2 through 6 are shown below. Match each
transaction with its related concept by entering the appropriate letter in the space provided.
Use only one letter for each blank space.

Concepts	Transactions
_____ (1) Users of financial statements	A. Recorded a $1,000 sale of merchandise on credit.
	B. Counted (inventoried) the unsold items at the end of the period and valued them in dollars.
_____ (2) Objective of financial statements	C. Acquired a vehicle for use in operating the business.
	D. Reported the amount of amortization expense because it likely will affect important decisions of statement users.
Qualitative Characteristics	E. Identified as the investors, creditors, and others interested in the business.
_____ (3) Relevance	F. Used special accounting approaches because of the uniqueness of the industry.
_____ (4) Reliability	
Assumptions	G. Issued bonds payable of $1 million.
_____ (5) Separate entity	H. Paid a contractor for an addition to the building with $10,000 cash and $20,000 market value of the company's shares ($30,000 was deemed to be the cash equivalent price).
_____ (6) Continuity	
_____ (7) Unit of measure	
_____ (8) Periodicity	I. Engaged an outside independent accountant to audit the financial statements.
Elements of Financial Statements	J. Sold merchandise and rendered services for cash and on credit during the year; then determined the cost of those goods sold and the cost of rendering those services.
_____ (9) Revenues	
_____ (10) Expenses	
_____ (11) Gains	K. Established an accounting policy that sales revenue shall be recognized only when ownership of the goods sold passes to the customer.
_____ (12) Losses	
_____ (13) Assets	L. To design and prepare the financial statements to assist the users in making decisions.
_____ (14) Liabilities	
_____ (15) Accounting equation	M. Established a policy not to include in the financial statements the personal financial affairs of the owners of the business.
Principles	N. Sold an asset at a loss that was a peripheral or incidental transaction.
_____ (16) Cost	O. The value to users of a special financial report exceeds the cost of preparing it.
_____ (17) Revenue recognition	P. Valued an asset, such as inventory, at lower than its purchase cost because its market value is lower.
_____ (18) Matching	Q. Dated the income statement "For the Year Ended December 31, 2005."
_____ (19) Full disclosure	R. Used services from outsiders—paid cash for some and the remainder on credit.
Constraints of Accounting	S. Acquired an asset (a pencil sharpener that will have a useful life of five years) and recorded it as an expense when purchased for $1.99.
_____ (20) Materiality threshold	
_____ (21) Cost–benefit constraint	T. Disclosed in the financial statements all relevant financial information about the business; necessitated the use of notes to the financial statements.
_____ (22) Conservatism constraint	U. Sold an asset at a gain that was a peripheral or incidental transaction.
_____ (23) Industry peculiarities	V. Assets of $500,000 − Liabilities of $300,000 = Shareholders' Equity of $200,000.
	W. Accounting and reporting assume a "going concern."

■ LO3

P6–2   Matching Definitions with Balance Sheet–Related Terms

Selected terms related to the balance sheet, which were discussed in Chapters 2 through 5, are listed below. Match each definition with its related term by entering the appropriate letter in the space provided.

Terms

_____ (1) Retained earnings

_____ (2) Current liabilities

_____ (3) Liquidity

_____ (4) Contra-asset account

_____ (5) Accumulated amortization

_____ (6) Intangible assets

_____ (7) Other assets

_____ (8) Shares outstanding

_____ (9) Normal operating cycle

_____ (10) Book value

_____ (11) Contributed surplus

_____ (12) Liabilities

_____ (13) Long-term assets

_____ (14) Shareholders' equity

_____ (15) Current assets

_____ (16) Assets

_____ (17) Long-term liabilities

Definitions

A. A miscellaneous category of assets.

B. Amount of contributed capital for which shares were not issued.

C. Total assets minus total liabilities.

D. Nearness of assets to cash (in time).

E. Assets expected to be collected in cash within one year or the operating cycle, if longer.

F. Same as carrying value; cost less accumulated amortization to date.

G. Accumulated earnings minus accumulated dividends.

H. Asset offset account (subtracted from asset).

I. Balance of the Common Shares account divided by the issue price per share.

J. Assets that do not have physical substance.

K. Probable future economic benefits owned by the entity from past transactions.

L. Liabilities expected to be paid out of current assets, normally within the next year.

M. The average cash-to-cash time involved in the operations of the business.

N. Sum of the annual amortization expense on an asset from the date of its acquisition to the current date.

O. All liabilities not classified as current liabilities.

P. Property, plant, and equipment.

Q. Debts or obligations from past transactions to be paid with assets or services.

R. None of the above.

■ LO3

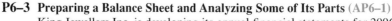

P6–3   Preparing a Balance Sheet and Analyzing Some of Its Parts (AP6–1)

King Jewellers Inc. is developing its annual financial statements for 2006. The following amounts were correct at December 31, 2006: cash, $42,000; accounts receivable, $51,300; merchandise inventory, $110,000; prepaid insurance, $800; investment in shares of Z Corporation (long term), $26,000; store equipment, $48,000; used store equipment held for disposal, $7,000; accumulated amortization, store equipment, $9,600; accounts payable, $42,000; long-term note payable, $30,000; income taxes payable, $7,000; retained earnings, $86,500; and common shares, 100,000 shares outstanding (originally issued at $1.10 per share).

Required:

1. Based on these data, prepare the company's balance sheet at December 31, 2006. Use the following major captions (list the individual items under these captions):

   a. Assets: Current Assets; Long-Term Investments; Property, Plant and Equipment; and Other Assets.

   b. Liabilities: Current Liabilities and Long-Term Liabilities.

   c. Shareholders' Equity: Share Capital and Retained Earnings.

2. What is the net book value of the

   a. Inventory?

   b. Accounts receivable?

   c. Store equipment?

   d. Note payable (long term)?

Explain what these values mean.

P6–4 **Preparing Both an Income Statement and Balance Sheet from a Trial Balance** (AP6–2)

■ **LO3**

Juan Real Estate Company (organized as a corporation on April 1, 2004) has completed the accounting cycle for the second year, ended March 31, 2006. Juan also has completed a correct trial balance as follows:

JUAN REAL ESTATE COMPANY
Trial Balance
At March 31, 2006

Account Titles	Debit	Credit
Cash	$ 53,000	
Accounts receivable	44,800	
Office supplies inventory	300	
Automobiles (company cars)	30,000	
Accumulated amortization, automobiles		$ 10,000
Office equipment	3,000	
Accumulated amortization, office equipment		1,000
Accounts payable		20,250
Salaries and commissions payable		1,500
Note payable, long term		30,000
Share capital (30,000 shares)		30,000
Contributed surplus		5,000
Retained earnings (on April 1, 2005)		7,350
Dividends declared	8,000	
Sales commissions earned		77,000
Management fees earned		13,000
Operating expenses (detail omitted to conserve your time)	48,000	
Amortization expense (including $500 on office equipment)	5,500	
Interest expense	2,500	
Totals	$195,100	$195,100

Required:

1. Prepare an income statement for the reporting year ended March 31, 2006. Include income tax expense, assuming a 30-percent tax rate. Use the following major captions: Revenues, Expenses, Income before Income Taxes, Income Tax, Net Income, and Earnings per Share (list each item under these captions as appropriate).

2. Prepare the journal entry to record income taxes for the year (not yet paid).

3. Prepare a balance sheet at the end of the reporting year, March 31, 2006. Use the following captions (list each item under these captions as appropriate).

Assets

Current Assets

Non-Current Assets

Liabilities

Current Liabilities

Long-Term Liabilities

Shareholders' Equity

Share Capital

Retained Earnings

P6–5 **Determining and Interpreting the Effects of Transactions on Income Statement Categories and Return on Equity** (AP6–3)

■ **LO3, 4**

Apple Computer

Apple Computer popularized both the personal computer and the easy-to-use graphic interface. Today it competes against many companies that rely on Intel microprocessors and the Windows operating system. Presented here is an income statement (in millions).

Net sales	$5,941
Costs and expenses	
Cost of sales	4,462
Research and development	310
Selling, general, and administrative	908
Operating income	261
Interest and other income, net	68
Income before provision for income taxes	329
Provision for income taxes	20
Net income	$ 309

Required:

1. Assume that the following hypothetical *additional* transactions occurred during the fiscal year. Complete the following tabulation, indicating the sign of the effect of each *additional* transaction (+ for increase, − for decrease, and NE for no effect). Consider each item independently and ignore income taxes.
   a. Recorded sales on account of $500 and related cost of goods sold of $475.
   b. Incurred additional research and development expense of $100, which was paid in cash.
   c. Issued additional common shares for $200 cash.
   d. Declared and paid dividends of $90.

Transaction	Gross Profit	Operating Income (Loss)	Return on Equity
a.			
b.			
c.			
d.			

2. Assume that during the next period, Apple does not pay any dividends, does not issue or retire common shares, and earns the same income as during the current period. Will Apple's ROE next period be higher, lower, or the same as the current period? Why?

ALTERNATE PROBLEMS

■ **LO3** **AP6–1 Preparing a Balance Sheet and Analyzing Some of Its Parts** (P6–3)

Carpet Bazaar is developing its annual financial statements for 2006. The following amounts were correct at December 31, 2006: cash, $35,000; investment in shares of ABC Corporation (long term), $32,000; store equipment, $51,000; accounts receivable, $47,500; carpet inventory, $118,000; prepaid insurance, $1,300; used store equipment held for disposal, $3,500; accumulated amortization, store equipment, $10,200; income taxes payable, $6,000; long-term note payable, $26,000; accounts payable, $45,000; retained earnings, $76,100; and common shares, (100,000 shares outstanding, originally sold and issued at $1.25 per share).

Required:

1. Based on these data, prepare the company's balance sheet at December 31, 2006. Use the following major captions (list the individual items under these captions):
   a. Assets: Current Assets; Long-Term Investments; Property, Plant, and Equipment; and Other Assets.
   b. Liabilities: Current Liabilities and Long-Term Liabilities.
   c. Shareholders' Equity: Share Capital and Retained Earnings.

2. What is the net book value of the
   a. Inventory?
   b. Accounts receivable?
   c. Store equipment?
   d. Note payable (long term)?

Explain what these values mean.

AP6–2 **Preparing Both an Income Statement and Balance Sheet from a Trial Balance** (P6–4) ■ **LO3**
ACME Pest Control Services (organized as a corporation on September 1, 2004) has
completed the accounting cycle for the second year, ended August 31, 2006. ACME Pest
Control also has completed a correct trial balance as follows:

ACME PEST CONTROL SERVICES
Trial Balance
At August 31, 2006

Account Titles	Debit	Credit
Cash	$ 26,000	
Accounts receivable	30,800	
Supplies inventory	1,300	
Service vehicles (company vans)	60,000	
Accumulated amortization, automobiles		$ 20,000
Equipment	14,000	
Accumulated amortization, equipment		4,000
Accounts payable		16,700
Salaries payable		1,100
Note payable, long term		34,000
Share capital (10,000 shares)		10,000
Contributed surplus		30,000
Retained earnings (on September 1, 2005)		4,300
Dividends declared	2,000	
Sales revenue		38,000
Maintenance contract revenue		17,000
Operating expenses (detail omitted to conserve your time)	27,000	
Amortization expense (including $2,000 on equipment)	12,000	
Interest expense	2,000	
Totals	$175,100	$175,100

Required:

1. Prepare an income statement for the reporting year ended August 31, 2006. Include
    income tax expense, assuming a 30-percent tax rate. Use the following major captions:
    Revenues, Expenses, Income before Income Tax, Income Tax, Net Income, and Earnings
    per Share (list each item under these captions as appropriate).

2. Prepare the journal entry to record income taxes for the year (not yet paid).

3. Prepare a balance sheet at the end of the reporting year, August 31, 2006. Use the
    following captions (list each item under these captions as appropriate).

Assets
Current Assets
Non-Current Assets

Liabilities
Current Liabilities
Long-Term Liabilities

Shareholders' Equity
Share Capital
Retained Earnings

AP6–3 **Determining and Interpreting the Effects of Transactions on Income Statement** ■ **LO3, 4**
Categories and Return on Equity (P6–5)
Barnes & Noble, Inc., revolutionized bookselling by making its stores public spaces and
community institutions where customers may browse, find a book, relax over a cup of coffee,
talk with authors, and join discussion groups. Today it is fighting increasing competition not
only from traditional sources but also from online booksellers. Presented here is a recent
income statement (in millions).

Barnes & Noble

Net sales	$2,448
Costs and expenses	
Cost of sales	1,785
Selling, general, and administrative	466
Depreciation and amortization	60
Preopening expenses	18
Operating income	119
Interest and other income (expenses), net	(38)
Income before provision (benefit) for income taxes	81
Provision for income taxes	30
Net income	$ 51

Its beginning and ending shareholders' equity amounts were $400 and $446, respectively.

Required:

1. Assume that the following hypothetical *additional* transactions occurred during the fiscal year. Complete the following tabulation, indicating the sign of the effect of each *additional* transaction (+ for increase, − for decrease, and NE for no effect). Consider each item independently and ignore income taxes.
   a. Recorded and received additional interest income of $4.
   b. Purchased $25 of additional inventory on open account.
   c. Recorded and paid additional advertising expense of $9.
   d. Issued additional common shares for $50 cash.

Transaction	Operating Income	Net Income	Return on Equity
a.			
b.			
c.			
d.			

2. Assume that during the next period, Barnes & Noble does not pay any dividends, does not issue or retire common shares, and earns 20 percent more than during the current period. Will Barnes & Noble's ROE next period be higher, lower, or the same as in the current period? Why?

CASES AND PROJECTS

FINDING AND INTERPRETING FINANCIAL INFORMATION

■ LO2, 3   **CP6–1** **Finding Financial Information**

Van Houtte

Refer to the financial statements of Van Houtte Inc., given in Appendix B at the end of this book. At the bottom of each statement, the company warns readers to "See accompanying notes to consolidated financial statements." The following questions illustrate the types of information that you can find in the financial statements and accompanying notes.

Required:

1. The company spent $23,116,000 on capital expenditures (fixed assets) this year. Were operating activities or financing activities the major source of cash for these expenditures?

2. What was the company's largest asset (net) at the end of the year?

3. What was the amount of interest expense for the most recent year?

CP6–2 Finding Financial Information

Refer to the Online Learning Centre at **www.mcgrawhill.ca/college/libby/student/resources** for the financial statements of The Forzani Group Ltd. (FGL). The following questions illustrate the types of information that you can find in the financial statements and accompanying notes. (*Hint:* Use the notes.)

■ LO2, 3

The Forzani Group

Required:

1. What was the highest stock price for the company during the current year?

2. How much land did the company own at the end of the current year?

3. What was the amortization expense for the current year?

4. What amount of goodwill did the company report at the end of the current year?

CP6–3 Comparing Companies

Refer to the Online Learning Centre at **www.mcgrawhill.ca/college/libby/student/resources** for the financial statements of The Forzani Group Ltd. and to Appendix B for the financial statements of Van Houtte Inc.

■ LO4

Van Houtte vs. The Forzani Group

Required:

1. Compute the return on equity for the current year. Which company provided the higher return to shareholders during the current year?

2. How might the ownership versus the rental of property, plant, and equipment affect the return on equity?

FINANCIAL REPORTING AND ANALYSIS CASES

CP6–4 Interpreting the Financial Press

The Committee of Sponsoring Organizations (COSO) published a research study that examined financial statement fraud occurrences between 1987 and 1997. A summary of the findings by M. S. Beasley, J. V. Carcello, and D. R. Hermanson, "Fraudulent Financial Reporting: 1987–1997: An Analysis of U.S. Public Companies," *The Auditor's Report*, Summer 1999, pp. 15–17, is available on the Online Learning Centre at **www.mcgrawhill.ca/college/libby/students/resources.*** Read the article and then write a short memo outlining the following:

■ LO4

The Auditor's Report

1. The size of the companies involved.

2. The extent of top management involvement.

3. The specific accounting fraud techniques involved.

4. What might lead managers to introduce misstatements into the income statement near the end of the accounting period.

*Reprinted with permission from *The Auditor's Report*, copyright © 1999 by American Institute of Certified Public Accountants, Inc.

CP6–5 Using Financial Reports: Financial Statement Inferences

The following amounts were selected from the annual financial statements for Genesis Corporation at December 31, 2006 (end of the third year of operations):

■ LO2, 3

From the 2006 income statement:	
Sales revenue	$275,000
Cost of goods sold	(170,000)
All other expenses (including income tax)	(95,000)
Net income	10,000
From the December 31, 2006, balance sheet:	
Current assets	$ 90,000
All other assets	212,000
Total assets	302,000
Current liabilities	40,000
Long-term liabilities	66,000

Common shares*	100,000
Contributed surplus	16,000
Retained earnings	80,000
Total liabilities and shareholders' equity	$302,000

*10,000 shares issued and outstanding throughout the year.

Required:

Analyze the data on the 2006 financial statements of Genesis by answering the questions that follow. Show computations.

1. What was the gross margin on sales?
2. What was the amount of earnings per share?
3. If the income tax rate was 25 percent, what was the amount of pretax income?
4. What was the average issuance price per common share?
5. Assuming that no dividends were declared or paid during 2006, what was the beginning balance (January 1, 2006) of retained earnings?

■ **LO3, 4**   **CP6–6**   **Using Financial Reports: Interpreting Financial Statement Information, Analyzing**

WestJet Airlines
                  and Interpreting Ratios

WestJet Airlines Ltd. was founded in 1996 by four Calgary entrepreneurs, and has grown from serving Western Canadian destinations to being Canada's largest coast-to-coast low-fare airline.

WestJet's financial statements for 2002 and 2003 and excerpts from selected notes to its financial statements are shown below.

WestJet Airlines Ltd.
Consolidated Balance Sheets
Years ended December 31, 2003 and 2002
(stated in thousands of dollars)

	2003	2002
Assets		
Current assets:		
Cash and cash equivalents	$ 241,384	$ 100,410
Accounts receivable	11,781	20,532
Prepaid expenses and deposits	19,928	19,759
Inventory	3,764	2,314
	276,857	143,015
Property and equipment (note 2)	1,140,226	605,124
Other long-term assets (note 3)	59,775	36,066
	$ 1,476,858	$ 784,205
Liabilities and Shareholders' Equity		
Current liabilities:		
Accounts payable and accrued liabilities	$ 82,822	$ 67,008
Income taxes payable	9,820	7,982
Advance ticket sales	58,086	44,195
Non-refundable guest credits	21,718	15,915
Current portion of long-term debt (note 4)	59,334	32,674
Current portion of obligations under capital lease (note 5)	6,297	7,290
	238,077	175,064
Long-term debt (note 4)	589,531	198,996
Obligations under capital lease (note 5)	7,015	16,352
Future income tax (note 7)	61,423	38,037
	896,046	428,449
Shareholders' equity:		
Share capital (note 6)	376,081	211,564
Retained earnings	204,731	144,192
	580,812	355,756
Commitments and contingencies (notes 5 and 8)		
	$ 1,476,858	$ 784,205

WestJet Airlines Ltd.
Consolidated Statements of Earnings and Retained Earnings
Years ended December 31, 2003 and 2002
(stated in thousands of dollars, except per share data)

	2003	2002
Revenues:		
Guest revenues	$ 794,450	$ 643,174
Charter and other	65,146	36,822
	859,596	679,996
Expenses:		
Aircraft fuel	155,756	111,737
Airport operations	116,135	88,586
Flight operations and navigational charges	104,955	75,759
Maintenance	75,718	81,973
Amortization	63,208	52,637
Sales and marketing	57,871	44,707
General and administration	46,105	39,791
Aircraft leasing	44,179	35,822
Inflight	38,077	27,284
Reservations	22,213	20,106
Employee profit share (note 8(b))	15,855	15,233
	740,072	593,635
Earnings from operations	119,524	86,361
Non-operating income (expense):		
Interest income	4,003	3,078
Interest expense	(24,915)	(7,038)
Gain (loss) on foreign exchange	(1,848)	346
Gain on disposal of property and equipment	631	97
	(22,129)	(3,517)
Earnings before income taxes	97,395	82,844
Income taxes (note 7):		
Current	11,264	12,626
Future	25,592	18,438
	36,856	31,064
Net earnings	60,539	51,780
Retained earnings, beginning of year	144,192	92,412
Retained earnings, end of year	$ 204,731	$ 144,192
Earnings per share (note 6(d)):		
Basic	$ 0.79	$ 0.70
Diluted	$ 0.77	$ 0.69

See accompanying notes to consolidated financial statements.

WestJet Airlines Ltd.
Consolidated Statements of Cash Flows
Years ended December 31, 2003 and 2002
(stated in thousands of dollars)

	2003	2002
Cash provided by (used in):		
Operations:		
Net earnings	$ 60,539	$ 51,780
Items not involving cash:		
Amortization	63,208	52,637
Gain on disposal of property and equipment	(631)	(97)
Issued from treasury stock	3,063	—
Future income tax	25,592	18,438
	151,771	122,758
Decrease in non-cash working capital	40,646	38,866
	192,417	161,624
Financing:		
Increase in long-term debt	466,353	190,366
Repayment of long-term debt	(49,158)	(8,471)
Issuance of common shares	165,545	84,634
Share issuance costs	(6,297)	(3,672)
Increase in other long-term assets	(25,101)	(32,257)
Decrease in obligations under capital lease	(6,498)	(6,088)
	544,844	224,512
Investments:		
Aircraft additions	(564,130)	(320,871)
Other property and equipment additions	(34,249)	(24,031)
Other property and equipment disposals	2,092	234
	(596,287)	(344,668)
Increase in cash	140,974	41,468
Cash, beginning of year	100,410	58,942
Cash, end of year	$ 241,384	$ 100,410

Cash is defined as cash and cash equivalents.
See accompanying notes to consolidated financial statements.

NOTES TO CONSOLIDATED FINANCIAL STATEMENTS

1. Significant accounting policies:

. . .

(c) Revenue recognition:
Guest revenue is recognized when air transportation is provided. Tickets sold but not yet used are included in the balance sheet as advance ticket sales under current liabilities.

(g) Deferred costs:
Sales and marketing and reservation expenses attributed to advance ticket sales are deferred and expensed in the period the related revenue is recognized. Included in pre-paid expenses are $5,334,000 (2002—$4,161,000) of deferred costs.

(i) Maintenance costs:
Costs related to the acquisition of an aircraft and preparation for service are capitalized and included in aircraft costs. Heavy maintenance ("D" check) costs incurred on aircraft are capitalized and amortized over the remaining useful service life of the "D" check. All other maintenance costs are expensed as incurred.

Required:

1. Examine WestJet's balance sheets. The company's assets increased significantly in 2003. Which asset shows the largest increase? How did the company finance the increase in this asset?

2. Compute and interpret the debt-to-equity ratios for 2002 and 2003.

3. WestJet's current liabilities include the account *Advanced ticket sales* with a balance of $58,086. What does this account represent, and what type of transactions would cause an increase or a decrease in the account balance? Explain.

4. Note 1 (g) refers to deferred costs. What is the nature of this item and why is it shown on the balance sheet? What would cause the amount of deferred costs to change over time? Explain.

5. WestJet increased its investment in aircraft during 2003, but its maintenance expense decreased from $81,973 in 2002 to $75,718 in 2003. How does the company account for its maintenance costs, and why has the amount of maintenance expense decreased in 2003? Does the company provide any information on this issue in the Management Discussion and Analysis section of the annual report? (www.westjet.com/pdffile/WestJet2003AR.pdf)

6. Compute the total asset turnover ratio, return on assets, return on equity, and net profit margin for both years 2002 and 2003. Comment on the profitability of WestJet's operations in both years. WestJet's total assets and shareholders' equity at December 31, 2001 amounted to $393,903 and $222,170, respectively.

7. WestJet's operations generated significant amounts of cash during both the years 2002 and 2003. The company also made significant investments in new aircraft in 2003. How did the company finance the acquisition of additional aircraft?

8. Compute and interpret the quality of income ratio and the capital acquisitions ratio for both 2002 and 2003.

9. Access www.investor.reuters.com, search for WestJet Airlines Ltd. (WJA.TO) under Stock Information, and look up "Estimates" under "Analysis." (You will be asked to sign in to access the information—access is free.) What is the average analysts' estimate of WestJet's earnings per share (EPS) for the next two fiscal years? Do analysts expect WestJet's EPS to increase or decrease in the future? What information did the analysts take into consideration in computing their EPS estimates for the next two years?

CP6–7 Using Financial Reports: Interpreting Financial Statement Information, Analyzing and Interpreting Ratios

■ **LO3, 4**

RONA Inc.

RONA Inc. (www.rona.ca), founded in 1939, is Canada's leading distributor and retailer of hardware, home improvement, and gardening products. It has a network that exceeds 500 stores across Canada. Its sales grew from $478 million in 1993 to $2,710 million in 2003. Its financial statements for 2002 and 2003 are shown below.

RONA Inc.
Consolidated Balance Sheets
December 28, 2003 and December 29, 2002
(in thousands of dollars)

	2003	2002
Assets		
Current assets		
Cash	$	$ 475
Accounts receivable (note 7)	139,070	131,910
Inventory	528,680	347,276
Prepaid expenses	7,787	7,246
Future income taxes (note 4)	8,942	6,260
	684,479	493,167
Investments (note 8)	25,124	34,359
Fixed assets (note 10)	360,036	201,176
Goodwill	160,449	19,469
Other assets (note 11)	13,636	7,967
Future income taxes (note 4)	18,298	10,296
	$1,262,022	$ 766,434

(continued)

RONA Inc.
Consolidated Balance Sheets
December 28, 2003 and December 29, 2002 *(continued)*

	2003	2002
Liabilities		
Current liabilities		
Outstanding cheques	$ 3,031	$
Bank loans (note 12)	19,945	13,568
Accounts payable and accrued liabilities	327,914	234,194
Income taxes payable	18,451	196
Future income taxes (note 4)	426	4,395
Instalments on long-term debt (note 13)	102,997	20,803
	472,764	273,156
Long-term debt (note 13)	163,925	99,337
Deferred revenue	2,154	
Future income taxes (note 4)	8,259	8,239
Non-controlling interest	4,637	
	651,739	380,732
Shareholders' equity		
Capital stock (note 14)	403,382	250,667
Retained earnings	205,448	133,843
Contributed surplus	1,453	1,192
	610,283	385,702
	$1,262,022	$ 766,434

The accompanying notes are an integral part of the consolidated financial statements.

RONA Inc.
Consolidated Earnings
Years ended December 28, 2003 and December 29, 2002
(in thousands of dollars, except earnings per share)

	2003	2002
Net sales	$2,710,268	$2,332,119
Earnings before the following items	175,063	128,784
Interest on long-term debt	14,244	23,982
Interest on bank loans	3,249	3,118
Depreciation and amortization (notes 10 and 11)	35,530	32,034
	53,023	59,134
Earnings before income taxes	122,040	69,650
Income taxes (note 4)	44,093	26,536
Net earnings	$ 77,947	$ 43,114
Earnings per share (note 21)	$ 1.47	$ 1.12
Diluted earnings per share (note 21)	$ 1.44	$ 1.08

The accompanying notes are an integral part of the consolidated financial statements.

RONA Inc.
Consolidated Cash Flows
Years ended December 28, 2003 and December 29, 2002
(in thousands of dollars)

	2003	2002
Operating activities		
Net earnings	$ 77,947	$ 43,114
Non-cash items		
Capitalized interest on debentures		6,101
Depreciation and amortization	35,530	32,034
Future income taxes	(4,442)	1,701
Other items	15	(88)
	109,050	82,862
Changes in working capital items (note 5)	5,085	395
Cash flows from operating activities	114,135	83,257
Investing activities		
Business acquisitions (note 6)	(331,850)	
Advances to joint ventures and other advances	2,419	1,212
Other investments	(2,780)	(2,527)
Fixed assets	(72,341)	(35,308)
Other assets	(12,003)	(2,665)
Disposal of assets	15,643	9,198
Cash flows from investing activities	(400,912)	(30,090)
Financing activities		
Bank loans and revolving credit	50,064	(118,620)
Other long-term debt	117,203	595
Repayment of other long-term debt and redemption of preferred shares	(29,433)	(72,529)
Issue of common shares	152,715	149,259
Purchase of common shares		(785)
Expenses relating to the issue of common shares	(7,278)	(9,510)
Cash flows from financing activities	283,271	(51,590)
Net increase (decrease) in cash	(3,506)	1,577
Cash (outstanding cheques), beginning of year	475	(1,102)
Cash (outstanding cheques), end of year	$ (3,031)	$ 475

The accompanying notes are an integral part of the consolidated financial statements.

Required:

1. Examine RONA's balance sheets. Why did the company's assets increase significantly in 2003? Which sections of the annual reports would include information that helps the reader answer this question? Which assets show the largest increases, and how did the company finance the increase in these assets?

2. Compute and interpret the debt-to-equity ratios for 2002 and 2003.

3. RONA's current liabilities include the account *Outstanding cheques* with a balance of $3,031. What does this account represent, and what type of transactions would cause an increase or a decrease in the account balance? Explain.

4. RONA's income statement does not include information related to cost of goods sold and general, selling, and administrative expenses. Why did the company exclude such details from its income statement? Explain.

5. Compute the total asset turnover ratio, return on assets, return on equity, and net profit margin for both years 2002 and 2003. Comment on the profitability of RONA's operations in both years. RONA's total assets and shareholders' equity at December 31, 2001 amounted to $744,076 and $211,820, respectively.

6. RONA's operations generated significant amounts of cash during both the years 2002 and 2003. The company also made significant investments in 2003. How did the company finance these investments?

7. Compute and interpret the quality of income ratio for both 2002 and 2003.

8. Access www.investor.reuters.com, search for RONA Inc. (RON.TO) under Stock Information, and look up "Estimates" under "Analysis." (You may be asked to sign in to access the information—access is free.) What is the average analysts' estimate of RONA's Earnings per share (EPS) for the next two years? Do analysts expect RONA's EPS to increase or decrease in the future? What information did the analysts take into consideration in computing their EPS estimates for the next two years?

■ LO3, 4   **CP6–8**

Danier Leather

Using Financial Reports: Interpreting Financial Statement Information, Analyzing and Interpreting Ratios

Danier Leather Inc. (DL) is one of the largest publicly traded specialty leather apparel retailers in the world. It designs, manufactures, and sells high-quality, fashionable leather clothing and accessories to customers. Its products are sold in stores at shopping malls, through its corporate sales division, and online through its Web site, www.danier.com. Since entering the retail business in 1974, the company has produced a strong, long-term track record of growth and profits from continuing operations. DL's financial statements for 2003 and 2004 and Note 9 to its 2004 financial statements are shown below.

Danier Leather, Inc.
Consolidated Balance Sheets
(thousands of dollars)

	June 26, 2004	June 28, 2003
Assets		
Current Assets		
Cash	$ 23,000	$ 7,254
Accounts receivable	634	600
Income taxes recoverable	—	83
Inventories (note 2)	29,915	37,029
Prepaid expenses	923	889
Future income tax asset (note 8)	107	368
	54,579	46,223
Other Assets		
Capital assets (note 3)	30,212	34,246
Goodwill (note 4)	342	342
Future income taxes asset	4,736	676
	$ 89,869	$ 81,487
Liabilities		
Current Liabilities		
Accounts payable and accrued liabilities	$ 9,425	$ 9,350
Income taxes payable	952	—
	10,377	9,350
Accrued litigation provision and related expenses (note 9)	15,450	1,209
Deferred lease inducements	2,283	2,238
Future income tax liability (note 8)	472	696
	28,582	13,493
Shareholders' Equity		
Share capital (note 6)	24,166	23,995
Contributed surplus (note 6)	219	—
Retained earnings	36,902	43,999
	61,287	67,994
	$ 89,869	$ 81,487

Danier Leather, Inc.
Consolidated Statements of Earnings (Loss)
(thousands of dollars, except per share amounts)

	For the Years Ended	
	June 26, 2004	June 28, 2003
Revenue	$ 178,115	$ 175,487
Cost of sales (note 7)	90,060	88,788
Gross profit	88,055	86,699
Selling, general and administrative expenses (note 7)	80,526	74,617
Interest (income) expense—net	(18)	66
Earnings before undernoted item and income taxes	7,547	12,016
Litigation provision and related expenses (note 9)	15,450	2,773
Earnings (loss) before income taxes	(7,903)	9,243
Provision for income taxes (note 8)		
Current	3,217	4,353
Future	(4,023)	(504)
	(806)	3,849
Net earnings (loss)	$ (7,097)	$ 5,394
Net earnings (loss) per share (note 6(c))		
Basic	($1.03)	$0.78
Diluted	n/a	$0.76

NOTE 9: LITIGATION PROVISION AND RELATED EXPENSES

	June 26, 2004	June 28, 2003
Provision for damages, costs and interest	$ 15,000	$ —
Legal and professional fees	$ 450	$ 1,209
Accrued litigation provision and related expenses	$ 15,450	$ 1,209

In fiscal 1999, the Company and certain of its directors and officers were served with a Statement of Claim under the Class Proceedings Act (Ontario) concerning the accuracy and disclosure of certain information contained in a financial forecast issued by the Company during its initial public offering ("IPO") in 1998. The suit sought damages be paid equal to the alleged diminution in value of the shares.

In October 2001, a motion to certify the action as a class action was granted. The trial commenced in the Superior Court of Justice (Ontario) during May 2003 and was completed in January 2004. On May 7, 2004 the Judge issued a judgment in favour of the Plaintiffs and awarded damages to Canadian shareholders who purchased subordinate voting shares in the IPO. The Judge concluded that at the time of pricing of the IPO, which was two weeks before the closing, the forecast was reasonable and that the Company's CEO and CFO had an honest belief at the time the IPO closed that the forecast could be achieved. The Judge further held that the forecast was, in fact, substantially achieved. Despite these findings, the Court decided that management's judgment that the forecast was still achievable at the time of closing was not reasonable. The Company is contesting this decision and has filed a Notice of Appeal as discussed below.

For those shareholders who sold their shares between June 4 and 9, 1998, the Court awarded them the difference between the IPO price and the price at which they sold their shares. For those shareholders who sold or still hold those shares after June 9, 1998, the Court awarded $2.35 per share.

Based solely on the information available at year-end, if the award had been paid at year-end the Company estimates the damages to be about $10 million. Interest and costs have not been dealt with by the Court but if awarded, the Company estimates the total aware could increase by approximately $5 million. During the fourth quarter of 2004, the Company recorded an expense and set up a provision of $15 million pursuant to this judgment. The judgment is a joint and several responsibility of the Company and two of its Senior Officers. The Company carries directors and officers insurance and it expects that the insurance will cover the two Senior Officers' portion of the total award but the amount of insurance is not reasonably determinable at this time and its recovery has therefore not been accrued. The provision for recovery of income taxes related to the award is based on the entire $15 million provision and does not take account of the potential results of the appeal discussed in the next paragraph, any possible insurance recoveries or future tax adjustments. The damages award and income tax recovery is based on management's best estimate and is subject to adjustment when all facts are known and all issues are resolved. The possible adjustment could be significant.

In June 2004, a Notice of Appeal was filed by the Company and two of its Senior Officers. Payment of any damages will be deferred as the award and the judgment are stayed by the filing of the appeal.

During fiscal 2003, the Company expensed legal and professional fees of approximately $2.8 million of which approximately $1.6 million related to legal and professional fees actually incurred during fiscal 2003 and approximately $1.2 million was set up as a provision for future legal and professional fees. As at June 26, 2004, $0.5 million was set up as a provision for future legal fees in connection with the appeal.

Required:

1. Examine Danier Leather's balance sheets. Identify the four largest changes in the book value of assets, liabilities, and shareholders' equity between the balance sheet dates. What type of transactions could have caused the changes in the book value of these items?

2. The company's liabilities include the account *Accrued litigation provision and related expenses* with a balance of $15,450. Note 9 to the 2004 financial statements provides a brief description of the events that led to the recognition of this liability. Review the content of the note and explain the nature of these events. Why did the company disclose such details?

3. Using information from the company's balance sheets and income statement for 2004, can you determine the amount of cash flow generated from operations? If not, where can one find such information?

4. Compute the following ratios for fiscal years 2003 and 2004: debt-to-equity, total asset turnover, return on assets, return on equity, and net profit margin. Use the results of your computations to comment on the company's financial situation and profitability of its operations in both years. DL's total assets and shareholders' equity at June 29, 2002 amounted to $75,695 and $62,522, respectively.

5. Suppose that you are evaluating DL's financial statements for a potential investment in the company's shares. To what extent is the information contained in these financial statements relevant for your decision? What additional information would you require before making your decision?

■ LO3

Diageo

CP6–9 **Using Financial Reports: Interpreting International Financial Statement Classifications (Challenging)**

As the economy becomes more international in scope, users of financial statements may be expected to analyze companies that are not incorporated in Canada. Diageo is a major world corporation located in London, England. It is a worldwide consumer goods company that owns a number of well-known businesses such as Guinness and the Pillsbury Company.

Required:

Based on the concepts presented in this book, explain the meaning of the various account classifications shown on the portion of the Diageo annual report presented here. (*Note:* There are three reserve accounts and a minority interests account. These accounts are discussed in advanced accounting courses.)

DIAGEO
Consolidated Balance Sheet
At 30th September, Current Year and Prior Year

	Notes	Current Year £m	Current Year £m	Prior Year £m	Prior Year £m
Fixed assets					
Intangible assets	11		2,652		588
Tangible assets	12		3,839		3,280
Investments	13		144		206
			6,635		4,074
Current assets					
Stocks	14	1,269		761	
Debtors	15	1,451		873	
Cash at bank and in hand		215		138	
		2,935		1,772	
Creditors—due within one year					
Borrowings	17	(362)		(187)	
Other creditors	19	(2,316)		(1,301)	
		(2,678)		(1,488)	
Net current assets	15		257		284
Total assets less current liabilities			6,892		4,358
Creditors—due after more than one year					
Borrowings	17	(3,494)		(702)	
Other creditors	20	(231)		(163)	
			(3,725)		(865)
Provisions for liabilities and charges	21		(325)		(55)
			2,842		3,438
Capital and reserves					
Called-up share capital	22		506		443
Reserves	23				
Share premium account		436		7	
Revaluation reserve		(944)		649	
Special reserve		—		282	
Related companies' reserves		10		16	
Profit and loss account		2,802		2,010	
			2,304		2,964
			2,810		3,407
Minority interests			32		31
			2,842		3,438

LO1, 2

CP6–10 Using Financial Reports: Analyzing Income Statement–Based Executive Bonuses

Callaway Golf

Callaway Golf believes in tying executives' compensation to the company's performance as measured by accounting numbers. In a recent year, Callaway had agreed to pay its five executive officers bonuses of up to 200 percent of base salary if sales growth and pretax earnings as a percentage of sales (computed here) met or exceeded target amounts. Callaway's income statements for the relevant years are presented here.

(in thousands, except per share data)	Year Ended December 31			
	Current Year		Prior Year	
Net sales	$254,645	100%	$132,058	100%
Cost of goods sold	115,458	45%	62,970	48%
Gross profit	139,187	55%	69,088	52%
Selling expenses	38,485	15%	19,810	15%
General and administrative expenses	28,633	11%	14,990	11%
Research and development costs	3,653	1%	1,585	1%
Income from operations	68,416	27%	32,703	25%
Other income				
Interest income, net	1,024		403	
Other income, net	160	—	69	—
Income before income taxes and cumulative effect of accounting change	69,600	27%	33,175	25%
Provision for income taxes	28,396	—	13,895	—
Income before cumulative effect of accounting change	41,204	16%	19,280	15%
Cumulative effect of accounting change	1,658	—		
Net income	$42,862	17%	$19,280	15%

Callaway executives will receive bonuses if *sales growth* and *pretax earnings as a percentage of sales* meet or exceed target amounts (35.1 percent and 21.1 percent, respectively). Meeting these goals in the current year would result in bonuses ranging from $400,000 to $700,000 for each of the five executive officers.

Required:
Use the preceding information to determine whether Callaway executives earned their bonuses in the most recent year presented.

CRITICAL THINKING CASES

LO4

CP6–11 **Making Decisions as a Manager: Evaluating the Effects of Business Strategy on Return on Equity**

Sony

Sony is a world leader in the manufacture of consumer and commercial electronics as well as the entertainment and insurance industries. Its ROE has increased from 9 percent to 14 percent over the last three years.

Required:
Using the table below, indicate the most likely effect of each of the following changes in business strategy on Sony's ROE for the next period and future periods (+ for increase, − for decrease, and NE for no effect), assuming all other things are unchanged. Explain your answer for each. Treat each item independently.

a. Sony decreases its investment in research and development aimed at products to be brought to market in more than one year.

b. Sony begins a new advertising campaign for a movie to be released during the next year.

c. Sony issues additional shares for cash, the proceeds to be used to acquire other high-technology companies in future periods.

Strategy Change	Current Period ROE	Future Periods' ROE
a.		
b.		
c.		

CP6–12 **Making a Decision as an Auditor: Effects of Errors on Income, Assets, and Liabilities**
Megan Company (not a corporation) was careless about its financial records during its first
year of operations, 2005. It is December 31, 2005, the end of the company's fiscal year.
An external auditor examined the records and discovered numerous errors, all of which are
described below. Assume that each error is independent of the others.

■ **LO1**

Megan Company

		Effect On				
	Net Income		**Assets**		**Liabilities**	
Independent Errors	2005	2006	2005	2006	2005	2006
1. Amortization expense for 2005, not recorded in 2005, $950.	O $950	NE	O $950	O $950	NE	NE
2. Wages earned by employees during 2005 not recorded in 2005 but will be paid in 2006, $500.						
3. Revenue earned during 2005 but not collected or recorded until 2006, $600; will be collected in 2006.						
4. Amount paid in 2005 and recorded as expense in 2005, but it is not an expense until 2006, $200.						
5. Revenue collected in 2005 and recorded as revenue in 2005, but it is not earned until 2006, $900.						
6. Sale of services for cash in 2005. Recorded as a debit to Cash and as a credit to Accounts Receivable, $300.						
7. On December 31, 2005, bought land on credit for $8,000, but did not record the transaction until payment was made on February 1, 2006.						

Required:
Analyze each error and indicate its effect on 2005 and 2006 income, assets, and liabilities if
not corrected. Do not assume any other errors. Use these codes to indicate the effect of each
dollar amount: O = overstated, U = understated, and NE = no effect. Write an explanation
of your analysis of each transaction to support your response. (The answer for the first item
is given as an example.)

A sample explanation of analysis of errors that are not corrected is provided below, using
the first error as an example:

1. Failure to record amortization in 2005 caused amortization expense to be too low;
   therefore, income was overstated by $950. Accumulated amortization also is too low by
   $950, which causes assets to be overstated by $950 until the error is corrected.

CP6–13 **Evaluating an Ethical Dilemma: Management Incentives and Fraudulent**
Financial Statements
Mercury Finance Co. was a fast-growing auto-finance and insurance company. In January
1997, however, the auditors discovered that recently announced 1996 earnings had been
grossly overstated and prior years' earnings had been overstated to a lesser extent. The
estimated size of the earnings overstatement for 1996 is described in the following excerpt:

■ **LO3**

Mercury Finance

BUSINESS BRIEF—MERCURY FINANCE CO.

Estimates for 1996 Revised Again, Now to a Big Loss

Mercury Finance Co., which previously warned that it had grossly overstated earlier
years' earnings, said it now expects to report up to a $55 million loss for 1996. In January,
the Lake Forest, Ill., auto-finance company initially reported earnings of $120.7 million
for 1996. Soon afterward, however, Mercury disclosed the accounting "irregularities"
and estimated that last year's earnings probably would be about $56.7 million. Yesterday,

Mercury said in an "update" that 1996 results will include an additional $125 million in loss provisions, as well as a $25 million reserve to cover the planned sale of its Lyndon insurance unit. As a result, the company anticipates a 1996 net loss of between $48 million and $55 million. In New York Stock Exchange composite trading, Mercury closed down 25 cents, or 13%, at $1.75.

The Wall Street Journal,
April 24, 1997, A8.

Required:
Using more recent news reports (*Wall Street Journal Index, Dow Jones Interactive,* and *Bloomberg Business News* are good sources), answer the following questions.

1. What were Mercury's closing stock prices on the day before (January 28, 1997) and the day after (January 30, 1997) the announcement of the misstatement?

2. How might executive compensation plans that tied bonuses to accounting earnings motivate unethical conduct in this case?

FINANCIAL REPORTING AND ANALYSIS TEAM PROJECT

■ **LO2, 3**

CP6–14 **Team Project: Analyzing the Accounting Communication Process**
As a team, select an industry to analyze. *Reuters* provides lists of industries and their make-up at www.investor.reuters.com. Each team member should acquire the annual report for one publicly traded company in the industry, with each member selecting a different company. (Library files, the SEDAR service at www.sedar.com, or the company itself are good sources.)

Required:
On an individual basis, each team member should write a short report answering the following questions about the selected company.

1. What formats are used to present the balance sheet and income statement?

2. Find one note that describes an accounting principle applied in the company's statements, one note that presents additional detail about a reported financial statement number, and one note that reports financial statement information not listed in the statements. What information is provided in each case?

3. Using the company's Web site, the periodicals and newspapers indexes in the library at your school, or an instructor-assigned resource, find one article reporting the company's annual earnings announcement. How does the date of the announcement compare with the date on the annual report? Why is there a difference?

4. Compute return on equity for the current year. Which company provided the highest return to shareholders during the current year?

Discuss any patterns across the companies that you as a team observe. Then, as a team, write a short report comparing and contrasting your companies using these attributes. Provide potential explanations for any differences discovered.

After studying this chapter, you should be able to:

1. Apply the revenue principle to determine the appropriate time for revenue recognition for typical retailers, wholesalers, manufacturers, and service companies. p. 345

2. Analyze the impact of credit card sales, sales discounts, and sales returns on the amounts reported as net sales. p. 346

3. Compute and interpret the gross profit percentage. p. 350

4. Estimate, report, and evaluate the effects of uncollectable accounts receivable (bad debts) on financial statements. p. 352

5. Compute and interpret the accounts receivable turnover ratio and the effects of accounts receivable on cash flows. p. 360

6. Report, control, and safeguard cash. p. 363

Reporting and Interpreting Sales Revenue, Receivables, and Cash

O ver the past several years, casual wear has become increasingly acceptable in the workplace as employers adopt flexible dress codes. Gildan Activewear Inc., which is based in Montreal, Québec, took advantage of this trend and became a significant producer and marketer of high-quality casual wear, including T-shirts, sports shirts, and sweatshirts. Gildan started as a family operation, and grew to become a publicly traded company in both Canada and the United States.

Gildan's sales grew from US$224 million for fiscal year 1999 to US$533.4 million for fiscal 2004*. Such a growth in sales could not happen if the company did not pursue specific business strategies to produce quality products and market them to its customers. The company's focus on low-cost manufacturing of premium-quality casual wear and its marketing philosophy of controlled distribution have been important factors in its success. The company's management recognized that its dedication to being the lowest-cost producer and leading marketer of branded basic casual wear to wholesale channels of distribution required the adoption of a set of objectives and principles such as (1) nurturing and strengthening the Gildan Activewear brand, (2) remaining price-competitive by constantly reinvesting in state-of-the-art facilities, and (3) maintaining strong relationships with the distributors of the company's products. These objectives and related action plans are aimed at increasing net sales and/or decreasing the cost of sales, thereby increasing gross profit.

*Gildan uses the U.S. dollar as a reporting currency because a significant portion of its revenues, expenses, assets, and liabilities are denominated in U.S. dollars.

UNDERSTANDING THE BUSINESS

Planning Gildan's strategy requires careful coordination of marketing, production, and financing activities. The success of each element of Gildan's strategy can be seen in the information presented in the comparative statements of earnings presented in Exhibit 7.1. Following the multiple-step format that we discussed in Chapter 3, Revenues (Sales) are reported first, and Cost of Sales (an expense) is set out separately from the remaining expenses. Similar account titles sometimes used are Cost of Goods Sold and Cost of Products Sold. Next, the income statement shows *gross profit* (*gross margin*), which is net sales revenue minus cost of goods sold. Revenues, gross profit, and net income for 2004 were at an all-time high.

To assess the effectiveness of Gildan's strategy, we need to know how net sales and cost of goods sold are determined. In this chapter, we will focus on the transactions that affect *net sales revenue* on the income statement and *cash* and *accounts receivable* on the balance sheet. We will also introduce the gross profit percentage as a basis for evaluating changes in gross profit, as well as the receivables turnover ratio as a measure of the efficiency of credit-granting and collection activities.

Generating operating cash flow is also one of Gildan's financial goals. The primary source of operating cash for most organizations is the collection of accounts receivable, and a primary use is payment for inventory. As a consequence, careful management of receivables and inventory can be the key to avoiding a business failure driven by cash shortages. Since cash is a tempting target for fraud and embezzlement, we will discuss how accounting systems commonly include controls to prevent and detect these misdeeds.

Lenders, shareholders, and analysts also carefully monitor these accounts because of their importance as predictors of the future success of companies. Their importance is supported by the fact that the majority of shareholder lawsuits and enforcement actions by securities regulators against companies for misleading financial statements relate to these accounts.

EXHIBIT **7.1**

Consolidated Statements of Earnings

REAL WORLD EXCERPT

Gildan Activewear Inc.

ANNUAL REPORT

Consolidated Statements of Earnings
Years ended October 3, 2004, October 5, 2003, and September 29, 2002
(in U.S. dollars)

	2004	2003	2002
Sales	$533,367,537	$431,194,602	$382,312,228
Cost of Sales	378,695,819	301,340,580	274,838,307
Gross Profit	154,671,718	129,854,022	107,473,921
Selling, General and Administrative			
Expenses	62,897,875	48,403,267	40,698,461
Earnings Before the Undernoted Items	91,773,843	81,450,755	66,775,460
Depreciation and Amortization	22,274,524	16,088,028	11,199,462
Interest	6,170,071	6,418,683	8,473,366
	28,444,595	22,506,711	19,672,828
Earnings Before Income Taxes	63,329,248	58,944,044	47,102,632
Income Taxes (Note 11)	3,078,000	5,788,346	4,666,046
Net Earnings	$ 60,251,248	$ 53,155,698	$ 42,436,586
Earnings Per Share (Note 12):			
Basic	$ 2.04	$ 1.82	$ 1.49
Diluted	2.02	1.79	1.45

See accompanying notes to consolidated financial statements

ORGANIZATION OF THE CHAPTER

• Accounting for Sales Revenue	• Measuring and Reporting Receivables	• Reporting and Safeguarding Cash
Sales to Consumers	Classifying Receivables	Cash and Cash Equivalents Defined
Sales Discounts to Businesses	Accounting for Bad Debts	Cash Management
Sales Returns and Allowances	Reporting Accounts Receivable	Internal Control of Cash
Reporting Net Sales	Estimating Bad Debts	Reconciliation of the Cash Accounts and the Bank Statements
Gross Profit Percentage	Receivables Turnover Ratio	
	Internal Control and Management Responsibility	
	Control over Accounts Receivable	

ACCOUNTING FOR SALES REVENUE

As indicated in Chapter 3, the *revenue principle* requires recording revenues when earned (an exchange has taken place, the earnings process is nearly complete, and collection is probable). For sellers of goods, these criteria are most often met when the goods pass from the seller to the buyer; the seller then records sales revenue on that date. This is when title and risks of ownership pass to the buyer.[1] Service companies most often record sales revenue when they have provided services to the buyer. Companies disclose the specific revenue recognition rule they follow in the footnote to their financial statements entitled Summary of Significant Accounting Policies. In that note, Gildan reports the following:

■ **LEARNING OBJECTIVE 1**

Apply the revenue principle to determine the appropriate time for revenue recognition for typical retailers, wholesalers, manufacturers, and service companies.

NOTES TO CONSOLIDATED FINANCIAL STATEMENTS

1. Summary of significant accounting policies

Revenue Recognition

Sales are recognized upon shipment of products to customers, since title passes upon shipment. At the time of sale, estimates are made based upon existing programs for customer price discounts and rebates. Accruals required for new programs which relate to prior sales, are recorded at the time the new program is introduced. Sales are recorded net of these program costs.

REAL WORLD EXCERPT

Gildan Activewear Inc.

ANNUAL REPORT

---

[1] The point at which title (ownership) changes hands is determined by the shipping terms in the sales contract. When goods are shipped *F.O.B. (free on board) shipping point*, title changes hands at shipment, revenue is recognized at that time, and the buyer normally pays for shipping. When they are shipped *F.O.B. destination*, title changes hands on delivery, revenue is recognized at the date of delivery, and the seller normally pays for shipping. Auditors expend a lot of effort ensuring that revenue recognition rules are applied consistently and revenues are recognized in the proper period.

Like Gildan, many manufacturers, wholesalers, and retailers recognize revenue at shipment. The appropriate *amount* of revenue to record is the *cash equivalent* sales price. Both the form of payment (cash, credit card, or credit) and returns and allowances affect the amount recorded as *net sales* on the income statement. If the sale involves the trade-in of a non-cash asset (such as the trade-in of an old car for a new car), the amount of revenue is the cash equivalent of the goods received or given up, whichever is the more clearly determinable.

Companies use different business practices concerning sales to businesses and consumers. For example, Gildan sells its products primarily through wholesale distributors, a strategy that enables the company to use a small sales force and avoid the costs and complexities of selling to the retail channel and to consumers. Gildan sells its products to a network of more than 100 distributors in over 20 countries, who in turn resell the blank products to garment decorators. These companies sell the decorated garments to corporate promotional buyers, retailers, and customers.

Companies use a variety of methods to motivate customers to buy their products and make payment for their purchases. The principal methods include (1) allowing customers to use credit cards to pay for purchases, (2) providing direct credit and discounts for early payment, and (3) allowing returns under certain circumstances. These methods in turn affect the way we compute net sales revenue.

SALES TO CONSUMERS

■ **LEARNING OBJECTIVE 2**

Analyze the impact of credit card sales, sales discounts, and sales returns on the amounts reported as net sales.

Sales to consumers are for cash or credit card (mainly Visa, MasterCard, and American Express). The seller accepts credit cards as payment for a variety of reasons:

1. Increasing customer traffic at its stores.

2. Avoiding the costs of providing credit directly to customers, including record keeping and bad debts (discussed later).

3. Lowering losses due to bad cheques.

4. Avoiding losses from fraudulent credit card sales. (Normally, the credit card company absorbs any losses if the seller follows the credit card company's verification procedure.)

5. Faster receipt of its money. (Since credit card receipts can be directly deposited in its bank account, the seller receives its money faster than it would if it provided credit directly to consumers.)

A **CREDIT CARD DISCOUNT** is the fee charged by the credit card company for services.

The credit card company charges a fee for the service it provides. For example, when a seller deposits its credit card receipts in the bank, it might receive credit for an amount equal to only 97 percent of the sales price. The credit card company is charging a 3-percent fee (the **credit card discount**) for its service. If credit card sales were $3,000 on January 2, the seller reports the following:

Sales revenue	$3,000
Less: Credit card discounts (0.03 × $3,000)	90
Net sales (reported on the income statement)	$2,910

SALES DISCOUNTS TO BUSINESSES

Most of Gildan's sales to businesses are credit sales on open account; that is, there is no formal written promissory note indicating the amount owed to Gildan by the customer. When Gildan sells T-shirts to wholesalers on credit, credit terms are printed on each sales document and invoice (bill) sent to the customer. Often credit terms are abbreviated, using symbols. For example, if the full amount of the invoice is due within 30 days of the invoice date, the credit terms would be noted as *n/30*. Here, the *n* means the sales amount *net* of or less any sales returns.

In other cases, a **sales discount** (often called a **cash discount**) is granted to the purchaser to encourage early payment. For example, let us assume that Gildan offers standard credit terms of 2/10, n/30, which means that the customer may deduct 2 percent from the invoice amount if cash payment is made within 10 days from the date of sale. If cash payment is not made within the 10-day discount period, however, the full invoice amount (less any returns) is due within a maximum of 30 days from date of sale.

A **SALES (OR CASH) DISCOUNT** is a cash discount offered to encourage prompt payment of an account receivable.

Early Payment Incentive

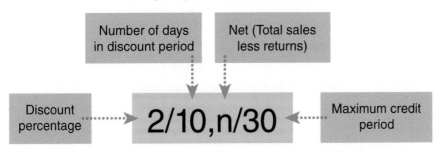

Gildan offers this sales discount to encourage customers to pay more quickly. This provides two benefits to Gildan:

1. Prompt receipt of cash from customers reduces the necessity to borrow money to meet operating needs.
2. Since customers tend to pay bills providing discounts first, a sales discount also decreases the chances that the customer will run out of funds before Gildan's bill is paid.

Companies commonly record sales discounts taken by subtracting the discount from sales if payment is made *within* the discount period (the usual case).[2] For example, if credit sales are recorded with terms 2/10, n/30 ($1,000 × 0.98 = $980) and payment is made within the discount period, net sales of the following amount would be reported:

Sales revenue	$1,000
Less: Sales discounts (0.02 × $1,000)	20
Net sales (reported on the income statement)	$ 980

If the payment is made after the discount period, the full $1,000 would be reported as net sales.

Note that both the purpose of sales discounts and the accounting for sales discounts are very similar to the purpose of and the accounting for credit card discounts. Both sales discounts and credit card discounts provide an attractive service to customers while promoting faster receipt of cash, reducing recordkeeping costs, and minimizing bad debts.[3] Accounting for sales discounts is discussed in more detail in Supplement A.

[2]We use the gross method in all examples in this textbook. Some companies use the alternative net method, which records sales revenue after deducting the amount of the cash discount. Since the choice of method has little effect on the financial statements, discussion of this method is left for an advanced course.

[3]It is important not to confuse a cash discount with a trade discount. Vendors sometimes use a *trade discount* for quoting sales prices; the list or printed catalogue price *less* the trade discount is the sales price. For example, an item may be quoted at $10 per unit subject to a 20-percent trade discount on orders of 100 units or more; thus, the price for the large order is $8 per unit. Similarly, the price on a slow-moving product line can be lowered simply by increasing the trade discount. Sales revenue should always be recorded net of trade discounts.

FINANCIAL **ANALYSIS**

TO TAKE OR NOT TO TAKE THE DISCOUNT, THAT IS THE QUESTION

Usually customers pay within the discount period because the savings are substantial. With terms 2/10, n/30, 2 percent is saved by paying 20 days early (the 10th day instead of the 30th), which is equivalent to an annual interest rate of 37 percent. This annual interest rate is obtained by first computing the interest rate for the discount period. When the 2-percent discount is taken, the customer pays only 98 percent of the gross sales amount. Thus, the interest rate for the 20-day discount period is

(Amount saved ÷ Amount paid) = Interest rate for 20 days

(2% of the bill ÷ 98% of the bill) = 2.04% for 20 days or 0.102% per day

Given that there are 365 days in a year, the annual interest rate is then computed in the following manner:

Annual interest rate = 0.102% × 365 days = 37.23%

Credit customers would save a lot of money even if they had to borrow cash from a bank at 10 percent to take advantage of cash discounts. Normally, the bank's interest rate is less than the high interest rate associated with failing to take cash discounts.

A QUESTION OF **ETHICS**

STRETCHING OUT THE PAYABLES

Hoffa Shoes has been incurring significant interest charges (12 percent) on short-term borrowing from its bank.* Hoffa normally purchases shoes from suppliers on terms 1/10, n/30. The annual rate of interest earned by taking the discount is 18.43 percent computed as follows:

(Amount saved ÷ Amount paid) = Interest rate for 20 days

(1% ÷ 99%) = 1.01% for 20 days or 0.0505 per day

Annual interest rate = 0.0505% × 365 days = 18.43%

Hoffa's policy had been to take all purchase discounts even if it had to borrow at 12 percent to make the early payment. Management reasoned that the company earned 6.43 percent more than it paid in interest (18.43 percent − 12 percent).

A new employee suggested a new plan. Records indicated that, even though the terms of Hoffa's agreement with its suppliers (1/10, n/30) required payment of the full amount within a maximum of 30 days, the suppliers would not complain as long as payment was made within 55 days of the purchase date, since they normally did not send out a second bill until 60 days after the purchase date. She reasoned that Hoffa would be better off forgoing the discount and paying on the 55th day after the purchase date. She argued that since Hoffa would now be paying in 55 days instead of 10 days of the purchase, not taking the discount would be borrowing for 45 days, not the 20 days used in the former analysis. The analysis supporting the proposal is as follows:

(Amount saved ÷ Amount paid) = Interest rate for 45 days

(1% ÷ 99%) = 1.01% for 45 days or 0.02244%

Annual interest rate = 0.02244% × 365 days = 8.19%

*Hoffa Shoes is a fictitious company, but most companies face this dilemma.

In effect, her plan allows Hoffa to borrow from suppliers at 8.19 percent instead of the bank's rate of 12 percent, saving 3.81 percent. When she presented this plan to the management for discussion, the purchasing manager agreed with the arithmetic presented but objected nonetheless. Since the plan violated its agreement with suppliers, the purchasing manager thought it was unethical. Many ethical dilemmas in business involve trade-offs between monetary benefits and potential violations of moral values.

SALES RETURNS AND ALLOWANCES

For Gildan, prompt delivery of exactly what the customer ordered is a key to maintaining good relations with the customers to whom it sells. Delivery of incorrect or damaged merchandise may cost the customer sales and can destroy these relationships. When this occurs, the customers have a right to return unsatisfactory or damaged merchandise and receive a refund or an adjustment to the bill.

Such returns are often accumulated in a separate account called **Sales Returns and Allowances** and must be deducted from gross sales revenue in determining net sales. This account has an important purpose because it informs Gildan's management of the volume of returns and allowances and thus provides a measure of the quality of service provided to customers. Assume that a customer bought 40 dozen T-shirts from Gildan for $2,000 on account. Before paying for the T-shirts, the customer discovered that 10 dozen T-shirts were not the colour ordered and returned them to Gildan.[4] Gildan would compute net sales as follows:

SALES RETURNS AND ALLOWANCES is a reduction of sales revenues for return of or allowances for unsatisfactory goods.

Sales revenue	$2,000
Less: Sales returns (0.25 × $2,000)	500
Net sales (reported on the income statement)	$1,500

The cost of goods sold related to the 10 pairs would also be reduced.

REPORTING NET SALES

On the company's books, credit card discounts, sales discounts, and sales returns and allowances are accounted for separately to allow monitoring of the costs of the related activities (allowing use of credit cards, offering sales discounts, returns of incorrect or damaged merchandise, respectively). The amount of net sales reported on the income statement is computed in the following manner:[5]

Sales revenue
Less: Credit card discounts (a contra revenue)
Sales discounts (a contra revenue)
Sales returns and allowances (a contra revenue)
Net sales (reported on the income statement)

Companies rarely disclose the determinants of net sales in the annual report so it often is difficult to determine the effects of these items, even for well-educated external users. As we noted earlier, net sales less cost of goods sold equals the subtotal *gross profit* or *gross margin*. Analysts often examine gross profit as a percentage of net sales, called the *gross profit* or *gross margin percentage*.

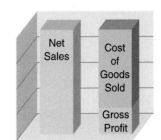

---

[4]Alternatively, Gildan might offer the customer a $200 allowance to keep the wrong-colour T-shirts. If the customer accepts the offer, Gildan reports $200 as sales returns and allowances.

[5]Sales and credit card discounts may also be reported as expenses on the income statement.

KEY **RATIO ANALYSIS:**

■ **LEARNING OBJECTIVE 3**

Compute and interpret the gross profit percentage.

GROSS PROFIT PERCENTAGE

ANALYTICAL QUESTION → By what amount (percentage) did sales prices exceed the costs to purchase or produce the goods or services sold?

RATIO AND COMPARISONS → The gross profit percentage is helpful in answering this question. It is computed as follows:

$$\text{Gross Profit Percentage} = \frac{\text{Gross Profit}}{\text{Net Sales}}$$

The 2004 ratio for Gildan is:

$$\frac{\$154,671,718}{\$533,367,537} = 0.29 \ (29.0\%)$$

Comparisons over Time			Comparisons with Competitors	
Gildan			Russell Corporation	Anvil Holdings
2002	2003	2004	2004	2004
28.1%	30.1%	29.0%	28.0%	25.0%

INTERPRETATIONS

Selected Focus Company Comparisons

Van Houtte 51%

Dell Computer 18%

Sleeman Breweries 48%

In General → The gross profit percentage measures the ability to charge premium prices and produce goods and services at lower cost. All other things being equal, a higher gross profit results in higher net income. Business strategy, as well as competition, affects the gross profit percentage. Companies pursuing a product-differentiation strategy use research and development and product promotion activities to convince customers of the superiority or distinctiveness of the company's products. This allows them to charge premium prices, producing higher gross profit percentages. Companies following a low-cost strategy rely on more efficient management of production to reduce costs and increase the gross profit percentage. Managers, analysts, and creditors use this ratio to assess the effectiveness of the company's product development, marketing, and production strategy.

Focus Company Analysis → Gildan's gross profit percentage was relatively stable over the three-year period, 2002–2004, surpassing those of its U.S. competitors in 2004. At the beginning of the chapter, we discussed key elements of Gildan's business strategy that focused on low-cost manufacturing of premium-quality products and its marketing philosophy of controlled distribution. According to Gildan's annual report for fiscal year 2003, the improvement in the gross profit percentage is the result of "manufacturing efficiencies generated through recent capital investments together with lower raw-material costs, and a more favourable product mix." In 2004, Gildan's gross profit percentage decreased slightly because of higher cotton costs as well as the effect of changing its reporting currency from the Canadian dollar to the U.S. dollar.

A Few Cautions → Understanding the sources of any change in gross profit percentage is necessary to assess the company's ability to sustain its new gross margins. For example, an increase in margin resulting from increases in seasonal sales of high-margin products would be judged to be less sustainable than one resulting from introducing new products. Also, higher prices must often be sustained with higher R&D and advertising costs, which can eat up any increase in gross margin. Finally, be aware that a small change in gross profit percentage can lead to a large change in net income.

SELF-STUDY **QUIZ 7-1**

1. Assume that the T-shirt company sold $30,000 worth of T-shirts to various retailers with terms 1/10, n30, and half of that amount was paid within the discount period. Gross sales at company-owned stores were $5,000 for the same period, 80 percent being paid using credit cards with a 3-percent discount and the rest in cash. Compute net sales for the period.

2. During the third quarter of the year, the company's net sales were $150,000 and cost of sales was $110,000. Verify that its gross profit percentage was 26.66 percent.

_____

_____

After you have answered the questions, check your answers with the solutions on page 376.

MEASURING AND REPORTING RECEIVABLES

CLASSIFYING RECEIVABLES

Receivables may be classified in three common ways. First, the receivable may be either an account receivable or a note receivable. An **account receivable** is created when there is a credit sale. For example, an account receivable is created when Gildan sells on account to a wholesaler. A **note receivable** is a written promise made by another party (e.g., a customer) to pay the company a specified amount of money, called *principal*, at a definite future date, known as the *maturity date*. In addition, the company receives *interest* on the principal at one or more future dates. Notes receivable also require periodic recording of interest revenue. We discuss the computation of interest when we discuss notes payable in a later chapter.

Second, receivables may be classified as trade or non-trade receivables. A *trade receivable* is created in the normal course of business when there is a sale of merchandise or services on credit. A *non-trade receivable* arises from transactions other than the normal sale of merchandise or services. For example, if Gildan loaned money to key employees to assist them in financing the purchase of their first homes, the loans would be classified as non-trade receivables. Third, in a classified balance sheet, receivables also are classified as either *current* or *non-current* (short term or long term), depending on when the cash is expected to be collected. Like many companies, Gildan reports only one type of receivable account, Accounts Receivable from customers (trade receivables), and classifies the asset as a current asset (short term) because the accounts receivable should be collected within one year.

Gildan allows its customers (the wholesalers that buy and then resell its casual wear) to purchase goods on open account because it believes that providing this service will result in more sales. Providing this service to customers also has a cost. Gildan must pay to maintain a credit-granting and collection system, and it must realize that not all customers will pay their debts. Credit policies should be set based on the *trade-off* between profits on additional sales and any additional bad debts. In fact, an extremely low rate of bad debts may not be good because it may indicate a credit policy that is too tight. If the credit policy is too restrictive, the company will turn away many good credit customers, causing a loss of sales volume.

ACCOUNTS RECEIVABLE (TRADE RECEIVABLES, RECEIVABLES) are open accounts owed to the business by trade customers.

A **NOTE RECEIVABLE** is a written promise that requires another party to pay the business a specified amount at a specific future date.

INTERNATIONAL **PERSPECTIVE**

FOREIGN CURRENCY RECEIVABLES

Export (international) sales are an increasing aspect of the Canadian economy. For example, international sales amounted to 92 percent of Gildan's revenues in 2004. As is the case with domestic sales to other businesses, most export sales to businesses are on credit. When the buyer has agreed to pay in its local currency instead of Canadian dollars, Gildan cannot add these accounts receivable, which are denominated in foreign currency, directly to its Canadian-dollar accounts receivable. Gildan must first convert them into Canadian dollars using the end-of-period exchange rate between the two currencies. For example, if a European distributor purchased goods from Gildan for €20,000 (European currency units or

Selected Foreign Currency Exchange Rates (in C$)

Mexican Peso $0.12

Singapore Dollar $0.76

Euro $1.61

euros) on September 20, 2004, and each euro was worth $1.50 ($Cdn) on that date, Gildan would add $30,000 to its accounts receivable on that date. If Gildan has not collected the €20,000 by October 3, 2004, the end of its fiscal year, then the receivable should be adjusted for the change in the value of the euro, and an exchange gain or loss would be reported on the income statement.

ACCOUNTING FOR BAD DEBTS

■ LEARNING OBJECTIVE 4

Estimate, report, and evaluate the effects of uncollectable accounts receivable (bad debts) on financial statements.

The **ALLOWANCE METHOD** bases bad debt expense on an estimate of uncollectable accounts.

BAD DEBT EXPENSE (DOUBTFUL ACCOUNTS EXPENSE, UNCOLLECTABLE ACCOUNTS EXPENSE) is the expense associated with estimated uncollectable accounts receivable.

ALLOWANCE FOR DOUBTFUL ACCOUNTS (ALLOWANCE FOR BAD DEBTS, ALLOWANCE FOR UNCOLLECTABLE ACCOUNTS) is a contra-asset account containing the estimated uncollectable accounts receivable.

Businesses that extend credit to customers know that a certain amount of credit sales may not be collected in the future. The matching principle requires the recording of bad debt expense in the *same* accounting period in which the related sales are made. However, Gildan may not learn that particular customers will not pay until the *next* accounting period.

Gildan resolves this problem and satisfies the matching principle by using the **allowance method** to estimate the expected amount of bad debts. There are two primary steps in applying the allowance method: (1) the estimation of bad debts expense and (2) writing off specific accounts determined to be uncollectable during the period.

Recording Bad Debt Expense Estimates **Bad debt expense (doubtful accounts expense, uncollectable accounts expense)** is the expense associated with estimated uncollectable accounts receivable. It is recorded through an *adjusting journal entry at the end of the accounting period*. Assume that for the year ended October 3, 2004, Gildan estimated bad debt expense to be $2,383,000 and made the following adjusting entry.[6]

Bad debt expense (E)	2,383,000	
Allowance for doubtful accounts (XA)		2,383,000

Assets	=	Liabilities	+	Shareholders' Equity
Allowance for doubtful accounts −2,383,000				Bad debt expense −2,383,000

The bad debt expense of $2,383,000 is reported on the income statement. It is normally included in Selling Expenses on the income statement. The credit in the preceding journal entry was made to a *contra-asset account* called **Allowance for Doubtful Accounts** (also called **Allowance for Bad Debts** or **Allowance for Uncollectable Accounts**). Thus, the entry decreases net income and total assets. Accounts Receivable cannot be credited because the specific customers who may not pay in the future are not identifiable at this date. As a contra asset, the balance in Allowance for Doubtful Accounts is *always* subtracted from the balance of Accounts Receivable. Thus, it is treated exactly like Accumulated Amortization, the first contra-asset account we discussed in Chapter 4.

Writing Off Specific Uncollectable Accounts Throughout the year, when it is determined that a customer will not pay its debt (e.g., due to bankruptcy), the write-off of that individual debt is recorded through a journal entry. Now that the specific uncollectable account receivable has been identified, it can be removed from Accounts

---

[6]Gildan did not disclose in its annual report any information about its bad debt expense or the allowance for doubtful accounts. Hence, the amounts used in this example are assumed.

Receivable. At the same time, the related estimate of bad debt is no longer needed and is removed from the Allowance for Doubtful Accounts. The following journal entry summarizes the write-offs of $2,356,000 during the year 2004:

Allowance for doubtful accounts (XA)	2,356,000	
Accounts receivable (A)		2,356,000

Assets	=	Liabilities	+	Shareholders' Equity
Allowance for doubtful accounts +2,356,000				
Accounts receivable −2,356,000				

Notice that this journal entry *did not affect any income statement accounts*. The estimated bad debt expense was already recorded in the period of sale. Also, the entry *did not change the net book value of Accounts Receivable*, since the decrease in the asset account (Accounts Receivable) was offset by an equal decrease in the contra-asset account (Allowance for Doubtful Accounts) and thus did not affect total assets.

Recovery of Accounts Previously Written Off When a customer makes a payment on an account previously written off, the initial journal entry to write off the account is reversed for the amount that is collected, and another journal entry is made to record the collection of cash. Assume that of the $2,356,000 receivables that were written off during fiscal year 2004, $48,000 was recovered from a customer that faced financial difficulties but was able to arrange for long-term financing to restart the business. The journal entries and transaction effects related to the recovery of bad debts are shown below:

Accounts receivable (A)	48,000	
Allowance for doubtful accounts (XA)		48,000
Cash (A)	48,000	
Accounts receivable (A)		48,000

Assets	=	Liabilities	+	Shareholders' Equity
Accounts receivable +48,000				
Allowance for doubtful accounts −48,000				
Cash +48,000				
Accounts receivable −48,000				

Notice that the net effect of the recovered amount on Accounts Receivable is zero. The recovered amount is first recorded in Accounts Receivable in order to show that the customer has honoured its previous commitment to pay Gildan $48,000.

Summary of the Accounting Process It is important to remember that accounting for bad debts is a two-step process:

Step	Timing	Accounts Affected	Financial Statement Effects
1. Record estimated bad debts adjustment	End of period in which sales are made	Bad Debt Expense (E) ↑	Net Income ↓
		Allowance for Doubtful Accounts (XA) ↑	Assets (Accounts Receivable, Net) ↓
2. Identify and write off actual bad debts	Throughout period as bad debts become known	Accounts Receivable (A) ↓	Net Income ⎫
		Allowance for Doubtful Accounts (XA) ↓	Assets (Accounts Receivable, Net) ⎭ No effect

The complete accounting process for bad debts can now be summarized in terms of the changes in Accounts Receivable and the Allowance for Doubtful Accounts (in thousands):[7]

Accounts Receivable (A)

Beginning balance	64,260	Collections on account	509,955
Sales on account	533,368	Write-offs	2,356
Ending balance	85,317		

Allowance for Doubtful Accounts (XA)

		Beginning balance	1,742
Write-offs	2,356	Bad debt expense adjustment	2,383
		Ending balance	1,769

REPORTING ACCOUNTS RECEIVABLE

In Exhibit 7.2, Gildan reports accounts receivable, net of allowance for doubtful accounts, of $85,317 and $64,260 for fiscal years 2004 and 2003, respectively.

Accounts Receivable (Gross) includes the total accounts receivable, both collectible and uncollectible. The balance in the Allowance for Doubtful Accounts is the portion of the accounts receivable balance the company estimates to be uncollectible. Accounts Receivable (Net) reported on the balance sheet is the portion of the accounts the company expects to collect (or its estimated net realizable value).

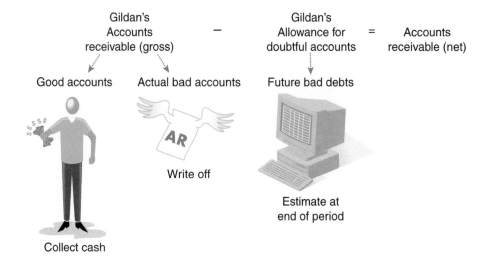

Gildan did not disclose any information about its Allowance for Doubtful Accounts.[8] *Financial Reporting in Canada 2004* indicates that the majority of companies (166 out of 200) did not disclose or refer to an allowance for doubtful accounts in their 2003 annual reports. In contrast, many U.S. companies disclose in their annual reports information about their bad debt expense and the related allowance for doubtful accounts.

ESTIMATING BAD DEBTS

The bad debt expense amount recorded in the end-of-period adjusting entry often is estimated in each accounting period based on either (1) the total credit sales for the period or (2) an aging of accounts receivable.

---

[7]This assumes that all sales to businesses (wholesale sales) are on account.

[8]Canadian companies are not required to disclose such information. The *CICA Handbook* (section 3020.01) states: "Since it is to be assumed that adequate allowance for doubtful accounts has been made if no statement is made to the contrary, it is not considered necessary to refer to such an allowance."

EXHIBIT **7.2**

Accounts Receivable on the
Balance Sheet

REAL WORLD EXCERPT

*Gildan
Activewear Inc.*

ANNUAL REPORT

Gildan Activewear Inc.
Consolidated Balance Sheets
October 3, 2004 and October 5, 2003
(in U.S. dollars)

	2004	2003
Assets		
Current assets:		
Cash and cash equivalents	$ 60,670,810	$ 69,339,953
Accounts receivable	85,317,148	64,259,826
Inventories	116,614,770	103,502,919
Prepaid expenses and deposits	3,432,435	3,849,180
Future income taxes (note 11)	8,148,893	4,681,900
	274,184,056	245,633,778

Percentage of Credit Sales Method Many companies make their estimates using the **percentage of credit sales method**, which bases bad debt expense on the historical percentage of credit sales that result in bad debts. This method is also called the *income statement method* because it involves the direct computation of the income statement number, *bad debt expense,* based on the income statement number *credit sales.*

The average percentage of credit sales that result in bad debts can be computed by dividing total bad debts by total *credit* sales. A company that has been operating for some years has sufficient experience to estimate probable future bad debts. For example, assume that Amar and Ciero (a hypothetical company) had experienced the following in three recent years:

PERCENTAGE OF CREDIT SALES METHOD bases bad debt expense on the historical perspective of credit sales that result in bad debts.

Year	Bad Debts	Credit Sales
2004	$ 900	$190,000
2005	1,200	220,000
2006	1,400	290,000
Total	$3,500	$700,000

The average bad debt rate equals 0.005 ($3,500 ÷ $700,000) or 0.5% for the three-year period 2004–2006.

If net credit sales in the current year were approximately $268,000 and the company used this method, then the bad debt expense is $1,340, computed as follows:

Bad debt expense = Credit sales × Bad debt rate
= $268,000 × 0.5% = $1,340

This amount is directly recorded as Bad Debt Expense in the current year, with a corresponding increase in Allowance for Doubtful Accounts. New companies often rely on the experience of similar companies that have been operating for a number of years. A company usually adjusts the historical average bad debt rate to reflect future expectations. For example, if retail sales were rising, the company might decrease its rate to 0.4 percent, reasoning that fewer of its business customers (retailers) will become bankrupt.

Allowance for Doubtful Accounts (XA)

	Beginning balance	1,455
Write-offs (throughout the year) 1,267		
	Unadjusted balance	188
Based on percentage of credit sales →	→ Bad debt expense (compute)	1,340
	Ending balance	1,528

FINANCIAL **ANALYSIS**

REAL WORLD EXCERPT

The Wall Street Journal

JUDGING THE ACCURACY OF BAD DEBT ESTIMATES

Without access to detailed information concerning any changes in customer mix and credit terms, an outside financial analyst would have little basis for judging the accuracy of the current period's bad debt estimates. For example, *The Wall Street Journal* reported:

FORMER T2 EXECUTIVES SETTLE SEC
LAWSUIT OVER EARNINGS REPORTS

NEW YORK—Four former executives of T2 Medical Inc. agreed to pay a total of more than $456,000 to settle Securities and Exchange Commission allegations that they artificially inflated the company's reported earnings. . . . According to the suit, which the SEC filed against the four in federal court here, they improperly accelerated recognition of revenues and product-delivery schedules and deferred bad debt write-offs, all in order to overstate earnings.

In this case, the company had increased its recognized bad debt expense from 5.4 percent of sales in the prior year to 6.5 percent of sales in recognition of an increase in the risk of bad debts. After the accounting irregularities were investigated, however, the accurate bad debt rate was determined to be 11 percent of sales. Although the financial community expected an increase in the bad debt rate, a doubling of the rate surprised most analysts because they were not aware of the dramatic changes in the company's credit sales policies.

Source: *The Wall Street Journal*, June 12, 1997, B12.

AGING OF ACCOUNTS RECEIVABLE METHOD
estimates uncollectable accounts based on the age of each account receivable.

Aging of Accounts Receivable Method   As an alternative to the percentage of credit sales method, many companies estimate bad debt expense by examining the age of accounts receivable that are outstanding. The **aging of accounts receivable method** relies on the fact that, as accounts receivable become older and overdue, they usually are less likely to be collectable. For example, a receivable that has not been paid after 60 days is more likely to be collected, on average, than a similar receivable that still remains unpaid after 120 days. Based on its prior experience, the company could estimate the percentage of receivables of different ages that may not be paid.

This method is also called the *balance sheet method* because it involves the direct computation of the balance of the *allowance for doubtful accounts* based on the ending balance of *accounts receivable*. Suppose that Amer and Ciero split its receivables into five age categories, as presented in Exhibit 7.3. Management of the company might then *estimate* the following probable bad debt rates: 1 percent of receivables not yet due; 3 percent of receivables that are past due by 1 to 30 days; 6 percent of receivables that are past due by 31 to 60 days; and so on. The total of the amounts estimated to be uncollectable under the aging method is the balance that *should be* in the allowance for doubtful accounts at the end of the period. This is called the *estimated balance*.

The approach to recording bad debt expense using the aging method is different from that for the percentage of credit sales method. Recall that, using the percentage

EXHIBIT **7.3**

Aging Schedule

Customer	Not Yet Due	1–30 Days Past Due	31–60 Days Past Due	61–90 Days Past Due	Over 90 Days Past Due	Total
			AMER AND CIERO Aging Anaysis of Accounts Receivable, December 31, 2005			
Adams, Inc.	$ 600					$ 600
Baker Stores	300	$ 900	$ 100			1,300
Cox Co.			400	$ 900	$ 100	1,400
Zoe Stores	2,000		1,000			3,000
Total	$17,200	$12,000	$8,000	$1,200	$1,600	$40,000
Estimated % uncollectable	1%	3%	6%	10%	25%	
Estimated uncollectable accounts	$ 172	$ 360	$ 480	$ 120	$ 400	$ 1,532

of credit sales, we *directly computed* the amount to be recorded as bad debt expense on the income statement for the period. Alternatively, when using the aging method, we are computing the *final ending balance* we would like to have in the allowance for doubtful accounts on the balance sheet after we make the necessary entry. Thus, the amount of bad debt expense for the period is the *difference* between the estimated uncollectable accounts (just calculated) and the balance of the allowance for doubtful accounts at the end of the period *before the adjusting entry* has been made.

Computation	
Estimated balance (from aging schedule)	$1,532
Less: Current balance (preadjustment balance from ledger account)	188
Bad debt expense to be recorded for the current year (solve)	$1,344

This computation also can be illustrated in T-account form. The current credit balance in the allowance account, before the end-of-period adjustment, is $188. We insert the new ending balance from the aging schedule and then solve for the current amount of bad debt expense.

Allowance for Doubtful Accounts (XA)

		Beginning balance	1,455
Write-offs (throughout the year)	1,267		
		Unadjusted balance	188
		Bad debt expense (solve)	1,344 ◄——— Step 2: Adjustment inferred
		Estimated balance (from aging)	1,532 ◄——— Step 1: Ending balance estimated from aging of accounts receivable

The end-of-period adjusting entry to Bad Debt Expense and Allowance for Doubtful Accounts is made on December 31 for $1,344.

The percentage of credit sales method focuses on an income statement valuation (bad debt expense matched to the period's credit sales), whereas the aging method focuses on a balance sheet valuation (estimated net realizable value of accounts receivable). In both cases, the objective is to estimate the amount of bad debt expense related to the period's credit sales. The computation of bad debt expense under the two methods are contrasted below, where the computed amounts are highlighted. Both methods are acceptable under GAAP if the resulting allowance is reasonable, and are widely used in practice, but do not produce the same estimate of bad debts.

Percentage of Credit Sales	Aging of Accounts Receivable
Beginning balance of Allowance account	Beginning balance of Allowance account
− Write-offs throughout the year	− Write-offs throughout the year
+ Bad debt expense (computed)	+ Bad debt expense (inferred)
= Ending balance of Allowance account (inferred)	**= Ending balance of Allowance account (computed)**

Actual Write-Offs Compared with Estimates   The amount of uncollectable accounts actually written off seldom equals the estimated amount previously recorded. This error in estimating bad debts is taken into consideration in determining the bad debt expense at the end of the next accounting period. When estimates are found to be incorrect, financial statement values for *prior* annual accounting periods are *not* corrected.

FINANCIAL ANALYSIS

SALES VERSUS COLLECTIONS—THE MARKETING/FINANCIAL MANAGEMENT CONFLICT

Company managers often forget that extending credit increases sales volume but it may also increase the volume of bad debts if proper credit checks of the customers are not made or if the company relaxes its credit policy. Marketing-oriented companies that emphasize sales without monitoring the collection of credit sales will soon find much of their current assets tied up in accounts receivable. On the other hand, the absence of bad debts may be the result of a very tight credit policy that reduces both sales and net income.

In the late 1990s, the leading telecommunications companies, such as Nortel Networks Corporation, Cisco Systems Inc., and Lucent Technologies Inc., contributed to sales growth by providing short- and medium-term financing to their telecommunications equipment customers in order to encourage them to purchase such equipment. Financing of sales by the seller, called *vendor financing*, had become common industry practice until the risks of vendor financing came to light when demand for telecommunications equipment and services weakened. Customers started to default on their debts and vendors were forced to absorb credit losses and increase their allowances for doubtful accounts. In their recent annual reports, Cisco Systems, Lucent Technologies, and Nortel Networks reported allowances for doubtful accounts that equalled 23 percent, 16.5 percent, and 19 percent of their accounts receivable, respectively.

When credit losses are relatively high because of vendor financing, financial analysts should be cautious in their analysis of companies' sales growth.

Conservatism in the Valuation of Accounts Receivable   Creditors and analysts prefer that companies follow *conservative* financial strategies that result in reporting lower amounts for net income and assets and higher amounts for liabilities. Accountants and auditors are also cautious about reporting optimistic values that overstate the company's operating performance and its financial position. For accounts receivable, the amount reported on the balance sheet should reflect the amount expected to be collected from customers. In this context, conservatism suggests that the allowance for doubtful accounts be commensurate with the creditworthiness of the company's customers. A conservative measure of accounts receivable means a larger amount of bad debt expense and a larger allowance for doubtful accounts. However, it is better to err on the side of having a larger allowance than having a smaller one that may not be adequate to cover future bad debts.

FOCUS ON **CASH FLOWS**

ACCOUNTS RECEIVABLE

The change in accounts receivable can be a major determinant of a company's cash flow from operations. The income statement reflects the revenues of the period, whereas the cash flow from operating activities must reflect the cash collections from customers for the same period. As explained in Chapter 5, credit sales increase the balance in accounts receivable, and cash collections from customers decrease the balance in accounts receivable. The change in accounts receivable from the beginning to the end of the period is the difference between sales and cash collections.

EFFECT ON CASH FLOW STATEMENT

IN GENERAL → When a net *decrease in accounts receivable* for the period occurs, the amount of cash collected from customers exceeds revenue; thus, the decrease must be *added* to revenue or to net income (since revenue is a component of net income) in computing cash flows from operations.

When a net *increase in accounts receivable* occurs, cash collected from customers is less than revenue; thus, the increase must be *subtracted* from net income in computing cash flows from operations.

	Effect on Cash Flows
Operating activities (indirect method)	
Net income	$xxx
Adjusted for	
Decrease in accounts receivable	+
or	
Increase in accounts receivable	−

FOCUS COMPANY ANALYSIS → Exhibit 7.4 is the Operating Activities section of Gildan's cash flow statement. When the accounts receivable balance increases during the period, as was the case at Gildan in 2003, and 2004, the company recorded more net sales than it collected in cash from customers during the period. Thus, the increase is subtracted from net earnings in the computation of Gildan's cash flow from operations. In fiscal year 2004, Gildan's sales totalled $533 million. Accounts receivable also increased during the same period, indicating that the company did not collect this whole amount in 2004. For this reason, the increase in accounts receivable is subtracted from sales revenue (hence, net income) in computing the cash received from operating activities.

EXHIBIT **7.4**

Accounts Receivable on the Cash Flow Statement

REAL WORLD EXCERPT

Gildan Activewear Inc.

ANNUAL REPORT

Gildan Activewear, Inc.
Consolidated Statements of Cash Flows
Years ended October 3, 2004, October 5, 2003, and September 29, 2002
(in U.S. dollars)

	2004	2003	2002
Cash Flows from Operating Activities:			
Net earnings	$ 60,251,248	$ 53,155,698	$ 42,436,586
Adjustments for:			
Depreciation and amortization	22,274,524	16,088,028	11,199,462
Stock-based compensation charges	476,586	—	—
Future income taxes	2,946,671	4,196,389	3,214,691
Loss on disposal of fixed assets	1,949,648	243,954	611,607
Unrealized foreign exchange loss (gain)	585,946	(33,654)	2,218,771
Changes in non-cash working capital balances:			
Accounts receivable	(20,236,219)	(7,319,605)	24,460,403
Inventories	(13,111,851)	(16,130,657)	42,015,362
Prepaid expenses and deposits	419,745	(996,062)	409,216
Accounts payable and accrued liabilities	5,436,007	12,818,249	(13,242,389)
Income taxes payable	(2,072,617)	1,698,540	921,720
	58,919,688	63,720,880	114,245,429

To assess the effectiveness of overall credit granting and collection activities, managers and analysts often compute the *receivables turnover* ratio.

KEY **RATIO ANALYSIS:**

■ LEARNING OBJECTIVE 5

Compute and interpret the accounts receivable turnover ratio and the effects of accounts receivable on cash flows.

RECEIVABLES TURNOVER

ANALYTICAL QUESTION → How effective are credit-granting and collection activities?
RATIO AND COMPARISONS → An answer to this question is provided by the receivables turnover ratio, which is computed as follows:

$$\text{Receivables Turnover} = \frac{\text{Net Sales*}}{\text{Average Net Trade Accounts Receivable}^\dagger}$$

*Since the amount of net credit sales is normally not reported separately, most analysts use net sales in this equation.
†Average Net Trade Accounts Receivable = (Beginning Net Trade Accounts Receivable + Ending Net Trade Accounts Receivable) ÷ 2

The 2004 ratio for Gildan is:

$$\frac{\$533,367}{(\$64,260 + 85,317) \div 2} = 7.13$$

This ratio can be stated in a more intuitive manner by dividing the average trade accounts receivable by the average credit sales per day:

$$\text{Average Collection Period} = \frac{\text{Average Trade Accounts Receivable}}{\text{Credit Sales}/365}$$

The 2004 average collection period for Gildan is:

$$\text{Average Collection Period} = \frac{\$74,789}{\$533,367/365} = 51.2 \text{ days}$$

An equivalent computation is

$$\text{Average Collection Period} = \frac{365}{\text{Receivables Turnover}} = \frac{365}{7.13} = 51.2 \text{ days}$$

Comparisons over Time			Comparisons with Competitors	
Gildan			Russell Corporation	Anvil Holdings
2002	2003	2004	2004	2004
5.54	7.19	7.13	6.69	7.89

INTERPRETATIONS

Selected Industry Comparisons: Receivables Turnover Ratio

Variety stores 98.6

Malt beverages 14.9

Lumber and building materials 12.7

In General → The receivables turnover ratio reflects how many times average trade receivables were recorded and collected during the period. A higher ratio indicates faster collection of receivables. This benefits the company because it can invest the cash collected, earning interest income, or reduce borrowings, thus reducing interest expense. Granting credit with later payment deadlines and using ineffective collection methods cause this ratio to be low. Analysts and creditors watch this ratio because a sudden decline in it may mean that a company is extending payment deadlines in an attempt to prop up lagging sales or even is recording sales that later will be returned by customers.

Focus Company Analysis → Gildan's receivables turnover increased from 5.54 in 2002 to 7.13 in 2004. Its ratio is higher than Russell's but lower than that of Anvil Holdings Inc. This indicates that Gildan is exceeding Russell in its ability to collect receivables from customers. Gildan's sales increased from $382 million in 2002 to $533 million in 2004. This significant increase in sales was accompanied by a decrease in the average collection period, from 66 days in 2002 to 51 days in 2004. Thus, it appears that Gildan tightened its credit policy as it achieved this sizeable increase in sales.

A Few Cautions → Since differences across industries in the manner in which customer purchases are financed cause dramatic differences in the ratio, a particular firm's ratio should be compared only with its prior years' figures or with other firms in the same industry. Many managers and analysts compute the related *average collection period* or *average days' sales in receivables,* which indicates the average time it takes a customer to pay its accounts.

SELF-STUDY **QUIZ 7-2**

1. Indicate whether *granting longer payment deadlines* (e.g., 60 days instead of 30 days) will most likely *increase* or *decrease* the accounts receivable turnover ratio. Explain.

2. Assume that Kleer Company reported beginning and ending balances in the Allowance for Doubtful Accounts of $723 and $904, respectively. It also reported that write-offs of bad debts amounted to $648 (all numbers in thousands). Assuming that the company did not collect any amounts that were written off previously, what amount did the company record as bad debt expense for the period? (*Solution approach:* Use the Allowance for Doubtful Accounts T-account to solve for the missing value.)

Allowance for Doubtful Accounts (XA)

3. Kleer Company reported an increase in accounts receivable for the period. Was that increase added to or subtracted from net income in the computation of cash flow from operations? Explain your answer.

After you complete your work, check your answers with the solution on page 376.

INTERNAL CONTROL AND MANAGEMENT RESPONSIBILITY

The term **internal control** refers to the process by which a company's board of directors, audit committee, management, and other personnel provide reasonable assurance regarding the reliability of the company's financial reporting, the effectiveness and efficiency of its operations, and its compliance with applicable laws and regulations.[9] Internal control procedures should extend to all aspects of the company's financial reporting process. A well-designed system of internal controls prevents inadvertent errors and removes opportunities for individuals to steal, misrepresent, defraud, or embezzle assets from a company.

Recent high-profile scandals in the United States, such as Enron and WorldCom, led the U.S. Congress to approve the Sarbanes-Oxley Act in July 2002. This Act, commonly known as SOX, requires public companies to take measures that are intended to provide better protection for investors by improving the accuracy and reliability of financial reporting. Specifically, the new legislation requires top executives to certify the accuracy of the financial statements released by their companies. It also places greater emphasis on internal control systems and procedures to prevent, detect, and remediate fraud and misconduct by management and other employees. The Sarbanes-Oxley Act also requires that external auditors vouch for the accuracy of management's

INTERNAL CONTROLS are the processes by which the company's board of directors, management, and other personnel provide reasonable assurance regarding the reliability of the company's financial reporting, the effectiveness and efficiency of its operations, and its compliance with applicable laws and regulations.

---

[9]According to the *CICA Handbook* (section 5200.05), "internal control comprises the plan of organization and all the co-ordinate systems established by the management of an enterprise to assist in achieving management's objective of ensuring, as far as practical, the orderly and efficient conduct of its business, including the safeguarding of assets, the reliability of accounting records and the timely preparation of reliable financial information."

statements concerning the company's financial results. Furthermore, auditors are required to audit the company's internal controls.

Because of the interdependence between the U.S. and Canadian financial markets, and the listing of major Canadian companies on U.S. stock exchanges, the Canadian Securities Administrators proposed in February 2005 new internal-control regulations for companies listed on Canadian stock exchanges that are consistent with the U.S. regulations.[10] The new Canadian regulations require both the chief executive officer and the chief financial officer to certify that the annual financial statements together with the other financial information included in the annual reports *fairly present* in all material respects the company's financial condition, results of operations, and cash flows. Furthermore, the certifying officers should declare their responsibility for internal control over financial reporting, and for establishing and maintaining disclosure controls and procedures to ensure that the company's accounting policies are in accordance with GAAP, that information technology is not misused, and that anti-fraud programs are in place.[11]

Compliance with the requirements of the Sarbanes-Oxley Act has cost companies billions of dollars, which prompted the top executives of many companies to question whether the expected benefits from implementing the new requirements are worth the additional costs of compliance. Furthermore, some have questioned whether such measures will effectively prevent future corporate scandals.[12] Nevertheless this law restored authority to the accounting profession and raised the profile of the auditing function in ensuring that information conveyed in financial reports has a high degree of reliability. It also has helped companies to identify material weaknesses and significant deficiencies in their internal control procedures. For example, Revlon Inc., which provides cosmetics and personal-care products, reported that review of its internal control procedures revealed that a US$1.2-million error was made in estimating the allowance for sales returns.[13]

A QUESTION OF **ETHICS**

ETHICS AND THE NEED FOR INTERNAL CONTROL

Some people are bothered by the recommendation that all well-run companies should have strong internal control procedures. These people believe that control procedures suggest that the company's management does not trust its employees. Although the vast majority of employees are trustworthy, an unfortunate fact of life is that employee theft costs businesses billions of dollars each year. Interviews with convicted felons indicate that, in many cases, they stole from their employers because they thought that it was easy and that no one cared (internal control procedures were not present).

---

[10] Reporting on Internal Control over Financial Reporting, Multilateral Instrument 52-111, Canadian Securities Administrators, February 4, 2005, as posted on CSA's website at www.csa-acvm.ca, accessed on March 11, 2005.

[11] In anticipation of these new regulations, the Canadian Auditing and Assurance Standards Board approved new recommendations designed to provide standards and guidance to auditors who are engaged to perform an audit of internal control over financial reporting. The objective of the new *Handbook* section is to promote a high quality of reporting on internal control. In this vein, auditors are required to express an opinion on management's assessment of the effectiveness of internal control over financial reporting. See Assurance and Auditing Recommendations, "An Audit of Internal Control over Financial Reporting Performed in Conjunction with an Audit of Financial Statements," in *CICA Handbook* (Toronto: Canadian Institute of Chartered Accountants, revised to February 2005.)

[12] See, for example, J. Gray, "Down the drain? The costs of regulatory compliance are soaring" *Canadian Business*, July 19–August 15, 2004, pp. 67–68, and T. Tedesco, "Audit rules called no cure for fraud" *National Post*, May 31, 2004, FP1, 9.

[13] The company's stock declined by 2.7 percent pursuant to the company's announcement of this error. *National Post*, March 11, 2005, FP13.

A recent survey of actual fraud committed by company employees, managers, and executives revealed that internal controls were not effective in detecting the fraud.[14] In fact, internal control procedures were identified as the primary source of fraud detection in fewer than 20 percent of the cases. The reported weaknesses in internal control systems explain why the Sarbanes-Oxley Act requires companies to strengthen their internal controls.

Many companies give their employees a formal code of ethics that includes high standards of behaviour in dealing with customers, suppliers, fellow employees, and the company's assets. Although each employee is ultimately responsible for his or her own ethical behaviour, internal control procedures can be thought of as important value statements from management. Preventing theft through strong internal controls prevents people from destroying their lives if they steal and are subsequently caught and penalized for their unethical behaviour.

CONTROL OVER ACCOUNTS RECEIVABLE

Many managers forget that extending credit will increase sales volume but unless the related receivables are collected they do not increase net income. Companies that emphasize sales without monitoring the collection of credit sales will soon find much of their current assets tied up in accounts receivable. To guard against extending credit to non-worthy customers, the following practices can help minimize bad debts:

1. Require approval of customers' credit history by a person independent of the sales and collection functions.

2. Monitor the age of accounts receivable periodically and contact customers with overdue payments.

3. Reward both sales and collection personnel for speedy collections so that they work as a team.

REPORTING AND SAFEGUARDING CASH

CASH AND CASH EQUIVALENTS DEFINED

Cash is defined as money or any instrument that banks will accept for deposit and immediate credit to the company's account, such as a cheque, money order, or bank draft. Cash usually is divided into three categories: cash on hand, cash deposited in banks, and other instruments that meet the definition of cash.

Section 1540 of the *CICA Handbook* defines **cash equivalents** as short-term, highly liquid investments that are readily convertible to known amounts of cash and which are subject to an insignificant risk of change in value. Typical instruments included as cash equivalents are bank certificates of deposit and Treasury bills issued by the government to finance its activities.

Even though a company may have several bank accounts and several types of cash equivalents, all cash accounts and cash equivalents are usually combined as one amount for financial reporting purposes. Gildan reports a single account, Cash and Cash Equivalents. The company treats as cash equivalents all liquid investments with maturities of three months or less from the date of acquisition.

CASH MANAGEMENT

Many businesses receive a large amount of cash, cheques, and credit card receipts from their customers each day. Anyone can spend cash, so management must develop procedures to safeguard the cash it uses in the business. Effective cash management

■ LEARNING OBJECTIVE 6

Report, control, and safeguard cash.

CASH is money or any instrument that banks will accept for deposit and immediate credit to the company's account, such as a cheque, money order, or bank draft.

CASH EQUIVALENTS are short-term, highly liquid investments that are readily convertible to known amounts of cash and which are subject to an insignificant risk of change in value.

[14]*2004 Report to the Nation on Occupational Fraud and Abuse.* Certified Fraud Examiners, Austin: USA, 2004.

involves more than protecting cash from theft, fraud, or loss through carelessness. Other cash management responsibilities include the following:

1. Accurate accounting so that reports of cash flows and balances may be prepared.

2. Controls to ensure that enough cash is on hand to meet (a) current operating needs, (b) maturing liabilities, and (c) unexpected emergencies.

3. Prevention of the accumulation of excess amounts of idle cash. Idle cash earns no revenue; therefore, it is often invested in securities to earn a revenue (return) pending future need for the cash.[15]

INTERNAL CONTROL OF CASH

Because cash is the asset most vulnerable to theft and fraud, a significant number of internal control procedures should focus on cash. You have already observed internal control procedures for cash, although you may not have known it at the time. At most movie theatres, one employee sells tickets and another employee collects them. It would be less expensive to have one employee do both jobs, but it would also be easier for that single employee to steal cash and admit a patron without issuing a ticket. If different employees perform the tasks, a successful theft requires participation of both.

Effective internal control of cash should include the following:

1. *Separation of duties related to cash handling and record keeping*
   a. Complete separation of the tasks of receiving cash and disbursing cash ensures that the individual responsible for depositing cash has no authority to sign cheques.
   b. Complete separation of the procedures of accounting for cash receipts and cash disbursements ensures, for example, that those handling sales returns do not create fictitious returns to conceal cash shortages.
   c. Complete separation of the physical handling of cash and all phases of the accounting function ensures that those either receiving or paying cash have no authority to make accounting entries.

The following diagram illustrates how the separation of duties contributes to strong internal control:

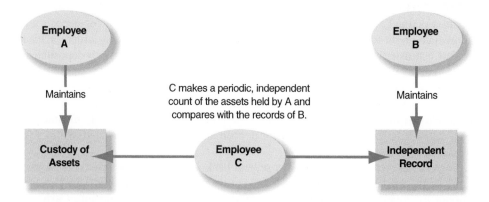

The separation of individual responsibilities deters theft because the collusion of two or more persons is needed to steal cash and then conceal the theft in the accounting records.

2. *Prescribed policies and procedures*
   Specific policies and procedures should be established so that the work done by one individual is compared to the results reported by other individuals. Exhibit 7.5 provides a summary of typical policies and procedures to control cash.

---

[15]An introduction to accounting for short-term investment in securities is available on the Online Learning Centre at www.mcgrawhill.ca/college/libby/student/resources.

EXHIBIT **7.5**

**Typical Internal Controls
for Cash**

Internal Control Component	Prescribed Policies or Procedures
Cash budget	Prepare a monthly forecast of cash receipts, disbursements, and balances for the year and require that managers document and justify any deviations from the budget each month.
Cash receipts	Prepare a listing of cash receipts on a daily basis. In practice this often takes the form of cash register receipts, or a descriptive list of incoming cheques. Require that all cash receipts be deposited in a bank daily. Keep any cash on hand under strict control.
Cash payments	Require separate approval of the purchases and other expenditures and separate approval of the actual cash payments. Assign the cash payment approval and the actual cheque-signing responsibilities to different individuals. Use pre-numbered cheques and pay special attention to payments by electronic funds transfers since the bank does not process controlled documents (cheques).
Independent internal verification	Require comparison of cash receipts to bank deposits, and cheques issued to invoices by an independent supervisor. Require monthly reconciliation of bank accounts with the cash accounts on the company's books (discussed in detail in the next section).
Rotation of duties	Require employees to take vacations, and rotate their duties.

When procedures similar to those described in Exhibit 7.5 are followed, concealing a fraudulent cash disbursement is difficult without the collusion of two or more persons. Reconciliation of cash accounts with bank statements provides an additional control on disbursements. The level of internal control, which is reviewed by the outside independent auditor, increases the reliability of the financial statements of the business.

RECONCILIATION OF THE CASH ACCOUNTS AND THE BANK STATEMENTS

Content of a Bank Statement   Proper use of the bank accounts of a business can be an important internal control procedure for cash. Each month, the bank provides the company (the depositor) with a **bank statement** that lists (1) each deposit recorded by the bank during the period, (2) each cheque cleared by the bank during the period, and (3) the balance in the company's account. The bank statement also shows the bank charges or deductions (such as service charges) made directly to the company's account by the bank. The bank statement may include copies of the deposit slips and all cheques that cleared through the bank during the period covered by the statement, although this practice is declining because it increases the bank's processing costs. A typical bank statement (excluding the deposit slips and cancelled cheques) is shown in Exhibit 7.6.

Exhibit 7.6 lists three items that need explanation. Notice that on June 20, listed under Debits, there is a deduction for $204.76 coded *NC*.[16] A cheque for $204.76 was received from a customer, R. Smith, and deposited by J. Doe Company with its bank, the Canadian Bank. The bank processed the cheque through banking channels to Smith's bank. Smith's account did not have sufficient funds to cover it; therefore, Smith's bank returned it to the Canadian Bank, which then charged it back to J. Doe Company. This type of cheque often is called an *NSF cheque* (not sufficient funds). The company needs to collect the amount of the cheque again from the customer. The NSF cheque is now a receivable; consequently, J. Doe Company must make an entry to debit Receivables (R. Smith) and credit Cash for the $204.76.

Notice the $10 listed on June 20 under Debits and coded *SC*. This is the code for bank service charges. The bank statement included a memo by the bank explaining this

A **BANK STATEMENT** is a monthly report from a bank that shows deposits recorded, cheques cleared, other debits and credits, and a running bank balance.

---

[16]These codes vary among banks.

EXHIBIT **7.6**

Example of a Bank Statement

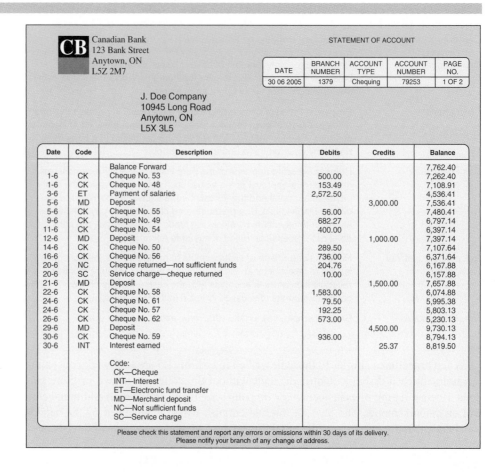

Date	Code	Description	Debits	Credits	Balance
		Balance Forward			7,762.40
1-6	CK	Cheque No. 53	500.00		7,262.40
1-6	CK	Cheque No. 48	153.49		7,108.91
3-6	ET	Payment of salaries	2,572.50		4,536.41
5-6	MD	Deposit		3,000.00	7,536.41
5-6	CK	Cheque No. 55	56.00		7,480.41
9-6	CK	Cheque No. 49	682.27		6,797.14
11-6	CK	Cheque No. 54	400.00		6,397.14
12-6	MD	Deposit		1,000.00	7,397.14
14-6	CK	Cheque No. 50	289.50		7,107.64
16-6	CK	Cheque No. 56	736.00		6,371.64
20-6	NC	Cheque returned—not sufficient funds	204.76		6,167.88
20-6	SC	Service charge—cheque returned	10.00		6,157.88
21-6	MD	Deposit		1,500.00	7,657.88
22-6	CK	Cheque No. 58	1,583.00		6,074.88
24-6	CK	Cheque No. 61	79.50		5,995.38
24-6	CK	Cheque No. 57	192.25		5,803.13
26-6	CK	Cheque No. 62	573.00		5,230.13
29-6	MD	Deposit		4,500.00	9,730.13
30-6	CK	Cheque No. 59	936.00		8,794.13
30-6	INT	Interest earned		25.37	8,819.50

Code:
  CK—Cheque
  INT—Interest
  ET—Electronic fund transfer
  MD—Merchant deposit
  NC—Not sufficient funds
  SC—Service charge

Please check this statement and report any errors or omissions within 30 days of its delivery.
Please notify your branch of any change of address.

service charge (which was not documented by a cheque). J. Doe Company must make an entry to reflect the $10 decrease in the bank balance as a debit to a relevant expense account, such as Bank Service Expense, and a credit to Cash.

Notice the $25.37 listed on June 30 under Credits and the code INT for interest earned. The bank pays interest on chequing account balances, which increased J. Doe Company's account for interest earned during the period. The Company must record the interest by making an entry to debit Cash and credit Interest Revenue for the $25.37.

A **BANK RECONCILIATION** is the process of verifying the accuracy of both the bank statement and the cash accounts of a business.

Need for Reconciliation   A **bank reconciliation** is the process of comparing (reconciling) the ending cash balance in the company's records and the ending cash balance reported by the bank on the monthly bank statement. A bank reconciliation should be completed for each separate chequing account (i.e., for each bank statement received from each bank) at the end of each month.

Usually, the ending cash balance as shown on the bank statement does not agree with the ending cash balance shown by the related Cash ledger account on the books of the company. For example, the Cash ledger account of J. Doe Company showed the following at the end of June (Doe has only one chequing account):

Cash

June 1 balance	6,637.14	Cheques written in June	8,714.45
June deposits	11,800.00		
Ending balance	9,722.69		

The $8,819.50 ending cash balance shown on the bank statement (Exhibit 7.6) is different from the $9,722.69 ending balance of cash shown on the books of J. Doe Company. This difference exists because (1) some transactions affecting cash were recorded in the books of J. Doe Company but were not shown on the bank statement, (2) some transactions were shown on the bank statement but had not been recorded in the books of the J. Doe Company, and (3) errors in recording transactions.

The flow of documents that have not reached either the company or the bank by the end of the accounting period is illustrated below:

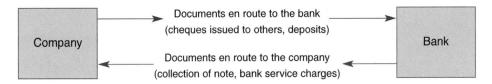

The most common causes of differences between the ending bank balance and the ending book balance of cash are as follows:

1. **Outstanding cheques.** Cheques written by the company and recorded in the company's ledger as credits to the Cash account. These cheques have not cleared the bank (they are not shown on the bank statement as a deduction from the bank balance). The outstanding cheques are identified by comparing the cancelled cheques that the bank returned with the record of cheques (such as cheque stubs or a journal) maintained by the company.

2. **Deposits in transit.** Deposits sent to the bank by the company and recorded in the company's ledger as debits to the Cash account. The bank has not recorded these deposits (they are not shown on the bank statement as an increase in the bank balance). Deposits in transit usually happen when deposits are made one or two days before the close of the period covered by the bank statement. Deposits in transit are determined by comparing the deposits listed on the bank statement with the copies of the deposit slips retained by the company or other company records.

3. **Bank service charges.** An expense for bank services listed on the bank statement. This expense must be recorded in the company's ledger by making a debit to a relevant expense account, such as Bank Service Expense, and a credit to Cash.

4. **NSF cheques.** A "bad cheque" that was deposited but must be deducted from the company's account. The company must make a journal entry to debit Accounts Receivable and credit Cash.

5. **Interest.** The interest paid by the bank to the company on its bank balance.

6. **Errors.** Both the bank and the company may make errors, especially when the volume of cash transactions is large.

Bank Reconciliation Illustrated The company should make a bank reconciliation immediately after receiving each bank statement. The general format for the bank reconciliation follows:

Ending cash balance per books	$xxx	Ending cash balance per bank statement	$xxx
+ Collections by bank	xx	+ Deposits in transit	xx
− NSF cheques/Service charges	xx	− Outstanding cheques	xx
± Company errors	xx	± Bank errors	xx
Ending correct cash balances	$xxx	Ending correct cash balance	$xxx

Exhibit 7.7 shows the bank reconciliation prepared by J. Doe Company for the month of June to reconcile the ending bank balance ($8,819.50) with the ending book balance ($9,722.69). On the completed reconciliation, the correct cash balance is $9,542.30. This balance is different from both the reported bank and book balances before the reconciliation with the bank statement. This correct balance is the amount that should be shown in the Cash account after the reconciliation. In this example, it is

EXHIBIT **7.7**

Bank Reconciliation Illustrated

J. DOE COMPANY
Bank Reconciliation
June 30, 2005

Company's Books		Bank Statement	
Ending cash balance per books	$9,722.69	Ending cash balance per bank statement	$ 8,819.50
Additions		Additions	
Interest earned	25.37	Deposit in transit	1,800.00
Error in recording cheque No. 55	9.00		
	9,757.06		10,619.50
Deductions		Deductions	
NSF cheque of R. Smith	204.76	Outstanding cheques	1,077.20
Bank service charges	10.00		
Ending correct cash balance	$9,542.30	Ending correct cash balance	$ 9,542.30

also the correct amount of cash that should be reported on the balance sheet (J. Doe Company has only one chequing account and no cash on hand). J. Doe Company followed these steps in preparing the bank reconciliation:

1. **Identify the outstanding cheques.** A comparison of the cancelled cheques returned by the bank with the company's records of all cheques drawn showed the following cheques still outstanding (not cleared) at the end of June:

Cheque No.	Amount
60	$ 145.00
63	815.00
64	117.20
Total	$1,077.20

This total was entered on the reconciliation as a deduction from the bank account. These cheques will be deducted by the bank when they clear the bank.

2. **Identify the deposits in transit.** A comparison of the deposit slips on hand with those listed on the bank statement revealed that a deposit of $1,800 made on June 30 was not listed on the bank statement. This amount was entered on the reconciliation as an addition to the bank account. It will be added by the bank when it records the deposit.

3. **Record bank charges and credits:**
   a. Interest received from the bank, $25.37—entered on the bank reconciliation as an addition to the book balance; it already has been included in the bank balance.
   b. NSF cheque of R. Smith, $204.76—entered on the bank reconciliation as a deduction from the book balance; it has been deducted from the bank statement balance.
   c. Bank service charges, $10—entered on the bank reconciliation as a deduction from the book balance; it has been deducted from the bank balance.

4. **Determine the impact of errors.** At this point, J. Doe Company found that the reconciliation did not balance by $9. Because this amount is divisible by 9, a transposition of numbers was suspected. (A transposition, such as writing 27 for 72, always will cause an error that is exactly divisible by 9.) Upon checking the journal entries made during the month, a cheque written for $56 to pay an account payable was found. The cheque was recorded in the company's accounts as $65. The incorrect

entry made was a debit to Accounts Payable and a credit to Cash for $65 (instead of $56). Therefore, $9 (i.e., $65 − $56) must be added to the book cash balance on the reconciliation; the bank cleared the cheque for the correct amount, $56.

Note that in Exhibit 7.7, both the Company's Books and the Bank Statement sections of the bank reconciliation now show a correct cash balance of $9,542.30. This amount will be reported as cash on a balance sheet prepared at June 30, 2005. If the company had cash on hand, it would be added to the $9,542.30, and the total would be reported on the balance sheet.

A bank reconciliation as shown in Exhibit 7.7 accomplishes two major objectives:

1. Checks the accuracy of the bank balance and the company cash records, which involves developing the correct cash balance. The correct cash balance (plus cash on hand, if any) is the amount of cash that is reported on the balance sheet.

2. Identifies any previously unrecorded transactions or changes that are necessary to cause the company's Cash account(s) to show the correct cash balance. Any transactions or changes on the Company's Books side of the bank reconciliation need journal entries. Therefore, the following journal entries based on the Company's Books side of the bank reconciliation (Exhibit 7.7) must be entered into the company's records.

Accounts of J. Doe Company

(a) Cash (A)	25.37	
Interest revenue (A)		25.37
To record interest from bank.		
(b) Accounts receivable (A)	204.76	
Cash (A)		204.76
To record NSF cheque.		
(c) Bank service expense (E)	10.00	
Cash (A)		10.00
To record service fees charged by bank.		
(d) Cash (A)	9.00	
Accounts payable (L)		9.00
To correct error made in recording a cheque payable to a creditor.		

Assets	=	Liabilities	+	Shareholders' Equity	
Cash (+25.37 − 204.76		Accounts		Bank service	
− 10.00 + 9.00)	−180.39	payable	+9.00	expense	−10.00
Accounts receivable	+204.76			Interest earned	+25.37

Cash Account of J. Doe Company

The Cash account prior to reconciliation was given earlier in this chapter. After the preceding journal entries are posted, the Cash account is as follows:

Cash					
June 1	Balance	6,637.14	June	Cheques written	8,714.45
June	Deposits	11,800.00	June 30	NSF cheque*	204.76
June 30	Interest earned*	25.37	June 30	Bank service charge*	10.00
June 30	Correcting entry*	9.00			
	Correct cash balance	9,542.30			

*Based on the bank reconciliation.

Notice that all of the additions and deductions on the Company's Books side of the reconciliation need journal entries to update the Cash account. The additions and deductions on the Bank Statement side do not need journal entries because they will work out automatically when they clear the bank.

SELF-STUDY QUIZ 7-3

Indicate which of the following items discovered while preparing a company's bank reconciliation will result in adjustment of the cash balance on the balance sheet.

1. Outstanding cheques.

2. Deposits in transit.

3. Bank service charges.

4. NSF cheques that were deposited.

After you complete your answers, check them with the solutions on page 376.

DEMONSTRATION CASE A

Wholesale Warehouse Stores sold $950,000 in merchandise during 2006, $400,000 of which was on credit with terms 2/10, n/30 (75 percent of these amounts were paid within the discount period), $500,000 was paid with credit cards (there was a 3-percent credit card discount), and the rest was paid in cash. On December 31, 2006, the Accounts Receivable balance was $80,000, and the Allowance for Doubtful Accounts was $3,000 (credit balance).

Required:

1. Compute net sales for 2006, assuming that sales and credit card discounts are treated as contra-revenue accounts.

2. Assume that Wholesale uses the percentage of sales method for estimating bad debt expense and that it estimates that 2 percent of credit sales will produce bad debts. Record bad debt expense for 2006.

3. Assume that Wholesale uses the aging of accounts receivable method and that it estimates that $10,000 worth of current accounts are uncollectable. Record bad debt expense for 2006.

We strongly recommend that you prepare your own answers to these requirements and then check your answers with the following suggested solution.

SUGGESTED SOLUTION

1. Both sales discounts and credit card discounts should be subtracted from sales revenues in the computation of net sales.

Sales Revenue	$950,000
Less: Sales discounts (0.02 × 0.75 × $400,000)	6,000
Credit card discounts (0.03 × $500,000)	15,000
Net sales	$929,000

2. The percentage estimate of bad debts should be applied to credit sales. Cash sales never produce bad debts.

Bad debt expense (E) (0.02 × $400,000)	8,000	
Allowance for doubtful accounts (XA)		8,000

Assets		=	Liabilities	+	Shareholders' Equity	
Allowance for doubtful					Bad debt	
accounts	−8,000				expense	−8,000

3. The entry made when using the aging of accounts receivable method is the estimated balance minus the unadjusted balance.

| Bad debt expense (E) ($10,000 − $3,000) .... | 7,000 | |
| Allowance for doubtful accounts (XA) .... | | 7,000 |

Assets		=	Liabilities	+	Shareholders' Equity	
Allowance for doubtful accounts	−7,000				Bad debt expense	−7,000

DEMONSTRATION **CASE B**

Heather Ann Long, a first-year university student, has just received her first chequing account statement. This was her first chance to attempt a bank reconciliation. She had the following information to work with:

Bank balance, September 1	$1,150
Deposits during September	650
Cheques cleared during September	900
Bank service charge	5
Bank balance, October 1	895

Heather was surprised that the deposit of $50 she made on September 29 had not been posted to her account and was pleased that her rent cheque of $200 had not cleared her account. Her chequebook balance was $750.

Required:

1. Complete Heather's bank reconciliation.
2. Why is it important for individuals such as Heather and businesses to do a bank reconciliation each month?

We strongly recommend that you prepare your own answers to these requirements and then check your answers with the following suggested solution.

SUGGESTED SOLUTION

1. Heather's bank reconciliation:

Heather's Books		Bank Statement	
October 1 cash balance	$750	October 1 cash balance	$895
Additions		Additions	
None		Deposit in transit	50
Deductions		Deductions	
Bank service charge	(5)	Outstanding cheque	(200)
Correct cash balance	$745	Correct cash balance	$745

2. Bank statements, whether personal or business, should be reconciled each month. This process helps ensure that a correct balance is reflected in the customer's books. Failure to reconcile a bank statement increases the chance that an error will not be discovered and may result in bad cheques being written. Businesses must reconcile their bank statements for an additional reason: the correct balance that is calculated during reconciliation is recorded on the balance sheet. A bank reconciliation is an important internal control measure.

Chapter Supplement A

Recording Discounts and Returns

In the chapter, both *credit card discounts* and *cash discounts* can be recorded either as contra revenues or as expenses. For example, if the credit card company is charging a 3-percent fee for its service and credit card sales were $3,000 at a factory store for January 2, the sales transaction is recorded as follows:

Cash (A)	2,910	
Credit card discount (XR or E)	90	
Sales revenue (R)		3,000

Assets		=	Liabilities	+	Shareholders' Equity	
Cash	+2,910				Sales revenue	+3,000
					Credit card discount	−90

Similarly, if credit sales are recorded with terms 2/10, n/30 ($1,000 × 0.98 = $980), and payment is made within the discount period, the selling company would record the following:

| Accounts receivable (A) .... | 1,000 | |
| Sales revenue (R) .... | | 1,000 |

Assets		=	Liabilities	+	Shareholders' Equity	
Accounts receivable	+1,000				Sales revenue	+1,000

Cash (A)	980	
Sales discount (XR or E)	20	
Accounts receivable (A)		1,000

Assets		=	Liabilities	+	Shareholders' Equity	
Cash	+980				Sales discount	−20
Accounts receivable	−1,000					

Sales returns and allowances should always be treated as a contra-revenue account. Assume that the T-shirt company bought 1,000 T-shirts for $6,000 on account. On the date of sale, the selling company makes the following journal entry:

| Accounts receivable (A) .... | 6,000 | |
| Sales revenue (R) .... | | 6,000 |

Assets		=	Liabilities	+	Shareholders' Equity	
Accounts receivable	+6,000				Sales revenue	+6,000

Before paying for the T-shirts, the T-shirt company discovered that 50 T-shirts were not the colour ordered and returned them to the seller. On that date, the seller records:

| Sales returns and allowances (XR) .... | 300 | |
| Accounts receivable (A) .... | | 300 |

Assets		=	Liabilities	+	Shareholders' Equity	
Accounts receivable	−300				Sales returns and allowances	+300

Chapter Supplement B

Applying the Revenue Principle in Special Circumstances

The revenue principle was introduced in Chapter 3. As noted earlier, application of this principle in the case of Gildan and similar companies was fairly straightforward. Such companies record revenue when goods or services are shipped or delivered. We now expand our discussion of the revenue principle and see how it is applied in business practice by companies other than typical manufacturers, wholesalers, and retailers.

DELAYED REVENUE RECOGNITION: INSTALMENT METHOD

Recall that to record revenue (1) an exchange must take place, (2) the earnings process must be nearly complete, and (3) collection must be probable. Failure to meet the third revenue recognition criterion (collection must be probable) requires that revenue recognition be delayed until after an initial exchange. When a high level of uncertainty concerning the collectability of the sales price exists, revenue recognition is postponed until *cash is collected from the customer*. This revenue recognition method, called the **instalment method**, is considered to be a very conservative method since it postpones revenue recognition, sometimes until long after goods have been delivered. The most common applications are in certain types of *retail* and *real estate transactions* in which payment is made over a multi-year period and a large proportion of customers stop making payments long before the final payment is due. Certain types of expensive equipment, such as supercomputers, are sometimes sold under contracts calling for payment to be made over a multi-year period and giving the customers the right to return the equipment and cease making payments if they are dissatisfied. The instalment method also is required here. Application of this specialized revenue recognition method is discussed in intermediate accounting courses.

> The **INSTALMENT METHOD** recognizes revenue on the basis of cash collection after the delivery of goods.

REVENUE RECOGNITION BEFORE THE EARNINGS PROCESS IS COMPLETE: LONG-TERM CONSTRUCTION CONTRACTS

An important exception to the usual criteria exists for companies involved in long-term construction projects such as building an office complex for a large corporation. These projects may take a number of years to complete. As a result, if the company recorded no revenue or expenses directly related to the project during the years that it worked on the project and then recorded a massive amount of revenue in the year that it delivered the product to the customer, the financial statements would not accurately represent the company's economic activities. This method of accounting is often referred to as the *completed contract method*.

To deal with this unique problem for long-term construction projects, many companies use the **percentage of completion method**, which records revenue based on the percentage of work completed during the accounting period, instead of the **completed contract method**, which records revenue when the completed product is delivered to the customer.

Under the percentage of completion method, revenues are based on the amount of work done each year. Typically, the amount of work accomplished each year is measured by the *percentage of total cost* that was incurred during the year. For example, assume that the total contract price was $50 million and the total cost for construction was $40 million. In 2005, the construction company spent $10 million, which was 25 percent of the contract cost ($10 million ÷ $40 million).[17] This percentage of completion is then multiplied by the total contract revenue to determine the amount of revenue to be reported in 2005 (25% × $50,000,000 = $12,500,000).

> The **PERCENTAGE OF COMPLETION METHOD** records revenue based on the percentage of work completed during the accounting period.
>
> The **COMPLETED CONTRACT METHOD** records revenue when the completed product is delivered to the customer.

---

[17]The difference between the expected cost and the actual cost of construction, which did not occur in this simple example, creates additional accounting problems.

The amount of expense reported each year is the actual cost incurred ($10,000,000 in 2005), and the amount of income is simply the difference between revenue and expense ($12,500,000 − $10,000,000 = $2,500,000 in 2005). It is important to note that the total revenue, expenses, and income for the two methods over the life of the contract are exactly the same. The methods differ only in terms of the accounting periods in which the various revenues and expenses are reported (their timing). The percentage of completion method recognizes income throughout the contract period; the completed contract method recognizes income only in the year of completion.

Notice that the percentage of completion method does not completely satisfy the second revenue recognition criterion because revenue is reported before the earnings process is complete. It is the preferred method, however, in cases such as this because the completed contract method makes it appear that the contractor was not able to generate any profits for the initial years of the contract but then became very profitable in the final year. In reality, the company was active in all years. Thus, the percentage of completion method better represents this type of underlying economic activity.

Companies may use the percentage of completion method when progress toward completion and costs to complete the contract can be reasonably estimated and they have a firm contract that guarantees payment to satisfy the cash collectability criterion.

REVENUE RECOGNITION FOR SERVICE CONTRACTS

Companies that provide services over more than one accounting period often follow revenue recognition policies similar to those followed for long-term construction contracts. They may record revenue after all services have been provided (after the contract is completed) or may recognize revenue from the completed portion of the services. Since the individual size of the contracts involved often is small (compared to construction contracts) and companies often are engaged in many service contracts with different beginning and ending dates, the distortion caused by the completed contract method is usually smaller than that of long-term construction contracts. Yet many service companies, such as Federal Express, which provides air delivery service, employ the percentage of completion revenue recognition policy as indicated in the following note:

REAL WORLD EXCERPT

Federal Express

ANNUAL REPORT

FEDERAL EXPRESS CORPORATION AND SUBSIDIARIES

Notes to Consolidated Financial Statements
NOTE 1. SUMMARY OF SIGNIFICANT ACCOUNTING POLICIES
  Revenue recognition. Revenue is generally recognized upon delivery of shipments. For shipments in transit, revenue is recorded based on the percentage of service completed.

For the services in progress at the end of the accounting period, Federal Express uses the percentage of completion method for revenue recognition, recognizing only a percentage of the revenues and related costs of providing the services based on the degree of completion of the service. This method is also called the *proportional performance* method. This form of revenue recognition is very similar to CanWest Global's accounting for its TV cable contracts and SNC-Lavalin's accounting for its construction contracts. Each company recognizes revenues and expenses related to the *completed portion* of its contract with the customer. The major difference is that CanWest Global is paid for the cable subscriptions in advance, SNC-Lavalin receives progress payments throughout the contract period, and Federal Express receives payment from its business customers after it provides the service.

FINANCIAL **ANALYSIS**

REVENUE RECOGNITION AND FINANCIAL STATEMENT ANALYSIS

Financial analysts cannot evaluate the income earned by a company if they do not understand how it applied the revenue recognition criteria. As a result, all companies disclose any special revenue recognition issues in the notes to their financial statements. For example, CAE, Inc., a provider of flight simulators and training to the aviation and marine transport industries, states the following in its annual report:

> Revenue from long-term contracts for building simulators and controls systems is recognized using the percentage-of-completion method, where revenue, earnings and unbilled accounts receivable are recorded as related costs are incurred on the basis of the percentage of actual costs incurred to date on a contract, relative to the estimated total costs to complete that contract. Revision in cost and earnings estimates during the term of the contract are reflected in the period in which the need for revision becomes known. Losses, if any, are recognized fully when first anticipated. Generally, the terms of long-term contracts provide for progress billings based on completion of certain phases of work. Warranty provisions are recorded at the time revenue is recognized, based on past experience. No right of return or complimentary upgrades are provided to customers. Post-delivery customer support is billed separately, and revenue is recorded ratably over the support period.

This succinct explanation of the percentage of completion method is an adequate explanation for someone who has read this chapter, but it is doubtful that someone who has not studied accounting would understand its meaning. This is an excellent example of the importance of careful study of accounting even if you do not major in accounting.

DEMONSTRATION **CASE C**

Assume that (1) Canada Post had shipments in transit involving fees totalling $20 million on December 31 of the current year, (2) none of the fees had been collected, and (3) on average, the shipments in transit were 60-percent completed.

Required:

1. Determine what amount related to the shipments in transit is recognized as revenue in the current year using the revenue recognition rule indicated in the Federal Express note that is shown in the prior section.
2. Indicate what asset(s) is(are) affected by recording revenue from the shipments in transit (accounts and amounts).

We strongly recommend that you prepare your own answers to these requirements and then check your answers with the suggested solution below.

SUGGESTED SOLUTION

1. Delivery revenue is recorded for $12,000,000 ($20,000,000 × 60%).
2. Accounts Receivable increases by $12,000,000.

SOLUTIONS TO **SELF-STUDY QUIZZES**

Self-Study Quiz 7-1

1. Gross Sales	$35,000
Less: Sales discounts (0.01 × 1/2 × $30,000)	150
Credit card discounts (0.03 × 0.8 × $5,000)	120
Net Sales	$34,730

2. Gross profit = $150,000 − $110,000 = $40,000

Gross profit percentage = $40,000 ÷ $150,000 = 26.66%

Self-Study Quiz 7-2

1. Granting longer payment deadlines will most likely *decrease* the accounts receivable turnover ratio because later collections from customers will increase the average accounts receivable balance (the denominator of the ratio), thus decreasing the ratio.

2.

Allowance for Doubtful Accounts (XA)

		Beginning balance	723
Write-offs	648	Bad debt expense (*solve*)	829
		Ending balance	904

Beginning + Bad debt expense − Write-offs = Ending; $723 + X − 648 = $904; X = $829

3. The amount would be subtracted from net income because an increase in the Accounts Receivable account indicates that sales revenue was in excess of cash collected from customers for the period.

Self-Study Quiz 7-3

3. Bank service charges are deducted from the company's account; thus, cash must be reduced and an expense must be recorded.

4. NSF cheques that were deposited were recorded on the books as increases in the Cash account; thus, cash must be decreased and the related account receivable increased if payment is still expected.

CHAPTER **TAKE-AWAYS**

1. **Apply the revenue principle to determine the appropriate time for revenue recognition for typical retailers, wholesalers, manufacturers, and service companies. p. 345**
   Revenue recognition policies are widely recognized as one of the most important determinants of the fair presentation of financial statements. For most merchandisers and manufacturers, the required revenue recognition point is the time of shipment or delivery of goods. For service companies, it is the time at which services are provided.

2. **Analyze the impact of credit card sales, sales discounts, and sales returns on the amounts reported as net sales. p. 346**
   Both *credit card discounts* and *cash discounts* can be recorded either as contra revenues or as expenses. When recorded as contra revenues, they reduce net sales. *Sales returns and allowances,* which should always be treated as contra revenues, also reduce net sales.

3. **Compute and interpret the gross profit percentage. p. 350**
   The gross profit percentage measures the ability to charge premium prices and produce goods and services at lower cost. Managers, analysts, and creditors use this ratio to assess the effectiveness of the company's product development, marketing, and production strategy.

4. **Estimate, report, and evaluate the effects of uncollectable accounts receivable (bad debts) on financial statements. p. 352**
   When receivables are material, companies must employ the allowance method to account for uncollectables. The steps in the process are
   1. Preparing the end-of-period adjusting entry to record an estimate of bad debt expense.
   2. Writing off specific accounts determined to be uncollectable during the period, and recovery of amounts written off.
   The adjusting entry reduces net income as well as net accounts receivable. The write-off of accounts receivable affects neither.

5. **Compute and interpret the accounts receivable turnover ratio and the effects of accounts receivable on cash flows. p. 360**
   Accounts receivable turnover ratio—Measures the effectiveness of credit granting and collection activities. It reflects how many times average trade receivables were recorded and collected during the period. Analysts and creditors watch this ratio because a sudden decline in it may mean that a company is extending collection

deadlines in an attempt to prop up lagging sales or even is recording sales that later will be returned by customers. Alternatively, the average age of receivables indicates the average number of days it takes to collect from customers.

Effects on cash flows—When a net decrease in accounts receivable for the period occurs, cash collected from customers exceeds revenue, and cash flows from operations increases. When a net increase in accounts receivable occurs, cash collected from customers is less than revenue; thus, the cash flow from operations declines.

6. **Report, control, and safeguard cash.   p. 363**
   Cash is the most liquid of all assets, flowing continually into and out of a business. As a result, a number of critical control procedures, including the reconciliation of bank accounts, should be applied. Also, management of cash may be critically important to decision makers who must have cash available to meet current needs yet must avoid excess amounts of idle cash that produce no revenue.

Closely related to recording revenue is recording the cost of what was sold. Chapter 8 will focus on transactions related to inventory and cost of goods sold. This topic is important because cost of goods sold has a major impact on a company's gross profit and net income, which are watched closely by investors, analysts, and other users of financial statements. Increasing emphasis on quality, productivity, and costs has further focused production managers' attention on cost of goods sold and inventory. Since inventory cost figures play a major role in product introduction and pricing decisions, they also are important to marketing and general managers. Finally, since inventory accounting has a major effect on many companies' tax liabilities, this is an important place to introduce the effect of taxation on management decision making and financial reporting.

KEY **RATIOS**

The gross profit percentage measures the excess of sales prices over the costs to purchase or produce the goods or services sold as a percentage. It is computed as follows (p. 350):

$$\text{Gross Profit Percentage} = \frac{\text{Gross Profit}}{\text{Net Sales}}$$

The receivables turnover ratio measures the effectiveness of credit-granting and collection activities. It is computed as follows (p. 360):

$$\text{Receivables Turnover} = \frac{\text{Net Sales}}{\text{Average Net Trade Accounts Receivable}}$$

FINDING **FINANCIAL INFORMATION**

BALANCE SHEET
Under Current Assets
  Accounts receivable (net of allowance for doubtful accounts)

INCOME STATEMENT
Revenues
  Net sales (sales revenue less discounts if treated as contra revenues and sales returns and allowances)
Expenses
  Selling expenses (including bad debt expense and discounts if treated as expenses)

CASH FLOW STATEMENT
Under Operating Activities (indirect method)
  Net income
  + decrease in accounts receivable (net)
  − increase in accounts receivable (net)

NOTES
Under Summary of Significant Accounting Policies
  Revenue recognition policy

KEY **TERMS**

Accounts Receivable (Trade Receivables or Receivables) p. 351

Aging of Accounts Receivable Method p. 356

Allowance for Doubtful Accounts (Allowance for Bad Debts or Allowance for Uncollectable Accounts) p. 352

Allowance Method p. 352

Bad Debt Expense (Doubtful Accounts Expense, Uncollectable Accounts Expense) p. 352

Bank Reconciliation p. 366

Bank Statement p. 365

Cash p. 363

Cash Equivalents p. 363

Completed Contract Method p. 373

Credit Card Discount p. 346

Instalment Method p. 373

Internal Controls p. 361

Note Receivable p. 351

Percentage of Completion Method p. 373

Percentage of Credit Sales Method p. 355

Sales (or Cash) Discount p. 347

Sales Returns and Allowances p. 349

QUESTIONS

1. Explain the difference between sales revenue and net sales.
2. What is gross profit or gross margin on sales? How is the gross profit ratio computed? In your explanation, assume that net sales revenue is $100,000 and cost of goods sold is $60,000.
3. What is a credit card discount? How does it affect amounts reported on the income statement?
4. What is a sales discount? Use credit terms 1/10, n/30 in your explanation.
5. What is the distinction between *sales allowances* and *sales discounts*?
6. Differentiate accounts receivable from notes receivable.
7. Which basic accounting principle is satisfied by using the allowance method of accounting for bad debts?
8. Using the allowance method, is bad debt expense recognized in (a) the period in which sales related to the uncollectable were made or (b) the period in which the seller learns that the customer is unable to pay?
9. What is the effect of the write-off of bad debts (using the allowance method) on (a) net income and (b) accounts receivable, net?
10. Does an increase in the receivables turnover ratio generally indicate faster or slower collection of receivables? Explain.
11. Define *cash* and *cash equivalents* in the context of accounting. Indicate the types of items that should be included.
12. Summarize the primary characteristics of an effective internal control system for cash.
13. Why should cash-handling and cash-recording activities be separated? How is this separation accomplished?
14. What are the purposes of a bank reconciliation? What balances are reconciled?
15. Briefly explain how the total amount of cash reported on the balance sheet is computed.
16. (Chapter Supplement A) Under the gross method of recording sales discounts, is the amount of sales discount taken recorded (a) at the time the sale is recorded or (b) at the time the collection of the account is recorded?
17. (Chapter Supplement B) When is it acceptable to use the percentage of completion method?

MULTIPLE-CHOICE QUESTIONS

1. What is the best description of a *credit card discount*?
   a. The discount offered by a seller to a consumer for using a national credit card such as Visa
   b. The fee charged by a seller to a consumer for the right to use a credit card, calculated as a percentage of the sale price
   c. The discount offered by a seller to a customer for early payment of an account receivable
   d. The percentage fee charged by a credit card company to a seller
2. Sales discounts with terms 2/10, n/30 mean:
   a. 10-percent discount for payment within 30 days.

b. 2-percent discount for payment within 10 days or the full amount (less returns) is due within 30 days.

c. Two-tenths of one percent discount for payment within 30 days.

d. None of the above.

3. A company has been successful in reducing the costs of its manufacturing process by relocating the factory to another locale. What effect will this factor have on the company's gross profit percentage, all other things equal?

a. The percentage will not change.   c. The percentage will decrease.

b. The percentage will increase.   d. It depends on the new location of the factory.

4. Indicate how many of the following statements are true when a company using the allowance method writes off a specific customer's account receivable.

- Total shareholders' equity remains the same.
- Total assets remain the same.
- Total expenses remain the same.

a. none   c. two

b. one   d. three

5. You have determined that Company X estimates bad debt expense with an aging of accounts receivable schedule. Company X's estimate of uncollectable receivables resulting from the aging analysis equals

a. bad debt expense for the current period.

b. the ending balance in the allowance for doubtful accounts at the end of the period.

c. the change in the allowance for doubtful accounts for the period.

d. the amount of receivables written off during the period.

6. Upon review of the most recent bank statement, you discover that you recently received an insufficient funds cheque from a customer. Which of the following describes the actions to be taken when preparing your next bank reconciliation?

Balance per Books	Balance per Bank
a. No change	Decrease
b. Decrease	Increase
c. Decrease	No change
d. Increase	Decrease

7. Which of the following is *not* a step toward effective internal control over cash?

a. Require signatures from a manager and one financial officer on all cheques

b. Require that cash be deposited daily at the bank

c. Require that the person responsible for removing the cash from the register have no access to the accounting records

d. Require only one person to sign cheques

8. When using the allowance method, as bad debt expense is recorded,

a. total assets remain the same and shareholders' equity remains the same.

b. total assets decrease and shareholders' equity decreases.

c. total assets increase and shareholders' equity decreases.

d. total liabilities increase and shareholders' equity decreases.

9. Which of the following best describes the proper presentation of accounts receivable in the financial statements?

a. gross accounts receivable plus the allowance for doubtful accounts in the asset section of the balance sheet

b. gross accounts receivable in the asset section of the balance sheet and the allowance for doubtful accounts in the expense section of the income statement

c. gross accounts receivable less bad debt expense in the asset section of the balance sheet

d. gross accounts receivable less the allowance for doubtful accounts in the asset section of the balance sheet

10. Which of the following is not a component of net sales?

a. sales returns and allowances   c. cost of goods sold

b. sales discounts   d. credit card discounts

For more practice with multiple-choice questions, go to our Web site at www.mcgrawhill.ca/college/libby, click on "Student Edition" in the upper left menu, click on this chapter's name and number from the list of contents, and then click on "Multiple-Choice Quiz" from the menu on the left.

EXERCISES

LO1

E7–1 Interpreting the Revenue Principle

Identify the *most likely* point in time when sales revenue should be recorded for each of the listed transactions.

Transaction	Point A	Point B
a. Airline tickets sold by an airline on a credit card	____ Point of sale	____ Completion of flight
b. Computer sold by mail-order company on a credit card	____ Shipment	____ Delivery to customer
c. Sale of inventory to a business customer on open account	____ Shipment	____ Collection from customers

LO2

E7–2 Reporting Net Sales with Credit Sales and Sales Discounts

During the months of January and February, Bronze Corporation sold goods to three customers. The sequence of events was as follows:

Jan.	6	Sold goods for $1,000 to S. Green and billed that amount subject to terms 2/10, n/30.
	9	Sold goods to M. Munoz for $800 and billed that amount subject to terms 2/10, n/30.
	14	Collected cash due from S. Green.
Feb.	8	Collected cash due from M. Munoz.
	28	Sold goods for $500 to R. Reynolds and billed that amount subject to terms 2/10, n/45.

Required:

Assuming that sales discounts are treated as contra revenues, compute net sales for the two months ended February 28.

LO2

E7–3 Reporting Net Sales with Credit Sales, Sales Discounts, and Credit Card Sales

The following transactions were selected from the records of Evergreen Company:

July	12	Sold merchandise to Rami, who charged the $1,000 purchase on his Visa credit card. Visa charges Evergreen a 2-percent credit card fee.
July	15	Sold merchandise to Steven at an invoice price of $5,000; terms 2/10, n/30.
	20	Sold merchandise to Tania at an invoice price of $3,000; terms 2/10, n/30.
	23	Collected payment from Steven from July 15 sale.
Aug.	25	Collected payment from Tania from July 20 sale.

Required:

Assuming that sales discounts are treated as contra revenues, compute net sales for the two months ended August 31.

LO2

E7–4 Reporting Net Sales with Credit Sales, Sales Discounts, Sales Returns, and Credit Card Sales

The following transactions were selected from among those completed by Hailey Retailers in 2006:

Nov.	20	Sold two items of merchandise to Brigitte, who charged the $400 sales amount on her Visa credit card. Visa charges Hailey a 2-percent credit card fee.
	25	Sold 20 items of merchandise to Clara for $4,000; terms 3/10, n/30.
	28	Sold 10 identical items of merchandise to David for $6,000; terms 3/10, n/30.
Nov.	30	David returned one of the items purchased on the 28th; the item was defective, and credit was given to the customer.
Dec.	6	David paid the account balance in full.
	30	Clara paid in full the amount due for the purchase on November 25, 2006.

Required:

Assume that sales discounts and credit card discounts are treated as contra revenues; compute net sales for the two months ended December 31, 2006.

E7–5 Determining the Effects of Credit Sales, Sales Discounts, Credit Card Sales, and Sales Returns and Allowances on Income Statement Categories ■ **LO2**

Rockland Shoe Company records sales returns and allowances as contra revenues, and sales discounts and credit card discounts as selling expenses. Complete the following tabulation, indicating the effect (+ for increase, − for decrease, and NE for no effect) of each transaction. Do not record the related cost of goods sold.

July 12 Sold merchandise to Rosa, who charged the $300 purchase on her American Express card. American Express charges a 3-percent credit card fee.
July 15 Sold merchandise to Thomas for $5,000; terms 2/10, n/30.
July 20 Collected the amount due from Thomas.
July 21 Lee returned shoes with an invoice price of $1,000, before paying for them.

Transaction	Net Sales	Gross Profit	Income from Operations
July 12			
July 15			
July 20			
July 21			

E7–6 Evaluating the Effects of Sales Returns and Allowances on Sales ■ **LO2**

Teen World, Inc. sells a wide selection of clothing items for teenage girls. The company imports merchandise from various international suppliers, and distributes its merchandise to retail stores in major shopping areas. The company sells merchandise on credit, allows retailers to return incorrect or damaged merchandise within a period of two months, and grants them sales allowances under certain circumstances. The company is currently reviewing its sales returns policy and provided you with the following information for the past six quarters:

Quarter	Gross Sales	Cost of Sales	Sales Returns and Allowances
Jan. 1–March 31, 2006	$1,346,300	$ 942,400	$ 53,852
April 1–June 30, 2006	1,474,500	1,042,100	76,674
July 1–Sept. 30, 2006	1,529,100	1,080,300	94,804
Oct. 1–Dec. 31, 2006	1,671,400	1,101,200	140,397
Jan. 1–March 31, 2007	1,708,800	1,103,600	153,792
April 1–June 30, 2007	1,992,700	$1,317,500	219,197

Required:

1. Compute the following percentages for each of the six quarters: (1) cost of sales to net sales, and (2) sales return and allowances to gross sales.

2. Comment on the ratios computed in requirement 1 and identify possible reasons for the increase in the amount of sales returns and allowances as well as your recommendations for controlling the amount of sales returns and allowances.

E7–7 Analyzing Gross Profit Percentage on the Basis of a Multiple-Step Income Statement ■ **LO3**

The following summarized data were provided by the records of Slate, Inc., for the year ended December 31, 2006:

Sales of merchandise for cash	$220,000
Sales of merchandise on credit	32,000
Cost of goods sold	147,000
Selling expense	40,200
Administrative expense	19,000
Sales returns and allowances	7,000
Items not included in the above amounts:	
Estimated bad debt, 2.5% of credit sales	
Average income tax rate, 30%	
Number of common shares outstanding, 5,000	

Required:

1. Based on these data, prepare a multiple-step income statement (showing both gross profit and income from operations). Include a Percentage Analysis column.

2. What was the amount of gross profit? What was the gross profit percentage? Explain what these two numbers mean.

■ **LO3**

Wolverine
World Wide

E7–8   Analyzing Gross Profit Percentage on the Basis of a Multiple-Step Income Statement and Within-Industry Comparison

Wolverine World Wide Inc. prides itself as being the "world's leading marketer of U.S. branded non-athletic footwear." The following data were taken from a recent annual report (in thousands):

Sales of merchandise	$413,957
Income taxes	10,047
Cash dividends declared	2,347
Selling and administrative expense	85,993
Cost of products sold	290,469
Interest expense	3,678
Other income	297
Number of common shares outstanding	17,114

Required:

1. Based on these data, prepare a multiple-step income statement for the year (showing both gross profit and income from operations). Include a Percentage Analysis column.

2. How much was the gross profit? What was the gross profit percentage? Explain what these two numbers mean.

■ **LO4**

E7–9   Comparing Two Methods of Estimating Bad Debts

Kwan Ltd. earned $328,000 in credit sales during its first year of operation. At year end, it had $79,636 in accounts receivable and estimated that 2.5 percent of its credit sales may not be collectible in the future.

Required:

1. Compute the balance of the Allowance for Doubtful Accounts at year end.

2. Assume that the company's estimate of uncollectible accounts was based on the balance of accounts receivable at a rate of 10 percent. Compute the balance of the Allowance for Doubtful Accounts at year end.

3. What are the main differences between the two methods of estimating bad debt expense?

■ **LO4**

E7–10   Recording and Determining the Effects of Bad Debt Transactions on Income Statement Categories

During 2005, Choi and Goldstein Furniture recorded credit sales of $650,000. Based on prior experience, the company estimates that the bad debt rate is 2 percent of credit sales.

Required:

1. Prepare journal entries to record the following transactions:
   a. The appropriate bad debt expense adjustment was recorded for the year 2005.
   b. On December 31, 2005, an account receivable for $1,600 from a prior year was determined to be uncollectable and was written off.

2. Complete the following tabulation, indicating the amount and effect (+ for increase, − for decrease, and NE for no effect) of each transaction.

Transaction	Net Sales	Gross Profit	Income from Operations
a.			
b.			

E7–11   Interpreting Bad Debt Disclosures

■ **LO4**

DaimlerChrysler AG

DaimlerChrysler is the largest industrial group headquartered in Germany. Best known as the manufacturer of Mercedes-Benz and Chrysler cars and trucks, it also manufactures products in the fields of rail systems, aerospace, propulsion, defence, and information technology. In a recent filing pursuant to its listing on the New York Stock Exchange, it disclosed the following information concerning its allowance for doubtful accounts (in millions of euros, denoted €):

Balance at Beginning of Period	Charged to Costs and Expenses	Amounts Written Off	Balance at End of Period
587	49	(160)	476

Required:

1. Record summary journal entries related to bad debts for the current year.

2. If DaimlerChrysler had written off an additional €10 million of accounts receivable during the period, how would net receivables and net income have been affected? Explain.

E7–12   Inferring Bad Debt Write-Offs and Cash Collections from Customers

■ **LO4**

Microsoft

Microsoft develops, produces, and markets a wide range of computer software including the Windows operating system. On a recent balance sheet, Microsoft reported the following information about accounts receivable and net sales revenue.

	Year 2	Year 1
Accounts receivable, net of allowances of $166 and $242	$ 5,890	$ 5,196
Net revenues	36,835	32,187

According to its annual report, Microsoft recorded bad debt expense of $120 and did not reinstate any previously written-off accounts during year 2.

Required:

1. What amount of bad debts was written off during year 2?

2. Assuming that all of Microsoft's sales during the period were on open account, compute the amount of cash collected from customers for year 2.

E7–13   Determining the Impact of Uncollectable Accounts on Income and Working Capital

■ **LO4**

Sears

An annual report for Sears contained the following information at the end of its fiscal year (in millions of dollars):

	Year 2	Year 1
Credit card receivable	$32,595	$29,321
Allowance for uncollectable accounts	(1,836)	(1,166)
	$30,759	$28,155

A footnote to the financial statements disclosed that uncollectable accounts amounting to $1,289 million were written off as bad during year 1 and $1,591 million during year 2. Assume that the tax rate for Sears was 30 percent.

Required:

1. Determine the bad debt expense for year 2 based on the preceding facts.

2. *Working capital* is defined as current assets minus current liabilities. How was Sears's working capital affected by the write-off of $1,591 million in uncollectable accounts during year 2? What impact did the recording of bad debt expense have on working capital in year 2?

3. How was net income affected by the $1,591 million write-off during year 2? What impact did recording bad debt expense have on net income for year 2?

■ **LO4**

E7–14   Computing Bad Debt Expense Using Aging Analysis

Brown Cow Dairy uses the aging approach to estimate bad debt expense. The balance of each account receivable is aged on the basis of three time periods as follows: (1) not yet due, $24,000; (2) up to 120 days past due, $10,000; and (3) more than 120 days past due, $6,000. Experience has shown that for each age group, the average bad debt rates on the amount of the receivable at year-end due to uncollectability are (1) 2 percent, (2) 10 percent, and (3) 30 percent, respectively. At December 31, 2006 (end of the current year), the Allowance for Doubtful Accounts balance was $600 (credit) before the end-of-period adjusting entry is made.

Required:

What amount should be recorded as bad debt expense for the current year?

■ **LO4**

E7–15   Recording, Reporting, and Evaluating a Bad Debt Estimate

Connor Company started business on January 1, 2005. During the year, the company's records indicated the following:

Sales on cash basis	$400,000
Sales on credit basis	150,000
Collections on accounts receivable	100,000

The company's manager is concerned about accounting for bad debts. At December 31, 2005, although no accounts were considered bad, several customers were considerably late in paying their accounts. A friend of the manager suggested a 1-percent bad debt rate on sales, which the manager decided to use at the start.

Required:

1. You have been employed on a part-time basis to assist with the company's record keeping. The manager told you to set up bad debt expense of $5,500. Prepare the required journal entry.

2. You are concerned about how the $5,500 was determined. The manager told you the figure was provided by another manager "who knew his business" and used 1 percent of sales. Do you agree with the estimate of bad debts? If you disagree, prepare the correct journal entry and explain the basis for your disagreement.

3. Show how the various accounts related to credit sales should be shown on the company's income statement for 2005 and its balance sheet at December 31, 2005.

■ **LO4**

E7–16   Recording, Reporting, and Evaluating a Bad Debt Estimate

During 2007, Gauthier's Camera Shop had sales revenue of $170,000, of which $85,000 was on credit. At the start of 2007, Accounts Receivable showed a $10,000 debit balance, and the Allowance for Doubtful Accounts showed a credit balance of $800. Collections of accounts receivable during 2007 amounted to $68,000. On December 31, 2007, an Account Receivable (J. Doe) of $1,500 from a prior year was determined to be uncollectable; therefore, it was written off immediately as a bad debt. On the basis of experience, a decision was made to continue the accounting policy of basing estimated bad debt at 2 percent of credit sales for the year.

Required:

1. Prepare the required journal entries on December 31, 2007 (end of the accounting period).

2. Show how the amounts related to Bad Debt Expense and Accounts Receivable would be reported on the income statement for 2007 and the balance sheet at December 31, 2007. Disregard income tax considerations.

3. On the basis of the data available, does the 2-percent rate appear to be reasonable? Explain.

4. There are two alternative methods that can be used to determine the amount of bad debt expense for the year. Do you have a preference for either of these methods? Explain.

E7–17 **Analyzing and Interpreting the Receivables Turnover Ratio**

An annual report for Federal Express contained the following data:

	(in millions)	
	Current Year	Previous Year
Accounts receivable	$ 3,178	$2,776
Less: Allowance for doubtful accounts	151	149
Net accounts receivable	$ 3,027	$2,627
Net sales (assume all on credit)	$24,710	

Required:

1. Determine the accounts receivable turnover ratio and average age of receivables for the current year.

2. Explain the meaning of the number that you calculated in requirement 1.

E7–18 **Determining the Effects of Bad Debts on the Receivables Turnover Ratio**

During 2005, Leung Enterprises Corporation recorded credit sales of $650,000. Based on prior experience, it estimates a 1-percent bad debt rate on credit sales. At the beginning of the year, the balance in Net Trade Accounts Receivable was $50,000. At the end of the year, the balance in Net Trade Accounts Receivable was $55,500 *before* the bad debt expense was recorded and *before* any bad debts had been written off.

Required:

1. Assume that on December 31, 2005, the appropriate bad debt expense was recorded for the year 2005 and accounts receivable totalling $6,000 for the year were determined to be uncollectable and written off. What was the receivables turnover ratio for 2005?

2. Assume instead that on December 31, 2005, the appropriate bad debt expense was recorded for the year 2005 and $7,000 of accounts receivable was determined to be uncollectable and written off. What was the receivables turnover ratio for 2005?

3. Explain why the answers to requirements 1 and 2 differ or do not differ.

E7–19 **Comparing Receivables Turnover Ratios of Two Companies**

The net sales and average balances of accounts receivable for Air Canada and WestJet Airlines for a recent fiscal year are shown below (in millions of dollars):

	Average Accounts Receivable	Sales
Air Canada	$600	$8,368
WestJet Airlines	16	859

Required:

1. Compute the following for each company:
   a. The receivable turnover ratio.
   b. The average collection period.

2. Based on your computations for requirement 1, which company's accounts receivable appear to be the more "liquid" asset? Explain.

E7–20 **Interpreting the Effects of Sales Growth and Changes in Receivables on Cash Flow from Operations**

Nike, Inc. is the best-known sports apparel and equipment company in the world. Three recent years produced a combination of dramatic increases in sales revenue and net income. Cash flows from operations declined during the period, however. Contributing to that declining cash flow was the change in accounts receivable. The current and prior year balance sheets reported the following:

	(in millions)	
	Current Year	Previous Year
Accounts receivable, less allowance for doubtful accounts	$2,120	$2,083

Required:

1. How would the change in accounts receivable affect cash flow from operations for the current year? Explain why it would have this effect.

2. Explain how increasing sales revenue often leads to (a) increasing accounts receivable and (b) an excess of sales revenue over collections from customers.

◼ LO6   **E7–21   Identifying Strengths and Weaknesses of Internal Control**

You have been engaged to review the internal control procedures used by Data Flow Inc. During the course of your review, you note the following practices:

a. The credit manager maintains the accounts receivable records and handles all collections from customers, because the accounting department personnel are not authorized to handle cash receipts.

b. All cash received from customers is deposited daily in the company's bank account.

c. Employees who handle cash receipts are not permitted to write off accounts receivable as uncollectable.

d. Invoices that require payment are first verified by the accounting personnel for accuracy. An accounting clerk stamps them "paid" if they are cleared for payment and sends them to the treasurer, who issues and signs the cheques.

e. The cheques issued by the company treasurer are not pre-numbered.

f. After preparing the bank reconciliation, any difference between the adjusted cash balance per the company's books and the adjusted balance per the bank statement is debited (or credited) to the Cash account.

Required:

Indicate whether each of these six practices reflects a strength or a weakness of the internal control system. Provide justification for your answer.

◼ LO6   **E7–22   Reporting Cash and Cash Equivalents When There Are Several Bank Accounts**

Singh Corporation has manufacturing facilities in several cities and has cash on hand at several locations as well as in several bank accounts. The general ledger at the end of 2005 showed the following accounts:

Cash on Hand—Home Office	$ 700	Cash on Hand—Location C	200
City Bank—Home Office	58,600	National Bank—Location C	965
Cash on Hand—Location A	100	Petty Cash Fund	300
National Bank—Location A	3,350	Credit Suisse—3-month Certificate	
Cash on Hand—Location B	200	of Deposit	5,800
National Bank—Location B	785	FransaBank—6-month Certificate	
		of Deposit	4,500

The bank balances given represent the current cash balances as reflected on the bank reconciliations.

Required:

What amount of cash and cash equivalents should be reported on the company's 2005 balance sheet? Explain the basis for your decisions on any questionable items.

◼ LO6   **E7–23   Preparing Bank Reconciliation, Entries, and Reporting**

The June 30, 2006, bank statement for Zoltan Company and the June ledger accounts for cash are summarized below:

Bank Statement			
	Cheques	Deposits	Balance
Balance, June 1, 2006			$ 7,200
Deposits during June		$17,000	24,200
Cheques cleared through June	$18,100		6,100
Bank service charges	50		6,050
Balance, June 30, 2006			6,050

Cash in Bank					
June 1	Balance	6,800	June	Cheques written	18,400
June	Deposits	19,000			

Cash on hand		
June 30 Balance	300	

Required:

1. Reconcile the bank balance to the book balance at June 30, 2006. A comparison of the cheques written with the cheques that have cleared the bank shows outstanding cheques of $700. Some of the cheques that cleared in June were written prior to June. No deposits in transit were carried over from May, but a deposit is in transit at the end of June.

2. Prepare any journal entries that should be made as a result of the bank reconciliation.

3. What is the balance in the Cash account after the reconciliation entries?

4. What is the total amount of cash that should be reported on the balance sheet at June 30, 2006?

E7–24 Preparing Bank Reconciliation, Entries, and Reporting   ■ **LO6**

The September 30, 2008, bank statement for Russell Company and the September ledger accounts for cash are summarized here:

Bank Statement			
	Cheques	Deposits	Balance
Balance, September 1, 2008			$ 6,300
Deposits recorded during September		$27,000	33,300
Cheques cleared during September	$28,500		4,800
NSF cheque—Betty Brown	150		4,650
Bank service charges	50		4,600
Balance, September 30, 2008			4,600

Cash					
Sept 1	Balance	6,300	Sept.	Cheques written	28,600
Sept.	Deposits	28,000			

Cash on hand		
Sept 30 Balance	400	

No outstanding cheques and no deposits in transit were carried over from August; however, there are deposits in transit and cheques outstanding at the end of September.

Required:

1. Reconcile the balance in the bank account with the cash balance in the books at September 30, 2008.

2. Prepare any journal entries that should be made as a result of the bank reconciliation.

3. What should be the balance in the Cash account after the reconciliation entries?

4. What total amount of cash should the company report on the balance sheet at September 30, 2008?

E7–25 Recording Credit Sales, Sales Discounts, Sales Returns, and Credit Card Sales (Supplement A)

The following transactions were selected from among those completed by Hailey Retailers in 2006:

Nov. 20   Sold two items of merchandise to Baja, who charged the $400 sales amount on her Visa credit card. Visa charges Hailey a 2-percent credit card fee.

25   Sold 20 items of merchandise to Christine for $4,000; terms 2/10, n/30.

28   Sold 10 identical items of merchandise to Daoud for $6,000; terms 2/10, n/30.

30   Daoud returned one of the items purchased on the 28th; the item was defective, and credit was given to the customer.

Dec. 6   Daoud paid the account balance in full.

30   Christine paid in full the amount due for the purchase on November 25, 2006.

Required:

Prepare the appropriate journal entry for each of these transactions, assuming the company uses the gross method to record sales revenue. Do not record the cost of goods sold.

E7–26 Determining Income Using the Percentage of Completion Method (Supplement B)

Blanchard Construction Company entered into a long-term construction contract with the government to build a special landing strip at an Air Force base in Saint Hubert, Québec. The project took three years and cost the government $12 million. Blanchard spent the following amounts each year: 2005, $2 million; 2006, $5 million; 2007, $3 million. The company uses the percentage of completion method. Cost estimates equalled actual costs.

Required:

Determine the amount of net income that Blanchard can report each year for this project. Ignore income taxes.

PROBLEMS

LO1

P7–1 Applying the Revenue Principle (AP7–1)

At what point should revenue be recognized in each of the following independent cases? Explain your answers.

Case A. For December holiday presents, a fast-food restaurant sells coupon books for $10. Each of the $1 coupons may be used in the restaurant at any time during the following 12 months. The customer must pay cash when purchasing the coupon book.

Case B. Howard Land Development Corporation sold a lot to Quality Builders to construct a new home. The price of the lot was $50,000. Quality made a down payment of $10,000 and agreed to pay the balance in six months. After making the sale, Howard learned that Quality Builders often entered into these agreements but refused to pay the balance if it did not find a customer who wanted a house built on the lot.

Case C. Driscoll Corporation has always recorded revenue at the point of sale of its refrigerators. Recently, it has extended its warranties to cover all repairs for a period of seven years. One young accountant with the company now questions whether Driscoll has completed its earning process when it sells the refrigerators. She suggests that the warranty obligation for seven years means that a significant amount of additional work must be performed in the future.

LO2, 4

P7–2 Reporting Net Sales and Expenses with Discounts, Returns, and Bad Debts (AP7–2)

The following data were selected from the records of May Company for the year ended December 31, 2007.

Balances January 1, 2007	
Accounts receivable (various customers)	$110,000
Allowance for doubtful accounts	5,000

The company sells merchandise for cash and on open account with credit terms 2/10, n/30. Assume a unit sales price of $500 in all transactions, and use the gross method to record sales revenue.

Transactions during 2007

a. Sold merchandise for cash, $225,000.

b. Sold merchandise to R. Agostino; invoice amount, $12,000.

c. Sold merchandise to K. Black; invoice amount, $26,000.

d. Two days after purchase, R. Agostino returned one of the units purchased in (b) and received account credit.

e. Sold merchandise to B. Assaf; invoice amount, $24,000.

f. R. Agostino paid his account in full within the discount period.

g. Collected $98,000 cash from customers for credit sales made in 2006, all within the discount periods.

h. K. Black paid the invoice in (c) within the discount period.

i. Sold merchandise to R. Fong; invoice amount, $17,000.

j. Three days after paying the account in full, K. Black returned seven defective units and received a cash refund.

k. After the discount period, collected $7,000 cash on an account receivable on sales made in 2006.

l. Wrote off an old account of $2,900 after deciding that the amount would never be collected.

m. The estimated bad debt rate used by the company was 1 percent of credit sales net of returns.

Required:

1. Using the following categories, indicate the dollar effect (increase, decrease, no effect) of each listed transaction, including the write-off of the uncollectable account and the adjusting entry for estimated bad debts (ignore cost of goods sold).

Sales Revenue	Sales Discounts (taken)	Sales Returns and Allowances	Bad Debt Expense

2. Show how the accounts related to the preceding sale and collection activities should be reported on the income statement for 2007. (Treat sales discounts as contra revenues.)

P7–3 Understanding the Income Statement Based on the Gross Profit Percentage
The following data were taken from the year-end records of Nomura Export Company.

■ LO3

Income Statement Items	Independent Cases	
	Case A	Case B
Gross sales revenue	$160,000	$232,000
Sales returns and allowances	?	18,000
Net sales revenue	?	?
Cost of goods sold	68%	?
Gross profit	?	30%
Operating expenses	18,500	?
Income before income taxes	?	20,000
Income tax expense (20%)	?	?
Income before extraordinary items	?	?
Extraordinary items, net of tax	8,000 (gain)	1,600 (loss)
Net income	?	?
EPS (10,000 shares outstanding)	3.00	?

Required:
Fill in all of the missing amounts. Show computations.

P7–4 Interpreting Disclosure of Allowance for Doubtful Accounts (AP7–3)
Kimberly-Clark manufactures and markets a variety of paper and synthetic fibre products, including well-known Kleenex tissues. It recently disclosed the following information concerning the allowance for doubtful accounts in its annual report.

■ LO4

Kimberly-Clark

SCHEDULE VIII
Valuation and Qualifying Accounts
For the Years Ended December 31, 2003, 2002, and 2001
(millions of dollars)

Description: Allowances for Doubtful Accounts	Balance at Beginning of Period	Charged to Costs and Expenses	Charged to Other Accounts*	Write-Offs	Balance at End of Period
December 31, 2003	$48.4	$11.9	$6.5	$18.9	$47.9
December 31, 2002	49.8	10.4	0	?	48.4
December 31, 2001	53.2	?	3.1	18.5	49.8

*These are primarily bad debt recoveries. *Hint:* These require a reversal of the previous entry made when they were written off.

Required:

1. Record summary journal entries related to bad debts for 2003.
2. Supply the missing dollar amounts noted by (?) for 2001 and 2002.

■ **LO4**

P7–5   Determining Bad Debt Expense Based on Aging Analysis (AP7–4)

Green Pastures Equipment Company uses the aging approach to estimate bad debt expense at the end of each accounting year. Credit sales occur frequently on terms n/60. The balance of each account receivable is aged on the basis of three time periods as follows: (1) not yet due, (2) up to one year past due, and (3) more than one year past due. Experience has shown that for each age group, the average bad debt rate on the amounts receivable at year-end due to uncollectability are (a) 1 percent, (b) 5 percent, and (c) 30 percent, respectively.

At December 31, 2006 (end of the current accounting year), the Accounts Receivable balance was $41,000, and the unadjusted balance of the Allowance for Doubtful Accounts was $1,020 (credit). To simplify, the accounts of only five customers are used; the details of each follow:

B. Brown—Account Receivable

Date	Explanation	Debit	Credit	Balance
3/11/2005	Sale	14,000		14,000
6/30/2005	Collection		5,000	9,000
1/31/2006	Collection		4,000	5,000

D. Di Lella—Account Receivable

Date	Explanation	Debit	Credit	Balance
2/28/2006	Sale	22,000		22,000
4/15/2006	Collection		10,000	12,000
11/30/2006	Collection		8,000	4,000

N. Gidda—Account Receivable

Date	Explanation	Debit	Credit	Balance
11/30/2006	Sale	9,000		9,000
12/15/2006	Collection		2,000	7,000

S. Kavouris—Account Receivable

Date	Explanation	Debit	Credit	Balance
3/2/2004	Sale	5,000		5,000
4/15/2004	Collection		5,000	0
9/1/2005	Sale	10,000		10,000
10/15/2005	Collection		8,000	2,000
2/1/2006	Sale	19,000		21,000
3/1/2006	Collection		5,000	16,000
12/31/2006	Sale	3,000		19,000

T. Patel—Account Receivable

Date	Explanation	Debit	Credit	Balance
12/30/2006	Sale	6,000		6,000

Required:

1. Prepare an aging analysis schedule and complete it.
2. Compute the estimated uncollectable amount for each age category and in total.
3. Prepare the adjusting entry for bad debt expense at December 31, 2006.

4. Show how the amounts related to accounts receivable should be presented on the income statement for 2006 and the balance sheet at December 31, 2006.

P7–6 Determining Bad Debts and Reporting Accounts Receivable   ■ **LO4**

The bookkeeper of Vital Inc. has asked you to assist him with the preparation of information about the company's accounts receivable for presentation in the financial statements at December 31, 2006, the end of the company's fiscal year. The following details have been extracted from the company's files.

	Debit	Credit
Accounts Receivable, January 1, 2006	$500,000	
Allowance for Doubtful Accounts, January 1, 2006		$35,000

Sales for 2006 totalled $1,300,000; $300,000 were in cash and the rest on account. The company collected $800,000 from credit customers during 2006, and wrote off $40,000 of accounts receivable as uncollectable.

Required:

1. Determine the balance of Accounts Receivable at December 31, 2006.
2. Vital uses the balance sheet method to estimate the net realizable value of accounts receivable at year end, and estimates that 6 percent of the ending balance of its accounts receivable may not be collected in the future. Prepare the journal entries to record the write-off of accounts receivable and the bad debt expense for 2006.
3. Show how the information related to accounts receivable is presented on the company's balance sheet as at December 31, 2006.
4. After you finished helping the bookkeeper with the journal entries and the balance sheet presentation, he said: "These calculations seem to be complicated. Would it not be simpler to treat the $40,000 as bad debt expense when the company is certain that the customers are not able to pay the amount owed? That way, you record the exact amount of bad debt when it happens, and you do not have to estimate an amount of doubtful accounts and risk being incorrect." Prepare a response to the bookkeeper.

P7–7 Preparing a Multiple-Step Income Statement and Computing the Gross Profit   ■ **LO2, 3, 4**
Percentage with Discounts, Returns, and Bad Debts (AP7–5)

Builders Company, Inc., sells heavy construction equipment. It has 10,000 common shares outstanding and its fiscal year ends on December 31. The adjusted trial balance was taken from the general ledger on December 31, 2006.

Account Titles	Debit	Credit
Cash	$ 42,000	
Accounts receivable	18,000	
Inventory, ending	65,000	
Long-term assets	51,000	
Accumulated amortization		$ 21,000
Liabilities		30,000
Common shares		90,000
Retained earnings, January 1, 2006		11,600
Sales revenue		182,000
Sales returns and allowances	5,000	
Cost of goods sold	98,000	
Selling expenses	17,000	
Administrative expenses	18,000	
Bad debt expense	3,000	
Sales discounts	8,000	
Income tax expense	9,600	
Totals	$334,600	$334,600

Required:

1. Beginning with net sales, prepare a multiple-step income statement (showing both gross profit and income from operations). Treat sales discounts as contra revenues.
2. Compute the gross profit percentage and explain its meaning.

■ **LO6**

P7–8 Evaluating Internal Controls

Cripple Creek Company has one trusted employee who, as the owner said, "handles all of the bookkeeping and paperwork for the company." This employee is responsible for counting, verifying, and recording cash receipts and payments, making the weekly bank deposit, preparing cheques for major expenditures (signed by the owner), making small expenditures from the cash register for daily expenses, and collecting accounts receivable. The owner asked the local bank for a $20,000 loan. The bank asked that an audit be performed covering the year just ended. The independent auditor, in a private conference with the owner, presented some evidence of the following activities of the trusted employee during the past year:

a. Cash sales sometimes were not entered in the cash register, and the trusted employee pocketed approximately $50 per month.

b. Cash taken from the cash register (and pocketed by the trusted employee) was replaced with expense memos with fictitious signatures (approximately $12 per day). Cripple Creek is open five days per week throughout the year.

c. A $300 collection on an account receivable of a valued out-of-town customer was pocketed by the trusted employee and was covered by making a $300 entry as a debit to Sales Returns and a credit to Accounts Receivable.

d. An $800 collection on an account receivable from a local customer was pocketed by the trusted employee and was covered by making an $800 entry as a debit to Allowance for Doubtful Accounts and a credit to Accounts Receivable.

Required:

1. What was the approximate amount stolen during the past year?
2. What would be your recommendations to the owner about the company's internal controls?

■ **LO6**

P7–9 Preparing a Bank Reconciliation and Related Journal Entries (AP7–6)

The bookkeeper at Hopkins Company has not reconciled the bank statement with the Cash account, saying, "I don't have time." You have been asked to prepare a reconciliation and review the procedures with the bookkeeper.

The April 30, 2007, bank statement and the April ledger accounts for cash showed the following (summarized):

	Bank Statement		
	Cheques	Deposits	Balance
Balance, April 1, 2007			$25,850
Deposits during April		$36,000	61,850
Notes collected for company (including $70 interest)		1,070	62,920
Cheques cleared during April	$44,200		18,720
NSF cheque—A. B. Wright	140		18,580
Bank service charges	50		18,530
Balance, April 30, 2004			18,530

Cash in Bank					
Apr. 1	Balance	23,250	Apr.	Cheques written	43,800
Apr.	Deposits	42,000			

Cash on hand		
Apr. 30	Balance	100

A comparison of cheques written before and during April with the cheques cleared through the bank showed that cheques of $2,200 are still outstanding at April 30. No deposits in transit were carried over from March, but a deposit was in transit at April 30.

Required:

1. Prepare a detailed bank reconciliation at April 30, 2007.
2. Prepare any required journal entries as a result of the reconciliation. Why are they necessary?
3. What were the balances in the cash accounts in the ledger on May 1, 2007?
4. What total amount of cash should be reported on the balance sheet at April 30, 2007?

P7–10 Computing Outstanding Cheques and Deposits in Transit and Preparing a Bank Reconciliation and Journal Entries

■ **LO6**

The August 2005 bank statement for Martha Company and the August 2005 ledger accounts for cash follow:

PB Provincial Bank		STATEMENT OF ACCOUNT			
594 Water Street					
Faubourg, ON					
L2G 4S6					

DATE	BRANCH NUMBER	ACCOUNT TYPE	ACCOUNT NUMBER	PAGE NO.
31 08 2005	815	Chequing	85157	1 OF 1

Martha Company
2784, 7th Avenue
Faubourg, ON
L3G 3B5

Date	Description	Debits	Credits	Balance
Aug. 1	Balance Forward			17,470
2	Cheque No. 103	300		17,170
3	Deposit		12,000	29,170
4	Cheque No. 101	400		28,770
5	Cheque No. 105	250		28,520
9	Cheque No. 102	900		27,620
10	Cheque No. 104	300		27,320
15	Deposit		4,000	31,320
21	Cheque No. 106	400		30,920
24	Cheque No. 108	21,000		9,920
25	Deposit		7,000	16,920
30	Cheque No. 109	800		16,120
30	Collection of note		2,180	18,300
30	Service charge	10		18,290
31	Interest earned		80	18,370

The amount collected on August 30 includes interest of $180.

Cash in Bank

Aug. 1 Balance	16,520	Cheques written		
Deposits		Aug. 2		300
Aug. 2	12,000	4		900
12	4,000	15		290
24	7,000	17		550
31	5,000	18		800
		20		400
		23		21,000

Cash on hand

Aug. 31 Balance	200

Outstanding cheques at the end of July were for $250, $400, and $300. No deposits were in transit at the end of July.

Required:

1. Compute the amount of deposits in transit at August 31, 2005.

2. Compute the amount of outstanding cheques at August 31, 2005.

3. Prepare a bank reconciliation at August 31, 2005.

4. Prepare any journal entries that the company should make as a result of the bank reconciliation. Why are they necessary?

5. After the reconciliation journal entries are posted, what balances would be reflected in the cash accounts in the ledger?

6. What total amount of cash should be reported on the August 31, 2005, balance sheet?

ALTERNATE PROBLEMS

AP7–1 Applying the Revenue Principle

■ **LO1**

Review the revenue recognition practices of the following companies, and indicate at what point in time revenue should be recognized in each of these independent cases. Explain your answer.

Case A. The sales representatives of Computec Corporation are under intense pressure to achieve very high sales levels. To achieve their specific objectives, the sales representatives ask customers to order computer equipment in advance with payment to be made later. In many cases, the company records sales on the basis of customers' orders, even though the ordered equipment may have not been manufactured yet.

Case B. Scenic Trails, Inc. is a campground operator that sells annual memberships to interested campers. Members are allowed to pay the annual memberships fees over a period of six months. The company records revenue from membership fees as soon as a new member signs the membership agreement. Members are allowed 10 days to cancel their memberships and many members cancel their memberships within days of signing.

Case C. Educational Toys, Inc. sells a wide variety of toys to distributors and allows them to return unsold merchandise within a period of three months. The company's policy encourages distributors to buy products and keep them for three months knowing they could return any unsold merchandise during this period. The company recognizes revenue as soon as it delivers its products to distributors.

■ **LO2, 4** **AP7–2** **Reporting Net Sales and Expenses with Discounts, Returns, and Bad Debts** (P7–2)
The following data were selected from the records of Fluwars Company for the year ended December 31, 2006.

> Balances January 1, 2006:
> Accounts receivable (various customers) $103,000
> Allowance for doubtful accounts   6,000

The company sold merchandise for cash and on open account with credit terms 1/10, n/30. Assume a unit sales price of $400 in all transactions and use the gross method to record sales revenue.

Transactions during 2006

a. Sold merchandise for cash, $118,000.

b. Sold merchandise to Abbey Corp; invoice amount, $6,800.

c. Sold merchandise to Brown Company; invoice amount, $14,000.

d. Abbey paid the invoice in (b) within the discount period.

e. Sold merchandise to Cavendish Inc; invoice amount, $12,400.

f. Two days after paying the account in full, Abbey returned four defective units and received a cash refund.

g. Collected $99,000 cash from customers for credit sales made in 2005, all within the discount periods.

h. Three days after the purchase date, Brown returned two of the units purchased in (c) and received account credit.

i. Brown paid its account in full within the discount period.

j. Sold merchandise to Decca Corporation; invoice amount, $9,000.

k. Cavendish paid its account in full after the discount period.

l. Wrote off an old account of $1,600 after deciding that the amount would never be collected.

m. The estimated bad debt rate used by the company was 2 percent of credit sales net of returns.

Required:

1. Using the following categories, indicate the dollar effect (increase, decrease, no effect) of each listed transaction, including the write-off of the uncollectable account and the adjusting entry for estimated bad debts (ignore the cost of goods sold).

Sales Revenue	Sales Discounts (taken)	Sales Returns and Allowances	Bad Debt Expense

2. Show how the accounts related to the preceding sale and collection activities should be reported on the income statement for 2006. (Treat sales discounts as contra revenues.)

AP7–3 Interpreting Disclosure of Allowance for Doubtful Accounts (P7–4)

■ **LO4**

Dell Computer Corporation is the leading direct-sales computer systems company and a provider of products and services for customers to build their information technology and Internet infrastructures. Dell recently disclosed the following information concerning the allowance for doubtful accounts in its annual report:

Dell Computer

| **SCHEDULE II** **VALUATION AND QUALIFYING ACCOUNTS** **(dollars in millions)** | | | | | |
Fiscal Year	Description	Balance at Beginning of Period	Charged to Bad Debt Expense	Write-Offs Charged to Allowance	Balance at End of Period
Year 3	Allowance for doubtful accounts	$71	$48	$35	?
Year 2	Allowance for doubtful accounts	68	?	36	$71
Year 1	Allowance for doubtful accounts	69	39	?	68

Required:

1. Record summary journal entries related to bad debts for year 1.

2. Supply the missing dollar amounts noted by (?) for year 2, year 3, and year 4.

AP7–4 Determining Bad Debt Expense Based on Aging Analysis (P7–5)

■ **LO4**

Briggs & Stratton Engines Inc. uses the aging approach to estimate bad debt expense at the end of each fiscal year. Credit sales occur frequently on terms n/45. The balance of each account receivable is aged on the basis of four time periods as follows: (1) not yet due, (2) up to 6 months past due, (3) 6 to 12 months past due, and (4) more than one year past due. Experience has shown that for each age group, the average bad debt rate on the amounts receivable at year-end due to uncollectability is (a) 1 percent, (b) 5 percent, (c) 20 percent, and (d) 50 percent, respectively.

At December 31, 2006 (end of the current fiscal year), the Accounts Receivable balance was $39,500, and the Allowance for Doubtful Accounts balance was $1,550 (debit). To simplify, the accounts of only five customers are used; the details of each follow:

Date	Explanation	Debit	Credit	Balance
	R. Aouad—Account Receivable			
3/13/2006	Sale	19,000		19,000
5/12/2006	Collection		10,000	9,000
9/30/2006	Collection		7,000	2,000
	C. Chronis—Account Receivable			
06/01/2005	Sale	31,000		31,000
11/01/2005	Collection		20,000	11,000
12/01/2006	Collection		5,000	6,000
	D. McClain—Account Receivable			
10/31/2006	Sale	12,000		12,000
12/10/2006	Collection		8,000	4,000
	T. Skibinski—Account Receivable			
05/02/2006	Sale	15,000		15,000
06/01/2006	Sale	10,000		25,000
06/15/2006	Collection		15,000	10,000
07/15/2006	Collection		10,000	0
10/01/2006	Sale	26,000		26,000
11/15/2006	Collection		16,000	10,000
12/15/2006	Sale	4,500		14,500
	H. Wu—Account Receivable			
12/30/2006	Sale	13,000		13,000

Required:

1. Set up an aging analysis schedule and complete it.

2. Compute the estimated uncollectable amount for each age category and in total.

3. Prepare the adjusting entry for bad debt expense at December 31, 2006.

4. Show how the amounts related to accounts receivable should be presented on the income statement for 2006 and the balance sheet at December 31, 2006.

■ **LO2, 3, 4**   **AP7–5**   **Preparing a Multiple-Step Income Statement and Computing the Gross Profit Percentage with Discounts, Returns, and Bad Debts** (P7–7)

Big Tommy Corporation is a local grocery store organized seven years ago as a corporation. At that time, 6,000 common shares were issued to the three organizers. The store is in an excellent location, and sales have increased each year. At the end of 2007, the bookkeeper prepared the following statement (assume that all amounts are correct; note the incorrect terminology and format):

BIG TOMMY CORPORATION **Profit and Loss** **December 31, 2007**		
	Debit	**Credit**
Sales		$420,000
Cost of goods sold	$279,000	
Sales returns and allowances	8,000	
Selling expenses	58,000	
Administrative and general expenses	16,000	
Bad debt expense	3,000	
Sales discounts	6,000	
Income tax expense	15,000	
Net profit	35,000	
Totals	$420,000	$420,000

Required:

1. Beginning with net sales, prepare a multiple-step income statement (showing both gross profit and income from operations). Treat sales discounts as an expense.

2. Compute the gross profit percentage and explain its meaning.

■ **LO6**   **AP7–6**   **Preparing a Bank Reconciliation and Related Journal Entries**

The president of Kostas Fashions Ltd., Joan Kostas, has just received the monthly bank statement for June, which shows a balance of $10,517. She remembers seeing a different balance for Cash at June 30 when the company accountant, Peter Wong, presented to her the monthly balance sheet. She checks the balance sheet and finds a Cash balance of $6,518. She is not sure which amount is correct. She calls Peter and asks him why the two amounts are different. Peter takes the bank statement and related documents and promises to provide his boss with an explanation within a few hours. He then proceeds to prepare a bank reconciliation report for the month of June.

A review of the documents that accompanied the bank statement shows the following:

a. A credit memorandum for the collection of a note for $2,080, including $80 of interest on the note. The bank charged the company a collection fee of $25.

b. A debit memorandum for an NSF cheque for $286 from customer Rami Cossette.

c. Total service charges for June amounting to $39.

When comparing the bank statement with the company's records, Peter discovers the following discrepancies:

d. A deposit of $1,145 was not recorded on the bank statement.

e. Three cheques had not been presented to the bank for payment yet. The amounts of these cheques are $1,573, $679, and $1,252.

f. A deposit of $2,340 was recorded incorrectly in the books at $2,430.

Required:

1. Explain to Joan Kostas why the two balances for cash are not equal, and why it is important to prepare a bank reconciliation statement.

2. Prepare a bank reconciliation statement at June 30 and the related journal entries.

CASES AND PROJECTS

FINDING AND INTERPRETING FINANCIAL INFORMATION

CP7–1 Finding Financial Information
Refer to the financial statements of Van Houtte Inc. given in Appendix B of this book.

■ LO1, 3, 4, 6

Van Houtte

Required:

1. How much cash and cash equivalents does the company hold at the end of the current year?

2. Does the company report an allowance for doubtful accounts on the balance sheet or in the notes? Explain why it does or does not.

3. Compute the company's gross profit percentage for the most recent two years. Has it risen or fallen? Explain the meaning of the change.

4. Does the company disclose its revenue recognition policy? What point in time does it use to recognize revenue?

CP7–2 Finding Financial Information
Refer to the Online Learning Centre Web site at **www.mcgrawhill.ca/college/libby/student/ resources** for the financial statements of The Forzani Group Ltd.

■ LO2, 5, 6

The Forzani Group

Required:

1. The company sells to both consumers and business customers. What items would you expect to be subtracted from sales revenue in the computation of net sales?

2. What expenses does The Forzani Group subtract from net sales in the computation of income before income taxes? How does this differ from Van Houtte's practice?

3. Compute The Forzani Group's receivables turnover ratio for the year ended January 30, 2005. What characteristics of its business might cause it to be so high?

4. What was the change in accounts receivable and how did it affect the cash provided by operating activities for the current year?

CP7–3 Comparing Companies
Refer to the Online Learning Centre Web site at **www.mcgrawhill.ca/college/libby/student/ resources** for the financial statements of The Forzani Group Ltd. and to Appendix B for the financial statements of Van Houtte Inc.

■ LO3, 5

Van Houtte vs.
The Forzani Group

Required:

1. Compute the gross profit percentage for both companies for the current year. Does The Forzani Group comment on the company's gross profit percentage in its Management's Discussion and Analysis?

2. Compute the accounts receivable turnover ratio for both companies for fiscal years 2004 and 2005. The Forzani Group had $38,275,000 in accounts receivable (net) at February 2, 2003, and Van Houtte had $33,652,000 in accounts receivable (net) at March 29, 2003. What accounts for the change in these ratios?

FINANCIAL REPORTING AND ANALYSIS CASES

CP7–4 Interpreting the Financial Press
Knight-Ridder Tribune Business News recently interviewed a number of managers and asked, "How do you structure a credit policy that encourages sales without sending yourself to the poorhouse?"* The article is available on the Online Learning Centre Web site at **www.mcgrawhill.ca/college/libby/students/resources**.

Knight-Ridder Tribune Business News

Required:
Read the article, organize the recommendations into categories, and write a short memo outlining the key recommended steps.

---

*Reprinted with permission of Knight-Ridder/Tribune Information Services.

■ **LO4, 5**   **CP7–5**   **Using Financial Reports: International Bad Debt Disclosure**

Foster's Brewing

Foster's Brewing controls more than 50 percent of the beer market in Australia. As an Australian company, it follows Australian GAAP and uses Australian accounting terminology. In the footnotes to a recent annual report, it discloses information on receivables (all numbers are reported in thousands of Australian dollars).

Note 3: Receivables	Year 2	Year 1
Current		
Trade debtors	792,193	999,159
Provision for doubtful debts	(121,449)	(238,110)
Other debtors	192,330	130,288
Provision for doubtful debts	(384)	(2,464)
Non-current		
Trade debtors	164,808	200,893
Other debtors	15,094	16,068
Provision for doubtful debts	(7,920)	(7,400)
Note 15: Operation Profit	Year 2	Year 1
Amounts set aside to provisions for		
Doubtful debts—trade debtors	(21,143)	(53,492)
Doubtful debts—other debtors	(228)	(2,570)

Required:

1. The account titles used by Foster's are different from those normally used by Canadian companies. What account titles does it use in place of Allowance for Doubtful Accounts and Bad Debt Expense?

2. Sales on account for year 2 were $9,978,875. Compute the accounts receivable (trade debtors) turnover ratio for year 2 (ignore uncollectable accounts).

3. Compute the provision for doubtful debts as a percentage of current receivables separately for receivables from trade debtors and receivables from others. Explain why these percentages might be different.

4. What was the total amount of receivables written off in year 2, net of recoveries?

■ **LO4**   **CP7–6**   **Canadian Banks**

In June 2001, the shares of Toronto-Dominion Bank lost 8 percent of their market value in two days after the bank increased its provisions for credit losses on loans to companies operating in the telecommunications industry. The telecom companies were facing weak demand for their products and services, and a number of companies in this sector were facing financial difficulties. In fact, the other major Canadian banks were similarly affected by the downturn of activity in the telecom industry, as they had loaned sizeable amounts of money to companies in this sector.

Using your Web browser, contact the Web sites and consult the annual reports of three of the following banks: Bank of Montreal, Scotiabank, Canadian Imperial Bank of Commerce, National Bank of Canada, Royal Bank of Canada, and Toronto-Dominion Bank.

Required:

1. How much did each bank report as "provision for credit losses"?

2. Compute the following percentage: Provision for credit losses/Net interest income. Which bank has the largest ratio?

3. How much did each bank report as "allowance for credit losses"?

4. Compute the following percentage: Allowance for credit losses/Total loans receivable. Which bank has the largest ratio? Is it the same bank identified in requirement 2 above? Identify reasons why this bank has a higher ratio than the other two. (*Hint*: The notes to the financial statements and Management's Discussion and Analysis are useful sources of information.)

CRITICAL THINKING CASES

CP7–7 Making Decisions as an Independent Accountant

■ **LO6**

Lane Manufacturing Company is a relatively small local business that specializes in the repair and renovation of antique furniture. The owner is an expert craftsperson. Although a number of skilled workers are employed, there is always a large backlog of work to be done. A long-time employee who serves as clerk-bookkeeper handles cash receipts, keeps the records, and writes cheques for disbursements. The owner signs the cheques. The clerk-bookkeeper pays small amounts in cash, subject to a month-end review by the owner. Approximately 80 regular customers are extended credit that typically amounts to less than $1,000. Although credit losses are small, in recent years the bookkeeper had established an allowance for doubtful accounts, and all write-offs were made at year-end. During January 2006 (the current year), the owner decided to start as soon as possible the construction of a building for the business that would provide many advantages over the currently rented space and would allow space to expand facilities. As a part of the considerations in financing, the financing institution asked for 2005 audited financial statements. The company statements had never been audited. Early in the audit, the independent accountant found numerous errors and one combination of amounts, in particular, that caused concern.

There was some evidence that a $2,500 job completed by Lane had been recorded as a receivable (from a new customer) on July 15, 2005. The receivable was credited for a $2,500 cash collection a few days later. The new account was never active again. The auditor also observed that shortly thereafter, three write-offs of accounts receivable balances had been made to Allowance for Doubtful Accounts as follows: Jones, $800; Blake, $750; and Sellers, $950—all of whom were known as regular customers. These write-offs drew the attention of the auditor.

Required:

1. Explain what caused the auditor to be concerned. Should the auditor report the suspicions to the owner?

2. What recommendations would you make with respect to internal control procedures for this company?

CP7–8 Making a Decision as a Manager: Choosing among Alternative Recognition Points

■ **LO1**

UPS, Federal Express, and Airborne

UPS, Federal Express, and Airborne are three of the major players in the highly competitive package delivery industry. Comparability is a key qualitative characteristic of accounting information that allows analysts to compare similar companies. The revenue recognition footnotes of the three competitors reveal three different revenue recognition points for package delivery revenue: package delivery, percentage of service completed, and package pick-up. These points correspond to the end, continuous recognition, and the beginning of the earnings process, respectively.

UNITED PARCEL SERVICE OF AMERICA, INC.

Revenue is recognized upon delivery of a package.

FEDERAL EXPRESS CORPORATION

Revenue is generally recognized upon delivery of shipments. For shipments in transit, revenue is recorded based on the percentage of service completed.

AIRBORNE FREIGHT CORP.

Domestic revenues and most domestic operating expenses are recognized when shipments are picked up from the customer . . .

The Airborne footnote goes on to say, however: "The net revenue resulting from existing recognition policies does not materially differ from that which would be recognized on a delivery date basis."

Required:

1. Do you believe that the difference between Airborne's and UPS's revenue recognition policies materially affects their reported earnings? Why or why not?

2. Assume that all three companies pick up packages from customers and receive payment of $1 million for services each day of the year and that each package is delivered the next day. What would be each company's service revenue for a year, given its stated revenue recognition policy?

3. Given your answer to requirement 2, under what conditions would that answer change?

4. Which revenue recognition rule would you prefer as a manager? Why?

■ **LO1**

CP7–9 **Evaluating an Ethical Dilemma: Management Incentives, Revenue Recognition, and Sales with the Right of Return**

Platinum Software was a fast-growing maker of accounting software. According to the federal charges, when business slowed and the company was unable to meet the stock market's expectation for continued growth, the former chairman and CEO (the company's founder), former CFO, and former controller responded by improperly recording revenue and allowances for returns, resulting in overstatement of net income by $18 million. The three recently settled both federal charges brought by the SEC and a shareholder suit by paying nearly $2.8 million in restitution and fines and being suspended from practice for differing periods. The exact nature of the fraud is described in the excerpt below:

Required:

1. What facts, if any, presented in the article suggest that Platinum violated the revenue principle?

2. What do you think may have motivated management to falsify the statements? Why was management concerned with reporting continued growth in net income?

3. Explain who was hurt by management's unethical conduct.

4. Assume that you are the auditor for other software licensing firms. After reading about the fraud, to what types of transactions would you pay special attention in the audit of your clients in this industry?

THREE EX-OFFICERS OF O.C. SOFTWARE FIRM SANCTIONED; SEC:

Platinum founder Gerald Blackie agrees to 10-year ban as officer of public company to settle suit over falsifying books. Two other former executives are fined.

JOHN O'DELL TIMES STAFF WRITER

Los Angeles Times Orange County Edition 5/10/96

. . .

The SEC suit charged that Blackie, Tague and Erickson began falsifying sales records in 1993 and early 1994 in order to pump up Platinum's quarterly sales figures and make the company's financial situation appear stronger than it was.

For a period of at least nine months, ending early in 1994, the men backdated sales orders and reported as actual revenue fees that had not yet been received and were subject to secret cancellation agreements that the customers often exercised, the suit said.

In one case in 1993, the suit alleges, Blackie personally closed a $1.5-million software licensing deal with the Wackenhut Corp. on the day the fiscal year ended. He also executed a separate letter giving Wackenhut a 60-day right to cancel. Blackie then instructed Erickson to enter the $1.5 million as revenue in the just-completed fiscal year, even though the money had not been received.

Wackenhut later cancelled the contract, the suit says, but Platinum did not disclose the cancellation or adjust for it when it later filed its annual report with the SEC.

In August 1993, with the company's stock price rising on the strength of the falsified financial reports, Blackie, Tague, and Erickson all sold large amounts of stock. Blackie profited again with a stock sale in November 1993, the SEC suit says. After the company revealed the accounting irregularities and announced Blackie's resignation in April 1994, the stock price plummeted 64 percent.

The suit also says Blackie received $128,125 in performance bonuses for the nine-month period in which he was falsifying financial reports; Erickson got $50,000 and Tague received $6,000. "If they had been any lower in the company they would never have gotten away with this for as long as they did," said SEC attorney Nathan.

Copyright 1996, *Los Angeles Times.* Reprinted by permission.

CP7–10 **Evaluating the Effects of Credit Policy Changes on the Receivables Turnover Ratio and Cash Flows from Operating Activities**

■ **LO5**

V. R. Rao and Company has been operating for five years as a software consulting firm specializing in the installation of industry standard products. During this period, it has experienced rapid growth in sales revenue and in accounts receivable. Ms. Rao and her associates all have computer science backgrounds. This year, the company hired you as its first corporate controller. You have put into place new credit-granting and collection procedures that are expected to reduce receivables by approximately one-third by year-end. You have gathered the following data related to the changes:

	(in thousands)	
	Beginning of Year	End of Year (projected)
Accounts receivable	$1,000,608	$660,495
Less: Allowance for doubtful accounts	36,800	10,225
Net accounts receivable	$ 963,808	$650,270
		Current Year (projected)
Net sales (assume all on credit)		$7,015,069

Required:

1. Compute the accounts receivable turnover ratio based on two different assumptions:
   a. Those presented in the preceding table (a decrease in the balance in accounts receivable, net).
   b. No change in the balance of net accounts receivable; the balance was $963,808 at year-end.

2. Compute the effect (sign and amount) of the projected change in net accounts receivable on cash flow from operating activities for the year.

3. On the basis of your findings in requirements 1 and 2, write a brief memo explaining how an increase in the accounts receivable turnover ratio can result in an increase in cash flow from operating activities. Also explain how this increase can benefit the company.

■ **LO6**   **CP7–11 Evaluating Internal Controls**

Cory Magnum has been working for Matrix Products Inc. for five years and has gained the respect of his peers for his exemplary behaviour and work ethic. His job includes receiving cash and cheques from customers, depositing the cash receipts in the company's account at the local bank, and recording the transactions in the company's computerized accounting program. Cory was faced with personal financial problems and decided to make use of $2,000 of the company's available cash to solve them. He planned to return the money as soon as his financial situation improved. The $2,000 he took was part of the total cash sales to customers during the previous two business days. At the same time, Cory had received a cheque for $2,000 from PLC, Ltd. as a partial payment on its account receivable.

To hide his theft, Cory deposited the cheque in the company's bank account instead of the cash, and made the following journal entry:

Cash in Bank	2,000	
Cash on Hand		2,000

In addition, he recorded the following journal entry to credit the account of PLC, Ltd. to avoid any questions from that company in the future.

Sales Returns and Allowances	2,000	
Accounts Receivable—PLC, Ltd.		2,000

Required:

1. Assume that Matrix Products prepares financial statements on a monthly basis. Would any items on the income statement or the balance sheet be incorrect? Explain.

2. Identify the weaknesses that exist in the company's internal control system. What changes should be made to strengthen internal control over cash receipts?

FINANCIAL REPORTING AND ANALYSIS TEAM PROJECT

■ **LO1, 4, 5**   **CP7–12 Team Project: Analyzing Revenues and Receivables**

As a team, select an industry to analyze (industry lists can be found at **www.market guide.com/mgi/industry/industry.html** and **www.hoovers.com**; click on "Companies and Industries"). Each team member should acquire the annual report for one publicly traded company in the industry, with each member selecting a different company. (Library files, the SEC EDGAR service at **www.freeedgar.com**, the SEDAR service at **www.sedar.com**, or the company Web sites are good sources.) On an individual basis, each team member should then write a short report answering the following questions about the selected company.

1. What specific revenue recognition policy does the company follow?

2. What is the receivables turnover ratio?

3. If the annual report is available, determine what additional disclosures are available concerning the allowance for doubtful accounts. If the necessary information is provided, what is bad debt expense as a percentage of sales?

4. What was the effect of the change in accounts receivable on cash flows from operations? Explain your answer.

Discuss any patterns across the companies that you as a team observe. Then, as a group, write a short report comparing and contrasting your companies using these attributes. Provide potential explanations for any differences discovered.

Reporting and Interpreting Cost of Goods Sold and Inventory

8

FOCUS COMPANY:

Dell Inc.

SELLING DIRECTLY TO THE CUSTOMER

If you shopped for a personal computer recently, you probably considered buying one of the well-known and long-standing brand names in the computer industry such as Apple, Hewlett-Packard, or IBM. You also may have considered buying a desktop computer or a notebook computer directly from Dell Inc. through the Internet.

Dell Inc. was founded in 1984 by Michael Dell on a simple concept: selling personal computer systems directly to customers. The company designs, develops, manufactures, markets, and sells a wide range of computer systems, including desktop and notebook computers, servers, workstations, networking products, and printing and imaging systems. It also offers software, peripherals, and service and support programs. The company sells its products and services directly to large corporate, government, health care, and education customers, as well as to individuals. In 2004, Dell was the leading seller of computer systems worldwide.

The company's business strategy is based on its direct business model. The direct model is based on the principle that delivering custom-built computer systems is the best business model for providing solutions that are relevant to end-user needs. The company believes that the direct model provides it with several distinct competitive advantages. This model eliminates the need to support an extensive network of wholesale and retail dealers, thereby avoiding dealer mark-ups. It also avoids the higher inventory costs associated with the wholesale and retail channels, and the competition for retail shelf space. In addition, Dell's build-to-order manufacturing process is designed to allow the company to quickly produce customized computer systems and to reduce the high risk of obsolescence associated with products in a rapidly changing technological market.

UNDERSTANDING THE BUSINESS

Concerns about the cost and quality of inventory face all modern manufacturers and merchandisers and turn our attention to *cost of goods sold (cost of sales, cost of products sold)* on the income statement and *inventory* on the balance sheet. Exhibit 8.1 presents the relevant excerpts from Dell's financial statements that include these accounts. The Cost of Goods Sold is subtracted from net sales to produce gross profit on its income statement. Inventory is a current asset on the balance sheet; it is reported below Cash and Accounts Receivable because it is less liquid than those two current assets.

Dell's successful expansion of production and management of cost of goods sold and inventory require a combined effort by human resource managers, engineers, production managers, marketing managers, and accounting and financial managers. It is truly a multidisciplinary task. The primary goals of inventory management are to have sufficient quantities of high-quality inventory available to serve customers' needs while minimizing the costs of carrying inventory (production, storage, obsolescence, financing, etc.). Low quality leads to customer dissatisfaction, returns, and a decline in future sales. Also, purchasing or producing too *few* units of a hot-selling item causes stockouts that mean lost sales revenue and potential customer dissatisfaction. Conversely, purchasing or producing too *many* units of a slow-selling item increases the storage costs and interest costs on short-term borrowings to finance the production or purchases. It may even lead to losses if the merchandise cannot be sold at normal prices.

To meet these inventory management goals, marketing, financial, and production managers must work together to forecast customer demand for different computer models or peripheral items and provide feedback so that production or purchasing

EXHIBIT **8.1**

**Income Statement and
Balance Sheet Excerpts**

REAL WORLD EXCERPT

Dell Inc.

ANNUAL REPORT

DELL INC.
CONSOLIDATED STATEMENTS OF INCOME
Fiscal Years Ended January 28, 2005, January 30, 2004, and January 31, 2003
(in millions, except per share amounts)

	Fiscal Year Ended		
	January 28, 2005	January 30, 2004	January 31, 2003
Net revenue	$49,205	$41,444	$35,404
Cost of revenue (cost of goods sold)	40,190	33,892	29,055
Gross margin	9,015	7,552	6,349

DELL INC.
CONSOLIDATED STATEMENTS OF FINANCIAL POSITION
January 28, 2005 and January 30, 2004
(in millions, except per share amounts)

	January 28, 2005	January 30, 2004
ASSETS		
Current assets:		
Cash and cash equivalents	$ 4,747	$ 4,317
Short-term investments	5,060	835
Accounts receivable, net	4,414	3,635
Inventories	459	327
Other	2,217	1,519
Total current assets	16,897	10,633

adjustments can be made. Production, human resource, and purchasing managers also must work to control the cost of goods sold to improve gross profit margin. As a consequence, managers, investors, and financial analysts emphasize cost of goods sold and inventory because they are such important determinants of a company's success.

The accounting system plays three roles in the inventory management process. First, the system must provide accurate information necessary for preparation of periodic financial statements and reports to tax authorities.[1] Second, it must provide up-to-date information on inventory quantities and costs to facilitate ordering and manufacturing decisions. Third, since inventories are subject to theft and other forms of misuse, the system also must provide the information necessary to help protect and control these important assets. First we discuss the makeup of inventory, the important choices management must make in the financial and tax reporting process, and how these choices affect taxes paid. Then we will briefly discuss how accounting systems are organized to keep track of inventory quantities and costs for decision making and control. This topic will be the principal subject matter of your managerial accounting course. Finally, we discuss how managers and analysts evaluate the efficiency of inventory management.

ORGANIZATION OF THE CHAPTER

• Nature of Inventory and Costs of Goods Sold	• Control of Inventory	• Inventory Costing Methods	• Valuation at Lower of Cost or Market	• Evaluating Inventory Management
Items Included in Inventory	Perpetual and Periodic Inventory Systems	Specific Identification Method		Measuring Efficiency in Inventory Management
Inventory Cost	Perpetual Inventory Records in Practice	Cost Flow Assumptions (FIFO, LIFO, Weighted Average)		Inventory Turnover Ratio
Flow of Inventory Costs	Methods for Estimating Inventory	Financial Statement Effects of Inventory Methods		Inventory and Cash Flows
Nature of Cost of Goods Sold	Errors in Measuring Ending Inventory	Managers' Choice of Inventory Costing Methods		
		Inventory Costing Methods and Financial Statement Analysis		

NATURE OF INVENTORY AND COST OF GOODS SOLD

ITEMS INCLUDED IN INVENTORY

Inventory is tangible property that (1) is held for sale in the normal course of business or (2) is used to produce goods or services for sale. Inventory is reported on the balance sheet as a current asset because it usually is used or converted into cash within one year or within the next operating cycle of the business, whichever is longer. Goods in inventory are initially recorded at cost, which is the price paid or consideration given to acquire the asset. Inventory cost includes the sum of the costs incurred in bringing an article to a usable or saleable condition and location. The types of inventory normally held depend on the characteristics of the business.

■ **LEARNING OBJECTIVE 1**

Apply the cost principle to identify the amounts that should be included in inventory and the matching principle to determine the cost of goods sold for typical retailers, wholesalers, and manufacturers.

INVENTORY is tangible property held for sale in the normal course of business or used in producing goods or services for sale.

---

[1]Tax reports often differ from the statements prepared for shareholders and other external users.

MERCHANDISE INVENTORY includes goods held for resale in the ordinary course of business.

RAW (OR PRODUCTION) MATERIALS INVENTORY includes items acquired for the purpose of processing into finished goods.

WORK-IN-PROCESS INVENTORY includes goods in the process of being manufactured.

FINISHED GOODS INVENTORY includes manufactured goods that are completed and ready for sale.

STORES INVENTORY includes parts held for repair or replacement of productive or service machinery.

Merchandisers (wholesale or retail businesses) hold the following:

Merchandise inventory Goods (or merchandise) held for resale in the normal course of business. The goods usually are acquired in a finished condition and are ready for sale without further processing.

Dell manufactures most of the products it sells, but it also purchases products from other manufacturers and resells them to customers.

Manufacturing businesses hold the following types of inventory:

Raw (or production) materials inventory Items acquired by purchase, growth (such as food products), or extraction (natural resources) for processing into finished goods. Such items are included in raw materials inventory until used, at which point they become part of work-in-process inventory.

Work-in-process inventory Goods in the process of being manufactured but not yet completed. When completed, work-in-process inventory becomes finished goods inventory.

Finished goods inventory Goods manufactured by the business, completed and ready for sale.

Stores inventory Parts held for repair or replacement of productive or service machinery.

Inventories related to Dell's manufacturing operations are recorded in these accounts. Dell's recent inventory note reports the following:

NOTE 10 — Supplemental Consolidated Financial Information

	January 28, 2005	January 30, 2004
	(in millions)	
Inventories:		
Production materials	$228	$161
Work-in-process	58	69
Finished goods	173	97
	$459	$327

INVENTORY COST

Goods in inventory are recorded in conformity with the *cost principle*. The primary basis of accounting for inventory is cash equivalent cost, which is the price paid or consideration given to acquire an asset. Inventory cost includes, in principle, the sum of the applicable expenditures and charges directly or indirectly incurred in bringing an article to a usable or saleable condition and location.

When Dell purchases raw materials for the computer products line and software for resale to customers, it follows similar accounting practices. Theoretically, the amount recorded for purchase of raw materials or merchandise should include the invoice price and indirect expenditures related to the purchase, such as freight charges to deliver the items to its warehouses (freight-in) and inspection and preparation costs. In general, the company should cease accumulating costs of purchases when the raw materials are *ready for use* or when the merchandise inventory is in a condition and location *ready for shipment* to customers. Any additional costs related to selling the merchandise inventory to customers, such as salaries of marketing personnel, should be included in Selling, General, and Administrative Expenses of the period of sale since they are incurred after the inventory is ready for use in the normal course of business. Direct sales to customers, by telephone or through the Internet, have reduced the need to stock inventory for long periods and help reduce inventory storage costs and the cost of obsolescence.

FINANCIAL **ANALYSIS**

APPLYING THE MATERIALITY CONSTRAINT IN PRACTICE

Incidental costs such as inspection and preparation costs often are not material in amount (see the discussion of the materiality constraint in Chapter 4) and do not have to be assigned to the inventory cost. Thus, for practical reasons, many companies use the invoice price, less returns and discounts, to assign a unit cost to raw materials or merchandise and record other indirect expenditures as a separate cost that is reported as an expense. Invoice price may or may not include transportation charges (freight-in) for shipment to the warehouse.

FLOW OF INVENTORY COSTS

The flow of inventory costs for merchandisers, both wholesalers and retailers, is relatively simple, as shown in Exhibit 8.2A. When merchandise is purchased, the Merchandise Inventory account is increased. When the goods are sold, the merchandise inventory is decreased and the cost of goods sold is increased.

The flow of inventory costs in a manufacturing environment is more complex, as diagrammed in Exhibit 8.2B. First *raw materials* (also called *direct materials*) must be purchased. For Dell, these raw materials include memory chips, processors, hard disks, and graphic cards, among others. When they are used, the cost of each material is removed from the raw materials inventory and added to the work-in-process inventory.

Two other components of manufacturing costs, direct labour and factory overhead, are also added to the work-in-process inventory when incurred in the manufacturing process. **Direct labour** cost represents the earnings of employees who work directly on the products being manufactured. **Factory overhead** costs include all other

DIRECT LABOUR refers to the earnings of employees who work directly on the products being manufactured.

FACTORY OVERHEAD comprises manufacturing costs that are not raw material or direct labour costs.

EXHIBIT **8.2**

Flow of Inventory Costs

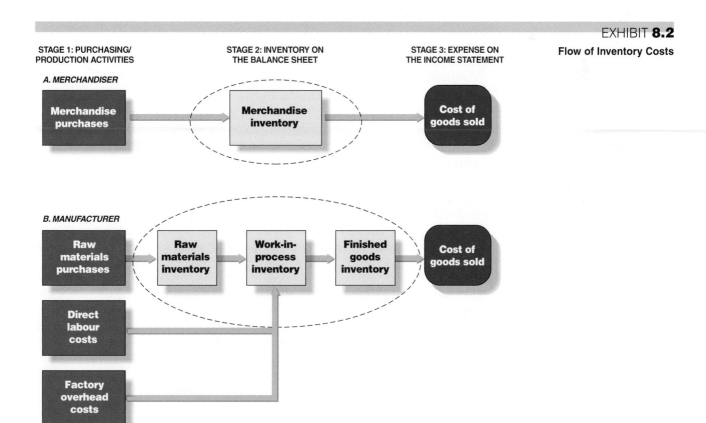

manufacturing costs. For example, the salary of the factory supervisor and the cost of heat, light, and power to operate the factory are included in factory overhead. When the computers are completed and ready for sale, the related amounts in work-in-process inventory are transferred to finished goods inventory. When the finished goods are sold, cost of goods sold increases and the finished goods inventory decreases.

Note in Exhibit 8.2 that there are three stages to inventory cost flows for *both* merchandisers and manufacturers. The first involves purchasing and/or production activities. In the second, these activities result in additions to inventory accounts on the balance sheet. At the third stage, the inventory items are sold and the amounts become cost of goods sold expense on the income statement. Since the flow of inventory costs for merchandise inventory and finished goods to cost of goods sold are very similar, we will focus the rest of our discussion on merchandise inventory.

FINANCIAL **ANALYSIS**

MODERN MANUFACTURING TECHNIQUES AND INVENTORY COSTS

The flows of inventory costs diagrammed in Exhibit 8.2 represent the keys to manufacturing cost and quality control. Since the company must pay to finance and store raw materials and purchased parts, minimizing these inventories in keeping with projected manufacturing demand is the first key to the process. This requires that Dell work closely with its suppliers in design, production, and delivery of manufactured parts and in planning raw materials deliveries. (This approach to inventory management is called *just-in-time.*) To reduce the costs of work-in-process and finished goods, companies redesign and simplify manufacturing processes and retrain their manufacturing personnel to minimize both the direct labour and factory overhead costs. Simplified product design and production processes often lead to higher product quality and reduced scrap and rework costs. Dell's build-to-order manufacturing process is designed to allow it to quickly produce customized computer systems and to achieve rapid inventory turnover and reduced inventory levels, which reduces the company's exposure to the risk of declining inventory values.

Dell's management accounting system is designed to monitor the success of these changes and provide information to allow continuous improvements in manufacturing. The design of such systems is the subject matter of management accounting and cost accounting courses.

NATURE OF COST OF GOODS SOLD

Cost of goods sold (CGS) is a major expense item for most non-service businesses and is directly related to sales revenue. The amount of sales revenue during an accounting period is the number of units sold multiplied by the sales price. Cost of goods sold is the same number of units multiplied by their unit costs; it includes the cost of all merchandise and finished goods sold during the period. The measurement of cost of goods sold is an excellent example of the application of the matching principle.

Let us examine the relationship between cost of goods sold on the income statement and inventory on the balance sheet. Dell starts each accounting period with a stock of inventory called *beginning inventory* (BI). During the accounting period, new *purchases* (P) are added to inventory. The sum of the cost of beginning inventory and the cost of purchases is the **cost of goods available for sale** during that period. What remains unsold at the end of the period becomes *ending inventory* (EI) on the balance sheet. The portion of the cost of goods that are sold becomes *cost of goods sold* on the income statement. The ending inventory for one accounting period then becomes the beginning inventory for the next period. These relationships are represented visually in Exhibit 8.3.

The **COST OF GOODS AVAILABLE FOR SALE** refers to the sum of the cost of beginning inventory and the cost of purchases (or transfers to finished goods) for the period.

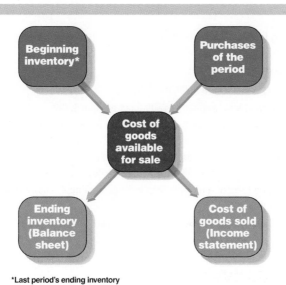

EXHIBIT **8.3**

**Nature of Cost of Goods Sold
for Merchandise Inventory**

*Last period's ending inventory

From these relationships, we can compute the cost of goods sold as follows:

$$\underbrace{\text{Beginning Inventory} + \text{Purchases during the Period}}_{\text{Cost of Goods Available for Sale}} - \underbrace{\text{Ending Inventory}}_{\text{Cost of Goods Not Sold}} = \underbrace{\text{Cost of Goods Sold}}_{\text{Cost of Goods Sold}}$$

Later in the chapter, this **cost of goods sold equation** serves as a basic tool for analyzing the effects of inventory errors and different accounting methods on the financial statements. To illustrate the relationships represented by this equation, assume that Dell began the period with $40 million of software in beginning inventory, purchased additional software during the period for $55 million, and had $35 million in inventory at the end of the period. These amounts are combined as follows to compute the cost of goods sold of $60 million:

COST OF GOODS SOLD EQUATION:
BI + P − EI = CGS

Beginning inventory	$40 million
Add: Purchases of merchandise during the year	+55 million
Cost of goods available for sale	$95 million
Deduct: Ending inventory	−35 million
Cost of goods sold	$60 million

These same relationships can be represented in the merchandise inventory T-account as follows (amounts in millions):

Merchandise Inventory (A)			
Beginning inventory	40		
Purchases of inventory	55	Cost of goods sold	60
Ending inventory	35		

If three of these four amounts are known, either the equation or the inventory T-account can be used to solve for the fourth amount.

SELF-STUDY **QUIZ 8-1**

Assume the following facts for computer monitor model PE1500 that Dell purchased and sold to customers during the year:

> Beginning inventory: 500 units at unit cost of $200.
>
> Ending inventory: 600 units at unit cost of $200.
>
> Sales: 1,100 units at a sales price of $300 (cost per unit $200).

1. Using the cost of goods sold equation, compute the dollar amount of purchases of model PE1500 for the period.

$$\underset{\text{Inventory}}{\text{Beginning}} + \underset{\text{the Period}}{\text{Purchases of}} - \underset{\text{Inventory}}{\text{Ending}} = \underset{\text{Goods Sold}}{\text{Cost of}}$$

2. Prepare the first three lines of a multiple-step income statement (showing gross profit) for the PE1500 monitor for the year.

After you complete your answers, check them with the solutions presented on page 436.

CONTROL OF INVENTORY

PERPETUAL AND PERIODIC INVENTORY SYSTEMS

■ LEARNING OBJECTIVE 2

Compare methods of keeping track of inventory, and analyze the effects of inventory errors on financial statements.

To compute cost of goods sold, three amounts must be known: (1) beginning inventory, (2) purchases of merchandise (or transfers to finished goods) during the period, and (3) ending inventory. The amount of purchases for the period is always accumulated in the accounting system. The amount of the ending inventory can be determined by using one of two different inventory systems: perpetual or periodic. To simplify the discussion of how accounting systems keep track of these amounts, we will focus this discussion on the monitors that Dell sells. Although the same general principles apply, the more complex details of manufacturing accounting systems are discussed in management accounting and cost accounting courses.

In a **PERPETUAL INVENTORY SYSTEM**, a detailed inventory record is maintained, recording each purchase and sale during the accounting period.

Perpetual Inventory System In a **perpetual inventory system**, a detailed record is maintained for each type of merchandise stocked, showing (1) units and cost of the beginning inventory, (2) units and cost of each purchase, (3) units and cost of the goods for each sale, and (4) the units and cost of the goods on hand at any point in time. This up-to-date record is maintained on a transaction-by-transaction basis throughout the period. In a complete perpetual inventory system, the inventory record gives both the amount of ending inventory and the cost of goods sold amount at any point in time. Under this system, a physical count must be performed from time to time to ensure that records are accurate in case errors or theft of inventory occur.

This system typically involves a computer system. Whether the accounting system is manual or computerized, the data that are recorded and reported are the same. The maintenance of a separate inventory record for each type of good stocked on a transaction-by-transaction basis usually is necessary for purchasing, manufacturing, and distribution decisions. Most companies rely heavily on this system and may even share some of this information electronically with their suppliers or customers.[2]

All journal entries for purchase and sale transactions discussed in the text so far have been recorded using a perpetual inventory system. In a perpetual inventory system, purchase transactions are directly recorded in an inventory account. In addition, when each sale is recorded, a companion cost of goods sold entry is made, decreasing inventory and recording cost of goods sold. As a result, information on cost of goods sold and ending inventory is available on a continuous (perpetual) basis.

---

[2]Gildan Activewear Inc., the focus company in Chapter 7, provides product information to its current and potential customers. The Web site www.gildanfinder.com allows the customer to find out how many units of each product are available at each location that distributes its products in Canada, the United States, or Europe.

Periodic Inventory System Under the **periodic inventory system,** no up-to-date record of inventory is maintained during the year. An actual physical count of the goods remaining on hand is required at the *end of each period.* The number of units of each type of merchandise on hand is multiplied by their unit cost to compute the dollar amount of the ending inventory. Cost of goods sold is calculated using the cost of goods sold equation. Because the amount of inventory is not known until the end of the period when the inventory count is taken, the amount of cost of goods sold cannot be determined reliably until the inventory count is completed.

Inventory purchases are debited to a temporary account called Purchases. Revenues are recorded at the time of each sale. However, cost of goods sold is not recorded until after the inventory count is completed. At other times, companies using a periodic system must estimate the amount of inventory on hand. We briefly discuss the estimation of inventory amounts later in the chapter.

Before affordable computers and bar code readers were available, the primary reason for using the periodic inventory system was its low cost. The primary disadvantage of a periodic inventory system is the lack of inventory information. Managers do not receive timely information to help them respond to low stock or overstocked situations. Most modern companies could not survive without this information. As noted at the beginning of the chapter, cost and quality pressures brought on by increasing competition, combined with dramatic declines in the cost of computers, have made sophisticated perpetual inventory systems a minimum requirement at all but the smallest companies.

Comparison of Perpetual and Periodic Systems The differences between the perpetual and periodic inventory systems are highlighted in italics in Exhibit 8.4:

In a **PERIODIC INVENTORY SYSTEM**, ending inventory and cost of goods sold are determined at the end of the accounting period based on a physical count.

EXHIBIT **8.4**

Comparison of Perpetual and Periodic Inventory Systems

Perpetual	Periodic
Beginning inventory (carried over from prior period)	Beginning inventory (carried over from prior period)
+ Purchases for the period (accumulated in an *Inventory* account	+ Purchases for the period (accumulated in *Purchases** account)
= Cost of goods available for sale	= Cost of goods available for sale
− *Cost of goods sold (measured at every sale, based on perpetual record)*	− *Ending inventory (measured at end of period, based on physical inventory count)*
= *Ending inventory (perpetual record updated at every sale)*	= *Cost of goods sold (computed as a residual amount)*

*Purchases is a temporary account (T) closed to cost of goods sold at the end of the period.

Assume, for this illustration only, that Dell stocks and sells only one item, its PE1500 monitor, and that only the following events occur in 2005:

Jan. 1: Beginning inventory: 800 units, at unit cost of $200.

April 14: Purchased 1,100 additional units, at unit cost of $200.

Nov. 30: Sold 1,300 units, at unit sales price of $279.

In the two types of inventory systems, the following sequential steps would take place:

Perpetual Records	Periodic Records
1. Record all purchases in the *Inventory* account and in a detailed perpetual inventory record. April 14, 2005:	1. Record all purchases in an account called *Purchases.* April 14, 2005:

Inventory (A) (1,100 units at $200)* 220,000
   Accounts payable (L) (or Cash)   220,000
	Purchases* (T) (1,100 units at $200) 220,000
	   Accounts payable (L) (or Cash) 220,000

*Also entered in the detailed perpetual inventory record as 1,100 units at $200 each.	*Purchases is a temporary account (T) closed to cost of goods sold at the end of the period. <div align="right">*(continued)*</div>

Perpetual Records	Periodic Records

2. Record all sales in the Sales Revenue account and record the cost of goods sold.
 	
November 30, 2005:
 	
Accounts receivable (A) (or Cash) 362,700
    Sales revenue (R) (1,300 units at $279) ..   362,700
Cost of goods sold (E) 260,000
    Inventory (A) (1,300 units at $200)*   260,000
 	
*Also entered in the perpetual inventory record as a reduction of 1,300 units at $200 each.
	2. Record all sales in a Sales Revenue account.
	
	November 30, 2005:
	
	Accounts receivable (A) (or Cash) 362,700
	    Sales revenue (R) (1,300 units at $279) .. 362,700

3. Use the cost of goods sold and inventory amounts. At the end of the accounting period, the balance in the Cost of Goods Sold account is reported on the income statement. It is not necessary to compute the cost of goods sold because, under the perpetual inventory system, the Cost of Goods Sold account is up to date. Also, the Inventory account shows the ending inventory amount reported on the balance sheet. The sum of all of the inventory balances in the various perpetual inventory records should equal the balance in the Inventory account in the ledger at any point in time. A physical inventory count is still necessary to assess the accuracy of the perpetual records and to assess theft and other forms of misuse (called *shrinkage*).
 	
            No entry
	3. At end of period:
	    a. Count the number of units on hand.
	    b. Compute the dollar value of the ending inventory.
	    c. Compute and record the cost of goods sold.

Beginning inventory (last period's ending inventory)	$160,000
Add purchases (balance in the Purchases account)	220,000
Cost of goods available for sale	380,000
Deduct ending inventory (physical count—600 units at $200)	$120,000
Cost of goods sold	$260,000

December 31, 2005:

Transfer beginning inventory and purchases to the Cost of Goods Sold account:

Cost of goods sold (E) 380,000
    Inventory (A) (beginning)   160,000
    Purchases (T)   220,000

Transfer the ending inventory amount out of the Cost of Goods Sold account to establish the ending inventory balance and complete the computation of the cost of goods sold:

Inventory (A) (ending) 120,000
    Cost of goods sold (E)   120,000

Note that the effects of the entries on the accounting equation are the same under both systems. Only the timing of the recording of amounts changes.

PERPETUAL INVENTORY RECORDS IN PRACTICE

The decision to use a perpetual versus a periodic inventory system is based primarily on management's need for timely information for use in operating decisions and on the cost of the perpetual system. Further, the specific manner in which the perpetual system is designed will also be determined with these trade-offs in mind. Many inventory ordering and production decisions require exact information only on inventory quantities, not costs, which provides the information necessary for efficient management of inventory, providing delivery information to dealers, and quality control.

METHODS FOR ESTIMATING INVENTORY

When a periodic inventory system is used and detailed perpetual inventory records are not kept, the cost of goods sold and the amount of ending inventory can be directly computed only when a physical inventory count is taken. Because taking a physical inventory is expensive, it is normally done only once each year. In these circumstances, managers who wish to prepare monthly or quarterly financial statements for internal use often estimate the cost of goods sold and ending inventory using the *gross profit method*. The gross profit method uses the historical gross profit percentage (introduced in Chapter 7) to estimate cost of goods sold.

For example, if Dell's historical gross profit percentage on monitors is 30 percent and $500,000 worth of monitors were sold in January, it would estimate the cost of goods sold to be $350,000 ($500,000 × [100% − 30%]) for the month. If Dell keeps track of purchases and other additions to inventory, it could then use the cost of goods sold equation to solve for an estimate of ending inventory. Retailers often take their physical inventory counts based on the retail price instead of cost and then use a similar method (called the *retail method*) to estimate cost.[3]

ERRORS IN MEASURING ENDING INVENTORY

As the cost of goods sold equation indicates, a direct relationship exists between the cost of ending inventory and cost of goods sold because items not in the ending inventory are assumed to have been sold. Thus, the measurement of ending inventory quantities and costs affects both the balance sheet (assets) and the income statement (cost of goods sold, gross profit, and net income). The measurement of ending inventory affects not only the net income for that period but also the net income for the *next accounting period*. This two-period effect occurs because the ending inventory for one period is the beginning inventory for the next accounting period.

Greeting card maker Gibson Greetings had overstated its current year profits by 20 percent because one division had overstated ending inventory for the year. You can compute the effects of the error on both the current year's and next year's income before taxes using the cost of goods sold equation. Assume that ending inventory is overstated by $10,000 due to a clerical error that is not discovered the next year. It would have the following effects:

Current Year

Beginning Inventory	+	Purchases during the Period	−	Ending Inventory	=	Cost of Goods Sold
				Overstated $10,000		Understated $10,000

Because cost of goods sold was *understated*, income before taxes would be *overstated* by $10,000 in the *current year*. Since the current year's ending inventory becomes the next year's beginning inventory, it would have the following effects next year:

Next Year

Beginning Inventory	+	Purchases during the Period	−	Ending Inventory	=	Cost of Goods Sold
Overstated $10,000						Overstated $10,000

Because cost of goods sold was *overstated*, income before taxes would be *understated* by the same amount in the *next year*. Each of these errors would flow into retained earnings so that at the end of the current year, retained earnings would be overstated by $10,000 (less the related income tax expense). This error would be offset in the next year, and retained earnings and inventory at the end of next year would be correct.

Exhibit 8.5 shows how an error that understates the cost of ending inventory affects other elements of financial statements during the year of the error and the following year.

---

[3]Methods for estimating inventory and cost of goods sold are discussed in detail in intermediate accounting courses.

EXHIBIT 8.5

Effect of Understatement in Ending Inventory on Selected Financial Statement Items

ERROR: UNDERSTATEMENT OF ENDING INVENTORY

	Year of the Error	Following Year
Beginning inventory	NE	U*
Ending inventory	U	NE
Cost of goods sold	O	U
Gross profit	U	O
Income before income tax	U	O
Income tax expense	U	O
Net income	U	O
Retained earnings, end of year	U	NE

* U = Understated; O = Overstated; NE = No Effect

An error that overstates ending inventory would have exactly the opposite effects on the financial statement items shown in Exhibit 8.5.

SELF-STUDY **QUIZ 8-2**

Sarlos Ltd. provided the following summary income statements for fiscal years 2004 and 2005. Assume that an error in the inventory count at December 31, 2004, resulted in an overstatement of ending inventory by $10,000.

	SARLOS LTD. **INCOME STATEMENTS** **For the Years Ended December 31**			
	With Inventory Error		**Without Inventory Error**	
	2005	**2004**	**2005**	**2004**
Sales	$600,000	$500,000	$600,000	$500,000
Cost of goods sold	350,000	300,000	?	?
Gross profit	250,000	200,000	?	?
Selling, general, and administrative expenses	120,000	100,000	?	?
Income before income tax	130,000	100,000	?	?
Income tax expense (at 40%)`	52,000	40,000	?	?
Net income	$ 78,000	$ 60,000	?	?

1. Complete the income statements above for 2004 and 2005 assuming that the inventory error was discovered at the end of 2005.

2. Compute the combined net income for both years 2004 and 2005. Would the inventory error at December 31, 2004, affect the financial statements for year 2006? Explain.

After you complete your answers, check them with the solutions provided on page 436.

INVENTORY COSTING METHODS

■ LEARNING OBJECTIVE 3

Report inventory and cost of goods sold using four inventory costing methods.

In the example presented earlier, the cost of all units of computer monitor model PE1500 was the same—$200. If inventory costs do not change, this would be the end of our discussion of inventory costs. As we are all aware, the prices of most goods often change. The costs of many manufactured items such as automobiles and motorcycles have risen in recent years, but only at a moderate rate. In other industries, such as computers, however, costs of production have dropped dramatically along with retail prices.

When inventory costs change, the determination of the cost of goods sold and the cost of ending inventory can turn profits into losses (and vice versa) and cause companies to pay or save hundreds of millions of dollars in taxes. A simple example will illustrate these dramatic effects. Do not let the simplicity of our example mislead you. It applies broadly to actual company practices.

The example is based on the following data for Dell during the first quarter of the current year, assuming for simplicity that Dell buys and sells only computer monitor model PE1500.

Date	Transaction or Event	Number of Monitors	Number of Monitors on Hand	Cost per Monitor	Sale Price Per Monitor
January 1	Beginning inventory	800	800	$200	
January 31	Sale to customers	(600)	200		$279
February 5	Purchase from supplier	800	1,000	210	
February 28	Sale to customers	(900)	100		$295
March 10	Purchase from supplier	900	1,000	220	
March 31	Sale to customers	(200)	800		$299

Total number of monitors sold = 600 + 900 + 200 = 1,700
Ending inventory = 800 monitors

Given the rising cost of model PE1500, the challenge for the accountant is to determine the cost of goods sold and the gross profit from the three sale transactions. Which unit cost should the accountant use? **The answer depends on which specific goods we assume are sold.** Four generally accepted inventory costing methods are available for doing so:

1. Specific identification.
2. First-in, first-out (FIFO).
3. Last-in, first-out (LIFO).
4. Weighted average.

The four inventory costing methods are alternative ways to assign the total cost of goods available for sale between (1) ending inventory and (2) cost of goods sold. Generally accepted accounting principles (GAAP) require only that the inventory costing method used be rational and systematic. The selected inventory costing method should be the method that provides the best matching of expenses with revenues. The first method identifies individual items that remain in inventory or are sold. The remaining three methods assume that inventory items follow a certain physical flow.

SPECIFIC IDENTIFICATION METHOD

When the **specific identification method** is used, the cost of each item sold is individually identified and recorded as cost of goods sold. This method requires keeping track of the purchase cost of each item. This is done by either (1) coding the purchase cost on each unit before placing it in stock or (2) keeping a separate record of the unit and identifying it with a serial number. The technology of bar code scanning is a simple and cost-effective process of keeping track of inventory items at all times, even for items with low unit costs. The scanner transmits cost and quantity information to a company's central database, thereby creating a perpetual record of inventory costs. In the Dell example, any combination of the 1,700 monitors could be sold to customers. This affects the computation of the cost of goods sold and the cost of ending inventory. To compute the cost of goods sold, the bar code identifies the specific monitor that is sold and matches it to the recorded cost through the scanning process. The recorded cost of all monitors that remain unsold at March 31 represents the cost of ending inventory.

The specific identification method is impractical when large numbers of similar items are stocked, especially if inventory tracking technology, such as bar coding or radio frequency identification, is not used to keep track of inventory. On the other hand, when dealing with expensive items such as houses or fine jewellery, this method is appropriate because each item tends to differ from the other items. The method may

The **SPECIFIC IDENTIFICATION METHOD** identifies the cost of the specific item that was sold.

be manipulated when the units are *identical* because one can affect the cost of goods sold and the ending inventory accounts by picking and choosing from among the several available unit costs. For example, the manager of a textbook store could either increase or decrease the store's net income by choosing from among the identical textbooks that have been sold. As a consequence, most inventory items are accounted for using one of the following three cost flow assumptions.

COST FLOW ASSUMPTIONS

The following three inventory costing methods are not based on the physical flow of goods on and off the shelves. That is why the methods are called *cost flow assumptions*. A useful visual learning tool for representing inventory cost flows is a stack of inventory units. The different inventory costing methods then can be visualized as flows of inventory in and out of the stack. We use this concept to illustrate inventory flow throughout the following sections. We assume that Dell uses a periodic inventory system, where the costs of goods sold and ending inventory are determined at the end of the accounting period.[4] The oldest monitors are placed at the top of the stack because they are typically sold first.

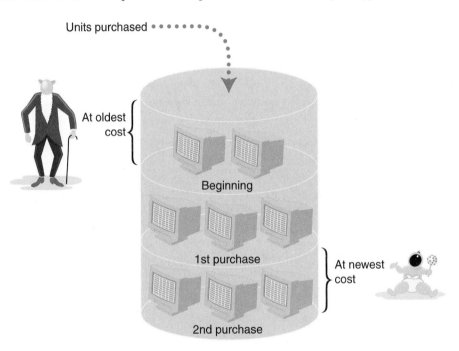

First-In, First-Out Method   The **first-in, first-out method,** frequently called **FIFO,** assumes that the earliest goods purchased (the first ones in) are the first units sold (the first ones out) and the last goods are left in ending inventory. First, each purchase is treated as if it were added to the stack in sequence (800 monitors at $200 each, 800 monitors at $210 each, and 900 monitors at $220 each). The 1,700 monitors sold are then removed from the stack in the same sequence they were added (800 units at $200, 800 units at $210, and 100 units at $220); *first in is first out*. These flows are summarized in Exhibit 8.6. FIFO allocates the *oldest* unit costs to *cost of goods sold* and the *newest* unit costs to the *ending inventory*.

The **FIRST-IN, FIRST-OUT (FIFO) METHOD** assumes that the oldest units (the first costs in) are the first units sold.

Last-In, First-Out Method   The **last-in, first-out method,** often called **LIFO,** assumes that the most recently acquired goods (the last ones in) are sold first and the oldest units are left in ending inventory, as illustrated in Exhibit 8.7. Unlike the FIFO

The **LAST-IN, FIRST-OUT (LIFO) METHOD** assumes that the most recently acquired units are sold first.

[4]This assumption, though unrealistic, allows us to focus our attention on the fundamental differences among the three inventory costing methods, without introducing the complex calculations associated with the use of a perpetual inventory system. Those complexities are covered in Chapter Supplement A.

EXHIBIT **8.6**

FIFO Inventory Flows

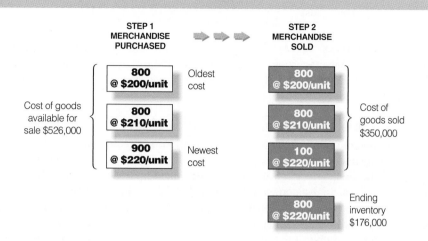

EXHIBIT **8.7**

LIFO Inventory Flows

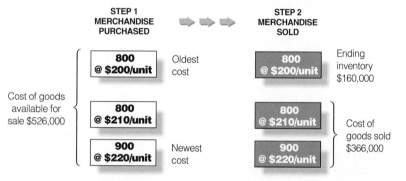

case, the monitors sold are then removed in the following sequence (900 units at $220 and 800 units at $210); *last in is first out.*

LIFO allocates the *most recent* unit costs to *cost of goods sold* and the *oldest* unit costs to the *ending inventory.* The LIFO flow assumption is the exact opposite of the FIFO flow assumption. These relationships are summarized as follows:

	FIFO	LIFO
Cost of goods sold on income statement	Oldest unit costs	Most recent unit costs
Inventory on balance sheet	Most recent unit costs	Oldest unit costs

Weighted-Average Cost Method The **weighted-average cost method** requires computation of the weighted-average unit cost of the goods available for sale. For our example, the weighted-average unit cost is computed as follows:

Number of Monitors	×	Unit Cost	=	Total Cost
800	×	$200	=	$160,000
800	×	$210	=	168,000
900	×	$220	=	198,000
2,500				$526,000

$$\text{Average Cost} = \frac{\textbf{Cost of Goods Available for Sale}}{\textbf{Number of Monitors Available for Sale}}$$

The **WEIGHTED-AVERAGE COST METHOD** uses the weighted-average unit cost of the goods available for sale for both cost of goods sold and ending inventory.

$$\text{Average Cost} = \frac{\$526,000}{2,500 \text{ Monitors}} = \$210.40^5 \text{ per Monitor}$$

In these circumstances, the cost of goods sold and the ending inventory are assigned the same weighted-average cost of $210.40 per monitor. The cost of goods sold is $357,680 (1,700 monitors at $210.40 each) and the cost of the ending inventory is $168,320 (800 monitors at $210.40 each).

FINANCIAL STATEMENT EFFECTS OF INVENTORY METHODS

Each of the four alternative inventory costing methods is in conformity with GAAP. To understand why managers choose different methods in different circumstances, we must first understand their effects on the income statement and balance sheet. Exhibit 8.8 summarizes the financial statement effects of FIFO, LIFO, and weighted average methods in our example. Remember that the methods differ only in the portion of goods available for sale allocated to cost of goods sold versus ending inventory. For that reason, the method that gives the highest ending inventory amount also gives the lowest cost of goods sold and the highest gross profit, income tax expense, and income amounts, and vice versa. The weighted average cost method gives income and inventory amounts that are between the FIFO and LIFO extremes.

EXHIBIT **8.8**

Financial Statement Effects of Inventory Costing Methods

	FIFO	LIFO	Weighted Average
Cost of Goods Sold Calculation			
Beginning inventory	$160,000	$160,000	$160,000
Add: Purchases	366,000	366,000	366,000
Cost of goods available for sale	526,000	526,000	526,000
Deduct: Ending inventory (to balance sheet)	176,000	160,000	168,320
Cost of goods sold (to income statement)	$350,000	$366,000	$357,680
Effect on the Income Statement			
Sales	$492,700*	$492,700	$492,700
Cost of goods sold	350,000	366,000	357,680
Gross profit	$142,700	$126,700	$134,820
Effect on the Balance Sheet			
Inventory	$176,000	$160,000	$168,320

*600 × $279 + 900 × $295 + 200 × $299

In the comparison in Exhibit 8.8, unit costs were increasing. When unit costs are *rising, LIFO* produces *lower income* and a *lower inventory valuation* than FIFO. However, some companies' costs decline even in inflationary periods of time. When unit costs are *declining, LIFO* produces *higher income* and *higher inventory* valuation than FIFO. These effects, *which hold as long as inventory quantities are constant or rising,* are summarized in the following table:

---

[5]Notice that the simple average of the unit costs is $210 [($200 + $210 + $220)/3], but the weighted-average is $210.40 because the latter considers the number of monitors purchased at each unit cost. Beware of using a simple average.

| | Normal Financial Statement Effects of | | | |
| | Rising Costs | | Declining Costs | |
	FIFO	LIFO	FIFO	LIFO
Cost of goods sold	Lower	Higher	Higher	Lower
Gross profit	Higher	Lower	Lower	Higher
Net income	Higher	Lower	Lower	Higher
Ending inventory	Higher	Lower	Lower	Higher

These effects occur because LIFO causes the newer unit costs to be reflected in cost of goods sold on the income statement, which is a realistic measurement of the current cost of items that were sold; FIFO causes the older unit costs to be reflected in cost of goods sold on the income statement. In contrast, on the balance sheet, the ending inventory amount under LIFO is based on the oldest unit costs, which may be an unrealistic valuation, whereas FIFO ending inventory is based on the newest costs, thus assisting the user in predicting the amount of cash needed to replace the inventory.

Consistency in Use of Inventory Costing Methods   It is important to remember that regardless of the physical flow of goods, a company can use any of the inventory costing methods. Furthermore, a company is not required to use the same inventory costing method for all inventory items, and no particular justification is needed for the selection of one or more of the acceptable methods. *Financial Reporting in Canada* shows[6] that 26 of the companies surveyed used different inventory costing methods for different inventory items. For example, in a recent annual report, Finning International Inc., which sells Caterpillar equipment, disclosed that it used specific identification to account for the cost of equipment it sells to customers, but it used FIFO for two-thirds of parts and supplies, and average cost for the remainder of its inventory.

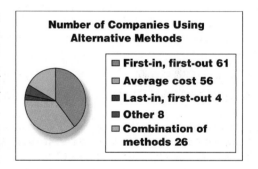

Number of Companies Using Alternative Methods

- First-in, first-out 61
- Average cost 56
- Last-in, first-out 4
- Other 8
- Combination of methods 26

INTERNATIONAL **PERSPECTIVE**

DIFFERENT METHODS FOR DIFFERENT TYPES OF INVENTORY

Asahi Chemical Industry Co., Ltd., is a major Japanese manufacturer of chemicals, plastics, fibres and textiles, and housing and construction materials. Most of its inventories are accounted for using average cost, which is very common in Japan. In addition, its housing and construction materials division constructs and sells homes. It accounts for both residential lots and dwellings under construction, which are expensive, distinguishable items, by using specific identification.

Asahi Chemical Industry Co., Ltd.

To enhance comparability, accounting rules require companies to apply their accounting methods on a consistent basis. A company is not permitted to use FIFO one period, LIFO the next, and then go back to FIFO. A change in method is allowed only if the change will improve the measurement of financial results and financial position. Changing from one inventory costing method to another is a significant event. Such a change requires full disclosure about the reason for the change and the accounting effects.

---

[6]C. Byrd, I. Chen, and J. Smith, *Financial Reporting in Canada 2004*. Toronto: Canadian Institute of Chartered Accountants, 2004, p. 210.

MANAGERS' CHOICE OF INVENTORY COSTING METHODS

Financial Reporting in Canada reported that 4 of the surveyed companies used LIFO in 2004, compared to 56 companies that used weighted-average cost and 61 companies that used FIFO. This raises one important question: What motivates companies to choose different inventory costing methods? Our discussion in Chapter 6 suggests that management should choose the method allowed by GAAP that most reflects its economic circumstances for financial reporting purposes. Management must also make a second choice of inventory costing method to use on its tax return (tax purposes). In general, the choice from among the acceptable methods for use on the company's tax return should be the one that allows payment of the least amount of taxes as late as possible—the "least-latest rule."

The income tax effects associated with LIFO and FIFO for companies facing rising costs can be illustrated by continuing our simple Dell example. Using the data from Exhibit 8.8 and assuming that expenses other than cost of goods sold were $42,700 and a tax rate of 25 percent, the following differences in taxes result:

Inventory Costing Method		
	FIFO	LIFO
Sales revenue	$492,700	$492,700
Cost of goods sold	350,000	366,000
Gross profit	142,700	126,700
Other expenses	42,700	42,700
Income before income tax	100,000	84,000
Income tax expense (at 25%)	25,000	21,000
Net income	$ 75,000	$ 63,000

In this situation, the cost of goods sold and the income before income taxes differed by $16,000, which was caused by the differences between the FIFO and LIFO methods. Costs were rising, and a significant difference existed between the old and new unit costs. When multiplied by the 25-percent income tax rate, the difference in pretax income generates cash tax savings of $4,000. It is important to remember that this choice is independent of the actual physical flow of goods. This example illustrates the primary motivations for the choice of LIFO. Given the tax benefits of using LIFO, why then do Canadian companies not use LIFO for inventory costing? In Canada, the LIFO method is rarely permitted for tax purposes, so Canadian companies typically use FIFO or average cost for financial reporting to external financial statement users and for tax purposes.

Another factor that should be taken into consideration is the effect of the inventory costing method on the company's productive capacity. Proponents of LIFO argue that the use of FIFO during periods of rising prices may lead to the erosion of the company's productive capacity if net income is distributed as cash dividends.

Assume, for illustration purposes, that all sales were for cash and all expenses were paid in cash. Consequently, net income equals net cash flow from operations. Assume further that the company's board of directors declared a cash dividend equal to net income. Under FIFO, $75,000 would be distributed in cash to shareholders, whereas only $63,000 would be distributed under LIFO. In this particular situation, there were 800 monitors at January 1 and 800 monitors at March 31. Thus, the company maintained its physical productive capacity as represented by its inventory of monitors. The increase in the cost per monitor, from $200 to $220, required the use of an additional amount of $16,000 (800 monitors × $20) to maintain the company's productive capacity. This additional cost that was incurred to replace the original 800 monitors is included in the cost of goods sold under LIFO, thus reducing the amount of net income that is distributable to shareholders as cash dividends. For this reason, it is argued that the higher net income under FIFO reflects an overstatement of the amount that is distributable to shareholders as cash dividends, thus causing an erosion of the company's physical productive capacity.

Alternatively, many high-technology companies are facing declining costs. In such circumstances, the FIFO method, in which the oldest, most expensive goods become cost of goods sold, produces the largest cost of goods sold, the lowest gross profit, and thus the lowest income tax liability. Dell and two of its competitors, Apple Computer and Gateway Inc., account for inventories using FIFO.

As indicated earlier, most Canadian companies use either FIFO or average cost for inventory costing. The choice of either method affects both the reported value on the balance sheet as well as net income and cash flows. The reported amounts also affect the calculation of several financial ratios. When prices are rising, companies that wish to minimize their income taxes would logically choose average cost rather than FIFO because the average cost method produces lower income before income taxes. The lower net income reduces profitability and other ratios. However, management may be interested in maximizing net income and the reported inventory value to satisfy restrictions imposed by creditors in lending agreements. While companies are expected to adopt the inventory costing method that provides the best matching of costs to revenues, the choice of a specific accounting method is influenced, in some cases, by management's objectives and the effects of the chosen method on the reported results.

A QUESTION OF **ETHICS**

INVENTORY COSTING AND CONFLICTS BETWEEN MANAGERS' AND OWNERS' INTERESTS

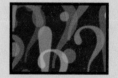

As discussed earlier in this chapter, the selection of an inventory method can have significant effects on financial statements. Company managers may have incentives to select a particular method that may not be consistent with the objectives of the owners. For example, the use of weighted-average cost during a period of rising prices may be in the best interests of the owners because the weighted-average method often reduces the company's tax liability. On the other hand, managers may prefer FIFO because it typically results in higher profits, and the compensation of most managers is affected by reported profits.

A well-designed compensation plan should reward managers for acting in the best interests of the owners, but unfortunately, this is not always the case. Clearly, a manager who selects an accounting method that is not optimal for the company solely to increase his or her compensation has engaged in questionable ethical behaviour.

SELF-STUDY **QUIZ 8-3**

Assume that a company began operations this year. Its purchases for the year included:

January	10 units @ $ 6 each
May	5 units @ $10 each
November	5 units @ $12 each

During the year, 15 units were sold for $20 each and other operating expenses totalled $100.

1. Compute cost of goods sold and pretax income for the year under FIFO and LIFO accounting methods.

2. Which method would you recommend that the company adopt? Why?

After you complete your answers, check them with the solutions presented on page 437.

FINANCIAL **ANALYSIS**

INVENTORY COSTING METHODS AND FINANCIAL STATEMENT ANALYSIS

Critics of GAAP argue that the existence of alternative accounting methods is inconsistent with the *comparability* characteristic of useful information. This quality is needed so that analysts can compare information for a company with that of other companies for the same period. These types of comparisons are more difficult if companies use different accounting methods, since one company's statements must be converted to a comparable basis before meaningful comparisons can be made.

Users of financial statements must be certain that their decisions are based on real differences, not artificial differences created by alternative accounting methods. For this reason, users must be knowledgeable about alternative accounting methods and how they affect statements.

VALUATION AT LOWER OF COST OR MARKET

■ LEARNING OBJECTIVE 5

Report inventory at the lower of cost or market (LCM).

NET REALIZABLE VALUE is the expected sales price less selling costs (e.g., repair and disposal costs).

REPLACEMENT COST is the current purchase price for identical goods.

LOWER OF COST OR MARKET (LCM) is a valuation method departing from the cost principle; it serves to recognize a loss when replacement cost or net realizable value drops below cost.

Inventories should be measured at their acquisition cost in conformity with the cost principle. When the market value of ending inventory drops below cost, the lower amount should be used as the inventory valuation. This is consistent with conservatism, which suggests that care should be taken not to overstate inventory values. *Market value* refers to a number of alternative measures, depending on whether the company is considering the cost of replacing an asset in its present condition or selling it to another party. For the purpose of inventory valuation, market value usually refers to the **net realizable value** of the inventory, which is essentially an estimate of the amount that a company expects to receive for selling its inventory on a specific date. An alternative measure of market value is **replacement cost**, which reflects the current purchase price for identical inventory items. *Financial Reporting in Canada 2004* indicates that 78 of the 200 companies included in the survey used net realizable value, seven companies used replacement cost, while 69 companies used a combination of valuation methods.[7] Damaged, obsolete, and deteriorated items in inventory should be assigned a unit cost that represents their current estimated net realizable value if that is below cost. This rule is known as measuring inventories at the **lower of cost or market (LCM).**

This departure from the cost principle is based on the conservatism constraint, which requires special care to avoid overstating assets and income. It is particularly important for two types of companies: (1) high-technology companies such as Dell that manufacture goods for which the cost of production and the selling price are declining and (2) companies such as The Gap that sell seasonal goods such as clothing, the value of which drops dramatically at the end of each selling season (fall or spring).

Under LCM, companies recognize a "holding" loss in the period in which the net realizable value of an item drops rather than in the period in which the item is sold. The holding loss is the difference between the purchase cost and the net realizable value, and is added to the cost of goods sold of the period. To illustrate, assume that Dell had the following in the current period's ending inventory:

Item	Quantity	Cost per Item	Net Realizable Value (NRV) per Item	Lower of Cost or NRV per Item	Total Lower of Cost or NRV
Pentium chips	1,000	$250	$200	$200	1,000 × $200 = $200,000
Disk drives	400	100	110	100	400 × $100 = 40,000

[7]C. Byrd, I. Chen, and J. Smith, *Financial Reporting in Canada 2004*. Toronto: Canadian Institute of Chartered Accountants, 2004, p. 211.

The 1,000 Pentium chips should be recorded in the ending inventory at the current market ($200), which is lower than the cost ($250). Dell makes the following journal entry to record the write-down:

| Cost of goods sold (E) (1,000 × $50) . . . . | 50,000 | |
| Inventory (A) . . . . | | 50,000 |

Assets		=	Liabilities	+	Shareholders' Equity	
Inventory	−50,000				Cost of Goods Sold	−50,000

Since the market value of the disk drives ($110) is higher than the original cost ($100), no write-down is necessary. The drives remain on the books at their cost of $100 per unit ($40,000 in total). Recognition of holding gains on inventory is not permitted by GAAP.

The write-down of the Pentium chips to market produces the following financial statement effects:

Effects of LCM Write-Down	Current Period	Period of Sale
Cost of goods sold	Increase $50,000	Decrease $50,000
Pretax income	Decrease $50,000	Increase $50,000
Ending inventory on balance sheet	Decrease $50,000	Unaffected

The LCM rule accounts for the added expense in the current period, not in the period of sale. Consequently, pretax income is reduced by $50,000 in the period in which the market value drops rather than in the next period when the chips will be used in the production of computers that are sold. Since the cost of goods sold for the current period *increases* by $50,000 and the cost of goods sold for the next period *decreases* by $50,000, the total cost of goods sold (and income before taxes) for the two periods combined does not change. On the balance sheet, the $50,000 loss in the current period reduces the amount of inventory reported at year-end.

In the case of seasonal goods such as clothing, obsolete goods, or damaged goods, if the net realizable value (sales price less selling costs) drops below cost, this difference is subtracted from ending inventory and added to the cost of goods sold of the period. This has the same effect on current and future periods' financial statements as the write-down to replacement cost.

Under generally accepted accounting principles, the lower-of-cost-or-market rule can be applied to inventories the cost of which is determined using any of the four acceptable inventory costing methods. Notice that in the two excerpts that follow, both IBM, which uses the weighted-average cost, and Dell, which is a FIFO company, report the use of lower of cost or market for financial statement purposes.

DELL COMPUTER CORPORATION
NOTES TO CONSOLIDATED FINANCIAL STATEMENTS
NOTE 1—Description of Business and Summary of Significant Accounting Policies
Inventories—Inventories are stated at the lower of cost or market, with cost being determined on a first-in, first-out basis.

REAL WORLD EXCERPT

Dell Inc.

ANNUAL REPORT

INTERNATIONAL BUSINESS MACHINES
NOTES TO CONSOLIDATED FINANCIAL STATEMENTS
1. Significant Accounting Policies
Inventories
Raw materials, work in process and finished goods are stated at the lower of average cost or net realizable value.

REAL WORLD EXCERPT

IBM

ANNUAL REPORT

EVALUATING INVENTORY MANAGEMENT

MEASURING EFFICIENCY IN INVENTORY MANAGEMENT

■ **LEARNING OBJECTIVE 6**

Evaluate inventory management using the inventory turnover ratio and the effects of inventory on cash flows.

As noted at the beginning of the chapter, the primary goals of inventory management are to have sufficient quantities of high-quality inventory available to serve customers' needs while minimizing the costs of carrying inventory (production, storage, obsolescence, and financing). The inventory turnover ratio is an important measure of the company's success in balancing these conflicting goals.

KEY **RATIO ANALYSIS:**

INVENTORY TURNOVER

ANALYTICAL QUESTION → How efficient are inventory management activities?

RATIO AND COMPARISONS → The answer to this question is facilitated by the computation of the inventory turnover ratio as follows:

$$\text{Inventory Turnover} = \frac{\text{Cost of Goods Sold}}{\text{Average Inventory*}}$$

*Average Inventory = (Beginning Inventory + Ending Inventory) ÷ 2

The 2004 inventory turnover ratio for Dell is:

$$\frac{\$40,190}{(\$327 + \$459) \div 2} = 102.3$$

Comparisons over Time			Comparisons with Competitors	
Dell			**Gateway**	**IBM**
2002	2003	2004	2004	2004
99.5	108.1	102.8	21.5	20.6

Dell's fiscal year ends in late January/early February, so its financial statements essentially cover Dell's activities during the previous calendar year.

INTERPRETATIONS

In General → The inventory turnover ratio reflects how many times the average inventory was produced and sold during the period. A higher ratio indicates that inventory moves more quickly through the production process to the ultimate customer, reducing storage and obsolescence costs. Because less money is tied up in inventory, the excess can be invested to earn interest income or to reduce borrowings, which reduces interest expense. More efficient purchasing and production techniques such as just-in-time inventory, as well as high product demand, cause this ratio to be high. Inefficient purchasing and production techniques and declining product demand cause this ratio to be low. Analysts and creditors watch this ratio because a sudden decline may mean that a company is facing an unexpected decline in demand for its products or is becoming sloppy in its production management. Many managers and analysts compute the related number of average days to sell inventory, which is equal to average inventory ÷ (cost of goods sold ÷ 365 days), or 3.57 days for Dell. It indicates the average time it takes the company to produce and deliver inventory to customers.

Focus Company Analysis → Dell has maintained a relatively high inventory turnover during the period 2002–2004. This high turnover is the result of the company's direct business model, which enables it to operate with reduced levels of components and finished goods inventories. Dell's inventory turnover is much higher than that of its competitors: Gateway, a Dell competitor that has adopted the direct business model of sales to customers, and IBM, which continues to rely on wholesalers and retailers to sell its products and services to customers. As indicated earlier, comparisons may not be appropriate if companies use different accounting methods. Both Dell and Gateway use the FIFO method of inventory costing, but IBM uses the

SELECTED FOCUS COMPANY INVENTORY TURNOVER	
Gildan Activewear	3.5
Home Depot	5.1
Van Houtte	10.5

weighted-average cost method. Given that the computer industry has faced declining prices in the past few years, the average cost method would produce lower cost of goods sold and higher inventory values than FIFO. Consequently, IBM's inventory turnover would be higher under FIFO compared to average cost, but this difference in inventory costing methods would not account for the sizeable difference between Dell's and IBM's ratios.

Dell's impressive inventory turnover ratio is greatly influenced by its method of classifying product shipments that are in transit to customers at year-end. Dell includes these in-transit shipments in Other Current Assets instead of Inventories, whereas its competitors treat them as inventory. If in-transit shipments ($430 and $387 million as of January 28, 2005 and January 30, 2004, respectively) were added to Dell's ending inventory, its inventory turnover ratio for 2004 would decrease to 52.0, about half the initial computation. Careful reading of the notes to financial statements is often essential for proper analysis.

A Few Cautions → Differences across industries in purchasing, production, and sales processes cause dramatic differences in the ratio. For example, restaurants such as Pizza Hut, which must turn over their perishable inventory very quickly, tend to have much higher inventory turnover than automakers such as Toyota. A particular firm's ratio should be compared only with its prior years' figures or with other firms in the same industry.

INVENTORY AND CASH FLOWS

When companies expand production to meet increases in demand, this increases the amount of inventory reported on the balance sheet. However, when companies overestimate demand for a product, they usually produce too many units of the slow-moving item. This increases storage costs as well as the interest costs on short-term borrowings that finance the inventory. It may even lead to losses if the excess inventory cannot be sold at normal prices. The cash flow statement often provides the first sign of such problems.

FOCUS ON **CASH FLOWS**

INVENTORY

As with the change in accounts receivable, the change in inventories can be a major determinant of a company's cash flow from operations. The income statement reflects the cost of goods sold during the period, whereas the cash flow statement should reflect the cash payments to suppliers for the same period. Cost of goods sold may be more or less than the amount of cash paid to suppliers during the period. Since most inventory is purchased on open credit (the borrowing from a supplier is normally called *accounts payable*), reconciling cost of goods sold with cash paid to suppliers requires consideration of the changes in both the Inventory and Accounts Payable accounts, as explained in Chapter 5.

The simplest way to think about the effects of changes in inventory is that buying (increasing) inventory eventually decreases cash, and selling (decreasing) inventory eventually increases cash. Similarly, borrowing from suppliers, which increases accounts payable, increases cash; paying suppliers, which decreases accounts payable, decreases cash.

EFFECT ON CASH FLOW STATEMENT

IN GENERAL → A *decrease in inventory* for the period indicates that the cost of goods sold exceeded the cost of goods purchased; thus, the decrease in inventory must be *added* to net income to reflect the cost of goods purchased.

An *increase in inventory* for the period indicates that the cost of goods purchased exceeded the cost of goods sold; thus, the increase in inventory must be *subtracted* from net income to reflect the cost of goods purchased.

A *decrease in accounts payable* for the period indicates that the payments to suppliers exceeded the cost of goods purchased; thus, the decrease in accounts payable must be *subtracted* from net income in computing cash flows from operations.

An *increase in accounts payable* for the period indicates that the cost of goods purchased exceeded the payments to suppliers; thus, the increase in accounts payable must be *added* to net income in computing cash flows from operations.

	Effect on Cash Flows
Operating activities (indirect method)	
Net income	$xxx
Adjusted for	
Add inventory *decrease*	+
or	
Subtract inventory *increase*	−
Add accounts payable *increase*	+
or	
Subtract accounts payable *decrease*	−

> **SELECTED FOCUS COMPANY COMPARISONS: 3-YEAR CHANGE IN CASH FLOWS RELATED TO INVENTORY CHANGES (IN MILLIONS)**
>
> | | |
> |---|---|
> | Gildan Activewear | +39 |
> | Home Depot | −2,351 |
> | Van Houtte | −3 |

FOCUS COMPANY ANALYSIS → Exhibit 8.9 is the Operating Activities section of Dell's cash flow statement. When the inventory balance increases during the period, as was the case at Dell in fiscal years 2004 and 2005, the company purchased or produced more inventory than it sold during the period. Thus, the increase is subtracted from net income in the computation of cash flow from operations. When the accounts payable balance increased during these periods, the company borrowed more from its suppliers than it

EXHIBIT 8.9

Inventories on the Cash Flow Statement

REAL WORLD EXCERPT

Dell Inc.

ANNUAL REPORT

DELL INC.
CONSOLIDATED STATEMENT OF CASH FLOWS
Fiscal Years Ended January 28, 2005, January 30, 2004, and January 31, 2003
(in millions)

	Fiscal Year Ended		
	January 28, 2005	January 30, 2004	January 31, 2003
Cash flows from operating activities:			
Net income	$3,043	$2,645	$2,122
Adjustments to reconcile net income to net cash provided by operating activities:			
Depreciation and amortization	334	263	211
Tax benefits of employee stock plans	249	181	260
Effects of exchange rate changes on monetary assets and liabilities denominated in foreign currencies	(602)	(677)	(537)
Other	78	113	60
Changes in:			
Operating working capital	1,755	872	1,210
Non-current assets and liabilities	453	273	212
Net cash provided by operating activities	5,310	3,670	3,538

NOTE 10: Supplemental Consolidated Financial Information

Supplemental Consolidated Statement of Cash Flows Information

	Fiscal Year Ended		
	January 28, 2005	January 30, 2004	January 31, 2003
Changes in operating working capital accounts:			
Accounts receivable, net	$ (837)	$ (813)	$ 190
Inventories	(130)	(53)	(21)
Accounts payable	1,595	1,283	844
Accrued and other liabilities	1,583	867	585
Other, net	(411)	(412)	(388)
	$1,755	$ 872	$1,210
Income taxes paid	$ 575	$ 699	$ 607
Interest paid	$ 31	$ 30	$ 20

paid back during the period. Thus, the increase is added to net income in the computation of cash flow from operations.*

---

*For companies with foreign currency or business acquisitions/dispositions, the amount of the change reported on the cash flow statement will not equal the change in the accounts reported on the balance sheet.

When sales rise quickly, as they have at Dell in fiscal year 2005, inventories usually rise, decreasing cash flow from operations. However, the highlighted section of Exhibit 8.9 indicates that increases in borrowing from suppliers have more than offset the inventory increases in 2004 and 2003.

SELF-STUDY **QUIZ 8-4**

1. Refer to the Key Ratio Analysis for Dell's inventory turnover. Based on the computations for 2004, answer the following question. If Dell had been able to manage its inventory more efficiently and *decrease* purchases and ending inventory by $100, would its inventory turnover ratio increase or decrease? Explain.

_____

_____

_____

2. Based on the Focus on Cash Flows section, answer the following question. If Dell had been able to manage its inventory more efficiently and *decrease* ending inventory, would its cash flow from operations increase or decrease?

_____

_____

After you complete your answers, check them with the solutions presented on page 437.

DEMONSTRATION **CASE A**

This case reviews the application of the inventory costing methods and the inventory turnover ratio.

Balent Appliances distributes a number of high-cost household appliances. One product, microwave ovens, has been selected for case purposes. Assume that the following summarized transactions were completed during the accounting period in the order given:

	Units	Unit Cost
a. Beginning inventory	11	$200
b. Inventory purchases	9	220
c. Sales (at $420 per unit)	8	?
d. Inventory purchases	10	210
e. Sales (at $420 per unit)	11	?

Required:

1. Compute the following amounts in accordance with each of the inventory costing methods, assuming that a periodic inventory system is used.

	Ending Inventory		Cost of Goods Sold	
	Units	Dollars	Units	Dollars
1. FIFO				
2. LIFO				
3. Weighted Average				

2. Compute the inventory turnover ratio for the current period using each of the inventory costing methods. What does this ratio mean? Which inventory costing method provides the highest ratio? Is this true in all situations? Explain.

We strongly recommend that you prepare your own answers to these requirements and then check your answers with the suggested solution.

SUGGESTED SOLUTION

1.

	Ending Inventory		Cost of Goods Sold	
	Units	Dollars	Units	Dollars
1. FIFO	11	$2,320	19	$3,960
2. LIFO	11	2,200	19	4,080
3. Weighted Average	11	2,303	19	3,977

Computations

Cost of goods available for sale = Beginning Inventory + Purchases
= (11 units × $200) + (9 units × $220 + 10 units × $210)
= $6,280

FIFO Cost

Ending inventory   = (10 units × $210 + 1 unit × $220) = $2,320
Cost of goods sold = $6,280 − $2,320 = $3,960

LIFO Cost

Ending inventory   = 11 units × $200 = $2,200
Cost of goods sold = $6,280 − $2,200 = $4,080

Weighted-Average Cost

Average cost = $6,280/30 units = $209.33

Ending inventory = 11 units × $209.33 = $2,303

Cost of goods sold = $6,280 − $2,303 = $3,977

2. Inventory turnover ratio = Cost of Goods Sold ÷ Average Inventory

FIFO $3,960 ÷ [($2,200 + $2,320) ÷ 2] = 1.75

LIFO $4,080 ÷ [($2,200 + $2,200) ÷ 2] = 1.85

Weighted Average $3,977 ÷ [($2,200 + $2,303) ÷ 2] = 1.77

The inventory turnover ratio reflects how many times the average inventory was purchased and sold during the period. Thus, Balent Appliances purchased and sold its average inventory less than two times during the period.

The LIFO inventory costing method provides the highest inventory turnover ratio. This is generally true when the prices of inventory items increase over time, because the cost of goods sold reflects current prices and ending inventory reflects older, lower prices.

DEMONSTRATION **CASE B**

Metal Products, Incorporated, has been operating for three years as a distributor of a line of metal products. It is now the end of 2006, and for the first time, the company will undergo an audit by an external auditor. The company uses a *periodic* inventory system. The annual income statements prepared by the company are as follows:

	For the Year Ended December 31			
	2006		**2005**	
Sales revenue		$800,000		$750,000
Cost of goods sold				
Beginning inventory	$ 40,000		$ 45,000	
Add purchases	484,000		460,000	
Cost of goods available for sale	524,000		505,000	
Less ending inventory	60,000		40,000	
Cost of goods sold		464,000		465,000
Gross margin on sales		336,000		285,000
Operating expenses		306,000		275,000
Pretax income		30,000		10,000
Income tax expense (20%)		6,000		2,000
Net income		$ 24,000		$ 8,000

During the early stages of the audit, the external auditor discovered that the ending inventory for 2005 was understated by $15,000.

Required:

1. Based on the preceding income statement amounts, compute the gross profit percentage on sales for each year. Do the results suggest an inventory error? Explain.
2. Correct and reconstruct the two income statements.
3. Answer the following questions:
   a. What are the correct gross profit percentages?
   b. What effect did the $15,000 understatement of the ending inventory have on the pretax income for 2005? Explain.
   c. What effect did the inventory error have on the pretax income for 2006? Explain.
   d. How did the inventory error affect the income tax expense?

We strongly recommend that you prepare your own answers to these requirements and then check your answers with the suggested solution.

SUGGESTED SOLUTION

1. The gross profit percentages as reported are:
   2005: $285,000 ÷ $750,000 = 0.38
   2006: $336,000 ÷ $800,000 = 0.42
   The change in the gross profit percentage from 0.38 to 0.42 suggests the possibility of an inventory error in the absence of any other explanation.

2. The corrected income statements follow:

	For the Year Ended December 31	
	2006	2005
Sales revenue	$800,000	$750,000
Cost of goods sold		
Beginning inventory	$55,000*	$45,000
Add purchases	484,000	460,000
Cost of goods available for sale	539,000	505,000
Less ending inventory	60,000	55,000*
Cost of goods sold	479,000	450,000
Gross margin on sales	321,000	300,000
Operating expenses	306,000	275,000
Pretax income	15,000	25,000
Income tax expense (20%)	3,000	5,000
Net income	$12,000	$20,000

*Increased by $15,000.

3. *a.* The correct gross profit percentages are:
   2005: $300,000 ÷ $750,000 = 0.400
   2006: $321,000 ÷ $800,000 = 0.401
   The inventory error of $15,000 was responsible for the difference in the gross profit percentages reflected in requirement 1. The error in the 2005 ending inventory affected the gross margin for both years 2005 and 2006 by the same amount, $15,000, but in the opposite direction.

   b. Effect on pretax income in 2005: The *understatement* ($15,000) of ending inventory caused an *understatement* of pretax income by the same amount.

   c. Effect on pretax income in 2006: The *understatement* of beginning inventory (by the same $15,000 since the inventory amount is carried over from the prior period) caused an *overstatement* of pretax income by the same amount.

   d. The total income tax expense for 2005 and 2006 combined was the same ($8,000) regardless of the error. However, there was a shift of $3,000 ($15,000 × 20%) in income tax expense from 2005 to 2006.

OBSERVATION An ending inventory error in one year affects pretax income by the amount of the error. It affects pretax income again in the following year by the same amount but in the opposite direction.

Chapter Supplement A

Perpetual Inventory Systems and Inventory Costing Methods

The previous computations of the cost of goods sold and ending inventory have so far assumed that Dell uses a periodic inventory system. But would the computation of cost of goods sold and ending inventory change if Dell used a perpetual inventory system? The answer depends on which inventory costing method is used. The perpetual inventory system produces the same results for FIFO and specific identification, but different results for LIFO and the weighted-average costing methods. Let us use the example shown on pages 417–420 to illustrate the computation of cost of goods sold and ending inventory under a perpetual system.

Date	Transaction or Event	Number of Monitors	Number of Monitors in Store	Cost per Monitor	Sale Price Per Monitor
January 1	Beginning inventory	800	800	$200	
January 31	Sale to customers	(600)	200		$279
February 5	Purchase from supplier	800	1,000	210	
February 28	Sale to customers	(900)	100		$295
March 10	Purchase from supplier	900	1,000	220	
March 31	Sale to customers	(200)	800		$299

Total number of monitors sold = 600 + 900 + 200 = 1,700
Ending inventory = 800 monitors

First-In, First-Out Method   FIFO assumes that the oldest items are sold first. Exhibit 8.10 shows the computation of cost of goods sold and ending inventory as the units sold flow out of the inventory stack. When a perpetual inventory system is used, the inventory records are updated after every purchase and sale transaction in order to keep track of the number of inventory items on hand. This process of continuous updating of the inventory records requires computation of the cost of goods sold for each sales transaction. Hence, the computation of the cost of goods sold is done throughout the accounting period, but it is done only once at the end of the accounting period if a periodic inventory system is used.

In Exhibit 8.10, the cost of goods sold is computed after each sales transaction. The 600 monitors sold on January 31 are taken from the beginning inventory of 800 monitors at a cost of $200 per monitor. When Dell sold 900 monitors on February 28, the company shipped to customers the remaining 200 monitors at a cost of $200 each, plus 700 monitors from the 800 units purchased on February 5 at a cost of $210 each. The remaining 100 monitors were then sold on March 31 in addition to 100 monitors that were purchased earlier on March 10 at a cost of $220 each. The total cost of goods sold is $350,000, the same amount computed under a periodic inventory system. This is not surprising because the old units that are in inventory at any date are assumed to be sold first before the new units are sold. Under both the periodic and perpetual systems, the 800 units in the beginning inventory, the 800 units purchased on February 5, and 100 of the 900 units purchased on March 10 are assumed to be sold.

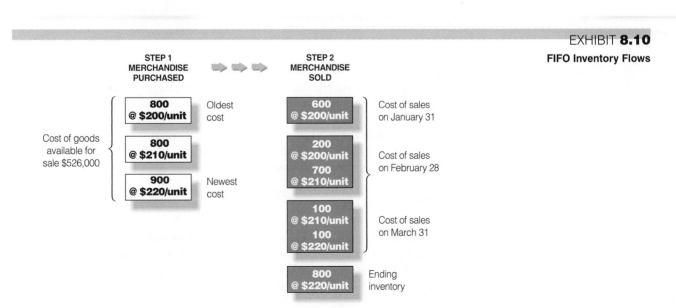

EXHIBIT **8.10**

FIFO Inventory Flows

Last-In, First-Out Method The LIFO method assumes that the most recently acquired items are sold first. In Exhibit 8.11, the monitors purchased last are assumed to be removed from the stack when a sale occurs. The 600 monitors sold on January 31 are taken from the beginning inventory of 800 monitors at a cost of $200 per monitor, the 900 monitors sold on February 28 are taken first from the 800 monitors purchased on February 5 at a cost of $210 each, and an additional 100 monitors are taken from the remaining inventory at $200 each. The 200 monitors sold on March 31 are taken from the 900 monitors that were purchased on March 10 at a cost of $220 each. The 800 monitors left in ending inventory consist of two layers of units purchased on different dates at different costs per unit. The total cost of goods sold is $352,000, compared to $366,000 under the periodic inventory system. When unit costs increase over time, periodic LIFO produces a higher cost of goods sold than does perpetual LIFO, and vice versa. As we noted earlier in this chapter, perpetual records are rarely kept on a LIFO basis because of the complexity and cost of such systems.

EXHIBIT **8.11**

LIFO Inventory Flows

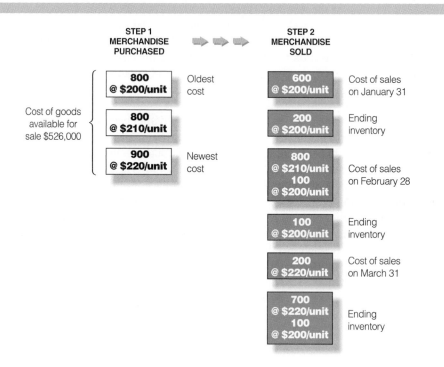

Moving Weighted-Average Cost Method The weighted-average method requires the computation of the weighted-average unit cost of the monitors available for sale every time Dell sells monitors to customers. The 600 monitors sold on January 31 are taken from the beginning inventory of 800 monitors at an average cost of $200 per monitor, for a total cost of $120,000. The cost of the remaining 200 monitors is then added to the cost of the 800 monitors purchased on February 5 to compute a new weighted-average unit cost as follows:

$$\text{Weighted-Average Cost} = \frac{200 \text{ units} \times \$200 + 800 \text{ units} \times \$210}{1{,}000 \text{ units}} = \$208$$

This average cost is then used to compute the cost of the 900 monitors sold on February 28; that is, 900 × $208 or $187,200. The cost of the remaining 100 monitors is then added to the cost of the 900 monitors purchased on March 10 to compute another weighted-average unit cost as follows:

$$\text{Weighted-Average Cost} = \frac{100 \text{ units} \times \$208 + 900 \text{ units} \times \$220}{1{,}000 \text{ units}} = \$218.80$$

This average cost is then used to compute the cost of the 200 monitors sold on March 31; that is 200 × $218.80, or $43,760. Since the average cost changed three times, this method is called the *moving average cost* method.

The total cost of goods sold during the quarter is $350,960 ($120,000 + $187,200 + $43,760), compared to $357,880 under the periodic inventory system. The periodic average cost is always higher than the perpetual average cost in a period of rising prices because the periodic average cost per unit includes the cost of all units available for sale during the accounting period, whereas the perpetual average cost method considers only the cost of units available for sale at different dates in the accounting period.

The cost of goods sold and ending inventory that have been computed using any combination of inventory system and costing method are summarized below.

	Cost of Goods Available for Sale	Periodic System		Perpetual System	
		Cost of Goods Sold	Ending Inventory	Cost of Goods Sold	Ending Inventory
FIFO	$526,000	$350,000	$176,000	$350,000	$176,000
LIFO	526,000	366,000	160,000	352,000	174,000
Weighted Average	526,000	357,880	168,120	350,960	175,040

The various methods produce different results. The differences in the cost of goods sold and ending inventory could be significant in periods of changing prices. However, if unit prices are relatively stable, all of the methods produce costs that are not materially different.

Chapter Supplement B

Additional Issues in Measuring Purchases

PURCHASE RETURNS AND ALLOWANCES

Goods purchased may be returned to the vendor if they do not meet specifications, arrive in damaged condition, or otherwise are unsatisfactory. When the goods are returned or when the vendor makes an allowance because of the circumstances, the effect on the cost of purchases must be measured. The purchaser normally receives a cash refund or a reduction in the liability to the vendor for a return. Assume that Dell returned to a supplier unsatisfactory monitors that cost $1,000. The return would be recorded by Dell as follows:

Accounts payable (L) (or Cash)	1,000	
Inventory* (A)		1,000

Assets		=	Liabilities		+	Shareholders' Equity
Inventory	−1,000		Accounts Payable	−1,000		

*Purchase Returns and Allowances (T) may be credited when the periodic inventory system is used. It is subtracted in the calculation of cost of goods sold.

Purchase returns and allowances are treated as a reduction in the cost of inventory purchases associated with unsatisfactory goods.

PURCHASE DISCOUNTS

Cash discounts must be accounted for by both the seller and the buyer (accounting by the seller was discussed in Chapter 7). When merchandise is bought on credit, terms such as 2/10, n/30 are sometimes specified. This means that if payment is made within 10 days from date of purchase, a 2-percent cash discount known as the **purchase discount** is granted. If payment is not made within the discount period, the full invoice cost is due 30 days after the date of purchase. Assume that on January 17, Dell bought

PURCHASE RETURNS AND ALLOWANCES are a reduction in the cost of purchases associated with unsatisfactory goods.

A **PURCHASE DISCOUNT** is a cash discount received for prompt payment of an account.

goods that had a $1,000 invoice price with terms 2/10, n/30. Assuming that the company uses the gross method, the purchase should be recorded as follows:

Date of Purchase

| Jan. 17 | Inventory* (A) .... | 1,000 | |
| | Accounts payable (L) .... | | 1,000 |

Assets		=	Liabilities	+	Shareholders' Equity
Inventory	+1,000		Accounts Payable +1,000		

*Purchases (T) is debited when a periodic inventory system is used.

Date of Payment, within the Discount Period

Jan. 26	Accounts payable (L)	1,000	
	Inventory* (A)		20
	Cash (A)		980

Assets		=	Liabilities	+	Shareholders' Equity
Inventory	−20		Accounts Payable −1,000		
Cash	−980				

*Purchase Discounts (T) is credited when a periodic inventory system is used. Purchase Discounts would be reported as a deduction from the cost of purchases in the calculation of cost of goods sold.

If for any reason Dell did not pay within the 10-day discount period, the following entry would be needed:

| Feb. 1 | Accounts payable (L) .... | 1,000 | |
| | Cash (A) .... | | 1,000 |

Assets		=	Liabilities	+	Shareholders' Equity
Cash	−1,000		Accounts Payable −1,000		

SOLUTIONS TO **SELF-STUDY QUIZZES**

Self-Study Quiz 8-1

1. BI = 500 × $200 = $100,000   BI   + P − EI   = CGS
    EI = 600 × $200 = $120,000   100,000 + P − 120,000 = 220,000
    CGS = 1,100 × $200 = $220,000   P = 240,000

2. Net sales $330,000
    Cost of goods sold   220,000
    Gross profit $110,000

Self-Study Quiz 8-2

1.

SARLOS LTD.
INCOME STATEMENTS
For the Years Ended December 31

	With Inventory Error		Without Inventory Error	
	2005	2004	2005	2004
Sales	$600,000	$500,000	$600,000	$500,000
Cost of goods sold	350,000	300,000	*340,000*	*310,000*
Gross profit	250,000	200,000	*260,000*	*190,000*
Selling, general, and administrative expenses	120,000	100,000	*120,000*	*100,000*
Income before income tax	130,000	100,000	*140,000*	*90,000*
Income tax expense (at 40%)	52,000	40,000	*56,000*	*36,000*
Net income	$ 78,000	$ 60,000	*$ 84,000*	*$ 54,000*

2. The combined net income for each of the years 2004 and 2005 is $138,000. The effects of the inventory error at the end of 2004 cancel out after two years. The 2004 error would not affect the financial statements for 2006.

Self-Study Quiz 8-3

1. FIFO cost of goods sold = $(10 \times \$6) + (5 \times \$10) = \$110$

   LIFO cost of goods sold = $(5 \times \$12) + (5 \times \$10) + (5 \times \$6) = \$140$

	FIFO	LIFO
Sales revenue (15 × $20)	$300	$300
Cost of goods sold	110	140
Gross profit	190	160
Other expenses	100	100
Pretax income	90	60

2. LIFO would be recommended because it produces lower pretax income and lower taxes.

Self-Study Quiz 8-4

1. Inventory turnover will increase because the denominator of the ratio will decrease by $50.

$$\frac{\$40,190}{(\$327 + \$359) \div 2} = 117.2$$

2. A decrease in inventory would increase cash flow from operations. (See the Focus on Cash Flows section of the chapter.)

CHAPTER **TAKE-AWAYS**

1. **Apply the cost principle to identify the amounts that should be included in inventory and the matching principle to determine the cost of goods sold for typical retailers, wholesalers, and manufacturers. p. 407**
   Inventory should include all of the items held for resale that the entity owns. Costs flow into inventory when goods are purchased or manufactured, and they flow out (as an expense) when the goods are sold or otherwise disposed of. In conformity with the matching principle, the total cost of the goods sold during the period must be matched with the sales revenue earned during the period.

2. **Compare methods for keeping track of inventory, and analyze the effects of inventory errors on financial statements. p. 412**
   A company can keep track of the ending inventory and cost of goods sold for the period using: (1) the perpetual inventory system, which is based on the maintenance of detailed and continuous inventory records for each kind of inventory stocked, and (2) the periodic inventory system, which is based on a physical inventory count of ending inventory and the costing of those goods to determine the proper amounts for cost of goods sold and ending inventory. An error in the measurement of ending inventory affects the cost of goods sold on the current period's income statement and ending inventory on the balance sheet. It also affects the cost of goods sold in the following period by the same amount, but in the opposite direction, because this year's ending inventory becomes next year's beginning inventory. These relationships can be seen through the cost of goods sold equation (BI + P − EI = CGS).

3. **Report inventory and cost of goods sold using four inventory costing methods. p. 416**
   The chapter discussed four different inventory costing methods and their applications in different economic circumstances. The methods discussed were FIFO, LIFO, weighted-average cost, and specific identification. Each of the inventory costing methods is in conformity with GAAP. Remember that the cost flow assumption need not match the physical flow of inventory.

4. **Decide when the use of different inventory costing methods is beneficial to a company. p. 422**
   The selection of a method of inventory costing is important because it will affect reported income, income tax expense (and, hence, cash flow), and the inventory valuation reported on the balance sheet. In a period of rising prices, FIFO normally results in a higher income than does LIFO; in a period of falling prices, the opposite result occurs.

5. **Report inventory at the lower of cost or market (LCM). p. 424**
   Ending inventory should be measured based on the lower of actual cost or market value (LCM basis). This practice can have a major effect on the statements of companies

facing declining costs. Damaged, obsolete, and out-of-season inventory also should be written down to their current estimated net realizable value if that is below cost. The LCM adjustment increases cost of goods sold, decreases income, and decreases reported inventory.

6. **Evaluate inventory management using the inventory turnover ratio and the effects of inventory on cash flows. p. 426**
   The inventory turnover ratio measures the efficiency of inventory management. It reflects how many times the average inventory was produced and sold during the period. Analysts and creditors watch this ratio because a sudden decline in this ratio may mean that a company is facing an unexpected decline in demand for its products or is becoming sloppy in its production management. When a net *decrease in inventory* for the period occurs, sales are more than purchases; thus, the decrease must be *added* to net income in computing cash flows from operations. When a net *increase in inventory* for the period occurs, sales are less than purchases; thus, the increase must be *subtracted* from net income in computing cash flows from operations.

In this and previous chapters, we discussed the current assets of a business. These assets are critical for the operations of a business, but many of them do not directly produce value. In Chapter 9, we will discuss the noncurrent assets property, plant, and equipment; natural resources; and intangibles that are the elements of *productive capacity.* Many of the non-current assets produce value, such as a factory that manufactures cars. These assets present some interesting accounting problems because they benefit a number of accounting periods.

KEY **RATIO**

> **Inventory turnover ratio** measures the efficiency of inventory management. It reflects how many times the average inventory was produced and sold during the period (p. 426):
>
> $$\text{Inventory Turnover} = \frac{\text{Cost of Goods Sold}}{\text{Average Inventory}}$$

FINDING **FINANCIAL** INFORMATION

BALANCE SHEET
Under Current Assets
   Inventories

INCOME STATEMENT
Expenses
   Cost of goods sold

CASH FLOW STATEMENT
Under Operating Activities (indirect method):
   Net income
      + decreases in inventory
      − increases in inventory
      + increases in accounts payable
      − decreases in accounts payable

NOTES
Under Summary of Significant Accounting Policies:
   Description of management's choice of inventory accounting policy (FIFO, Average cost, LCM, etc)
Under a Separate Note
   If not listed on the balance sheet, components of inventory (merchandise, raw materials, work-in-process, finished goods)

KEY **TERMS**

Cost of Goods Available for Sale p. 410

Cost of Goods Sold Equation p. 411

Direct Labour p. 409

Factory Overhead p. 409

Finished Goods Inventory p. 408

First-In, First-Out (FIFO) Method p. 418

Inventory p. 407

Last-In, First-Out (LIFO) Method p. 418

Lower of Cost or Market (LCM) p. 424

Merchandise Inventory p. 408

Net Realizable Value p. 424

Periodic Inventory System p. 413

Perpetual Inventory System p. 412

Purchase Discount p. 435

Purchase Returns and Allowances p. 435

Raw (or Production) Materials
   Inventory p. 408

Replacement Cost p. 424

Specific Identification Method p. 417

Stores Inventory p. 408

Weighted-Average Method p. 419

Work-in-Process Inventory p. 408

QUESTIONS

1. Why is inventory an important item to both internal (management) and external users of financial statements?
2. What are the general guidelines for deciding which items should be included in inventory?
3. Explain the application of the cost principle to an item in the ending inventory.
4. Define *cost of goods available for sale*. How does it differ from cost of goods sold?
5. Define *beginning inventory* and *ending inventory.*
6. When a perpetual inventory system is used, unit costs of the items sold are known at the date of each sale. In contrast, when a periodic inventory system is used, unit costs are known only at the end of the accounting period. Why are these statements correct?
7. The periodic inventory calculation is BI + P − EI = CGS. The perpetual inventory calculation is BI + P − CGS = EI. Explain the significance of the difference between these two calculations.
8. The chapter discussed four inventory costing methods. List the four methods and briefly explain each.
9. Explain how income can be manipulated when the specific identification inventory costing method is used.
10. Contrast the effects of LIFO versus FIFO on reported assets (i.e., the ending inventory) when (a) prices are rising and (b) prices are falling.
11. Contrast the income statement effect of LIFO versus FIFO (i.e., on income before income taxes) when (a) prices are rising and (b) prices are falling.
12. Contrast the effects of LIFO versus FIFO on cash outflow and inflow.
13. Explain briefly the application of the LCM concept to the ending inventory and its effect on the income statement and balance sheet when the market value of inventory is lower than its cost.

MULTIPLE-CHOICE QUESTIONS

1. How many of the following statements are true regarding *cost of goods sold*?
    - Cost of goods sold represents the cost that a company incurred to purchase or produce inventory in the current period.
    - Cost of goods sold is an expense on the income statement.
    - Cost of goods sold is affected by the inventory method selected by a company (FIFO, LIFO, etc.).
    - a. none of the statements
    - b. one statement
    - c. two statements
    - d. all three statements
2. The inventory costing method selected by a company will affect
    - a. the balance sheet.
    - b. the income statement.
    - c. the statement of retained earnings.
    - d. all of the above.
3. Which of the following is *not* a component of the cost of inventory?
    - a. administrative overhead
    - b. direct labour
    - c. raw materials
    - d. factory overhead

4. Each period, the cost of goods available for sale is allocated between
   a. assets and liabilities.
   b. assets and expenses.
   c. assets and revenues.
   d. expenses and liabilities.

5. A Montréal bridal dress designer makes high-end custom wedding dresses. Which inventory costing method would he most likely use?
   a. FIFO
   b. LIFO
   c. Weighted average
   d. Specific identification

6. An increasing inventory turnover ratio
   a. indicates a longer time span between the ordering and receiving of inventory.
   b. indicates a shorter time span between the ordering and receiving of inventory.
   c. indicates a shorter time span between the purchase and sale of inventory.
   d. indicates a longer time span between the purchase and sale of inventory.

7. If the ending balance in accounts payable decreases from one period to the next, which of the following is true?
   a. Cash payments to suppliers exceeded current period purchases.
   b. Cash payments to suppliers were less than current period purchases.
   c. Cash receipts from customers exceeded cash payments to suppliers.
   d. Cash receipts from customers exceeded current period purchases.

8. How many of the following statements are true?
   • The lower of cost or market rule is consistent with the historical cost principle.
   • When the replacement cost of inventory drops below the cost shown in the financial records, net income is reduced.
   • When the replacement cost of inventory drops below the cost shown in the financial records, total assets are reduced.
   a. none of the statements
   b. one statement
   c. two statements
   d. three statements

9. Which inventory method provides a better matching of current costs with sales revenue on the income statement and outdated values for inventory on the balance sheet?
   a. FIFO
   b. weighted average
   c. LIFO
   d. specific identification

10. Which of the following is false regarding a perpetual inventory system?
    a. Physical counts are not needed since records are maintained on a transaction-by-transaction basis.
    b. The balance in the inventory account is updated with each inventory purchase and sale transaction.
    c. Cost of goods sold is increased as sales are recorded
    d. The account Purchases is not used as inventory is acquired.

For more practice with multiple-choice questions, go to our Web site at www.mcgrawhill.ca/college/libby, click on "Student Edition" in the upper left menu, click on this chapter's name and number from the list of contents, and then click on "Multiple-Choice Quiz" from the menu on the left.

EXERCISES

■ **LO1**

E8–1 Recording the Cost of Purchases for a Merchandiser

Elite Apparel purchased 80 new shirts for cash and recorded a total cost of $3,140 determined as follows:

Invoice amount	$2,600
Shipping charges	165
Import taxes and duties	115
Interest paid in advance (10%) on $2,600 borrowed to finance the purchase	260
	$3,140

Required:

Make the needed corrections in this calculation. Prepare the journal entry(ies) to record this purchase in the correct amount, assuming a perpetual inventory system. Show computations.

E8–2 Inferring Missing Amounts Based on Income Statement Relationships ▬ **LO1**

Supply the missing dollar amounts for the 2006 income statement of Laurin Retailers for each of the following independent cases:

Cases	Sales Revenue	Beginning Inventory	Purchases	Total Available	Ending Inventory	Cost of Goods Sold	Gross Profit	Operating Expenses	Pretax Income or (Loss)
A	$ 650	$100	$700	$?	$500	$?	$?	$200	$?
B	900	200	800	?	?	?	?	150	0
C	?	150	?	?	300	200	400	100	?
D	800	?	600	?	250	?	?	250	100
E	1,000	?	900	1,100	?	?	500	?	(50)

E8–3 Inferring Missing Amounts Based on Income Statement Relationships ▬ **LO1**

Supply the missing dollar amounts for the 2008 income statement of Kwan Company for each of the following independent cases:

	Case A	Case B	Case C
Sales revenue	$ 8,000	$ 6,000	$?
Sales returns and allowances	150	?	275
Net sales revenue	?	?	5,920
Beginning inventory	11,000	6,500	4,000
Purchases	5,000	?	9,420
Transportation-in	?	120	170
Purchase returns	350	600	?
Cost of goods available for sale	?	14,790	13,370
Ending inventory	10,000	10,740	?
Cost of goods sold	?	?	5,400
Gross profit	?	1,450	?
Expenses (operating)	1,300	?	520
Pretax income (loss)	$ 800	$ (500)	$ 0

E8–4 Inferring Merchandise Purchases ▬ **LO1**

The Gap, Inc., is a specialty retailer that operates stores selling clothes under the trade names Gap, GapKids, BabyGap, and Banana Republic. Assume that you are employed as a stock analyst and your boss has just completed a review of the new Gap annual report. She provided you with her notes, but they are missing some information that you need. Her notes show that the ending inventory for Gap in the current year was $243,482,000 and in the previous year was $193,268,000. Net sales for the current year were $1,586,596,000. Gross profit was $540,360,000; net income was $97,628,000. For your analysis, you determine that you need to know the amount of purchases and the cost of goods sold for the year.

The Gap, Inc.

Required:
Do you need to ask your boss for her copy of the annual report, or can you develop the information from her notes? Explain and show calculations.

E8–5 Analyzing the Effects of an Error in Recording Purchases ▬ **LO2**

Garraway Ski Company mistakenly recorded purchases of inventory on account received during the last week of December 2005 as purchases during January of 2006 (this is called a *purchases cut-off error*). Garraway uses a periodic inventory system, and ending inventory was correctly counted and reported each year. Assuming that no correction was made in 2005 or 2006, indicate whether each of the following financial statement amounts will be understated, overstated, or correct.

1. Net Income for 2005.

2. Net Income for 2006.

3. Retained Earnings at December 31, 2005.

4. Retained Earnings at December 31, 2006.

■ **LO2**

E8–6 **Recording Purchases and Sales Using a Perpetual and Periodic Inventory System**
Demski Company reported beginning inventory of 100 units at a unit cost of $25. It engaged in the following purchase and sale transactions during 2005:

Jan. 14   Sold 25 units at unit sales price of $45 on open account.

April 9   Purchased 15 additional units at unit cost of $25 on open account.

Sept. 2   Sold 50 units at sales price of $50 on open account.

At the end of the 2005, a physical count showed that Demski Company had 40 units of inventory still on hand.

Required:
Record each transaction, assuming that Demski Company uses (a) a perpetual inventory system and (b) a periodic inventory system (including any necessary entries at December 31, the end of the accounting period).

■ **LO2**

Gibson
Greeting Cards

E8–7 **Analyzing the Effect of an Inventory Error Disclosed in an Actual Note to a Financial Statement**
Several years ago, the financial statements of Gibson Greeting Cards contained the following note:

> On July 1, the Company announced that it had determined that the ending inventory . . . had been overstated. . . . The overstatement of inventory . . . was $8,806,000.

Gibson reported an incorrect net income amount of $25,852,000 for the year in which the error occurred and the income tax rate was 39.3 percent.

Required:

1. Compute the amount of net income that Gibson reported after correcting the inventory error. Show computations.

2. Assume that the inventory error was not discovered. Identify the financial statement accounts that would have been incorrect for the year the error occurred and for the subsequent year. State whether each account was understated or overstated.

■ **LO2**

E8–8 **Analyzing and Interpreting the Impact of an Inventory Error**
Dalez Corporation prepared the following two income statements (simplified for illustrative purposes):

	Second Quarter 2006		First Quarter 2006	
Sales revenue		$18,000		$17,000
Cost of goods sold				
Beginning inventory	$ 4,000		$ 3,000	
Purchases	12,000		7,000	
Cost of goods available for sale	16,000		10,000	
Ending inventory	9,000		4,000	
Cost of goods sold		7,000		6,000
Gross profit		11,000		11,000
Expenses (operating)		6,000		5,000
Pretax income		$ 5,000		$ 6,000

During the third quarter, it was discovered that the ending inventory for the first quarter should have been $4,400.

Required:

1. What effect did this error have on the combined pretax income of the two quarters? Explain.

2. Did this error affect the EPS amounts for each quarter? (See the discussion of EPS in Chapter 6.) Explain.

3. Prepare corrected income statements for each quarter.

4. Set up a schedule with the following headings to reflect the comparative effects of the correct and incorrect amounts on the income statement:

	2nd Quarter			1st Quarter		
Income Statement Item	Incorrect Amount	Correct Amount	Error (if any)	Incorrect Amount	Correct Amount	Error (if any)

E8–9 **Analyzing and Interpreting the Financial Statement Effects of LIFO and FIFO**   ■ **LO3**

Lunar Company uses a periodic inventory system. The company's accounting records provided the following information for Product 2:

Transactions	Units	Unit Cost
a. Inventory, December 31, 2005	3,000	$12
For the year 2006:		
b. Purchase, April 11	9,000	10
c. Sale, May 1 ($30 each)	5,000	
d. Purchase, June 1	8,000	13
e. Sale, July 3 ($30 each)	6,000	
f. Operating expenses (excluding income tax expense), $85,000		

Required:

1. Prepare an income statement for 2006 through pretax income, showing the detailed computation of cost of goods sold for
   a. Case A: FIFO.
   b. Case B: LIFO.
   For each case, show the computation of the ending inventory. (*Hint:* Set up adjacent columns, one for each case.)

2. Compare the pretax income and the ending inventory amounts between the two cases. Explain the similarities and differences.

E8–10 **Evaluating the Choice among Three Alternative Inventory Methods Based on Cash Flow and Income Effects**   ■ **LO3, 4**

Courtney Company uses a periodic inventory system. Data for 2006: beginning merchandise inventory (December 31, 2005), 2,000 units at $35; purchases, 8,000 units at $38; operating expenses (excluding income taxes), $142,000; ending inventory per physical count at December 31, 2006, 1,800 units; sales price per unit, $70; and average income tax rate, 30 percent.

Required:

1. Prepare income statements under the FIFO, LIFO, and weighted-average costing methods. Use a format similar to the following:

		Inventory Costing Method		
Income Statement	Units	FIFO	LIFO	Weighted Average
Sales revenue	_____	$_____	$_____	$_____
Cost of goods sold	_____			
Beginning inventory	_____			
Purchases	_____			
Cost of goods available for sale	_____			
Ending inventory	_____			
Cost of goods sold	_____			
Gross profit				
Expenses (operating)				
Pretax income				
Income tax expense				
Net income				

2. Which method, FIFO or LIFO, is preferable in terms of (a) net income and (b) cash flow? Explain.

3. What would be your answer to requirement 2, assuming that prices were falling? Explain.

LO3, 4   **E8–11** **Evaluating the Choice among Three Alternative Inventory Methods Based on Cash Flow Effects**

Following is partial information for the income statement of Timber Company under three different inventory costing methods, assuming the use of a periodic inventory system:

	FIFO	LIFO	Weighted Average
Unit sales price, $50			
Cost of goods sold			
Beginning inventory (330 units)	$11,220	$11,220	$11,220
Purchases (475 units)	17,100	17,100	17,100
Cost of goods available for sale			
Ending inventory (510 units)			
Cost of goods sold			
Operating expenses, $1,600			

Required:

1. Compute the cost of goods sold under the FIFO, LIFO, and weighted-average inventory costing methods.

2. Prepare an income statement through pretax income for each method.

3. Rank the three methods in order of favourable cash flow and explain the basis for your ranking. Assume that LIFO is acceptable for tax purposes.

LO4   **E8–12** **Analyzing Notes to Adjust Inventory from LIFO to FIFO**

Ford Motor Company

The following note was contained in a Ford Motor Company annual report:

Inventory Valuation—Automotive. Inventories are stated at the lower of cost or market. The cost of most US inventories is determined by the last-in, first-out ("LIFO") method. The cost of the remaining inventories is determined substantially by the first-in, first-out ("FIFO") method.

If FIFO were the only method of inventory accounting used by the company, inventories would have been $1,235 million higher than reported this year and $1,246 million higher than reported last year.

The major classes of inventory for the company's automotive business segment at December 31 were as follows:

	Inventory (in $ millions)	
	Current Year	Previous Year
Finished products	$3,413.8	$3,226.7
Raw material and work in process	2,983.9	2,981.6
Supplies	419.1	429.9
Total	$6,816.8	$6,638.2

Required:

1. Determine the ending inventory that would have been reported in the current year if Ford had used only FIFO.

2. The cost of goods sold reported by Ford for the current year was $74,315 million. Determine the cost of goods sold that would have been reported if Ford had used only FIFO for both years.

E8–13 Reporting Inventory at Lower of Cost or Market

Peterson Company is preparing the annual financial statements dated December 31, 2006. Ending inventory information about the five major items stocked for regular sale follows:

■ **LO5**

	Ending Inventory, 2006		
Item	Quantity on Hand	Unit Cost When Acquired (FIFO)	Net Realizable Value at Year-End
A	50	$15	$13
B	75	40	40
C	10	50	52
D	30	30	30
E	400	8	6

Required:

Compute the valuation that should be used for the 2006 ending inventory using the LCM rule applied on an item-by-item basis. (*Hint:* Set up columns for Item, Quantity, Total Cost, Total Market, and LCM Valuation.)

E8–14 Analyzing and Interpreting the Inventory Turnover Ratio

Gateway, Inc., competes with Dell in manufacturing and selling personal computers directly to customers. In recent years, it reported the following amounts (in millions).

■ **LO6**

Gateway, Inc.

Net sales revenue	$6,079
Cost of sales	5,241
Beginning inventory	315
Ending inventory	120

Required:

1. Determine the inventory turnover ratio and average days to sell inventory for the current year.

2. Explain the meaning of each of the amounts computed in requirement 1.

E8–15 Analyzing and Interpreting the Effects of the LIFO/FIFO Choice on Inventory Turnover Ratio

The records at the end of January 2006 for All Star Company showed the following for a particular kind of merchandise:

■ **LO6**

Inventory, December 31, 2005, at FIFO: 19 units @ $14 = 266

Inventory, December 31, 2005, at LIFO: 19 units @ $10 = 190

Transactions	Units	Unit Cost	Total Cost
Purchase, January 9, 2006	25	15	$375
Purchase, January 20, 2006	50	16	800
Sale, January 11, 2006 (at $38 per unit)	40		
Sale, January 27, 2006 (at $39 per unit)	28		

Required:

Compute the inventory turnover ratio under the FIFO and LIFO inventory costing methods and a periodic inventory system (show computations and round to the nearest dollar). Which method is the more accurate indicator of the liquidity of inventory? Explain.

E8–16 Interpreting the Effect of Changes in Inventories and Accounts Payable on Cash Flow from Operations

First Team Sports, Inc., is engaged in the manufacture (through independent contractors) and distribution of in-line roller skates, ice skates, street hockey equipment, and related accessory products. Its recent annual report included the following on its balance sheet:

■ **LO6**

First Team Spors, Inc.

CONSOLIDATED BALANCE SHEETS
February 29, 2006, and February 28, 2005

	2006	2005
. . . .		
Inventory (Note 3)	22,813,850	20,838,171
. . . .	. . .	. . .
Trade accounts payable	9,462,883	9,015,376

Required:

Explain the effects of the changes in inventory and trade accounts payable in 2006 on cash flow from operating activities for 2006.

E8–17 **(Chapter Supplement A) Analyzing the Financial Statement Effects of Inventory Costing Methods in a Perpetual Inventory System**

Refer to the information related to Product 2 in E8–9. Assume that Lunar Company uses a perpetual inventory system.

Required:

1. Prepare an income statement for 2006 through pretax income, showing the detailed computation of cost of goods sold under each of the following inventory costing methods:
   a. Case A: FIFO.
   b. Case B: LIFO.
   c. Case C: Moving average.
   For each case, show the computation of the ending inventory. (*Hint:* Set up adjacent columns, one for each case.)

2. Compare the pretax income and the ending inventory amounts among the three cases. Explain the similarities and differences.

E8–18 **(Chapter Supplement B) Recording Sales and Purchases with Cash Discounts**

A. The Cycle Shop sells merchandise on credit terms of 2/10, n/30. Merchandise that cost $500 was sold to Claudette Labelle on February 1, 2006, at $800. The company uses the gross method of recording sales discounts.

Required:

1. Prepare the journal entry to record the credit sale. Assume that the company uses the perpetual inventory system.

2. Prepare the journal entry to record the collection of cash from C. Labelle. Assume that the cash was received on (a) February 9, 2006, and (b) March 2, 2006.

B. On March 4, 2006, the Cycle Shop purchased bicycles and accessories from a supplier on credit for $8,000; the terms were 1/15, n/30. The company uses the gross method to record purchases.

Required:

3. Prepare the journal entry to record the purchase on credit. Assume that the company uses the perpetual inventory system.

4. Prepare the journal entry to record the payment of the invoice, assuming that the cash was paid on (a) March 12, 2006, and (b) March 28, 2006.

PROBLEMS

LO1

P8–1 **Analyzing Items to Be Included in Inventory**

Reggie Company has just completed a physical inventory count at year-end, December 31, 2007. Only the items on the shelves, in storage, and in the receiving area were counted and costed on a FIFO basis. The inventory amounted to $55,000. During the audit, the auditor developed the following additional information:

a. Goods costing $500 were being used by a customer on a trial basis and were excluded from the inventory count at December 31, 2007.

b. Goods costing $600 were in transit on December 31, 2007, with terms F.O.B. destination. Because these goods had not arrived, they were excluded from the physical inventory count.

c. On December 31, 2007, goods in transit to customers, with terms F.O.B. shipping point, amounted to $1,000 (the expected delivery date was January 10, 2008). Because the goods had been shipped, they were excluded from the physical inventory count.

d. On December 28, 2007, a customer purchased goods for $2,000 cash and left them "for pick-up on January 3, 2008." The cost of goods sold totalled $1,200 and was included in the physical inventory count because the goods were still on hand.

e. On the date of the inventory count, the company received notice from a supplier that goods ordered earlier at a cost of $2,200 had been delivered to the transportation company on December 27, 2007; the terms were F.O.B. shipping point. Because the shipment had not arrived by December 31, 2007, it was excluded from the physical inventory count.

f. On December 31, 2007, the company shipped goods to a customer, F.O.B. destination. The goods, which cost $950, are not expected to arrive at their destination before January 8, 2008. Because the goods were not on hand, they were not included in the physical inventory count.

g. One of the items sold by the company has such a low volume that the management planned to drop it last year. To induce Reggie Company to continue carrying the item, the manufacturer-supplier provided the item on a "consignment basis." This means that the manufacturer-supplier retains ownership of the item, and Reggie Company (the consignee) has no responsibility to pay for the items until they are sold to customers. Each month, Reggie Company sends a report to the manufacturer on the number sold and remits cash for the cost. At the end of December 2007, Reggie Company had five of these items on hand; therefore, they were included in the physical inventory count at $1,000 each.

Required:
Assume that Reggie's accounting policy requires including in inventory all goods for which it has title. Note that the point where title (ownership) changes hands is determined by the shipping terms in the sales contract. When goods are shipped "F.O.B. shipping point," title changes hands at shipment and the buyer normally pays for shipping. When they are shipped "F.O.B. destination," title changes hands on delivery, and the seller normally pays for shipping. Begin with the $55,000 inventory amount and compute the correct amount for the ending inventory. Explain the basis for your treatment of each of the preceding items. (*Hint:* Set up three columns: Item, Amount, and Explanation.)

P8–2 **Analyzing and Interpreting the Effects of Inventory Errors** (AP8–1)   ■ **LO2**

The income statements for four consecutive years for Clement Company reflected the following summarized amounts:

	2008	2007	2006	2005
Sales revenue	$58,000	$62,000	$51,000	$50,000
Cost of goods sold	37,000	43,000	35,000	32,500
Gross profit	21,000	19,000	16,000	17,500
Operating expenses	12,000	14,000	12,000	10,000
Pretax income	$ 9,000	$ 5,000	$ 4,000	$ 7,500

Subsequent to the development of these amounts, it has been determined that the physical inventory taken on December 31, 2006, was understated by $3,000.

Required:
1. Revise the income statements to reflect the correct amounts, taking into consideration the inventory error.

2. Compute the gross profit percentage for each year (a) before the correction and (b) after the correction. Do the results lend confidence to your corrected amounts? Explain.

3. What effect would the error have had on the income tax expense, assuming an average tax rate of 30 percent?

■ **LO3**

P8–3 Analyzing the Effects of Four Alternative Inventory Methods (AP8–2)

Allsigns Company uses a periodic inventory system. The company's accounting records for the most popular item in inventory showed the following details:

Transactions	Units	Unit Cost
Beginning inventory, January 1, 2008	400	$30
Transactions during 2008:		
a. Purchase, February 20	600	32
b. Sale, April 1 ($46 each)	(700)	
c. Purchase, June 30	500	36
d. Sale, August 1 ($46 each)	(100)	
e. Sales return, August 5 (related to Transaction [*d*])	20	

Required:

Compute (a) the cost of goods available for sale during 2008, (b) the cost of ending inventory at December 31, 2008, and (c) the cost of goods sold for 2008, under each of the following inventory costing methods (show computations and round to the nearest dollar):

1. Weighted-average cost.

2. First-in, first-out.

3. Last-in, first-out.

4. Specific identification, assuming that the sale on April 1, 2008, was selected one-fifth from the beginning inventory and four-fifths from the purchase of February 20, 2008. Assume that the sale of August 1, 2008, was selected from the purchase of June 30, 2008.

■ **LO3, 4**

P8–4 Evaluating Four Alternative Inventory Methods Based on Income and Cash Flow

At the end of January 2006, the records of Regina Company showed the following for a particular item that sold at $18 per unit:

Transactions	Units	Amount
Inventory, January 1, 2006	500	$2,500
Sale, January 10	(400)	
Purchase, January 12	600	3,600
Sale, January 17	(300)	
Purchase, January 26	160	1,280
Purchase return, January 28	(10)	Out of Jan. 26 purchase

Required:

1. Assuming the use of a periodic inventory system, prepare a summarized income statement through gross profit on sales under each of the following inventory costing methods: (a) weighted-average cost, (b) FIFO, (c) LIFO, and (d) specific identification. For specific identification, assume that the first sale was out of the beginning inventory and the second sale was out of the January 12 purchase. Show the inventory computations in detail.

2. Which method, FIFO or LIFO, would result in the highest pretax income? Which method would result in the highest EPS?

3. If LIFO were acceptable for income tax purposes:
   a. Which method, FIFO or LIFO, would result in the lowest income tax expense? Explain, assuming a 30-percent average tax rate.
   b. Which method, FIFO or LIFO, would produce the more favourable cash flow? Explain.

■ **LO3, 4**

P8–5 Analyzing and Interpreting Income Manipulation Under the LIFO Inventory Method

Pacific Company sells electronic test equipment that it acquires from a foreign source. During the year 2007, the inventory records reflected the following:

	Units	Unit Cost	Total Cost
Beginning inventory	15	$12,000	$180,000
Purchases	40	13,000	520,000
Sales (45 units at $25,000 each)			

Inventory is valued at cost using the LIFO inventory method. On December 28, 2007, the unit cost of the test equipment increased to $14,000. The cost will increase again during the first quarter of the next year.

Required:

1. Complete the following income statement summary and ending inventory using the LIFO method and the periodic inventory system (show computations):

Sales revenue	$ _____
Cost of goods sold	_____
Gross profit	_____
Operating expenses	300,000
Pretax income	$ _____
Ending inventory	$ _____

2. Pacific's management is considering the purchase of 20 additional units before December 31, 2007, at $14,000 each. Restate the income statement for the year, assuming the purchase of these 20 units.

3. Assume that you are the manager responsible for purchasing these 20 additional units, and that your annual bonus is based on Pacific's net income for the year. Would you purchase these 20 units before the end of 2007? Explain.

4. Assume that Pacific did not purchase additional test equipment, and that the market price per unit dropped suddenly to $12,500 because of oversupply. At what amount would the ending inventory be shown on the company's balance sheet? Would this amount be different if Pacific used FIFO instead of LIFO? Explain.

P8–6 Evaluating the FIFO to LIFO Change from a Shareholder's Perspective ■ **LO4**
Allendale Corporation reported the following summarized annual data at the end of 2008:

	(millions)
Sales revenue	$850
Cost of goods sold*	400
Gross profit	450
Operating expenses	310
Pretax income	$140

*Based on ending FIFO inventory of $120 million. On a LIFO basis, this ending inventory would have been $75 million.

Before issuing the preceding statement, the company decided to change from FIFO to LIFO for 2008 because "it better reflects our operating results." The company has always used FIFO.

Required:

1. Restate the summary income statement on a LIFO basis.

2. How much did pretax income change due to the LIFO decision for 2008? What caused the change in pretax income?

3. If you were a shareholder, what would be your reaction to this change? Explain.

P8–7 Evaluating the LIFO and FIFO Choice When Costs Are Rising and Falling ■ **LO4**
Income is to be evaluated under four different situations as follows:

a. Prices are rising:
    1. Situation A: FIFO is used.
    2. Situation B: LIFO is used.

b. Prices are falling:
1. Situation C: FIFO is used.
2. Situation D: LIFO is used.

The basic data common to all four situations are sales, 500 units for $12,500; beginning inventory, 300 units; purchases, 400 units; ending inventory, 200 units; and operating expenses, $4,000. The following tabulated income statements for each situation have been set up for analytical purposes:

	Prices Rising		Prices Falling	
	Situation A FIFO	Situation B LIFO	Situation C FIFO	Situation D LIFO
Sales revenue	$12,500	$12,500	$12,500	$12,500
Cost of goods sold				
Beginning inventory	3,600	?	?	?
Purchases	5,200	?	?	?
Cost of goods available for sale	8,800	?	?	?
Ending inventory	2,600	?	?	?
Cost of goods sold	6,200	?	?	?
Gross profit	6,300	?	?	?
Operating expenses	4,000	4,000	4,000	4,000
Pretax income	2,300	?	?	?
Income tax expense (30%)	690	?	?	?
Net income	$ 1,610			

Required:

1. Complete the preceding tabulation for each situation. In Situations A and B (prices rising), assume the following: beginning inventory, 300 units at $12 = $3,600; purchases, 400 units at $13 = $5,200. In Situations C and D (prices falling), assume the opposite; that is, beginning inventory, 300 units at $13 = $3,900; purchases, 400 units at $12 = $4,800. Use periodic inventory procedures.

2. Analyze and discuss the relative effects on pretax income and on net income as demonstrated by requirement 1 when prices are rising and when prices are falling.

3. Discuss the relative effects, if any, on the cash position for each situation.

4. Would you recommend FIFO or LIFO? Explain.

■ LO4   **P8–8 Evaluating the Effects of Inventory Costing Methods on Financial Statement Elements** (AP8–3)

Neverstop Corporation sells item A as part of its product line. Information about the beginning inventory, purchases, and sales of item A are given in the following table for the first six months of 2008. The company uses a periodic inventory system.

	Purchases		Sales	
Date	Number of Units	Unit Cost	Number of Units	Sales Price
January 1 (beginning inventory)	500	$2.50		
January 24			300	$4.00
February 8	600	$2.60		
March 16			560	$4.20
June 11	300	$2.75		

Required:

1. Compute the cost of ending inventory using the weighted-average costing method.
2. Compute the gross profit for the first six months of 2008 using the FIFO costing method.

3. Would the gross profit be higher, lower, or the same if Neverstop used the LIFO costing method rather than the FIFO method? Explain. No calculations are required.

4. Assume that due to a clerical error, the ending inventory is reported to be 440 units rather than the actual number of units (540) on hand. If FIFO is used, calculate the amount of the understatement or overstatement in
   a. the cost of goods sold for the first six months of 2008.
   b. the current assets at June 30, 2008.

P8–9 Evaluating the Income Statement and Cash Flow Effects of Lower of Cost or Market

■ **LO5**

Smart Company prepared its annual financial statements dated December 31, 2006. The company applies the FIFO inventory costing method; however, the company neglected to apply LCM to the ending inventory. The preliminary 2006 income statement follows:

Sales revenue		$280,000
Cost of goods sold		
Beginning inventory	$ 30,000	
Purchases	182,000	
Cost of goods available for sale	212,000	
Ending inventory (FIFO cost)	44,000	
Cost of goods sold		168,000
Gross profit		112,000
Operating expenses		61,000
Pretax income		51,000
Income tax expense (30%)		15,300
Net income		$ 35,700

Assume that you have been asked to restate the 2006 financial statements to incorporate the LCM inventory valuation rule. You have developed the following data relating to the ending inventory at December 31, 2006:

		Acquisition Cost		Net Realizable Value
Item	Quantity	Unit	Total	(Market)
A	3,000	$3	$ 9,000	$4
B	1,500	4	6,000	2
C	7,000	2	14,000	4
D	3,000	5	15,000	3
			$44,000	

Required:

1. Restate the income statement to reflect the valuation of the ending inventory on December 31, 2006, at the lower of cost or market. Apply the LCM rule on an item-by-item basis and show computations.

2. Compare and explain the LCM effect on each amount that was changed in requirement 1.

3. What is the conceptual basis for applying LCM to merchandise inventories?

4. What effect (increase, decrease, no effect) did the LCM rule have on the cash flow for 2006? What will be the long-term effect on cash flow (increase, decrease, no effect)? Computations are not necessary.

P8–10 Evaluating the Effects of Manufacturing Changes on Inventory Turnover Ratio and Cash Flows from Operating Activities (AP8–4)

■ **LO6**

H.–T. Tan and Company has been operating for five years as an electronics component manufacturer specializing in cellular phone components. During this period, it has experienced rapid growth in sales revenue and in inventory. Mr. Tan and his associates have hired you as the company's first corporate controller. You have put into place new purchasing and manufacturing procedures that are expected to reduce inventories by approximately one-third by year-end. You have gathered the following data related to the changes:

	(in thousands)	
	Beginning of Year	End of Year (projected)
Inventory	$463,808	$310,270
		Current Year (projected)
Cost of goods sold		$7,015,069

Required:

1. Compute the inventory turnover ratio based on two different assumptions:
   a. Those presented in the preceding table (a decrease in the balance in inventory).
   b. No change from the beginning of the year in the inventory balance.

2. Compute the effect of the projected change in the balance in inventory on cash flow from operating activities for the year (show the sign and amount of the effect).

3. On the basis of the preceding analysis, write a brief memo explaining how an increase in inventory turnover can result in an increase in cash flow from operating activities. Also explain how this increase can benefit the company.

P8–11 **(Chapter Supplement A) Evaluating the Effects of Perpetual Inventory Costing Methods on Financial Statement Elements**

This problem is an extension of P8–8. Neverstop Corporation sells item A as part of its product line. Information about the beginning inventory, purchases, and sales of item A are given in the following table for the first six months of 2008. The company uses a perpetual inventory system.

	Purchases		Sales	
Date	Number of Units	Unit Cost	Number of Units	Sales Price
January 1 (beginning inventory)	500	$2.50		
January 24			300	$4.00
February 8	600	$2.60		
March 16			560	$4.20
June 11	300	$2.75		

Required:

1. Compute the cost of ending inventory using the moving average costing method.

2. Compute the gross profit for the first six months of 2008 using the FIFO costing method.

3. Would the gross profit be higher, lower, or the same if Neverstop used the LIFO costing method rather than the FIFO method? Explain. No calculations are required.

4. Compare your answers to the requirements above to your answers to the corresponding requirements in P8-8 and comment on the differences, if any. Explain why the gross profit under perpetual LIFO differs from the gross profit under periodic LIFO.

P8–12 **(Chapter Supplement B) Recording Sales and Purchases with Cash Discounts and Returns** (AP8–5)

Campus Stop, Incorporated, is a student co-op. On January 1, 2007, the beginning inventory was $150,000, the Accounts Receivable balance was $4,000, and the Allowance for Doubtful Accounts had a credit balance of $800. Campus Stop uses a perpetual inventory system and records inventory purchases using the gross method.

The following transactions (summarized) occurred during 2007:

a. Sold merchandise for cash (cost of sales $137,500) $275,000

b. Received merchandise returned by customers as unsatisfactory and paid a cash refund (cost of sales $800) 1,600

c. Purchased merchandise from vendors on credit; terms 3/10, n/30 as follows:

　(i) August Supply Company invoice price before deduction of cash discount 5,000

　(ii) Other vendors, invoice price before deduction of cash discount 120,000

d. Purchased equipment for use in store; paid cash 2,200

e. Purchased office supplies for future use in the store; paid cash 700

f. Freight on merchandise purchased; paid cash 400

g. Paid accounts payable in full during the period as follows:

　(i) Paid August Supply Company after the discount period 5,000

　(ii) Paid other vendors within the 3% discount period 116,400

Required:
Prepare journal entries for each of the preceding transactions.

ALTERNATE PROBLEMS

AP8–1 **Analyzing and Interpreting the Effects of Inventory Errors** (P8–2) ■ **LO2**

The income statement for Sherwood Company summarized for a four-year period shows the following:

	2008	2007	2006	2005
Sales revenue	$3,000,000	$2,500,000	$2,400,000	$2,000,000
Cost of goods sold	2,100,000	1,780,000	1,630,000	1,400,000
Gross profit	900,000	720,000	770,000	600,000
Operating expenses	550,000	520,000	500,000	450,000
Pretax income	350,000	200,000	270,000	150,000
Income tax expense (30%)	105,000	60,000	81,000	45,000
Net income	$ 245,000	$ 140,000	$ 189,000	$ 105,000

An audit revealed that in determining these amounts, the ending inventory for 2006 was overstated by $20,000. The company uses a periodic inventory system.

Required:

1. Revise these income statements to reflect the correct amounts.

2. Did the error affect the cumulative net income for the four-year period? Explain.

3. What effect would the error have had on the income tax expense, assuming a 30-percent tax rate?

AP8–2 **Analyzing the Effects of Four Alternative Inventory Methods** (P8–3) ■ **LO3**

Yared Company uses a periodic inventory system. The company's accounting records for the most popular item in inventory showed the following details:

Transactions	Units	Unit Cost
Beginning inventory, January 1, 2007	1,800	$2.50
Transactions during 2007:		
a. Purchase, January 30	2,500	3.10
b. Sale, March 14 ($5 each)	(1,450)	
c. Purchase, May 1	1,200	4.00
d. Sale, August 31 ($5 each)	(1,900)	
e. Sales return, September 5 (related to Transaction [d])	150	

Required:

Compute (a) the cost of goods available for sale during 2007, (b) the cost of ending inventory at December 31, 2007, and (c) the cost of goods sold for 2007, under each of the following inventory costing methods (show computations and round to the nearest dollar):

1. Weighted-average cost.

2. First-in, first-out.

3. Last-in, first-out.

4. Specific identification, assuming that the sale of March 14, 2007, was selected two-fifths from the beginning inventory and three-fifths from the purchase of January 30, 2007. Assume that the sale of August 31, 2007, was selected from the remainder of the beginning inventory, with the balance from the purchase of May 1, 2007. The returned merchandise relates to the sale on August 31, but Yared bought the returned merhandise on May 1.

■ LO4   **AP8–3** **Evaluating the Effects of Inventory Costing Methods on Financial Statement Elements** (P8–8)

The Sportex Company, a diversified distribution outlet for sporting goods, purchases cartons of tennis balls from the Ball Corporation and markets the balls under the Sportex name. Purchases and sales data for January 2005, the first month of operations, are provided below.

	Date	Number of Cartons	Total Cost	Amount of Invoice
Purchases:	January 2	800	$16,000	
	January 19	600	13,200	
	January 29	500	11,000	
Sales:	January 5	500		$20,000
	January 21	700		29,200

Sportex uses a periodic inventory system.

Required:

1. Compute the cost of goods sold in January 2005 using FIFO.

2. Compute the change in income before income taxes for January 2005 that would result from using LIFO instead of FIFO.

3. Compute the cost of ending inventory at January 31, 2005, assuming that Sportex uses the weighted-average cost method. (Round your calculation of the average cost to the nearest cent.)

4. Some people argue that LIFO should always be used by Canadian companies because it increases the cost of goods sold and reduces income before taxes as well as the amount of taxes payable to the Canada Revenue Agency. In addition, LIFO produces a valuation of inventory that reflects current market prices. Comment on the previous statements, and provide justification for agreeing or disagreeing with the above-mentioned reasons for using LIFO.

■ LO6   **AP8–4** **Evaluating the Effects of Failed Expansion Plans on Inventory Turnover Ratio and Cash Flows from Operating Activities** (P8–10)

Arctic Enterprises

Arctic Enterprises, Inc., was the world's second-largest manufacturer of snowmobiles and had experienced exceptional growth in recent years. It planned for a major increase in sales in the following period by increasing production dramatically. Unfortunately, North America experienced less snow that year than in any of the preceding 20 years. As a consequence, sales remained flat, and Arctic reported a small profit of $1.9 million. However, its inventory balance increased by $24 million. Based on the following information, answer the questions that follow:

	(in thousands)	
	Beginning of Year	End of Year
Inventory	$23,808	$47,270
		Current Year
Cost of goods sold		$161,069

Required:

1. Compute the inventory turnover ratio based on two different assumptions:
   a. Those presented in the preceding table.
   b. No change from the beginning of the year in the inventory balance.

2. Compute the effect of the change in the balance in inventory on cash flow from operating activities for the year (show the sign and amount of the effect).

3. On the basis of your analysis, write a brief memo explaining how a decrease in inventory turnover can result in a decrease in cash flow from operating activities.

AP8–5 **(Chapter Supplement B) Recording Sales and Purchases with Cash Discounts and Returns** (P8–12)

The following transactions were selected from those occurring during the month of January 2008 for Dan's Store, Incorporated. A wide line of goods is offered for sale. Credit sales are extended to a few select customers; the usual credit terms are n/EOM. The cost of sales is always one-half of the gross sales price.

a. Sales to customers:

Cash	$228,000
On credit	72,000

b. Unsatisfactory merchandise returned by customers:

Cash	3,000
Credit	2,000

c. Purchased merchandise from vendors on credit; terms 2/10, n/30:

(*i*) Amount billed by Amy Supply Company	4,000
(*ii*) Amount billed by other vendors	68,000

d. Freight on merchandise purchased; paid cash — 1,500

e. Collections on accounts receivable — 36,000

f. Paid accounts payable in full during the period as follows:

(*i*) Amy Supply Company after the discount period	4,000
(*ii*) Paid other vendors within the discount period	66,640

g. Purchased two new typewriters for the office; paid cash — 1,000

Required:

Prepare journal entries for these transactions, assuming that a perpetual inventory system is used. Record inventory purchases using the gross method.

CASES AND PROJECTS

FINDING AND INTERPRETING FINANCIAL INFORMATION

CP8–1 **Finding Financial Information**

Refer to the Online Learning Centre Web site at www.mcgrawhill.ca/college/libby/student/ resources for the financial statements of The Forzani Group Ltd. (FGL).

■ **LO1, 3**

The Forzani Group

1. How much inventory does the company own at the end of the current year?

2. Estimate the amount of inventory that the company purchased and produced during the current year. (*Hint:* Use the cost of goods sold equation.)

3. What method does the company use to determine the cost of its inventory?

4. What was the change in inventory? How did it affect net cash provided by operating activities for the current year?

CP8–2 **Finding Financial Information**

Refer to the financial statements of Van Houtte Inc. given in Appendix B at the end of this book.

■ **LO1, 3, 6**

Van Houtte

1. What method does the company use to determine the cost of its inventory?

2. What are the components of the company's inventory balance? What aspects of its operations might determine why the first component is much smaller than the second?

3. Compute Van Houtte's inventory turnover ratio for the year ended April 2, 2005. Assume that Van Houtte's cost of sales is $177.9 million.

■ **LO6**

Van Houtte vs.
The Forzani Group

CP8–3   **Comparing Companies**

Refer to the Online Learning Centre Web site at **www.mcgrawhill.ca/college/libby/student/resources** for the financial statements of The Forzani Group Ltd. and to Appendix B of this book for the financial statements of Van Houtte Inc.

Required:

1. Compute the inventory turnover ratio for both companies for the current year. What would you infer from the difference? Assume that Van Houtte's cost of sales is $177.9 million.

2. Both companies measure inventory at the lower of cost or market. However, one of the companies determines cost of inventory using the average cost method while the other uses FIFO. Would you expect the different methods to cause a large difference in cost of goods sold? Why?

FINANCIAL REPORTING AND ANALYSIS CASES

■ **LO2**

The Wall Street Journal

CP8–4   **Interpreting the Financial Press**

In an article entitled "Convenient Fiction: Inventory Chicanery Tempts More Firms, Fools More Auditors," *The Wall Street Journal* outlined a series of cases in which companies used inventory fraud to overstate earnings. The article is available on the Online Learning Centre Web site at **www.mcgrawhill.ca/college/libby/student/resources**. Read the article and then write a short memo outlining the cases involved and how each of the inventory misstatements inflated earnings. Each case involved inflating ending inventory quantities or values. Indicate how doing so increases earnings. Also discuss the steps the author suggests that auditors should take to avoid such misstatements in the future.

Diageo

CP8–5   **Using Financial Reports: An International Perspective**

As the economy becomes more international in scope, users of financial statements are often expected to analyze companies that are not incorporated in Canada. Diageo is a major world corporation located in London. It owns many businesses, such as The Pillsbury Company.

DIAGEO
CONSOLIDATED PROFIT AND LOSS ACCOUNT
Years ended 30 June

(in millions of British pounds)	Notes	Current Year	Prior Year
Turnover	2	8,891	9,281
Operating costs	4/7	(7,020)	(7,494)
Operating profit	2	1,871	1,787
Share of profits of associates	6	438	457
Trading profit		2,309	2,244
Disposal of fixed assets	7	(35)	(43)
Sale of businesses	7	(10)	(1,254)
Interest payable (net)	8	(295)	(315)
Profit before taxation		1,969	632
Taxation	9	(487)	(491)
Profit after taxation		1,482	141
Minority interests			
Equity		(58)	(56)
Non-equity		(32)	(35)
Profit for the year		1,392	50
Dividends	10	(833)	(786)
Transferred to reserves		559	(736)
Earnings per share	11		
Basic		45.9p	1.6p
Diluted		45.9p	1.6p

Required:
Based on the concepts presented in this book, explain the meaning of the various
account classifications shown on the portion of the Diageo annual report presented here.
(Note: "Share of profits of associates" and "Minority interests," "Equity," and "Non-equity"
pertain to topics introduced in subsequent chapters.)

CRITICAL THINKING CASES

CP8–6 Making a Decision as a Financial Analyst: Analysis of the Effect of a Change to LIFO
An annual report for Quaker Oats included the following information:

■ **LO4**

Quaker Oats

> The company adopted the LIFO cost flow assumption for valuing the majority of remain-
> ing U.S. Grocery Products inventories. The Company believes that the use of the LIFO
> method better matches current costs with current revenues. The cumulative effect of this
> change on retained earnings at the beginning of the year is not determinable, nor are the
> pro forma effects of retroactive application of LIFO to prior years. The effect of this change
> on the current year was to decrease net income by $16.0 million, or $0.20 per share.

Required:
As a new financial analyst at a leading investment banking firm, you are assigned to write a
memo outlining the effects of the accounting change on Quaker's financial statements.
Assume a 34-percent tax rate. In your report, be sure to discuss the following issues:

1. In addition to the reason that was cited, why did management adopt LIFO?

2. As an analyst, how would you react to the $0.20 per share decrease in income caused by
   the adoption of LIFO?

**CP8–7 Evaluating an Ethical Dilemma: Earnings, Inventory Purchases, and Management
Bonuses**
Micro Warehouse is a computer software and hardware online and catalogue sales company.
A *Wall Street Journal* article disclosed the following:

■ **LO2**

Micro Warehouse

> ### MICRO WAREHOUSE IS REORGANIZING TOP MANAGEMENT
>
> Micro Warehouse Inc. announced a "significant reorganization" of its management,
> including the resignation of three senior executives.
>
> The move comes just a few weeks after the Norwalk, Conn., computer catalogue sales
> company said it overstated earnings by $28 million since 1992 as a result of accounting
> irregularities. That previous disclosure prompted a flurry of shareholder lawsuits against
> the company. In addition, Micro Warehouse said it is cooperating with an "informal inquiry"
> by the Securities and Exchange Commission.
>
> Source: Stephan E. Frank, *The Wall Street Journal*, November 21, 1996, p. B2.

Its quarterly report filed with the Securities and Exchange Commission two days before
indicated that inaccuracies involving understatement of purchases and accounts payable
in current and prior periods amounted to $47.3 million. It also indicated that, as a result,
$2.2 million of executive bonuses for 1995 would be cancelled. Micro Warehouse's effective
tax rate is approximately 40.4 percent. Both cost of goods sold and executive bonuses are
fully deductible for tax purposes.

Required:
As a new staff member at Micro Warehouse's auditing firm, you are assigned to write a
memo outlining the effects of the understatement of purchases and the cancellation of the
bonuses. In your report, be sure to include the following:

1. The total effect on pretax and after-tax earnings of the understatement of purchases.

2. The total effect on pretax and after-tax earnings of the cancellation of the bonuses.

3. An estimate of the percentage of after-tax earnings that management is receiving in bonuses.

4. A discussion of why Micro Warehouse's board of directors may have decided to tie managers' compensation to reported earnings and the possible relationship between this type of bonus scheme and the accounting errors.

FINANCIAL REPORTING AND ANALYSIS TEAM PROJECT

LO3, 4

CP8–8 **Team Project: Analyzing Inventories**

As a team, select an industry to analyze (industry lists can be found at www.investor.reuters.com and www.hoovers.com; click on "Companies and Industries"). Each team member should acquire the annual report for one publicly traded company in the industry, with each member selecting a different company. (Library files, the SEDAR service at www.sedar.com, or the company Web sites are good sources.) On an individual basis, each team member should then write a short report answering the following questions about the selected company.

1. What inventory costing method is applied to its inventories? What do you think motivated this choice?

2. If the company used LIFO, how much higher or lower would net income before taxes be if it had used FIFO or a similar method instead?

3. What is the inventory turnover ratio?

4. What was the effect of the change in inventories on cash flow from operations? Explain your answer.

Discuss any patterns across the companies that you as a team observe. Then, as a team, write a short report comparing and contrasting your companies using these attributes. Provide potential explanations for any differences discovered.

After studying this chapter, you should be able to:

1. Define, classify, and explain the nature of long-term assets and interpret the fixed asset turnover ratio. p. 464

2. Apply the cost principle to measure the acquisition and maintenance of property, plant, and equipment. p. 465

3. Apply various cost allocation methods as assets are held and used over time. p. 474

4. Explain the effect of asset impairment on the financial statements. p. 482

5. Analyze the disposal of property, plant, and equipment. p. 483

6. Apply measurement and reporting concepts for natural resources and intangible assets. p. 485

7. Explain the impact on cash flows of the acquisition, use, and disposal of long-term assets. p. 491

Reporting and Interpreting Property, Plant, and Equipment; Natural Resources; and Intangibles

FOCUS COMPANY:

WestJet Airlines

MANAGING PROFITS THROUGH
CONTROL OF PRODUCTIVE CAPACITY

WestJet Airlines, Canada's second largest airline, provides low-fare, friendly service to 34 North American cities. Clive Beddoe, along with a small team of Calgary entrepreneurs, started up WestJet in 1996 with three Boeing 737-200 aircraft. In 1999, the company completed its initial public offering on the Toronto Stock Exchange. By the end of 2003, the company's fleet had grown to 44 aircraft, its property and equipment reached a value of $1.14 billion, and it had captured 25 percent of the travellers (or guests, as the company prefers to call its passengers) in the markets it serves. As the company purchases new aircraft it increases the number of available seat miles,[1] or capacity to serve its customers' travel requirements.

The average age of its aircraft is six years and will decrease as WestJet completes its fleet renewal and expansion plan. WestJet will retire its old fleet of 737-200s by March 2006 and will replace them with newer, quieter, more fuel-efficient Boeing 737 aircraft. WestJet has agreements to acquire 26 Boeing 737s between January 2005, and August 2006, with options to buy additional aircraft.

Its expansion plan is part of a long-term strategy of controlled growth, financed by a combination of debt, equity, and cash generated from its operations. In September 2003, the company started a two-year program to retrofit its aircraft with Blended Winglet Technology to improve the aerodynamic performance and handling design of the 737-700s, extend the aircraft's flight

[1] An available seat mile is the number of miles a seat travels in a given period of time, whether or not it contains a passenger.

range, and reduce fuel consumption. This move is part of WestJet's strategy to enhance its position as the low-cost and innovation leader in the aviation industry.

UNDERSTANDING THE BUSINESS

Running a business such as an airline, a resource extraction and processing organization, or a pharmaceuticals company means acquiring adequate property, plant facilities, and equipment that will provide the capacity to serve the customers' current and future needs. Airlines require aircraft, spare engines and parts, flight simulators, buildings, and equipment. Resource extraction, processing, and distribution companies such as Petro-Canada, the focus company in Chapter 10, require the property from which they extract raw resources, the plant facilities to process raw materials into refined products, and a distribution system to bring the refined products to the point of sale.

In contrast, pharmaceutical and biotechnology companies require the property, plant, and equipment to conduct research and manufacture their products, but more importantly, they require the know-how to discover and apply scientific information. The most prominent assets on a pharmaceutical company's balance sheet are usually intangible assets such as licences, brand names, and patents.

One of the major challenges facing managers of most businesses is forecasting the level of long-term productive capacity (that is, the size of the company's plant and equipment) it will need to produce specified revenue streams. If managers underestimate the level of capacity needed in the future, the company will not be able to produce goods or services that are in demand and will miss the opportunity to earn revenue. On the other hand, if managers overestimate the productive capacity needed, the company will incur excessive costs that will reduce its profitability.

The airline industry provides an outstanding example of the difficulty associated with planning for and analyzing its capacity to produce revenue. If an airline takes off from Calgary to Toronto with empty seats, the economic value associated with these seats is lost for that flight. There is obviously no way to sell the seat to a customer after the airplane has left the gate. Unlike a manufacturer, an airline cannot place seats in inventory for use on future flights.

Likewise, if a large number of people want to board a flight, the airline must turn away some customers if seats are not available. You might be willing to buy a television set from Future Shop even if you are told that it is out of stock and there will be a one-week delay in delivery. You probably won't fly home for a holiday on an airline that would have you wait one week because no seats were available on its flights when you wanted to fly. You would simply pick another airline or use a different mode of transportation.

Much of the battle for passengers in the airline industry is fought in terms of property, plant, and equipment. Passengers want convenient schedules (which require a large number of aircraft) and they want to fly in new, modern equipment. Because airlines have such a large investment in equipment with no opportunity to hold unused seats in inventory, they work hard to fill aircraft to capacity for each flight. The importance of filling aircraft with passengers is highlighted in the following excerpt from WestJet's annual report for 2004 (pages 21–22).

REAL WORLD EXCERPT

WestJet Airlines

ANNUAL REPORT

MANAGEMENT'S DISCUSSION AND ANALYSIS OF FINANCIAL RESULTS
Revenues

In 2004, we increased our available seat miles ("ASMs") by 30.4% and revenue passenger miles ("RPMs") by 29.4% to 9.0 billion and 6.3 billion respectively. This increase in capacity was achieved through the acquisition of 11 new 737-700 aircraft, and the replacement of one 737-200 aircraft during the year... Even with a 30.4% increase in ASMs, we were still able to maintain a load factor of 70.0% in 2004.[2]

---

[2]The load factor is a measure of total capacity utilization, calculated as the proportion of total available seats occupied by revenue passengers.

Each flight not only generates revenue but also creates wear and tear on the equipment, no matter how many seats are filled. In pricing an airline ticket for a specific flight, WestJet's management includes an amount to cover this daily wear and tear that is part of the cost of operating an aircraft. The wear and tear is estimated and recorded as annual amortization expense. Industry practice is to assume that the lifetime of an aircraft is 20 years, during which companies like WestJet recover the acquisition cost of the aircraft and the related maintenance, operating, and financing costs, and turn a profit.

As you can see from this brief discussion, issues related to property, plant, and equipment have a pervasive impact on a company in terms of strategy, pricing decisions, and profitability. Business managers devote considerable time planning optimal levels of productive capacity adequate to meet expected future demand. Accountants estimate and report the cost of using these assets throughout their productive lives, taking into consideration applicable income tax laws and regulations, and financial analysts closely review financial statements to determine the impact of management decisions on the company's profitability and financial condition.

This chapter is organized according to the life cycle of long-lived assets—acquisition, use, and disposal. First we will discuss the measuring and reporting issues related to land, buildings, and equipment. Then we will discuss the measurement and reporting issues for natural resources and intangible assets. Among the issues we will discuss are maintaining, using, and disposing of property and equipment over time and measuring and reporting assets considered impaired in their ability to generate future cash flows.

ORGANIZATION OF THE CHAPTER

• Acquisition and Maintenance of Plant and Equipment	• Use, Impairment, and Disposal of Plant and Equipment	• Natural Resources and Intangible Assets
Classification of Long-Term Assets	Amortization Concepts	Acquisition and Depletion of Natural Resources
Fixed Asset Turnover Ratio	Alternative Amortization Methods	Acquisition and Amortization of Intangible Assets
Measuring and Recording Acquisition Cost	Managers' Selection Among Accounting Alternatives	Examples of Intangible Assets
Various Acquisition Methods	Measuring Asset Impairment	
Repairs, Maintenance, and Betterments	Disposal of Property, Plant, and Equipment	

ACQUISITION AND MAINTENANCE OF PLANT AND EQUIPMENT

Exhibit 9.1 shows the asset section of WestJet's balance sheet at December 31, 2004. Nearly 77 percent of WestJet's total assets are property and equipment. The company's annual report contains additional information about the cost of property, plant, and equipment owned or controlled by WestJet and related amortization; the amount of new investment in equipment during the year; and the amount of equipment that was sold or retired, as well as details of other long-term assets owned or controlled by WestJet. Let us begin by classifying these long-term assets.

Plant and Equipment as a Percentage of Total Assets for Selected Focus Companies

Dell Inc. 7.9%

Sleeman Breweries 31.4%

BCE Inc. 83.7%

CLASSIFICATION OF LONG-TERM ASSETS

■ **LEARNING OBJECTIVE 1**

Define, classify, and explain the nature of long-term assets and interpret the fixed asset turnover ratio.

LONG-TERM (OR LONG-LIVED OR CAPITAL) ASSETS are tangible and intangible resources owned by a business and used in its operations over several years.

TANGIBLE ASSETS (or fixed assets) have physical substance.

INTANGIBLE ASSETS have property ownership rights but not physical substance.

Accountants use the terms **long-term assets, long-lived assets, or capital assets** to identify property, plant, equipment, and intangible properties held for production, rental to others, or administrative purposes, or for the development, construction, maintenance, or repair of other assets. Long-term assets are acquired, constructed, or developed for long-term use on a continuing basis. They are not normally sold to generate revenue, although the normal course of business for real estate companies such as Intrawest Corporation is the purchase and sale of long-term assets such as land and buildings. Long-term assets can be tangible or intangible, and have the following characteristics:

1. **Tangible assets** can be touched because they have physical substance. This classification is most often called *property, plant, and equipment*. The three kinds of tangible assets held for use in operations are:

   a. *Land*, which is reported on the balance sheet as a separate item if it has a material value. Unlike aircraft or patents on pharmaceutical products, land does not become obsolete; therefore, it is never amortized.

   b. *Buildings, fixtures, and equipment* that are reported as a separate item on the balance sheet or in the notes. WestJet reports the details of such assets in Note 2, separating buildings from computer hardware, equipment, aircraft, and flight simulators.

   c. *Natural resources*, which include mineral deposits such as gold or iron ore, oil wells and reserves, and timber tracts. Corporations such as Barrick Gold, Suncor Energy Inc., and Noranda Mining and Exploration extract natural resources.

2. **Intangible assets** have no physical substance. Historically, they were called *Intangibles and Other Nothings*. Often, intangible assets arise from intellectual effort and are known as *intellectual property*. Examples include copyrights, patents, licences, trademarks, software, franchises, and subscription lists. In Canada, the cost of intangible assets with limited lives is allocated over the asset's legal or economic life. Intangibles that have indefinite lives, such as goodwill, must be tested annually for impairment to their value.

EXHIBIT **9.1**

WestJet Airlines Asset Section of the Balance Sheet

REAL WORLD EXCERPT

WestJet Airlines

ANNUAL REPORT

WESTJET AIRLINES LTD.
CONSOLIDATED BALANCE SHEETS
December 31, 2004 and 2003
(in thousands of dollars)

	2004	2003
Assets		
Current assets:		
Cash and cash equivalents	$ 148,532	$ 241,384
Accounts receivable	12,814	11,781
Income taxes recoverable	2,854	—
Prepaid expenses and deposits	25,493	19,928
Inventory	5,382	3,764
	195,075	276,857
Property and equipment (note 2)	1,601,546	1,140,226
Other assets (note 3)	80,733	59,775
	$1,877,354	$1,476,858

KEY **RATIO ANALYSIS:**

FIXED ASSET TURNOVER

ANALYTICAL QUESTION → How effectively is management utilizing its property, plant, and equipment or fixed assets to generate revenues?

RATIO AND COMPARISONS → The fixed asset turnover ratio is useful in answering this question. It is computed as follows:

$$\text{Fixed Asset Turnover} = \frac{\text{Net Sales (or operating revenues)}}{\text{Average Net Fixed Assets*}}$$

*Beginning + Ending Fixed Asset Balance (net of accumulated amortization) ÷ 2

The 2004 ratio for WestJet is:

$$\$1,057,990 \div [(\$1,140,226 + \$1,601,546) \div 2] = 0.77 \text{ times}$$

Comparisons over Time			Comparisons with Competitors	
WestJet Airlines			Southwest	Jet Blue
2002	2003	2004	2004	2004
1.50	0.99	0.77	0.83	0.71

INTERPRETATIONS

In General → The fixed asset turnover ratio measures how many times average fixed assets generated revenues. A high rate normally suggests effective management. An increasing rate over time signals more efficient fixed asset use. Creditors and security analysts use this ratio to assess a company's effectiveness in generating sales from its long-term assets.

Focus Company Analysis → WestJet's fixed assets turnover ratio has decreased significantly over the last three years, suggesting that there might be a decline in asset efficiency. When compared to two other companies in the industry, WestJet appears to be as efficient in utilizing its fixed assets as Jet Blue, but less efficient than Southwest Airlines. However, one has to be cautious in interpreting these ratios. One reason for the reduced turnover ratio is the renewal and growth in WestJet's fleet, from 27 in 2001 to 54 in 2004. WestJet also reported commitments to buy another 15 aircraft in 2005. Future turnover rates will remain low unless WestJet can either (1) dispose of older aircraft quicker than it has in the past, or (2) increase its revenues from flights, either by increasing the number of flights, increasing the number of paying passengers for existing flights, or increasing the revenue per paying passenger.

A Few Cautions → A lower or declining rate may indicate that a company is expanding (by acquiring additional productive assets) in anticipation of higher sales in the future. An increasing ratio could also signal that a firm has cut back on capital expenditures due to anticipation of a downturn in business. As a consequence, appropriate interpretation of the fixed asset turnover ratio requires an investigation of related activities.

Selected Focus Companies' Fixed Asset Turnover Ratios for 2004

Sleeman Breweries 2.43

Gildan Activewear 2.72

Dell 30.7

MEASURING AND RECORDING ACQUISITION COST

The *cost principle* requires that all reasonable and necessary costs incurred in acquiring a long-term asset, placing it in its operational setting, and preparing it for use should be recorded in a designated asset account (that is, the costs should be capitalized). These costs, including any sales taxes, legal fees, transportation costs, and installation costs, are added to the purchase price of the asset. Any financing (interest) charges associated with the purchase should not, however, be included in the cost of the asset. Financing charges should be reported as interest expense.

The cash flow statement of WestJet for fiscal year 2004 shows that WestJet acquired additional aircraft for $546.2 million. Although details of these purchases are not

■ **LEARNING OBJECTIVE 2**

Apply the cost principle to measure the acquisition and maintenance of property, plant, and equipment.

The **ACQUISITION COST** is the net cash equivalent amount paid or to be paid for the asset.

publicly available, we can make assumptions for illustration purposes. Let us assume that the net invoice amount for one aircraft is $59 million and that WestJet paid for transportation charges of $500,000 and preparation costs of $1,000,000 to make the airplaine ready for use. The amount recorded for the purchase is called the **acquisition cost**, which is the net cash equivalent amount paid or to be paid for the asset. WestJet calculates the acquisition cost of the airplane as follows:

Net invoice amount	$59,000,000
Add: Transportation charges paid by WestJet	500,000
Installation (preparation) costs paid by WestJet	1,000,000
Cost of the aircraft (added to the asset account)	$60,500,000

In addition to purchasing buildings and equipment, a company may acquire undeveloped land, typically with the intent to build a new factory or office building. When land is purchased, all of the incidental costs paid by the purchaser, such as title fees, sales commissions, legal fees, title insurance, delinquent taxes, and surveying fees, should be included in the cost of the land. Because land is not subject to amortization, it must be recorded as a separate asset.

Sometimes an old building or used machinery is purchased for operational use in the business. Renovation and repair costs incurred by the purchaser prior to use should be included in the asset account as a part of the cost of the asset.

VARIOUS ACQUISITION METHODS

For Cash   Assuming that WestJet paid cash for the aircraft and related transportation and preparation costs, the transaction affects WestJet's records as follows:

Aircraft (A)	60,500,000	
Cash (A)		60,500,000

Assets		=	Liabilities	+	Shareholders' Equity
Aircraft	+60,500,000				
Cash	−60,500,000				

It might seem unusual for WestJet to pay cash to purchase new assets that cost $60.5 million, but this is often the case. When it acquires productive assets, a company may pay with cash that was generated from operations or cash that was recently borrowed. Notice that WestJet's cash balance at December 31, 2004 exceeds $148.5 million. It also is possible for the seller to finance the purchase on credit.

For Debt   Now let us assume that WestJet signed a note payable for the aircraft and paid cash for the transportation and preparation costs. WestJet records the following journal entry:

Aircraft (A)	60,500,000	
Cash (A)		1,500,000
Note payable (L)		59,000,000

Assets		=	Liabilities		+	Shareholders' Equity
Aircraft	+60,500,000		Note payable	+59,000,000		
Cash	− 1,500,000					

For Equity (or Other Non-Cash Consideration)   A non-cash consideration, such as a company's common shares or a right given by the company to the seller to purchase the company's goods or services at a special price, might be part of the transaction. When a non-cash consideration is included in the purchase of an asset, the cash-equivalent cost is measured as any cash paid plus the current market value of the non-cash consideration given. Alternatively, if the market value of the non-cash consideration given cannot be determined, the current market value of the asset purchased is used for measurement purposes.

Assume that WestJet gave 2,000,000 of its common shares, with a market value of $25 per share (the approximate stock price on the date of the transaction), and paid the balance in cash, including cash for the transportation and preparation costs. The journal entry and transaction effects follow:

Aircraft (A)	60,500,000	
Cash (A)		10,500,000
Common shares (SE)		50,000,000

Assets		=	Liabilities	+	Shareholders' Equity	
Aircraft	+60,500,000				Common shares	+50,000,000
Cash	−10,500,000					

By Construction   In some cases, a company may construct an asset for its own use instead of buying it from a manufacturer. For example, in 2003, WestJet expanded a hangar facility in Calgary to shelter its aircraft. Because the company expanded the asset for its own use, the hangar's cost includes necessary costs of construction such as labour and materials, as well as overhead costs directly attributable to the construction activity. The costs also include the interest expense incurred during the construction period, based on the amount of funds invested in the construction of the hangar. WestJet can add the interest incurred to the other construction costs of the hangar until it is ready for use in operations. The amount of interest that is included in the cost of the hangar is called **capitalized interest**, which reduces the company's total interest expense every year until the hanger is in use. The complex computation of interest capitalization is discussed in other accounting courses.

WestJet described its policy on capitalized interest in note 1 to its financial statements:

CAPITALIZED INTEREST represents interest on borrowed funds directly attibutable to construction until the asset is substantially complete.

NOTES TO CONSOLIDATED FINANCIAL STATEMENTS

1. Significant Accounting Policies

...

(k) Capitalized costs:

Costs associated with assets under construction are capitalized from inception through to commencement of commercial operations. Interest attributable to funds used to finance capital assets is capitalized to the related asset. Legal and financing costs for the loan facilities are capitalized to other long-term assets and amortized on a straight-line basis over the term of the related loan.

Costs of new route development are expensed as incurred.

As a Basket Purchase of Assets   When several long-term assets, such as land, building, and equipment, are acquired in a single transaction and for a single lump sum, known as a **basket purchase**, the cost of each asset must be measured and recorded separately. This is true because land is not amortized, but buildings and equipment are, although at different rates. The purchase price must be apportioned among the land, the building, and the equipment on a rational basis.

Accountants use relative market values of the acquired assets on the date of acquisition to apportion the single lump sum to the various assets in the basket. Assume that WestJet paid $300,000 cash to purchase a building and the land on which the building is located. The separate, current market values of the building and land were not known; therefore, a professional appraisal was obtained. This appraisal, totalling

BASKET PURCHASE is an acquisition of two or more assets in a single transaction for a single lump sum.

$315,000, showed the following estimated market values: $189,000 for the building and $126,000 for the land. The apportioned purchase price based on a percentage of the relative market values is computed as follows:

Building	Land
$\dfrac{\text{Market Value}}{\text{Total Market Value}} = \dfrac{\$189,000}{\$315,000} = 60\%$	$\dfrac{\text{Market Value}}{\text{Total Market Value}} = \dfrac{\$126,000}{\$315,000} = 40\%$
$60\% \times \$300,000$ Total Cost $= \$180,000$	$40\% \times \$300,000$ Total Cost $= \$120,000$

The ratio of the market value of the land to the total market value ($126,000 ÷ $315,000 = 40 percent) is multiplied by the total cost to measure the cost of the land ($300,000 × 40 percent). Similarly, the ratio of the market value of the building to the total market value ($189,000 ÷ $315,000 = 60 percent) is multiplied by the total cost to measure the cost of the building ($300,000 × 60 percent). Assuming that WestJet purchases the assets with cash, the entry and effects are as follows:

Land (A)	120,000	
Building (A)	180,000	
Cash (A)		300,000

Assets		=	Liabilities	+	Shareholders' Equity
Land	+120,000				
Building	+180,000				
Cash	−300,000				

SELF-STUDY **QUIZ 9-1**

McDonald's Corporation

In a recent year, McDonald's Corporation purchased property, plant, and equipment priced at $1.8 billion. Assume that the company also paid $70 million for sales tax; $8 million for transportation costs; $1.3 million for installation and preparation of the property, plant, and equipment before use; and $100,000 in maintenance contracts to cover repairs to the property, plant, and equipment during use.

1. Compute the acquisition cost for the buildings and equipment.

2. For each situation below, indicate the effects of this acquisition on the following financial statement categories. Use + for increase and − for decrease and indicate the accounts and amounts:

	Assets	Liabilities	Shareholders' Equity
a. Paid 30% in cash and signed a note payable for the balance.			
b. Issued 10 million shares at a market price of $45 per share and paid the balance in cash.			

After you complete your answers, check them with the solutions presented on page 496.

REPAIRS, MAINTENANCE, AND BETTERMENTS

Most assets require substantial expenditures during their useful lives to maintain or enhance their productive capacity. These expenditures include cash outlays for ordinary repairs and maintenance, major repairs, replacements, and additions. Remember that the terms *expenditure* and *expense* are not synonymous. An expenditure is the payment of money to acquire goods or services. These goods and services may be recorded as either assets or expenses, depending on whether they benefit future periods or only the current period. Expenditures made after an asset is acquired are classified as follows:

1. **Revenue expenditures**—expenditures that maintain the productive capacity of the asset during the current accounting period only. Therefore, they are added to the appropriate *expense* accounts in the current period. **Ordinary repairs and maintenance** costs are for normal maintenance and upkeep of long-term assets and are necessary to keep the assets in their usual condition. These costs are recurring in nature, involve relatively small amounts at each occurrence, and do not directly lengthen the useful life of the asset.

   In the case of WestJet, examples of ordinary repairs include changing oil in engines, replacing lights in the control panels, and fixing scuffed leather on a passenger seat. Although each expenditure for ordinary repairs is relatively small, in the aggregate these expenditures can be substantial. In the year 2004, WestJet incurred more than $78.3 million for ordinary aircraft maintenance and repairs. This amount was reported as an expense on its income statement.

2. **Capital expenditures**—expenditures that increase the productive life, operating efficiency, or capacity of the asset. Capital expenditures are added to the appropriate **asset** accounts. **Extraordinary repairs** and **betterments** occur infrequently, involve large amounts of money, and increase an asset's economic usefulness in the future through either increased efficiency or longer life. Examples include additions, major overhauls, complete reconditioning, and major replacements and improvements, such as the complete replacement of an engine on an aircraft.

   For example, one betterment that Transport Canada requires is periodic maintenance of aircraft called *D checks*, whereby the aircraft is stripped to its airframe and every component is repaired, reconditioned, or replaced. An older 737-200 must undergo a D check about every seven years. The frequency of a D check, however, increases with the increasing age of an aircraft. The older the aircraft, the fewer years it can safely fly before a D check is completed. The cost of a D check is a betterment because it enhances the performance, increases the resale value, and extends the useful life of an aircraft.

   An example of an extraordinary repair has also arisen in the airline industry from a change in Transport Canada's regulation to reduce the acceptable level of engine noise. WestJet had to undertake an unplanned, very expensive, one-time repair that extended the economic life of its aircraft. It installed hushkits on all of its old aircraft engines that did not meet new noise-abatement regulations. Without hushkits, WestJet would not be able to fly these planes. This extraordinary repair is a one-time cost that certainly increased the aircraft's future economic usefulness.

REVENUE EXPENDITURES maintain the productive capacity of the asset during the current accounting period only and are recorded as expenses.

ORDINARY REPAIRS AND MAINTENANCE are costs for normal operating upkeep of long-term assets.

CAPITAL EXPENDITURES increase the productive life, operating efficiency, or capacity of the asset and are recorded as increases in asset accounts, not as expenses.

EXTRAORDINARY REPAIRS are infrequent expenditures that increase the asset's economic usefulness in the future.

BETTERMENTS are costs incurred to enhance the productive or service potential of a long-term asset.

In many cases, no clear line distinguishes capital expenditures (assets) from revenue expenditures (expenses). In these situations, accountants must exercise professional judgment and make subjective decisions. Many managers prefer to classify an item as a capital expenditure for financial reporting because net income for the period is higher by not reporting the total amount as an expense in the current period. Of course, most managers prefer to classify the expenditure as a deductible expense on the income tax return to pay lower taxes in the current period. Because these decisions are subjective, auditors closely review the items reported as capital and revenue expenditures.

To avoid spending too much time on classifying capital and revenue expenditures, some companies develop simple policies that govern the accounting for these expenditures. For example, one large computer company expenses all individual items that cost less than $1,000. These policies are acceptable because of the *materiality constraint.*

FINANCIAL **ANALYSIS**

HIDING BILLIONS IN EXPENSES THROUGH CAPITALIZATION

When expenditures that should be recorded as current period expenses are improperly capitalized as part of the cost of an asset, the effects on the financial statements can be enormous. In one of the largest accounting frauds in history, WorldCom inflated its income and cash flows from operations by billions of dollars in just such a scheme. Over five quarters in 2001 and 2002, the company initially announced that it had capitalized $3.8 billion that should have been recorded as operating expenses. This amount was later raised to an estimated $7.2 billion in false profits reported in 1999 through 2002. This fraud turned World-Com's actual losses into large profits. Accounting for expenses as capital expenditures increases current income because it spreads a single period's operating expenses over many future periods as amortization expense. It increases cash flows from operations by moving cash outflows from the operating section to the investing section of the cash flows statement. A full report about this accounting scandal totalling 340 pages was submitted by the company to the Securities and Exchange Commission in June 2003.

SELF-STUDY **QUIZ 9-2**

A building that originally cost $400,000 has been used over the past 10 years and needs continuous maintenance and repairs. For each of the following expenditures, indicate whether it should be expensed in the current period or capitalized as part of **the cost of the asset.**

	EXPENSE OR CAPITALIZE?
1. Replacing electrical wiring throughout the building.	_____
2. Repairs to the front door of the building.	_____
3. Annual cleaning of the filters on the building's air conditioning system.	_____
4. Significant repairs due to damage from an unusual and infrequent flood.	_____

After you have completed your answers, check them with the solutions on page 497.

USE, IMPAIRMENT, AND DISPOSAL OF PLANT AND EQUIPMENT

AMORTIZATION CONCEPTS

All long-term assets, except land, have limited useful lives (such as aircraft purchased by WestJet). They represent the prepaid cost of a bundle of future services or benefits.

The matching principle requires that a portion of an asset's cost be allocated as an expense to the periods in which revenue is earned as a result of its use. Thus, the cost of long-term assets is matched in a systematic and rational manner with the revenues that are earned by using them. WestJet earns revenue by flying its aircraft and incurs an expense when using its aircraft to generate the revenue.

The term used to identify the matching of the cost of buildings and equipment with revenues generated by the assets is **amortization**.

Amortization: The process of *allocating the acquisition cost* of tangible long-term assets, other than land, over their productive lives using a systematic and rational method.

The amount of amortization recorded during each period is reported on the income statement as an expense for that period. WestJet reported in its income statement an amortization expense of $3.2 million for the year 2003. The journal entry and transaction effects, including the contra-asset account (XA) follow:

AMORTIZATION is the process of allocating the acquisition cost of property, plant, and equipment (but not land) over their useful lives using a systematic and rational method.

Amortization expense (E)	63,208,000	
Accumulated amortization (XA)		63,208,000

Assets	=	Liabilities	+	Shareholders' Equity
Accumulated amortization −63,208,000				Amortization expense −63,208,000

The periodic amortization expenses throughout the asset's useful life are accumulated in the contra-asset account Accumulated Amortization. The acquisition cost minus accumulated amortization is called **net book value or net carrying value** and appears on the balance sheet. In addition, companies like WestJet disclose, in a note to the financial statements for 2004, information about the long-term assets they own or control and the related accumulated amortization.

NET BOOK (OR NET CARRYING) VALUE is the acquisition cost of an asset less accumulated amortization.

REAL WORLD EXCERPT

WestJet Airlines

ANNUAL REPORT

NOTES TO CONSOLIDATED FINANCIAL STATEMENTS

2. Property and Equipment

2004	Cost	Accumulated depreciation	Net book value
Aircraft—700 series	$1,282,308	$ 46,180	$1,236,128
Aircraft—200 series	142,657	121,182	21,475
Ground property and equipment	109,334	34,586	74,748
Spare engines and parts—700 series	52,641	4,777	47,864
Buildings	39,636	2,840	36,796
Aircraft under capital lease	31,304	26,781	4,523
Spare engines and parts—200 series	24,397	16,523	7,874
Leasehold improvements	5,655	3,104	2,551
	1,687,932	255,973	1,431,959
Deposits on aircraft	156,943	—	156,943
Assets under construction	12,644	—	12,644
	$1,857,519	$255,973	$1,601,546

FINANCIAL **ANALYSIS**

NET BOOK VALUE AS AN APPROXIMATION OF REMAINING LIFE

Some analysts compare the net book value of assets to their original cost as an approximation of their remaining life. If the net book value of an asset is 100 percent of its cost, it is a new asset; if the net book value is 25 percent of its cost, the asset has about 25 percent of its estimated life remaining. In WestJet's case, the net book value of its aircraft is 90 percent of its original cost. This compares with 70 percent for Southwest Airlines and 96 percent for Jet Blue. This comparison suggests that the aircraft used by WestJet may have more of its estimated life remaining than those of some other major airlines.

Book Value/ Original Cost

WestJet 90%

Southwest 70%

Jet Blue 96%

Based on the information WestJet provided in its note 1 (h) and note 2, the net book value can be used to estimate the asset's remaining useful life. You simply calculate the ratio of net book value to acquisition cost and multiply it by the asset's estimated useful life. Consider, for example, WestJet's spare engines and parts for the 700 series.

$$\frac{\text{Net book value}}{\text{Acquisition cost}} \times \text{Estimated useful life} = \frac{\$47,864,000}{\$52,641,000} \times 20 = 18.2 \text{ years}$$

The useful life of WestJet's important assets can be analyzed in this manner and comparisons can be made to other companies in the industry. This is, however, only a rough approximation because the net book value of long-term assets depends on the estimates of useful life and residual value, as well as the specific amortization method used.

Students are often confused about the concept of amortization as accountants define it. Amortization in accounting is a process of *cost allocation*. It is not a process of determining the current market value or worth of the asset. When an asset is amortized, the net book value *does not* represent the current market value of the asset. Under the cost principle, the cost of a long-term asset is recorded at its current market value only on the acquisition date. At subsequent balance sheet dates, the unamortized cost is not measured on a market value basis. Instead, the acquisition cost is reduced by accumulated amortization.

The need for amortization can be illustrated with a simple example. If you were the president of WestJet in a year when it acquired a new aircraft for $45 million in cash, you probably would object strongly if the accountant tried to charge the entire cost as an expense in the year of acquisition. You would argue that the aircraft should produce revenue for several years, so the cost of the asset should be allocated to expense over the periods in which it will earn revenue. Failure to do so would understate income in the year of acquisition and overstate income in each year that the aircraft was used. This explains why accountants amortize tangible long-term assets and why amortization is an important part of measuring a company's profitability.

The calculation of amortization expense requires three amounts for each amortizable asset:

1. Acquisition cost.
2. *Estimated* useful life to the company.
3. *Estimated* residual (or salvage) value at the end of the asset's useful life to the company.

Two of these three amounts are estimates. Therefore, *amortization expense is an estimate*.

Useful life represents management's estimate of the asset's useful *economic life* to the company rather than the total economic life to all potential users. For example, WestJet has estimated the useful life of a typical 737-200 at 17,500 flight hours and that of a typical 737-700 at 86,500 flight hours. Furthermore, let us assume that West-Jet estimates the number of flight hours per year at 2,500 for the 737-200 and at 3,460 hours for the 737-700. The older 737-200 must be repaired more frequently than the newer 737-700 and therefore will not fly as many hours each year. Dividing the total estimated useful life by the annual use provides an estimate of 7 years for the 737-200 and 25 years for the new 737-700.

The determination of estimated useful life of a long-term asset must conform to the *continuity assumption*. This assumption holds that the business will continue indefinitely to pursue its commercial objectives and will not liquidate in the foreseeable future.

WestJet, similar to other companies, discloses in note 1 to its financial statements the useful lives of its long-term assets and the methods used to amortize them. We will use the same estimates in our illustrations, where appropriate.

> **USEFUL LIFE** is the expected service life of an asset to the present owner.

> **REAL WORLD EXCERPT**
>
> *WestJet Airlines*
>
> ANNUAL REPORT

NOTES TO CONSOLIDATED FINANCIAL STATEMENTS

1. Significant Accounting Policies

.....

(i) Property and equipment:

Property and equipment are recorded at cost and depreciated to their estimated residual values. Aircraft under capital lease are initially recorded at the present value of minimum lease payments at the inception of the lease.

Asset	Basis	Rate
Aircraft net of estimated residual value—700 series	Cycles	Cycles flown
Aircraft net of estimated residual value—200 series	Flight hours	Hours flown
Ground property and equipment	Straight-line	5 to 25 years
Spare engines and parts net of estimated residual value—700 series	Straight-line	20 years
Buildings	Straight-line	40 years
Aircraft under capital lease	Straight-line	Term of lease
Spare engines and parts net of estimated residual value—200 series	Flight hours	Fleet hours flown
Leasehold improvements	Straight-line	Term of lease

Residual (or salvage) value represents management's estimate of the amount the company expects to recover upon disposal of the asset at the end of its estimated useful life. The residual value is not necessarily the value of the asset as salvage or scrap. Rather, it may be the value to another user at the date on which the current owner intends to dispose of it.

Residual value is the estimated amount to be recovered less any estimated costs of dismantling, disposal, and sale. In many cases, disposal costs may approximately equal the gross residual value. Therefore, many amortizable assets are assumed to have no residual value.

In the case of aircraft owned by WestJet, the company uses a conservative approach by estimating only the residual value of the aircraft's engines, which is approximately $1,400,000. Other companies such as Delta Air Lines estimate the residual value at 5 percent of the acquisition cost, which is greater than $1,400,000.

> **RESIDUAL (OR SALVAGE) VALUE** is the estimated amount to be recovered, less disposal costs, at the end of the estimated useful life of an asset.

FINANCIAL **ANALYSIS**

DIFFERENCES IN ESTIMATED LIVES WITHIN A SINGLE INDUSTRY

Notes to actual financial statements of companies in the airline industry reveal the following estimates for lives of flight equipment:

Company	Estimated Life (in years)
WestJet Airlines	7 to 25
Delta Air Lines	20 to 25
U•S Airways	11 to 30
Singapore Airlines	15
Southwest Airlines	20 to 25

The differences in estimated lives may be attributable to a number of factors such as type of aircraft used by each company, equipment replacement plans, differences in operations, and the degree of management conservatism. In addition, given the same type of aircraft, companies that plan to use the equipment over fewer years may estimate higher residual values than do companies that plan to use the equipment longer. For example, Singapore Airlines uses a residual value of 20 percent over a relatively short useful life, as compared to 5 percent for Delta Air Lines over a 25-year useful life.

Differences in estimated lives and residual values of assets used by specific companies can have a significant impact on the comparison of the profitability of the companies. Analysts must be certain that they identify the causes for the differences in amortizable lives.

■ **LEARNING OBJECTIVE 3**

Apply various cost allocation methods as assets are held and used over time.

ALTERNATIVE AMORTIZATION METHODS

Accountants have not been able to agree on a single, best method of amortization because matching the cost of using long-term assets to the revenue they generate differs significantly among companies. As a result, managers may choose from several different acceptable amortization methods, basing their decision on how they believe the asset will generate revenues over time. Once selected, the method should be applied consistently over time to enhance comparability of financial information to users. We will discuss the three most common amortization methods:

1. Straight-line.
2. Units-of-production.
3. Declining-balance.

The facts shown in Exhibit 9.2 will be used to illustrate each of the three methods of calculating amortization expense for one 737-700 aircraft purchased on January 1, 2006.[3]

---

[3]Most of the examples that we discuss in this chapter assume that assets were acquired on the first day of the year and amortized for the entire year. In practice, assets are purchased at various times during the year. Most companies adopt a policy to cover partial-year amortization, such as "to the nearest full month" or "half year in the year of acquisition."

EXHIBIT **9.2**

Illustrative Data for Computing Amortization under Alternative Methods

WESTJET AIRLINES	
Acquisition cost of aircraft, purchased on January 1, 2006	$45,000,000
Estimated life (in years)	25
Estimated residual value	$1,400,000
Estimated life in flight hours	86,500 flight hours
Actual flight hours in: Year 2006	3,460 flight hours
Year 2007	3,600 flight hours
Year 2008	3,350 flight hours

Straight-Line Method   More companies, including WestJet, use **straight-line amortization** in their financial statements than all other methods combined. Under the straight-line method, an equal portion of an asset's amortizable cost is allocated to each accounting period over its estimated useful life. The formula to estimate annual amortization expense follows:

STRAIGHT-LINE AMORTIZATION is the method that allocates the cost of an asset in equal periodic amounts over its useful life.

Straight-Line Method	
Amortizable Amount	**Straight-Line Rate**

(Cost − Residual Value) × 1/Useful Life = Amortization Expense

"Cost minus residual value" is the amortizable amount. "1 ÷ Useful life" is the straight-line rate. Using the data provided in Exhibit 9.2, the amortization expense is measured as follows:

$$(\$45,000,000 - \$1,400,000) \times 1/25 = \$1,744,000$$

An *amortization schedule* for the first three years of the aircraft's useful life follows (in thousands of dollars):

Year	Computations	Amortization Expense (Reported on the income statement)	Accumulated Amortization (Reported on the balance sheet at year-end)	Net Book Value (Cost − Accumulated Amortization at year-end)
At acquisition				$45,000
2006	($45,000 − $1,400) × 1/25	$1,744	$1,744	43,256
2007	($45,000 − $1,400) × 1/25	1,744	3,488	41,512
2008	($45,000 − $1,400) × 1/25	1,744	5,232	39,768
	Total	$5,232		

Notice that

(1) amortization expense is a constant amount for each year,

(2) accumulated amortization increases by an equal amount each year, and

(3) net book value decreases by the same amount each year. This is the reason for the name *straight-line method*.

Also notice that, from this schedule, the adjusting entry can be prepared and the effects on the income statement and ending balance on the balance sheet are known. WestJet uses the straight-line method for all of its long-term assets, except for aircraft and spare engines and parts. WestJet reported amortization expense in the amount of $126,338,000 for 2004. Most companies in the airline industry use the straight-line method.

UNITS-OF-PRODUCTION AMORTIZATION is the method that allocates the cost of a long-term asset over its useful life based on the relation of its periodic output to its total estimated output.

Units-of-Production (Activity) Method   WestJet uses the **units-of-production amortization** method to relate amortizable cost to the total estimated productive service of its aircraft. The formula to estimate annual amortization expense under this method follows:

Units-of-Production Method

Amortization Rate
per Unit

$$\underbrace{\frac{(\text{Cost} - \text{Residual Value})}{\text{Estimated Total Production}}} \times \frac{\text{Actual}}{\text{Production}} = \text{Amortization Expense}$$

Dividing the amortizable amount by the estimated total production yields the amortization rate per unit of production (or activity), which then is multiplied by the actual annual production (or activity) to determine amortization expense. Using the information in Exhibit 9.2, the computation of the amortization rate per unit follows:

$$\frac{\$45,000,000 - \$1,400,000}{86,500 \text{ flight hours}} = \$504 \text{ per Flight Hour}$$

For every flight hour that the aircraft flies, WestJet records amortization expense of $504. The amortization schedule for the years 2006, 2007, and 2008 under the units-of-production method follows (amounts in thousands of dollars):

Year	Computations	Amortization Expense	Accumulated Amortization	Net Book Value
At acquisition				$45,000
2006	$504 × 3,460 flight hours	$1,744	$1,744	43,256
2007	504 × 3,600 flight hours	1,814	3,558	41,442
2008	504 × 3,350 flight hours	1,688	5,246	39,754
	Total	$5,246		

Notice that amortization expense, accumulated amortization, and net book value vary from period to period directly with the number of flight hours. When the units-of-production method is used, amortization expense is said to be a *variable expense* because it varies directly with production or use.

The units-of-production method is based on an estimate of an asset's total productive capacity or output that is difficult to estimate. This is another example of the degree of subjectivity that is inherent in accounting.

Declining-Balance Method   Under the declining-balance amortization method, amortization expense amounts are higher in the early years of an asset's useful life than in the later years. This method results in **accelerated amortization**. Accelerated amortization is used for the following reasons:

1. An amortizable asset produces more revenue in its early life because it is more efficient in earlier years than in later years. Therefore, accelerated amortization better matches the cost of using the asset to the revenue it generates.

2. Repair costs increase in later years; therefore, the total cost of use per period should include a decreasing amortization expense to offset the increasing repair expense each period.

The relationship between accelerated amortization expense, repair expense, and the total expense of using the asset is shown in Exhibit 9.3.

Accelerated methods are seldom used for financial reporting purposes. The accelerated method used more frequently than others is the declining-balance method, which is illustrated here.

Units of Production Annual Amortization Expense (in millions)

$1.74 $1.81 $1.69

Year   2006   2007   2008

ACCELERATED AMORTIZATION methods result in higher amortization expense in the early years of an asset's life and lower expense in the later years.

Declining-balance amortization is based on multiplying the asset's net book value by a fixed rate that exceeds the straight-line (SL) rate. The declining-balance (DB) rate is found by (1) computing the SL rate, ignoring residual value, and then (2) multiplying that SL rate by a selected acceleration rate. The rate is often double (two times) the straight-line rate and is called the *double-declining-balance rate*. For example, if the estimated useful life is 10 years, the straight-line rate is 10 percent (1 ÷ 10), then the declining-balance rate is 20 percent (2 × the straight-line rate of 10 percent). Other typical acceleration rates are 1.5 times and 1.75 times. The *double-declining-balance (DDB) rate* is adopted most frequently by companies utilizing the accelerated method and will be used in our illustration.

To calculate amortization expense under the double-declining-balance method, the net book value of the asset is multiplied by the DDB rate as follows:

DECLINING-BALANCE AMORTIZATION is the method that allocates the cost of an asset over its useful life based on a multiple of (often two times) the straight-line rate.

Double-Declining-Balance Method	
Net Book Value	**Declining-Balance Rate**

(Cost − Accumulated Amortization) × 2/Useful Life = Amortization Expense

Note that the residual value is not subtracted from acquisition cost in computing amortization expense at this stage. However, an asset's net book value cannot be amortized below residual value. Therefore, if the annual computation reduces net book value below residual value, a lower amount of amortization expense must be recorded so that net book value equals residual value. No additional amortization expense is computed in subsequent years. Computation of DDB amortization expense is illustrated using the data given in Exhibit 9.2 (amounts in thousands of dollars):

Year	Computations	Amortization Expense	Accumulated Amortization	Net Book Value
At acquisition				$45,000
2006	($45,000 − $0) × 2/25	$3,600	$3,600	41,400
2007	($45,000 − $3,600) × 2/25	3,312	6,912	38,088
2008	($45,000 − $6,912) × 2/25	3,047	9,959	35,041
	Total	$9,959		

Double-Declining-Balance Annual Amortization Expense

$3,600 $3,312 $3,047

Year   2006 2007 2008

The calculated amortization expense for this asset differs depending upon the amortization method used. Using the straight-line method, the annual expense is $1,744,000 each year of the aircraft's 25-year useful life. Using the units-of-production method, annual amortization expense varies each year from a low of $1,688,400 in year 2008 to a high of $1,814,400 in year 2007. Finally, using the DDB method, amortization expense declines every year from $3,600,000 in 2006 to $3,047,000 in year 2008. This, in part, explains why an analyst must be careful when using net book value to estimate the remaining useful life of an asset. Using our example, we obtain different estimates for the remaining useful life for the same aircraft after three years, depending on the amortization method used:

Amortization Method	Estimated Remaining Useful Life
Straight line	($39,768/$45,000) $\times$ 25 = 22.24 years or approximately 22 years
Units of production	($39,753/$45,000) $\times$ 25 = 22.09 years or approximately 22 years
Double declining balance	($35,041/$45,000) $\times$ 25 = 19.47 years or approximately 20 years

This example illustrates why care must be taken to read the notes to the financial statements of any company and identify the accounting policies it uses before comparing its financial results to those of other companies.

Companies in industries that expect fairly rapid obsolescence of their equipment use the declining-balance method. Sony is one of the companies that uses this method.

REAL WORLD EXCERPT

Sony

ANNUAL REPORT

2. Summary of significant accounting policies:

Property, plant, and equipment and depreciation

Property, plant, and equipment are stated at cost. Depreciation of property, plant, and equipment is primarily computed on the declining-balance method for Sony Corporation and Japanese subsidiaries, except for certain semiconductor manufacturing facilities whose depreciation is computed on the straight-line method, and on the straight-line method for foreign subsidiaries at rates based on estimated useful lives of the assets, principally, ranging from 15 years up to 50 years for buildings and from 2 years up to 10 years for machinery and equipment. Significant renewals and additions are capitalized at cost. Maintenance and repairs, and minor renewals and betterments are charged to income as incurred.

As this note indicates, companies may use different amortization methods for different classes of assets. Under the consistency principle, they are expected to apply the same methods to those assets over time.

In the previous illustration, we assumed that the aircraft was purchased at the beginning of the year. In reality, however, companies purchase assets at any date during the year, which complicates the computation of amortization expense for the first year of acquisition. For practical purposes, acquisitions made during the year are amortized in a convenient manner during the asset's first year of operation. Amortization expense can be computed for the number of months the asset is actually in use, or it can be computed for half a year using the half-year convention.

For example, if WestJet acquired the aircraft on May 1, 2006 instead of January 1, 2006, the annual straight-line amortization expense could be prorated by determining the monthly amortization expense and multiplying the monthly amortization by the number of months WestJet flew this aircraft during 2006 (eight months in this case):

$$\text{Amortization expense} = (\$1,744,000 \div 12) \times 8 \text{ months} = \$1,162,667$$

Alternatively, companies that acquire many long-term assets during the year may use the half-year rule, which implies that similar long-term assets, such as office equipment, that are acquired at different dates throughout the year can be assumed to have been purchased around the middle of the year. Thus, all the office equipment acquired during the fiscal year is amortized for half a year at the end of the year of acquisition. This practical rule is acceptable as long as the amount of amortization expense for the year is not materially misstated.

In Summary The following table summarizes the three amortization methods and computations and shows graphically the differences in amortization expense over time for each method. The units-of-production method varies with the amount of actual production or service activity during the period (see Exhibit 9.4).

Method	Computation
Straight line	(Cost − Residual Value) × 1/Useful Life
Units of production	(Cost − Residual Value)/Estimated Total Production × Annual Production
Double declining balance	(Cost − Accumulated Amortization) × 2/Useful Life

EXHIBIT **9.4**

Differences in Amortization Methods over Time

Amortization Expense / Years

- Straight line
- Units of production
- Declining balance (typical pattern)

FINANCIAL **ANALYSIS**

IMPACT OF ALTERNATIVE AMORTIZATION METHODS

Assume that you are analyzing two companies that are exactly the same except for the fact that one uses accelerated amortization and the other uses the straight-line method. Which company would you expect to report higher net income? Actually, the question is a bit tricky. The answer is that you cannot say for certain which company's income would be higher.

The accelerated methods report higher amortization and therefore lower net income during the early years of the life of an asset. As the age of the asset increases, this effect reverses. Therefore, companies that use accelerated amortization report lower amortization expense and higher net income during the later years of an asset's life. The preceding graph shows the pattern of amortization over the life of an asset for the two methods discussed in this chapter. When the curve for the accelerated method falls below the curve for the straight-line method, the accelerated method produces a higher net income than the straight-line method. While the annual amortization expense varies with the method used, the total amortization of the asset over its useful life should be the same, irrespective of the method used.

Users of financial statements must understand the impact of alternative amortization methods used over time. Differences in amortization methods rather than real economic differences can cause significant variations in reported net incomes.

SELF-STUDY **QUIZ 9-3**

Assume that WestJet acquired new computer equipment at a cost of $240,000. The equipment has an estimated life of six years (and an estimated operating life of 50,000 hours) with an estimated residual value of $30,000. Determine the amortization expense for the first full year under each of the following methods:

1. Straight-line

2. Double-declining-balance

3. Units-of-production (assuming the equipment ran for 8,000 hours in the first year)

After you complete your answers, check them with the solutions presented on page 497.

Amortization Methods Commonly Used

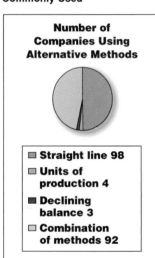

Number of Companies Using Alternative Methods

- Straight line 98
- Units of production 4
- Declining balance 3
- Combination of methods 92

MANAGERS' SELECTION AMONG ACCOUNTING ALTERNATIVES

Financial Reporting   For financial reporting purposes, corporate managers must select the amortization method that provides the best matching of revenues and expenses for any given asset. If the asset is expected to provide benefits evenly over time, then the straight-line method is preferred. Managers also find this method to be easy to use and to explain. If no other method is more systematic or rational, then the straight-line method is selected. Also, during the early years of an asset's life, the straight-line method reports higher income than the accelerated methods do. For these reasons, the straight-line method is far and away the most common.

On the other hand, certain assets produce more revenue in their early lives because they are more efficient then than in later years. In this case, managers select an accelerated method to allocate cost. In addition, as the asset ages, repair costs are likely to increase. Thus, the total of the amortization expense and repair expense for any given period is likely to provide a nearly constant amount charged to income each period.

The 2004 edition of *Financial Reporting in Canada* reported the amortization methods used by 200 companies in 2003.[4] More than 50 percent of the companies surveyed used a single amortization method. The majority of companies (98) used the straight-line method, followed by four companies that used the units-of-production method. In addition, 92 companies used at least two different amortization methods. Most of these companies used straight-line amortization and either the units-of-production method or the declining-balance method.

Tax Reporting   WestJet Airlines, like most public companies, must prepare two sets of reports. One set of reports is prepared under GAAP for shareholders. The other set of reports is prepared to determine the company's tax obligation under the Income Tax Act. When they first learn that companies prepare two sets of reports, some people question the ethics or the legality of the practice. In reality, **it is both legal and ethical to prepare separate reports for tax and financial reporting purposes** because the objectives of GAAP and the Income Tax Act differ.

Financial Reporting (GAAP)	Tax Reporting
The primary objective of financial reporting is to provide economic information about a business to help external parties make sound financial decisions. GAAP allows a business to choose, from a menu of acceptable methods, those that most closely reflect its particular economic circumstances. In this way, financial reporting provides information that, among other things, is useful in projecting the future cash flows of a business.	The objective of the Income Tax Act is to raise sufficient revenues to pay for the expenditures of the federal government, with many provisions designed to encourage certain behaviours that are thought to benefit society (e.g., contributions to charities are tax-deductible to encourage people to support worthy programs).

---

[4]C. Byrd, I. Chen, and J. Smith, *Financial Reporting in Canada 2004*. Toronto: Canadian Institute of Chartered Accountants, 2004, pp. 239–240.

It is easy to understand why two sets of accounting reports are permitted, but perhaps the more interesting aspect concerns the reason why managers incur the extra cost of preparing two sets of reports. In some cases, differences between the Income Tax Act and GAAP leave the manager no choice but to have separate reports. In other cases, the explanation is an economic one. It is often called the *least and the latest rule*. All taxpayers want to pay the lowest amount of tax that is legally permitted, and they want to pay it at the latest possible date. If you had the choice of paying $100,000 to the federal government at the end of this year or the end of next year, you would choose the end of next year. By doing so, you would be able to invest the money for an extra year and earn a return on the investment.

By complying with the requirements of the Income Tax Act, corporations are able to defer (delay) paying taxes in the amount of millions and sometimes billions of dollars. The following companies reported significant gross future income tax obligations in a recent year by choosing accounting methods that delay tax payments. Much of the deferral is due to differences in amortization methods:

Company	Future Tax Liabilities	Percentage Due to Applying Different Amortization Methods
Gildan Activewear Inc.	$ 11,504,699	70%
Potash Corp.	844,200,000	95
Intrawest Corporation	105,605,000	79

The amortization methods discussed in the previous section are not acceptable for federal income tax reporting. Corporations that are subject to taxation in Canada must apply Capital Cost Allowance (CCA) to tangible assets, as determined by the schedules provided by the tax authorities. These schedules are used to calculate the maximum annual expense that is used in computing taxable income according to the tax rules and regulations. CCA schedules classify capital assets into different classes and stipulate the maximum CCA rate (a declining-balance rate) for each class. For example, aircraft is currently Class 9, with a CCA rate of 25 percent per year.

CCA does not attempt to match the cost of an asset with the revenue it produces over its useful life in conformity with the matching principle. Instead, CCA provides for accelerated amortization of an asset over a period that is usually much shorter than the asset's estimated useful life. The intent of CCA is to provide an incentive for corporations to invest in modern property, plant, and equipment to be competitive in world markets. The high amortization expense reported under CCA reduces a corporation's taxable income and therefore the amount it must pay in taxes.

INTERNATIONAL **PERSPECTIVE**

AMORTIZATION METHODS IN OTHER COUNTRIES

The various amortization methods discussed in this chapter are widely used by corporations in most countries. Some methods used in other countries are not generally used in Canada. German companies may amortize costs based on the number of hours that an asset is used, and British companies may use the annuity method, which results in lower amortization during the early years of the life of an asset (contrasted with accelerated amortization, which results in higher amortization during the early years).

Many countries, including Australia, Brazil, England, Hong Kong, Mexico, and Singapore, also permit the revaluation of property, plant, and equipment to their current cost as of the balance sheet date. The primary argument in favour of such revaluation is that the historical cost of an asset purchased 15 or 20 years ago is not meaningful because of the impact of inflation. For example, most people would not compare the original price of a 1965 Ford to the original price of a 2006 Ford because the purchasing power of the dollar changed dramatically during the intervening period. Revaluation to current cost is prohibited (under GAAP) in Canada, the United States, Germany, and Japan. A primary argument against restatement is the lack of objectivity involved in estimating the current cost of an asset.

MEASURING ASSET IMPAIRMENT

■ **LEARNING OBJECTIVE 4**

Explain the effect of asset impairment on the financial statements.

A recent accounting standard (*CICA Handbook*, section 3063) requires that corporations review the net book value of their long-term assets for impairment. *Impairment* occurs when events or changed circumstances cause the net book value of these assets to be higher than estimates of future cash flows (future benefits). If impairment occurs, then an impairment loss should be recognized and the assets should be *written down*. The revised book value of assets should not be increased subsequent to an increase in their market value. Total impairment losses and the methods used to calculate impairments should also be disclosed.

As part of its significant accounting policies, Van Houtte Inc. stated its impairment policy in note 2(d) to its financial statements. A write-down may occur whenever events or conditions indicate that the net carrying (book) value of a long-term asset may not be recoverable from estimated future cash flows. If it is determined that the estimated net recoverable amount of the asset is less than its net carrying value, then the asset is written down and a loss is recognized. In note 4 to its consolidated financial statements, Van Houtte Inc. reported the following:

REAL WORLD EXCERPT

Van Houtte Inc.

ANNUAL REPORT

4. Non-recurring charges

	2003	2002
Write-down of fixed assets (i)	$ —	$11,850
Write-off of fixed assets (i) (ii)	2,911	6,933
Loss on disposal of investments and of a business unit (ii)	1,740	—
Other restructuring charges	523	1,235
	$5,174	$20,018

(i) In 2002, following changes in market conditions and evolution of the technology, the management of the Company did an in-depth review of the future use of its coffee service equipment and of its vending machines. Therefore, certain pieces of equipment have been written off and others have been written down.

(ii) In 2003, to reflect the new organizational structure and the integration of its Canadian operations, the Company wrote off certain assets related to the integration of its information management systems and the divestiture of a marginal non-strategic unit.

A QUESTION OF **ETHICS**

REAL WORLD EXCERPT

Fortune

FIERCE PRESSURE TO REPORT SMOOTH, EVER-HIGHER EARNINGS

Corporate executives have been under intense pressure over the past decade to keep earnings rising smoothly to meet the consensus expectations of analysts. As the expectations have become more explicit, so too have the mechanisms executives use to manage earnings and hit their targets. Long-term assets can play a significant role in the ability of companies to meet or beat the estimates, as indicated in the financial press:

"Learn to Play the Earnings Game (and Wall Street will love you)"

How the pros do it

Plan ahead: Time store openings or asset sales to keep earnings rising smoothly. In most cases, this is earnings management at its least controversial. The master of it is General Electric.

Capitalize it: Usually it's pretty clear which costs you capitalize and which you expense. But there are gray areas—software R & D is one—and you can get creative about the length of time an asset should be depreciated. America Online was, until it stopped in October, a noted aggressive capitalizer.

Write it off: Take a "big bath" and charge a few hundred million in restructuring costs, and meeting future earnings targets will be easier. Among the biggest restructurers in the 1990s: IBM.

Source: *Fortune*, March 31, 1997, pp. 77–80. © 1997 *Time, Inc.* All rights reserved.

DISPOSAL OF PROPERTY, PLANT, AND EQUIPMENT

In some cases, a business may *voluntarily* decide not to hold a long-term asset for its entire life. The company may drop a product from its line and no longer need the equipment that was used to produce the product, or managers may want to replace a machine with a more efficient one. These disposals include sale, trade-in, or retirement. When WestJet disposes of an old aircraft, it may sell it to a cargo airline or regional airline. A business may also dispose of an asset *involuntarily* as a result of a casualty, such as a storm, fire, or accident.

Disposals of long-term assets seldom occur on the last day of the accounting period. Therefore, amortization must be updated to the date of disposal. The disposal of an amortizable asset usually requires two entries:

(1) an adjusting entry to update the amortization expense and accumulated amortization accounts and

(2) an entry to record the disposal. Then the cost of the asset and any accumulated amortization at the date of disposal must be removed from the accounts. The difference between any resources received on disposal of an asset and its net book value at the date of disposal is a gain or loss on disposal of the asset. This gain (or loss) is revenue (or expense) from "peripheral or incidental" activities rather than from normal operations. Gains and losses from disposals are usually shown separately on the income statement after income from operations.

Assume that at the end of year 2004, WestJet sold a 737-200 aircraft and replaced it with a newer 737-700 model. The original cost of the aircraft was $2.6 million, with an estimated useful life of 17,500 flight hours and no residual value. The unrecorded amortization expense for the year was $371,000.[5] The aircraft was sold for $1.6 million in cash and had accumulated amortization of $595,000 at the end of 2004. The loss on the sale of this aircraft is $405,000, calculated as follows:

■ **LEARNING OBJECTIVE 5**

Analyze the disposal of property, plant, and equipment.

---

[5]Sale of the aircraft during the year requires updating the accumulated amortization account to the date of sale by computing amortization for a fraction of the year. The amortization expense could be based on the number of months of amortization or 50 percent of the annual amortization if the company uses the half-year rule.

Cash received		$1,600,000
Original cost	$2,600,000	
Less: Accumulated amortization	595,000	
Net book value		2,005,000
Loss on disposal		$ (405,000)

The entries and effects of the transaction on the date of the sale follow:

① Amortization expense (E) 371,000
    Accumulated amortization—Aircraft (XA)   371,000
② Cash (A) 1,600,000
    Accumulated amortization—Aircraft (XA) 595,000
    Loss on sale of asset (+Loss, −SE) 405,000
    Aircraft (A)   2,600,000

Assets		=	Liabilities	+	Shareholders' Equity	
① Accumulated amortization	− 371,000				① Amortization expense	−371,000
② Cash	+1,600,000				② Loss on sale of asset	−405,000
Accumulated amortization	+ 595,000					
Aircraft	−2,600,000					

A gain or loss on disposal occurs because (1) amortization expense is based on estimates that may differ from actual experience and (2) amortization is based on original cost, not current market value. Because the gain or loss on disposal is not part of the continuing operating activities of a company, it usually is shown as a separate line item on the income statement. In 2004, for example, WestJet sold property and equipment and reported a net gain of $63,000 as a separate item on its income statement.

SELF-STUDY **QUIZ 9-4**

Now let us assume the same facts as above except that the asset was sold for $2,300,000 cash. Prepare the two entries on the date of the sale.

1. Update the amortization expense for the year.

2. Record the sale.

After you have completed your answers, check them with the solutions on page 497.

Companies may also trade in an old asset in exchange for a new asset and pay cash to cover the difference in the assets' values. Let us assume that an old vehicle, originally acquired at $20,000 with $16,000 of accumulated amortization, has a fair market value of $3,000. The company exchanges this vehicle in partial payment for computer hardware, and pays an additional amount of $1,600 in cash. This trade-in transaction includes a non-cash consideration. Hence, the computer hardware is recorded at its fair market value, unless the fair market value of the old vehicle is more objectively determinable. Notice that the net book value of the vehicle is $4,000 and the total payment for the computer hardware is $4,600, which is equal to the fair market value of the vehicle plus the cash consideration. Assuming that the fair market value of the vehicle is more objectively determinable, the journal entry and effects of the trade-in transaction would be as follows:[6]

---

[6]The same analysis applies when a company exchanges an old asset for a new asset of the same kind, such as an old vehicle for a newer model.

Computer hardware (A)	4,600	
Accumulated amortization—Delivery van (XA)	16,000	
Loss on disposal of assets (Loss, −SE)	1,000	
Delivery van (A)		20,000
Cash (A)		1,600

In certain situations, the company may dispose of an old, unusable asset if it cannot sell it to another party. The abandonment or retirement of an asset results in a loss that is equal to the asset's net book value. The journal entry to record the retirement of an asset is similar to the case of a sale or a trade-in, except that the cash account is not affected.

FINANCIAL **ANALYSIS**

TAKING A DIFFERENT STRATEGY TO SUCCESS

Singapore Airlines, formed in 1972, has recognized continued profitability as one of the world's largest operators of the most technologically advanced "jumbo jets," the Boeing 747-400. Unlike the rest of the airline industry with an average fleet age of more than 12 years, Singapore Airlines uses its aircraft for an average of just under six years. This strategy for managing the company's productivity has a dual effect. Amortization expense is significantly higher due to the shorter estimated useful life, thus reducing net income. Singapore Airlines sells its used aircraft, however—an activity that has resulted in gains reported on the income statement. Both the amortization computations (through the use of estimates) and asset sales (through choosing the timing of the sales) provide management with the flexibility to **manage earnings**.

For example, Singapore Airlines' 2003 annual report shows a gain on disposal of aircraft of $102.7 million, representing 12.5 percent of pretax income. This is compared to $144.9 million in 2002, or 14.8 percent of pretax income. These gains on disposals increase the company's normal operating profits.

How can this lead to earnings management? Singapore Airlines amortizes its aircraft faster than most other airlines. Therefore, when it sells its aircraft, the book value used to record the sale is quite low relative to the actual proceeds from the sale, resulting in a gain. Because management can decide to sell more or fewer aircraft in any given year, when ordinary earnings are low, management has the ability simply to retire more aircraft, recognize the gains, and increase net income.

In general, the practice of using conservative accounting policies (in this case, high amortization from conservative useful life estimates) to increase subsequent net income is called creating a "cookie jar." These "cookies" (aircraft whose sale will result in a large gain) are available as needed to boost net income.

NATURAL RESOURCES AND INTANGIBLE ASSETS

ACQUISITION AND DEPLETION OF NATURAL RESOURCES

You are probably most familiar with large companies that are involved in manufacturing goods (Bombardier, Dell), distribution of goods (Sears Canada, Home Depot), or performing a service (Canada Post, Holiday Inn). A number of large companies, some of which are less well known, develop raw materials and products from **natural resources**, which include mineral deposits such as gold or iron ore (Placer Dome), oil wells (Suncor Energy), and timber tracts. These resources are often called *wasting assets* because they are depleted (i.e., physically used up). Companies involved with natural resources are critical to the economy because they produce such essential items as lumber for construction, fuel for heating and transportation, and food for consumption. Companies involved with natural resources also attract considerable public attention because of the significant effect they can have on the environment. Concerned citizens often read financial statements from companies involved in exploration for oil, coal, and various ores to determine the amount of money spent to protect the environment.

■ **LEARNING OBJECTIVE 6**

Apply measurement and reporting concepts for natural resources and intangible assets.

NATURAL RESOURCES

are assets that occur in nature, such as mineral deposits, timber tracts, oil, and gas.

DEPLETION is the systematic and rational allocation of the cost of a natural resource over the period of exploitation.

When natural resources are acquired or developed, they are recorded in conformity with the *cost principle*. As a natural resource is used up, its acquisition cost must be apportioned among the various periods in which the resulting revenues are earned, in conformity with the *matching principle*. The term **depletion** refers to the systematic and rational allocation of the acquisition cost of natural resources to future periods in which the use of those natural resources contributes to revenue. The concept of depletion is exactly the same as amortization; the only difference is the type of asset that is being accounted for.[7] The units-of-production method is often applied to compute depletion.

To illustrate, Suncor Energy Inc. is a Canadian integrated petroleum explorer, developer, and refiner. The company depletes the acquisition cost of its natural gas reserves based on engineering estimates of the proven quantity of natural gas in the reserve, known as *proved reserves*. Proved reserves are considered to be recoverable under current technology and existing economic conditions. Suncor also explores and develops its own reserves and produces natural gas primarily from three areas in western Alberta and northeastern British Columbia. Note 1 to its consolidated financial statements included the following:

REAL WORLD EXCERPT

Suncor Energy Inc.

ANNUAL REPORT

Depreciation, depletion and amortization

Natural Gas:

. . . Acquisition costs of proved properties are depleted using the unit of production method based on proved reserves. Capitalized exploratory drilling costs and development costs are depleted on the basis of proved developed reserves. For purposes of the depletion calculation, production and reserves volumes for oil and natural gas are converted to a common unit of measure on the basis of their approximate relative energy content. Gas plants, support facilities and equipment are depreciated on a straight-line basis over their useful lives, which average 12 years.

Example: Assume that the depletion of Suncor's proved and proved developed reserves is $6,000,000 for the current year. The journal entry to record depletion expense and the transaction effects are:

Natural gas inventory (A)	6,000,000	
Natural gas reserves (A)		6,000,000
(or Accumulated depletion XA)		

Assets	=	Liabilities	+	Shareholders' Equity
Natural gas inventory +6,000,000				
Natural gas reserves −6,000,000				
(or Accumulated depletion)				

Note that the amount of the natural resource that is depleted is capitalized as inventory, not expensed. When the inventory is sold, the cost of goods sold is then included as an expense on the income statement.

A *depletion rate* is computed by dividing the total acquisition and development cost (less any estimated residual value, which is rare) by the estimated units that can be withdrawn economically from the resource. The depletion rate is multiplied each period by the actual number of units withdrawn during the accounting period. This procedure is the same as the units-of-production method of calculating amortization.

---

[7]Consistent with the procedure for recording amortization, an accumulated depletion account may be used. In practice, most companies credit the asset account directly for the periodic depletion. This procedure is also typically used for intangible assets, which are discussed in the next section.

When buildings and similar improvements are acquired for the development and exploitation of a natural resource, they should be recorded in separate asset accounts and *amortized*—not depleted. Their estimated useful lives cannot be longer than the time needed to exploit the natural resource unless they have a significant use after the source is depleted.

ACQUISITION AND AMORTIZATION OF INTANGIBLE ASSETS

An intangible asset, like any other asset, has value because of certain rights and privileges conferred by law on the owner of the asset. An intangible asset has no material or physical substance as do tangible assets such as land and buildings. Examples include patents, trademarks, and licences. Most intangible assets usually are evidenced by a legal document. The growth in the importance of intangible assets has resulted from the tremendous expansion in computer information systems and web technologies. These technological developments led some companies to purchase other companies at high prices, with the expectation that the intangible resources will provide significant future benefits to the purchasing companies.

Intangible assets are recorded at historical cost only if they are purchased. If an intangible asset is developed internally, the cost of development normally is recorded as an expense. In August 2001, the Accounting Standards Board approved a new handbook section (3062) dealing with goodwill and other intangible assets. The new recommendations require companies to differentiate intangible assets that have an indefinite life from those that have limited lives. Intangibles acquired after July 1, 2001 that have indefinite lives will no longer be amortized. Intangible assets with a definite life will continue to be amortized over their useful lives. Upon acquisition of intangible assets, managers determine whether the separate intangibles have definite or indefinite lives.

Definite Life: The cost of an intangible with a definite life is allocated on a straight-line basis each period over its useful life in a process similar to amortization of long-term assets. However, most companies do not estimate a residual value for their intangible assets. Let us assume a company purchases a patent for $800,000 and intends to uses it for 20 years. The adjusting entry to record $40,000 in patent amortization expense ($800,000 ÷ 20 years) is as follows:

Patent amortization expense (E)	40,000	
Patent (A) (or Accumulated amortization (XA)		40,000

Amortization expense is included on the income statement each period and the intangible assets are reported at cost less accumulated amortization on the balance sheet.

Indefinite Life: Intangible assets with indefinite lives are **not amortized**. Instead, these assets are to be tested at least annually for possible impairment, and the asset's book value is written down (decreased) to its fair value if impaired. The process is similar to that used for other long-term assets including intangibles with definite lives.

Let us assume a company purchases for $120,000 cash a copyright that is expected to have an indefinite life. At the end of the current year, management determines that the fair value of the copyright is $90,000. The $30,000 loss ($120,000 book value less $90,000 fair value) is recorded as follows:

Loss due to impairment (+Loss, −SE)	30,000	
Copyright (A)		30,000

EXAMPLES OF INTANGIBLE ASSETS

The 2004 edition of *Financial Reporting in Canada* reported that 132 of the 200 companies included in the survey disclosed information about goodwill in their 2003 annual reports. This compares to 92 companies that disclosed information about intangibles other than goodwill. These intangibles include broadcast rights, publishing rights, trademarks, patents, licences, customer lists, franchises, and purchased research and development.

For example, CAE Inc., a Canadian provider of flight simulators and training, acquired the following intangible assets as part of its acquisition of a number of companies in fiscal years 2002 and 2003.

REAL WORLD EXCERPT

CAE Inc.

ANNUAL REPORT

(amounts in millions of Canadian dollars)	2003	2002				
	HiTec Marine Automation	BAE Systems	Valmarine	Schreiner	SimuFlite	Total
Intangible assets						
Trade names	—	—	3.2	—	37.1	40.3
Customer relations	—	—	9.8	66.0	29.2	105.0
Customer contractual agreements	—	—	2.3	2.2	3.6	8.1
Other intangibles	1.2	2.5	3.1	—	7.0	12.6
Goodwill	1.6	104.2	40.4	102.8	106.3	353.7

For accounting purposes, **GOODWILL** is the excess of the purchase price of a business over the market value of the business's identifiable assets and liabilities.

Goodwill   By far, the most frequently reported intangible asset is **goodwill**. The term goodwill, as used by most businesspeople, means the favourable reputation that a company has with its customers. Goodwill arises from factors such as customer confidence, reputation for good service and quality products, and financial standing. For example, WestJet's promise to deliver no-frills, friendly, reliable transportation combines factors that produce customer loyalty and repeated travel.

From its first day of operations, a successful business continually builds its own goodwill through a combination of factors that cannot be sold separately. In this context, goodwill is said to be *internally generated* and is not reported as an asset. The only way to report goodwill as an asset is to purchase another business. Often, the purchase price of a business exceeds the fair market value of all of the identifiable assets owned by the business minus all of the identifiable liabilities owed to others. Why would a company pay more to acquire a business as a whole than it would pay if it bought the assets individually? The answer is to obtain the acquired company's goodwill. It may be easy for the acquiring company to buy a fleet of aircraft, but a new business would not generate the same level of revenue flying the same routes as if it acquired WestJet's goodwill.

For accounting purposes, goodwill is defined as the difference between the purchase price of a company as a whole and the fair market value of all of its identifiable assets minus the fair market value of its identifiable liabilities.

```
  Purchase price
− Fair market value of identifiable assets and liabilities
  Goodwill to be reported
```

Both parties to the sale estimate an acceptable amount for the goodwill of the business and add it to the appraised fair value of the business's assets and liabilities. Then the sale price of the business is negotiated. The resulting amount of goodwill is recorded as an intangible asset only when it actually is purchased at a measurable cost, in conformity with the *cost principle*.

Companies that reported goodwill related to acquisitions prior to July 1, 2001, were required to amortize it over an estimated useful life (not to exceed 40 years) using the straight-line method. Revised Canadian and U.S. accounting standards consider goodwill arising from acquisitions after January 1, 2002 to have an indefinite life, but any subsequent impairment in its value should be written down. This leads to the recognition of a loss that is reported as a separate item on the income statement in the year the impairment occurs.

Trademarks A **trademark** is a special name, image, or slogan identified with a product or a company. For example, banks such as the Bank of Montreal, auto manufacturers such as Toyota and General Motors, and fast-food restaurant chains such as Pizza Hut have familiar trademarks. Trademarks are protected by law when they are registered at the Canadian Intellectual Property Office of Industry Canada. The protection of a trademark provides the registered holder with exclusive rights to the trademark and can be renewed every 15 years throughout its life. Trademarks are often some of the most valuable assets that a company can own, but they are rarely seen on balance sheets. The reason is simple: intangible assets are not recorded unless they are purchased. Companies often spend millions of dollars developing trademarks, but these expenditures are recorded as expenses and not capitalized. Purchased trademarks that have definite lives are amortized on a straight-line basis over their estimated useful life, up to a maximum period of 40 years.

> A **TRADEMARK** is an exclusive legal right to use a special name, image, or slogan.

Patents A **patent** is an exclusive right granted by the Canadian Intellectual Property Office of Industry Canada for a period of 20 years. It is typically granted to a person who invents a new product or discovers a new process. The patent enables the owner to use, manufacture, and sell the subject of the patent and the patent itself. Without the protection of a patent, inventors likely would be unwilling to search for new products. The patent prevents a competitor from simply copying a new invention or discovery until the inventor has had a period of time to earn an economic return on the new product.

A patent that is *purchased* is recorded at cost. An *internally developed* patent is recorded at only its registration and legal cost because GAAP require the immediate expensing of research and development costs. In conformity with the *matching principle,* the cost of a patent must be amortized over the shorter of its economic life or its remaining legal life. Amortization usually is recorded with a debit to Amortization Expense and a credit directly to the asset account instead of a contra account Accumulated Amortization.

> A **PATENT** is granted by the federal government for an invention; it is an exclusive right given to the owner to use, manufacture, and sell the subject of the patent.

Copyrights **Copyright** protection is granted by the Canadian Intellectual Property Office. It gives the owner the exclusive right to publish, use, and sell a literary, musical, or artistic piece of work for a period not exceeding 50 years after the author's death. The book that you are reading has a copyright to protect the publisher and the authors. It would be against the law, for example, if an instructor copied several chapters from this book and handed them out in class. The same principles, guidelines, and procedures used in accounting for the cost of patents also are used for copyrights.

> A **COPYRIGHT** is the exclusive right to publish, use, and sell a literary, musical, or artistic work.

Franchises **Franchises** may be granted by either the government or other businesses for a specified period and purpose. A city may grant one company a franchise to distribute gas to homes for heating purposes, or a company may sell franchises, such as the right for a local outlet to operate a Harvey's restaurant. Franchise agreements are contracts that can have a variety of provisions. Franchises usually require an investment by the franchisee to acquire them; therefore, they should be accounted for as intangible assets. The life of the franchise agreement depends on the contract and may be for a single year or an indefinite period. Blockbuster Video is a popular company in the home video rental business. To expand rapidly, the company enters into franchise agreements with local operators. The franchise agreement requires the payment of a franchise fee and covers a period of 20 years. Blockbuster has more than 900 stores under franchise agreements.

> A **FRANCHISE** is a contractual right to sell certain products or services, use certain trademarks, or perform activities in a geographical region.

Technology The number of companies reporting a *technology* intangible asset has increased significantly in recent years. Computer software and web development costs are becoming increasingly significant as companies modernize their processes and make greater use of advances in information and communication technology. In 2004, IBM Corporation reported a net amount of $158 million in *completed technology* in a note to its balance sheet and disclosed the following in its accounting policies:

REAL WORLD EXCERPT

International Business Machines Corporation

ANNUAL REPORT

The company capitalizes certain costs that are incurred to purchase or to create and implement internal-use computer software, which includes software coding, installation, testing, and data conversion. Capitalized costs are amortized on a straight-line basis over two years.

Licences and Operating Rights   Licences and *operating rights* are typically obtained through agreements with governmental units or agencies, and permit the holders to use public property in performing their services. For airline companies, the operating rights are authorized landing slots that are regulated by the government and are in limited supply at many airports. They are intangible assets that can be bought and sold by the airlines. Other types of *licences* that grant permission to companies include air waves for radio and television broadcasts, and land for cable and telephone lines.

Research and Development Expense—*Not an Intangible Asset*   If an intangible asset is developed internally, the cost of development normally is recorded as **research and development expense**. For example, QLT, Inc. (a manufacturer of pharmaceutical products) recently spent more than $42.6 million on research to discover new products. This amount was reported as an expense, not an asset, because research and development expenditures typically do not possess sufficient probability of resulting in measurable future cash flows. If QLT had spent an equivalent amount to purchase patents for new products from other drug companies, it would have recorded the expenditure as an asset.

LEASEHOLDS are rights granted to a lessee under a lease contract.

Leaseholds   A **leasehold** is the right granted in a contract called a *lease* to use a specific asset. Leasing is a common type of business contract. For a consideration called *rent,* the owner (lessor) extends to another party (lessee) certain rights to use specified property. Leases may vary from simple arrangements, such as the month-to-month (*operating*) lease of an office or the daily rental of an automobile, to long-term (*capital*) leases having complex contractual arrangements.

Lessees sometimes make significant improvements to a leased property when they enter into a long-term lease agreement. A company that agrees to lease office space on a 15-year lease may install new fixtures or move walls to make the space more useful. These improvements are called *leasehold improvements* and are recorded as an asset by the lessee despite the fact that the lessor usually owns the leasehold improvements at the end of the term of the lease. The cost of leasehold improvements should be amortized over the estimated useful life of the related improvements or the remaining life of the lease, whichever is shorter.

WestJet has made leasehold improvements to the administrative building, two training centres, warehousing buildings, and numerous airport stations and maintenance facilities across Canada. These leasehold improvements had a net book value of $2,551,000 at December 31, 2004, as reported in note 2 to WestJet's financial statements. WestJet amortizes this intangible asset on a straight-line basis over the term of the lease.

FOCUS ON **CASH FLOWS**

PRODUCTIVE ASSETS AND AMORTIZATION

Amortization expense is commonly called a *non-cash expense* because it does not directly affect cash flows. The cash outflow associated with amortization occurs when the related asset is acquired. When amortization is recorded, no cash payment is made (i.e., there is not a credit to Cash). Most other expenses cause an immediate or subsequent outflow of cash. The recording of salary expense, for example, is associated with either the immediate payment of cash or a subsequent payment when the Salaries Payable account is paid.

EFFECT ON CASH FLOW STATEMENT

■ **LEARNING OBJECTIVE 7**

Explain the impact on cash flows of the acquisition, use, and disposal of long-term assets.

IN GENERAL → Acquiring, selling, and amortizing long-term assets affect a company's cash flows as indicated in the following table:

	Effect on Cash Flows
Operating activities (indirect method)	
Net income	$xxx
Adjusted for: Amortization expense	+
Gains on disposition of long-term assets	−
Losses on disposition of long-term assets	+
Losses due to asset impairment write-downs	+
Investing activities	
Purchase of long-term assets	−
Sale of long-term assets	+

Gains and losses on disposition of long-term assets represent the difference between cash proceeds and the book value of the assets disposed of. Hence, gains and losses are non-cash amounts that do not relate to operating activities, but they are included in the computation of net income. Therefore, gains are deducted from net income and losses are added to net income in the computation of cash flow from operations.

FOCUS COMPANY ANALYSIS → Exhibit 9.5 shows WestJet's cash flow statements prepared using the indirect method. Buying and selling long-term assets are investing activities. In 2004, WestJet used $546 million in cash to purchase aircraft and other property and equipment. WestJet did not sell aircraft during 2004, but it sold other long-term assets. Since selling long-term assets is not an operating activity, any gains (losses) on sales of long-term assets that are included in net income are deducted from (added to) net income in the operating activities section to eliminate the effect of the sale. Unless they are large, these gain and loss adjustments are normally not specifically highlighted on the cash flow statement. WestJet lists a gain of $63,000 in its cash flow statement for 2004.

SELECTED FOCUS COMPANY COMPARISONS: PERCENTAGE OF AMORTIZATION TO CASH FLOWS FROM OPERATIONS	
WestJet Airlines	88%
Intrawest Corp.	55%
Van Houtte	42%

EXHIBIT **9.5**

WestJet Cash Flow Statements

REAL WORLD EXCERPT

WestJet Airlines

ANNUAL REPORT

WESTJET AIRLINES LTD.
CONSOLIDATED STATEMENTS OF CASH FLOWS
Years ended December 31, 2004 and 2003
(in thousands of dollars)

	2004	2003
Cash provided by (used in):		
Operations:		
Net earnings (loss)	$ (17,168)	$ 60,539
Items not involving cash:		
Amortization	126,338	63,208
Gain on disposal of property and equipment	(63)	(631)
Other (summarized)	18,268	28,655
	127,375	151,771
Decrease in non-cash working capital	16,697	40,646
	144,072	192,417
Investing activities:		
Aircraft additions	(546,242)	(564,130)
Other property and equipment additions	(41,545)	(34,249)
Other property and equipment disposals	2,945	2,092
	(584,842)	(596,287)

Finally, in capital-intensive industries such as airlines, amortization is a significant non-cash expense included in net income. In WestJet's case, amortization expense is the single largest adjustment to net income in determining cash flows from operations. It has averaged approximately 30 percent of operating cash flows over the years 2002 and 2003 and reached almost 90 percent in 2004 when WestJet renewed its fleet. Other focus companies that are more capital-intensive, such as Intrawest Corporation and Van Houtte, have significantly higher amortization adjustments as a percentage of cash flows from operations.

FINANCIAL **ANALYSIS**

A MISINTERPRETATION

Some analysts misinterpret the meaning of a non-cash expense and often say that "cash is provided by amortization." Although amortization is added in the operating section of the cash flow statement, it is not a source of cash. Cash from operations can be provided only by selling goods and services. A company with a large amount of amortization expense does not generate more cash compared with a company that reports a small amount of amortization expense, assuming that they are exactly the same in every other respect. Amortization expense reduces the amount of reported net income for a company, but it does not reduce the amount of cash generated by the company because it is a non-cash expense. Remember that the effects of recording amortization are a reduction in shareholders' equity and in long-term assets, not in cash. That is why, on the cash flow statement, amortization expense is added back to net income (on an accrual basis) to compute cash flows from operations (income on a cash basis). Note that the amortization expense on WestJet's cash flow statement is listed under the subtitle "Items not involving cash."

Although amortization is a non-cash expense, the amortization method used for tax purposes can affect a company's cash flows. Amortization, in the form of Capital Cost Allowance (CCA), is a deductible expense for income tax purposes. The higher the amount of CCA reported by a company for tax purposes, the lower the taxable income and the taxes it must pay. Because taxes must be paid in cash, a reduction in the tax obligation of a company reduces the company's cash outflows.

The maximum deduction for CCA for each class of assets is based on rates specified by Canada Revenue Agency, but corporations may choose to deduct lower amounts for CCA during periods of losses or low income before taxes and postpone CCA deductions to future years to minimize their tax obligations.

DEMONSTRATION **CASE**

Diversified Industries has been operating for a number of years. It started as a residential construction company. In recent years, it expanded into heavy construction, ready-mix concrete, sand and gravel, construction supplies, and earth-moving services.

The following transactions were selected from those completed during year 2006. They focus on the primary issues discussed in this chapter. Amounts have been simplified for case purposes.

2006

Jan. 1   The management decided to buy a building that was about 10 years old. The location was excellent, and there was adequate parking space. The company bought the building and the land on which it was situated for $305,000. It paid $100,000 in cash and signed a mortgage note payable for the rest. A reliable appraiser provided the following market values: land, $126,000; and building, $174,000.

Jan. 12   Paid renovation costs on the building of $38,100 prior to use.

June 19   Bought a third location for a gravel pit (designated No. 3) for $50,000 cash. The location had been carefully surveyed. It was estimated that 100,000 cubic yards of gravel could be removed from the deposit.

July 10   Paid $1,200 for ordinary repairs on the building.

Aug. 1   Paid $10,000 for costs of preparing the new gravel pit for exploitation.

Dec. 31   Year-end adjustments:
  a. The building will be amortized on a straight-line basis over an estimated useful life of 30 years. The estimated residual value is $35,000.
  b. During 2006, 12,000 cubic yards of gravel were removed from gravel pit No. 3 and sold.
  c. The company owns a patent right that is used in operations. On January 1, 2006, the patent account had a balance of $3,300. The patent has an estimated remaining useful life of six years (including 2006).
  d. At the beginning of the year, the company owned equipment with a cost of $650,000 and a book value of $500,000. The equipment is being amortized using the double-declining-balance method, with a useful life of 20 years with no residual value.
  e. At year-end, the company identified a piece of old excavation equipment with a cost of $156,000 and remaining book value of $120,000. Due to its smaller size and lack of safety features, the old equipment has limited use. The company reviewed the asset for possible impairment of value. The future cash flows are expected to be $40,000.

Required:

1. Indicate the accounts affected and the amount and direction (+ for increase and − for decrease) of the effect for each of the preceding events on the balance sheet equation. Use the following headings:

Date	Assets	=	Liabilities	+	Shareholders' Equity

2. Record the adjusting journal entries based on the information for December 31 ([a] and [b] only).
3. Show the December 31, 2006, balance sheet classifications and amount for each of the following items:

   Fixed assets—land, building, equipment, and gravel pit

   Intangible asset—patent

4. Assuming that the company had sales of $1,000,000 for the year and a net book value of $500,000 for fixed assets at the beginning of the year, compute the fixed asset turnover ratio. Explain its meaning.

We strongly recommend that you attempt to answer the requirements on your own and then check your answers with the suggested solution.

SUGGESTED SOLUTION

1. Effects of events (with computations):

Date	Assets		Liabilities		Shareholders' Equity	
Jan. 1 (1)	Cash Land Building	−100,000 +128,100 +176,900	Note payable	+205,000		
Jan. 12	Cash Building	−38,100 +38,100				
June 19	Cash Gravel pit No. 3	−50,000 +50,000				
July 10	Cash	−1,200			Repairs expense	−1,200

Date	Assets		Liabilities	Shareholders' Equity	
Aug. 1	Cash	−10,000			
	Gravel pit No. 3	+10,000			
Dec. 31 *a* (2)	Accumulated amortization	−6,000		Amortization expense	−6,000
Dec. 31 *b* (3)	Gravel pit No. 3	−7,200			
	Gravel inventory	+7,200			
Dec. 31 *c* (4)	Patent	−550		Amortization expense	−550
Dec. 31 *d* (5)	Accumulated amortization	−50,000		Amortization expense	−50,000
Dec. 31 *e* (6)	Accumulated amortization	−80,000		Loss due to asset impairment	−80,000

(1)

	Land		Building		Total
Market	$126,000	+	$174,000	=	$300,000
Percentage of total	42%	+	58%	=	100%
Cost	$128,100	+	$176,900	=	$305,000

(2) **Cost of building**

Initial payment	$176,900
Repairs prior to use	38,100
Acquisition cost	$215,000

Straight-line amortization

($215,000 cost − $35,000 residual value) ×
1/30 years = $6,000 annual amortization

(3) **Cost of gravel pit**

Initial payment	$ 50,000
Preparation costs	10,000
Acquisition cost	$ 60,000

Units-of-production depletion

($60,000 cost/100,000 estimated production) ×
12,000 actual production = $7,200 annual depletion

(4) **Straight-line amortization**

Unamortized cost of patent	$3,300
÷ Remaining useful life	÷ 6 years
	$ 550

(5) **Double-declining-balance amortization**

($650,000 cost − $150,000 accumulated amortization) × 2/20 = $50,000 annual amortization

(6) **Asset impairment**

Book value of old equipment	$120,000
Expected future cash flows	40,000
Loss due to impairment	$ 80,000

2. Adjusting entries Dec. 31, 2006:

a. Amortization expense, building (E)	6,000	
Accumulated amortization (XA)		6,000
b. Gravel inventory (A)	7,200	
Gravel pit No. 3 (A)		7,200

3. Balance sheet, December 31, 2006:

Assets		
Fixed assets		
Land		$128,100
Building	$215,000	
Less: Accumulated amortization	6,000	209,000
Equipment	650,000	
Less: Accumulated amortization ($150,000 + 50,000 + 80,000)	280,000	370,000
Gravel pit		52,800
Total fixed assets		$759,900
Intangible asset		
Patent ($3,300 − $550)		$ 2,750

4. Fixed asset turnover ratio:

$$\frac{\text{Net Sales}}{\text{Average Net Fixed Assets}} = \frac{\$1,000,000}{(\$500,000 + \$759,900) \div 2} = 1.59$$

This construction company is capital-intensive. The fixed asset turnover ratio measures the company's efficiency at using its investment in property, plant, and equipment to generate sales.

Chapter Supplement A

Changes in Amortization Estimates

Amortization is based on two estimates—useful life and residual value. These estimates are made at the time an amortizable asset is acquired. One or both of these initial estimates may have to be revised as experience with the asset accumulates. In addition, extraordinary repairs and betterments may be added to the original acquisition cost at some time during the asset's use. When it is clear that either estimate should be revised to a material degree or the asset's cost has been changed, the unamortized asset balance (less any residual value at that date) should be apportioned, based on the new estimate, over the remaining estimated life. This is called a *change in estimate*.

To compute the new amortization expense due to a change in estimate for any of the amortization methods described in this chapter, substitute the net book value for the original acquisition cost, the new residual value for the original amount, and estimated remaining life in place of the original estimated life. As an illustration, the computation using the straight-line method is as follows.

Assume the following for an aircraft owned by WestJet:

Cost of aircraft when acquired	$45,000,000
Estimated useful life	20 years
Estimated residual value	$ 1,400,000
Accumulated amortization through year 5	
($45,000,000 − $1,400,000) × 1/20 = $ 2,180,000 per year	
× 5 years	
= $10,900,000	

Shortly after the start of year 6, WestJet changed the initial estimated life to 25 years and lowered the estimated residual value to $750,000. At the end of year 6, the computation of the new amount for amortization expense is as follows:

Acquisition cost	$45,000,000
Less: Accumulated amortization (years 1–5)	10,900,000
Net book value	$34,100,000
Less: New residual value	750,000
New amortizable amount	$33,350,000
Annual amortization based on remaining life:	
$33,350,000 ÷ 20 years (25 − 5 years) =	$ 1,667,500 per year

Companies may also change amortization methods (for example, from declining-balance to straight-line), although such change requires significantly more disclosure since the consistency principle is violated. Under GAAP, changes in accounting estimates and amortization methods should be made only when the new estimate or accounting method "better measures" the periodic income of the business.

SELF-STUDY **QUIZ 9-5**

Assume that WestJet Airlines owned a service truck that originally cost $100,000. When purchased, the truck had an estimated useful life of 10 years, with no residual value. After operating the truck for five years, WestJet determined that the remaining life was only two more years. Based on this change in estimate, what amount of amortization should be recorded over the remaining life of the asset? WestJet uses the straight-line method.

After you complete your answer, check it with the following solution:

$50,000 (book value after 5 years) ÷ 2 years (remaining life) = $25,000 amortization expense per year.

FINANCIAL **ANALYSIS**

INCREASED PROFITABILITY DUE TO AN ACCOUNTING ADJUSTMENT? READING THE FOOTNOTES

Financial analysts are particularly interested in changes in accounting estimates because they can have a large impact on a company's before-tax operating income. As an example, in its news release, TransAlta Power, a power transmission limited partnership headquartered in Calgary, Alberta, announced first quarter earnings of $4.9 million for 2001, up from $3.6 million in the first quarter of 2000. Naturally, the president and director of TransAlta is "very pleased with the first quarter results . . . " and notes that "our operating performance continues at industry leading levels . . ."

However, in examining the information presented in the notes to the financial statements, the following disclosure is found: "Effective January 1, 2001, the estimated useful life of the power plant has increased to 27 years from 17 years." This change in estimate—a 59 percent increase in the estimated useful life of the plant—had the effect of increasing TransAlta's net income by $1.35 million.

Therefore, if the change in estimate had not been made, TransAlta's results for the first quarter of 2001 would be $3.55 million, a slight decrease from the first quarter of 2000. TransAlta may still be operating at industry leading levels, but without a convenient change in estimates, its bottom line would not have improved from the prior year.

Source: "TransAlta Power, L.P. announces first quarter results," CNN Newswire, April 19, 2001.

SOLUTIONS TO **SELF-STUDY QUIZZES**

Self-Study Quiz 9-1

1.

Property, Plant, and Equipment (PPE)	
Acquisition cost	$1,800,000,000
Sales tax	70,000,000
Transportation	8,000,000
Installation	1,300,000
Total	$1,879,300,000

The maintenance contracts are not necessary for making the assets ready for use and therefore are not included in the acquisition cost.

2.

	Assets		Liabilities		Shareholders' Equity	
a. PPE	+1,879,300,000	Note payable	+1,315,510,000			
Cash	− 563,790,000					
b. PPE	+1,879,300,000				Share capital	+450,000,000
Cash	−1,429,300,000					

Self-Study Quiz 9-2

1. Capitalize   2. Expense   3. Expense   4. Capitalize

Self-Study Quiz 9-3

1. ($240,000 − $30,000) × ⅙ = $35,000
2. ($240,000 − 0) × ⅔ = $80,000
3. [($240,000 − $30,000) ÷ 50,000] × 8,000 = $33,600

Self-Study Quiz 9-4

1. Amortization expense (E)   371,000
    Accumulated amortization—aircraft (XA)   371,000
2. Cash (A)   2,300,000
    Accumulated amortization—aircraft (XA)   595,000
        Gain on sale of asset (+Gain, +SE)   295,000
        Aircraft (A)   2,600,000

CHAPTER **TAKE-AWAYS**

1. **Define, classify, and explain the nature of long-term assets and interpret the fixed asset turnover ratio.   p. 464**
    a. Noncurrent assets are those that a business retains for long periods of time for use in the course of normal operations rather than for sale. They may be divided into tangible assets (land, buildings, equipment, natural resources) and intangible assets (including goodwill, patents, and franchises).
    b. The cost allocation method utilized affects the amount of net property, plant, and equipment that is used in the computation of the fixed asset turnover ratio. Accelerated methods reduce book value and increase the turnover ratio.

2. **Apply the cost principle to measure the acquisition and maintenance of property, plant, and equipment.   p. 465**
    Acquisition cost of property, plant, and equipment is the cash-equivalent purchase price plus all reasonable and necessary expenditures made to acquire and prepare the asset for its intended use. These assets may be acquired using cash, debt, equity, or through self-construction. Expenditures made after the asset is in use are either capital expenditures or revenue expenditures:
    a. **Capital expenditures** provide benefits for one or more accounting periods beyond the current period. Amounts are debited to the appropriate asset accounts and amortized or depleted over their useful lives.
    b. **Revenue expenditures** provide benefits during the current accounting period only. Amounts are debited to appropriate current expense accounts when the expenses are incurred.

3. **Apply various cost allocation methods as assets are held and used over time.   p. 474**
    Cost allocation methods: In conformity with the matching principle, cost (less any estimated residual value) is allocated to periodic expense over the periods benefited. Because of amortization, the net book value of an asset declines over time and net income is reduced by the amount of the expense. Common amortization methods include straight-line (a constant amount over time), units-of-production (a variable amount over time), and double-declining-balance (a decreasing amount over time).
    • Amortization—buildings and equipment, intangibles.
    • Depletion—natural resources.

4. **Explain the effect of asset impairment on the financial statements.   p. 482**
    When events or changes in circumstances reduce the estimated future cash flows of long-term assets below their book value, the book values should be written down (by recording a loss) to the fair value of the assets.

5. **Analyze the disposal of property, plant, and equipment.   p. 483**
    When assets are disposed of through sale or abandonment,
    • Record additional amortization since the last adjustment was made.
    • Remove the cost of the old asset and its related accumulated amortization, or depletion.
    • Recognize the cash proceeds.
    • Recognize any gains or losses when the asset's net book value is not equal to the cash received.

6. **Apply measurement and reporting concepts for natural resources and intangible assets.** p. 485

The cost principle should be applied in recording the acquisition of natural resources and intangible assets. Natural resources should be depleted (usually by the units-of-production method) usually with the amount of the depletion expense capitalized to an inventory account. Intangibles with definite useful lives are amortized using the straight-line method. Intangibles with indefinite useful lives, including goodwill, are not amortized, but are reviewed at least annually for impairment. Report intangibles at net book value on the balance sheet.

7. **Explain the impact on cash flows of the acquisition, use, and disposal of long-term assets.** p. 491

Amortization expense is a noncash expense that has no effect on cash. It is added back to net income on the cash flow statement to determine cash from operations. Acquiring and disposing of long-term assets are investing activities.

In the previous chapters, we discussed business and accounting issues related to the assets a company holds. In Chapters 10, 11, and 12, we shift our focus to the other side of the balance sheet to see how managers finance the operations of their business and the acquisition of productive assets. We discuss various types of liabilities in Chapters 10 and 11 and examine owners' equity in Chapter 12.

KEY **RATIO**

The **fixed asset turnover ratio** measures how efficiently a company utilizes its investment in property, plant, and equipment over time. Its ratio can be compared to the ratio of its competitors. It is computed as follows (p. 465):

$$\text{Fixed Asset Turnover} = \frac{\text{Net Sales (or operating revenues)}}{\text{Average Net Fixed Assets}}$$

FINDING **FINANCIAL INFORMATION**

BALANCE SHEET

Under Non-Current Assets

Property, plant, and equipment (net of accumulated amortization)

Natural resources (net of accumulated depletion)

Intangibles (net of accumulated amortization)

INCOME STATEMENT

Under Operating Expenses

Amortization and depletion expense or as part of

Selling, general, and administrative expenses and

Cost of goods sold (with the amount of amortization expense disclosed in a note)

CASH FLOW STATEMENT

Under Operating Activities (indirect method)

Net income

+ Amortization expense

– Gains on sales of assets

+ Losses on sales of assets

Under Investing Activities

+ Sales of assets for cash

– Purchases of assets for cash

NOTES

Under Summary of Significant Accounting Policies

Description of management's choice for amortization methods, including useful lives, and the amount of annual amortization expense, if not listed on the income statement.

Under a Separate Footnote

If not specified on the balance sheet, a listing of the major classifications of long-term assets at cost and the balance in accumulated amortization and depletion.

KEY **TERMS**

Accelerated Amortization p. 476

Acquisition Cost p. 466

Amortization p. 471

Basket Purchase p. 467

Betterments p. 469

Capital Expenditures p. 469

Capitalized Interest p. 467

Copyright p. 489

Declining-Balance Amortization p. 477

Depletion p. 486

Extraordinary Repairs p. 469

Franchise p. 489

Goodwill p. 488

Intangible Assets p. 464

Leaseholds p. 490

Long-Term (or Long-Lived or Capital) Assets p. 464

Natural Resources p. 485

Net Book (or Net Carrying) Value p. 471

Ordinary Repairs and Maintenance p. 469

Patent p. 489

Residual (or Salvage) Value p. 473

Revenue Expenditures p. 469

Straight-Line Amortization p. 475

Tangible Assets p. 464

Trademark p. 489

Units-of-Production Amortization p. 475

Useful life p. 473

QUESTIONS

1. Define *long-term assets*. Why are they considered a "bundle of future services"?
2. How is the fixed asset turnover ratio computed? Explain its meaning.
3. What are the classifications of long-term assets? Explain each.
4. Relate the cost principle to accounting for long-term assets. Under the cost principle, what amounts usually should be included in the acquisition cost of a long-term asset?
5. Describe the relationship between the matching principle and accounting for long-term assets.
6. What is a basket purchase? What measurement problem does it pose?
7. Distinguish between
    a. Capital expenditures and revenue expenditures. How is each accounted for?
    b. Ordinary and extraordinary repairs. How is each accounted for?
8. Distinguish between amortization and depletion.
9. In computing amortization, three values must be known or estimated; identify and explain the nature of each.
10. Estimated useful life and residual value of a long-term asset relate to the current owner or user rather than all potential users. Explain this statement.
11. What type of amortization expense pattern is provided under each of the following methods? When is the use of each method appropriate?
    a. Straight line.
    b. Units of production.
    c. Double declining balance.
12. Over what period should an addition to an existing long-term asset be amortized? Explain.
13. What is an *asset impairment?* How is it accounted for?
14. Define *intangible asset.* What period should be used to amortize an intangible asset?
15. Define *goodwill.* When is it appropriate to record goodwill as an intangible asset?
16. Distinguish between a leasehold and a leasehold improvement. Over what period should a leasehold improvement be amortized? Explain.
17. Why is amortization expense added to net income on the cash flow statement?

MULTIPLE-CHOICE QUESTIONS

1. Simon Company and Allen Company both bought a new delivery truck on January 1, 2003. Both companies paid exactly the same cost, $30,000 for their respective vehicles. As of December 31, 2006, the net book value of Simon's truck was less than the net book value of Allen's truck. Which of the following is an acceptable explanation for the difference in net book values?
    a. Both companies used straight-line amortization, but Simon Company used a longer estimated useful life.

b. Simon Company estimated a lower residual value, but both estimated the same useful life and both chose straight-line amortization.

c. Because GAAP specifies rigid guidelines regarding the calculation of amortization, this situation is not possible.

d. Simon Company is using the straight-line method of amortization, and Allen Company is using the double-declining-balance method of amortization.

2. Barber, Inc., followed the practice of amortizing its building on a straight-line basis. A building was purchased in 2005 and had an estimated useful life of 20 years and a residual value of $20,000. The company's amortization expense for 2005 was $20,000 on the building. What was the original cost of the building?

a. $360,000   c. $400,000
b. $380,000   d. $420,000

3. ACME, Inc., uses straight-line amortization for all of its amortizable assets. ACME sold a used piece of machinery on December 31, 2005, that it purchased on January 1, 2004, for $10,000. The asset had a five-year life, zero residual value, and $2,000 accumulated amortization as of December 31, 2004. If the sales price of the used machine was $7,500, the resulting gain or loss is

a. $500 (loss)   d. $1,500 (gain)
b. $500 (gain)   e. Not determinable from these data.
c. $1,500 (loss)

4. Which method of amortization produces a *net book value* that equals the amortizable base?

a. Straight-line   c. Declining-balance
b. Units-of-production   d. All of the above

5. What assets should be amortized using the straight-line method?

a. Natural resources   c. Intangible assets with indefinite lives
b. Intangible assets with definite lives   d. All of the above

6. A company wishes to report the highest earnings possible for financial reporting purposes. Therefore, when calculating amortization,

a. it will follow the Capital Cost Allowance tables prescribed by the taxation authorities.
b. it will select the shortest lives possible for its assets.
c. it will select the longest lives possible for its assets.
d. it will estimate higher residual values for its assets.

7. How many of the following statements are true?

• Goodwill is not reported unless purchased in an exchange.
• Goodwill must be reviewed annually for possible impairment.
• Impairment of goodwill results in a decrease in net income.

a. none of these statements   c. two statements
b. one statement   d. all three statements

8. Company X is going to retire equipment that is fully amortized. The equipment will simply be disposed of, not sold. Which of the following statements is false?

a. Total assets will not change as a result of this transaction.
b. Net income will not be impacted as a result of this transaction.
c. This transaction will not impact cash flow.
d. All of the above statements are true.

9. When recording amortization, which of the following statements is true?

a. Total assets increase and shareholders' equity increases.
b. Total assets decrease and total liabilities increase.
c. Total assets decrease and shareholders' equity increases.
d. None of the above statements are true.

10. (Supplement) Thornton Industries purchased a machine for $45,000 and is amortizing it with the straight-line method over a life of 10 years, using a residual value of $3,000. At the beginning of the sixth year, a major overhaul was made costing $5,000, and the estimated useful life was extended by 3 years. Amortization expense for Year 6 is:

a. $1,885.   d. $3,625.
b. $2,000.   e. $4,200.
c. $3,250.

For more practice with multiple-choice questions, go to our Web site at **www.mcgrawhill.ca/college/libby**, click on "Student Edition" in the upper left menu, click on this chapter's name and number from the list of contents, and then click on "Multiple-Choice Quiz" from the menu on the left.

EXERCISES

E9–1 Classifying Long-Term Assets and Related Cost Allocation Concepts

LO1

For each of the following long-term assets, indicate its nature and related cost allocation concept. Use the following symbols:

Nature		Cost Allocation Concept	
L	Land		
B	Building	DP	Depletion
E	Equipment	A	Amortization
NR	Natural resource	NO	No cost allocation
I	Intangible	O	Other
O	Other		

Asset	Nature	Cost Allocation	Asset	Nature	Cost Allocation
(1) Copyright	_____	_____	(6) Operating licence	_____	_____
(2) Land held for use	_____	_____	(7) Land held for sale	_____	_____
(3) Warehouse	_____	_____	(8) Delivery vans	_____	_____
(4) Oil well	_____	_____	(9) Timber tract	_____	_____
(5) New engine for old machine	_____	_____	(10) Production plant	_____	_____

E9–2 Preparing a Classified Balance Sheet

LO1

Ballard Power Systems Inc.

The following is a list of account titles and amounts (in thousands) reported by Ballard Power Systems Inc., a leading developer and manufacturer of fuel cells, an alternative power source for automobiles:

Materials	$ 15,613	Deposits on manufacturing equipment	$ 4,943
Leasehold improvements	9,152	Accumulated amortization	28,262
Long-term receivables	1,700	Fuel cell technoogy acquired	42,760
Manufacturing equipment	14,151	Work in progress	1,291
Accounts receivable	23,054	Cash and cash equivalents	288,729
Finished goods	739	Computer equipment	12,974
Furniture and fixtures	5,428	Building	15,240
Land	5,706	Short-term investments`	480,944
Investments	117,370	Pilot production and test equipment	47,433

Required:

Prepare the asset section of the balance sheet for Ballard Power Systems Inc., classifying the assets into Current Assets; Property, Plant, and Equipment (net); and Other Assets.

E9–3 Identifying Capital and Revenue Expenditures

LO2

For each of the following items, enter the correct letter to the left to show the type of expenditure. Use the following:

Type of Expenditure

C Capital expenditure **R** Revenue expenditure **N** Neither

Transactions

_____ (1) Paid $400 for ordinary repairs.

_____ (2) Paid $6,000 for extraordinary repairs.

_____ (3) Paid cash, $20,000, for addition to old building.

_____ (4) Paid for routine maintenance, $200, on credit.

_____ (5) Purchased a machine, $7,000; signed a long-term note.

_____ (6) Paid $2,000 for organization costs.

_____ (7) Paid one-year insurance premium in advance, $900.

_____ (8) Purchased a patent, $4,300 cash.

_____ (9) Paid $10,000 for monthly salaries.

_____ (10) Paid cash dividends, $20,000.

■ **LO1**

E9–4 Computing and Evaluating the Fixed Asset Turnover Ratio

The following information was reported by Cutter's Air Cargo Service for 2004:

Net fixed assets (beginning of year)	$1,450,000
Net fixed assets (end of year)	2,250,000
Net sales for the year	3,250,000
Net income for the year	1,700,000

Compute the company's fixed asset turnover ratio for the year. What can you say about Cutter's ratio when compared to WestJet's ratio for 2004, as computed in the chapter?

■ **LO1**

QLT Inc.

E9–5 Computing and Interpreting the Fixed Asset Turnover Ratio from a Financial Analyst's Perspective

The following data were disclosed in the annual reports of QLT Inc., a Canadian biotechnology company that has recently developed a product to treat macular degeneration of the eyes. If left untreated, this medical condition causes blindness.

(in thousands of dollars)	2004	2003	2002	2001
Net sales	$186,072	$146,750	$110,513	$83,375
Net fixed assets	81,674	43,262	35,281	36,121

Required:

1. Compute QLT's fixed asset turnover ratio for the three years 2002, 2003, and 2004.

2. How might a financial analyst interpret the results?

■ **LO2**

E9–6 Determining Financial Statement Effects of Acquisition of Several Assets in a Basket Purchase

Kline Corporation acquired additional land and a building that included several pieces of equipment for $600,000. The acquisition was settled as follows: cash, $120,000; issuance of Kline's common shares, $120,000; and signing a long-term note for $360,000. An appraiser estimated the market values to be $200,000 for the land, $500,000 for the building, and $100,000 for the equipment. Indicate the accounts affected and the amount and direction (+ for increase and − for decrease) of the effect of this acquisition on the balance sheet equation. Use the following headings:

Assets	=	Liabilities	+	Shareholders' Equity

■ **LO2, 3**

E9–7 Computing and Recording Cost and Amortization of Assets in a Basket Purchase (Straight-Line Amortization)

Zeidler Company bought a building and the land on which the building is located for a total cash price of $178,000. The company paid transfer costs of $2,000. Renovation costs on the building were $23,000. An independent appraiser provided market values for the building, $150,000, and land, $50,000.

Required:

1. Apportion the cost of the property on the basis of the appraised values. Show computations.

2. Prepare the journal entry to record the purchase of the building and land, including all expenditures. Assume that all transactions were for cash and that all purchases occurred at the start of the year.

3. Compute amortization of the building at the end of one year, using the straight-line method. Assume an estimated useful life of 12 years and an estimated residual value of $14,000.

4. What would be the book value of the property (building and land) at the end of year 2?

E9–8 Determining Financial Statement Effects of an Asset Acquisition and Amortization (Straight-Line Amortization)   ■ **LO2, 3**

Vicario Company purchased a machine on March 1, 2005, at an invoice price of $22,000. On the date of delivery, March 2, 2005, the company paid $6,000 on the machine, and signed a note for the balance at 12-percent interest. On March 3, 2005, it paid $250 for freight on the machine. On March 5, Vicario paid installation costs of $1,200 relating to the machine. On October 1, 2005, the company paid the balance due on the machine plus the interest. On December 31, 2005 (the end of the accounting period), Vicario recorded straight-line amortization on the machine based on an estimated useful life of 10 years and an estimated residual value of $3,450.

Required (round all amounts to the nearest dollar):

1. Indicate the accounts affected and the amount and direction (+ for increase and − for decrease) of the effect of each transaction (on March 1, 2, 3, 5, and October 1) on the accounting equation. Use the following headings:

Date	Assets	=	Liabilities	+	Shareholders' Equity

2. Compute the acquisition cost of the machine.

3. Compute the amortization expense to be reported for 2005.

4. What is the impact on the cost of the machine of the interest paid on the 12-percent note? Under what circumstances can interest expense be included in an asset's cost?

5. What would be the net book value of the machine at the end of 2006?

E9–9 Evaluating the Impact of Capitalized Interest on Cash Flows and Fixed Asset Turnover from an Analyst's Perspective   ■ **LO1, 2**

You are a financial analyst charged with evaluating the asset efficiency of companies in the airline industry. The financial statements for Air Canada include the following note:

Air Canada

(l) Interest Capitalized

Interest on funds used to finance the acquisition of new flight equipment and other property and equipment is capitalized for periods preceding the dates the assets are available for service.

Required:

1. Assume that Air Canada followed this policy for a major construction project this year. What is the sign of the effect of Air Canada's policy on the following? Use + for increase, − for decrease, and NE for no effect.
   a. Cash flows.
   b. Fixed asset turnover ratio.

2. Normally, how would your answer to requirement 1(b) affect your evaluation of Air Canada's effectiveness in utilizing property, plant, and equipment?

3. If the fixed asset turnover ratio decreases due to interest capitalization, does this change indicate a real decrease in efficiency? Why or why not?

E9–10 Recording Amortization and Repairs (Straight-Line Amortization) and Determining Financial Statement Effects   ■ **LO3**

Stevie-Lane Company operates a small manufacturing facility as a supplement to its regular service activities. At the beginning of 2007, an asset account for the company showed the following balances:

Manufacturing equipment	$78,000
Accumulated amortization through 2006	55,000

In early January 2007, the following expenditures were incurred for repairs and maintenance:

Routine maintenance and repairs on the equipment	$ 850
Major overhaul of the equipment	10,500

The equipment is being amortized on a straight-line basis over an estimated life of 15 years with a $3,000 estimated residual value. The company's fiscal year ends on December 31.

Required:

1. Prepare the adjusting entry to record the amortization of the manufacturing equipment on December 31, 2006.

2. Prepare the journal entries to record the two expenditures that occured during 2007.

3. Prepare the adjusting entry at December 31, 2007, to record the amortization of the manufacturing equipment, assuming no change in the estimated life or residual value of the equipment. Show computations.

4. Indicate the accounts affected and the amount and direction (+ for increase and − for decrease) of the balance sheet effects of the journal entries you prepared for requirements 1 to 3. Use the following headings:

Date	Assets	=	Liabilities	+	Shareholders' Equity

■ **LO3**

E9–11   Computing Amortization under Alternative Methods

Mardig Corporation bought a machine at the beginning of the year at a cost of $6,400. The estimated useful life was four years, and the residual value was $800. Assume that the estimated productive life of the machine is 80,000 units. Yearly production was 26,000 units in year 1; 22,000 units in year 2; 18,000 units in year 3; and 14,000 units in year 4.

Required:

1. Determine the amount for each cell in the following schedule. Show your computations, and round to the nearest dollar.

Year	Amortization Expense		
	Straight Line	Units of Production	Double Declining Balance
1			
2			
3			
4			
Totals			

2. Assuming that the machine was used directly in the production of one of the products that the company manufactures and sells, what factors might management consider in selecting a preferable amortization method in conformity with the matching principle?

■ **LO3**

E9–12   Computing Amortization under Alternative Methods

Hawkins Inc. purchased a machine on January 1, 2006 at a cost of $21,500. The machine has an estimated residual value of $1,500, and an estimated useful life of four years or 20,000 machine hours. Compute the net book value of the machine at December 31, 2008 under each of the following amortization methods:

1. Straight-line.

2. Double-declining balance. Round your computations to the nearest dollar.

3. Units-of-production. The machine ran 3,000 hours in 2006, 8,000 hours in 2007, and 7,000 hours in 2008.

■ **LO3**

E9–13   Explaining Depreciation Policy

Eastman Kodak

An annual report for Eastman Kodak contained the following note:

Significant Accounting Policies

Depreciation. Depreciation expense is provided based on historical cost and the estimated useful lives of the assets. The Company generally uses the straight-line method for calculating the provision for depreciation. For assets in the United States acquired prior to January 1, 1992, the provision for depreciation is generally calculated using accelerated methods.

Required:

1. Explain the term *historical cost*. What is the meaning of *provision for depreciation*?

2. Why do you think the company changed its amortization method for assets acquired in 1992 and subsequent years? What impact did the change have on net income?

E9–14 **Interpreting Management's Choice of Different Depreciation Methods for Tax and Financial Reporting**

■ **LO3**

Federal Express

An annual report for Federal Express Corporation included the following information:

For financial reporting purposes, depreciation and amortization of property and equipment is provided on a straight-line basis over the asset's service life. For income tax purposes, depreciation is generally computed using accelerated methods.

Required:

Explain why Federal Express uses different methods of depreciation for financial reporting and tax purposes.

E9–15 **Computing Amortization and Book Value for Two Years Using Alternative Amortization Methods, and Interpreting the Impact on Cash Flows**

■ **LO3, 7**

Cotton Company bought a machine for $65,000 cash. The estimated useful life was five years, and the estimated residual value was $5,000. Assume that the estimated useful life is 150,000 units. Units actually produced were 40,000 in year 1 and 45,000 in year 2.

Required:

1. Determine the appropriate amounts to complete the following schedule. Show computations, and round to the nearest dollar.

	Amortization Expense for		Book Value at the End of	
Method of Amortization	Year 1	Year 2	Year 1	Year 2
Straight line				
Units of production				
Double declining balance				

2. Which method would result in the lowest earnings per share for year 1? For year 2?

3. Which method would result in the highest amount of cash outflows in year 1? Why?

4. Indicate the effects of (a) acquiring the machine and (b) recording annual amortization on the operating and investing activities on the cash flow statement for year 1. Assume that straight-line amortization is used.

E9–16 **Inferring Asset Impairment**

■ **LO4**

Sunglass Hut International

Sunglass Hut International is the world's largest specialty retailer of sunglasses, with stores located in a wide variety of high-traffic shopping and tourist destinations. The following note and data were reported in an annual report:

NOTE 1—ORGANIZATION AND SUMMARY OF SIGNIFICANT ACCOUNTING POLICIES

Property and Equipment

The Company performed an analysis of the recoverability of the net book value of property and equipment for underperforming operations. As a result of the analysis, the Company reduced property and equipment by . . . .

	In millions
Cost of property and equipment (beginning of year)	$192
Cost of property and equipment (end of year)	178
Capital expenditures during the year	29
Accumulated amortization (beginning of year)	63
Accumulated amortization (end of year)	77
Amortization expense during the year	27

Required:

Based on the preceding information, compute the amount of property and equipment (both cost and accumulated amortization) that Sunglass Hut wrote off as impaired during the year. (*Hint:* Set up T-accounts.)

■ **LO5**

Sears Canada Inc.

E9–17   **Recording the Disposal of an Asset and Financial Statement Effects**

Sears Canada Inc. has developed a consolidated distribution network in Vaughan, Ontario, and in Calgary, Alberta. As part of its distribution service, Sears trucks transport inventory to its various department, furniture, appliance, automotive, and outlet stores, as well as to individual customers. Assume that Sears sold a small delivery truck that had been used in the business for three years. The records of the company reflect the following:

Delivery truck	$18,000
Accumulated amortization	13,000

Required:

Prepare the journal entry to record the disposal of the truck and the related transaction effects, assuming that the sales price was: (a) $5,000; (b) $5,600; or (c) $4,600.

■ **LO5**

E9–18   **Inferring Asset Age and Recording Accidental Loss on a Long-Term Asset (Straight-Line Amortization)**

On January 1, 2007, the records of Barken Corporation showed the following:

Truck (estimated residual value, $2,000)	$12,000
Accumulated amortization (straight line, two years)	4,000

On September 30, 2007, the delivery truck was a total loss as a result of an accident. As the truck was insured, the company collected $5,600 cash from the insurance company on October 5, 2007.

Required:

1. Based on the data given, compute the estimated useful life of the truck.

2. Prepare all journal entries to record the events that occurred on September 30 and October 5, 2007, and the related adjustments to the accounts. Show computations.

■ **LO6**

Freeport-McMoran

E9–19   **Computing the Acquisition and Depletion of a Natural Resource**

Freeport-McMoran is a natural resources company involved in the exploration, development, and extraction of natural resources. Annual revenues exceed $1 billion. Assume that in February 2005, Freeport-McMoran paid $700,000 for a mineral deposit in Wyoming. During March, it spent $65,000 in preparing the deposit for exploitation. It was estimated that

900,000 total cubic yards could be extracted economically. During 2005, 60,000 cubic yards were extracted. During January 2006, the company spent another $6,000 for additional developmental work. After conclusion of the latest work, the estimated remaining recovery was increased to 1,200,000 cubic yards over the remaining life. During 2006, 50,000 cubic yards were extracted.

Required:

1. Compute the acquisition cost of the deposit in 2005.

2. Compute the depletion expense for 2005.

3. Compute the acquisition cost of the deposit after payment of the January 2006 developmental costs.

4. Compute the depletion expense for 2006.

E9–20 Computing Goodwill and Patents　　　　　　　　　　　　　　　■ **LO6**

Elizabeth Pie Company has been in business for 30 years and has developed a large group of loyal restaurant customers. Vaclav's Foods made an offer to buy Elizabeth Pie Company for $5,000,000. The book value of Elizabeth Pie's recorded assets and liabilities on the date of the offer is $4,400,000, with a market value of $4,600,000. Elizabeth Pie holds a patent for a piecrust fluting machine that the company invented (the patent, with a market value of $200,000, was never recorded by Elizabeth Pie because it was developed internally). The company estimates goodwill from loyal customers to be $300,000 (also never recorded by the company). Should Elizabeth Pie Company management accept Vaclav's Foods' offer of $5,000,000? If so, compute the amount of goodwill that Vaclav's Foods should record on the date of the purchase.

E9–21 Computing and Reporting the Acquisition and Amortization of Three Different　■ **LO6**
Intangible Assets

Wyatt Company had three intangible assets at the end of 2006 (end of the fiscal year):

a. A patent purchased from R. Jay on January 1, 2006, for a cash cost of $5,640. Jay had registered the patent with the Canadian Intellectual Property Office seven years earlier on January 1, 1999. The cost of the patent is amortized over its legal life.

b. A franchise acquired from the local community to provide certain services for five years starting January 1, 2006. The franchise cost $25,000 cash.

c. A lease on some property for a five-year term beginning January 1, 2006. The company immediately spent $7,800 cash for long-term improvements (estimated useful life, eight years; no residual value). At the termination of the lease, there will be no recovery of these improvements.

Required:

1. What is the acquisition cost of each intangible asset?

2. Compute the amortization of each intangible asset at December 31, 2006. The company does not use contra accounts.

3. Show how these assets and any related expenses should be reported on the balance sheet at December 31, 2006, and on the income statement for 2006.

E9–22 Recording Rent Paid in Advance, Leasehold Improvements, Periodic Rent, and　■ **LO6**
Related Amortization

Starbucks Coffee Company is a rapidly expanding retailer of specialty coffee with more than 1,650 stores. Assume that Starbucks planned to open a new store on St. George Street near the University of Toronto and obtained a 15-year lease starting January 1, 2006. Although a serviceable building was on the property, the company had to build an additional structure for storage. The 15-year lease required a $12,000 cash advance payment plus cash payments of $4,000 per month during occupancy. During January 2006, the company spent $60,000 cash building the structure. The new structure has an estimated life of 18 years with no residual value.

Starbucks Coffee Company

Required:

1. Prepare the journal entries for the company to record the payment of the $12,000 advance on January 1, 2006, and the first monthly rental.

2. Prepare the journal entry to record the construction of the new structure.

3. Prepare any adjusting entries required at December 31, 2006, the end of the company's fiscal year, with respect to (a) the advance payment and (b) the new structure. Assume that straight-line amortization is used. Show computations.

4. Compute the total expense resulting from the lease for 2006.

■ **LO3, 4, 5, 6** **E9–23** **Finding Financial Information as a Potential Investor**

You are considering investing the cash gifts you received for graduation in shares of various companies. You visit the Web sites of major companies, searching for relevant information.

Required:

For each of the following, indicate where you would locate the information in an annual report (*Hint:* The information may be in more than one location):

1. The detail on major classifications of long-term assets.

2. The accounting method(s) used for financial reporting purposes.

3. Whether the company has had any capital expenditures for the year.

4. Net amount of property, plant, and equipment.

5. Policies on amortizing intangibles.

6. Amortization expense.

7. Any significant gains or losses on disposals of long-term assets.

8. Accumulated amortization of property, plant, and equipment at the end of the last fiscal year.

9. The amount of assets written off as impaired during the year.

■ **LO2** **E9–24** **(Supplement A) Recording and Explaining Amortization, Extraordinary Repairs, and Changes in Estimated Useful Life and Residual Value (Straight-Line Amortization)**

The records of Luci Company reflected the following details for Machine A at December 31, 2007, the end of the company's fiscal year.

Cost when acquired	$28,000
Accumulated amortization	10,000

During January 2008, the machine was renovated at a cost of $10,000. As a result, the estimated life increased from five years to eight years, and the residual value increased from $3,000 to $4,000. The company uses straight-line amortization.

Required:

1. Prepare the journal entry to record the renovation.

2. How old was the machine at the end of 2007?

3. Prepare the adjusting entry at the end of 2008 to record straight-line amortization for the year.

4. Explain the rationale for your entries in requirements 1 and 3.

■ **LO3** **E9–25** **(Supplement A) Computing the Effect of a Change in Useful Life and Residual Value on Financial Statements and Cash Flows (Straight-Line Amortization)**

Dustin Company owns the office building occupied by its administrative office. The office building was reflected in the accounts at the end of last year as follows:

Acquisition cost	$450,000
Accumulated amortization (based on straight-line amortization, an estimated life of 30 years, and residual value of $30,000)	196,000

Following a careful study, management decided in January of this year that the total estimated useful life should be changed to 25 years (instead of 30) and the residual value reduced to $23,000 (from $30,000). The amortization method will not change.

Required:

1. Compute the annual amortization expense prior to the change in estimates.

2. Compute the annual amortization expense after the change in estimates.

3. What will be the net effect of changing the estimates on the balance sheet, net income, and cash flows for the year?

PROBLEMS

P9–1 **Understanding the Nature of Amortization** ■ LO3, 5

At the beginning of his first year at university, Georgio Labos bought a used combination colour television and stereo system for $960. He estimates that these two items will be almost worthless by the time he graduates in four years, and plans to abandon them then.

Required:

1. Assume that Georgio expects to receive four years of entertainment services for the $960. What is the book value of these items after one year? Use straight-line amortization with no residual value.

2. The university's academic year lasts a total of 30 weeks, from early September to late April. Georgio does not take the TV and stereo system with him on vacations. During the academic year, he participates in many activities, so he averages three hours per week of television viewing and listening to music. What is the average cost per hour of use? (Ignore costs of electricity and repairs.)

3. Georgio is disturbed by the answer to requirement 2. He complains to a friend that this amount exceeds the hourly cost of going to the movies on specific days of the week. His friend suggests that he could lower the average cost by leaving the TV set on whenever he goes to class. Georgio attends classes for 12 hours per week. Comment on this suggestion.

4. After owning the TV set and stereo system for one year, Georgio became curious about the price he could get for selling these items. He discovered that the most he could receive is $600. He does not plan to sell them but the information distresses him. What amount should he associate with the TV set and stereo system after one year? Explain.

P9–2 **Explaining the Nature of a Long-Term Asset and Determining the Financial Statement** ■ LO1, 2
Effects of Its Purchase (AP9–1)

On January 2, 2005, Athol Company bought a machine for use in operations. The machine has an estimated useful life of eight years and an estimated residual value of $1,500. The company provided the following information:

a. Invoice price of the machine, $70,000.

b. Freight paid by the vendor per sales agreement, $800.

c. Installation costs, $2,000 cash.

d. Payment of the machine's price was made as follows:

On January 2:

- Issued 2,000 common shares of Athol Company at $3 per share.

- Signed a $40,000 note payable due April 16, 2005, plus 12-percent interest.

- Balance of the invoice price to be paid in cash. The invoice allows for a 2-percent cash discount if the cash payment is made by January 11.

On January 15:

- Athol Company paid the balance due.

Required:

1. What are the classifications for long-term assets? Explain their differences.

2. Prepare the journal entries to record the purchase of the machine and subsequent cash payment on January 15.

3. Indicate the accounts affected and the amounts and direction (+ for increase and − for decrease) of the effects of the purchase and subsequent cash payment on the accounting equation. Use the following headings:

Date	Assets	=	Liabilities	+	Shareholders' Equity

4. Explain the basis you used for any questionable items.

P9–3 **Analyzing the Effects of Repairs, a Betterment, and Amortization** (AP9–2) ■ LO2, 3

Assume that Sears Canada Inc. acquired the Eaton's retail store in downtown Toronto, purchasing the space at the beginning of 1998 for 50 percent of its net book value. The purchased property cost $75 million when it was purchased by Eaton's at the beginning of 1990, and was amortized on a straight-line basis over a 20-year useful life, with no residual

Sears Canada Inc.

value. Since early 1998, Sears has been amortizing the building over its estimated useful life of 12 years on a straight-line basis (no residual value). Of the $445 million that Sears spent upgrading all of its facilities, the betterment for the Eaton's store cost $125 million, paid in cash. During the year 1999, the following expenditures related to the building were made:

a. Ordinary repairs and maintenance expenditures for the year, $585,000 paid in cash.

b. Extensive and major repairs to the roof of the building, $850,000 paid in cash. These repairs were completed on June 30, 1999.

c. The betterment was completed on June 30, 1999, has an estimated useful life of 20 years, and no residual value. The company intends to sell the building, including the betterment, at the end of the building's useful life (in 10½ years from June 30, 1999).

Required:

1. Applying the policies of Sears Canada Inc., complete the following schedule, indicating the effects of the preceding expenditures. If there is no effect on an account, write NE on the line:

	Building	Accumulated Amortization	Amortization Expense	Repairs Expense	Cash
Balance January 1, 1999	$22,500	_____	_____		
Amortization Jan. 1–June 30		_____	_____		_____
Balance prior to expenditures	22,500	_____	_____		
a.	_____	_____	_____	_____	_____
b.	_____	_____	_____	_____	_____
c.	_____	_____	_____	_____	_____
Amortization July 1–December 31:					
Existing building		_____	_____	_____	_____
Major repairs and betterments		_____	_____	_____	_____
Balance December 31, 1999	_____	_____	_____	_____	_____

2. What was the book value of the building on December 31, 1999?

3. Explain the effect of amortization on cash flows.

LO2, 3

P9–4   Computing a Basket Purchase Allocation and Recording Amortization under Three Alternative Methods (AP9–3)

At the beginning of the year, Dittman Company bought three used machines from Hangar, Inc., for a total cash price of $38,000. Transportation costs on the machines were $2,000. The machines immediately were overhauled, installed, and started operating. The machines were different; therefore, each had to be recorded separately in the accounts. An appraiser was requested to estimate their market value at date of purchase (prior to the overhaul and installation). The net book values shown on Hangar's books also are available. The book values, appraisal results, installation costs, and renovation expenditures follow:

	Machine A	Machine B	Machine C
Net book value—Hangar	$8,000	$12,000	$6,000
Appraisal value	9,500	32,000	8,500
Installation costs	300	500	200
Renovation costs prior to use	2,000	400	600

By the end of the first year, each machine had been operating 8,000 hours.

Required:

1. Compute the cost of each machine by making a supportable allocation. Explain the rationale for the allocation basis used.

2. Prepare the entry to record amortization expense at the end of year 1, assuming the following:

| Machine | Estimates | | Amortization Method |
	Life	Residual Value	
A	5	$1,500	Straight line
B	40,000 hours	900	Units of production
C	4	2,000	Double declining balance

P9–5   Inferring Amortization Amounts and Determining the Effects of an Amortization Error on Key Ratios (AP9–4)

REX Stores Corporation, headquartered in Dayton, Ohio, is one of the leading consumer electronics retailers in the United States, operating more than 234 stores in 37 states. The following is a note from a recent annual report:

■ **LO1, 3**

REX Stores
Corporation

(1) SUMMARY OF SIGNIFICANT ACCOUNTING POLICIES—

(g) Property and Equipment—Property and equipment is recorded at cost. Depreciation is computed using the straight-line method. Estimated useful lives are 15 to 40 years for buildings and improvements and 3 to 12 years for fixtures and equipment. Leasehold improvements are depreciated over the initial lease term and one renewal term when exercise of the renewal term is assured. The components of property and equipment at January 31, 2005 and 2004, are as follows:

	2005	2004
	(in thousands)	
Land	$ 38,598	$ 38,519
Buildings and improvements	102,210	101,448
Fixtures and equipment	17,979	18,567
Leasehold improvements	8,886	9,797
	167,673	168,331
Less: Accumulated depreciation	(39,023)	(36,922)
	$128,650	$131,409

Required:

1. Assuming that REX Stores did not sell any property, plant, and equipment in 2005, what was the amount of amortization expense recorded in 2005?

2. Assume that REX Stores failed to record amortization in 2005. Indicate the effect of the error (i.e., overstated or understated) on the following ratios: (*a*) earnings per share, (*b*) fixed asset turnover, and (*c*) return on equity. Computations are not required.

P9–6   Evaluating the Effect of Alternative Amortization Methods on Key Ratios from an Analyst's Perspective

Pratt & Whitney is one of the largest aircraft engine manufacturers in the world. The company's assets exceed $27 billion. As a result, amortization is a significant item on Pratt & Whitney's income statement. You are a financial analyst for Pratt & Whitney and have been asked to determine the impact of alternative amortization methods. For your analysis, you have been asked to compare methods based on a machine that cost $68,225. The estimated useful life is 10 years, and the estimated residual value is $2,225. The machine has an estimated useful life in productive output of 88,000 units. Actual output was 10,000 in year 1 and 8,000 in year 2.

■ **LO1, 3**

Pratt & Whitney

Required:

1. Determine the appropriate amounts for the following table. Show your computations.

	Amortization Expense for		Net Book Value at End of	
Method of Amortization	Year 1	Year 2	Year 1	Year 2
Straight line				
Units of production				
Double declining balance				

2. Evaluate each method in terms of its effect on cash flow, fixed asset turnover, and earnings per share (EPS). Assuming that Pratt & Whitney is most interested in reducing taxes and maintaining a high EPS for year 1, which method of amortization would you recommend to management? Would your recommendation change for year 2? Why or why not?

■ LO5, 7

Mattel Inc.

P9–7 Inferring Asset Age and Determining Financial Statement Effects of a Long-Term Asset Disposal (Challenging) (AP9–5)

Mattel Inc. is the leading toy maker in the world. The company's revenues exceed $5 billion. In the toy business, it is very difficult to determine the life expectancy of a product. Products that children love one year may sit on the shelf the following year. As a result, companies in the toy business often sell productive assets that are no longer needed. Assume that on December 31, 2007, the end of the company's fiscal year, Mattel's records showed the following data about a machine that was no longer needed to make a toy that was popular last year:

Machine, original cost	$52,000
Accumulated amortization	27,500*

*Based on an estimated useful life of eight years, a residual value of $8,000, and straight-line amortization.

On April 1, 2008, the machine was sold for $26,000 cash.

Required:

1. How old was the machine on January 1, 2008? Show computations.

2. Indicate the effect (i.e., the amount and direction—increase or decrease) of the sale of the machine on April 1, 2008, on
   a. Total assets.
   b. Net income.
   c. Cash flows (by each section of the statement: Operating, Investing, and Financing Activities).

■ LO5, 7

Singapore Airlines

P9–8 Inferring Activities Affecting Fixed Assets from Notes to the Financial Statements and Analyzing the Impact of Amortization on Cash Flows

Singapore Airlines reported the following information in the notes to a recent annual report (in Singapore dollars):

SINGAPORE AIRLINES
Notes to the Accounts
17. Fixed Assets (in $ Million)
The Company

	Beginning of Year	Additions	Disposals/ Transfers	End of Year
Cost				
Aircraft	17,256.5	1,834.5	2,030.5	17,060.5
Other fixed assets (summarized)	6,373.9	2,236.8	2,224.7	6,386.0
	23,630.4	4,071.3	4,255.2	23,446.5
Accumulated amortization				
Aircraft	5,672.2	923.1	1,279.2	5,316.1
Other fixed assets (summarized)	2,735.3	285.5	194.9	2,825.9
	8,407.5	1,208.6	1,474.1	8,142.0

Singapore Airlines also reported the following cash flow details:

Cash Flow from Operating Activities (in $ Million)	The Company	
	Current Year	Prior Year
Operating Profit	1,829.4	820.9
Adjustments for:		
Amortization of fixed assets	1,208.6	1,180.2
Gain on disposal of fixed assets	(223.9)	(108.2)
Other adjustments (summarized)	(27.5)	(132.4)
Net Cash Provided by Operating Activities	2,786.6	1,760.5

Required:

1. Reconstruct the information in Note 17 into T-accounts for Fixed Assets and Accumulated Amortization:

Fixed Assets			Accumulated Amortization	
Beg. balance				Beg. balance
Acquisitions	Disposals/transfers	Disposals/transfers		Amortization expense
End. balance				End. balance

2. Compute the amount of cash the company received for disposals and transfers. Show computations.

3. Compute the percentage of amortization expense to cash flows from operations. How do you interpret this percentage?

P9–9 **Recording and Interpreting the Disposal of Three Long-Term Assets** (AP9–6)   ■ **LO5**

During 2007, Coté Company disposed of three different assets. On January 1, 2007, prior to their disposal, the accounts reflected the following:

Asset	Original Cost	Residual Value	Estimated Life	Accumulated Amortization (straight line)
Machine A	$20,000	$3,000	8 years	$12,750 (6 years)
Machine B	42,600	4,000	10 years	30,880 (8 years)
Machine C	76,200	4,200	15 years	57,600 (12 years)

The machines were disposed of in the following ways:

a. Machine A: Sold on January 1, 2007, for $8,200 cash.

b. Machine B: Sold on April 1, 2007, for $9,000; received cash, $3,000, and a $6,000 interest-bearing (12%) note receivable due at the end of 12 months.

c. Machine C: Suffered irreparable damage from an accident on July 2, 2007. On July 10, 2007, a salvage company removed the machine immediately at no cost. The machine was insured, and $18,000 cash was collected from the insurance company.

Required:

1. Prepare all journal entries related to the disposal of each machine.

2. Explain the accounting rationale for the way that you recorded each disposal.

P9–10 **Determining Financial Statement Effects of Activities Related to Various Long-Term**   ■ **LO6**
Assets (AP9–7)

During the 2008 fiscal year, Boyd Company completed the following transactions:

a. On January 10, 2008, paid $7,000 for a complete reconditioning of each of the following machines acquired on January 1, 2004 (total cost, $14,000). Although the reconditioning of the machines was necessary, it did not extend their useful lives.

(1) Machine A: Original cost, $26,000; accumulated amortization (straight line) to December 31, 2007, $18,400 (residual value, $3,000).

(2) Machine B: Original cost, $32,000; accumulated amortization (straight line) $13,000 (residual value, $6,000).

b. On July 1, 2008, purchased a patent for $19,600 cash (estimated useful life, seven years).

c. On January 1, 2008, purchased another business for cash $70,000, including $16,000 for goodwill. The company assumed no liabilities. The company follows the new Canadian accounting standards for goodwill.

d. On September 1, 2008, constructed a storage shed on land leased from A. Kumar. The cost was $10,800, paid in cash; the estimated useful life was five years with no residual value. The company uses straight-line amortization. The lease will expire in three years.

e. Total expenditures during 2008 for ordinary repairs and maintenance were $5,200.

f. On July 1, 2008, sold Machine A for $6,500 cash.

Required:

1. Indicate the accounts, amounts, and direction of the effects of each transaction on the accounting equation. Use the following structure:

Date	Assets	=	Liabilities	+	Shareholders' Equity

2. For each of the long-term assets, compute the amortization expense for 2008 to the nearest month.

■ **LO6**

P9–11 **Computing Goodwill from the Purchase of a Business and Related Amortization**

Biovail Corporation

Biovail Corporation is a fully integrated pharmaceutical company whose objective is the scientific and technological advancement of medications for the treatment of chronic medical conditions and the successful commercialization of these superior pharmaceutical products. The notes to the company's financial statements for the year 2000 indicate that it acquired the net assets of DJ Pharma Inc. on October 6, 2000. The purchase price was $164,561,000 and the fair market value of identifiable assets acquired and liabilities assumed are as follows (in thousands of dollars):

Current assets	$ 14,705
Equipment	672
Brand names and product rights	130,500
Other assets	13,468
Current liabilities	(22,844)
Future income tax liability	(32,892)
Other liabilities	(42,437)

Required:

1. Compute the amount of goodwill resulting from the purchase.

2. Compute the adjustments that Biovail would make at the end of its fiscal year, December 31, 2000, for amortization of all long-term assets (straight line), assuming an estimated remaining useful life of 15 years and no residual value. The company does not amortize goodwill.

■ **LO6**

P9–12 **Determining the Financial Statement Effects of the Acquisition and Amortization of Intangibles**

Figg Company, with a fiscal year ending December 31, acquired three intangible assets during 2007. For each of the following transactions, indicate the accounts and amounts affected and the direction of the effect (+ for increase, − for decrease, and NE for no effect). Use the following headings:

Date	Assets	=	Liabilities	+	Shareholders' Equity

a. On January 1, 2007, the company purchased a patent from Ullrich Ltd. for $6,000 cash. Ullrich had developed the patent and registered it with the Canadian Intellectual Property Office on January 1, 2002.

b. On January 1, 2007, the company purchased a copyright for a total cash cost of $12,000; the remaining legal life was 25 years. Company executives estimated that the copyright would have no value by the end of 20 years.

c. The company purchased another company in January 2007 at a cash cost of $130,000. Included in the purchase price was $30,000 for goodwill; the balance was for plant, equipment, and fixtures (no liabilities were assumed).

d. On December 31, 2007, amortized the patent over its remaining legal life.

e. On December 31, 2007, amortized the copyright over the appropriate period.

P9–13 Computing Amortization, Net Book Value, and Asset Impairment Related to Different Intangible Assets (AP9–8)

■ **LO4, 6**

Havel Company has five different intangible assets to be accounted for and reported on the financial statements. The management is concerned about the amortization of the cost of each of these intangibles. Facts about each intangible follow:

a. *Patent.* The company purchased a patent at a cash cost of $54,600 on January 1, 2006. The patent had a legal life of 20 years from the date of registration with the Canadian Intellectual Property Office, which was January 1, 2002. It is amortized over its remaining legal life.

b. *Copyright.* On January 1, 2006, the company purchased a copyright for $22,500 cash. The legal life remaining from that date is 30 years. It is estimated that the copyrighted item will have no value by the end of 25 years.

c. *Franchise.* The company obtained a franchise from Terwilliger Company to make and distribute a special item. It obtained the franchise on January 1, 2006, at a cash cost of $14,400 for a 12-year period.

d. *Licence.* On January 1, 2005, the company secured a licence from the city to operate a special service for a period of five years. Total cash expended to obtain the licence was $14,000.

e. *Goodwill.* The company started business in January 2004 by purchasing another business for a cash lump sum of $400,000. Included in the purchase price was "Goodwill, $60,000." Company executives stated that "the goodwill is an important long-term asset to us."

Required:

1. Compute the amount of amortization that should be recorded for each intangible asset at the end of the fiscal year, December 31, 2006.

2. Compute the net book value of each intangible asset on *January 1, 2008.*

3. Assume that on January 2, 2008, the copyrighted item was impaired in its ability to continue to produce strong revenues. The other intangible assets were not affected. Havel estimated that the copyright will be able to produce future cash flows of $15,000. Compute the amount, if any, of the impairment loss to be recorded.

P9–14 (Supplement A) Analyzing and Recording Entries Related to a Change in Estimated Life and Residual Value

■ **LO3**

Reader's Digest

Reader's Digest is a global publisher of magazines, books, and music and video collections, and is one of the world's leading direct-mail marketers. Many direct-mail marketers use high-speed Didde press equipment to print their advertisements. These presses can cost more than $1 million. Assume that Reader's Digest owns a Didde press acquired at an original cost of $400,000. It is being amortized on a straight-line basis over a 20-year estimated useful life and has a $50,000 estimated residual value. At the end of 2007, the press had been amortized for eight years. In January 2008, a decision was made, on the basis of improved maintenance procedures, that a total estimated useful life of 25 years and a residual value of $73,000 would be more realistic. The fiscal year ends December 31.

Required:

1. Compute (a) the amount of amortization expense recorded in 2007 and (b) the net book value of the printing press at the end of 2007.

2. Compute the amount of amortization that should be recorded in 2008. Show computations.

3. Prepare the adjusting entry to record amortization expense at December 31, 2008.

ALTERNATE PROBLEMS

■ **LO1, 2**

AP9–1 Explaining the Nature of a Long-Term Asset and Determining the Financial Statement Effects of Its Purchase (P9–2)

On June 1, 2006, the Fitzgerald Corp. bought a machine for use in operations. The machine has an estimated useful life of six years and an estimated residual value of $2,000. The company provided the following information:

a. Invoice price of the machine, $60,000.

b. Freight paid by the vendor per sales agreement, $650.

c. Installation costs, $1,500 cash.

d. Payment of the machine's price was made as follows:

On June 1:

- Fitzgerald Corp. issued 2,000 common shares at $5 per share.

- Signed an interest-bearing note for the balance of the invoice price, payable on September 2, 2006, plus 12-percent interest.

On September 2:

- Fitzgerald Corp. paid the balance and interest due on the note payable.

Required:

1. What are the classifications of long-term assets? Explain their differences.

2. Prepare the journal entries to record the purchase of the machine and subsequent cash payment.

3. Indicate the accounts affected and the amounts and direction (+ for increase and − for decrease) of the balance sheet effects of the purchase and subsequent cash payment. Use the following headings:

Date	Assets	=	Liabilities	+	Shareholders' Equity

4. Explain the basis you used for any questionable items.

■ **LO2, 3**

AMERCO

AP9–2 Analyzing the Effects of Repairs, a Betterment, and Amortization (P9–3)

A recent annual report for AMERCO, the holding company for U-Haul International, Inc., included the following note:

> **PROPERTY, PLANT, AND EQUIPMENT**
>
> Property, plant, and equipment are carried at cost and are amortized on the straight-line and accelerated methods over the estimated useful lives of the assets. . . . Maintenance is charged to operating expenses as incurred, while renewals and betterments are capitalized. Major overhaul costs are amortized over the estimated period benefited.

AMERCO subsidiaries own property, plant, and equipment that are utilized in the manufacture, repair, and rental of U-Haul equipment and that provide offices for U-Haul. Assume that AMERCO made extensive repairs on an existing building and added a new wing. The building is a garage and repair facility for rental trucks that serve the Seattle area. The existing building originally cost $230,000, and by the end of 2007 (5 years), it was one-quarter amortized on the basis of a 20-year estimated useful life and no residual value. Assume straight-line amortization computed to the nearest month. During 2008, the following expenditures related to the building were made:

a. Ordinary repairs and maintenance expenditures for the year, $3,000 paid in cash.

b. Extensive and major repairs to the roof of the building, $15,000 paid in cash. These repairs were completed on June 30, 2008.

c. The new wing was completed on June 30, 2008, at a cash cost of $86,500. By itself, the wing had an estimated useful life of 15 years and no residual value. The company intends to sell the building and wing at the end of the building's useful life (in 14½ years from June 30, 2008).

Required:

1. Applying the policies of AMERCO, complete the following schedule, indicating the effects of the preceding expenditures. If there is no effect on an account, write NE on the line:

	Building	Accumulated Amortization	Amortization Expense	Repairs Expense	Cash
Balance January 1, 2008	$230,000	————	————		
Amortization Jan. 1–June 30		————	————		————
Balance prior to expenditures	230,000	————	————		
a.	————	————	————	————	————
b.	————	————	————	————	————
c.	————	————	————	————	————
Amortization July 1–December 31:					
Existing building		————	————	————	————
Major repairs and betterments		————	————	————	————
Balance December 31, 2008	————	————	————	————	

2. What was the net book value of the building on December 31, 2008?

3. Explain the effect of amortization on cash flows.

AP9–3 **Computing a Basket Purchase Allocation, and Recording Amortization under Three Alternative Methods** (P9–4)

■ **LO2, 3**

At the beginning of the year, Kohler Inc. bought three used machines from Lucas Corporation, for a total cash price of $62,000. Transportation costs on the machines were $3,000. The machines immediately were overhauled, installed, and started operating. The machines were different; therefore, each had to be recorded separately in the accounts. An appraiser was requested to estimate their market value at the date of purchase (prior to the overhaul and installation). The net book values shown on Lucas's books also are available. The net book values, appraisal results, installation costs, and renovation expenditures follow:

	Machine A	Machine B	Machine C
Net Book value—Lucas	$10,500	$22,000	$16,000
Appraisal value	11,500	32,000	28,500
Installation costs	800	1,100	1,100
Renovation costs prior to use	600	1,400	1,600

By the end of the first year, each machine had been operating 7,000 hours.

Required:

1. Compute the cost of each machine by making a supportable allocation (round your calculations to two decimal places). Explain the rationale for the allocation basis used.

2. Prepare the entry to record amortization expense at the end of year 1, assuming the following:

	ESTIMATES		
Machine	Life	Residual Value	Amortization Method
A	4	$1,000	Straight line
B	35,000 hours	2,000	Units of production
C	5	1,500	Double declining balance

■ **LO3, 7**

The Forzani
Group Ltd.

AP9–4 Inferring Amortization Amounts and Determining the Effects of an Amortization Error on Key Ratios (P9–5)

The Forzani Group Ltd. (FGL) franchises several specialty sports retail clothing and sports equipment stores. Its stores include SportChek, Coast Mountain Sports, Sport Mart, and National Sports. Its franchises are Intersport, RnR, Atmosphere, and Sports Experts. As at January 30, 2005, its fiscal year-end, the company operated 232 corporate stores and sold merchandise to 195 franchises. Its retail and franchise operations network spans Canada. The following is a note from a recent annual report:

1. Significant Accounting Policies

(c) Capital Assets

Capital assets are recorded at cost and are amortized using the following methods and ratios:

Building	—4% declining-balance basis
Building on leased land	—straight-line basis over the lesser of the length of the lease and estimated useful life of the building, not exceeding 20 years
Furniture, fixtures, equipment, and automotive	—straight line over 3–5 years
Leasehold improvements	—straight-line over the lesser of the length of the lease and estimated useful life of the improvements, not exceeding 10 years

Capital assets at January 30, 2005, and February 1, 2004, are as follows (in thousands of dollars):

	2005	2004
Land	$ 3,173	$ 1,994
Building	17,637	16,501
Building on leased land	3,159	3,159
Furniture, fixtures, equipment, and automotive	143,234	113,495
Leasehold improvements	187,141	170,972
Construction in progress	369	2,667
	$354,713	$308,788
Less accumulated amortization	175,011	141,072
Net capital assets	$179,702	$167,716

Required:

1. Assuming that FGL did not have any asset impairment write-offs and did not sell any property, plant, and equipment in fiscal year 2005, what was the amount of amortization expense recorded in 2005?

2. Assume that FGL failed to record amortization in 2005. Indicate the effect of the error (i.e., overstated or understated) on the following ratios: (*a*) earnings per share, (*b*) fixed asset turnover, and (*c*) return on equity. Computations are not required.

■ **LO5, 7**

Hasbro, Inc.

AP9–5 Inferring Asset Age and Determining Financial Statement Effects of a Long-Term Asset Disposal (Challenging) (P9–7)

Hasbro, Inc., designs, manufactures, and markets high-quality toys, games, and infant products. The company's revenues exceed $3.0 billion. In the toy business, it is very difficult to determine the life expectancy of a product. Products that children love one year may sit on the shelf the following year. As a result, companies in the toy business often sell productive assets that are no longer needed. Assume that on December 31, 2006, the end of the company's fiscal year, Hasbro's records showed the following data about a machine that was no longer needed to make a toy that was popular last year:

Machine, original cost	$107,000
Accumulated amortization	64,000*

*Based on an estimated useful life of six years, a residual value of $11,000, and straight-line amortization.

On July 1, 2007, the machine was sold for $38,000 cash.

Required:

1. How old was the machine on January 1, 2007? Show computations.

2. Indicate the effect (i.e., the amount and direction—increase or decrease) of the sale of the machine on July 1, 2007, on
   a. Total assets.
   b. Net income.
   c. Cash flows (by each section of the statement: Operating, Investing, and Financing Activities).

AP9–6 **Recording and Interpreting the Disposal of Three Long-Term Assets** (P9–9)   ■ **LO5**
During 2005, Callaway Company disposed of three different assets. On January 1, 2005, prior to their disposal, the accounts reflected the following:

Asset	Original Cost	Residual Value	Estimated Life	Accumulated Amortization (straight line)
Machine A	$24,000	$2,000	5 years	$17,600 (4 years)
Machine B	16,500	5,000	10 years	8,050 (7 years)
Machine C	59,200	3,200	14 years	48,000 (12 years)

The machines were disposed of in the following ways:

a. Machine A: Sold on January 1, 2005, for $6,250 cash.

b. Machine B: Sold on July 1, 2005, for $9,500; received cash, $4,500, and a $5,000 interest-bearing (10%) note receivable due at the end of 12 months.

c. Machine C: Suffered irreparable damage from an accident on October 2, 2005. On October 10, 2005, a salvage company removed the machine immediately at no cost. The machine was insured, and $11,500 cash was collected from the insurance company.

Required:

1. Prepare all journal entries related to the disposal of each machine.

2. Explain the accounting rationale for the way that you recorded each disposal.

AP9–7 **Determining Financial Statement Effects of Activities Related to Various Long-Term**   ■ **LO6**
Assets (P9–10)
During the 2008 fiscal year, Zhou Corporation completed the following transactions:

a. On January 1, 2008, paid $8,000 for a complete reconditioning of each of the following machines acquired on January 1, 2005 (total cost, $16,000). Although the reconditioning of the machines was necessary, it did not extend their useful lives.
   (1) Machine A: Original cost, $21,500; accumulated amortization (straight line) to December 31, 2007, $13,500 (residual value, $3,500).
   (2) Machine B: Original cost, $18,000; accumulated amortization (straight line) to December 31, 2007, $10,200 (residual value, $1,000).

b. On July 1, 2008, purchased a licence for $6,300 cash (estimated useful life, three years).

c. On July 1, 2008, purchased another business for cash $120,000, including $29,000 for goodwill. The company assumed $24,000 of liabilities from the other business. The company does not amortize goodwill.

d. On July 1, 2008, sold Machine A for $11,000 cash.

e. On October 1, 2008, repaved the parking lot of the building leased from J. Caldwell. The cost was $7,800, paid in cash; the estimated useful life was five years with no residual value. The company uses straight-line amortization. The lease will expire on December 31, 2011.

f. Total expenditures during 2008 for ordinary repairs and maintenance were $6,700.

Required:

1. For each of these transactions, indicate the accounts, amounts, and direction of the effects (+ for increase and − for decrease) on the accounting equation. Use the following structure:

Date	Assets	=	Liabilities	+	Shareholders' Equity

2. For each of the long-term assets, compute the amortization expense for 2008 to the nearest amount.

LO4, 6   **AP9–8** **Computing Amortization, Net Book Value, and Asset Impairment Related to Different Intangible Assets** (P9–13)

Theriault Corporation has five different intangible assets to be accounted for and reported on the financial statements. The management is concerned about the amortization of the cost of each of these intangibles. Facts about each intangible follow:

a. *Patent.* The company purchased a patent at a cash cost of $20,400 on January 1, 2007. The patent had a legal life of 20 years from date of registration with the Canadian Intellectual Property Office, which was January 1, 2005. It is amortized over its remaining legal life.

b. *Copyright.* On January 1, 2007, the company purchased a copyright for $23,250 cash. The legal life remaining from that date is 30 years. It is estimated that the copyrighted item will have no value by the end of 15 years.

c. *Franchise.* The company obtained a franchise from Farrell Company to make and distribute a special item. It obtained the franchise on January 1, 2007, at a cash cost of $19,200 for a 12-year period.

d. *Licence.* On January 1, 2006, the company secured a licence from the city to operate a special service for a period of seven years. Total cash expended to obtain the licence was $17,500.

e. *Goodwill.* The company started business in January 2005 by purchasing another business for a cash lump sum of $650,000. Included in the purchase price was "Goodwill, $75,000." Company executives stated that "the goodwill is an important long-term asset to us."

Required:

1. Compute the amount of amortization expense that should be recorded for each intangible asset at the end of the fiscal year, December 31, 2007.

2. Compute the net book value of each intangible asset on *January 1, 2010*.

3. Assume that on January 2, 2010, the franchise was impaired in its ability to continue to produce strong revenues. The other intangible assets were not affected. Theriault estimated that the franchise will be able to produce future cash flows of $14,500. Compute the amount, if any, of the impairment loss to be recorded.

CASES AND PROJECTS

FINDING AND INTERPRETING FINANCIAL INFORMATION

LO1, 3   **CP9–1** **Finding Financial Information**

Van Houtte

Refer to the financial statements and accompanying notes of Van Houtte Inc. given in Appendix B at the end of this book.

Required:

1. What method of depreciation and amortization does the company use?

2. What is the amount of accumulated depreciation and amortization at the end of the current year?

3. For depreciation purposes, what is the estimated useful life of the coffee-service equipment?

4. What amount of depreciation and amortization was reported as expense for the current year?

5. What is the fixed asset turnover ratio? What does it suggest?

6. For each of the preceding questions, where did you locate the information?

CP9–2 Comparing Companies within an Industry

■ **LO1, 3**

WestJet Airlines vs.
Southwest Airlines

Southwest Airlines is an exuberant, no-frills airline that was started more than 30 years ago. WestJet Airlines has followed Southwest's successful corporate strategy, which is based on "keeping airplanes in the air." Selected data from Southwest's annual reports appear below (in millions of dollars):

	December 31 2004	2003
Property and equipment, at cost	$11,921	$10,550
Less allowance for depreciation	3,198	3,107
	8,723	7,443
Total assets	11,337	9,878
Total operating revenues for the year	6,530	5,937
Southwest uses the straight-line amortization method.		

Similar data for WestJet Airlines for fiscal year 2004 were provided earlier in this chapter.

Required:

1. Compute the percentage of net capital assets to total assets for both companies each year. Why might the two ratios differ?

2. Compute the percentage of the capital assets that has been amortized for each company for the most recent year. Why do you think the percentages differ?

3. Compute the fixed asset turnover ratio for the most recent year presented for both companies. Which has the higher efficiency in using assets? Why?

4. Would you expect Southwest's ratios to increase or decrease over time? Why? What about WestJet's ratios?

FINANCIAL REPORTING AND ANALYSIS CASES

CP9–3 Broadening Financial Research Skills: Identifying Competitors in an Industry

Reuters provides lists of industries and the competitors in each at www.investor.reuters.com/ Industries.aspx.

Required:

Using your Web browser, contact Reuters and identify three competitors for the following industries:

1. Airline.

2. Hotels and motels.

3. Footwear.

4. Computer hardware.

CP9–4 Interpreting the Financial Press

■ **LO4**

The October 5, 1998, edition of *Business Week* includes the article, "Earnings Hocus-Pocus." You can access the article on the Online Learning Centre Web site at www.mcgrawhill.ca/ college/libby/student/resources.

Required:

Read pages 1 through 9 of the article (stopping at the paragraph beginning with "Meanwhile, the SEC...." Then answer the following questions:

1. What is meant by the concept that many companies take a "big bath"?

2. List several companies mentioned in the article that have taken a big bath by writing down fixed assets or intangibles. Indicate for each the nature of the earnings manipulation.

■ **LO3**

Papa John's
International

CP9–5   Using Financial Reports: Analyzing the Age of Assets

A note to a recent annual report for PapaJohn's International contained the following information (in thousands of dollars):

	Current Year	Previous Year
Land	$ 30,449	$ 25,798
Buildings and improvements	78,970	66,494
Leasehold improvements	70,838	60,763
Equipment and other	136,410	121,414
Construction in progress	12,642	23,089
	329,309	297,558
Less accumulated depreciation and amortization	(83,435)	(69,745)
Net property and equipment	$245,874	$227,813

Depreciation and amortization expense (in thousands of dollars) charged to operations was $34,172 in the current year and $24,827 in the previous year. Depreciation generally is computed using the straight-line method for financial reporting purposes.

Required:

1. What is your best estimate of the average expected life for PapaJohn's depreciable assets?

2. What is your best estimate of the average age of PapaJohn's depreciable assets?

■ **LO1, 3, 6, 7   CP9–6   Using Financial Reports: Analyzing Fixed Asset Turnover Ratio and Cash Flows**

CanWest Global
Communications
Corp.

CanWest Global Communications Corp., with headquarters in Winnipeg, Manitoba, is one of Canada's largest media conglomerates and the owner of many Canadian newspapers, television stations, and cable channels, as well as several stations in Australia, Ireland, and New Zealand. During 2000, CanWest acquired additional companies, adding more than $800 million to its intangible assets. Selected data from a recent annual report are as follows (in thousands of dollars):

Property and equipment, and intangibles From the consolidated balance sheet	Current Year	Prior Year
Investment in film and television program rights	$ 251,114	$ 45,503
Property and equipment, net	185,224	110,011
Broadcast licences and goodwill	1,095,066	287,452
From the consolidated income statement		
Revenue	731,848	602,344
From the consolidated statement of cash flows		
Net earnings for the year	162,680	146,103
Adjustments:		
Amortization of broadcast licences and goodwill	28,871	22,833
Amortization of other assets	9,575	8,425
Other adjustments, net	(173,226)	(71,238)
Cash provided by operations	27,900	106,123
From the notes to the financial statements		
Accumulated amortization on property and equipment	$135,865	$126,290

Required:

1. Compute the cost of the property and equipment at the end of the current year. Explain your answer.

2. What is your best estimate of the average expected life of CanWest's property and equipment? What was the approximate age of the property and equipment at the end of the current year? Assume that CanWest uses straight-line amortization.

3. Compute the fixed asset turnover ratio for the current year. Explain your results.

4. Compute an estimate of the amortization expense of broadcast licences and goodwill for the next year.

5. On the consolidated cash flow statement, why are the amortization amounts added to net earnings for the year?

CP9–7 Using Financial Reports: Inferring the Sale of Assets

■ **LO5**

Eastman Kodak

An annual report for Eastman Kodak reported that the balance of property, plant, and equipment at the end of the current year was $16,774 million. At the end of the previous year, it had been $15,667 million. During the current year, the company bought $2,118 million worth of new equipment. The balance of accumulated amortization at the end of the current year was $8,146 million and at the end of the previous year was $7,654 million. Amortization expense for the current year was $1,181 million. The annual report did not disclose any gain or loss on the disposition of property, plant, and equipment, so you may assume that the amount was zero.

Required:

What amount of proceeds did Eastman Kodak receive when it sold property, plant, and equipment during the current year? (*Hint:* Set up T-accounts.)

CP9–8 Using Financial Reports: Comparing Amortization Methods in Different Countries

■ **LO3**

Diageo

Diageo is a major international company located in London, England. An annual report contained the following information concerning its accounting policies.

Fixed assets and amortization

Fixed assets are stated at cost or at professional valuation. Cost includes interest, net of any tax relief, on capital employed in major developments.

No amortization is provided on freehold land. Other leaseholds are amortized over the unexpired period of the lease. All other buildings, plant, equipment, and vehicles are amortized to residual values over their estimated useful lives within the following ranges:

Industrial buildings	25 to 100 years
Plant and machinery	3 to 25 years
Fixtures and fittings	3 to 17 years

Required:

Compare accounting for fixed assets and amortization in England with procedures used in this country.

CRITICAL THINKING CASES

CP9–9 Making a Decision as a Financial Analyst: Interpreting the Impact of the Capitalization of Interest on an Accounting Ratio

■ **LO3**

WestJet Airlines

The capitalization of interest associated with self-constructed assets was discussed in this chapter. A recent annual report for WestJet Airlines disclosed the following information concerning capitalization of interest:

1. Significant accounting policies (continued):

(i) Capitalized interest costs:

Costs associated with the introduction of new aircraft and other assets under construction are capitalized from inception through to commencement of commercial operations. Interest attributable to funds used to finance the acquisition of new aircraft and construction of major ground facilities is capitalized as an additional cost of the asset.

Assume that WestJet capitalized interest in the amount of $500,000 and disclosed $2.2 million of interest expense in its income statement for the year. One useful accounting ratio is the interest coverage ratio (Income before interest and taxes divided by Interest Expense).

Required:

1. Explain why an analyst would calculate this ratio.

2. Did WestJet include the $500,000 in the reported interest expense of $2.2 million? If not, should an analyst include it when calculating the interest coverage ratio? Explain.

■ **LO3, 7**   **CP9–10** **Evaluating an Ethical Dilemma: Analyzing an Accounting Change**

Ford Motor Company

An annual report for Ford Motor Company included the following information:

> **Note 6. Net Property, Amortization and Amortization—Automotive**
>
> Assets placed in service before January 1, 1993, are depreciated using an accelerated method. Assets placed in service beginning in 1993 will be depreciated using the straight-line method of amortization. This change in accounting principle is being made to reflect improvements in the design and flexibility of manufacturing machinery and equipment and improvements in maintenance practices. These improvements have resulted in more uniform productive capacities and maintenance costs over the useful life of an asset. Straight-line is preferable in these circumstances. The change is expected to improve 1993 after-tax results by $80 to $100 million.

Required:

1. What was the stated reason for the change in method? What other factors do you think management considered when it decided to make this accounting change?

2. Do you think this is an ethical decision?

3. Who were affected by the change and how were they benefited or harmed?

4. What impact did this change have on cash flows for Ford?

5. As an investor, how would you react to the fact that Ford's net income will increase by $80 to $100 million as the result of this change?

FINANCIAL REPORTING AND ANALYSIS TEAM PROJECT

■ **LO3, 7**   **CP9–11** **Team Project: Analysis of Long-Term Assets**

MarketGuide provides lists of industries and the competitors in each at www.marketguide.com/mgi/industry/industry.html.

Using your Web browser, contact *MarketGuide*. As a group, select an industry to analyze. Each team member should then, using the Web browser, obtain the annual report for one publicly traded company in the industry, with each member selecting a different company.

Required:

1. On an individual basis, each team member should write a short report listing the following:
   a. The accounts and amounts of the company's long-term assets (property, plant, and equipment; intangible assets; and natural resources).
   b. The cost allocation method(s) and estimates used for each type of long-term asset.
   c. The approximate average life of the assets.
   d. The fixed asset turnover ratio.

2. Discuss any patterns that you as a team observe. Then, as a team, write a short report comparing and contrasting your companies according to the preceding attributes.

LEARNING OBJECTIVES

Reporting and Interpreting Liabilities

10

Petro-Canada was established in 1975 by the Government of Canada to create a strong Canadian presence in the oil industry and identify new Canadian energy sources. In 2004, the Government of Canada sold its remaining ownership of Petro-Canada to other investors. Petro-Canada is an integrated oil and gas company, a leader in the Canadian petroleum industry, with a portfolio of businesses spanning both the upstream and downstream sectors of the industry. In the upstream businesses, the company explores for, develops, produces, and markets crude oil, natural gas liquids (NGL), and natural gas in Canada and internationally. The downstream business refines crude oil and other feedstocks and markets petroleum products and related goods and services, primarily in Canada. It also offers services such as convenience stores, car washes, and automotive repair and maintenance services through a network of more than 1,600 wholesale and retail outlets across Canada. For 2005, it planned to spend $3.6 billion on a number of projects including modification of refineries to produce cleaner-burning diesel fuels, exploration activities, and establishing new ventures for the long run. Achieving these plans requires the investment of large amounts of capital, some of which will be borrowed from creditors.

Financial analysts consider a number of factors when they assess the strength of a company's financial position. One of the key areas they examine is how the company has financed its operations. Managing a company's liabilities is often as important as managing its assets.

UNDERSTANDING THE BUSINESS BACKGROUND

Businesses finance the acquisition of their assets from two sources: funds supplied by creditors (debt) and funds provided by owners (equity). The mixture of debt and equity used by a business is called its **capital structure**. In addition to selecting a capital structure, management can select from a variety of sources from which to borrow money. The liabilities and shareholders' equity of Petro-Canada's balance sheet (Exhibit 10.1) shows that its capital structure at December 31, 2004, was composed of approximately 52 percent debt and 48 percent equity. This proportional mix of debt and equity reflects management's financing strategy to achieve the company's goals.

In deciding how best to finance its projects, Petro-Canada's management must consider two key factors: the risk associated with the source of financing, and the return to shareholders on their investment in the company. Debt capital is riskier than equity because interest payments on debt are legal obligations that must be paid. If a company cannot meet a required interest payment because of a temporary cash shortage, creditors may force the company into bankruptcy and require the sale of assets to satisfy the debt obligations. In contrast, dividend payments to shareholders are not a legal obligation until declared by the board of directors, which means that equity offers lower financial risk to the issuing corporation. As with any business transaction, borrowers and lenders attempt to negotiate the most favourable terms possible. Managers devote considerable effort to analyzing alternative borrowing arrangements.

Companies that include debt in their capital structure also must make strategic decisions concerning the proper balance between short-term debt and long-term debt.

EXHIBIT **10.1**

Petro-Canada Energy's Balance Sheet

REAL WORLD EXCERPT

Petro-Canada

ANNUAL REPORT

PETRO-CANADA
CONSOLIDATED BALANCE SHEETS
As at December 31

(in millions of Canadian dollars)	2004	2003 (Note 2)
Assets		
Current assets		
Cash and cash equivalents (note 13)	$ 170	$ 635
Accounts receivable (note 11)	1,254	1,503
Inventories (note 14)	549	551
Prepaid expenses	13	16
Total current assets	1,986	2,705
Property, plant and equipment, net (note 15)	14,783	10,943
Goodwill (note 12)	986	810
Deferred charges and other assets (note 16)	345	316
Total assets	$18,100	$14,774
Liabilities and Shareholders' Equity		
Current liabilities		
Accounts payable and accrued liabilities	$ 2,223	$ 1,822
Income taxes payable	370	300
Short-term notes payable	299	—
Current portion of long-term debt (note 17)	6	6
Total current liabilities	2,898	2,128
Long-term debt (note 17)	2,275	2,223
Other liabilities (note 18)	646	306
Asset retirement obligations (note 19)	834	773
Future income taxes (note 7)	2,708	1,756
Commitments and contingent liabilities (note 25)		
Shareholders' equity (note 20)	8,739	7,588
Total liabilities and shareholders' equity	$18,100	$14,774

Financial analysts calculate a number of accounting ratios to evaluate a company's capital structure and the balance between short-term and long-term debt. In this chapter, we discuss both short-term and long-term debt as well as some important accounting ratios. We will also introduce you to present value concepts. In the next chapter, we discuss a special category of long-term debt, bonds payable.

ORGANIZATION OF THE CHAPTER

• **Liabilities Defined and Classified**	• **Current Liabilities**	• **Long-Term Liabilities**	• **Present and Future Value Concepts**
Current Ratio	Accounts Payable	Long-Term Notes Payable and Bonds	Future and Present Values of a Single Amount
	Accounts Payable Turnover Ratio	Lease Liabilities	Future and Present Values of an Annuity
	Accrued Liabilities		Accounting Applications of Future and Present Values
	Notes Payable		
	Current Portion of Long-Term Debt		
	Deferred Revenues		
	Estimated Liabilities Reported on the Balance Sheet		
	Contingent Liabilities and Commitments		

LIABILITIES DEFINED AND CLASSIFIED

Most people have a reasonable understanding of the definition of the word *liability*. Accountants formally define **liabilities** as probable future sacrifices of economic benefits. Liabilities are obligations arising from an entity's past transactions that will be settled in the future by some transfer or use of assets or provision of service. As Exhibit 10.1 shows, Petro-Canada reported short-term and long-term liabilities amounting to $9,361 million. Petro-Canada has borrowed money in the past from creditors and purchased goods and services on credit (past transactions), promising its creditors to pay cash (an asset) at some point in the future, based on the terms of its debt agreements.

When a liability is first recorded, it is measured in terms of its current cash equivalent, which is the cash amount that a creditor would accept to settle the liability immediately. Petro-Canada's long-term debt is $2,275 million, but it will repay much more than that because the company must also pay interest on the debt. Interest that will be paid in the future is not included in the amount of the liability because it accrues and becomes a liability with the passage of time. For fiscal year 2004, the company reported $142 million of interest expense on its income statement.

Like most businesses, Petro-Canada has several kinds of liabilities and a wide range of creditors. The list of liabilities on the balance sheet differs for almost every company that you study because different operating activities result in different types of liabilities. The liability section of Petro-Canada's balance sheet begins with the caption Current Liabilities. **Current liabilities** are defined as short-term obligations that will be paid within the normal operating cycle of the business or within one year of the balance sheet date, whichever is longer. Because most companies have an operating cycle that is shorter than one year, current liabilities can be defined simply as liabilities that are due within one year. Non-current liabilities include all other liabilities. Information about current liabilities is important to managers and analysts because these

■ **LEARNING OBJECTIVE 1**

Define, measure, and report current liabilities.

LIABILITIES are obligations arising from past transactions that will be settled in the future by some transfer or use of assets or provision of service.

CURRENT LIABILITIES are short-term obligations that will be paid within the normal operating cycle or one year, whichever is longer.

LIQUIDITY is the ability to pay current obligations.

obligations must be paid in the near future. Analysts say that a company has **liquidity** if it has the ability to meet its current obligations. A number of financial ratios are useful in evaluating liquidity, including the current ratio.

KEY **RATIO ANALYSIS:**

■ **LEARNING OBJECTIVE 2**

Compute and interpret the current ratio.

CURRENT RATIO

ANALYTICAL QUESTION → Does the company currently have the resources to pay its short-term debt?

RATIO AND COMPARISONS → Analysts use the *current ratio* as an indicator of the amount of current assets available to satisfy current liabilities. It is computed as follows:

Current Ratio = Current Assets ÷ Current Liabilities

The 2004 ratio for Petro-Canada is:

$1,986 ÷ 2,898 = 0.69

Comparisons over Time				Comparisons with Competitors	
Petro-Canada				Suncor Energy	Imperial Oil
2002	2003	2004		2004	2004
0.97	1.27	0.69		0.85	0.84

INTERPRETATIONS

In General → A high ratio normally suggests good liquidity, but too high a ratio suggests inefficient use of resources. An old guideline was that companies should have a current ratio between 1 and 2. Today, many strong companies use sophisticated management techniques to minimize funds invested in current assets, and as a result have current ratios below 1.

Focus Company Analysis → Petro-Canada's current ratio for 2004 indicates that the company has $0.69 to pay each $1.00 in current liabilities. The decrease in Petro-Canada's current ratio from 2003 to 2004 signals that Petro-Canada's liquidity position is deteriorating. However, in the notes to its financial statements, Petro-Canada discloses that it has $1,500 million available in various short-term credit facilities, enough to repay more than half of its current liabilities in full if they suddenly become due. The industry comparison indicates that Petro-Canada's current ratio in 2004 was lower than those of Suncor and Imperial Oil.

A Few Cautions → The current ratio may be a misleading measure of liquidity if significant funds are tied up in assets that will not be easily converted into cash. A company with a high current ratio might still have liquidity problems if the majority of its current assets comprised slow-moving inventory. Analysts recognize that managers can manipulate the current ratio by engaging in certain transactions just before the close of the fiscal year. In most cases, for example, the current ratio can be improved by paying creditors immediately prior to the preparation of financial statements.

FINANCIAL **ANALYSIS**

BALANCE SHEET RATIOS AND DEBT CONTRACTS

When firms borrow money, they agree to make specific payments of interest and principal in the future. To provide protection for the creditors, they also often agree to other restrictions on their activities. For example, Petro-Canada has issued long-term notes for US$600 million payable in the year 2035, along with semi-annual interest payments. The agreement between the company and the creditors puts some limitations on the company's issuance of additional debt. Other types of debt contracts require companies to maintain a minimum specified current ratio and a maximum debt-to-equity ratio.

Maintaining a specified level of the current ratio assures creditors that the company has sufficient *liquidity* (liquid assets, after the payment of other current liabilities) to pay its current debts. The debt-to-equity ratio measures the portion of the company that is financed with debt as opposed to equity. By limiting the debt-to-equity ratio, the company agrees to limit the amount of its additional borrowing, which limits additional demands by these new creditors on the company's cash.

SELF-STUDY **QUIZ 10-1**

Refer to the balance sheet of Petro-Canada presented in Exhibit 10.1. Assume that the long-term debt contracts require Petro-Canada to maintain a minimum current ratio of 0.75 and a maximum debt-to-equity ratio of 1.50.

1. Compute the current ratio and the debt-to-equity ratio at December 31, 2003 and December 31, 2004, to verify if Petro-Canada violated these conditions of its lending agreement.
2. Should the company's management be concerned about the level of these two ratios? Explain.

After you complete the quiz, check your answers with the solution on page 560.

As you study companies, you will often hear people talk about both the current ratio and a closely related concept called **working capital**, which is the dollar amount of the difference between current assets and current liabilities. Working capital is important to both managers and financial analysts because it has a significant impact on the health and profitability of a company. The working capital accounts are actively managed to achieve a balance between costs and benefits. If a business has too little working capital, it runs the risk of not being able to meet its obligations to creditors. On the other hand, too much working capital may tie up resources in unproductive assets and incur additional costs.

WORKING CAPITAL is the dollar difference between total current assets and total current liabilities.

The current ratio and working capital are measures of a company's liquidity. Petro-Canada's working capital of $217 million confirms that if all current liabilities had to be repaid immediately, the company would have excess cash of $217 million, assuming that all current assets can be readily converted into cash at their book value.

SELF-STUDY **QUIZ 10-2**

Assume that the current ratio for Petro-Canada is 2.0. For each of the following events, indicate whether the current ratio and working capital will increase or decrease:

1. Petro-Canada incurs an account payable of $250,000, with no change in current assets.
2. The company borrows $1,000,000 in long-term debt.
3. The company pays taxes payable in the amount of $750,000.
4. The company finances a new building with long-term debt.

After you complete your answers, check them with the solutions on page 561.

Liabilities are very important from an analytical perspective because they affect a company's future cash flows and risk characteristics. Current liabilities are usually grouped according to type of creditor, separating liabilities owed to suppliers and other trade creditors (accounts payable) from those owed to banks (short-term borrowings), providers of services (accrued liabilities), governments (taxes payable), and others. For many types of liabilities, the amount of the debt is determined based on contractual agreements between the company and suppliers of goods, services, or funds. Most of these liabilities are recorded as they occur during the accounting period, as in the case of trade payables for merchandise purchases, loans from banks, and notes payable to creditors. However, specific liabilities that can be determined with accuracy, such as salaries payable and interest payable, require accrual through adjusting entries at the end of the accounting period prior to the preparation of financial statements.

For other types of liabilities, the exact amount will not be known with certainty until a future event, but they must be estimated and recorded if they relate to transactions that occurred during the accounting period. For example, a liability for product warranty will not be known until the repair work is carried out in the future. But the matching principle requires that warranty costs be matched to the related sales revenue that is recorded in the period of sale. As these costs and the related liability are not known, they must be estimated based on past experience or some reasonable basis, and recorded through adjusting entries prior to the preparation of the financial statements.

In certain cases, it may not be possible to provide a reasonable estimate of a potential future liability that is contingent on a future event. In those cases, relevant information about contingent liabilities must be disclosed to readers in the financial statement notes.

Most analysts devote a considerable amount of time to reviewing a company's liabilities. We discuss them in the order in which they appear on a balance sheet.

CURRENT LIABILITIES

ACCOUNTS PAYABLE

Most companies do not produce all the goods and services that they use in their basic operations. Instead, they purchase goods and services from other businesses. Typically, these transactions are made on credit with cash payments occurring after the goods and services have been provided. As a result, these transactions create *accounts payable,* also called *trade accounts payable.* Journal entries associated with accounts payable were discussed in Chapter 8.

For many companies, trade credit is a relatively inexpensive way to finance the purchase of inventory, because interest does not normally accrue on accounts payable. As an incentive to encourage more sales, some suppliers may offer very generous credit terms that may give the buyer the opportunity to resell merchandise and collect cash before payment must be made to the original supplier. For example, Dell Inc. reported the following details in its annual report for fiscal year 2005:

	2005	2004	2003
Average age of receivables (days)	29	31	28
Average age of payables (days)	73	70	68

Dell maintains an efficient cash management system as it collects from customers within one month of the sale, but pays its suppliers 73 days after the date of purchase.

Some managers may be tempted to delay payment to suppliers for as long as possible to conserve cash. This strategy normally is not advisable. Most successful companies develop positive working relationships with their suppliers to ensure quality goods and services. Managers can destroy good supplier relationships if they are slow to pay. In addition, financial analysts become concerned if a business does not meet its obligations to trade creditors on a timely basis because such slowness often indicates that the company is experiencing financial difficulties.

KEY **RATIO ANALYSIS:**

■ **LEARNING OBJECTIVE 3**

Compute and interpret the accounts payable turnover ratio.

ACCOUNTS PAYABLE TURNOVER RATIO

ANALYTICAL QUESTION → How efficient is management in meeting its obligations to suppliers?

RATIO AND COMPARISONS → The *accounts payable turnover ratio* is a measure of how quickly management is paying trade creditors. Analysts use this ratio as a measure of liquidity. It is computed as follows:

    Accounts Payable Turnover = Cost of Goods Sold ÷ Average Accounts Payable

The 2004 ratio for Petro-Canada is:

$$\$6,740 \div \$2,023^* = 3.33$$

*($1,822 + $2,223) ÷ 2 = $2,023

In the oil and gas industry, companies report the cost of purchases of crude oil and products instead of cost of goods sold. In addition, the company reported its accounts payable along with accrued liabilities without a separate disclosure of accounts payable. Consequently, the denominator of the computed ratio overstates the average accounts payable, and understates the computed ratio. This observation applies to the ratios computed for Petro-Canada over time and its two competitors, Suncor Energy Inc. and Imperial Oil Limited.

Comparisons over Time			Comparisons with Competitors	
Petro-Canada			Suncor Energy	Imperial Oil
2002	2003	2004	2004	2004
2.98	3.02	3.33	2.52	5.52

INTERPRETATIONS

In General → A high ratio normally suggests that a company is paying its suppliers in a timely manner. The ratio can be stated in a more intuitive manner by dividing average accounts payable by the cost of goods sold per day:

Average Age of Payables = Average Accounts Payable ÷ (Cost of Goods Sold ÷ 365)

The 2004 ratio for Petro-Canada is:

$$\$2,023 \div (\$6,740 \div 365) = 109.6 \text{ Days}$$

Alternatively, the average age of payables can be computed by dividing the accounts payable turnover by 365 (365 ÷ 3.33 = 109.6 days).

Focus Company Analysis → The accounts payable turnover for Petro-Canada has increased over the past three years, from 2.98 in 2002 to 3.33 in 2004. Petro-Canada's 2004 ratio is lower than that of Imperial Oil, which may indicate that Petro-Canada is more aggressive than Imperial Oil in its cash management policy. By conserving cash (with slower payments to suppliers), the company is able to minimize the amount of money it must borrow and pay back with interest.

A Few Cautions → The accounts payable turnover ratio is an average associated with all accounts payable. The ratio might not reflect reality if a company pays some creditors on time but is late with others. The ratio is also subject to manipulation. Managers could be late with payments to creditors during the entire year but "catch up" at year-end so that the ratio is at an acceptable level. As our focus company analysis indicates, a low ratio can indicate either liquidity problems or aggressive cash management. The first is a problem; the second is a strength. Analysts would have to study other factors (such as the current ratio and the amount of cash flows generated from operating activities) to determine which is the case.

ACCRUED LIABILITIES

In many situations, a business incurs an expense in one accounting period and makes cash payment for the expense in a subsequent period. **Accrued liabilities** are expenses that have been incurred before the end of an accounting period but have not yet been paid. They are recorded as adjusting entries at year-end. These expenses include such items as employee salaries and wages, rent, interest, and income taxes.

ACCRUED LIABILITIES are expenses that have been incurred but have not been paid at the end of the accounting period.

Income Taxes Payable Like individuals, corporations must pay tax at the appropriate federal and provincial rates on income from active business operations, property income, and capital gains arising from the sale of assets. Based on data from the 200 corporations that participated in the survey for *Financial Reporting in Canada 2004*, combined statutory tax rates ranged from a low combined federal and provincial rate of 37 percent to a high of 42.6 percent.[1] Petro-Canada reported a combined statutory tax rate of 38 percent in the year 2004, and discloses its income tax expense for 2004 in note 9 to its financial statements:

REAL WORLD EXCERPT

Petro-Canada

ANNUAL REPORT

INCOME STATEMENT for the years ended December 31			
($ millions)	2004	2003	2002
Earnings before income taxes	3,245	2,960	1,798
Provision for income taxes (note 7)			
Current	1,461	1,247	959
Future	27	63	(116)
	1,488	1,310	843
Net earnings	$1,757	$1,650	$ 955

Notice that the income taxes expense is composed of two components: (1) a current portion of $1,461 million and (2) a future portion of $27 million. The current portion is payable within prescribed time limits, but the future portion will eventually be payable based on future events. The basic reason for dividing the income tax expense into current and future portions is explained in Chapter Supplement A.

Taxes Other than Income Taxes   In addition to paying taxes on income, companies are often required to pay other types of taxes and fees, depending on the specific industry in which they operate. These taxes add to the cost of producing and selling goods and services, and are eventually passed on to customers through higher sales prices.[2] Companies serve as agents of the federal and provincial governments in collecting taxes that are charged to customers for their purchases of goods and services. Sales of most goods and services in Canada are subject to sales taxes at both the federal and provincial levels. Typically, the prices of goods and services are increased by the federal Goods and Services Tax (GST), which is currently set at 7 percent, and a Provincial Sales Tax (PST) that varies between zero and 10 percent, depending on the province.

The GST and PST amounts are added to the sales price, collected from customers, and then remitted to the federal and provincial governments. In this respect, the seller acts as an intermediary between the customer and the government and facilitates the collection of sales taxes from customers. When a company sells goods and services, the applicable sales taxes, if any, are added to the sales price, but they do not constitute revenue for the seller. The sales taxes collected from customers represent liabilities that are remitted periodically (monthly or quarterly) to the respective governments. For example, when a Petro-Canada gas station sells gasoline to a customer for $40, the total cash paid by the customer would include a GST of $2.80 ($40 × 7%) and another amount for PST, for example, $3.20 ($40 × 8%). The journal entry to record this transaction and the transaction effects would be:

---

[1]C. Byrd, I. Chen, and J. Smith, *Financial Reporting in Canada 2004*. Toronto: Canadian Institute of Chartered Accountants, 2004, pp. 395–406.

[2]To highlight the relative significance of the taxes and fees imposed on the airlines industry, WestJet Airlines offered to sell one-way tickets for $3 on flights between Calgary and Edmonton on June 30, 2002. However, the price of a $6 return ticket quickly rose to $89.27 when all of the applicable fees and taxes were added! See P. Fitzpatrick, "WestJet Launches $3 Ticket Protest." *National Post* (*Financial Post*), June 21, 2002, p. FP1.

Cash	46.00	
Sales revenue		40.00
GST payable		2.80
PST payable		3.20

Assets		=	Liabilities		+	Shareholders' Equity	
Cash	+46.00		GST payable	+2.80		Sales revenue	+40.00
			PST payable	+3.20			

All of the GST and PST collected from customers are accumulated in these two liability accounts. The balance of the account GST payable is reduced by the amount of GST that the company pays on its own purchases of goods and services, and the net amount is then remitted to the federal government. Provincial governments follow different practices for collecting provincial sales taxes from companies, and for reimbursing them for the PST they pay on their purchases. The unpaid amounts at year-end are included in current liabilities. The following note to the 2004 financial statements of Imperial Oil Limited shows an assortment of taxes that Imperial Oil pays to the federal, provincial, and local governments:

Notes to the Consolidated Financial Statements

17. Net payments/payables to governments

millions of dollars	2004	2003	2002
Current income tax expense (note 4)	1,103	610	718
Federal excise tax	1,264	1,254	1,231
Property taxes included in expenses	85	80	85
Payroll and other taxes included in expenses	50	52	51
GST/QST/HST collected (a)	2,297	2,015	1,717
GST/QST/HST input tax credits (a)	(1,948)	(1,705)	(1,368)
Other consumer taxes collected for governments	1,670	1,662	1,589
Crown royalties	472	418	314
Total paid or payable to governments	4,993	4,386	4,337
Less investment tax credits and other receipts	14	30	12
Net paid or payable to governments	4,979	4,356	4,325
Net payments to:			
Federal government	2,472	2,061	2,171
Provincial governments	2,422	2,215	2,069
Local governments	85	80	85
Net paid or payable to governments	4,979	4,356	4,325

(a) The abbreviations refer to the federal goods and services tax, the Quebec sales tax and the federal/provincial harmonized sales tax, respectively. The HST is applicable in the provinces of Nova Scotia, New Brunswick and Newfoundland and Labrador.

Note that the provincial sales tax in Quebec is referred to as Quebec Sales Tax, and that the Atlantic Provinces have combined the GST and PST into one Harmonized Sales Tax of 15 percent.

Payroll Liabilities At the end of each accounting period, employees usually will have earned salaries that have not been paid. Unpaid salaries may be reported as a separate item or as part of accrued liabilities, as is the case with Petro-Canada. In addition to reporting salaries that have been earned but unpaid, companies also must report the cost of benefits, which include retirement programs, vacation time, employment insurance, health insurance, and many others. In addition to the current liability arising directly from wages and salaries payable, employers must also remit income tax and other social benefit contributions on behalf of their employees to the appropriate government agencies.

Employee Deductions   Employee income tax is usually the largest amount withheld from wages and salaries by the employer. Federal and provincial laws require the employer to deduct an appropriate amount of income tax each period from the gross earnings of each employee. The amount of income tax withheld from the employee's salary is recorded by the employer as a current liability between the date of deduction and the date on which the amount held is remitted to the government.

If you have been employed and received a pay cheque, you would have noticed that additional amounts were deducted from your gross earnings for employment insurance (EI), contributions to the Canada Pension Plan (CPP) for future retirement benefits, health insurance, and other contributions that you and your employer must remit to the appropriate agencies. In general, employers match the employee's CPP remittance, but pay $1.40 for every $1.00 remitted by the employee for employment insurance. Other deductions such as union dues and workers' compensation will depend on the terms of employment and will result in a future obligation for the employer to remit these amounts to the legal recipient. In total, the employer's share of contributions remitted by a corporation on behalf of its employees to other parties can add up to 20 percent of the employee's gross earnings. This is one reason why corporations prefer to have existing employees work overtime rather than hire new ones.

Compensation expense for employee services includes all funds earned by the employee as well as funds that must be paid to others on behalf of employees (i.e., benefits). To illustrate, let us assume that Petro-Canada accumulated the following information in its detailed payroll records for the first two weeks of June 2005:

Salaries and wages earned	$1,800,000
Income taxes withheld	450,000
CPP contributions	31,000
EI contributions	15,000

Remember that the employer must also contribute an equal amount of CPP contributions and $1.40 times the employees' contributions to employment insurance. As a result, the total liability associated with CPP and EI contributions is $98,000 ($31,000 + $31,000 + $15,000 + $21,000). The entry to record the payroll and employee deductions, and the related transaction effects, follow:

Compensation expense (E)	1,852,000	
Liability for income taxes withheld (L)		450,000
CPP payable (L)		62,000
EI payable (L)		36,000
Cash (A)		1,304,000

Assets		=	Liabilities		+	Shareholders' Equity	
Cash	−1,304,000		Liability for income taxes withheld	+450,000		Compensation expense	−1,852,000
			CPP payable	+62,000			
			EI payable	+36,000			

Notice in the journal entry that compensation expense ($1,800,000 + $52,000) includes salary and wages earned, as well as the employer's share of CPP and EI contributions because these are fringe benefits earned by the employees. The cash paid to employees ($1,304,000) is not the total amount earned ($1,800,000) because the employer must withhold both income taxes ($450,000) and the employees' share of CPP and EI contributions ($46,000). The CPP and EI payable reflect both the employees' share and the employer's share.

FOCUS ON **CASH FLOWS**

ACCOUNTS PAYABLE AND ACCRUED LIABILITIES

The change in accounts payable can be a major determinant of a company's cash flow from operations. While the income statement reflects the expenses of the period, the cash flow from operating activities reflects cash payments to suppliers. Since purchases on account increase the balance in accounts payable, the change in accounts payable from the beginning to the end of the period is the difference between purchases and cash payments to suppliers. As explained in Chapter 5, the amount of purchases equals the cost of goods sold adjusted for the change in the balances of inventories from the beginning to the end of the period.

■ **LEARNING OBJECTIVE 4**

Explain the impact of changes in accounts payable and accrued liabilities on cash flows.

EFFECT ON THE CASH FLOW STATEMENT

IN GENERAL → When there is a net *increase in accounts payable* for the period, cash paid to suppliers is less than purchases; thus, the increase must be *added* to net income in computing cash flow from operations.

When there is a net *decrease in accounts payable* for the period, cash paid to suppliers is more than purchases; thus, the decrease must be *subtracted* from net income in computing cash flow from operations.

Changes in accrued liabilities, which are usually reported together with accounts payable, have similar effects on cash flow as accounts payable.

SELECTED FOCUS COMPANY COMPARISONS: CHANGE IN CASH FLOW RELATED TO ACCOUNTS PAYABLE AND ACCRUED LIABILITIES (IN MILLIONS)

Gildan Activewear	5.4
WestJet Airlines	9.0
Intrawest Corp.	28.4

	Effect on Cash Flows
Operating activities (indirect method)	
Net income	$xxx
Adjusted for:	
Add increase in accounts payable and accrued liabilities	+
Subtract decrease in accounts payable and accrued liabilities	−

FOCUS COMPANY ANALYSIS → A segment of Petro-Canada's cash flow statement for 2004 and related note 10 follow.

REAL WORLD EXCERPT

Petro-Canada

ANNUAL REPORT

PETRO-CANADA
CONSOLIDATED STATEMENT OF CASH FLOWS
(stated in millions of Canadian dollars)
For the years ended December 31

	2004	2003 (Note 2)	2002 (Note 2)
Operating activities			
Net earnings	$1,757	$1,650	$ 955
Items not affecting cash flow from operating activities			
before changes in non-cash working capital (note 9)	1,755	1,451	1,020
Exploration expenses (note 15)	235	271	301
Cash flow from operating activities before changes in non-cash working capital	3,747	3,372	2,276
Proceeds from sale of accounts receivable (note 11)	399	—	—
(Increase) decrease in other non-cash working capital related to operating activities (note 10)	133	(164)	(226)
Cash flow from operating activities	4,279	3,208	2,050

Note 10 (increase) decrease in non-cash working capital

	2004	2003	2002
Operating activities			
Accounts receivable	$(88)	$93	$(268)
Inventories	4	34	(74)
Prepaid expenses	6	3	9
Accounts payable and accrued liabilities	247	(219)	467
Income taxes payable	71	37	(313)
Current portion of long-term liabilities and other	(107)	(112)	(47)
	$ 133	$(164)	$(226)
Investing activities			
Accounts payable and accrued liabilities	$ 10	$ 94	$ (16)
Financing activities			
Accounts payable and accrued liabilities	$ (26)	$ —	$ —

Recall from our previous discussions of the cash flow statement that revenues and expenses reported on the income statement include both cash and non-cash components, and that changes in working capital accounts (other than cash and cash equivalents) reflect non-cash revenues and expenses during the accounting period. The disclosed information shows that changes in non-cash working capital items increased cash flows from operating activities by $133 million. Petro-Canada's note 10 shows further that changes in accounts payable and accrued liabilities during 2004 increased cash flows from operations by $247 million simply because of delayed payments related to operating activities. Notice that changes in accounts payable and accrued liabilities resulted not only from operating activities, but from investing and financing activities as well.

NOTES PAYABLE

■ LEARNING OBJECTIVE 5

Report notes payable and explain the time value of money.

The **TIME VALUE OF MONEY** is interest that is associated with the use of money over time.

Most companies need to borrow money to finance their operations. When a company borrows money, a formal written document is usually prepared. Obligations supported by these written notes are typically called *notes payable*. A note payable specifies such items as the amount borrowed, when it must be paid, and the interest rate associated with the borrowing.

Creditors are willing to lend cash because they will earn interest to compensate them for giving up the use of their money for a period. This simple concept is called the **time value of money**. The longer borrowed money is held, the larger is the total dollar amount of interest expense. Interest at a given interest rate on a two-year loan is more than interest on a one-year loan. To the *borrower*, interest is an expense; to the *creditor*, interest is a revenue.

To calculate interest, three variables must be considered: (1) the principal (i.e., the cash that was borrowed), (2) the annual interest rate, and (3) the time period for the loan. The interest formula is

$$\textbf{Interest} = \textbf{Principal} \times \textbf{Annual Interest Rate} \times \textbf{Time}$$

To illustrate the accounting for a note payable, assume that on November 1, 2005, Petro-Canada borrowed $100,000 cash on a one-year, 12-percent note payable. The interest is payable on April 30, 2006, and October 31, 2006. The principal is payable at the maturity date of the note, October 31, 2006. The note is recorded in the accounts as follows:

Cash (A)	100,000	
Note payable, short term (L)		100,000

Assets		=	Liabilities	+	Shareholders' Equity
Cash	+100,000		Notes payable +100,000		

Interest on this note is incurred as long as the debt is outstanding. Under the matching concept, interest expense is recorded when it is incurred rather than when the cash actually is paid. Because the company uses the money for two months during 2005, it records interest expense in 2005 for two months, even though cash is not paid until April 30.

The computation of interest expense for 2005 is as follows:

$$\textbf{Interest} = \textbf{Principal} \times \textbf{Annual Interest Rate} \times \textbf{Time}$$

$$\textbf{Interest} = \textbf{\$100,000} \times \quad\quad \textbf{12\%} \quad\quad \times \textbf{2/12} = \textbf{\$2,000}$$

Note that interest expense is calculated for a specific accounting period, which varies from one month up to one year. The entry to record interest expense on December 31, 2005, is

Interest expense (E)	2,000	
Interest payable (L)		2,000

Assets	=	Liabilities	+	Shareholders' Equity
		Interest payable +2,000		Interest expense −2,000

On April 30, 2006, Petro-Canada would pay $6,000 in interest, which includes the $2,000 accrued and reported in 2005 plus the $4,000 interest accrued in the first four months of 2006. The following journal entry would be made:

Interest expense (E)	4,000	
Interest payable (L)	2,000	
Cash (A)		6,000

Assets	=	Liabilities	+	Shareholders' Equity
Cash −6,000		Interest payable −2,000		Interest expense −4,000

SELF-STUDY **QUIZ 10-3**

In the previous example, we assumed that the $100,000 note payable by Petro-Canada required payment of interest on April 30 and October 31. Assume that the note required the payment of interest on January 31 and July 31.

1. What adjusting entry should Petro-Canada make at December 31, 2005, the end of its fiscal year?

2. What entry should the company make on January 31, 2006?

3. What entry should the company make on July 31, 2006?

After you complete your answers, check them with the solutions on page 561.

CURRENT PORTION OF LONG-TERM DEBT

The distinction between current and long-term debt is important for both managers and analysts because current debt must be paid within the next year. The company must have sufficient cash to repay currently maturing debt. To provide accurate information concerning current liabilities, a company must reclassify long-term debt within a year of its maturity date as a current liability. Assume that Petro-Canada signed a note payable of $5 million on January 1, 2005. Repayment is required on December 1, 2007. The December 31, 2006 and 2007 balance sheets report the following:

December 31, 2006

Long-term liabilities	
Note payable	$5,000,000

December 31, 2007

Current liabilities	
Current portion of long-term note	5,000,000

An example of this type of disclosure can be seen in Exhibit 10.1. Notice that Petro-Canada reported $6 million as the current portion of long-term debt at December 2004 that is payable in full during 2005.

DEFERRED REVENUES

In most business transactions, cash is paid after the product or service has been delivered. In some cases, cash is paid before delivery. You have probably paid for several magazines that you will receive at some time in the future. The publisher collects money for your subscription in advance of publishing the magazine. When a company collects cash before the related revenue has been earned, this cash is called **deferred revenues** (or *unearned revenues* or *revenues collected in advance*). Under the revenue principle, revenue cannot be recognized until it has been earned.

Deferred revenues are reported as a liability because cash has been collected but the related revenue has not been earned by the end of the accounting period. The obligation to provide the services or goods in the future still exists. These obligations are classified as current or long-term, depending on when they must be satisfied.

DEFERRED REVENUES are revenues that have been collected but not earned; they are liabilities until the goods or services are provided.

ESTIMATED LIABILITIES REPORTED ON THE BALANCE SHEET

Some recorded liabilities are based on estimates because the exact amount will not be known until a future date. For example, an estimated liability is created when a company offers a warranty with the products it sells. The cost of providing repair work must be estimated and recorded as a liability (and expense) in the period in which the product is sold. Most companies quickly refund money for any defective products that they sell. To illustrate, Dell Inc., which sells computer products, has included the following in a recent annual report:

REAL WORLD EXCERPT

Dell Inc.

ANNUAL REPORT

NOTE 7 — Deferred Revenue and Warranty Liability

Revenue from extended warranty and service contracts, for which Dell is obligated to perform, is recorded as deferred revenue and subsequently recognized over the term of the contract or when the service is completed. Dell records warranty liabilities at the time of sale for the estimated costs that may be incurred under its basic limited warranty. Changes in Dell's aggregate deferred revenue and warranty liability (basic and extended warranties), which are included in other current and non-current liabilities on Dell's consolidated statement of financial position, are presented in the following table:

	Fiscal Year Ended	
	January 28, 2005	January 30, 2004
	(in millions)	
Aggregate deferred revenue and warranty liability at beginning of period	$2,694	$2,042
Revenue deferred and costs accrued for new warranties	3,435	2,547
Service obligations honoured	(1,176)	(983)
Amortization of deferred revenue	(1,359)	(912)
Aggregate deferred revenue and warranty liability at end of period	$3,594	$2,694
Current portion	$1,893	$1,333
Non-current portion	1,701	1,361
Aggregate deferred revenue and warranty liability at end of period	$3,594	$2,694

Dell determines its warranty liability based on the number of units sold, historical and anticipated rates of warranty claims on those units, and the cost per claim to satisfy Dell's warranty obligation. Assuming that Dell's costs of new warranties is $1,000 million, the journal entry to record the estimated liability at year end follows:

Warranty expense (E)	1,000	
Estimated warranty liability (L)		1,000

Assets	=	Liabilities	+	Shareholders' Equity
		Estimated warranty		Warranty
		liability +1,000		expense −1,000

When the company receives units that require repair under the warranty, its computer technicians repair the defective product, replace component parts as needed, and return the units to customers. If repairs during the year total $983 million, the entry to record the repairs would be:

Estimated warranty liability (L)	983	
Inventories (A), Wages payable (L)		983

Notice that the cost of repairs affects two accounts: Inventories for the cost of parts replaced, and Wages Payable for the cost of labour needed to replace or repair the defective products. If Dell paid cash to satisfy the warranty, then the cash account would be credited instead of Inventories.

Notice that the warranty expense is not affected by the costs incurred under the warranty because the expense was recognized in the same period of sale of the products, which is consistent with the matching principle.

Another type of future service obligation that has generated a considerable public interest is the adverse impact that business activities have on the environment. Some companies incur significant obligations associated with the environmental impact of their operations. In this regard, Petro-Canada's liabilities include an Asset Retirement Obligation of $834 million as at December 31, 2004. This liability reflects those legal obligations where the company will be required to retire long-term assets such as producing well sites, offshore production platforms, and natural gas processing plants and marketing sites.

Liabilities associated with future service obligations are often based on estimates that are very difficult to develop accurately. The future cost of cleaning up pollution depends on a number of factors, including changing technology and legal standards. Many companies have faced bankruptcy because they underestimated the cost of environmental regulations. Managers and analysts must be very cautious in evaluating potential costs associated with activities that impact the environment.

CONTINGENT LIABILITIES AND COMMITMENTS

Each of the liabilities that we have discussed is reported on the balance sheet with a specific dollar amount because each involves the *probable* future sacrifice of economic benefits. Some transactions or events create only a *potential* (but not probable) future sacrifice of economic benefits. These situations create **contingent liabilities**, which are potential liabilities that are created as a result of a past event. A contingent liability may or may not become a recorded liability depending on future events. A situation that produces a contingent liability also causes a contingent loss.

■ **LEARNING OBJECTIVE 6**

Report contingent liabilities and commitments.

A **CONTINGENT LIABILITY** is a potential liability that is created as a result of a past event; it is not an effective liability until some future event occurs.

Contingent Liability Examples

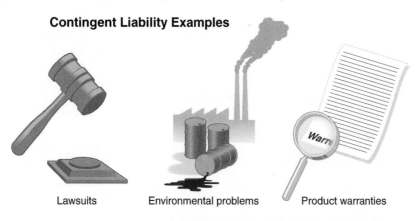

Lawsuits   Environmental problems   Product warranties

Whether a situation produces a recorded or a contingent liability depends on two factors: the probability of the future economic sacrifice and the ability of management to estimate the amount of the liability. The following table illustrates the various possibilities:

	Likely	Unlikely	Not Currently Determinable
Subject to reasonable estimate	Record as liability	Disclosure not required	Disclose in note
Not subject to estimate	Disclose in note	Disclosure not required	Disclose in note

The probabilities of occurrence are defined in the following manner:

1. Likely—the chance that the future event or events will occur is high.
2. Unlikely—the chance that the future event or events will occur is low.
3. Not currently determinable—the chance that the future event or events will (or will not) occur cannot be determined.

When recording liabilities, a company must determine whether the amount of any liability can be reasonably estimated. The general accounting guidelines are (1) a liability that is *both* likely and can be reasonably estimated must be recorded and reported on the balance sheet, (2) a liability that is reasonably possible (whether it can be estimated or not) must be disclosed in a note in the financial statements if the occurrence of the confirming event is not determinable, or if the event is likely to occur but the amount of the loss cannot be reasonably estimated, and (3) disclosure of unlikely contingencies is desirable but not required.

The notes to Petro-Canada's 2004 annual report include the following:

REAL WORLD EXCERPT

Petro-Canada

ANNUAL REPORT

Notes to the Consolidated Financial Statements

25. COMMITMENTS AND CONTINGENT LIABILITIES

....

(a) The Company has leased property and equipment under various long-term operating leases for periods up to 2013. The minimum annual rentals for non-cancellable operating leases are estimated at $122 million in 2005, $102 million in 2006, $80 million in 2007, $68 million in 2008, $61 million in 2009 and $217 million thereafter.

(b) The Company is involved in litigation and claims in the normal course of operations. In addition, the Company may provide indemnifications, in the course of normal operations, that are often standard contractual terms to counterparties in certain transactions such as purchase and sale agreements. The terms of these indemnifications will vary based upon the contract, the nature of which prevents the Company from making a reasonable estimate of the maximum potential amounts that may be required to be paid. Management is of the opinion that any resulting settlements relating to the litigation matters or indemnification would not materially affect the financial position of the Company.

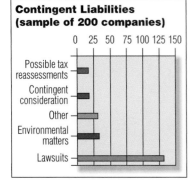

Contingent Liabilities (sample of 200 companies)

Petro-Canada reported not only its contingencies, but also its commitments to pay specific amounts in the future. Commitments reflect contractual agreements to enter into a transaction with another party. Commitments to buy or sell goods and services or to make specific payments are not normally recorded in the accounting system as long as there is no exchange transaction. Commitments to pay or receive cash are relevant to financial statement users and help them in predicting the company's future cash flows.

Financial Reporting in Canada surveyed the financial statements of 200 companies and found that litigation was the most common type of contingent liability in 2003.

LONG-TERM LIABILITIES

Long-term liabilities include all of the entity's obligations that are not classified as current liabilities, such as long-term notes and bonds payable. These liabilities are long-term contracts that specify the terms of the borrowing agreement (e.g., interest rate and repayment schedule). Typically, a long-term liability will require payment more than one year in the future. These obligations may be created by borrowing money, or they may result from other activities.

Most companies borrow money on a long-term basis in order to purchase operational assets. To reduce risk for creditors who are willing to lend money for a long period (which, in turn, reduces the interest rate that must be paid), some companies contractually agree that specific assets will be used as security for the liability. If the liability is not satisfied, the creditor may take ownership of the asset. A liability supported by this type of agreement is called *secured debt*. An *unsecured debt* is one for which the creditor relies primarily on the borrower's integrity and general earning power.

Long-term liabilities are reported on the balance sheet immediately following current liabilities. Notice the example for Petro-Canada in Exhibit 10.1. The accounts Long-term debt, Other liabilities, Asset retirement obligations, and Future income taxes are disclosed separately and explained in notes.

LONG-TERM NOTES PAYABLE AND BONDS

Companies can raise long-term debt directly from a number of financial service organizations, including banks, insurance companies, and pension plans. Raising debt from one of these organizations is known as *private placement*. This type of debt often is called a *note payable*, which is a written promise to pay a stated sum at one or more specified future dates, called the *maturity date(s)*.

In many cases, a company's need for debt capital exceeds the financial ability of any single creditor. In these situations, the company may issue publicly traded debt called *bonds*. The bonds can be traded in established markets that provide bondholders with liquidity (i.e., the ability to sell the bond and quickly receive cash). They can sell their bonds to other investors prior to maturity if they have an immediate need for cash. Both notes and bonds are written promises to pay a debt. Long-term notes are discussed later in this chapter and bonds will be discussed in detail in the next chapter.

Petro-Canada borrows billions of dollars in long-term debt to explore for oil and natural gas and bring these natural resources to the market. In exchange for the borrowed money, Petro-Canada signs debt agreements in the form of a loan, a note, or a mortgage note with banks and other institutional lenders. Loans and notes are often for terms of five years or less while mortgage terms can exceed twenty-five years.

Lenders often protect their interests by requesting that the debt be secured rather than unsecured. If you have a credit card, a student loan, or perhaps an automobile loan, you may have read the terms of the debt contract, which indicates if the debt is secured or not. In the case of a personal credit card the debt is unsecured, which means if a debtor fails to make the required payment, or *defaults,* the lender cannot repossess any specific asset of the cardholder.

In the case of a large, personal, long-term loan such as an automobile loan, lenders will insist on the right to repossess the automobile in the event of default. Repossession allows the lender to sell the automobile and recover all or part of the unpaid loan. Corporations such as Petro-Canada can secure both their notes and bonds payable using revenue, inventory, property, equipment, and buildings. Secured debt provides the creditor with the right to foreclose on the debt and repossess the assets, or collateral, pledged by the company as security should the company violate the terms of its debt contract.

Exhibit 10.2 shows note 17 to Petro-Canada's financial statements, which lists the different types of long-term debt that the company has issued in the past—mostly unsecured notes and debentures that are denominated in U.S. dollars.

■ **LEARNING OBJECTIVE 7**

Report long-term liabilities.

LONG-TERM LIABILITIES
are all of the entity's obligations not classified as current liabilities.

EXHIBIT **10.2**

Long-term Debt

Note 17 Long-term debt

	Maturity	2004	2003
Debentures and notes			
5.35% unsecured senior notes[1] ($300 million US)	2033	$ 361	$ 388
7.00% unsecured debentures ($250 million US)	2028	301	323
7.875% unsecured debentures ($275 million US)	2026	331	355
9.25% unsecured debentures ($300 million US)	2021	361	388
5.00% unsecured senior notes[2] ($400 million US)	2014	481	—
4.00% unsecured senior notes[1] ($300 million US)	2013	361	388
Capital leases (note 15)[3]	2007–2017	85	94
Acquisition credit facilities[4]	2005	—	293
		2,281	2,229
Current portion		(6)	(6)
		$2,275	$2,223

[1] In anticipation of issuing these senior notes, the Company entered into interest rate derivatives which resulted in effective interest rates of 6.073% for the 5.35% notes due in 2033 and 4.838% for the 4.00% notes due in 2013.

[2] The Company established a $400 million US underwritten credit facility to partially fund the acquisition of Prima Energy Corporation (see note 12 to the Consolidated Financial Statements). On November 8, 2004, the Company issued these senior notes, the proceeds of which were used to repay the credit facility.

[3] The Company is party to a transportation agreement to transport bitumen from the MacKay River production facilities to the Athabasca Pipeline Terminal. The agreement is for an initial term of 15 years ending in 2017 and is extendable at the Company's option for an additional 10 years.

The Company is party to an agreement for the time charter and operation of a vessel for the transportation of East Coast Oil crude oil production. The agreement is for an initial term of 10 years ending in 2007 and extendable at the Company's option for up to an additional 15 years.

The transportation and time charter agreements are accounted for as capital leases and have implicit rates of interest of 14.65% and 11.90%, respectively. The aggregate remaining repayments under the transportation and time charter agreements are $85 million, including the following amounts in the next five years: 2005—$6 million; 2006—$7 million; 2007—$7 million; 2008—$2 million; and 2009—$3 million.

[4] The Company established two unsecured credit facilities with certain banks for the acquisition of the oil and gas operations of Veba Oil & Gas GmbH (see Note 12 to the Consolidated Financial Statements). The credit facilities totaled $3,320 million, of which $2,100 million was drawn in the form of floating rate Canadian dollar bankers' acceptances in 2002. At December 31, 2003, the amount of the facilities was $743 million, of which $293 million was outstanding. During 2004, the Company sold $400 million under a new accounts receivable securitization program (see Note 11 to the Consolidated Financial Statements) and a portion of the proceeds was used to repay the remaining $293 million of advances.

Interest on long-term debt, net of capitalized interest, was $132 million in 2004 (2003—$177 million; 2002—$182 million).

The Company's syndicated operating credit facilities totaled $1,500 million to be used for general corporate purposes.

Over the past years, business operations have become more global. Successful corporations market their products in many countries and locate manufacturing facilities around the world, based on cost and productivity. The financing of corporations also has become international, even for companies that do not have international operations.

INTERNATIONAL **PERSPECTIVE**

BORROWING IN FOREIGN CURRENCIES

Many corporations with foreign operations elect to finance those operations with foreign debt to lessen the exchange rate risk. This type of risk exists because the relative value of each nation's currency varies virtually on a daily basis due to various economic factors. As this book is being written, the U.S. dollar is worth approximately $1.23. A year earlier, it was worth $1.30. A Canadian company that owed debt denominated in U.S. dollars would experience a gain from this decrease in the value of the U.S. dollar.

A Canadian corporation that conducts business operations in the United States might decide to borrow U.S. dollars to finance its operations. The profits from the business will be in U.S. dollars, which can be used to pay off the debt, which is in U.S. dollars. If the business earned profits in U.S. dollars but paid off debt in Canadian dollars, it would be exposed to exchange rate risk because the value of the Canadian dollar fluctuates relative to the U.S dollar.

Foreign corporations face this same problem. A note to an annual report from Toyota (a Japanese company) stated:

> Earnings declined in the current year ended, as the appreciation of the yen aggravated the adverse effects of sluggish demand. . . . The movement in exchange rates reduced operating income of the company. Losses on currency exchange thus offset most of the cost savings we achieved.

Even if a company does not have international operations, it may elect to borrow in foreign markets. When a country is experiencing a recession, interest rates often are low. These situations give corporations the opportunity to borrow money at a lower cost.

For reporting purposes, accountants must convert, or translate, foreign debt into Canadian dollars. Conversion rates for all major currencies are published in most newspapers and on the Internet. To illustrate foreign currency translation, assume that Petro-Canada borrowed 1 million U.S. dollars. For the Petro-Canada annual report, the accountant must use the conversion rate as of the balance sheet date, which we assume was $1.00 ($US) = $1.23 ($Cdn). The dollar equivalent of the debt is $1,230,000 ($Cdn) ($1,000,000 [$US] × 1.23). As you can see, the dollar equivalent of foreign debt may change if the conversion rate changes even when no additional borrowings or repayments occur. The changes in conversion rates result in foreign exchange gains or losses that are covered in advanced accounting courses.

The notes to the balance sheet for Petro-Canada indicate that the company has borrowed money primarily in Canada and the United States. In contrast, consider the following note from a recent annual report of Bombardier Inc. (in millions):

	$	Currency Component	Average Rate	Maturity
Bombardier				
Debentures	1,527.6	€500.0	6.4%	2004–2027
		£175.0		
Notes	315.4	$167.3 (US)	6.6%	2004–2012
Other loans	237.7	$ 64.9 (US)	4.0%	2003–2029
		€ 32.6		
	2,080.7			

Bombardier is an international company with more than 90 percent of its sales outside Canada. The company borrows heavily in international markets in euros (€) and British pounds (£) to minimize the risk associated with variations in exchange rates. This is typical for most large corporations and is further justification for business executives to develop an understanding of international markets.

LEASE LIABILITIES

An **OPERATING LEASE** does not meet any of the four criteria established by GAAP and does not cause the recording of an asset and liability.

Companies often lease assets rather than purchasing them. For example, renting extra delivery trucks during a busy period is more economical than owning them if they are not needed during the rest of the year. When a company leases an asset on a short-term basis, the agreement is called an **operating lease**. No liability is recorded when an operating lease is created. Instead, a company records rent expense as it uses the asset. Assume that on December 15, 2005, Petro-Canada signed an operating lease contract to rent five large trucks during January 2006. No liability is recorded in 2005. Rent expense is recorded during January 2006 as the trucks are actually used.

A **CAPITAL LEASE** meets at least one of the four criteria established by GAAP and results in the recording of an asset and liability.

For a number of reasons, a company may prefer to lease an asset on a long-term basis rather than purchase it. This type of lease is called a **capital lease**. In essence, a capital lease contract represents the purchase and financing of an asset even though it is legally a lease agreement. Unlike an operating lease, capital leases are accounted for as if an asset has been purchased by recording an asset and a liability. Because of the significant differences between operating and capital leases, GAAP have specified criteria to distinguish between them. If a lease meets any of the following criteria, it is considered a capital lease:

- The lease term is 75 percent or more of the asset's expected economic life.
- Ownership of the asset is transferred to the lessee at the end of the lease term.
- The lease contract permits the lessee to purchase the asset at a price that is lower than its fair market value.
- The present value of the lease payments is 90 percent or more of the fair market value of the asset when the lease is signed.

Note 17 to Petro-Canada's 2004 annual report indicates that the balance sheet includes $85 million in long-term debt associated with capital leases. The recorded value of debt associated with a capital lease is the present value of the required lease payments. The next section, on present value concepts, shows how this amount is actually computed.

The accounting for leases as capital leases reflects the substance of the transaction, which is in essence a purchase of an asset with long-term financing, rather than the legal form of the commitment to make specific payments in the future. In the absence of accounting rules governing the distinction between operating and capital leases, companies would prefer to report all lease contracts as operating leases because the commitment to make future payments on the lease contract would not be reported as liabilities on the balance sheet (a form of off–balance sheet financing). In contrast, the accounting for capital leases requires the reporting of a long-term liability, thereby increasing the debt-to-equity ratio. Furthermore, the current portion of the lease liability increases current liabilities, reduces working capital and lowers the current ratio. Companies would avoid these undesirable consequences if capital leases are accounted for as operating leases. It is important to note, however, that the cash outflows would not be affected by the classification of leases.

PRESENT AND FUTURE VALUE CONCEPTS

■ **LEARNING OBJECTIVE 8**

Apply the concepts of present and future values.

Our discussion of capital leases raised an interesting question about liabilities: Is the recorded amount of the liability the actual amount of cash that will be paid in the future? For example, if I agree to pay you $10,000 five years from now, should I report a liability of $10,000 on my personal balance sheet? To answer such questions, we will now introduce some relatively simple mathematics called **present** and **future value concepts**. These concepts will provide a foundation for measuring and reporting long-term notes and bonds.

The concepts of present value (PV) and future value (FV) focus on the time value of money. Money received today is worth more than money to be received one year from today (or at any other future date) because it can be used to earn interest. If you invest $1,000 today at 10 percent, you will have $1,100 in one year. In contrast, if you receive $1,000 one year from today, you will lose the opportunity to earn the $100 interest revenue. The difference between the $1,000 and the $1,100 is interest that can be earned during the year.

In some business situations, you know the dollar amount of a cash flow that will occur in the future and need to determine its value now. This is known as a **present value** situation. The opposite situation occurs when you know the dollar amount of a cash flow that occurs today and need to determine its value at some point in the future. This is called a **future value** situation. The value of money changes over time because money can earn interest. The following illustrates the basic difference between present value and future value problems:

	Now	Future
Present value	?	$1,000
Future value	$1,000	?

PRESENT VALUE is the current cash equivalent of an amount to be received in the future; a future amount discounted for compound interest.

FUTURE VALUE is the sum to which an amount will increase as a result of compound interest.

Present and future value problems may involve two types of cash flow: a single payment or an annuity (a series of cash payments).[3] Thus, four different situations are related to the time value of money:

1. Future value of a single payment.

2. Present value of a single payment.

3. Future value of an annuity.

4. Present value of an annuity.

Many inexpensive hand-held calculators, as well as spreadsheet and financial software, can perform the detailed arithmetic computations required in computing present value and future value problems. In subsequent courses and in all business situations, you will probably use a calculator to solve these problems. At this stage, it is convenient to solve problems using Tables A.1 through A.4 in Appendix A at the end of this book. They give the value of $1 (single payment or annuity) for different periods of time (*n*) and at different rates of interest (*i*). The present value or future value factors are multiplied by the amount of the payment.

FUTURE AND PRESENT VALUES OF A SINGLE AMOUNT

Future Value of a Single Amount   In situations involving future value of a single amount, you are asked to calculate how much money you will have in the future as a result of investing a certain amount at the present time. If you were to receive a gift of $10,000, for instance, you might decide to put it in a savings account and use the money as a down payment on a house when you graduate. The future value computation will tell you how much money would be available when you graduate.

To solve a future value problem, you need to know three items:

1. the amount to be invested,

2. the interest rate (*i*) that the amount will earn, and

3. the number of periods (*n*) in which the amount will earn interest.

Since the future value concept is based on compound interest, the amount of interest for each period is calculated by multiplying the principal plus any interest not paid

---

[3]Present value and future value problems involve cash flows. The basic concepts are the same for cash inflows (receipts) and cash outflows (payments). No fundamental differences exist between present value and future value calculations for cash payments versus cash receipts.

out in prior periods. Graphically, the calculation of the future value of $1 for three periods and an interest rate of 10 percent may be represented as follows:

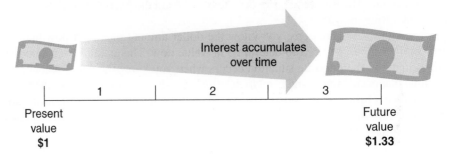

Assume that on January 1, 2005, you deposit $1,000 in a savings account at 10 percent annual interest, compounded annually. At the end of three years, the $1,000 will have increased to $1,331 as follows:

Year	Amount at Start of Year	+	Interest During the Year	=	Amount at End of Year
1	$1,000	+	$1,000 × 10% = $100	=	$1,100
2	1,100	+	1,100 × 10% = $110	=	1,210
3	1,210	+	1,210 × 10% = $121	=	1,331

We can avoid the detailed arithmetic by referring to Table A-1, Future Value of $1. For $i = 10\%$, $n = 3$, we find the value 1.331. We then compute the balance at the end of year 3 as follows:

$$\$1,000 \times 1.3310 = \$1,331$$

From Table A-1,
Interest rate = 10%
N = 3

Note that the increase of $331 is due to the time value of money. It is interest revenue to the owner of the savings account and interest expense to the savings institution.

Present Value of a Single Amount   The present value of a single amount is the amount of cash that you are willing to accept today in lieu of a cash receipt at some date in the future. You might be offered the opportunity to invest in a debt instrument that would pay you $10,000 in 10 years. Before you decided whether to invest, you would want to determine the present value of the instrument.

To compute the present value of an amount to be received in the future, we discount the amount at i interest rate for n periods (a procedure that is opposite to compounding). In discounting, the interest is subtracted from the amount rather than added to the amount (as is the case with compounding).

Graphically, the present value of $1 due at the end of the third period with an interest rate of 10 percent can be represented as follows:

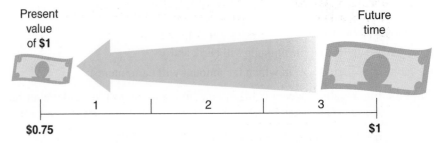

Assume that today is January 1, 2005, and you have the opportunity to receive $1,000 cash on December 31, 2007. At an interest rate of 10 percent per year, how much is the $1,000 payment worth to you on January 1, 2005? You could discount the amount year by year,[4] but it is easier to use Table A-2, Appendix A, Present Value of $1. For $i = 10\%$, $n = 3$, we find that the present value of $1 is 0.7513. The present value of $1,000 to be received at the end of three years can be computed as follows:

$$\$1,000 \times 0.7513 = \$751.30$$

| From Table A-2, |
| Interest rate = 10% |
| N = 3 |

In other words, if you invest $751.30 today at an annual interest rate of 10 percent, it will grow to $1,000 after three years as follows:

$$\$751.30 \times 1.331 = \$1,000 \text{ (rounded)}$$

| From Table A-1, |
| Interest rate = 10% |
| N = 3 |

It is not difficult to learn how to compute a present value amount, but it is more important that you understand what it means. The $751.30 is the amount that you would pay to have the right to receive $1,000 at the end of three years, assuming an interest rate of 10 percent. Conceptually, you would be indifferent about having $751.30 today and receiving $1,000 in three years, because you can use financial institutions to convert dollars from the present to the future and vice versa. If you had $751.30 today but preferred $1,000 in three years, you could simply deposit the money into a savings account that paid annual interest at 10% and it would grow to $1,000 in three years. Alternatively, if you had a contract that promised you $1,000 in three years, you could sell it to an investor for $751.30 cash today because it would permit the investor to earn 10 percent on his or her money.

SELF-STUDY **QUIZ 10-4**

1. If the interest rate in a present value problem increases from 10 percent to 11 percent, will the present value increase or decrease? Explain.

2. What is the present value of $10,000 to be received 10 years from now if the interest rate is 5 percent compounded annually?

Check your answers with those on page 561.

FUTURE AND PRESENT VALUES OF AN ANNUITY

Many business problems involve multiple cash payments over a number of periods instead of a single payment. An **annuity** is a series of consecutive payments characterized by

An **ANNUITY** is a series of equal amounts of cash that are paid or received at equally distant points in time.

1. An equal dollar amount each interest period.

2. Interest periods of equal length (year, semi-annual, quarter, or month).

3. An equal interest rate each interest period.

Examples of annuities include monthly payments on an automobile or home loan, yearly contributions to a savings account, and monthly retirement benefits.

Future Value of an Annuity   If you are saving money for some purpose, such as a new car or a trip to Europe, you might decide to deposit a fixed amount of money in a

---

[4]The detailed discounting is as follows:

Periods	Interest for the Year	Present Value*
1	$1,000 − ($1,000 × 1/1.10) = $90.91	$1,000 − $90.91 = $909.09
2	$909.09 − ($909.09 × 1/1.10) = $82.65	$909.09 − $82.65 = $826.44
3	$826.44 − ($826.44 × 1/1.10) = $75.14[†]	$826.44 − $75.14 = $751.30

*Verifiable in Table A-2.

[†]Adjusted for rounding.

savings account each month. The future value of an annuity computation will tell you how much money will be in your savings account at some point in the future.

The future value of an annuity includes *compound interest* on each payment from the date of payment to the end of the term of the annuity. Each new payment accumulates less interest than prior payments only because the number of periods remaining to accumulate interest decreases. The future value of an annuity of $1 for three periods at 10 percent may be represented graphically as:

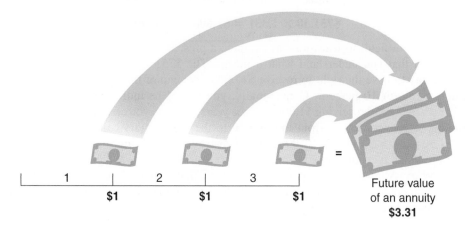

Assume that you deposit $1,000 cash in a savings account each year for three years at 10 percent interest per year (i.e., a total principal of $3,000). You make the first $1,000 deposit on December 31, 2005, the second deposit on December 31, 2006, and the third and last one on December 31, 2007. The first deposit earns compound interest for two years (for a total principal and interest of $1,210); the second deposit earns interest for one year (for a total principal and interest of $1,100); and the third deposit earns no interest because it was made on the day that the balance is computed. Thus, the total amount in the savings account at the end of three years is $3,310 ($1,210 + $1,100 + $1,000).

To derive the future value of this annuity, we could compute the interest on each deposit. However, we can refer to Table A-3, Appendix A, Future Value of an Annuity of $1 for $i = 10\%$, $n = 3$ to find the value 3.3100. The future value of your three deposits of $1,000 each can be computed as follows:

From Table A-3,
Interest rate = 10%
N = 3

$$\mathbf{\$1,000 \times 3.3100 = \$3,310.}$$

The Power of Compounding   Compound interest is a remarkably powerful economic force. The ability to earn interest on interest is the key to building economic wealth. If you start your career on your twenty-second birthday and save $1,000 per year for 10 years that earns an interest rate of 5 percent compounded annually until you retire at the end of your sixty-fifth year of age, you will accumulate a total of $69,390. The money saved is $10,000 and the rest is interest that accumulated over the 44-year period from the time you started saving until the time you retired. If the money saved earns 6 percent instead of 5 percent throughout the 44-year period, then the total amount increases to $101,309 on your sixty-sixth birthday, a hefty birthday present! However, if you continue to save $1,000 per year for 44 years and earn 5 percent interest per year, then your retirement fortune jumps to $158,700; $44,000 is money saved and the rest is compound interest. The power of compounding in this specific case is illustrated in the graph. The lesson associated with compound interest is clear: even though it's hard to do, you should start saving money now.

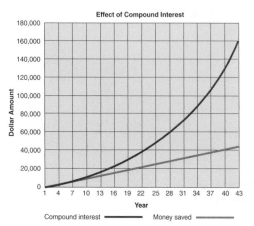

Present Value of an Annuity   The present value of an annuity is the value now of a series of equal amounts to be received (or paid) each period for some specified number of periods in the future. It is computed by discounting each of the equal periodic amounts. A good example of this type of problem is a retirement program that offers the retiree a monthly income after retirement. The present value of an annuity of $1 for three periods at 10 percent may be represented graphically as follows:

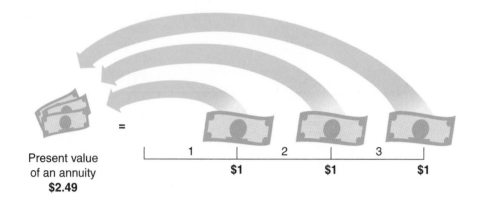

Present value
of an annuity
$2.49

    Assume you are to receive $1,000 cash on each December 31, 2005, 2006, and 2007. How much would the sum of these three $1,000 future amounts be worth on January 1, 2005, assuming an interest rate of 10 percent per year? We could use Table A-2, Appendix A to calculate the present value as follows:

Year	Amount		Factor from Table A-2, Appendix A, $i = 10\%$		Present Value
1	$1,000	×	0.9091 ($n = 1$)	=	$ 909.10
2	$1,000	×	0.8264 ($n = 2$)	=	826.40
3	$1,000	×	0.7513 ($n = 3$)	=	751.30
			Total present value	=	$2,486.80

    We can compute the present value of this annuity more easily however, by using Table A-4, Appendix A, as follows:

$$\$1{,}000 \times 2.4869 = \$2{,}487 \text{ (rounded)}$$

From Table A-4,
Interest rate = 10%
N = 3

Exhibit 10.3 provides a graphical illustration of the present value and future value computations discussed above.

Interest Rates and Interest Periods   The preceding illustrations assumed annual periods for compounding and discounting. Although interest rates almost always are quoted on an annual basis, most interest-compounding periods encountered in business are less than one year (such as semi-annually or quarterly). When interest periods are less than a year, the values of n and i must be restated to be consistent with the length of the interest period.

    To illustrate, 12-percent interest compounded annually for five years requires use of $n = 5$ and $i = 12\%$. If compounding is quarterly, the interest period is one-quarter of a year (i.e., four periods per year), and the quarterly interest rate is one-quarter of the annual rate (i.e., 3 percent per quarter). Therefore, 12-percent interest compounded quarterly for five years requires use of $n = 20$ and $i = 3\%$.

EXHIBIT **10.3**

Overview of Future and Present Value Computations

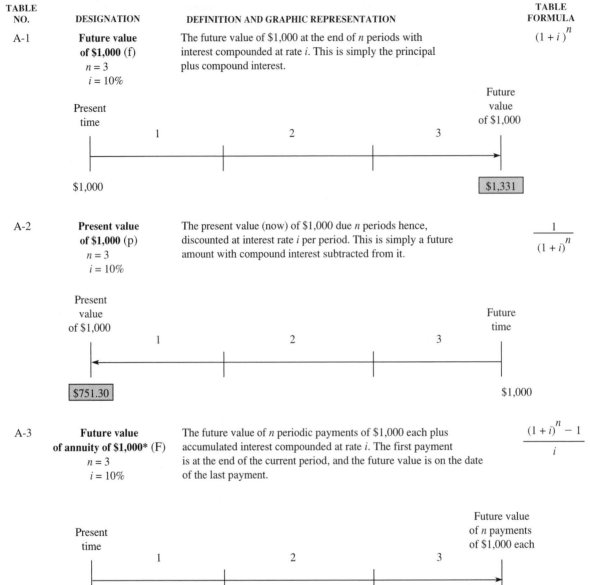

TABLE NO.	DESIGNATION	DEFINITION AND GRAPHIC REPRESENTATION	TABLE FORMULA
A-1	**Future value of $1,000** (f) $n = 3$ $i = 10\%$	The future value of $1,000 at the end of n periods with interest compounded at rate i. This is simply the principal plus compound interest.	$(1 + i)^n$
A-2	**Present value of $1,000** (p) $n = 3$ $i = 10\%$	The present value (now) of $1,000 due n periods hence, discounted at interest rate i per period. This is simply a future amount with compound interest subtracted from it.	$\dfrac{1}{(1 + i)^n}$
A-3	**Future value of annuity of $1,000*** (F) $n = 3$ $i = 10\%$	The future value of n periodic payments of $1,000 each plus accumulated interest compounded at rate i. The first payment is at the end of the current period, and the future value is on the date of the last payment.	$\dfrac{(1 + i)^n - 1}{i}$
A-4	**Present value of annuity of $1,000*** (P) $n = 3$ $i = 10\%$	The present value (now) of n periodic payments of $1,000 each to be received (or paid) each period, discounted at interest rate i per period. The first payment is at the end of the first period.	$\dfrac{1 - \dfrac{1}{(1 + i)^n}}{i}$

*Notice that these are ordinary annuities; that is, they are often called *end-of-period annuities*. Thus, the table values for F, the future amount, are on the date of the last payment, and for P, the present value, are at the beginning of the period of the first payment. Annuities due assume the opposite; that is, they are *beginning-of-period annuities*. Ordinary annuity values can be converted into annuities due simply by multiplication of (1 + *i*).

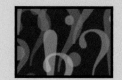

A QUESTION OF **ETHICS**

TRUTH IN ADVERTISING

A number of advertisements in newspapers and magazines and on television easily can be misinterpreted if the consumer does not understand present value concepts. We discuss two examples.

Most car companies offer seasonal promotions with special financing incentives. A car dealer may advertise 1.9-percent interest on car loans when banks are charging 10 percent. Typically, the lower interest rate is not a special incentive because the dealer simply charges a higher price for cars that the dealership finances. It may be better to borrow from the bank and "pay cash" at the dealership to negotiate a lower price. Customers should use the present value concepts illustrated in this chapter to compare financing alternatives.

Another misleading advertisement is seen every January and promises a chance to become an instant millionaire. The fine print discloses that the winner will receive $25,000 for 40 years, which is $1,000,000 (40 × $25,000), but the present value of this annuity at 8 percent is only $298,000. Most winners are happy to get the money, but they are not really millionaires.

Some consumer advocates criticize businesses that use these types of advertisements. They argue that consumers should not have to study present value concepts to understand advertisements. Some of these criticisms may be valid, but the quality of information contained in advertisements that include interest rates has improved during the past few years.

ACCOUNTING APPLICATIONS OF FUTURE AND PRESENT VALUES

Many business transactions require the use of future and present value concepts. We illustrate two such cases so that you can test your understanding of these concepts:

CASE A On January 1, 2005, Petro-Canada bought some new equipment. The company signed a note and agreed to pay $200,000 for the equipment on December 31, 2006. The market interest rate for this note was 12 percent. The $200,000 represents the cash equivalent price of the equipment and the interest that will be earned for two years.

1. How should the accountant record the purchase?
Answer: This case requires application of the present value of a single amount. In conformity with the cost principle, the cost of the equipment is its current cash equivalent price, which is the present value of the future payment. The problem can be shown graphically as follows:

■ **LEARNING OBJECTIVE 9**

Apply present value concepts to liabilities.

January 1, 2005	December 31, 2005	December 31, 2006
?		$200,000

The present value of the $200,000 is computed as follows:

$200,000 × 0.7972 = $159,440

From Table A-2,
Interest rate = 12%
N = 2

Therefore, the journal entry is as follows:

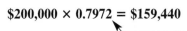

Equipment (A)	159,440	
Note payable (L)		159,440

Assets	=	Liabilities	+	Shareholders' Equity
Equipment +159,440		Note payable +159,440		

Some companies prefer to record the following journal entry:

Equipment (A)	159,440	
Discount on notes payable (XL)	40,560	
Note payable (L)		200,000

Assets	=	Liabilities	+	Shareholders' Equity
Equipment +159,440		Note payable +200,000		
		Discount −40,560		

The discount account is a contra-liability account that represents the interest that will accrue on the note over its life.

2. What journal entry should be made at the end of the first and second years for interest expense?

Answer: The following schedule shows the computation of interest expense for the two years.

Date	Interest Expense Unpaid Balance × 12%	Unpaid Balance of Note payable
January 1, 2005		$159,440
December 31, 2005	$159,440 × 12% = $19,132	178,572
December 31, 2006	178,573 × 12% = 21,428	200,000

Each year's interest expense is recorded in an adjusting entry as follows:

Dec. 31, 2005 Interest expense (E)	19,132	
Note payable (L)		19,132

Assets	=	Liabilities	+	Shareholders' Equity
		Note payable +19,132		Interest expense −19,132

Dec. 31, 2006 Interest expense (E)	21,428	
Note payable (L)		21,428

Assets	=	Liabilities	+	Shareholders' Equity
		Note payable +21,428		Interest expense −21,428

Notice that interest of $19,132 accrued during 2005, but was not paid. It is therefore added to the balance of the note payable account. This interest amount has itself earned interest during 2006.

3. What journal entry should be made on December 31, 2006, to record the payment of the debt?

Answer: At this date, the amount to be paid is the balance of Note Payable, which is the same as the maturity amount on the due date. The journal entry to record full payment of the debt follows:

Note payable (L)	200,000	
Cash (A)		200,000

Assets	=	Liabilities	+	Shareholders' Equity
Cash −200,000		Note payable −200,000		

CASE B   On January 1, 2005, Petro-Canada bought new drilling equipment. The company elected to finance the purchase with a note payable to be paid in three equal annual instalments of $163,686. Each instalment includes principal plus interest on the unpaid balance at 11 percent per year. The annual instalments are due on December 31, 2005, 2006, and 2007. This problem can be shown graphically as follows:

January 1, 2005	December 31, 2005	December 31, 2006	December 31, 2007
?	$163,686	$163,686	$163,686

1. What is the amount of the note?

Answer: The note is the present value of each instalment payment, $i = 11\%$ and $n = 3$. This is an annuity because payment is made in three equal instalments. The amount of the note is computed as follows:

$$\$163,686 \times 2.4437 = \$400,000$$

From Table A-4,
Interest rate = 11%
N = 3

The acquisition is recorded as follows:

Drilling equipment (A)	400,000	
Note payable (L)		400,000

Assets	=	Liabilities	+	Shareholders' Equity
Drilling equipment +400,000		Note payable +400,000		

2. What was the total amount of interest expense in dollars?

Answer:

$$\$163,686 \times 3 \ (= \$491,058) - \$400,000 = \$91,058$$

3. Prepare a debt payment schedule that shows the entry for each payment and the effect on interest expense and the unpaid amount of principal each period.

Answer:

Debt Payment Schedule

Date	Cash Payment (Credit)	Interest Expense (Unpaid Principal × 11%) (Debit)	Decrease in Principal (Debit)	Unpaid Principal
1/1/2005				$400,000
12/31/2005	$163,686	$400,000 × 11% = $44,000	$119,686[a]	280,314[b]
12/31/2006	163,686	280,314 × 11% = $30,835	132,851	147,463
12/31/2007	163,686	147,463 × 11% = $16,223*	147,463	0
Total	$491,058	$91,058*	$400,000	

*To accommodate rounding error.
Computations:
[a]$163,686 − $44,000 = $119,686, etc.   [b]$400,000 − $119,686 = $280,314, etc.

Notice in the debt payment schedule that for each successive payment, the payment on principal increases and interest expense decreases. This effect occurs because the interest each period is based on a lower amount of the unpaid principal. When an annuity is involved, schedules such as this one often are useful analytical tools.

4. What journal entry should be made at the end of each year to record the payments on this note?

Answer:

Dec. 31, 2005 Note payable (L)	119,686	
Interest expense (E)	44,000	
Cash (A)		163,686

Assets	=	Liabilities	+	Shareholders' Equity
Cash −163,686		Note payable −119,686		Interest expense −44,000

Dec. 31, 2006	Note payable (L)	132,851	
	Interest expense (E)	30,835	
	Cash (A)		163,686

Assets		=	Liabilities	+	Shareholders' Equity	
Cash	−163,686		Note payable	−132,851	Interest expense	−30,835

Dec. 31, 2007	Note payable (L)	147,463	
	Interest expense (E)	16,223	
	Cash (A)		163,686

Assets		=	Liabilities	+	Shareholders' Equity	
Cash	−163,686		Note payable	−147,463	Interest expense	−16,223

In the next chapter, we will use the present value techniques that you have just learned to understand how to account for bonds.

Chapter Supplement A

Future Income Tax Assets and Liabilities

In previous chapters, we made simplifying assumptions concerning income tax expense. We often provided the amount of income tax expense (e.g., $100,000) and prepared a journal entry similar to the following:

| Income tax expense (E) .... | 100,000 | |
| Income tax payable (L) .... | | 100,000 |

Assets	=	Liabilities		+	Shareholders' Equity	
		Income tax			Income tax	
		payable	+100,000		expense	−100,000

However, separate rules govern the preparation of financial statements (GAAP) and tax returns (Income Tax Act). Specifically, some types of revenue are exempt from tax while other types of expenses are not deductible in computing taxable income. These *permanent differences* do not cause much complication in accounting for income taxes. Examples of such permanent differences appear in the upper part of Exhibit 10.4. However, *temporary differences* of the following types result in complex accounting:

1. Revenue that is recognized in financial statements (e.g., rent revenue) when the goods are sold or the services are rendered, but is taxable only when the cash is received.

2. Product warranty costs that are recognized as a liability and an expense for financial reporting purposes when the related products are sold, but are deductible for tax purposes only when payments under the warranty are made.

3. Long-term assets, including development costs, that are usually amortized using the straight-line method for financial reporting purposes, but are amortized on an accelerated basis (Capital Cost Allowance) for tax purposes.

The differences between amortization expense and CCA are by far the most common source of temporary differences, which disappear over the long run. Assuming the corporation is a going concern, a specific long-term asset will eventually be unable to generate further benefits to the corporation and will be fully amortized. Similarly, the cost of this asset would have been deducted over the years as CCA for tax purposes. So the main issue is timing of the recognition of revenues and expenses for financial reporting versus tax purposes. These temporary differences cause the income tax expense (that is based on the income before taxes reported on the income statement)

EXHIBIT **10.4**

**Disclosures Made by
Petro-Canada**

REAL WORLD EXCERPT

Petro-Canada

ANNUAL REPORT

Note 7 Income Taxes

The computation of the provision for income taxes, which requires adjustment to earnings before income taxes for non-taxable and non-deductible items, is as follows:

	2004	2003	2002
Earnings before income taxes	$3,245	$2,960	$1,798
Add (deduct):			
Non-deductible royalties and other payments to provincial governments, net	352	392	277
Resource allowance	(512)	(542)	(467)
Equity in earnings of affiliates	(15)	(11)	(9)
Non-taxable foreign exchange	(40)	(237)	52
Other	5	28	(3)
Earnings as adjusted before income taxes	$3,035	$2,590	$1,648
Canadian Federal income tax rate	38.0%	38.0%	38.0%
Income tax on earnings as adjusted at Canadian Federal income tax rate	$1,153	$984	$626
Large Corporations Tax	17	16	16
Provincial income taxes	271	194	130
Federal—abatement and other credits	(274)	(167)	(102)
Future income taxes (decrease) increase due to federal and provincial rate changes	(13)	(45)	4
Higher foreign income tax rates	357	337	176
Income tax credits and other	(23)	(9)	(7)
Provision for income taxes	$1,488	$1,310	$843
Effective income tax rate on earnings before income taxes	45.9%	44.3%	46.9%

Future income taxes consists of the following future income tax liabilities (assets) relating to temporary differences for:

	2004	2003
Property, plant and equipment	$2,961	$2,010
Partnership income[1]	404	381
Inventories	(184)	(134)
Asset retirement obligations and other liabilities	(318)	(333)
Deferred charges and other assets	55	43
Resource allowance and other	(210)	(211)
	$2,708	$1,756

[1]Taxable income for certain Canadian upstream activities are generated by a partnership and the related taxes will be included in current income taxes in the next year.

to be different from the income tax payable (that is based on the taxable income computed on the income tax return).

This difference creates an interesting accounting problem: Should the tax liability reported on the balance sheet be the amount of income taxes currently payable based on the tax return or should the liability include future tax effects that exist because of differences between GAAP and the income tax rules? Accountants have resolved this issue by recording the "economic" liability, which includes income taxes currently payable adjusted for the effects of differences between GAAP and the income tax rules.

The difference between the amounts of *income tax expense* and *income taxes payable* is called *Future Income Taxes*. Future income tax items exist because of temporary differences caused by reporting revenues and expenses according to GAAP on a company's income statement and according to the Income Tax Act on the tax return. In practice, future income taxes can be either assets (such as taxes related to cash collected from a customer, which is taxable before it is reported as a revenue on the income statement) or liabilities (such as taxes related to amortization, reported on the tax return on an accelerated basis and on the income statement on a straight-line basis).

To illustrate, let us consider one item that gives rise to future income taxes. Petro-Canada uses straight-line amortization for its financial statements and the capital cost allowance (CCA) for its tax return. As a result, it reports lower income on its tax return than on its income statement because of the higher amount of amortization expense (CCA) on the tax return. Assume that Petro-Canada computed income taxes payable of $8,000,000 based on the numbers reported on the tax return, and income tax expense of $10,000,000 based on the income statement. The company records its tax obligation as follows:

Income tax expense (E)	10,000,000	
Future income taxes (L)		2,000,000
Income tax payable (L)		8,000,000

Assets	=	Liabilities		+	Shareholders' Equity	
		Future income			Income tax	
		taxes	+2,000,000		expense	−10,000,000
		Income tax				
		payable	+8,000,000			

The future income tax amount is paid when amortization expense "reverses" in the future. This happens when the CCA recorded on the tax return becomes lower than the straight-line amortization reported on the income statement (remember from Chapter 9 that accelerated amortization, such as CCA, causes higher amortization expense than straight-line amortization in the early years of an asset's life and lower amortization in the later years). When a temporary difference reverses, the future income tax amount is reduced.

In reality, although temporary differences reverse in theory, new temporary differences are created and offset the reversing differences. As a result, the future income tax liabilities reported by most companies may not result in significant cash outflows in the foreseeable future. For Petro-Canada, its future income tax liability actually increased by $952 million during 2004, indicating that new originating temporary differences exceeded the reversing temporary differences.

As indicated earlier, the future income tax liability arises primarily from differences between amortization expense and CCA. But, what if companies used CCA for reporting purposes instead of straight-line amortization? In this case, most of the temporary differences would disappear and the future income tax asset or liability would be reduced to a relatively small amount, thus reducing the significance of this item on the balance sheets of most companies. However, the use of CCA for financial reporting purposes increases the amortization expense, thus reducing income before taxes and net income. This outcome may not be desirable by managers if it affects their remuneration and the market value of the company's shares, even though the use of CCA instead of straight-line amortization does not affect cash outflows for income tax purposes.

CURRENT INCOME TAX REPORTING REQUIREMENTS

The *CICA Handbook,* section 3465, describes in considerable detail the concepts and principles that are the foundation of accounting standards for the recognition, measurement, presentation, and disclosure of income tax. This section of the *Handbook* affects all audited corporate financial disclosure beginning January 2001 and amends previous Canadian accounting disclosure practices to match those in effect in the U.S. since 1992. The approach currently recommended is called the Future Income Tax Asset/Liability (FITAL) approach.

Using the FITAL approach, the accountant must identify and disclose the sources of the temporary differences that give rise to probable future income tax benefits (i.e., reduction of future income taxes) or liabilities (taxes that are deferred to some future period). In general, the accountant must measure, record, and disclose these future assets and liabilities, as well as their cause in a format that informs the readers about the type of transactions that resulted in temporary differences and the related future tax effects.

Exhibit 10.4 shows the disclosures made by Petro-Canada in the notes to its financial statements for 2004. The disclosures include a detailed account of the components of the income tax expense (or provision for income taxes) for 2004, as well as a listing of the items that caused temporary differences between financial reporting and income tax reporting. Note that the temporary difference between amortization expense and CCA resulted in the largest effect on the future income tax liabilities reported on Petro-Canada's balance sheet.

The computation of future income taxes involves some complexities that are discussed in advanced accounting courses.

Chapter Supplement B

Accrued Retirement Benefits

Most employers provide retirement programs for their employees. In a *defined contribution* program, the employer makes cash payments to an investment fund. When employees retire, they are entitled to a portion of the fund. If the investment strategy of the fund is successful, the retirement income for the employees will be larger. If the strategy is not successful, it will be lower. In other words, the employees bear the risk associated with the investments in the plan. The employer's only obligation is to make the required annual payments to the fund, which are recorded as pension expense.

Other employers offer *defined benefit* programs. Under these programs, an employee's retirement benefits are based on a percentage of his or her pay at retirement or a certain number of dollars for each year of employment. In these cases, the amount of pension expense that must be accrued each year is the change in the current cash value of the employee's retirement package. The current cash value changes each year for a variety of reasons. For example, it changes (1) as employees get closer to receiving benefits, (2) as employees' retirement benefits increase because of higher pay or longer service, or (3) if the employees' life expectancies change. The company must report a pension liability based on any portion of the current cash value of the retirement program that has not actually been funded. For example, if the company transferred $8 million to the pension fund manager but the current cash value of the pension program was $10 million, the company reports a $2-million pension liability on its balance sheet.

For many corporations, especially those with unionized work forces, the financial obligation associated with defined benefit retirement programs can be very large because the risk associated with investments in the pension plan is borne by the employer, which must cover any shortfall between the investment earnings and the payments to retirees. For this reason, companies are moving away from defined benefit pension plans in favour of defined contribution pension plans.

Petro-Canada has set up both a defined benefit pension plan and a defined contribution pension plan for its eligible employees. In addition, Petro-Canada provides post-retirement benefits, including certain health and life insurance benefits for its retired employees and eligible surviving dependants.

REAL WORLD EXCERPT

Petro-Canada

ANNUAL REPORT

Notes to the Consolidated Financial Statements

Note 22. EMPLOYEE FUTURE BENEFITS

The Company maintains pension plans with defined benefit and defined contribution provisions, and provides certain health care and life insurance benefits to its qualifying retirees. The actuarially determined cost of these benefits is accrued over the estimated service life of employees. The defined benefit provisions are generally based upon years of service and average salary during the final years of employment. Certain defined benefit options require employee contributions and the balance of the funding for the registered plans is provided by the Company, based upon the advice of an independent actuary. The accrued benefit obligations and the fair value of plan assets are measured for accounting purposes at December 31 of each year. The most recent actuarial valuation of the pension plan for funding purposes was as of December 31, 2002 and the next required valuation will be as of December 31, 2004.

The defined contribution option provides for an annual contribution of 5% to 8% of each participating employee's pensionable earnings.

Petro-Canada's obligations under these various plans totalled $1,487 million as at December 31, 2004. The company has set aside funds that had a fair value of $1,157 million at that date. The shortfall of $330 million is important to analysts who forecast Petro-Canada's future cash flows, and to employees who may be concerned about the availability of money in the pension fund to pay them cash during their retirement. However, Petro-Canada disclosed in note 22 to its financial statements an accrued benefit asset of $71 million, which does not reflect the net unfunded obligation. The computation of the pension asset or liability is complex and covered in advanced accounting courses.

In recent years, employer-provided health care benefits have been the subject of much discussion. Many large companies pay for a portion of their employees' health insurance costs. The payments are recorded as an expense in the current accounting period. Some employers agree to continue to pay for health care costs after employees retire. The cost of these future benefits must be estimated and recorded as an expense in the periods when the employees perform services. The recording of future health care costs for retired employees is an excellent example of the use of estimates in accounting. Imagine the difficulty of estimating future health care costs when you do not know how long employees will live, how healthy they will be during their lives, and how much doctors and hospitals will charge for their services in the future.

Accounting for retirement benefits is a complex topic that is discussed in detail in subsequent accounting courses. This topic is introduced at this point as another example of the application of the matching concept, which requires that expenses be recorded in the year in which the benefit is received. The benefit in this case is the work performed by the employees, and all costs incurred to compensate employees for their work, must be recorded regardless of the timing of pension payments.

It also illustrates how accounting avoids the creation of improper incentives for managers. If the future cost of retirement benefits was not included in the period in which work was performed, managers might have the incentive to offer employees increases in their retirement benefits instead of increases in their salaries. In this manner, managers could understate the true cost of employee services and make their companies appear more profitable. Many economists argue that the local, provincial, and federal governments have fallen into this trap. Government officials can give large pensions to current workers without the cost being recognized until the employee retires. By doing this, governments can appear to be very efficient when in reality they are simply deferring costs to the future.

SOLUTIONS TO **SELF-STUDY QUIZZES**

Self-Study Quiz 10-1

1.

	December 31, 2003	**December 31, 2004**
Current ratio	$\dfrac{\$2,705}{\$2,128} = 1.27$	$\dfrac{\$1,986}{\$2,898} = 0.69$
Debt-to-equity ratio	$\dfrac{\$7,186}{\$7,588} = 0.95$	$\dfrac{\$9,361}{\$8,739} = 1.07$

The current ratio at December 31, 2004 is below the minimum level required, but the debt-to-equity ratio is above 1.50 at both dates.

2. Management should be concerned about the decrease in the current ratio and must take the necessary steps to increase this ratio in the future.

Self-Study Quiz 10-2

Current ratio	Working capital
1. Decrease	Decrease
2. Increase	Increase
3. Increase	No change
4. No change	No change

Self-Study Quiz 10-3

1. Interest expense	2,000	
Interest payable		2,000
2. Interest expense	1,000	
Interest payable	2,000	
Cash		3,000
3. Interest expense	6,000	
Cash		6,000

Self-Study Quiz 10-4

1. The present value will decrease. With a higher interest rate, more interest will accumulate over time, so the initial amount needed at the start would be smaller because the interest component will be larger.
2. $\$10,000 \times 0.6139 = \$6,139$

CHAPTER **TAKE-AWAYS**

1. **Define, measure, and report current liabilities. p. 529**
   Strictly speaking, accountants define liabilities as obligations arising from past transactions that will be settled in the future by some transfer or use of assets or provision of a service. They are classified on the balance sheet as either current or long term. Current liabilities are short-term obligations that will be paid within the normal operating cycle of the business or within one year of the balance sheet date, whichever is longer. Long-term liabilities are all obligations not classified as current.

2. **Compute and interpret the current ratio. p. 530**
   The current ratio is a comparison of current assets to current liabilities. Analysts use this ratio to assess the liquidity of a company.

3. **Compute and interpret the accounts payable turnover ratio. p. 532**
   This ratio is computed by dividing cost of goods sold by accounts payable. It shows how quickly management is paying its trade creditors and is considered to be a measure of liquidity.

4. **Explain the impact of changes in accounts payable and accrued liabilities on cash flows. p. 536**
   Changes in accounts payable and accrued liabilities affect cash flows from operating activities. Cash flows are increased by increases in accounts payable and accrued liabilities, and vice versa.

5. **Report notes payable and explain the time value of money. p. 538**
   A note payable specifies the amount borrowed, when it must be repaid, and the interest rate associated with the debt. Accountants must report the debt and the interest as it accrues. The time value of money refers to the fact that interest accrues on borrowed money with the passage of time.

6. **Report contingent liabilities and commitments. p. 541**
   A contingent liability is a potential liability that has arisen as a result of a past event. Such liabilities are disclosed in a note if the obligation is reasonably possible but not currently determinable. A commitment is a contractual agreement to enter into a transaction with another party in the future.

7. **Report long-term liabilities. p. 543**
   Usually, long-term liabilities will be paid more than one year in the future. Accounting for long-term debt is based on the same concepts used in accounting for short-term debt.

8. **Apply the concepts of present and future values. p. 546**
   These concepts are based on the time value of money. Simply stated, a dollar to be received in the future is worth less than a dollar available today (present value).

Alternatively, a dollar invested today will grow to a larger amount in the future (future value). These concepts are applied either to a single payment or multiple payments called *annuities*. Tables, calculators, spreadsheets, or financial software can be used to determine present and future values.

9. **Apply present value concepts to liabilities.   p. 553**
   Accountants use present value concepts to determine the reported amounts of liabilities. A liability involves the payment of some amount at a future date. The reported liability is not the amount of the future payment. Instead, the liability is reported at the amount of the present value of the future payment.

In this chapter, we focused on current liabilities and introduced you to present value concepts. In the next chapter, we will use present value concepts to measure bonds. We will also discuss long-term liabilities in the context of the capital structure of the company.

KEY **RATIOS**

Current ratio measures the ability of a company to pay its current obligations. It is computed as follows (p. 530):

$$\text{Current Ratio} = \frac{\text{Current Assets}}{\text{Current Liabilities}}$$

Accounts payable turnover and its companion **average age of payables** are measures of how quickly a company pays its creditors. They are computed as follows (p. 532):

$$\text{Accounts Payable Turnover} = \frac{\text{Cost of Goods Sold}}{\text{Average Accounts Payable}}$$

$$\text{Average Age of Payables} = \frac{\text{Average Accounts Payable}}{\text{Cost of Goods Sold} \div 365}$$

FINDING **FINANCIAL INFORMATION**

BALANCE SHEET
Under Current Liabilities
Liabilities listed by account title, such as
  Accounts payable
  Accrued liabilities
  Notes payable
Under Non-Current Liabilities
Liabilities listed by account title, such as
  Long-term debt
  Future income taxes

INCOME STATEMENT
Liabilities are shown only on the balance sheet, never on the income statement. Transactions affecting liabilities often affect an income statement account. For example, accrued salary compensation affects an income statement account (compensation expense) and a balance sheet account (salaries payable).

CASH FLOW STATEMENT
Under Operating Activities (indirect method)
Net income
  + Increases in most current liabilities
  − Decreases in most current liabilities
Under Financing Activities
  + Increases in long-term liabilities
  − Decreases in long-term liabilities

NOTES
Under Summary of Significant Accounting Policies
Description of pertinent information concerning the accounting treatment of liabilities. Normally, there is minimal information.
Under a Separate Note
If not listed on the balance sheet, a listing of the major classifications of liabilities with information about maturities and interest rates appears in a note. Information about contingent liabilities is reported in the notes.

KEY **TERMS**

Accrued Liabilities p. 533

Annuity p. 549

Capital Lease p. 546

Capital Structure p. 528

Contingent Liability p. 541

Current Liabilities p. 529

Deferred Revenues p. 540

Future Value p. 547

Liabilities p. 529

Liquidity p. 530

Long-Term Liabilities p. 543

Operating Lease p. 546

Present Value p. 547

Time Value of Money p. 538

Working Capital p. 531

QUESTIONS

1. Define *liability*. Differentiate between a current liability and a long-term liability.
2. How can external parties be informed about the liabilities of a business?
3. Liabilities are measured and reported at their current cash equivalent amount. Explain.
4. A *liability* is a known obligation of either a definite or an estimated amount. Explain.
5. Define *working capital*. How is it computed?
6. What is the current ratio? How is it related to the classification of liabilities?
7. Define *accrued liability*. What type of entry usually reflects an accrued liability?
8. Define *deferred revenue*. Why is it a liability?
9. Define *note payable*. Differentiate between a secured and an unsecured note.
10. What is a contingent liability? How is a contingent liability reported?
11. Compute 2006 interest expense for the following note: face, $4,000; 12-percent interest; date of note, April 1, 2006. Assume that the fiscal year ends on December 31.
12. Explain the concept of the time value of money.
13. Explain the basic difference between future value and present value.
14. If you deposited $10,000 in a savings account that earns 10 percent compounded annually, how much would you have at the end of 10 years? Show your computations.
15. What is the present value of a contract that will pay you $8,000 cash 10 years hence if the going rate of interest is 10 percent? Show your computations.
16. What is an annuity?
17. Complete the following schedule:

Table Values				
Concept	Symbol	$n = 4, i = 5\%$	$n = 7, i = 10\%$	$n = 10, i = 14\%$
FV of $1				
PV of $1				
FV of annuity of $1				
PV of annuity of $1				

18. If you deposit $1,000 for each of 10 interest periods (ordinary annuity) that earns 8 percent interest per period, how much would you have at the end of period 10? Show your computations.
19. You purchased an XIT auto for $18,000 by making a $3,000 cash payment and six semi-annual instalment payments for the balance at 12-percent annual interest. Show your computation of the amount of each payment.
20. As a result of a slowdown in operations, Mercantile Stores is offering to employees who have been terminated a severance package of $100,000 cash; another $100,000 to be paid in one year; and an annuity of $30,000 to be paid each year for 20 years. What is the present value of the package, assuming an interest rate of 8 percent?

MULTIPLE-CHOICE QUESTIONS

1. You and your spouse are planning your retirement. In addition to other savings, you have opened an account with a bank. Your goal is to deposit $15,000 at the end of each year,

starting in 12 months and continuing for 10 years. You expect to earn 5 percent each year. What would be the balance in your account at the end of 10 years?

a. $24,433   c. $188,668

b. $150,000   d. $495,990

2. The university spirit organization needs to buy a new trailer in which to haul the team mascot to the football games. A dealership in Newtown has agreed to the following terms: $2,000 down plus monthly payments of $365 for 4 years, which includes interest at 6 percent. A dealership in Oldtown will agree to a $1,000 down payment, plus payments of $380 per month for four years, which includes interest at 12 percent. Which is the better deal, *and why?*

a. The Oldtown offer is better because the total payments of $19,240 are less than the total payments of $19,520 to be made to the Newtown dealership.

b. The Newtown offer is better because the cost in terms of present value is less than the cost of the Oldtown offer.

c. The Newtown offer is better because the financing rate is less.

d. The Oldtown offer is better because the cash down payment is less.

e. The Oldtown offer is better because the cost in terms of present value is less than the cost of the Newtown offer.

3. Which of the following best describes *accrued liabilities?*

a. Long-term liabilities.

b. Current amounts owed to suppliers of inventory.

c. Current liabilities to be recognized as revenue in a future period.

d. Current amounts owed to various parties excluding suppliers of inventory.

4. Company X has borrowed $100,000 from the bank to be repaid over the next five years with payments beginning next month. Which of the following best describes the presentation of this debt in the balance sheet as of today (the date of borrowing)?

a. $100,000 in the Long-Term Liabilities section.

b. $100,000 plus the interest to be paid over the five-year period in the Long-Term Liabilities section.

c. A portion of the $100,000 in the Current Liabilities section and the remainder of the principal in the Long-Term Liabilities section.

d. A portion of the $100,000 plus interest in the Current Liabilities section and the remainder of the principal plus interest in the Long-Term Liabilities section.

5. A company is facing a class-action lawsuit in the upcoming year. It is possible, but not probable, that the company will have to pay a settlement of approximately $2,000,000. How would this fact be reported in the financial statements to be issued at the end of the current month?

a. $2,000,000 in the Current Liabilities section.

b. $2,000,000 in the Long-Term Liabilities section.

c. In a descriptive narrative in the footnote section.

d. Disclosure in this case is not required.

6. Which of the following transactions would usually cause accounts payable turnover to increase?

a. Collection of cash from a customer.   c. Purchase of merchandise on credit.

b. Payment of cash to a supplier.   d. None of the above.

7. How is working capital calculated?

a. Current assets multiplied by current liabilities.

b. Current assets plus current liabilities.

c. Current assets minus current liabilities.

d. Current assets divided by current liabilities.

8. Which of the following is least likely to be an annuity?

a. Monthly payments to a savings account.   c. Monthly payments on a home mortgage.

b. Monthly receipts from a pension plan.   d. Monthly utility bill payments.

9. On October 1, 2005, SLC Inc. borrowed $50,000 from a local bank and signed a two-year note, payable on September 30, 2007. The company is required to pay interest semi-annually on March 30 and September 30 at an annual rate of 8 percent. SLC's fiscal year ends on December 31. The interest expense that should be reported on the company income statement for 2005 equals:

a. $4,000   c. $1,000

b. $8,000   d. $2,000

10. Fred wants to save enough money each year so that he can purchase a sports car in January 2008. Fred receives a large bonus from his employer every December 31. He anticipates that the car will cost $54,000 on January 1, 2008. In order for Fred to calculate how much he needs to save each December 31, he will need to have which of the following?
    a. The anticipated interest rate and the present value of $1 table.
    b. The anticipated interest rate and the future value of $1 table.
    c. The anticipated interest rate and the present value table for annuities,
    d. The anticipated interest rate and the future value table for annuities.

For more practice with multiple-choice questions, go to our Web site at www.mcgrawhill.ca/college/libby, click on "Student Edition" in the upper left menu, click on this chapter's name and number from the list of contents, and then click on "Multiple-Choice Quiz" from the menu on the left.

EXERCISES

E10–1 **Computing Shareholders' Equity and Working Capital; Explaining the Current Ratio and Working Capital**

■ **LO1, 2**

Flair Corporation is preparing its 2006 balance sheet. The company records show the following related amounts at the end of the fiscal year, December 31, 2006:

Total current assets	$170,100
Total all other assets	575,000
Liabilities:	
Notes payable (9%, due in 5 years)	28,000
Accounts payable	60,000
Income taxes payable	12,000
Liability for withholding taxes	3,000
Rent revenue collected in advance	4,000
Bonds payable (due in 15 years)	110,000
Wages payable	7,800
Property taxes payable	2,000
Note payable (10%; due in 6 months)	10,000
Interest payable	400

Required:

1. Compute the amount of shareholders' equity.

2. Compute (a) the amount of working capital and (b) the current ratio (show computations). Why is working capital important to management? How do financial analysts use the current ratio?

3. Compute the amount of interest expense for 2006 on the long-term note. Assume that it was dated October 1, 2006.

E10–2 **Recording a Note Payable through Its Time to Maturity with Discussion of Management Strategy**

■ **LO1, 5**

Hudson's Bay

Many businesses borrow money during periods of increased business activity to finance inventory and accounts receivable. Hudson's Bay is one of Canada's largest general merchandise retailers. Each year, Hudson's Bay builds up its inventory to meet the needs of December holiday shoppers. A large portion of these holiday sales are on credit. As a result, Hudson's Bay often collects cash from the sales several months after the December holidays. Assume that on November 1, 2005, Hudson's Bay borrowed $4.5 million cash from Provincial Bank for working capital purposes and signed an interest-bearing note due in six months. The interest rate was 10 percent per annum, payable at maturity. Assume that the Hudson's Bay fiscal year ends on December 31.

Required:

1. Prepare the journal entry to record the note on November 1, 2005.

2. Prepare any adjusting entry required at December 31, 2005.

3. Prepare the journal entry to record payment of the note and interest on the maturity date, April 30, 2006.

4. If Hudson's Bay needs extra cash for every December holiday season, should management borrow money on a long-term basis to avoid the necessity of negotiating a new short-term loan each year?

■ **LO1, 5**

Hudson's Bay

E10–3   Determining Financial Statement Effects of Transactions Involving Notes Payable

Using the data from the previous exercise, complete the following:

Required:

Determine the financial statement effects for each of the following: (a) issuance of the note on November 1, 2005, (b) impact of the adjusting entry at December 31, 2005, and (c) the payment of the note and interest on April 30, 2006. Indicate the accounts, amounts, and direction of the effects (+ for increases and − for decreases) on the balance sheet equation. Use the following headings:

Date	Assets	Liabilities	Shareholders' Equity

■ **LO1**

E10–4   Recording Payroll Costs with Discussion

Matyas Company completed the salary and wage payroll for March 2005. The payroll provided the following details:

Salaries and wages earned	$224,000
Employee income taxes withheld	46,000
Union dues withheld	3,000
Insurance premiums withheld	1,000
CPP contibutions*	16,445
EI contributions†	9,611

*$16,445 each for employer and employees.
†Employment insurance, employees' share.

Required:

1. Prepare the journal entry to record the payroll for March, including employee deductions.

2. Prepare the journal entry to record the employer's additional payroll expenses.

3. Prepare a combined journal entry to show the payment of amounts owed to governmental agencies and other organizations.

4. What was the total compensation expense for the company? Explain. What percentage of the payroll was take-home pay? From the employers' perspective, does an economic difference between the cost of salaries and the cost of fringe benefits exist? From the employees' perspective, does a difference exist?

■ **LO1**

E10–5   Computing Payroll Costs; Discussion of Labour Costs

Town Lake Company has completed the payroll for January 2006, reflecting the following data:

Salaries and wages earned	$79,000
Employee income taxes withheld	8,900
Union dues withheld	1,200
CPP contibutions*	6,013
EI contributions†	3,514

*$6,013 each for employer and employee.
†Employment insurance, employees' share.

Required:

1. What amount of additional compensation expense must be paid by the company? What was the amount of the employees' take-home pay?

2. List the liabilities and related amounts that are reported on the company's January 31, 2006, balance sheet.

3. Would employers react differently to a 10-percent increase in the employer's share of CPP than to a 10-percent increase in the basic level of salaries? Would financial analysts react differently?

E10–6 Reporting Warranty Liability

Gonzales Co. provides warranties for many of its products. Its Estimated Warranty Liability account had a balance of $35,200 at January 1, 2006. Based on an analysis of warranty claims during the past several years, the warranty expense for 2006 was established at 0.4 percent of sales. During 2006, the actual cost of servicing products under warranty was $15,600, and sales were $3,600,000.

LO1

Required:

1. Compute the warranty expense that should appear on the company's income statement for the year ended December 31, 2006.

2. What amount will be reported in the Estimated Warranty Liability account on the balance sheet as at December 31, 2006?

E10–7 Determining the Impact of Transactions, Including Analysis of Cash Flows

Mawani Company sells a wide range of goods through two retail stores operated in adjoining cities. Most purchases of goods for resale are on invoices. Occasionally, a short-term note payable is used to obtain cash for current use. The following transactions were selected from those occurring during 2006:

LO1, 2, 4

a. On January 10, 2006, purchased merchandise on credit, $18,000; the company uses a periodic inventory system.

b. On March 1, 2006, borrowed $50,000 cash from Local Bank and signed an interest-bearing note payable: face amount, $50,000, due at the end of six months, with an annual interest rate of 8 percent payable at maturity.

c. On April 5, 2006, sold merchandise on credit, $34,500; this amount included GST of $2,100 and PST of $2,400. Ignore the related cost of goods sold.

Required:

1. Describe the impact of each transaction on the balance sheet equation. Indicate the accounts, amounts, and direction of the effects (+ for increases and − for decreases) on the balance sheet equation. Use the following headings:

Date	Assets	Liabilities	Shareholders' Equity

2. What amount of cash is paid on the maturity date of the note?

3. Discuss the impact of each transaction on Mawani's cash flows.

4. Discuss the impact of each transaction on the current ratio. Assume that the current ratio is greater than 1 before considering each transaction.

E10–8 Reporting Contingent Liabilities

Buzz Coffee Shops is famous for its large servings of hot coffee. After a famous case involving McDonald's, the lawyer for Buzz warned management (during 2003) that it could be sued if someone were to spill hot coffee and be burned: "With the temperature of your coffee, I can guarantee it's just a matter of time before you're sued for $1,000,000." Unfortunately, in 2005, the prediction came true when a customer filed suit. The case went to trial in 2006, and the jury awarded the customer $400,000 in damages, which the company immediately appealed. During 2007, the customer and the company settled their dispute for $150,000. What is the proper reporting each year of the events related to this liability?

LO6

E10–9 Evaluating Lease Alternatives

As the new vice president for consumer products at Acme Manufacturing, you are attending a meeting to discuss a serious problem associated with delivering merchandise to customers. Bob Vargas, director of logistics, summarized the problem: "It's easy to understand, we just don't have enough delivery trucks given our recent growth." Barb Bader from the accounting department responded: "Maybe it's easy to understand but it's impossible to do anything. Because of Bay Street's concern about the amount of debt on our balance sheet, we're under a freeze and can't borrow money to acquire new assets. There's nothing we can do."

On the way back to your office after the meeting, your assistant offers a suggestion: "Why don't we just lease the trucks we need? That way we can get the assets we want without having to record a liability on the balance sheet."

How would you respond to this suggestion?

LO1

■ **LO1, 7**   **E10–10 Reporting a Liability**

Carnival Cruise Lines

Carnival Cruise Lines provides exotic vacations on board luxurious passenger ships. In 1998, the company moved its offices and included the following note in its current annual report:

> **Leases**
>
> On March 27, 1998, the Company entered into a ten-year lease for 230,000 square feet of office space located in Miami, Florida. The Company moved its operation to this location in October 1998. The total rent payable over the ten-year term of the lease is approximately $24 million.

Required:

Based on these facts, do you think the company should report this obligation on its balance sheet? Explain. If the obligation should be reported as a liability, how should the amount be measured?

■ **LO8**   **E10–11 Computing Four Kinds of Present and Future Values**

On January 1, 2005, Wesley Company completed the following transactions (assume an 11-percent annual compound interest rate):

a. Deposited $12,000 in Fund A.

b. Established Fund B by agreeing to make six annual deposits of $2,000 each. Deposits are made each December 31.

c. Established Fund C by depositing a single amount that will increase to $40,000 by the end of year 7.

d. Decided to deposit a single sum in Fund D that will provide 10 equal annual year-end payments of $15,000 to a retired employee (payments starting December 31, 2005).

Required (show computations and round to the nearest dollar):

1. What will be the balance of Fund A at the end of year 9?

2. What will be the balance of Fund B at the end of year 6?

3. What single amount must be deposited in Fund C on January 1, 2005?

4. What single sum must be deposited in Fund D on January 1, 2005?

■ **LO8**   **E10–12 Computing Growth in a Savings Account: A Single Amount**

On January 1, 2005, you deposited $6,000 in a savings account. The account will earn 10 percent annual compound interest, which will be added to the fund balance at the end of each year.

Required (round to the nearest dollar):

1. What will be the balance in the savings account at the end of 10 years?

2. What is the interest for the 10 years?

3. How much interest revenue did the fund earn in 2005? 2006?

■ **LO8**   **E10–13 Recording Growth in a Savings Account with Equal Periodic Payments**

You plan to deposit $2,000 in a savings account on each December 31. The account will earn 9 percent annual interest, which will be added to the fund balance at year-end. The first deposit will be made December 31, 2005 (end of period).

Required (show computations and round to the nearest dollar):

1. Prepare the required journal entry on December 31, 2005, assuming you keep books to account for your personal finances.

2. What will be the balance in the savings account at the end of the tenth year (i.e., after 10 deposits)?

3. What is the interest earned on the 10 deposits?

4. How much interest revenue did the fund earn in 2006? 2007?

5. Prepare all required journal entries at the end of 2006 and 2007.

E10–14 Computing Growth for a Savings Fund with Periodic Deposits   ■ **LO8**

On January 1, 2005, you plan to take a trip around the world upon graduation four years from now. Your grandmother wants to deposit sufficient funds for this trip in a savings account for you. You estimate that the trip would cost $15,000. To be generous, your grandmother decided to deposit $3,500 in the fund at the end of each of the next four years, starting on December 31, 2005. The savings account will earn 6 percent annual interest, which will be added to the savings account at each year-end.

Required (show computations and round to the nearest dollar):

1. How much money will you have for the trip at the end of year 4 (i.e., after four deposits)?

2. What is the interest for the four years?

3. How much interest revenue did the fund earn in 2005, 2006, 2007, and 2008?

E10–15 Computing Value of an Asset Based on Present Value   ■ **LO8**

Quetario Company is considering purchasing a machine that would save the company $13,500 in cash per year for six years, at the end of which the machine would be retired with no salvage value. The firm wishes to earn a minimum of 12 percent interest, compounded annually, on any such investment. Assume that the cash savings occur at year-end and ignore taxes.

Required:

1. What is the maximum amount that the firm should be willing to pay for this machine? Show your computations.

2. Would the maximum amount be different if the machine is expected to have a salvage value of $4,000 at the end of six years? Explain.

3. As an alternative to the scenario in requirement 2, the company could buy a machine that had no salvage value and offered no cost savings for the first five years, but this machine would offer cost savings of $113,561 at the end of the sixth year. If the company can buy only one machine, which one should it be? Defend your answer.

E10–16 Reporting a Mortgage Note   ■ **LO1, 9**

On January 1, 2006, Wong Corporation signed a mortgage note for $5,000,000 at 8 percent for a term of 5 years. Mortgage payments are made semi-annually on June 30 and on December 31. Each mortgage payment is a blend of interest on the unpaid amount and a partial repayment of the principal loan.

Required:

1. Compute the amount of each mortgage payment.

2. Record the mortgage payments on June 30, 2006 and on December 31, 2006.

3. What is the current portion of the mortgage at December 31, 2006? What portion of the mortgage would appear as long-term debt on the balance sheet at that same date?

E10–17 (Supplement B) Reporting a Liability, with Discussion   ■ **LO1**

An annual report for Ford Motor Company contained the following information: Ford Motor Company

> **Postretirement Health Care and Life Insurance Benefits**
>
> The company and certain of its subsidiaries sponsor unfunded plans to provide selected health care and life insurance benefits for retired employees. The company's employees may become eligible for those benefits if they retire while working for the company. However, benefits and eligibility rules may be modified from time to time.

Required:

Should Ford report a liability for these benefits on its balance sheet? Explain.

E10–18 (Supplement A) Computing Future Income Tax: One Temporary Difference, with Discussion   ■ **LO1, 7**

The comparative income statements of Martin Corporation at December 31, 2006, showed the following summarized pretax data:

	Year 2005	Year 2006
Sales revenue	$65,000	$72,000
Expenses (excluding income tax)	50,000	54,000
Pretax income	$15,000	$18,000

The expenses for 2006 included an amount of $2,800 that was deductible only in the 2005 income tax return (rather than in 2006). The average income tax rate was 40 percent. Taxable income from the income tax returns was $14,000 for 2005, and $17,400 for 2006.

Required:

1. For each year compute (a) the income taxes payable and (b) the future income tax. Is the future income tax a liability or an asset? Explain.

2. Show what amounts related to income taxes should be reported each year on the income statement and the balance sheet. Assume that the income tax is paid on March 1 of the next year.

3. Explain why tax expense is not simply the amount of cash paid during the year.

■ **LO1, 7**   **E10–19** **(Supplement A) Recording Future Income Tax: One Temporary Difference; Discussion of Management Strategy**
The comparative income statement for Chung Corporation at the end of December 31, 2006, provided the following summarized pretax data:

	Year 2005	Year 2006
Revenue	$80,000	$88,000
Expenses (excluding income tax)	65,000	69,000
Pretax income	$15,000	$19,000

The revenue for 2006 included an amount of $5,000 that was taxable only in the 2005 income tax return. The average income tax rate was 35 percent. Taxable income shown in the tax returns was $13,000 for 2005, and $18,500 for 2006.

Required:

1. For each year compute (a) the income taxes payable and (b) the future income tax. Is the future income tax a liability or an asset? Explain.

2. Prepare the journal entry for each year to record income taxes payable, the future income tax, and the income tax expense.

3. Show the tax-related amounts that should be reported each year on the income statement and the balance sheet. Assume that income tax is paid on March 1 of the next year.

4. Why would management want to incur the cost of preparing separate tax and financial accounting reports to defer the payment of taxes?

■ **LO1, 7**   **E10–20** **(Supplement A) Computing and Reporting Future Income Tax: Amortization**
Amber Corporation reported the following summarized pretax data at the end of each year:

Income Statement at December 31	2005	2006	2007
Revenues	$170,000	$182,000	$195,000
Expenses (including amortization)*	122,000	126,000	130,000
Pretax income	$ 48,000	$ 56,000	$ 65,000

*Straight-line amortization expense on a machine purchased January 1, 2005, for $75,000. The machine has a three-year estimated life and no residual value. The company used accelerated amortization on the income tax return as follows: 2005, $37,500; 2006, $25,000; and 2007, $12,500. The average income tax rate is 28 percent for each of the three years.

Taxable income from the income tax return was as follows: 2005, $32,000; 2006, $56,000; and 2007, $85,000.

Required:

1. For each year, compute (a) the income taxes payable and (b) the future income tax. Is the future income tax a liability or an asset? Explain.

2. Show the tax-related amounts that should be reported each year on the income statement and the balance sheet.

PROBLEMS

P10–1 **Recording and Reporting Current Liabilities with Discussion of Cash Flow Effects** (AP10–1)

■ LO1, 2, 3

Uzma Company completed the following transactions during 2006. The company's fiscal year ends on December 31, 2006.

Jan.	8	Purchased merchandise for resale at a cost of $12,420. The company uses a periodic inventory system.
	17	Paid the invoice received on January 8.
Mar.	10	Sold merchandise on credit for a total amount of $11,500, which included GST at 7 percent and PST at 8 percent.
Apr.	1	Borrowed $40,000 from National Bank for general use; signed a 12-month, 12-percent interest-bearing note payable.
June	3	Purchased merchandise for resale at a cost of $17,820.
July	5	Paid the invoice received on June 3.
Aug.	1	Rented a small office in a building owned by the company and collected $5,400 for six months' rent in advance. (Record the collection in a way that will not require an adjusting entry at year-end.)
Dec.	20	Received a $100 deposit from a customer as a guarantee to return a large trailer "borrowed" for 30 days.
	31	Determined that wages earned but not yet paid on December 31 amounted to $7,200. Ignore payroll taxes.

Required:

1. Prepare journal entries for each of these transactions.

2. Prepare the adjusting entry (entries) required on December 31, 2006.

3. Show how all of the liabilities arising from these transactions are reported on the balance sheet at December 31, 2006.

4. For each transaction and related adjusting entry, state whether the current ratio is increased, decreased, or remains the same. Assume that the current ratio is greater than 1 before considering each transaction.

P10–2 **Determining Financial Effects of Transactions Affecting Current Liabilities with Discussion of Cash Flow Effects** (AP10–2)

■ LO1, 2, 3

Using data from the previous problem, complete the following requirements.

Required:

1. For each transaction (including adjusting entries) listed in the previous problem, indicate the accounts, amounts, and direction of the effects (+ for increases and − for decreases) on the balance sheet equation. Use the following headings:

Date	Assets	Liabilities	Shareholders' Equity

2. For each transaction and related adjusting entry, state whether cash flow from operating activities is increased, decreased, or remains unchanged.

P10–3 **Recording and Reporting Accrued Liabilities and Deferred Revenue, Financial Statement Effects with Discussion**

■ LO1

During 2006, Riverside Company completed the following two transactions. The company's fiscal year ends on December 31.

a. Paid and recorded wages of $130,000 during 2006; however, at the end of December 2006, wages of $5,100 for three days are unpaid and unrecorded because the next weekly pay day is January 6, 2007.

b. Rented office space to another party and collected $3,000 on December 10, 2006. The rent collected was for 30 days from December 12, 2006, through January 10, 2007, and was credited in full to Rent Revenue.

Required:

1. Prepare (*a*) the adjusting entry required on December 31, 2006, and (*b*) the journal entry on January 6, 2007, to record the payment of any unpaid wages from December 2006.

2. Prepare (*a*) the journal entry for the collection of rent on December 10, 2006, and (*b*) the adjusting entry on December 31, 2006.

3. Determine the financial statement effects for each of the journal entries you prepared in requirements 1 and 2. Indicate the accounts, the amounts, and direction of the effects (+ for increases and − for decreases) on the balance sheet equation. Use the following headings:

Date	Assets	Liabilities	Shareholders' Equity

4. Show how any liabilities related to these transactions should be reported on the company's balance sheet at December 31, 2006.

5. Explain why the accrual method of accounting provides more relevant information to financial analysts than the cash method.

LO1, 5   **P10–4 Determining Financial Statement Effects of Various Liabilities** (AP10–3)

Polaroid

1. Polaroid designs, manufactures, and markets products primarily in instant image recording. Its annual report contained the following note:

> **Product Warranty**
>
> Estimated product warranty costs are accrued at the time products are sold.

Required:
Assume that estimated warranty costs for 2005 were $2 million and that the warranty work was performed during 2006. Describe the financial statement effects for each year.

Reader's Digest Association

2. Reader's Digest Association is a publisher of magazines, books, and music collections. The following note is from its annual report:

> **Revenues**
>
> Sales of subscriptions to magazines are recorded as unearned revenue at the time the order is received. Proportional shares of the subscription price are recognized as revenues when the subscription is fulfilled.

Required:
Assume that Reader's Digest collected $10 million in 2005 for magazines that will be delivered in future years. During 2006, the company delivered $8 million worth of magazines on those subscriptions. Describe the financial statement effects for each year.

Brunswick Corporation

3. Brunswick Corporation is a multinational company that manufactures and sells marine and recreational products. Its annual report contained the following information:

> **Litigation**
>
> A jury awarded $44.4 million in damages in a suit brought by Independent Boat Builders, Inc., a buying group of boat manufacturers and its 22 members. Under the antitrust laws, the damage award has been trebled, and the plaintiffs will be entitled to their attorney's fees and interest.
>
>   The Company has filed an appeal contending the verdict was erroneous as a matter of law, both as to liability and damages.

Required:

How should Brunswick report this litigation in its financial statements?

4. A recent annual report for The Coca-Cola Company reported current assets of $4,247,677 and current liabilities of $5,303,222 (dollars in thousands). Based on the current ratio, do you think that Coca-Cola is experiencing financial difficulty?

The Coca-Cola Company

5. Alcoa is involved in the mining and manufacturing of aluminum. Its products can become an advanced alloy for the wing of a Boeing 777 or a common recyclable Coca-Cola can. The annual report for Alcoa stated the following:

Alcoa

> **Environmental Expenditures**
>
> Liabilities are recorded when remedial efforts are probable and the costs can be reasonably estimated.

Required:

In your own words, explain Alcoa's accounting policy for environmental expenditures. What is the justification for this policy?

P10–5 Recording and Reporting Product Warranties (AP10–4) ■ **LO1**

Bombardier Inc. specializes in manufacturing transportation products (aircraft, railway equipment, snowmobiles, and watercraft). The company offers warranties on all of its products. Note 12 to Bombardier's financial statements for fiscal year 2004 stated the following:

> Product warranties in the aerospace segment typically range from one to five years, except for structural warranties which extend up to 20 years, and from one to five years in the transportation segment.

Selected information from Bombardier's annual reports follows (amounts in millions of dollars).

	2004	2003	2002
Revenues	21,329	23,665	21,633
Estimated warranty liability at year end	1,236	1,289	1,199

During fiscal year 2004, Bombardier paid $942 million to customers in exchange for returned products under the warranty.

Required:

1. Compute the amount of warranty expense for 2004.

2. Prepare journal entries to record both the warranty expense for the year and the payments made under the warranty.

3. Compute the ratio of the warranty liability to revenues for the three years. Has the ratio increased or decreased during the three-year period?

4. Based on the limited information available about the warranty expense and payments in 2004, should Bombardier reduce the balance of the warranty liability in future years? Explain.

P10–6 Determining Financial Statement Effects of Deferred (Unearned) Revenues ■ **LO1**

A. Unearned revenues—customer deposits

Eastern Brewing Company (EBC) distributes its products in an aluminium keg. Customers are charged a deposit of $25 per keg, and deposits received from customers are recorded in the Keg Deposits account.

Required:

1. Where on the balance sheet will the Keg Deposits account be found? Explain.

2. A production specialist who works for EBC estimates that 50 kegs for which deposits were received during the year will never be returned. How would the deposits related to these 50 kegs be reflected in the company's financial statements?

B. Unearned revenues—rent

On September 1, 2006, Noreen Ltd. collected $9,000 in cash from its tenant as an advance rent payment on its store location. The six-month lease period ends on February 28, 2007, at which time the lease contract may be renewed. Noreen's fiscal year ends on December 31.

Required:

1. Prepare journal entries to record the collection of rent on September 1, 2006, and the related adjustment for the amount of rent earned during 2006.

2. If the amount received on September 1, 2006, had covered a period of 18 months, how should Noreen report the unearned rent amount on its balance sheet as at December 31, 2006?

C. Unearned revenues—subscription fees

Tremblay Inc. publishes a monthly newsletter for retail marketing managers and requires its subscribers to pay $60 in advance for a one-year subscription. During the month of April 2007, Tremblay Inc. sold 150 one-year subscriptions and received payments in advance from all new subscribers. Only 70 of the new subscribers paid their fees in time to receive the April newsletter. The other subscribers received the newsletter in May.

Required:

1. Prepare journal entries to record the subscription fees received in advance during April 2007, and the related adjusting entry to recognize the subscription revenue earned during April 2007.

2. The company is now considering the possibility of offering a lifetime membership option to its subscribers. Under this proposal, subscribers would receive the monthly newsletter throughout their life by paying a one-time subscription fee of $550. The one-year subscription rate of $60 would continue to apply to new and existing subscribers who choose to subscribe on an annual basis. Assume that the average age of Tremblay's current subscribers is 40 and their life expectancy is 80 years. Tremblay Inc.'s average interest rate on long-term debt is 12 percent. Determine whether it would be profitable for the company to sell lifetime subscriptions.

■ LO4

P10–7 Determining Cash Flow Effects (AP10–5)

For each of the following transactions, determine whether cash flows from operating activities will increase, decrease, or remain the same:

a. Purchased merchandise on credit.

b. Paid an account payable.

c. Accrued payroll for the month but did not pay it.

d. Borrowed money from the bank. The term of the note is 90 days.

e. Reclassified a long-term note as a current liability.

f. Paid accrued interest expense.

g. Recorded a contingent liability based on a pending lawsuit.

h. Paid back the bank for money borrowed in *d*, along with related interest.

i. Collected cash from a customer for services that will be performed in the next accounting period.

j. Paid GST to the federal government. The amount was previously collected from customers.

■ LO8

P10–8 Computing Present and Future Values (AP10–6)

On January 1, 2005, Perrakis Company completed the following transactions and events (use an 8-percent annual interest rate for all transactions and assume annual compounding unless otherwise stated):

a. Deposited $60,000 in a debt retirement fund. Interest will be computed at six-month intervals and added to the fund at those times (i.e., semi-annual compounding). (*Hint:* Think carefully about *n* and *i*.)

b. Established a plant addition fund of $400,000 to be available at December 31, 2009. A single sum that will grow to $400,000 will be deposited on January 1, 2005.

c. Established a pension retirement fund of $1,000,000 to be available by December 31, 2010 by making six equal annual deposits at year-end, starting on December 31, 2005.

d. Purchased a $180,000 machine on January 1, 2005, and paid cash, $80,000. A four-year note payable is signed for the balance. The note will be paid in four equal year-end amounts starting on December 31, 2005.

Required (show computations and round to the nearest dollar):

1. In Transaction (*a*), what will be the balance in the fund at the end of year 4? What is the total amount of interest revenue that will be earned during the first four years?

2. In Transaction (*b*), what amount must the company deposit on January 1, 2005? What is the total amount of interest revenue that will be earned by the end of year 5?

3. In Transaction (*c*), what is the required amount of each of the six equal annual deposits? What is the total amount of interest revenue that will be earned over the six years?

4. In Transaction (*d*), what is the amount of each of the equal annual payments that will be paid on the note? What is the total amount of interest expense that will be incurred during the four years? Prepare journal entries to record the purchase of the machine and the payments on December 31, 2005, and 2006.

P10–9 Comparing Options Using Present Value Concepts (AP10–7) ■ **LO8**
After hearing a knock at your front door, you are surprised to see the Prize Patrol from a large, well-known magazine subscription company. It has arrived with the good news that you are the big winner, having won $20 million. Later, after consulting with a lawyer, you discover that you have three options: (1) you can receive $1 million per year for the next 20 years (starting one year from now), (2) you can have $8 million today, or (3) you can have $2 million today and receive $700,000 for each of the next 20 years. Your investment adviser tells you that it is reasonable to expect to earn 10 percent compound interest on investments. Which option do you prefer? What factors influence your decision?

P10–10 Computing Amounts for a Debt Fund with Journal Entries (AP10–8) ■ **LO9**
On December 31, 2005, Post Company set aside in a fund the cash to pay the principal amount of a $160,000 debt due on December 31, 2008. The company will make four equal annual deposits on December 31 of the years 2005 through 2008. The fund will earn 7 percent compound annual interest, which will be added to the balance at each year-end. The fund trustee will pay the loan principal (to the creditor) upon receipt of the last fund deposit. The company's fiscal year ends on December 31.

Required (show computations and round to the nearest dollar):

1. How much cash must be deposited each December 31?

2. What amount of interest will be earned on the four deposits until December 31, 2008?

3. How much interest revenue will the fund earn each year?

4. Prepare journal entries for the company on the following dates:
   a. For the first deposit on December 31, 2005.
   b. For all amounts at the end of 2006 and 2007.
   c. For payment of the debt on December 31, 2008.

5. Show how the effect of the fund will be reported on the income statement for 2006 and the balance sheet at December 31, 2006.

P10–11 Computing Equal Periodic Debt Payments and Completing a Schedule (AP10–9) ■ **LO9**
On January 1, 2005, you bought a new Toyota Corolla automobile for $24,000. You made a $5,000 cash down payment and signed a $19,000 note, payable in four equal instalments on each December 31, the first payment to be made on December 31, 2005. The interest rate is 12 percent per year on the unpaid balance. Each payment will include payment on principal plus the interest.

Required:

1. Compute the amount of the equal payments that you must make.

2. What is the total amount of interest that you will pay during the four years?

3. Complete the following schedule:

Debt Payment Schedule				
Date	Cash Payment	Interest Expense	Decrease in Principal	Unpaid Principal
1/1/2005				
12/31/2005				
12/31/2006				
12/31/2007				
12/31/2008				
Totals				

4. Explain why the amount of interest expense decreases each year.

5. To reduce the total amount of interest paid on this note, you considered the possibility of making equal payments every three months (four payments per year). Compute the amount of the equal payments that you must make, and the amount of interest that will be saved over the life of the note.

■ LO8

P10–12 Computing the Present Value of Contract for Basketball Player with Alternatives
In August 2001, star basketball player Vince Carter signed a six-year contract to extend his association with the Raptors, a basketball team based in Toronto. The contract price was estimated at $140 million, one of the largest in professional basketball history. The new contract started in the 2002–2003 season and continues until the 2007–2008 season. Vince's salary for 2002–2003 was $15 million and will increase annually by 12.5 percent until 2007–2008. Assume that Vince's net pay is 60 percent of his gross salary, which he has received at the end of May each year, starting in 2003.

Required:

1. Compute the cash equivalent of Vince's contract (future cash receipts) on June 1, 2002. Assume that Vince can earn an 8-percent after-tax rate of return on his investments. Show your computations.

2. Recompute the cash equivalent of Vince's contract on June 1, 2002, assuming that his salary is spread equally over the 12 months each year and that his first pay date is June 30, 2002. The present value factor for the monthly annuity is 11.4958.

3. Before signing the contract with the Raptors, Vince was considering another, equally lucrative offer from a U.S. basketball team. That contract was for a similar duration and would have resulted in fixed payments of $22 million (Cdn) per year for six years. Assume again that Vince receives 60 percent of his gross salary on May 31 each year, starting in 2003. Did Vince make the most beneficial financial decision by accepting the contract with the Raptors instead of the U.S. basketball team? Show your computations.

4. List some of the assumptions that you made in answering the three requirements above.

■ LO1, 6

P10–13 (Supplement A) Recording and Reporting Future Income Tax: Amortization (AP10–10)
At December 31, 2005, the records of Pearson Corporation provided the following information:

Income statement	
Revenues	$160,000
Amortization expense (straight line)	(11,000)
Other expenses (excluding income tax)	(90,000)
Income before income taxes	$ 59,000

Additional information:

a. Revenues include $20,000 interest on tax-free municipal bonds.

b. Amortization expense relates to equipment acquired on January 1, 2005, at a cost of $44,000, with no salvage value and an estimated useful life of four years.

c. The accelerated amortization (capital cost allowance) used on the tax return is as follows: 2005, $17,600; 2006, $13,200; 2007, $8,800: and 2008, $4,400.

d. The company is subject to an income tax rate of 30 percent. Assume that 85 percent of the income tax liability is paid in the year incurred.

e. The income tax return for 2005 shows a taxable income of $32,400.

Required:

1. Compute the income taxes payable and the future income tax for 2005. Is the future income tax a liability or an asset? Explain.

2. Prepare the journal entry to record income taxes for 2005.

3. Show how the tax-related amounts should be reported on the income statement for 2005 and the balance sheet at December 31, 2005.

ALTERNATE PROBLEMS

AP10–1 **Recording and Reporting Current Liabilities, with Discussion of Cash Flow Effects** (P10–1)   ■ **LO1, 4**

Fontaine Company completed the following transactions during 2006. The company's fiscal year ends on December 31, 2006.

Jan.	2	Paid accrued interest in the amount of $45,000.
Apr.	30	Borrowed $550,000 from Commerce Bank; signed a 12-month, 10-percent interest-bearing note payable.
May	20	Sold merchandise for $5,000 cash plus Harmonized Sales Tax at 15 percent.
June	3	Purchased merchandise for resale at a cost of $75,800, terms 2/10, n/30.
July	5	Paid the invoice received on June 3.
Aug.	31	Signed a contract to provide security service to a small apartment complex and collected $12,000 of fees for six months in advance. (Record the collection in a way that will not require an adjusting entry at year-end.)
Dec.	31	Reclassified a long-term liability in the amount of $120,000 to a current liability.
	31	Determined that salary and wages earned but not yet paid on December 31 totalled $85,000. Ignore payroll taxes.
	31	Recorded income tax expense for the year in the amount of $116,000. The current income taxes payable were $93,000.

Required:

1. Prepare journal entries to record each of these transactions.

2. Prepare all adjusting and reclassification entries required on December 31, 2006.

3. Show how all of the current liabilities arising from these transactions are reported on the balance sheet at December 31, 2006.

4. For each transaction and entry, state whether the current ratio is increased, decreased, or remains unchanged. Assume that the current ratio is less than 1 prior to each transaction/entry.

AP10–2 **Determining Financial Effects of Transactions Affecting Current Liabilities, with Discussion of Cash Flow Effects** (P10–2)   ■ **LO1, 4**

Using data from the previous problem, complete the following requirements.

Required:

1. For each transaction (including adjusting and reclassification entries) listed in the previous problem, indicate the accounts, amounts, and direction of the effects (+ for increases and − for decreases) on the balance sheet equation. Use the following headings:

Date	Assets	Liabilities	Shareholders' Equity

2. For each transaction, state whether cash flow from operating activities is increased, decreased, or remains unchanged.

AP10–3 **Determining Financial Statement Effects of Various Liabilities** (P10–4)   ■ **LO1, 5**

Pulte

1. Pulte Corporation is a national builder of homes, doing more than $2 billion in business each year. Its annual report contained the following note:

Allowance for Warranties

Home purchasers are provided with warranties against certain building defects. Estimated warranty cost is provided in the period in which the sale is recorded.

Required:

Assume that estimated warranty costs for 2005 were $8.5 million and that the warranty work was performed during 2006. Describe the financial statement effects for each year.

Carnival Cruise Lines **2.** Carnival Cruise Lines operates cruise ships in Alaska, the Caribbean, the South Pacific, and the Mediterranean. Some cruises are brief; others can last for several weeks. The company does more than $1 billion in cruise business each year. The following note is from its annual report:

Revenues

Customer cruise deposits, which represent unearned revenue, are included in the balance sheet when received and are recognized as cruise revenue upon completion of voyages of a duration of 10 days or less and on a pro rata basis computed using the number of days completed for voyages in excess of 10 days.

Required:

In your own words, explain how unearned revenue is reported on the balance sheet for Carnival. Assume that Carnival collected $19 million in 2006 for cruises that will be completed in the following year. Of that amount, $4 million was related to cruises of 10 or fewer days that were not complete; $8 million to cruises of more than 10 days that, on average, were 60 percent complete; and $7 million was related to cruises that had not yet begun. What is the amount of unearned revenue that should be reported on the 2006 balance sheet?

Sunbeam **3.** Sunbeam Corporation is a consumer products company that manufactures and markets a number of familiar brands, including Mr. Coffee, Osterizer, First Alert, and Coleman. Annual revenues for the company exceed $2 billion. Its annual report contained the following information:

Litigation

The Company and its subsidiaries are involved in various lawsuits arising from time to time that the Company considers to be ordinary routine litigation incidental to its business. In the opinion of the Company, the resolution of these routine matters will not have a material adverse effect upon the financial position, results of operations, or cash flows of the Company. At the end of the current year, the Company had established accruals for litigation matters of $31.2 million.

In 1996, the Company recorded a $12.0 million charge related to a case for which an adverse development arose. In the fourth quarter of this year, the case was favorably resolved and, as a result, $8.1 million of the charge was reversed into income.

Required:

Explain the meaning of this note in your own words. Describe how litigation has affected the financial statements for Sunbeam.

Exxon **4.** An annual report for Exxon reported a current ratio of 0.90. For the previous year, the ratio was 1.08. Based on this information, do you think that Exxon is experiencing financial difficulty? What other information would you want to consider in making this evaluation?

Brunswick **5.** Brunswick Corporation is a multinational company that manufactures and sells marine and recreational products. Its annual report contained the following information:

Legal and Environmental

The company is involved in numerous environmental remediation and clean-up projects with an aggregate estimated exposure of approximately $21 million to $42 million. The Company accrues for environmental remediation-related activities for which commitments or clean-up plans have been developed and for which costs can be reasonably estimated.

Required:

In your own words, explain Brunswick's accounting policy for environmental expenditures. What is the justification for this policy?

AP10–4 **Recording and Reporting Warranty Liabilities** (P10–5) ■ **LO1**

Gateway Inc. makes desktop and portable PCs and network servers for individual and enterprise customers. The company also offers third-party peripherals including printers, as well as consumer electronics such as digital music players and plasma televisions. Gateway provides standard warranties with the sale of its products. The company's note on significant accounting policies states:

> The estimated cost of providing the product warranty is recorded at the time revenue is recognized. Gateway maintains product quality programs and processes including actively monitoring and evaluating the quality of its suppliers. Estimated warranty costs are affected by ongoing product failure rates, specific product class failures outside of experience and material usage and service delivery costs incurred in correcting a product failure or in providing customer support. Gateway has experienced a decline in its required levels of accrued warranties in recent years due to the shortening of warranty periods coupled with the increasing assumption of warranty repair costs by the original design manufacturers who produce the Company's products.

In addition, Gateway offers its customers an option to purchase extended warranties. Revenue related to sales of extended warranties sold on behalf of third parties is recognized at the time of sale. Revenue from sales of extended warranties where Gateway is the legal obligor is deferred and recognized on a straight-line basis over the warranty service period.

Selected information related to warranties provided by Gateway follows (in thousands of dollars):

	2004	2003	2002
Net sales	3,649,734	3,402,364	4,171,325
Accrued warranty, end of year	19,291	26,897	67,141
Settlements made during the year	62,984	154,286	167,252
Extended warranty deferred revenue, end of year	178,381	216,790	147,599
Additions to extended warranty deferred revenue during the year	93,839	163,265	138,188

Required:

1. Compute the amount of warranty expense for 2003 and 2004.

2. Prepare journal entries to record both the warranty expense for 2004 and the payments made under the warranty during the year.

3. Compute the ratio of the warranty expense to net sales for the three years. Assume that the warranty expense is $131,687 for 2002. Has the ratio increased or decreased during the three-year period? Provide possible reasons for the changes in the ratio.

4. Based on the limited information available about the warranty expense and settlements during these three years, should Gateway reduce the ratio of the warranty expense to net sales in future years? Explain.

5. Compute the extended warranty revenue recognized during 2003 and 2004, and prepare the journal entry to record the revenue recognized in 2004.

AP10–5 **Determining Cash Flow Effects** (P10–7) ■ **LO4**

For each of the following transactions, determine whether cash flows from operating activities will increase, decrease, or remain the same:

a. Purchased merchandise for cash.

b. Paid salaries and wages for the last month of the previous accounting period.

c. Paid PST to the provincial government, based on collections from customers.

d. Borrowed money from the bank. The term of the note is two years.

e. Withheld CPP contributions from employees' paycheques and immediately paid them to the government.

f. Recorded accrued interest expense.

g. Paid cash as a result of losing a lawsuit. A contingent liability associated with the liability had been recorded.

h. Paid salaries and wages for the current month.

i. Performed services for a customer who had paid for them in the previous accounting period.

■ LO8   **AP10–6** **Computing Present and Future Values** (P10–8)

On January 1, 2005, Nader Company completed the following transactions (use a 10-percent annual interest rate for all transactions):

a. Deposited $300,000 in a debt retirement fund. Interest will be computed at six-month intervals and added to the fund at those times (i.e., semi-annual compounding). (*Hint:* Think carefully about *n* and *i*.)

b. Established a plant addition fund of $800,000 to be available at the end of year 10. A single sum that will grow to $800,000 will be deposited on January 1, 2005.

c. Established a pension retirement fund of $600,000 to be available by the end of year 10 by making 10 equal annual deposits at year-end, starting on December 31, 2005.

d. Purchased a $750,000 machine on January 1, 2005, and paid cash, $350,000. A four-year note payable is signed for the balance. The note will be paid in four equal year-end amounts, starting on December 31, 2005.

Required (show computations and round to the nearest dollar):

1. In Transaction (*a*), what will be the balance in the fund at the end of year 5? What is the total amount of interest revenue that will be earned during the first five years?

2. In Transaction (*b*), what amount must the company deposit on January 1, 2005? What is the total amount of interest revenue that will be earned by the end of year 10?

3. In Transaction (*c*), what is the required amount of each of the 10 equal annual deposits? What is the total amount of interest revenue that will be earned over the 10 years?

4. In Transaction (*d*), what is the amount of each of the equal annual payments that will be paid on the note? What is the total amount of interest expense that will be incurred during the four years? Prepare journal entries to record the purchase of the machine and the payments on December 31, 2005 and 2006?

■ LO8   **AP10–7** **Comparing Options Using Present Value Concepts** (P10–9)

After completing a long and successful career as senior vice-president for a large bank, you are preparing for retirement. After visiting the human resources office, you have found that you have several retirement options: (1) you can receive an immediate cash payment of $600,000, (2) you can receive $60,000 per year for life (you have a life expectancy of 20 years), or (3) you can receive $50,000 per year for 10 years and then $70,000 per year for life (this option is intended to give you some protection against inflation). You have determined that you can earn 8 percent compounded annually on your investments. Which option do you prefer and why?

■ LO9   **AP10–8** **Computing Amounts for a Fund with Journal Entries** (P10–10)

On January 1, 2005, Jalopy Company decided to accumulate a fund to build an addition to its plant. The company will deposit $230,000 in the fund at each year-end, starting on December 31, 2005. The fund will earn 9-percent interest, which will be added to the fund balance at each year-end. The fiscal year ends on December 31.

Required:

1. What will be the balance in the fund immediately after the December 31, 2007, deposit?

2. Complete the following fund accumulation schedule:

Date	Cash Payment	Interest Revenue	Increase In Fund	Fund Balance
12/31/2005				
12/31/2006				
12/31/2007				
Total				

3. Prepare adjusting journal entries on December 31 of each of the three years.

4. The plant addition was completed on January 1, 2008, for a total cost of $749,000. Prepare the journal entry, assuming that this amount is paid in full to the contractor.

AP10–9 Computing Equal Periodic Debt Payments and Completing a Schedule with Journal Entries (P10–11)

■ **LO9**

On January 1, 2005, Ontario Company sold a new machine to Canada Company for $80,000. Canada Company made a cash down payment of $20,000 and signed a $60,000, 8-percent note for the balance due. The note is payable in three equal instalments due on December 31, 2005, 2006, and 2007. Each payment includes principal plus interest on the unpaid balance. Canada Company recorded the purchase as follows:

Jan. 1, 2005	Machinery	80,000	
	Cash		20,000
	Note payable		60,000

Required (show computations and round to the nearest dollar):

1. What is the amount of the equal annual payments that Canada Company must make?

2. What is the total interest on the note over the three years?

3. Complete the following debt payment schedule:

Date	Cash Payment	Interest Expense	Decrease in Principal	Unpaid Principal
1/1/2005				
12/31/2005				
12/31/2006				
12/31/2007				
Total				

4. Prepare the journal entries for each of the three payments.

5. Explain why interest expense decreased in amount each year.

AP10–10 (Supplement A) Recording and Reporting Future Income Taxes: Two Temporary Differences (P10–13)

■ **LO1, 6**

The records of Calib Corporation provided the following summarized data for 2005 and 2006:

Year-End December 31		
	2005	2006
Income statement		
Revenues	$210,000	$218,000
Expenses (excluding income tax)	130,000	133,000
Income before income taxes	$ 80,000	$ 85,000

a. Calib is subject to an income tax rate of 35 percent. Assume that 80 percent of the income taxes payable are paid in the current year and 20 percent on February 28 of the next year.

b. The temporary differences resulted from the following:
  (1) The 2006 expenses include an amount of $8,000 that must be deducted only in the 2005 tax return.
  (2) The 2006 revenues include an amount of $6,000 that was taxable only in 2007.

c. The taxable income shown in the tax returns was $72,000 for 2005, and $87,000 for 2006.

Required:

1. For each year compute (a) the income taxes payable and (b) the future income taxes. Identify whether the future income tax amounts are assets or liabilities. Explain.

2. Prepare the journal entry for each year to record income taxes payable, future income taxes, and income tax expense.

3. Show the tax-related amounts that should be reported each year on the income statement and the balance sheet.

4. As a financial analyst, would you evaluate differently a future income tax liability compared with income taxes currently payable?

CASES AND PROJECTS

FINDING AND INTERPRETING FINANCIAL INFORMATION

■ **LO1, 3, 5**   **CP10–1**   **Finding Financial Information**

Van Houtte

Refer to the financial statements of Van Houtte Inc. in Appendix B of this book.

Required:

1. Does Van Houtte report income taxes payable as a separate account at the end of the current year? If not, where would this account be included on Van Houtte's balance sheet?

2. How did changes in accounts payable and accrued liabilities affect cash flows from operating activities in the current year?

3. What is the amount of long-term debt at the end of the current year?

4. What amounts of future income tax assets and liabilities are reported on the balance sheet at the end of the current year?

5. Does the company have a post-retirement or a defined benefit pension program?

■ **LO1, 5**   **CP10–2**   **Finding Financial Information**

The Forzani Group

Refer to the Online Learning Centre Web site at **www.mcgrawhill.ca/college/libby/student/ resources** for the financial statements of The Forzani Group Ltd.

Required:

1. What is the amount of accounts payable and accrued liabilities at the end of the current year?

2. How did changes in accounts payable and accrued liabilities affect cash flows from operating activities in the current year?

3. What is the amount of long-term debt at the end of the current year?

4. Does the company have any contingent liabilities?

■ **LO2, 3**   **CP10–3**   **Comparing Companies within an Industry**

Van Houtte Inc. vs. The Forzani Group

Refer to the Online Learning Centre Web site at **www.mcgrawhill.ca/college/libby/student/ resources** for the financial statements of The Forzani Group Ltd. and to Appendix B of this book for the financial statements of Van Houtte Inc.

Required:

1. Compute the current ratio for each company for each year shown in the financial statements.

2. Compute the accounts payable turnover ratio for each company for each year. What is the amount of long-term debt at the end of the current year? Assume that Van Houtte's cost of sales for the current year is $177,900.

3. Using this information and any other data from the annual report, write a brief assessment of the liquidity of the two companies.

FINANCIAL REPORTING AND ANALYSIS CASES

■ **LO1**   **CP10–4**   **Explaining a Note: Accrued Liability for a Frequent Flyer Program**

Southwest Airlines

Most major airlines have frequent flyer programs that permit passengers to earn free tickets based on the number of reward miles they have flown. A Southwest Airlines annual report contained the following note:

Frequent Flyer Awards

The Company accrues the estimated incremental cost to provide transportation for travel awards when earned under its Company Club frequent flyer program.

The phrase *incremental cost* refers to additional expense associated with an extra passenger taking the flight (e.g., the cost of a soft drink and a snack).

Required:

1. What cost measures other than incremental cost could Southwest use?

2. What account should Southwest debit when it accrues this liability?

CP10–5 **Reporting Short-Term Borrowings**

■ **LO1**

PepsiCo. Inc.

PepsiCo, Inc., engages in a number of activities that are part of our daily lives. Its businesses include Pepsi-Cola, Slice, Mountain Dew, and Fritos. The company's annual revenues exceed $25 billion. A recent PepsiCo annual report contained the following information:

> At the end of the current year, $3.6 billion of short-term borrowings were classified as long term, reflecting PepsiCo's intent and ability to refinance these borrowings on a long-term basis, through either long-term debt issuances or rollover of existing short-term borrowings. The significant amount of short-term borrowings classified as long term, as compared to the end of the previous year when no such amounts were reclassified, primarily reflects the large commercial paper issuances in the current year, but also resulted from a refined analysis of amounts expected to be refinanced beyond one year.

Required:

As an analyst, comment on the company's classification of short-term borrowings as long-term liabilities. What conditions should exist to permit a company to make this type of classification?

CP10–6 **Interpreting the Financial Press**

■ **LO5**

Increasingly, companies are becoming sensitive to environmental issues surrounding their business operations. They recognize that some of their actions can have detrimental impacts on the environment in ways that may not be fully understood for years or even decades. Environmental issues present complex problems for companies that must report contingent liabilities. A related article, Munter, Sacasas, and Garcia, "Accounting and Disclosure of Environmental Contingencies," January 1996, pp. 36–37, 50–52, from the *CPA Journal* (www.cpaj.com) is available on the Web site at **www.mcgrawhill.ca/college/libby/student/resources**. Read the article and prepare a brief memo concerning how companies should report environment issues on their financial statements.

CP10–7 **Computing the Present Value of Lease Obligations**

■ **LO8**

Petro-Canada

The 2004 annual report for Petro-Canada indicated that the company has made the following commitments in relation to non-cancellable operating leases during the next five years:

Years	Minimum Payments (in millions)
2005	122
2006	102
2007	80
2008	68
2009	61

You are a lending officer for a large commercial bank and for comparative purposes want to compute the present values of these leases.

Required:

Determine the present value of the lease payments shown as of December 31, 2004. You may assume an interest rate of 7 percent.

CP10–8 **Interpreting Contingent Liabilities: Litigation**

■ **LO6**

Research In Motion

Research In Motion (RIM) is a leading designer, manufacturer, and marketer of innovative wireless solutions for the worldwide mobile communications market. RIM's products include the BlackBerry wireless platform, software development tools, and software/hardware licensing agreements.

The following excerpt from the company's balance sheet as at February 26, 2005 shows Accrued litigation and related expenses for US$455,610,000. Note 15 to the company's financial statements provides an explanation for the nature of this liability (refer to http://www.rim.com/investors/pdf/2005rim_ar.pdf).

Consolidated Balance Sheets

As at	February 26, 2005	February 28, 2004
	(in thousands of US dollars)	
Liabilities		
Current		
Accounts payable	$ 68,464	$ 35,570
Accrued liabilities (notes 13 and 18(c))	87,133	70,538
Accrued litigation and related expenses (note 15)	455,610	84,392
Income taxes payable (note 9)	3,149	1,684
Deferred revenue	16,235	16,498
Current portion of long-term debt (note 10)	223	193
	630,814	208,875
Long-term debt (note 10)	6,504	6,240
	637,318	215,115

Required:

1. Review note 15 to RIM's financial statements and identify the main reason for the reported liability as well as the specific amounts that the company recorded as liabilities during each of the fiscal years 2003, 2004, and 2005.

2. Search the financial press following the publication of the 2005 annual report and identify any developments related to the litigation in question.

3. Has the amount of this liability changed in subsequent quarterly reports issued by the company? If so, explain the reason for the change.

4. Does the company's annual report include information about other litigation during the past few years? If so, has the company provided an estimate of the liabilities that it may have to pay in the future? Explain.

CRITICAL THINKING CASES

■ **LO1, 2**   **CP10–9** **Making Decisions as a Manager: Liquidity**
In some cases, a manager can engage in transactions that improve the appearance of financial reports without affecting the underlying economic reality. In this chapter, we discussed the importance of liquidity as measured by the current ratio and working capital. For each of the following transactions, (a) determine whether reported liquidity (as measured by the current ratio and working capital) is improved and (b) state whether you believe that the fundamental liquidity of the company has been improved. Assume that the company has positive working capital and a current ratio of 2 immediately prior to each transaction event.

a. Borrowed $1 million from the bank, payable in 90 days.

b. Borrowed $10 million with a long-term note, payable in five years.

c. Reclassified the current portion of long-term debt as long term as a result of a new agreement with the bank that guarantees the company's ability to refinance the debt when it matures.

d. Paid $100,000 of the company's accounts payable.

e. Entered into a borrowing agreement that allows the company to borrow up to $10 million when needed.

f. Required all employees to take accrued vacation to reduce its liability for vacation compensation.

CP10–10 Evaluating an Ethical Dilemma: Managing Reported Results

The president of a regional wholesale distribution company planned to borrow a significant amount of money from a local bank at the beginning of the next fiscal year. He knew that the bank placed a heavy emphasis on the liquidity of potential borrowers. To improve the company's current ratio, the president told his employees to stop shipping new merchandise to customers and to stop accepting merchandise from suppliers for the last three weeks of the fiscal year. Is this behaviour ethical? Would your answer be different if the president had been concerned about reported profits and asked all of the employees to work overtime to ship out merchandise that had been ordered at the end of the year?

CP10–11 Making a Decision as a Financial Analyst: Cash Flows

As a young analyst at a large mutual fund, you have found two companies that meet the basic investment criteria of the fund. One company has a very high current ratio but a relatively low amount of cash flow from operating activities reported on the cash flow statement. The other company has a very low current ratio but very significant cash flows from operating activities. Which company would you tend to prefer?

CP10–12 Making a Decision as an Auditor: Contingent Liabilities

For each of the following situations, determine whether the company should (a) report a liability on the balance sheet, (b) disclose a contingent liability, or (c) not report the situation. Justify and explain your conclusions.

1. An automobile company introduces a new car. Past experience demonstrates that lawsuits will be filed as soon as the new model is involved in any accidents. The company can be certain that at least one jury will award damages to people injured in an accident.

2. A research scientist determines that your company's best-selling product may infringe on another company's patent. If the other company discovers the infringement and files suit, your company could lose millions.

3. As part of land development for a new housing project, your company has polluted a natural lake. Under provincial law, you must clean up the lake once you complete the development. The development project will take five to eight years to complete. Current estimates indicate that it will cost $2 to $3 million to clean up the lake.

4. Your company has just been notified that it lost a product liability lawsuit for $1 million that it plans to appeal. Management is confident that the company will win on appeal, but the lawyers believe that it will lose.

5. A key customer is unhappy with the quality of a major construction project. The company believes that the customer is being unreasonable but, to maintain goodwill, has decided to do $250,000 in repairs next year.

CP10–13 Assessing Contingent Liabilities

If a liability is both likely and subject to reasonable estimate, it must be recorded as a liability on the balance sheet. The *CICA Handbook* has defined *likely* as "the chance of the occurrence (or non-occurrence) of the future event(s) is high." Working in a small group, decide on a specific probability that is appropriate for this standard. (For example, is an 80 percent chance of occurrence likely?) Be prepared to justify your determination.

CP10–14 Evaluating an Ethical Dilemma: Fair Advertising

The New York State Lottery Commission ran the following advertisement in a number of New York newspapers:

> The Lotto jackpot for Wednesday, August 25, 1999, will be $3 million including interest earned over a 20-year payment period. Constant payments will be made each year.

Explain the meaning of this advertisement in your own words. Evaluate the "fairness" of this advertisement. Could anyone be misled? Do you agree that the lottery winner has won $3 million? If not, what amount is more accurate? State any assumptions that you make.

FINANCIAL REPORTING AND ANALYSIS TEAM PROJECT

■ **LO1, 3, 5** **CP10–15**

Team Project: Examining an Annual Report

As a team, select an industry to analyze. Each team member should acquire the annual report for one publicly traded company in the industry, with each member selecting a different company. (Library files, the SEDAR service at www.sedar.com, or the company itself are good sources.) On an individual basis, each team member should then write a short report answering the following questions about the selected company.

1. Review the liabilities for your selected company. What strategy has the company followed with respect to borrowed funds?

2. Compare the individual liability accounts over several years. How have they changed?

3. Does the company have any contingent liabilities? If so, evaluate the risk associated with the contingency or contingencies.

4. Compare the selected company's liabilities to its assets, income, and cash flows. Do you have any concerns?

Discuss any patterns across the companies that you as a team observe. Then, as a team, write a short report comparing and contrasting your companies using these attributes. Provide potential explanations for any differences discovered.

After studying this chapter, you should be able to:

1. Describe the basic characteristics of bonds payable and use the financial leverage ratio. p. 592

2. Report bonds payable and related interest expense, with bonds sold at par, at a discount, and at a premium. p. 598

3. Compute and interpret the times interest earned ratio. p. 605

4. Understand the difference between effective-interest and straight-line amortization. p. 606

5. Report the early retirement of bonds. p. 609

6. Explain how financing activities are reported on the cash flow statement. p. 610

Reporting and Interpreting Bonds

11

P
lacer Dome Inc., with its head office in Vancouver, is one of the world's leading gold producers. In 2004, the company operated 17 mines, employing 13,000 people on five continents. It is principally engaged in exploration for gold, and the acquisition, development, and operation of gold mineral properties. Its major mining operations are located in Canada, the United States, Australia, Papua New Guinea, South Africa, Tanzania, and Chile. In 2004, Placer Dome's mines produced 3.65 million ounces of gold, which is

FOCUS COMPANY:

Placer Dome Inc.

FINANCING GROWTH WITH BOND PAYABLE

used in the fabrication of jewellery. In addition, gold bullion is held by governments as a store of value and safeguard against the collapse of paper assets such as stocks, bonds, and other financial instruments. The company also produces copper, which is used primarily in telecommunications, automobiles, construction, and consumer durables. In 2004, revenues from copper sales accounted for 25 percent of the company's total revenues.

Placer Dome and its competitors spend hundreds of millions of dollars exploring for gold deposits, purchasing properties, and developing mines on those few that are most likely to return a profit. To sustain its profitability and replace depleted gold reserves, the company planned to spend at least $110 million in 2005 on exploration alone. Building a mine, however, costs in excess of $970 million, and to finance this level of exploration and development Placer Dome has issued in excess of $1.1 billion in various types of long-term debt, including $140 million in notes, $700 million in bonds, and $230 million in debentures.

In this chapter, we will examine Placer Dome's issuance of various types of bonds and debentures. We will study the accounting rules that govern the recording of bonds payable, and examine the related financial statement disclosures. We will also examine the reasons for which management raises money through long-term debt, and how the reported debt and supplementary disclosures are used by financial statement analysts to make informed judgments about investment and/or credit risk.

UNDERSTANDING THE BUSINESS

In Chapter 10, we introduced the term *capital structure*, the mix of debt and equity that is used to finance a company's growth. Almost all companies employ some debt in their capital structure. In this chapter, we focus on long-term debt, which simply reflects a contractual obligation whereby the borrower receives cash or other assets in exchange for a promise to pay the lender a fixed or determinable amount of money at a specific date in the future.

The types of long-term debt available to a company of Placer Dome's size are not available to students and professors, or even to small- and medium-sized corporations. Because of its size and the predictability of its revenue, Placer Dome can choose to borrow from a single lender or it can choose to issue debt to many lenders. Single-lender debt is typically in the form of a note or a mortgage note, whereas multiple-lender debt is typically in the form of a debenture or a bond.

The use of long-term debt offers significant advantages to companies such as Placer Dome:

1. Debt does not dilute ownership and control of the company because debtholders participate neither in the management of operations nor in the distribution of accumulated earnings that are eventually distributed to shareholders.

2. Cash payments to the debtholders are limited to the scheduled payments of interest and the repayment of the principal amount of the debt.

3. Interest expense is deductible for tax purposes but dividends paid to shareholders are not. The deductibility of interest for tax purposes reduces the net cost of borrowing, as shown in the following simplified example where net income is calculated under two scenarios: (1) a company that uses 100-percent equity financing ($600,000) and (2) a similar company that uses a mix of 50-percent debt ($300,000) and 50-percent equity ($300,000). Assume that both companies earned $100,000 of income before interest and taxes, that the interest rate on the debt is 10 percent, and that both companies are subject to a tax rate of 40 percent.

	Capital Structure	
	100% Equity	50% Debt 50% Equity
Income before interest and income taxes	$100,000	$100,000
Interest expense	0	30,000
	100,000	70,000
Income tax expense (at 40%)	40,000	28,000
Net income	$ 60,000	$ 42,000
Owners' equity	$600,000	$300,000
Return on equity (Net income/Owners' equity)	10%	14%

FINANCIAL LEVERAGE is the use of borrowed funds to increase the rate of return on owners' equity; it occurs when the interest rate on debt is lower than the rate of return on total assets.

It is evident from this simplified illustration that borrowing reduces net income but the deductibility of interest expense for tax purposes increases the return on the owners' investment. This example also illustrates the use of positive **financial leverage**, whereby a company borrows funds at a specified interest rate and invests them in productive assets. Shareholders benefit from borrowing when the rate of return on assets exceeds the after-tax interest rate on the debt.

However, the issuance of long-term debt has some disadvantages. The primary disadvantage is that the required interest and principal payments must be made at specific dates in the future, whether the corporation earns income or incurs a loss. These payments, which are legally enforceable, increase the financial risk of the company. In contrast, dividends are usually paid to shareholders only if the corporation has generated earnings from its past operations. Each year, some companies go bankrupt because of their inability to make required debt payments to their creditors.[1] Sound business practice requires maintaining an appropriate balance between debt and equity capital.

This chapter provides a basic understanding of the management, accounting, and financing issues associated with bonds. We will refer to the bonds reported on Placer Dome's balance sheet at December 31, 2004, and related note disclosures in order to illustrate the accounting for and the reporting of bonds payable. We also show how readers can use this information to analyze and assess the financial health of Placer Dome. Exhibit 11.1 shows note 14 of Placer Dome's financial statements. It discloses information concerning the company's long-term debt.

EXHIBIT **11.1**
Long-Term Debt

REAL WORLD EXCERPT
Placer Dome Inc.
ANNUAL REPORT

14. Debt

(a) Consolidated long-term debt and capital leases comprise the following:

December 31	2004	2003
Placer Dome Inc.		
Bonds, unsecured (vii)		
June 15, 2007 at 7.125% per annum	$ 100	$ 100
June 15, 2015 at 7.75% per annum	100	100
March 3, 2033 at 6.375% per annum(i)	200	200
October 15, 2035 at 6.45% per annum(ii)	300	300
Preferred Securities unsecured(iii)(viii)		
Series B, December 31, 2045 at 8.5% per annum	77	77
Medium-term notes, unsecured(iv)	140	140
Senior Convertible Debentures, unsecured,		
October 15, 2023 at 2.75%(ii)	230	230
East African Gold, non-recourse (note 3(b))(v)	—	36
Capital leases(vi)	7	6
	1,154	1,189
Current portion	(45)	(10)
	$1,109	$1,179

(i) On March 3, 2003, Placer Dome completed a private placement of $200 million 30 year debentures. The debentures carry an interest rate of 6.375%. The Corporation has prepared and filed registration documentation that permits the debentures to be resold to the public.

(ii) On October 10, 2003, Placer Dome completed two private debenture offerings totaling $530 million in aggregate principal amount. Of the aggregate principal amounts, $300 million was raised as unsecured 32-year senior debentures with interest payable at a rate of 6.45% per year. An additional $230 million was raised as unsecured 20-year senior convertible debentures with interest payable at 2.75% per year. Upon occurrence of certain prescribed conditions, holders of the convertible debentures will have the right to convert each $1,000 principal amount into 47.7897 common shares of Placer Dome, representing a conversion price of $20.925 per common share. As at December 31, 2004, none of these prescribed conditions had occurred....

(continued)

---

[1]Recent examples include Enron Corp. and WorldCom Inc., which received extensive coverage in the financial press because they used aggressive accounting methods and stretched the interpretation and application of GAAP to hide their poor financial performances. These companies were unable to repay sizeable amounts of debt to their creditors and could not overcome their financial difficulties, which led to their inevitable collapse.

EXHIBIT **11.1**

(Continued)

(iii) Series B Preferred Securities are redeemable by the Corporation, in whole or in part, on or after December 17, 2006, respectively, at the principal amount plus accrued and unpaid interest to the date of redemption (hereafter referred to as the "Maturity Amount"). The Corporation may, at its option, pay the Maturity Amount by delivering Common Shares, in which event the holder of the securities shall be entitled to receive a cash payment equal to the Maturity Amount from proceeds of the sale of the Common Shares on behalf of the holder. Holders of the securities are not entitled to receive any Common Shares in satisfaction of the obligation to pay the Maturity Amount.

(iv) The interest rates range from 6.6% to 8.1% and the notes mature between 2005 and 2026.

(v) This loan relates to project financing for the North Mara mine and was non-recourse to Placer Dome. It bore interest at LIBOR plus 2.75% and was repayable over 5 years. This was repaid on July 29, 2004.

(vi) The Corporation is obligated under capital leases for mobile mining equipment for remaining terms ranging from two to four years. All capital lease agreements provide that the Corporation can purchase the leased equipment at fair value at the end of the lease term. At December 31, 2004 and 2003, $6 million and $4 million, respectively, of leased property was included in plant and equipment, net of $3 million and $11 million, respectively, of accumulated depreciation and depletion.

(vii) Anticipated requirements to meet long-term debt and capital lease repayments over the next five years from December 31, 2004 are as follows:

	Long-term debt	Capital leases	Total
2005	$43	$2	$45
2006	—	2	2
2007	100	2	102
2008	—	2	2
2009	16	—	16
Thereafter	988	—	988
Long-term debt and capital lease obligations	1,147	8	1,155
Less amount representing interest	—	(1)	(1)
	$1,147	$7	$1,154

(viii) On January 31, 2003, Placer Dome repaid, from cash, the $137 million of unsecured debt assumed in the purchase of AurionGold.
On April 24, 2003, Placer Dome redeemed, for cash, all of the Corporation's outstanding $185 million 8.625% Series A Preferred Securities. A loss of $5 million was recorded on redemption.
On May 15, 2003, Placer Dome, as scheduled, repaid $200 million of 7.125% unsecured bonds.

ORGANIZATION OF THE CHAPTER

• **Characteristics of Bonds Payable**	• **Reporting Bond Transactions**	• **Additional Topics**
Players in the Bond Market	Bonds Issued at Par	Effective-Interest Amortization
Financial Leverage Ratio	Bonds Issued at a Discount	Early Retirement of Debt
	Bonds Issued at a Premium	Financing Activities on the Cash Flow Statement
	Times Interest Earned Ratio	

CHARACTERISTICS OF BONDS PAYABLE

LEARNING OBJECTIVE 1

Describe the basic characteristics of bonds payable and use the financial leverage ratio.

A bond usually requires the payment of interest over its life, with the repayment of principal on the maturity date. The **bond principal** is (1) the amount payable at the maturity date and (2) the basis for computing periodic cash interest payments. The principal also is called the **par value, face amount,** and *maturity value.* All bonds have a par value, which is the amount that will be paid when the bond matures. For most bonds the par value is $1,000, but it can be any amount.

A bond always specifies a **stated rate** of interest and the timing of periodic cash interest payments, usually annually or semi-annually. Each periodic interest payment is equal to the principal times the stated interest rate. The selling price of a bond does not affect the periodic cash payment of interest. For example, a $1,000, 8-percent bond always pays cash interest of (1) $80 on an annual basis or (2) $40 on a semi-annual basis.

Different types of bonds have different characteristics for good economic reasons. Different types of creditors have different types of risk-and-return preferences. A retired person, for example, may be willing to receive a lower interest rate in return for having more security. This type of creditor might want a mortgage bond that pledges a specific asset as security if the company is unable to repay the bond. Another creditor might be willing to accept a low interest rate and an unsecured status if the company provides the opportunity to convert the bond into common shares at some point in the future. A bond that is not secured with the pledge of a specific asset is called a **debenture**. Companies try to design bond features that are attractive to different groups of creditors, just as automobile manufacturers try to design cars that appeal to different groups of consumers. Some key types of bonds are shown below.

The **BOND PRINCIPAL** is the amount payable at the maturity of the bond. It is also the basis for computing periodic cash interest payments.

PAR VALUE and **FACE AMOUNT** are other names for bond principal or the maturity amount of a bond.

The **STATED RATE** is the rate of cash interest per period specified in the bond contract.

A **DEBENTURE** is an unsecured bond; no assets are specifically pledged to guarantee repayment.

Unsecured bond
(or debenture) → No assets are pledged as a guarantee of repayment at maturity.

Secured bond → Specific assets are pledged as a guarantee of repayment at maturity.

Term bond → Principal is payable in full at a single specified maturity date in the future.

Serial bond → Principal is payable in instalments on a series of specified maturity dates in the future.

Callable bond → Bond may be called for early retirement by the issuer.

Convertible bond → Bond may be converted to common shares of the issuer.

Companies like Placer Dome often need to undertake massive mining projects to explore for and produce gold. One possibility is for Placer Dome to finance the project by issuing bonds that are secured by the assets that will be in place once the project is finished. Another possibility is to issue bonds secured by the amount of revenues expected from the completed project. The company could also issue debentures that are unsecured, depending on how much risk the debenture holders are willing to take.

An **INDENTURE** is a bond contract that specifies the legal provisions of a bond issue.

When a company decides to issue new bonds, it prepares a bond **indenture** (bond contract) that specifies the legal provisions of the bonds. These provisions include the maturity date, rate of interest to be paid, date of each interest payment, and any conversion privileges. The indenture also contains covenants designed to protect the creditors. These include limitations on new debt that the company might issue in the future, limitations on the payment of dividends, and required minimum levels of certain accounting ratios, such as the current ratio. Managers prefer covenants that are least restrictive because they may limit the company's future actions. Creditors, however, prefer more restrictive covenants that reduce the risk of losing their investment. As with any business transaction, the final result is achieved through a process of negotiation. Bond covenants are usually reported in the notes to the financial statements.

Placer Dome disclosed the following information in Note 14 to its financial statements:

REAL WORLD EXCERPT

Placer Dome Inc.

ANNUAL REPORT

Notes to the Consolidated Financial Statements

14. Debt

....

(e) Certain of Placer Dome's debt facilities contain various common public debt covenants and default provisions including payment defaults, limitation on liens, limitation on sale and leaseback transactions and merger restrictions. These debt instruments include the Corporation's unsecured Bonds, Preferred Securities, Medium-Term Notes, Senior Convertible Debentures, and bank lines of credit. In addition, Placer Dome's metal and foreign currency contracts and options (note 17) require it to maintain a consolidated tangible net worth of $1.0 billion.

As at December 31, 2004, Placer Dome was in compliance with all debt covenants and default provisions.

The bond issuer also prepares a *prospectus*, which is a legal document that is given to potential buyers of the bonds. The prospectus describes the company, the bond, and how the proceeds of the bonds will be used. For example, in April 2004, Placer Dome filed a prospectus with the securities commissions offering to exchange an aggregate principal amount of up to US$300 million of 6.45-percent debentures due October 15, 2035 for the same aggregate principal amount of the 6.45-percent debentures that are referred to in Exhibit 11.1, item (a)(ii).[2] These debentures were sold initially to private U.S. investors along with another offering of US$200 million of unsecured senior convertible debentures. The company intended to use the net proceeds from these debentures to refinance costs associated with the July 2003 acquisition of East African Gold Mines, and the associated capital for expansion of the North Mara mine. Remaining proceeds were to be used to fund capital expenditures and development projects, and for general corporate purposes.

A **BOND CERTIFICATE** is the bond document that each bondholder receives.

When a bond is issued, the investor receives a **bond certificate**. All of the bond certificates for a single bond issue are identical. The face of each certificate shows the same maturity date, interest rate, interest dates, and other provisions. An independent party, called the **trustee**, is usually appointed to represent the bondholders. A trustee's duties are to ascertain whether the issuing company fulfils all of the provisions of the bond indenture.

A **TRUSTEE** is an independent party appointed to represent the bondholders.

As mentioned earlier, each bond issue has characteristics that are specified in the bond indenture. The issuing company often adds special characteristics to a bond to make it more attractive to investors, who normally have a large number of investment alternatives from which to select.

---

[2]A copy of this prospectus is available on the SEDAR system (www.sedar.com). Access the Web site, search for Placer Dome Inc. under the letter P, view the documents filed by the company, and select Final short-form prospectus – English, dated April 14, 2004.

Bonds sometimes offer different features with respect to early retirement:

Redeemable (callable) bonds may be called for early retirement at the option of the issuer.

Retractable bonds may be turned in for early retirement at the option of the bondholder.

Convertible bonds may be converted to other securities of the issuer (usually common shares) at the option of the bondholder. For example, Exhibit 11.1, item (a)(ii) shows that, under specific conditions, holders of Placer Dome's convertible debenture will have the right to convert each $1,000 principal amount into 47.7897 common shares of the company. The converted debt would be equivalent in value to the common shares if the share price is $20.925. At the time of writing this text, the share price was $15.22, so it would not have been advantageous to debenture holders to convert the debentures even if the specific condition were met.[3]

These features are normally present for debt issues that are marketable. Of 136 companies that reported marketable debt in their 2003 annual reports, 64 companies disclosed details of the redemption features and 41 companies provided details of the conversion features of their bonds.[4]

Bonds also differ in terms of their status in relationship to other debt:

Senior debt receives preference over other debt in the event of bankruptcy or default.

Subordinated debt is paid off after payment is made to some other group of creditors. Obviously, subordinated debt is riskier than senior debt.

Each year, corporations introduce new features that are included with their bonds. For example, The Walt Disney Company issued the first bond with a 100-year maturity. Despite an increase in unusual features, the basics that we discuss in this chapter permit you to understand most types of bonds.

PLAYERS IN THE BOND MARKET

Most companies work with an underwriter, who either buys the entire issue of bonds and then resells them to individual creditors (called a *firm commitment underwriter*), or simply sells the bonds or notes without any obligation to purchase them (called a *best efforts underwriter*). It is not uncommon for companies to use several underwriters to sell a large bond issue. For example, Placer Dome deals with underwriters like CIBC World Markets Inc., Scotia Capital Inc., HSBC Securities (Canada) Inc., Merrill Lynch Canada Inc., and BMO Nesbitt Burns Inc.

Bonds dealers sell bonds typically to institutional investors such as banks, insurance companies, and mutual and pension funds. They also create a secondary market for bonds by trading them for their own account in response to supply and demand by institutional investors. Almost all trades occur by telephone, known as an over the counter (OTC) market, not through a formal bond exchange. The market in bonds exceeds by far the value of stocks traded on a typical day because of the high value of each trade. A bond trade of $200 million would not be unusual in this market.[5]

Because of the complexities associated with bonds, several agencies exist to evaluate the probability that a bond issuer will not be able to meet the requirements

REDEEMABLE (CALLABLE) BONDS may be called for early retirement at the option of the issuer.

RETRACTABLE BONDS may be turned in for early retirement at the option of the bondholder.

CONVERTIBLE BONDS may be converted to other securities of the issuer (usually common shares).

---

[3]If all the convertible debentures are converted into shares, then the company will have to issue a total of 10,991,631 shares ($230 million × 47.7897). These additional shares will increase the total number of shares outstanding and cause a dilution (or reduction) of the company's earnings per share. Even if the debentures are not converted into shares, the disclosed information informs the reader of the potential dilution to the existing number of common shares, and helps them estimate the potential dilution in earnings per share.

[4]C. Byrd, I. Chen, and J. Smith, *Financial Reporting in Canada 2004*. Toronto: Canadian Institute of Chartered Accountants, 2004, p. 304.

[5]Further details about the bond market are available at http://www.investinginbonds.com.

specified in the indenture. This risk is called *default risk*. In general, the higher the risk of default, the higher will be the interest rate required to successfully persuade investors to purchase the bond and the more restrictive will be the covenants protecting the bondholder. Dominion Bond Rating Service (DBRS), Fitch Investor Service, Moody's, and Standard and Poor's (S&P) each assess the default risk for every issue of corporate debentures and bonds.[6] Their ratings range from investment grade to extremely speculative junk bonds. If it becomes apparent that there has been a change in default risk for any debt already issued, each rating service will issue a public bulletin that upgrades or downgrades the credit rating, along with reasons for the change.[7]

Companies such as Placer Dome and Barrick Gold Corporation, which rely on bonds to expand their operations, will often publish the various debt ratings in their annual reports.

Credit rating

Credit ratings at December 31, 2004, from major rating agencies

Standard and Poor's	A
Moody's	Baa1
DBRS	A

Our ability to access unsecured debt markets and the related cost of debt financing is, in part, dependent upon maintaining an acceptable credit rating. A deterioration in our credit rating would not adversely affect existing debt securities or the terms of gold sales contracts, but could impact funding costs for any new debt financing. The key factors that are important to our credit rating include the following: our market capitalization; the strength of our balance sheet, including the amount of net debt and our debt-to-equity ratio; our net cash flow, including cash generated by operating activities and expected capital expenditure requirements; the quantity of our gold reserves; and our geo-political risk profile.

Bond prices change for two main reasons: the creditworthiness of the bond issuer and changes in interest rates. The company's creditworthiness depends on the operating, investing and financing decisions made by management. However, interest rates are not within the control of corporations. They are rather controlled by governments. The most important interest rate is the rate at which the federal government can borrow money for the long term. This is the benchmark, risk-free rate of return on bonds because purchasers believe that the federal government will never fail to repay, or default on its debts. The interest rates of all other debt instruments are established relative to this risk-free rate. The difference between the interest rate on other bonds and the risk-free rate is called the spread. The size of the spread depends upon the perceived additional risk that the company will default on either its interest or principal payments on the bonds.

---

[6]Standard & Poor's (S&P) acquired Canadian Bond Rating Service in October of 2000. S&P has a useful Web site at http://www.standardandpoors.com for those interested in learning about the credit ratings used by Standard & Poor's.

[7]The details of how default risk is rated vary slightly from one agency to another. You can view a sample of these descriptions in detail at http://www.dbrs.com.

KEY **RATIO ANALYSIS:**

FINANCIAL LEVERAGE RATIO

ANALYTICAL QUESTION → How is management using debt to increase the amount of assets the company employs to earn income for shareholders?

RATIO AND COMPARISONS → The financial leverage ratio is useful in addressing this issue. It is computed as follows:

$$\text{Financial Leverage Ratio} = \frac{\text{Average Total Assets}}{\text{Average Shareholders' Equity}}$$

The 2004 ratio for Placer Dome is:

$$\frac{(\$4{,}585 + \$5{,}544)/2}{(\$2{,}399 + \$3{,}154)/2} = 1.82$$

Comparisons over Time			Comparisons with Competitors	
Placer Dome			**Barrick Gold Corporation**	**Newmont Mining Corporation**
2002	2003	2004	2004	2004
1.89	1.84	1.82	1.60	1.55

INTERPRETATIONS

In General → The financial leverage ratio measures the relationship between total assets and the shareholders' equity that finances the assets. As noted, companies finance their assets with shareholders' equity and debt. The higher the proportion of assets financed by debt, the higher the financial leverage ratio. Conversely, the higher the proportion of assets financed with shareholders' equity, the lower the ratio. Increasing debt (and the leverage ratio) increases the amount of assets the company employs to earn income for shareholders, which increases the chances of earning higher income. However, it also increases *risk*. Debt financing is riskier than financing with shareholders' equity because the interest payments on debt must be made every period (they are legal obligations), whereas dividends on shares can be postponed. An increasing ratio over time signals more reliance on debt financing and more risk.

Creditors and security analysts use this ratio to assess a company's risk level, while managers use the ratio in deciding whether to expand by adding debt. As long as the interest on borrowing is less than the additional earnings generated, utilizing debt will enhance the shareholders' earnings.

Focus Company Analysis → Placer Dome's financial leverage has been relatively stable over the three-year period 2002–2004. For every $1 of equity, the company had $0.82 of debt during 2004. The company's financial leverage for 2004 is higher than those of its competitors. This suggests that Placer Dome is following a slightly riskier (less conservative) financing strategy than are other companies in the gold-mining industry. Placer Dome's use of debt has been beneficial to its shareholders as the company's return on equity for both 2003 and 2004 reached 10 percent, exceeding the return on equity achieved by its competitors.

A Few Cautions → A financial leverage ratio near 1:1 indicates a company that is choosing not to utilize debt to expand. This suggests the company has lower risk but is not enhancing the return to shareholders. When comparing competitors, the ratio may be influenced by differences in business strategies, such as whether the company rents or buys facilities.

SELECTED FOCUS COMPANY LEVERAGE RATIOS

WestJet Airlines	2.41
Gildan Activewear	1.72
Intrawest Corp.	3.37

REPORTING BOND TRANSACTIONS

■ **LEARNING OBJECTIVE 2**

Report bonds payable and related interest expense, with bonds sold at par, at a discount, and at a premium.

Exhibit 11.1 shows that Placer Dome has issued unsecured bonds for a total face value of $930 million as at December 31, 2004. Each bond indenture specifies two types of cash payments:

1. *Principal.* This is usually a single payment made when the bond matures. It is also called the *par,* or *face, value.*

2. *Cash interest payments.* These payments represent an annuity and are computed by multiplying the principal amount times the interest rate, called the *contract, stated,* or **coupon rate** of interest stated in the bond contract. The bond contract specifies whether these payments are made quarterly, semi-annually, or annually.

The **COUPON RATE** is the stated rate of interest on bonds.

Neither the company nor the underwriter determines the price at which the bonds sell. Instead, the market determines the price using the present value concepts that were introduced in the previous chapter. To determine the present value of the bond, you compute the present value of the principal (a single payment) and the present value of the interest payments (an annuity) and add the two amounts.

Creditors demand a certain rate of interest to compensate them for the risks related to bonds, called the **market interest rate** (also known as the **yield**, or **effective-interest rate**). Because the market rate is the interest rate on a debt when it is incurred, it should be used in computing the present value of the bond.

MARKET INTEREST RATE is the current rate of interest on a debt when incurred; also called the **YIELD**, or **EFFECTIVE-INTEREST RATE**.

The present value of a bond may be the same as par, above par (**bond premium**), or below par (**bond discount**). If the stated and the market interest rates are the same, a bond sells at par. If a bond pays a stated interest rate that is lower than the market rate that creditors demand, they will not buy it unless its price is reduced (i.e., a discount must be provided). If a bond pays a stated rate that is higher than the market rate that creditors demand, they will be willing to pay a premium to buy it.

BOND PREMIUM is the difference between the selling price and par when the bond is sold for more than par.

This relationship can be shown graphically as follows:[8]

BOND DISCOUNT is the difference between the selling price and par when the bond is sold for less than par.

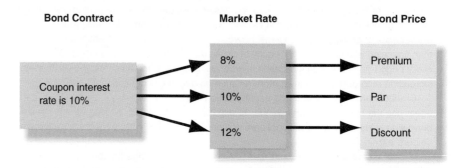

Basically, corporations and creditors are indifferent to whether a bond is issued at par, at a discount, or at a premium because bonds are always priced to provide the market rate of interest. To illustrate, consider a corporation that issues three separate bonds on the same day. The bonds are exactly the same except that one has a stated interest rate of 6 percent, another 7 percent, and a third 8 percent. If the market rate of interest was 7 percent, the first would be issued at a discount, the second at par, and the third at a premium, but a creditor who bought any one of the bonds would earn the market interest rate of 7 percent.

---

[8]The difference between the coupon interest rate and the market interest rate is often very small, usually a fraction of 1 percent, when the bonds are sold. Companies try to sell their bonds at prices close to their par value. However, the market rate of interest continually changes as a result of such factors as inflation expectations and the level of business activity. It is therefore virtually impossible to issue a bond at a point when the coupon rate and the market rate are exactly the same.

PLACER DOME INC.

$100,000 Bonds

7% Interest
payable June 30 and December 31

Due on December 31, 2014

Issued: January 1, 2005

7%
Sells at
par
$100,000

Market Rate?

6%
Sells at a
premium
$107,441

8%
Sells at a
discount
$92,206

FINANCIAL **ANALYSIS**

BOND INFORMATION FROM THE BUSINESS PRESS

Bond prices are reported each day in the business press based on transactions that occurred in the market on the previous trading day. The following is typical of the information that you will find:

| Bond | Coupon | Mat. Date | September 9, 2004 | | July 23, 2005 | |
			Bid $	Yld	Bid $	Yld
Bell	6.10	Mar. 16/35	95.51	6.44	106.34	5.66
Domtar	10.00	Apr. 15/11	123.23	5.71	121.41	5.67
Royal Bank	5.45	Nov. 14/13	101.40	5.25	108.22	4.26

The highlighted listing means that Bell's bond has a coupon rate of 6.10 percent and will mature on March 16, 2035. The bond's yield was 6.44 percent on September 9, 2004, and its price was 95.51 percent of its par value, or $955.10. Market conditions caused the yield to decrease to 5.66 percent by July 23, 2005, but notice that the coupon rate remains fixed at 6.10 percent. As the yield decreased relative to the fixed coupon rate, the price increased from $95.51 on September 9, 2004, to $106.34 on July 23, 2005, which illustrates the inverse relationship between the yield and the bond price.

Bell's bond sold on September 9, 2004, at a discount because the market rate demanded by buyers is higher than the coupon rate offered by the company. By comparison, Domtar's bond sold at a premium of 23.23 percent of its face value on the same date because it offers a 10-percent coupon rate that exceeded by far the market interest rate of 5.71 percent.

Although analysts may study the daily price changes of bonds, remember that these changes do not affect the company's financial statements. For financial reporting purposes, the company uses the interest rates that existed when the bonds were first sold to the public in conformity with the historical cost principle. Subsequent changes do not affect the company's accounting for the bonds.

SELF-STUDY **QUIZ 11-1**

Your study of bonds will be easier if you understand the terminology that has been introduced in this chapter. Let us review some of those terms. Define the following:

1. Market interest rate. Identify synonyms for *market interest rate*.
2. Coupon interest rate. Identify synonyms for *coupon interest rate*.
3. Bond discount.
4. Bond premium.

After you complete your work, check your answers with the solution on page 613.

BONDS ISSUED AT PAR

Bonds sell at their par value when buyers are willing to invest in them at the interest rate stated on the bond. To illustrate, let us assume that on January 1, 2005, Placer Dome issued 10-percent bonds with a par value of $400,000 and received $400,000 in cash (which means that the bonds sold at par). The bonds were dated to start interest on January 1, 2005, and will pay interest each June 30 and December 31. The bonds mature in 10 years on December 31, 2014.

The amount of money a corporation receives when it sells bonds is the present value of the future cash flows associated with them. When Placer Dome issued its bonds, it agreed to make two types of payments in the future: a single payment of $400,000 when the bond matures in 10 years and an annuity of $20,000 payable twice each year for 10 years. The bond payments can be shown graphically as follows:

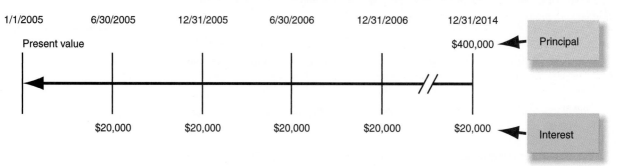

The present value of the bond payments can be computed with the tables contained in Appendix A using the factor for 20 periods and an interest rate of 5 percent (10 percent ÷ 2):

	Present Value
a. Single payment: $400,000 × 0.3769	$150,760
b. Annuity: $20,000 × 12.4622	249,240*
Issue price of Placer bonds	$400,000

*Rounded.

If the effective rate of interest equals the stated rate of interest, the present value of the future cash flows associated with a bond always equals the bond's par value. Remember that a bond's selling price is determined by the present value of its future cash flows, not the par value. On the date of issue, bond liabilities are recorded at the present value of future cash flows as follows:

Cash (A)	400,000	
Bonds payable (L)		400,000

Assets		=	Liabilities		+	Shareholders' Equity
Cash	+400,000		Bonds payable	+400,000		

Reporting Interest Expense on Bonds Issued at Par The creditors who bought the bonds did so with the expectation that they would earn interest over the life of the bond. Placer Dome will pay interest at 5 percent (i.e., 10 percent per year) on the par value of the bonds each June 30 and December 31 until the bond's maturity date. The amount of interest each period will be $20,000 (5% × $400,000). The entry to record the interest payments follows:

Bond interest expense (E)	20,000	
Cash (A)		20,000

Assets	=	Liabilities	+	Shareholders' Equity
Cash −20,000				Interest expense −20,000

Bond interest payment dates rarely coincide with the last day of a company's fiscal year. Under the matching concept, interest expense that has been incurred but not paid must be accrued with an adjusting entry. If Placer Dome's fiscal year ended on May 31, the company would accrue interest for five months and record interest expense and interest payable.

Notice in the preceding journal entry that interest expense and cash interest paid are the same amount. This is the case when the effective interest rate and the stated rate are the same. When bonds are sold at a discount or a premium, this is not the case, as shown below.

BONDS ISSUED AT A DISCOUNT

Bonds sell at a discount when the market rate of interest demanded by the buyers is higher than the stated interest rate offered by the issuer. Assume that the market rate of interest was 12 percent when Placer Dome sold its bonds (which have a par value of $400,000). The bonds have a stated rate of 10 percent, payable semi-annually, which is less than the market rate on that date. Therefore, the bonds sold at a discount.

To compute the issue price of the bonds, we need to compute the present value of the future cash flows specified on the bond. As in the previous example, the number of periods is 20, but we must use an interest rate of 6 percent (12 percent ÷ 2), which is the market rate of interest. Thus, the issue price of Placer Dome's bonds is computed as follows:

	Present Value
a. Principal: $400,000 × 0.3118	$124,720
b. Interest: $20,000 × 11.4699	229,398
Issue (sale) price of Placer Dome's bonds	$354,118*

*Discount: $400,000 − $354,118 = $45,882.

The price of the bonds issued by Placer Dome is $354,118. Some people refer to this price as 88.5, which means that the bonds were sold at 88.5 percent of their par value ($354,118 ÷ $400,000).

When a bond is sold at a discount, the Bonds Payable account is credited for the par value, and the discount is recorded as a debit to Discount on Bonds Payable. The issuance of Placer Dome's bonds at a discount is recorded as follows:

Cash (A)	354,118	
Discount on bonds payable (XL)	45,882	
Bonds payable (L)		400,000

Assets	=	Liabilities	+	Shareholders' Equity
Cash +354,118		Bonds payable +400,000		
		Discount on bonds		
		payable −45,882		

Note that the discount is recorded in a separate contra-liability account (Discount on Bonds Payable) as a debit. The balance sheet reports the bonds payable at their book value, which is their maturity amount less any unamortized discount. Placer Dome, like most companies, does not separately disclose the amount of unamortized discount (or premium) when the amount is small relative to other balance sheet amounts.

The following excerpt from the financial statements of Teck Cominco Limited for 2003 provides an example of the reporting of debt issued at a discount. Note that the convertible debenture pays interest at the rate of 3.75 percent but its yield was 6 percent at the date of issuance.

REAL WORLD EXCERPT

*Teck Cominco
Limited*

ANNUAL REPORT

6. LONG-TERM DEBT

	2003	2002
	($ in millions)	
Convertible debenture due 2006 (a)	$202	$241
6.875% debenture due February 2006 (US$150 million)	194	237
7% debenture due September 2012 (US$200 million)	255	312

(a) In 1994 the company received net proceeds of $186 million on the issue of US$137 million deep discount convertible subordinated debentures, with a stated amount of US$170 million, due in 2006. The debentures bear interest on the issue price at 6% per annum, computed on a semi-annual basis. The cash interest payment is 3.75% of the stated value, with the balance deferred to maturity in 2006. Conversion is at the option of the holder at any time on or prior to maturity into Class B Subordinate Voting Shares at a conversion rate of 46.551 shares per US$1,000 of stated amount at maturity. The debentures are redeemable at any time at the option of the company. In December 2001, the company entered into interest rate swaps with respect to US$100 million of this debt. The 3.75% cash portion of the interest rate has been exchanged for a floating interest rate of LIBOR less 1.0%.

Reporting Interest Expense on Bonds Issued at a Discount   During the 10-year term of the bonds, Placer Dome must make 20 semi-annual cash interest payments of $20,000 (i.e., $400,000 × 5%) and pay the $400,000 principal at the maturity date. Therefore, in addition to the cash interest, Placer Dome must repay more money than it received when it sold the bonds (i.e., it borrowed $354,118 but must repay $400,000). This extra cash that must be paid is an adjustment to the interest payments to ensure that creditors earn the market rate of interest on the bonds. To compute the interest expense, the bond discount must be apportioned (*amortized*) to each semi-annual interest period and be added to the interest payment.

The bond discount can be allocated over the life of the bond using two amortization methods: (1) straight line and (2) effective interest. Because straight-line amortization is easy to compute, we will discuss it first. The effective-interest method is discussed later in this chapter.

Straight-Line Amortization   To amortize the $45,882 bond discount over the life of Placer Dome's bonds using **straight-line amortization**, an equal dollar amount is allocated to each interest period. Placer Dome's bonds have 20 six-month interest periods. Therefore, the amount amortized on each semi-annual interest date is $2,294 ($45,882 ÷ 20 periods). This amount is added to the interest paid ($20,000) to compute interest expense for the period ($22,294). The interest payments on Placer Dome's bonds each period are as follows:

STRAIGHT-LINE AMORTIZATION of a bond discount or premium is a simplified method that allocates an equal dollar amount to each interest period.

Bond interest expense (E)	22,294	
Discount on bonds payable (XL)		2,294
Cash (A)		20,000

Assets		=	Liabilities		+	Shareholders' Equity	
Cash	−20,000		Discount on bonds payable	+2,294		Bond interest expense	−22,294

Bonds payable are reported on the balance sheet at their *book value*; that is, the maturity amount less any unamortized bond discount (or plus any unamortized bond premium). Therefore, on June 30, 2005, the book value of Placer Dome's bonds is $356,412 ($354,118 + $2,294).

$$\textbf{Book Value of Bonds} = \frac{\textbf{Maturity Amount}}{\textbf{(or Face Value)}} - \frac{\textbf{Unamortized Bond Discount}}{\textbf{(+ Unamortized Bond Premium)}}$$

In each interest period, the unamortized discount decreases by $2,294; therefore, the book value of the bonds increases by $2,294 each interest period. At the maturity date of the bonds, the unamortized discount (i.e., the balance in the Discount on Bonds Payable account) is *zero*. At that time, the maturity amount of the bonds and the book value are the same (i.e., $400,000).

A note from an annual report for Ames Department Stores effectively summarizes our discussion of this point:

Debt

Debt obligations that carried face interest rates significantly less than market were discounted to their present values using estimated market rates. The discount amount will be amortized to interest expense over the term of the related obligation. The determination of appropriate interest rates was based upon evaluation of Ames' credit standing, the nature of the collateral, if any, and other terms pertaining to the debt, and the prevailing rates for similar instruments or issues with similar credit rating.

Bonds are recorded at the present value of their future cash flows using an interest rate determined by the market on the date the bonds were sold. The accounting for the bonds is not affected by subsequent changes in the market rate of interest. This interest rate is based on the terms of the debt issue and the risk characteristics of the debt.[9]

BONDS ISSUED AT A PREMIUM

Bonds sell at a premium when the market rate of interest is *lower* than the stated interest rate. Assume that the market rate of interest was 8 percent while Placer Dome's bonds paid interest of 10 percent. In this case, the bonds sell at a premium. The issue price for Placer Dome's bonds is computed as follows:

	Present Value
a. Principal: $400,000 × 0.4564	$182,560
b. Interest: $20,000 × 13.5903	271,806
Issue (sale) price of Placer Dome's bonds	$454,366

---

[9]While most companies issue bonds that pay interest on a semi-annual basis, certain bond issues do not pay interest on a regular basis. These bonds are often called *zero coupon bonds* because the coupon interest rate is zero. Why would an investor buy a bond that does not pay interest? Our discussion of bond discounts has probably given you a good idea of the right answer. The coupon interest rate on a bond can be virtually any amount and the price of the bond will be adjusted so that investors earn the market rate of interest. A bond with a zero coupon interest rate is a *deep discount bond* that will sell for substantially less than its maturity value.

When a bond is sold at a premium, the Bonds Payable account is credited for the par value, and the premium is recorded as a credit to Premium on Bonds Payable, an adjunct-liability account. The issuance of Placer Dome's bonds at a premium is recorded as follows:

Cash (A)	454,366	
Premium on bonds payable (L)		54,366
Bonds payable (L)		400,000

Assets	=	Liabilities	+	Shareholders' Equity
Cash +454,366		Premium on bonds payable +54,366		
		Bonds payable +400,000		

The book value of the bond is the sum of the two accounts, Premium on Bonds Payable and Bonds Payable, or $454,366.

Reporting Interest Expense on Bonds Issued at a Premium   The premium of $54,366 recorded by Placer Dome must be apportioned to each of the 20 interest periods. Using the straight-line method, the premium that is amortized in each semi-annual interest period is $2,718 ($54,366 ÷ 20 periods). This amount is subtracted from the interest payment ($20,000) to calculate the interest expense ($17,282). Therefore, amortization of the bond premium decreases interest expense. The payment of interest on the bonds is recorded as follows:

Bond interest expense (E)	17,282	
Premium on bonds payable (L)	2,718	
Cash (A)		20,000

Assets	=	Liabilities	+	Shareholders' Equity
Cash −20,000		Premium on bonds payable −2,718		Bond interest expense −17,282

Notice that the $20,000 cash paid each period includes $17,282 interest expense and $2,718 premium amortization. Thus, the cash payment to the investors includes the current interest they have earned plus a return of part of the premium they paid when they bought the bonds.

The book value of the bonds is the amount in the Bonds Payable account plus any unamortized premium. On June 30, 2005, the book value of the bonds is $451,648 ($400,000 + $54,366 − $2,718).

At the maturity date, after the last interest payment, the bond premium is fully amortized, and the maturity amount of the bonds and their book value is the same (i.e., $400,000). At the maturity date, December 31, 2014, the bonds are paid off in full, resulting in the same entry whether the bond was originally sold at par, at a discount, or at a premium. Exhibit 11.2 compares the effects of the amortization of bond discount and bond premium on a $1,000 bond.

SELF-STUDY **QUIZ 11-2**

Assume that Placer Dome issued $100,000 bonds that will mature in 10 years. The bonds pay interest twice each year at an annual rate of 9 percent. They were sold when the market rate was 8 percent. Determine the bonds' selling price.

After you complete your work, check your answer with the solution on page 613.

EXHIBIT **11.2**

**Amortization of Bond Discount
and Premium Compared—
Straight-Line Amortization**

Bond
Issue
Price

Acquisition
Date

Maturity
Date

Book (Carrying) Value at End of Year
(straight-line amortization)

At a
premium → $1,050

1,040

1,030

1,020

1,010

At par → 1,000

990

980

970

960

At a
discount → 950

Year 1   Year 2   Year 3   Year 4   Year 5

$1,000
maturity
amount

KEY **RATIO ANALYSIS:**

TIMES INTEREST EARNED

ANALYTICAL QUESTION → Is the company generating sufficient resources (added value) from its profit-making activities to meet its current obligations associated with debt?

RATIO AND COMPARISONS → The *times interest earned ratio* is helpful in answering this question. It is computed as follows:

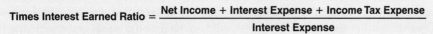

$$\text{Times Interest Earned Ratio} = \frac{\text{Net Income} + \text{Interest Expense} + \text{Income Tax Expense}}{\text{Interest Expense}}$$

The 2004 ratio for Placer Dome is:

$$(\$284,000 + \$77,000 + \$130,000) \div \$77,000 = 6.38$$

■ **LEARNING OBJECTIVE 3**

Compute and interpret the times interest earned ratio.

Comparisons over Time			Comparisons with Competitors	
Placer Dome			**Barrick Gold Corporation**	**Newmont Mining Corporation**
2002	2003	2004	2004	2004
2.27	5.04	6.38	24.7	8.36

INTERPRETATIONS

In General → A high ratio is viewed more favourably than a low ratio. Basically, the ratio shows the amount of income before interest and income tax that is generated for each dollar of interest expense. A high ratio shows an extra margin of protection in case profitability deteriorates. Analysts are particularly interested in a company's ability to meet its required interest payments because failure to do so could result in bankruptcy.

Focus Company Analysis → Placer Dome's profit-making activities generated $6.38 for each dollar of interest in 2004. Placer Dome's income could fall substantially before the company would appear to have trouble meeting its interest obligations with resources generated by normal operations. Placer Dome's ability to repay its creditors has strengthened steadily over the last three years, but it fell short of its competitors' ratios. This is consistent with the fact that Placer Dome uses proportionally more debt than its competitors.

A Few Cautions → The times interest earned ratio is often misleading for new or rapidly growing companies that tend to invest considerable resources to build capacity for future operations. In such cases, the times interest earned ratio will reflect significant amounts of interest expense associated with the acquired capacity but current operations do not yet include the levels of expected future profitability. Analysts should consider the company's long-term strategy when using this ratio. While this ratio is widely used, some analysts prefer to compare interest expense to the amount of cash that a company is able to generate, because creditors cannot be paid with "income" that is generated. The cash coverage ratio addresses this concern and is discussed in Chapter 13.

ADDITIONAL TOPICS

In the following sections, we discuss four additional topics commonly encountered in accounting for bonds payable[10]:

- Effective-interest amortization of bond discounts and premiums.
- Early retirement of debt.
- Reporting of financing activities on the cash flow statements.

EFFECTIVE-INTEREST AMORTIZATION

■ **LEARNING OBJECTIVE 4**

Understand the difference between effective-interest and straight-line amortization.

The **EFFECTIVE-INTEREST METHOD** amortizes a bond discount or premium on the basis of the effective-interest rate; it is theoretically preferred to the straight-line method.

Earlier in this chapter, we discussed the straight-line method for amortizing a bond discount or premium. The only advantage of the straight-line method is its simplicity. Under generally accepted accounting principles (GAAP), the straight-line method may be used only if the reported results are not materially different from those of the **effective-interest method**, a conceptually superior method to amortize a bond discount or premium. We believe this method provides a better understanding of why the amortization of a bond discount or premium is an adjustment to the interest payment.[11]

Under the effective-interest method, interest expense for a bond is computed by multiplying the current unpaid balance (i.e., the amount that was actually borrowed) times the market rate of interest that existed on the date the bonds were sold. The periodic amortization of a bond premium or discount is then calculated as the difference between interest expense and the amount of cash paid or accrued.

Effective Interest Amortization of a Bond Discount Earlier in this chapter, we illustrated accounting for bonds issued at a discount. Let us expand that example to see how the discount is amortized under the effective-interest method. The previous example involved 10-percent Placer Dome bonds with a par value of $400,000, issued when the market rate was 12 percent. The issue price of the bonds was $354,118, and the bond discount was $45,882.

The first interest payment on Placer Dome's bonds is on June 30, 2005. The journal entry to record interest expense is basically the same as the one shown earlier in this chapter under the straight-line method. The only difference is the amount. Interest expense at the end of the first six months is calculated by multiplying the amount that

---

[10]One additional topic commonly encountered in accounting for long-term debt is the reporting of financial instruments and related disclosures. This topic is discussed in the Online Learning Centre Web site at **www.mcgrawhill.ca/college/libby/student/resources**.

[11]At the time of writing this text, the Accounting Standards Board proposed a new standard requiring companies to use the effective interest method to account for investments in bonds.

was actually borrowed by the market rate of interest for six months ($354,118 × 12% × $\frac{6}{12}$ = $21,247). The amount of cash paid is calculated by multiplying the principal by the stated rate of interest for six months ($400,000 × 10% × $\frac{6}{12}$ = $20,000). The difference between the interest expense and the cash paid (or accrued) is the amount of discount that has been amortized ($21,247 − $20,000 = $1,247).

> Effective-interest amortization causes these amounts to change each period.

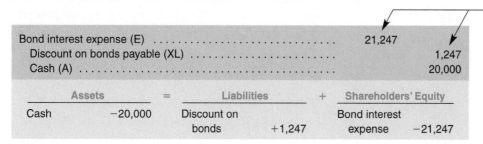

Bond interest expense (E)	21,247	
Discount on bonds payable (XL)		1,247
Cash (A)		20,000

Assets		=	Liabilities		+	Shareholders' Equity	
Cash	−20,000		Discount on bonds	+1,247		Bond interest expense	−21,247

The amortization of the bond discount reduces the balance of the Discount on Bonds Payable account. A reduction of a contra-liability account increases the book value of the liability, as shown:

	January 1, 2005	June 30, 2005
Bonds payable	$400,000	$400,000
Discount on bonds payable	45,882	44,635*
Book value	$354,118	$355,365

*$45,882 − $1,247 = $44,635.

Each period, the amortization of the bond discount increases the bond's book value (or unpaid balance). The amortization of bond discount can be thought of as interest that was earned by the bondholders but not paid to them. During the first six months of 2005, the bondholders earned interest of $21,247 but received only $20,000 in cash. The additional $1,247 was added to the principal of the bond and will be paid when the bond matures.

The interest expense for the second half of 2005 is calculated by multiplying the unpaid balance on June 30, 2005, by the market rate of interest for six months ($355,365 × 12% × $\frac{6}{12}$ = $21,322). The amortization of the bond discount in the second period is $1,322.

Bond interest expense (E)	21,322	
Discount on bonds payable (XL)		1,322
Cash (A)		20,000

Assets		=	Liabilities		+	Shareholders' Equity	
Cash	−20,000		Discount on bonds	+1,322		Bond interest expense	−21,322

Notice that interest expense for the second half of 2005 is more than the amount for the first six months of 2005. This is logical because Placer Dome effectively borrowed more money during the second half of the year (i.e., the $1,247 unpaid interest). Interest expense increases each year during the life of the bond because the amortized bond discount reflects unpaid interest on an increasing amount.

Some companies use a bond amortization schedule to assist them with the detailed computations required under the effective-interest amortization method. The following schedule shows the computations for the first two years and the last year of the bond's life.

Comparison of Discount Amortization Methods

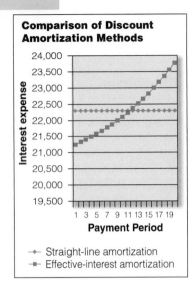

- ◆ Straight-line amortization
- ■ Effective-interest amortization

Amortization Schedule: Bond Discount

Date	(a) Interest Paid (Par Value × 5%)	(b) Interest Expense (Book Value × 6%)	(c) Amortization of Bond Discount [(b) − (a)]	(d) Book Value
1/1/2005				$354,118
6/30/2005	$20,000	$21,247	$1,247	355,365
12/31/2005	20,000	21,322	1,322	356,687
6/30/2006	20,000	21,401	1,401	358,088
12/31/2006	20,000	21,485	1,485	359,573
.				
.				
6/30/2014	20,000	23,560	3,560	396,226
12/31/2014	20,000	23,774	3,774	400,000

Interest expense (column b) is computed by multiplying the market rate of interest by the book value at the beginning of the period (column d). Amortization is computed by subtracting interest paid (column a) from interest expense (column b). The book value (column d) is computed by adding amortization of bond discount (column c) to the book value at the beginning of the period.

Under the effective-interest method, interest expense changes each accounting period as the effective amount of the liability changes. Under the straight-line method, interest expense remains constant over the life of the bond. The graph illustrates these differences. The effective-interest method produces a book value that reflects the present value of remaining payments using the effective interest rate at the date of issue. However, both methods amortize the same historic discount and do not reflect current market values.

Effective-Interest Amortization of Bond Premium The effective-interest method is basically the same for a discount or a premium. In either case, interest expense for a bond is computed by multiplying the book value (i.e., the unpaid balance) times the market rate of interest on the date the bonds were sold. The periodic amortization of a bond premium or discount is then calculated as the difference between interest expense and the amount of cash paid or accrued. Let us use our earlier example of a bond premium to illustrate the similarity. The example involved 10-percent Placer Dome bonds with a par value of $400,000 issued when the market rate was 8 percent. The issue price of the bonds was $454,366, and the bond premium was $54,366.

The first interest payment on Placer Dome's bonds is made on June 30, 2005. The interest expense at the end of the first six months is calculated by multiplying the amount actually borrowed by the market rate of interest for six months ($454,366 × 8% × $\frac{6}{12}$ = $18,175). The amount of cash paid is calculated by multiplying the principal by the stated rate of interest for six months ($400,000 × 10% × $\frac{6}{12}$ = $20,000). The difference between the interest expense and the cash paid (or accrued) is the amount of premium that has been amortized ($20,000 − $18,175 = $1,825).

Comparison of Premium Amortization Methods

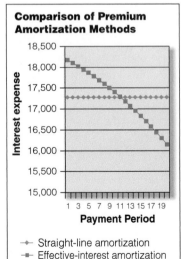

- ◆ Straight-line amortization
- ■ Effective-interest amortization

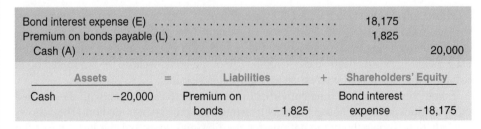

Bond interest expense (E)	18,175	
Premium on bonds payable (L)	1,825	
Cash (A)		20,000

Assets	=	Liabilities	+	Shareholders' Equity
Cash −20,000		Premium on bonds −1,825		Bond interest expense −18,175

The basic difference between effective-interest amortization of a bond discount and a bond premium is that the amortization of a discount increases the book value of the liability and the amortization of a premium reduces it. An amortization schedule for the first year of this example follows. Compare it to the amortization schedule for a discount shown previously.

Amortization Schedule: Bond Premium

Date	(a) Interest Paid (Par Value × 6%)	(b) Interest Expense (Book Value × 4%)	(c) Amortization of Bond Premium [(a) − (b)]	(d) Book Value
1/1/2005				$454,366
6/30/2005	$20,000	$18,175	$1,825	452,541
12/31/2005	20,000	18,102	1,898	450,642
6/30/2006	20,000	18,026	1,974	448,668
12/31/2006	20,000	17,947	2,053	446,615
.				
.				
6/30/2014	20,000	16,444	3,556	403,846
12/31/2014	20,000	16,154	3,846	400,000

FINANCIAL **ANALYSIS**

UNDERSTANDING ALTERNATIVE AMORTIZATION METHODS

Although the effective-interest method is preferred conceptually, some companies use the straight-line method. Under the materiality constraint, accounting for various transactions should conform with GAAP unless the amounts involved are immaterial and will not affect the decisions made by users of the statements. The straight-line method is permitted when the difference in periodic amortization between the two methods is not material in amount. Because differences are immaterial, most financial statements do not disclose which method the company uses. Even if the method were disclosed, the analysts cannot quantify the impact of using one method versus the other. As a result, most analysts are not concerned about which method a company chooses.

SELF-STUDY **QUIZ 11-3**

Refer to the amortization schedule on the previous page and answer the following requirements:

1. Complete the schedule for three additional semi-annual payments of interest until June 30, 2008.

2. Compute the unpaid balance of the bonds at June 30, 2008. Can you think of another way of computing this balance? If so, show your computations.

After you complete your work, check your answers with the solution on page 613.

EARLY RETIREMENT OF DEBT

Bonds are normally issued for long periods, such as 20 or 30 years. As mentioned earlier, bondholders who need cash prior to the maturity date can simply sell the bonds to another investor. This transaction does not affect the books of the company that issued the bonds.

In several situations, a corporation may decide to retire bonds before their maturity date. A bond with a call feature may be called in for early retirement at the issuer's option. Typically, the bond indenture includes a call premium for bonds retired before the maturity date, which often is stated as a percentage of par value. The prospectus for Placer Dome's 6.45% debentures included the following:

■ LEARNING OBJECTIVE 5

Report the early retirement of bonds.

We may redeem the exchange debentures in whole, at any time, or in part, from time to time, at the redemption prices described under "Description of Debentures—Optional Redemption." In addition, we may redeem all, but not less than all, of the exchange debentures at a redemption price equal to 100 percent of the principal amount thereof plus accrued and unpaid interest to the date of redemption.

Assume that in 1994, Placer Dome issued bonds in the amount of $1 million and that the bonds sold at par. If Placer Dome called the bonds in 2005 at 102 percent of par, the company's accountants would make the following journal entry:

Bonds payable (L)	1,000,000	
Loss on redemption of bonds (Loss)	20,000	
Cash (A)		1,020,000

Assets	=	Liabilities	+	Shareholders' Equity
Cash −1,020,000		Bonds payable −1,000,000		Loss −20,000

If the bonds are issued at either a discount or at a premium, then the loss or gain on redemption would be the difference between the redemption amount and the book value of the bonds, which reflects the unamortized portion of the discount or premium.

In some cases, a company may elect to retire debt early by purchasing it on the open market, just as an investor would. This approach is necessary when the bonds do not have a call feature. It might also be an attractive approach if the price of the bonds fell after the date of issue. What could cause the price of a bond to fall? The most common cause is a rise in interest rates. As you may have noticed during our discussion of present value concepts, bond prices move in the opposite direction of interest rates. If interest rates go up, bond prices fall, and vice versa. When interest rates go up, a company that wants to retire a bond before maturity may find buying the bond on the open market to be less expensive than paying a call premium.

When interest rates increase, the market value of the bonds would decrease, and the redemption or repurchase of the bonds in the open market would result in a gain. The gain increases the company's net income, which reflects positively on the performance of management. However, if the company needs to reissue bonds at a higher interest rate, then the gain on redemption or repurchase of the bonds is misleading, because the company will need to make higher interest payments on the refinanced debt. In contrast, when interest rates decrease the refinancing of long-term debt by retiring old debt and issuing new debt will result in a loss on debt retirement, but will reduce the amount of periodic interest payments. Hence, management may be inclined to retire debt prematurely in order to show improved financial performance, but this decision may affect cash flows negatively in the future.

FOCUS ON **CASH FLOWS**

■ LEARNING OBJECTIVE 6

Explain how financing activities are reported on the cash flow statement.

FINANCING ACTIVITIES ON THE CASH FLOW STATEMENT

BONDS PAYABLE

The *Financing Activities* section of the cash flow statement reports both cash inflows and outflows that relate to how cash was obtained from external sources (owners and creditors) to finance the enterprise and its operations. The issuance of a bond payable is reported as a cash inflow from financing activities. The repayment of principal is reported as an outflow from financing activities. Many students are surprised to learn that the payment of bond interest is *not* reported in the Financing Activities section of the cash flow statement. Interest payments are directly related to earning income and are therefore reported in the *Cash Flows from Operating Activities* section of the statement. In addition, companies are required to report the amount of cash paid for interest each accounting period. *Financial Reporting in Canada 2004* shows that companies reported this information in a variety of locations in their 2003 annual reports.

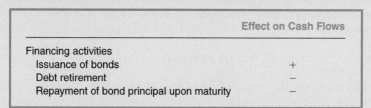

Disclosure of Interest Payments (sample of 200 companies)

EFFECT ON CASH FLOW STATEMENT

IN GENERAL → As we saw in the previous chapter, transactions involving short-term creditors (e.g., accounts payable) affect working capital, and are therefore reported in the operating activities section of the cash flow statement. Cash received from long-term creditors is reported as an inflow from financing activities. Cash payments made to long-term creditors (with the exception of interest expense) are reported as outflows from financing activities. Examples are shown in the following table:

	Effect on Cash Flows
Financing activities	
Issuance of bonds	+
Debt retirement	−
Repayment of bond principal upon maturity	−

FOCUS COMPANY ANALYSIS → A segment of Placer Dome's cash flow statements for the years 2003 and 2004 follows. Only two of the items listed pertain to the issues discussed in this chapter. Other items will be discussed in Chapter 12.

In 2003, the company raised a substantial amount of long-term debt ($715 million) to finance its operating and investing activities. It also reduced its long-term debt by $534 million in 2003 and another $39 million in 2004. Repayments of long-term debt are made when the debt matures or when a company decides to redeem the outstanding debt prematurely in order to take advantage of lower interest rates. In this case, long-term debt that pays a high interest rate was redeemed and new debt with a lower interest rate was issued. Such refinancing of long-term debt results in annual savings in interest payments.

Analysts are particularly interested in the Financing Activities section of the cash flow statement because it provides important insights about the future capital structure for the company. Rapidly growing companies typically report significant amounts of funds in this section of the cash flow statement.

SELECTED FOCUS COMPANY COMPARISONS: CASH FLOWS FROM FINANCING ACTIVITIES (IN MILLIONS)

Placer Dome	$419
Intrawest Corp.	−326
Gildan Activewear	−14

REAL WORLD EXCERPT

Placer Dome

ANNUAL REPORT

CONSOLIDATED STATEMENTS OF CASH FLOWS
For the Year ended December 31

(in millions of United States dollars)	2004	2003	2002
Financing activities			
Short-term debt (note 14(b))	113	—	(2)
Restricted cash (note 14(b))	(110)	—	—
Long-term debt and capital leases			
Borrowings, net of issue costs	4	715	2
Repayments	(39)	(534)	(34)
Redemption of minority interest	—	(1)	(5)
Common shares issued, net of issue costs (note 16(a))	492	31	24
Dividends paid			
Common shares	(41)	(41)	(34)
Minority interests	—	(3)	(13)
	419	167	(62)

DEMONSTRATION **CASE**

To raise funds to build a new plant, Reed Company management issued bonds. The bond indenture specified the following:

Par value of the bonds ($1,000 bonds): $600,000.

Date of issue: February 1, 2006; due in 10 years on January 31, 2016.

Interest: 10 percent per annum, payable 5 percent on each July 31 and January 31.

All of the bonds were sold on February 1, 2006, at 102.5. The fiscal year for Reed Company ends on December 31.

Required:

1. How much cash did Reed Company receive from the sale of the bonds on February 1, 2006? Show your computations.
2. What was the amount of premium on the bonds payable? Over how many months should it be amortized?
3. Compute the amount of amortization of the premium per month and for each six-month interest period; use straight-line amortization. Round to the nearest dollar.
4. Prepare the journal entry on February 1, 2006, to record the sale and issuance of the bonds payable.
5. Prepare the journal entry for the payment of interest and amortization of the premium for the first interest payment on July 31, 2006.
6. Prepare the adjusting entry required on December 31, 2006, at the end of the fiscal year.
7. Prepare the journal entry to record the second interest payment and the amortization of the premium on January 31, 2006.
8. Show how bond interest expense and bonds payable are reported on the financial statements at December 31, 2006.

We highly recommend that you attempt to answer the requirements on your own before consulting the suggested solution below.

SUGGESTED SOLUTION

1. Sale price of the bonds: $600,000 × 102.5% = $615,000.
2. Premium on the bonds payable: $600,000 × 2.5% = $15,000.
   Months of amortization: From date of sale, February 1, 2006, to maturity date, January 31, 2016 = 120 months.
3. Premium amortization: $15,000 ÷ 120 months = $125 per month, or $750 each six-month interest period (straight line).
4. February 1, 2006 (issuance date):

Cash (A)	615,000	
Premium on bonds payable (L)		15,000
Bonds payable (L)		600,000
To record sale of bonds payable at 102.5.		

5. July 31, 2006 (first interest payment date):

Bond interest expense (E) ($30,000 − $750)	29,250	
Premium on bonds payable (L)	750	
Cash (A) ($600,000 × 5%)		30,000
To record payment of semi-annual interest.		

6. December 31, 2006 (end of the accounting period):

Bond interest expense (E)	24,375	
Premium on bonds payable (L) ($125 × 5 months)	625	
Bond interest payable (L) ($600,000 × 10% × $\frac{5}{12}$)		25,000
Adjusting entry for five months' interest accrued plus amortization of the premium, August 1 to December 31, 2006.		

7. January 31, 2007 (second interest date):

Bond interest payable (L)	25,000	
Premium on bonds payable (L)	125	
Bond interest expense (E)	4,875	
Cash (A)		30,000

To record payment of semi-annual interest.

8. Interest expense reported on the 2006 income statement should be for the period outstanding during the year (i.e., for 11 months, February 1 through December 31). Interest expense, per these entries, is $29,250 + $24,375 = $53,625; alternatively ($600,000 × 10% × ^{11}/$_{12}$ = $55,000) − ($125 × 11 months = $1,375) = $53,625.

Income statement for 2006:

Interest expense	$ 53,625

Balance sheet, December 31, 2006:

Long-term liabilities:

Bonds payable, 10% (due January 31, 2016)	600,000
Add unamortized premium*	13,625
	$613,625

*$15,000 − ($750 + $625) = $13,625.

SOLUTIONS TO **SELF-STUDY QUIZZES**

Self-Study Quiz 11-1

1. The market rate is the interest rate demanded by creditors. It is the rate used in the present value computations to discount future cash flows. The market interest rate is also called *yield* or *effective-interest rate*.

2. The coupon interest rate is the stated rate on the bonds. It is also called *stated rate* and *contract rate*.

3. A bond that sells for less than par is sold at a discount. This occurs when the stated rate is lower than the market rate.

4. A bond that sells for more than par is sold at a premium. This occurs when the coupon rate is higher than the market rate.

Self-Study Quiz 11-2

Principal:	$100,000 ×	0.4564	=	$ 45,640
Interest:	4,500 ×	13.5903	=	$ 61,156
				$106,796

Self-Study Quiz 11-3

1.

Date	(a) Interest Paid (Par Value × 5%)	(b) Interest Expense (Book Value × 6%)	(c) Amortization of Bond Discount [(b) − (a)]	(d) Book Value
				$359,573
6/30/2007	$20,000	$21,574	$1,574	361,147
12/31/2007	20,000	21,669	1,669	362,816
6/30/2008	20,000	21,769	1,769	364,585

2. The book value at June 30, 2008, is $364,585. This amount is the unpaid balance of the bonds, and represents the present value of the remaining payments using the market rate of interest when the bonds were issued. At June 30, 2008, there are 13 interest payments remaining and the principal of the bonds. Their present value is:

$$\text{Present value} = \$400,000 \times 0.4688 \text{ (Table A-2, Appendix A)}$$
$$+ \$20,000 \times 8.8527 \text{ (Table A-4, Appendix A)}$$
$$= \$364,574 \text{ (The difference of } \$11 \text{ is due to rounding.)}$$

CHAPTER **TAKE-AWAYS**

1. **Describe the basic characteristics of bonds payable and use the financial leverage ratio. p. 592**
Bonds payable have a number of characteristics designed to meet the needs of the issuing corporation and the creditor.

Corporations use debt to raise long-term capital. Bonds payable offer a number of advantages compared to equity, including financial leverage, the tax deductibility of interest, and the fact that control of the company is not diluted. Bonds payable carry additional risk because interest and principal payments are not discretionary.

The financial leverage ratio compares the amount of capital supplied by creditors to the amount supplied by owners. It is a measure of a company's debt capacity. It is an important ratio because high risk is associated with debt capital because of obligatory payments.

2. **Report bonds payable and related interest expense, with bonds sold at par, at a discount, and at a premium. p. 598**
Three types of events must be recorded over the life of a typical bond: (1) the receipt of cash when the bond is first sold, (2) the periodic payment of cash interest, and (3) the repayment of principal upon the maturity of the bond.

Bonds are sold at a discount whenever the coupon interest rate is less than the market rate of interest. A discount is the difference between the par value of the bond and its selling price. The discount is recorded as a contra liability when the bond is sold and is amortized over the life of the bond as an adjustment to interest expense.

Bonds are sold at a premium whenever the coupon interest rate is higher than the market rate of interest. A premium is the difference between the selling price of the bond and its par value. The premium is recorded as a liability when the bond is sold and is amortized over the life of the bond as an adjustment to interest expense.

3. **Compute and interpret the times interest earned ratio. p. 605**
This ratio measures the ability of a company to meet its interest obligations with resources from its profit-making activities. The ratio is computed by comparing interest expense to income before interest expense and income taxes.

4. **Understand the difference between effective-interest and straight-line amortization. p. 606**
There are two methods to amortize bond discounts and premiums: (1) the straight-line method and (2) the effective-interest method. Under the effective-interest method, interest expense is computed by multiplying the book value of the bond liability by the market rate of interest that existed when the bonds were first issued.

5. **Report the early retirement of bonds. p. 609**
A corporation may retire bonds before their maturity date. The difference between the book value and the amount paid to retire the bonds is reported as a gain or loss, depending on the circumstances.

6. **Explain how financing activities are reported on the cash flow statement. p. 610**
Cash flows associated with transactions involving long-term creditors are reported in the Financing Activities section of the cash flow statement. Interest expense is reported in the Operating Activities section.

The capital structure of a business is made up of funds supplied by both the creditors and the owners. In this chapter, we discussed the role of bonds payable in the capital structure of a business. In the next chapter, we will discuss shareholders' equity.

KEY **RATIOS**

The **financial leverage ratio** measures the relationship between total assets and the shareholders' equity that finances the assets. The ratio is computed as follows:

$$\text{Financial Leverage} = \frac{\text{Average Total Assets}}{\text{Average Shareholders' Equity}}$$

Times interest earned ratio measures a company's ability to generate resources from current operations to meet its interest obligations. The computation of this ratio follows:

$$\text{Times Interest Earned} = \frac{\text{Net Income} + \text{Interest Expense} + \text{Income Tax Expense}}{\text{Interest Expense}}$$

BALANCE SHEET

Under Current Liabilities

Bonds and debentures are normally listed as long-term liabilities. An exception occurs when these liabilities are within one year of maturity. Such debts are reported as current liabilities with the following title:

Current portion of long-term debt

Under Non-Current Liabilities

Bonds and debentures are listed under a variety of titles, depending on the characteristics of the debt. Titles include

Bonds payable

Debentures

Convertible bonds

INCOME STATEMENT

Interest expense associated with bonds is reported on the income statement. Most companies report interest expense in a separate category on the income statement.

CASH FLOW STATEMENT

Under Financing Activities

+ Cash inflows from long-term creditors
− Cash outflows to long-term creditors

Under Operating Activities

The cash outflow associated with interest expense is reported as an operating activity.

NOTES

Under Summary of Significant Accounting Policies

Description of pertinent information concerning accounting treatment of liabilities. Normally, there is minimal information. Some companies report the method used to amortize bond discounts and premiums.

Under a Separate Note

Most companies include a separate note called "Long-Term Debt" that reports information about each major debt issue, including amount and interest rate. The note also provides detail concerning debt covenants.

KEY **TERMS**

Bond Certificate p. 594

Bond Discount p. 598

Bond Premium p. 598

Bond Principal p. 592

Convertible Bonds p. 595

Coupon Rate p. 598

Debenture p. 593

Effective-Interest Method p. 606

Effective-Interest Rate p. 598

Face Amount p. 593

Financial Leverage p. 590

Indenture p. 594

Market Interest Rate p. 598

Par Value p. 593

Redeemable (Callable) Bonds p. 595

Retractable Bonds p. 595

Stated Rate p. 593

Straight-Line Amortization p. 602

Trustee p. 594

Yield p. 598

QUESTIONS

1. What are the primary characteristics of a bond? For what purposes are bonds usually issued?
2. What is the difference between a bond indenture and a bond certificate?
3. Differentiate secured bonds from unsecured bonds.
4. Differentiate among redeemable, retractable, and convertible bonds.
5. From the perspective of the issuer, what are some advantages of using bonds instead of issuing shares?

6. As the tax rate increases, the net cost of borrowing money decreases. Explain.
7. Explain financial leverage. Can it be negative?
8. At the date of issuance, bonds are recorded at their current cash equivalent amount. Explain.
9. What is the nature of the discount and premium on bonds payable? Explain.
10. What is the difference between the stated interest rate and the effective-interest rate on a bond?
11. Differentiate between the stated and effective rates of interest on a bond sold (a) at par, (b) at a discount, and (c) at a premium.
12. What is the book value of a bond payable?
13. Explain the basic difference between straight-line amortization and effective-interest methods of amortizing bond discount or premium. Explain when each method should or may be used.
14. If a company issues a bond at a discount, will interest expense each period be more or less than the cash payment for interest? If another company issues a bond at a premium, will interest expense be more or less than the cash payment for interest? Is your answer to either question affected by the method used to amortize the discount or premium?

MULTIPLE-CHOICE QUESTIONS

1. Which of the following statements explains the increase in the annual interest expense for a single bond issue over the life of the bonds?
   a. The market rate of interest has increased since the bonds were sold.
   b. The coupon rate of interest has increased since the bonds were sold.
   c. The bonds were sold at a discount.
   d. The bonds were sold at a premium.
2. Which of the following is *not* an advantage of issuing bonds when compared to issuing shares in order to obtain additional capital?
   a. Shareholders maintain proportionate ownership percentages.
   b. Interest expense reduces taxable income.
   c. Flexibility associated with the timing of interest payments.
   d. All of the above are advantages associated with bonds.
3. Which of the following does not impact the calculation of the cash interest payments to be made to bondholders?
   a. par value of the bond   c. market rate of interest
   b. coupon rate of interest   d. the frequency of the payments
4. Which account would be included in the calculation of the financial leverage ratio?
   a. Unearned Revenue   c. Income Taxes Payable
   b. Retained Earnings   d. All of the above are included
5. Which of the following is false when a bond is issued at a premium?
   a. The bond will sell for an amount above its par value.
   b. "Bonds payable" will be credited for the par value of the bond.
   c. Interest expense will exceed the cash interest payments.
   d. All of the above are false
6. When the issuing corporation has the right to terminate the relationship with the bondholder early and repay the amount borrowed ahead of schedule, we say that the bond is
   a. convertible   c. amortizable
   b. secured   d. callable
7. To determine whether a bond will be sold at a premium, discount, or at face value, one must know the following pieces of information:
   a. the par value and the coupon rate on the date the bonds were issued
   b. the par value and the market rate on the date the bonds were issued
   c. the coupon rate and the market rate on the date the bonds were issued
   d. the coupon rate and the stated rate on the date the bonds were issued
8. When using the effective-interest method of amortization, interest expense reported in the income statement is impacted by the
   a. par value of the bonds
   b. coupon rate of interest stated in the bond certificate
   c. market rate of interest on the date the bonds were issued
   d. all of the above

9. Which of the following would not appear in the Financing section of the cash flow statement?
    a. cash interest payments to bondholders
    b. principal repayments to bondholders
    c. amounts borrowed from bondholders
    d. all of the above appear in the Financing section of the statement
10. Which of the following causes a change in the book value of the bonds on each interest payment date when the effective-interest method of amortization is used?
    a. interest expense
    c. amortization of the discount or premium
    b. cash interest payment
    d. none of the above

For more practice with multiple-choice questions, go to our Web site at
www.mcgrawhill.ca/college/libby, click on "Student Edition" in the upper left
menu, click on this chapter's name and number from the list of contents, and
then click on "Multiple-Choice Quiz" from the menu on the left.

EXERCISES

E11–1 Recording Bonds Based on an Annual Report

Lennar Corporation is a builder of new homes that has constructed more than 140,000
single-family residences since its founding in 1954. Lennar's annual report contained the
following information (in thousands):

LO1, 2

Lennar Corporation

	2004	2003	2002
Interest expense	$ 134,193	$ 141,347	$ 145,567
Bonds payable	2,021,014	1,552,217	1,585,309

Required:

1. Record interest expense using a single journal entry for each year.

2. Record the issuance of bonds payable during 2004, assuming that they were issued at par
   and no repayment of bonds issued in prior years.

3. Recognizing that Lennar is a home builder, why do you think that the amounts of bonds
   payable increased so much during this period?

**E11–2 Determining Financial Statement Effects for Bond Issue and First Interest Payment,
with Premium**

Grocery Corporation sold a $500,000, 11-percent bond issue on January 1, 2005, at a market
rate of 8 percent. The bonds were dated January 1, 2005, with interest to be paid each
December 31; they mature 10 years from January 1, 2005. Use straight-line amortization.

LO1, 2, 4

Required:

1. How are the financial statements affected by the issuance of the bonds? Describe the
   impact on the financial leverage and times interest earned ratios, if any.

2. How are the financial statements affected by the payment of interest on December 31?
   Describe the impact on the financial leverage and times interest earned ratios, if any.

3. Show how the bond interest expense, interest payment, and the bonds payable should be
   reported on the December 31, 2005, annual financial statements.

E11–3 Explaining Why Debt Is Sold at a Discount

The annual report of Apple Computer, Inc., contained the following note:

LO1

Apple Computer

Long-Term Debt

On February 10, 1994, the Company issued $300 million aggregate principal amount of
its 6.5% unsecured notes. The notes were sold at 99.925% of par, for an effective yield
of 6.51%. The notes pay interest semi-annually and mature on February 15, 2004.

After reading this note, one student asked why Apple didn't simply sell the notes for an effective yield of 6.5 percent and avoid having to account for a very small discount over the next 10 years. Prepare a written response to this question.

■ LO2

Carnival Cruise Lines

E11–4   Explaining Bond Terminology

The balance sheet for Carnival Cruise Lines includes "zero coupon convertible subordinated notes." In your own words, explain the features of this debt. The balance sheet does not report a premium or a discount associated with this debt. Do you think it is recorded at par?

■ LO1

Bell Canada Inc.

E11–5   Interpreting Information Reported in the Business Press

The business press reported the following information concerning a bond issued by Bell Canada Inc.:

Bonds	Coupon	Maturity	Bid	Yield
Bell	6.55	May 01/29	111.29	5.68

Required:

1. Explain the meaning of the reported information. If you bought Bell Canada Inc. bonds with $10,000 face value, how much would you pay (based on the preceding information reported)? Assume that the bond was originally sold at par. What impact would the decline in value have on the financial statements for Bell Canada Inc.?

2. Check the business press and find out the bid price and the yield for this bond issue.

3. Refer to Bell Canada's annual report for 2004 at its Web site (www.bell.ca). Does the company provide information about this bond issue? If so, what are the features of this debt?

■ LO1

PepsiCo, Inc.

The Walt Disney Company

E11–6   Evaluating Bond Features

You are a personal financial planner working with a married couple in their early 40s who have decided to invest $100,000 in corporate bonds. You have found two bonds that you think will interest your clients. One is a zero coupon bond issued by PepsiCo with an effective interest rate of 9 percent and a maturity date of 2015. It is callable at par. The other is a Walt Disney bond that matures in 2093. It has an effective interest rate of 9.5 percent and is callable at 105 percent of par. Which bond would you recommend and why? Would your answer be different if you expected interest rates to fall significantly over the next few years? Would you prefer a different bond if the couple's ages were in the late 60s and they were retired?

■ LO1, 2

E11–7   Computing the Issue Price of a Bond, with Discussion

Charger Corporation issued a $250,000 bond that matures in five years. The bond has a stated interest rate of 8 percent and pays interest on February 1, May 1, August 1, and November 1. When the bond was issued, the market rate of interest was 12 percent. Record the issuance of the bond on February 1. Also record the payment of interest on May 1 and August 1. Use the straight-line method for amortization of any discount or premium. Explain why someone would buy a bond that did not pay the market rate of interest.

■ LO1, 2

The Walt Disney Company

E11–8   Explaining an International Transaction

A Walt Disney annual reported contained the following note:

The Company issued Yen 100 billion (approximately $920 million) of Japanese yen bonds through a public offering in Japan. The bonds are senior, unsecured debt obligations of the Company, which mature in June 1999. Interest on the bonds is payable semi-annually at a fixed interest rate of 5% per year through maturity. The bonds provide for principal payments in dollars and interest payment in Japanese yen.

Required:

1. Describe how this bond would be reported on the balance sheet.

2. Explain why management borrowed money in this manner.

E11–9 **Analyzing Financial Ratios**
■ **LO1, 3**

You have just started your first job as a financial analyst for a large investment company. Your boss, a senior analyst, has finished a detailed report evaluating bonds issued by two different companies. She stopped by your desk and asked for help: "I have compared two ratios for the companies and found something interesting." She went on to explain that the financial leverage ratio for Applied Technologies, Inc., is much lower than the industry average and that the one for Innovative Solutions, Inc., is much higher. On the other hand, the times interest earned ratio for Applied Technologies is much higher than the industry average, and the ratio for Innovative Solutions is much lower. Your boss then asked you to think about what the ratios indicate about the two companies so that she could include the explanation in her report. How would you respond to your boss?

E11–10 **Computing the Issue Price of a Bond**
■ **LO2**

On January 1, 2006, Kaizen Corporation issued a $500,000 bond that matures in 10 years. The bond has a stated interest rate of 10 percent. When the bond was issued, the market rate was 10 percent. The bond pays interest twice per year on June 30 and December 31. At what price was the bond issued?

E11–11 **Computing the Issue Price of a Bond with Analysis of Income and Cash Flow Effects**
■ **LO2, 6**

Imai Company issued a $1-million bond that matures in five years. The bond has a 9-percent coupon rate. When the bond was issued, the market rate was 8 percent. The bond pays interest twice per year on June 30 and December 31. Record the issuance of the bond on June 30. Was the bond issued at a discount or at a premium? How will the discount or premium affect future income and future cash flows?

E11–12 **Computing Issue Prices of Bonds for Three Cases**
■ **LO2**

Thompson Corporation is planning to issue $100,000, five-year, 8-percent bonds. Interest is payable semi-annually each June 30 and December 31. All of the bonds will be sold on July 1, 2007; they mature on June 30, 2011.

Required:
Compute the issue (sale) price on July 1, 2005, if the yield is: (a) 8 percent, (b) 7.5 percent, and (c) 8.5 percent. Show computations.

E11–13 **Recording Bond Issue and First Interest Payment with Discount**
■ **LO2**

On January 1, 2005, Seton Corporation sold a $1,000,000, 8.5-percent bond issue. The bonds were dated January 1, 2005, had a yield of 9 percent, pay interest each December 31, and mature 10 years from January 1, 2005.

Required:

1. Prepare the journal entry to record the issuance of the bonds.

2. Prepare the journal entry to record the interest payment on December 31, 2005. Use straight-line amortization.

3. Show how the bond interest expense and the bonds payable should be reported on the annual financial statements for 2005.

E11–14 **Recording Bond Issue: Entries for Issuance and Interest**
■ **LO2**

Northland Corporation had $400,000, 10-year coupon bonds outstanding on December 31, 2006 (end of the accounting period). Interest is payable each December 31. The bonds were issued (sold) on January 1, 2006. The 2006 annual financial statements showed the following:

Income statement
Bond interest expense (straight-line amortization) $ 33,200
Balance sheet
Bonds payable (net liability)   389,200

Required (show computations):

1. What was the issue price of the bonds? Prepare the journal entry to record the issuance of the bonds on January 1, 2006.

2. What was the coupon rate on the bonds? Prepare the entry to record interest expense for 2006.

■ **LO3** **E11–15** **Determining Financial Statement Balance with the Effective-Interest Amortization of a Bond Discount**

Eagle Corporation issued $10,000,000, 6.5 percent bonds dated April 1, 2005. The market rate of interest was 7 percent, with interest paid each March 31. The bonds mature in three years on March 31, 2008. Eagle's fiscal year ends on December 31.

Required:

1. What was the issue price of these bonds?
2. Compute the bond interest expense for fiscal year 2005. The company uses the straight-line method of amortization.
3. Show how the bonds should be reported on the balance sheet at December 31, 2005.
4. What amount of interest expense will be reported on March 31, 2006? Is this amount different from the amount of cash that is paid? If so, why?

■ **LO2** **E11–16** **Analyzing a Bond Amortization Schedule: Reporting Bonds Payable**

Stein Corporation issued a $1,000 bond on January 1, 2005. The bond specified an interest rate of 9 percent payable at the end of each year. The bond matures at the end of 2007. It was sold at a market rate of 11 percent per year. The following schedule was completed:

	Cash	Interest	Amortization	Balance
January 1, 2005 (issuance)				$ 951
End of year 2005	?	$105	$15	966
End of year 2006	?	106	16	982
End of year 2007	?	108	18	1,000

Required:

1. What was the bond's issue price?
2. Did the bond sell at a discount or a premium? How much was the premium or discount?
3. What amount of cash was paid each year for bond interest?
4. What amount of interest expense should be shown each year on the income statement?
5. What amount(s) should be shown on the balance sheet for bonds payable at each year-end? (For year 2007, show the balance just before repayment of the bond.)
6. What method of amortization was used?
7. Show how the following amounts were computed for year 2006: (a) $106, (b) $16, and (c) $982.
8. Is the method of amortization that was used preferable? Explain why.

■ **LO2, 4** **E11–17** **Preparing a Debt Payment Schedule with Effective-Interest Method of Amortization and Determining Reported Amounts**

Shuttle Company issued $1,000,000, three-year 10-percent bonds on January 1, 2005. The bond interest is paid each December 31. The bond was sold to yield 9 percent.

Required:

1. Complete a bond payment schedule. Use the effective interest method.
2. What amounts will be reported on the financial statements for the years 2005, 2006, and 2007?

■ **LO6** **E11–18** **Determining Effects on the Cash Flow Statement**

A number of events over the life of a bond have effects that are reported on the cash flow statement. Determine whether each of the following events affects the cash flow statement. If so, describe the impact and specify where the effect is reported on the statement.

1. A $1,000,000 bond is issued at a discount in 2005. The book value of the bond reported on the balance sheet on that date is $985,000, before any amortization of bond discount.
2. At year-end, accrued interest amounted to $50,000 and $1,000 of the bond discount is amortized using the straight-line method.
3. Early in 2006, the accrued interest is paid. At the same time, $8,000 of interest that accrued in 2006 is paid.

PROBLEMS

P11–1 **Recording Issuance of Note and Computation of Interest** (AP11–1)

■ LO1, 2

On November 24, 2000, Aliant Telecom issued medium-term notes with the following specifications:

Principal amount:	$150 million
Maturity date:	November 24, 2005
Issue price:	99.925% of principal amount
Coupon rate:	6.70%
Interest payment dates:	May 24 and November 24

The underwriters that sold these notes to investors received a commission of $525,000 and remitted to the company the net proceeds of $149,362,500 from the sale of these notes.

Required:

1. Prepare a journal entry to record the sale of these notes on November 24, 2000.

2. Compute the interest expense that accrued from November 24, 2000, to December 31, 2000, the end of Aliant Telecom's fiscal year.

3. Prepare the adjusting journal entry on December 31, 2000 to record amortization of the discount on the notes. The company uses the straight-line method of amortization.

4. Prepare the journal entry to record the payment of interest on May 24, 2001.

5. Show the amounts that should be reported on Aliant Telecom's financial statements for the year 2000.

6. Compute the total amount of interest expense over the five-year life of the notes.

7. After looking at the issue price, a student asked why Aliant Telecom did not simply sell the notes at 100 percent of the principal amount instead of selling them at a discount. How would you respond to this question?

P11–2 **Comparing Bonds Issued at Par, Discount, and Premium**

■ LO1, 2

Sikes Corporation, whose fiscal year ends on December 31, issued the following bonds:

Date of bonds: January 1, 2007.
Maturity amount and date: $10 million due in 10 years (December 31, 2014).
Interest: 10 percent per annum payable each December 31.
Date of sale: January 1, 2007.

Required:

1. Provide the following amounts to be reported on the 2007 financial statements (use straight-line amortization and show amounts in thousands):

	Issued at Par Case A	at 96 Case B	at 102 Case C
a. Interest expense	$	$	$
b. Bonds payable			
c. Unamortized premium or discount			
d. Net book value of bonds			
e. Stated rate of interest			
f. Cash paid for interest			

2. Explain why items (*a*) and (*f*) in requirement 1 are different for cases B and C.

3. Assume that you are an investment adviser and a retired person has written to you asking, "Why should I buy a bond at a premium when I can find one at a discount? Isn't that stupid? It's like paying the list price for a car instead of negotiating a discount." Write a brief letter in response to the question.

P11–3 **Analyzing the Reclassification of Debt** (AP11–2)

■ LO1

PepsiCo, Inc.

PepsiCo, Inc., is a $25-billion company in the beverage, snack food, and restaurant businesses. PepsiCo's annual report included the following note:

At year-end, $3.5 billion of short-term borrowings were reclassified as long-term, reflecting PepsiCo's intent and ability to refinance these borrowings on a long-term basis, through either long-term debt issuances or rollover of existing short-term borrowings.

As a result of this reclassification, PepsiCo's current ratio improved from 0.51 to 0.79. Do you think the reclassification was appropriate? Why do you think management made the reclassification? As a financial analyst, would you use the current ratio before the reclassification or after the reclassification to evaluate PepsiCo's liquidity?

■ **LO2, 3, 4**   **P11–4 Recording Bond Issuance and Interest Payment with Discussion of Management Strategy** (AP11–3)

On March 1, 2006, Chung Corporation issued $40 million in bonds that mature in 10 years. The bonds have a stated interest rate of 8.2 percent and pay interest on March 1 and September 1. When the bonds were sold, the market rate of interest was 8 percent. Chung uses the effective-interest method. By December 31, 2006, the market interest rate had increased to 10 percent.

Required:

1. Record the issuance of the bond on March 1, 2006.

2. Record the payment of interest on September 1, 2006.

3. Record the adjusting entry for accrued interest on December 31, 2006.

4. As a manager of a company, would you prefer the straight-line method or the effective-interest method to amortize the bond discount or premium?

5. Determine the impact of these transactions at year-end on the financial leverage ratio and the times interest earned ratio.

■ **LO2**   **P11–5 Completing Schedule Comparing Bonds Issued at Par, Discount, and Premium** (AP11–4)

Quartz Corporation sold a $50 million, 7-percent bond issue on January 1, 2007. The bonds pay interest each December 31 and mature 10 years from January 1, 2007. For comparative study and analysis, assume three independent selling scenarios: Case A, bonds sold at par; Case B, bonds sold at 98; Case C, bonds sold at 102. Use straight-line amortization and disregard income tax unless specifically required.

Required:

1. Complete the following schedule to analyze the differences among the three cases.

	Case A (Par)	Case B (at 98)	Case C (at 102)
a. Cash inflow at the date of issue (sale).			
b. Total cash outflow through the maturity date.			
c. Net cash outflow—total interest expense over the life of the bonds.			
d. Total interest expense, net of income tax (25 percent).			

Income statement for 2007
   e. Bond interest expense.

Balance sheet at December 31, 2007, long-term liabilities
   f. Bonds payable, 7 percent.
   g. Unamortized discount.
   h. Unamortized premium.
   i. Net liability.

2. For each case, explain why the amounts in items (*c*), (*d*), and (*e*) of requirement 1 are the same or different.

■ **LO2**   **P11–6 Recording Bond Issuance and Interest Payments** (AP11–5)

West Company issued bonds with the following provisions:

Maturity value: $60,000,000.
Interest: 9 percent per annum payable semi-annually each June 30 and December 31.
Terms: Bonds dated January 1, 2006, due five years from that date.

The company's fiscal year ends on December 31. The bonds were sold on January 1, 2006, at a yield of 8 percent.

Required:

1. Compute the issue (sale) price of the bonds (show computations).

2. Prepare the journal entry to record the issuance of the bonds.

3. Prepare the journal entries at the following dates: June 30, 2006; December 31, 2006; and June 30, 2007. Use the straight-line method to amortize bond discount or premium.

4. How much interest expense would be reported on the income statement for 2006? Show how the liability related to the bonds should be reported on the balance sheet at December 31, 2006.

P11–7 Completing an Amortization Schedule   ■ **LO2**
Berj Corporation issued bonds and received cash in full for the issue price. The bonds were dated and issued on January 1, 2005. The coupon rate was payable at the end of each year. The bonds mature at the end of four years. The following schedule has been partially completed (amounts in thousands):

Date	Cash	Interest	Amortization	Balance
January 1, 2005				$6,101
End of year 2005	$450	$427	$23	6,078
End of year 2006	450	?	?	6,053
End of year 2007	450	?	?	?
End of year 2008	450	?	?	6,000

Required:

1. Complete the amortization schedule.

2. What was the maturity amount of the bonds?

3. How much cash was received at the date of issuance (sale) of the bonds?

4. What was the amount of discount or premium on the bond?

5. How much cash will be disbursed for interest each period and in total for the full life of the bond issue?

6. What method of amortization is being used? Explain.

7. What is the coupon rate of interest?

8. What is the effective rate of interest?

9. What amount of interest expense should be reported on the income statement each year?

10. Show how the bonds should be reported on the balance sheet at the end of each year (show the last year immediately before repayment of the bonds).

11. Why is the method of amortization being used preferable to other methods? When must it be used?

P11–8 Computing Amounts for Bond Issue and Comparing Amortization Methods (AP11–6)   ■ **LO2, 4**
Dektronik Corporation manufactures electrical test equipment. The company's board of directors authorized a bond issue on January 1, 2005, with the following terms:

Maturity (par) value: $800,000.
Interest: 7.5 percent per annum payable each December 31.
Maturity date: December 31, 2009.
Effective-interest rate when sold: 8 percent.

Required:

1. Compute the bond issue price. Explain why both the stated and effective-interest rates are used in this computation.

2. Assume that the company used the straight-line method to amortize the discount or premium on the bond issue. Compute the following amounts for each year (2005–2009):

    a. Cash payment for bond interest.

    b. Amortization of bond discount or premium.

    c. Bond interest expense.

    d. Net book value of the bond.

    e. Interest expense as a percentage of net book value (item [*c*] ÷ item [*d*]).

    f. The straight-line method is theoretically deficient when interest expense is related to the net book value of the debt. Explain.

3. Assume instead that the company used the effective-interest method to amortize the discount or premium. Prepare an effective-interest bond amortization schedule similar to the one in the text (see p. 608). The effective-interest method provides a constant interest rate when interest expense is related to the net book value (unpaid balance). Explain by referring to the bond amortization schedule.

4. Which method should the company use to amortize the bond discount or premium? As a financial analyst, would you prefer one method over the other? If so, why?

■ **LO1, 5**   **P11–9 Comparing Carrying Value and Market Value** (AP11–7)

The name Hilton is well known in the hotel industry. The Hilton annual report contained the following information concerning long-term debt:

REAL WORLD
EXCERPT

Hilton Hotels

ANNUAL REPORT

> **Long-Term Debt**
>
> The estimated current market value of long-term debt is based on the quoted market price for the same or similar issues. The current carrying value for long-term debt is $1,132.5 (million) and the current market value is $1,173.5 (million).

Required:

Explain why there is a difference between the carrying value and the current market value of the long-term debt for Hilton. Assume that Hilton decided to retire all of its long-term debt for cash (a very unlikely event). Prepare the journal entry to record the transaction.

ALTERNATE PROBLEMS

■ **LO1, 2**   **AP11–1 Recording Issuance of Note and Computation of Interest** (P11–1)

On January 15, 2002, Aliant Telecom issued medium-term notes with the following specifications:

Principal amount:	$100 million
Maturity date:	January 15, 2007
Issue price:	99.97% of principal amount
Coupon rate:	5.35%
Interest payment dates:	January 15 and July 15

The underwriters that sold these notes to investors received a commission of $350,000 and remitted to the company the net proceeds of $99,620,000 from the sale of these notes.

Required:

1. Prepare a journal entry to record the sale of these notes on January 15, 2002.

2. Compute the interest expense that accrued from July 15, 2002, to December 31, 2002, the end of Aliant Telecom's fiscal year.

3. Prepare the adjusting journal entry to record amortization of the discount on the notes. The company uses the straight-line method of amortization.

4. Prepare the journal entry to record the payment of interest on January 15, 2003.

5. Show the amounts that should be reported on Aliant Telecom's financial statements for the year 2002.

6. Compute the total amount of interest expense over the five-year life of the notes.

AP11–2 Analyzing the Reclassification of Debt (P11–3)

■ **LO1**

General Mills is a multibillion-dollar company that makes and sells products used in the kitchens of most North American homes. The Company's annual report included the following note:

General Mills

> We have a revolving credit agreement expiring in two years that provides for a credit line (which permits us to borrow money when needed). This agreement provides us with the opportunity to refinance short-term borrowings on a long-term basis.

Should General Mills classify the short-term borrowings as current or non-current debt based on this ability to borrow money to refinance the debt if needed? If you were a member of the management team, explain what you would want to do and why. If you were a financial analyst, would your answer be different?

AP11–3 Using the Effective-Interest Method with Discussion of Management Strategy (P11–4)

■ **LO2, 4**

Carter Corporation issued $5,000,000 in bonds that mature in 10 years. The bonds have a coupon rate of 6.3 percent and pay interest on March 1 and September 1. When the bonds were sold, the market rate of interest was 6 percent. Carter uses the effective-interest method to amortize bond discount or premium. By December 31, 2007, the market interest rate of interest had increased to 7 percent.

Required:

1. Record the issuance of the bond on March 1, 2007.

2. Record the payment of interest on September 1, 2007.

3. Record the adjusting entry for accrued interest on December 31, 2007.

4. As a manager of a company, would you prefer the straight-line or the effective-interest method of amortization?

5. Determine the impact of these transactions at year-end on the financial leverage ratio and the times interest earned ratio.

AP11–4 Completing a Schedule That Involves a Comprehensive Review of the Issuance of Bonds at Par, Discount, and Premium, Including Cash Flows (P11–5)

■ **LO2, 6**

On January 1, 2005, Ontec Corporation sold and issued $100 million, five-year, 10-percent bonds. The bond interest is payable annually each December 31. Assume three separate and independent selling scenarios: Case A, bonds sold at par; Case B, bonds sold at 90; and Case C, bonds sold at 110.

Required:

1. Complete a schedule similar to the following for each separate case, assuming straight-line amortization of discount and premium. Disregard income tax. Show all dollar amounts in millions.

2. For each separate case, calculate each of the following:
   a. Total cash outflow.
   b. Total cash inflow.
   c. Net cash outflow.
   d. Total interest expense over the life of the bonds.

						At End of 2009	
	At Start of 2005	At End of 2005	At End of 2006	At End of 2007	At End of 2008	Prior to Payment of Principal	Payment of Principal
Case A: sold at par (100)	$	$	$	$	$	$	$
Cash inflow							
Cash outflow							
Interest expense on income statement							
Net book value on balance sheet							
Case B: sold at a discount (90)							
Cash inflow							
Cash outflow							
Interest expense on income statement							
Net book value on balance sheet							
Case C: sold at a premium (110)							
Cash inflow							
Cash outflow							
Interest expense on income statement							
Net book value on balance sheet							

3. *a.* Explain why the net cash outflows differ among the three cases.

   b. For each case, explain why the net cash outflow is the same as total interest expense.

■ **LO2**

AP11–5 Computing Issue Price of Bonds and Recording Issuance and Interest Payments (P11–6)
Jaymar Company issued bonds with the following provisions:

> **Maturity value: $100,000,000.**
> Interest: 9 percent per annum payable semi-annually each June 30 and December 31.
> Terms: Bonds dated January 1, 2007, due 10 years from that date.

The company's fiscal year ends on December 31. The bonds were sold on January 1, 2005, at a yield of 10 percent.

Required:

1. Compute the issue (sale) price of the bonds (show computations).

2. Prepare the journal entry to record the issuance of the bonds.

3. Prepare the journal entries at the following dates: June 30, 2005; December 31, 2007; and June 30, 2008. Use the straight-line method to amortize bond discount or premium.

4. How much interest expense would be reported on the income statement for 2007? Show how the liability related to the bonds should be reported on the balance sheet at December 31, 2007.

■ **LO2, 4**

AP11–6 Straight-Line versus Effective-Interest Methods of Amortizing Bond Discount, with Discussion (P11–8)
Canadian Products Corporation manufactures office equipment and supplies. The company authorized a bond issue on January 1, 2005, with the following terms:

> **Maturity (par) value: $120,000,000.**
> Interest: 7.9 percent per annum payable each December 31.
> Maturity date: December 31, 2009.
> Effective-interest rate when sold: 8 percent.

Required:

1. Compute the bond issue price. Explain why both the stated and effective-interest rates are used in this computation.

2. Prepare the entry to record this bond issue.

3. Assume that the company used the straight-line method to amortize the discount or premium on the bond issue. Compute the following amounts for each year (2005–2009):

    a. Interest paid.

    b. Amortization of bond discount or premium.

    c. Bond interest expense.

    d. Net book value of the bond.

    e. Interest expense as a percentage of the net book value (item [*c*] ÷ item [*d*]).

    f. The straight-line method is theoretically deficient when interest expense is related to the net book value of the debt. Explain.

4. Assume instead that the company used the effective-interest method to amortize the discount or premium. Prepare an effective-interest bond amortization schedule similar to the one in the text (see p. 608). The effective-interest method provides a constant interest rate when interest expense is related to the net liability. Explain by referring to the bond amortization schedule.

5. Which method should the company use to amortize the bond discount or premium? As a financial analyst, would you prefer one method over the other? If so, why?

AP11–7 **Understanding the Difference between Carrying Value and Market Value** (P11–9)

■ LO1, 5

Quaker Oats is a well-known name at most breakfast tables. The company does more than $6 billion in sales revenue each year. The Quaker annual report contained the following information concerning long-term debt:

REAL WORLD EXCERPT

Quaker Oats

ANNUAL REPORT

> **Long-Term Debt**
>
> The fair value of long-term debt was $779.7 million at the end of the current fiscal year, which was based on market prices for the same or similar issues or on the current rates offered to the Company for similar debt of the same maturities. The carrying value of long-term debt as of the same date was $759.5 million.

Required:

What is meant by "fair value"? Explain why there is a difference between the carrying value and the fair value of the long-term debt for Quaker Oats. Assume that Quaker Oats decided to retire all of its long-term debt for cash (a very unlikely event). Prepare the journal entry to record the transaction.

CASES AND PROJECTS

FINDING AND INTERPRETING FINANCIAL INFORMATION

CP11–1 **Finding Financial Information**

■ LO2, 6

Van Houtte

Refer to the financial statements of Van Houtte Inc. given in Appendix B of this book.

Required:

1. How much cash was paid for interest during the fiscal year ended April 2, 2005?

2. Review the company's note on long-term debt and identify the characteristics of each debt issue.

3. Describe the company's established arrangements, if any, that permit it to borrow money if needed.

CP11–2 **Finding Financial Information**

■ LO2, 6

The Forzani Group Ltd.

Refer to the financial statements of The Forzani Group Limited provided on the Web site **www.mcgrawhill.ca/college/libby/student/resources**.

Required:

1. How much cash was paid for interest during the fiscal year ended January 30, 2005?

2. Review the company's note on long-term debt and identify the characteristics of each debt issue.

3. Describe the company's established arrangements, if any, that permit it to borrow money if needed.

■ **LO1, 3**   **CP11–3**   **Comparing Companies**

Van Houtte vs.
The Forzani
Group Ltd.

Refer to the Online Learning Centre Web site at **www.mcgrawhill.ca/college/libby/student/ resources** for the financial statements of The Forzani Group Ltd. and to Appendix B of this textbook for the financial statements of Van Houtte Inc.

Required:

1. Based on your analysis of the reports and your understanding of the industry, explain why The Forzani Group has built a rather unusual capital structure.

2. Two financial ratios (the financial leverage ratio and the times interest earned ratio) are discussed in this chapter. Are they relevant for these companies? Explain.

FINANCIAL REPORTING AND ANALYSIS CASES

■ **LO1**   **CP11–4**   **Analyzing Financial Leverage**

Cricket Corporation's financial statements for 2006 showed the following:

Income Statement	
Revenues	$300,000
Expenses	(198,000)
Interest expense	(2,000)
Pretax income	100,000
Income tax (30%)	(30,000)
Net income	$ 70,000
Balance Sheet	
Assets	$300,000
Liabilities (average interest rate, 10%)	$ 20,000
Share capital	200,000
Retained earnings	80,000
	$300,000

Notice that the company had a debt of only $20,000 compared with share capital of $200,000. A consultant recommended the following: debt, $100,000 (at 10 percent) instead of $20,000 and share capital of $120,000 (12,000 shares) instead of $200,000 (20,000 shares). That is, the company should finance the business with more debt and less owner contribution.

Required (round to nearest percent):

1. You have been asked to develop a comparison between (a) the actual results and (b) the results based on the consultant's recommendation. To do this, you decided to develop the following schedule:

Item	Actual Results for 2006	Results with an $80,000 Increase in Debt
a. Total debt.		
b. Total assets.		
c. Total shareholders' equity.		
d. Interest expense.		
e. Net income.		
f. Return on total assets.		
g. Earnings available to shareholders:		
(1) Amount.		
(2) Per share.		
(3) Return on shareholders' equity.		

2. Based on the completed schedule in requirement 1, provide a comparative analysis and interpretation of the actual results and the consultant's recommendation.

CP11–5 Analyzing Zero Coupon Bonds from an Actual Company

In July 2001, Shaw Communications issued a convertible zero coupon debt and raised $790 million. The debt is called a *liquid yield option note* or LYON. The LYONs were issued at $639.23 per $1,000 and the maturity date is May 1, 2021. The yield to maturity is 2.25 percent over 20 years. The LYONs are both redeemable after May 1, 2007, and convertible by the holders at any time into 8.82988 common shares per LYON. When this debt was issued, the yield ranged between 6 and 7 percent. A magazine article has noted, "It's easy to see why corporations like to issue debt that does not pay interest. But why would anybody want to buy that kind of paper?"

LO1

Shaw Communications Inc.

Required:

Explain why an investor would buy a LYON with a zero interest rate.

CP11–6 Explaining Bond Premiums and Effective-Interest Rate Amortization

Times Company issued a $100-million bond with a stated interest rate of 6.3 percent. When the bond was issued, the market rate was 6 percent. The bond matures in 10 years and pays interest on December 31 each year. The bond was issued on January 1, 2005.

LO4

Required:

1. Compute the present value of the difference between the interest paid each year ($6.3 million) and the interest demanded by the market ($100 million × 6% = $6 million). Use the market rate of interest and the 10-year life of the bond in your present value computation. What does this amount represent? Explain.

2. Why does interest expense change each year when the effective-interest method is used?

3. Compute the present value of the Times Company bonds, assuming that they had a 7-year life instead of 10-year life. Compare this amount to the net book value of the bond at the end of year 2007. What does this comparison demonstrate?

CP11–7 Interpreting the Financial Press

In this chapter, we talked about bonds primarily from the perspective of the issuing corporation. To understand bonds, it is also necessary to develop an understanding of why investors buy bonds. An article on this topic is available on the Web site at **www.mcgrawhill.ca/college/libby/student/resources**. You should read the article, "It's time for bonds to get some respect," January 19, 1998, and then write a short memo summarizing the article in your own words. What type of investors are interested in buying bonds? Describe the impact of inflation on bonds.

LO1

CP11–8 International Financing

Access the Web site of BCE Inc. at **www.bce.ca** and retrieve the most recent annual report. The note related to long-term debt discloses that BCE has borrowed money in a currency other than the dollar. Write a brief memo explaining why the company borrowed money in a foreign currency.

LO1

CRITICAL THINKING CASES

CP11–9 Making a Decision as a Financial Analyst

You are working for a large mutual fund company as a financial analyst. You have been asked to review two competitive companies in the same industry. Both have similar cash flows and net income, but one has no debt in its capital structure and the other has a financial leverage ratio of 3.2. Based on this limited information, which would you prefer? Justify your conclusion. Would your preference be influenced by the companies' industry?

LO1

CP11–10 Evaluating an Ethical Dilemma

You work for a small company considering investing in a new Internet business. Financial projections suggest that the company will be able to earn in excess of $40 million per year on an investment of $100 million. The company president suggests borrowing the money by issuing bonds that will carry a 7-percent interest rate. He says, "This is better than printing money! We won't have to invest a penny of our own money, and we get to keep $33 million per year after we pay interest to the bondholders." As you think about the proposed transaction, you feel a little uncomfortable about taking advantage of the creditors in this fashion. You feel that it must be wrong to earn such a high return by using money that belongs to other people. Is this an ethical business transaction?

LO1

LO1 **CP11–11 Evaluating an Ethical Dilemma**

Many retired people invest a significant portion of their money in bonds of corporations because of their relatively low level of risk. During the 1980s, significant inflation caused some interest rates to rise to as high as 15 percent. Retired people who bought bonds that paid only 6 percent continued to earn at the lower rate. During the 1990s, inflation subsided and interest rates declined. Many corporations took advantage of call options on bonds and refinanced high interest rate debt with low interest rate debt. In your judgment, is it ethical for corporations to continue paying low interest rates when rates increase but to call bonds when rates decrease?

LO1 **CP11–12 Evaluating an Ethical Dilemma**

Assume that you are a portfolio manager for a large insurance company. The majority of the money you manage is from retired school teachers who depend on the income you earn on their investments. You have invested a significant amount of money in the bonds of a large corporation and have just received a call from the company's president explaining that it is unable to meet its current interest obligations because of deteriorating business operations related to increased international competition. The president has a recovery plan that will take at least two years. During that time, the company will not be able to pay interest on the bonds and, she admits, if the plan does not work, bondholders will probably lose more than half of their money. As a creditor, you can force the company into immediate bankruptcy and probably get back at least 90 percent of the bondholders' money. You also know that your decision will cause at least 10,000 people to lose their jobs if the company ceases operations. Given only these two options, what should you do?

LO1 **CP11–13 Analyzing Risk and Return**

As explained in this chapter, the use of financial leverage offers shareholders the opportunity to earn higher returns, but it also creates higher risk. Different individuals have different preferences for risk and return, so determining the optimal balance of risk and return is not an easy matter. To illustrate the problem, conduct the following exercise in a small group.

You are offered the opportunity to participate in one of the following lotteries that require an investment of $10,000:

1. There is a 100-percent probability that you will get back $10,500 at the end of one year.

2. There is a 50-percent probability that you will get back $10,000 at the end of one year and a 50 percent probability that you will get $12,000.

3. There is a 50-percent probability that you will get back $8,000 at the end of one year and a 50-percent probability that you will get $16,000.

Determine which of the three lotteries you prefer and then attempt to reach a group consensus as to which lottery the group will accept.

FINANCIAL REPORTING AND ANALYSIS TEAM PROJECT

LO1, 2, 3, 6   **CP11–14 Team Project: Examining an Annual Report**

As a team, select an industry to analyze. Each group member should acquire the annual report for one publicly traded company in the industry, with each member selecting a different company. (Library files, the SEDAR service at www.sedar.com, and the company itself are good sources.) On an individual basis, each team member should then write a short report answering the following questions about his or her selected company.

1. Review the types of long-term debt issued by the company. Do you observe any unusual features?

2. Compute and analyze the financial leverage and the times interest earned ratios.

3. Review the cash flow statement. Has the company either issued or repaid money associated with a debt? If so, can you determine the reason?

4. Has the company issued debt denominated in a foreign currency? Can you determine why?

5. Were bonds issued at either a premium or a discount? If so, does the company use the straight-line or effective-interest amortization method?

Discuss any patterns across the companies that you as a team observe. Then, as a team, write a short report comparing and contrasting your companies using these attributes. Provide potential explanations for any differences discovered. (*Hint:* Large Canadian companies such as BCE Inc., Intrawest Corporation, Placer Dome Inc., Shaw Communications Inc., and Suncor Energy Inc. have debt structures that provide enough material to complete this project, although there are many other companies from which to choose.)

LEARNING OBJECTIVES

Reporting and Interpreting Owners' Equity

12

B ell Canada Enterprises (BCE) Inc. is Canada's largest communications company. BCE has focused its communications services on three Cs: connectivity, content, and commerce. BCE provides voice, data, and image communications services to millions of customers in Canada and abroad through its investments in companies such as Bell Canada, Aliant, and Bell ExpressVu. BCE's investment in Bell Globemedia brings content to its customers through broadcaster CTV, Internet portal Sympatico, and *The Globe and Mail* newspaper. BCE competes with companies such as AT&T Canada, Rogers Telecommunications, Telus, and similar companies to provide telecommunications services to millions of people.

The investments that BCE made to bring these communications services to customers required a sizeable amount of capital. At December 31, 2004, BCE had $39.1 billion in assets. About one-third of this amount was financed by owners and the rest was financed by creditors. In fact, BCE has one of the largest numbers of registered owners of any Canadian corporation. At December 31, 2004, holders of BCE common shares collectively owned almost 926 million shares.

In the previous chapter, we discussed the role of bonds in the capital structure of a company. In this chapter, we will focus on share capital. Like debt, shares provide many different features. Managers of businesses must identify the best mixture of features to attract investors.

UNDERSTANDING THE BUSINESS

To some people, the words *corporation* and *business* are almost synonymous. You have probably heard friends refer to business careers as "the corporate world." Equating business and corporations is understandable because corporations are the dominant form of business organization in terms of volume of operations. If you were to write the names of 50 familiar companies on a piece of paper, probably all of them would be corporations.

The popularity of the corporate form can be attributed to a critical advantage that corporations have over sole proprietorships and partnerships. They can raise large amounts of capital because both large and small investors can easily participate in the ownership of corporations. This ease of participation is related to three important factors:

- Shares can be purchased in small amounts. You could buy a single share of BCE for about $29 and become one of the owners of this company.

- Ownership interest can easily be transferred through the sale of shares on established markets such as the Toronto Stock Exchange.

- Stock ownership provides investors with limited liability.[1]

Many Canadians own shares, either directly or indirectly through a mutual fund or pension program. Share ownership offers them the opportunity to earn higher returns than they could on deposits to bank accounts or investments in corporate bonds. Unfortunately, share ownership also involves higher risk. The proper balance between risk and the expected return on an investment depends on individual preferences.

Exhibit 12.1 presents the shareholders' equity section of BCE's balance sheet, as well as consolidated statements of deficit (negative retained earnings). We use this exhibit to illustrate our discussion of shareholders' equity.

EXHIBIT **12.1**

Shareholders' Equity Sections of Consolidated Balance Sheets and Statements of Retained Earnings (Deficit)

REAL WORLD EXCERPT

BCE Inc.

ANNUAL REPORT

CONSOLIDATED BALANCE SHEETS
At December 31, 2004 and 2003

($ millions)	Notes	2004	2003
Shareholders' Equity			
Preferred shares	21	1,670	1,670
Common shareholders' equity			
Common shares	21	16,781	16,749
Contributed surplus		1,061	1,037
Deficit		(5,424)	(5,837)
Currency translation adjustment		(56)	(46)
Total common shareholders' equity		12,362	11,903
Total shareholders' equity		14,032	13,573

(continued)

---

[1]In the case of a corporation's insolvency, the creditors have recourse for their claims only to the corporation's assets. Thus, the shareholders stand to lose, as a maximum, only their equity in the corporation. In the case of a partnership or sole proprietorship, creditors have recourse to the owners' personal assets if the assets of the business are insufficient to meet its outstanding debts.

EXHIBIT **12.1**

(Continued)

CONSOLIDATED STATEMENTS OF DEFICIT
For the year ended December 31

(in $ millions)	Notes	2004	2003	2002
Balance at beginning of year, as previously reported		(5,830)	(6,435)	(7,686)
Accounting policy change for asset retirement obligations	1	(7)	(7)	(7)
Balance at beginning of year, as restated		(5,837)	(6,442)	(7,693)
Consolidation of variable interest entity	1	—	(25)	—
Net earnings		1,593	1,815	2,407
Dividends declared on common shares		(1,110)	(1,105)	(1,031)
Dividends declared on preferred shares		(70)	(64)	(59)
Costs relating to the issuance of common shares, net of $22 million of taxes		—	—	(62)
Premium on redemption of preferred shares		—	(7)	(6)
Other		—	(9)	2
Balance at end of year		(5,424)	(5,837)	(6,442)

ORGANIZATION OF THE CHAPTER

• **Ownership of a Corporation**	• **Types of Share Capital**	• **Accounting for Share Capital**	• **Accounting for Stock Dividends and Stock Splits**
Benefits of Share Ownership	Common Shares	Initial Sale of Shares	Stock Dividends
Authorized, Issued, and Outstanding Shares	Preferred Shares	Sale of Shares in Secondary Markets	Stock Splits
		Shares Issued for Non-Cash Assets or Services	
		Shares Issued for Employee Compensation	

• **Accounting for Cash Dividends**	• **Retained Earnings**	• **Accounting and Reporting for Unincorporated Businesses**
Dividend Yield Ratio	Restrictions on Retained Earnings	
Dividends on Preferred Shares	Dividend Payout Ratio	

OWNERSHIP OF A CORPORATION

■ **LEARNING OBJECTIVE 1**

Explain the role of share capital in the capital structure of a corporation.

The corporation is the only business form that the law recognizes as a separate entity. As a distinct entity, the corporation enjoys a continuous existence separate and apart from its owners. It may own assets, incur liabilities, expand and contract in size, sue others, be sued, and enter into contracts independently of the shareholders.

To protect everyone's rights, the creation and governance of corporations are tightly regulated by law. Corporations are created by making application to the federal government or a specific provincial government. The Canada Business Corporations Act (CBCA) outlines all of the legal requirements of federal incorporation (http://www.laws. justice.gc.ca).

To create a corporation, an application for a charter must be submitted to the appropriate government authorities. The application must specify the name of the corporation, the purpose (type of business), the types and number of shares authorized, and a minimum amount of capital that the owners must invest at the date of organization. Upon approval of the application, the government issues a *charter,* sometimes called the *articles of incorporation.* Each corporation is governed by a board of directors elected by the shareholders.

BENEFITS OF SHARE OWNERSHIP

When you invest in a corporation, you are known as a *shareholder* or *stockholder.* As a shareholder, you receive shares (a share certificate) that you can subsequently sell on established stock exchanges without affecting the corporation. The share certificate states the name of the shareholder, date of purchase, type of shares, number of shares represented, and their characteristics. The back of the certificate has instructions and a form to be completed when the shares are sold or transferred to another party.

Owners of common shares receive the following benefits:

1. **A voice in management.** You may vote at the shareholders' meeting (or by proxy) on major issues concerning management of the corporation.[2]

2. **Dividends.** You receive a proportionate share of the distribution of the corporation's profits.

3. **Residual claim.** You may receive a proportionate share of the distribution of remaining assets upon the liquidation of the company.

Owners, unlike creditors, are able to vote at the annual shareholders' meeting. The following notice of annual and special meeting of shareholders was sent to all shareholders of BCE Inc. in April 2005.

REAL WORLD EXCERPT

BCE Inc.

NOTICE OF SHAREHOLDERS'
ANNUAL AND SPECIAL MEETING

NOTICE OF 2005 ANNUAL SHAREHOLDER MEETING

You are invited to our annual shareholder meeting

When
Wednesday, May 25, 2005
9:30 a.m. (Eastern time)

Where
Metro Toronto Convention Centre
South Building
222 Bremner Blvd.
Toronto, Ontario

---

[2]A voting proxy is written authority given by a shareholder that gives another party the right to vote the shareholder's shares in the annual meeting of the shareholders. Typically, proxies are solicited by, and given to, the president of the corporation.

Webcast

A simultaneous webcast of the meeting will be available on our website at www.bce.ca.

What the meeting is about

We will be covering four items at the meeting:

1. receiving BCE's financial statements for the year ended December 31, 2004, including the auditor's report
2. electing directors who will serve until the end of the next annual shareholder meeting
3. appointing the auditor who will serve until the end of the next annual shareholder meeting
4. considering the shareholder proposals described in Schedule A. The meeting may also consider other business that properly comes before the meeting.

You have the right to vote

You are entitled to receive notice of and vote at our annual shareholder meeting, or any adjournment, if you were a holder of BCE common shares on March 27, 2005.

You have the right to vote your shares on electing directors, appointing the auditor, all shareholder proposals and any other items that may properly come before the meeting or any adjournment.

Your vote is important

As a shareholder of BCE, it is very important that you read this material carefully and then vote your shares, either by proxy or in person at the meeting.

The notice of the annual meeting was accompanied by an *information circular* that contained several pages of information concerning the people who were nominated to be members of the board of directors. Since most owners do not actually attend the annual meeting, the notice included a proxy card, which is similar to an absentee ballot. Each owner may complete the proxy and mail it to the company, which will include it in the votes at the annual meeting.

Shareholders have ultimate authority in a corporation, as shown in Exhibit 12.2. The board of directors and, indirectly, all the employees are accountable to the shareholders. The organizational structure shown in Exhibit 12.2 is typical of most corporations, but the specific structure depends on the nature of the company's business.

AUTHORIZED, ISSUED, AND OUTSTANDING SHARES

When a corporation is created, its corporate charter specifies the type and maximum number of shares that it can sell to the public. This maximum is called the **authorized number of shares**. Typically, the corporate charter authorizes a larger number of shares than the corporation expects to issue initially. This strategy provides future flexibility for the issuance of additional shares without the need to amend the charter. In the case of BCE, the number of authorized common shares is unlimited.[3]

The number of **issued shares** and the number of **outstanding shares** are determined by the corporation's equity transactions. For BCE, the number of issued shares and of outstanding shares is the same; at December 31, 2004, this number was 925,935,682. The number of issued shares may differ from the number of outstanding shares if the company has bought back some of its shares from shareholders. If a corporation needs to sell more shares than its charter authorizes, it must seek permission from the current shareholders to modify the charter.

Exhibit 12.3 defines and illustrates the terms usually used in relation to corporate shares.

The **AUTHORIZED NUMBER OF SHARES** is the maximum number of shares that a corporation can issue, as specified in the charter.

The term **ISSUED SHARES** refers to the number of shares that have been issued.

The term **OUTSTANDING SHARES** refers to the total number of shares that are owned by shareholders on any particular date.

---

[3]*Three-quarters of the 200 companies surveyed in Financial Reporting in Canada 2004 have corporate charters that authorize them to issue an unlimited number of shares. C. Byrd, I. Chen, and J. Smith, Financial Reporting in Canada 2004. Toronto: Canadian Institute of Chartered Accountants, 2004, p. 317.*

EXHIBIT **12.2**

Typical Organizational Structure of a Corporation

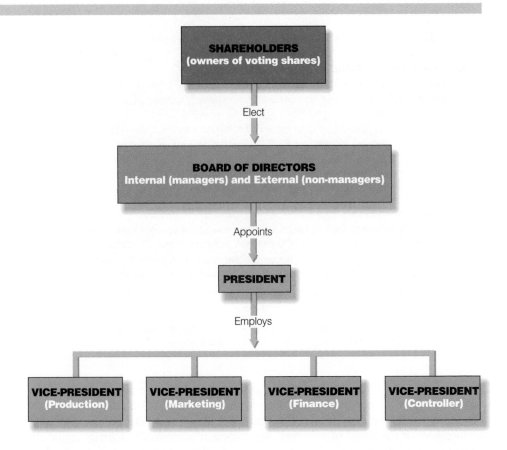

EXHIBIT **12.3**

Authorized, Issued, and Outstanding Shares

Definitions	Illustrations
Authorized number of shares: The maximum number of shares that can be issued, as specified in the charter of the corporation.	The charter specifies "an unlimited number of common shares."
Issued number of shares: The total number of shares that the corporation has issued to date.	To date, XYZ Corporation has sold and issued 30,000 common shares.
Unissued number of shares: The number of authorized shares that have never been issued to date.	Authorized shares 100,000 Issued shares 30,000 Unissued shares 70,000
Treasury shares:* Shares that have been issued to investors and then reacquired by the issuing corporation.	To date, XYZ Corporation has repurchased 1,000 previously issued shares.
Outstanding number of shares: The number of shares currently owned by shareholders; that is, the number of shares authorized minus the total number of unissued shares and minus the number of treasury shares.	Authorized shares 100,000 Treasury shares (1,000) Unissued shares (70,000) Outstanding shares 29,000

*Treasury shares will be discussed later. Notice that when treasury shares are held, the number of shares issued and the number outstanding differ by the number of treasury shares held (treasury shares are included in "issued" but not in "outstanding").

TYPES OF SHARE CAPITAL

Most corporations issue two types of shares, common shares and preferred shares. All corporations issue common shares, while only some issue preferred shares, which grant preferences that the common shares do not have.

In Chapter 11, we mentioned that corporations issue many different types of bonds to appeal to the risk and return preferences of individual creditors. The same is true of shares. In this chapter, we introduce you to many features that are used to encourage investors to buy shares.

COMMON SHARES

Common shares are the basic voting shares issued by a corporation. They are often called the *residual equity* because they rank after the preferred shares for dividends and assets distributed upon liquidation of the corporation. The dividend rate for common shares is determined by the board of directors based on the company's profitability, unlike the dividend rate on preferred shares, which is determined by contract. In the jargon of Bay Street, common equity has more "upside potential" than preferred equity and more "downside risk." This means that if the company is profitable, dividends on common shares may grow to be more than dividends on preferred shares, and in fact may increase each year (upside potential). When the company is not profitable, the board may cut or eliminate dividends on common shares, but in most cases it cannot reduce preferred dividends. As a result, common share dividends may be less than preferred share dividends during troubled times (downside risk).

The fact that dividends on common shares may increase with increases in the company's profitability helps explain why investors can make money on the stock market. Basically, you can think of the price of a share as the present value of all of its future dividends. If a company's profitability improves so that it can pay out higher dividends, the present value of its common share will increase. In this situation, you would not expect the value of the preferred share to change significantly because preferred dividends may change only if the share contract provides for some flexibility.

No Par Value and Par Value Shares **Par value** is the nominal value per share established in the charter of a corporation. It has no relationship to the market value per share. The Canada Business Corporations Act (CBCA) and most provincial corporations Acts prohibit the issuance of par value shares. The few Canadian companies that still have par value shares outstanding issued them before the CBCA was amended in 1985. According to *Financial Reporting in Canada 2004*, only 3 of the 200 companies surveyed have reported use of par value shares, 88 companies issued shares without par value, and 109 companies made no reference to par value of their shares.[4] For this reason, the remainder of this chapter focuses on **no par value shares**, which do not have an amount per share specified in the corporate charter. In contrast, most U.S. corporations issue par value shares.[5]

The original purpose of requiring corporations to specify a par value per share was to establish a minimum permanent amount of capital that the owners could not withdraw as long as the corporation existed. Thus, owners could not withdraw all of their capital in anticipation of a bankruptcy, which would leave creditors with an empty corporate shell. This permanent amount of capital is called **legal capital**. The requirement that shares not be issued for less than their par value often resulted in par values that were too small to be effectively meaningful. This notion of legal capital has lost its significance over time because the par values of shares have been set at very low amounts by issuing corporations. In contrast, when a corporation issues no par value shares, the legal capital is the initial amount received from shareholders.

■ **LEARNING OBJECTIVE 2**

Describe the characteristics of shares and analyze transactions affecting share capital.

COMMON SHARES are the basic, normal, voting shares issued by a corporation; called *residual equity* because they rank after preferred shares for dividend and liquidation distributions.

PAR VALUE is the nominal value per share specified in the charter; it serves as the basis for legal capital.

NO PAR VALUE SHARES are shares that have no par value specified in the corporate charter.

LEGAL CAPITAL is the permanent amount of capital, defined by law, that must remain invested in the business; it serves as a cushion for creditors.

---

[4]C. Byrd, I. Chen, and J. Smith, *Financial Reporting in Canada 2004*. Toronto: Canadian Institute of Chartered Accountants, 2004, p. 317.

[5]Accounting for par value shares is covered on the Online Resource Centre Web site at www.mcgraw hill.ca/college/libby/student/resources.

BCE's corporate charter authorizes the issue of no par value common shares. However, its preferred shares have a stated value upon which the dividend payments are based. This stated value has no relationship to the market value of the preferred shares.

FINANCIAL **ANALYSIS**

LEGAL CAPITAL

Legal capital represents the amount of capital that must remain invested in the corporation until it is liquidated. It is usually viewed as the par value of the shares outstanding. In the case of no par value shares, legal capital is viewed as either the stated value set by the company or the amount for which the shares were sold originally.

In most situations, financial analysts do not include par value and legal capital in their review of a company. Although these concepts have important legal implications, they are usually of no analytical significance.

PREFERRED SHARES are shares that have specified rights over common shares.

PREFERRED SHARES

In addition to common shares, some corporation issue preferred shares. **Preferred shares** differ from common shares because of a number of rights granted to the preferred shareholders. The most significant differences are:

- **Preferred shares do not grant voting rights.** As a result, they do not appeal to investors who want some control over the operations of the corporation. Indeed, this is one of the main reasons why some corporations issue preferred shares to raise equity capital. Preferred shares permit them to raise funds without diluting common shareholders' control of the company. The chart in the margin shows the percentage of companies surveyed by *Financial Reporting in Canada 2004* that include preferred shares in their capital structure.

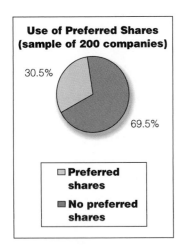

Use of Preferred Shares (sample of 200 companies)

30.5%

69.5%

☐ **Preferred shares**

☐ **No preferred shares**

- **Preferred shares are less risky than common shares.** Preferred shareholders have a priority over common shareholders for the receipt of dividends and in the distribution of assets if the corporation goes out of business. Usually a specified amount per share must be paid to preferred shareholders upon dissolution before any remaining assets can be distributed to the common shareholders.

- **Preferred shares typically have a fixed dividend rate.** Preferred shares typically have no par value but, unlike common shares, they often carry a nominal value called the *stated value*. BCE's preferred shares have a stated value of $25 per share. Most preferred shares have fixed dividend rates or amounts per share. For example, BCE's Preferred Shares, Series AC, pay an annual dividend of $1.385 per share.

CONVERTIBLE PREFERRED SHARES are preferred shares that are convertible to common shares at the option of the holder.

Special Features of Preferred Shares Some corporations issue **convertible preferred shares**, which provide preferred shareholders the option to exchange their preferred shares for a different series of preferred shares or common shares of the corporation. The terms of the conversion specify the conversion dates and a conversion ratio.

The classification of preferred shares as equity or debt depends upon the terms of the preferred equity issue. Preferred shares may be *redeemable* or *callable* at some future date at the option of the issuing corporation. Corporations are unlikely to redeem preferred shares if conditions are financially unfavourable to the company. Such redeemable shares are classified as equity because the issuing corporation can choose to not redeem the shares. However, preferred shares that have fixed redemption dates are classified as debt because the issuing corporation has a future financial liability. Moreover, dividends on these shares are treated as expenses, much like the interest expense related to long-term debt.

Some preferred share issues are *retractable* at the option of the shareholder. In that case, preferred shareholders have the right to receive the redemption price from the corporation at a specific future date. Thus, retractable preferred shares represent a contractual obligation to deliver cash or another financial asset at a future date under conditions that may be unfavourable to the issuing corporation. Consequently, retractable preferred shares are classified as debt.

The notes to BCE's consolidated financial statements for the year 2004 provide a considerable amount of detail regarding its preferred shares.

REAL WORLD EXCERPT

BCE Inc.

ANNUAL REPORT

NOTE 21: SHARE CAPITAL

Preferred Shares

BCE Inc.'s articles of amalgamation provide for an unlimited number of First Preferred Shares and Second Preferred Shares. The terms set out in the articles authorize BCE Inc.'s

directors to issue the shares in one or more series and to set the number of shares and conditions for each series.

The table below is a summary of the principal terms of BCE Inc.'s First Preferred Shares. There were no Second Preferred Shares issued and outstanding at December 31, 2004. BCE Inc.'s articles of amalgamation describe the terms and conditions of these shares in detail.

Series	Annual Dividend Rate	Convertible into	Conversion Date	Redemption Date	Redemption Price	Number of Shares Authorized	Issued and Outstanding	Stated Capital at December 31 2004	2003
Q	floating	Series R	December 1, 2010	At any time	$25.50	8,000,000	—	—	—
R	$1.5435	Series Q	December 1, 2005	December 1, 2005	$25.00	8,000,000	8,000,000	200	200
S	floating	Series T	November 1, 2006	At any time	$25.50	8,000,000	8,000,000	200	200
T	fixed	Series S	November 1, 2011	November 1, 2011	$25.00	8,000,000			
Y	floating	Series Z	December 1, 2007	At any time	$25.50	10,000,000	1,147,380	29	29
Z	$1.3298	Series Y	December 1, 2007	December 1, 2007	$25.00	10,000,000	8,852,620	221	221
AA	$1.3625	Series AB	September 1, 2007	September 1, 2007	$25.00	20,000,000	20,000,000	510	510
AB	floating	Series AA	September 1, 2012	At any time	$25.50	20,000,000	—	—	—
AC	$1.3850	Series AD	March 1, 2008	March 1, 2008	$25.00	20,000,000	20,000,000	510	510
AD	floating	Series AC	March 1, 2013	At any time	$25.50	20,000,000	—	—	—
								1,670	1,670

SELF-STUDY **QUIZ 12-1**

Refer to the previous table showing a summary of BCE's preferred shares, and answer the following questions related to First Preferred Shares, Series Z.

1. How much did BCE receive per share when it sold the Series Z shares to investors?

2. What is the total amount of dividends payable on Series Z per year?

3. What is meant by redemption date?

4. Why is the redemption date for this series, December 1, 2007, the same as the conversion date?

After you complete your answers, check them with the solutions on page 659.

ACCOUNTING FOR SHARE CAPITAL

The shareholders' equity section of BCE's balance sheet reports five different accounts, as shown in Exhibit 12.1. These accounts represent the two primary sources of shareholders' equity:

1. *Contributed capital*, which reflects the amount invested by shareholders. Contributed capital has two distinct components: (a) amounts initially received from the

sale of shares, and (b) contributed surplus that reflects contributions made by shareholders in excess of the amounts credited to share capital accounts. The contributed capital accounts for BCE are preferred shares, common shares, and contributed surplus. (The account *currency translation adjustment* relates to transactions involving foreign currencies, which are discussed in advanced accounting courses.)

2. *Retained earnings* generated by the profit-making activities of the company. This is the *cumulative* amount of net income earned since the organization of the corporation less the cumulative amount of dividends paid by the corporation since organization.

Most companies generate a significant part of their shareholders' equity from retained earnings rather than from capital raised through the sale of shares. In the case of BCE, however, the retained earnings amount is negative. BCE's deficit resulted from the implementation in 2002 of a new standard related to the valuation of the company's goodwill, which resulted in an impairment write-off of $8,180 billion.

INITIAL SALE OF SHARES

Two names are applied to transactions involving the initial sale of a company's shares to the public. An *initial public offering,* or *IPO,* involves the very first sale of a company's shares to the public (i.e., when the company first "goes public"). You have probably heard stories of Internet companies that had their shares increase dramatically in value the day of their IPO. While investors sometimes earn significant returns on IPOs, they also take significant risks. Once the shares of a company are traded on established markets, additional sales of new shares to the public are called *seasoned new issues.*

As was the case with debt (discussed in Chapter 11), most companies use an underwriter to assist in the sale of shares. The underwriter is usually an investment bank that acts as an intermediary between the corporation and the investors. The underwriter advises the corporation on matters concerning the sale and is directly involved in the sale of shares to the public.

Most sales of shares to the public are cash transactions. To illustrate accounting for an initial sale of shares, assume that BCE sold 100,000 common shares for $22 per share. The company records the following journal entry:

Cash (A) (100,000 × $22)		2,200,000	
Common shares			2,200,000

Assets	=	Liabilities	+	Shareholders' Equity
Cash	+2,200,000			Common shares	+2,200,000

The sale of common shares is reported on the balance sheet in the format shown in Exhibit 12.1.

SALE OF SHARES IN SECONDARY MARKETS

When a company sells shares to the public, the transaction is between the issuing corporation and the buyer. Subsequent to the initial sale, investors can sell shares to other investors without directly affecting the corporation. For example, if investor Jon Drago sold 1,000 of BCE's common shares to Jennifer Lea, BCE does not record a journal entry on its books. Mr. Drago received cash for the shares he sold, and Ms. Lea received shares for the cash she paid. BCE itself did not receive or pay anything because of this transaction.

Each business day, the *National Post* and other newspapers report the results of thousands of transactions between investors in the secondary markets, where trading of shares among investors takes place. These markets include the Toronto Stock Exchange and CDNX (in Canada), the New York Stock Exchange, the American Stock Exchange, and NASDAQ (in the United States), and similar markets in other countries.

Managers of corporations follow very closely the movements in the price of their company's shares. Shareholders expect to earn money on their investment from both

SELECTED FOCUS COMPANY COMPARISONS: RETAINED EARNINGS AS A PERCENTAGE OF SHAREHOLDER'S EQUITY

Placer Dome	18.6%
Intrawest Corp.	40.4%
Petro Canada	61.9%

dividends and increases in the share (or stock) price. In many instances, senior management has been replaced because of poor performance of the shares in the secondary markets. Although managers watch the share price on a daily basis, it is important to remember that the transactions between investors do not directly affect the company's financial statements.

FINANCIAL **ANALYSIS**

GOING PUBLIC

As noted earlier, an initial public offering (IPO) is the first sale of shares to the public. Prior to that sale, the company is a private company. A company might want to go public for two common reasons. For it to grow and meet consumer demand, it must expand its productive capacity. The need for new capital may be beyond the capability of the private owners. By going public, the company can raise the funds needed to expand.

In some cases, the company may not need significant funds, but the current owners may want to create a market for its shares. Often, selling shares is difficult if the company is not listed on a major stock exchange. By going public, a company can increase the marketability of its shares.

Initial public offerings often create a lot of interest among investors. Some good opportunities are available to earn excellent returns by investing in growing companies. Substantial risk also is associated with many IPOs.

In recent years, much interest has surrounded Internet companies that have gone public. Virtually any company with ".com" in its name has received significant attention from investors. Recently, Google Inc., which operates one of the most popular search engines, had an initial public offering of its shares at an initial price of $85. Since the IPO in August 2004, Google's share price increased significantly, reaching $300 by July 2005 due to investors' expectations of the company's future profitability.

There are countless stories of people in their twenties and thirties who have become instant millionaires after the IPO of a new Internet company. Less well publicized, however, are the stories of individuals who have lost money investing in new and unproven businesses.

SHARES ISSUED FOR NON-CASH ASSETS OR SERVICES

Small companies are playing an increasingly important role in the North American economy. They account for a large percentage of the new jobs that have been created in the past decade. Many of today's corporate giants were small start-up companies just a few years ago. Companies such as Dell, Microsoft, and Amazon.com began literally as basement operations in the homes of their founders.

One feature common to all start-up companies is a shortage of cash. Because these companies often cannot afford to pay cash for needed assets and services, they sometimes issue shares to people who can supply these assets and services. Many executives, for instance, will join start-up companies for very low salaries because they also earn compensation in the form of common shares. An executive who was granted BCE shares during its early days would be very wealthy today.

When a company issues shares to acquire assets or services, the acquired items are recorded at the *market value* of the shares issued at the date of the transaction in accordance with the *cost principle*. If the market value of the shares issued cannot be determined, the market value of the consideration received should be used.

To illustrate, assume that during its early years of operations, BCE was unable to pay cash for needed legal services. The company issued 10,000 shares to a law firm when the share was selling for $15. At that time, the company recorded the following journal entry:

| Legal fees (E) | 150,000 | |
| Common shares | | 150,000 |

Assets	=	Liabilities	+	Shareholders' Equity	
				Legal fees	−150,000
				Common shares	+150,000

Notice that the value of the legal services received is assumed to be the same as the value of the shares that were issued. This assumption is reasonable because two independent parties usually keep negotiating a deal until the value of what is given up equals the value of what is received.

SHARES ISSUED FOR EMPLOYEE COMPENSATION

One of the advantages of the corporate form is the possibility to separate the management of a business from its ownership. This separation also can be a disadvantage because some managers may not act in the shareholders' best interests. This problem can be overcome in a number of ways. Compensation packages can be developed to reward managers for meeting goals that are important to shareholders. Another strategy is to offer managers *stock options,* which permit them to buy shares at a fixed price.

The holder of a stock option has an interest in a company's performance in the same manner as a shareholder. Stock option plans have become an increasingly common form of compensation over the past years. Indeed, 196 of the 200 companies surveyed by *Financial Reporting in Canada 2004* reported stock option plans for their employees.[6] However, the excessive use of stock options as a form of compensating key executives led the executives of some companies to manipulate reported financial information in an effort to increase the share price so they can benefit by buying shares at a fixed price and selling them at a higher price.

The BCE annual report provides the following disclosures:

REAL WORLD EXCERPT

BCE Inc.

ANNUAL REPORT

Note 22. STOCK-BASED COMPENSATION PLANS

The table below shows you more about BCE Inc.'s stock option programs at December 31, 2004.

Range of Exercise Prices	Options Outstanding			Options Exercisable	
	Number	Weighted Average Remaining Life	Weighted Average Exercise Price ($)	Number	Weighted Average Exercise Price ($)
Below $20	1,609,697	3 years	$14	1,609,697	$14
$20–$30	12,377,141	7 years	$29	2,052,600	$28
$30–$40	8,123,342	7 years	$34	5,419,524	$34
Over $40	6,371,499	6 years	$41	5,551,612	$41
	28,481,679		$32	14,633,433	$34

The options issued by BCE specify that shares could be bought at a predetermined exercise price. Granting a stock option is a form of compensation even if the exercise price and the current share price are the same. If someone gives you a stock option, you

---

[6]C. Byrd, I. Chen, and J. Smith, *Financial Reporting in Canada 2004.* Toronto: Canadian Institute of Chartered Accountants, 2004, p. 490.

could think of it as a risk-free investment. If you hold a stock option when the share price declines, you have lost nothing. If the share price increases, you can exercise your option at the specified price and sell the shares at a higher price for a profit.

Stock options are a widely used form of executive compensation. Most companies offer them with an exercise price equal to the current market price per share.

For example, in 2004 BCE granted its key employees options to purchase a total of 5,911,576 common shares in the future at an average price of $30, which equals the market price per share on the date of the grant. The option holders would benefit from the stock option in a few years if the market price per share exceeds $30, presumably because the increase in BCE's market value is partially attributed to their managerial skills. Undoubtedly, the difference between the increased market price and the exercise price of $30 is a form of compensation to the key employees. When the options are exercised, BCE receives $30 per common share, while it could obtain a higher price if it sold the same shares in the market to other investors. Clearly, the exercise of employee stock options entails a cost to BCE that should be measured and reported. The more interesting issue, however, is whether BCE incurs a cost at the time of granting the options, even if the exercise price equals the market price at the grant date. In general, a fair value of the options can be estimated using complex mathematical formulae, and then compared to the exercise price to determine the additional compensation expense for the period.

The measurement and reporting of the cost of stock options has been hotly debated by accounting standard setters and company executives. Many companies rely on stock options to compensate their employees and key executives, especially in the technology, energy, and gold mining sectors. Companies in these sectors have lobbied against reporting the cost of stock options as an expense on the income statement because it would lower their net income, and may even turn the net income into a net loss.

Recent changes in Canadian accounting standards require Canadian companies to measure the cost of their stock option plans using a conventional but complex present value calculation, then include the result as a compensation expense in the computation of net income. The application of this new standard is likely to cause significant reductions in the net incomes of many companies. For example, the 2004 net income of Research In Motion Limited, best known for its production and sale of the BlackBerry wireless platform, would have been reduced by 40 percent had the company reported the cost of its stock option plan as a compensation expense.

ACCOUNTING FOR CASH DIVIDENDS

LEARNING OBJECTIVE 3

Discuss dividends and analyze related transactions.

Investors buy common shares because they expect a return on their investment. This return can come in two forms: appreciation of the share price and dividends. Some investors prefer to buy shares that pay little or no dividends because companies that reinvest the majority of their earnings tend to increase their future earnings potential, along with their stock price. Wealthy investors in high tax brackets prefer to receive their return on equity investments in the form of higher stock prices because capital gains may be taxed at a lower rate than dividend income. Other investors, such as retired people who need a steady income, prefer to receive their return on an investment in the form of dividends. These people often seek shares that will pay very high dividends, such as shares of utility companies.

A corporation does not have a legal obligation to pay dividends. Creditors can force a company into bankruptcy if it does not meet required interest payments on debt, but shareholders do not have a similar right if a corporation is unable to pay dividends.

Without a qualifier, the term *dividend* means a cash dividend, but dividends can also be paid in assets other than cash or by issuing additional shares. The most common type of dividend is a cash dividend.

Although a corporation does not have a legal obligation to pay a dividend, a liability is created when the board of directors approves (i.e., declares) a dividend.

BCE pays cash dividends on its outstanding preferred and common shares on a quarterly basis. The company provides details of the quarterly dividends on its preferred and common shares on its Web site. For example, the cash dividends on common shares and First Preferred, Series Z shares for the last quarter of 2005 follow.

REAL WORLD EXCERPT

BCE Inc.

DIVIDEND INFORMATION

www.bce.ca

Type of Share	Amount of Dividend	Declaration Date	Date of Record	Payment Date
Common share	$0.30	Nov. 30, 2005	Dec. 15, 2005	Jan. 15, 2006
First Preferred, Series Z	$0.33245	Nov. 30, 2005	Feb. 1, 2006	Mar. 1, 2006

A dividend declaration includes three important dates:

The **DECLARATION DATE** is the date on which the board of directors officially approves a dividend.

The **DATE OF RECORD** is the date on which the corporation prepares the list of current shareholders as shown on its records; dividends can be paid only to the shareholders who own shares on that date.

The **PAYMENT DATE** is the date on which a cash dividend is paid to the shareholders of record.

1. **Declaration date.** The **declaration date** is the date on which the board of directors officially approved the dividend. As soon as it makes the declaration, it creates a dividend liability.

2. **Date of record.** The **date of record** follows the declaration; it is the date on which the corporation prepares the list of current shareholders, based on its shareholder records. The dividend is payable only to those names listed on the record date. No journal entry is made on this date.

3. **Payment date.** The **payment date** is the date on which the cash is disbursed to pay the dividend liability. It follows the date of record as specified in the dividend announcement.

For instructional purposes, the time lag between the date of declaration and the date of payment may be ignored because it does not pose any substantive issues. When all three dates fall in the same accounting period, a single entry on the date of payment may be made in practice for purely practical reasons.

Assume, for simplicity, that BCE had 900 million common shares and 1 million First Preferred—Series 2 shares outstanding on the declaration date. The amounts of cash dividends on these two classes of shares are computed as follows:

First Preferred—Series 2: $1,000,000 \times \$0.33245 = \$\ \ \ \ \ 332,450$

Common: $900,000,000 \times \$0.30\ \ \ = \$270,000,000$

The declaration of dividends creates a liability on November 30, 2005, that is recorded as follows:

Retained earnings (SE)	270,332,450	
Dividend payable—Preferred (L)		332,450
Dividend payable—Common (L)		270,000,000

Assets	=	Liabilities		+	Shareholders' Equity	
		Dividends payable—P	332,450		Retained	
		Dividends payable—C	270,000,000		earnings	−270,332,450

The payment of the dividends on common shares on January 15, 2006 and the payment of dividends on the First Preferred—Series 2 shares on March 1, 2006 are recorded as follows:

| Dividend payable—Common (L) | . . . . | 270,000,000 | |
| Cash (A) | . . . . | | 270,000,000 |

Assets	=	Liabilities	+	Shareholders' Equity
Cash −270,000,000		Dividends payable—C −270,000,000		

| Dividend payable—Preferred (L) | . . . . | 332,450 | |
| Cash (A) | . . . . | | 332,450 |

Assets	=	Liabilities	+	Shareholders' Equity
Cash −332,450		Dividends payable—P −332,450		

Notice that the declaration and payment of a cash dividend have two impacts: they reduce assets (cash) and shareholders' equity (retained earnings) by the same amount. This observation explains the two fundamental requirements for the payment of a cash dividend:

1. *Sufficient retained earnings.* The corporation must have accumulated a sufficient amount of retained earnings to cover the amount of the dividend. Incorporation laws usually place restrictions on cash dividends. For example, federal and provincial laws often limit cash dividends to the balance in the Retained Earnings account.

2. *Sufficient cash.* The corporation must have access to sufficient cash to pay the dividend and to meet the operating needs of the business. The mere fact that the Retained Earnings account has a large credit balance does not mean that the board of directors can declare and pay a cash dividend. The cash generated in the past by earnings represented in the Retained Earnings account may have been expended to acquire inventory, buy operational assets, and pay liabilities. Consequently, no necessary relationship exists between the balance of retained earnings and the balance of cash on any particular date. Quite simply, retained earnings is not cash.

FINANCIAL **ANALYSIS**

IMPACT OF DIVIDENDS ON SHARE PRICE

An additional date is important in understanding dividends, but it has no accounting implications. The date two business days before the date of record is known as the *ex-dividend date.* This date is established by the stock exchanges to make certain that dividend cheques are sent to the right people. If you buy shares before the ex-dividend date, you receive the dividend. If you buy the shares on the ex-dividend date or later, the previous shareholder receives the dividend.

If you follow share prices, you will notice that the price of a company's common share often falls on the ex-dividend date. The reason is simple. On that date, the share is worth less because it no longer includes the right to receive the next dividend.

Because of the importance of dividends to many investors, analysts often compute the dividend yield ratio to evaluate a corporation's dividend policy.

KEY **RATIO ANALYSIS:**

■ **LEARNING OBJECTIVE 4**

Analyze the dividend yield ratio.

DIVIDEND YIELD RATIO

ANALYTICAL QUESTION → Investors in common shares expect to earn a return on their investment. A portion of this return comes in the form of dividends. How much do investors earn on their investment based on dividends?

RATIO AND COMPARISONS → The *dividend yield ratio* is a measure of the percentage return that owners are earning from the dividends they receive. Potential investors often use this ratio to help select from alternative investment opportunities. It is computed as follows:

Dividend Yield Ratio = Dividends per Share ÷ Market Price per Share

The 2004 ratio for BCE is:

$1.20 ÷ $28.92 = 4.1%

Comparisons over Time			Comparisons with Competitors	
BCE			**Shaw Communications**	**Telus**
2002	2003	2004	2004	2004
4.5%	4.2%	4.1%	0.8%	1.66%

INTERPRETATIONS

In General → Investors in common shares earn a return from dividends and capital appreciation (increases in the market price of the shares they own). Growth-oriented companies often pay out very small amounts of dividends and rely on increases in their market price to provide a return to investors. Others pay out large dividends but have more stable market prices. Each type of share appeals to different types of investors with different risk and return preferences.

Focus Company Analysis → During the three years 2002, 2003, and 2004, BCE distributed annual dividends of $1.20 per share, yet its dividend yield decreased from 4.5 percent to 4.1 percent. This is because the market price of BCE's common shares increased slightly during this period. In comparison with BCE, both Shaw Communications and Telus paid a low dividend per share relative to their share prices; hence, their low dividend yields.

A Few Cautions → Remember that the dividend yield ratio tells only part of the return on investment story. Often, potential capital appreciation is a much more important consideration. When analyzing changes in the ratio, it is important to understand the cause. For example, a company might pay out $2 per share in dividends each year. If the market price of its shares is $100 per share, the yield is 2 percent. If the market price per share falls to $25 the following year and the company continues to pay out $2 per share in dividends, the dividend yield ratio will "improve" to 8 percent. Most analysts would not interpret this change as being favourable.

DIVIDENDS ON PREFERRED SHARES

Investors who purchase preferred shares give up certain advantages that are available to investors in common shares. Generally, preferred shareholders do not have the right to vote at the annual meeting, nor do they share in increased earnings if the company becomes more profitable. To compensate these investors, preferred shares offer some advantages not available to common shareholders. Perhaps the most important advantage is dividend preference. The two most common dividend preferences are:

1. Current dividend preference.
2. Cumulative dividend preference.

CURRENT DIVIDEND PREFERENCE is the feature of preferred shares that grants preferred shareholders priority for dividends over common shareholders.

Current Dividend Preference Preferred shares always carry a **current dividend preference**, which requires that the current preferred dividend be paid before any dividends are paid on the common shares. When the current dividend preference has been met and there are no other preferences, dividends can then be paid to the common shareholders.

Declared dividends must be allocated between the preferred and common shares. First, dividends are allocated to the preferred shares, and then the remainder of the total dividend is allocated to the common shares. Exhibit 12.4, Case A, illustrates the allocation of the current dividend preference under three different assumptions concerning the total amount of dividends to be paid.

Cumulative Dividend Preference The **cumulative dividend preference** states that if all or a part of the current dividend is not paid in full, the unpaid amount, known as **dividends in arrears**, must be paid in the future before any common dividends can be paid. Of course, if the preferred shares are non-cumulative, dividends cannot be in arrears; any dividends that are not declared are lost permanently by the preferred shareholders. Because preferred shareholders are not willing to accept this unfavourable feature, preferred shares are usually cumulative.

Dividends are never an actual liability until the board of directors declares them. Dividends in arrears are not reported on the balance sheet but are disclosed in the notes to the statements.

The allocation of dividends between cumulative preferred shares and common shares is illustrated in Exhibit 12.4, Case B, under four different assumptions concerning the total amount of dividends to be paid. Notice that the dividends in arrears are paid first, then the current dividend preference is paid, and, finally, the remainder is paid to the common shareholders.

CUMULATIVE DIVIDEND PREFERENCE is the feature of preferred shares that requires specified current dividends not paid in full to accumulate for every year in which they are not paid. These cumulative preferred dividends must be paid before any common dividends can be paid.

DIVIDENDS IN ARREARS are dividends on cumulative preferred shares that have not been declared in prior years.

EXHIBIT **12.4**

Dividends on Preferred Shares

Case A—Current dividend preference only

Preferred shares outstanding, $1.20; 2,000 shares.

Common shares outstanding, 5,000 shares.

Allocation of dividends between preferred and common shares assuming current dividend preference only:

Assumptions	Total Dividends Paid	$1.20 Preferred Shares (2,000 shares)*	Common Shares (5,000 shares)
No. 1	$ 2,000	$2,000	0
No. 2	3,000	2,400	$ 600
No. 3	18,000	2,400	15,600

*Preferred dividends = 2,000 × $1.20 = $2,400.

Case B—Cumulative dividend preference

Preferred and common shares outstanding—same as in Case A. Dividends in arrears for the two preceding years.

Allocation of dividends between preferred and common shares, assuming cumulative preference:

Assumptions (dividends in arrears, 2 years)	Total Dividends Paid	$1.20 Preferred Shares (2,000 shares)*	Common Shares (5,000 shares)
No. 1	$ 2,400	$2,400	0
No. 2	7,200	7,200	0
No. 3	8,000	7,200	$ 800
No. 4	30,000	7,200	22,800

*Current dividend preference, 2,000 × $1.20 = $2,400; dividends in arrears preference, $2,400 × 2 years = $4,800; and current dividend preference plus dividends in arrears = $7,200.

FINANCIAL **ANALYSIS**

REAL WORLD EXCERPT

Lone Star Industries

ANNUAL REPORT

IMPACT OF DIVIDENDS IN ARREARS

The existence of dividends in arrears is important information because they limit a company's ability to pay dividends to its common shareholders and has implications for the company's future cash flows. The following note from Lone Star Industries is typical if a company has dividends in arrears:

> The total of dividends in arrears on the $13.50 preferred shares at the end of the year was $11,670,000. The aggregate amount of such dividend must be paid before any dividends are paid on common shares.

Remember that various issues of preferred shares can offer different features. Most preferred shares have the cumulative dividend preference to provide shareholders with extra security. Companies can offer additional features to provide even more security. Many companies offer the feature described in the following note from Bally Manufacturing:

REAL WORLD EXCERPT

Bally Manufacturing

ANNUAL REPORT

> The holders of preferred shares do not have voting rights except that the holders would have the right to elect two additional directors of Bally if dividends on the preferred shares are in arrears in an amount equal to at least six quarterly dividends.

By electing two members of the board of directors, preferred shareholders have specific individuals to represent their interests. Bally included this feature with its preferred shares to make the shares more attractive to potential shareholders.

SELF-STUDY **QUIZ 12-2**

Answer the following questions concerning dividends:

1. On which dividend date is a liability created?
2. On which dividend date does a cash outflow occur?
3. When are dividends in arrears reported on the balance sheet as a liability?
4. What are the two fundamental requirements for the payment of a dividend?

After you complete your answers, check them with the solutions on page 659.

ACCOUNTING FOR STOCK DIVIDENDS AND STOCK SPLITS

STOCK DIVIDENDS

■ **LEARNING OBJECTIVE 5**

Discuss the purpose of stock dividends, stock splits, and report transactions.

A **STOCK DIVIDEND** is a distribution of additional shares of a corporation's own equity.

A **stock dividend** is a distribution of additional shares of a corporation's own share capital to its shareholders on a pro rata basis at no cost. Stock dividends usually consist of additional common shares issued to the holders of common shares. *Pro rata basis* means that each shareholder receives additional shares equal to the percentage of shares already held. A shareholder with 10 percent of the outstanding shares receives 10 percent of any additional shares issued as a stock dividend.

The term *stock dividend* is sometimes misused in annual reports and news articles. A recent *Wall Street Journal* headline announced that a particular company had just declared a "stock dividend." A close reading of the article revealed that the company had declared a cash dividend on the shares.

The value of a stock dividend is the subject of much debate. In reality, a stock dividend has no economic value, as such. All shareholders receive a pro rata distribution of shares, which means that each owns exactly the same portion of the company both before and after the stock dividend. The value of an investment is determined by the percentage of the company that is owned, not the number of shares that are held. If you get change for a dollar, you are not wealthier because you hold *four* quarters instead of only *one* dollar. Similarly, if you own 10 percent of a company, you are not wealthier simply because the company declares a stock dividend and gives you (and all other shareholders) more shares. At this point, you may still wonder why having extra shares does not make an investor wealthier. The reason is simple: the stock market reacts immediately when a stock dividend is issued, and the share price falls proportionally. Theoretically, if the share price was $60 before a stock dividend, normally (in the absence of events affecting the company) the price falls to $30 if the number of shares is doubled. Thus, an investor could own 100 shares worth $6,000 before the stock dividend (100 × $60) and 200 shares worth $6,000 after the stock dividend (200 × $30).

In reality, the fall in price is not exactly proportional to the number of new shares that are issued. In some cases, the stock dividend makes the stock more attractive to new investors. Many investors prefer to buy shares in *round lots,* which are multiples of 100 shares. An investor with $10,000 might not buy a share selling for $150 because she cannot afford to buy 100 shares. She might buy the share, however, if the price is less than $100 as a result of a stock dividend. In other cases, stock dividends are accompanied by an announcement of increases in cash dividends, which are attractive to some investors.

When a common stock dividend occurs, the company must transfer an additional amount into the Common Shares account to reflect the additional shares that have been issued. The amount transferred should reflect the fair market value per share at the declaration date, as recommended in the Canada Business Corporations Act.

For small stock dividends that are less than 20–25 percent of the outstanding shares, the amount transferred from the Retained Earnings account to the Common Shares account is based on the market price per share at the date of declaration. If the company declared a cash dividend instead of a stock dividend and the shareholders used the cash they receive to buy additional shares, the shareholders would be paying the market price to acquire additional shares. This assumption is valid if the stock dividend is relatively small, so that it will not cause a significant change in the market price. For larger stock dividends, the market price per share will drop significantly, so it will not be an appropriate basis for transferring an amount from Retained Earnings to Common Shares. In this case, the amount transferred is based on the average issue price per share. In either situation, the stock dividend does not change total shareholders' equity. It changes only the balances of specific shareholders' equity accounts.

Let us assume that a company declared on July 25, 2005, a 10-percent stock dividend on common shares to be issued on August 25, 2005, to shareholders of record on August 10, 2005. The company had 100,000 shares outstanding and the market price per share was $20 on the date of declaration. The declaration of the stock dividend requires the following journal entry on July 25, 2005:

Retained earnings (SE) (100,000 × 10% × $20)	200,000	
Stock dividend to be issued (SE)		200,000

Assets	=	Liabilities	+	Shareholders' Equity	
				Retained earnings	−200,000
				Stock dividend to be issued	+200,000

The equity account, Stock Dividend To Be Issued, is credited, instead of Common Shares, until the shares are issued. The issuance and distribution of the additional shares on August 25, 2005 is recorded as follows:

| Stock dividend to be issued (SE) .... | 200,000 | |
| Common shares (SE) .... | | 200,000 |

Assets	=	Liabilities	+	Shareholders' Equity	
				Stock dividend to be issued	−200,000
				Common shares	+200,000

If the company had declared a 50-percent stock dividend, the average price received for issuing all of the common shares would be used instead of the market price per share as a basis for the reduction of retained earnings. If the average issue price per share is $15,[7] the Retained Earnings account would be reduced by $750,000 (100,000 × 50% × $15) and the Common Shares account would be increased by the same amount.

STOCK SPLITS

Stock splits are *not* dividends. They are similar to a stock dividend but are quite different in terms of their impact on the shareholders' equity accounts. In a **stock split**, the *total* number of authorized shares is increased by a specified number, such as a 2-for-1 split. In this instance, each share held is called in, and two new shares are issued in its place. When BCE executed a 2-for-1 stock split on May 14, 1997, it doubled the number of common shares outstanding. In contrast to a stock dividend, a stock split does *not* result in a transfer of a dollar amount to the Common Shares account.

A **STOCK SPLIT** is an increase in the total number of authorized shares by a specified ratio; it does not decrease retained earnings.

Over the years, BCE's common shares split three times. A 4-for-1 split occurred on October 4, 1948, followed by a second 3-for-1 split on April 26, 1979. The last split was a 2-for-1, executed on May 14, 1997. In summary, a common share issued prior to October 4, 1948, has already split into 24 shares. If these stock splits did not occur, BCE's share price would have been $707.50 at the time of writing this book.

In both a stock dividend and a stock split, the shareholder receives more shares but does not pay to acquire the additional shares. A stock dividend requires a journal entry; a stock split does not require one but is disclosed in the notes to the financial statements. The comparative effects of a stock dividend versus a stock split may be summarized as follows:

Shareholders' Equity	Before	After a 100% Stock Dividend	After a Two-for-One Stock Split
Contributed capital			
Number of shares outstanding	30,000	60,000	60,000
Issue price per share	$ 10	$ 10	$ 5
Common shares	300,000	600,000	300,000
Retained earnings	650,000	350,000	650,000
Total shareholders' equity	$950,000	$950,000	$950,000

SELF-STUDY **QUIZ 12-3**

Barton Corporation issued 100,000 new common shares as a result of a stock dividend when the market value was $30 per share. The average issue price is $10 per share.

1. Record this transaction, assuming that it was a small stock dividend.

2. Record this transaction, assuming that it was a large stock dividend.

3. What journal entry is required if the transaction is a stock split?

After you complete your answers, check them with the solutions on page 659.

---

[7]The average issue price per share equals the balance of the Common Shares account divided by the number of common shares outstanding.

RETAINED EARNINGS

Retained earnings represent income that has been earned less dividends that have been declared since the first day of operations for the company. BCE has reported a deficit for the three years 2002, 2003, and 2004. The main reason for this deficit is the implementation in 2002 of the requirements of *CICA Handbook* section 3062, *Goodwill and Other Intangible Assets,* which came into effect on January 1, 2002. It requires that goodwill and indefinite-life intangible assets be assessed for impairment each year according to the new standards. Initial application of this new standard caused BCE to charge an impairment of $8,180 million to its retained earnings, which turned the credit balance of retained earnings into a debit balance, hence the deficit. Since the deficit did not result from unprofitable operations, BCE continued to declare and pay dividends to shareholders on a quarterly basis. During the three-year period 2002–2004, BCE retained more than $2 billion, which helped reduce the deficit from $7,686 million as at January 1, 2002 to $5,424 million as at December 31, 2004, as shown in Exhibit 12.1.

Under rare circumstances, you may see a statement that includes an adjustment to the beginning balance of retained earnings. This adjustment is called a **prior period adjustment**, which is the correction of an accounting error that occurred in the financial statements of a prior period.

If an accounting error from a previous period is corrected by making an adjustment to the current income statement, net income for the current period would be improperly measured. To avoid this problem, prior period adjustments are reported as an adjustment of the beginning balance of Retained Earnings because the incorrect amount of net income from the earlier year was closed to Retained Earnings in the year the error was made. Prior period adjustments are not reported on the income statement.

Several years ago, the financial statements of Lafayette Radio Electronics Corporation contained the following note:

> Subsequent to the issuance of its financial statements the company discovered a computational error in the amount of $1,046,000 in the calculation of its year-end inventory which resulted in an overstatement of ending inventory.

Lafayette Radio's overstatement of inventory resulted in an overstatement of pretax income by $1,046,000. If the company corrected the error in the year it was discovered and included its effect in that year's income statement, then pretax income would have been understated by $1,046,000. The incorrect measurement of income for each year could mislead some users of financial statements.

RESTRICTIONS ON RETAINED EARNINGS

Several types of business transactions may cause restrictions to be placed on retained earnings that limit a company's ability to pay dividends. The most typical example is borrowing money from a bank. For additional security, some banks include a loan covenant that limits the amount of dividends that a corporation can pay.[8] In addition, debt covenants often include a limit on borrowing and required minimum balances of cash or working capital. If debt covenants are violated, the creditor can demand immediate repayment of the debt.

The *full-disclosure principle* requires that restrictions on retained earnings be reported on the financial statements or in a separate note to the financial statements.

Most companies report restrictions on retained earnings in the notes to the statements. An example of such a note from an annual report of the May Department Store follows:

■ **LEARNING OBJECTIVE 6**
Measure and report retained earnings.

A **PRIOR PERIOD ADJUSTMENT** is an amount debited or credited directly to retained earnings to correct an accounting error of a prior period.

REAL WORLD EXCERPT

Lafayette Radio Electronics Corporation
ANNUAL REPORT

---

[8]In 2003, only eight of the 200 companies surveyed in *Financial Reporting in Canada 2004* indicated that there were conditions that affected their ability to pay dividends.

REAL WORLD EXCERPT

May Department Store

ANNUAL REPORT

Under the most restrictive covenants of long-term debt agreements, $1.2 billion of retained earnings was restricted as to the payment of dividends and/or common share repurchase.

Analysts are particularly interested in information concerning these restrictions because of the impact they have on the company's dividend policy.

KEY **RATIO ANALYSIS:**

■ **LEARNING OBJECTIVE 7**

Analyze the dividend payout ratio.

DIVIDEND PAYOUT RATIO

ANALYTICAL QUESTION → What proportion of earnings does the company pay in dividends?

RATIO AND COMPARISONS → The *dividend payout ratio* is the portion of current earnings that is paid to owners in the form of dividends. It is computed as follows:

$$\text{Dividend Payout Ratio} = \frac{\text{Dividends}}{\text{Net Income}}$$

The 2004 ratio for BCE is:

$$1{,}180 \div 1{,}593 = 0.74 \text{ or } 74\%$$

Comparisons over Time			Comparisons with Competitors	
BCE			Shaw Communications	Telus
2002	2003	2004	2004	2004
45%	64%	74%	40%	41%

INTERPRETATIONS

In General → The level of the dividend payout ratio (high or low) is not inherently good or bad; it simply gives you an insight into the strategy of a company. Low payout ratios are typically associated with rapidly growing companies that fund much of their growth with cash generated by operating activities. Companies with high payout ratios are often in lines of business that do not offer profitable growth opportunities. Rather than investing in these opportunities, such companies distribute earnings to the owners, who are free to invest them in other more profitable opportunities.

Focus Company Analysis → Prior to 2001, the dividend payout for BCE was a fairly low percentage of its net income. The company has maintained a dividend payout of $1.36 per share for years because the company's operations have been relatively stable over time. In 2001, BCE reduced its dividend payout to $1.20, because some of its investments in the telecommunications sector were not as profitable as expected. In 2004, BCE's dividend payout ratio increased significantly, not because the company distributed more dividends to its shareholders but because its net income declined significantly. In both 2003 and 2004, BCE's net income decreased as shown in Exhibit 12.1, causing an increase in the dividend payout ratio. This underscores the importance of analyzing ratios over time to avoid making incorrect inferences. BCE's ratio for 2004 is higher than those of Telus and Shaw Communications, indicating that these BCE competitors are retaining a higher percentage of their net income than BCE.

A Few Cautions → Most companies try to maintain a stable or increasing amount of dividends per share instead of maintaining a fixed dividend payout ratio. This means that in an unusually profitable year, the payout ratio will be low and in a year when profits are low, the ratio could be very high and might exceed 100 percent of the current year's earnings. The advantage of maintaining level dividends is that owners are able to plan and budget for a certain amount of dividend income each year, which may be important for some investors. As a result, analysts should review this ratio over a number of years to understand management's strategy.

FOCUS ON **CASH FLOWS**

FINANCING ACTIVITIES

Transactions involving share capital have a direct impact on the capital structure of a business. Because of the importance of these transactions, they are reported in a separate section of the statement called *Cash Flows from Financing Activities.* Examples of cash flows associated with share capital are included in the 2004 cash flow statement for BCE shown in Exhibit 12.5.

■ **LEARNING OBJECTIVE 8**

Discuss the impact of share capital transactions on cash flows.

EXHIBIT **12.5**

Excerpt from Statements of Cash Flows for BCE Inc.

REAL WORLD EXCERPT

BCE Inc.

ANNUAL REPORT

CONSOLIDATED STATEMENTS OF CASH FLOWS
For the Year Ended December 31

($ million)	2004	2003
Cash flows from financing activities		
Increase (decrease) in notes payable and bank advances	130	(295)
Issue of long-term debt	1,521	1,986
Repayment of long-term debt	(2,391)	(3,472)
Issue of common shares	32	19
Costs relating to the issuance of common shares	—	—
Issue of preferred shares	—	510
Redemption of preferred shares	—	(357)
Issue of equity securities by subsidiaries to non-controlling interest	8	132
Redemption of equity securities by subsidiaries from non-controlling interest	(58)	(108)
Cash dividends paid on common shares	(1,108)	(1,029)
Cash dividends paid on preferred shares	(85)	(61)
Cash dividends paid by subsidiaries to non-controlling interest	(188)	(184)
Other	(51)	(46)
Cash provided by (used in) financing activities	(2,190)	(2,905)

EFFECT ON CASH FLOW STATEMENT

IN GENERAL → Cash received from owners is reported as an inflow. Cash paid to owners is reported as an outflow. Examples are shown in the following table:

	Effect on Cash Flows
Financing activities	
Issuance of shares	+
Repurchase of shares	−
Payment of cash dividends	−

SELECTED FOCUS COMPANY COMPARISONS: CASH FLOWS FROM FINANCING ACTIVITIES (IN MILLIONS)

WestJet Airlines	$347
Intrawest Corp.	−326
Van Houtte	−5.9

FOCUS COMPANY ANALYSIS → During the last two years, BCE issued new common and preferred shares. At the same time, it redeemed previously issued preferred shares, paid dividends on both common and preferred shares, and repurchased its own common shares.

In both 2003 and 2004, BCE's equity transactions resulted in net cash outflows; the payment of dividends offset the relatively smaller amounts raised by issuing share capital.

ACCOUNTING AND REPORTING FOR UNINCORPORATED BUSINESSES

In this book, we emphasize the corporate form of business because it plays a dominant role in our economy. In fact, there are three forms of business organizations: corporations, sole proprietorships, and partnerships. As we have seen in this chapter, a *corporation* is a legal entity, separate and distinct from its owners. It can enter into contracts in its own name, be sued, and is taxed as a separate entity. A *sole proprietorship* is an unincorporated business owned by one individual. If you started a lawn care business in the summer by yourself, it would have been a sole proprietorship. It is not necessary to file any legal papers to create a proprietorship. A *partnership* is a business owned by two or more people. Again, it is not necessary to file legal papers to create a partnership, but it is certainly a good idea to have a lawyer draw up a contract between the partners.

Neither partnerships nor proprietorships are separate legal entities. As a result, owners may be directly sued and are individually taxed on the earnings of the business.

The fundamentals of accounting and reporting for unincorporated businesses are the same as for a corporation, except for owners' equity. Typical account structures for the three forms of business organizations are outlined in Exhibit 12.6.

EXHIBIT **12.6**

Comparative Account Structure among Types of Business Entities

Typical Account Structure		
Corporation (Shareholders' Equity)	Sole Proprietorship (Owner's Equity)	Partnership (Partners' Equity)
Share Capital Contributed Surplus	Doe, Capital	Able, Capital Baker, Capital
Retained Earnings	Not used	Not used
Dividends Paid	Doe, Drawings	Able, Drawings Baker, Drawings
Revenues, expenses, gains, and losses	Same	Same
Assets and liabilities	Same	Same

Accounting for sole proprietorships and partnerships is discussed in Chapter Supplement B.

DEMONSTRATION CASE

This case focuses on the organization and operations for the first year of Mera Corporation, which was organized on January 1, 2005. The laws specify that the legal capital for no par value shares is the full amount of the shares. The corporation was organized by 10 local entrepreneurs for the purpose of operating a business to sell various supplies to hotels. The charter authorized the following share capital:

Common shares, no par value, unlimited number of shares.
Preferred shares, 5 percent, $25 par value, 10,000 shares (cumulative, non-convertible, and non-voting; liquidation value, $26).

The following summarized transactions, selected from 2005, were completed during the months indicated:

a. Jan. Sold a total of 7,500 shares of no par value common shares to the 10 entrepreneurs for cash at $52 per share. Credit the Common Shares account for the total issue amount.

b. Feb. Sold 7,560 preferred shares at $25 per share; cash collected in full.

c. Mar. Purchased land for a store site and made full payment by issuing 400 preferred shares. Early construction of the store is planned. Debit Land (store site). The preferred share is selling at $25 per share.

d. Apr. Paid $2,000 cash for organization costs. Debit the intangible asset account Organization Costs.

e. May Issued 40 preferred shares to A.B. Cain in full payment of legal services rendered in connection with organization of the corporation. Assume that the preferred share is selling regularly at $25 per share. Debit Organization Costs.

f. June Sold 500 no par value common shares for cash to C.B. Abel at $54 per share.

g. Dec. 31 Purchased equipment for $600,000; paid cash. No amortization expense should be recorded in 2005.

h. Dec. 31 Borrowed $20,000 cash from the City Bank on a one-year, interest-bearing note. Interest is payable at a 12-percent rate at maturity.

i. Dec. 31 Calculated the following for the year: gross revenues, $129,300; expenses, including corporation income tax but excluding amortization of organization costs, $98,000. Assume that these summarized revenue and expense transactions involved cash. Because the equipment and the bank loan transactions were on December 31, no related adjusting entries at the end of 2005 are needed.

j. Dec. 31 Decided that a reasonable amortization period for organization costs, starting as of January 1, 2005, is 10 years. This intangible asset must be amortized to expense.

Required:

1. Prepare appropriate journal entries, with a brief explanation for each of these transactions.
2. Prepare the required adjusting entry for 2005 to amortize organization costs.
3. Prepare appropriate closing entries at December 31, 2005.
4. Prepare a balance sheet for Mera Corporation at December 31, 2005. Emphasize full disclosure of shareholders' equity.

We strongly recommend that you prepare your own answers to these requirements and then check your answers with the suggested solution.

SUGGESTED SOLUTION

1. Journal entries:

a. Jan. Cash (A) 390,000
          Common shares (7,500 shares) (SE)   390,000
          Sale of no par value common shares
          ($52 × 7,500 shares = $390,000).

b. Feb. Cash (A) 189,000
          Preferred shares, 5% (par $25, 7,560 shares) (SE)   189,000
          Sale of preferred shares ($25 × 7,560 shares = $189,000).

c.   Mar.   Land (SE)   10,000
            Preferred shares, 5% (par $25, 400 shares) (SE)   10,000
            Purchased land for future store site; paid in full by issuance
            of 100 preferred shares ($25 × 400 shares = $10,000.)

d.   Apr.   Organization costs (A)   2,000
            Cash (A)   2,000
            Paid organization costs.

e.   May   Organization costs (A)   1,000
            Preferred shares 5% (par $25, 40 shares) (SE)   1,000
            Organization costs (legal services) paid by issuance of
            40 preferred shares. The implied market value is
            $25 × 40 shares = $1,000.

f.   June   Cash (A)   27,000
            Common shares (500 shares) (SE)   27,000
            Sold 500 no par value common shares
            ($54 × 500 shares = $27,000).

h.   Dec. 31 Equipment (A)   600,000
            Cash (A)   600,000
            Purchased equipment.

i.   Dec. 31 Cash (A)   20,000
            Note payable (L)   20,000
            Borrowed cash and signed a one-year, 12 percent
            interest-bearing note.

j.   Dec. 31 Cash (A)   129,300
            Revenues (E)   129,300
            Expenses (E)   98,000
            Cash (A)   98,000
            To record summarized revenues and expenses.

2.   Dec. 31 Expenses (E)   300
            Organization costs (A)   300
            Adjusting entry to amortize organization cost for one year
            [($2,000 + $1,000) ÷ 10 years = $300].

3. Closing entries:

Dec. 31   Revenues (R)   129,300
          Retained earnings   129,300
          Retained earnings   98,300
          Expenses ($98,000 + $300) (E)   98,300

4. Balance sheet:

MERA CORPORATION
Balance Sheet
At December 31, 2005

Assets

Current assets		
Cash		$ 55,300
Tangible assets		
Land	$ 10,000	
Equipment (no depreciation assumed in the problem)	600,000	610,000
Intangible assets		
Organization cost (cost, $3,000 less amortization, $300)		2,700
Total assets		$668,000

Liabilities

Current liabilities	
Note payable, 12%	$ 20,000

Shareholders' Equity

Contributed capital	
Preferred shares, 5% (par value $25; authorized 10,000 shares, issued and outstanding 7,900 shares)	$200,000

(continued)

Common shares (no par value; authorized unlimited, issued and outstanding 8,000 shares)	417,000	
Total contributed capital	$617,000	
Retained earnings	31,000	
Total shareholders' equity		$648,000
Total liabilities and shareholders' equity		$668,000

SOLUTIONS TO **SELF-STUDY QUIZZES**

Self-Study Quiz 12-1

1. Amount received per share = Stated capital / Number of shares issued and outstanding
   = $221,000,000 / 8,852,620 = $24.96

   This amount should be $25.00, but we get $24.96 because the stated capital is rounded to the nearest $1 million.

2. Total annual dividends = Number of shares × Dividend per share = 8,852,620 × $1.3298 = $11,772,214.

3. The redemption date, December 1, 2007, is the earliest date when BCE can call Series Z back from shareholders and pay them $25.00 per share.

4. The redemption date is set on the same day as the conversion date so that shareholders who do not want to have their shares redeemed by BCE can choose to convert them to Series Y shares, provided that BCE has not redeemed Series Y shares at an earlier date.

Self-Study Quiz 12-2

1. Declaration date.

2. Date of payment.

3. Dividends are reported as a liability only after the date of declaration.

4. Dividends can be paid only if sufficient retained earnings and sufficient cash are both available.

Self-Study Quiz 12-3

1.	Retained earnings	3,000,000	
	Common shares		3,000,000
2.	Retained earnings	1,000,000	
	Common shares		1,000,000

3. No journal entry is required in the case of a stock split.

CHAPTER **TAKE-AWAYS**

1. **Explain the role of share capital in the capital structure of a corporation.   p. 636**
   The law recognizes corporations as separate legal entities. Owners invest in a corporation and receive shares that can be traded on established stock exchanges. Shares provide a number of rights, including the right to receive dividends.

2. **Describe the characteristics of shares and analyze transactions affecting share capital.   p. 639**
   A common share is the basic voting share issued by a corporation. Usually it has no par value, but par value shares also can be issued. Preferred shares are issued by some corporations. These shares contain some special rights and may appeal to certain investors.
   A number of key transactions involve share capital: (1) initial sale of shares, (2) cash dividends, and (3) stock dividends and stock splits. Each is illustrated in this chapter.

3. **Discuss dividends and analyze related transactions.   p. 645**
   The return associated with an investment in shares comes from two sources: appreciation of share price and dividends. Dividends are recorded as a liability when they are declared by the board of directors (i.e., on the date of declaration). The liability is satisfied when the dividends are paid (i.e., the date of payment).

4. **Analyze the dividend yield ratio.   p. 648**
   The dividend yield ratio measures the percentage of return on investment from dividends. For most companies, the return associated with dividends is very small.

5. **Discuss the purpose of stock dividends, stock splits, and report transactions.   p. 650**
   Stock dividends are distributions of a company's shares to existing shareholders on a pro rata basis. The transaction involves transferring an additional amount into the Common

Shares account from the Retained Earnings account. A stock split also involves the distribution of additional shares to shareholders but no additional amount is transferred into the Common Shares account from the Retained Earnings account.

6. **Measure and report retained earnings.   p. 653**
The Retained Earnings account includes income that has been earned since a company began its operations minus any dividends that have been distributed to shareholders. The amount of retained earnings is important because dividends normally can be paid only if there is a sufficient balance in this account (and in the cash account).

7. **Analyze the dividend payout ratio.   p. 654**
Dividends represent a distribution of the income earned by a corporation. The dividend payout ratio measures the percentage of income that is paid out each year. This percentage differs significantly among companies. Most companies that are growing rapidly pay out a small percentage of their earnings.

8. **Discuss the impact of share capital transactions on cash flows.   p. 655**
Both inflows (e.g., issuance of share capital) and outflows (e.g., repurchase of shares) are reported in the Financing Activities section of the cash flow statement. The payment of dividends is reported as an outflow in this section.

Throughout the preceding chapters, we emphasized the conceptual basis of accounting. An understanding of the rationale underlying accounting is important for both preparers and users of financial statements. In Chapter 13, we bring together our discussion of the major users of financial statements and how they analyze and use them. We discuss and illustrate many widely used analytical techniques discussed in earlier chapters, as well as additional techniques. As you study Chapter 13, you will see that an understanding of accounting rules and concepts is essential for effective analysis of financial statements.

Chapter Supplement A

Repurchase of Shares

TREASURY SHARES are a corporation's own shares that have been issued but were subsequently reacquired and held by that corporation.

A corporation may want to purchase its own shares from existing shareholders for a number of strategic reasons. A common reason is the existence of an employee bonus plan that provides workers with the company's shares as part of their compensation. Because of provincial securities regulations concerning newly issued shares, most companies find that it is less costly to give their employees shares that were purchased from shareholders than to issue new shares.

Shares that were issued to shareholders and then subsequently *reacquired* and held by that corporation are called **treasury shares**. While these shares are held by the issuing corporation, they have no voting, dividend, or other shareholder rights.

Most Canadian companies cancel their shares when they buy them back from shareholders, as indicated in *Financial Reporting in Canada 2004*.[9] When shares are cancelled, the appropriate share capital account is reduced by an amount that reflects the average issuance price per share. If the purchase price is less than the average issuance price, the difference is credited to Contributed Surplus. For example, if BCE purchased 100,000 common shares in the open market at $15 per share and the average price of all of the previously issued common shares is $17, the journal entry and the transaction effects would be as follows:

Companies Reporting Repurchase of Shares (sample of 200 companies)

- Treasury shares held 3
- Cancellation of shares 55
- No repurchase of shares 142

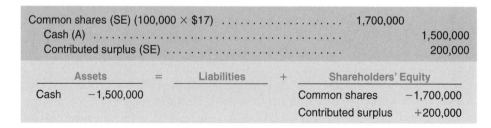

Common shares (SE) (100,000 × $17)	1,700,000	
Cash (A)		1,500,000
Contributed surplus (SE)		200,000

Assets		=	Liabilities	+	Shareholders' Equity	
Cash	−1,500,000				Common shares	−1,700,000
					Contributed surplus	+200,000

[9]C. Byrd, I. Chen, and J. Smith, *Financial Reporting in Canada 2004*. Toronto: Canadian Institute of Chartered Accountants, 2004, p. 319.

Assume further that BCE subsequently purchased 50,000 of its own common shares when the price per share was $23. In this case, the excess of the purchase price over the issuance price is $6 per share for a total of $300,000. This difference is debited first to Contributed Surplus to the extent of $200,000 (the account balance) and the remaining amount, $100,000, is debited to Retained Earnings. The Retained Earnings account is reduced because the excess of the purchase price over the contribution made previously by shareholders reflects the company's profitable operations, which resulted in net income and increased retained earnings; hence, the debit to Retained Earnings. The journal entry and the transaction effects follow:

Common shares (SE) (50,000 × $17)	850,000	
Contributed surplus (SE)	200,000	
Retained earnings (SE)	100,000	
Cash (A)		1,150,000

Assets		=	Liabilities	+	Shareholders' Equity	
Cash	−1,150,000				Common shares	−850,000
					Contributed surplus	−200,000
					Retained earnings	−100,000

Chapter Supplement B

Accounting for Owners' Equity for Sole Proprietorships and Partnerships

OWNER'S EQUITY FOR A SOLE PROPRIETORSHIP

A sole proprietorship is an unincorporated business owned by one person. Only two owner's equity accounts are needed: (1) a capital account for the proprietor (J. Doe, Capital), and (2) a drawing (or withdrawal) account for the proprietor (J. Doe, Drawings).

The capital account of a sole proprietorship serves two purposes: to record investments by the owner and to accumulate periodic income or loss. The drawing account is used to record the owner's withdrawals of cash or other assets from the business. The drawing account is closed to the capital account at the end of each accounting period. The capital account reflects the cumulative total of all investments by the owner plus all earnings of the entity less all withdrawals of resources from the entity by the owner.

In most respects, the accounting for a sole proprietorship is the same as for a corporation. Exhibit 12.7 presents the recording of selected transactions and the owner's equity section of the balance sheet of Doe Retail Store to illustrate the accounting for owner's equity for a sole proprietorship.

EXHIBIT **12.7**

Accounting for Owner's Equity for a Sole Proprietorship

Selected Transactions during 2005

January 1, 2005

J. Doe started a retail store by investing $150,000 of personal savings. The journal entry for the business is as follows:

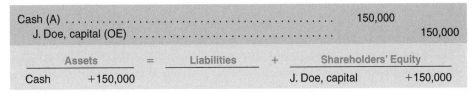

Cash (A)	150,000	
J. Doe, capital (OE)		150,000

Assets		=	Liabilities	+	Shareholders' Equity	
Cash	+150,000				J. Doe, capital	+150,000

During 2005

Each month during the year, Doe withdrew $1,000 cash from the business for personal living expenses. Accordingly, the following journal entry was made each month:

| J. Doe, drawings (OE) .... | 1,000 | |
| Cash (A) .... | | 1,000 |

Assets	=	Liabilities	+	Shareholders' Equity	
Cash −1,000				J. Doe, drawings	−1,000

Note: At December 31, 2005, after the last withdrawal, the drawings account will reflect a debit balance of $12,000.

December 31, 2005

The store's operations for the year resulted in revenues of $128,000 and expenses of $110,000. The revenue and expense accounts are closed to the capital account at the end of the year. The closing entry follows:

Individual revenue accounts (R)	128,000	
Individual expense account (E)		110,000
J. Doe, capital (OE)		18,000

Assets	=	Liabilities	+	Shareholders' Equity	
				Revenues	−128,000
				Expenses	+110,000
				J. Doe, capital	+18,000

December 31, 2005

The journal entry required to close the drawings account follows:

| J. Doe, capital (OE) .... | 12,000 | |
| J. Doe, drawings (OE) .... | | 12,000 |

Assets	=	Liabilities	+	Shareholders' Equity	
				J. Doe, capital	−12,000
				J. Doe, drawings	+12,000

Balance Sheet December 31, 2005 (partial)

Owner's equity	
J. Doe, capital, January 1, 2005	$150,000
Add: Net income for 2005	18,000
Total	168,000
Less: Withdrawals for 2005	(12,000)
J. Doe, capital, December 31, 2005	$156,000

A sole proprietorship does not pay income taxes. Therefore, its financial statements do not reflect income tax expense or income taxes payable. Instead, the net income of a sole proprietorship is taxed when it is included on the owner's *personal* income tax return. Because an employer/employee contractual relationship cannot exist with only one party involved, a "salary" to the owner is not recognized as an expense of a sole proprietorship. The owner's salary is accounted for as a distribution of profits (i.e., a withdrawal).

OWNERS' EQUITY FOR A PARTNERSHIP

Small businesses and professionals such as accountants, doctors, and lawyers use the partnership form of business. It is formed by two or more persons reaching mutual agreement about the terms of the partnership. The law does not require an application for a charter as it does in the case of a corporation. Instead, the agreement between the partners constitutes a partnership contract. The agreement should specify matters such as division of periodic income, management responsibilities, transfer or sale of partnership interests, disposition of assets upon liquidation, and procedures to be followed in case of the death of a partner. If the partnership agreement does not specify these matters, the applicable provincial laws are binding.

The primary advantages of a partnership are (1) ease of formation, (2) complete control by the partners, and (3) lack of income taxes on the business itself. The primary disadvantage is the unlimited liability of each partner for the partnership's liabilities. If the partnership does not have sufficient assets to satisfy outstanding debt, its creditors can seize the partners' personal assets.

As with a sole proprietorship, accounting for a partnership follows the same underlying fundamentals of accounting as any other form of business organization, except for those entries that directly affect owners' equity. Accounting for partners' equity follows the same pattern as illustrated earlier for a sole proprietorship, except that separate partner capital and drawings accounts must be established for each partner. Investments by each partner are credited to the partner's capital account, and withdrawals from the partnership by each partner are debited to the respective drawings account. The net income for a partnership is divided between the partners in the profit ratio specified in the partnership agreement and credited to each partner's account. The respective drawings accounts also are closed to the partner capital accounts. After the closing process, each partner's capital account reflects the cumulative total of all investments of that individual partner plus the partner's share of all partnership earnings less all the partner's withdrawals.

Exhibit 12.8 presents selected journal entries and partial financial statements for AB Partnership to illustrate the accounting for the distribution of income and partners' equity.

Selected Transactions during 2005

EXHIBIT **12.8**

Accounting for Partners' Equity

January 1, 2005

A. Able and B. Baker organized AB Partnership on this date. Able contributed $60,000 and Baker $40,000 cash to the partnership and agreed to divide net income (and net loss) 60% and 40%, respectively. The journal entry for the business to record the investment follows:

Cash (A)	100,000	
A. Able, capital (OE)		60,000
B. Baker, capital (OE)		40,000

Assets		=	Liabilities	+	Shareholders' Equity	
Cash	+100,000				A. Able, capital	+60,000
					B. Baker, capital	+40,000

During 2005

The partners agreed that Able would withdraw $1,000 and Baker $650 per month in cash. Accordingly, the following journal entry for the withdrawals was made each month:

A. Able, drawings (OE)	1,000	
B. Baker, drawings (OE)	650	
Cash (A)		1,650

Assets		=	Liabilities	+	Shareholders' Equity	
Cash	−1,650				A. Able, drawings	−1,000
					B. Baker, drawings	−650

December 31, 2005

Assume that the normal closing entries for the revenue and expense accounts resulted in a net income of $30,000 that was distributed between the two partners. The closing entry is as follows:

Individual revenue accounts (R)	150,000	
Individual expense accounts (E)		120,000
A. Able, capital (OE)		18,000
B. Baker, capital (OE)		12,000

Assets	=	Liabilities	+	Shareholders' Equity	
				Revenues	−150,000
				Expenses	+120,000
				A. Able, capital	+18,000
				B. Baker, capital	+12,000

Net income is divided as follows:

A. Able, $30,000 × 60%	$18,000
B. Baker, $30,000 × 40%	12,000
Total	$30,000

December 31, 2005

The journal entry required to close the drawings accounts follows:

A. Able, capital (OE)	12,000	
B. Baker, capital (OE)	7,800	
A. Able, drawings (OE)		12,000
B. Baker, drawings (OE)		7,800

Assets	=	Liabilities	+	Shareholders' Equity	
				A. Able, capital	−12,000
				B. Baker, capital	−7,800
				A. Able, drawings	+12,000
				B. Baker, drawings	+7,800

A separate statement of partners' capital similar to the following is customarily prepared to supplement the balance sheet:

AB PARTNERSHIP
Statement of Partners' Capital
For the Year Ended December 31, 2005

	A. Able	B. Baker	Total
Investment, January 1, 2005	$60,000	$40,000	$100,000
Add: Additional investments during the year	0	0	0
Net income for the year	18,000	12,000	30,000
Totals	78,000	52,000	130,000
Less: Drawings during the year	(12,000)	(7,800)	(19,800)
Partners' equity, December 31, 2005	$66,000	$44,200	$110,200

The financial statements of a partnership follow the same format as those for a corporation except that (1) the income statement includes an additional section entitled Distribution of Net Income, (2) the partners' equity section of the balance sheet is detailed for each partner, (3) a partnership has no income tax expense because partnerships do not pay income tax (each partner must report his or her share of the partnership profits on his or her individual tax return), and (4) salaries paid to partners are not recorded as expense but are treated as a distribution of earnings (withdrawals).

KEY **RATIOS**

The **dividend yield ratio** measures the dividend return on the current share price. The ratio is computed as follows (p. 648):

$$\text{Dividend Yield Ratio} = \frac{\text{Dividend per Share}}{\text{Market Price per Share}}$$

The **dividend payout ratio** measures the portion of net income that is paid to common shareholders in the form of dividends. The ratio is computed as follows (p. 654):

$$\text{Dividend Payout Ratio} = \frac{\text{Dividends}}{\text{Net income}}$$

FINDING **FINANCIAL INFORMATION**

BALANCE SHEET

Under Current Liabilities
Dividends, once declared by the board of directors, are reported as a liability (usually current).

Under Non-Current Liabilities
Transactions involving share capital do not usually generate non-current liabilities.

Under Shareholders' Equity
Typical accounts include
Preferred shares
Common shares
Contributed surplus
Retained earnings

STATEMENT OF SHAREHOLDERS' EQUITY

This statement reports detailed information concerning shareholders' equity, including
(1) amounts in each equity account,
(2) number of shares outstanding,
(3) impact of transactions such as earning income, declaration of dividends, and repurchase of shares.

INCOME STATEMENT

Share capital is never shown on the income statement. Dividends are not an expense. They are a distribution of income and are, therefore, not reported on the income statement.

CASH FLOW STATEMENT

Under financing activities:
+Cash inflows from initial sale of shares
−Cash outflows for dividends
−Cash outflows for repurchase of shares

NOTES

Under Summary of Significant Accounting Policies:
Usually, very little information concerning share capital is provided in this summary.

Under a separate note:
Most companies report information about their stock option plans and information about major transactions such as stock dividends. A historical summary of dividends paid per share is typically provided.

KEY **TERMS**

Authorized Number of Shares p. 637

Common Shares p. 639

Convertible Preferred Shares p. 640

Cumulative Dividend Preference p. 649

Current Dividend Preference p. 648

Declaration Date p. 646

Dividends in Arrears p. 649

Issued Shares p. 637

Legal Capital p. 639

No Par Value Shares p. 639

Outstanding Shares p. 637

Par Value p. 639

Payment Date p. 646

Preferred Shares p. 640

Prior Period Adjustment p. 653

Record Date p. 646

Stock Dividend p. 650

Stock Split p. 652

Treasury Shares p. 660

QUESTIONS

1. Define *corporation* and identify its primary advantages.
2. What is the charter of a corporation?
3. Explain each of the following terms: (a) *authorized capital shares*, (b) *issued capital shares*, and (c) *outstanding capital shares*.
4. Name three rights of shareholders. Which of these is most important in your mind? Why?
5. Differentiate between common shares and preferred shares.
6. Explain the distinction between par value shares and no par value shares.
7. What are the usual characteristics of preferred shares?
8. What are the two basic sources of shareholders' equity? Explain each.
9. Owners' equity is accounted for by source. What does *source* mean?
10. What are the two basic requirements to support a cash dividend? What are the effects of a cash dividend on assets and shareholders' equity?
11. Differentiate between cumulative and non-cumulative preferred shares.
12. Define *stock dividend*. How does it differ from a cash dividend?
13. What are the primary purposes of issuing a stock dividend?
14. Identify and explain the three important dates with respect to dividends.
15. Define *retained earnings*. What are the primary components of retained earnings at the end of each period?
16. Define *prior period adjustments*. How are they reported?
17. What does the term *restrictions on retained earnings* mean?
18. Your parents have just retired and have asked you for some financial advice. They have decided to invest $100,000 in a company very similar to BCE Inc. The company has issued both common and preferred shares. What factors would you consider in giving them advice? Which type of shares would you recommend?

MULTIPLE-CHOICE QUESTIONS

1. Which feature is not applicable to common share ownership?
   a. right to receive dividends before preferred shareholders
   b. right to participate in management through voting
   c. right to receive residual assets upon liquidation of the company
   d. All of the above are features of common share ownership.
2. Which one of the following would not be considered an advantage of the corporate form of organization?
   a. Limited liability of shareholders
   b. Separate legal existence
   c. Continuous life
   d. Government regulation
3. Which of the following statements about stock dividends is true?
   a. Stock dividends are reported on the cash flow statement.
   b. Stock dividends are reported on the statement of retained earnings.
   c. Stock dividends increase total equity.
   d. Stock dividends decrease total equity.
4. Which order best describes the largest number of shares to the smallest number of shares?
   a. shares authorized, shares issued, shares outstanding
   b. shares issued, shares outstanding, shares authorized
   c. shares outstanding, shares issued, shares authorized
   d. The order does not matter because the three numbers are equal.
5. Which combination would be the best for an investor when shopping for a new stock?
   a. high dividend yield ratio, high earnings per share
   b. low dividend yield ratio, high earnings per share
   c. high dividend yield ratio, low earnings per share
   d. low dividend yield ratio, low earnings per share
6. Which of the following events decreases a corporation's shareholders' equity?
   a. A payment of a previously declared cash dividend.
   b. A declaration of a 5-percent stock dividend.
   c. A $100,000 restriction of retained earnings.
   d. A declaration of a cash dividend for preferred shares.
7. The statement of retained earnings:
   a. is a basic financial statement that shows the change in retained earnings during a year.

b. indicates the amount of cash available for the payment of dividends.

c. includes cash dividends but not stock dividends.

d. shows revenue, expenses, and dividends for the accounting period.

8. Which statement regarding dividends is false?

a. Dividends represent a sharing of corporate profits with owners.

b. Both stock and cash dividends reduce retained earnings.

c. Cash dividends paid to shareholders reduce net income.

d. None of the above statements are false.

9. The statements below refer to dividends on cumulative preferred shares. Select the **incorrect** statement.

a. Dividends in arrears are recorded as a liability since the company is obligated to pay these dividends in future periods.

b. No dividends can be paid to common shareholders until all dividends on preferred shares are paid.

c. All dividends in arrears should be disclosed in a note to the financial statements.

d. Corporations are not obligated to pay dividends on preferred shares every year.

10. In what situation does an investor's personal wealth increase immediately?

a. when receiving a cash dividend

b. when receiving a stock dividend

c. when a stock split is announced

d. in all of these situations

EXERCISES

E12–1 Reporting Shareholders' Equity and Determining Dividend Policy   ■ **LO1, 2**

Sampson Corporation was organized in 2005 to operate a financial consulting business. The charter authorized the issue of 12,000 common shares. During the first year, the following selected transactions were completed:

a. Issued 5,000 common shares for cash at $20 per share.

b. Issued 600 common shares for a piece of land to be used for a facilities site; construction began immediately. Assume that the market price per share was $20 on the date of issuance. Debit Land.

c. Issued 2,000 common shares for cash at $21 per share.

d. At year-end, the accounts reflected a loss of $7,000. Because a loss was incurred, no income tax expense was recorded.

Required:

1. Prepare the journal entry required for each of these transactions.

2. Prepare the shareholders' equity section as it should be reported on the balance sheet at year-end, December 31, 2005.

3. Can Sampson pay dividends at year-end? Explain.

E12–2 Analyzing the Impact of Dividend Policy   ■ **LO3**

McDonald and Associates is a small manufacturer of electronic connections for local area networks. Consider three independent situations.

Case 1: McDonald increases its cash dividends by 50 percent, but no other changes occur in the company's operations.

Case 2: The company's income and cash flows increase by 50 percent but this does not change its dividends.

Case 3: McDonald issues a 50-percent stock dividend, but no other changes occur.

Required:

1. How do you think each situation would affect the company's stock price?

2. If the company changed its accounting policies and reported higher net income, would the change have an impact on the stock price?

E12–3 Determining the Effects of Transactions on Shareholders' Equity   ■ **LO1, 2**

Nguyen Corporation was organized in January 2005 by 10 shareholders to operate an air-conditioning sales and service business. The charter issued by the government authorized the following no par value shares:

Common shares, 200,000 shares.

Preferred shares, 50,000 shares.

During January and February 2005, the following transactions were completed:

a. Collected $50,000 cash from each of the 10 organizers and issued 2,500 common shares to each of them.

b. Issued 12,000 preferred shares at $25 per share; collected the cash.

The company's operations resulted in net income of $40,000 for 2005. The board of directors declared cash dividends of $20,000 that were paid in December 2005. The preferred shares have a dividend rate of $1 per share.

Required:

1. Prepare the shareholders' equity section of the balance sheet at December 31, 2005.

2. Why would an investor prefer to buy a preferred share rather than a common share?

■ **LO1, 2**   **E12–4**   **Determining the Effects of the Issuance of Common and Preferred Shares**

Kelly, Incorporated, was issued a charter on January 15, 2005, that authorized the following share capital:

Common shares, no par value, 100,000 shares.

Preferred shares, $1.50, no par value, 5,000 shares. (*Note*: $1.50 is the dividend rate.)

During 2005, the following selected transactions occurred:

a. Issued 15,000 common shares at $18 cash per share.

b. Issued 2,000 preferred shares at $22 cash per share.

At the end of 2005, the company's net income equalled $38,000.

Required:

1. Prepare the shareholders' equity section of the balance sheet at December 31, 2005.

2. Assume that you are a common shareholder. If Kelly needed additional capital, would you prefer to have it issue additional common or preferred shares? Explain.

■ **LO1, 2**   **E12–5**   **Recording Shareholders' Equity Transactions, Including Non-Cash Consideration: Write a Brief Memo**

Teacher Corporation obtained a charter at the start of 2005 that authorized 50,000 no par value common shares and 20,000, $2, no par value preferred shares. The corporation was organized by four individuals who "reserved" 51 percent of the common shares for themselves. The remaining shares were to be sold to other individuals at $40 per share on a cash basis. During 2005, the following selected transactions occurred:

a. Collected $25 per share cash from three of the organizers and received two adjoining lots of land from the fourth organizer. Issued 3,000 common shares to each of the four organizers and received title to the land.

b. Issued 5,000 common shares to an outsider at $40 cash per share.

c. Issued 8,000 preferred shares at $25 cash per share.

d. At the end of 2005, the accounts reflected net income of $36,000.

Required:

1. Prepare the journal entries to record each of these transactions.

2. Write a brief memo to explain the basis that you used to determine the cost of the land.

■ **LO3**   **E12–6**   **Computing Dividends on Preferred Shares and Analyzing Differences**

The records of Hoffman Company reflected the following balances in the shareholders' equity accounts at December 31, 2006:

Common shares, no par value, 40,000 shares outstanding	$800,000
Preferred shares, $2, no par value, 6,000 shares outstanding	$150,000
Retained earnings	$235,000

On September 1, 2006, the board of directors was considering the distribution of a $62,000 cash dividend. No dividends were paid during 2004 and 2005. You have been asked to determine dividend amounts under two independent assumptions (show computations):

a. The preferred shares are non-cumulative.

b. The preferred shares are cumulative.

Required:

1. Determine the total amounts that would be paid to the preferred shareholders and to the common shareholders under the two independent assumptions.

2. Write a brief memo to explain why the dividend per common share was less under the second assumption.

3. Why would an investor buy Hoffman's common shares instead of its preferred shares if they pay lower dividends per share? Explain. The market prices of the preferred and common shares were $25 and $40, respectively, on December 31, 2006.

E12–7 Analyzing Dividends in Arrears

■ LO3

Mission Critical Software, Inc., is listed on the NASDAQ and is a leading provider of systems management software for Windows NT network and Internet infrastructure. Like many start-up companies, Mission Critical struggled with cash flows as it developed new business opportunities. A student found a financial statement for Mission Critical that included the following:

Mission Critical
Software, Inc.

> 1998 increase in dividends in arrears on redeemable convertible preferred shares was $264,000.

The student who read the note suggested that the Mission Critical preferred shares would be a good investment because of the large amount of dividend income that would be earned when the company started paying dividends again: "As the owner of the shares, I'll get dividends for the period I hold the shares plus some previous periods when I didn't even own the shares." Do you agree? Explain.

E12–8 Determining the Impact of Dividends

■ LO3

Average Corporation has the following shares outstanding at the end of 2006:

Preferred shares, $4, no par value; 8,000 outstanding shares.

Common shares, no par value; 30,000 outstanding shares.

On October 1, 2006, the board of directors declared dividends as follows:

Preferred shares: Full dividend amount, payable December 20, 2006.

Common shares: 10 percent common stock dividend (i.e., one additional share for each 10 held), issuable December 20, 2006.

On December 20, 2006, the market prices were $50 per preferred share and $32 per common share.

Required:

Explain the effect of each of the dividends on the assets, liabilities, and shareholders' equity of the company at each of the specified dates.

E12–9 Recording the Payment of Dividends

■ LO3

An annual report for Sears Canada Inc. disclosed that the company paid preferred dividends in the amount of $25.6 million. It declared and paid dividends of $0.24 per common share. During the year, Sears had 106,783,847 common shares issued and outstanding. Assume that the transaction occurred on July 15.

Sears Canada Inc.

Required:

Prepare a journal entry to record the declaration and payment of dividends.

E12–10 Analyzing Stock Dividends

■ LO5

On December 31, 2007, the shareholders' equity section of the balance sheet of R & B Corporation reflected the following:

Common shares (no par value, authorized 60,000 shares, outstanding 25,000 shares)	$250,000
Contributed surplus	12,000
Retained earnings	75,000

On February 1, 2008, the board of directors declared a 12-percent stock dividend to be issued April 30, 2008. The market value per share was $18 on the declaration date.

Required:

1. For comparative purposes, prepare the shareholders' equity section of the balance sheet (a) before the stock dividend and (b) after the stock dividend. (*Hint:* Use two columns for this requirement.)

2. Explain the effects of this stock dividend on the company's assets, liabilities, and shareholders' equity.

■ LO7   **E12–11   Determining the Impact of Stock Dividends and Stock Splits**

Milano Tools, Inc., announced a 100-percent stock dividend. Determine the impact (increase, decrease, no change) of this dividend on the following:

1. Total assets.

2. Total liabilities.

3. Common shares.

4. Total shareholders' equity.

5. Market value per common share.

Now assume that the company announced a 2-for-1 stock split. Determine the impact of the stock split on the five items above. Explain why the accounting for stock dividends differs from that of the stock split.

■ LO1, 3   **E12–12   Preparing a Statement of Retained Earnings and Evaluating Dividend Policy**

The following account balances were selected from the records of Blake Corporation at December 31, 2007, after all adjusting entries were completed:

Common shares (no par value; authorized 100,000 shares, issued 36,000 shares)	$540,000
Contributed surplus	150,000
Dividends declared and paid in 2007	18,000
Retained earnings, January 1, 2007	67,000
Correction of prior period accounting error (a debit, net of income tax)	8,000
Income summary for 2007 (credit balance)	28,000

The stock price was $22.43 per share on that date.

Required:

1. Prepare the statement of retained earnings for 2007.

2. Prepare the shareholders' equity section of the balance sheet at December 31, 2007.

3. Compute and evaluate the dividend yield ratio.

■ LO3   **E12–13   Recording Dividends**

Suncor Energy Inc.

Suncor Energy Inc. is an integrated energy company that explores for, develops, and markets natural gas, and refines oil into products that people use to heat their homes and to power their vehicles. Suncor distributes its gasoline through Sunoco gas stations. A recent press release contained the following announcement:

> Calgary, Alberta (April 28, 2005)—Suncor Energy Inc. has declared a cash dividend of six cents per share on its common shares, payable June 24, 2005, to shareholders of record at the date of close of business on June 3, 2005.

At the time of this announcement, Suncor had 455 million shares issued and outstanding.

Required:

Prepare journal entries as appropriate for each date mentioned in the press release.

■ LO3   **E12–14   Evaluating Dividend Policy**

H & R Block

H&R Block is a well-known name, especially during income tax time each year. The company serves more than 18 million taxpayers in more than 10,000 offices in Canada,

Australia, England, and the United States. A 1999 press release contained the following information:

> H&R Block today reported that revenues for the first quarter ended July 31, 1999, climbed 72 percent to $121 million. The company reported a first quarter net loss of $37 million, or 38 cents per share. The Board of Directors declared a quarterly dividend of 27 cents per share payable October 1, 1999, to shareholders of record on September 10, 1999.

Required:

1. Explain why H&R Block can pay dividends despite its loss.
2. What factors did the board of directors consider when it declared the dividends?

E12–15 Explaining Cash Flows and the Dividend Payout Ratio

■ **LO5**

You are a stockbroker for a major firm and have just received a telephone call from a major client, Bob Smith. You sent him a report about a stock you are recommending. Bob says he has one concern, "I don't understand this dividend payout ratio. You're showing me the percentage of net income that is paid out but given that dividends are paid in cash, shouldn't you be calculating the percentage of cash flow from operating activities that is paid out?" How do you respond to Bob's question?

E12–16 (Chapter Supplement A) Analyzing the Repurchase of Shares

Winnebago is a familiar name on vehicles travelling North American highways. The company manufactures and sells large motor homes for vacation travel. These motor homes can be quickly recognized because of the company's "flying W" trademark. A news article contained the following information:

> The Company's profits have been running double a year ago, revenues were up 27 percent in the May quarter and order backlog stands at 2,229 units. Those are the kind of growth statistics that build confidence in the boardroom. The Company has announced plans to spend $3.6 million to expand its manufacturing facilities and it recently authorized repurchase of $15 million worth of its own shares, the third buyback in two years. The Company's stock is now selling for $25 per share.

Winnebago

Required:

1. Determine the impact of this transaction on the financial statements.
2. Why do you think the board decided to repurchase the company's shares?
3. What impact will this purchase have on Winnebago's future dividend obligations?

E12–17 (Chapter Supplement A) Repurchase of Shares

Danier Leather

Danier Leather Inc. manufactures and retails leather products, earning international recognition as a leader in leather and suede design. The company's annual report for the fiscal year ended June 30, 2001, included the following (all amounts are in thousands):

> b) The Company purchased for cancellation 197.5 (June 24, 2000—232) Subordinate Voting Shares at prevailing market prices for cash consideration of $2,231 (June 24, 2000—$2,006). The excess of $1,407 (June 24, 2000—$1,038) over the average paid-in value of the shares was charged to retained earnings.

Required:

1. What was the average price that the company paid to repurchase these shares?
2. Prepare the journal entry to record a summary of the 2001 repurchase transactions.

PROBLEMS

LO1, 2, 3, 5   **P12–1**   **Finding Missing Amounts** (AP12–1)

At December 31, 2006, the records of Nortech Corporation provided the following selected and incomplete data:

> Common shares, no par value
>   Shares authorized, 200,000.
>   Shares issued, ____?___; issue price $17 per share; cash collected in full, $2,125,000.
> Net income for 2006, $118,000.
> Dividends declared and paid during 2006, $75,000.
> Prior period adjustment, correction of 2003 accounting error, $9,000 (a credit, net of income tax).
> Retained earnings balance, January 1, 2006, $155,000.

Required:

1. Complete the following tabulation:

    Shares authorized _____.

    Shares issued _____.

    Shares outstanding _____.

2. Earnings per share is $ _____.

3. Dividend paid per common share is $ _____.

4. The prior period adjustment should be reported on the _____ as an addition to _____ (or a deduction from _____).

5. The amount of retained earnings available for dividends on January 1, 2006, was $_____.

6. Assume that the board of directors voted a 100-percent stock split (the number of shares will double). After the stock split, the average issue price per share will be $_____, and the number of outstanding shares will be _____.

7. Assume that the company declared a 100-percent stock dividend instead of the 100-percent stock split. Compare and contrast the stock dividend and the stock split with regard to their effects on shareholders' equity components.

LO1, 2   **P12–2**   **Recording Transactions Affecting Shareholders' Equity** (AP12–2)

Pappas Corporation began operations in January 2005. The charter authorized the following share capital:

Preferred shares: 9 percent, $25 par value, authorized 40,000 shares.

Common shares: no par value, authorized 80,000 shares.

During 2005, the following transactions occurred in the order given:

a. Issued 20,000 common shares to each of the three organizers. Collected $9 cash per share from two of the organizers and received a plot of land with a small building on it in full payment for the shares of the third organizer and issued the shares immediately. Assume that 30 percent of the non-cash payment received applies to the building.

b. Sold 2,400 preferred shares at $25 per share. Collected the cash and issued the shares immediately.

c. Sold 2,000 preferred shares at $25 and 1,000 common shares at $12 per share. Collected the cash and issued the shares immediately.

d. The operating results at the end of 2005 were as follows:

> | Revenues | $220,000 |
> |---|---|
> | Expenses, including income taxes | 160,000 |

Required:

1. Prepare the journal entries to record each of these transactions and to close the accounts.

2. Write a brief memo explaining how you determined the cost of the land and the building in the first journal entry.

P12–3 **Preparing the Shareholders' Equity Section after Selected Transactions** (AP12–3)

■ **LO1, 2, 3**

Eddie Edwards Limited, a public company, was formed on January 2, 2006 with the following authorized capital structure:

Preferred shares: No par value, $1.00 per share quarterly cumulative dividend, callable at 103, 100,000 shares authorized.

Common shares: Unlimited number of shares authorized.

The following selected transactions occurred during the first six months of operations:

January 2: Issued 100,000 common shares in exchange for land and building with a combined appraised value of $2,200,000. Sixty percent of the acquisition cost is attributable to the building.

January 3 Issued 50,000 preferred shares for $1,250,000 cash.

April 1 Declared the quarterly cash dividend on the preferred shares, payable on April 25.

April 10 Declared and distributed a 10-percent common stock dividend on all outstanding common shares as of March 31. The market price of the common shares on March 31 was $24 per share.

April 25 Paid the preferred dividend that was declared on April 1.

Required:

1. Prepare journal entries to record the above transactions.

2. Prepare the shareholders' equity section of the balance sheet for Eddie Edwards Limited as at June 30, 2006. Assume that the company recorded net income of $4,400,000 for its first six months.

P12–4 **Comparing Stock and Cash Dividends** (AP12–4)

■ **LO4, 5**

Water Tower Company had the following shares outstanding and retained earnings at December 31, 2007:

Preferred shares, 7% (par value $25;	
outstanding, 2,400 shares)	$ 60,000
Common shares (outstanding, 30,000 shares)	240,000
Retained earnings	280,000

The board of directors is considering the distribution of a cash dividend to the two groups of shareholders. No dividends were declared during 2005 or 2006. Three independent cases are assumed:

Case A: The preferred shares are non-cumulative; the total amount of dividends is $30,000.

Case B: The preferred shares are cumulative; the total amount of dividends is $12,600.

Case C: Same as Case B, except the amount is $66,000.

Required:

1. Compute the amount of dividends, in total and per share, that would be payable to each class of shareholders for each case. Show computations.

2. Assume that the company issued a 10-percent common stock dividend on the outstanding common shares when the market value per share was $24. Complete the following comparative schedule, including explanation of the differences.

	Amount of Dollar Increase (decrease)	
Item	Cash Dividend— Case C	Stock Dividend
Assets	$_____	$_____
Liabilities	$_____	$_____
Shareholders' equity	$_____	$_____

■ **LO3**

P12–5 **Analyzing Dividend Policy**

Dana and David, two young financial analysts, were reviewing financial statements for Compaq, a manufacturer of personal computers. Dana noted that the company did not report any dividends in the financing activity section of the cash flow statement and said, "Just a few years ago, *Forbes* magazine named that company as one of the best-performing companies. If it's so good, I wonder why it isn't paying any dividends." David wasn't convinced that Dana was looking in the right place for dividends but didn't say anything.

Dana continued the discussion by noting, "When *Forbes* selected it as a best-performing company, its sales doubled over the previous two years, just as they doubled over the prior two years. Its income was only $789 million that year, compared with $867 million the previous year, but cash flow from operating activities was $943 million, compared to an outflow of $101 million the prior year."

At that point, David noted that the cash flow statement reported that the company had invested $703 million in new property this year, compared with $408 million the prior year. He also was surprised to see that inventory and accounts receivable had increased by $1 billion and nearly $2 billion, respectively, the previous year. "No wonder it can't pay dividends; it generated less than $1 billion from operating activities and had to put it all back into accounts receivable and inventory."

Required:

1. Correct any misstatements that either Dana or David made. Explain.
2. Which of the factors presented in the case help you understand the company's dividend policy?

■ **LO3**

P12–6 **Determining the Financial Statement Effects of Dividends**

Legrand Company has outstanding 45,000 common shares and 25,000, $4, preferred shares. On December 1, 2007, the board of directors voted to distribute a $4 cash dividend per preferred share and a 5 percent common stock dividend on the common shares. At the date of declaration, the common share was selling at $40 and the preferred share at $50. The dividends are to be paid, or issued, on February 15, 2008. The company's fiscal year ends on December 31.

Required:

Explain the comparative effects of the two dividends on the assets, liabilities, and shareholders' equity (a) through December 31, 2007, (b) on February 15, 2008, and (c) the overall effects from December 1, 2007, through February 15, 2008. A schedule similar to the following might be helpful:

	Comparative Effects Explained	
Item	Cash Dividend on Preferred	Stock Dividend on Common
1. Through December 31, 2007:		
Assets, etc.		

■ **LO4, 5**

Adobe Systems

P12–7 **Recording Dividends**

Adobe Systems develops and markets computer software, including Adobe Acrobat, that enables users to access information across all print and electronic media. A 1999 news article contained the following information:

September 16, 1999

Adobe Systems reported record revenue and operating profit for the third quarter of fiscal 1999. The Board of Directors announced a 100% stock dividend will occur on October 26, 1999, for shareholders of record on October 4, 1999. The Board also declared this quarter's cash dividend of $0.05 per share, payable on October 12, 1999, to shareholders of record as of September 28, 1999.

Required:

1. Prepare any journal entries that Adobe should make as the result of information in the preceding report. Assume that the company has 1 million shares outstanding and the market value is $40 per share and an average issue price of $0.50.

2. What do you think happened to the company's stock price after the September 16 announcement?

3. What factors did the board of directors consider in making this decision?

P12–8 **(Chapter Supplement A) Analyzing the Repurchase of Shares**
Petro-Canada is one of the largest integrated oil and gas companies in Canada, offering a variety of petroleum products and services. Its annual report for fiscal year 2004 included the following (amounts are in millions of dollars):

Changes in common shares and contributed surplus were as follows:

			2004
	Shares	**Amount**	**Contributed Surplus**
Balance at beginning of year	265,586,093	$1,308	$2,147
Issued for cash under employee stock option and share purchase plans	1,246,000	39	—
Repurchases of common shares	(6,868,082)	(34)	(413)
Stock-based compensation	—	1	9
Balance at end of year	259,964,011	$1,314	$1,743

Under the terms of a normal course issuer bid (NCIB), the Company is entitled to purchase up to 21 million of its common shares during the period from June 22, 2004 to June 21, 2005, subject to certain conditions. During 2004, the Company repurchased 6,868,082 common shares under the NCIB at an average price of $65.02 per common share for a total cost of approximately $447 million. The excess of purchase cost over the carrying amount of the shares purchased was recorded as a reduction of contributed surplus.

Required:

1. Why do you think Petro-Canada's board of directors decided to repurchase the company's shares?

2. Prepare the journal entry to record a summary of the repurchase transactions.

3. Compute the average issuance price per common share, and explain why Petro-Canada paid a much higher price for repurchasing its own shares.

4. What impact will this transaction have on Petro-Canada's future dividend obligations?

P12–9 **(Chapter Supplement B) Comparing Owners' Equity Sections for Alternative Forms of Organization**

■ **LO1**

Assume for each of the following independent cases that the accounting period for NewBiz ends on December 31, 2006, and that the Income Summary account at that date reflected a debit balance (loss) of $20,000.

Case A: Assume that NewBiz is a *sole proprietorship* owned by Proprietor A. Prior to the closing entries, the capital account reflected a credit balance of $50,000 and the drawings account a balance of $8,000.

Case B: Assume that NewBiz is a *partnership* owned by Partner A and Partner B. Prior to the closing entries, the owners' equity accounts reflected the following balances: A, Capital, $40,000; B, Capital, $38,000; A, Drawings, $5,000; and B, Drawings, $9,000. Profits and losses are divided equally.

Case C: Assume that NewBiz is a *corporation.* Prior to the closing entries, the shareholders' equity accounts showed the following: Share Capital, authorized 30,000 shares, outstanding 15,000 shares, $150,000; Contributed Surplus, $5,000; Retained Earnings, $65,000.

Required:

1. Prepare all of the closing entries indicated at December 31, 2006, for each of the three separate cases.

2. Show for each case how the owners' equity section of the balance sheet would appear at December 31, 2006.

ALTERNATE PROBLEMS

LO1, 2, 3, 4   **AP12–1**   **Finding Missing Amounts** (P12–1)

At December 31, 2007, the records of Kozmetsky Corporation provided the following selected and incomplete data:

> Common shares, no par value.
>   Shares authorized, unlimited.
>   Shares issued, ____?___; issue price $75 per share.
> Net income for 2007, $4,800,000.
>   Common shares account $1,500,000.
> Dividends declared and paid during 2007, $2 per share.
> Retained earnings balance, January 1, 2007, $82,900,000.

Required:

1. Complete the following tabulation:

   Shares issued _____.

   Shares outstanding _____.

2. Earnings per share is $_____.

3. Total dividends paid on common shares during 2007 equal $_____.

4. Assume that the board of directors voted a 100-percent stock split (the number of shares will double). After the stock split, the average issue price per share will be $_____, and the number of outstanding shares will be _____.

5. Disregard the stock split (assumed in requirement 4). Assume instead that a 10-percent stock dividend was declared and issued when the market price of the common shares was $91. Explain how the shareholders' equity will change.

LO1, 2   **AP12–2**   **Recording Transactions Affecting Shareholders' Equity** (P12–2)

Arnold Company was granted a charter that authorized the following share capital:

   Preferred shares: 8 percent, par value $25, 20,000 shares.

   Common shares: No par value, 100,000 shares.

During the first year, 2005, the following selected transactions occurred in the order given:

a. Sold 20,000 common shares at $40 cash per share and 5,000 preferred shares at $25 per share. Collected cash and issued the shares immediately.

b. Issued 2,500 preferred shares as full payment for a plot of land to be used as a future plant site. Assume that the share was selling at $25.

c. Declared and paid the quarterly cash dividend on the preferred shares.

d. At December 31, 2005, the accounts reflected net income of $33,500.

Required:

1. Prepare the journal entries to record each of these transactions.

2. Explain the economic difference between acquiring an asset for cash compared with acquiring it by issuing shares. Is it "better" to acquire a new asset without having to give up another asset?

AP12–3 Preparing the Shareholders' Equity Section After Selected Transactions (P12–3)   ■ **LO1, 2, 3**

The shareholders' equity accounts of Freeman Inc. at January 2, 2007, are as follows:

Preferred shares, no par value, cumulative, 6,000 shares issued	$300,000
Common shares, no par value, 250,000 shares issued	500,000
Retained earnings	600,000

The following transactions occurred during the year:

March 10	Purchased a building for $1,000,000. The seller agreed to receive 14,000 preferred shares and 30,000 common shares of Freeman in exchange for the building. The preferred shares were trading in the market at $50 per share on that day.
July 1	Declared a semi-annual cash dividend of $0.50 per common share and the required amount of dividends on preferred shares, payable on August 1, 2007 to shareholders of record on July 21, 2007. The annual dividend of $4 per preferred share had not been paid in either 2006 or 2007.
August 1	Paid the cash dividend declared on July 1 to both common and preferred shareholders.
December 31	Determined that net income for the year was $385,000.

Required:

1. Prepare journal entries to record the above transactions.

2. Prepare the shareholders' equity section of Freeman's balance sheet as at December 31, 2007.

AP12–4 Comparing Stock and Cash Dividends (P12–4)   ■ **LO4, 5**

Ritz Company had the following shares outstanding and retained earnings at December 31, 2008:

Preferred shares, 8% (par value $25; outstanding, 8,400 shares)	$210,000
Common shares (outstanding, 50,000 shares)	500,000
Retained earnings	900,000

The board of directors is considering the distribution of a cash dividend to the two groups of shareholders. No dividends were declared during 2006 or 2007. Three independent cases are assumed:

Case A: The preferred shares are non-cumulative; the total amount of dividends is $25,000.

Case B: The preferred shares are cumulative; the total amount of dividends is $25,000.

Case C: Same as Case B, except the amount is $75,000.

Required:

1. Compute the amount of dividends, in total and per share, payable to each class of shareholders for each case. Show computations.

2. Assume that the company issued a 15-percent common stock dividend on the outstanding shares when the market value per share was $50. Complete the following comparative schedule, including explanation of the differences.

	Amount of Dollar Increase (decrease)	
Item	Cash Dividend— Case C	Stock Dividend
Assets	$_____	$_____
Liabilities	$_____	$_____
Shareholders' equity	$_____	$_____

CASES AND PROJECTS

FINDING AND INTERPRETING FINANCIAL INFORMATION

■ **LO1, 2, 3**   **CP12–1**   **Finding Financial Information**

Van Houtte

Refer to the financial statements of Van Houtte given in Appendix B of this book.

Required:

1. Identify the types of shares that Van Houtte is authorized to issue and their characteristics. Do all types of shares have the same voting rights? If not, explain why.
2. What is the number of shares outstanding on April 2, 2005?
3. Did the company pay dividends during fiscal year 2005? If so, how much per share?
4. Has the company ever issued a stock dividend or declared a stock split? If so, describe.
5. What is the average price received per each class of shares?

■ **LO1, 2, 3**   **CP12–2**   **Finding Financial Information**

The Forzani Group Ltd.

Refer to the Online Learning Centre Web site at **www.mcgrawhill.ca/college/libby/student/ resources** for the financial statements of The Forzani Group Ltd. (FGL).

Required:

1. Identify the types of shares that FGL is authorized to issue and their characteristics.
2. What was the highest price for the company's Class A shares during the past 12 years?
3. Did the company purchase any of its own shares during the period covered by the financial statements?
4. Describe the company's dividend policy, if any.

FINANCIAL REPORTING AND ANALYSIS CASES

■ **LO2, 3, 7**   **CP12–3**   **Financial Reporting and Analysis Cases**

Andrés Wines Ltd.

Andrés Wines Ltd. is a leading producer and marketer of quality wines in Canada. With wineries located in British Columbia, Ontario, and Nova Scotia, the Company markets wines produced from grapes grown in British Columbia's Okanagan Valley, Ontario's Niagara Peninsula, and vineyards around the world. Andrés sells its ultra-premium wines and icewines throughout the United States, Asia, and Europe.

The company's annual report for fiscal year 2005 includes the following details about its share capital (amounts in thousands of dollars):

9   Capital stock

		2005		2004	
		Issued		Issued	
	Authorized	Shares	Amounts	Shares	Amounts
Class A shares, non-voting	Unlimited	3,954,302	$6,844	3,921,092	$6,414
Class B shares, voting	Unlimited	1,001,772	400	1,001,972	400
		4,956,074	$7,244	4,923,064	$6,814

Class A shares are non-voting and are entitled to a dividend in an amount equal to 115% of any dividend paid or declared on Class B shares. Class B shares are voting and convertible into Class A shares on a one-for-one basis. During 2005, 200 Class B shares were converted into Class A shares (2004—1,000).

Selected information about the company's net income, dividends, and retained earnings for the five-year period 2001–2005 has been extracted from its annual reports:

	3/31/2005	3/31/2004	3/31/2003	3/31/2002	3/31/2001
Net income	$ 8,538	$ 9,570	$ 6,929	$ 5,325	$ 4,053
Dividends on Class A and Class B shares	3,108	3,086	2,971	2,967	2,966
Retained earnings, end of year	79,924	74,494	69,010	64,052	61,694

Required:

1. The note indicates that 200 Class B shares were converted into Class A shares. What is the apparent reason for the share conversion? Explain.

2. Prepare the journal entry to record the conversion. (Note that the book value of the shares is rounded to the nearest thousand).

3. How much of the dividends for 2005 were paid to Class A shareholders?

4. Compute the dividend payout ratio for each of the five years. What does the trend in the payout ratio suggest about the company's dividend policy? Explain.

CP12–4 Characteristics of Preferred Securities

■ **LO2**

Suncor Energy

Suncor Energy Inc. is an integrated energy company that explores for, develops, and markets natural gas, in addition to refining its oil into products that people use to heat their homes and to power their vehicles. Suncor distributes its gasoline through Sunoco gas stations. Suncor's 2001 annual report included the following information about an unsecured debenture that the company classified as share capital:

> **15. Preferred Securities**
>
> During 1999, the company completed a Canadian offering of $276 million of 9.05% preferred securities and a U.S. offering of US$162.5 million of 9.125% preferred securities, the proceeds of which totalled Cdn$507 million after issue costs of $17 million ($10 million after income tax credits of $7 million). The preferred securities are unsecured junior subordinated debentures, due in 2048 and redeemable at the company's option on or after March 15, 2004. Subject to certain conditions, the company has the right to defer payment of interest on the securities for up to 20 consecutive quarterly periods. Deferred interest and principal amounts are payable in cash, or, at the option of the company, from the proceeds on the sale of equity securities of the company delivered to the trustee of the preferred securities. Accordingly, the preferred securities are classified as share capital in the consolidated balance sheet and the interest distributions thereon, net of income taxes, are classified as dividends. Proceeds from the offerings were used to repay commercial paper borrowings.

Identify the various characteristics of these "preferred securities" and explain why the company classified these debentures as share capital.

CP12–5 Analyzing Dividend Policy

■ **LO4, 5**

General Mills

General Mills is a very successful company, with substantial growth in revenues and earnings during the past 11 years. The following information was contained in a recent annual report:

	2004	2003	2002	2001	2000	1999	1998	1997	1996	1995	1994
Dividend payout ratio	34%	44%	78%	47%	62%	62%	80%	72%	63%	81%	64%
Dividend yield ratio	2.4%	2.4%	2.4%	2.6%	2.7%	2.7%	3.1%	3.2%	3.3%	3.1%	3.5%
Dividends per share (dollars)	1.1	1.1	1.1	1.1	1.1*	2.16	2.12	2.03	1.91	1.88	1.88

*The company had a 2-for-1 stock split in 2000.

Assume that you are a financial analyst preparing a forecast of next year's operating results for General Mills. Net earnings for 2004 were $1,055 million, and the company paid out $358 million in dividends. Due to a number of factors, you believe that net income for next year will increase substantially and will be in the range of $1,300 to $1,400 million. To complete your financial forecast, you now need to estimate the total amount of dividends that

General Mills will pay. Based on this information, describe the dividend policy of General Mills, and estimate the dividends that the company will pay in 2005.

LO2, 3 **CP12–6** **(Chapter Supplement A) Interpreting the Financial Press**
As discussed in this chapter, companies buy back their own shares for a number of reasons. An article on this topic is available on the Web site at www.mcgrawhill.ca/college/libby/student/resources. Read the article, "Stock market time bomb,"[10] November 15, 1999, and then write a short memo summarizing its contents. In general, do you think large stock buy-backs are good for investors?

CRITICAL THINKING CASES

LO3, 4 **CP12–7** **Making a Decision as a Financial Analyst**
Assume that you are a stockbroker with two clients. One is a recent university graduate and the other is a retired couple. You have recently reviewed the annual report for Philip Morris, which sells popular tobacco and beer products along with Kraft-brand foods. You were impressed with a 22-percent increase in net income for Philip Morris in a recent year. You noticed that the company generated more than $8 billion in cash flows from operating activities and paid $1.68 per share in dividends. The dividend yield was 6.7 percent, one of the highest you have been able to find for large, well-known companies. Based on this information and your current knowledge of Philip Morris, would you recommend this stock for either of your clients?

LO3, 4, 5 **CP12–8** **Making a Decision as an Investor**
You have retired after a long and successful career as a business executive and now spend a good portion of your time managing your retirement portfolio. You are considering three basic investment alternatives. You can invest in (1) corporate bonds currently paying 7 percent interest, (2) conservative stocks with an average dividend yield of 5 percent and dividend payout ratios in excess of 80 percent, and (3) growth-oriented technology stocks that pay no dividends. Analyze each of these alternatives and select one. Justify your selection.

LO4, 5 **CP12–9** **Evaluating an Ethical Dilemma**
You are a member of the board of directors of a large company that has been in business for more than 100 years. The company is proud of the fact that it has paid dividends every year that it has been in business. Because of this stability, many retired people have invested large portions of their savings in the company's common stock. Unfortunately, the company has struggled for the past few years as it tries to introduce new products and is considering not paying a dividend this year. The president wants to skip the dividend in order to have more cash to invest in product development: "If we don't invest this money now, we won't get these products to market in time to save the company. I don't want to risk thousands of jobs." One of the most senior board members speaks next: "If we don't pay the dividend, thousands of retirees will be thrown into financial distress. Even if you don't care about them, you have to recognize our stock price will crash when they all sell." The company treasurer proposes an alternative: "Let's skip the cash dividend and pay a stock dividend. We can still say we've had a dividend every year." The entire board now turns to you for your opinion. What should the company do?

LO3 **CP12–10** **Evaluating an Ethical Dilemma**
You are the president of a very successful Internet company that has had a remarkably profitable year. You have determined that the company has more than $10 million in cash generated by operating activities not needed in the business. You are thinking about paying it out to shareholders as a special dividend. You discuss the idea with your vice-president, who reacts angrily to your suggestion: "Our stock price has gone up by 200 percent in the last year alone. What more do we have to do for the owners? The people who really earned that money are the employees who have been working 12 hours a day, six or seven days a week to make the company successful. Most of them didn't even take vacations last year. I say we have to pay out bonuses and nothing extra for the shareholders." As president, you know that

---

[10]Reprinted from November 15, 1999 issue of *BusinessWeek* by special permission, copyright © 1999 by the McGraw-Hill Companies, Inc.

you are hired by the board of directors, which is elected by the shareholders. What is your responsibility to both groups? To which group would you give the $10 million?

FINANCIAL REPORTING AND ANALYSIS
TEAM PROJECTS

CP12–11 **Team Project: Evaluating Stock Compensation**

Break into two teams. One team should play the role of labour union representatives and the other the role of senior management. The labour union wants all of its employees to receive an additional 10 percent of their compensation in the form of company shares. The union president argues that the shareholders will benefit from this proposal because the employees will work harder for the company if they are also owners. Management believes that this proposal is too expensive and that the board of directors would probably fire the management team if it ever approved the proposal. Outline the points to support your position and enter a negotiation to resolve the conflict. As a team, write a final recommendation to present to the board.

LO1

CP12–12 **Team Project: Studying the Impact of Dividend Announcements**

LO3

Each member of the team should find dividend announcements for different companies. Using a source such as *The Globe and Mail,* determine the stock price for the company for each day one week before and one week after the announcement. Using spreadsheet software, prepare a chart of the stock price movement. Compare the charts for each company.

Required:

The team should summarize what a comparison of the charts indicates. Review the dividend announcements. Do they help explain any of the differences observed? Write a brief statement explaining how you think the stock market reacts to dividend announcements.

After studying this chapter, you should be able to:

1. Explain how a company's business strategy affects financial analysis. p. 689

2. Discuss how analysts use financial statements. p. 691

3. Compute and interpret component percentages. p. 692

4. Compute and interpret profitability ratios. p. 694

5. Compute and interpret liquidity ratios. p. 702

6. Compute and interpret solvency ratios. p. 707

7. Compute and interpret market test ratios. p. 709

Analyzing Financial Statements

13

The history of Home Depot is an unusual success story. Founded in 1978 in Atlanta, Home Depot has grown to be North America's largest home improvement retailer. Its stores are located in major cities in Canada, the United States, Mexico, and Puerto Rico. Home Depot's financial statements are presented in Exhibit 13.1.

Home Depot operates more than 1,800 stores and design centres that sell building materials, decor, lawn and garden products, and home remodelling services. In Canada, Home Depot has 117 stores employing over 18,000 people. During the previous 10 years, Home Depot's revenues grew at an average rate of 19.3 percent per year and its earnings grew at an average annual rate of 23.5 percent.

Financial analysts evaluate Home Depot's historical performance to determine if they should recommend that their clients purchase its shares. The analysts want to have some reasonable assurance that the company will continue to thrive, causing the company's share price to increase and thereby benefit their clients. However, two analysts looking at the same company may arrive at different conclusions, and this depends in part on investors' objectives for their investments: growth or safety. Some analysts may reject Home Depot because it is too risky relative to other investment opportunities, whereas others may recommend investment because Home Depot is growing quickly relative to the risk in its business.

EXHIBIT 13.1

Home Depot Financial Statements

THE HOME DEPOT, INC., AND SUBSIDIARIES

Consolidated Balance Sheets

(amounts in millions, except per share data)

	January 30, 2005	February 1, 2004
Assets		
Current Assets:		
Cash and Cash Equivalents	$ 506	$ 1,103
Short-Term Investments	1,659	1,749
Receivables, net	1,499	1,097
Merchandise Inventories	10,076	9,076
Other Current Assets	450	303
Total Current Assets	14,190	13,328
Property and Equipment, at cost:		
Land	6,932	6,397
Buildings	12,325	10,920
Furniture, Fixtures and Equipment	6,195	5,163
Leasehold Improvements	1,191	942
Construction in Progress	1,404	820
Capital Leases	390	352
	28,437	24,594
Less Accumulated Depreciation and Amortization	5,711	4,531
Net Property and Equipment	22,726	20,063
Notes Receivable	369	84
Cost in Excess of the Fair Value of Net Assets Acquired, net of accumulated amortization of $56 at January 30, 2005 and $54 at February 1, 2004	1,394	833
Other Assets	228	129
Total Assets	$38,907	$34,437
Liabilities and Stockholders' Equity		
Current Liabilities:		
Accounts Payable	$ 5,766	$ 5,159
Accrued Salaries and Related Expenses	1,055	801
Sales Taxes Payable	412	419
Deferred Revenue	1,546	1,281
Income Taxes Payable	161	175
Current Installments of Long-Term Debt	11	509
Other Accrued Expenses	1,578	1,210
Total Current Liabilities	10,529	9,554
Long-Term Debt, excluding current installments	2,148	856
Other Long-Term Liabilities	763	653
Deferred Income Taxes	1,309	967
Stockholders' Equity		
Common Stock, par value $0.05; authorized: 10,000 shares; issued 2,385 shares at January 30, 2005 and 2,373 shares at February 1, 2004; outstanding 2,185 shares at January 30, 2005 and 2,257 shares at February 1, 2004	119	119
Paid-In Capital	6,650	6,184
Retained Earnings	23,962	19,680
Accumulated Other Comprehensive Income	227	90
Unearned Compensation	(108)	(76)
Treasury Stock, at cost, 200 shares at January 30, 2005 and 116 shares at February 1, 2004	(6,692)	(3,590)
Total Stockholders' Equity	24,158	22,407
Total Liabilities and Stockholders' Equity	$38,907	$34,437

See accompanying Notes to Consolidated Financial Statements.

EXHIBIT **13.1**

(continued)

THE HOME DEPOT, INC., AND SUBSIDIARIES
Consolidated Statements of Earnings
(amounts in millions, except per share data)

	Fiscal Year Ended[1]		
	January 30, 2005	February 1, 2004	February 2, 2003
Net Sales	$73,094	$64,816	$58,247
Cost of Merchandise Sold	48,664	44,236	40,139
Gross Profit	24,430	20,580	18,108
Operating Expenses:			
Selling and Store Operating	15,105	12,588	11,276
General and Administrative	1,399	1,146	1,002
Total Operating Expenses	16,504	13,734	12,278
Operating Income	7,926	6,846	5,830
Interest Income (Expense):			
Interest and Investment Income	56	59	79
Interest Expense	(70)	(62)	(37)
Interest, net	(14)	(3)	42
Earnings Before Provision for Income Taxes	7,912	6,843	5,872
Provision for Income Taxes	2,911	2,539	2,208
Net Earnings	$ 5,001	$ 4,304	$ 3,664
Weighted Average Common Shares	2,207	2,283	2,336
Basic Earnings Per Share	$ 2.27	$ 1.88	$ 1.57
Diluted Weighted Average Common Shares	2,216	2,289	2,344
Diluted Earnings Per Share	$ 2.26	$ 1.88	$ 1.56

(1) Fiscal years ended January 30, 2005, February 1, 2004 and February 2, 2003 include 52 weeks.

See accompanying Notes to Consolidated Financial Statements.

THE HOME DEPOT, INC., AND SUBSIDIARIES
Consolidated Statements of Cash Flows
(amounts in millions)

	Fiscal Year Ended[1]		
	January 30, 2005	February 1, 2004	February 2, 2003
Cash Flows from Operating Activities:			
Net Earnings	$ 5,001	$ 4,304	$ 3,664
Reconciliation of Net Earnings to Net Cash Provided by Operating Activities:			
Depreciation and Amortization	1,319	1,076	903
Stock-Based Compensation Expense	125	67	15
Changes in Assets and Liabilities, net of the effects of acquisitions:			
(Increase) Decrease in Receivables, net	(266)	25	(38)
Increase in Merchandise Inventories	(849)	(693)	(1,592)
Increase in Accounts Payable and Accrued Liabilities	917	790	1,394
Increase in Deferred Revenue	263	279	147
Increase (Decrease) in Income Taxes Payable	2	(27)	83
Increase in Deferred Income Taxes	319	605	173
Increase in Other Long-Term Liabilities	119	33	66
Other	(46)	86	(13)
Net Cash Provided by Operating Activities	6,904	6,545	4,802

EXHIBIT **13.1**

(concluded)

| | Fiscal Year Ended[1] | | |
	January 30, 2005	February 1, 2004	February 2, 2003
Cash Flows from Investing Activities:			
Capital Expenditures, net of $38, $47 and $49 of non-cash capital expenditures in fiscal 2004, 2003 and 2002, respectively	(3,948)	(3,508)	(2,749)
Purchase of Assets from Off-Balance Sheet Financing Arrangement	—	(598)	—
Payments for Businesses Acquired, net	(727)	(215)	(235)
Proceeds from Sales of Businesses, net	—	—	22
Proceeds from Sales of Property and Equipment	96	265	105
Purchases of Investments	(25,890)	(38,649)	(38,367)
Proceeds from Sales and Maturities of Investments	25,990	38,534	38,623
Net Cash Used in Investing Activities	(4,479)	(4,171)	(2,601)
Cash Flows from Financing Activities:			
Proceeds from Long-Term Borrowings, net of discount	995	—	1
Repayments of Long-Term Debt	(510)	(9)	—
Repurchase of Common Stock	(3,106)	(1,554)	(2,000)
Proceeds from Sale of Common Stock, net	285	227	326
Cash Dividends Paid to Stockholders	(719)	(595)	(492)
Net Cash Used in Financing Activities	(3,055)	(1,931)	(2,165)
(Decrease) Increase in Cash and Cash Equivalents	(630)	443	36
Effect of Exchange Rate Changes on Cash and Cash Equivalents	33	20	8
Cash and Cash Equivalents at Beginning of Year	1,103	640	596
Cash and Cash Equivalents at End of Year	$ 506	$ 1,103	$ 640
Supplemental Disclosure of Cash Payments Made For:			
Interest, net of interest capitalized	$ 78	$ 70	$ 50
Income Taxes	$ 2,793	$ 2,037	$ 1,951

(1) Fiscal years ended January 30, 2005, February 1, 2004 and February 2, 2003 include 52 weeks.

See accompanying Notes to Consolidated Financial Statements.

As you analyze Home Depot's financial results, it is important to remember that any analysis is understood in the context of what an investor wants to accomplish. Your analysis, in itself, will present neither a good nor a bad picture of Home Depot's performance. This assessment must be made in the context not only of the investor's goals but also of the industry's performance and the economic environment.

Would you want to buy shares in Home Depot? To make a rational decision, you would want to consider more factors than just the company's rapid growth in profitability and the recommendation of a financial analyst. The information contained in Home Depot's financial statements and the analytical tools discussed in this chapter provide an important basis to help you decide whether to invest in Home Depot shares.

UNDERSTANDING THE BUSINESS

In Canada and the United States, companies spend billions of dollars each year preparing, auditing, and publishing their financial statements. These statements are mailed to current and prospective investors. Most companies also make financial information available on the Internet. Home Depot has a particularly interesting Web site (www.homedepot.ca) that contains current financial statements, recent news articles about the company, and a variety of relevant information.

The reason that Home Depot and other companies spend so much money to provide information to investors is simple: Financial statements help people make better economic decisions. Two broad groups of people use financial statements. One group is the management of the business; it relies on accounting data to make important operating decisions, such as the pricing of products or expansion of productive capacity. The second group comprises external decision makers. In fact, published financial statements are designed primarily to meet the needs of external decision makers, including present and potential owners, investment analysts, and creditors.

Users of financial statements are interested in three types of information:

1. *Information about past performance.* Information concerning items such as income, sales volume, cash flows, and return earned on the investment helps people to assess the success of the business and the effectiveness of its management. Such information also helps the decision maker compare one company with others.

2. *Information about the present condition of a business.* This type of information helps answer questions such as: What types of assets are owned? How much debt does the business owe, and when is it due? What is its cash position? What are its EPS, return on investment, and debt-to-equity ratios? What is the inventory position? Answers to these and similar questions help people assess the successes and failures of the past; more importantly, they provide information useful in assessing the cash flow and profit potentials of the business.

3. *Information about the future performance of the business.* Decision makers select from among several alternative courses of action. All decisions are future-oriented. As you know, financial statements based on historical cost are not an ideal basis upon which to forecast future performance. Investors are most interested in risk and the potential rewards for accepting risk. In general, as risk in the business environment increases, investors demand a higher future return on their investments to compensate them for the increased riskiness of their investments. Investors prefer to earn maximum return for minimum risk when choosing companies in which to invest.

   Reliable accounting measures of past performance are one source of information upon which investors base their assessments of risk and potential return. Analysis of reliable measures that indicate financial trends for each company is therefore very important. If investors can reasonably assume that important business factors will be very similar in future to the current situation, then a reliable historical trend is often a satisfactory basis upon which to predict future financial performance. For example, the recent sales and earnings trends of a business are usually good indicators of what might be expected in the future. In other words, investors must know where the company has been in order to predict where it is likely to go.

ORGANIZATION OF THE CHAPTER

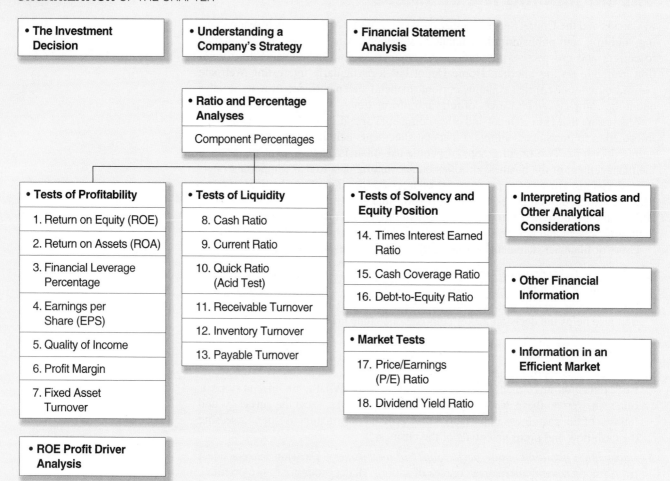

THE INVESTMENT DECISION

Of the people who use financial statements, current and potential investors are perhaps the single largest group. They often rely on the advice of professional analysts, who develop recommendations on widely held stocks such as Home Depot. Most individual investors use analysts' reports and track their recommendations. As this book was being written, professional analysts issued the following investment recommendations for Home Depot:

Analyst Ratings: Home Depot	Today	1 Month Ago	2 Months Ago	3 Months Ago
1—Strong Buy	**13**	12	10	9
2—Buy	**9**	9	7	9
3—Hold	**3**	4	5	5
4—Sell	**0**	0	0	0
5—Strong Sell	**0**	0	0	0
Average Rating	**1.56**	1.64	1.73	1.78

Source: Quicken.com/investments/

When considering an investment in shares, the investor should evaluate the future income and growth potential of the business on the basis of three factors:

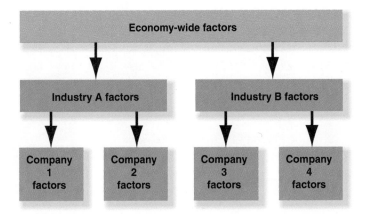

1. *Economy-wide factors.* Often the overall health of the economy has a direct impact on the performance of an individual business. Investors should consider data such as the unemployment rate, general inflation rate, and changes in interest rates. For example, increases in interest rates often slow economic growth because consumers are less willing to buy merchandise on credit when interest rates are high. Furthermore, companies that wish to expand their operations will find it too expensive to borrow funds.

2. *Industry factors.* Certain events have a major impact on each company within an industry, but have only a minor impact on other companies. For example, a major drought may be devastating for food-related industries but may have no effect on the electronics industry.

3. *Individual company factors.* To properly analyze a company, you should learn as much as you can about it. Good analysts do not rely only on the information contained in the financial statements. They visit the company, buy its products, and read about it in the business press. If you evaluate McDonald's, it is equally important to assess the quality of its balance sheet and the quality of its McChicken® sandwich. An example of company-specific information is contained in a research report on Home Depot written by Lehman Brothers, a large investment banking firm:

New Products Increase Profitability. Home Depot continues to add new product assortments to its stores. Its latest product addition is major appliances. Although well behind Sears, this year will be the first major step to potentially overtaking the No. 1 position.

REAL WORLD EXCERPT

Home Depot

LEHMAN BROTHERS
RESEARCH REPORT

UNDERSTANDING A COMPANY'S STRATEGY

Financial statement analysis involves more than just "crunching numbers." Before you start looking at numbers, you should know what you are looking for. While financial statements report on transactions, each of these transactions is the result of a company's operating decisions as it implements its business strategy.

■ **LEARNING OBJECTIVE 1**

Explain how a company's business strategy affects financial analysis.

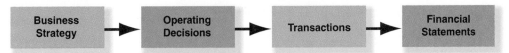

A useful starting point for financial statement analysis is the return on equity (ROE) profit driver analysis (also called *ROE decomposition* or *DuPont analysis*), which shows a logical relationship among the three ratios presented in Exhibit 13.2. These ratios are based on financial statement elements that are often called *profit drivers* or *profit levers* because they describe the three ways that management can improve ROE. The DuPont model helps us understand that a number of business strategies affect the profitability of a business. The model follows:

EXHIBIT **13.2**
ROE Profit Driver Analysis

Businesses can earn a high rate of return for the owners (i.e., a high ROE) by following different strategies. Two fundamental strategies follow:

1. *Product differentiation.* Under this strategy, companies offer products that are unique in some manner, such as being of high quality or offering unusual features or style. These unique benefits allow a company to charge higher prices. In general, higher prices result in higher profit margins, which lead to higher returns on equity (as shown in the ROE model).

2. *Cost advantage.* Under this strategy, companies attempt to operate more efficiently than their competitors, which permit them to offer lower prices to attract customers. The efficient use of resources is captured in the asset turnover ratio, and as the ROE model illustrates, a high asset turnover ratio leads to higher return on investment.

You can probably think of a number of companies that have followed one of these two basic strategies.

The best place to start your analysis is with a solid understanding of a company's business strategy. To evaluate how a company is doing, you must know what it is trying to do. You can learn a lot about a company's strategy by reading its complete annual report, especially the letter from the president. It also is useful to read articles about the company in the business press.

Home Depot's business strategy is described in its annual report as follows:

REAL WORLD EXCERPT

Home Depot

ANNUAL REPORT

OPERATING STRATEGY. The operating strategy for Home Depot stores is to offer a broad assortment of high-quality merchandise and services at competitive prices using highly knowledgeable, service-oriented personnel and aggressive advertising. We believe that our associates' knowledge of products and home improvement techniques and applications is very important in our marketing approach and our ability to maintain customer satisfaction. We regularly check our competitors' prices to ensure that our prices are competitive within each market.

Source: The Home Depot

This strategy has several implications for our analysis of Home Depot:

1. Cost control is critical. Home Depot must be able to purchase merchandise at low prices to beat competitors.

2. Stores must be able to generate high volume of business to cover the cost of operating large stores.

3. To offer a high level of service, Home Depot must incur employee compensation and training costs that are higher than competitors' costs. This puts pressure on Home Depot to control costs in other areas.

With these implications in mind, we can attach more meaning to the information contained in the financial statements.

As the preceding discussion indicates, a company can take different actions to try to affect each of its profit drivers. To understand the impact of these actions, financial analysts disaggregate each of the profit drivers into more detailed ratios. For example, the asset turnover ratio is further disaggregated into turnover ratios for specific assets such as accounts receivable, inventory, and fixed assets. We have developed our understanding of these ratios in previous chapters but we will bring them together in the next few sections as part of a comprehensive review of ratio analysis.

FINANCIAL STATEMENT ANALYSIS

Analyzing financial data without a basis of comparison is impossible. For example, would you be impressed with a company that earned $1 million last year? You are probably thinking, "It depends." A $1-million profit might be very good for a company that lost money the year before but not good for a company that made $500 million during the previous year. It might be good for a small company but not good for a very large company. And, it might be good if all the other companies in the industry lost money but not good if they all earned much larger profits.

As you can see from this simple example, financial results cannot be evaluated in isolation. To properly analyze the information reported in financial statements, you must develop appropriate comparisons. The task of finding appropriate benchmarks requires judgment and is not always an easy task. For this reason, financial analysis is a sophisticated skill, not a mechanical process.

There are two types of benchmarks for making financial comparisons, time series and comparisons with other companies.

1. *Time series analysis.* In this type of analysis, information for a single company is compared over time. For example, a key measure of performance for a retail company is the change in sales volume each year for its existing stores. The following time series chart shows that the percentage increase in sales volume for existing Home Depot stores fell from 1999 to 2001, but increased in both 2003 and 2004.[1]

■ **LEARNING OBJECTIVE 2**

Discuss how analysts use financial statements.

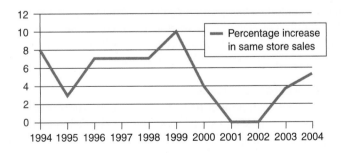

---

[1]The percentage change in sales for existing stores is computed as follows:

$$\text{Percentage change} = \left[\frac{\text{Sales}_{\text{Current Year}} - \text{Sales}_{\text{Previous Year}}}{\text{Sales}_{\text{Previous Year}}} \right] \times 100$$

Similar percentage changes can be computed for various elements of financial statements.

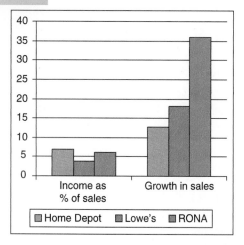

2. *Comparison with similar companies.* Financial results are often affected by industry and economy-wide factors. By comparing a company with another one in the same line of business, an analyst can obtain better insight into its performance. For example, the comparison of profit margin (income as a percentage of sales) for 2004, and growth in 2004 sales over 2003 sales for Home Depot, Lowe's, and RONA, shows that RONA had the highest increase in sales in 2004. However, Home Depot achieved a higher profit margin than RONA, which highlights its operating strength.

Finding comparable companies often is very difficult. Magna International Inc. is a well-known company that supplies automotive components and owns a subsidiary that is the largest operator of thoroughbred race tracks in North America. No other company sells exactly that group of products. Care must be exercised when selecting comparable companies from the same basic industry. Days Inn, Hilton, Holiday Inn, Marriott, and Intrawest are all in the hotel industry but not all could be considered comparable companies for purposes of financial analysis. These hotels offer different levels of quality and appeal to different types of customers.

The governments of the United States, Canada, and Mexico developed the North American Industry Classification System for use in reporting economic data. The system assigns a specific industry code to each corporation based on its business operations. Analysts often use these six-digit codes to make industry comparisons for various companies. Financial information services, such as Standard & Poor's, provide averages for many common accounting ratios for various industries as defined by the industrial classification codes. Because of the diversity of companies included in each industry classification, these data should be used with great care. For this reason, some analysts prefer to compare two companies that are very similar instead of using industry-wide comparisons.

RATIO AND PERCENTAGE ANALYSES

RATIO (PERCENTAGE) ANALYSIS is an analytical tool designed to identify significant relationships; it measures the proportional relationship between two financial statement amounts.

All financial analysts use **ratio analysis**, or **percentage analysis**, when they review companies. A ratio or percentage expresses the proportionate relationship between two different amounts by dividing one amount by another amount or number. Assessing a company's profitability is difficult if you know only that it earned a net income of $500,000. If shareholders' equity is $5 million, the relationship of earnings to shareholder investment is $500,000 ÷ $5,000,000 = 10 percent. This measure indicates a different level of performance than would be the case if shareholders' equity were $50 million. Ratio analysis condenses the large volume of raw financial data and helps decision makers to identify significant relationships and make meaningful comparisons between companies.

Ratios may be computed using amounts in one statement, such as the income statement, or in two different statements, such as the income statement and the balance sheet. In addition, amounts on a single statement may be expressed as a percentage of a base amount.

COMPONENT PERCENTAGES

■ LEARNING OBJECTIVE 3

Compute and interpret component percentages.

A **COMPONENT PERCENTAGE** expresses each item on a particular financial statement as a percentage of a single base amount.

Analysts often compute **component percentages**, which express each item on a financial statement as a percentage of a single *base amount*, the denominator of the ratio. To compute component percentages for the income statement, the base amount is net sales revenue. Each expense is expressed as a percentage of net sales revenue. On the balance sheet, the base amount is total assets; each balance sheet account is divided by total assets. This is also known as creating a common-size financial statement.

Discerning important relationships and trends in the Home Depot income statement shown in Exhibit 13.1 is difficult without using component percentages. Income

EXHIBIT **13.3**

**Component Percentages
for Home Depot**

Income Statement	Component Percentages		
	2004	2003	2002
Net sales	100.0%	100.0%	100.0%
Cost of merchandise sold	66.6	68.2	69.8
Gross profit	33.4	31.8	31.2
Operating expenses			
Selling and store operating	20.7	19.4	19.4
General and administrative	1.9	1.8	1.7
Total operating expenses	22.6	21.2	21.1
Operating income	10.8	10.6	10.1
Interest income	0.1	0.1	0.1
Interest expense	(0.1)	(0.1)	(0.0)
Interest, net	—	—	0.1
Earnings, before taxes	10.8	10.6	10.2
Income taxes	(4.0)	(4.0)	3.8
Net earnings	6.8	6.6	6.4

increased by more than 36.4 percent between 2002 and 2004,[2] which appears to be very good, but it is difficult for an analyst to evaluate the operating efficiency of Home Depot based on the reported numbers on the income statement.

Exhibit 13.3 shows a component percentage analysis for Home Depot's income statement (from Exhibit 13.1). If you simply reviewed the dollar amounts on the income statement, you might be concerned about several significant differences. For example, cost of goods sold increased by almost $4.4 billion between 2003 and 2004. Is this increase reasonable? Should you be concerned as an analyst? The component percentage indicates that cost of goods sold actually decreased as a percentage of sales revenue during that period. In other words, cost of goods sold has increased primarily because of the increase in sales revenue.

The component analysis for Home Depot (in Exhibit 13.3) helps highlight several additional issues:

1. Income increased by $1.34 billion between February 2, 2003, and January 30, 2005. A significant portion of this increase can be attributed to an increase in sales revenue but a portion is attributable to increased efficiency in operations. In fact, the cost of goods sold as a percentage of sales decreased during the period, and the gross profit increased from 31.2 percent to 33.4 percent.

2. Some of the changes in percentages may seem immaterial, but they involve very significant amounts of money. The increase in the ratio of selling and store operating expenses as a percentage of sales from 19.4 percent in 2003 to 20.7 percent in 2004 reduced earnings before taxes by $950 million [$73,094 × (20.7% − 19.4%)].

3. The cost of goods sold as a percentage of sales declined between 2002 and 2004. As we mentioned earlier, a key part of the strategy for Home Depot is selling merchandise at low prices. The annual report indicates that the improvement in the ratio of the cost of goods sold to sales revenue is a positive indication of the successful implementation of the company's strategy.

---

[2]The fiscal year of Home Depot ends in January, so its income statement covers essentially the results of the previous calendar year.

4. Significant stability in all of the income statement relationships indicates a well-run company. Notice that most of the individual income statement items changed by approximately one percentage point over a three-year period.

Many analysts use graphics software in their study of financial results. Graphic representation is especially useful when communicating findings during meetings or in printed form. A graphic summary of key 2004 data from Exhibit 13.3 is shown in the chart in the margin.

Of the many ratios that can be computed from a single set of financial statements, analysts use only those that can be helpful in a given situation. Comparing cost of goods sold to property, plant, and equipment is never useful because these items have no natural relationship. Instead, an analyst will often compute certain widely used ratios and then decide which additional ratios are relevant to the particular decision. For example, research and development costs as a percentage of sales is not a common ratio, but it is useful when analyzing companies that depend on new products, such as pharmaceutical or technology firms.

When you compute ratios, remember a basic fact about financial statements: Balance sheet amounts relate to an instant in time, and income statement amounts relate to a specified period. Therefore, when an income statement account is compared with a balance sheet amount, you should express the balance sheet amount as an average of the beginning and ending balances. In practice, many analysts simply use the ending balance sheet amount. This approach is appropriate only if no significant changes have occurred in balance sheet amounts. For consistency, we always use average amounts.

Financial statement analysis is a judgmental process. Not all ratios are helpful in a given situation. We will discuss several ratios that are appropriate to most situations. They can be grouped into the five categories shown in Exhibit 13.4.

TESTS OF PROFITABILITY

■ **LEARNING OBJECTIVE 4**

Compute and interpret profitability ratios.

TESTS OF PROFITABILITY compare income with one or more primary activities.

Profitability is a primary measure of the overall success of a company. Indeed, it is necessary for a company's survival. Investors and creditors prefer a single measure of profitability that is meaningful in all situations. Unfortunately, no single measure can be devised to meet this comprehensive need. Several **tests of profitability** focus on measuring the adequacy of income by comparing it to other items reported on the financial statements.

1. RETURN ON EQUITY (ROE)

Return on equity (also called *return on owners' investment*) relates income to the investment made by the owners. It reflects the simple fact that investors expect to earn more money if they invest more money. Two investments that offer a return of $10,000 are not comparable if one requires an investment of $100,000 and the other requires an investment of $250,000. The return on equity ratio is computed as follows:[3]

$$\text{Return on Equity} = \frac{\text{Income*}}{\text{Average Owners' Equity}}$$

$$\text{Home Depot, 2004} = \frac{\$5,001}{\$23,283^\dagger} = 21.5\%$$

*Income **before** extraordinary items should be used.
†($22,407 + $24,158) ÷ 2

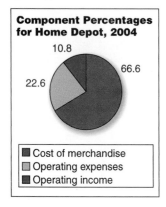

Component Percentages for Home Depot, 2004

10.8

66.6

22.6

■ Cost of merchandise
■ Operating expenses
■ Operating income

---

[3]The figures for Home Depot used throughout the following ratio examples are taken from the financial statements in Exhibit 13.1.

EXHIBIT **13.4**

Widely Used Accounting Ratios

Ratio	Basic Computation

Tests of Profitability

1. Return on equity (ROE)
   (Chapter 6)

$$\frac{\text{Income}}{\text{Average Owners' Equity}}$$

2. Return on assets (ROA)
   (Chapter 3)

$$\frac{\text{Income} + \text{Interest Expense (net of tax)}}{\text{Average Total Assets}}$$

3. Financial leverage percentage
   (Chapter 11)

Return on Equity − Return on Assets

4. Earnings per share
   (Chapter 4)

$$\frac{\text{Income Available to Common Shareholders}}{\text{Weighted-Average Number of Common Shares Outstanding}}$$

5. Quality of income
   (Chapter 5)

$$\frac{\text{Cash Flows from Operating Activities}}{\text{Net Income}}$$

6. Profit margin
   (Chapter 4)

$$\frac{\text{Income (before extraordinary items)}}{\text{Net Sales Revenue}}$$

7. Fixed asset turnover
   (Chapter 9)

$$\frac{\text{Net Sales Revenue}}{\text{Average Net Fixed Assets}}$$

Tests of Liquidity

8. Cash ratio
   (Chapter 13)

$$\frac{\text{Cash} + \text{Cash Equivalents}}{\text{Current Liabilities}}$$

9. Current ratio
   (Chapter 10)

$$\frac{\text{Current Assets}}{\text{Current Liabilities}}$$

10. Quick ratio
    (Chapter 13)

$$\frac{\text{Quick Assets}}{\text{Current Liabilities}}$$

11. Receivable turnover
    (Chapter 7)

$$\frac{\text{Net Credit Sales}}{\text{Average Net Trade Receivables}}$$

12. Inventory turnover
    (Chapter 8)

$$\frac{\text{Cost of Goods Sold}}{\text{Average Inventory}}$$

13. Payable turnover
    (Chapter 10)

$$\frac{\text{Net Credit Purchases}}{\text{Average Net Trade Payables}}$$

Tests of Solvency

14. Times interest earned
    (Chapter 11)

$$\frac{\text{Net Income} + \text{Interest} + \text{Income Tax Expense}}{\text{Interest Expense}}$$

15. Cash coverage
    (Chapter 13)

$$\frac{\text{Cash Flows from Operating Activities (before interest and tax expense)}}{\text{Interest Paid}}$$

16. Debt-to-equity
    (Chapter 2)

$$\frac{\text{Total Liabilities}}{\text{Owners' Equity}}$$

Market Tests

17. Price/earnings ratio
    (Chapter 1)

$$\frac{\text{Current Market Price per Share}}{\text{Earnings per Share}}$$

18. Dividend yield
    (Chapter 12)

$$\frac{\text{Dividends per Share}}{\text{Market Price per Share}}$$

Note: Most of these ratios have been discussed in previous chapters. The specific chapter appears below the ratio.

Home Depot earned 21.5 percent on the owners' investment. Was that return high or low? We can answer this question by comparing its ROE with the ROE of similar companies. The return on equity for two of Home Depot's competitors follows:

Canadian Tire	13.7%
RONA	20.3
Home Depot	21.5

RETURN ON EQUITY FOR SELECTED INDUSTRIES, 2004

Retailing	14.75%
Paper and Forest Products	13.42%
Telecommunication Services	3.47%
Gold	−5.11%

Clearly, Home Depot produced a better return than its competitors.

We gain additional insight by examining Home Depot's ROE over time:

	2004	2003	2002
ROE	21.5%	20.4%	18.8%

This comparison shows that Home Depot's performance as measured by ROE improved over the three-year period. In the annual report, management attributes this increase to changing customer preferences and continuing benefits from the company's centralized purchasing approach, which improved inventory management.

2. RETURN ON ASSETS (ROA)

Another test of profitability compares income to the total assets (i.e., total investment) used to earn the income. Many analysts consider the *return on assets ratio* to be a better measure of management's ability to utilize assets effectively because it is not affected by the way in which the assets were financed. For example, the return on equity could be very large for a company that has borrowed a large amount of debt compared to a company that earned the same return based on the same amount of assets but borrowed less money. The return on equity measures profitability from the perspective of the shareholders, whereas the return on assets takes into consideration the resources contributed by both shareholders and creditors. For this reason, the return to shareholders, net income, is augmented by the return to creditors, which is interest expense. Interest expense is measured net of income tax because it represents the net cost of the funds provided by the creditors to the corporation.[4]

The return on assets is computed as follows:

$$\text{Return on Assets} = \frac{\text{Income* + Interest Expense (net of tax)}}{\text{Average Total Assets}^\dagger}$$

$$\text{Home Depot, 2004} = \frac{\$5,001 + (\$70 \times 63\%)}{\$36,672^\dagger} = 13.8\%$$

*Income before extraordinary items should be used. This illustration uses a corporate tax rate of 37 percent.
†($34,437 + $38,907) ÷ 2

---

[4]To illustrate the net cost of using debt, assume that a company earned $100 in revenue and incurred $70 in operating expenses. Consider two scenarios: (1) the company uses long-term debt that cost $10 in interest expense, and (2) the company does not use debt.

	Debt Financing	Equity Financing
Income before interest and taxes	$30	$30
Interest expense	(10)	0
Income before income taxes	$20	$30
Income tax expense (@40 percent)	(8)	(12)
Net income	$12	$18

The deduction of interest expense from income reduced the income tax expense from $12 to $8, and net income decreased by only $6. Therefore, the net cost of using debt in this case is $6, or $10 × (1 − 0.4, the tax rate).

Home Depot earned 13.8 percent on the total resources it used during the year. The return on assets for Home Depot's competitors is shown below. This comparison indicates that Home Depot utilizes its assets more effectively than its competitors.

Canadian Tire	6.8%
RONA	11.4
Home Depot	13.8

3. FINANCIAL LEVERAGE PERCENTAGE

The *financial leverage percentage* measures the advantage or disadvantage that occurs when a company's return on equity differs from its return on assets (i.e., ROE − ROA). In the ROE profit driver analysis discussed earlier in this chapter, financial leverage was defined as the proportion of assets acquired with funds supplied by owners. The *financial leverage percentage* measures a related but different concept. It describes the relationship between the return on equity and the return on assets. Leverage is positive when the rate of return on a company's assets exceeds the average after-tax interest rate on its borrowed funds. Basically, the company borrows at one rate and earns a higher rate of return on its investments. Most companies have positive leverage.

Financial leverage percentage can be measured by comparing the two return on investment ratios as follows:

Financial Leverage = Return on Equity − Return on Assets

Home Depot, 2004 =   21.5%   −   13.8%   = 7.7%

When a company is able to borrow funds at an after-tax interest rate and invest those funds to earn a higher after-tax rate of return, the difference benefits the owners. The notes to Home Depot's annual report indicate that the company has borrowed money at rates ranging from 3.75 percent to 6.5 percent and invested this money in assets earning 13.8 percent. The difference between the income earned on the money it borrows and the interest it paid to creditors is available for the owners of Home Depot. This benefit of financial leverage is the primary reason that most companies obtain a significant amount of their resources from creditors rather than from the sale of shares. Notice that financial leverage can be enhanced either by investing effectively (i.e., earning a high return on investment) or borrowing effectively (i.e., paying a low rate of interest).

If the financial leverage percentage for Home Depot is negative, it could mean that ROE has decreased relative to ROA or that ROA has increased relative to ROE. The return on equity decreases when net income decreases, which signals a deterioration in the company's profitability, or when equity increases through the issuance of additional shares. An inflow of cash from a new equity issue may indicate that the company is entering a growth phase that is expected to increase profits. Without careful interpretation of all of the reliable and relevant information available on a specific company, investors cannot accurately interpret a decrease in ROE as either good news or bad news.

The second possibility is that the return on assets may have increased substantially relative to the return on equity. Again, an increase in ROA may reflect an increase in after-tax interest expense and in the cost of debt financing.

In general, if a decrease in ROE signals future growth despite a temporarily negative financial leverage percentage, investors may not be too alarmed by negative leverage. If, however, an increase in ROA is the result of borrowing at high interest rates, investors could well interpret negative leverage as reflecting bad news. It is therefore important for investors to be cautious when interpreting any increase or decrease in ratios.

4. EARNINGS PER SHARE (EPS)

Some analysts are critical of the return on investment ratios because they are based on historical cost data. The amount of owners' investment represents their original investment plus retained earnings, not the current market value of that investment. The same concern applies to the return on assets.

Earnings per share is based on the number of shares outstanding instead of dollar amounts reported on the balance sheet. Investors easily can interpret EPS in terms of their personal circumstances. An investor with 1,000 shares can quickly compute the return on his or her investment using EPS. The investor would not be able to compute the dollar amount of this return based only on the information that the company had earned 21.5 percent return on equity. Basically, EPS is computed as follows:

$$\text{Earnings per Share} = \frac{\text{Income Available to Common Shareholders}}{\substack{\text{Weighted-Average Number of} \\ \text{Common Shares Outstanding}}}$$

$$\text{Home Depot, 2004} = \frac{\$5{,}001}{\$2{,}207*} = \$2.27 \text{ per share}$$

*Reported on the income statement.

This computation of EPS is based on information provided in note 7 of the company's consolidated financial statements. The additional complexities in the computation of EPS are discussed in advanced accounting courses.

Earnings per share is probably the single most widely watched ratio. Companies' announcements of their net earnings each quarter during the fiscal year are normally reported in the business press. The following news story by Associated Press concerning Home Depot's earnings results for the second quarter of 2004 illustrates the importance of earnings per share.

REAL WORLD EXCERPT

Home Depot

EARNINGS ANNOUNCEMENT
BY ASSOCIATED PRESS

ATLANTA (AP)—The Home Depot Inc. raised its full-year earnings outlook on Tuesday after posting a 19 percent increase in net income as store and customer-service upgrades continued to buoy sales.

The results sent shares of Home Depot, a component of the Dow Jones industrials, up more than 3 percent and easily surpassed Wall Street expectations.

The nation's largest home improvement store chain said it earned $1.55 billion, or 70 cents a share, in the three months ending Aug. 1, compared to a profit of $1.30 billion, or 56 cents a share, in the same period a year ago.

Excluding the effect of an accounting change, Home Depot said it earned $1.57 billion, or 71 cents a share, in the quarter. Analysts surveyed by Thomson First Call were expecting earnings of 64 cents a share.

5. QUALITY OF INCOME

Most financial analysts are concerned about the quality of a company's earnings because some accounting procedures can be used to report higher income. For example, a company that uses LIFO and short estimated lives for long-term assets will report lower earnings than a similar company that uses FIFO and longer estimated lives. One method of evaluating the quality of a company's earnings is to compare its reported earnings to its cash flows from operating activities, as follows:

$$\text{Quality of Income} = \frac{\text{Cash Flows from Operating Activities}}{\text{Net Income}}$$

$$\text{Home Depot, 2004} = \frac{\$6{,}904}{\$5{,}001} = 1.38$$

A quality of income ratio higher than 1 is considered to indicate higher-quality earnings because each dollar of income is supported by at least one dollar of cash flow. A ratio below 1 represents lower-quality earnings.

6. PROFIT MARGIN

The *profit margin* measures the percentage of each sales dollar, on average, that represents profit. It is computed as follows:

$$\text{Profit Margin} = \frac{\text{Income (before Extraordinary Items)}}{\text{Net Sales Revenue}}$$

$$\text{Home Depot, 2004} = \frac{\$5,001}{\$73,094} = 6.8\%$$

During 2004, each dollar of Home Depot's sales generated 6.8 cents of profit. Care must be used in analyzing the profit margin because it does not consider the amount of resources employed (i.e., total investment) to earn income. For example, the hypothetical income statements of Home Depot and Canadian Tire might show the following:

		Home Depot	Canadian Tire
a.	Sales revenue	$500,000	$150,000
b.	Income	$25,000	$ 7,500
c.	Profit margin (b ÷ a)	5%	5%
d.	Total investment	$250,000	$125,000
e.	Return on total investment* (b ÷ d)	10%	6%

*Assuming no interest expense.

In this example, both companies reported the same profit margin (5 percent). Home Depot, however, appears to be performing much better because it is earning a 10 percent return on the total investment versus the 6 percent earned by Canadian Tire. The profit margin percentages do not reflect the effect of the $250,000 total investment in Home Depot compared to the $125,000 total investment in Canadian Tire. Thus, the profit margin omits one of the two important factors that should be used in evaluating return on the investment.

It is very difficult to compare profit margins for companies in different industries. For example, profit margins are low in the food industry, but they are high in the jewellery business. Both types of businesses can be quite profitable, however, because a high sales volume can compensate for a low profit margin. Grocery stores have low profit margins, but generate a large sales volume from their relatively inexpensive stores and inventory. Although jewellery stores earn more profit from each sales dollar, they require a large investment in luxury stores and very expensive inventory.

The trade-off between profit margin and sales volume can be stated in very simple terms: Would you prefer to have 5 percent of $1,000,000 or 10 percent of $100,000? As you can see, a larger percentage is not always better.

The operating strength of Home Depot comes more clearly into focus when you compare its profit margin with that of major competitors:

Canadian Tire	4.1%
RONA	6.0
Home Depot	6.8

7. FIXED ASSET TURNOVER

Another measure of operating efficiency is the fixed asset turnover ratio, which compares sales volume with a company's investment in fixed assets. The term *fixed assets* is synonymous with *property, plant, and equipment*. The ratio is computed as follows:

$$\text{Fixed Asset Turnover} = \frac{\text{Net Sales Revenue}}{\text{Average Net Fixed Assets}}$$

$$\text{Home Depot, 2004} = \frac{\$73,094}{\$21,395^*} = 3.42$$

*($20,063 + $22,726) ÷ 2

The fixed asset turnover ratio for Home Depot is lower than RONA's (11.10) but higher than Canadian Tire's (2.84). In simple terms, this means that Home Depot has a competitive advantage over Canadian Tire in terms of its ability to effectively utilize its fixed assets to generate revenue. For each dollar that Home Depot invested in property, plant, and equipment, it was able to earn $3.42 in sales revenue while RONA earned $11.10 and Canadian Tire earned only $2.84. This comparison is extremely important because it indicates that management of Home Depot is able to operate more efficiently than Canadian Tire's, but not RONA's.

The fixed asset turnover ratio is widely used to analyze capital-intensive companies such as airlines and electric utilities. For companies that have large amounts of inventory and accounts receivable, analysts often prefer to use the asset turnover ratio, which is based on total assets rather than fixed assets:

$$\text{Asset Turnover} = \frac{\text{Net Sales Revenue}}{\text{Average Total Assets}}$$

$$\text{Home Depot, 2004} = \frac{\$73,094}{\$36,672^*} = 1.99$$

*($34,437 + $38,907) ÷ 2

In 2004, Home Depot was able to generate $1.99 in revenue for each dollar invested in the company's assets. This ratio does not compare favourably to RONA's ratio of 2.83 but exceeds Canadian Tire's ratio of 1.41. Both turnover ratios show that Home Depot was able to operate more efficiently than Canadian Tire, but less efficiently than RONA.

As we showed with the ROE model earlier in this chapter, one strategy to improve return on equity is to generate more sales dollars from the company's assets. Many analysts consider this type of improvement to be an important indication of the quality of the company's management.

SELF-STUDY **QUIZ 13-1**

Canadian Tire Corporation Ltd. reported the following data in a recent annual report (in millions of dollars):

	Current Year	Last Year
Net income	$ 148	
Sales	5,207	
Interest expense (net of tax)	58	
Shareholders' equity	1,459	$1,345
Total assets	3,748	3,871

The company did not report any extraordinary items in the current year.

Compute the following ratios:

1. Return on equity.

2. Return on assets.

3. Profit margin.

After you complete your work, check your answers with the solutions on page 714.

ROE PROFIT DRIVER ANALYSIS

Exhibit 13.5 shows a decomposition of Home Depot's ROE profit driver analysis that was presented earlier in Exhibit 13.2. This analysis shows the sources of the change in ROE and can provide useful insights into Home Depot's business strategy.

EXHIBIT **13.5**

Home Depot ROE Profit Driver Analysis

	Fiscal Year Ending		
	Jan. 30, 2005	**Feb. 1, 2004**	**Feb. 2, 2003**
ROE Profit Drivers			
Net income	$ 5,001	$ 4,304	$ 3,664
Net sales	73,094	64,816	58,247
Average total assets	36,672	32,224	28,203
Average shareholders' equity	23,283	21,105	18,942
ROE Profit Driver Analysis			
Net income / Net sales	0.068	0.066	0.063
× Net sales / Avg. total assets	1.993	2.016	2.065
× Avg. total assets / Avg. shareholders' equity	1.575	1.527	1.489
= Net income / Avg. shareholders' equity	0.215	0.204	0.193

Exhibit 13.5 shows an increase in profit margin over the three-year period. The component percentages (see Exhibit 13.3) suggest that this increase was caused mainly by the decrease in the cost of goods sold relative to net sales. The analysis also shows a steady decline in asset turnover, indicating that Home Depot utilized increasing amounts of assets to generate each dollar of sales. Home Depot can increase asset turnover by increasing sales volume or by decreasing less-productive assets. Home Depot's balance sheet at January 30, 2005, reported about $2.2 billion in cash and cash equivalents and short-term investments, representing approximately 5 percent of total assets. These assets can be used to (1) expand the business in accordance with the company's business strategy, (2) reduce the company's debt, which improves the asset turnover ratio, since the average total assets are reduced with the payment of cash, or (3) use the idle cash to repurchase some of the company's outstanding shares, which reduces shareholders' equity and increases both financial leverage and the return on equity.

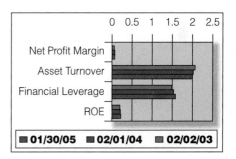

In summary, the improvement in Home Depot's return on equity during the fiscal years 2002–2004 was essentially due to increasing net profit margins as well as financial leverage, suggesting that Home Depot's use of additional debt to finance its operations and investments benefited the company's shareholders.[5] The decline in the asset turnover was not significant enough to offset the effects of the other components of the DuPont model.

---

[5]An expanded version of the ROE profit driver analysis is provided by the Scott formula. Interested readers are referred to the Online Learning Centre Web site at **www.mcgrawhill.ca/college/libby/student/ resources** for a detailed application of the Scott formula to the financial statements of Home Depot, Inc.

SELF-STUDY **QUIZ 13-2**

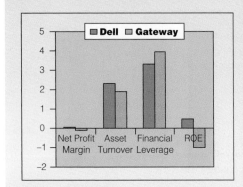

We used ROE analysis in Exhibit 13.5 to understand why Home Depot's ROE had changed over the fiscal years 2002–2004. This type of analysis is often called *time series analysis*. ROE analysis can also be used to explain why a company has an ROE different from its competitors at a single point in time. This type of analysis is called *cross-sectional analysis*. Dell Inc. and Gateway Inc. are the largest computer manufacturers that employ mail-order/Internet distribution. Both of these companies have followed a low-cost strategy, developing reputations for good products and service at low prices. The following is an analysis of their ROEs for the year 2004. Dell produced higher ROE in the previous two years, and its shareholders were amply rewarded with a significant increase in the value of their shares, whereas Gateway's share price declined during the same period because of net losses. Using ROE analysis, explain how Dell produced its higher ROE.

ROE Profit Drivers	Dell	Gateway
Net Income/Net Sales	0.061	−0.13
× Net Sales/Average Total Assets	2.31	1.92
× Avg. Total Assets/Average Shareholders' Equity	3.33	3.93
= Net Income/Average Shareholders' Equity	0.48	−0.98

After you complete your analysis, check your answers with the solutions on page 714.

TESTS OF LIQUIDITY

■ LEARNING OBJECTIVE 5

Compute and interpret liquidity ratios.

TESTS OF LIQUIDITY are ratios that measure a company's ability to meet its currently maturing obligations.

Liquidity refers to a company's ability to meet its currently maturing debts. **Tests of liquidity** focus on the relationship between current assets and current liabilities. A company's ability to pay its current liabilities is an important factor in evaluating its short-term financial strength. For example, a company that does not have cash available to pay for purchases on a timely basis will lose its cash discounts and run the risk of having its credit discontinued by vendors. Three ratios are used to measure liquidity: the cash ratio, the current ratio, and the quick ratio.

8. CASH RATIO

Cash is the lifeblood of a business. Without cash, a company cannot pay its employees or meet obligations to its creditors. Even a profitable business will fail without sufficient cash. One measure of the adequacy of available cash, called the *cash ratio*, is computed as follows:

$$\text{Cash Ratio} = \frac{\text{Cash} + \text{Cash Equivalents}}{\text{Current Liabilities}}$$

$$\text{Home Depot, 2004} = \frac{\$2,165}{\$10,529} = 0.21$$

Analysts often use this ratio to compare similar companies. The cash ratios for Canadian Tire and RONA indicate that Canadian Tire has a larger cash reserve compared to its current liabilities.

Canadian Tire	0.54
RONA	0.01
Home Depot	0.21

Would analysts be concerned about the lower ratio for Home Depot? Probably not, because there are other factors to consider. The cash flow statement for Home Depot shows that the company generates a very large amount of cash from operating activities each year. As a result, it does not have to keep a large amount of cash on reserve to meet unexpected needs. Indeed, most analysts believe that the cash ratio should not be too high, because holding excess cash usually is uneconomical. It is far better to invest the cash in productive assets or reduce debt.

The cash ratio for Home Depot has fluctuated over recent years, but remains high. However, a deteriorating ratio might be a cause for concern. It could be an early warning that the company is experiencing financial difficulty. Given the strong performance of Home Depot, the cash ratio is more likely the result of aggressive efforts by managers to minimize the amount of cash used to operate the business.

Some analysts do not use this ratio because it is very sensitive to small events. The collection of a large account receivable, for example, may have a significant impact on the cash ratio. The current ratio and the quick ratio are much less sensitive to the timing of such transactions.

9. CURRENT RATIO

The *current ratio* measures the relationship between current assets and current liabilities at a specific date. It is computed as follows:

$$\text{Current Ratio} = \frac{\text{Current Assets}}{\text{Current Liabilities}}$$

$$\text{Home Depot, 2004} = \frac{\$14,190}{\$10,529} = 1.35$$

The current ratio measures the cushion of working capital that companies maintain to allow for the inevitable unevenness in the flow of funds through the working capital accounts. At the end of 2004, Home Depot had $1.35 in current assets for each $1 of liabilities. Most analysts would judge the ratio to be very strong, given Home Depot's ability to generate cash. By comparison, both Canadian Tire and RONA have higher current ratios than Home Depot.

Canadian Tire	1.62
RONA	1.94
Home Depot	1.35

To properly use the current ratio, analysts must understand the nature of a company's business. Many manufacturing companies have developed sophisticated systems to minimize the amount of inventory they must hold. These systems, called *just-in-time inventory*, are designed to have an inventory item arrive just as it is needed. While these systems work well in manufacturing processes, they do not work as well in retailing. Customers expect to find merchandise when they want it, and it has proven difficult to precisely forecast consumer behaviour. As a result, most retailers have comparatively large current ratios because they must carry large inventories. To illustrate this issue, Home Depot maintains an inventory of 45,000 different products in each store.

Analysts consider a current ratio of 2 to be financially conservative. Indeed, most companies have current ratios that are below 2. The optimal level for a current ratio depends on the business environment in which a company operates. If cash flows are predictable and stable (as they are for a utility company), the current ratio can even be lower than 1. For a business with highly variable cash flows (such as an airline), a ratio exceeding 1 may be desirable.

Analysts become concerned if a company's current ratio is high compared to that of other companies. A firm is operating inefficiently when it ties up too much money in inventory or accounts receivable. There is no reason, for instance, for a Home Depot store to hold 100 refrigerators in stock if it sells only 10 refrigerators a month.

CURRENT RATIO FOR SELECTED INDUSTRIES, 2004	
Gold	5.12
Pharmaceuticals	3.90
Software	2.88
Retailing	2.27
Paper and Forest Products	1.89
Telecommunication Services	1.29

10. QUICK RATIO (ACID TEST)

The *quick ratio* is a more stringent test of short-term liquidity than the current ratio. The quick ratio compares quick assets, defined as *cash and near-cash assets*, to current liabilities. Quick assets include cash, short-term investments, and accounts receivable (net of the allowance for doubtful accounts). Inventories are omitted from quick assets because of the uncertainty of the timing of cash flows from their sale. Prepaid expenses are also excluded from quick assets. Thus, the quick, or acid test, ratio is a more severe test of liquidity than is the current ratio. It is computed as follows:

$$\text{Quick Ratio} = \frac{\text{Quick Assets}}{\text{Current Liabilities}}$$

$$\text{Home Depot, 2004} = \frac{\$3,664}{\$10,529} = 0.35$$

The quick ratio is a measure of the safety margin that is available to meet a company's current liabilities. Home Depot has 35 cents in cash and near-cash assets for every $1 in current liabilities. This ratio is below the threshold of 0.40 that is considered appropriate for this ratio. Analysts should not be concerned about the magnitude of this ratio because of the large amount of cash that Home Depot generates from operating activities. By comparison, the quick ratios for Canadian Tire and RONA are 1.19 and 0.39, respectively.

SELF-STUDY **QUIZ 13-3**

The current ratios for six industries appear in the margin on page 703. The following quick ratios, presented in a random order, pertain to the same six industries:

	Industries					
	1	2	3	4	5	6
Quick ratio	3.34	1.06	0.96	0.91	4.32	2.52

Two of these six industries are gold and retailing. Identify the ratio associated with each of these two industries. On average, the quick assets for the retailing industry represent 40 percent of the industry's current assets.

After you complete your work, check your answers with the solutions on page 714.

11. RECEIVABLE TURNOVER

Accounts receivable are closely related to both short-term liquidity and operating efficiency. A company that can quickly collect cash from its customers has good liquidity and does not needlessly tie up funds in unproductive assets. The receivable turnover ratio is computed as follows:

$$\text{Receivable Turnover} = \frac{\text{Net Credit Sales*}}{\text{Average Net Trade Receivables}}$$

$$\text{Home Depot, 2004} = \frac{\$73,094}{\$1,298^\dagger} = 56 \text{ Times}$$

*When the amount of credit sales is not known, total sales may be used as a rough approximation.
†($1,097 + $1,499) ÷ 2

This ratio is called a *turnover* because it reflects how many times the trade receivables were recorded, collected, and then recorded again during the period (i.e., "turnover"). Receivable turnover expresses the relationship of the average balance in Accounts Receivable to the transactions (i.e., credit sales) that created those receivables. This ratio measures the effectiveness of the company's credit-granting and collection activities. A high receivable turnover ratio suggests effective collection activities. Granting credit to poor credit risks and making ineffective collection efforts cause this ratio to be low. A very low ratio obviously is a problem, but a very high ratio also can be troublesome because it suggests an overly stringent credit policy that could cause lost sales and profits.

The receivable turnover ratio often is converted to a time basis known as the *average age of trade receivables*. The computation is as follows:

$$\textbf{Average Age of Trade Receivables} = \frac{\textbf{Days in a Year}}{\textbf{Receivable Turnover}}$$

$$\textbf{Home Depot, 2004} = \frac{365}{56} = \textbf{6.5 Average Days to Collect}$$

This computation is equivalent to dividing the average net trade receivables by the average net credit sales per day; that is:

$$\textbf{Average Collection Period} = \$1,298 \div (\$73,094 \div 365) = \textbf{6.5 days}$$

The effectiveness of credit and collection activities sometimes is judged by the general rule that the average collection period should not exceed 1.5 times the credit terms. For example, if the credit terms require payment in 30 days, the average collection period should not exceed 45 days (i.e., not more than 15 days past due). Like all rules, this one has many exceptions.

When you evaluate financial statements, you should always think about the reasonableness of the numbers you compute. We computed the average age of receivables for Home Depot as 6.5 days. Is that number reasonable? Probably not. It is very unlikely that Home Depot collects cash from its credit customers on average in just six days. Because we did not know the amount of Home Depot's credit sales, we used total sales as an approximation. Think about the last time you watched a customer buying merchandise on credit in a retail store. Most customers use a bank credit card such as MasterCard or Visa. From the seller's perspective, a sales transaction involving a bank credit card is recorded in virtually the same manner as a cash sale. A credit sale involving a credit card does not create an account receivable on the seller's books. Instead, the account receivable is recorded on the books of the credit card company. In practice, the majority of Home Depot's credit sales involve bank credit cards. As a result, Home Depot's accounts receivable turnover ratio is not meaningful.

12. INVENTORY TURNOVER

Like the receivable turnover, *inventory turnover* is a measure of both liquidity and operating efficiency. It reflects the relationship of inventory to the volume of goods sold during the period. It is computed as follows:

$$\textbf{Inventory Turnover} = \frac{\textbf{Cost of Goods Sold}}{\textbf{Average Inventory}}$$

$$\textbf{Home Depot, 2004} = \frac{\$48,664}{\$9,576*} = \textbf{5.1 Times}$$

*($9,076 + $10,076) ÷ 2

Because a company normally realizes a profit each time the inventory is sold, an increase in the ratio is usually favourable. If the ratio is too high, however, it may be an indication that sales were lost because desired items were not in stock.

On average, Home Depot's inventory was acquired and sold to customers 5.1 times during the year.[6] The inventory turnover ratio is critical for companies that have adopted the Home Depot strategy. They want to be able to offer the customer the right product when it is needed at a price that beats the competition. If Home Depot does not effectively manage its inventory levels, it will incur extra costs that must be passed on to the customer.

---

[6]The inventory turnover ratios for both RONA and Canadian Tire cannot be computed because neither company disclosed its cost of goods sold on its income statement.

Turnover ratios vary significantly from one industry to the next. Companies in the food industry (grocery stores and restaurants) have high inventory turnover ratios because their inventory is subject to rapid deterioration in quality. Companies that sell expensive merchandise (automobiles and high-fashion clothes) have much lower ratios because sales of these items are infrequent but customers want to have a selection to choose from when they do buy.

The turnover ratio often is converted to a time basis called *the average day's supply in inventory*. The computation is

$$\text{Average Day's Supply in Inventory} = \frac{\text{Days in Year}}{\text{Inventory Turnover}}$$

$$\text{Home Depot, 2004} = \frac{365}{5.1}$$

$$= 72 \text{ Average Day's Supply in Inventory}$$

Equivalently, the average day's supply in inventory can be computed by dividing the average inventory by the cost of goods sold per day; that is:

Average Day's Supply in Inventory = \$9,576 ÷ (\$48,664 ÷ 365) = 72 days

13. PAYABLE TURNOVER

The payable turnover ratio evaluates the company's effectiveness in managing payables to trade creditors. It is computed as follows:

$$\text{Payable Turnover} = \frac{\text{Net Credit Purchases}}{\text{Average Net Trade Payables}}$$

Credit purchases are not usually reported in financial statements; hence, we can use total purchases of merchandise inventory as a rough approximation. However, purchases are usually not reported separately in financial statements, but can be calculated by adjusting the cost of goods sold for the change in inventory during the period.

Purchases = Cost of Goods Sold + Ending Inventory − Beginning Inventory

The computation of the payable turnover for Home Depot follows:[7]

$$\text{Home Depot, 2004} = \frac{\$48,664 + \$10,076 - \$9,076}{\$5,463*} = 9.09 \text{ Times}$$

*(\$5,159 + \$5,766) ÷ 2

This ratio reflects how many times the trade payables were recorded, paid, and then recorded again during the period. The payable turnover expresses the relationship of the average balance in accounts payable to the purchase transactions that created those payables. Usually, a low ratio raises questions concerning a company's liquidity. It could also reflect aggressive cash management. By conserving cash with slow payment to trade suppliers, the company minimizes the amount of money it must borrow, and the related interest.

The payable turnover ratio is often converted to a time basis known as the *average age of payables*. The computation is:

$$\text{Average Age of Payables} = \frac{\text{Days in a Year}}{\text{Payable Turnover}}$$

$$\text{Home Depot, 2004} = \frac{365}{9.09} = 40 \text{ Average Days to Pay}$$

---

[7]The payable turnover ratios for both RONA and Canadian Tire cannot be computed because neither company disclosed its cost of goods sold on its income statement.

This computation is equivalent to dividing the average net trade payables by the average net credit purchases per day.

The payable turnover can be subject to manipulation. Managers may delay payment to creditors during the entire year, but catch up at year end so that the ratio is at an acceptable level.

A useful measure of liquidity and efficient cash management is the cash conversion cycle, which compares the average period of converting inventory into cash to the average period of payment for purchases. For Home Depot, the cash conversion cycle decreased by 15 days from 2000 to 2004 by extending the period of payments to suppliers.

	Fiscal Year				
	2004	2003	2002	2001	2000
Days of supply in inventory	72	72	69	65	69
Average collection period*	6	6	6	6	6
Average age of payables	(41)	(40)	(36)	(26)	(22)
Cash conversion cycle	37	38	39	45	53

*This computation assumes that all sales are on credit. In reality, a small proportion of the company's sales are on credit; hence, the average collection period would be close to zero and the cash conversion cycle would be reduced accordingly.

In contrast, companies that sell products through the Internet may not need to stock merchandise for long periods. In fact, Dell Inc. disclosed in its annual report for fiscal 2004 that its cash conversion cycle was −37 days during that year, indicating that Dell paid suppliers, on average, 37 days after it sold its products and collected from customers. While Home Depot needs money to finance the purchase of inventory, Dell has relied on suppliers to provide the necessary financing.

SELF-STUDY **QUIZ 13-4**

Canadian Tire Corporation Ltd. reported the following data in a recent annual report (in millions of dollars):

Net income	$ 148
Cash and short-term investments	131
Accounts receivable	515
Credit card receivables	453
Current liabilities	1,128
Cash flows from operating activities	502

Compute the following ratios:

1. Quality of income.

2. Quick ratio.

3. Cash ratio.

After you complete your work, check your answers with the solutions on page 714.

TESTS OF SOLVENCY

Solvency refers to a company's ability to meet its long-term obligations. **Tests of solvency** measure a company's ability to meet these obligations. Certain critical relationships can be identified by analyzing how a company has financed its assets and activities.

14. TIMES INTEREST EARNED RATIO

Interest payments are a fixed obligation of the borrowing company. If a company fails to make required interest payments, creditors may force it into bankruptcy. Because of

■ **LEARNING OBJECTIVE 6**

Compute and interpret solvency ratios.

TESTS OF SOLVENCY are ratios that measure a company's ability to meet its long-term obligations.

the importance of interest payments, analysts often compute a ratio called *times interest earned:*

$$\text{Times Interest Earned} = \frac{\text{Net Income + Interest Expense +}}{\text{Interest Expense}}$$

$$\text{Home Depot, 2004} = \frac{\$5,001 + \$70 + \$2,911}{\$70} = 114 \text{ Times}$$

This ratio compares the income that a company generated during one period to its interest obligation for the same period. It represents a margin of protection for the creditors. In 2004, Home Depot generated more than $114 in income for each $1 of interest expense, a high ratio that indicates a secure position for creditors.

Some analysts prefer to calculate this ratio based on all contractually required payments, including principal payments and rent obligations under lease contracts. Other analysts believe that this ratio is flawed because interest expense and other obligations are paid in cash, not with net income. These analysts prefer to use the cash coverage ratio.

15. CASH COVERAGE RATIO

Given the importance of cash flows and required interest payments, it is easy to understand why many analysts use the *cash coverage ratio*. It is computed as follows:

$$\text{Cash Coverage} = \frac{\text{Cash Flows from Operating Activities before Interest and Taxes}}{\text{Interest Paid (from cash flow statement)}}$$

$$\text{Home Depot, 2004} = \frac{\$6,904 + \$78 + \$2,793}{\$78} = 125$$

The cash coverage ratio compares the cash generated with the cash obligations of the period. Analysts are concerned about a company's ability to make required interest payments. The cash coverage ratio for Home Depot shows that the company generated $125 in cash from operations for every $1 of interest paid, which is very strong coverage. Notice that we used cash payments for interest and taxes, as disclosed in the cash flow statement. Accrued interest and interest payments are normally similar in amount, but not always the same. Note that the numerator and the denominator of the cash coverage ratio use *interest paid* from the cash flow statement instead of *interest expense* from the income statement.

16. DEBT-TO-EQUITY RATIO

The *debt-to-equity ratio* expresses a company's debt as a proportion of its owners' equity.[8] It is computed as follows:

$$\text{Debt-to-Equity Ratio} = \frac{\text{Total Liabilities}}{\text{Owners' Equity}}$$

$$\text{Home Depot, 2004} = \frac{\$14,749}{\$24,158} = 0.61 \text{ (or 61\%)}$$

In 2004, for each $1 of owners' equity, Home Depot had 61 cents of liabilities. By comparison, RONA and Canadian Tire's debt-to-equity ratios were 0.78 and 1.18, respectively.

---

[8]The relationship between debt and owners' equity alternatively may be calculated with the following ratio:

$$\text{Total Liabilities to Total Equities} = \frac{\text{Total Liabilities}}{\text{Total Liabilities and Owners' Equity}}$$

$$\text{Home Depot, 2004} = \frac{\$14,749}{\$38,907} = 37.9\%$$

Debt is risky for a company because specific interest payments must be made even if the company has not earned sufficient income to pay them. In contrast, dividends are always at the company's discretion and are not legally enforceable until they are declared by the board of directors. Owners' equity is "permanent" capital that does not have a maturity date. Thus, equity capital is usually considered much less risky than debt.

Despite the risk associated with debt, most companies obtain significant amounts of resources from creditors because of the advantages of financial leverage discussed earlier. In addition, interest expense is a deductible expense on the corporate income tax return. In selecting a capital structure, a company must balance the higher returns available through leverage against the higher risk associated with debt. Because of the importance of this risk–return relationship, most analysts consider the debt-to-equity ratio to be a key part of any company evaluation.

DEBT-TO-EQUITY RATIO FOR SELECTED INDUSTRIES, 2004	
Paper and Forest Products	1.50
Telecommunication Services	0.85
Gold	0.20
Retailing	0.18
Software	0.08

MARKET TESTS

Several ratios, often called **market tests**, relate the current market price per share to the return that accrues to investors. Many analysts prefer these ratios because they are based on the current value of an owner's investment in a company.

■ **LEARNING OBJECTIVE 7**

Compute and interpret market test ratios.

MARKET TESTS are ratios that tend to measure the market worth of a common share.

17. PRICE/EARNINGS (P/E) RATIO

The *price/earnings (P/E) ratio* measures the relationship between the current market price per share and its earnings per share. Recently, when the price of a Home Depot common share was $40.08, EPS was $2.27, as calculated earlier. The P/E ratio for the company is computed as follows:

$$\text{Price/Earnings Ratio} = \frac{\text{Current Market Price per Share}}{\text{Earnings per Share}}$$

$$\text{Home Depot, 2004} = \frac{\$40.08}{\$2.27} = 17.7$$

The P/E ratio indicates that Home Depot's shares were selling at a price that was 17.7 times its earning per share. The P/E ratio reflects the stock market's assessment of the company's future business performance. A high ratio indicates that the market expects earnings to grow rapidly. Home Depot's P/E ratio is reasonable and comparable to the ratios of its competitors.

Canadian Tire	15.9
RONA	10.1
Home Depot	17.7

Sometimes the components of the P/E ratio are inverted, giving the *capitalization rate*, a rate at which the stock market apparently is capitalizing the current earnings. The capitalization rate for Home Depot is $2.27 ÷ $40.08 = 5.7 percent.

In economic terms, the share price is related to the present value of the company's future earnings. Thus, a company that expects to increase its earnings in the future is worth more than one that cannot grow its earnings (assuming other factors are the same). But while a high P/E ratio and good growth prospects are considered favourable, there are risks. When a company with a high P/E ratio does not meet the level of earnings expected by the market, the negative impact on its share price can be dramatic. Home Depot's share price fell 28 percent on October 13, 2000, after the announcement that its rate of earnings growth had slowed. Clearly, the company share price had been based on an assessment of significant growth in future earnings.

AVERAGE P/E RATIO FOR SELECTED INDUSTRIES, 2004	
Transportation	11.3
Telecommunications	21.0
Gold	35.7
Retailing	12.4
Software	38.0

18. DIVIDEND YIELD RATIO

When investors buy shares, they expect returns from two sources: price appreciation and dividend income. The *dividend yield ratio* measures the relationship between the

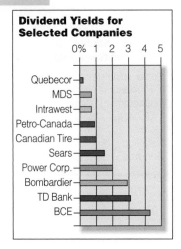

Dividend Yields for Selected Companies

dividends per share paid to shareholders and the current market price per share. Home Depot paid dividends of 17 cents per share when the market price per share was $40.08. Its dividend yield ratio is computed as follows:

$$\text{Dividend Yield Ratio} = \frac{\text{Dividend per Share}}{\text{Market Price per Share}}$$

$$\text{Home Depot, 2004} = \frac{\$0.35}{\$40.08} = 0.87\%$$

It might seem surprising that Home Depot's dividend yield was below 1 percent, given that an investor could earn higher returns on alternative investments. In fact, the dividend yield for shares of most companies is not high compared to returns on alternative investments. Investors may accept low dividend yields if they expect that the price of a company's shares will increase while they own it. Clearly, investors who bought Home Depot's common shares did so with the expectation that their price would increase. In contrast, companies with low growth potential tend to offer much higher dividend yields than do companies with high growth potential. These latter companies usually appeal to retired investors who need current income rather than future growth potential. The chart in the margin shows dividend yields for a selection of companies.

SELF-STUDY **QUIZ 13-5**

Canadian Tire Corporation Ltd. reported the following data in a recent annual report (in millions of dollars):

	Current Year	Last Year
Current assets	$1,528	
Current liabilities	1,128	
Cost of goods sold (assumed)	3,645	
Inventory	412	$473
Earnings per share	1.89	
Share price at year-end	19	

Compute the following ratios:

1. Current ratio.

2. Inventory turnover.

3. Price/earnings ratio.

After you complete your work, check your answers with the solutions on page 714.

INTERPRETING RATIOS AND OTHER ANALYTICAL CONSIDERATIONS

Except for earnings per share, the computation of financial ratios has not been standardized by the accounting profession or security analysts. Thus, users of financial statements should compute the various ratios in accordance with their decision objectives. Before using ratios computed by others, the analyst should determine the computational approach that was used.

Ratios can best be interpreted only by comparing them to other ratios or to some threshold value. For example, a very low current ratio may indicate an inability to meet maturing debts, and a very high current ratio may indicate an unprofitable use of funds. Furthermore, an optimal ratio for one company may not be optimal for another. Comparisons of ratios for different companies are appropriate only if the companies are indeed comparable in terms of industry, nature of operations, size, and accounting policies.

Because ratios are based on the aggregation of information, they may obscure underlying factors that are of interest to the analyst. To illustrate, a current ratio that is considered optimal may obscure a short-term liquidity problem if the company has a very large amount of inventory but a minimal amount of cash with which to pay debts as they mature. Careful analysis can uncover this type of problem.

In other cases, analysis cannot uncover obscured problems. For example, consolidated statements include financial information about the parent and its subsidiaries. The parent company may have a high current ratio and the subsidiary a low ratio. When the statements are consolidated, the current ratio may fall within an acceptable range. The fact that the subsidiary could have a serious liquidity problem is obscured in this case.

Despite limitations, ratio analysis is a useful analytical tool. For instance, financial ratios are effective for predicting bankruptcy. Exhibit 13.6 gives the current and debt-to-equity ratios for Braniff International Corporation for each year before it filed for bankruptcy. Notice the deterioration of these ratios each year. Analysts who studied the financial ratios probably were not surprised by Braniff's bankruptcy. After selling many of its assets and undergoing a complete financial restructuring, Braniff was able to resume limited flight operations but was forced to file for bankruptcy for a second time after additional financial difficulty.

	Years before Bankruptcy					EXHIBIT **13.6**
	5	4	3	2	1	**Selected Financial Ratios for Braniff International**
Current ratio	1.20	0.91	0.74	0.60	0.49	
Debt-to-equity ratio	2.03	2.45	4.88	15.67	N/A*	

*In the year before bankruptcy, Braniff reported negative owners' equity as a result of a large net loss that produced a negative balance in retained earnings. Total liabilities exceeded total assets.

Financial statements provide information to all investors, both sophisticated and unsophisticated. However, users who understand basic accounting principles and terminology are able to more effectively analyze the information contained in financial statements.

For example, some unsophisticated users who do not understand the cost principle believe that assets are reported on the balance sheet at their fair market value. Interpreting accounting numbers without an understanding of the concepts that were used to develop them is impossible.

In analyzing different companies, you will find that they rarely use exactly the same accounting policies. Comparisons among companies are appropriate only if the analyst who is making them understands the impact of various accounting alternatives. For example, one company may use conservative accounting alternatives such as accelerated amortization and LIFO, while another may use income-maximizing alternatives such as straight-line amortization and FIFO. Those who do not understand the different effects of accounting methods are very likely to misinterpret financial results. Perhaps the most important first step in analyzing financial statements is a review of the company's accounting policies, which are disclosed in a note to the statements.

OTHER FINANCIAL INFORMATION

The ratios we have discussed are useful for most analytical purposes. Because each company is different, you must exercise professional judgment when you conduct each financial analysis.

To illustrate, let us look at some special factors that might affect our analysis of Home Depot.

1. *Rapid growth.* Growth in total sales volume does not always indicate that a company is successful. Sales volume from new stores may obscure the fact that existing stores are not meeting customer needs and are experiencing declining sales. The

family pizza chain Chuck-E-Cheese appeared to be a success when it reported rapid growth in total sales revenue by opening new restaurants. Unfortunately, the novelty of the Chuck-E-Cheese stores proved to be a short-lived fad, and same-store sales volume fell quickly. Because its older restaurants were unprofitable, the company was forced to reorganize. In contrast, the Home Depot's annual report shows that the company posted same-store sales increases ranging from zero percent to 10 percent during the previous 10 years, which indicates that it is able to generate increases in sales volume from both new and existing stores.

2. *Uneconomical expansion.* Some growth-oriented companies open stores in less desirable locations if good locations cannot be found. These poor locations can cause the company's average productivity to decline. One measure of productivity in the retail industry is sales volume per square foot of selling space. For Home Depot, productivity has declined steadily since 1999. Management explains the slowdown in growth as the direct result of its strategy.

Year	Sales per Square Foot
2004	$375
2003	371
2002	370
2001	388
2000	415
1999	423

REAL WORLD EXCERPT

Home Depot

ANNUAL REPORT

We continue our cannibalization strategy, whereby we take the pressure off a busy store by opening another one nearby. While some challenge this approach because it tends to lower sales productivity, this strategy results in better service and greater customer satisfaction, which ultimately translates into higher sales and profits.

Source: The Home Depot

3. *Subjective factors.* Remember that vital information about a company is not contained in the annual report. The best way to evaluate Home Depot's strategy of being a price leader, for instance, is to visit its stores and those of competitors. An analyst who studied Home Depot for Salomon Smith Barney did exactly that:

REAL WORLD EXCERPT

Home Depot

SALOMON SMITH BARNEY
RESEARCH REPORT

On July 15, we surveyed the Boca Raton, Florida, market. The Home Depot store is about two years old and was particularly impressive with respect to its in-stock position, customer service and total store presentation. We were able to compare Home Depot's pricing on 20 sample items. Our price analysis revealed that Home Depot is the price leader in the market by an average of 11 percent below the average total price of our 20-item market basket. Given the Home Depot's low cost structure, we believe that it will remain the price leader in this important market.

Source: The Home Depot

As these examples illustrate, no single approach can be used to analyze all companies. Furthermore, an effective analyst will look beyond the information contained in an annual report.

INFORMATION IN AN EFFICIENT MARKET

Considerable research has been performed on the way in which stock markets react to new information. Much of this evidence supports the view that the markets react very quickly to new information in an unbiased manner (that is, the market does not systematically overreact or underreact to new information). A market that reacts to information in this manner is called an **efficient market**. In an efficient market, the price of a security fully reflects all publicly available information.

It is not surprising that the stock markets react quickly to new information. Many professional investors manage stock portfolios valued in the hundreds of millions of dollars. These investors have a large financial incentive to discover new information about a company and to trade quickly based on that information.

There are three versions of market efficiency, depending on the level of information available to investors. The *weak form* suggests that the current market price of a specific security reflects the information contained in past market prices of that security, and that knowledge of such publicly available information does not allow investors to outperform the market. The *semi-strong form* of market efficiency states that all publicly available information, including information disclosed by companies in their financial statements and through press releases, is fully incorporated into the current market price of the security. This suggests that investors cannot earn abnormal returns on their investment by analyzing a company's financial statements. Finally, the *strong form* of market efficiency indicates that information available only to insiders (e.g., management) cannot be used to earn abnormal profits because such information gets incorporated quickly in the security's current market price. It is argued that sophisticated market participants build rational expectations about the company's future cash flows, so that the information that becomes available to insiders is already incorporated into the security's market price in an objective manner.

The semi-strong and strong forms of the efficient market hypothesis suggest that investors would not benefit from financial statement analysis. However, these notions of market efficiency have been challenged by researchers who were able to achieve abnormal returns based on simple trading strategies.

The research on efficient markets has important implications for financial analysis. It probably is not beneficial to study old information (for example, an annual report that was released six months earlier) in an effort to identify an undervalued stock. In an efficient market, the price of the stock reflects all of the information contained in the report shortly after it was released. Furthermore, a company cannot manipulate the price of its stock by manipulating its accounting policy. The market should be able to differentiate between a company with increasing earnings due to improved productivity and one that has increased its earnings by changing from conservative to liberal accounting policies.

EFFICIENT MARKETS are securities markets in which prices fully reflect all publicly available information.

A QUESTION OF **ETHICS**

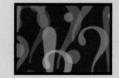

INSIDER INFORMATION

Financial statements are an important source of information for investors. Announcement of an unexpected earnings increase or decrease can cause a substantial movement in the price of a company's shares.

A company's accountants are often aware of important financial information before it is made available to the public. This type of data is called *insider information*. Some people may be tempted to buy or sell shares based on insider information, but to do so is a serious criminal offence. Securities commissions have brought charges against a number of individuals who traded on insider information. Their conviction resulted in large fines and time served in jail.

In some cases, it may be difficult to determine whether something is insider information. For example, an individual may simply overhear a comment made in the company elevator by two executives. A well-respected Wall Street investment banker gave good advice when dealing with such situations: "If you are not sure if something is right or wrong, apply the newspaper headline test. Ask yourself how you would feel to have your family and friends read about what you had done in the newspaper." Interestingly, many people who spent time in jail and lost small fortunes in fines because of insider trading convictions say that the most difficult part of the process was telling their families.

To uphold the highest ethical standard, many public accounting firms have rules that prevent members of their professional staff from investing in companies that the firm audits. These rules are designed to ensure that the company's auditors cannot be tempted to engage in insider trading.

SOLUTIONS TO **SELF-STUDY QUIZZES**

Self-Study Quiz 13-1

1. $\dfrac{\text{Income}}{\text{Average Owners' Equity}} = \dfrac{\$148}{(\$1,459 + \$1,345)/2} = 0.106,\text{ or } 10.6\%$

2. $\dfrac{\text{Income} + \text{Interest Expense (net of tax)}}{\text{Average Total Assets}} = \dfrac{\$148 + \$58}{(\$3,748 + \$3,871)/2} = 0.054,\text{ or } 5.4\%$

3. $\dfrac{\text{Income (before extraordinary items)}}{\text{Net Sales Revenue}} = \dfrac{\$148}{\$5,207} = 0.028,\text{ or } 2.8\%$

Self-Study Quiz 13-2

Dell has an edge over Gateway in the efficiency of its operations, as reflected in its high asset turnover ratio. Dell's major edge is its significantly higher net profit margin. This reflects Dell's success with its primary market segment, business customers. They often purchase in large quantities, which decreases order processing and production costs. They also often purchase higher-end, higher–net profit margin machines than customers in Gateway's primary market segment, individuals. The effect of this edge in net profit margin is multiplied further by Dell's greater reliance on leverage (debt financing). However, this greater leverage could come back to haunt Dell if there is a downturn in the personal computer market.

Self-Study Quiz 13-3

The quick ratio should be lower than the current ratio because the numerator of the quick ratio includes only part of the current assets. The quick ratio of 4.32 is greater than the current ratios of five of the six industries, so it cannot be associated with any of these five industries. Consequently, this quick ratio must be associated with the gold industry. Since the quick assets for the retailing industry equal 40 percent of its current assets, the quick ratio of this industry must equal 2.27 $\times$ 40 percent, or 0.91.

Self-Study Quiz 13-4

1. $\dfrac{\text{Cash Flows from Operating Activities}}{\text{Net Income}} = \dfrac{\$502}{\$148} = 3.39$

2. $\dfrac{\text{Quick Assets}}{\text{Current Liabilities}} = \dfrac{\$131 + \$515 + \$453}{\$1,128} = 0.97$

3. $\dfrac{\text{Cash} + \text{Cash Equivalents}}{\text{Current Liabilities}} = \dfrac{\$131}{\$1,128} = 0.12$

Self-Study Quiz 13-5

1. $\dfrac{\text{Current Assets}}{\text{Current Liabilities}} = \dfrac{\$1,528}{\$1,128} = 1.35$

2. $\dfrac{\text{Cost of Goods Sold}}{\text{Average Inventory}} = \dfrac{\$3,645}{(\$412 + \$473)/2} = 8.24$

3. $\dfrac{\text{Current Market Price per Share}}{\text{Earnings per Share}} = \dfrac{\$19}{\$1.89} = 10.1$

CHAPTER **TAKE-AWAYS**

1. Explain how a company's business strategy affects financial analysis.   p. 689
In simple terms, a business strategy establishes the objectives a business is trying to achieve. Performance is best evaluated by comparing the financial results to the objectives that the business was working to achieve. In other words, an understanding of a company's strategy provides the context for conducting financial statement analysis.

2. **Discuss how analysts use financial statements.** **p. 691**

Analysts use financial statements to understand present conditions and past performance as well as to predict future performance. Financial statements provide important information to help users understand and evaluate corporate strategy. The data reported on statements can be used for either time-series analysis (evaluating a single company over time) or in comparison with similar companies at a single point in time. Most analysts compute component percentages and ratios when using statements.

3. **Compute and interpret component percentages.** **p. 692**

To compute component percentages for the income statement, the base amount is net sales revenue. Each expense is expressed as a percentage of net sales revenue. On the balance sheet, the base amount is total assets; each balance sheet account is divided by total assets. Component percentages are evaluated by comparing them over time for a single company or by comparing them with percentages for similar companies.

4. **Compute and interpret profitability ratios.** **p. 694**

Several tests of profitability focus on measuring the adequacy of income by comparing it to other items reported on the financial statements. Exhibit 13.4 lists these ratios and shows how to compute them. Profitability ratios are evaluated by comparing them over time for a single company or by comparing them with ratios for similar companies.

5. **Compute and interpret liquidity ratios.** **p. 702**

Tests of liquidity measure a company's ability to meet its current maturing debt. Exhibit 13.4 lists these ratios and shows how to compute them. Liquidity ratios are evaluated by comparing them over time for a single company or by comparing them with ratios for similar companies.

6. **Compute and interpret solvency ratios.** **p. 707**

Solvency ratios measure a company's ability to meet its long-term obligations. Exhibit 13.4 lists these ratios and shows how to compute them. Solvency ratios are evaluated by comparing them over time for a single company or by comparing them with ratios for similar companies.

7. **Compute and interpret market test ratios.** **p. 709**

Market test ratios relate the current price per share to the return that accrues to investors. Exhibit 13.4 lists these ratios and shows how to compute them. Market test ratios are evaluated by comparing them over time for a single company or by comparing them with ratios for similar companies.

FINDING
**FINANCIAL
INFORMATION**

BALANCE SHEET

Ratios are not reported on the balance sheet, but analysts use balance sheet information to compute many ratios. Most analysts use an average of the beginning and ending amounts for balance sheet accounts when comparing the account to an income statement account.

INCOME STATEMENT

Earnings per share is the only ratio that is required to be reported on the financial statements. It is usually reported at the bottom of the income statement.

CASH FLOW STATEMENT

Ratios are not reported on this statement, but some ratios use amounts from this statement.

STATEMENT OF RETAINED EARNINGS

Ratios are not reported on this statement.

NOTES

Under Summary of Significant Accounting Policies

This note has no information pertaining directly to ratios, but it is important to understand accounting differences if you are comparing two companies.

Under a Separate Note

Most companies include a 5-year or a 10-year financial summary as a separate note. These summaries include data for significant accounts, some accounting ratios, and non-accounting information.

KEY **TERMS**

Component Percentage p. 692

Efficient Markets p. 713

Market Tests p. 709

Ratio (Percentage) Analysis p. 692

Tests of Liquidity p. 702

Tests of Profitability p. 694

Tests of Solvency p. 707

QUESTIONS

1. What are three fundamental uses of external financial statements by decision makers?
2. What are some of the primary items on financial statements about which creditors usually are concerned?
3. Why are the notes to the financial statements important to decision makers?
4. What is the primary purpose of comparative financial statements?
5. Why are statement users interested in financial summaries covering several years? What is the primary limitation of long-term summaries?
6. What is *ratio analysis?* Why is it useful?
7. What are *component percentages?* Why are they useful?
8. Explain the two concepts of return on investment.
9. What is *financial leverage?* How is it measured as a percentage?
10. Is profit margin a useful measure of profitability? Explain.
11. Compare and contrast the current ratio and the quick ratio.
12. What does the debt-to-equity ratio reflect?
13. What are market tests?
14. Identify two factors that limit the effectiveness of ratio analysis.
15. A large retailer reported revenue of $1,680,145,000. The company's gross profit percentage was 55.9 percent. What amount of cost of goods sold did the company report?
16. A manufacturer reported an inventory turnover ratio of 8.6 during 2005. During 2006, management introduced a new inventory control system that was expected to reduce average inventory levels by 25 percent without affecting sales volume. Given these circumstances, would you expect the inventory turnover ratio to increase or decrease during 2006? Explain.
17. Doritos Company has prepared draft financial results now being reviewed by the accountants. You notice that the financial leverage percentage is negative. You also note that the current ratio is 2.4 and the quick ratio is 3.7. You remember that these financial relationships are unusual. Does either imply that a mistake has been made? Explain.
18. An Internet company earned $5 per share and paid dividends of $2 per share. The company reported a dividend yield of 5 percent. What was the price per share?
19. Lexis Corporation is considering changing its inventory method from FIFO to weighted average and wants to determine the impact on selected accounting ratios. In general, what impact would you expect on the following ratios, assuming that prices have been increasing over time: profit margin, fixed asset turnover, current ratio, and quick ratio?

MULTIPLE-CHOICE QUESTIONS

1. Which of the following ratios is *not* used to analyze profitability?
   a. quality of income ratio
   b. return on assets
   c. quick ratio
   d. return on equity
2. Which of the following would *not* change the receivables turnover ratio for a retail company?
   a. increases in the retail prices of inventory
   b. a change in credit policy
   c. increases in the cost incurred to purchase inventory
   d. none of the above would change the ratio
3. Which of the following ratios is used to analyze liquidity?
   a. earnings per share
   b. debt-to-equity
   c. current ratio
   d. both (a) and (c)
4. Positive financial leverage indicates
   a. positive cash flow from financing activities.
   b. a debt-to-equity ratio higher than 1.
   c. a rate of return on assets exceeding the interest rate on debt.
   d. a profit margin in one year exceeding the previous year's profit margin.

5. If a potential investor is analyzing three companies in the same industry and wishes to invest in only one, which ratio is least likely to affect the investor's decision?
   a. quick ratio
   b. earnings per share
   c. price/earnings ratio
   d. dividend yield

6. Analysts use ratios to
   a. compare different companies in the same industry.
   b. track a company's performance over time.
   c. compare a company's performance to industry averages.
   d. Do all of the above.

7. Which of the following ratios incorporates cash flows from operations?
   a. inventory turnover
   b. earnings per share
   c. quality of income
   d. all of the above

8. Given the following ratios for four companies, which company is least likely to experience problems paying its current liabilities promptly?

	Quick ratio	Receivable turnover
a.	1.2	58
b.	1.2	45
c.	1.0	55
d.	0.5	60

9. A decrease in selling and administrative expenses would not impact the following ratio:
   a. fixed asset turnover ratio
   b. times interest earned ratio
   c. debt-to-equity ratio
   d. current ratio

10. A creditor is least likely to use the following ratio when analyzing a company that has borrowed funds on a long-term basis:
   a. cash coverage ratio
   b. debt-to-equity ratio
   c. times interest earned ratio
   d. profit margin

For more practice with multiple-choice questions, go to our Web site at **www.mcgrawhill.ca/college/libby**, click on "Student Edition" in the upper left menu, click on this chapter's name and number from the list of contents, and then click on "Multiple-Choice Quiz" from the menu on the left.

EXERCISES

E13–1 Matching Each Ratio with Its Computational Formula   ■ **LO3, 4, 5, 6, 7**

Match each ratio or percentage with its computation by entering the appropriate letters in the blanks.

Ratios or Percentages	Definitions
_____ 1. Profit margin	A. Income (before extraordinary items) ÷ Net Sales
_____ 2. Inventory turnover ratio	B. Days in Year ÷ Receivable Turnover
_____ 3. Average collection period	C. Income ÷ Average Owners' Equity
_____ 4. Dividend yield	D. Income ÷ Average Number of Common Shares Outstanding
_____ 5. Return on equity	E. Return on Equity − Return on Assets
_____ 6. Current ratio	F. Quick Assets ÷ Current Liabilities
_____ 7. Debt-to-equity ratio	G. Current Assets ÷ Current Liabilities
_____ 8. Price/earnings ratio	H. Cost of Goods Sold ÷ Average Inventory
_____ 9. Financial leverage percentage	I. Net Credit Sales ÷ Average Net Trade Receivables
_____ 10. Receivable turnover ratio	J. Days in Year ÷ Inventory Turnover
_____ 11. Average day's supply of inventory	K. Total Liabilities ÷ Owners' Equity
_____ 12. Owners' equity to total equities	L. Dividends per Share ÷ Market Price per Share
_____ 13. Earnings per share	M. Owners' Equity ÷ Total Equities
_____ 14. Return on assets	N. Current Market Price per Share ÷ Earnings per Share
_____ 15. Quick ratio	O. Owners' Equity ÷ Common Shares Outstanding
_____ 16. Times interest earned	P. Income + Interest Expense (net of tax) ÷ Average Total Assets
_____ 17. Cash coverage ratio	Q. Cash from Operating Activities (before interest and taxes) ÷ Interest Paid
_____ 18. Fixed asset turnover	R. Net Sales Revenue ÷ Average Net Fixed Assets
	S. (Net Income + Interest Expense + Income Tax Expense) ÷ Interest Expense

■ **LO3**

Le Groupe
Jean Coutu

E13–2 Preparing a Schedule Using Component Percentages

Le Groupe Jean Coutu is one of the fastest-growing retailers in North America. It claims to lead the Canadian chain drugstore industry in sales and profits. Complete the component percentage analysis on the company's income statement that follows. Discuss the insights provided by this analysis.

Le Groupe Jean Coutu	2004	2003
Income Statement (amounts in millions)		
Net sales	$4,096	$4,047
Cost of sales	3,179	3,107
Operating expenses	638	683
Interest expense	20	27
Income tax expense	81	70
Net income	178	160

■ **LO5**

E13–3 Analyzing the Impact of Selected Transactions on the Current Ratio

Current assets totalled $54,000, and the current ratio was 1.8. Assume that the following transactions were completed: (1) purchased merchandise for $6,000 on short-term credit and (2) purchased a delivery truck for $20,000, paid $4,000 cash, and signed a two-year interest-bearing note for the balance.

Required:
Compute the current ratio after each transaction.

■ **LO5**

Sunbeam

E13–4 Analyzing the Impact of Selected Transactions on the Current Ratio

Sunbeam is a leading designer, manufacturer, and marketer of branded consumer products, including Mr. Coffee, Oster, First Alert, and Coleman camping gear. A few years ago, the company experienced significant financial difficulties and was named in a number of lawsuits alleging material misstatements in its financial statements. The company's financial statements acknowledge that actions pending against the company "could have a material adverse impact on the Company's financial position." As a result, management must pay close attention to the impact that each operating decision has on the company's liquidity.

Sunbeam reported current assets of $1,090,068,000 and current liabilities of $602,246,000. Determine the impact of the following transactions on the current ratio for Sunbeam: (1) sold long-term assets that represented excess capacity for cash, (2) accrued severance pay and fringe benefits for employees who will be terminated, (3) wrote down the carrying value of certain inventory items that were deemed to be obsolete, and (4) acquired new inventory; the supplier was not willing to provide normal credit terms, so an 18-month interest-bearing note was signed.

■ **LO5**

Procter & Gamble

E13–5 Analyzing the Impact of Selected Transactions on Accounts Receivable and Inventory Turnover

Procter & Gamble is a multinational corporation that manufactures and markets many products that are probably in your home. Last year, sales for the company were $51,407 (all amounts in millions). The annual report did not disclose the amount of credit sales, so we will assume that 30 percent of sales was on credit. The average gross margin rate was 45 percent on sales. Account balances follow:

	Beginning	Ending
Accounts receivable (net)	$3,038	$4,062
Inventory	3,640	4,400

Required:
Compute the turnover for the accounts receivable and inventory, the average age of receivables, and the average day's supply of inventory.

E13–6 Computing Financial Leverage

■ **LO4**

Motorola

Motorola is a global leader in providing integrated communications and electronic solutions for businesses. Its financial statements reported the following at year-end (in millions):

Total assets	$30,889
Total debt (average 8% interest)	17,558
Net income (average tax rate 30%)	1,532

Required:

Compute the financial leverage percentage. Was it positive or negative?

E13–7 Analyzing the Impact of Selected Transactions on the Current Ratio

■ **LO5**

Current assets totalled $100,000, and the current ratio was 1.5. Assume that the following transactions were completed: (1) paid $6,000 for merchandise purchased on short-term credit, (2) purchased a delivery truck for $20,000 cash, (3) wrote off a bad account receivable for $1,000, and (4) paid previously declared dividends in the amount of $20,000.

Required:

Compute the current ratio after each transaction.

E13–8 Inferring Financial Information

■ **LO3**

Dollar General
Corporation

Dollar General Corporation operates general merchandise stores that feature quality merchandise at low prices. All stores are located predominantly in small towns in 24 midwestern and southeastern states. For one year, the company reported average inventories of $1,276 million and an inventory turnover of 4.2. Average total fixed assets were $1,019 million, and the fixed asset turnover ratio was 7.6. Determine the gross margin for Dollar General.

E13–9 Computing Selected Ratios

■ **LO5**

Sales for the year were $600,000, of which one-half was on credit. The average gross margin rate was 40 percent on sales. Account balances follow:

	Beginning	Ending
Accounts receivable (net)	$50,000	$70,000
Inventory	50,000	30,000

Required:

Compute and comment on the turnover for the accounts receivable and inventory, the average age of receivables, and the average day's supply of inventory.

E13–10 Analyzing the Impact of Selected Transactions on the Current Ratio

■ **LO5**

Current assets totalled $500,000, the current ratio was 2.0, and the company uses the periodic inventory method. Assume that the following transactions were completed: (1) sold $13,000 in merchandise on short-term credit, (2) declared but did not pay dividends of $20,000, (3) paid prepaid rent in the amount of $12,000, (4) paid previously declared dividends in the amount of $20,000, (5) collected an account receivable in the amount of $10,000, and (6) reclassified $45,000 of long-term debt as a short-term liability.

Required:

Compute the current ratio after each transaction.

E13–11 Computing Liquidity Ratios

■ **LO5**

Cintas

Cintas designs, manufactures, and implements corporate identity uniform programs that it rents or sells to customers throughout the United States and Canada. The company's stock is traded on the NASDAQ and has provided investors with significant returns over the past few years. Selected information from the company's balance sheet follows. The company reported revenue of $2,201,405,000 and cost of goods sold of $1,222,638,000 for fiscal year 2004.

Cintas	2004	2003
Balance Sheet (amounts in thousands)		
Cash and cash equivalents	$ 87,357	$ 32,239
Marketable securities	166,964	25,420
Accounts receivable, less allowance of $8,354 ($7,737)	285,592	278,147
Inventories	185,585	228,410
Prepaid expenses	7,395	7,607
Accounts payable	53,451	53,909
Accrued compensation and related liabilities	31,804	25,252
Future income taxes, current	47,042	53,018
Long-term debt due within one year	10,523	28,251

Required:

Compute the current ratio, quick ratio, inventory turnover, and accounts receivable turnover (assuming that 60 percent of sales was on credit), and comment on the liquidity position of the company.

■ **LO5**   **E13–12**   **Determining the Impact of Selected Transactions on Measures of Liquidity**

Three commonly used measures of liquidity are the current ratio, the quick ratio, and working capital. For each of the following transactions, determine whether the measure will increase, decrease, or not change. Assume that both ratios are higher than 1 and that working capital is positive.

a. The company purchased $100,000 of inventory on credit.

b. Merchandise, which cost $35,000, was sold on credit for $50,000. The company uses the periodic inventory method.

c. Previously declared dividends are paid in cash.

d. Amortization expense is recorded.

e. A customer pays money on his account receivable.

■ **LO3, 5, 6**   **E13–13**   **Using Financial Information to Identify Mystery Companies**

The following selected financial data pertain to four unidentified companies:

	Companies			
	1	2	3	4
Balance Sheet Data				
(component percentage)				
Cash	3.5	4.7	8.2	11.7
Accounts receivable	16.9	28.9	16.8	51.9
Inventory	46.8	35.6	57.3	4.8
Property and equipment	18.3	21.7	7.6	18.7
Income Statement Data				
(component percentage)				
Gross profit	22.0	22.5	44.8	N/A*
Profit before taxes	2.1	0.7	1.2	3.2
Selected Ratios				
Current ratio	1.3	1.5	1.6	1.2
Inventory turnover	3.6	9.8	1.5	N/A
Debt to equity	2.6	2.6	3.2	3.2

*N/A = Not applicable

This financial information pertains to the following companies:

a. Retail fur store.

b. Advertising agency.

c. Wholesale candy company.

d. Car manufacturer.

Required:

Match each company with its financial information.

E13–14 **Using Financial Information to Identify Mystery Companies**

▨ **LO3, 5, 6**

The following selected financial data pertain to four unidentified companies:

	Companies			
	1	2	3	4
Balance Sheet Data				
(component percentage)				
Cash	7.3	21.6	6.1	11.3
Accounts receivable	28.2	39.7	3.2	22.9
Inventory	21.6	0.6	1.8	27.5
Property and equipment	32.1	18.0	74.6	25.1
Income Statement Data				
(component percentage)				
Gross profit	15.3	N/A*	N/A	43.4
Profit before taxes	1.7	3.2	2.4	6.9
Selected Ratios				
Current ratio	1.5	1.2	0.6	1.9
Inventory turnover	27.4	N/A	N/A	3.3
Debt to equity	1.7	2.2	5.7	1.3
*N/A = Not applicable				

This financial information pertains to the following companies:

a. Travel agency.

b. Hotel.

c. Meat packer.

d. Drug company.

Required:

Match each company with its financial information.

E13–15 **Using Financial Information to Identify Mystery Companies**

▨ **LO3, 5, 6**

The following selected financial data pertain to four unidentified companies:

	Companies			
	1	2	3	4
Balance Sheet Data				
(component percentage)				
Cash	5.1	8.8	6.3	10.4
Accounts receivable	13.1	41.5	13.8	4.9
Inventory	4.6	3.6	65.1	35.8
Property and equipment	53.1	23.0	8.8	35.7
Income Statement Data				
(component percentage)				
Gross profit	N/A*	N/A	45.2	22.5
Profit before taxes	0.3	16.0	3.9	1.5
Selected Ratios				
Current ratio	0.7	2.2	1.9	1.4
Inventory turnover	N/A	N/A	1.4	15.5
Debt to equity	2.5	0.9	1.7	2.3
*N/A = Not applicable				

This financial information pertains to the following companies:

a. Cable TV company.

b. Grocery store.

c. Accounting firm.

d. Retail jewellery store.

Required:
Match each company with its financial information.

■ **LO3, 5, 6**   **E13–16   Using Financial Information to Identify Mystery Companies**
The selected financial data on the next page pertain to four unidentified companies:

a. Full-line department store.

b. Wholesale fish company.

c. Automobile dealer (both new and used cars).

d. Restaurant.

Required:
Match each company with its financial information.

	Companies			
	1	2	3	4
Balance Sheet Data				
(component percentage)				
Cash	11.6	6.6	5.4	7.1
Accounts receivable	4.6	18.9	8.8	35.6
Inventory	7.0	45.8	65.7	26.0
Property and equipment	56.0	20.3	10.1	21.9
Income Statement Data				
(component percentage)				
Gross profit	56.7	36.4	14.1	15.8
Profit before taxes	2.7	1.4	1.1	0.9
Selected Ratios				
Current ratio	0.7	2.1	1.2	1.3
Inventory turnover	30.0	3.5	5.6	16.7
Debt to equity	3.3	1.8	3.8	3.1

■ **LO1**   **E13–17   Inferring Information from the ROE Model**
In this chapter, we discussed the ROE profit driver (or DuPont) model. Using that framework, find the missing amount in each case below:

Case 1: ROE is 10 percent, net income is $200,000; asset turnover is 5, and net sales are $1,000,000. What is the amount of average shareholders' equity?

Case 2: Net income is $1,500,000; net sales are $8,000,000; average shareholders' equity is $12,000,000; ROE is 22 percent and asset turnover is 8. What is the amount of average total assets?

Case 3: ROE is 15 percent; net profit margin is 10 percent; asset turnover is 5; and average total assets are $1,000,000. What is the amount of average shareholders' equity?

Case 4: Net income is $500,000; ROE is 15 percent; asset turnover is 5; net sales are $1,000,000; and financial leverage is 2. What is the amount of average total assets?

PROBLEMS

P13–1 Analyzing Comparative Financial Statements Using Percentages (AP13–1) ■ **LO3**

The comparative financial statements prepared at December 31, 2006, for Goldfish Company showed the following summarized data:

	2006	2005
Income Statement		
Sales revenue	$195,000*	$165,000
Cost of goods sold	120,000	100,000
Gross margin	75,000	65,000
Operating expenses and interest expense	60,000	53,000
Pretax income	15,000	12,000
Income tax	4,000	3,000
Net income	$ 11,000	$ 9,000
Balance Sheet		
Cash	$ 4,000	$ 8,000
Accounts receivable (net)	15,000	18,000
Inventory	40,000	35,000
Property, plant, and equipment (net)	45,000	38,000
	$104,000	$ 99,000
Current liabilities (no interest)	$ 16,000	$ 19,000
Long-term liabilities (10% interest)	45,000	39,000
Common shares (6,000 shares)	30,000	30,000
Retained earnings†	13,000	11,000
	$104,000	$ 99,000

*One-third was credit sales.
†During 2006, cash dividends amounting to $9,000 were declared and paid.

Required:

1. Complete the following columns for each item in the preceding comparative financial statements:

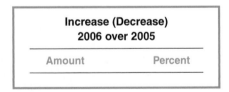

Increase (Decrease) 2006 over 2005	
Amount	Percent

2. Answer the following:
   a. By what amount did working capital change?
   b. What was the percentage change in the average income tax rate?
   c. What was the amount of cash inflow from revenues for 2006?
   d. What was the percentage change for the average mark-up realized on goods sold?

P13–2 Analyzing Comparative Financial Statements Using Percentages and Selected Ratios ■ **LO3, 4, 5, 6, 7**
(AP13–2)
Use the data given in P13–1 for Goldfish Company.

Required:

1. Present component percentages for 2006 only.

2. Answer the following for 2006:
   a. What was the average percentage mark-up on sales?
   b. What was the average income tax rate?

   c. Compute the profit margin. Was it a good or poor indicator of performance? Explain.

   d. What percentage of total resources was invested in property, plant, and equipment?

   e. Compute the following ratios and comment on their levels:
- debt to equity
- return on equity
- return on assets
- financial leverage percentage.

   f. Compute additional ratios not covered in requirement e above, and explain the meaning of each. Assume a stock price of $28 per share.

■ **LO3, 4, 5,**   **P13–3** **Analyzing Ratios** (AP13–3)
6, 7

Sears Canada Inc. and Hudson's Bay Company

Sears Canada Inc. and Hudson's Bay Company are two giants of the Canadian retail industry. Both offer full lines of moderately priced merchandise. Annual sales for Sears total $6.2 billion. Hudson's Bay is somewhat larger, with $7.4 billion in revenues. Compare the two companies as a potential investment based on the following ratios:

Ratio	Sears Canada	Hudson's Bay
P/E	12.8	17.0
Profit margin	2.2%	0.9%
Quick ratio	1.0	0.7
Current ratio	1.8	2.2
Debt to equity	1.4	0.7
Return on equity	6.0%	3.0%
Return on assets	4.1%	2.0%
Dividend yield	1.5%	11.2%
Dividend payout ratio	19.0%	36.0%
Earnings per share	$1.26	$0.82
Price per share at year end	$16.06	$12.82
Dividends per share	$0.24	$1.44

■ **LO3, 4, 5,**   **P13–4** **Analyzing a Financial Statement Using Several Ratios**
6, 7

Summer Corporation has just completed its comparative statements for the year ended December 31, 2006. At this point, certain analytical and interpretive procedures are to be undertaken. The completed statements (summarized) are as follows:

	2006	2005
Income Statement		
Sales revenue	$480,000*	$420,000*
Cost of goods sold	270,000	230,000
Gross margin	210,000	190,000
Operating expenses		
(including interest on bonds)	171,000	168,000
Pretax income	39,000	22,000
Income tax	12,000	6,000
Net income	$ 27,000	$ 16,000
Balance Sheet		
Cash	$ 6,800	$ 3,900
Accounts receivable (net)	42,000	28,000
Merchandise inventory	25,000	20,000
Prepaid expenses	200	100
Property, plant,and equipment (net)	130,000	120,000
	$204,000	$172,000
Accounts payable	$ 17,000	$ 18,000
Income taxes payable	1,000	2,000
Bonds payable (10% interest rate)	70,000	50,000
Common shares (20,000 shares)	100,000†	100,000
Retained earnings	16,000‡	2,000
	$204,000	$172,000

*Credit sales totalled 40 percent of total sales.
†The market price of the stock at the end of 2006 was $18 per share.
‡During 2006, the company declared and paid a cash dividend of $13,000.

Required:

1. Compute appropriate ratios and explain the meaning of each.

2. Answer the following for 2006:
   a. Evaluate the financial leverage. Explain its meaning using the computed amount(s).
   b. Evaluate the profit margin ratio and explain how a shareholder might use it.
   c. Explain to a shareholder why the current ratio and the quick ratio are different. Do you observe any liquidity problems? Explain.
   d. Assuming that credit terms are 1/10, n/30, do you perceive an unfavourable situation for the company related to credit sales? Explain.

P13–5 **Comparing Alternative Investment Opportunities** (AP13–4)

■ **LO3, 4, 5, 6, 7**

The 2006 financial statements for Armstrong and Blair companies are summarized below:

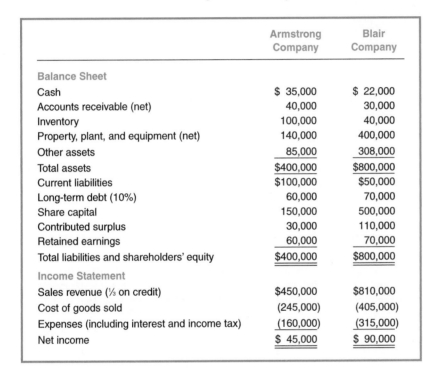

	Armstrong Company	Blair Company
Balance Sheet		
Cash	$ 35,000	$ 22,000
Accounts receivable (net)	40,000	30,000
Inventory	100,000	40,000
Property, plant, and equipment (net)	140,000	400,000
Other assets	85,000	308,000
Total assets	$400,000	$800,000
Current liabilities	$100,000	$50,000
Long-term debt (10%)	60,000	70,000
Share capital	150,000	500,000
Contributed surplus	30,000	110,000
Retained earnings	60,000	70,000
Total liabilities and shareholders' equity	$400,000	$800,000
Income Statement		
Sales revenue (⅓ on credit)	$450,000	$810,000
Cost of goods sold	(245,000)	(405,000)
Expenses (including interest and income tax)	(160,000)	(315,000)
Net income	$ 45,000	$ 90,000

Selected data from the 2005 statements:

Accounts receivable (net)	$ 20,000	$ 40,000
Inventory	92,000	48,000
Long-term debt	60,000	70,000

Other data:

Share price at end of 2006	$ 18	$ 15
Income tax rate	30%	30%
Dividends declared and paid in 2006	$ 36,000	$150,000
Number of common shares during 2006	15,000	50,000

The companies are in the same line of business and are direct competitors in a large metropolitan area. Both have been in business approximately 10 years, and each has had steady growth. The management of each has a different viewpoint in many respects. Blair is more conservative, and as its president said, "We avoid what we consider to be undue risk." Neither company is publicly held. Armstrong Company has an annual audit by an independent auditor but Blair Company does not.

Required:

1. Complete a schedule that reflects a ratio analysis of each company. Compute the ratios discussed in the chapter.

2. A client of yours has the opportunity to buy 10 percent of the shares in one or the other company at the share prices given and has decided to invest in one of the companies.

Based on the data given, prepare a comparative written evaluation of the ratio analyses (and any other available information) and give your recommended choice with the supporting explanation.

■ LO4, 5   **P13–6   Analyzing the Impact of Alternative Inventory Methods on Selected Ratios**

Company A uses the FIFO method to cost inventory, and Company B uses the LIFO method. The two companies are exactly alike except for the difference in inventory costing methods. Costs of inventory items for both companies have been rising steadily in recent years, and each company has increased its inventory each year. Each company has paid its tax liability in full for the current year (and all previous years), and each company uses the same accounting methods for both financial reporting and income tax reporting, except for inventory valuation.

Required:

Identify which company will report the higher amount for each of the following ratios. If it is not possible, explain why.

1. Current ratio.

2. Quick ratio.

3. Debt-to-equity ratio.

4. Return on equity.

5. Earnings per share.

■ LO3, 4, 5, 6, 7   **P13–7   Analyzing Financial Statements Using Appropriate Ratios** (AP13–5)

Sears Canada Inc.

Sears Canada Inc. offers Canadian consumers a diverse array of shopping options through department and specialty stores, catalogues, and the Internet. The following information was reported in a recent annual report.

Required:

1. Compute the ratios discussed in this chapter for the last two years. If there is not sufficient information, describe what is missing and explain what you would do.

2. Assume that you work in the loan department of the Provincial Bank, and you are evaluating an application from Sears for a two-year loan of $200 million that would be used to purchase the shares of another competing company. What specific ratios would you consider in your evaluation, and would you lend Sears the requested amount?

SEARS CANADA INC.
Consolidated Statements of Earnings
(in millions, except per share amounts)

	52 Weeks Ended January 1, 2005	53 Weeks Ended January 3, 2004	52 Weeks Ended December 28, 2002
Total Revenues	$6,230.5	$6,222.7	$6,535.9
Cost of merchandise sold, operating, administrative and selling expenses	5,816.9	5,771.3	6,107.9
Depreciation and amortization	166.0	166.2	148.7
Interest expense, net	55.0	59.5	59.8
Unusual items—expense (Note 12)	3.2	5.0	189.1
Earnings before income taxes	189.4	220.7	30.4
Income taxes (Note 4)			
Current	41.3	7.5	49.3
Future	19.4	88.7	(71.1)
	60.7	96.2	(21.8)
Net earnings	$ 128.7	$ 124.5	$ 52.2
Earnings per share (Note 19)	$ 1.21	$ 1.17	$ 0.49
Diluted earnings per share (Note 19)	$ 1.20	$ 1.16	$ 0.49

SEARS CANADA INC.
Consolidated Statements of Retained Earnings
(in millions)

	52 Weeks Ended January 1, 2005	53 Weeks Ended January 3, 2004	52 Weeks Ended December 28, 2002
Opening Balance	$1,321.7	$1,168.6	$1,142.0
Adoption of new accounting policy for Business Combinations (Note 1)	—	54.2	—
Net earnings	128.7	124.5	52.2
Dividends declared	(25.6)	(25.6)	(25.6)
Repurchase of shares (Note 10)	(6.9)	—	—
Closing Balance	$1,417.9	$1,321.7	$1,168.6

SEARS CANADA INC.
Consolidated Statements of Financial Position

(in millions)	As at January 1, 2005	As at January 3, 2004	As at December 28, 2002
ASSETS			
Current Assets			
Cash and short-term investments	$ 78.0	$ 82.6	$ 142.8
Accounts receivable (Notes 2 and 3)	1,526.3	1,249.1	1,322.5
Income taxes recoverable	—	11.8	4.1
Inventories	789.8	801.3	754.0
Prepaid expenses and other assets	132.4	110.6	109.4
Current portion of future income tax assets (Note 4)	85.0	151.0	183.1
	2,611.5	2,406.4	2,515.9
Investments and other assets (Note 5)	83.9	76.8	59.7
Capital assets (Note 6)	1,065.8	1,099.9	1,036.9
Deferred charges (Note 7)	270.5	293.6	309.3
Future income tax assets (Note 4)	79.3	32.6	77.8
Other long-term assets	115.4	229.9	61.7
	$4,226.4	$4,139.2	$4,061.3
LIABILITIES			
Current liabilities			
Accounts payable	$ 735.2	$ 728.2	$ 799.0
Accrued liabilities	434.7	451.1	517.3
Income and other taxes payable	101.7	95.9	99.1
Principal payments on long-term obligations due within one year (Note 9)	21.3	7.3	6.2
Current portion of deferred credit (Note 4)	—	—	30.0
	1,292.9	1,282.5	1,451.6
Long-term obligations (Note 9)	734.6	763.1	770.2
Accrued benefit liability (Note 8)	180.5	173.9	168.4
Other long-term liabilities	141.0	139.2	24.2
	2,349.0	2,358.7	2,414.4
SHAREHOLDERS' EQUITY			
Capital stock (Note 10)	459.5	458.8	458.1
Retained earnings	1,417.9	1,321.7	1,188.8
	1,877.4	1,780.5	1,646.9
	$4,226.4	$4,139.2	$4,061.3

■ **LO5, 6, 7**   **P13–8** **Analyzing an Investment by Comparing Selected Ratios** (AP13–6)

You have the opportunity to invest $10,000 in one of two companies from a single industry. The only information you have follows. The word *high* refers to the top third of the industry; *average* is the middle third; *low* is the bottom third. Which company would you select? Write a brief report justifying your recommendation.

Ratio	Company A	Company B
Current	High	Average
Quick	Low	Average
Debt to equity	High	Average
Inventory turnover	Low	Average
Price/earnings	Low	Average
Dividend yield	High	Average

■ **LO3, 4**   **P13–9** **Analyzing an Investment by Comparing Selected Ratios** (AP13–7)

You have the opportunity to invest $10,000 in one of two companies from a single industry. The only information you have is shown below. The word *high* refers to the top third of the industry; *average* is the middle third; *low* is the bottom third. Which company would you select? Write a brief report justifying your recommendation.

Ratio	Company A	Company B
Current	Low	Average
Quick	Average	Average
Debt to equity	Low	Average
Inventory turnover	High	Average
Price/earnings	High	Average
Dividend yield	Low	Average

ALTERNATE PROBLEMS

■ **LO3, 4,**   **AP13–1** **Analyzing Financial Statements Using Ratios and Percentage Changes** (P13–1)
5, 6, 7

Taber Company has just prepared the following comparative annual financial statements for 2006:

TABER COMPANY		
Comparative Income Statement		
For the Years Ended December 31, 2006 and 2005		
	2006	2005
Sales revenue (one-half on credit)	$110,000	$100,000
Cost of goods sold	52,000	49,000
Gross margin	58,000	51,000
Expenses (including $4,000 interest expense each year)	40,000	37,000
Pretax income	18,000	14,000
Income tax on operations (30%)	5,400	4,200
Income before extraordinary items	12,600	9,800
Extraordinary loss (net of tax)	1,400	
Extraordinary gain (net of tax)		2,100
Net income	$ 11,200	$ 11,900

TABER COMPANY
Comparative Balance Sheet
At December 31, 2006 and 2005

	2006	2005
Assets		
Cash	$ 49,500	$ 18,000
Accounts receivable (net; terms 1/10, n/30)	37,000	32,000
Inventory	25,000	38,000
Property, plant, and equipment (net)	95,000	105,000
Total assets	$206,500	$193,000
Liabilities		
Accounts payable	$ 42,000	$ 35,000
Income taxes payable	1,000	500
Note payable, long term	40,000	40,000
Shareholders' equity		
Share capital (9,000 shares)	90,000	90,000
Retained earnings	33,500	27,500
Total liabilities and shareholders' equity	$206,500	$193,000

Required (round percentage and ratios to two decimal places):

1. For 2006, compute the tests of (a) profitability, (b) liquidity, (c) solvency, and (d) market. Assume that the quoted price of the stock was $23 per share for 2006. Dividends declared and paid during 2006 were $5,200.

2. Answer the following for 2006:
   a. Compute the percentage changes in sales, income before extraordinary items, net income, cash, inventory, and debt.
   b. What appears to be the pretax interest rate on the note payable?

3. Identify at least two problems facing the company that are suggested by your responses to requirements 1 and 2.

AP13–2 **Using Ratios to Analyze Several Years of Financial Data** (P13–2)   ■ **LO3, 4, 5**

The following information was contained in the annual financial statements of Pine Company, which started business January 1, 2005 (assume account balances only in Cash and Share Capital on this date; all amounts are in thousands of dollars).

	2005	2006	2007	2008
Accounts receivable (net; terms n/30)	$11	$12	$18	$ 24
Merchandise inventory	12	14	20	30
Net sales (¾ on credit)	44	66	80	100
Cost of goods sold	28	40	55	62
Net income (loss)	(8)	5	12	11

Required (show computations and round to two decimal places):

1. Complete the following tabulation:

Items	2005	2006	2007	2008
a. Profit margin—percentage				
b. Gross margin—ratio				
c. Expenses as percentage of sales, excluding cost of goods sold				
d. Inventory turnover				
e. Days' supply in inventory				
f. Receivable turnover				
g. Average collection period				

2. Evaluate the results of the related ratios *a, b,* and *c* to identify the favourable or unfavourable factors. Give your recommendations to improve the company's operations.

3. Evaluate the results of the last four ratios (*d, e, f,* and *g*) and identify any favourable or unfavourable factors. Give your recommendations to improve the company's operations.

■ **LO3, 4**   **AP13–3** **Analyzing Ratios** (P13–3)

Coca-Cola and PepsiCo

Coke and Pepsi are well-known international brands. Coca-Cola sells more than $22 billion worth of beverages each year, while annual sales of Pepsi products exceed $29 billion. Compare the two companies as a potential investment based on the following ratios:

Ratio	Coca-Cola	PepsiCo
P/E	65.0	26.5
Gross profit margin	69.3	58.4
Profit margin	12.2%	8.8%
Quick ratio	0.4	0.7
Current ratio	0.6	1.1
Debt to equity	0.7	0.4
Return on equity	27.4%	29.1%
Return on assets	28.0%	16.6%
Dividend yield	1.0%	1.6%
Dividend payout ratio	65.0%	41.0%

■ **LO3, 4**   **AP13–4** **Comparing Loan Requests from Two Companies Using Several Ratios** (P13–5)

The 2006 financial statements for Rand and Tand companies are summarized below:

	Rand Company	Tand Company
Balance Sheet		
Cash	$ 25,000	$ 45,000
Accounts receivable (net)	55,000	5,000
Inventory	110,000	25,000
Property, plant, and equipment (net)	550,000	160,000
Other assets	140,000	57,000
Total assets	$880,000	$292,000
Current liabilities	$120,000	$ 15,000
Long-term debt (12%)	190,000	55,000
Share capital	480,000	210,000
Contributed surplus	50,000	4,000
Retained earnings	40,000	8,000
Total liabilities and shareholders' equity	$880,000	$292,000
Income Statement		
Sales revenue (on credit)	(½) $800,000	(¼) $280,000
Cost of goods sold	(480,000)	(150,000)
Expenses (including interest and income tax)	(240,000)	(95,000)
Net income	$ 80,000	$ 35,000
Selected Data from the 2005 Statements		
Accounts receivable, net	$ 47,000	$ 11,000
Long-term debt (12%)	190,000	55,000
Inventory	95,000	38,000
Other Data		
Share price at end of 2006	$ 14.00	$ 11.00
Income tax rate	30%	30%
Dividends declared and paid in 2006	$ 20,000	$ 9,000
Number of common shares during 2006	24,000	10,500

These two companies are in the same line of business and in the same province but in different cities. Each company has been in operation for about 10 years. Rand Company is audited by one of the national accounting firms; Tand Company is audited by a local accounting firm. Both companies received an unqualified opinion (i.e., the independent auditors found nothing wrong) on the financial statements. Rand Company wants to borrow $75,000 cash, and Tand Company needs $30,000. The loans will be for a two-year period and are needed for "working capital purposes."

Required:

1. Complete a schedule that reflects a ratio analysis of each company. Compute the ratios discussed in the chapter.

2. Assume that you work in the loan department of a local bank. You have been asked to analyze the situation and recommend which loan is preferable. Based on the data given, your analysis prepared in requirement 1, and any other information, give your choice and provide a supporting explanation.

AP13–5 Analyzing Financial Statements Using Appropriate Ratios (P13–7)

Hudson's Bay Company provides Canadians with a wide selection of goods and services through its retail channels, led by its two major divisions: The Bay and Zellers. The following information was reported in a recent annual report.

■ **LO3**

Hudson's Bay Company

Required:

1. Compute the ratios discussed in this chapter for the last two years. If there is not sufficient information, describe what is missing and explain what you would do.

2. Assume the role of an investment adviser. A client of yours has the opportunity to invest $1 million in shares of Canadian companies. Prepare a written evaluation of relevant ratios and indicate whether you would recommend to your client that the $1 million be invested in the shares of Hudson's Bay Company.

HUDSON'S BAY COMPANY
Consolidated Statements of Earnings
Years Ended January 31

(thousands of dollars except per share amounts)	Notes	2005	2004	2003
Sales and revenue				
The Bay		2,681,587	2,689,478	2,648,339
Zellers		4,301,128	4,519,706	4,656,274
Other		87,021	85,881	79,200
		7,069,736	7,295,065	7,383,813
Earnings before interest expense and income taxes				
The Bay		67,856	75,778	104,941
Zellers		84,644	126,257	120,401
Other		(23,133)	(37,388)	(26,022)
		129,367	164,647	199,310
Interest expense	16	(45,681)	(60,962)	(45,428)
Earnings before income taxes		83,686	103,685	153,882
Income taxes	4	(23,948)	(43,732)	(42,421)
Net earnings		59,738	59,953	111,461
Earnings per share—basic	17	$ 0.86	$ 0.87	$ 1.40
Earnings per share—diluted	17	$ 0.86	$ 0.86	$ 1.34

(See accompanying notes to the Consolidated Financial Statements)

HUDSON'S BAY COMPANY
Consolidated Statements of Retained Earnings
Years Ended January 31

(thousands of dollars)	Notes	2005	2004	2003
Retained earnings at beginning of year, as reported		772,904	740,853	668,304
Impact of new accounting standards				
—consideration received from vendors	2	(63,904)	(68,789)	
—reclassification of convertible debentures	2	(5,730)	(5,509)	
Lease accounting adjustment	2	(19,825)	(18,117)	
Retained earnings at beginning of year, as restated		683,445	648,438	668,304
Net earnings		59,738	59,953	111,461
Dividends—common shares		(24,963)	(24,946)	(25,070)
Dividends and accretion—convertible debentures				(13,842)
Retained earnings at end of year		718,220	683,445	740,853

(See accompanying notes to the Consolidated Financial Statements)

HUDSON'S BAY COMPANY
Consolidated Balance Sheets
January 31

(thousands of dollars)	Notes	2005	2004	2003
Current assets				
Cash in stores		7,713	8,033	7,308
Short-term deposits		254,908	168,943	51,418
Credit card receivables	3	427,443	538,734	559,151
Other accounts receivable		119,497	64,811	117,412
Merchandise inventories		1,412,320	1,386,097	1,551,104
Prepaid expenses and other current assets		65,439	115,086	122,860
		2,287,320	2,281,704	2,409,253
Fixed assets	5	1,049,505	1,058,789	1,205,333
Goodwill	1(i)	143,215	152,294	152,294
Pensions	6	365,196	365,175	349,549
Other assets	7	163,585	164,074	159,258
		4,008,821	4,022,036	4,275,687
Current liabilities				
Short-term borrowings	9	124,710	1,309	24,744
Trade accounts payable		417,376	415,350	436,368
Other accounts payable and accrued liabilities		455,699	520,581	541,599
Long-term debt due within one year	9	101,660	125,436	258,870
		1,099,445	1,062,676	1,261,581
Long-term debt	9	492,622	567,882	388,543
Employee future benefits other than pensions	6	57,964	59,112	59,709
Future income taxes	4	158,126	167,328	171,115
Shareholders' equity				
Capital stock	10	1,402,756	1,402,563	1,402,007
Convertible debentures	9	20,000	20,000	199,231
Contributed surplus		59,688	59,030	52,648
Retained earnings		718,220	683,445	740,853
		2,200,664	2,165,038	2,394,739
		4,008,821	4,022,036	4,275,687

(See accompanying notes to the Consolidated Financial Statements)

AP13–6 Analyzing an Investment by Comparing Selected Ratios (P13–8)

You have the opportunity to invest $10,000 in one of two companies from a single industry. The only information you have is shown below. The word *high* refers to the top third of the industry; *average* is the middle third; *low* is the bottom third. Which company would you select? Write a brief report justifying your recommendation.

■ LO4, 5, 6, 7

Ratio	Company A	Company B
EPS	High	Low
ROA	Low	High
Debt to equity	High	Average
Current	Low	Average
Price/earnings	Low	High
Dividend yield	High	Average

AP13–7 Analyzing an Investment by Comparing Selected Ratios (P13–9)

You have the opportunity to invest $10,000 in one of two companies from a single industry. The only information you have is shown below. The word *high* refers to the top third of the industry; *average* is the middle third; *low* is the bottom third. Which company would you select? Write a brief report justifying your recommendation.

■ LO4, 5, 6, 7

Ratio	Company A	Company B
ROA	High	Average
Profit margin	High	Low
Financial leverage	High	Low
Current	Low	High
Price/earnings	High	Average
Debt to equity	High	Low

CASES AND PROJECTS

FINDING AND INTERPRETING FINANCIAL INFORMATION

CP13–1 Analyzing Financial Statements

Refer to the financial statements of Van Houtte Inc. given in Appendix B of this book. From the list of ratios that were discussed in this chapter, select and compute the ratios that help you evaluate the company's operations for fiscal year 2005. Assume a market price of $23.50 per share.

■ LO4, 5, 6, 7

Van Houtte

CP13–2 Analyzing Financial Statements

Refer to the Online Learning Centre Web site at **www.mcgrawhill.ca/college/libby/student/ resources** for the financial statements of The Forzani Group Ltd. From the list of ratios that were discussed in this chapter, select and compute the ratios that help you evaluate the company's operations for fiscal year 2005.

■ LO4, 5, 6, 7

The Forzani
Group Ltd.

FINANCIAL REPORTING AND ANALYSIS CASES

CP13–3 Interpreting Financial Results Based on Corporate Strategy

In this chapter, we discussed the importance of analyzing financial results based on an understanding of the company's business strategy. Using the ROE model, we illustrated how different strategies could earn high returns for investors. Assume that two companies in the same industry adopt fundamentally different strategies. One manufactures high-quality

■ LO1

consumer electronics. Its products employ state-of-the-art technology, and the company offers a high level of customer service both before and after the sale. The other company emphasizes low cost with good performance. Its products utilize well-established technology but are never innovative. Customers buy these products at large, self-service warehouses and are expected to install the products using information contained in printed brochures. Which of the ratios discussed in this chapter would you expect to differ for these companies as a result of their different business strategies?

■ **LO4, 5, 6, 7**

Nordstrom and JCPenney

CP13–4 Interpreting Financial Results Based on Corporate Strategy

In this chapter, we discussed the importance of analyzing financial results based on an understanding of the company's business strategy. Using the ROE model, we illustrated how different strategies could earn high returns for investors. Both Nordstrom and JCPenney are in the retail industry. Nordstrom is a specialty apparel retailer operating in 23 states. Annual revenues exceed $5 billion. The store is well known for high-quality merchandise and a high level of customer service. JCPenney is a full-line retailer appealing to middle-income shoppers. Its merchandise is moderately priced, and customers receive a lower level of service. The following are several ratios from each company. Identify which company is Nordstrom and which is JCPenney. Which of these ratios do you think are affected by the different strategies? Explain.

Ratio	Company A	Company B
Gross margin	34.4%	23.1%
Profit margin	4.0%	1.7%
Current ratio	1.8	1.6
Debt to equity	0.8	1.4
Return on equity	15.9%	7.5%
Return on assets	6.5%	2.3%
Dividend payout	22.1	117.0
Price/earnings	15.3	9.3

CRITICAL THINKING CASES

■ **LO4, 5, 6, 7**

CP13–5 Analyzing the Impact of Alternative Amortization Methods on Ratio Analysis

Speedy Company uses the double-declining-balance method to amortize its property, plant, and equipment, and Turtle Company uses the straight-line method. Both companies use declining-balance amortization for income tax purposes. The two companies are exactly alike except for the difference in amortization methods.

Required:

1. Identify the financial ratios discussed in this chapter that are likely to be affected by the difference in amortization methods.

2. Which company will report the higher amount for each ratio that you have identified? If you cannot be certain, explain why.

■ **LO4**

CP13–6 Evaluating an Ethical Dilemma

Almost Short Company requested a sizeable loan from Provincial Bank to acquire a large tract of land for future expansion. Almost Short reported current assets of $1,900,000 ($430,000 in cash) and current liabilities of $1,075,000. Provincial denied the loan request for a number of reasons, including the fact that the current ratio was below 2. When Almost Short was informed of the loan denial, the comptroller of the company immediately paid $420,000 that was owed to several trade creditors. The comptroller then asked Provincial to reconsider the loan application. Based on these abbreviated facts, would you recommend that Provincial approve the loan request? Why? Are the comptroller's actions ethical?

FINANCIAL REPORTING AND ANALYSIS TEAM PROJECT

CP13–7 **Team Project: Examining an Annual Report**

■ **LO3, 4, 5, 6, 7**

As a team, select an industry to analyze. Each team member should acquire the annual report for one publicly traded company in the industry, with each member selecting a different company. (Library files, the SEDAR service at www.sedar.com, or the company itself are good resources.) On an individual basis, each team member should write a brief report analyzing his or her company using the techniques discussed in this chapter.

Discuss any patterns across the companies that you as a team observe. Then, as a team, write a short report comparing and contrasting your companies. Provide potential explanations for any difference discovered.

Appendix A—Present and Future Value Tables

TABLE A.1

Future Value of $1, $f = (1 + i)^n$

Periods	2%	3%	3.75%	4%	4.25%	5%	6%	7%	8%
0	1.	1.	1.	1.	1.	1.	1.	1.	1.
1	1.02	1.03	1.0375	1.04	1.0425	1.05	1.06	1.07	1.08
2	1.0404	1.0609	1.0764	1.0816	1.0868	1.1025	1.1236	1.1449	1.1664
3	1.0612	1.0927	1.1168	1.1249	1.1330	1.1576	1.1910	1.2250	1.2597
4	1.0824	1.1255	1.1587	1.1699	1.1811	1.2155	1.2625	1.3108	1.3605
5	1.1041	1.1593	1.2021	1.2167	1.2313	1.2763	1.3382	1.4026	1.4693
6	1.1262	1.1941	1.2472	1.2653	1.2837	1.3401	1.4185	1.5007	1.5869
7	1.1487	1.2299	1.2939	1.3159	1.3382	1.4071	1.5036	1.6058	1.7138
8	1.1717	1.2668	1.3425	1.3686	1.3951	1.4775	1.5938	1.7182	1.8509
9	1.1951	1.3048	1.3928	1.4233	1.4544	1.5513	1.6895	1.8385	1.9990
10	1.2190	1.3439	1.4450	1.4802	1.5162	1.6289	1.7908	1.9672	2.1589
20	1.4859	1.8061	2.0882	2.1911	2.2989	2.6533	3.2071	3.8697	4.6610

Periods	9%	10%	11%	12%	13%	14%	15%	20%	25%
0	1.	1.	1.	1.	1.	1.	1.	1.	1.
1	1.09	1.10	1.11	1.12	1.13	1.14	1.15	1.20	1.25
2	1.1881	1.2100	1.2321	1.2544	1.2769	1.2996	1.3225	1.4400	1.5625
3	1.2950	1.3310	1.3676	1.4049	1.4429	1.4815	1.5209	1.7280	1.9531
4	1.4116	1.4641	1.5181	1.5735	1.6305	1.6890	1.7490	2.0736	2.4414
5	1.5386	1.6105	1.6851	1.7623	1.8424	1.9254	2.0114	2.4883	3.0518
6	1.6771	1.7716	1.8704	1.9738	2.0820	2.1950	2.3131	2.9860	3.8147
7	1.8280	1.9487	2.0762	2.2107	2.3526	2.5023	2.6600	3.5832	4.7684
8	1.9926	2.1436	2.3045	2.4760	2.6584	2.8526	3.0590	4.2998	5.9605
9	2.1719	2.3579	2.5580	2.7731	3.0040	3.2519	3.5179	5.1598	7.4506
10	2.3674	2.5937	2.8394	3.1058	3.3946	3.7072	4.0456	6.1917	9.3132
20	5.6044	6.7275	8.0623	9.6463	11.5231	13.7435	16.3665	38.3376	86.7362

TABLE A.2

Present Value of $1, $p = 1/(1 + i)^n$

Periods	2%	3%	3.75%	4%	4.25%	5%	6%	7%	8%
1	0.9804	0.9709	0.9639	0.9615	0.9592	0.9524	0.9434	0.9346	0.9259
2	0.9612	0.9426	0.9290	0.9246	0.9201	0.9070	0.8900	0.8734	0.8573
3	0.9423	0.9151	0.8954	0.8890	0.8826	0.8638	0.8396	0.8163	0.7938
4	0.9238	0.8885	0.8631	0.8548	0.8466	0.8227	0.7921	0.7629	0.7350
5	0.9057	0.8626	0.8319	0.8219	0.8121	0.7835	0.7473	0.7130	0.6806
6	0.8880	0.8375	0.8018	0.7903	0.7790	0.7462	0.7050	0.6663	0.6302
7	0.8706	0.8131	0.7728	0.7599	0.7473	0.7107	0.6651	0.6227	0.5835
8	0.8535	0.7894	0.7449	0.7307	0.7168	0.6768	0.6274	0.5820	0.5403
9	0.8368	0.7664	0.7180	0.7026	0.6876	0.6446	0.5919	0.5439	0.5002
10	0.8203	0.7441	0.6920	0.6756	0.6595	0.6139	0.5584	0.5083	0.4632
20	0.6730	0.5534	0.4789	0.4564	0.4350	0.3769	0.3118	0.2584	0.2145

Periods	9%	10%	11%	12%	13%	14%	15%	20%	25%
1	0.9174	0.9091	0.9009	0.8929	0.8850	0.8772	0.8696	0.8333	0.8000
2	0.8417	0.8264	0.8116	0.7972	0.7831	0.7695	0.7561	0.6944	0.6400
3	0.7722	0.7513	0.7312	0.7118	0.6931	0.6750	0.6575	0.5787	0.5120
4	0.7084	0.6830	0.6587	0.6355	0.6133	0.5921	0.5718	0.4823	0.4096
5	0.6499	0.6209	0.5935	0.5674	0.5428	0.5194	0.4972	0.4019	0.3277
6	0.5963	0.5645	0.5346	0.5066	0.4803	0.4556	0.4323	0.3349	0.2621
7	0.5470	0.5132	0.4817	0.4523	0.4251	0.3996	0.3759	0.2791	0.2097
8	0.5019	0.4665	0.4339	0.4039	0.3762	0.3506	0.3269	0.2326	0.1678
9	0.4604	0.4241	0.3909	0.3606	0.3329	0.3075	0.2843	0.1938	0.1342
10	0.4224	0.3855	0.3522	0.3220	0.2946	0.2697	0.2472	0.1615	0.1074
20	0.1784	0.1486	0.1240	0.1037	0.0868	0.0728	0.0611	0.0261	0.0115

TABLE **A.3**

Future Value of Annuity of $1 (ordinary), $F = (1 + i)^n - 1/i$

Periods*	2%	3%	3.75%	4%	4.25%	5%	6%	7%	8%
1	1.	1.	1.	1.	1.	1.	1.	1.	1.
2	2.02	2.03	2.0375	2.04	2.0425	2.05	2.06	2.07	2.08
3	3.0604	3.0909	3.1139	3.1216	3.1293	3.1525	3.1836	3.2149	3.2464
4	4.1216	4.1836	4.2307	4.2465	4.2623	4.3101	4.3746	4.4399	4.5061
5	5.2040	5.3091	5.3893	5.4163	5.4434	5.5256	5.6371	5.7507	5.8666
6	6.3081	6.4684	6.5914	6.6330	6.6748	6.8019	6.9753	7.1533	7.3359
7	7.4343	7.6625	7.8386	7.8983	7.9585	8.1420	8.3938	8.6540	8.9228
8	8.5830	8.8923	9.1326	9.2142	9.2967	9.5491	9.8975	10.2598	10.6366
9	9.7546	10.1591	10.4750	10.5828	10.6918	11.0266	11.4913	11.9780	12.4876
10	10.9497	11.4639	11.8678	12.0061	12.1462	12.5779	13.1808	13.8164	14.4866
20	24.2974	26.8704	29.0174	29.7781	30.5625	33.0660	36.7856	40.9955	45.7620

Periods*	9%	10%	11%	12%	13%	14%	15%	20%	25%
1	1.	1.	1.	1.	1.	1.	1.	1.	1.
2	2.09	2.10	2.11	2.12	2.13	2.14	2.15	2.20	2.25
3	3.2781	3.3100	3.3421	3.3744	3.4069	3.4396	3.4725	3.6400	3.8125
4	4.5731	4.6410	4.7097	4.7793	4.8498	4.9211	4.9934	5.3680	5.7656
5	5.9847	6.1051	6.2278	6.3528	6.4803	6.6101	6.7424	7.4416	8.2070
6	7.5233	7.7156	7.9129	8.1152	8.3227	8.5355	8.7537	9.9299	11.2588
7	9.2004	9.4872	9.7833	10.0890	10.4047	10.7305	11.0668	12.9159	15.0735
8	11.0285	11.4359	11.8594	12.2997	12.7573	13.2328	13.7268	16.4991	19.8419
9	13.0210	13.5975	14.1640	14.7757	15.4157	16.0853	16.7858	20.7989	25.8023
10	15.1929	15.9374	16.7220	17.5487	18.4197	19.3373	20.3037	25.9587	33.2529
20	51.1601	57.2750	64.2028	72.0524	80.9468	91.0249	102.4436	186.6880	342.9447

*There is one payment each period.

TABLE **A.4**

Present Value of Annuity of $1, $P = 1 - 1/(1 + i)^n/i$

Periods*	2%	3%	3.75%	4%	4.25%	5%	6%	7%	8%
1	0.9804	0.9709	0.9639	0.9615	0.9592	0.9524	0.9434	0.9346	0.9259
2	1.9416	1.9135	1.8929	1.8861	1.8794	1.8594	1.8334	1.8080	1.7833
3	2.8839	2.8286	2.7883	2.7751	2.7620	2.7232	2.6730	2.6243	2.5771
4	3.8077	3.7171	3.6514	3.6299	3.6086	3.5460	3.4651	3.3872	3.3121
5	4.7135	4.5797	4.4833	4.4518	4.4207	4.3295	4.2124	4.1002	3.9927
6	5.6014	5.4172	5.2851	5.2421	5.1997	5.0757	4.9173	4.7665	4.6229
7	6.4720	6.2303	6.0579	6.0021	5.9470	5.7864	5.5824	5.3893	5.2064
8	7.3255	7.0197	6.8028	6.7327	6.6638	6.4632	6.2098	5.9713	5.7466
9	8.1622	7.7861	7.5208	7.4353	7.3513	7.1078	6.8017	6.5152	6.2469
10	8.9826	8.5302	8.2128	8.1109	8.0109	7.7217	7.3601	7.0236	6.7101
20	16.3514	14.8775	13.8962	13.5903	13.2944	12.4622	11.4699	10.5940	9.8181

Periods*	9%	10%	11%	12%	13%	14%	15%	20%	25%
1	0.9174	0.9091	0.9009	0.8929	0.8550	0.8772	0.8696	0.8333	0.8000
2	1.7591	1.7355	1.7125	1.6901	1.6681	1.6467	1.6257	1.5278	1.4400
3	2.5313	2.4869	2.4437	2.4018	2.3612	2.3216	2.2832	2.1065	1.9520
4	3.2397	3.1699	3.1024	3.0373	2.9745	2.9137	2.8550	2.5887	2.3616
5	3.8897	3.7908	3.6959	3.6048	3.5172	3.4331	3.3522	2.9906	2.6893
6	4.4859	4.3553	4.2305	4.1114	3.9975	3.8887	3.7845	3.3255	2.9514
7	5.0330	4.8684	4.7122	4.5638	4.4226	4.2883	4.1604	3.6046	3.1611
8	5.5348	5.3349	5.1461	4.9676	4.7988	4.6389	4.4873	3.8372	3.3289
9	5.9952	5.7590	5.5370	5.3282	4.1317	4.9464	4.7716	4.0310	3.4631
10	6.4177	6.1446	5.8892	5.6502	5.4262	5.2161	5.0188	4.1925	3.5705
20	9.1285	8.5136	7.9633	7.4694	7.0248	6.6231	6.2593	4.8696	3.9539

*There is one payment each period.

DISCOVER

ANNUAL REPORT 2005

From Bean to your Cup

VAN HOUTTE
CAFÉ

A taste of
EUROPE
in your cup

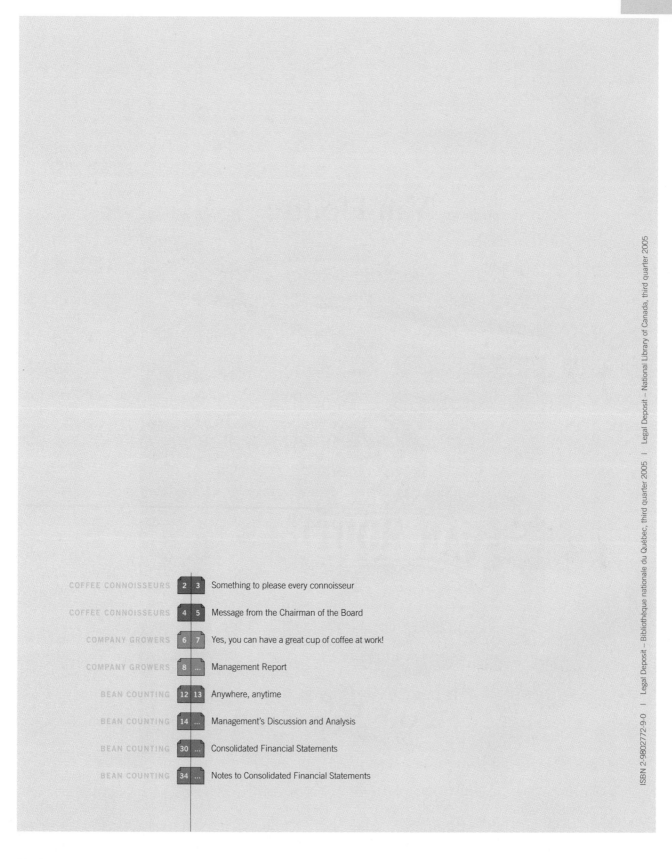

ISBN 2-9802772-9-0 | Legal Deposit – Bibliothèque nationale du Québec, third quarter 2005 | Legal Deposit – National Library of Canada, third quarter 2005

Note: Non-essential pages from the 2005 Van Houtte Annual Report have been omitted from this text, but are available on the Online Learning Centre, www.mcgrawhill.ca/college/libby.

Message from the Chairman of the Board

Dear fellow shareholders,

Fiscal 2005 was a good year. Under the leadership of president and CEO Jean-Yves Monette, Van Houtte's executive team, managers and employees drove earnings up 17%, outperforming the 10% to 15% target set a year ago.

This performance not only confirms that our business plan is sound but that we chose the right people to execute it. And so for 2006, we are once again projecting earnings growth of 10% to 15%.

This plan seeks sustainable gains, and it is on this basis that the Board evaluates the strategy and its implementation. Still, we are pleased to see that investors have already begun to acknowledge its merits. This is excellent news for those who share my expectations for an enduring return on their investment.

Your Board of Directors is not only responsible for supervising the design and execution of Van Houtte's strategy but also for prudently assuming its fiduciary responsibility vis-à-vis your investment. In this regard, we have finished updating our corporate governance rules to reflect Canada's new legislative and regulatory environment.

Thus in 2005 we revised and formalized the mandates of each Board committee and set up the appropriate performance evaluation mechanisms. We also developed effective controls and procedures for communicating information so as to guarantee the quality and timely presentation of financial information to shareholders.

During the year, we welcomed a new director to the Board. Roger Desrosiers, FCA, brings with him more than 40 years' auditing and strategic consulting experience. I would once again like to welcome Mr. Desrosiers.

Jean-Yves Monette and his colleagues on the management committee, Gérard Geoffrion and Roger Cohen, must be commended for their achievements this past year. Solidly backed by Van Houtte's employees, Jean-Yves and his team are the skilled, enthusiastic architects of Van Houtte's success. They can continue to rely on our full support.

I would also like to thank my colleagues on the Board of Directors for their commitment to the Company's development. In this regard, the work of the Board's committees deserves special mention. The shareholders, including myself, are grateful for their extensive and invaluable input.

Paul-André Guillotte
Chairman of the Board

Management's Discussion and Analysis

Company profile

Van Houtte Inc. ("Van Houtte," the "Company," "we") is the most integrated gourmet coffee roaster and distributor in North America. By "integrated roaster and distributor" we mean that our business activities, carried out directly or through our subsidiaries, affiliates or franchisees cover just about the entire supply chain, starting with the purchase of green coffee, followed by roasting, retail marketing and distribution in the retail food network, to total coffee solutions that include the coffee, the brewer, condiments and other related products, designed for wherever the drink is consumed: the workplace, commercial spaces, institutions, hotels and restaurants.

Our beginnings date back to 1919 when Albert-Louis Van Houtte launched an imported coffee and fine grocery store in Montreal.

At the time of writing, Van Houtte and its subsidiaries employed 1,887 people, including 1,792 on a full time basis.

Additional information

This MD&A was prepared on June 2, 2005. Additional information relating to the Company, including its Annual Information Form, is available on the SEDAR Web site at www.sedar.com. Unless otherwise indicated, the information contained herein is current as at June 2, 2005.

Main activities

The Company groups its activities into two broad categories: Manufacturing and Marketing, and Coffee Services.

Manufacturing and Marketing

The Manufacturing and Marketing segment encompasses coffee roasting and distribution for home consumption through retail channels, the production and distribution of coffeemakers and related equipment as well as the franchising and operation of café bistros. Canadian and American consumers can also buy our products online at www.vanhoutte.com.

Coffee roasting and distribution

Van Houtte is Canada's leading gourmet coffee roaster. We purchase our green coffee—almost exclusively Arabica—from the main producing countries located in the equatorial areas of Latin America, Africa and Asia. Because we buy gourmet coffee beans, we pay a premium over the prices published on the various coffee exchanges. And although we deal primarily with Canadian brokers, we pay for our purchases in U.S. dollars.

We operate four roasting plants: two in Montreal, Quebec, one in Vancouver, British Columbia, and one in Henderson, Kentucky. Accounting for more than 90% of our production capacity, the main plant in Montreal and the Henderson plant are state-of-the-art facilities with equipment that carefully controls the roasting process according to the specific profile required for each recipe. To ensure superior roasting worthy of the best roasting and blending traditional methods, we roast the coffee in small batches of 450 lbs. (204 kg). And thanks to our cutting-edge technology, this hand-made quality is carefully reproduced in each batch. Van Houtte uses a "cold grinding" process for its ground coffees in order to preserve bean aroma and ensure a uniform grind.

Van Houtte coffees are available in some 4,300 retail points of sale across Canada and on the East Coast of the United States, compared with 4,015 a year ago. This increase is essentially the result of an agreement signed with some Canadian retail food chains that added 250 points of sale in Ontario and Western Canada.

Although sold mainly under the Van Houtte brand, our coffees are also marketed under the Orient Express and other brand names. We offer more than 100 blends, roasting profiles and different packaging to suit the discriminating tastes of fine coffee lovers and connoisseurs everywhere. The Company is constantly developing new blends, profiles and packaging in response to a changing market. For example, in 2005, we launched JAVANATION™, a line of single origin coffees and espresso blends designed to meet the expectations of discriminating and demanding consumers.

Finally, we also roast and package coffee under private labels for supermarket chains who distribute our Van Houtte branded products.

TABLE 1
Breakdown of Retail Points of Sale Offering Van Houtte Products

	Number of points of sale
Canada	3,575
United States	725
Total	**4,300**

We usually negotiate directly with the supermarket chains and design, set up and stock the gourmet coffee department in a majority of their stores.

Coffeemaker manufacturing

Through our subsidiary VKI Technologies Inc. ("VKI"), we design, manufacture and market hopper-based, single-cup coffeemakers that brew coffee one cup at a time. At its plant in the Montreal suburb of Longueuil, VKI produces several models of single-cup coffeemakers adapted to various purposes and intensity of use. These machines can be equipped with an electronic control system, a liquid crystal display, a coffee/hot chocolate option and a paperless brewer.

In addition to the hopper-based coffeemaker, VKI has designed and produces the Espresso Café™, which uses pre-packaged pods of coffee to prepare a consistently high-quality espresso, cappuccino, latte or americano in just 45 seconds.

VKI is also a licensed manufacturer of a coffee machine that uses a pre-packaged cup-based technology, developed by Keurig, Inc., a Massachusetts-based company in which Van Houtte holds 23.5% of the diluted common shares. Marketed under the name K-Cup®, the small cups contain a hermetically sealed individual portion of coffee and an individual filter.

Other VKI products include a single-cup tea brewer, produced for an American client, and Scalehammer™, a hard water treatment system for residential and institutional use. Two Canadian hardware chains recently began selling this product.

Although our Coffee Services network (see next section) is VKI's primary market, the company also sells to other coffee service providers and vending machine manufacturers in North America, Japan and Europe.

Cafés bistros

We operate a network of 74 franchised café bistros in Quebec and in the Ottawa region. For several years, we owned a number of these establishments. Thus a year ago, we owned seven out of 67 Van Houtte café bistros. During the 2005 fiscal year we sold all of them to franchisees. Now all café bistros are franchised.

Although they represent a very small portion of our consolidated revenues, the bistros are nevertheless an integral part of our development strategy since they help maintain our brand image with consumers. Measuring from 70 to 200 square metres, the café bistros offer their clientele an extensive range of regular and specialty coffees as well as light meals and snacks.

Coffee Services

Our other major sphere of activity, Coffee Services focuses on the sale of coffee for consumption at work and other public places. In Canada this segment includes vending machine operations.

Coffee Services offer "Total Coffee Solutions" that guarantee a fresh cup of coffee at the office and increasingly in other public locations. To this end we designed coffee bars. Coffee bars provide a bistro ambiance in a smaller space. They carry a more limited range of products and are integrated into high-traffic areas such as supermarkets, hospitals and university campuses. They are found across all Canadian regions.

With this service, a company or operator typically leases the type and quantity of coffeemakers it requires and we supply the coffee and condiments. We also provide a variety of drinks and snacks. Van Houtte has a broad range of brewers priced for every budget and coffees designed to suit every taste. Our flexibility and size therefore allows us to meet the needs of all companies, large or small.

As the largest Coffee Services network in North America, we have 79 branches and franchised establishments in 77 cities across most of Canada and the U.S. We wholly own our Canadian branches except for three that are joint ventures. In the U.S., our Coffee Services operations are carried out through our subsidiary Filterfresh Coffee Service, Inc. ("Filterfresh"). Headquartered in the Boston, Massachusetts region, Filterfresh has wholly-owned and franchised branches, as well as branches that are jointly owned with local partners.

TABLE 2
Breakdown of Coffee Services Branches in Canada and the U.S. by Method of Ownership and Operation

	Wholly- or Jointly-Owned Branches	Franchised Branches	Total
Canada	35	–	35
United States	30	14	44
Total	**65**	**14**	**79**

We built this network primarily through acquisitions, driving most of the consolidation in the Canadian coffee services market. However, in the U.S. the market remains highly fragmented with many founder-led businesses in search of a successor and therefore presenting strong consolidation potential. Our strategy involves acquiring businesses or forming joint ventures with local entrepreneurs in regions where we already have a footprint. We integrate these acquisitions into our network or, as the case may be, integrate our own establishment into a joint venture. In both cases, we are densifying our network, enabling us to offer better service at a lower cost.

In fiscal 2005, we completed 22 acquisitions and formed two new joint ventures. Between the end of the fiscal year and the time of writing, we had completed four more acquisitions.

Thanks to our network – the only one of its kind in North America – we can serve clients with continental operations in Canada and the U.S. For example, in 2005 we signed the largest agreement in our history in terms of the number of establishments, installing Caffè Mio™ coffeemakers in more than 1,000 Lowe's stores, America's second largest home improvement chain.

Our Coffee Services branches operate vending machines that sell snacks, candies and hot and cold drinks in eight Canadian cities. We have spent the past two years streamlining this aspect of our business, selling the vending business units in nine cities where the current or projected profitability no longer justified the investment. The disposal of these nine business units represented a total of $8.6 million in annual sales.

Fiscal Year

Van Houtte's fiscal year ends on the Saturday closest to March 31 of each year. Rather than 365 days, it therefore comprises full weeks, usually 52 but sometimes 53. Thus, fiscal 2004 had 53 weeks, one week more than 2003 and 2005. Disregarding the seasonal nature of sales, this additional week alone added 1.9% to sales and EBITDA in 2004. A comparative analysis for 2005 and 2004 must therefore take this factor into account. The last fiscal year to have 53 weeks before 2004 was 1999.

The additional week in fiscal 2004 was added to the fourth quarter, which therefore had 13 rather than 12 weeks. This additional week had a significant impact on the sales, coffee shipments and EBITDA in last year's fourth quarter. To eliminate the impact of this additional week, we present the change in average weekly sales, coffee shipments and EBITDA.

In this analysis, unless otherwise indicated, "2005" means the 52-week fiscal year ended April 2, 2005, "2004" means the 53-week fiscal year ended April 3, 2004, and "2003" means the 52-week fiscal year ended March 29, 2003.

Effect of currency fluctuations

The high volatility of the U.S. dollar over the past two years has had a significant impact on sales and operating results. The U.S. dollar lost an average of 13% against the Canadian dollar between fiscal 2003 and 2004, and about 6% between 2004 and 2005, adversely affecting U.S. sales and operating income when converted into Canadian dollars. This MD&A indicates these impacts where possible. However, while difficult to accurately measure, the effect of currency fluctuations on the Company's consolidated net earnings is minimal since some of the Canadian operating costs, specifically, the purchase of green coffee and a portion of the depreciation and financial expenses are incurred in U.S. dollars and are also sensitive to currency fluctuations.

Non-GAAP financial measures

The Company defines EBITDA as earnings before amortization, financial expenses and income taxes. Equity in net earnings of companies subject to significant influence and non-controlling interest are not considered in the computation of EBITDA. The Company defines operating cash flows as cash flow from operating activities before changes in non-cash working capital related to operations.

EBITDA and operating cash flows as defined above are not measures of results that are consistent with generally accepted accounting principles in Canada, nor are they intended to be regarded as an alternative to other financial operating performance measures or to the statement of cash flows as a measure of liquidity. They are not intended to represent funds available for debt service, dividend payments, reinvestment or other discretionary uses, and should not be considered separately or as a substitute for measures of performance prepared in accordance with generally accepted accounting principles in Canada. EBITDA and operating cash flows are used by the Company because management believes they are meaningful measures of performance. EBITDA and operating cash flows are commonly used by the investment community to analyze and compare the performance of companies in the industries in which the Company is active. The Company's definition of EBITDA and operating cash flows may not be identical to similarly titled measures reported by other companies.

Three-year highlights

Van Houtte recorded net earnings of $21.7 million or $1.01 per share (basic and diluted) in fiscal 2005, a 52-week year ended April 2. This performance is a 16.9% increase over the $18.6 million and $0.87 ($0.86 diluted) recorded in the 53-week year ended April 3, 2004.

Revenues in fiscal 2005 were $348.8 million or 5.5% more than last year. On an average weekly basis, sales growth was 7.5%.

This improvement in earnings stems from the following main factors:

- Sales growth, to which our two main segments contributed and which is partly organic and partly attributable to the net impact of acquired and divested business units in 2004 and 2005;

- Improved operating efficiency: the operating ratio (EBITDA/sales), which was 18.0% in 2004, advanced to 18.8% in 2005;

- A slight decrease in financial expenses, attributable to another reduction in our debt load;

- Fiscal 2004 contained a non-recurring charge of $0.04 per share recorded in the first quarter related to the departure of the Company's CEO.

TABLE 3

Financial highlights fiscal 2003, 2004, 2005
(In thousands of dollars, except per share amounts and coffee shipments)

	Fiscal years ended:		
	April 2, 2005	April 3, 2004*	March 29, 2003
Revenues	348,755	330,548	316,768
Earnings from continuing operations	21,706	18,564	15,988
Earnings per share from continuing operations ($)			
Basic	1.01	0.87	0.74
Diluted	1.01	0.86	0.74
Net earnings	21,706	18,564	14,728
Earnings per share ($)			
Basic	1.01	0.87	0.68
Diluted	1.01	0.86	0.68
Total assets	370,683	369,977	363,097
Long-term liabilities	69,688	95,063	90,898
Dividend per share ($)	0.24	0.22	0.20
Coffee shipments *(millions of lbs.)*	25.3	24.9	23.1

* The fiscal year ended April 3, 2004 had 53 weeks.

Revenues increased 3.7% (1.7% on a weekly basis) in 2004 while net earnings advanced 26.0%. Besides the fact that 2004 had 53 weeks, this increase stemmed mainly from the following factors:

■ Steady growth in Canadian earnings.

■ Fiscal 2003 gave rise to non-recurring charges of $5.2 million or $3.6 million after taxes or $0.17 per share, related primarily to the integration of information and management systems. In 2003, Van Houtte also recorded an after-tax charge of $1.3 million or $0.06 per share as a loss from discontinued operations following the disposal of a European coffee services company.

Over the past three years, we have been managing our balance sheet more closely, limiting the growth of our total assets, and thanks to a strong operating cash flow, substantially reducing our debt load and increasing our dividend rate.

Review of operations – 2005

Van Houtte's financial statements have been prepared in accordance with Canadian generally accepted accounting principles ("GAAP") and in Canadian dollars. Unless expressly stated, the additional financial data appearing in this MD&A are also in Canadian dollars. Van Houtte has filed its 2005 audited consolidated financial statements with Canadian securities regulators, and these statements may be accessed through www.sedar.com or on the Van Houtte Web site at www.vanhoutte.com. This MD&A should be read in conjunction with these financial statements and related notes. In addition, once filed, Van Houtte's Annual Information Form for the fiscal year ended April 2, 2005 will be available through www.sedar.com.

Sales up 5.5%

For the fiscal year ended April 2, 2005, Van Houtte recorded consolidated sales of $348.8 million, compared with $330.5 million last year, an increase of 5.5% (7.5% on an average weekly basis).

This gain stems both from organic growth and the positive impact of coffee services acquisitions. It also reflects the negative impact of currency fluctuations and the disposal of certain vending business units in 2004 and 2005.

Moreover, the price of green coffee increased substantially during the fiscal year and part of this increase was passed on downstream. Without the impact of these price increases, 2005 sales growth for the year would have been 3.3% (5.2% on a weekly basis).

TABLE 4
Sources of Revenue Change, Fiscal 2005
(In thousands of dollars)

Revenues, fiscal 2004	**330,548**
Organic growth	12,087
Impact of acquisitions completed in 2004 and 2005	12,587
Impact of divestitures	(7,391)
Impact of selling price increases	7,500
Impact of currency fluctuations	(6,576)
Revenues, fiscal 2005	**348,755**

Consolidated earnings before interest, taxes, depreciation and amortization (EBITDA) for the year were $65.7 million, versus $59.6 million a year ago, an increase of 10.3%. The operating ratio (EBITDA/sales) was 18.8%, against 18.0% last year. Most of this improvement is attributable to Coffee Services.

TABLE 5
Sources of EBITDA Change, Fiscal 2005
(In thousands of dollars)

EBITDA, fiscal 2004	**59,562**
Impact of revenue growth	3,277
Impact of improved operating ratio	2,834
EBITDA, fiscal 2005	**65,673**

At $31.0 million, amortization and depreciation remained unchanged from last year.

Financial expenses amounted to $3.9 million or $1.0 million less than the $4.9 million recorded in 2004. This decrease, the second in as many years, stems from a reduction in the Company's debt load, made possible by disciplined balance sheet management and substantial cash flows.

Taxes were $7.0 million, for an effective tax rate of 22.8%, compared with $4.7 million and 19.7%. The increase in the effective tax rate is the result of our tax planning. Although optimal, some of our deductions are fixed and their relative impact decreases as taxable income increases.

Segmented analysis

TABLE 6
Segmented information
(In thousands of dollars, except for percentage change)

	Fiscal year ended April 2, 2005	Fiscal year ended April 3, 2004*	Change (%)
Sales			
Manufacturing and Marketing	155,948	142,257	9.6
Coffee Services	243,828	230,273	5.9
Inter-segment	(51,021)	(41,982)	21.5
Total sales	348,755	330,548	5.5
EBITDA			
Manufacturing and Marketing	32,213	31,442	2.5
Coffee Services	38,949	33,890	14.9
General expenses	(5,489)	(5,770)	(4.9)
Total EBITDA	65,673	59,562	10.3

* 53-week year.

Manufacturing and Marketing

Sales in the Manufacturing and Marketing segment reached $155.9 million in 2005, up 9.6% (11.7% on a weekly basis) over the $142.3 million recorded in 2004 on the strength of the entire segment. Currency fluctuations have a minimal impact on sales in this segment.

Coffee shipments were 25.3 million pounds, a 1.5% increase over 2004, which had one more week. Growth was 3.4% on an average weekly basis.

TABLE 7
Coffee Shipments by Distribution Channel and Brand, Fiscal 2004 and 2005
(In thousands of pounds)

	Fiscal 2005	(%)	Fiscal 2004*	(%)	Change (000 lbs)	Change (%)	Adjusted Change ** (%)
Retail networks							
Van Houtte brand	7,345	29.0	7,254	29.1	91	1.3	3.2
Other brands	9,119	36.1	9,426	37.8	(307)	(3.3)	(1.4)
Sub-total	16,464	65.1	16,679	66.9	(215)	(1.3)	0.6
Coffee Services							
Van Houtte brand	6,071	24.0	5,771	23.1	300	5.2	7.2
Other brands	2,768	10.9	2,487	10.0	281	11.3	13.4
Sub-total	8,838	34.9	8,257	33.1	581	7.0	9.1
Total	**25,303**	**100.0**	**24,937**	**100.0**	**366**	**1.5**	**3.4**

* 53-week year.
** The adjusted growth rates are determined based on the average weekly shipments each year.

Shipments to the growing Coffee Services segment advanced 7.0% in 2005 to 581,000 pounds. On a weekly basis, growth was 9.1%.

Retail shipments slipped from 16.7 to 16.5 million pounds in 2005. However, weekly shipments advanced 0.6%. Retail sales of the Van Houtte brand gained 3.2% on a weekly basis. Most of the decrease is attributable to our own brands other than Van Houtte, in particular Gold Cup and Orient Express labels, and to a lesser extent to the private labels produced for the supermarket chains that distribute our products.

The sales growth in the Manufacturing and Marketing segment is explained by the following factors:

■ An increase in the weighted average selling price of coffee due to:

  ➤ Price adjustments following increases in the price of green coffee, which has climbed back to its year 2000 level;

  ➤ A change in the product mix, namely, the relative increase in the Van Houtte brand as a proportion of sales to the detriment of our other brands and private labels;

Excluding the increase in the price of green coffee, sales in this segment would have advanced 4.3% (6.4% on a weekly basis).

■ An increase of more than 26% in VKI sales due to the execution of two major Coffee Services contracts for some 500 Suprema® coffeemakers for the Couche-Tard stores in Quebec and 1,000 Caffè Mio™ brewers for the Lowe's stores in the U.S. VKI's other activities also contributed to this growth, i.e., sales of VKI single-cup brewers and the Keurig-licensed coffeemaker to outside accounts.

Manufacturing and Marketing EBITDA was $32.2 million, up 2.5% (4.4% on a weekly basis) over the $31.4 million recorded last year. The operating ratio was 20.7% in 2005, compared with 22.1% in 2004. For the year overall, the gross margin rate on coffee remained unchanged as the increases in the price of green coffee were passed downstream in the distribution chain.

Three factors explain the decrease in operating ratio:

- The Manufacturing and Marketing segment stepped up its promotion and marketing efforts to further increase the awareness and equity of the Van Houtte brand outside Quebec, particularly in the Greater Toronto area. Following this investment, retail coffee shipments outside Quebec improved significantly but on a smaller growth base than in Quebec. Our products still have tremendous unexploited retail potential outside Quebec, especially in Ontario, the largest market in Canada.

- The corporate café bistros generated operating losses before they were sold. As well, we recorded as an operating expense a write-off of $272,425 in goodwill on the books of a number of corporate bistros.

- The increase in the price of fuel affected shipping costs.

Coffee Services

Coffee Services sales advanced 5.9% (7.9% on a weekly basis) in 2005 to $243.8 million, up from the $230.3 million recorded in 2004. This growth must be analyzed in light of the combined effect of the exchange rate on U.S. sales and the planned reduction in vending machine sales stemming from the disposal of certain business units in 2004 and 2005. On a constant exchange rate basis and excluding vending sales, sales advanced 13.6% (15.8% on a weekly basis).

In Canada, Coffee Services sales increased 6.7% (8.8% on a weekly basis). This growth was almost entirely organic, reflecting improved account retention and recruitment, as well as selling deeper to existing accounts.

In the U.S., sales climbed 16.5% after conversion to Canadian dollars and 23.7% (26.1% on a weekly basis) when expressed in U.S. dollars. Part of this growth is attributable to acquisitions made in 2004 and 2005.

EBITDA was up 14.9% over last year (17.1% on a weekly basis) to $39.0 million. This strong performance was achieved despite the erosion of the U.S. dollar and losses incurred on the disposal of certain vending business units. On a constant exchange rate basis and excluding vending machine operations, EBITDA rose 19.6%.

The operating ratio was 16.0% compared with 14.7% last year. Two factors explain this improvement: first, changes made to processes generated substantial operating savings, particularly in terms of selling expenses, and second, our network densification strategy produced the expected operating leverage – when our sales increase, costs increase less than proportionately.

These improvements more than offset the slight decrease in gross margin following stronger sales of coffee in K-Cups® for Keurig coffeemakers where the gross margin is lower than on other coffees offered by Coffee Services. However, since the Keurig machines require less capital than the other single-cup brewers, the return on investment is comparable.

TABLE 8
Installed Base of Single-Cup Brewers in Van Houtte's Coffee Services Network

	April 3, 2004	July 24, 2004	October 16, 2004	January 8, 2005	April 2, 2005
Canada	22,730	23,173	23,274	23,545	24,057
United States	17,681	18,997	19,275	19,410	20,082
Total	**40,411**	**42,170**	**42,549**	**42,955**	**44,139**

The number of single-cup coffeemakers installed in our Coffee Services network rose 9.2% during the year to 44,139 units at April 2, 2005. Acquisitions contributed to the good performance in the U.S. Organic growth was strong both in the U.S. and Canada, driven in large part by the agreement signed with Lowe's in the U.S.

On April 2, the Coffee Services segment had 70,919 active accounts, an increase of 8.3% over the 65,499 accounts active on April 3, 2004. The number of active accounts is greater than the number of single-cup coffeemakers as many clients still prefer the traditional pour-over brewing systems.

Intersegment sales and general corporate expenses

Intersegment climbed 21.5%, outpacing consolidated sales due to three main factors: 1) strong sales by VKI to Coffee Services; 2) coffee sales resulting from the growth of our Coffee Services network; and 3) the growing importance of our own coffees in this segment's sales.

General corporate expenses declined slightly. Last year, these expenses comprised non recurring charges related to the departure of the Company's CEO. However, certain general corporate expenses increased permanently in 2005, namely, the cost of complying with new governance and continuous disclosure rules, even if certain transitional costs in this regard will not recur, and the recording of executive stock-based compensation plans. This figure was $413,000 in 2005. In the past, this type of compensation was presented in a note to the financial statements but not included in the income statement.

Capital resources, financial position and outlook

Liquidity

Van Houtte's strong operating cash flows continue to grow, ending the year at $57.0 million, compared with $46.7 million in 2004. The main elements behind this gain were the increase in net earnings and a decline in future income taxes.

Cash flow per share stood at $2.65 ($2.64 diluted) compared with $2.18 ($2.17 diluted) a year ago. Changes in non-cash working capital generated $3.7 million in 2005 whereas they used $1.1 million in 2004.

Van Houtte spent $28.0 million on fixed asset acquisitions during the year, against $23.1 million in 2004. These investments were made chiefly in coffeemakers, the roasting plants and in information technology. They were financed out of operating cash flows.

The Company spent $9.3 million on acquisitions in 2005, compared with $13.9 million a year earlier. Most of these transactions took place in the U.S.

As a result of disciplined balance sheet management and strong cash flows, Van Houtte was able to increase its dividend payout to $5.2 million in 2005 versus $4.7 million a year ago and trim its long-term debt by $15.8 million.

Financial position and cash requirements

Working capital (not including the short-term portion of long-term debt) stood at $38.1 million on April 2, 2005, against $43.1 million a year earlier. This decrease, the second in as many years, is in line with the Company's strict capital management policy, developed in 2003. The increase in payables and accrued liabilities more than offset the increase in receivables and inventory.

Long-term assets consist of investments, fixed assets, goodwill, other assets and long-term future income taxes. Fixed assets declined slightly for the second year in a row. Depreciation of Coffee Services equipment and vending machines was greater than the net additions to fixed assets due notably to the divestiture of some vending business units in Canada.

Goodwill rose by $0.8 million. Although acquisitions added $5.9 million to goodwill, the decline in the U.S. dollar resulted in a devaluation of $4.8 million.

The Company's debt load (including the short-term portion of long-term debt) shrank for the third consecutive year, from $107.5 million to $88.4 million following the decrease of $15.8 million in long-term debt and the impact of exchange rate fluctuations on long-term debt. The debt/capital ratio stood at 26.8% at April 2, 2005, against 31.9% a year earlier.

Non-controlling interest was $6.5 million at April 2, 2005, compared with $5.6 million at the end of fiscal 2004.

The Company will continue with its disciplined investment policy. Set at approximately $28 million, the capital budget for fiscal 2006 is similar to that of fiscal 2005.

TABLE 9
Contractual Obligations by Term at April 2, 2005

	Payments Due by Term (Thousands of dollars)				
Contractual Obligations	Total	Less than 1 year	1-2 years	3-4 years	5 and more
Long-term debt	88,356	28,024	59,753	579	–
Net capital leases	21,229	5,855	8,041	2,546	4,787
Purchasing contracts – green coffee	10,094	10,094	–	–	–
Total	119,679	43,973	67,794	3,125	4,787

Van Houtte's operations generate substantial cash flows. Depreciation for fiscal 2006 is projected at $32 million. As at April 2, 2005, Van Houtte had unused credit facilities of $65 million.

In management's opinion, the Company has the necessary financial resources to pursue its operations and implement its business plan. Moreover, it has the financial flexibility to seize interesting acquisition opportunities that are consistent with its business plan.

Quarterly information

As is typical in our industry, particularly in the Coffee Services segment, business slows in the summer, which overlaps Van Houtte's first and second quarters. However, this fluctuation is tempered by the fact that the first quarter has 16 weeks whereas each of the other three has 12. Consequently, we record the strongest sales of the year in the first quarter but not necessarily the highest earnings.

TABLE 10
Unaudited quarterly results
(In thousands of dollars, except per share amounts)

| | 16 weeks ended: | 12 weeks ended: | | | 16 weeks ended: | 12 weeks ended: | | |
	July 19, 2003	October 11, 2003	January 3, 2004	April 3, 2004*	July 24, 2004	October 16, 2004	January 8, 2005	April 2, 2005*
Sales	94,054	72,521	77,671	86,302	102,574	77,695	82,542	85,943
EBITDA	14,143	13,063	14,787	17,569	18,508	15,107	16,313	15,745
Net earnings	3,302	4,025	4,773	6,464	5,345	4,673	5,487	6,201
Earnings per share ($)	0.16	0.19	0.22	0.30	0.25	0.22	0.25	0.29

* The quarter and fiscal year ended April 3, 2004 had 13 and 53 weeks respectively. The quarter and fiscal year ended April 2, 2005 had 12 and 52 weeks respectively.

Fiscal 2004 began on a relatively positive economic note in Canada but less so in the U.S. where the job market remained sluggish, particularly in the regions and sectors where our Coffee Services are concentrated. It was at this time that we began streamlining our vending machine operations, selectively disposing of business units whose performance fell below expectations. This streamlining continued into 2005. As well, in 2004 the U.S. dollar tumbled on the currency markets, which had a significant impact on the conversion of our U.S. sales into Canadian dollars.

Moreover, the departure of the Company's chief executive officer gave rise to non-recurring charges of approximately $0.04 per share.

These factors help explain the downturn in sales and earnings in the first quarter. However, despite the impact of many exogenous factors, we promptly took measures to revitalize sales and reorganize our operations with the result that sales rebounded in the second quarter. Fiscal 2004 ended with a very strong fourth quarter, notably because it had 13 rather than the usual 12 weeks but also because of the measures implemented since the beginning of the year.

These measures had a ripple effect into 2005 as both Coffee Services and the Company in general confirmed their return to growth. Still, sales growth continued to be hampered by the erosion of the U.S. dollar and the divestiture of the vending business units undertaken as part of a streamlining effort for this network. However, the operating ratio improved from quarter to quarter, reflecting greater operating efficiency and the positive impact of the growth on our operating leverage.

Fourth Quarter 2005

The last quarter of the year ended with net earnings of $6.2 million or $0.29 per share (basic and diluted), compared with $6.5 million and $0.30 per share (basic and diluted) for the same period in 2004. The fourth quarter of 2005 had 12 weeks, one week less than the comparable year-earlier quarter. The disposal of a number of vending business units had a downward impact on sales.

The slight decrease in sales from $86.3 million in the fourth quarter of 2004 to $85.9 million in 2005 is largely explained by this thirteenth week and to a lesser extent by the effect of the lower U.S. dollar and the divestiture of some vending business units. On a constant exchange rate basis and excluding vending operations, sales for the quarter advanced 4.3% or 13.0% on a weekly basis.

EBITDA fell by 10.4% to $15.7 million. On a constant exchange rate basis and excluding vending operations, EBITDA decreased 8.2% or 0.5% on a weekly basis.

TABLE 11
Quarterly segmented results
(In thousands of dollars, except for percentage change)

	Quarter ended April 2, 2005*	Quarter ended April 3, 2004*	Change * (%)
Sales			
Manufacturing and Marketing	39,411	35,390	11.4
Coffee Services	60,471	62,052	(2.5)
Inter-segment	(13,939)	(11,140)	25.1
Total sales	85,943	86,302	(0.4)
EBITDA			
Manufacturing and Marketing	6,913	8,207	(15.8)
Coffee Services	10,146	10,285	(1.4)
General expenses	(1,316)	(923)	42.5
Total EBITDA	15,743	17,569	(10.4)

* The quarter ended April 2, 2005 had 12 weeks; the quarter ended April 3, 2004 had 13 weeks.

Manufacturing and Marketing

Sales reached $39.4 million during the quarter, up 11.4% or 20.6% on an average weekly basis, mainly on the strength of coffee and VKI sales. Currency fluctuations have a minimal impact on sales in this segment.

Up 2.0% or 10.5% on a weekly basis over the fourth quarter in 2004, coffee shipments reached 6.1 million pounds.

TABLE 12
Coffee Shipments by Distribution Channel and Brand, Fourth Quarter, Fiscal 2004 and 2005
(In thousands of pounds)

	Quarter ended April 2, 2005*	(%)	Quarter ended April 3, 2004*	(%)	Change (000 lbs)	Change (%)	Adjusted Change** (%)
Retail networks							
Van Houtte brand	1,757	28.9	1,801	30.2	(44)	(2.4)	5.7
Other brands	2,033	33.4	2,014	33.8	19	0.9	9.4
Sub-total	3,790	62.3	3,815	64.0	(25)	(0.7)	7.6
Coffee Services							
Van Houtte brand	1,548	25.5	1,529	25.7	19	1.2	9.7
Other brands	744	12.2	616	10.3	128	20.8	30.8
Sub-total	2,292	37.7	2,146	36.0	146	6.8	15.7
Total	6,082	100.0	5,961	100.0	121	2.0	10.5

* The quarter ended April 2, 2005 has 12 weeks; the quarter ended April 3, 2004 has 13 weeks.
** The adjusted growth rate is calculated based on the average weekly shipments in each quarter.

■ Sales growth in the Manufacturing and Marketing segment reflect higher VKI and coffee sales, which increased in both volume and price. Some of the increase in volume is due to inventory building by some accounts in anticipation of the announced price hikes.

■ EBITDA for the Manufacturing and Marketing segment was $6.9 million, compared with $8.2 million in the year-ago quarter. The operating ratio stood at 17.5%, against 23.2% last year. The gross margin rate on intersegment and external coffee sales decreased during the quarter due to the magnitude and suddenness of the greater-than-expected increases in the price of green coffee. The impact of this change will be gradually eliminated over the first and second quarters of fiscal 2006. The operating ratio was also adversely affected by the increase in promotional and marketing expenses outside Quebec. Higher oil prices had an effect on shipping costs.

Coffee Services

Coffee Services sales were $60.5 million in the last quarter, down 2.5% over the $62.1 million recorded a year earlier. On an average weekly basis, sales advanced 5.6%. On a constant currency basis and excluding vending machine sales, sales grew 3.7% or 12.3% on an average weekly basis.

In Canada, sales slipped 1.6% but advanced 6.6% on an average weekly basis on the strength of organic growth.

In the U.S., sales improved 3.1% (11.7% on an average weekly basis) after conversion to Canadian dollars or 14.5% (24.1% on a weekly basis) in U.S. dollars. This performance was due in part to acquisitions made in 2004 and 2005.

EBITDA for the Coffee Services segment stood at $10.1 million, down 1.4% over the year-ago period. On a constant exchange rate basis and excluding vending operations, EBITDA rose 2.7%.

The operating ratio was 16.8% for the quarter, compared with 16.6% a year ago.

Outlook

For the past two years, Van Houtte has been executing a three-pronged strategy: 1) accelerate sales growth in the retail and Coffee Services networks in order to improve profitability; 2) exercise disciplined cost management; and 3) optimize capital management.

This strategy, however, poses different challenges depending on the region.

■ In Eastern Canada, where the Van Houtte brands are well established, we have successfully improved our operating efficiency in order to enhance both the service quality in the Coffee Services segment and our profitability. We must continue to be proactive and vigilant to maintain our market share and leadership in the retail sector, particularly in Quebec.

■ In the West, we have established ourselves as the market leader in coffee services. Our challenge in this region is to use this segment as a springboard to accelerate the penetration of the Van Houtte brand across all the distribution channels, especially retail. We have made great strides in terms of brand awareness, and retail sales have grown significantly in the last two years.

■ In absolute terms, Ontario offers the best potential for growth, both in retail and coffee services. The fact that per capita sales in Ontario are lower than in the other regions of Canada bespeaks untapped growth potential. However, because it is also the most competitive market in Canada, we will continue to invest heavily to boost penetration both in the retail and Coffee Services networks.

■ The job market has strengthened in the U.S. where we will continue implementing our organic and acquisition growth strategy in our current territories with a view to increasing the network's density.

We do not expect uniform quarterly growth in 2006. More specifically, the adjustments to our sourcing and pricing strategy that we made in the last quarter of 2005 in response to the recent increases in green coffee prices will only be fully effective from the second half of the first quarter of 2006. Consequently, this quarter will not perform up to potential. Nevertheless, Van Houtte expects net earnings for fiscal 2006 to increase between 10% and 15%, which will be fuelled equally by organic growth and acquisitions.

Dividend policy

The dividend policy established by the Board of Directors calls for deciding at mid-year whether dividends should be paid, and if so, the payout amount based on the Company's financial position and investment plans. Thus, a dividend of $0.24 per share was paid in fiscal 2005 for a total payout of $5.2 million, corresponding to approximately 10% of the previous year's cash flow.

Risks and uncertainties

Van Houtte's main product is coffee, a commodity subject to considerable price fluctuations. An increase in the price of coffee can adversely affect sales, profit margins or both. Van Houtte specializes in gourmet coffee, and past experience has shown that price sensitivity is less pronounced in the gourmet coffee segment since consumers are already prepared to pay more for a superior product. However, there is no assurance that this behaviour will continue.

Coffee destined for the retail sector represents nearly 25% of Van Houtte's total sales. Our access to this market depends on agreements signed with retailers, mostly supermarket chains. In most of their stores, we design, set up and stock the gourmet coffee department. However, some of these agreements allow the retailers to vary the number of Van Houtte products they carry, or even to decide whether or not they offer our products at all. As well, some chains have Van Houtte roast and package their coffee under private label. There is no assurance that these agreements and the related coffee volumes will be renewed.

Coffee Services account for more than 70% of sales and almost 60% of EBITDA. Because these services are offered mainly to workplaces, particularly offices, demand varies with the general economic and employment situation. A large portion of our Coffee Services costs are fixed in the near term, thereby creating significant operating leverage. When sales decrease, the corresponding decrease in EBITDA will be higher. Conversely, when sales increase, the corresponding decrease in EBITDA will be higher.

Our subsidiary VKI and affiliate Keurig have both developed cutting-edge brewing technology, providing us with a strategic edge in the coffee services market. Should equally advanced technologies be developed and offered on the market, our strategic position and development capacity would be weakened.

Finally, most of our loans are at variable interest rates determined according to the bankers' acceptance rates or the prime rate. Since our loans are both in Canadian and U.S. dollars, the interest rates could fluctuate based on the monetary policies of the Bank of Canada and the U.S. Federal Reserve. A sudden major increase in interest rates would reduce our profitability.

Changes in accounting policies

In fiscal 2005, Van Houtte began recording the cost of executive compensation in the form of stock options. Previously, this compensation was disclosed in a note to the financial statements but was not included in the computation of the Company's results, and therefore had no impact on earnings calculation.

Significant estimates

Some amounts in the financial statements or in this MD&A are estimates by management based on knowledge of current or anticipated events.

Goodwill

Goodwill is the difference between the acquisition cost of an enterprise over the fair value of its tangible and intangible net assets at the time of acquisition. Goodwill is revised downward if the fair value of an operating unit is less than its book value. This fair value is estimated annually. In 2005, Van Houtte recorded a write-off of $272,425 related to some corporate café bistros.

Others

Management uses other estimates when preparing financial statements but these have no material impact on the Company's earnings or value and consequently are not relevant.

Related party transactions

There were no material related party transactions in 2005.

Disclosure controls and procedures

We have evaluated the effectiveness of the disclosure controls and procedures as of the end of the period covered by the annual filings and concluded about its effectiveness.

Forward-looking information

This analysis contains forward-looking statements reflecting Van Houtte's objectives, estimates and expectations. Such statements may be marked by the use of verbs such as "believe," "anticipate," "estimate" and "expect" as well as the use of the future or conditional tense. By their very nature, such statements involve risks and uncertainty. Consequently, results could differ materially from the Company's projections or expectations.

Management's Responsibility for Financial Statements

These financial statements have been prepared by management in conformity with Canadian generally accepted accounting principles and include amounts that are based on best estimates and judgments.

Management of the Company and of its subsidiaries, in furtherance of the integrity and objectivity of the data in the financial statements, has developed and maintains systems of internal accounting controls and supports a program of internal audit. Management believes that these systems of internal accounting controls provide reasonable assurance that financial records are reliable and form a proper basis for the preparation of the financial statements and that assets are properly accounted for and safeguarded, and that the preparation and presentation of other financial information are consistent with the financial statements.

The Board of Directors carries out its responsibility for the financial statements principally through its Audit Committee, consisting solely of outside directors. The Audit Committee reviews the Company's annual consolidated financial statements, and management's discussion and analysis and recommends them to the Board of Directors for approval. The Audit Committee meets with the Company's management, internal and external auditors to discuss internal controls over the financial reporting process, auditing matters and financial reporting issues and formulates the appropriate recommendations to the Board of Directors. The auditors appointed by the shareholders have full access to the Audit Committee, with and without management being present.

These financial statements have been examined by the auditors appointed by the shareholders, KPMG LLP, chartered accountants, and their report is presented hereafter.

Jean-Yves Monette
President and Chief Executive Officer

Gérard Geoffrion
Executive Vice-President and Chief Financial Officer

May 20, 2005

Auditors' Report to the Shareholders

We have audited the consolidated balance sheets of Van Houtte Inc. as at April 2, 2005 and April 3, 2004 and the consolidated statements of earnings, retained earnings and cash flows for the years then ended. These financial statements are the responsibility of the Company's management. Our responsibility is to express an opinion on these financial statements based on our audits.

We conducted our audits in accordance with Canadian generally accepted auditing standards. Those standards require that we plan and perform an audit to obtain reasonable assurance whether the financial statements are free of material misstatement. An audit includes examining, on a test basis, evidence supporting the amounts and disclosures in the financial statements. An audit also includes assessing the accounting principles used and significant estimates made by management, as well as evaluating the overall financial statement presentation.

In our opinion, these consolidated financial statements present fairly, in all material respects, the financial position of the Company as at April 2, 2005 and April 3, 2004 and the results of its operations and its cash flows for the years then ended in accordance with Canadian generally accepted accounting principles.

Chartered Accountants

KPMG LLP

Montreal, Canada
May 20, 2005

759

Consolidated Statements of Earnings

Years ended April 2, 2005 and April 3, 2004
(In thousands of dollars, except for earnings per share data)

	2005	2004
Revenues	$348,755	$ 330,548
Cost of goods sold and operating expenses	283,082	270,986
	65,673	59,562
Depreciation and amortization	31,016	31,030
Financial expenses *(note 3)*	3,886	4,860
Operating profit before the undernoted	30,771	23,672
Income taxes *(note 4)*	7,012	4,671
Earnings before the undernoted	23,759	19,001
Share in net earnings of companies subject to significant influence	72	39
Share of non-controlling interest in subsidiary companies	(2,125)	(476)
Net earnings	$ 21,706	$ 18,564
EARNINGS PER SHARE *(note 5)*:		
Basic:		
Net earnings	$ 1.01	$ 0.87
Diluted:		
Net earnings	$ 1.01	$ 0.86
Weighted average number of shares outstanding *(in thousands)*	21,519	21,428
Diluted weighted average number of shares *(in thousands)*	21,598	21,532

See accompanying notes to consolidated financial statements.

Consolidated Statements of Retained Earnings

Years ended April 2, 2005 and April 3, 2004
(In thousands of dollars)

	2005	2004
Retained earnings, as stated, beginning of year	$ 99,757	$ 86,184
Change in accounting policy – stock-based compensation *(note 1 c))*	(1,630)	–
Restated retained earnings, beginning of year	98,127	86,184
Net earnings	21,706	18,564
Dividends	(5,176)	(4,719)
Premium paid on redemption of subordinate voting shares *(note 12)*	(54)	(272)
Retained earnings, end of year	$114,603	$ 99,757

See accompanying notes to consolidated financial statements.

Consolidated Balance Sheets

April 2, 2005 and April 3, 2004
(In thousands of dollars)

	2005	2004
ASSETS		
Current assets:		
Cash	$ 5,338	$ 7,341
Accounts receivable	41,298	36,396
Income taxes receivable	–	576
Inventories *(note 6)*	28,045	26,775
Prepaid expenses	3,310	3,301
Future income taxes *(note 4)*	1,681	1,859
	79,672	76,248
Investments *(note 7)*	18,939	18,128
Fixed assets *(note 8)*	115,805	116,963
Goodwill *(note 9)*	141,631	140,781
Other assets *(note 10)*	7,526	7,315
Future income taxes *(note 4)*	7,110	10,542
	$ 370,683	$ 369,977
LIABILITIES AND SHAREHOLDERS' EQUITY		
Current liabilities:		
Accounts payable and accrued liabilities	38,937	32,541
Income taxes payable	1,965	–
Deferred income	692	576
Current portion of long-term debt *(note 11)*	28,024	22,710
	69,618	55,827
Long-term debt *(note 11)*	60,332	84,796
Employee future benefits	1,764	1,562
Future income taxes *(note 4)*	1,075	3,083
Non-controlling interest	6,517	5,622
Shareholders' equity:		
Capital stock *(note 12)*	128,250	127,076
Contributed surplus *(notes 1 c) and 12))*	2,043	–
Retained earnings	114,603	99,757
Currency translation adjustment *(note 13)*	(13,519)	(7,746)
	231,377	219,087
Commitments and guarantees *(note 14)*		
Contingencies *(note 15)*		
	$ 370,683	$ 369,977

See accompanying notes to consolidated financial statements.

On behalf of the Board:

Jean-Yves Monette
Director

Robert Parizeau
Director

Consolidated Statements of Cash Flows

Years ended April 2, 2005 and April 3, 2004
(In thousands of dollars)

	2005	2004
CASH FLOWS FROM OPERATING ACTIVITIES		
Net earnings from continuing operations:	$ 21,706	$ 18,564
Adjustments for:		
Depreciation of fixed assets	28,536	28,881
Amortization of other assets	2,480	2,149
Amortization of financial expenses *(note 3)*	271	478
Future income taxes	1,308	(3,194)
Non-controlling interest	2,125	476
Equity in net earnings of companies subject to significant influence	(72)	(39)
Stock-based compensation *(note 12)*	413	–
Loss on write-off of other assets	272	–
Gain on disposal of fixed assets	(254)	(91)
Loss (gain) on disposal of businesses	304	(393)
Gain on foreign exchange	(103)	(126)
	56,986	46,705
Net change in non-cash balances related		
to working capital items *(note 16)*	3,698	(1,141)
	60,684	45,564
CASH FLOWS FROM INVESTING ACTIVITIES		
Business acquisitions *(note 17)*	(9,330)	(13,884)
Additions to fixed assets	(27,986)	(23,116)
Proceeds from disposal of fixed assets	1,043	1,503
Disposal of investments	(944)	(1,139)
Increase in other assets	(2,187)	(2,801)
	(39,404)	(39,437)
CASH FLOWS FROM FINANCING ACTIVITIES		
Issue of subordinate voting shares *(note 12)*	1,214	285
Redemption of subordinate voting shares for cancellation *(note 12)*	(94)	(710)
(Decrease) increase in long-term debt	(15,804)	51
Dividends	(5,176)	(4,719)
Dividends paid to non-controlling shareholders of subsidiaries	(1,817)	(830)
	(21,677)	(5,923)
Effect of exchange rate changes on cash denominated		
in foreign currency	(1,606)	(2,011)
Net decrease in cash	(2,003)	(1,807)
Cash, beginning of year	7,341	9,148
Cash, end of year	$ 5,338	$ 7,341

See accompanying notes to consolidated financial statements.

Notes to Consolidated Financial Statements

Years ended April 2, 2005 and April 3, 2004 (Tabular amounts are expressed in thousands of dollars)

Van Houtte Inc. is incorporated under the Canada Business Corporations Act. The Company is an important gourmet coffee roaster, marketer and distributor. It markets its gourmet coffees across Canada and the US through distribution channels that include coffee services, retail stores, cafés-bistros, on-line shopping and food service networks.

Note 1
Changes in accounting policies

The Company has made certain changes in accounting policies to conform to the new accounting standards issued and applicable to the Company.

a) Long-lived assets

Effective April 4, 2004, the Company adopted the CICA Handbook Section 3063, "Impairment of Long-Lived Assets". Long-lived assets, including fixed assets and intangible assets with finite useful lives, are amortized over their useful lives. The Company reviews long-lived assets for impairment whenever events or changes in circumstances indicate that the carrying amount of a group of assets may not be recoverable. If the sum of undiscounted net cash flows expected to result from the use and eventual disposition of a group of assets is less than its carrying amount, it is considered to be impaired. An impairment loss is measured as the amount by which the carrying amount of the group of assets exceeds its fair value. At April 2, 2005, no such impairment had occurred.

b) Asset retirement obligations

Effective April 4, 2004, the Company retroactively adopted CICA Handbook Section 3110 "Asset Retirement Obligations". The standard provides guidance for the recognition, measurement and disclosure of liabilities for asset retirement obligations and the associated asset retirement costs. The standard applies to legal obligations associated with the retirement of a tangible long-lived asset that result from acquisition, construction, development or normal operations.

The standard requires the Company to record the fair value of a liability for an asset retirement obligation in the year in which it is incurred and when a reasonable estimate of fair value can be made. The asset retirement cost is capitalized as part of the related asset and is amortized to earnings over time. The standard describes the fair value of a liability for an asset retirement obligation as the amount at which that liability could be settled in a current transaction between willing parties, that is, other than in forced or liquidation transaction and is adjusted for any changes resulting from passage of time and any changes to the timing or the amount of the original estimate or undiscounted cash flows. The Company is subsequently required to allocate the asset retirement cost to expense using a systematic and rational method over the assets' useful life.

The adoption of this standard had no impact on the Company's financial position, results of operations or cash flows.

c) Stock-based compensation and other stock-based payments

In 2003, The Canadian Institute of Chartered Accountants ("CICA") amended its pronouncement relating to stock-based compensation requiring companies to measure and expense all equity instruments awarded to employees and directors starting in the fiscal year beginning on or after January 1, 2004 in accordance with the fair value method. The fair value of stock options to employees and directors is determined at the date of grant using the Black-Scholes option pricing model, and the

Note 1: Changes in accounting policies (continued)

compensation charge is expensed over the vesting period of the options. The transitional provisions provide for a prospective treatment to this change in accounting policy for those companies who adopt this new pronouncement for fiscal years commencing before January 1, 2004, and a retroactive treatment for those companies adopting this new pronouncement after January 1, 2004.

Effective April 4, 2004, the Company applied the retroactive treatment without restatement, for options granted since March 31, 2002. The adoption by the Company of this standard did not have any effect on its results, financial position or cash flows, except for the following reclassifications included in shareholders' equity, an increase in contributed surplus of $1,630,000 and a decrease in retained earnings of $1,630,000. For the year ended April 2, 2005, the compensation expense of $413,000 was recorded in the statement of earnings and credited to contributed surplus.

Prior to April 4, 2004, no compensation expense was recognized when stock options were granted to employees and directors. However, the Company provided pro forma information as if the fair value method had been applied.

d) Hedging relationships

Effective April 4, 2004, the Company applied Accounting Guideline ("AcG") AcG-13, "Hedging Relationships", that presents its view on the identification, designation, documentation and effectiveness of hedging relationships, for the purpose of applying hedge accounting, as well as on the discontinuance of hedge accounting. The adoption of this new standard had no material impact on the Company's consolidated financial statements.

Note 2
Significant accounting policies

The consolidated financial statements are prepared in accordance with Canadian generally accepted accounting principles.

a) Consolidation and long-term investments

The consolidated financial statements include the accounts of Van Houtte Inc. and all its subsidiaries (the "Company"). The major subsidiaries are Red Carpet Food Systems Inc., Selena Coffee Inc., Filterfresh Coffee Service, Inc., including its principal subsidiaries (Corporate Coffee Services, LLC and Potomac Coffee, LLC), VKI Technologies Inc. and Les Cafés Orient Express Ltée.

Investments in joint ventures are accounted for using the proportionate consolidation method. Joint ventures represent a negligible portion of the Company's operations. Investments in companies subject to significant influence are accounted for by the equity method. Portfolio investments are recorded at cost and would be written down in the case of a permanent impairment. Investments in companies in which the Company believes it does not exercise a significant influence are classified as portfolio investments.

b) Inventories

Raw materials are stated at the lower of cost, based on the first-in, first-out method, and replacement value. Finished goods and work-in-process are stated at the lower of average cost and net realizable value.

Raw materials purchased using commodity contracts are accounted for at the purchase price set out under the terms and conditions of these contracts.

c) Fixed assets

Fixed assets are stated at cost, net of any investment tax credits which are accounted for when qualified expenditures are incurred. Interest expense and other direct costs relating to major capital projects are capitalized to the cost of fixed assets until the commercial production stage.

Note 2: Significant accounting policies (continued)

Depreciation is calculated using the straight-line method over the following periods:

Asset	Period
Buildings	20 to 30 years
Coffee service equipment	7 years
Vending equipment	12 years
Machinery and equipment	5 to 15 years
Furniture	10 years
Computer equipment	3 years
Rolling stock	3 to 15 years
Leasehold improvements	Term of lease

d) Goodwill and other intangible assets

Goodwill and intangible assets with indefinite useful lives are not amortized.

Goodwill is tested for impairment annually, or more frequently if events or changes in circumstances indicate that the asset might be impaired. The impairment test is carried out in two steps. In the first step, the carrying amount of the reporting unit is compared with its fair value. When the fair value of a reporting unit exceeds its carrying amount, then goodwill of the reporting unit is considered not to be impaired and the second step of the impairment test is not required. The second step is carried out when the carrying amount of a reporting unit exceeds its fair value, in which case the implied fair value of the reporting unit's goodwill is compared with its carrying amount to measure the amount of the impairment loss, if any. When the carrying amount of the reporting unit's goodwill exceeds the implied fair value of the goodwill, an impairment loss is recognized in an amount equal to the excess and is presented as a separate line item in the statement of earnings before extraordinary items and discontinued operations.

Intangible assets acquired in business combinations which have an indefinite useful life, are also tested for impairment annually, or more frequently if events or changes in circumstances indicate that the asset might be impaired. The impairment test compares the carrying amount of the intangible asset with its fair value, and an impairment loss is recognized in the statement of earnings for the excess of the carrying value over the fair value.

Intangible assets with finite useful lives such as non-compete agreements, are amortized using the straight-line method over the term of the agreement.

e) Other assets

Deferred development costs, net of applicable research and development tax credits, represent costs incurred to develop new coffee brewing equipment, brewers and other. Deferred costs are amortized on a straight-line basis over three years.

Patents and rights are recorded at cost and are amortized using the straight-line method over 17 years.

The deferred financing costs related to long-term financing are amortized using the straight-line method over the term of the related long-term debt.

Other assets, which include start-up costs, are primarily amortized over a period of 3 years.

Management reviews periodically the value and amortization period of other assets. A permanent decline, if such be the case, will be determined based on future undiscounted cash flows.

f) Income taxes

The Company follows the asset and liability method of accounting for income taxes. Under this method, future income tax assets and liabilities are recognized for the estimated future tax consequences attributable to differences between the financial statements carrying amounts of existing assets and liabilities and their respective tax bases. Future income tax assets and

Note 2: Significant accounting policies (continued)

liabilities are measured using enacted or substantively enacted tax rates expected to apply when the assets are realized or the liabilities settled. Future income tax assets are recognized and, if realization is not considered "more likely than not" a valuation allowance is provided. The effect on future income tax assets and liabilities of a change in tax rates is recognized in income in the period that substantive enactment or enactment occurs.

g) Employee future benefits

The Company accrues the estimated cost of the contractual termination benefits, when it is probable that employees will be entitled to benefits and the amount can be reasonably estimated.

h) Foreign currency translation

Net assets of self-sustaining foreign operations are translated using the current rate method. Adjustments arising from this translation are deferred and recorded as a separate item under shareholders' equity and are included in income only when a reduction in the net investment in these foreign operations is realized. Gains or losses on foreign currency balances or trans-actions that are designated as hedges of a net investment in self-sustaining foreign operations are offset against exchange losses or gains included in the currency translation adjustment account included in shareholders' equity.

Other foreign currency transactions entered into by the Company are translated using the temporal method. Translation gains and losses are included in the statement of earnings.

i) Derivative financial instruments

The Company uses various derivative financial instruments to manage its exposure to fluctuations in interest rates, foreign currency exchange rates and commodity pricing. The Company does not hold or use any derivative instruments for speculative trading purposes.

The Company documents all relationships between hedging instruments and hedged items, as well as its risk management objective and strategy for undertaking various hedge transactions. This process includes linking all derivatives to specific assets and liabilities or to specific firm commitments or forecasted transactions.

The Company enters into interest rate swaps in order to manage the impact of fluctuating interest rates on its long-term debt. These swap agreements require the periodic exchange of payments without the exchange of the notional principal amount on which the payments are based. The Company designates its interest rate swap agreements as hedges of the underlying debt. Interest expense on the debt is adjusted to include the payments made or received under the interest rate swaps.

Realized and unrealized gains or losses associated with derivative instruments, which have been terminated or cease to be effective prior to maturity, are deferred under other current or non-current assets or liabilities on the balance sheet and recognized in earnings in the period in which the underlying hedged transaction is recognized. In the event a designated hedged item is sold, extinguished or matures prior to the termination of the related derivative instrument, any realized or unrealized gain or loss on such derivative instrument is recognized in earnings.

j) Revenue recognition

Revenue is recognized when goods are delivered or when services are provided. Rental fees are billed on a periodic or a monthly basis and recognized when services are provided. When clients are invoiced, the portion of unearned revenues is recorded under deferred revenues.

k) Use of estimates

The preparation of financial statements requires management to make estimates and assumptions that affect the reported amounts of assets and liabilities, related amounts of revenues and expenses and disclosure of contingent assets and liabilities. Significant areas requiring the use of management estimates relate to the determination of the useful life of assets for amortiza-tion and evaluation of net recoverable amounts, the determination of the fair value of portfolio investments, the determination of the fair value of assets acquired and liabilities assumed in business combinations, implied fair value of goodwill, provisions for income taxes and determination of future income tax assets and liabilities and the determination of the fair value of financial instruments. Actual results could differ from those estimates.

Note 3
Financial expenses

	2005	2004
Interest on long-term debt	$ 3,615	$ 4,382
Amortization of financial expenses	271	478
	$ 3,886	$ 4,860

Note 4
Income taxes

Income tax expense is detailed as follows:

	2005	2004
Current	$ 5,704	$ 7,865
Future	1,308	(3,194)
	$ 7,012	$ 4,671

The following table reconciles the statutory tax rate with the effective tax rate:

	2005	2004
Combined statutory tax rate	31.9%	33.2%
Earnings taxed (losses recovered) at a different rate than the statutory rate	(5.8)	(9.5)
Manufacturing and processing deduction	–	0.2
Adjustment to future income tax assets and liabilities for enacted changes in tax laws and rates	(0.1)	(1.1)
Other items	(3.2)	(3.1)
Effective tax rate	22.8%	19.7%

The tax effects of temporary differences that give rise to significant portion of the future tax assets and future tax liabilities are as follows:

	2005	2004
Future income tax assets – current:		
Employee future benefits	$ 574	$ 624
Reserve deductible next year	1,107	1,235
	1,681	1,859
Future income tax assets – non-current:		
Tax losses carried forward	17,393	16,954
Differences between book and tax bases of fixed assets	2,438	1,676
Differences between book and tax bases of other assets	177	135
Valuation allowance	(1,622)	–
Total future income tax assets – non-current	18,386	18,765
Future income tax liabilities – non-current:		
Differences between book and tax bases of fixed assets	4,069	4,301
Differences between book and tax bases of other assets	8,282	7,005
Total future income tax liabilities	12,351	11,306
Net future income tax assets	$ 7,716	$ 9,318

Note 4: Income taxes (continued)

These future tax assets and liabilities are presented as follows in the consolidated balance sheet:

	2005	2004
Future income tax assets:		
Current	$ 1,681	$ 1,859
Long-term	7,110	10,542
	8,791	12,401
Future income tax liabilities	1,075	3,083
Net future income tax assets	$ 7,716	$ 9,318

The Company has not recognized a future tax liability for the undistributed earnings of its subsidiaries in 2005 and in prior years because the Company does not expect those unremitted earnings to reverse and become taxable to the Company in the foreseeable future. A future tax liability will be recognized when the Company expects that it will recover these undistributed earnings in a taxable manner.

As at April 2, 2005, the Company had net operating loss carryforwards for income tax purposes available to reduce future federal, provincial and US federal taxable income of approximately $14,895,000, $15,726,000 and $30,877,000, respectively. These losses will expire as follows:

	Federal	Provincial	US Federal
2008	$ 255	$ 294	$ 85
2009	1,311	1,308	–
2010	5,837	8,012	246
2014	6,168	4,439	1,051
2015	1,324	1,673	377
2018 to 2024	–	–	29,118
	$ 14,895	$ 15,726	$ 30,877

As at April 2, 2005, the Company also had capital losses to carry forward of $1,514,000 without expiry dates. The future tax asset related to these operating losses is recorded in the financial statements.

Note 5
Earnings per share

Basic earnings per share is calculated by dividing the net earnings attributable to the common shareholders by the weighted average daily number of common shares outstanding during the year.

Diluted earnings per share is calculated by dividing the net earnings attributable to the common shareholders by the weighted average number of common shares outstanding restated to take into account the potential dilutive impact of the exercise of the stock options under the treasury stock method.

	2005	2004
	(in thousands)	*(in thousands)*
Weighted average number of outstanding common shares	21,519	21,428
Potential dilutive impact	79	104
Weighted average number of common and dilutive shares	21,598	21,532

Note 6
Inventories

	2005	2004
Raw materials	$ 11,008	$ 10,685
Work-in-process	564	657
Finished goods	16,473	15,433
	$ 28,045	$ 26,775

Note 7
Investments

	2005	2004
Shares in companies subject to significant influence, voting and participating, at equity value	$ 427	$ 383
Advances to companies subject to significant influence and to minority shareholders, with various interest rates and payment terms	3,092	2,325
Portfolio investment	15,420	15,420
	$ 18,939	$ 18,128

Note 8
Fixed assets

	2005		
	Cost	Accumulated depreciation	Net book value
Land	$ 1,571	$ –	$ 1,571
Buildings	15,229	5,098	10,131
Coffee service equipment and vending equipment	153,020	84,644	68,376
Machinery and equipment	41,107	22,394	18,713
Furniture, computer equipment and leasehold improvements	25,844	16,412	9,432
Rolling stock	18,164	10,582	7,582
	$ 254,935	$ 139,130	$ 115,805

	2004		
	Cost	Accumulated depreciation	Net book value
Land	$ 1,571	$ –	$ 1,571
Buildings	14,893	4,628	10,265
Coffee service equipment and vending equipment	145,138	74,300	70,838
Machinery and equipment	40,269	22,907	17,362
Furniture, computer equipment and leasehold improvements	26,839	17,170	9,669
Rolling stock	17,247	9,989	7,258
	$ 245,957	$ 128,994	$ 116,963

Note 9
Goodwill

For the year ended April 2, 2005, the changes in the carrying amounts of goodwill are as follows for each of the two business segments:

	Manufacturing and marketing	Coffee services	Total
Balance as at April 3, 2004	$ 29,414	$ 111,367	$ 140,781
Purchases (disposals) of businesses	–	5,922	5,922
Write-off following discontinuance of several bistro operations	(273)	–	(273)
Translation adjustments	–	(4,799)	(4,799)
Balance as at April 2, 2005	$ 29,141	$ 112,490	$ 141,631

Note 10
Other assets

			2005
	Cost	Accumulated amortization	Net book value
Patents and rights	$ 914	$ 615	$ 299
Start-up costs	1,163	687	476
Deferred development costs	7,785	4,611	3,174
Deferred financing costs	1,453	1,153	300
Other assets	5,048	1,771	3,277
	$ 16,363	$ 8,837	$ 7,526

			2004
	Cost	Accumulated amortization	Net book value
Patents and rights	$ 918	$ 515	$ 403
Start-up costs	1,163	440	723
Deferred development costs	6,318	3,260	3,058
Deferred financing costs	1,889	1,562	327
Other assets	4,010	1,206	2,804
	$ 14,298	$ 6,983	$ 7,315

Note 11
Long-term debt

	2005	2004
Revolving bank credit facility (i)	$ 85,928	$ 104,681
Other	2,428	2,825
	88,356	107,506
Less current portion	28,024	22,710
	$ 60,332	$ 84,796

40 | 41

Note 11: Long-term debt (continued)

(i) As at April 2, 2005, these borrowings were drawn on a bank credit facility of $150 million. The bank credit facility is composed of two tranches. The first tranche of $60 million is a 364-day revolving facility that can be extended on a yearly basis, and the second tranche of $90 million is a three-year revolving facility maturing in October 2005. As at April 2, 2005, Cdn$18,900,000 was borrowed under the first tranche, and $67,028,400 (Cdn$33,000,000 and US$28,000,000) under the second tranche. The borrowed amounts of the first tranche are to be reimbursed in full in October 2007 at the latest or if the facility is not extended, while the borrowed amounts of the second tranche will be converted, in October 2005, into a two-year term loan repayable in eight quarterly installments beginning three months following the effective date of the term loan.

The credit agreement governing this bank credit facility contains certain covenants, among which is the obligation to maintain certain financial ratios. During the year, the Company satisfied the covenants pertaining to these ratios. The borrowed amounts bear interest at floating rates based on Bankers' Acceptances or the bank prime rate. The bank credit facility is unsecured by the assets of Van Houtte Inc.

In accordance with the terms of various borrowing agreements and excluding any refinancing options, the Company will make the following repayments over the next five years:

2006	$ 28,024
2007	34,163
2008	25,590
2009	200
2010	379

Note 12
Capital stock

	2005	2004
Authorized		
Unlimited number of multiple voting shares with voting rights of five votes per share, participating and without par value		
Unlimited number of subordinate voting shares with voting rights of one vote per share, participating and without par value		
Unlimited number of Classes A and B preferred shares, issuable only in series, non-voting and without par value		
Issued and paid		
5,300,000 multiple voting shares	$ 353	$ 353
16,303,331 subordinate voting shares (16,130,481 shares in 2004)	127,897	126,723
	$ 128,250	$ 127,076

a) Share issue and repurchase – 2005

During the year, 5,000 subordinate voting shares were redeemed for a cash consideration of $94,000. The excess of the price paid over the average cost of these shares as well as the redemption expenses of $54,000 were recorded as a reduction of retained earnings.

During the year, 177,850 subordinate voting shares were issued upon the exercise of stock options, for a cash consideration of $1,213,613.

Note 12: Capital stock (continued)

b) Share issue and repurchase – 2004

During the year, 55,700 subordinate voting shares were redeemed for a cash consideration of $710,000. The excess of the price paid over the average cost of these shares as well as the redemption expenses of $272,000 were recorded as a reduction of retained earnings.

During the year, 46,500 subordinate voting shares were issued upon the exercise of stock options, for a cash consideration of $284,675.

c) Stock option plan

Under a stock option plan, 1,650,000 subordinate voting shares are reserved for certain management employees of the Company. The exercise price of each option is determined based on the average of the daily high and low board lot trading prices of the Company's shares on the TSX stock exchange for the last five trading days for which there have been transactions immediately preceding the date on which the option is granted. Each option may be exercised during a period not exceeding ten years from the date it was granted.

The following table provides details regarding changes to outstanding options for the years ended April 2, 2005 and April 3, 2004.

	2005		2004	
	Options	Weighted average exercise price	Options	Weighted average exercise price
Balance at beginning	1,033,023	$ 18.11	1,181,674	$ 20.26
Granted	42,000	16.15	243,921	14.22
Cancelled	(52,486)	16.49	(346,072)	24.32
Exercised	(177,850)	6.82	(46,500)	6.12
Balance at end of year	844,687	$ 20.49	1,033,023	$ 18.11
Vested options at end of year	593,033	$ 21.81	714,515	$ 18.08

The following table provides summary information regarding outstanding options as at April 2, 2005:

	Options outstanding			Options exercisable	
Range of exercise prices	Number of outstanding options as at April 2, 2005	Weighted average years to maturity	Weighted average exercise price	Number exercisable as at April 2, 2005	Weighted average exercise price
$ 10 to 15	206,201	7.3	$ 14.19	133,500	$ 14.17
15 to 20	322,390	5.4	18.31	153,500	18.48
20 to 25	133,000	4.3	23.17	133,000	23.17
25 to 30	183,096	3.3	29.48	173,033	29.61
$ 10 to 30	844,687	5.2	$ 20.49	593,033	$ 21.81

During the year 2005, the Company granted 42,000 stock options to senior executives and management at a weighted average exercise price of $16.15 and cancelled 52,486 options, of which 38,019 were granted after March 31, 2002 at a weighted average exercise price of $14.11. The weighted average fair value of stock options granted was $4.99 while that of cancelled options was $3.95. The fair value of each option granted was determined using the Black-Scholes option pricing model and the following weighted average assumptions:

Risk-free interest rate	3.93%
Expected life	7.1 years
Expected volatility	27%
Expected dividend yield	1.5%

Note 12: Capital stock (continued)

The compensation expense for the year ended April 2, 2005 was $413,000. The total consideration was recorded under contributed surplus.

If the stock options had been accounted for based on the fair value based method, pro forma net earnings and pro forma net earnings per share would have been as follows for the year ended April 3, 2004:

	As reported	Pro forma
Net earnings	$ 18,564	$ 17,841
Earnings per share:		
Basic	$ 0.87	$ 0.83
Diluted	$ 0.86	$ 0.83

The pro forma figures omit the effect of stock options granted prior to March 31, 2002.

Note 13
Currency translation adjustment

	2005	2004
Balance at beginning	$ (7,746)	$ (1,172)
Effect of exchange rate variation on translation		
of net assets of U.S. self-sustaining subsidiaries	(5,773)	(6,574)
Balance at end	$ (13,519)	$ (7,746)

Furthermore, gain (loss) on foreign exchange transactions recorded in the consolidated statement of earnings amounted to ($667,000) in 2005 and ($1,563,000) in 2004.

Note 14
Commitments and guarantees

a) Commitments

The Company rents premises and equipment under operating leases which expire at various dates up to 2017 and for which gross rents total $26,411,000. Of this amount, a portion of $5,182,000 is assumed by the franchisees of the Company. Annual payments under these leases for the next five years are as follows:

	Gross	Franchisees	Net
2006	$ 6,953	$ 1,098	$ 5,855
2007	5,500	861	4,639
2008	4,149	747	3,402
2009	3,142	596	2,546
2010 and thereafter	6,667	1,880	4,787

b) Disclosure of guarantees

Capital leases

A subsidiary of the Company, VKI Technologies Inc., has guaranteed lease obligations to third parties by franchisees of its Filterfresh Coffee Service, Inc. subsidiary. As security for the guarantees provided, the Company has a lien on the franchisees' licenses and assets. As at April 2, 2005, the Company guarantees a total of US$13,030 for lease obligations to third parties. The Company also guarantees lease obligations to third parties for a total of US$59,472. In the opinion of management, the security for the guarantees provided is adequate.

Note 14: Commitments and guarantees (continued)

Directors' and officers' indemnification agreements

The Company indemnifies its directors and officers, former directors and officers and individuals who act or who have acted at the Company's request as a director or officer of an entity in which the Company is a shareholder or creditor, to the extent permitted by law, against any and all charges, costs, expenses, amounts paid in settlement or investigative damages incurred by the directors and officers as a result of any lawsuit, or any judicial, administrative or investigating proceeding in which the directors and officers are sued as a result of their service. These indemnification claims are subject to any statutory or other legal limitation period. The nature of the indemnification agreements prevents the Company from making a reasonable estimate of the maximum potential amount it could be required to pay to counterparties.

The Company has purchased directors' and officers' liability insurance coverage in the amount of $30,000,000 which carries a $250,000 deductible. No amount has been accrued in the consolidated balance sheet with respect to these indemnifications. To the knowledge of the Company, there is no such claim against directors and officers.

Operating leases

The Company has guaranteed lease obligations for its franchisees expiring between 2006 and 2007. If a franchisee defaults under its contractual obligation, the Company must, under certain conditions, compensate the lessor for the default. The maximum exposure in respect of these guarantees is $542,497 (2004 - $737,651). As at April 2, 2005, the Company has not recorded a liability associated with these guarantees, since it is not probable that a franchisee will default under the agreement.

Note 15
Contingencies

The Company is involved in various lawsuits and claims. Management is of the opinion that the resolution of these claims would have no material impact on the Company's financial position or results of operations.

Note 16
Additional information on cash flows

	2005	2004
Operating activities		
Changes in non-cash operating working capital items:		
(Increase) decrease in the undernoted items:		
Accounts receivable	$ (4,850)	$ (2,744)
Income taxes payable	2,542	1,655
Inventories	(1,270)	(2,372)
Prepaid expenses	(9)	384
(Decrease) increase in the undernoted items:		
Accounts payable and accrued liabilities	6,058	2,865
Employee future benefits	(173)	(1,212)
Working capital acquired	1,400	283
	$ 3,698	$ (1,141)
Cash payments of interest and income taxes were as follows		
Cash interest payments	$ 3,786	$ 4,765
Cash payments for income taxes	$ 3,163	$ 6,211
Purchase of fixed assets financed by accounts payable	$ 1,147	$ 1,644
Purchase of fixed assets financed by capital lease	$ 236	$ –

44 **45**

Note 17
Business acquisitions and disposals

The business combinations are accounted for using the purchase method. Results of the businesses acquired are included from the date of the acquisition in the consolidated financial statements of the Company.

a) 2005

During the year, the Company acquired twenty-two coffee service businesses, seventeen in the United States and five in Canada, and sold three of its vending branches in Canada for a total net cash consideration of $9,330,000. The principal acquisitions of the year are:

United States

On June 26, 2004, concurrent with a partnership agreement of which the Company holds a 67.5% interest, the Company purchased the business of Potomac Coffee LLC.

On December 21, 2004, the Company purchased the business of North America Coffee (Manteno).

Canada

On October 22, 2004, the Company purchased the business of Café de Marc inc.

b) 2004

During the year, the Company acquired fifteen coffee service businesses, twelve in the United States and three in Canada, and sold six of its vending branches in Canada for a total net cash consideration of $13,884,000. The principal acquisitions of the year are:

United States

On March 30, 2003, concurrent with a partnership agreement of which the Company holds a 74% interest, the Company purchased the businesses of Coffee Time Inc. and Mocha Men West Inc.

On December 15, 2003, concurrent with a partnership agreement of which the Company holds a 56% interest, the Company purchased the business of Corporate Coffee Systems, Inc.

On June 26, 2003, the Company acquired the remaining 75% ownership of Caffe Satisfaction LLC.

The acquisitions and disposals are summarized as follows:

	2005	2004
Assets acquired and disposed		
Non-cash operating working capital	$ 1,400	$ 283
Fixed assets	2,642	4,183
Other assets	917	1,831
Goodwill [1]	5,922	14,737
	10,881	21,034
Liabilities assumed		
Long-term debt	–	549
Non-controlling interest	1,088	4,070
(Loss) gain on disposal	(304)	393
Net assets acquired at fair value	$ 10,097	$ 16,022
Consideration		
Cash	$ 9,330	$ 13,884
Portion of purchase price paid in a prior year	767	2,138
	$ 10,097	$ 16,022
[1] Tax base of goodwill acquired	$ 4,854	$ 13,796

Note 18
Financial instruments

a) Fair value

The carrying value of cash, accounts receivable, accounts payable and accrued liabilities approximates their fair value because of the near-term maturity of these instruments. The carrying value of the revolving term loan and other debt approximates its fair value, as the interest rates vary based on market rate.

b) Management of interest risk

The Company has entered into interest rate swaps to manage its interest rate exposure on a portion of the revolving bank credit. The Company is committed to exchange, at specific intervals, the difference between the fixed and floating interest rates calculated by reference to the notional amounts. As at April 2, 2005 and April 3, 2004, the Company pays a fixed interest rate of 4.86% on a notional amount of $30,000,000 and receives a floating interest based on Bankers' Acceptance having a three-month maturity. The swap will expire in July 2007. The negative fair value of the interest rate swap is $1,070,316 (2004 - $1,884,907).

The Company does not foresee any failure by the counterparties to these contracts as they are financially-sound Canadian banks.

c) Foreign exchange risk

The Company makes several purchases in US dollars and enters into various types of foreign exchange forward contracts in order to manage its foreign exchange risk. The Company does not hold nor issue such financial instruments for trading purposes. As at April 2, 2005, there were forward exchange contracts outstanding for a notional amount of US$32,500,000 (2004 - US$4,500,000). The positive fair value of the forward exchange contracts is $151,439 as at April 2, 2005 and there was a negative fair value of $61,000 as at April 3, 2004.

d) Credit risk

The Company does not have a significant exposure to any individual customer nor counter-party. The Company reviews a new customer's credit history before extending credit and conducts regular reviews of its existing customers' credit performance. An allowance for doubtful accounts is established based upon factors such as the credit risk for specific customers, historical trends and other information.

e) Other risk

The Company also has a significant exposure toward the fluctuation of the price of green coffee. The Company purchases, from time to time, coffee contracts on a public commodities market in order to manage its price risk. As at April 2, 2005, the Company had contracts for 6.3 million pounds of green coffee having a negative fair value of $358,141 and as at April 3, 2004, the Company had contracts for 2.4 million pounds of green coffee having a positive fair value of $309,094.

Note 19
Segmented information

In order to better distinguish the unique dynamics of the coffee services market from the Company's other activities, the segmented information is now presented as follows:

a) The "Manufacturing and Marketing" segment encompasses coffee roasting and distribution for home consumption through retail channels such as supermarkets. It also includes café-bistros and the manufacture of coffeemakers.

b) The "Coffee Services" segment focuses on the sale of coffee for consumption in the workplace and other public locations. Van Houtte's coffee services network also distributes complementary products such as condiments, snacks, drinks, water and point-of-use water systems. Moreover, this segment includes vending machine operations.

46 | 47

Note 19: Segmented information (continued)

These segments are managed separately, since they require different marketing strategies and are assessed individually based on operating income before depreciation, amortization and financial expenses.

The accounting policies of each segment are identical to those policies used for the consolidated financial statements.

Segment income includes income from sales to third parties and inter-segment sales. These sales are accounted for at prevailing market prices.

	2005	2004
Business segments		
Revenues:		
Manufacturing and Marketing	$155,948	$ 142,257
Coffee Services	243,828	230,273
	399,776	372,530
Intersegment	(51,021)	(41,982)
	$348,755	$ 330,548
Operating earnings before depreciation and amortization, financial expenses:		
Manufacturing and Marketing	$ 32,213	$ 31,442
Coffee Services	38,949	33,890
	71,162	65,332
General corporate expenses	(5,489)	(5,770)
	$ 65,673	$ 59,562
Fixed assets and goodwill:		
Manufacturing and Marketing	$ 63,360	$ 62,565
Coffee Services	194,076	195,179
	$257,436	$ 257,744
Additions to fixed assets and other assets:		
Manufacturing and Marketing	$ 9,537	$ 6,926
Coffee Services	20,370	19,704
	29,907	26,630
General corporate	5	300
	$ 29,912	$ 26,930
Depreciation and amortization of fixed assets and other assets:		
Manufacturing and Marketing	$ 8,165	$ 8,007
Coffee Services	22,697	22,920
	30,862	30,927
General corporate	154	103
	$ 31,016	$ 31,030

Note 20
Comparative figures

Certain comparative figures have been reclassified to conform with the financial statement presentation adopted in the current year.

Index